Visual Basic for Applications

Diane Zak
College of DuPage

COURSE
TECHNOLOGY

Thomson Learning™

ONE MAIN STREET, CAMBRIDGE, MA 02142

Australia • Canada • Mexico • Singapore • Spain • United Kingdom • United States

Visual Basic for Applications by Diane Zak

Associate Publisher:	Kristen Duerr
Senior Product Manager:	Jennifer Muroff
Development Editors:	Kim Crowley and Amanda Brodkin
Production Editor:	Jean Bermingham
Associate Product Manager:	Tricia Coia
Editorial Assistant:	Elizabeth Wessen
Associate Marketing Manager:	Meagan Walsh
Cover Designer:	MaryAnn Southard

ISBN 0-619-00020-1

Printed in Canada
1 2 3 4 5 WC 03 02 01 00

Preface

Visual Basic for Applications (VBA) is a programming language found in many Microsoft and non-Microsoft products. VBA allows users to customize their applications by creating more convenient ways to perform common tasks. VBA is fast becoming a standard as more and more third-party software publishers license VBA to include in their applications. As a result, rather than learning a separate language for each software application, as users once had to do, you need only to learn one—in this case, VBA.

Visual Basic for Applications is designed to guide the beginning programmer in writing procedures using the VBA language. The procedures that you will create in this book will allow you to customize the applications included in Microsoft Office 2000 so that the applications work the way you want them to work. This book assumes that you have a basic knowledge of the applications included in Microsoft Office 2000. However, no prior programming experience is necessary.

Organization and Coverage

Visual Basic for Applications contains 15 tutorials that present hands-on instruction. In these tutorials, students with no previous programming experience learn how to plan and create well-structured procedures. By the end of the book, students will have learned how to access the objects contained in object models, as well as how to write procedures using the sequence, selection, and repetition programming structures. Students also will learn how to create dialog boxes and perform automation.

Each tutorial includes a Concept lesson, which introduces the programming concept that is presented in the tutorial, and three Application lessons: Excel, Word, and Access. Each Application lesson provides an opportunity for the student to apply the knowledge learned in the Concept lesson within his or her choice of applications. The book can be used to learn VBA in one application, or in all three. This flexible presentation of VBA allows the instructor to customize course content to his or her specifications. It also provides the student with learning opportunities beyond what might be taught in the classroom.

Approach

Visual Basic for Applications distinguishes itself from other books because of its unique approach, which motivates students by demonstrating why they need to learn the concepts and skills. This book teaches programming concepts using a task-driven, rather than a command-driven, approach. By working through the tutorials—which are each motivated by a realistic case—students learn how to create programs that solve problems they are likely to encounter in the workplace. This is much more effective than memorizing a list of commands out of context.

Features

Visual Basic for Applications is an exceptional book because it also includes the following features:

- **"Read This Before You Begin" Section** This section is consistent with Course Technology's unequaled commitment to helping instructors introduce technology into the classroom. Technical considerations and assumptions about hardware, software, and default settings are listed in one place to help instructors save time and eliminate unnecessary aggravation.
- **Lessons** Each tutorial is divided into four lessons—Concept, Excel, Word, and Access. The Concept lesson introduces the programming concepts that will be explored in the remaining three lessons. In the Excel, Word, and Access lessons, the student creates the procedures that solve the lesson's Case problem.
- **Case Approach** Each tutorial addresses programming-related problems that students could reasonably expect to encounter in the real world. Fictional case scenarios are presented in each Application lesson. In completing each lesson, the student develops functional solutions to the challenges posed in each case.
- **Step-by-Step Methodology** The unique Course Technology methodology keeps students on track. They write program code always within the context of solving the problems posed in the lessons. The text constantly guides students, letting them know where they are in the process of solving the problem. The numerous figures include labels that direct students' attention to what they should look at on the screen.
- **Help?s** These paragraphs anticipate the problems students might encounter and help them resolve these problems on their own. This feature facilitates independent learning and frees the instructor to focus on substantive conceptual issues, rather than on common procedural errors.
- **Tips** Tips provide additional information about a procedure—for example, an alternative method of performing the procedure. Tips also inform students where they can find more information on the current topic.
- **Summaries and Review Questions** Following the Concept lesson is a Summary, which recaps the programming concepts covered in the lesson. The Summary is followed by meaningful, conceptual Review Questions that test students' understanding of what they learned in the lesson.
- **Exercises** Each lesson concludes with Exercises, which provide students with additional practice of the skills and concepts they learned in the lesson.
- **PowerPoint Exercises** Each Concept lesson includes one PowerPoint Exercise, which allows students to apply the tutorial's programming concept in a PowerPoint presentation. PowerPoint Exercises are designated by the word "powerpoint" in the margin.

- **Discovery Exercises** The Discovery Exercises, which are designated by the word "discovery" in the margin, encourage students to challenge and independently develop their own programming skills.
- **Debugging Exercises** One of the most important programming skills a student can learn is the ability to correct problems, called "bugs," in existing code. The Debugging Exercises, which are designated by the word "debugging" in the margin, provide an opportunity for students to detect and correct errors in existing procedures.

Teaching Tools

The following teaching tools are available when this book is used in a classroom setting. All of the teaching tools available with this book are provided to the instructor on a single CD-ROM.

Electronic Instructor's Manual The Instructor's Manual that accompanies this textbook includes:

- Additional instructional material to assist in class preparation, including suggestions for lecture topics.
- Solutions to all end-of-chapter materials. (Due to the nature of programming, students' solutions may differ from these solutions and still be correct.)
- **Data Files** Data Files, containing all of the data that students will use for the tutorials and exercises in this book, are provided through Course Technology's Online Companion and on the Instructor's Resource Kit CD-ROM. See the "Read This Before You Begin" section preceding the Overview for more information on Data Files.

Course Test Manager 1.2 Accompanying this book is a powerful assessment tool known as the Course Test Manager. Designed by Course Technology, this cutting-edge Windows-based testing software helps instructors design and administer tests and pre-tests. In addition to being able to generate tests that can be printed and administered, this full-featured program also has an online testing component that allows students to take tests at the computer and have their exams graded automatically.

PowerPoint Presentations This book comes with Microsoft PowerPoint slides for each chapter. These are included as a teaching aid for classroom presentation, to make available to students on the network for chapter review, or to be printed for classroom distribution. Instructors can add their own slides for additional topics they introduce to the class.

Acknowledgments

I would like to thank all of the people who helped to make this book a reality, especially Kim Crowley and Amanda Brodkin (my fantastic Development Editors), Jennifer Muroff (the best Product Manager any author could have), and Jean Bermingham (the greatest Production Editor there is). Thank you for your hard work, and for being so kind, patient, understanding, helpful, and fun. I know I could not have made it through this project without the four of you by my side.

Thanks also to Kristen Duerr, Associate Publisher; John Bosco, Quality Assurance Manager; Nicole Ashton, Quality Assurance Engineer; and Alex White, Quality Assurance Project Leader. I am grateful to the many reviewers who provided invaluable comments on the manuscript, in particular: Ginny Alvis, Virginia Highlands Community College; Jamie Bates, DeVry Institute; Paula Baxter, San Juan College; Peg Byers; Debi Griggs, San Jacinto College; Linda Kieffer, Eastern Washington University; Meg Littlefield, Maine Area Technical College; Mark Shellman, Gaston College; and Kim Stewart, McHenry County College.

A special thanks goes to my husband, Charles, whose help and constant encouragement make all of this possible.

Diane Zak

Contents

tutorial 2

THE OBJECT MODEL *81*

tutorial 3

OBJECT VARIABLES *153*

tutorial 4

STRING VARIABLES *207*

DATE VARIABLES *267*

tutorial 8

THE SELECT CASE STATEMENT AND THE MSGBOX FUNCTION 449

t u t o r i a l   9

THE REPETITION STRUCTURE AND THE WITH STATEMENT *509*

tutorial 10

MORE ON THE REPETITION STRUCTURE AND STRING FUNCTIONS 575

tutorial 11

BUILT-IN DIALOG BOXES AND THE OFFICE ASSISTANT 627

tutorial 12

CUSTOM DIALOG BOXES *697*

OPTION BUTTON, CHECK BOX, AND LIST BOX CONTROLS 787

t u t o r i a l   1 4

AUTOMATION *861*

t u t o r i a l   1 5

AUTOMATION AND ERROR TRAPPING *913*

Read This Before You Begin

To the User

Data Disks

To complete the tutorials and exercises in this book, you will need a Data Disk. The term "Data Disk" does not refer to a floppy disk; instead, it refers to a collection of files that reside on your hard drive. The Data Disk contains all of the source files you will need. You will also save the files that you create while completing the tutorials onto your Data Disk. Because of the size and quantity of the files you will be working with, you will need to store your Data Disk on your local workstation or on a network file server to which you can connect.

If you are going to copy the Data Disk source files from a file server, your instructor will tell you the drive letter and folder that contains the source files that you need. To create your Data Disk, navigate to the Data Disk folder provided by your instructor, select all of the subfolders, and copy them to the folder on the hard drive where you want to store your Data Disk files. There are folders for Tutorials 1 through 15 in the book. Each of the tutorial folders contains subfolders for the lessons in each tutorial, for example, Tut 11\Access. Many of the code examples in this book require you to enter a folder path to your Data Disk. Figures that accompany these instructions often reference a folder path that shows the Data Disk as being on the C drive. Unless you are working from the root directory of a C drive, the folder path you will enter will be different from the one shown in the figure.

Using Your Own Computer

If you are going to work through this book using your own computer, you will need:

- **Computer System and Software** Microsoft Office 2000 and Microsoft Windows 95, 98, NT, or higher must be installed on your computer. For further information about installing Microsoft Office 2000 and setting up your computer's environment, see the "Installing Microsoft Office 2000 and setting up your environment" section on the facing page.
- **Data Disk** You will not be able to complete the tutorials or exercises in this book using your own computer until you have a Data Disk. You can get the files for your Data Disk from your instructor. The files also may be obtained electronically through the Internet at www.course.com.

Visit Our World Wide Web Site

Additional materials designed especially for your course might be available on the World Wide Web. Go to **www.course.com**. Search for this book title periodically on the Course Technology Web site for more details.

Installing Microsoft Office 2000 and setting up your environment:

This book assumes a custom installation of Microsoft Office 2000. You will need to perform a custom installation in order to install the Visual Basic Help files and the Genius.acs file. After installing Microsoft Office 2000, you will need to set the Macro Security level in Word, Excel, and/or PowerPoint to either Medium or Low. Additionally, you will need to set the appropriate environment settings in the Visual Basic Editor's Options dialog box, and copy the data folders and files to your computer's hard drive, which is typically the C drive.

To install Microsoft Office 2000 and set up your environment so that your screens match the figures shown in the book, do the following:

1. When installing Microsoft Office 2000, click the Custom button to perform a custom installation.

2. In the Microsoft Office 2000: Selecting Features dialog box, click the plus box that appears to the left of Office Tools.

3. To install the Visual Basic Help files, click the Visual Basic Help list arrow, and then click Run from My Computer in the list.

4. To install the Genius.acs file, click the plus box that appears to the left of Office Assistant, then click the Genius list arrow, and then click Run from My Computer in the list.

5. Click the Install Now button to complete the installation process.

6. After installing Microsoft Office 2000, you will need to set the macro security level in Word, Excel, and PowerPoint (if you will be completing the PowerPoint exercises in this book) to either Medium or Low. To do so, start the application whose security level you want to change. Click Tools on the Standard menu bar, point to Macro, and then click Security. Click either the Medium or Low option button, then click the OK button.

7. To set up the Visual Basic environment, start either Word, Excel, PowerPoint, or Access. Press Alt+F11 to open the Visual Basic Editor. Click Tools on the Standard menu, then click Options. Click the Editor tab on the Options dialog box, then select the following check boxes, if necessary: Auto Syntax Check, Require Variable Declaration, Auto List Members, Auto Quick Info, and Auto Data Tips. If necessary, deselect the Default to Full Module View check box. Click the OK button to close the Options dialog box, then press Alt+F11 to return to the application. Close the application without saving the document, workbook, presentation, or database.

8. This book assumes that the data folders and files that are needed to complete the tutorials and exercises are stored on the computer's hard drive, which is typically the C drive.

To the Instructor

To complete the tutorials and exercises in this book, your students must use a set of data files, referred to throughout the book as the Data Disk. These files are included in the Instructor's Resource Kit. They also may be obtained electronically through the Internet at **http://www.course.com**.

Once the files are copied, you will need to inform your students where to find the files so they can make their own Data Disks. Make sure the files get copied correctly to the Data Disks by following the instructions in the Data Disks section.

Course Technology Data Disk Files

You are granted a license to copy the Data Disk files to any computer or computer network used by students who have purchased this book.

A Brief History of BASIC, Microsoft, and Visual Basic for Applications

objectives

This overview contains basic definitions and background information, including:

- A brief history of BASIC and Microsoft Corporation
- A discussion of the advantages of learning VBA
- Information on using the tutorials effectively

BASIC and Microsoft Corporation

In 1964, Professors John Kemeny and Thomas Kurtz, both of Dartmouth College in Hanover, New Hampshire, developed a simple language for teaching students how to program a computer. They called the language BASIC (Beginner's All-purpose Symbolic Instruction Code). Since its inception, the BASIC language has changed considerably, and many versions of BASIC have emerged, each extending the language through new commands and features.

Although BASIC began as a simple teaching aid, later versions of BASIC—for example, QuickBASIC and Visual Basic—now can be used to create large-scale business applications. You also will find a version of the BASIC language, called Visual Basic for Applications (VBA), in Microsoft's Office suite software. VBA also is licensed to other software vendors and is included in a wide range of products, such as Autodesk, Inc.'s AutoCAD, Corel Corporation's CorelDRAW, and Peachtree's Office Accounting software.

How does a language designed to be a mere teaching aid become not only a powerful programming language, but also an integral part of some of the most popular application software in the world? A brief history of the relationship between BASIC, Bill Gates, and Microsoft Corporation will help you understand how this phenomenon occurred.

You can find a more thorough discussion of the life and achievements of Bill Gates and Microsoft in _The Making of Microsoft_ by Daniel Ichbiah and Susan L. Knepper, published by Prima Publishing. Although the book's coverage of Bill Gates and Microsoft ends with the early 1990s, it provides insight into how Microsoft came to be the powerful software giant it is today. You also can find some very interesting historical information about Microsoft, from its inception in 1975 through the present, by visiting the Microsoft Museum at www.microsoft.com/MSCorp/Museum/exhibits/pastpresent/intro.asp.

The Beginning of Microsoft

William Henry (Bill) Gates III was born in Seattle, Washington, on October 28, 1955. He was the only son of William Henry Gates Jr., a successful attorney, and his wife, Mary, a schoolteacher. Bill Gates' love affair with computer programming began as early as January 1969 when, while attending eighth grade, he and his 10th-grade friend, Paul Allen, first used a Teletype machine to communicate with a minicomputer located at nearby General Electric. It was not unusual for both friends to sneak into their school at night to hone their programming skills. Paul Allen enjoyed working with assembly language, while Bill Gates was more interested in the BASIC programming language.

In 1975, Gates and Allen formed a partnership named Micro-Soft (the hyphen was later dropped) and implemented a version of BASIC for the first personal computer—the Altair—which was developed in 1974 by Ed Roberts at MITS (Micro Instrumentation and Telemetry Systems). In its contract with MITS, Microsoft retained ownership of its BASIC language, while granting MITS a license only to distribute the language (but not sell it as its own product).

From 1976 through 1979, many other computer companies—such as Commodore, Tandy, and Apple—also were granted licenses to distribute BASIC with their computers. By the end of 1979, BASIC was the most popular programming language for personal computers. It was during this time that IBM negotiated secretly with Microsoft to create a version of BASIC for the first IBM personal computers, which entered the marketplace in 1981.

In 1982, Microsoft released its first software application—a DOS-based spreadsheet named Multiplan—followed most notably by the operating system software Windows and application software such as Word, Excel, Access, and PowerPoint. Microsoft Word for Windows, which first shipped in 1989, was the first application to contain a version of the BASIC language, called WordBasic, which was modeled after Microsoft QuickBASIC—a descendent of the original BASIC. WordBasic allowed the user to automate repetitive tasks by creating small procedures called macros. A **macro** is simply a series of instructions grouped together as a single command that then can be executed by the user with one keystroke.

Microsoft introduced Visual Basic, Programming Edition in 1992; it contained a version of BASIC called Visual Basic. When Microsoft Access, a database software application, was released in 1992, it contained its own version of BASIC, called Access Basic. Surprisingly, the initial versions of Microsoft's spreadsheet software, Excel, did not contain the BASIC language; rather, they contained a macro language named XLM (Excel Macro). It wasn't until the 1994 release of Excel Version 5.0 that Microsoft, in an effort to standardize the programming languages used in its software applications, replaced XLM with VBA (Visual Basic for Applications). Shortly thereafter, in 1995, Microsoft replaced Access Basic with VBA, and it integrated VBA into the Programming Edition of Visual Basic, allowing the Programming Edition to communicate with other applications supporting VBA. By the time Office 97, a suite of Microsoft's most popular business software applications, was released, VBA had made its way into four of the five Office applications: Word, Excel, Access, and PowerPoint (a presentation graphics software). The fifth Office 97 application, Outlook 97, an e-mail and information management software, contained VBScript—a subset of the Visual Basic language.

▶ tip

Many people refer to the Programming Edition of Visual Basic simply as Visual Basic. Technically, however, Visual Basic is a programming language, whereas the Programming Edition is the development environment in which you use the Visual Basic language to create stand-alone applications. A stand-alone application is one that can be run directly from Windows.

Unlike Word, PowerPoint, and Excel, the Access component of Office 97 did not contain the Visual Basic Editor, a convenient editor in which VBA procedures can be created and modified. However, in the latest version of Microsoft Office, Office 2000, each of the five Office suite components now contains VBA and each has access to the Visual Basic Editor. As you can see, BASIC has come a long way since 1964.

Why Should You Learn VBA?

VBA is the programming language found in many Microsoft and non-Microsoft products, and it is fast becoming a standard as more and more third-party software publishers license VBA to include in their applications. Therefore, rather than learning a separate language for each software application, as users once had to do, you need only to learn one—in this case, VBA. Once you learn VBA, you then can apply your knowledge to any software that includes VBA.

You can view a listing of non-Microsoft companies licensing VBA at www.msdn.microsoft.com/vba/license/vbawho.asp.

One of the advantages of VBA is that it allows you to customize an application so that the application works the way you want it to work. For example, you can customize Word so that the Office Assistant displays the current date when a new document is opened. Or, you can use VBA to automate your Excel worksheet for a novice user, allowing you to enjoy your vacation worry-free while a coworker enters data into the worksheet.

VBA also allows you to create macros that use components found in more than one application. For example, you can create an Excel macro that generates an Excel chart from the sales amounts entered in an Access database, and then includes the chart in a report created in Word—all without leaving Excel.

The tutorials in this book will help you learn Microsoft Visual Basic for Applications 6.0. Tutorials 1 and 2 cover the Visual Basic Editor (VBE) and the Object Browser. It might take a little time to get comfortable with both features, but once you do, you are well on your way to learning VBA.

Using the Tutorials Effectively

Each tutorial in this book is divided into four lessons titled Concept, Excel, Word, and Access. The Concept lesson introduces one or more important programming concepts, and the remaining three lessons walk you through implementation of the concepts using Excel, Word, and Access. The Application lessons use examples illustrated by three fictitious organizations.

The material in this book can be covered in two ways: tutorial-by-tutorial or application-by-application. If your instructor chooses the tutorial-by-tutorial approach, you will be required to complete a tutorial in its entirety before moving on to the next tutorial. If your instructor chooses the application-by-application approach, you will need to read the Concept lesson and the appropriate Application lesson(s)—either Excel, Word, and/or Access—in each tutorial.

The Excel, Word, and Access lessons are designed to be used at your computer. The lessons contain a combination of explanatory text and numbered steps. Begin by reading the explanatory text. Then, when you come to the numbered steps, follow the steps on your computer. Read each step carefully and completely before you try it.

As you work, compare your screen with the figures in the book to verify your results. Don't worry if your screen display differs slightly from the figures. The important parts of the screen display are labeled in each figure. Just be sure you have these parts on your screen.

Don't worry about making mistakes; that's part of the learning process. Help notes identify common problems and explain how to get back on track. You should complete the steps in the Help notes only if you are having the problem described. Tip notes provide additional information about a procedure—for example, an alternative method of performing the procedure or some interesting background information.

Following the Concept lesson in each tutorial is a Summary section, as well as questions and exercises designed to review and reinforce the lesson's material. You also will find exercises at the end of each of the three Application lessons. You should complete all of the end-of-lesson questions and exercises before going on to the next lesson. Learning VBA requires practice, and future tutorials assume that you have mastered the information found in the previous tutorials.

Some of the end-of-lesson exercises are Discovery Exercises that allow you to "discover" the solutions to problems on your own and also to experiment with material that is not covered in the lesson. The Concept lesson also contains one or more PowerPoint Exercises, which are designated by the word "powerpoint" in the margin. These exercises allow you to practice the tutorial's programming concepts using the PowerPoint application. Still other end-of-lesson exercises are Debugging Exercises that are designed to let you practice **debugging**—meaning "finding the errors in"—VBA code. Debugging Exercises are designated by the word "debugging" in the margin.

Before you begin the tutorials, you should know how to use one or more of the following Office 2000 applications: Excel, Word, Access, and/or PowerPoint. Which applications you need to know depends on which Application lessons you will be covering and whether you will be completing the PowerPoint Exercises. You can learn about the Office 2000 applications using one of the following Course Technology books: *New Perspectives on Office 2000*, *New Perspectives on Microsoft Access 2000*, *New Perspectives on Microsoft Excel 2000*, and/or *New Perspectives on Microsoft Word 2000*.

Using the Visual Basic Editor

Concept Lesson

Procedures

As you learned in the Overview, Visual Basic for Applications (VBA) is the programming language found in many Microsoft and non-Microsoft products, and it is fast becoming a standard as more and more third-party vendors license VBA to include in their applications. As a result, rather than learning a separate language for each software application, as users once had to do, you need only to learn one—in this case, VBA. Once you learn VBA, you then can apply your knowledge to any software that includes VBA.

You can use VBA to customize an application to fit your needs. You do so by creating a **procedure**, which is simply a series of VBA instructions grouped together as a single unit for the purpose of performing a specific task. For example, you can create a procedure that directs Microsoft Word to automatically perform a mail merge operation when the Send Letters document is opened. Or, you can create a procedure that builds a Microsoft Excel chart from the sales data entered in a Microsoft Access database. Rather than you having to perform the time-consuming, repetitive actions necessary to accomplish these tasks, you need simply to run the appropriate procedure, which will do the work for you.

You can run some procedures, called **macros**, directly from the Macros dialog box, which is available in many of the Office 2000 applications. Other procedures, called **event procedures**, are not run from the Macros dialog box; rather, these procedures run in response to specific actions you perform on an object. Those actions—such as opening a document, activating a worksheet, or clicking a command button—are called **events**.

In Excel, the Macros dialog box is called the Macro dialog box. In Access, you run a macro from either the Macro window or the Database window.

You also can create procedures that are neither macros nor event procedures. Such procedures run in response to being called, or executed, by macros or event procedures.

You can use the Visual Basic Editor, which is available in the Office 2000 applications and in many other VBA-enabled applications, to create new procedures and edit existing ones.

The Visual Basic Editor

To open the Visual Basic Editor, click Tools on the host application's menu bar, point to Macro, and then click Visual Basic Editor. The **host application** is the application in which you are working. Figure 1-1, for example, shows the Visual Basic Editor opened in the host application Microsoft Excel.

name of the
open file

indicates that
you are
working in the
Visual Basic
Editor

main window

Project Explorer
window

View Code
button

View Object
button

Toggle Folders
button

properties

default values

Properties
window

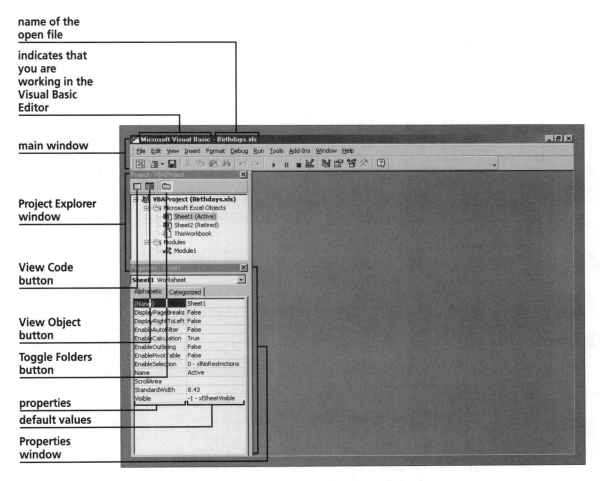

Figure 1-1: The Visual Basic Editor opened in Microsoft Excel

 tip

You also can open the Visual Basic Editor by pressing Alt+F11.

As Figure 1-1 indicates, the Visual Basic Editor contains three separate windows: the main window, the Project Explorer window, and the Properties window. The

Visual Basic Editor will have a similar interface in every application in which it is contained; only the contents of the windows will vary from application to application.

The **main window**, at the top of the screen, contains the title bar, the menu bar, and the Standard toolbar. The text Microsoft Visual Basic – Birthdays.xls, which appears in the title bar, indicates that you are working in the Visual Basic Editor and that the open file is named Birthdays.xls.

> If the Standard toolbar is not displayed in the main window upon opening the Visual Basic Editor, click View on the Visual Basic Editor menu bar, point to Toolbars, and then click Standard.

The **Project Explorer window** displays a list of the open projects and their components. The Project Explorer window shown in Figure 1-1 indicates that one project, named VBAProject, is open. The Birthdays.xls text that appears in parentheses after the project name is the name of the file that contains the project.

Notice that the VBAProject project contains a Microsoft Excel Objects folder and a Modules folder. The Microsoft Excel Objects folder contains two Worksheet objects, named Sheet1 (Active) and Sheet2 (Retired), and one ThisWorkbook object, which represents the current Workbook object. The Modules folder contains one Module object named Module1. A **Module object** is simply a container that stores macros and other procedures that are not associated with any specific object in the project.

> As you will learn in this tutorial's Application lessons, event procedures are contained in the objects to which they pertain. For example, a Workbook object's Open event procedure is contained in the Workbook object itself.

> If the Project Explorer window is not displayed upon opening the Visual Basic Editor, click View on the Visual Basic Editor menu bar and then click Project Explorer. You also can click the Project Explorer button 🖾 on the Visual Basic Editor's Standard toolbar, or you can press Ctrl+R.

As you will learn in Tutorial 2, almost every part of an application is considered an object in VBA. Examples of VBA objects include modules; Excel workbooks, worksheets, and charts; Word documents and paragraphs; PowerPoint slides; and Access reports. Text boxes, check boxes, command buttons, and the dialog boxes in which they are contained also are treated as objects.

Every VBA object has a set of characteristics, called **properties**, associated with it that control the object's appearance and behavior. These properties, along with their values, are listed in the **Properties window**. Although each property is assigned a default value, you can use the Properties window to change to a different value. For example, Figure 1-1 shows that the current value of the Sheet1 (Active) worksheet's EnableCalculation property is True, which tells Excel to automatically recalculate the worksheet when necessary. Changing the EnableCalculation property to False in the Properties window tells Excel to recalculate the worksheet only at the user's request.

> **tip**
>
> If the Properties window is not displayed upon opening the Visual Basic Editor, click View on the Visual Basic Editor menu bar, and then click Properties Window. You also can click the Properties Window button 🔲 on the Visual Basic Editor's Standard toolbar, or you can press the F4 key.

In addition to the list of open projects and their components, notice in Figure 1-1 that the Project Explorer window also contains the View Code, View Object, and Toggle Folders buttons. The **Toggle Folders** button 🔲 controls the display of the folders in the Project Explorer window. The default view displays the folders, as well as the names of the objects contained within the folders. If you click 🔲 off, only the names of the objects contained within the folders, not the folders themselves, are displayed. Both options are shown in Figure 1-2.

Toggle Folders button toggled on

Toggle Folders button toggled off

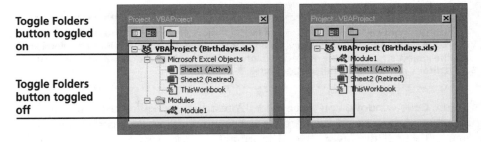

Figure 1-2: Project Explorer window with the Toggle Folders button toggled on and off

The Project Explorer window operates similarly to the Windows Explorer window in that a plus sign next to a folder indicates that the folder contains objects whose names are not displayed currently, and a minus sign indicates that you are viewing the names of all of the objects included in the folder. See Figure 1-3.

indicates that you are viewing all of the folders contents

indicates that the folder contains objects whose names are not currently displayed

View Code button

View Object button

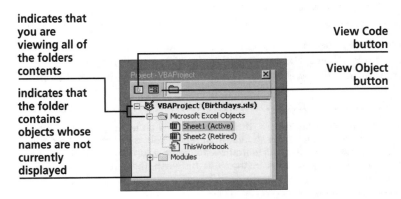

Figure 1-3: Project Explorer window showing minus and plus signs

You can use the **View Object** button ▣ to view the object whose name is selected in the Project Explorer window. For example, to display the Retired worksheet in Excel, you simply click Sheet2 (Retired) in the Project Explorer window and then click ▣.

> **tip**
> You also can right-click the object's name in the Project Explorer window and then click View Object on the shortcut menu to view an object. Additionally, you can click the object's name in the Project Explorer window, then click View on the Visual Basic Editor's menu bar, and then click Object.

When an object is selected in the Project Explorer window, you can use the **View Code** button ▣ to open its Code window. To open the Module1 object's Code window, for example, you click Module1 in the Project Explorer window and then click ▣.

> **tip**
> You also can right-click the object's name in the Project Explorer window and then click View Code on the shortcut menu to view an object's Code window. Additionally, you can click the object's name in the Project Explorer window, then click View on the Visual Basic Editor's menu bar, and then click Code.

In the **Code window**, you enter the VBA instructions, called **code**, that instruct a procedure on how to perform a task. For example, the VBA instructions shown in Figure 1-4 will display a "Good morning!" message when the MorningMsg procedure is run.

Notice that the Code window's title bar shows the name of both the current file (Birthdays.xls) and the current object (Module1). The title bar also contains the word (Code), which identifies the window as the Code window.

> **tip**
> When the Code window is maximized, the name of both the current file and the current object, as well as the word (Code), will appear in the Visual Basic Editor's title bar. You can refer to Figure 1-7 to see how a maximized Code window looks.

You enter your VBA instructions between the Public Sub and End Sub lines in the Code window. The Public Sub line denotes the beginning of the procedure whose name follows the word Sub, and the End Sub line marks the end of the procedure.

> **tip**
> As you will learn in the Application lessons, if the procedure is an event procedure, you enter your VBA instructions between the Private Sub and End Sub lines in the Code window. In the Access lesson, you also will learn how to create a function procedure. In a function procedure, you enter your VBA instructions between the Public Function and End Function lines.

identifies this
window as the
Code window

current
module's name

current file's
name

Object list box

Procedure list
box

Code window

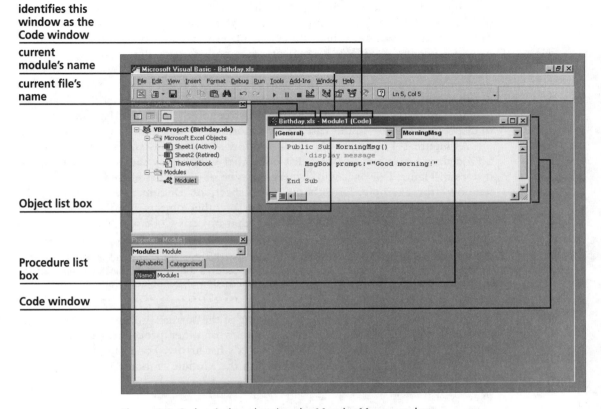

Figure 1-4: Code window showing the MorningMsg procedure

`Public`, `Sub`, and `End` are keywords in VBA. A **keyword** is a word that has a special meaning in a programming language. For example, the keyword `Sub`, which specifies the procedure's type, is an abbreviation of the term *sub procedure*. In programming terminology, a **sub procedure** refers to a block of code that performs a specific task but does not return a value. You also can create function procedures in VBA. **Function procedures**, which are designated by the keyword `Function`, are procedures that *can* return a value. You will learn how to create a function procedure in this tutorial's Access lesson.

The keywords `Public` and `Private` indicate the procedure's **scope**, which determines which objects can use the procedure. A `Public` scope indicates that the procedure can be used by all objects within the project. A `Private` scope, on the other hand, indicates that the procedure can be used only by the object in which the procedure is contained. An object's event procedures, for example, have a `Private` scope, indicating that they can be used only by the object.

The keyword `End` indicates the end of something. When combined with the keyword `Sub`, it indicates the end of a sub procedure. When combined with the keyword `Function`, it indicates the end of a function procedure.

Notice that the MorningMsg procedure shown in Figure 1-4 contains two lines of VBA code: `'display message` and `MsgBox prompt:="Good morning!"`. The `'display message` line is a **comment**. Programmers use comments to internally document a procedure. Comments serve both as reminders to the programmer and as explanatory information for anyone reading the procedure. You create a comment in VBA simply by typing an apostrophe (`'`) before the text you want treated as a comment; VBA will ignore everything after the apostrophe on that line. The `MsgBox prompt:="Good morning!"` instruction uses VBA's MsgBox statement to display a message—in this case, "Good morning!"—in a dialog box on the screen.

As Figure 1-4 indicates, the Code window also contains an Object list box and a Procedure list box. The **Object list box** either will display the word (General), as it does in Figure 1-4, or it will display the type of object associated with the Code window (for example, Workbook, Worksheet, or Document). By clicking the Object box's list arrow, you display a list of other objects from which you can select. When you select a different object, that object's Code window opens.

> Procedures that are not associated with any specific object are entered in the General section of a Module object's Code window. Procedures that are not associated with any of an object's events are entered in the General section of the object's Code window.

The **Procedure list box** displays the name of the current procedure—in this case, it displays MorningMsg. To view the names of other procedures stored in the Module object, you click the Procedure box's list arrow. For example, Figure 1-5 shows the listing of procedures contained in the Module1 module.

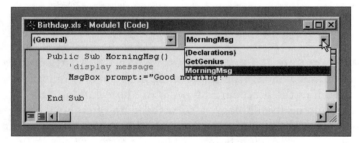

Figure 1-5: Listing of procedures contained in the Module1 module

Sometimes scroll bars will appear on the Procedure list box to indicate that not all of the procedures are currently displayed. In those cases, you would need to scroll the list box to see the remaining procedures. To select another procedure, you simply click the one you want in the list. For example, Figure 1-6 shows the Code window for the Module object's GetGenius procedure. Notice that the Procedure list box now shows that the GetGenius procedure is the current procedure.

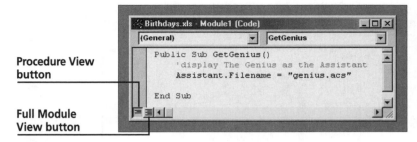

Procedure View button

Full Module View button

Figure 1-6: Code window showing the GetGenius procedure

The GetGenius procedure contains a comment and a VBA instruction that sets the Assistant object's FileName property. In VBA the **Assistant object** represents the Office Assistant, and its **FileName property** controls the character used to display the Office Assistant. The GetGenius procedure sets the FileName property to "genius.acs", which is the name of the file that contains the Office Assistant character named The Genius.

As Figure 1-6 indicates, in addition to the Object and Procedure list boxes, the Code window also contains the Procedure View and Full Module View buttons; only one of these buttons can be selected at a time. When the **Procedure View** button 🔲 is selected, as it is in Figures 1-4 through 1-6, each procedure associated with the selected object appears in its own Code window. When the **Full Module View** button 🔲 is selected, all of the current object's code appears as a single listing in the Code window. Figure 1-7 on the next page shows the Module1 module's maximized Code window with the Full Module View button selected.

When an object's Code window is maximized, as it is in Figure 1-7, the object's name (in this case, Module1) and the word (Code) appear in the Visual Basic Editor's title bar; otherwise, that information appears in the Code window's title bar.

When the Full Module View button 🔲 is selected, notice that the Code window displays both the MorningMsg and GetGenius procedures. Whether you choose to display the Code window in procedure view or in full module view is really a matter of personal preference. Some programmers find it helpful to see all of an object's code at the same time, while others find the display of so much information to be confusing.

If you are viewing the Code window in full module view, as you are in Figure 1-7, notice that the Procedure list box displays the name of only the current procedure, which is the procedure that contains the insertion point. In Figure 1-7 the insertion point is located in the MorningMsg procedure, so MorningMsg appears in the Code window's Procedure list box. If you move the insertion point somewhere within the GetGenius procedure, the Code window's Procedure list box will display GetGenius.

Now that you are familiar with the components of the Visual Basic Editor, you will learn how to enter instructions in the Code window.

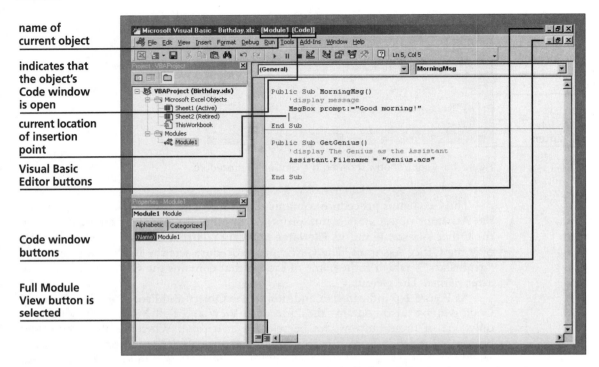

name of
current object

indicates that
the object's
Code window
is open

current location
of insertion
point

Visual Basic
Editor buttons

Code window
buttons

Full Module
View button is
selected

Figure 1-7: Maximized Code window with the Full Module View button selected

Entering Instructions in the Code Window

You can enter VBA instructions into a Code window by directly typing each instruction in its entirety—for example, you can type `Assistant.FileName = "genius.acs"`—or the Visual Basic Editor can assist you in entering the instructions. The Visual Basic Editor can provide assistance in two ways: by displaying a listing of an object's properties and methods after you type the object's name followed by a period in the Code window, and by displaying the syntax, or programming language rules, of a command as you are entering it in the Code window. As you learned earlier, a property is a characteristic of an object, and it controls the appearance and behavior of the object. A **method**, on the other hand, is a predefined VBA procedure, which is simply a procedure that the Microsoft programmers have already coded for you. A method tells an object to perform an action on its own—in other words, without user intervention. For example, the Print method tells an object to print itself and the Open method tells an object to open itself.

If your preference is to have the Visual Basic Editor assist you when entering instructions, you need to select both the Auto List Members and Auto Quick Info check boxes, which are located on the Editor tab in the Visual Basic Editor's Options dialog box. You open the Options dialog box by clicking Tools on the Visual Basic Editor menu bar, and then clicking Options. Figure 1-8 shows the Options dialog box.

when selected,
these options
tell the Visual
Basic Editor to
assist you in
entering your
VBA
instructions

this option
controls
whether the
Code window
opens in Full
Module View
or in Procedure
View

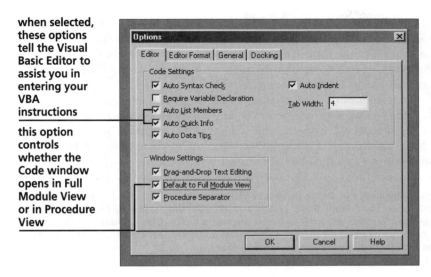

Figure 1-8: Options dialog box

When the **Auto List Members** check box is selected, the Visual Basic Editor will display an object's members—in other words, its properties and methods—after you type the object's name followed by a period. To use the member list to enter the `Assistant.FileName = "genius.acs"` instruction, for example, type the word `assistant` followed by a period(`.`). After you type the period, the Visual Basic Editor displays the properties and methods associated with the Assistant object, as shown in Figure 1-9.

method icon

property icons

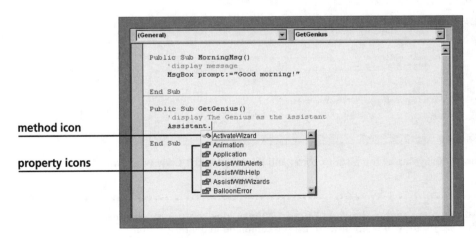

Figure 1-9: Member list for the Assistant object

The properties (designated by the icon) and methods (designated by the icon) are listed in alphabetical order, and the list contains a scroll bar, which indicates that not all of the members can be viewed at the same time. To select the FileName property, scroll down the list until you see the word FileName; then click FileName in the list. After selecting FileName in the list, type an equal sign followed by the name of the character file enclosed in quotation marks (`="genius.acs"`), then press the Enter key to move to the next line in the Code window. The period between the object (`Assistant`) and its property (`FileName`) is known as the **dot member selection operator** and it indicates that the FileName property is a member of the Assistant object.

> **tip**
>
> To find the names of the Office Assistant character files that come with Microsoft Office 2000, open the Visual Basic Editor and display the FileName property's Help screen. The character files are located in the Microsoft Office\Office folder on either the local hard drive or the network drive. To download additional assistants, visit Microsoft's Web site at http://officeupdate.microsoft.com/index.htm.

When the **Auto Quick Info** check box is selected on the Editor tab of the Options dialog box, the Visual Basic Editor displays the syntax of the command you are typing in the Code window. The term **syntax** refers to the rules of a programming language—in this case, they are the VBA rules you must follow in order to use the command. To use the Auto Quick Info option to enter the `MsgBox prompt:="Good morning!"` instruction in the Code window, type `msgbox` followed by a space. The Visual Basic Editor then displays the syntax of the MsgBox command, as shown in Figure 1-10.

Figure 1-10: Syntax of the MsgBox command displayed in the Code window

> **tip**
>
> Although the syntax shown in Figure 1-10 may look confusing right now, it won't look that way after you learn how to use the command in a later tutorial.

According to the syntax, you can include five items of information, called **arguments**, in the MsgBox command. The names of the arguments are Prompt, Buttons, Title, HelpFile, and Context. Only the Prompt argument, where you enter the message you want the dialog box to display, is required. The other four arguments are optional, as indicated by the square brackets ([]) in the syntax.

Arguments that have names are called, more specifically, named arguments.

To have the MsgBox command display the "Good morning!" message, type `prompt` followed by a colon and an equal sign (:=); then type `"Good morning!"`. You must use the := operator to separate the argument's name (Prompt) from the argument's value ("Good morning!"). The quotation marks around the "Good morning!" message identify the message as a string literal constant. You will learn about string literal constants in Tutorial 4. The quotation marks will not appear when the message is displayed in the dialog box.

Having the Visual Basic Editor display a command's syntax as you are typing is helpful in situations where you know how to use the command, but cannot remember its arguments. However, the syntax display may not give you enough information if you don't already know how to use the command. In those cases, you may need to display the command's Help screen. You can do so using the Help menu, or you can type the command in the Code window and then press the F1 key.

In addition to the Auto List Members and Auto Quick Info check boxes, the Editor tab on the Options dialog box also contains the Default to Full Module View check box. When this check box is selected, as it is in Figure 1-8, the Code window opens in full module view and displays all of the selected object's code. If the Default to Full Module View check box is not selected, the Code window opens in procedure view, in which case it displays only the selected object's current procedure. As mentioned earlier, the view you choose—full module or procedure—is a matter of personal preference. When you install Microsoft Office 2000, the Default to Full Module View check box is selected automatically.

After entering VBA instructions into a Code window, you need to save the instructions and then test them to see if they are working correctly.

Saving a Procedure

You save a VBA procedure by saving the file that contains the procedure. For example, you can save the MorningMsg and GetGenius procedures shown in Figure 1-7 by saving the Excel workbook Birthdays.xls, which contains both procedures. You can save a file while working in the Visual Basic Editor, or you can return to the host application to save the file. For example, you can use either the Visual Basic Editor or Microsoft Excel to save the Birthdays.xls file. You can use the Save command on the File menu, the Save button 🔲 on the Standard toolbar, or the key combination Ctrl+S to save the file.

tip

It is a good practice to save a file every 10 to 15 minutes so you won't lose a lot of work if the computer loses power. If you are using the host application to save a file and more than one project is open, you must activate the project you want to save before saving the file. If you are using the Visual Basic Editor to save a file and more than one project is open, you must select the appropriate project name in the Visual Basic Editor before saving the file.

After saving a procedure, you then run it to verify that it is working correctly.

Running a Procedure

The only way to verify that a procedure is working correctly is to run it. When you run a procedure, VBA executes the instructions contained within the procedure. As you will learn in this tutorial's Application lessons, you can run a procedure from either the Visual Basic Editor or the host application. While in the Visual Basic Editor, you can use either the Run menu or the Tools menu to run a procedure; you also can click the Run *procedureType* button on the Standard toolbar or you can press the F5 key. The method you use to run a procedure from the host application depends on the type of procedure being run. For example, macros are run using either the host application's Tools menu or the key combination Alt+F8. (In Access, you use the Run button 🔳 to run a macro.) Event procedures, on the other hand, run automatically in response to the occurrence of an event, such as the opening of a document or the clicking of a command button.

When you are sure that a procedure is working correctly, you should print a copy of the procedure for documentation purposes.

Printing a Procedure

You should always provide both internal and external documentation for the procedures you create. As you learned earlier, you document a procedure internally by entering comments in the Code window. You provide external documentation by printing a copy of the procedure's code; you can do so by right-clicking the project's name in the Project Explorer window and then clicking Print on the shortcut menu. You also can use the Print command on the Visual Basic Editor's File menu, or you can press Ctrl+P. Either of these methods will display a Print dialog box similar to the one shown in Figure 1-11.

prints only the code selected in the Code window

prints only the current object's code

prints the code for the entire project

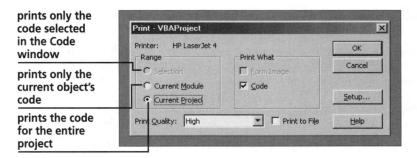

Figure 1-11: Print dialog box

When the Code check box is selected in the Print What section, as it is in Figure 1-11, the Visual Basic Editor prints the code for the range selected in the Range section of the dialog box. Notice that the Range section contains three option buttons: Selection, Current Module, and Current Project. You use the Current Module option button to print the code for the current object only. You could use this option, for example, to print just the Module1 object's code; or, you could use it to print only the Retired Worksheet object's code. The Current Module option button will be available in the Print dialog box only if the Code window is the active window—in other words, only if it contains the insertion point.

You use the Current Project option button to print the code for the entire project. You use the Selection option button to print either a specific procedure's code—for example, just the GetGenius procedure's code—or only a portion of the code shown in the Code window. Notice that the Selection option button shown in Figure 1-11 is dimmed. The Selection option button will be available only if you select the code you want to print before opening the Print dialog box.

You now have completed Tutorial 1's Concept Lesson. You can either take a break or complete the end-of-lesson questions and exercises before moving on to the next lesson.

 # S U M M A R Y

To open the Visual Basic Editor:

■ Click Tools on the host application's menu bar, point to Macro, and then click Visual Basic Editor. You also can press Alt+F11.

To open the Project Explorer window, which contains a listing of the open projects and their components:

■ Click View on the Visual Basic Editor menu bar and then click Project Explorer. You also can click the Project Explorer button 📄 on the Visual Basic Editor's Standard toolbar, or you can press Ctrl+R.

To open the Properties window, which contains a listing of properties along with their default values:

■ Click View on the Visual Basic Editor menu bar, and then click Properties Window. You also can click the Properties Window button ▣ on the Visual Basic Editor's Standard toolbar, or you can press the F4 key.

To view the Standard toolbar in the Visual Basic Editor main window:

■ Click View on the Visual Basic Editor menu bar, point to Toolbars, and then click Standard.

To control the display of the items in the Project Explorer window:

■ Click the Toggle Folders button ▣, as well as the minus and plus signs, in the Project Explorer window.

To display an object:

■ Click the object's name in the Project Explorer window and then click the View Object button ▣. You also can right-click the object's name in the Project Explorer window and then click View Object on the shortcut menu. Additionally, you can click the object's name in the Project Explorer window, then click View on the Visual Basic Editor menu bar, and then click Object.

To open an object's Code window:

■ Click the object's name in the Project Explorer window and then click the View Code button ▣. You also can right-click the object's name in the Project Explorer window and then click View Code on the shortcut menu. Additionally, you can click the object's name in the Project Explorer window, then click View on the Visual Basic Editor menu bar, and then click Code.

To have the Visual Basic Editor assist you when entering instructions in the Code window:

■ Click Tools on the Visual Basic Editor menu bar and then click Options. When the Options dialog box appears, select the Auto List Members check box and the Auto Quick Info check box, which are located on the Editor tab.

To document a procedure:

■ Provide internal documentation by entering comments in the Code window. You enter a comment by beginning the text with an apostrophe ('). VBA ignores everything after the apostrophe on that line.

■ Provide external documentation by printing a copy of the procedure's code.

To display each procedure in a separate Code window:

■ Click the Procedure View button ▤ in the Code window.

■ To have the Visual Basic Editor default to procedure view, click Tools on the menu bar, then click Options to open the Options dialog box. Click the Editor tab, if necessary, and then click the Default to Full Module View check box to deselect it.

To display an object's code as a single listing in the Code window:

■ Click the Full Module View button ▤ in the Code window.

■ To have the Visual Basic Editor default to full module view, click Tools on the menu bar, then click Options to open the Options dialog box. Click the Editor tab, if necessary, and then click the Default to Full Module View check box to select it.

To save a procedure:

■ You save a procedure by saving the file that contains the procedure. You can save a file from either the Visual Basic Editor or the host application. You can do so using the Save command on the File menu, the Save button ▣ on the Standard toolbar, or by pressing Ctrl+S.

To run a procedure in order to verify the accuracy of its instructions:

■ While in the Visual Basic Editor, you can use either the Run menu or the Tools menu to run a procedure; you also can use the Run *procedureType* button on the Standard toolbar or you can use the F5 key.

■ While in the host application, you can use either the Tools menu or Alt+F8 to run a macro procedure. You run an event procedure by causing the event to occur.

To print a procedure:

■ Display the Print dialog box by using the Print command on the Visual Basic Editor's File menu, or by pressing Ctrl+P, or by right-clicking the object's name in the Project Explorer window and then clicking Print on the shortcut menu.

■ Select the Code check box in the Print What section of the Print dialog box. To print only the current object's code, select the Current Module option button in the Range section. (The Code window must be the active window in order for the Current Module option button to be available in the Print dialog box.) To print the entire project's code, select the Current Project option button. To print a selection of code, select the code that you want to print before you display the Print dialog box, then select the Selection option button, if necessary.

R E V I E W   Q U E S T I O N S

Match each term shown in the box below to its correct definition. Write the term's letter on the line to the left of its definition.

A	Auto List Members check box	N	Object list box
B	Auto Quick Info check box	O	procedure
C	code	P	Procedure list box
D	Code window	Q	Procedure View button
E	comment	R	Project Explorer window
F	dot member selection operator	S	Properties window
G	event	T	property
H	Full Module View button	U	syntax
I	host application	V	Toggle Folders button
J	macro	W	View Code button
K	main window	X	View Object button
L	method	Y	Visual Basic Editor
M	Module object		

1 _____ The editor in which you create VBA procedures.

2 _____ The application that contains the Visual Basic Editor and is the application in which you are working.

3 _____ A container that stores procedures not associated with any specific object in the project.

4 _____ A characteristic of an object that controls the object's appearance and behavior.

5 _____ The VBA instructions entered into a Code window.

6 _____ A procedure that can be run from the Macros dialog box.

7 _____ When this is selected in the Code window, the Code window displays all of an object's code.

8 _____ When this is selected in the Options dialog box, it displays an object's member list when you type the object's name followed by a period.

9 _____ The rules of a programming language.

10 _____ Contains the title bar, menu bar, and Standard toolbar.

11 _____ The window in which you enter your VBA instructions.

12 _____ When selected in the Options dialog box, it displays the syntax of the current command in the Code window.

13 _____ A block of instructions that performs a task.

14 _____ The part of the Code window that displays the name of the current object and also allows you to select a different object.

15 _____ Provides internal documentation for a procedure.

16 _____ You can use this button to view the Code window for the object whose name is selected in the Project Explorer window.

17 _____ This button controls the display of the folders in the Project Explorer window.

18 _____ The part of the Code window that displays the name of the current procedure and also allows you to select a different procedure.

19 _____ When selected in the Code window, only one procedure appears in the Code window.

20 _____ This window displays the characteristics of the object whose name is selected in the Project Explorer window.

21 _____ This window lists the open projects and their components.

22 _____ You can use this button to view the object whose name is selected in the Project Explorer window.

23 _____ A predefined VBA procedure that tells an object to perform an action on its own.

24 _____ The period between an object's name and its property.

25 _____ The type of procedure that runs in response to an action, such as opening a workbook.

E X E R C I S E S

1. Refer to Figure 1-12, which shows the Visual Basic Editor opened in Microsoft Word. Identify the following Visual Basic Editor components by writing the appropriate letter on the line to the left of the component.

_____ Code window	_____ Procedure list box
_____ Code window's Close button	_____ Procedure View button
_____ Dot member selection operator	_____ Project Explorer window
_____ Full Module View button	_____ Properties window
_____ Method icon	_____ Property icon
_____ Object list box	_____ Visual Basic Editor's Close button

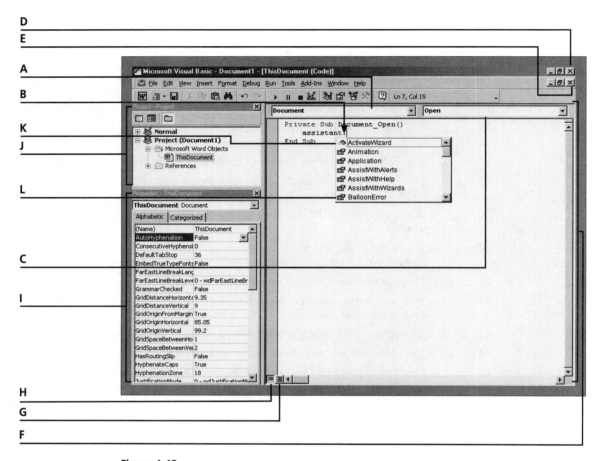

D
E
A
B
K
J
L
C
I
H
G
F

Figure 1-12

2. In the `Assistant.Left = 216` instruction, what is the period called and what does the name signify?

3. Explain how you document a procedure both internally and externally.

4. In this lesson, you learned about projects, modules, procedures, and VBA instructions. Figure 1-13 shows the hierarchy of a project. Based on what you learned in this lesson:
a. Which rectangles represent modules (A, B, or C)?
b. Which rectangles represent procedures (A, B, or C)?
c. Which rectangles represent VBA instructions (A, B, or C)?

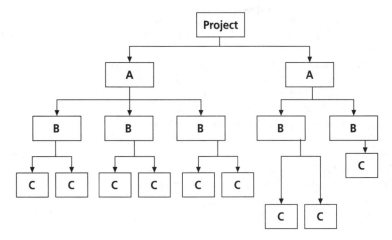

Figure 1-13

5. You can use the Assistant object's Visible property to show and hide the Office Assistant. The property can be set to either the keyword `True` or the keyword `False`. Write the VBA instruction that will show the Office Assistant.

Exercise 6 is a Discovery Exercise. Discovery Exercises, which may include topics that are not covered in this lesson, allow you to "discover" the solutions to problems on your own.

discovery ▶ 6. Visit the Microsoft Web site at www.microsoft.com. Look for some information on Visual Basic for Applications. Write a one-page summary of your findings.

You also can use VBA in PowerPoint to create procedures that enhance your presentations. Exercise 7 allows you to apply this tutorial's programming concept in a PowerPoint presentation.

powerpoint 7. In this exercise, you will create a procedure that displays your name in a message box on the screen.
    a. Start PowerPoint. Open the T1-PP-E7 (T1-PP-E7.ppt) file, which is located in the Tut01\Concept folder on your Data Disk. Click the Enable Macros button, if necessary, then save the file as T1-PP-E7D.
    b. Click Tools on the menu bar, point to Macro, then click Visual Basic Editor.
    c. Open the Project Explorer window, if necessary, and view the contents of the Modules folder. Right-click Module1 in the Modules folder, then click View Code on the shortcut menu. Use the Code window's Procedure box to view the DisplayName procedure.

d. In the DisplayName procedure, press the Tab key to indent the insertion point, then enter a MsgBox statement that will display your name in a message box on the screen.

e. Save and run the procedure. (If the procedure does not run correctly, click the OK button to remove the error dialog box, then click the Reset button ■ on the Visual Basic Editor's Standard toolbar. Save and then run the procedure again.)

f. When the DisplayName procedure displays your name in a message box, click the OK button to close the message box, then close the presentation.

A procedure is good only if it works. Errors in programming code can cause a procedure to run incorrectly. Therefore, a programmer needs to know how to locate and fix any errors in his or her code. Exercise 8 is a Debugging Exercise. Debugging Exercises allow you to practice recognizing and solving errors in code.

debugging **8.** What is wrong with the following VBA instruction?

```
Asistant.FileName = 'genius.acs'
```

Excel Lesson

Using the Visual Basic Editor in Excel

case ▶ Each morning Jasmine Webber, the office manager at Paradise Electronics, opens an Excel workbook that contains the tasks she needs to complete during the week. Jasmine has decided to create two procedures for this workbook. The first procedure will automatically display "Good morning!" in a dialog box when the workbook is opened. This procedure will be an event procedure because it will need to run in response to the action of Jasmine opening the workbook. The second procedure will allow Jasmine to display the Office Assistant and change its character from the default—Clippit—to another of her favorite characters—The Genius. Jasmine will make this procedure a macro so that she can run the procedure from the Macro dialog box in Excel whenever she chooses to do so.

Using the Visual Basic Editor in Microsoft Excel

As you learned in the Concept lesson, you can use VBA to customize an application to fit your needs. You do so by creating a procedure, which is simply a series of VBA instructions grouped together as a single unit for the purpose of performing a specific task. Recall that you create a procedure using the Visual Basic Editor.

To open the Visual Basic Editor in Excel:

1 Start Microsoft Excel. Open the **T1-EX-1** (T1-EX-1.xls) workbook, which is located in the Tut01\Excel folder on your Data Disk, and then save the workbook as **ToDo**. The workbook, along with the Clippit Office Assistant, appears on the screen. See Figure 1-14.

workbook
filename

your toolbars
might be
different

Clippit Office
Assistant (your
assistant, as
well as its
location, might
be different)

worksheet
name

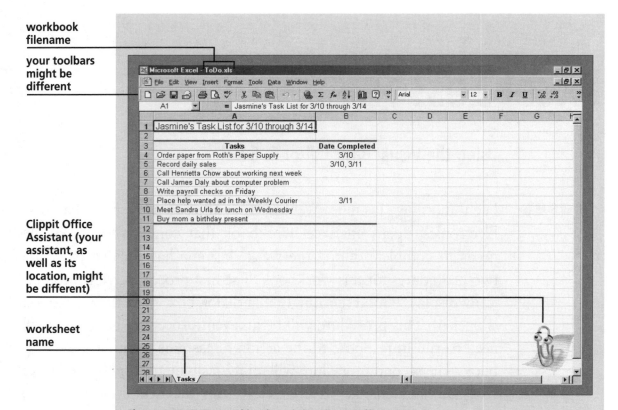

Figure 1-14: ToDo workbook and the Clippit Office Assistant

HELP? If the Office Assistant does not appear on your screen, click Help on the menu bar, then click Show the Office Assistant.

HELP? If the Office Assistant character is not Clippit, click the Office Assistant, then click Options in the Office Assistant's balloon. Click the Gallery tab on the Office Assistant dialog box, then use the Next or Back button to scroll through the different assistants. When you locate the Clippit assistant, click the OK button to close the dialog box.

Before opening the Visual Basic Editor, turn the Office Assistant feature off.

2 Click the **Office Assistant**, then click **Options** in the Office Assistant's balloon. Click the **Options** tab on the Office Assistant dialog box, if necessary, then click the **Use the Office Assistant** check box to deselect it. Click the **OK** button to close the Office Assistant dialog box. The Office Assistant is removed from the screen.

3 Click **Tools** on the menu bar, point to **Macro**, and then click **Visual Basic Editor** to open the Visual Basic Editor. The Visual Basic Editor appears, as shown in Figure 1-15.

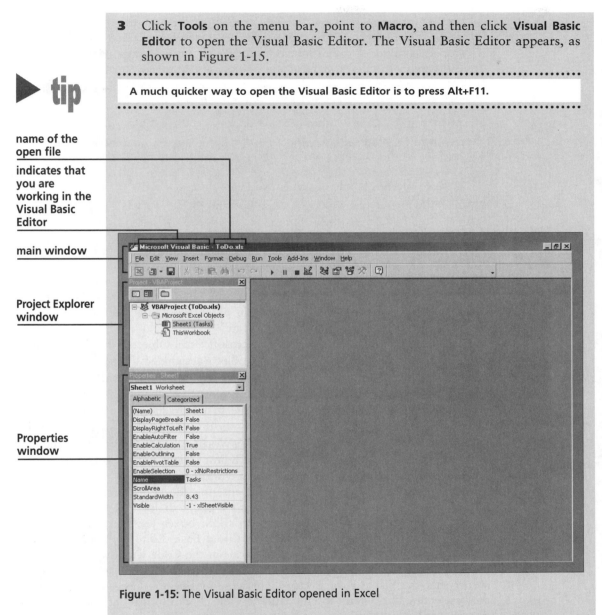

> tip
>
> A much quicker way to open the Visual Basic Editor is to press Alt+F11.

name of the open file

indicates that you are working in the Visual Basic Editor

main window

Project Explorer window

Properties window

Figure 1-15: The Visual Basic Editor opened in Excel

HELP? If necessary, you can use the mouse to drag the borders of the Project Explorer and Properties windows until the windows are the desired size.

HELP? If the Project Explorer window is not displayed, click View on the Visual Basic Editor menu bar and then click Project Explorer.

HELP? Although you won't need the Properties window in this lesson, you can display it by clicking View on the Visual Basic Editor menu bar, and then clicking Properties Window. If no properties appear in the Properties window, click ThisWorkbook in the Project Explorer window, and then click Sheet1 (Tasks).

HELP? If the Standard toolbar is not displayed, click View on the Visual Basic Editor menu bar, point to Toolbars, and then click Standard.

HELP? If the Code window is displayed, click its Close button ⊠ to close it.

HELP? If the Immediate window is displayed, click its Close button ⊠ to close it.

If the Properties window is open, you can close it.

4 Click the Properties window's **Close** button ⊠.

The text, Microsoft Visual Basic – ToDo.xls, that appears in the main window's title bar indicates that you are working in the Visual Basic Editor and that the name of the current file is ToDo.xls. The Project Explorer window shows that only one project (designated by the 🐝 icon) is open; the name of the project is VBAProject. The ToDo.xls that appears in parentheses after the project name is the name of the file that contains the project.

The VBAProject project contains a Microsoft Excel Objects folder that contains two Microsoft Excel objects: a Worksheet object (designated by the 🏢 icon) and a Workbook object (designated by the 📄 icon). You will notice that Sheet1 (Tasks) appears to the right of the 🏢 icon in the Project Explorer window. Sheet1 is the name the Visual Basic Editor assigns to the first worksheet in a workbook. The name enclosed in parentheses after Sheet1—in this case, Tasks—is the name that appears on the worksheet's tab in Excel. ThisWorkbook, which appears to the right of the 📄 icon, is the name the Visual Basic Editor assigns to the workbook itself; in this case, ThisWorkbook refers to the ToDo workbook.

Before opening a Code window and entering the appropriate VBA instructions, you will open the Visual Basic Editor's Options dialog box to verify that the Auto List Members and Auto Quick Info check boxes are selected. Recall that when these check boxes are selected, the Visual Basic Editor provides assistance while you are entering your VBA instructions in the Code window. You also will deselect the Default to Full Module View check box in the Options dialog box to ensure that the Visual Basic Editor Code window opens in procedure view. (You are deselecting the Default to Full Module View check box so that your Code windows agree with the ones in this book, which are displayed in procedure view.)

To view the status of the Options dialog box:

1 Click **Tools** on the menu bar, and then click **Options** to open the Options dialog box. Click the **Editor** tab in the Options dialog box, if necessary.

2   Click the **Auto List Members** and **Auto Quick Info** check boxes to select these options, if necessary. Click the **Default to Full Module View** check box to deselect it, if necessary. See Figure 1-16.

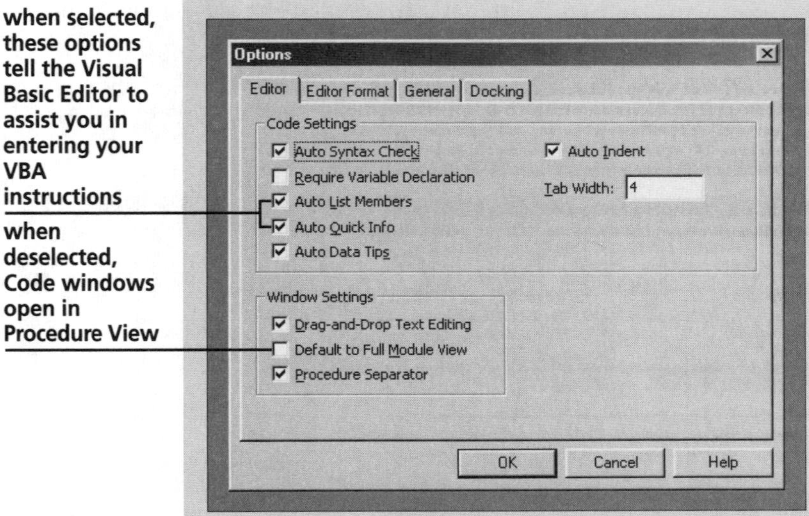

when selected, these options tell the Visual Basic Editor to assist you in entering your VBA instructions

when deselected, Code windows open in Procedure View

Figure 1-16: Options dialog box

3   Click the **OK** button to close the Options dialog box.

The first procedure you will code is the ToDo workbook's Open event procedure, which should display the message "Good morning!" in a dialog box.

Coding the Workbook Object's Open Event Procedure

As you learned in the Concept lesson, an event procedure runs in response to an action performed on an object by the user. A workbook's **Open event procedure**, for example, runs automatically when the user opens the workbook. You will code the Open event procedure so that it displays the message "Good morning!" in a dialog box.

To code the workbook's Open event procedure:

1   Right-click **ThisWorkbook** in the Project Explorer window. Recall that the ThisWorkbook object represents the workbook itself. Click **View Code** on the shortcut menu.

Notice that (General) appears in the Code window's Object list box and (Declarations) appears in its Procedure list box. This section of the Code window is referred to as the General Declarations section. Every object has its own **General Declarations section**, where you can enter code that is not associated with any of the object's events. For this lesson, you do not need to concern yourself with this section.

2   Click the **Object box list arrow**, then click **Workbook** in the list. The Workbook object's Open event procedure appears in the Code window, as shown in Figure 1-17.

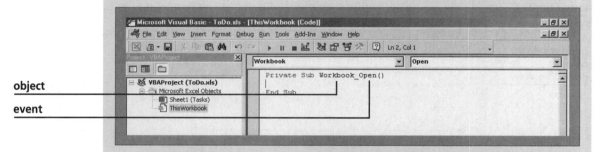

object

event

Figure 1-17: Code window showing the Workbook object's Open event procedure

HELP? If the Code window is not maximized, click its Maximize button ☐.

To help you follow the syntax, or rules of its language, VBA provides you with a **code template** for the procedure. Because the procedure is an event procedure, the code template begins with the keywords Private Sub followed by the name of the object, an underscore, the name of the event and, in this case, an empty set of parentheses. As you learned in the Concept lesson, the keyword Sub is an abbreviation of the term *sub procedure*, which refers to a block of code that performs a specific task but does not return a value. The keyword Private indicates that the event procedure can be used only by the object in which it is contained; in this case, the Open event procedure can be used only by the Workbook object. The code template ends with the keywords End Sub.

· ·

Some event procedures have arguments within the parentheses.

· ·

If you are using a color monitor, you will notice that Private Sub and End Sub appear in a different color from both the object's name and the name of the event. The Visual Basic Editor displays keywords in a different color to help you quickly identify these elements in the Code window. In this case, the color-coding helps you easily locate the beginning and end of the event procedure.

In the Open event procedure, you will enter a comment that describes the purpose of the procedure. Then you will enter the VBA instruction that will display the "Good morning!" message in a dialog box.

3 Verify that the insertion point is located between the `Private Sub` and `End Sub` lines in the Code window, then press the **Tab** key to indent the insertion point.

> It is a standard programming practice to indent the instructions that appear between the `Private Sub` and `End Sub` lines for readability.

4 Type **'display message** (be sure to type the apostrophe) and then press the **Enter** key to move the insertion point to the next line in the Code window.

Notice that when you press the Enter key, the Visual Basic Editor color-codes the comment and also indents the insertion point on the next line. If you want to remove the indentation, you simply press the Backspace key. In this case, however, you will keep the indentation.

As you learned in the Concept lesson, you can use VBA's MsgBox command to display a message in a dialog box.

5 Type **msgbox** and press the **spacebar**. Because the Auto Quick Info check box is selected in the Options dialog box, the Visual Basic Editor displays the syntax of the MsgBox command.

Recall that you need only to enter the Prompt argument in the MsgBox command; the remaining four arguments are optional. The Prompt argument specifies the message you want the dialog box to display.

6 Type **prompt:="Good morning!"** and press the **Enter** key. Although the message is enclosed in quotation marks in the Prompt argument, the quotation marks will not appear when the message is displayed in the dialog box. Figure 1-18 shows the completed Open event procedure.

comment

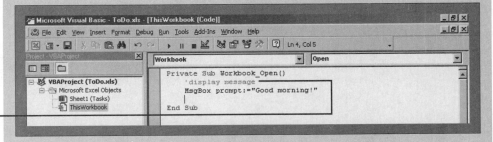

Figure 1-18: Code window showing the completed Open event procedure

Notice that the Visual Basic Editor changes the capitalization of the word `msgbox` to `MsgBox`. You can enter VBA commands in any case—uppercase, lowercase, or a combination of both cases. When you move the insertion point to another line in the Code window, the Visual Basic Editor changes the capitalization to match the capitalization used in the VBA language.

After entering the code in the Code window, you should save the procedure and then run it to verify that it is working correctly. Recall that you save a procedure by saving the file in which it is contained. You run an event procedure by causing the event—in this case, the workbook's Open event—to occur.

To save and run the workbook's Open event procedure:

1 Click the **Save ToDo.xls** button 🖫 on the Visual Basic Editor's Standard toolbar to save the procedure, then click the **View Microsoft Excel** button 🖾 on the Standard toolbar to return to Excel.

2 Close the ToDo workbook by clicking its **Close** button ☒. Be sure to leave Excel running.

To run the workbook's Open event procedure, you need simply to open the workbook.

3 Open the **ToDo** (ToDo.xls) workbook. Click the **Enable Macros** button, if necessary. The workbook's Open event procedure displays the "Good morning!" message in a dialog box, as shown in Figure 1-19.

HELP? If the Open event procedure does not display the dialog box, the macro security feature level in Excel may be set to High. Click Tools on the menu bar, point to Macro, and then click Security to open the Security dialog box. Click the Security Level tab, if necessary, then click the Medium option button to select it. Click the OK button to close the Security dialog box, then repeat Steps 2 and 3.

4 Click the **OK** button to close the dialog box.

Now return to the Visual Basic Editor and close the Code window.

5 Click **Tools** on the menu bar, point to **Macro**, and then click **Visual Basic Editor** to switch to the Visual Basic Editor. Close the Code window by clicking its **Close** button ☒.

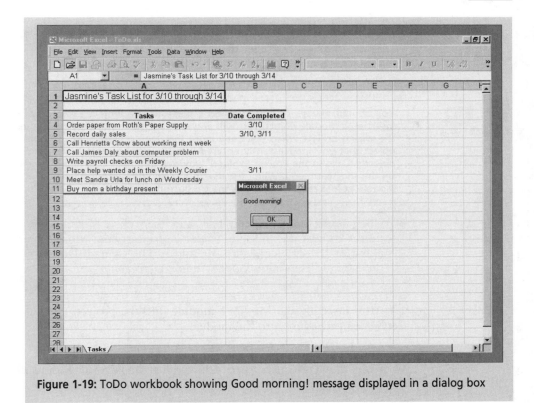

Figure 1-19: ToDo workbook showing Good morning! message displayed in a dialog box

The workbook's Open event procedure is working correctly. Now you can begin coding Jasmine's second procedure, the GetGenius procedure.

Coding the GetGenius Macro Procedure

Recall that Jasmine wants a procedure that she can use to both display the Office Assistant and change its character to The Genius. You will name this procedure GetGenius. Unlike the Open event procedure, which runs automatically when Jasmine opens the ToDo workbook, Jasmine wants to be able to run the GetGenius procedure whenever she chooses to do so. For that to happen, the GetGenius procedure will need to be a macro procedure. Recall that a macro procedure, more simply referred to as a macro, is a procedure that the user can run from the Macro dialog box in Excel.

Before you can create a macro, you first must insert a Module object into the current project. Recall that a Module object is a container for macros and other procedures that are not associated with any specific object in the project.

To insert a Module object into the VBAProject (ToDo.xls) project:

1 Click **VBAProject (ToDo.xls)** in the Project Explorer window to select the project. This will ensure that the Module object you want to insert goes into the VBAProject (ToDo.xls) project.

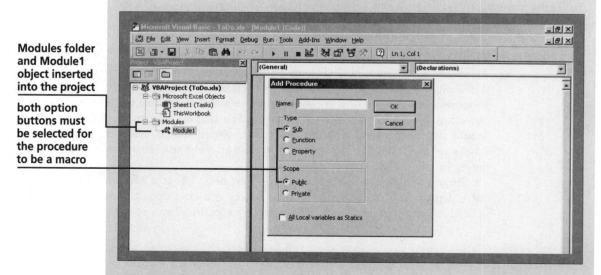

> You should always click the project's name in the Project Explorer window before inserting a Module object. This will prevent you from inserting the Module object into the wrong project when you have more than one project open. To remove a Module object that you inadvertently entered into the wrong project, right-click the Module object's name in the Project Explorer window, and then click Remove *<module name>* on the shortcut menu. When the dialog box appears asking if you want to export the module before removing it, click the No button.

2 Click **Insert** on the menu bar, and then click **Module**. The Visual Basic Editor creates the Modules folder and inserts the Module1 module (designated by the ⚙ icon) into the folder. The General Declarations section of the Module1 module's Code window appears.

After inserting the Module1 module into the project, you then can insert the GetGenius procedure into the module.

To insert the GetGenius procedure into the Module1 module, then code the procedure:

1 Verify that the title bar shows that you are viewing the Module1 module's Code window, and that the insertion point is located in the Code window. Click **Insert** on the menu bar and then click **Procedure**. The Add Procedure dialog box opens, as shown in Figure 1-20.

Modules folder and Module1 object inserted into the project

both option buttons must be selected for the procedure to be a macro

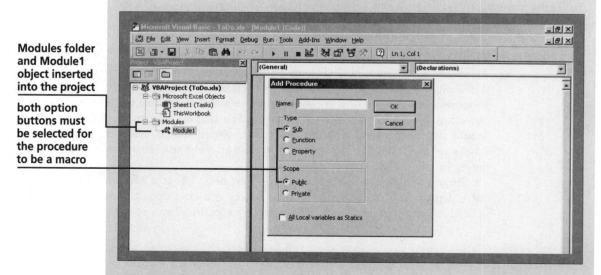

Figure 1-20: Add Procedure dialog box

HELP? If the Procedure option on the Insert menu is dimmed, close the Insert menu. Click inside the Code window to make it the active window, then repeat step 1.

▶ **tip**

Before inserting a procedure into a module, always verify that the module's Code window is open and that the insertion point is located in the Code window. You can verify that the module's Code window is open by noting the text either in the Visual Basic Editor's title bar when the Code window is maximized or in the Code window's title bar when the Code window is not maximized.

First you need to name the procedure.

2 Type **GetGenius** in the Name text box.

All macro procedures in Excel must begin with the keywords `Public Sub`. As you learned in the Concept lesson, `Public` specifies the procedure's scope and `Sub` specifies its type. Both the Sub and Public option buttons are already selected in the Add Procedure dialog box.

▶ **tip**

Procedures that do not begin with `Public Sub` are not considered macros in Excel; therefore, you will not be able to run these procedures from Excel's Macro dialog box.

3 Click the **OK** button to close the Add Procedure dialog box. The Visual Basic Editor inserts the GetGenius procedure into the Module1 module, and the code template for the GetGenius procedure appears in the Code window.

Between the `Public Sub` and `End Sub` lines, you will enter a comment that describes the purpose of the procedure. You also will enter the VBA instructions that will display the Office Assistant and change its character to The Genius.

4 Press the **Tab** key to indent the insertion point, then type **'display The Genius as the Assistant** (be sure to type the apostrophe) and then press the **Enter** key.

Before you can display the Office Assistant, you need to turn the Office Assistant feature on. You do so from code by setting the Assistant object's On property to the Boolean value True. The instruction you will use is `Assistant.On = True`.

▶ **tip**

`True` is a keyword in VBA; it means the Boolean value True. VBA also has a keyword, `False`, that represents the Boolean value False.

5 Type **assistant** and then type . (a period). Because you selected the Auto List Members check box in the Options dialog box, an alphabetical listing of the Assistant object's properties (designated by the 🖻 icon) and methods (designated by the 🔖 icon) appears.

6 Scroll down the members list until you locate the On property, then click **On**.

>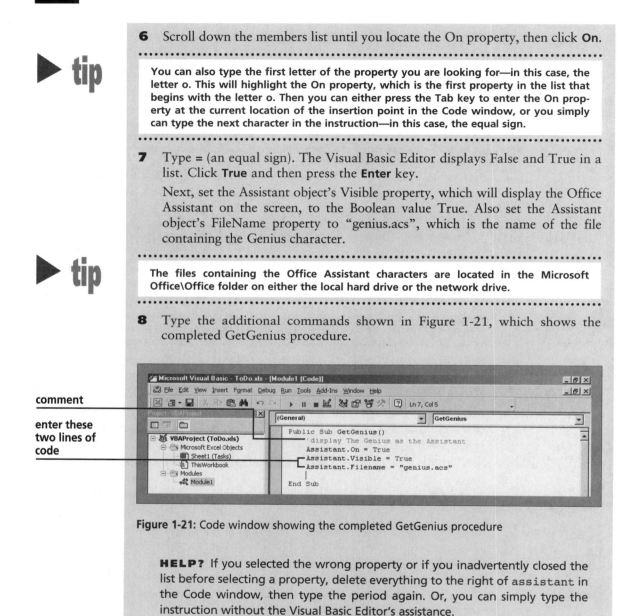
>
> **tip**
>
> You can also type the first letter of the property you are looking for—in this case, the letter o. This will highlight the On property, which is the first property in the list that begins with the letter o. Then you can either press the Tab key to enter the On property at the current location of the insertion point in the Code window, or you simply can type the next character in the instruction—in this case, the equal sign.

7 Type = (an equal sign). The Visual Basic Editor displays False and True in a list. Click **True** and then press the **Enter** key.

Next, set the Assistant object's Visible property, which will display the Office Assistant on the screen, to the Boolean value True. Also set the Assistant object's FileName property to "genius.acs", which is the name of the file containing the Genius character.

> **tip**
>
> The files containing the Office Assistant characters are located in the Microsoft Office\Office folder on either the local hard drive or the network drive.

8 Type the additional commands shown in Figure 1-21, which shows the completed GetGenius procedure.

comment

enter these two lines of code

Figure 1-21: Code window showing the completed GetGenius procedure

> **HELP?** If you selected the wrong property or if you inadvertently closed the list before selecting a property, delete everything to the right of `assistant` in the Code window, then type the period again. Or, you can simply type the instruction without the Visual Basic Editor's assistance.

Now save and run the GetGenius procedure to verify that it is working correctly; then print the project's code. Because the GetGenius procedure begins with the keywords `Public Sub`, you can run the procedure either from the Macros dialog box in the Visual Basic Editor or from the Macro dialog box in the host application, Excel.

To save and run the GetGenius procedure, then print the project's code:

1 Click the **Save ToDo.xls** button 🔲 on the Visual Basic Editor's Standard toolbar.

2 Click **Tools** on the menu bar, then click **Macros** to display the Macros dialog box in the Visual Basic Editor. (In Excel, this dialog box is called the Macro dialog box.) GetGenius is already selected in the Macro Name list box, so you just need to click the **Run** button to run the procedure. The Office Assistant appears on the screen as The Genius character, as shown in Figure 1-22.

The Genius Office Assistant ————

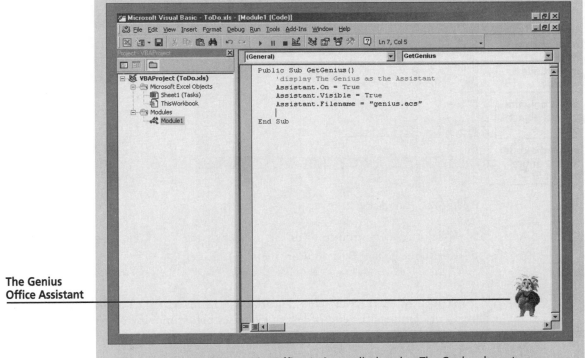

Figure 1-22: Screen showing the Office Assistant displayed as The Genius character

HELP? If a dialog box appears and displays the message "The Assistant file associated with your selection cannot be located or contains invalid data," click the End button to close the dialog box. Then, verify that you typed the `Assistant.Filename = "genius.acs"` instruction correctly. If you did not type the instruction correctly, correct the instruction and then repeat steps 1 and 2. However, if you did type the instruction correctly, it means that the genius.acs file is not installed on your computer. You can fix this problem by installing the file from the Office 2000 CD. You also can simply remove the `Assistant.Filename = "genius.acs"` instruction from the GetGenius procedure, or you can change the filename to one that is installed on your computer—for example, you can change it to "clippit.acs". If you make any changes, save your work.

▶ **tip**

•••

A much quicker way to run a macro is to click the Run *<procedureType>* button ▶ on the Visual Basic Editor's Standard toolbar.

•••

3 Close the GetGenius procedure's Code window.

Now provide external documentation for this project by printing its code.

4 Click **File** on the Visual Basic Editor menu bar, and then click **Print**. In the Print dialog box, verify that both the Current Project option button and the Code check box are selected, as shown in Figure 1-23.

prints only the code selected in the Code window

prints only the current object's code

prints the code for the entire project

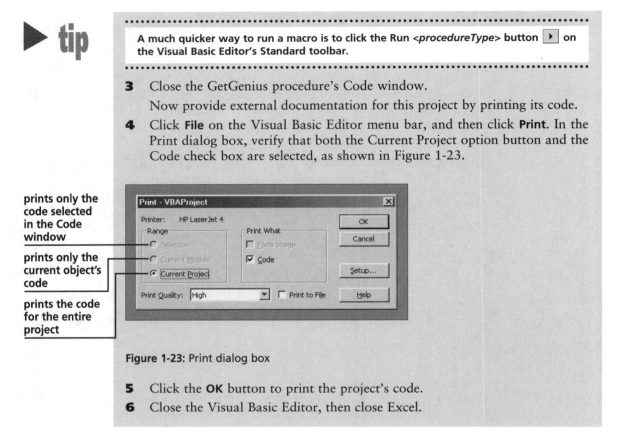

Figure 1-23: Print dialog box

5 Click the **OK** button to print the project's code.

6 Close the Visual Basic Editor, then close Excel.

You now have completed Tutorial 1's Excel lesson. You can either take a break or complete the end-of-lesson exercises before moving on to the next lesson.

E X E R C I S E S

1. In this exercise, you will run a macro from Excel.

   a. Open the ToDo (ToDo.xls) workbook that you completed in this lesson. The workbook is located in the Tut01\Excel folder on your Data Disk. Click the Enable Macros button, if necessary, then click the OK button to remove the "Good morning!" message.

   b. Turn the Office Assistant feature off, if necessary.

   c. To run the GetGenius macro from Excel, click Tools on Excel's menu bar, point to Macro, then click Macros. Click GetGenius in the Macro dialog box, if necessary, and then click the Run button.

   d. Close the ToDo workbook.

2. In this exercise, you will code the Workbook object's BeforeClose event procedure so that it displays the message "So long!" in a dialog box. You also will create a macro, named GetClippit, that will display the Office Assistant and also set its FileName property to "clippit.acs".

   a. Open the ToDo (ToDo.xls) workbook that you completed in this lesson. The workbook is located in the Tut01\Excel folder on your Data Disk. Click the Enable Macros button, if necessary, then click the OK button to remove the "Good morning!" message. Save the workbook as T1-EX-E2D.

   b. Turn the Office Assistant feature off, if necessary.

   c. Open the Visual Basic Editor. Insert a macro procedure named GetClippit into the Module1 module. (*Hint*: You will need to open the Module1 module's Code window before inserting the procedure.) Code the GetClippit macro so that it displays the Office Assistant and also sets the Assistant's FileName property to "clippit.acs". Include an appropriate comment for internal documentation.

   d. Save and run the procedure to verify that it is working correctly, then close the Code window.

   e. Open the Workbook object's BeforeClose event procedure. Code the procedure so that it displays the "So long!" message in a dialog box. Include an appropriate comment for internal documentation.

   f. Save the workbook, then close the Code window.

   g. Close the Visual Basic Editor. Run the BeforeClose event procedure by closing the workbook. Click the OK button to remove the "So long!" message.

   h. When both procedures are working correctly, open the T1-EX-E2D workbook and print the project's code, then close the workbook.

3. In this exercise, you will modify the GetGenius macro that you created in this lesson by setting the Office Assistant's Left and Top properties.

   a. Open the ToDo (ToDo.xls) workbook that you completed in this lesson. The workbook is located in the Tut01\Excel folder on your Data Disk. Click the Enable Macros button, if necessary, then click the OK button to remove the "Good morning!" message. Save the workbook as T1-EX-E3D.

   b. Modify the GetGenius macro so that, in addition to displaying the Assistant and setting its FileName property, the macro also sets the Assistant's Left and Top properties, which control the upper-left position of the Office Assistant on the screen; both property values are measured in points. (A point is a screen measurement. One point is equivalent to 1/72 of an inch.) Set the Left property to 144 points (2 inches) and set the Top property to 216 points (3 inches).

   c. Save and run the macro. When the macro is working correctly, print only the GetGenius procedure's code. Drag the Office Assistant to the lower-right corner of the screen, then close the Visual Basic Editor and the workbook.

Exercises 4 and 5 are Discovery Exercises. Discovery Exercises, which may include topics that are not covered in this lesson, allow you to "discover" the solutions to problems on your own.

discovery ▶ 4. In this exercise, you will create a macro procedure that displays the system date in a dialog box.

   a. Open a new workbook in Excel, then save the workbook as T1-EX-E4D in the Tut01\Excel folder on your Data Disk.

   b. Open the Visual Basic Editor. Use the Visual Basic Editor's Help menu to search for a VBA command that you can use to display the system date. (The system date is the current date maintained by your computer's internal clock.)

c. Insert a module into the project, then insert a macro procedure named DisplayDate. Code the macro so that it uses the appropriate VBA command, along with the MsgBox command, to display the system date. Include an appropriate comment for internal documentation.

d. Save and run the macro. When the macro is working correctly, close the Visual Basic Editor and the workbook.

discovery ▶ 5. In this exercise, you will code the Activate event procedure for two Worksheet objects.

a. Open the T1-EX-E5 workbook, which is located in the Tut01\Excel folder on your Data Disk. Save the workbook as T1-EX-E5D.

b. Open the Visual Basic Editor. Use the Help menu to research a Worksheet object's Activate event procedure. When does the Activate event occur?

c. Open the Active worksheet's Code window. Use the Object and Procedure list boxes to open the Worksheet object's Activate procedure. Code the Activate event procedure so that it displays "Active worksheet" in a dialog box when the Active worksheet is activated.

d. Code the Retired worksheet object's Activate event procedure so that it displays "Retired worksheet" in a dialog box when the Retired worksheet is activated.

e. Save the file, then press Alt+F11 to return to Excel. Test the procedures by switching between both worksheets. When the procedures are working correctly, close the workbook.

A computer program is good only if it works. Errors in programming code can cause a program to run incorrectly. Therefore, a programmer needs to know how to locate and fix any errors in his or her code. Exercise 6 is a Debugging Exercise. Debugging Exercises allow you to practice recognizing and solving errors in code.

debugging 6. What is wrong with the following macro procedure?

```
Private Sub RemoveAssistant()
    Assistant.On = False
End Sub
```

Word Lesson

Using the Visual Basic Editor in Word

case ▶ Pat Jones is the manager of Willowton Health Club. One of her responsibilities is to send a welcome letter and a temporary ID to each new member. Pat has decided to create two procedures for her welcome letter, which has been created and saved as a Word document. The first procedure will automatically display the Office Assistant and position it in the upper-right corner of the screen when the document is opened. This procedure will be an event procedure because it will run in response to the action of Pat opening the document. The second procedure will allow Pat to display the current date in a dialog box. Pat will make this procedure a macro so that she can run the procedure from the Macros dialog box in Word whenever she chooses to do so.

Using the Visual Basic Editor in Microsoft Word

As you learned in the Concept lesson, you can use VBA to customize an application to fit your needs. You do so by creating a procedure, which is simply a series of VBA instructions grouped together as a single unit for the purpose of performing a specific task. Recall that you create a procedure using the Visual Basic Editor.

To open the Visual Basic Editor in Word:

1 Start Microsoft Word. Open the **T1-WD-1** (T1-WD-1.doc) document, which is located in the Tut01\Word folder on your Data Disk, and then save the document as **New Member**. The document, along with the Clippit Office Assistant, appears on the screen. See Figure 1-24. (The Office Assistant character that appears on your screen might be different.)

document
filename

your toolbars
might be
different

Clippit Office
Assistant (your
assistant, as
well as its
location, might
be different)

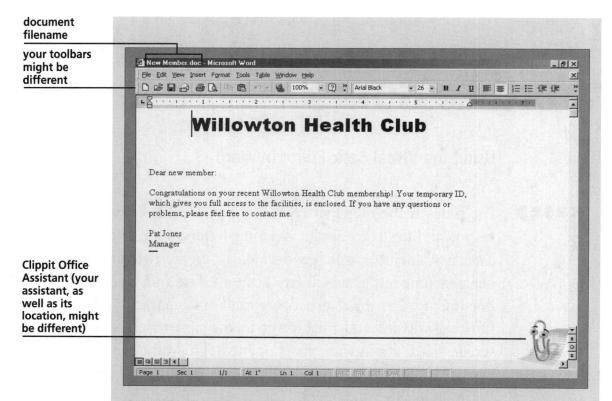

Figure 1-24: New Member document and the Clippit Office Assistant

HELP? If the Office Assistant does not appear on your screen, click Help on the menu bar, then click Show the Office Assistant.

HELP? It is not essential to use the Clippit Office Assistant in this lesson; any Assistant character will work. However, if you want to use Clippit, click the Office Assistant, then click Options in the Office Assistant's balloon. Click the Gallery tab on the Office Assistant dialog box, then use the Next or Back button to scroll through the different assistants. When you locate the Clippit assistant, click the OK button to close the dialog box.

Before opening the Visual Basic Editor, turn the Office Assistant feature off.

2 Click the **Office Assistant**, then click **Options** in the Office Assistant's balloon. Click the **Options** tab on the Office Assistant dialog box, if necessary, then click the **Use the Office Assistant** check box to deselect it. Click the **OK** button to close the Office Assistant dialog box. The Office Assistant is removed from the screen.

3 Click **Tools** on the menu bar, point to **Macro**, and then click **Visual Basic Editor** to open the Visual Basic Editor. The Visual Basic Editor appears, as shown in Figure 1-25. (You may need to click the plus signs in the Project Explorer window to view each folder's contents.)

▶ tip

A much quicker way to open the Visual Basic Editor is to press Alt+F11.

name of the open file

indicates that you are working in the Visual Basic Editor

main window

Project Explorer window

Properties window

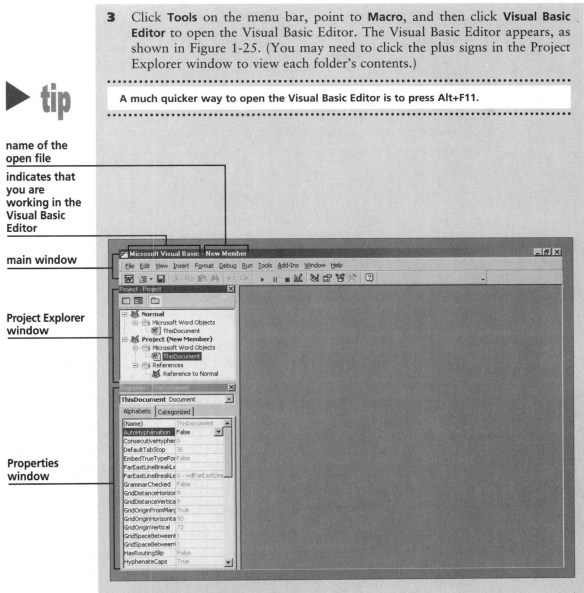

Figure 1-25: The Visual Basic Editor opened in Word

HELP? If necessary, you can use the mouse to drag the borders of the Project Explorer and Property windows until the windows are the desired size.

HELP? If the Project Explorer window is not displayed, click View on the Visual Basic Editor menu bar and then click Project Explorer.

> **HELP?** Although you won't need the Properties window in this lesson, you can display it by clicking View on the Visual Basic Editor menu bar, and then clicking Properties Window. If no properties appear in the Properties window, click the Microsoft Word Objects folder in the Project Explorer window, and then click ThisDocument.
>
> **HELP?** If the Standard toolbar is not displayed, click View on the Visual Basic Editor menu bar, point to Toolbars, and then click Standard.
>
> **HELP?** If the Code window is displayed, click its Close button ⊠ to close it.
>
> **HELP?** If the Immediate window is displayed, click its Close button ⊠ to close it.

If the Properties window is open, you can close it.

4   Click the Properties window's **Close** button ⊠.

The text, Microsoft Visual Basic – New Member, that appears in the main window's title bar indicates that you are working in the Visual Basic Editor and that the name of the current file is New Member. The Project Explorer window shows that two projects (designated by the 🔣 icon) are open; the names of the projects are Normal and Project. The New Member that appears in parentheses after the Project project name is the name of the file that contains that project.

Notice that the Normal and Project (New Member) projects each contain a Microsoft Word Objects folder that contains one document object (designated by the 📄 icon) named ThisDocument. The Project (New Member) project also contains a folder named References, which contains a reference (designated by the 🔣 icon) to the Normal project.

The ThisDocument object stored in the Normal project represents the Normal template document in Microsoft Word. As you may already know, when you start Word or open a new document, Word creates a blank document that is based on the settings in the Normal template. Word uses the Normal template to store such things as macros and custom menu settings that you want to routinely use and make available to every Word document. The ThisDocument object stored in the Project (New Member) project, on the other hand, represents the Word document in which you are currently working. The References folder contained in the Project (New Member) project allows the current document to access the settings stored in the Normal template.

You will not be making any changes to the Normal project, so you can close the display of its contents to avoid confusing the two ThisDocument objects. You also can close the References folder.

5   Click the **minus sign** that appears to the left of Normal in the Project Explorer window. Also click the **minus sign** that appears to the left of the References folder.

Before opening a Code window and entering the appropriate VBA instructions, you will open the Visual Basic Editor's Options dialog box to verify that the Auto List Members and Auto Quick Info check boxes are selected. Recall that when these check boxes are selected, the Visual Basic Editor provides assistance while you are entering your VBA instructions in the Code window. You also will deselect the Default to Full Module View check box in the Options dialog box to ensure that the Visual Basic Editor Code window opens in procedure view. (You are deselecting the Default to Full Module View check box so that your Code windows agree with the ones in this book, which are displayed in procedure view.)

To view the status of the Options dialog box:

1 Click **Tools** on the menu bar, and then click **Options** to open the Options dialog box. Click the Editor tab in the Options dialog box, if necessary.

2 Click the **Auto List Members** and **Auto Quick Info** check boxes to select these options, if necessary. Click the **Default to Full Module View** check box to deselect it, if necessary. See Figure 1-26.

when selected, these options tell the Visual Basic Editor to assist you in entering your VBA instructions

when deselected, Code windows open in Procedure View

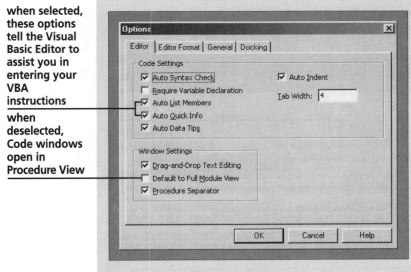

Figure 1-26: Options dialog box

3 Click the **OK** button to close the Options dialog box.

The first procedure you will code is the New Member document's Open event procedure, which should display the Office Assistant and position it in the upper-right corner of the screen.

Coding the Document Object's Open Event Procedure

As you learned in the Concept lesson, an event procedure runs in response to an action performed on an object by the user. A document's Open event procedure, for example, runs automatically when the user opens the document. You will code the Open event procedure so that it displays the Office Assistant and positions it in the upper-right corner of the screen.

To code the document object's Open event procedure:

1 In the Project Explorer window, right-click **ThisDocument** in the Project (New Member) project. Recall that the ThisDocument object represents the New Member document. Click **View Code** on the shortcut menu.

Notice that `(General)` appears in the Code window's Object list box and `(Declarations)` appears in its Procedure list box. This section of the Code window is referred to as the General Declarations section. Every object has its own **General Declarations section**, where you enter code that is not associated with any of the object's events. For this lesson, you do not need to concern yourself with this section.

2 Click the **Object box list arrow**, then click **Document** in the list. The Document object's New event procedure appears in the Code window. Click the **Procedure box list arrow**, then click **Open** in the list. The Code window now displays the Document object's Open event procedure, as shown in Figure 1-27.

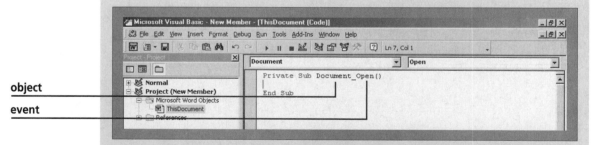

object

event

Figure 1-27: Code window showing the Document object's Open event procedure

HELP? If the Code window is not maximized, click its Maximize button ▢.

To help you follow the syntax, or rules of its language, VBA provides you with a **code template** for the procedure. Because the procedure is an event procedure, the code template begins with the keywords `Private Sub` followed by the name of the object, an underscore, the name of the event and, in this case, an empty set of parentheses. As you learned in the Concept lesson, the keyword `Sub` is an abbreviation of the term *sub procedure*, which refers to a block of code that performs a specific task but does not return a value. The keyword `Private` indicates that the event procedure can be used only by the object in which it is contained; in this case, the Open event procedure can be used only by the Document object. The code template ends with the keywords `End Sub`.

Some event procedures have arguments within the parentheses.

If you are using a color monitor, you will notice that `Private Sub` and `End Sub` appear in a different color from both the object's name and the name of the event. The Visual Basic Editor displays keywords in a different color to help you quickly identify these elements in the Code window. In this case, the color-coding helps you easily locate the beginning and end of the event procedure.

In the Open event procedure, you will enter a comment that describes the purpose of the procedure. Then you will enter the VBA instructions that display the Office Assistant and also position it in the upper-right corner of the screen.

3 Verify that the insertion point is located between the `Private Sub` and `End Sub` lines in the Code window, then press the **Tab** key to indent the insertion point.

It is a standard programming practice to indent the instructions that appear between the `Private Sub` **and** `End Sub` **lines for readability.**

4 Type **'display and position the Assistant** (be sure to type the apostrophe) and then press the **Enter** key to move the insertion point to the next line in the Code window.

Notice that when you press the Enter key, the Visual Basic Editor color-codes the comment and also indents the insertion point on the next line. If you want to remove the indentation, you simply press the Backspace key. In this case, however, you will keep the indentation.

Before you can display the Office Assistant, you need to turn the Office Assistant feature on. You do so from code by setting the Assistant object's On property to the Boolean value True. The instruction you will use is `Assistant.On = True`.

> `True` is a keyword in VBA; it means the Boolean value True. VBA also has a keyword, `False`, that represents the Boolean value False.

5 Type **assistant** and then type . (a period). Because you selected the Auto List Members check box in the Options dialog box, an alphabetical listing of the Assistant object's properties (designated by the 📇 icon) and methods (designated by the 🐭 icon) appears.

6 Scroll down the members list until you locate the On property, then click **On**.

> You can also type the first letter of the property you are looking for—in this case the letter o. This will highlight the On property, which is the first property in the list that begins with the letter o. Then you can either press the Tab key to enter the On property at the current location of the insertion point in the Code window, or you simply can type the next character in the instruction—in this case, the equal sign.

7 Type = (an equal sign). The Visual Basic Editor displays False and True in a list. Click **True** and then press the **Enter** key.

Next, set the Assistant object's Visible property, which will display the Office Assistant on the screen, to the Boolean value True.

8 Type **assistant.visible = true** and press the **Enter** key.

You position the Assistant by setting its **Left and Top properties**, which control the upper-left location of the Assistant on the screen. You will position the Office Assistant so that its left border is 650 points from the left side of the screen, and its top border is 0 points from the top of the screen. A **point** is a unit of measurement, typically used when specifying font sizes, such as 8 point and 10 point. One point is equivalent to 1/72 of an inch, so 650 points is approximately 9 inches.

9 Type the additional instructions shown in Figure 1-28, which shows the completed Open event procedure. (Be sure to set the Top property to the number 0 and not the letter O.)

enter these
two lines
of code

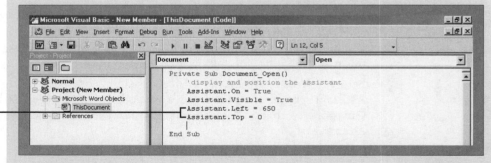

Figure 1-28: Code window showing the completed Open event procedure

HELP? If you selected the wrong property or if you inadvertently closed the list before selecting a property, delete everything to the right of `assistant` in the Code window, then type the period again. Or, you can simply type the instruction without the Visual Basic Editor's assistance.

After entering the code in the Code window, you should save the procedure and then run it to verify that it is working correctly. Recall that you save a procedure by saving the file in which it is contained. You run an event procedure by causing the event—in this case, the document's Open event—to occur.

To save and run the document's Open event procedure:

1 Click the **Save New Member** button 🖫 on the Visual Basic Editor's Standard toolbar to save the procedure, then click the **View Microsoft Word** button 🗒 on the Standard toolbar to return to Word.

2 Close the New Member document by clicking its **Close** button ☒. Be sure to leave Word running.

To run the document's Open event procedure, you need simply to open the document.

3 Open the **New Member** (New Member.doc) document. If necessary, click the **Enable Macros** button. The document's Open event displays the Office Assistant and also positions it in the upper-right corner of the screen, as shown in Figure 1-29.

current location of the Office Assistant

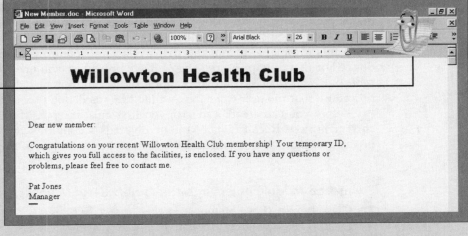

Figure 1-29: Office Assistant displayed in the upper-right corner of the screen

HELP? If the Open event procedure does not display the Office Assistant, the macro security level in Word may be set to High. Click Tools on the menu bar, point to Macro, and then click Security to open the Security dialog box. Click the Security Level tab, if necessary, then click the Medium option button to select it. Click the OK button to close the Security dialog box, then repeat Steps 2 and 3.

HELP? Don't be concerned if the Office Assistant is not positioned exactly as shown in the figure.

Now turn the Office Assistant feature off, and then return to the Visual Basic Editor and close the Code window.

4 Click the **Office Assistant,** then click **Options** in the Office Assistant's balloon. Click the **Options** tab on the Office Assistant dialog box, if necessary, then click the **Use the Office Assistant** check box to deselect it. Click the **OK** button to close the Office Assistant dialog box.

5 Click **Tools** on the menu bar, point to **Macro,** and then click **Visual Basic Editor** to switch to the Visual Basic Editor. Close the Code window by clicking its **Close** button ⊠.

The document object's Open event procedure is working correctly. Now you can begin coding Pat's second procedure, the DisplayDate procedure.

Coding the DisplayDate Macro Procedure

Recall that Pat wants a procedure that she can use to display the current date in a dialog box; you will name this procedure DisplayDate. Unlike the Open event procedure, which runs automatically when Pat opens the New Member document, Pat wants to be able to run the DisplayDate procedure whenever she chooses to do so. For that to happen, the DisplayDate procedure will need to be a macro procedure. Recall that a macro procedure, more simply referred to as a macro, is a procedure that the user can run from the Macros dialog box in Word.

Before you can create a macro, you first must insert a Module object into the current project. Recall that a Module object is a container for macros and other procedures that are not associated with any specific object in the project.

To insert a Module object into the Project (New Member) project:

1 Click **Project (New Member)** in the Project Explorer window to select the project. This will ensure that the Module object is inserted in the New Member project rather than in the Normal project.

tip

You should always click the project's name in the Project Explorer window before inserting a Module object. This will prevent you from inadvertently inserting the Module object into the wrong project when you have more than one project open. To remove a Module object that you inadvertently entered into the wrong project, right-click the Module object's name in the Project Explorer window, and then click Remove *<module name>* on the shortcut menu. When the dialog box appears asking if you want to export the module before removing it, click the No button.

2   Click **Insert** on the menu bar, and then click **Module**. The Visual Basic Editor creates the Modules folder and inserts the Module1 module (designated by the 🔍 icon) into the folder. The General Declarations section of the Module1 module's Code window appears.

After inserting the Module1 module into the project, you then can insert the DisplayDate procedure into the module.

To insert the DisplayDate procedure into the Module1 module, then code the procedure:

1   Verify that the title bar shows that you are viewing the Module1 module's Code window, and that the insertion point is located in the Code window. Click **Insert** on the menu bar and then click **Procedure**. The Add Procedure dialog box opens, as shown in Figure 1-30.

Modules folder and Module1 object inserted into the project

both options must be selected for the procedure to be a macro

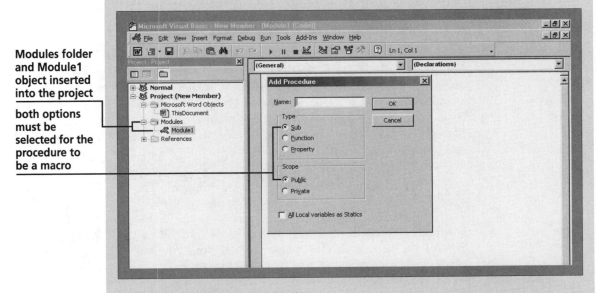

Figure 1-30: Add Procedure dialog box

HELP? If the Procedure option on the Insert menu is dimmed, close the Insert menu. Click inside the Code window to make it the active window, then repeat Step 1.

▶ **tip**

> Before inserting a procedure into a module, always verify that the module's Code window is open and that the insertion point is located in the Code window. You can verify that the module's Code window is open by noting the text either in the Visual Basic Editor's title bar when the Code window is maximized or in the Code window's title bar when the Code window is not maximized.

First you need to name the procedure.

2 Type **DisplayDate** in the Name text box.

All macro procedures in Word must begin with the keywords `Public Sub`. As you learned in the Concept lesson, `Public` specifies the procedure's scope and `Sub` specifies its type. Both the Sub and Public option buttons are already selected in the Add Procedure dialog box.

▶ **tip**

> Procedures that do not begin with `Public Sub` are not considered macros in Word; therefore, you will not be able to run these procedures from Word's Macros dialog box.

3 Click the **OK** button to close the Add Procedure dialog box. The Visual Basic Editor inserts the DisplayDate procedure into the Module1 module, and the code template for the DisplayDate procedure appears in the Code window.

Between the `Public Sub` and `End Sub` lines, you will enter a comment that describes the purpose of the procedure. You also will enter the VBA instruction that will display the current date in a dialog box.

4 Press the **Tab** key to indent the insertion point, then type **'display current date** (be sure to type the apostrophe) and then press the **Enter** key.

As you learned in the Concept lesson, you can use VBA's MsgBox command to display a message in a dialog box.

5 Type **msgbox** and press the **spacebar**. Because the Auto Quick Info check box is selected in the Options dialog box, the Visual Basic Editor displays the syntax of the MsgBox command.

Recall that you need only to enter the Prompt argument in the MsgBox command; the remaining four arguments are optional. The Prompt argument specifies the message you want the dialog box to display. You can use VBA's Date function to display the current date as the dialog box's message. A **function** is a procedure that can return a value. In this case, the **Date function** returns the current date as maintained by your computer system's internal clock; this date is referred to as the **system date**.

6 Type **prompt:=date** and press the **Enter** key. Figure 1-31 shows the completed DisplayDate procedure.

comment

displays the
system date

```
Microsoft Visual Basic - New Member - [Module1 (Code)]
File Edit View Insert Format Debug Run Tools Add-Ins Window Help
                                              Ln 5, Col 5
(General)                          DisplayDate

     Public Sub DisplayDate()
         'display current date
         MsgBox prompt:=Date

     End Sub
```

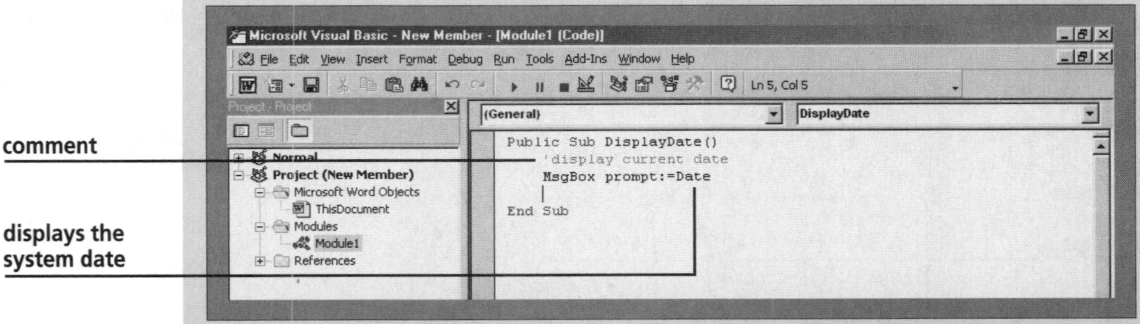

Figure 1-31: Code window showing the completed DisplayDate procedure

Notice that the Visual Basic Editor changes the capitalization of the words msgbox and date to MsgBox and Date. You can enter VBA commands in any case—uppercase, lowercase, or a combination of both cases. When you move the insertion point to another line in the Code window, the Visual Basic Editor changes the capitalization to match the capitalization used in the VBA language.

Now save and run the DisplayDate procedure to verify that it is working correctly; then print the project's code. Because the DisplayDate procedure begins with the keywords Public Sub, you can run the procedure from the Macros dialog box in either the Visual Basic Editor or the host application, Word.

To save and run the DisplayDate procedure, and then print the project's code:

1 Click the **Save New Member** button 🖫 on the Visual Basic Editor's Standard toolbar.

2 Click **Tools** on the menu bar, then click **Macros** to display the Macros dialog box in the Visual Basic Editor. DisplayDate is already selected in the Macro Name list box, so you just need to click the **Run** button to run the procedure. The New Member document appears with the current date displayed in a dialog box, as shown in Figure 1-32. (Your date might be different from that shown in Figure 1-32; it will reflect the current date maintained by your computer's internal clock.)

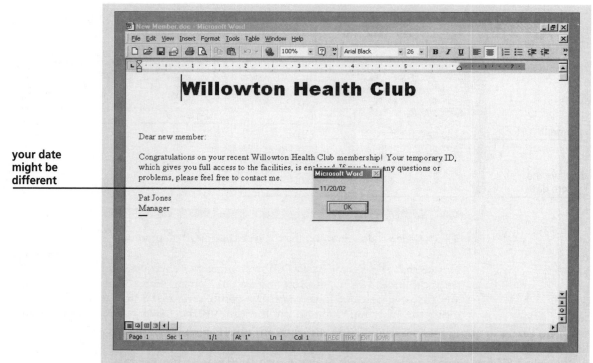

Figure 1-32: New Member document showing the current date displayed in a dialog box

A much quicker way to run a macro is to click the Run *<procedureType>* button ▶ on the Visual Basic Editor's Standard toolbar.

3 Click the **OK** button to close the dialog box.

4 Close the DisplayDate procedure's Code window.

Now provide external documentation for this project by printing its code.

5 Click **File** on the Visual Basic Editor menu bar, and then click **Print**. In the Print dialog box, verify that both the Current Project option button and the Code check box are selected, as shown in Figure 1-33.

6 Click the **OK** button to print the project's code.

7 Close the Visual Basic Editor, then close Word.

prints only the code selected in the Code window

prints only the current object's code

prints the code for the entire project

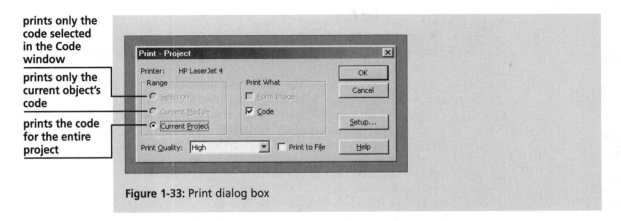

Figure 1-33: Print dialog box

You now have completed Tutorial 1's Word lesson. You can either take a break or complete the end-of-lesson exercises before moving on to the next lesson.

E X E R C I S E S

1. In this exercise, you will run a macro from Word.
   a. Open the New Member (New Member.doc) document that you completed in this lesson. The document is located in the Tut01\Word folder on your Data Disk. Click the Enable Macros button, if necessary.
   b. Turn the Office Assistant feature off.
   c. To run the DisplayDate macro from Word, click Tools on Word's menu bar, point to Macro, then click Macros. Click DisplayDate in the Macros dialog box, if necessary, and then click the Run button. Click the OK button to close the dialog box, then close the New Member document.

2. In this exercise, you will code the Document object's Close event procedure so that it turns the Office Assistant feature off when the document is closed. You also will create a macro, named GetGenius, that will display the Office Assistant and set its FileName property to "genius.acs".
   a. Open the New Member (New Member.doc) document that you completed in this lesson. The document is located in the Tut01\Word folder on your Data Disk. Click the Enable Macros button, if necessary. Save the document as T1-WD-E2D.
   b. Open the Visual Basic Editor. Insert a macro procedure named GetGenius into the Module1 module. (*Hint*: You will need to open the Module1 module's Code window before inserting the procedure.) Code the GetGenius macro so that it displays the Office Assistant and also sets the Assistant's FileName property to "genius.acs". Include an appropriate comment for internal documentation.
   c. Save and run the procedure to verify that it is working correctly, then close the Code window.
   d. Open the Document object's Close event procedure. Code the procedure so that it turns the Office Assistant feature off when the document is closed. Include an appropriate comment for internal documentation.

    e. Save the document, then close the Code window.

    f. Close the Visual Basic Editor. Run the Close event procedure by closing the document.

    g. When both procedures are working correctly, open the T1-WD-E2D document and print the project's code, then close the document.

3. In this exercise, you will modify the New Member document's Open event procedure so that it displays a message before positioning the Office Assistant.

    a. Open the New Member (New Member.doc) document that you completed in this lesson. The document is located in the Tut01\Word folder on your Data Disk. Click the Enable Macros button, if necessary. Save the document as T1-WD-E3D.

    b. Open the Visual Basic Editor. Modify the document's Open event procedure so that it displays the "Click OK to position the Assistant." message in a dialog box before the Assistant's Left and Top properties are set.

    c. Save and test the procedure. When the procedure is working correctly, print only the Open event procedure's code, then close the document.

Exercises 4 and 5 are Discovery Exercises. Discovery Exercises, which may include topics that are not covered in this lesson, allow you to "discover" the solutions to problems on your own.

discovery ▶ **4.** In this exercise, you will create a macro that displays the system time in a dialog box.

    a. Open a new document in Word, then save the document as T1-WD-E4D in the Tut01\Word folder on your Data Disk.

    b. Open the Visual Basic Editor. Use the Visual Basic Editor's Help menu to search for a VBA command that you can use to display the system time, which is the current time maintained by your computer system's internal clock.

    c. Insert a module into the T1-WD-E4D project, then insert a macro procedure named DisplayTime into the module. Code the DisplayTime procedure so that it uses the appropriate VBA command, along with the MsgBox command, to display the system time in a dialog box.

    d. Save and run the macro. When the macro is working correctly, close the document.

discovery ▶ **5.** In this exercise, you will use the Help feature in the Visual Basic Editor to learn how to create a macro that runs automatically when Word is started.

    a. Open a new document in Word. Open the Visual Basic Editor. Use the Visual Basic Editor's Help menu to learn how to create a macro that runs automatically when Word is started. Such a macro is referred to as an automatic macro or, more simply, an auto macro. Use the Help screen to answer the following questions:

       1) What is the name of the macro that runs automatically when you start Word?

       2) Where must the macro be stored in order to run automatically?

       3) How can you prevent an auto macro from running?

    b. Close the document.

A computer program is good only if it works. Errors in programming code can cause a program to run incorrectly. Therefore, a programmer needs to know how to locate and fix any errors in his or her code. Exercise 6 is a Debugging Exercise. Debugging Exercises allow you to practice recognizing and solving errors in code.

debugging **6.** What is wrong with the following macro procedure?

```
Sub Public DisplayName
     MsgBox message:="Pam"
End Sub
```

Access Lesson

Using the Visual Basic Editor in Access

case▶ Jose Martinez, an economics professor at Snowville College, uses a Microsoft Access database to manage the information he keeps on his Economics 100 students. Specifically, the database contains a table named Students, a form named StudentForm, and a report named StudentReport. Professor Martinez uses the form to enter each student's ID, name, and grade in the table, and he uses the report to print the contents of the table.

Professor Martinez has decided to create two procedures for his database. The first procedure will automatically display "Remember to print the grade report." in a dialog box when the entry form is closed. This procedure will be an event procedure because it will run in response to the action of Professor Martinez closing the form. The second procedure will display the message "So long" in a dialog box before it turns off the Office Assistant feature. Professor Martinez will make this procedure a macro so that he can run the procedure from the Database window in Access whenever he chooses to do so.

Using the Visual Basic Editor in Microsoft Access

As you learned in the Concept lesson, you can use VBA to customize an application to fit your needs. You do so by creating a procedure, which is simply a series of VBA instructions grouped together as a single unit for the purpose of performing a specific task. Recall that you create a procedure using the Visual Basic Editor.

To open the Visual Basic Editor in Access:

1 Start Microsoft Access. Open the **Econ100** (Econ100.mdb) database, which is located in the Tut01\Access folder on your Data Disk. The Database window, along with the Clippit Office Assistant, appears on the screen. Click the **Maximize** button ☐ on the Microsoft Access title bar to maximize the Microsoft Access window, if necessary. Click **Tables** in the Objects bar of the Database window to display the Tables list, if necessary. The Tables list box shows that the database contains one table, named Students. See Figure 1-34.

Clippit Office Assistant (your assistant, as well as its location, might be different)

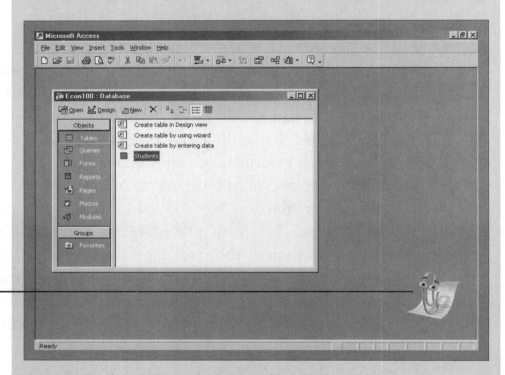

Figure 1-34: Database window and the Clippit Office Assistant

> **HELP?** If the Office Assistant does not appear on your screen, click Help on the menu bar, then click Show the Office Assistant.

> **HELP?** It is not essential to use the Clippit Office Assistant in this lesson; any Assistant character will work. However, if you want to use Clippit, click the Office Assistant, then click Options in the Office Assistant's balloon. Click the Gallery tab on the Office Assistant dialog box, then use the Next or Back button to scroll through the different assistants. When you locate the Clippit assistant, click the OK button to close the dialog box.

2 Click **Tools** on the menu bar, point to **Macro**, and then click **Visual Basic Editor** to open the Visual Basic Editor. The Visual Basic Editor appears, as shown in Figure 1-35.

▶ **tip**

A much quicker way to open the Visual Basic Editor is to press **Alt+F11**.

name of the
open file

indicates that
you are
working in the
Visual Basic
Editor

main window

Project Explorer
window

Properties
window

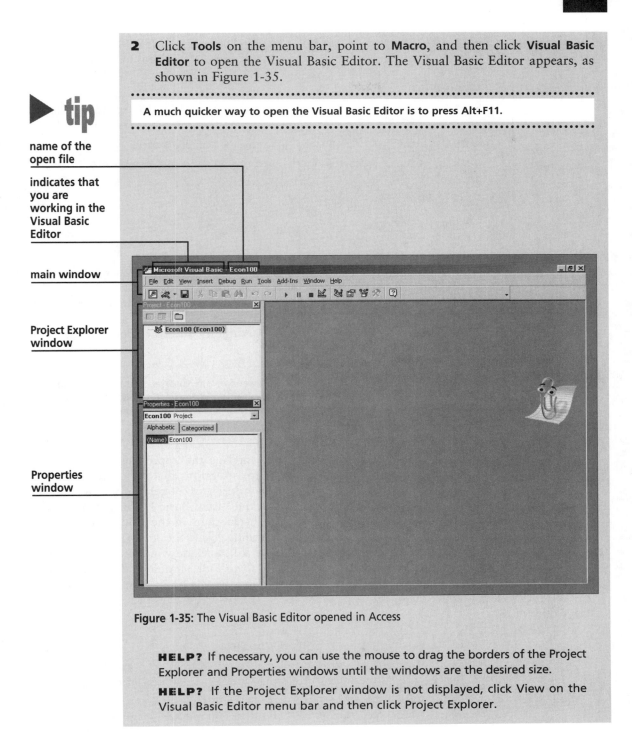

Figure 1-35: The Visual Basic Editor opened in Access

HELP? If necessary, you can use the mouse to drag the borders of the Project Explorer and Properties windows until the windows are the desired size.

HELP? If the Project Explorer window is not displayed, click View on the Visual Basic Editor menu bar and then click Project Explorer.

HELP? Although you won't need the Properties window in this lesson, you can display it by clicking View on the Visual Basic Editor menu bar, and then clicking Properties Window. Don't be concerned if the Properties window is empty.

HELP? If the Standard toolbar is not displayed, click View on the Visual Basic Editor menu bar, point to Toolbars, and then click Standard.

HELP? If the Code window is displayed, click its Close button ☒ to close it.

HELP? If the Immediate window is displayed, click its Close button ☒ to close it.

If the Properties window is open, you can close it.

3 Click the Properties window's **Close** button ☒.

The text, Microsoft Visual Basic – Econ100, that appears in the main window's title bar indicates that you are working in the Visual Basic Editor and that the name of the current file is Econ100. The Project Explorer window shows that one project (designated by the 🔲 icon) is open; the name of the project is Econ100. The Econ100 that appears in parentheses after the project name is the name of the file that contains the project.

• •

If you completed either the Word or Excel lessons in this tutorial, you might be surprised to see that the Project Explorer window shown in Figure 1-35 does not list the names of any folders or objects. In this lesson, you will learn how to add folder and object names to the Project Explorer window.

• •

Before opening a Code window and entering the appropriate VBA instructions, you will open the Visual Basic Editor's Options dialog box to verify that the Auto List Members and Auto Quick Info check boxes are selected. Recall that when these check boxes are selected, the Visual Basic Editor provides assistance while you are entering your VBA instructions in the Code window. You also will deselect the Default to Full Module View check box in the Options dialog box to ensure that the Visual Basic Editor Code window opens in procedure view. (You are deselecting the Default to Full Module View check box so that your Code windows agree with the ones in this book, which are displayed in procedure view.)

To view the status of the Options dialog box:

1 Click **Tools** on the menu bar, and then click **Options** to open the Options dialog box. Click the Editor tab in the Options dialog box, if necessary.

2 Click the **Auto List Members** and **Auto Quick Info** check boxes to select these options, if necessary. Click the **Default to Full Module View** check box to deselect it. See Figure 1-36.

when selected, these options tell the Visual Basic Editor to assist you in entering your VBA instructions

when deselected, Code windows open in Procedure View

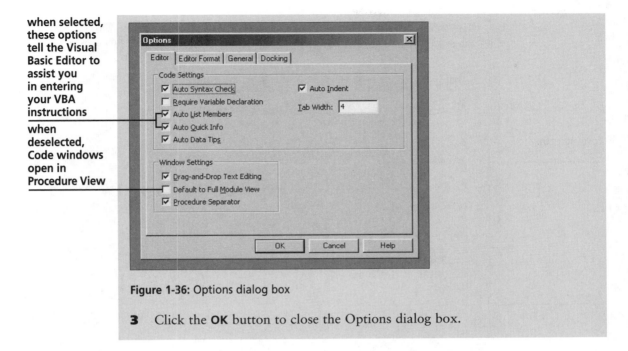

Figure 1-36: Options dialog box

3 Click the **OK** button to close the Options dialog box.

The first procedure you will code is the StudentForm form's Close event procedure, which will display the message "Remember to print the grade report." in a dialog box.

Coding the Form Object's Close Event Procedure

As you learned in the Concept lesson, an event procedure runs in response to an action performed on an object by the user. A form's **Close event procedure**, for example, runs automatically when the user closes the form. You will code the Close event procedure so that it displays the message "Remember to print the grade report." in a dialog box. Before you can open the form's Code window, however, you first need to include the form's name in the Project Explorer window.

To include the form's name in the Project Explorer window and then code its Close event procedure:

1 Click the **View Microsoft Access** button ⊞ on the Visual Basic Editor's Standard toolbar to return to Access. Click **Forms** in the Objects bar of the Database window to display the Forms list. The Forms list box shows that the database contains one form, named StudentForm.

2 Right-click **StudentForm** in the Forms list box and then click **Design View** on the shortcut menu. The form opens in design view, as shown in Figure 1-37.

form selector box

form

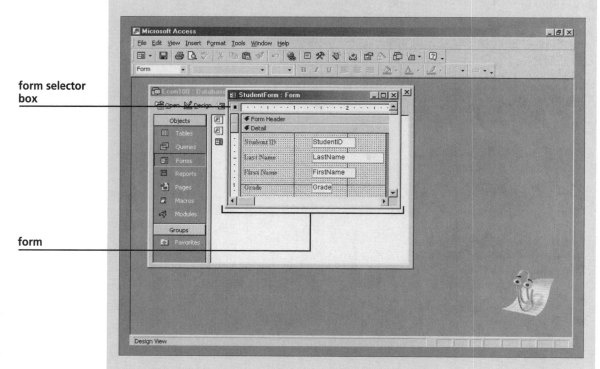

Figure 1-37: StudentForm opened in design view

HELP? If the Toolbox window is open, click its Close button ☒ to close it.

To include the form's name in the Project Explorer window, you simply need to set the form's Has Module property to Yes. You do so using the form's property sheet.

3 Locate the form selector box on the Design View window shown in Figure 1-37. Right-click the **form selector box** and then click **Properties** on the shortcut menu. If necessary, click the **Other** tab on the property sheet. You will notice that the Other tab contains the Has Module property. Click **Has Module**, then click the **Has Module list arrow**, and then click **Yes** in the list. See Figure 1-38.

when this property is set to Yes, the form's name will appear in the Project Explorer window

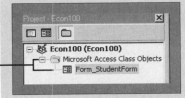

Figure 1-38: The current status of the Has Module property in the Form property sheet

HELP? If the property sheet's title bar says Section: FormHeader or Section: Detail, you inadvertently selected one of the selector boxes located below the form selector box. Locate the form selector box in Figure 1-37, and then repeat Step 3.

You will learn more about the property sheet in future tutorials.

4   Click the Form property sheet's **Close** button ☒, then click the **Save** button 🖫 on the Access Standard toolbar to save the change made to the form's Has Module property. Click the Design View window's **Close** button ☒ to close the window.

Now return to the Visual Basic Editor and open the form's Code window.

5   Click **Tools** on the menu bar, point to **Macro**, and then click **Visual Basic Editor** to return to the Visual Basic Editor. The Project Explorer window now contains a Microsoft Access Class Objects folder. Included in the folder is a Form object (designated by the 🖼 icon); the Form object's name is Form_StudentForm. See Figure 1-39.

folder and object added to the Project Explorer window

Figure 1-39: Current status of the Project Explorer window

HELP? You may need to click the plus sign that appears to the left of the Microsoft Access Class Objects folder to open the folder.

Now that the Form object is included in the Project Explorer window, you can open its Code window.

6 Right-click **Form_StudentForm** in the Project Explorer window, then click **View Code**.

Notice that (General) appears in the Code window's Object list box and (Declarations) appears in its Procedure list box. This section of the Code window is referred to as the General Declarations section. Every object has its own **General Declarations section**, where you can enter code that is not associated with any of the object's events. For this lesson, you do not need to concern yourself with this section, nor do you have to worry about the Option Compare Database instruction entered in the section.

▶ **tip**

The Option Compare statement designates the technique Access uses to compare and sort text data. The default, Database, means that Access compares and sorts letters in normal alphabetical order.

7 Click the **Object box list arrow**, then click **Form** in the list. The Form object's Load event procedure appears in the Code window. Click the **Procedure box list arrow**. Scroll up the procedure list until you see Close, then click **Close** in the list. The Code window now displays the Form object's Close event procedure, as shown in Figure 1-40.

object
event

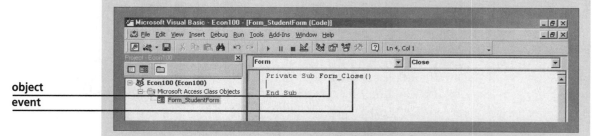

Figure 1-40: Code window showing the Form object's Close event procedure

HELP? If the Code window is not maximized, click its Maximize button ☐.

To help you follow the syntax, or rules of its language, VBA provides you with a **code template** for the procedure. Because the procedure is an event procedure, the code template begins with the keywords `Private Sub` followed by the name of the object, an underscore, the name of the event and, in this case, an empty set of parentheses. As you learned in the Concept lesson, the keyword `Sub` is an abbreviation of the term *sub proce-dure*, which refers to a block of code that performs a specific task but does not return a value. The keyword `Private` indicates that the event proce-dure can be used only by the object in which it is contained; in this case, the Close event procedure can be used only by the Form object. The code tem-plate ends with the keywords `End Sub`.

Some event procedures have arguments within the parentheses.

If you are using a color monitor, you will notice that `Private Sub` and `End Sub` appear in a different color from both the object's name and the name of the event. The Visual Basic Editor displays keywords in a different color to help you quickly identify these elements in the Code window. In this case, the color-coding helps you easily locate the beginning and end of the event procedure.

In the Close event procedure, you will enter a comment that describes the purpose of the procedure. Then you will enter the VBA instruction that will display the "Remember to print the grade report." message in a dialog box.

8 Verify that the insertion point is located between the `Private Sub` and `End Sub` lines in the Code window, then press the **Tab** key to indent the insertion point.

It is a standard programming practice to indent the instructions that appear between the `Private Sub` and `End Sub` lines for readability.

9 Type **'display message** (be sure to type the apostrophe) and then press the **Enter** key to move the insertion point to the next line in the Code window.

Notice that when you press the Enter key, the Visual Basic Editor color-codes the comment and also indents the insertion point on the next line. If you want to remove the indentation, you simply press the Backspace key. In this case, however, you will keep the indentation.

As you learned in the Concept lesson, you can use VBA's MsgBox com-mand to display a message in a dialog box.

10 Type **msgbox** and press the **spacebar**. Because the Auto Quick Info check box is selected in the Options dialog box, the Visual Basic Editor displays the syntax of the MsgBox command. Recall that you need only to enter the Prompt argument in the MsgBox command; the remaining four arguments are optional. The Prompt argument specifies the message you want the dialog box to display.

11 Type **prompt:="Remember to print the grade report."** and press the **Enter** key. Although the message is enclosed in quotation marks in the Prompt argument, the quotation marks will not appear when the message is displayed in the dialog box. Figure 1-41 shows the completed Close event procedure.

comment

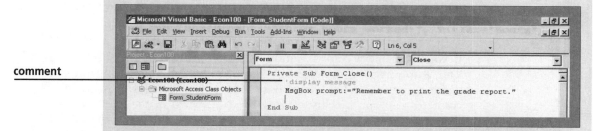

Figure 1-41: Code window showing the completed Close event procedure

Notice that the Visual Basic Editor changes the capitalization of the word `msgbox` to `MsgBox`. You can enter VBA commands in any case—uppercase, lowercase, or a combination of both cases. When you move the insertion point to another line in the Code window, the Visual Basic Editor changes the capitalization to match the capitalization used in the VBA language.

After entering the code in the Code window, you should save the procedure and then run it to verify that it is working correctly. Recall that you save a procedure by saving the file in which it is contained. You run an event procedure by causing the event—in this case, the form's Close event—to occur.

To save and run the form's Close event procedure:

1 Click the **Save Econ100** button 🖫 on the Visual Basic Editor's Standard toolbar to save the procedure. Close the Code window by clicking its **Close** button ✖, then close the Visual Basic Editor. You are returned to the Database window in Access.

HELP? Don't be concerned if the form appears behind the Database window.

2 Right-click **StudentForm** in the Forms list box and then click **Open** on the shortcut menu. Click the **Close** button ☒ on the Student Entry Form window to close the form. Before the form is closed, its Close event procedure displays the "Remember to print the grade report." message in a dialog box, as shown in Figure 1-42.

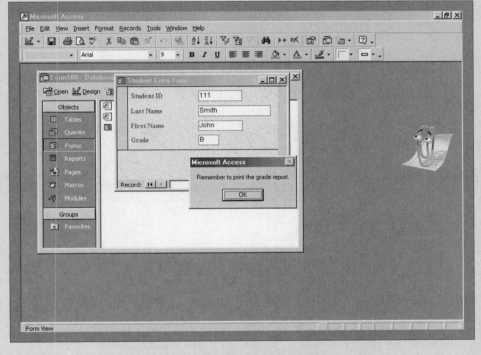

Figure 1-42: The form and the message displayed in a dialog box

3 Click the **OK** button to close the dialog box and the form.

The form's Close event procedure is working correctly. Now you can begin coding Professor Martinez's second procedure, the CancelAssistantMacro procedure.

Coding the CancelAssistantMacro Procedure

Recall that Professor Martinez wants a procedure that displays "So long" in a dialog box before it turns the Office Assistant feature off. Because Professor Martinez wants to be able to run the procedure whenever he chooses to do so, the procedure will need to be a macro procedure. Recall that a macro procedure is more simply referred to as a macro. In Access, you use the Macro window to create a macro, which then can be run from either the Macro window or the Database window in Access.

tip

> The way you create a macro in Access differs from the way you create a macro in the other Office 2000 applications.

To create a macro in Access:

1 Click **Macros** in the Objects bar of the Database window, then click the **New** button 🗗 in the Database window's toolbar. The Macro window opens, as shown in Figure 1-43.

Action combo box

Action arguments section

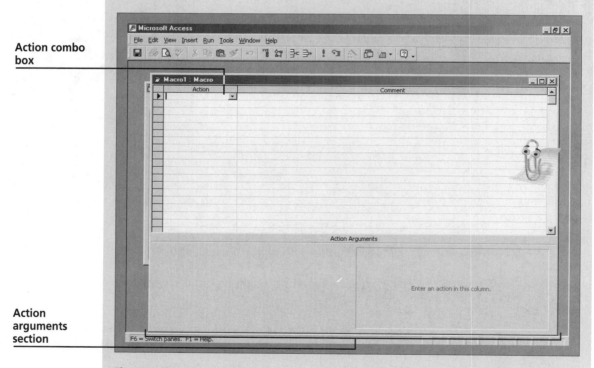

Figure 1-43: Macro window

In the Macro window, you record the tasks that you want the macro to perform. You do so by selecting one or more actions from the Action combo box. (Each line in the Macro window has its own Action combo box.) For example, to display the "So long" message in a dialog box, you select the MsgBox action in the Action combo box.

tip

A combo box is a combination of a text box and a list box. A combo box allows you to either type a value into its text box portion or select a value from its list box portion.

2 Click the **Action list arrow** that appears in the first line of the Macro window. Scroll down the list until you see MsgBox, then click **MsgBox**. The Action Arguments section of the Macro window shows a description of the MsgBox action. It also shows the names of the action's four arguments— Message, Beep, Type, and Title—and provides areas in which each argument's value can be entered.

3 Click **Message** in the Action Arguments section to place the insertion point in the Message text box. The description of the argument appears in the Action Arguments section, and it indicates that you enter the dialog box's message in this argument. Type **So long** and press the **Enter** key. See Figure 1-44.

Action Arguments section

message to display in the dialog box

description of the Beep action

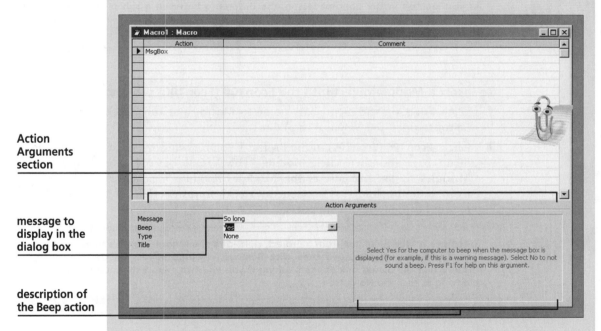

Figure 1-44: MsgBox action added to the Macro window

In addition to displaying the "So long" message, the macro also must turn the Office Assistant feature off. Unfortunately, the Action list does not contain a specific action for performing this task; however, you can use the Visual Basic Editor to create one. You create an action by creating a function procedure.

Before returning to the Visual Basic Editor to create the necessary function procedure, save the macro.

4 Click the **Save** button 🔲 on the Standard toolbar. When you are asked for the macro name, type **CancelAssistantMacro** and press the **Enter** key, then close the Macro window.

Creating a Function Procedure in Access

At times, you may want a macro to perform a task for which no action exists in the Macro window's Action list. In those cases, you need to use the Visual Basic Editor to create a function procedure, and then you use the Action list's RunCode action to include the procedure in the macro. The **RunCode action** tells the macro to run the code contained in the function procedure. Before you can create a function procedure, you need to insert a Module object into the project.

> As you learned in the Concept lesson, the difference between a sub procedure and a function procedure is that a function procedure *can* return a value, if necessary; whereas a sub procedure cannot.

To insert a Module object into the Econ100 (Econ100) project:

1 Click **Tools** on the menu bar, point to **Macro**, and then click **Visual Basic Editor** to open the Visual Basic Editor.

2 Click **Econ100 (Econ100)** in the Project Explorer window, click **Insert** on the menu bar, and then click **Module**. The Visual Basic Editor creates the Modules folder and inserts the Module1 module (designated by the 🔧 icon) into the folder. The General Declarations section of the Module1 module's Code window appears.

> To remove a Module object from a project, right-click the Module object's name in the Project Explorer window, and then click Remove *<module name>* on the shortcut menu. When the dialog box appears asking if you want to export the module before removing it, click the No button.

After inserting the Module1 module into the project, you then can insert the CancelAssistant function procedure into the module.

To insert the CancelAssistant function procedure into the Module1 module, then code the procedure:

1 Verify that the title bar shows that you are viewing the Module1 module's Code window, and that the insertion point is located in the Code window. Click **Insert** on the menu bar and then click **Procedure**. The Add Procedure dialog box opens.

>   **HELP?** If the Procedure option on the Insert menu is dimmed, close the Insert menu. Click inside the Code window to make it the active window, then repeat Step 1.

> Before inserting a procedure into a module, always verify that the module's Code window is open and that the insertion point is located in the Code window. You can verify that the module's Code window is open by noting the text either in the Visual Basic Editor's title bar when the Code window is maximized or in the Code window's title bar when the Code window is not maximized.

First you need to name the procedure.

2 Type **CancelAssistant** in the Name text box.

For a procedure to be run by the Action list's RunCode action, the procedure must begin with the keywords `Public Function`. As you learned in the Concept lesson, `Public` specifies the procedure's scope and `Function` specifies its type. The Public option button already is selected in the Add Procedure dialog box. You need only to select the Function option button.

3 Click the **Function** option button in the Type section of the dialog box, as shown in Figure 1-45.

Modules folder and Module1 object inserted into the project

both options must be selected for the procedure to be run by the RunCode action

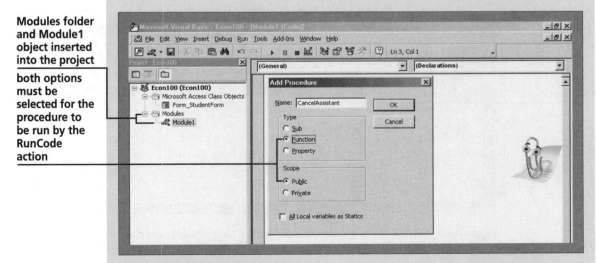

Figure 1-45: Add Procedure dialog box

4 Click the **OK** button to close the Add Procedure dialog box. The Visual Basic Editor inserts the CancelAssistant procedure into the Module1 module, and the code template for the CancelAssistant procedure appears in the Code window.

Between the `Public Function` and `End Function` lines, you will enter a comment that describes the purpose of the current procedure. Then you will enter the VBA instruction that will turn the Office Assistant feature off.

5 Press the **Tab** key to indent the insertion point. Type **'turn Office Assistant feature off** and then press the **Enter** key.

You turn the Office Assistant feature off from code by setting the Assistant object's On property to the Boolean value False. The instruction you will use is `Assistant.On = False`.

6 Type **assistant** and then type . (a period). Because you selected the Auto List Members check box in the Options dialog box, an alphabetical listing of the Assistant object's properties (designated by the 📑 icon) and methods (designated by the 🦴 icon) appears.

7 Scroll down the members list until you locate the On property, then click **On**.

tip

You also can type the first letter of the property you are looking for—in this case the letter o. This will highlight the On property, which is the first property in the list that begins with the letter o. Then you can either press the Tab key to enter the On property at the current location of the insertion point in the Code window, or you simply can type the next character in the instruction—in this case, the equal sign.

8 Type = (an equal sign). The Visual Basic Editor displays False and True in a list. Click **False** and then press the **Enter** key. Figure 1-46 shows the completed CancelAssistant procedure.

comment

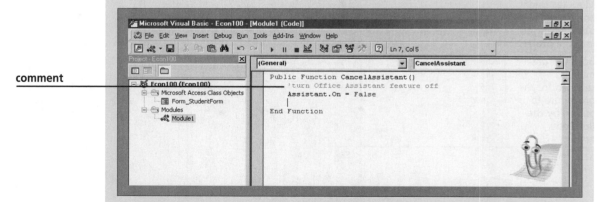

Figure 1-46: Code window showing the completed CancelAssistant procedure

9 Click the **Save Econ100** button 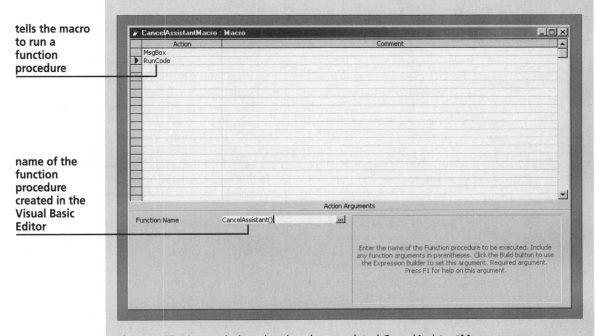 on the Standard toolbar. When the Save As dialog box appears, click the **OK** button to accept the default module name, Module1.

10 Close the Code window, then close the Visual Basic Editor.

Now return to the Macro window and complete the CancelAssistantMacro macro.

To return to the Macro window and complete the CancelAssistantMacro macro, then save and run the macro:

1 Right-click **CancelAssistantMacro** in the Macros list box, then click **Design View** to open the Macro window.

2 Click the **line immediately below MsgBox** in the Macro window.

The action that tells a macro to run a function procedure is called RunCode.

3 Click the **Action list arrow**. Scroll the list until you see RunCode, then click **RunCode**. Click **Function Name** in the Action Arguments section of the window. In the blank area to the right of Function Name, type **CancelAssistant()** (be sure to type the parentheses) as the function name. Figure 1-47 shows the completed CancelAssistantMacro macro.

tells the macro
to run a
function
procedure

name of the
function
procedure
created in the
Visual Basic
Editor

Figure 1-47: Macro window showing the completed CancelAssistantMacro macro

Next, save and run the macro to verify that it is working correctly.

4 Click the **Save** button 🖫 on the toolbar, then click the **Run** button ⚠ on the toolbar. The macro displays "So long" in a dialog box. Click the **OK** button to close the dialog box. The macro runs the CancelAssistant function procedure, which turns the Office Assistant feature off. The Office Assistant is removed from the screen.

5 Close the Macro window.

Before closing Access, you will compact the database so that it consumes less space on your Data Disk.

 tip

> As you are working in a database, its size increases and takes up more space on your disk. You can decrease the size of a database by compacting it.

6 Click **Tools** on the Standard toolbar, point to **Database Utilities**, and then click **Compact and Repair Database**.

7 Close Access.

You now have completed Tutorial 1's Access lesson. You can either take a break or complete the end-of-lesson exercises.

E X E R C I S E S

1. In this exercise, you will code the StudentForm form's Click event procedure so that it displays the current time in a dialog box when you click the form.
    a. Use Windows to make a copy of the Econ100 (Econ100.mdb) database that you completed in this lesson. The file is located in the Tut01\Access folder on your Data Disk. Rename the copy T1-AC-E1D.mdb.
    b. Open the T1-AC-E1D (T1-AC-E1D.mdb) file. Open the Visual Basic Editor, then open the form's Open event procedure. Code the Open event so that it displays the current time in a dialog box. You can use VBA's Time function to do so. A function is a procedure that returns a value. In this case, the Time function returns the current time as maintained by your computer system's internal clock; this time is referred to as the system time.
    c. Save the procedure, then close the Visual Basic Editor. Open the StudentForm form. When the dialog box showing the current time appears, click the OK button to close the dialog box, then close the form. Also close the "Remember to print the grade report." message box.
    d. When the procedure is working correctly, print the project's code, then compact and close the database.

2. In this exercise, you will create a macro that opens the Students table and then beeps.
    a. Use Windows to make a copy of the Econ100 (Econ100.mdb) database that you completed in this lesson. The file is located in the Tut01\Access folder on your Data Disk. Rename the copy T1-AC-E2D.mdb.

b. Open the T1-AC-E2D (T1-AC-E2D.mdb) file, then open the Visual Basic Editor. Add a function procedure named GetAssistant to the Module1 module. The procedure should display the Office Assistant by setting its On and Visible properties to the Boolean value True. Save the procedure, then close the Visual Basic Editor.

c. Use the Macro window to create a macro that opens the Students table, beeps, and then runs the GetAssistant procedure.

d. Save the macro, naming it OpenBeepShowMacro, then close the Macro window. Run the OpenBeepShowMacro macro from the Database window.

e. Close the table, then compact and close the database.

Exercise 3 is a Discovery Exercise. Discovery Exercises, which may include topics that are not covered in this lesson, allow you to "discover" the solutions to problems on your own.

discovery ▶ 3. In this exercise, you will code the StudentReport report's Open event procedure so that it displays the message "Print two copies" in a dialog box.

a. Use Windows to make a copy of the Econ100 (Econ100.mdb) database that you completed in this lesson. The file is located in the Tut01\Access folder on your Data Disk. Rename the copy, T1-AC-E3D.mdb.

b. Open the T1-AC-E3 (T1-AC-E3D.mdb) file. Open the StudentReport report in Design View, then display its property sheet. Set the report's Has Module property to Yes. Save the report, then close the report.

c. Open the Visual Basic Editor. Code the report's Open event procedure so that it displays the message "Print two copies" in a dialog box.

d. Save the procedure, then run the procedure by opening the report in Print Preview. When the procedure is working correctly, print only the code for the report's Open event procedure, then compact and close the database.

A computer program is good only if it works. Errors in programming code can cause a program to run incorrectly. Therefore, a programmer needs to know how to locate and fix any errors in his or her code. Exercise 4 is a Debugging Exercise. Debugging Exercises allow you to practice recognizing and solving errors in code.

debugging 4. What is wrong with the following event procedure?

```
Private Sub Form_Open()
    MsgBox prompt:="Hello"
End Form_Open
```

The Object Model

In this tutorial you will learn how to:

- Refer to the objects contained in an application's object model
- Use the Object Browser in the Visual Basic Editor
- Enter instructions in the Immediate window in the Visual Basic Editor
- Refer to the most commonly used objects in Excel, Word, and Access

Concept Lesson

Understanding the Object Model

As you learned in the Overview, Visual Basic for Applications (VBA) is the programming language included in Microsoft Office 2000, as well as in many non-Microsoft applications. The advantage of having the VBA language shared among many applications is that once you learn the language you can use that knowledge to customize many different applications.

Although all VBA-enabled applications share the same language, each contains its own unique set of objects, referred to as the application's **object model**. For example, the Excel object model includes workbook and worksheet objects, while the Word object model contains document and paragraph objects. Before you can write the VBA instructions needed to customize an application, you first must become familiar with the objects that comprise the application's object model, because you will need to refer to these objects in your VBA code.

Although you may not realize it, you already are familiar with object models. For example, Figure 2-1 shows a simplified object model for a library.

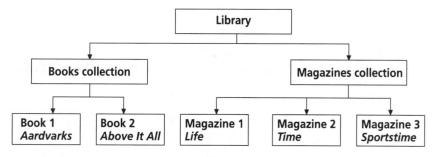

Figure 2-1: Simplified object model for a library

Similar to an application's object model, a library's object model shows the hierarchy of the objects included in the model.

All object models contain two types of objects: collection objects and individual objects. A **collection object**, typically referred to simply as a **collection**, is a group of one or more individual objects treated as one unit. A library, for example, has a books collection that contains the individual book objects owned by the library. It also has a magazines collection that contains the individual magazine objects. In most object models, a plural word (books and magazines) is used to designate a collection, while a singular word (book and magazine) indicates an individual object. The advantage of treating a group of related objects as a collection is that it allows you to conveniently refer to all of the individual objects at the same time—for example, the librarian can advise you simply to search the magazines collection.

In the next section, you will learn how to refer to the objects contained in an application's object model.

Referring to the Objects Contained in an Application's Object Model

You can refer to an individual object within a collection using either its name or its position number in the collection. For example, you can refer to the *Above It All* book shown in Figure 2-1 by its name (*Above It All*) or by its position number in the books collection. Because the *Above It All* book is the second book in the books collection, its position number is 2.

Just like a library, most VBA-enabled applications have object models that contain many objects, and the object model can seem a bit overwhelming when viewed. Fortunately, you routinely use only a small portion of an application's object model. For example, Figure 2-2 shows just a small portion of the PowerPoint object model. This figure includes only the most commonly used PowerPoint objects.

tip

••
You will learn how to view the full PowerPoint object model in this lesson's Exercise 6.
••

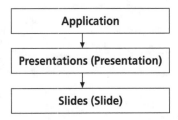

Figure 2-2: The most commonly used PowerPoint objects

Notice that the object model shown in Figure 2-2 includes three rectangles: Application, Presentations (Presentation), and Slides (Slide). The Application rectangle represents the Application object, which refers to the application in which you are working. In PowerPoint, for example, the Application object refers to the PowerPoint application; however, in Word the Application object refers to the Word application. The Application object is always the highest object in an application's object model.

Immediately below the Application rectangle is the Presentations (Presentation) rectangle, which represents both the Presentations collection and the individual Presentation objects within the collection. Notice that the name of the collection (Presentations) is plural, but the name of an individual object within the collection (Presentation) is singular. When a rectangle represents both a collection and its associated objects, the collection name is listed first, followed by the individual object name enclosed in parentheses. Presentations (Presentation) tells you that the Presentations collection is made up of individual Presentation objects.

The Slides (Slide) rectangle is one level down from the Presentations (Presentation) rectangle in the object model. In this case, the plural word *Slides* denotes the name of the collection, and the singular word *Slide* indicates the type of object included in the collection. In other words, a Slides collection is composed of Slide objects.

Figure 2-3 illustrates the PowerPoint objects and collections shown in Figure 2-2.

tip

All collection names in an object model are plural and, for the most part, all individual object names are singular; some exceptions do exist, however. For example, the plural words *LanguageSettings* and *DefaultWebOptions* in an object model refer to objects rather than collections. If you are not sure to what a name refers, you can view its Help screen.

both Presentation objects are included in the Presentations collection

Application object

January presentation's Slides collection

Slide object

February presentation's Slides collection

Slide object

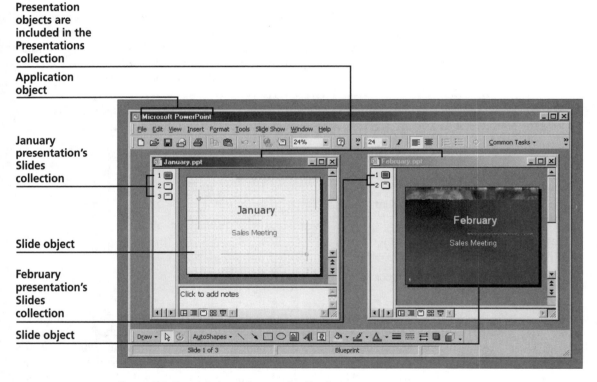

Figure 2-3: PowerPoint objects and collections

As Figure 2-3 indicates, the Application object is the PowerPoint application itself. Contained within the Application object is the Presentations collection, which includes two Presentation objects (January.ppt and February.ppt). The January.ppt Presentation object contains one Slides collection, composed of three Slide objects. The February.ppt Presentation object also contains one Slides collection, but its Slides collection contains two Slide objects.

Referring to Objects in VBA Code

You can use VBA to refer to any element in an application's object model, but to do so you must specify the object's exact location in the object model's hierarchy. When specifying the location, you begin at the top of the hierarchy, with the Application object, and then work your way down each level until you reach the desired element. You use the dot member selection operator (.) to separate the name of an element located on one level from the name of an element located on the next level. For example, you use `Application.Presentations` in a VBA instruction to refer to the Application object's Presentations collection.

▶ **tip**

> As you learned in Tutorial 1, the dot member selection operator indicates that the item to its right is a member of the item to its left. For example, `Application.Presentations` indicates that the Presentations collection is a member of the Application object.

As in the library example discussed earlier, you can refer to a specific object within a collection using either the object's name, enclosed in quotation marks, or its position number within the collection, referred to as its **index**. In most collections, the index of the first object in the collection is 1. In VBA code, you include the name or index in a pair of parentheses following the collection's name. For example, to refer to the first Presentation object shown in Figure 2-3, you use either `Application.Presentations("January.ppt")` or `Application.Presentations(1)`. Notice that the name of the object within a collection is enclosed in quotation marks, but its index is not.

To refer to the Slides collection contained within the January.ppt Presentation object, you use either `Application.Presentations("January.ppt").Slides` or `Application.Presentations(1).Slides`. You use either `Application.Presentations("January.ppt").Slides("Slide3")` or `Application.Presentations(1).Slides(3)` to refer to the third Slide object contained within the January.ppt Presentation object's Slides collection.

Every object in the object model has a set of properties and methods. In the next section, you will learn how to refer to these properties and methods in code.

Referring to an Object's Properties and Methods in VBA Code

As you learned in Tutorial 1, an object's properties and methods are referred to as members of the object. A property, you may remember, is a characteristic of an object, and a method is an action that an object can perform on its own. The Application object, for example, has a Name property that stores the Application object's name, and it has a Quit method that is used to end the application.

You use the *expression.property* syntax in a VBA instruction to access an object's property, and you use the *expression.method* syntax to invoke one of its methods. In the syntax, *expression* represents the location in the object model of the object whose *property* or *method* you want to access. In the `Application.Presentations.Count` instruction, for example, `Application.Presentations` is the *expression*, and it specifies that the desired object—in this case, the

Presentations collection—is located immediately below the Application object in the object model. `Count` is a *property* of the Presentations collection; it stores the number of presentations currently open. In the `Application.Quit` instruction, on the other hand, `Application` is the *expression*, and it refers to the top object in the hierarchy. `Quit` is a *method* of the Application object; `Quit` instructs the application to close itself. As you learned in Tutorial 1, you use the dot member selection operator (.) to separate an object from its property or method.

As mentioned earlier, before you can customize an application, you need to become familiar with the objects in its object model. One way to do so is to use the Object Browser, which is available in the Visual Basic Editor.

The Object Browser

The **Object Browser** allows you to browse through all available objects in an application and see their properties, methods, and events. You also can use the Object Browser to display an object's Help screen. You can open the Object Browser by clicking the Object Browser button 🔳 on the Visual Basic Editor's Standard toolbar. You also can select the Object Browser command on the View menu, or you can press the F2 key. The Object Browser appears in its own window, as shown in Figure 2-4.

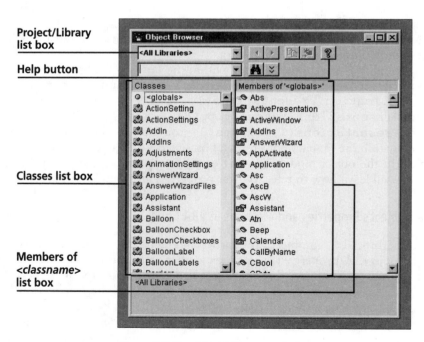

Figure 2-4: The Object Browser window

As Figure 2-4 indicates, the Object Browser includes a Help button 🔳, a Project/Library list box, a Classes list box, and a Members of *<classname>* list box.

A **class** is the formal definition of an object; it defines the properties that control the object's appearance and the methods and events that control the object's behavior. You can think of a class as being a pattern from which an object is created. For example, when you create a new PowerPoint presentation, VBA uses the PowerPoint Presentation class to create the appropriate Presentation object. The Presentation object will contain all of the properties, methods, and events defined in the Presentation class.

All of the information pertaining to an application's object model is stored in an **object library**, which is simply a file. Every VBA-enabled application comes with its own object library, which is copied to either the local hard drive or the network drive when the application is installed. Currently, the Project/Library list box contains <All Libraries>, which specifies that you want to view the contents of all the available libraries. To view the information stored only in the PowerPoint object library, you click the Project/Library list arrow and then select PowerPoint in the list. After you switch to the PowerPoint library, you will see only the PowerPoint classes listed in the Classes list box, as shown in Figure 2-5.

tip

Most object library file names have an .olb ("object library") extension. For example, in Office 2000, the Microsoft Access object library is stored in the msacc9.olb file and the Microsoft PowerPoint object library is stored in the msppt9.olb file. However, some object library file names have a .tlb ("type library"), .exe ("executable"), or .dll ("dynamic link library") extension.

displays only
PowerPoint's
object library

Help button

refers to
PowerPoint's
Application
object

PowerPoint's
object library
file

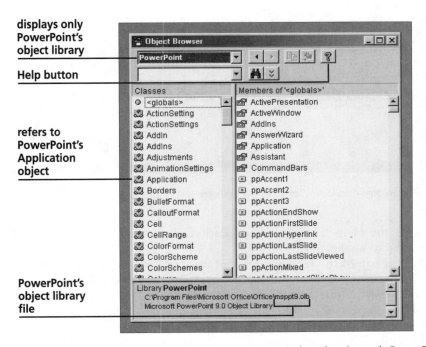

Figure 2-5: The Object Browser window showing only PowerPoint's classes

Next, you will learn how to use the Object Browser to display an object's Help screen.

Getting Help in the Object Browser

You can view an object's Help screen by clicking the object's class in the Classes list box, and then clicking the Help button [?] located at the top of the Object Browser window. For example, you can view the PowerPoint Application object's Help screen by clicking Application in the Classes list box, and then clicking [?]. Figure 2-6 shows the Help screen for the PowerPoint Application object.

represents a portion of PowerPoint's object model

the Application object represents the Microsoft PowerPoint application

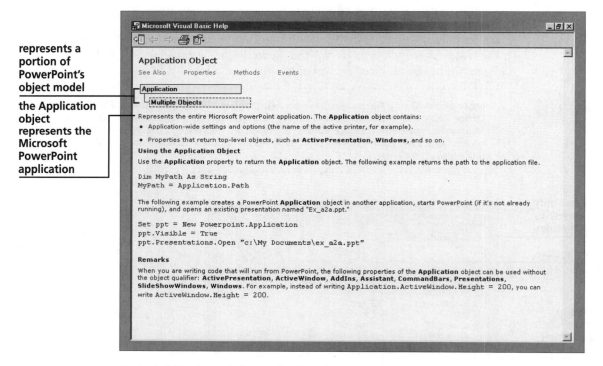

Figure 2-6: The PowerPoint Application object's Help screen

According to the Help screen, the Application object represents the entire Microsoft PowerPoint application.

Notice that the top of the Help screen contains two rectangles: Application and Multiple Objects. These two rectangles represent only a small portion of the PowerPoint object model, which, as you recall, always begins with the Application object.

As discussed earlier, the Application rectangle represents the Application object. The Multiple Objects rectangle represents the objects found at the next level in the object model hierarchy. To view a listing of these lower-level objects, you need simply to click the Multiple Objects rectangle; doing so will open the Topics Found dialog box shown in Figure 2-7.

listing of objects located below PowerPoint's Application object

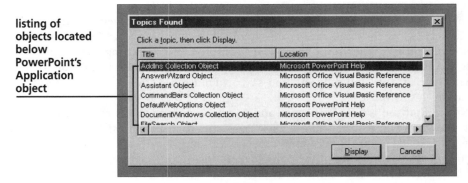

Figure 2-7: Topics Found dialog box

To view a Help screen for one of these objects, you select the object's name in the list, and then click the Display button. For example, Figure 2-8 shows the Help screen for the Presentations collection object. (Recall from Figure 2-2 that the Presentations collection is one level below the Application object in the PowerPoint object model.)

Back button

click here to display property listing

object model

click here to view the Presentation object Help screen

click here to display method listing

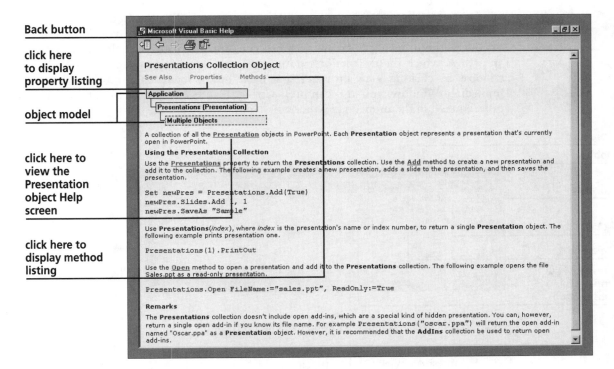

Figure 2-8: Presentations Collection Object Help screen

You can view the Help screen for an individual Presentation object by clicking <u>Presentation</u> in the Presentations Collection Object Help screen. You can use the Help screen's Back button ⟸ to return to a previously viewed Help screen.

As the diagram shown at the top of Figure 2-8's Help screen indicates, the Presentations collection and the Presentation objects are located on the level immediately below the Application object, which means that these objects are contained within the Application object. The Multiple Objects rectangle that appears below the Presentations (Presentation) rectangle represents the objects found on the next level in the hierarchy. As you saw in Figure 2-2, the Slides collection is located on this lower level.

Notice that the words Properties and Methods appear at the top of the Help screen shown in Figure 2-8. You can click Properties to display a listing of the properties associated with the Presentations collection object, and you can click Methods to display a listing of the object's methods.

The Object Browser and the Help screens are invaluable tools for learning an application's object model. Once you are familiar with the object model, you can use the Immediate window in the Visual Basic Editor to practice entering VBA instructions that access the properties and methods of the various objects.

Using the Immediate Window

In addition to the Code window, the Visual Basic Editor also provides an Immediate window into which you can enter VBA instructions. Unlike the Code window, the Immediate window is a temporary testing environment that allows you to try a line of code without having to create and then run an entire procedure. It also provides an area in which the instruction's output can be viewed. You open the Immediate window by clicking View on the Visual Basic Editor menu bar, and then clicking Immediate Window; you also can press Ctrl+g. Figure 2-9 shows two VBA instructions entered in the Immediate window.

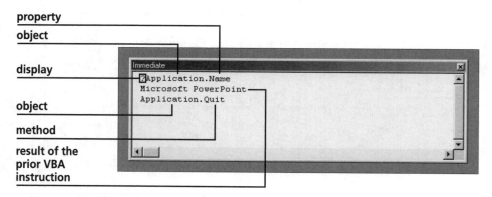

Figure 2-9: Immediate window showing two VBA instructions

The question mark (?) that appears at the beginning of the `?Application.Name` instruction causes the value of what follows the ? symbol to appear below the instruction in the Immediate window. In this case, VBA displays the value stored in the Application object's Name property (Microsoft PowerPoint) immediately below the `?Application.Name` instruction. Although other objects in the PowerPoint object model also have a Name property, the `Application.Name` instruction indicates that you are interested only in the Application object's Name property.

> **You also can use the keyword Print to display a value in the Immediate window. For example, you can use the `Print Application.Name` instruction to display in the Immediate window the value stored in the Application object's Name property.**

Notice that the `Application.Quit` instruction shown in Figure 2-9 does not begin with a question mark, nor does any result appear immediately below the instruction in the Immediate window. Because `Quit` is a method, which represents an action that an object can perform, it does not store a value that can be displayed, as does a property. The Quit method simply instructs the application to close itself. The PowerPoint application will close as soon as you press the Enter key after typing the `Application.Quit` instruction in the Immediate window.

Just as when entering instructions in a Code window, typing the period after an object's name in the Immediate window will display a listing of the object's members (its methods and properties). The icon that appears next to the member's name in the list indicates whether the member is a method 🔧 or a property 🖾.

> **As you learned in Tutorial 1, the member list appears only if the Auto List Members check box is selected in the Options dialog box of the Visual Basic Editor.**

Assume that you want to know how many Presentation objects are included in the Presentations collection shown earlier in Figure 2-3. You can display that information in the Immediate window by entering, in the window, an instruction that accesses the Presentations collection's Count property, as shown in Figure 2-10.

property

display

number of
Presentation
objects
contained in
Figure 2-3's
Presentation
collection

full reference
to the
Presentations
collection

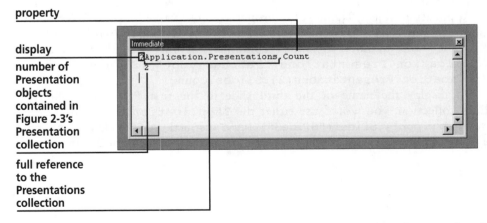

Figure 2-10: Immediate window displaying the number of Presentation objects within the Presentations collection

Recall that the syntax for referring to the property of an object is *expression.property*, where *expression* represents the location of the object in the object model. In the `?Application.Presentations.Count` instruction, `Application.Presentations` specifies the location of the Presentations collection in the object model, and `Count` specifies the desired property. (You may want to refer to Figure 2-2 to view the location of the Presentations collection in the PowerPoint object model.) The `Application.Presentations.Count` reference indicates that the Count property is a member of the Presentations collection, which is contained in the Application object.

Now assume that you want to know the name of the second Presentation object in the Presentations collection. You would use the instruction shown in Figure 2-11 to display that information in the Immediate window.

property

name of the second Presentation object

full reference to the second Presentation object

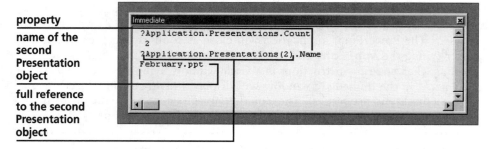

Figure 2-11: Immediate window displaying the name of the second Presentation object within the Presentations collection

Notice that the VBA instruction displays February.ppt as the name of the second Presentation object. In the instruction, `Application.Presentations(2)` is the *expression*, and it indicates that the object is the second Presentation object contained within the Presentations collection, which is contained within the Application object; Name is the *property* whose value you want to display. Following this logic, you would use either of the following two instructions to display the number of slides contained in the second presentation: `?Application.Presentations("February.ppt").Slides.Count` or `?Application.Presentations(2).Slides.Count`.

To display the name of the third slide in the first Presentation object's Slides collection, you would use either the `?Application.Presentations ("January.ppt").Slides("Slide3").Name` instruction or the `?Application. Presentations(1).Slides(3).Name` instruction, as shown in Figure 2-12.

full reference to second Presentation object's Slides collection

full reference to third Slide object contained in the first Presentation object's Slides collection

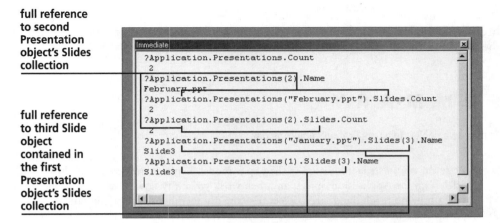

Figure 2-12: Immediate window showing additional VBA instructions and their results

Because the Application object always refers to the application in which you are working, you can omit the `Application` keyword from a VBA instruction. For example, the two instructions `Application.Presentations.Count` and `Presentations.Count` will produce equivalent results. In the latter instruction, VBA assumes that you are referring to the Presentations collection within the current Application object. However, it is recommended that you include the `Application` keyword in your instructions until you gain more experience with the application's object model.

Repeating and Deleting Instructions in the Immediate Window

If you want to repeat an instruction that you entered earlier, you can either retype the instruction after the last instruction in the Immediate window, or you can select the instruction in the Immediate window, copy it to the clipboard, and then paste it after the last instruction in the Immediate window.

If you want to remove one or more lines from the Immediate window, simply select the lines you want to remove and then press either the Delete key or the Backspace key; you also can use the Cut command on the Edit menu or Ctrl+x. When you close the application, the Visual Basic Editor automatically clears the contents of the Immediate window.

Printing Code from the Immediate Window

You can use either a text editor or a word processor—for example, WordPad or Word—to print the instructions entered in the Immediate window. First select the instructions in the Immediate window and then copy them to the clipboard. Open a new document in either a text editor or word processor and then paste the instructions in the document. You then can print the document for future reference.

Like the Object Browser and the Help screens, the Immediate window is an invaluable tool for learning an application's object model.

You now have completed Tutorial 2's Concept lesson. You can either take a break or complete the end-of-lesson questions and exercises before moving on to the next lesson.

SUMMARY

To refer to an object in an application's object model:

■ Specify the object's exact location in the object model. Begin at the top of the object model, with the Application object, and then work your way down each level in the model until you reach the desired object. Use the dot member selection operator (.) to separate the name of an object located on one level from the name of an object located on the next level.

■ If the object is a member of a collection, include either the object's name or its index in a set of parentheses following the collection's name. If you use the object's name, the name must be enclosed in quotation marks.

To access the property of an object:

■ Use the *expression.property* syntax, where *expression* represents the location of the object in the object model.

To invoke one of an object's methods:

■ Use the *expression.method* syntax, where *expression* represents the location of the object in the object model.

To view information about the various objects available to your application:

■ Open the Object Browser window by clicking the Object Browser button 📺 on the Visual Basic Editor's Standard toolbar. You also can use the Object Browser command on the View menu, or you can press the F2 key.

■ Select the appropriate object library from the Project/Library list box.

■ Click the appropriate keyword in the Classes list box, and then click the Help button 🔳 .

To use the Immediate window in the Visual Basic Editor:

■ Open the Immediate window in the Visual Basic Editor by clicking View on the Visual Basic Editor menu bar, and then clicking Immediate Window; you also can use Ctrl+g.

■ Enter the instruction in the Immediate window. If you want to display a value in the Immediate window, begin the instruction with a ? (question mark).

■ You can copy and paste instructions from one part of the Immediate window to another.

■ Remove one or more lines from the Immediate window by selecting the lines you want to remove and then pressing either the Delete key or the Backspace key; you also can use the Cut command on the Edit menu or Ctrl+x.

■ To print the instructions entered in the Immediate window, first select the instructions and then copy them to the clipboard. Open a new document in either a text editor or word processor and then paste the instructions in the document. You then can print the document.

REVIEW QUESTIONS

1. All VBA-enabled applications use the same object model.
   a. True
   b. False

2. A(n) _____ is a group of one or more individual objects treated as one unit.
   a. assortment
   b. collection
   c. compilation
   d. set

3. The names of collections are always _____, and the names of individual objects are typically _____.
   a. lowercase, uppercase
   b. plural, singular
   c. singular, plural
   d. uppercase, lowercase

4. The _____ object is the highest object in an application's object model.
   a. App
   b. Application collection
   c. Application
   d. Collection

5. Which of the following would you find in an object model rectangle that represents both a collection and its associated objects?
   a. Application
   b. Presentation (Presentations)
   c. Slides
   d. Slides (Slide)

6. Which of the following instructions will display the number of Presentation objects contained in the Presentations collection?
   a. `?Application.Count.Presentation`
   b. `?Application.Count.Presentations`
   c. `?Application.Presentation.Count`
   d. `?Application.Presentations.Count`

7. Which of the following instructions will display the name of the first Presentation object contained in the Presentations collection?
   a. `?Application.Name.Presentation(1)`
   b. `?Application.Name.Presentations(1)`
   c. `?Application.Presentations(1).Name`
   d. `?Application.Presentation(1).Name`

8. Which of the following instructions will display the number of slides contained in the third Presentation object, which is named "March.ppt"?
   a. `?Application.Presentations("March.ppt").Slides.Count`
   b. `?Application.Presentations.Slides(3).Count`
   c. `?Application.Slides.Presentations("March.ppt").Count`
   d. `?Application.Slides.Presentations(3).Count`

E X E R C I S E S

1. Figure 2-13 shows a simplified object model for a pet store.

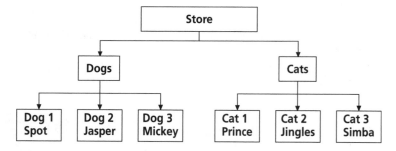

Figure 2-13

a. Which rectangles shown in Figure 2-13 represent collections?
b. Which rectangles shown in Figure 2-13 represent individual objects contained within a collection?
c. Use the appropriate collection and object names, along with the dot member selection operator, to write a reference to the following objects within the pet store object model. (For example, you would use the `Store.Dogs` reference to refer to the Dogs collection.)
   i)   The Cats collection
   ii) The Mickey object (use its index)
   iii) The Jingles object (use its name)
   iv) The Spot object (use its name)
   v)   The Prince object (use its index)

2. In this exercise, you will write references to the objects found in a portion of the Microsoft Excel object model, which is shown in Figure 2-14.

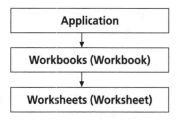

Figure 2-14

  a. What are the names of the collections shown in Figure 2-14? What type of objects are contained in the collections?
  b. How would you refer to the Application object in Excel?
  c. How would you refer to the Workbooks collection?
  d. How would you refer to the first Workbook object in the Workbooks collection?
  e. How would you refer to the second Worksheet object contained in the first Workbook object?

3. In this exercise, you will write references to the objects found in a portion of the Microsoft Word object model, which is shown in Figure 2-15.

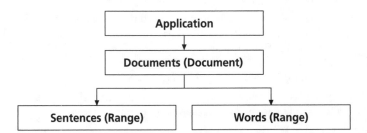

Figure 2-15

  a. What are the names of the collections shown in Figure 2-15? What type of objects are contained in the collections?
  b. How would you refer to the Application object in Word?
  c. How would you refer to the Documents collection?
  d. How would you refer to the third Document object in the Documents collection?
  e. How would you refer to the first sentence contained in the second Document object?
  f. How would you refer to the Words collection in the first Document object?
  g. How would you refer to the fifth word contained in the first Document object?

4. In this exercise, you will write references to the objects found in a portion of the Microsoft Access object model, which is shown in Figure 2-16.

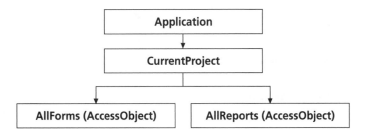

Figure 2-16

a. What are the names of the collections shown in Figure 2-16? What type of objects are contained in the collections?
b. How would you refer to the Application object in Access?
c. How would you refer to the CurrentProject object?
d. How would you refer to the AllForms collection?
e. How would you refer to the first form in the AllForms collection? The first form in the AllForms collection has an index of 0.

Exercise 5 is a Discovery Exercise. Discovery Exercises, which may include topics that are not covered in the lesson, allow you to "discover" the solutions to problems on your own.

discovery ▶ 5. In this exercise, you will learn how to search the Object Browser.
a. Start either PowerPoint, Excel, Access, or Word. Open the Visual Basic Editor. How can you use the Object Browser to search all of the available libraries for the word "Application"?
b. Close either PowerPoint, Excel, Access, or Word.

You also can use VBA in PowerPoint to create procedures that enhance your presentations. Exercise 6 allows you to apply this tutorial's programming concept in a PowerPoint presentation.

powerpoint 📁 6. In this exercise, you will learn how to display the entire object model for the PowerPoint application. You also will display Help screens for PowerPoint objects, properties, and methods.
a. Start PowerPoint and then open a new PowerPoint presentation. Open the Visual Basic Editor, and then open the Object Browser window. Display the Help screen for the Application object in the PowerPoint object library.
b. Click See Also in the Application Object Help screen. When the Topics Found dialog box appears, click Microsoft PowerPoint Objects in the list, and then click the Display button to display the full PowerPoint object model.
c. Display Help screens for the following:
   i) The Application object's ActivePresentation property
   ii) The Presentation collection's Open method
   iii) The Presentation object's Saved property
   iv) The Presentation object's PrintOut method
   v) The Slide object
d. Close PowerPoint.

A computer program is good only if it works. Errors in programming code can cause a program to run incorrectly. Therefore, a programmer needs to know how to locate and fix any errors in his or her code. Exercise 7 is a Debugging Exercise. Debugging Exercises allow you to practice recognizing and solving errors in code.

debugging **7.** The following instruction is supposed to display the name of the fourth slide contained in the December.ppt presentation, but it is not working correctly. Correct the instruction.

```
?Application.Presentation(December.ppt).Slide(4).Name
```

Excel Lesson

The Excel Object Model

case ▶ Martin Washington, the accountant at Paradise Electronics, uses Microsoft Excel to complete many of his daily tasks. For example, he uses an Excel workbook to track each store's inventory and sales. He would like to use VBA to customize his Excel workbooks to better suit his work style and needs. You tell him that before he can do so, he must become familiar with the objects included in the Excel object model. You agree to explain a portion of the model to him, and to show him how he can refer to these objects in VBA.

Understanding the Excel Object Model

As you learned in the Concept lesson, an application's object model depicts the hierarchy of objects available in the application. Before Martin can customize his Excel workbooks, he needs to understand how to refer to the objects included in the Excel object model.

Figure 2-17 shows the portion of the Microsoft Excel object model that includes the most commonly used Excel objects. (You will view the full Excel object model in this lesson's Exercise 3.)

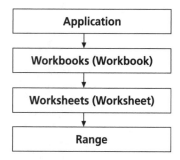

Figure 2-17: The most commonly used Excel objects

As Figure 2-17 indicates, the Excel object model begins with the Application object, which represents the Excel application. Contained within the Application object are the Workbooks collection and its associated Workbook objects. At the next level, you will find the Worksheets collection, made up of individual Worksheet objects. Included within a Worksheet object are Range objects. A **Range object** in Excel is defined as a cell, a row, a column, or a selection of cells containing one or more contiguous or noncontiguous blocks of cells. The Application, Workbook, Worksheet, and Range objects, as well as the Workbooks and Worksheets collections, are illustrated in Figure 2-18.

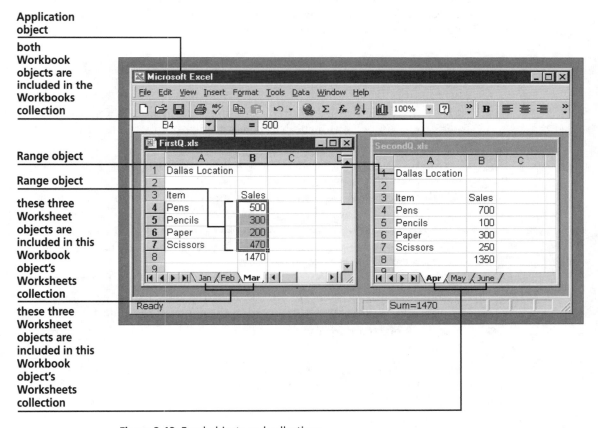

Figure 2-18: Excel objects and collections

In the next section, you will use the Object Browser in the Visual Basic Editor to display a Help screen for the Application object in Excel. You also will learn how to display the Help screens for other objects in the Excel object model.

Using the Object Browser in Excel

As you learned in the Concept lesson, you can use the Object Browser in the Visual Basic Editor to view information about the objects included in an application's object model. The Object Browser is a useful tool for understanding the structure of an object model and for studying the various objects included in the model, as well as the properties and methods of the objects.

To access the Object Browser in Excel:

1 Start Microsoft Excel. A new blank workbook appears.

In Tutorial 1, you learned how to open the Visual Basic Editor using the Tools menu on the Excel menu bar. A much quicker way to open the Visual Basic Editor is to press Alt+F11.

2 Press **Alt+F11** to open the Visual Basic Editor. Close any open Visual Basic windows, except for the Visual Basic Editor window.

3 Click the **Object Browser** button 🖼 on the Standard toolbar to open the Object Browser window. If necessary, maximize the Object Browser window.

· ·

You also can open the Object Browser by clicking View on the menu bar and then clicking Object Browser, or by pressing the F2 key.

· ·

As you learned in the Concept lesson, all of the information pertaining to an application's object model is stored in the application's object library.

4 Click the **Project/Library** list arrow, then click **Excel** in the list to display only the Excel object library. See Figure 2-19.

HELP? If the Object Browser window displays the Search Results section, click the Hide Search Results button ⊼ to close the section.

Project/Library list arrow

refers to the Excel Application object

Help button

the Excel object library file

your path might be different

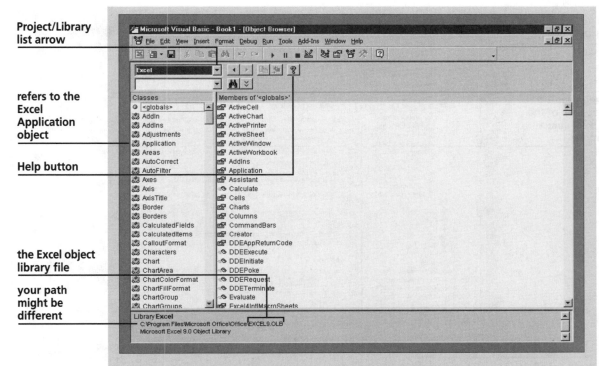

Figure 2-19: Object Browser window showing the Excel object library

5 Click **Application** in the Classes list box, and then click the **Help** button to open the Microsoft Visual Basic Help window, which displays the Application object's Help screen. Maximize the Microsoft Visual Basic Help window, then click the **Contents** tab, if necessary. See Figure 2-20.

HELP? If an error message appears indicating Help is not installed, see your instructor or technical support person.

HELP? If the Application Property Help screen appears, you inadvertently selected Application in the Members of *<classname>* list box. Close the Help window, then repeat Step 5; this time be sure to click Application in the Classes list box.

HELP? Don't be concerned if your Selection pane does not match the one shown in the figure.

Hide button

represents a portion of the Excel object model

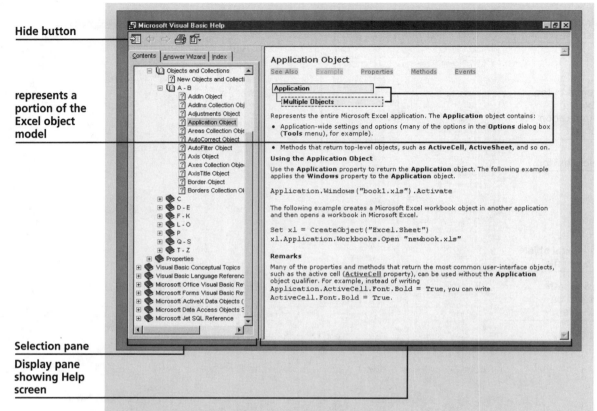

Selection pane

Display pane showing Help screen

Figure 2-20: Microsoft Visual Basic Help window

According to the Help screen, the Application object represents the entire Microsoft Excel application.

Notice that the Microsoft Visual Basic Help window is divided into two panes: the Selection pane and the Display pane. You use the Selection pane, which contains the Contents, Answer Wizard, and Index tabs, to select the topic whose Help screen you want to display in the Display pane. You also can hide the Selection pane so that you can view more of the information in the Display pane.

6 Click the **Hide** button 🔲 on the Microsoft Visual Basic Help toolbar to hide the Selection pane. Notice that 🔲 becomes a Show button 🔲, which you use to redisplay the Selection pane.

Next, view the Help screen for the Application object's Quit method.

7 Click **Methods** at the top of the Help screen. When the Topics Found dialog box appears, scroll down the list of methods until you see Quit Method. Click **Quit Method** in the list, and then click the **Display** button. The Quit Method Help screen appears, as shown in Figure 2-21.

Show button

purpose

syntax

click here to
view an
example of
using the Quit
method

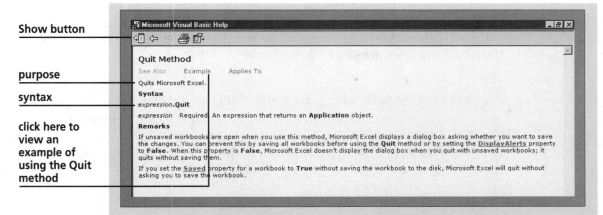

Figure 2-21: Quit Method Help screen

According to the Help screen, you use the Quit method to exit the
Microsoft Excel application. The syntax of the method is *expression*.**Quit**,
where *expression* refers to the Application object. You can click the word
Example at the top of the Help screen to view an example of using the Quit
method in a VBA instruction.

8 Click **Example** at the top of the Quit method's Help screen. See Figure 2-22.

Back button

instructs the
Excel
Application
object to
close itself

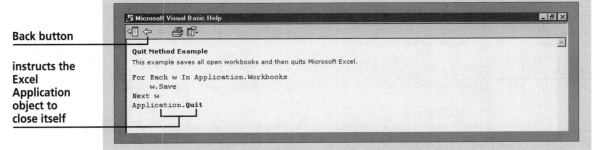

Figure 2-22: Example showing the Quit method in a VBA instruction

As the example shows, the `Application.Quit` instruction tells Excel
to close itself.

 tip

As you learned in Tutorial 1, a method is an action that an object can perform on
its own.

9 Click the **Back** button ⬅ on the Microsoft Visual Basic Help toolbar. The
Quit method's Help screen appears. Click ⬅ again to return to the
Application Object Help screen.

Notice that a Multiple Objects rectangle appears below the Application rectangle in the Application Object Help screen. As you learned in the Concept lesson, a Multiple Objects rectangle represents the next level of objects in the object model hierarchy. Now view a listing of these objects.

To view the next level of objects in the object model hierarchy:

1 Click the **Multiple Objects** rectangle in the Application Object Help screen. The Topics Found dialog box appears and lists the objects found on the next level of the Excel object model. Recall that the Workbooks collection and its Workbook objects are located on this lower level.

View the Help screen for the Workbooks collection object.

2 Scroll down the list of objects in the Topics Found dialog box until you see Workbooks Collection Object. Click **Workbooks Collection Object** and then click the **Display** button. The Workbooks Collection Object Help screen appears, as shown in Figure 2-23.

a yellow rectangle represents a collection and its associated objects

click here to display the Workbook Object Help screen

a blue rectangle represents an object

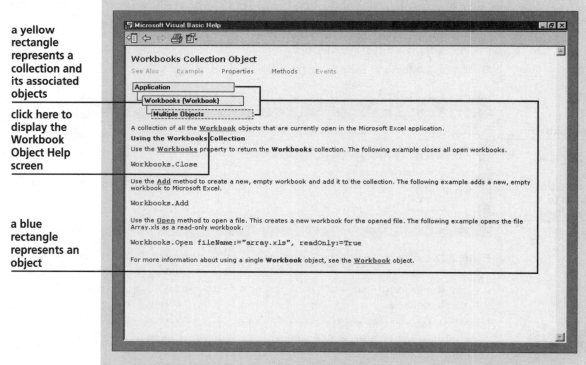

Figure 2-23: Workbooks Collection Object Help screen

If you are using a color monitor, you will notice that the object model diagram located at the top of the Help screen contains two blue rectangles and one yellow rectangle. A blue rectangle represents an object in the object model. A yellow rectangle represents a collection and its associated objects. In this case, the Application and Multiple Objects rectangles are colored blue because they represent objects. The Workbooks (Workbook) rectangle is colored yellow because it represents the Workbooks collection and its associated Workbook objects.

You can view a listing of the objects located on the next level of the object model by clicking the blue Multiple Objects rectangle located below the Workbooks (Workbook) rectangle. Recall that you will find the Worksheets collection and its Worksheet objects on this lower level.

As the Help screen shown in Figure 2-23 indicates, a Workbooks collection object is a collection of all the Workbook objects that are currently open in Excel. To display a Help screen for a Workbook object, you need simply to click <u>Workbook</u> in the first paragraph of the Help screen.

3   Click **<u>Workbook</u>** in the first paragraph of text in the Help screen. The Workbook Object Help screen appears, as shown in Figure 2-24.

Show button

click here to display the next level of objects

click here to display the object's properties, methods, and events

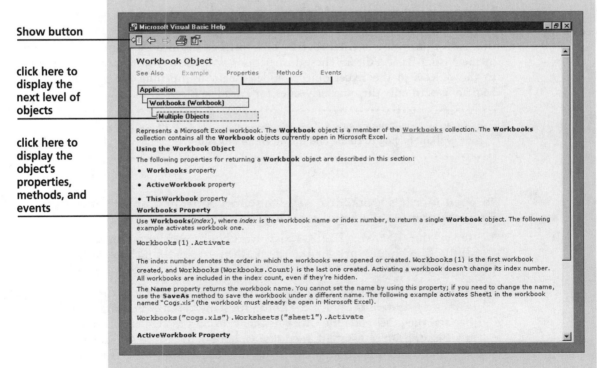

Figure 2-24: Workbook Object Help screen

You can use this Help screen to display a listing of the properties, methods, and events associated with a Workbook object. You also can use it to display a listing of the objects found on the next level of the object model.

You now are finished with the Microsoft Visual Basic Help window and the Object Browser, as well as the Visual Basic Editor, so you can close these three windows.

4 Click the **Show** button ⬛ on the Microsoft Visual Basic Help toolbar to display the Help window's Selection pane, then close the Microsoft Visual Basic Help window.

5 Close the Object Browser window, and then close the Visual Basic Editor to return to Microsoft Excel.

As you learned in the Concept lesson, once you are familiar with an application's object model, you can use the Immediate window in the Visual Basic Editor to practice entering VBA instructions that access the properties and methods of the various objects.

Using the Immediate Window in Excel

In this section, you will enter several VBA instructions into the Immediate window in the Visual Basic Editor. These instructions will allow you to practice referring to the objects in the Excel object model. Begin by opening the workbook that Martin uses to tally the quarterly sales for Paradise Electronics.

 tip

Recall that, unlike the Code window, the Immediate window allows you to test a line of code without having to create and run an entire procedure.

To open Martin's workbook, save the workbook, and enter several VBA instructions into the Immediate window:

1 Open the **T2-EX-1** (T2-EX-1.xls) workbook, which is located in the Tut02\Excel folder on your Data Disk, then save the workbook as QtrSales. See Figure 2-25.

HELP? If the Office Assistant appears, you can either hide it or turn the Office Assistant feature off. To hide the Office Assistant, click Help on the Excel menu bar and then click Hide the Office Assistant. To turn the Office Assistant feature off, click the Office Assistant, then click Options in the Office Assistant's balloon. Click the Options tab on the Office Assistant dialog box, if necessary, then click the Use the Office Assistant check box to deselect it. Click the OK button to close the Office Assistant dialog box.

name of the Application object

name of the Workbook object

names of the Worksheet objects

	A	B	C	D	E	F	G	H	I	J	K
1	**Item**	*January*	*February*	*March*	***Total***						
2	A123FG	$ 200.00	$ 300.00	$ 50.00	$ 550.00						
3	A344HY	130.00	700.00	600.00	1,430.00						
4	Q89755	90.00	400.00	200.00	690.00						
5	P234JJ	85.00	200.00	700.00	985.00						
6	Q34589	128.00	100.00	100.00	328.00						
7	L122MT	96.00	25.00	200.00	321.00						
8	*Totals*	$ 729.00	$1,725.00	$1,850.00	$4,304.00						

Microsoft Excel - QtrSales.xls

File Edit View Insert Format Tools Data Window Help

Arial ▾ 11 ▾ **B** *I* U

A1 = Item

Jackson / Glen Park /

Figure 2-25: QtrSales.xls workbook

The QtrSales Workbook object contains two Worksheet objects named Jackson and Glen Park.

2 Press **Alt+F11** to open the Visual Basic Editor. Maximize the Visual Basic Editor and, if necessary, close the Properties window, the Object Browser window, and any open Code windows. Click **View** on the menu bar, then click **Project Explorer** to open the Project Explorer window, if necessary.

3 Click **View** on the menu bar and then click **Immediate Window** to open the Immediate window, if necessary. See Figure 2-26.

HELP? Don't be concerned if the size and location of your Immediate window does not match the one shown in the figure. You can resize the Immediate window by dragging its borders. You can reposition the Immediate window by dragging the window by its title bar.

 tip

You also can press Ctrl+g to open the Immediate window.

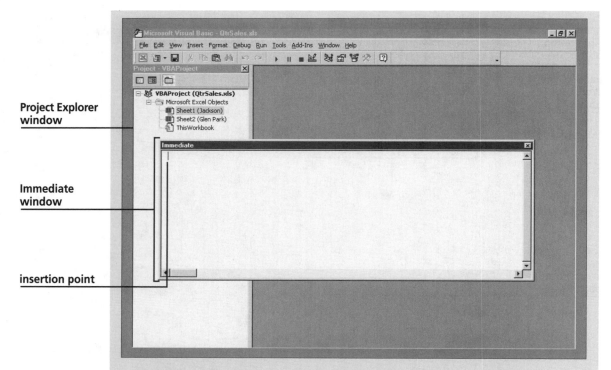

Project Explorer window

Immediate window

insertion point

Figure 2-26: Visual Basic Editor showing open Project Explorer and Immediate windows

The first VBA instruction you will enter into the Immediate window, **?Application.Name**, will display the value stored in the Application object's Name property. Recall that the question mark (**?**) at the beginning of the instruction tells VBA to display the value of what follows the question mark below the instruction in the Immediate window.

4   Type **?application.** (be sure to type the period) in the Immediate window. The Application object's member list appears.

HELP? If the member list does not appear, click Tools on the menu bar, then click Options to open the Options dialog box. Select the Auto List Members check box on the Editor tab, then click the OK button to close the Options dialog box.

Rather than scrolling down the member list until you locate the Name property, and then clicking Name in the list to select it, as you did in Tutorial 1, you will use a much quicker way to select the Name property.

5 Type **n** to select the Name property in the member list and then press the **Enter** key. The name of the Application object—Microsoft Excel—appears in the Immediate window.

Next, you will use a property of the Workbooks collection to display the number of open Workbook objects. Recall that you access an object's property using the *expression.property* syntax, where *expression* represents the location of the object in the object model. In this case, you will use `Application.Workbooks`, which represents the location of the Workbooks collection in the object model, as the *expression*, and you will use `Count` as the *property*. The instruction you will enter into the Immediate window is `?Application.Workbooks.Count`.

Important Note: When you are told to enter an instruction, you always will be shown the complete instruction to enter. You can enter the instruction either by typing it yourself or by using the listings that appear at various times in the Immediate window.

6 Type **?application.workbooks.count** and press the **Enter** key. The number 1 appears in the Immediate window because only one workbook is open at this time.

Now display the name of the open workbook. In this case, use `Application.Workbooks(1)`, which represents the location of the first Workbook object in the object model, as the *expression*, and use `Name` as the *property*. Notice that the *expression* begins with the Application object (the highest object in the object model). It then uses the dot member selection operator to separate the Application object from the object located in the next level of the hierarchy—in this case, the Workbooks collection. To refer to a specific object within a collection, recall that you enter either the object's index or its name in parentheses following the collection's name. In this case, because only one workbook is open, you will use the Workbook object's index of 1. (Recall that the index of the first object in most collections is 1.)

7 Type **?application.workbooks(1).name** and press the **Enter** key. QtrSales.xls, which is the name of the open workbook, appears in the Immediate window.

Now display the number of Worksheet objects contained in the QtrSales.xls workbook. Use `Application.Workbooks("QtrSales.xls").Worksheets` as the *expression*, and use `Count` as the property. The *expression* indicates that the Worksheets collection is contained in the QtrSales.xls Workbook object, which is a member of the Workbooks collection, which is contained in the Application object. Notice that you can refer to the QtrSales.xls Workbook object either by its index, as you did in Step 7, or by its name, as you will do in Step 8.

8 Type **?application.workbooks("qtrsales.xls").worksheets.count** and press the **Enter** key. The number 2 appears in the Immediate window because the QtrSales.xls workbook contains two worksheets.

Next, use the **?Application.Workbooks(1).Worksheets(2).Name** instruction to display the name of the second Worksheet object contained in the QtrSales.xls workbook, which is the only open workbook. Notice that this instruction specifies both a specific Workbook object (the first Workbook object within the Workbooks collection) and a specific Worksheet object (the second Worksheet object within the Worksheets collection).

9 Type **?application.workbooks(1).worksheets(2).name** and press the **Enter** key. Glen Park, the name of the second Worksheet object in the QtrSales.xls workbook, appears in the Immediate window. Figure 2-27 shows the VBA instructions you have entered in the Immediate window.

all of these instructions display the values stored in properties

insertion point

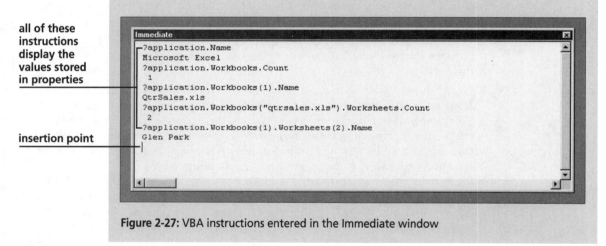

Figure 2-27: VBA instructions entered in the Immediate window

In the next section, you will learn how to refer to Range objects in a VBA instruction.

Referring to Range Objects

As you learned earlier, a Range object in Excel is defined as a cell, a row, a column, or a group of contiguous or noncontiguous cells. Figure 2-28 shows how you refer to each of these different Range objects.

To refer to a Range object consisting of:	Use the following expression in a VBA instruction:
One cell	*worksheetObject*.**Range("***cellAddress***")**
One row	*worksheetObject*.**Range("***rowNum:rowNum***")**
One column	*worksheetObject*.**Range("***colNum:colNum***")**
Contiguous cells	*worksheetObject*.**Range("***cellAddress:cellAddress***")**
Noncontiguous cells	*worksheetObject*.**Range("***cellAddress:cellAddress, cellAddress:cellAddress***")**

Figure 2-28: Referring to a Range object in Excel

In Figure 2-28, *worksheetObject* refers to the location in the object model of the Worksheet object that contains the Range object. *cellAddress* refers to the address of a cell—for example, "A1". *rowNum* and *colNum* refer to a row number and column number, respectively, in the worksheet—for example, "2:2" refers to row 2, and "B:B" refers to column B. Notice that *cellAddress*, *rowNum*, and *colNum* are enclosed in quotation marks.

In the next set of steps, you will enter several VBA instructions that will allow you to practice referring to Range objects in Excel.

To enter VBA instructions that contain references to Excel Range objects:

1   Verify that the insertion point is positioned after the last instruction in the Immediate window, as shown in Figure 2-27.

The first VBA instruction you will enter will display the value stored in a Range object consisting of one cell. According to Figure 2-28, you refer to a one-cell Range object using the *worksheetObject*.**Range("***cellAddress***")** syntax. In this case, you will use `Application.Workbooks(1).Worksheets(1).Range ("A1")` to refer to cell A1 in the first worksheet, and you will use the Range object's Value property to access the contents of the one-cell Range object.

2   Type **?application.workbooks(1).worksheets(1).range("a1").value** and press the **Enter** key. The content of cell A1, Item, appears immediately below the instruction in the Immediate window.

In addition to using the Value property to display the value stored in a one-cell Range object, you also can use it to change the value stored in either a one-cell or multiple-cell Range object. For example, you will use the Value property to enter the number 5 in a Range object consisting of cells B10 through C15. According to Figure 2-28, you use the *worksheetObject*.**Range("***cellAddress:cellAddress***")** syntax to refer to a Range object made up of contiguous cells.

3   Type **application.workbooks(1).worksheets(1).range("b10:c15").value = 5** and press the **Enter** key. Press **Alt+F11** to return to Excel. You will notice that the number 5 appears in the Range object consisting of cells B10 through C15.

As you learned in the Concept lesson, in addition to entering VBA instructions that access an object's properties, you also can enter VBA instructions that invoke an object's methods. For example, you will use the Range object's Select method to select row 2 in the first worksheet. According to Figure 2-28, you use the *worksheetObject*.**Range("*rowNum:rowNum*")** syntax to refer to a row in the worksheet.

4   Press **Alt+F11** to return to the Visual Basic Editor, then click the **Immediate window's title bar** to make this window active. Type **application.workbooks (1).worksheets(1).range("2:2").select** and press the **Enter** key. Press **Alt+F11** to return to Excel. Notice that row 2 is selected in the first worksheet.

Now use the Select method to select a Range object consisting of cells A1 through A8 and cells E1 through E8. According to Figure 2-28, you use the *worksheetObject*.**Range("*cellAddress:cellAddress, cellAddress:cellAddress*")** syntax to refer to a Range object that contains a group of noncontiguous cells.

5   Press **Alt+F11** to return to the Visual Basic Editor, then click the **Immediate window's title bar** to make this window active. Type the additional instruction shown in Figure 2-29 and press the **Enter** key.

```
Immediate                                                          ▢
  1
?application.Workbooks(1).Name
QtrSales.xls
?application.Workbooks("qtrsales.xls").Worksheets.Count
  2
?application.Workbooks(1).Worksheets(2).Name
Glen Park
?application.Workbooks(1).Worksheets(1).range("a1").value
Item
application.Workbooks(1).Worksheets(1).range("b10:c15").value = 5
application.Workbooks(1).Worksheets(1).range("2:2").select
application.Workbooks(1).Worksheets(1).range("a1:a8, e1:e8").select
|
```

scroll bar →

enter this
instruction →

Figure 2-29: Additional instruction entered in the Immediate window

> You can use the Immediate window's scroll bar to scroll through the instructions entered in the window.

6   Press **Alt+F11** to return to Excel. Notice that cells A1 through A8 and cells E1 through E8 are selected, as shown in Figure 2-30.

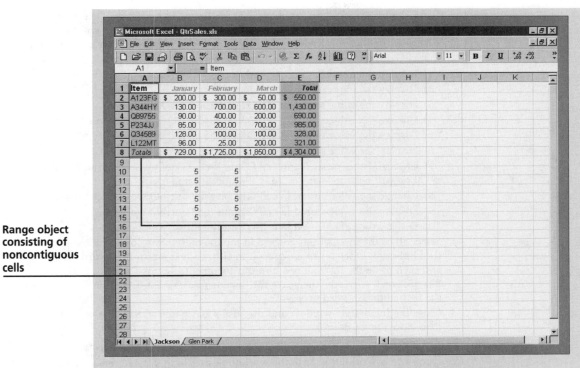

Figure 2-30: Jackson worksheet showing selection of a Range object consisting of noncontiguous cells

Finally, use the Application object's Quit method to close Excel.

7 Press **Alt+F11** to return to the Visual Basic Editor. Beneath the instruction you just entered, type **application.quit** and press the **Enter** key to close Excel. When you are asked if you want to save the changes made to the QtrSales workbook, click the **Yes** button.

You now have completed Tutorial 2's Excel lesson. You can either take a break or complete the end-of-lesson exercises before moving on to the next lesson.

 **E X E R C I S E S**

1. In this exercise, you will write VBA instructions that access Excel objects.
   a. Open the T2-EX-E1 (T2-EX-E1.xls) workbook, which is located in the Tut02\Excel folder on your Data Disk. Save the workbook as T2-EX-E1D.

b. Open the Visual Basic Editor, then open the Immediate window. Delete any instructions from the Immediate window, then use the Immediate window to enter VBA instructions that perform the following tasks. (After entering an instruction that changes the worksheet data, return to Excel to verify the results.)

1) Display the number of open workbooks.
2) Display the name of the second worksheet.
3) Display the value stored in cell D14 on the FirstQ worksheet.
4) Change the value stored in cell D5 on the FirstQ worksheet to 2200.
5) Display the value stored in cell D5 on the FirstQ worksheet.
6) Display the value stored in cell C12 on the ThirdQ worksheet.
7) Change the value stored in cell C3 on the SecondQ worksheet to May. (*Hint:* You will need to enclose "May" in quotation marks.)
8) Change the value stored in cell C11 on the FourthQ worksheet to 200.
9) Display the value stored in cell C12 on the FourthQ worksheet.
10) Display the value stored in cell D3 on the FirstQ worksheet.

c. Select all of the instructions entered in the Immediate window, then copy them to the clipboard. Open a new document in either a text editor or a word processor, and then paste the instructions into the document. Remove any instructions that did not work correctly, then save the document as T2-EX-E1D-Immediate. Close the text editor or word processor.

d. Close the Immediate window and the Visual Basic Editor. Save the workbook and then close the workbook.

2. In this exercise, you will write VBA instructions that access Excel objects.

a. Open a new workbook. Save the workbook as T2-EX-E2D in the Tut02\Excel folder on your Data Disk.

b. Open the Visual Basic Editor, then open the Immediate window. Delete any instructions from the Immediate window, then use the Immediate window to enter VBA instructions that perform the following tasks. (After entering an instruction that either selects or changes the data in the worksheet, return to Excel to verify the results.)

1) Display the path for the Application object. (*Hint:* Use the Application object's Path property.)
2) Display the number of worksheets in the current Workbook object's Worksheets collection.
3) Display the names of each worksheet. (*Hint:* You will need to use more than one instruction.)
4) Enter the number 2 in cells A3 through G3 in the first worksheet.
5) Display the value stored in cell D3 in the first worksheet.
6) Enter the number 4 in cells A1 through B3 and cells D1 through D10 in the second worksheet.
7) Select cells A3, C3, and F3 in the first worksheet.

c. Select all of the instructions entered in the Immediate window, then copy them to the clipboard. Open a new document in either a text editor or a word processor, and then paste the instructions into the document. Remove any instructions that did not work correctly, then save the document as T2-EX-E2D-Immediate. Close the text editor or word processor.

d. Close the Immediate window and the Visual Basic Editor. Save the workbook and then close the workbook.

3. In this exercise, you will view the entire object model for the Excel application.
   a. Open a new workbook. Open the Visual Basic Editor, and then open the Object Browser window. Display the Help screen for the Application object in the Excel object library. Click the Application rectangle to display the Microsoft Excel Objects Help screen.
   b. Close the Help window, the Object Browser, the Visual Basic Editor, and the workbook.

Exercises 4 and 5 are Discovery Exercises. Discovery Exercises, which may include topics that are not covered in the lesson, allow you to "discover" the solutions to problems on your own.

discovery ▶ 4. In this exercise, you will learn about the Activate and Printout methods, as well as the ActiveWorkbook, ActiveWorksheet, and ActiveCell properties.
   a. Open a new workbook. Save the workbook as T2-EX-E4D in the Tut02\Excel folder on your Data Disk. Open the Visual Basic Editor. Use the Object Browser to display the Help screens for a Workbook object's Printout method and a Worksheet object's Activate method. Also display the Help screens for the Application object's ActiveWorkbook, ActiveSheet, and ActiveCell properties. Study the Help screens. (You may want to print the Help screens for future reference.) Close the Help window and the Object Browser.
   b. Open the Immediate window. Delete any instructions from the Immediate window, then use the Immediate window to enter VBA instructions that perform the following tasks: (After entering each instruction, return to Excel to verify the results.)
      1) Use the Activate method to activate Sheet3.
      2) Use the ActiveWorkbook and ActiveSheet properties, and the Select method (which you learned about in this lesson) to select cell B5.
      3) Use the ActiveCell and Value properties to enter the number 10 in cell B5.
      4) Use the ActiveCell and Value properties to increase the contents of cell B5 by 1.
      5) Use the appropriate method to activate Sheet2.
      6) Use the appropriate method and properties to select cell C3 on the active worksheet.
      7) Use the appropriate properties to enter the word "Hello" in the active cell.
      8) Use the appropriate method to activate Sheet1.
      9) Use the appropriate method and properties to select cell A1 on the active worksheet.
      10) Use the appropriate method and properties to enter your name in the active cell.
      11) Use the Printout method to print the workbook.
   c. Select all of the instructions entered in the Immediate window, then copy them to the clipboard. Open a new document in either a text editor or a word processor, and then paste the instructions into the document. Remove any instructions that did not work correctly, then save the document as T2-EX-E4D-Immediate. Close the text editor or word processor.
   d. Close the Immediate window and the Visual Basic Editor, then save and close the workbook.

discovery ▶ 5. In this exercise, you will learn the difference between a Range object's Value property and its Text property.
   a. Open a new workbook. Enter the number 2 in cell A1 in the first worksheet. Use the Cells command on the Format menu to format cell A1 to Currency. $2.00 appears in cell A1.

b. Open the Visual Basic Editor. Use the Object Browser to display the Help screens for a Range object's Value and Text properties. Study the Help screens, then close the Help window and the Object Browser.

c. Open the Immediate window. Delete any instructions from the Immediate window, then enter two VBA instructions. The first instruction should display the value stored in cell A1's Value property, and the second instruction should display the value stored in its Text property. What is the difference between a Range object's Value property and its Text property?

d. Close the Immediate window and the Visual Basic Editor, then close the workbook without saving it.

A computer program is good only if it works. Errors in programming code can cause a program to run incorrectly. Therefore, a programmer needs to know how to locate and fix any errors in his or her code. Exercises 6 and 7 are Debugging Exercises. Debugging Exercises allow you to practice recognizing and solving errors in code.

debugging 6. The following VBA instruction is supposed to select cells A1 through B5 and cells C10 through C15, but it is not working correctly. (The cells are located in the first worksheet contained in the first workbook.) Correct the instruction.

```
Application.Workbook(1).Worksheet(1).Range("A1:B5",
"C10:C15").Selected
```

debugging 7. The following VBA instruction is supposed to enter the number 25 in column B of the first workbook's first worksheet, but it is not working correctly. Correct the instruction.

```
Application.Workbooks(1).Worksheets(1).Column("B:B").Value = 25
```

Word Lesson

The Word Object Model

case ▶ Pat Jones, the manager of Willowton Health Club, uses Microsoft Word to complete many of her daily tasks. For example, she uses Word to create a Welcome letter that is sent to new members, and also to create the club's promotional material. Pat would like to use VBA to customize her Word documents to better suit her work style and needs. You tell her that before she can do so, she must become familiar with the objects included in the Word object model. You agree to explain a portion of the model to her, and also to show her how she can refer to these objects in VBA.

Understanding the Word Object Model

As you learned in the Concept lesson, an application's object model depicts the hierarchy of objects available in the application. Before Pat can customize her Word documents, she needs to understand how to refer to the objects included in the Word object model.

Figure 2-31 shows the portion of the Microsoft Word object model that includes the most commonly used Word objects. (You will view the full Word object model in this lesson's Exercise 3.)

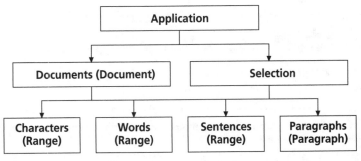

Figure 2-31: The most commonly used Word objects

As Figure 2-31 indicates, the Word object model begins with the Application object, which represents the Word application. Contained within the Application object are the Documents collection and its associated Document objects, and the Selection object, which represents the information currently selected in a document. On the third level of the hierarchy, you will find the Characters, Words, Sentences, and Paragraphs collections. As the figure shows, these collections are contained within the Documents collection and its associated Document objects, and also within the Selection object.

Notice in Figure 2-31 that the Paragraphs collection is made up of Paragraph objects, whereas the Characters, Words, and Sentences collections consist of Range objects. A **Range object** in Word is defined as a contiguous area in a document; it can be as small as the insertion point or as large as the entire document. The Application, Document, Selection, Character, Word, Sentence, and Paragraph objects, as well as the Documents, Characters, Words, Sentences, and Paragraphs collections, are illustrated in Figure 2-32.

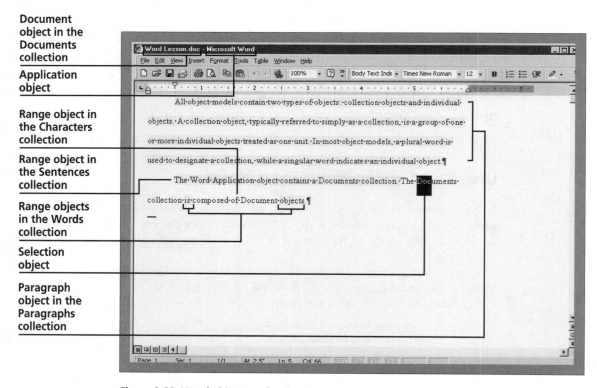

Document object in the Documents collection

Application object

Range object in the Characters collection

Range object in the Sentences collection

Range objects in the Words collection

Selection object

Paragraph object in the Paragraphs collection

Figure 2-32: Word objects and collections

Although a paragraph is a contiguous area in a document, it is considered a Paragraph object rather than a Range object.

The Application object, which refers to Microsoft Word, contains one Document object in its Documents collection. The Document object's name is Word Lesson.doc. The Word Lesson document contains two Paragraph objects in its Paragraphs collection. You can determine the number of Paragraph objects by counting the number of paragraph markers (¶) in the document. The first Paragraph object contains all of the characters from the first character in the document—in this case, the letter A—up to and including the first paragraph marker; this area is shaded in the figure. The second Paragraph object in the document begins with the character following the first paragraph marker, and it continues through the next paragraph marker.

The Word Lesson document also contains five sentences in its Sentences collection; each sentence is a Range object. Unlike a sentence in the English language, a sentence in Word does not end when a period, question mark, or exclamation point is encountered; rather, it includes any spaces and paragraph markers that appear after those punctuation marks. For example, notice that the document's fourth sentence, which is shaded in Figure 2-32, includes the space following the period.

Like the Sentences collection, the Words collection also consists of Range objects. For example, the two words—"is " and "objects"—that appear shaded in the document's last sentence are Range objects belonging to the document's Words collection. Notice that a word includes the space that follows it, but it does not include the punctuation mark that follows it.

The Characters collection also consists of Range objects, but each Range object in this collection is composed of exactly one character. The letter f, which is shaded in the last sentence shown in Figure 2-32, is an example of a Range object included in the Characters collection.

Recall that the Selection object represents the information currently selected in a document. The Word Lesson document contains one Selection object that consists of the three characters, Doc.

In the next section, you will use the Object Browser in the Visual Basic Editor to display a Help screen for the Application object in Word. You also will learn how to display the Help screens for other objects in the Word object model.

Using the Object Browser in Word

As you learned in the Concept lesson, you can use the Object Browser in the Visual Basic Editor to view information about the objects included in an application's object model. The Object Browser is a useful tool for understanding the structure of an object model, and for studying the various objects included in the model, as well as their properties and methods.

To access the Object Browser in Word:

1 Start Microsoft Word. A new document appears.

In Tutorial 1, you learned how to open the Visual Basic Editor using the Tools menu on the Word menu bar. A much quicker way to open the Visual Basic Editor is to press Alt+F11.

2 Press **Alt+F11** to open the Visual Basic Editor. Close any open Visual Basic windows, except for the Visual Basic Editor window.

3 Click the **Object Browser** button 📖 on the Standard toolbar to open the Object Browser window. If necessary, maximize the Object Browser window.

> ▶ **tip**
>
> You also can open the Object Browser by clicking View on the menu bar and then clicking Object Browser, or by pressing the F2 key.

As you learned in the Concept lesson, all of the information about an application's object model is stored in the application's object library.

4 Click the **Project/Library** list arrow, then click **Word** in the list to display the Word object library. See Figure 2-33.

Project/Library list arrow

Help button refers to the Word Application object

the Word object library file

your path might be different

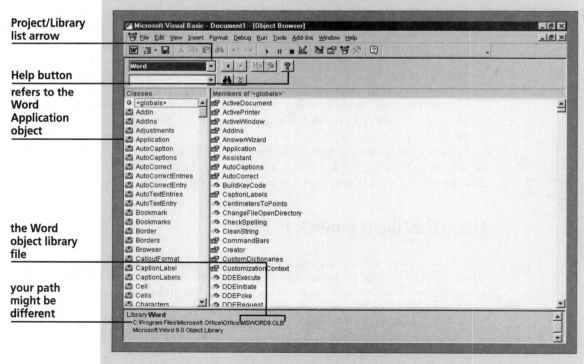

Figure 2-33: Object Browser window showing the Word object library

HELP? If the Object Browser window displays the Search Results section, click the Hide Search Results button ⌃ to close the section.

5 Click **Application** in the Classes list box, and then click the **Help** button ❓ to open the Microsoft Visual Basic Help window, which displays the Application object's Help screen. Maximize the Microsoft Visual Basic Help window, then click the **Contents** tab, if necessary. See Figure 2-34.

Hide button

represents a portion of the Word object model

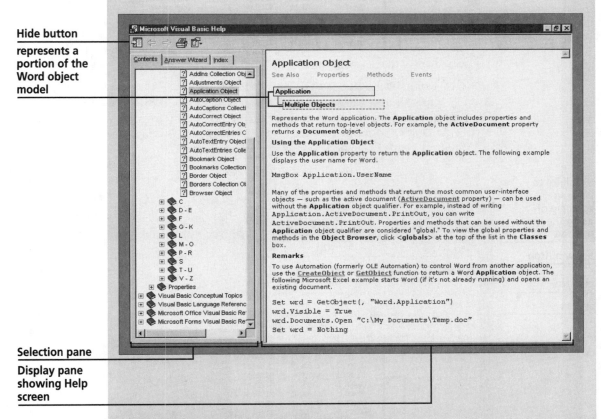

Selection pane

Display pane showing Help screen

Figure 2-34: Microsoft Visual Basic Help window

HELP? If an error message appears indicating that Help is not installed, see your instructor or technical support person.

HELP? If the Application Property Help screen appears, you inadvertently selected Application in the Members of *<classname>* list box. Close the Help window, then repeat Step 5; this time be sure to click Application in the Classes list box.

HELP? Don't be concerned if your Selection pane does not match the one shown in the figure.

According to the Help screen, the Application object represents the entire Word application.

Notice that the Microsoft Visual Basic Help window is divided into two panes: the Selection pane and the Display pane. You use the Selection pane, which contains the Contents, Answer Wizard, and Index tabs, to select the topic whose Help screen you want to display in the Display pane. You also can hide the Selection pane so that you can view more information in the Display pane.

6 Click the **Hide** button 🔲 on the Microsoft Visual Basic Help toolbar to hide the Selection pane. Notice that 🔲 becomes a Show button ◀🔲, which you use to redisplay the Selection pane.

Next, view the Help screen for the Application object's Quit method.

7 Click **Methods** at the top of the Help screen. When the Topics Found dialog box appears, scroll down the list of methods until you see Quit Method. Click **Quit Method** in the list, and then click the **Display** button. The Quit Method Help screen appears, as shown in Figure 2-35.

click here to view an example of using the Quit method

Show button

purpose

syntax

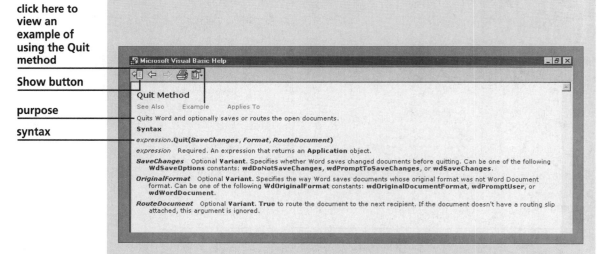

Figure 2-35: Quit Method Help screen

According to the Help screen, you use the Quit method to exit the Microsoft Word application. The syntax of the method is *expression*.**Quit**, where *expression* refers to the Application object. You can click Example at the top of the Help screen to view an example of using the Quit method in a VBA instruction.

8 Click **Example** at the top of the Quit method's Help screen. See Figure 2-36.

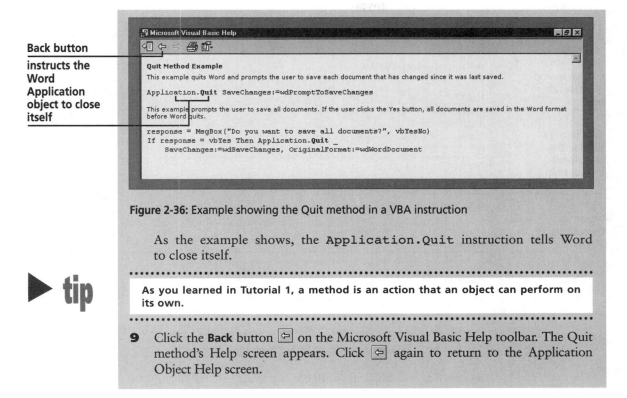

Back button
instructs the
Word
Application
object to close
itself

Figure 2-36: Example showing the Quit method in a VBA instruction

As the example shows, the `Application.Quit` instruction tells Word to close itself.

▶ **tip**

> As you learned in Tutorial 1, a method is an action that an object can perform on its own.

9   Click the **Back** button ⇦ on the Microsoft Visual Basic Help toolbar. The Quit method's Help screen appears. Click ⇦ again to return to the Application Object Help screen.

Notice that a Multiple Objects rectangle appears below the Application rectangle in the Application Object Help screen. As you learned in the Concept lesson, the Multiple Objects rectangle represents the next level of objects in the object model hierarchy. Now you will view a listing of these objects.

To view the next level of objects in the object model hierarchy:

1   Click the **Multiple Objects** rectangle in the Application Object Help screen. The Topics Found dialog box appears and lists the objects found on the next level of the Word object model. Recall that the Documents collection and its Document objects, as well as the Selection object, are located on this lower level.

View the Help screen for the Documents collection object.

2   Scroll down the list of objects in the Topics Found dialog box until you see Documents Collection Object. Click **Documents Collection Object** and then click the **Display** button. The Documents Collection Object Help screen appears, as shown in Figure 2-37.

a yellow rectangle represents a collection and its associated objects

click here to display the Document Object Help screen

a blue rectangle represents an object

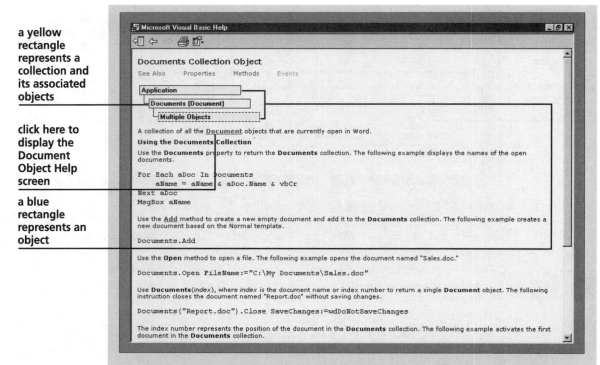

Figure 2-37: Documents Collection Object Help screen

If you are using a color monitor, you will notice that the object model diagram located at the top of the Help screen contains two blue rectangles and one yellow rectangle. A blue rectangle represents an object in the object model. A yellow rectangle represents a collection and its associated objects. In this case, the Application and Multiple Objects rectangles are colored blue because they represent objects. The Documents (Document) rectangle is colored yellow because it represents the Documents collection and its associated Document objects.

You can view a listing of the objects located on the next level of the object model by clicking the blue Multiple Objects rectangle located below the Documents (Document) rectangle. Recall that the Characters, Words, Sentences, and Paragraphs collections, as well as their associated Range and Paragraph objects, are on this lower level.

As the Help screen shown in Figure 2-37 indicates, a Documents collection object is a collection of all the Document objects that are currently open in Word. To display a Help screen for a Document object, you need simply to click Document in the first paragraph of the Help screen.

3 Click **Document** in the first paragraph of text in the Help screen. The Document Object Help screen appears, as shown in Figure 2-38.

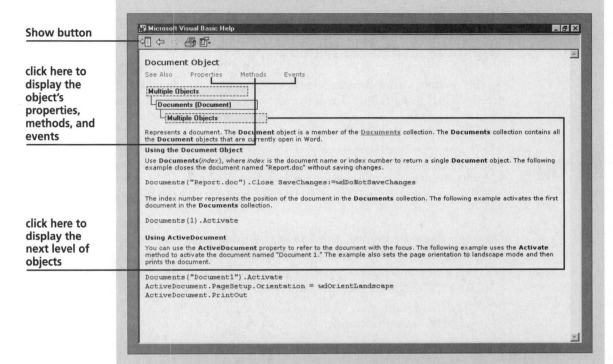

Show button

click here to display the object's properties, methods, and events

click here to display the next level of objects

Figure 2-38: Document Object Help screen

You can use this Help screen to display a listing of the properties, methods, and events associated with a Document object. You also can use it to display a listing of the objects found on the next level of the object model.

You now are finished with the Microsoft Visual Basic Help window and the Object Browser, as well as the Visual Basic Editor, so you can close these three windows.

4 Click the **Show** button ◀️ on the Microsoft Visual Basic Help toolbar to display the Help window's Selection pane, then close the Microsoft Visual Basic Help window.

5 Close the Object Browser, and then close the Visual Basic Editor to return to Microsoft Word.

As you learned in the Concept lesson, once you are familiar with an application's object model, you can use the Immediate window in the Visual Basic Editor to practice entering VBA instructions that access the properties and methods of the various objects.

Using the Immediate Window

In this section, you will enter several VBA instructions into the Immediate window in the Visual Basic Editor. These instructions will allow you to practice referring to the objects in the Word object model. Begin by opening the promotion document that Pat sends to club members.

> **tip** Recall that, unlike the Code window, the Immediate window allows you to test a line of code without having to create and run an entire procedure.

To open Pat's document, then save the document and enter several VBA instructions into the Immediate window:

1 Open the **T2-WD-1** (T2-WD-1.doc) document, which is located in the Tut02\Word folder on your Data Disk. Save the document as Offer.

View the nonprinting characters—for example, the spaces and paragraph markers—in the document.

2 Click **Tools** on the menu bar, then click **Options**. When the Options dialog box appears, click the **View** tab, if necessary, then click the **All** check box in the Formatting marks section, if necessary, to select that option. Click the **OK** button to close the Options dialog box. The Offer document appears as shown in Figure 2-39.

HELP? If the Office Assistant appears, you can either hide it or turn the Office Assistant feature off. To hide the Office Assistant, click Help on the Word menu bar and then click Hide the Office Assistant. To turn the Office Assistant feature off, click the Office Assistant, then click Options in the Office Assistant's balloon. Click the Options tab on the Office Assistant dialog box, if necessary, then click the Use the Office Assistant check box to deselect it. Click the OK button to close the Office Assistant dialog box.

name of the Document object

name of the Application object

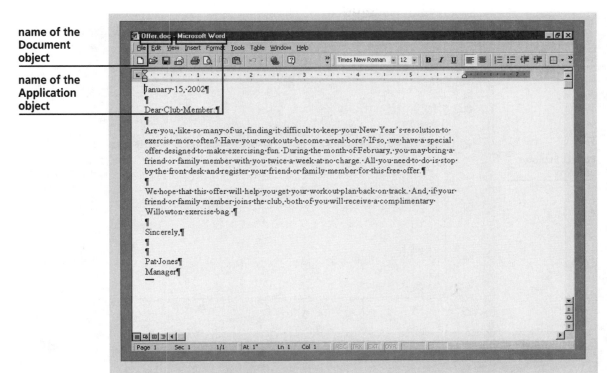

Figure 2-39: Offer document

3 Press **Alt+F11** to open the Visual Basic Editor. Maximize the Visual Basic Editor. If necessary, close the Properties window, the Object Browser window, and any open Code windows. Click **View** on the menu bar, then click **Project Explorer** to open the Project Explorer window, if necessary.

4 Click **View** on the menu bar and then click **Immediate Window** to open the Immediate window, if necessary. See Figure 2-40.

HELP? Don't be concerned if the size and location of your Immediate window does not match the one shown in the figure. You can resize the Immediate window by dragging its borders. You can reposition the Immediate window by dragging the window by its title bar.

 tip

You also can press Ctrl+g to open the Immediate window.

Immediate
window

Project Explorer
window

insertion point

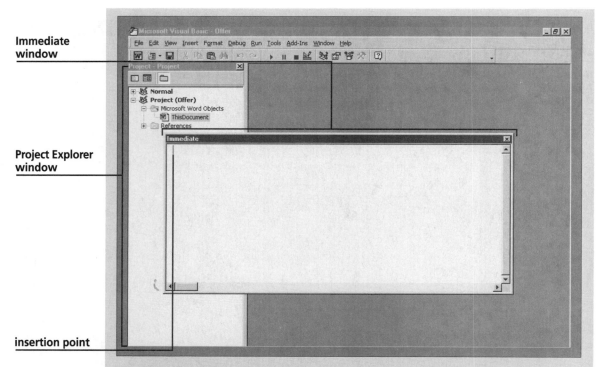

Figure 2-40: Visual Basic Editor showing open Project Explorer and Immediate windows

The first VBA instruction you will enter into the Immediate window, `?Application.Name`, will display the value stored in the Application object's Name property. Recall that the question mark (?) at the beginning of an instruction tells VBA to display the value of what follows the question mark below the instruction in the Immediate window.

5 Type **?application.** (be sure to type the period) in the Immediate window. The Application object's member list appears.

HELP? If the member list does not appear, click Tools on the menu bar, then click Options to open the Options dialog box. Select the Auto List Members check box on the Editor tab, then click the OK button to close the Options dialog box.

Rather than scrolling down the member list until you locate the Name property, and then clicking Name in the list to select it, as you did in Tutorial 1, you will use a much quicker way to select the Name property.

6 Type **n** to select the Name property in the member list and then press the **Enter** key. The name of the Application object—Microsoft Word—appears in the Immediate window.

Next, you will use a property of the Documents collection to display the number of open Document objects. Recall that you access an object's property using the *expression.property* syntax, where *expression* represents the location of the object in the object model. In this case, you will use `Application.Documents`, which represents the location of the Documents collection in the object model, as the *expression*, and you will use `Count` as the property. The instruction you will enter into the Immediate window is `?Application.Documents.Count`.

Important Note: When you are told to enter an instruction, you always will be shown the complete instruction to enter. You can enter the instruction either by typing it yourself or by using the listings that appear at various times in the Immediate window.

7 Type **?application.documents.count** and press the **Enter** key. The number 1 appears in the Immediate window because only one document is open at this time.

Now display the name of the open document. In this case, use `Application.Documents(1)`, which represents the location of the first Document object in the object model, as the *expression*, and use `Name` as the *property*. Notice that the *expression* begins with the Application object (the highest object in the object model). It then uses the dot member selection operator to separate the Application object from the object located in the next level of the hierarchy—in this case, the Documents collection. To refer to a specific object within a collection, recall that you can enter either the object's index or its name in parentheses following the collection's name. In this case, because only one document is open, you will use the Document object's index of 1. (Recall that the index of the first object in most collections is 1.)

8 Type **?application.documents(1).name** and press the **Enter** key. Offer.doc, which is the name of the open document, appears in the Immediate window.

Now display the number of Paragraph objects contained in the Offer.doc document. To do so, use `Application.Documents("Offer.doc").Paragraphs` as the *expression*, and use `Count` as the *property*. The *expression* indicates that the Paragraphs collection is contained in the Offer.doc Document object, which is a member of the Documents collection, which is contained in the Application object. Notice that you can refer to the Offer.doc Document object either by its index, as you did in Step 8, or by its name, as you will do in Step 9.

9 Type **?application.documents("offer.doc").paragraphs.count** and press the **Enter** key. The number 13 appears in the Immediate window because the Offer document contains 13 Paragraph objects.

tip

Recall that you can determine the number of Paragraph objects by counting the number of paragraph markers (¶) in the document.

Now display the number of sentences contained in the Offer.doc document.

10 Type **?application.documents("offer.doc").sentences.count** and press the **Enter** key. The number 12 appears in the Immediate window because the Offer document contains 12 sentences.

Next, display the fifth sentence in the Offer document. To do so, you will use `Application.Documents("Offer.doc").Sentences(5)` as the *expression*. As you learned earlier in Figure 2-31, the Sentences collection is composed of Range objects. You will need to use the Range object's Text property to display the fifth sentence.

11 Type **?application.documents("offer.doc").sentences(5).text** and press the **Enter** key. The "If so, we have a special offer designed to make exercising fun." sentence appears in the Immediate window. Figure 2-41 shows the VBA instructions you have entered in the Immediate window.

HELP? The date and the salutation are considered sentences. Specifically, they are sentences one and two in the document.

all of these
instructions
display the
values stored
in properties

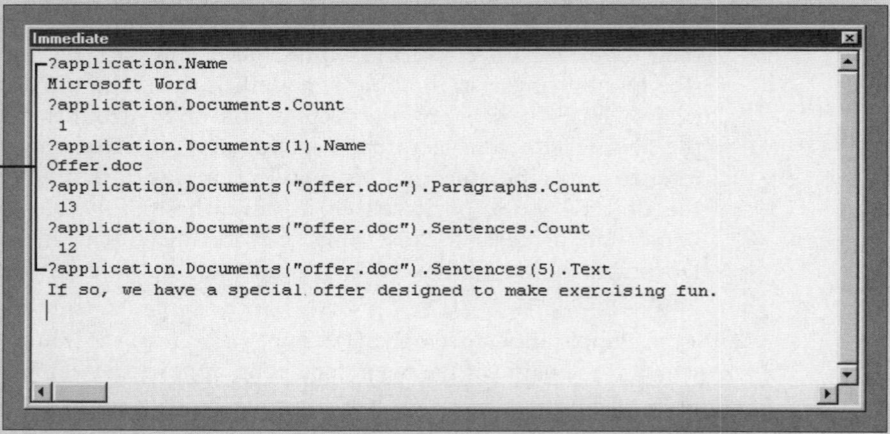

```
Immediate                                                    [x]
?application.Name
Microsoft Word
?application.Documents.Count
 1
?application.Documents(1).Name
Offer.doc
?application.Documents("offer.doc").Paragraphs.Count
 13
?application.Documents("offer.doc").Sentences.Count
 12
?application.Documents("offer.doc").Sentences(5).Text
If so, we have a special offer designed to make exercising fun.
|
```

Figure 2-41: VBA instructions entered in the Immediate window

Next, you will use the Selection object to display the information selected in the document. First, however, you will need to select some text.

To use the Selection object:

1 Press **Alt+F11** to return to Word. Select the three words **New Year's resolution** in the document. Press **Alt+F11** to return to the Visual Basic Editor, then click the **Immediate window's title bar** to make the window active.

2 Type **?application.selection.text** and press the **Enter** key. The text selected in the document—New Year's resolution—appears in the Immediate window.

Now display the second word in the selected text.

3 Type **?application. selection.words(2).text** and press the **Enter** key. The word Year's appears in the Immediate window.

In addition to displaying the value stored in a Range object's Text property, a VBA instruction also can change the value stored in the Text property. For example, the next instruction you will enter will change the first word in the document from January to Jan.

4 Type the additional instruction shown in Figure 2-42. (Be sure to include a space between the letter n and the ending quotation mark.) Press the **Enter** key.

HELP? Recall that a word includes the space that follows it; therefore, you must include the space in the replacement text.

include a
space here

enter this
instruction

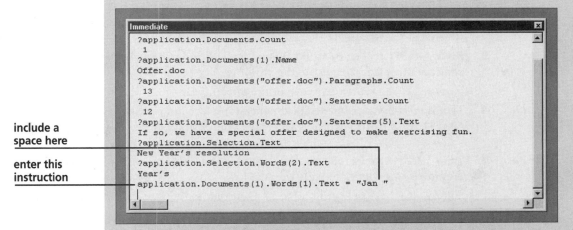

```
Immediate                                                                    ×
?application.Documents.Count
 1
?application.Documents(1).Name
Offer.doc
?application.Documents("offer.doc").Paragraphs.Count
 13
?application.Documents("offer.doc").Sentences.Count
 12
?application.Documents("offer.doc").Sentences(5).Text
If so, we have a special offer designed to make exercising fun.
?application.Selection.Text
New Year's resolution
?application.Selection.Words(2).Text
Year's
application.Documents(1).Words(1).Text = "Jan "
```

Figure 2-42: Additional instruction entered in the Immediate window

You can use the Immediate window's scroll bar to scroll through the instructions entered in the window.

5 Press **Alt+F11** to return to Word. You will notice that the VBA instruction replaced the first word, "January ", with the word "Jan ".

6 Press **Alt+F11** to return to the Visual Basic Editor.

In the next section, you will learn how to use the Select method to select portions of the document.

Using the Range Object's Select Method

You can use the Range object's Select method to select a word, sentence, paragraph, or character in a document. In the next set of steps, you will use the Select method to select a word and a sentence in the Offer document.

To use the Select method in the Offer document:

1   Click the **Immediate window's title bar** to activate the window.

First use the Range object's Select method to select the first word in the document.

2   Type **application.documents(1).words(1).select** and press the **Enter** key. Press **Alt+F11** to return to Word. The word Jan, along with its trailing space, appears selected in the document.

3   Press **Alt+F11** to return to the Visual Basic Editor, then click the **Immediate window's title bar** to activate the window.

Now select the fourth sentence in the document.

4   Type **application.documents(1).sentences(4).select** and press the **Enter** key. Press **Alt+F11** to return to Word. The "Have your workouts become a real bore?" sentence, along with its trailing space, appears selected in the document.

5   Press **Alt+F11** to return to the Visual Basic Editor. Click the **Immediate Window's title bar** to activate the window.

Finally, use the Application object's Quit method to exit Word.

6   Type **application.quit** and press the **Enter** key to exit Word. When you are asked if you want to save the changes made to the document, click the **Yes** button.

You now have completed Tutorial 2's Word lesson. You can either take a break or complete the end-of-lesson exercises before moving on to the next lesson.

E X E R C I S E S

1.   In this exercise, you will write VBA instructions that access Word objects.
    a. Open the T2-WD-E1 (T2-WD-E1.doc) document, which is located in the Tut02\Word folder on your Data Disk. Save the document as T2-WD-E1D.
    b. View the nonprinting characters in the document.

   c. Select the words "Microsoft Office 2000" that appear in the text below the <u>Object Models</u> heading.

   d. Open the Visual Basic Editor, then open the Immediate window. Delete any instructions from the Immediate window, then use the Immediate window to enter VBA instructions that perform the following tasks. (After entering an instruction that either selects or changes the data in the document, return to Word to verify the results.) (*Hint*: If you make a mistake when changing information in the document, use the Undo command on the Word Edit menu to undo the change.)

      1) Display the name of the open document.

      2) Display the number of paragraphs contained in the current document.

      3) Display the first sentence. (Recall that a sentence includes any paragraph markers following the sentence.)

      4) Display the second sentence.

      5) Display the ninth word.

      6) Display the tenth word.

      7) Display the second character.

      8) Display the selected text.

      9) Display the second word in the selected text.

      10) Use the Select method to select the third sentence.

      11) Display the selected text.

      12) Change the word "included", which is word number 19 in the document, to "contained ". (Be sure to include a space before the ending quotation mark in the replacement text.)

      13) Display word number 19.

      14) Change the word "Overview", which is the second word in the document, to "first tutorial". (*Hint*: Recall that a word includes its trailing space, but it does not include any punctuation marks.)

      15) Use the Document object's Select method to select the entire document.

   e. Select all of the instructions entered in the Immediate window, then copy them to the clipboard. Open a new document in Word, and then paste the instructions into the document. Remove any instructions that did not work correctly, then save the document as T2-WD-E1D-Immediate. Close the T2-WD-E1D-Immediate document.

   f. Close the Immediate window and the Visual Basic Editor. Save and then close the T2-WD-E1D document.

2. In this exercise, you will write VBA instructions that access Word objects.

   a. Open the T2-WD-E2 (T2-WD-E2.doc) document, which is located in the Tut02\Word folder on your Data Disk. Save the document as T2-WD-E2D.

   b. View the nonprinting characters in the document.

   c. Open the Visual Basic Editor, then open the Immediate window. Delete any instructions from the Immediate window, then use the Immediate window to enter VBA instructions that perform the following tasks. (After entering an instruction that either selects or changes the data in the document, return to Word to verify the results.) (*Hint*: If you make a mistake when changing information in the document, use the Undo command on the Word Edit menu to undo the change.)

      1) Display the path for the Application object. (*Hint*: Use the Application object's Path property.)

      2) Change the second word in the document from "you're" to "you are ". (Be sure to include the space after the word "are".)

3) Change the word "screen" in the first sentence to "monitor". (*Hint*: Recall that a word includes its trailing space, but it does not include any punctuation marks.)

4) Change the second sentence from "A blue rectangle is an object." to "A blue rectangle represents an object in the object model." (*Hint*: Recall that a sentence includes its trailing space.)

5) Select the fourth sentence in the document.

6) Remove the selection by assigning an empty string ("") to its Text property.

d. Select all of the instructions entered in the Immediate window, then copy them to the clipboard. Open a new document in Word, and then paste the instructions into the document. Remove any instructions that did not work correctly, then save the document as T2-WD-E2D-Immediate. Close the T2-WD-E2D-Immediate document.

e. Close the Immediate window and the Visual Basic Editor. Save and then close the T2-WD-E2D document.

3. In this exercise, you will learn how to display the entire object model for the Word application.

a. Open a new document. Open the Visual Basic Editor, and then open the Object Browser window. Display the Help screen for the Application object in the Word object library. Click the Application rectangle to display the Microsoft Word Objects Help screen.

b. Close the Help window, the Object Browser, the Visual Basic Editor, and the document.

Exercises 4 and 5 are Discovery Exercises. Discovery Exercises, which may include topics that are not covered in the lesson, allow you to "discover" the solutions to problems on your own.

discovery ▶ 4. In this exercise, you will select a paragraph in a document.

a. Open the Offer (Offer.doc) document, which you completed in this lesson. The document is located in the Tut02\Word folder on your Data Disk.

b. View the nonprinting characters in the document. Open the Visual Basic Editor, then open the Immediate window. Enter a VBA instruction that selects the seventh paragraph in the document. (*Hint*: Recall that the Paragraphs collection is composed of Paragraph objects. Also recall that the Select method is a method of a Range object; it is not a method of a Paragraph object.)

c. Close the document.

discovery ▶ 5. In this exercise, you will learn about the PrintPreview method, as well as the ActiveDocument and ActivePrinter properties.

a. Open a new document. Type your name in the document, and then save the document as T2-WD-E5D in the Tut02\Word folder on your Data Disk.

b. Open the Visual Basic Editor. Use the Object Browser to display the Help screens for the Application object's ActiveDocument and ActivePrinter properties. Also display the Help screen for the Document object's PrintPreview method. Study the Help screens. (You may want to print the Help screens for future reference.) Close the Help window and the Object Browser.

c. Open the Immediate window. Enter VBA instructions that perform the following tasks:

1) Use the ActiveDocument property to display the name of the active document.

2) Use the ActivePrinter property to display the name of the active printer.

3) Use the PrintPreview method to preview the document.

d. Select all of the instructions entered in the Immediate window, then copy them to the clipboard. Open a new document in Word, and then paste the instructions into the document. Remove any instructions that did not work correctly, then save the document as T2-WD-E5D-Immediate. Close the T2-WD-E5D-Immediate document.

e. Close the Immediate window and the Visual Basic Editor. Save and then close the T2-WD-E5D document.

A computer program is good only if it works. Errors in programming code can cause a program to run incorrectly. Therefore, a programmer needs to know how to locate and fix any errors in his or her code. Exercises 6 and 7 are Debugging Exercises. Debugging Exercises allow you to practice recognizing and solving errors in code.

debugging

6. The following VBA instruction is supposed to change the second word in the first document to "January", but it is not working correctly. Correct the instruction.

```
Application.Documents(1).Words(2).Value = "January"
```

debugging

7. The following VBA instruction is supposed to select the third sentence in the first Document object, but it is not working correctly. Correct the instruction.

```
Application.Documents(1).Range(3).Selection
```

Access Lesson

The Access Object Model

case ► Jose Martinez, a professor at Snowville College, uses Microsoft Access to maintain information on his students and courses. He would like to use VBA to customize his Access databases to better suit his work style and needs. Before he begins customizing his Access databases, you advise him that he must become familiar with the objects included in the Access object model. You agree to explain a portion of the model to him, and to show him how he can refer to these objects in VBA.

Understanding the Access Object Model

As you learned in the Concept lesson, an application's object model depicts the hierarchy of objects available in the application. Before Professor Martinez can customize his Access databases, he needs to understand how to refer to the objects included in the Access object model.

Figure 2-43 shows the portion of the Microsoft Access object model that includes several of the most commonly used Access objects. (You will view the full Access object model in this lesson's Exercise 3.)

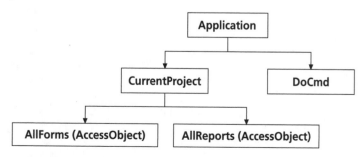

Figure 2-43: Several of the most commonly used Access objects

As Figure 2-43 indicates, the Access object model begins with the Application object, which represents the Access application. Contained within the Application object are the CurrentProject and DoCmd objects. The CurrentProject object represents the currently active Microsoft Access project. The DoCmd object is the Access object that allows you to perform tasks such as closing windows, opening forms, and printing reports. You will learn about the CurrentProject object in this lesson. You will practice with the DoCmd object in this lesson's Exercise 4.

Immediately below the CurrentProject rectangle in Figure 2-43 are the AllForms and AllReports collections. As the figure indicates, both of these collections are made up of individual AccessObject objects. In the AllForms collection, an AccessObject object is a form, while in the AllReports collection, it is a report.

In Access, forms and reports are considered AccessObject objects.

The Application, CurrentProject, and AccessObject objects, as well as the AllForms and AllReports collections, are illustrated in Figure 2-44.

AccessObject objects in the AllForms collection

Application object

each form and report is contained in the CurrentProject object

AccessObject objects in the AllReports collection

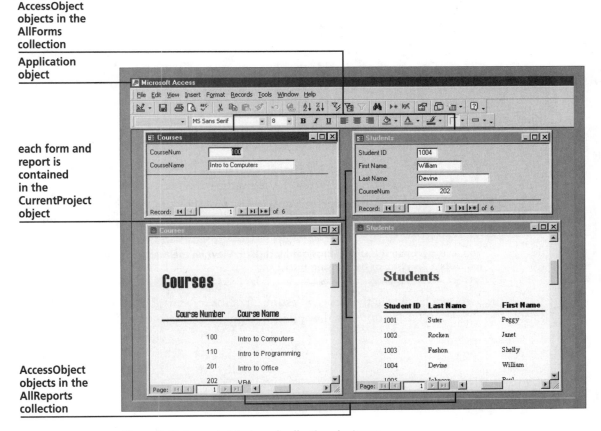

Figure 2-44: Several objects and collections in Access

In the next section, you will use the Object Browser in the Visual Basic Editor to display a Help screen for the Application object in Access. You also will learn how to display the Help screens for other objects in the Access object model.

Using the Object Browser in Access

As you learned in the Concept lesson, you can use the Object Browser in the Visual Basic Editor to view information about the objects included in an application's object model. The Object Browser is a useful tool for understanding the structure of an object model, and for studying the various objects included in the model, as well as their properties and methods.

To use the Object Browser in Access:

1 Start Microsoft Access. Open the **Jose** (Jose.mdb) database, which is located in the Tut02\Access folder on your Data Disk. The database contains two tables, two reports, and two forms. The Courses table is selected in the Database window. Click the **Maximize** button ▢ on the Microsoft Access title bar to maximize the Microsoft Access window, if necessary.

HELP? If the Office Assistant appears, you can either hide it or turn the Office Assistant feature off. To hide the Office Assistant, click Help on the Access menu bar, and then click Hide the Office Assistant. To turn the Office Assistant feature off, click the Office Assistant, and then click Options in the Office Assistant's balloon. Click the Options tab on the Office Assistant dialog box, if necessary, then click the Use the Office Assistant check box to deselect it. Click the OK button to close the Office Assistant dialog box.

2 Press **Alt+F11** to open the Visual Basic Editor. Close any open Visual Basic windows, except for the Visual Basic Editor window.

3 Click the **Object Browser** button 📺 on the Standard toolbar. The Object Browser window opens. If necessary, maximize the Object Browser window.

> You also can open the Object Browser by clicking View on the menu bar, and then clicking Object Browser, or by pressing the F2 key.

As you learned in the Concept lesson, all of the information for an application's object model is stored in the application's object library.

4   Click the **Project/Library** list arrow, then click **Access** in the list to display only the Access object library. See Figure 2-45.

Project/Library list arrow

Help button

Access object library file

your path might be different

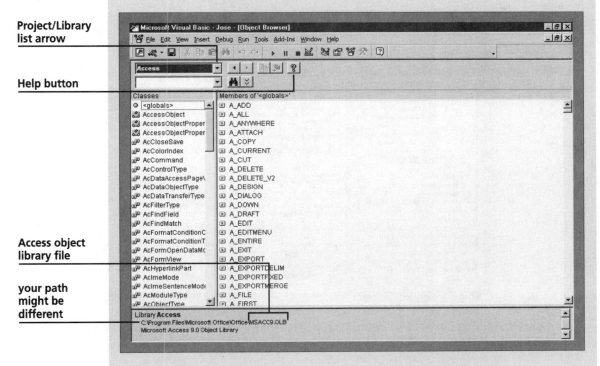

Figure 2-45: Object Browser window showing the Access object library

HELP? If the Object Browser window displays the Search Results section, click the Hide Search Results button ⌃ to close the section.

5   Scroll down the Classes list box until you see Application. Click **Application** in the list, and then click the **Help** button ⑧ to open the Microsoft Visual Basic Help window, which displays the Application object's Help screen. Maximize the Microsoft Visual Basic Help window, then click the **Contents** tab, if necessary. See Figure 2-46.

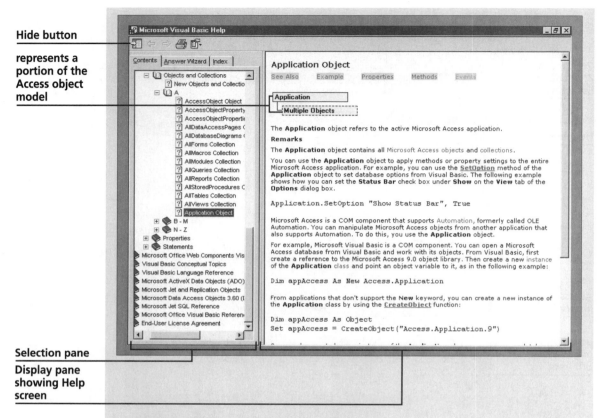

Hide button

represents a portion of the Access object model

Selection pane

Display pane showing Help screen

Figure 2-46: Microsoft Visual Basic Help window

HELP? If an error message appears indicating Help is not installed, see your instructor or technical support person.

HELP? If the Application Property Help screen appears, you inadvertently selected Application in the Members of <*classname*> list box. Close the Help window, then repeat Step 5; this time be sure to click Application in the Classes list box.

HELP? Don't be concerned if your Selection pane does not match the one shown in the figure.

According to the Help screen, the Application object represents the Microsoft Access application.

Notice that the Microsoft Visual Basic Help window is divided into two panes: the Selection pane and the Display pane. You use the Selection pane, which contains the Contents, Answer Wizard, and Index tabs, to select the topic whose Help screen you want to display in the Display pane. You also can hide the Selection pane so that you can view more of the information in the Display pane.

6 Click the **Hide** button 🔟 on the Microsoft Visual Basic Help toolbar to hide the Selection pane. Notice that 🔟 becomes a Show button 🔟, which you use to redisplay the Selection pane.

Next, view the Help screen for the Application object's Quit method.

7 Click **Methods**. When the Topics Found dialog box appears, scroll down the list of methods until you see Quit Method (Application Object). Click **Quit Method (Application Object)** in the list, and then click the **Display** button. The Quit Method Help screen appears, as shown in Figure 2-47.

click here to view an example of using the Quit method

Show button

purpose

syntax

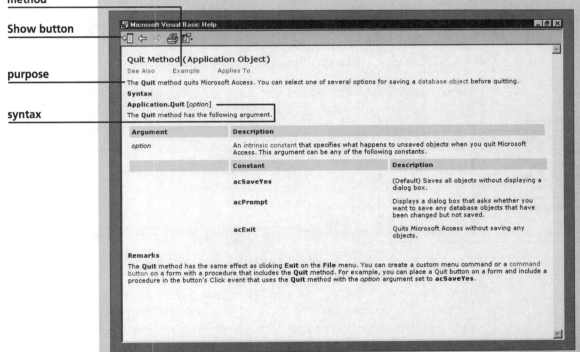

Figure 2-47: Quit Method (Application Object) Help screen

According to the Help screen, you use the Quit method to exit the Microsoft Access application. The syntax of the method is **Application.Quit** [*option*], where *option* indicates how Access should handle unsaved changes made to the database. According to the Help screen, the *option* argument can be either of the following intrinsic constants: `acSaveYes`, `acPrompt`, or `acExit`. However, when you enter the Quit method in either the Immediate or

Code windows, the Auto List Members list shows that the names of the constants are `acQuitPrompt`, `acQuitSaveAll`, and `acQuitSaveNone`. Don't be surprised if you find some inconsistencies in the Help screens. In this case, you can use either of the six constants as the *option* argument. The `acSaveYes` and `acQuitSaveAll` constants indicate that Access should save all changes, automatically, without prompting the user. The `acPrompt` and `acQuitPrompt` constants, on the other hand, indicate that the user should be prompted to save any changes. The `acExit` and `acQuitSaveNone` constants indicate that Access should simply close without saving any changes.

 tip

An intrinsic constant is a word, built into an application, that typically represents a numeric value. Constants are more meaningful than the numbers they represent, so they are easier to understand and remember. For example, the constant `acQuitSaveAll` is more meaningful than its numeric equivalent—the number 1.

You can click the word *Example* at the top of the Help screen to view an example of using the Quit method in a VBA instruction.

8 Click **Example** at the top of the Quit method's Help screen. See Figure 2-48.

Back button instructs the Access Application object to close itself

prompts user to save changes

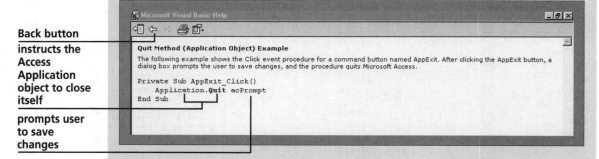

Figure 2-48: Example showing the Quit method in a VBA instruction

As the example shows, the `Application.Quit acPrompt` instruction prompts the user to save any changes before Access closes itself.

 tip

As you learned in Tutorial 1, a method is an action that an object can perform on its own.

9 Click the **Back** button ⇐ on the Microsoft Visual Basic Help toolbar. The Quit Method (Application Object) Help screen appears. Click ⇐ again to return to the Application Object Help screen.

Notice that a Multiple Objects rectangle appears below the Application rectangle in the Application Object Help screen. As you learned in the Concept lesson, a

Multiple Objects rectangle represents the next level of objects in the object model hierarchy. Now view a listing of these objects.

To view the next level of objects in the object model hierarchy:

1 Click the **Multiple Objects** rectangle in the Application Object Help screen. The Topics Found dialog box appears and lists the objects found on the next level of the Access object model. Recall that the CurrentProject object is located on this lower level.

View the Help screen for the CurrentProject object.

2 Scroll down the list of objects in the Topics Found dialog box until you see CurrentProject Object. Click **CurrentProject Object** and then click the **Display** button. The CurrentProject Object Help screen appears.

Notice that a Multiple Objects rectangle, which represents the objects located on the next level in the object model hierarchy, appears below the CurrentProject rectangle in the Help screen. Recall that the AllReports collection and its AccessObject objects are located on this lower level.

3 Click the **Multiple Objects** rectangle. When the Topics Found dialog box appears, click **AllReports Collection** in the list, then click the **Display** button. The AllReports Collection Help screen shown in Figure 2-49 appears.

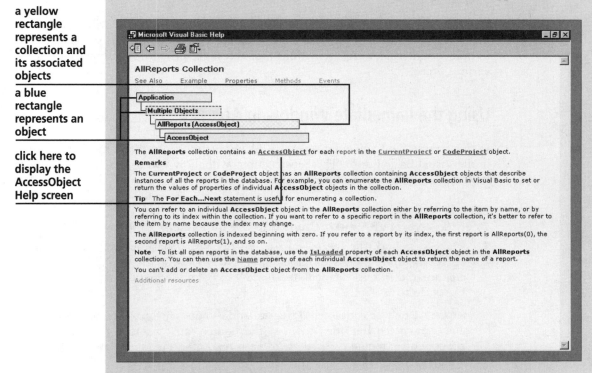

Figure 2-49: AllReports Collection Help screen

If you are using a color monitor, you will notice that the object model diagram located at the top of the Help screen contains three blue rectangles and one yellow rectangle. A blue rectangle represents an object in the object model. A yellow rectangle, on the other hand, represents a collection and its associated objects.

> **tip**
>
> Notice that AccessObject appears in both the yellow AllReports (AccessObject) rectangle and the blue AccessObject rectangle. Unlike the Help screens in PowerPoint, Excel, and Word, the Access Help screens include a separate blue rectangle for the type of object included in a collection.

To display the AccessObject Help screen, you click either the AccessObject rectangle in the diagram or the word AccessObject in the first paragraph of the Help screen.

You now are finished with the Microsoft Visual Basic Help window and the Object Browser, so you can close both windows.

4 Click the **Show** button ⬛ on the Microsoft Visual Basic Help toolbar to display the Help window's Selection pane, then close the Microsoft Visual Basic Help window and the Object Browser.

As you learned in the Concept lesson, once you are familiar with an application's object model, you can use the Immediate window in the Visual Basic Editor to practice entering VBA instructions that access the properties and methods of the various objects.

Using the Immediate Window in Access

In this section, you will enter several VBA instructions into the Immediate window in the Visual Basic Editor. These instructions will allow you to practice referring to the objects in the Access object model.

To enter several VBA instructions into the Immediate window:

1 Make sure both the Jose database and the Visual Basic Editor window are open. Maximize the Visual Basic Editor. Click **View** on the Visual Basic Editor menu bar, then click **Immediate Window** to open the Immediate window. See Figure 2-50.

> **HELP?** Don't be concerned if the size and location of your Immediate window does not match the one shown in the figure. You can resize the Immediate window by dragging its borders. You can reposition the Immediate window by dragging the window by its title bar.

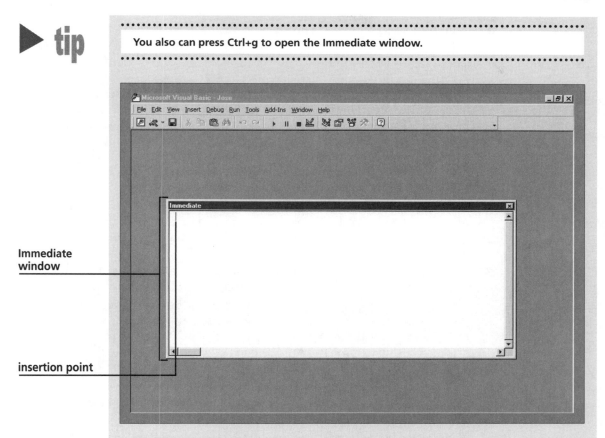

▶ **tip**

•••
You also can press **Ctrl+g** to open the Immediate window.
•••

Immediate
window

insertion point

Figure 2-50: Visual Basic Editor showing open Immediate window

The first VBA instruction you will enter into the Immediate window, **?Application.Name**, will display the value stored in the Application object's Name property. Recall that the question mark (**?**) at the beginning of an instruction tells VBA to display the value of what follows the question mark below the instruction in the Immediate window.

2   Type **?application.** (be sure to type the period) in the Immediate window. The Application object's member list appears.

HELP? If the member list does not appear, click Tools on the menu bar, then click Options to open the Options dialog box. Select the Auto List Members check box on the Editor tab, then click the OK button to close the Options dialog box.

Rather than scrolling down the member list until you locate the Name property, and then clicking Name in the list to select it, as you did in Tutorial 1, you will use a much quicker way to select the Name property.

3   Type **n** to select the Name property in the member list and then press the **Enter** key. The name of the Application object—Microsoft Access—appears in the Immediate window.

Next, you will use the CurrentProject object's `Name` property to display the name of the current project. Recall that you access an object's property using the *expression.property* syntax, where *expression* represents the location of the object in the object model. In this case, you will use `Application.CurrentProject`, which represents the location of the CurrentProject object in the object model, as the *expression*, and you will use `Name` as the property. The instruction you will enter into the Immediate window is `?Application.CurrentProject.Name`.

Important Note: When you are told to enter an instruction, you always will be shown the complete instruction to enter. You can enter the instruction either by typing it yourself or by using the listings that appear at various times in the Immediate window.

4   Type **?application.currentproject.name** and press the **Enter** key. The name of the current project, Jose.mdb, appears in the Immediate window.

Next, you will use the AllReports collection's `Count` property to display the number of reports in the current project. In this case, you will use `Application.CurrentProject.AllReports` as the *expression*. The *expression* indicates that the AllReports collection is contained in the CurrentProject object, which is contained in the Application object.

5   Type **?application.currentproject.allreports.count** and press the **Enter** key. The number 2 appears in the Immediate window because the current project (Jose.mdb) contains two reports.

Now display the name of the first report (AccessObject object) in the AllReports collection. To do so, you will use the `Application.CurrentProject.AllReports(0).Name` instruction. As you learned in the Concept lesson, you refer to a specific object within a collection by entering either the object's index or its name in parentheses following the collection's name. The first report (AccessObject object) in the AllReports collection has an index of 0.

> Unlike PowerPoint, Excel, and Word, Access assigns an index of 0 to the first object in most of its collections. The other Microsoft Office applications assign an index of 1.

6   Type **?application.currentproject.allreports(0).name** and press the **Enter** key. The name of the first report, StudentsReport, appears in the Immediate window.

You use the AccessObject object's IsLoaded property to determine if a report is open. Determine if the StudentsReport report is open.

7 Type **?application.currentproject.allreports("studentsreport").isloaded** and press the **Enter** key. The value False appears in the Immediate window because the StudentsReport report is not open currently.

HELP? If an error message appears in a dialog box, click the OK button to close the dialog box. Then retype the instruction shown in Step 7.

Notice that you can refer to an object in the AllReports collection either by its index, as you did in Step 6, or by its name, as you did in Step 7. Figure 2-51 shows the VBA instructions you have entered in the Immediate window.

index of the first object in the collection ⎯⎯⎯⎯⎯⎯⎯⎯⎯

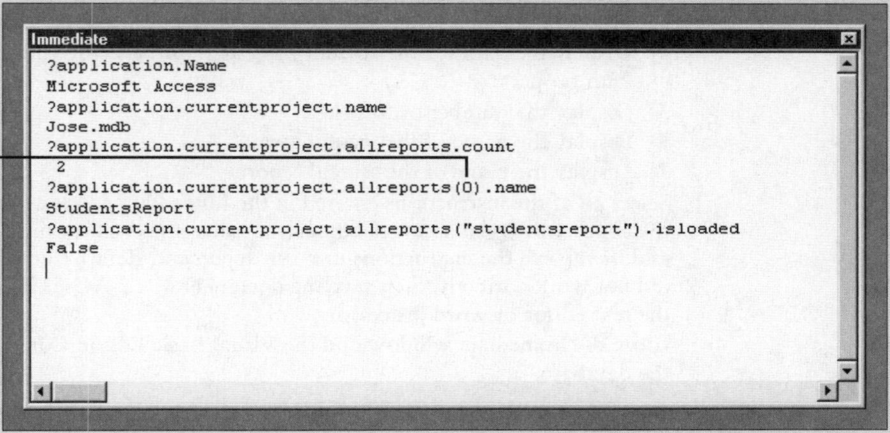

```
Immediate                                                                    ×
?application.Name
Microsoft Access
?application.currentproject.name
Jose.mdb
?application.currentproject.allreports.count
 2
?application.currentproject.allreports(0).name
StudentsReport
?application.currentproject.allreports("studentsreport").isloaded
False
|
```

Figure 2-51: VBA instructions entered in the Immediate window

As you learned in the Concept lesson, in addition to entering VBA instructions that access an object's properties, you also can enter VBA instructions that invoke an object's methods. Next, you will invoke the Access Application object's Quit method, which will close the application. Use the constant acQuitSaveNone as the Quit method's *option* argument. Recall that the acQuitSaveNone constant indicates that Access should simply close itself without saving any changes.

8 Type **application.quit acquitsavenone** and press the **Enter** key to close Microsoft Access.

You now have completed Tutorial 2's Access lesson. You can either take a break or complete the end-of-lesson exercises.

E X E R C I S E S

1. In this exercise, you will enter VBA instructions that refer to Access objects.

   a. Open the Jose (Jose.mdb) database, which is located in the Tut02\Access folder on your Data Disk. Open the Visual Basic Editor, then open the Immediate window. Delete any instructions from the Immediate window, then use the Immediate window to enter VBA instructions that perform the following tasks:

   1) Display the name of the application.
   2) Display the name of the current project.
   3) Display the full name of the current project. (*Hint*: Use the CurrentProject object's FullName property.)
   4) Display the path for the current project. (*Hint*: Use the CurrentProject object's Path property.)
   5) Display the number of forms.
   6) Display the name of the second form.
   7) Display the name of the second report.

   b. Select all of the instructions entered in the Immediate window, then copy them to the clipboard. Open a new document in either a text editor or a word processor, and then paste the instructions into the document. Remove any instructions that did not work correctly, then save the document as T2-AC-E1D-Immediate. Close the text editor or word processor.

   c. Close the Immediate window and the Visual Basic Editor. Compact and then close the database.

2. In this exercise, you will enter VBA instructions that refer to Access objects.

   a. Open the Sales (Sales.mdb) database, which is located in the Tut02\Access folder on your Data Disk. The Sales database contains one table, one report, one form, and two queries.

   b. Open the Visual Basic Editor, then open the Immediate window. Delete any instructions from the Immediate window, then use the Immediate window to enter VBA instructions that perform the following tasks:

   1) Display the name of the current project.
   2) Display the number of forms.
   3) Display the name of the form.
   4) Display the name of the report.

   c. Select all of the instructions entered in the Immediate window, then copy them to the clipboard. Open a new document in either a text editor or a word processor, and then paste the instructions into the document. Remove any instructions that did not work correctly, then save the document as T2-AC-E2D-Immediate. Close the text editor or word processor.

   d. Close the Immediate window and the Visual Basic Editor. Compact and then close the database.

3. In this exercise, you will learn how to display the entire object model for the Access application.

   a. Open the Jose (Jose.mdb) database. Open the Visual Basic Editor, and then open the Object Browser window. Display the Help screen for the Application object in the Access object library.

b. Click See Also in the Application Object Help screen. When the Topics Found dialog box appears, click Microsoft Access Objects in the list and then click the Display button to display the full Access object model.

c. Close the Help window, the Object Browser, the Visual Basic Editor, and the database.

Exercise 4 is a Discovery Exercise. Discovery Exercises, which may include topics that are not covered in the lesson, allow you to "discover" the solutions to problems on your own.

 4. In this exercise, you will practice with the DoCmd object in Access.

a. Open the Sales (Sales.mdb) database, which is located in the Tut02\Access folder on your Data Disk, then open the Visual Basic Editor. The Sales database contains one table, one report, one form, and two queries.

b. Display the Help screen for the DoCmd object. Also display the Help screens for the DoCmd object's OpenReport, OpenForm, and OpenQuery methods. (You may want to print the Help screens for future reference.) Study the Help screens, then close the Help screens.

c. Open the Immediate window. Delete any instructions from the Immediate window, then use the Immediate window to enter VBA instructions that perform the following tasks. After entering each instruction, return to Access to see the result of the instruction, then close the report, form, or query.

1) Open the report for previewing.
2) Open and then print the report.
3) Open the form.
4) Open the SalesQuery1 query.

d. Select all of the instructions entered in the Immediate window, then copy them to the clipboard. Open a new document in either a text editor or a word processor, and then paste the instructions into the document. Remove any instructions that did not work correctly, then save the document as T2-AC-E4D-Immediate. Close the text editor or word processor.

e. Close the Immediate window and the Visual Basic Editor. Compact and then close the database.

A computer program is good only if it works. Errors in programming code can cause a program to run incorrectly. Therefore, a programmer needs to know how to locate and fix any errors in his or her code. Exercise 5 is a Debugging Exercise. Debugging Exercises allow you to practice recognizing and solving errors in code.

 5. The following instruction is supposed to display the name of the first form in the current project, but it is not working correctly. Correct the instruction.

```
?Application.CurrentProject.AllForms.Forms(1).Name
```

TUTORIAL

3

Object Variables

Objectives

In this tutorial, you will learn how to:

- Explain how properties and variables are stored in memory
- Create an object variable using the Dim statement
- Select the appropriate name and data type for an object variable
- Use the Set statement to assign an object's address to an object variable
- Insert a row, value, and formula into an Excel worksheet using VBA code
- Format an Excel worksheet using VBA code
- Assign a theme to a Word document using VBA code
- Create a hyperlink in a Word document using VBA code
- Open an Access report using VBA code
- Order the records in an Access report using VBA code

Concept Lesson

Memory Cells

As you learned in prior tutorials, every object in a VBA-enabled application has a set of properties whose values control the object's appearance and behavior. For example, the Assistant object's Left property contains a numeric value that controls the position of the Office Assistant's left border on the screen. The Assistant object's FileName property, on the other hand, contains a value—in this case, a filename—that determines the character used to display the Office Assistant. VBA stores each property, along with its corresponding value, inside the computer in an area called **internal memory**, which is simply an ordered sequence of memory cells contained on computer chips (integrated circuits residing on silicon). It may be helpful to picture a memory cell as a tiny box inside the computer. When VBA creates an object—for example, when it creates the Assistant object—it reserves a group of boxes (memory cells) in which it stores information about the object. VBA assigns each memory cell in the group a name that corresponds to the name of a property, and VBA places each property's value in its corresponding memory cell. For example, VBA stores the value of the Assistant object's Left property in a memory cell named Left. It stores the value of the Assistant object's FileName property, on the other hand, in a memory cell named FileName, as illustrated in Figure 3-1.

Left	Filename			
144	clippit.acs			

Figure 3-1: Illustration of memory cells that store property values

Because different objects can have the same property—for example, the Document object in Word has a Name property, and so do the Workbook and Worksheet objects in Excel—VBA stores each object's properties in a separate section of internal memory, as illustrated in Figure 3-2.

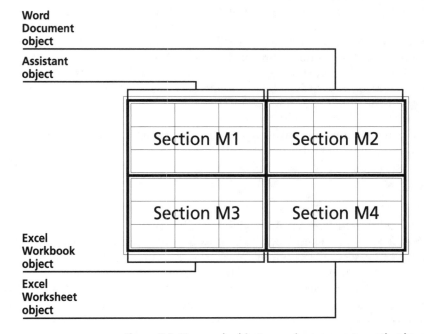

Figure 3-2: How each object occupies a separate section in memory

As shown in Figure 3-2, the properties pertaining to the Assistant object are stored in section M1 in internal memory, while the properties pertaining to the Document object in Word and Workbook and Worksheet objects in Excel are stored in sections M2, M3, and M4, respectively. By storing each object's properties in a separate section in memory, VBA can distinguish the memory cells associated with one object from the memory cells associated with a different object. For example, if a procedure refers to a property of the Document object, when the procedure is run, it will look for that property in section M2 in memory. However, if a procedure refers to the property of the Worksheet object, it will search section M4 for the property.

In addition to assigning both a name and a value to each property's memory cell, VBA also assigns a data type. The data type refers to the type of data the memory cell can store. For example, the Left property's memory cell can store only numbers, whereas the FileName property's memory cell can store both letters and numbers. You can determine the type of data that a property's memory cell can store by viewing the property's Help screen.

As you learned in Tutorial 2, you can assign a different value to the property of an object using a VBA instruction whose syntax is *expression.property = value*, where *expression* represents the location of the object in the object model. When you assign a different value to a property, VBA replaces the value currently contained in the property's memory cell with the new value, because a memory cell can contain only one value at a time. The `Assistant.FileName = "genius.acs"` instruction, for example, replaces the "clippit.acs" value, which is stored in the FileName memory cell shown in Figure 3-1, with the value "genius.acs". The `Assistant.Left = 72` instruction replaces the current value of the Assistant object's Left property (144) with the number 72.

When an object is closed—for example, when you close a Word document or an Excel workbook—VBA removes the contents of the memory cells that store the object's properties. In other words, VBA no longer reserves a section in the computer's memory for the object.

In addition to the memory cells that VBA automatically reserves when an object is created, internal memory also can contain memory cells that are reserved by the programmer. These memory cells are called variables.

Variables

Recall that when an object is created, VBA automatically reserves a memory cell for each of the object's properties, and VBA stores a value within each memory cell. A programmer also can reserve memory cells for storing information. For example, a programmer can reserve a memory cell to hold the result of a calculation made within a procedure, or he or she can reserve a memory cell to store the user's input from the keyboard. The memory cells reserved by the programmer are called **variables**.

> The term *variable* refers to the fact that the contents of these memory cells can *vary* as a procedure is running. Although the contents of property memory cells also can vary, the term *variable* refers only to memory cells not associated with properties.

Like all reserved memory cells, the variables that you create must have both a name and a data type. Recall that the data type refers to the type of data the memory cell can store. Numeric variables, for example, can store only numbers, while String variables can store numbers, letters, and special characters, such as the dollar sign ($). Date variables can store dates and times. You will learn about String variables in Tutorial 4, Date variables in Tutorial 5, and numeric variables in Tutorial 6. In this tutorial, you will learn about object variables, which store addresses of objects in memory. Programmers use object variables to make procedures easier to write and understand. Object variables also help to improve the performance of a procedure by allowing the procedure to run more quickly.

Object Variables

An **object variable** is a memory cell (box) that contains the address of an object in memory. The address tells VBA where—in other words, in what section of memory—the object is located. For example, the object variable shown in Figure 3-3 contains the address M2, which is the address (location) of the Word Document object in internal memory. The M2 address tells VBA that it can find all of the Document object's properties in section M2 of internal memory.

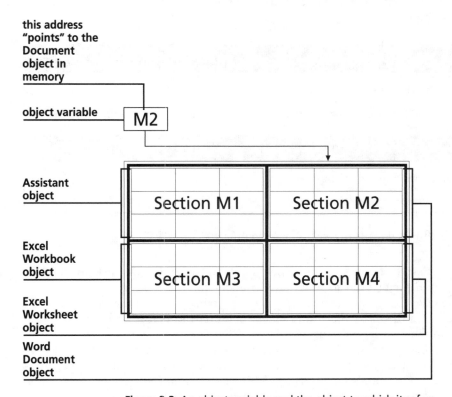

Figure 3-3: An object variable and the object to which it refers

An object variable does not store an object; rather, it stores the address of an object.

As shown in Figure 3-3, the address contained in an object variable "points" to the location of an object in memory. The M2 address stored in the object variable shown in Figure 3-3, for example, points to the Word Document object. Although the concept of using addresses to point to objects may sound confusing at first, it is one with which you are already familiar. For example, your street address "points" to your house—in other words, it tells everyone where your house is located. Your social security number is an address that "points" to you. When the grocery clerk tells you that canned vegetables are in aisle 5, he or she is using an address (the number 5) to point you to the location of canned vegetables in the store.

As mentioned earlier, object variables make your procedures easier to write and easier to understand; they also make them run more efficiently. For example, assume that a procedure needs to display the contents of the first Slide object's Name and Layout properties in PowerPoint. As you learned in Tutorial 2, you could use the first two instructions shown in Figure 3-4 to do so. An easier way, however, is to assign the address of the first Slide object to an object variable named sldFirst, and then use the last two instructions shown in Figure 3-4 to display the object's properties.

Without an object variable:

```
MsgBox Prompt:=Application.Presentations(1).Slides(1).Name

MsgBox Prompt:=Application.Presentations(1).Slides(1).Layout
```

With an object variable:

```
MsgBox Prompt:=sldFirst.Name

MsgBox Prompt:=sldFirst.Layout
```

Figure 3-4: Instructions to display the first Slide object's Name and Layout properties

Notice that the first two instructions shown in Figure 3-4 are fairly long, which makes them difficult both to write and to understand. The longer an instruction, the greater the chance of making a typing error when entering the instruction in a procedure, and the more the reader has to comprehend before he or she can fully understand the instruction's purpose.

Besides being difficult both to write and understand, the first two instructions also are inefficient. For example, when VBA processes the `MsgBox Prompt:=Application.Presentations(1).Slides(1).Name` instruction, first it must locate the appropriate Application object in memory, then it must locate the first Presentation object within the Presentations collection, followed by the first Slide object within the Slides collection. Only after taking this long and indirect path to the Slide object can VBA display the Slide object's Name property. VBA repeats this process when it executes the `MsgBox Prompt:=Application.Presentations(1).Slides(1).Layout` instruction—once again having to locate the appropriate Application, Presentation, and Slide objects in memory.

Because the first two instructions shown in Figure 3-4 provide an indirect path to the Slide object, rather than a direct one, the instructions will take longer to process. As you already know, a direct route to a destination is always quicker than an indirect one.

If you assign the Slide object's address to an object variable named sldFirst, you can use the last two instructions shown in Figure 3-4 to display the Slide object's

Name and Layout properties. The last two instructions are not only shorter, which makes them easier to enter and easier to understand, but they also are more efficient. This is because the sldFirst object variable contains an address that points directly to the location of the Slide object in memory. So, rather than having to locate the Application and Presentation objects before it can find the Slide object, as VBA needs to do when processing the first two instructions shown in Figure 3-4, the last two instructions allow VBA to go right to the Slide object in memory. In other words, unlike the first two instructions, the last two instructions provide VBA with a direct path to the Slide object, making these instructions much more efficient.

Before you can use an object variable, you first must declare, or reserve, the object variable in memory. The instruction you use to do so, as well as the location where you enter that instruction, determines the object variable's scope. A variable's **scope** refers to which procedures in the project can use the variable. Variables in VBA can have one of three scopes: procedure-level, module-level, or public. In this tutorial, you will learn how to reserve procedure-level variables only.

Both module-level and public variables are created outside of a procedure, in the General Declarations section of a module. A module-level variable can be used by any procedure in the module in which it is created. A public variable can be used by any of the procedures contained within any of the project's modules.

Reserving a Procedure-Level Variable

A **procedure-level variable** is reserved, or declared, within a procedure, and it can be used only by the procedure in which it is declared. It is customary to declare procedure-level variables at the beginning of the procedure, immediately below the `Private Sub` or `Public Sub` instruction or, in the case of Access, immediately below the `Public Function` instruction.

You use the VBA **Dim statement** to reserve a procedure-level variable. The syntax of the Dim statement is **Dim** *variablename* **As** *datatype*, where *variablename* represents the name of the variable (memory cell) and *datatype* represents its data type. Notice that the Dim statement includes the two items of information needed by every reserved memory cell—a name and a data type. When VBA processes the Dim statement in a procedure, it reserves a memory cell to which it assigns *variablename* as the name and *datatype* as the data type.

Dim comes from the word "dimension," which is how programmers in the 1960s referred to the process of allocating memory.

As you learned in Tutorial 1, *syntax* refers to the rules of a programming language—in this case, it is the VBA rules you must follow in order to use the Dim statement.

Notice that the words **Dim** and **As** appear in bold in the Dim statement's syntax, while *variablename* and *datatype* appear in italics. Words in bold are required parts of the syntax; you must include both Dim and As in the Dim statement. Items in *italics*, on the other hand, indicate that the programmer must supply information pertaining to the current procedure. In the Dim statement, the programmer must supply the variable's name and its data type.

Selecting the Appropriate Data Type and Name for an Object Variable

You must assign a data type to each of the variables (memory cells) that you reserve. In the case of an object variable, the data type that you select will depend on the type of object to which the object variable will point. For example, if an object variable will point to a Document object, then the object variable's data type will be Document. Similarly, if an object variable will contain the address of a Worksheet object, then the object variable's data type will be Worksheet. Figure 3-5 shows the data types that correspond to some of the most-used objects available in the Microsoft Office applications. Notice that, in most cases, the data type has the same name as its corresponding object.

Object	Data type
Microsoft Access	
AccessObject	AccessObject
Report	Report
Form	Form
Field	Field
Recordset	Recordset
Microsoft Excel	
Workbook	Workbook
Worksheet	Worksheet
Range	Range
Microsoft PowerPoint	
Presentation	Presentation
Slide	Slide
Microsoft Word	
Document	Document
Paragraph	Paragraph
Sentence	Range
Word	Range
Character	Range

Figure 3-5: Data types corresponding to some of the objects available in the Microsoft Office applications

tip

In addition to assigning a data type to a variable, recall that you also must assign a name to the variable. You should assign a descriptive name to each variable that you create. The name should help you remember both the data type and purpose of the variable. One popular naming convention is to have the first three characters in the name represent the data type, and the remainder of the name represent the variable's purpose. Figure 3-6 lists the three characters typically associated with the data types shown in Figure 3-5.

Data type	ID
Microsoft Access	
AccessObject	aob
Report	rpt
Form	frm
Field	fld
Recordset	rst
Microsoft Excel	
Workbook	wkb
Worksheet	sht
Range	rng
Microsoft PowerPoint	
Presentation	prs
Slide	sld
Microsoft Word	
Document	doc
Paragraph	par
Range	rng

Figure 3-6: Data types and their three-character IDs

It is a common practice to type the three-character ID in lowercase and capitalize the first letter in the part of the name that identifies the purpose. For example, a good name for an object variable that contains the address of the Smith document in memory is docSmith. Although S also could be used as the name for that variable, notice that it is not as descriptive as the name docSmith. In the latter case, the name reminds you that the object variable points to a Document object named Smith.

In addition to being descriptive, the name that a programmer assigns to a variable also must follow several specific rules. These rules are listed in Figure 3-7, along with examples of valid and invalid object variable names.

Rules for naming variables

1. The name must begin with a letter.

2. The name must contain only letters, numbers, and the underscore. No punctuation characters or spaces are allowed in the name.

3. The name cannot be more than 255 characters long.

4. The name cannot be a reserved word, such as Print, because reserved words have special meaning in VBA.

Valid object variable names:	Invalid object variable names:	
doc94Sales	94SalesDoc	(the name must begin with a letter)
rngRegionWest	rngRegion West	(the name cannot contain a space)
rptEast	rpt.East	(the name cannot contain punctuation)
sldTop	MsgBox	(the name cannot be a reserved word)

Figure 3-7: Rules and examples for variable names

Figure 3-8 shows examples of the Dim statement used to declare object variables.

Dim statement	Explanation
`Dim sldFirst As Slide`	Creates an object variable named sldFirst that can store the address of a Slide object
`Dim docSales As Document`	Creates an object variable named docSales that can store the address of a Document object
`Dim wkbPay As Workbook`	Creates an object variable named wkbPay that can store the address of a Workbook object
`Dim rngWest As Range`	Creates an object variable named rngWest that can store the address of a Range object
`Dim rptBonus As Report`	Creates an object variable named rptBonus that can store the address of a Report object

Figure 3-8: Examples of the Dim statement used to declare object variables

tip

Always be sure to include the As *datatype* portion of the Dim statement. If you neglect to assign a specific data type to a variable, VBA assigns a default data type, called Variant, to it. You should refrain from using the Variant data type because it is not as efficient as the data types listed in Figure 3-5.

When you use the Dim statement to declare an object variable, VBA reserves a memory cell to which it attaches *variablename* as the name and *datatype* as the data type. VBA also automatically stores the keyword `Nothing` in the object variable. This is referred to as **initializing** the variable—in other words, giving the variable a beginning value. When an object variable contains the keyword `Nothing`, it means that the object variable does not point to any object in memory.

After you use the Dim statement to create and initialize an object variable, you then use the Set statement to assign the address of an object to it.

Using the Set Statement

You use the **Set statement** to assign the address of an object to an object variable. The syntax of the Set statement is **Set** *objectVariableName* = *object*, where *objectVariableName* is the name of an object variable, and *object* is the object whose address you want to store in the variable. Figure 3-9 shows examples of the Set statement used to assign addresses to the object variables created in Figure 3-8.

Set statement

```
Set sldFirst = Application.Presentations(1).Slides(1)

Set docSales = Application.Documents(1)

Set shtPay = Application.Workbooks(1).Worksheets(1)

Set rngWest = Application.Documents("stock.doc").Sentences(4)

Set rptBonus = Application.Reports("bonus")
```

Figure 3-9: Examples of the Set statement

The Set statement locates the *object* in memory and then stores the object's address in the memory cell whose name is *objectVariableName*. The `Set sldFirst = Application.Presentations(1).Slides(1)` statement, for example, locates, in memory, the desired Slide object, and then it stores the object's address in the sldFirst object variable. After creating the object variable, you can use the sldFirst object variable, rather than the longer `Application.Presentations(1).Slides(1)`, in your instructions. For example, you can use the `sldFirst.Name = "Overview"` instruction to change the contents of the Slide object's Name property.

As you learned earlier, a procedure-level variable is declared within a procedure, and it can be used only by the procedure in which it is declared. A procedure-level variable remains in memory only while the procedure in which it is declared is running. When the procedure ends, the procedure level variable is removed from memory. For example, assume that the PrintSlide procedure in PowerPoint contains the following Dim statement: `Dim sldOver As Slide`. When VBA processes the Dim statement, it reserves the sldOver object variable in memory, and it initializes the object variable to `Nothing`. VBA also automatically creates a link between the

PrintSlide procedure and its sldOver variable. While the PrintSlide procedure is running, VBA maintains the connection between the procedure and the variable. When the PrintSlide procedure ends, VBA destroys the connection, leaving the memory cell unreserved.

You now have completed Tutorial 3's Concept lesson. You can either take a break or complete the end-of-lesson questions and exercises before moving on to the next lesson.

SUMMARY

To create a procedure-level object variable, and then assign an address to it:

■ Use the Dim statement to create the variable. The syntax of the Dim statement is **Dim** *variablename* **As** *datatype*, where *variablename* represents the name of the variable (memory cell) and *datatype* represents its data type.

■ Refer to Figure 3-5 for a listing of the data types corresponding to some of the objects available in the Microsoft Office applications. Refer to Figures 3-6 and 3-7 for information on naming a variable. Refer to Figure 3-8 for examples of the Dim statement.

■ Use the Set statement to assign the address of an object to an object variable. The syntax of the Set statement is **Set** *objectVariableName* = *object*, where *objectVariableName* is the name of an object variable and *object* is the object whose address you want to assign to the object variable. Refer to Figure 3-9 for examples of the Set statement.

REVIEW QUESTIONS

1. When VBA creates an object, it assigns a _____ to each of the memory cells associated with the object's properties.
   a. Data type
   b. Name
   c. Value
   d. All of the above

2. Which of the following assignment statements assigns the number 100 to the memory cell that contains the Assistant object's Top property?
   a. `Assistant.Memory(Top) = 100`
   b. `Assistant.Top = 100`
   c. `Memory.Assistant.Top = 100`
   d. `Top.Assistant = 100`

3. If an object variable will point to a Workbook object, you should use the _____ data type in the Dim statement that declares the object variable.
   a. Book
   b. Range
   c. Sheet
   d. Workbook

4. Which of the following is a valid name for a variable?
   a. docBonus
   b. 2000Sales
   c. shtPrice.Per.Unit
   d. January Sales

5. Which of the following is false?
   a. A procedure-level variable is created in a procedure.
   b. When you declare a variable using the Document data type, VBA initializes the variable to an empty document.
   c. A procedure-level variable can be used only by the procedure in which it is declared.
   d. You use the VBA Dim statement to create a procedure-level variable.

6. Which of the following is false?
   a. A procedure-level variable remains in memory only while the procedure in which it is declared is running.
   b. The variables created within a procedure remain in memory until you close the application.
   c. After an object variable is created and initialized, you use the Set statement to assign the address of an object to the variable.
   d. None of the above

Use the following instructions to answer questions 7 and 8.

```
Dim docSmith As Document
Set docSmith = Application.Documents(1)
```

7. What is the value stored in the docSmith object variable after the Dim statement is processed?
   a. the address of the docSmith object in memory
   b. the address of the first Document object in memory
   c. the keyword Empty
   d. the keyword Nothing

8. What is stored in the docSmith object variable after the Set statement has been processed?
   a. the address of the docSmith object in memory
   b. the address of the first Document object in memory
   c. the keyword Document
   d. the keyword Nothing

9. Which of the following is the three-character ID associated with the Presentation data type?
   a. ppt
   b. pps
   c. prs
   d. prt

10. Which of the following is the correct data type to use for an object variable that will point to a Worksheet object in Microsoft Excel?
   a. Sheet
   b. Sht
   c. Worksheet
   d. XlWorksheet

11. Which of the following is the correct data type to use for an object variable that will point to a sentence in Microsoft Word?
   a. Range
   b. Sentence
   c. ThisSentence
   d. None of the above

 **E X E R C I S E S**

1. Write a Dim statement that declares an object variable named docMemo. The object variable will store the address of a Document object. Then write a Set statement that assigns the address of the Application.Documents(1) object to the docMemo object variable.

2. Write a Dim statement that declares an object variable named shtInvent. The object variable will store the address of a Worksheet object. Then write a Set statement that assigns the address of the Application.Workbooks(1).Worksheets(1) object to the shtInvent object variable.

3. Write a Dim statement that declares an object variable named sldMain. The object variable will store the address of a Slide object. Then write a Set statement that assigns the address of the Application.Presentations(1).Slides(2) object to the sldMain object variable.

Use the following figure to complete Exercises 4 through 7.

Application.Workbooks(1).Worksheets(1)   Application.Documents(1)

	Section M1				Section M2	
	Section M3				Section M4	

Application.Presentations(1).Slides(1)   Application.Presentations(1).Slides(2)

Figure 3-10

4. In Exercise 1, you declared an object variable named docMemo, and then assigned the address of the Application.Documents(1) Document object to it. According to Figure 3-10, what address will be stored in the docMemo object variable?

5. In Exercise 2, you declared an object variable named shtInvent, and then assigned the address of the Application.Workbooks(1).Worksheets(1) object to it. According to Figure 3-10, what address will be stored in the shtInvent object variable?

6. In Exercise 3, you declared an object variable named sldMain, and then assigned the address of the Application.Presentations(1).Slides(2) object to it. According to Figure 3-10, what address will be stored in the sldMain object variable?

7. According to Figure 3-10, how many Slide objects are stored in memory?

Exercise 8 is a Discovery Exercise. Discovery Exercises, which may include topics that are not covered in the lesson, allow you to "discover" the solutions to problems on your own.

discovery ▶ 8. Start either Word, Excel, Access, or PowerPoint. Open the Visual Basic Editor. Display the Creating Object Variables Help screen. (*Hint*: Use the Help menu to open the Microsoft Visual Basic Help window, then use the Answer Wizard tab to search for the Help screen.) Use the Help screen to complete the following statements:

    a. If you use an object variable without declaring it first, the data type of the object variable is _____ by default.

    b. You can declare an object variable with the _____ data type when the specific object type is not known until the procedure runs.

    c. You can use the _____ keyword to refer to the current instance of the object where the code is running.

You also can use VBA in PowerPoint to create procedures that enhance your presentations. Exercise 9 allows you to apply this tutorial's programming concept in a PowerPoint presentation.

powerpoint 9. In this exercise, you will declare an object variable and assign the address of the active presentation to it.

    a. Start PowerPoint and open a new presentation, then open the Visual Basic Editor.

    b. Display a Help screen for the Application object's ActivePresentation property. What does this property return? Close PowerPoint.

    c. Write a Dim statement that declares an object variable named prsMain. The object variable will store the address of a Presentation object. Then write a Set statement that assigns the address of the active presentation to the prsMain object variable.

A computer program is good only if it works. Errors in programming code can cause a program to run incorrectly. Therefore, a programmer needs to know how to locate and fix any errors in his or her code. Exercise 10 is a Debugging Exercise. Debugging Exercises allow you to practice recognizing and solving errors in code.

debugging 🚫 10. The following code should create an object variable that can store a Workbook object. It also should assign the address of the first Workbook object to the object variable. What is wrong with the following code? Correct the error(s).

```
Dim wkbInventory as Workbook
wkbInventory = Application.Workbooks(1)
```

Excel Lesson

Creating and Using Object Variables in Excel

case ▶ At the end of each quarter, Martin Washington, the accountant at Paradise Electronics, enters the company's quarterly sales data into an Excel worksheet. He then sends a copy of the worksheet to the district sales manager and also to the regional sales manager. Unfortunately, because both sales managers want the worksheet set up in a different manner, Martin first must format and print the worksheet for the district sales manager, and then reformat it and print it for the regional sales manager. Martin has asked you to create a procedure that will handle this time-consuming task for him. You will make the procedure a macro so that Martin can run the procedure from the Macro dialog box in Excel whenever he chooses to do so.

Creating the FormatWorksheet Macro Procedure

Begin by opening Martin's quarterly sales workbook, which is located in the Tut03\Excel folder on your Data Disk.

To open Martin's workbook, and then insert a module and a procedure:

1 Start Microsoft Excel. Open the **T3-EX-1** (T3-EX-1.xls) workbook, which is located in the Tut03\Excel folder on your Data Disk, then save the workbook as

Sales. The Sales workbook contains one worksheet named First Quarter, as shown in Figure 3-11.

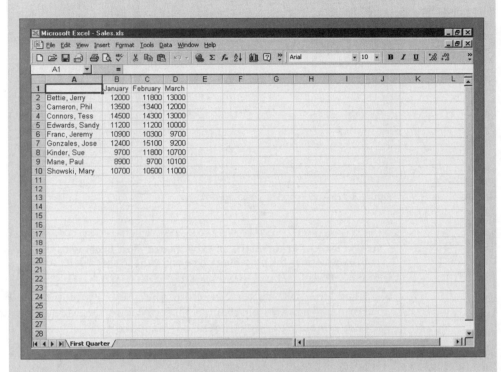

Figure 3-11: Sales workbook showing First Quarter worksheet

2   Press **Alt+F11** to open the Visual Basic Editor. If necessary, open the Project Explorer window and close the Properties window, the Immediate window, and any open Code windows.

3   Click **VBAProject (Sales.xls)** in the Project Explorer window, then click **Insert** on the menu bar, and then click **Module**. The Visual Basic Editor inserts the Modules folder and the Module1 module into the current project. The General Declarations section of the Module1 module appears in the Code window.

4   Click **Insert** on the menu bar and then click **Procedure**. When the Add Procedure dialog box appears, type **FormatWorksheet** in the Name text box. Also verify that the Sub option button and the Public option button are selected, as shown in Figure 3-12.

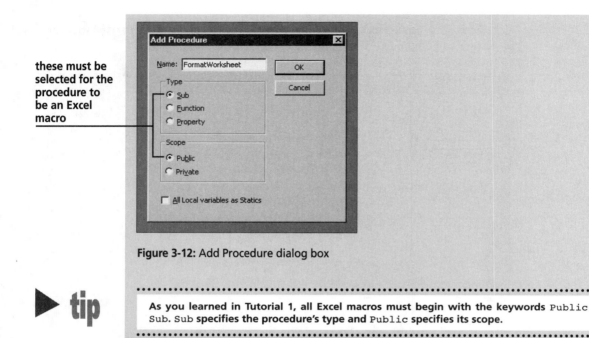

these must be selected for the procedure to be an Excel macro

Figure 3-12: Add Procedure dialog box

▶ **tip**

As you learned in Tutorial 1, all Excel macros must begin with the keywords `Public Sub`. `Sub` **specifies the procedure's type and** `Public` **specifies its scope.**

5   Click the **OK** button to close the Add Procedure dialog box. The FormatWorksheet procedure is inserted into the Module1 module, and its code template appears in the Code window.

Before entering instructions into a procedure, you should write down on a piece of paper what you want the procedure to accomplish, and the steps it will need to do so. For example, Martin wants the FormatWorksheet procedure to format and print the worksheet for the district and regional sales managers. Figures 3-13 and 3-14 show how the district and regional sales managers, respectively, want the worksheet to appear.

cell A1 contains the company's name

two new rows

=SUM (B4:B12) formula

=SUM (C4:C12) formula

=SUM (D4:D12) formula

Accounting2 format

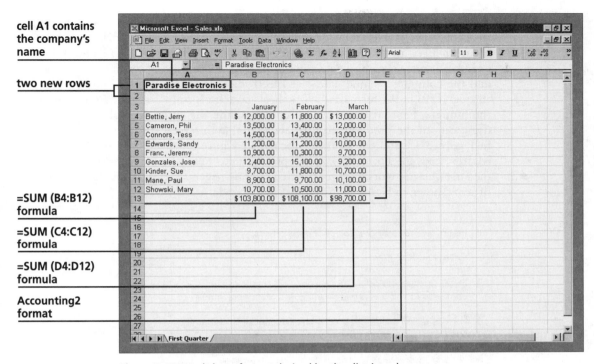

Figure 3-13: Worksheet format desired by the district sales manager

company name

two new rows

SUM (B4:B12) formula

SUM (C4:C12) formula

SUM (D4:D12) formula

Classic2 format

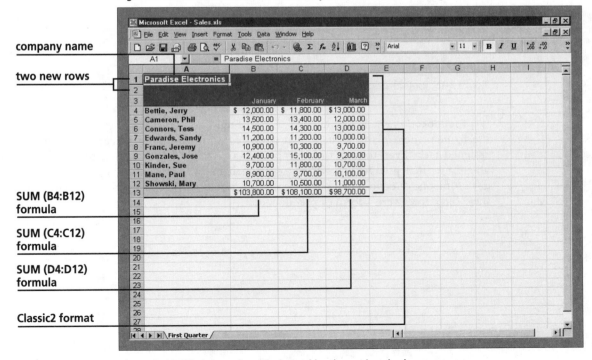

Figure 3-14: Worksheet format desired by the regional sales manager

You can determine the steps the FormatWorksheet procedure will need to take to accomplish its overall task simply by comparing the original worksheet shown in Figure 3-11 with the formatted worksheets shown in Figures 3-13 and 3-14. For example, notice that two new rows appear at the top of the formatted worksheets, and the company's name, Paradise Electronics, appears in cell A1. Also, cells B13 through D13 in the formatted worksheets contain formulas that add the contents of the January, February, and March columns, and the entire worksheet is formatted using one of the predesigned formats available in Excel—the Accounting2 format in Figure 3-13 and the Classic2 format in Figure 3-14. Figure 3-15 lists the steps Martin needs the FormatWorksheet procedure to follow in order to format and print the First Quarter worksheet for the two sales managers. In programming terms, the list of steps shown in Figure 3-15 is called pseudocode.

---

1. Insert two rows at the top of the worksheet.

2. Enter Paradise Electronics in cell A1.

3. Enter formulas in cells B13 through D13 that add the contents of the January, February, and March columns.

4. Format cells A1 through D13 to the Accounting2 format for the district sales manager.

5. Print the worksheet for the district sales manager.

6. Format cells A1 through D13 to the Classic2 format for the regional sales manager.

7. Print the worksheet for the regional sales manager.

Figure 3-15: Pseudocode for the FormatWorksheet procedure

Pseudocode, which is composed of short English statements, is a tool programmers use to help them plan the steps that a procedure must take in order to perform its assigned task. Even though the term *pseudocode* might be unfamiliar to you, you've already written pseudocode without even realizing it. Think about the last time you gave someone directions. You wrote each direction down on paper, in your own words; these directions were a form of pseudocode.

The programmer uses the pseudocode as a guide when coding the procedure. For example, the first step in Martin's pseudocode shown in Figure 3-15 is to insert two rows at the top of the worksheet.

Inserting Rows into a Worksheet

You insert a row into a worksheet using the syntax *worksheetObject*.**Rows** (*rowNumber*).**Insert**, where *worksheetObject* is the name of a Worksheet object and *rowNumber* is the number of the row above which the new row will be inserted. Figure 3-16 shows some examples of using this syntax to insert a row into a worksheet.

Syntax: *worksheetObject*.**Rows**(*rowNumber*).**Insert**

Without an object variable, you would need to use the following instructions to insert a row above row 1 and a row above row 5 in the First Quarter worksheet:

```
Application.Workbooks("sales.xls").Worksheets("first quarter").Rows(1).Insert
Application.Workbooks("sales.xls").Worksheets("first quarter").Rows(5).Insert
```

After creating an object variable named shtFirstQ that points to the First Quarter worksheet, you can use the following instructions to insert a row above row 1 and a row above row 5 in the First Quarter worksheet:

```
shtFirstQ.Rows(1).Insert
shtFirstQ.Rows(5).Insert
```

Figure 3-16: Examples of inserting a row into a worksheet

As you learned in the Concept lesson, instructions that use object variables to point to objects in memory are much more efficient, as well as easier to enter and understand, than are instructions that contain the full path to the object. In the next set of steps, you will create an object variable named shtFirstQ and assign the address of the First Quarter worksheet to it. You then will enter the instructions to insert two rows at the top of the worksheet.

To create an object variable and then use it to enter instructions:

1   In the Visual Basic Editor, the insertion point should be positioned in the blank line between the `Public Sub` and `End Sub` lines in the Code window. Press the **Tab** key, then type **'declare object variable and assign address** and press the **Enter** key. As you learned in Tutorial 1, good programmers both indent and document their code for readability.

2   Type **dim shtFirstQ as worksheet** and press the **Enter** key to create the shtFirstQ object variable. Recall that the Dim statement initializes the object variable to the keyword `Nothing`.

The *sht* in the shtFirstQ name represents the variable's data type (Worksheet), and the *FirstQ* represents the variable's purpose; in this case, the purpose is to store the address of the FirstQ worksheet. Recall that it is a common practice to type the three-character ID in lowercase and capitalize the first letter in the part of the name that identifies the purpose.

3   Type **set shtfirstq = application.workbooks("sales.xls").worksheets(1)** and press the **Enter** key to assign the address of the First Quarter worksheet, which is the first Worksheet object in the workbook, to the object variable.

HELP? If the Application object's member list does not appear when you type the period, click Tools on the menu bar, and then click Options to open the Options dialog box. Click the Editor tab's Auto List Members and Auto Quick Info check boxes to select each one, then click the OK button to close the Options dialog box.

After pressing the Enter key in Step 3, notice that the Visual Basic Editor changes the object variable's name to match the case used in the Dim statement. In other words, it changes the name from shtfirstq to shtFirstQ. Always type the variable's name using the correct case in the Dim statement. After that, you can type the name using any case. If the Visual Basic Editor does not correct the case in a subsequent instruction, it means that you mistyped the variable's name in that instruction.

Now that you have created the object variable and assigned the appropriate address to it, you can use the object variable in the instructions that tell VBA to insert two rows above row 1 in the worksheet.

4   Type **'insert two rows above row 1** and press the **Enter** key. Type **shtfirstq.rows(1).insert** and press the **Enter** key, then type **shtfirstq.rows(1).insert** and press the **Enter** key. See Figure 3-17.

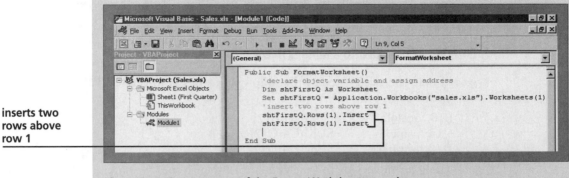

Figure 3-17: Current status of the FormatWorksheet procedure

HELP? If the Code window appears in Full Module View, click its Procedure View button ☰.

According to the pseudocode shown in Figure 3-15, the next step is to enter the company name in cell A1.

Entering a Value into a Range Object

In Tutorial 2, you learned that a cell in an Excel worksheet is considered a Range object. You may also recall that a row, a column, or a group of contiguous or non-contiguous cells in a worksheet also are Excel Range objects.

tip

....
You may want to refer to Tutorial 2's Figure 2-28, which shows examples of how to refer to Range objects in Excel.
....

Recall from Tutorial 2 that you can use a Range object's Value property to change the value stored in either a one-cell or multiple-cell Range object. For example, the `shtFirstQ.Range("A1").Value = "Paradise Electronics"` instruction replaces the value stored in cell A1 with "Paradise Electronics." The `shtFirstQ.Range("A1:C1").Value = "Paradise Electronics"` instruction, on the other hand, enters "Paradise Electronics" in cells A1, B1, and C1. In this case, you want to enter the company's name in cell A1 only.

To enter the instruction that will assign "Paradise Electronics" to cell A1:

1 Type **'enter company name** and press the **Enter** key.

2 Type **shtfirstq.range("a1").value = "Paradise Electronics"** and press the **Enter** key.

inserts two rows above row 1

The next step in the pseudocode shown in Figure 3-15 is to enter formulas in cells B13 through D13.

Entering a Formula into a Range Object

Recall that you need to enter the following formulas in cells B13 through D13 in the worksheet:

B13 formula	=SUM(B4:B12)
C13 formula	=SUM(C4:C12)
D13 formula	=SUM(D4:D12)

These formulas will add the contents of their respective columns. For example, the =SUM(B4:B12) formula entered in cell B13 will add the January sales amounts. The =SUM(C4:C12) formula entered in cell C13 will add the February sales amounts, and the =SUM(D4:D12) formula entered in cell D13 will add the March sales amounts. Figure 3-18 shows two ways you can enter the SUM formulas in the appropriate cells.

Using three instructions:

```
shtFirstQ.Range("b13").Formula = "=SUM(b4:b12)"

shtFirstQ.Range("c13").Formula = "=SUM(c4:c12)"

shtFirstQ.Range("d13").Formula = "=SUM(d4:d12)"
```

Using one instruction:

```
shtFirstQ.Range("b13:d13").Formula = "=SUM(b4:b12)"
```

Figure 3-18: Two ways of entering the SUM formulas into cells B13 through D13

You also can use the Range object's Value property to enter a formula into a cell. However, the Formula property is more indicative of what the instruction is doing, so it is the preferred property to use when entering a formula.

As shown in Figure 3-18, you can use three separate instructions to enter the SUM formulas in the appropriate cells. You also can use the one instruction, `shtFirstQ.Range("b13:d13").Formula = "=SUM(b4:b12)"`. This instruction enters the =SUM(b4:b12) formula in cell B13, which is the first cell in the range B13:D13. Because the cell addresses used in the formula (b4 and b12) are relative, VBA will adjust them when entering the formula in the other two cells in the range—cells C13 and D13. In this case, VBA will enter the =SUM(c4:c12) formula in cell C13, and it will enter the =SUM(d4:d12) formula in cell D13. Notice that whether you use three instructions or one instruction, the formula must be enclosed in quotation marks.

tip

Cell addresses can be relative, absolute, or mixed. A relative cell address is one that changes when copied. An absolute cell address is one that does not change when copied. A mixed cell address is one in which either the row number or the column letter, but not both, changes when copied.

To enter the appropriate formulas in cells B13, C13, and D13:

1 Type **'enter total formulas** and press the **Enter** key.

2 Type **shtfirstq.range("b13:d13").formula = "=sum(b4:b12)"** and press the **Enter** key.

The next step in Figure 3-15's pseudocode is to format cells A1 through D13 to the Accounting2 format.

Formatting a Range Object

A collection of predesigned worksheet formats is available in Excel. The names of some of these formats are shown in Figure 3-19.

```
xlRangeAutoFormatAccounting1
xlRangeAutoFormatAccounting2
xlRangeAutoFormatAccounting3
xlRangeAutoFormatAccounting4
xlRangeAutoFormatClassic1
xlRangeAutoFormatClassic2
xlRangeAutoFormatClassic3
```

Figure 3-19: Names of some of the Excel predesigned formats

tip

To view a complete listing of the Excel predesigned formats, display the **AutoFormat** method's Help screen.

You can use the Range object's AutoFormat method to format a Range object to one of the Excel predesigned formats. The syntax of the AutoFormat method is *rangeObject*.**AutoFormat Format:=** *format*, where *rangeObject* is the name of a Range object and *format* is the name of one of the Excel predesigned formats. As you learned in Tutorial 1, the word following the := operator in the syntax is called an argument, and the word preceding the := operator is the argument's name. In this case, Format is the name of the *format* argument, and it specifies that what follows the := operator is the name of a format.

The next instruction you will enter into the FormatWorksheet procedure is the `shtFirstQ.Range("a1:d13").AutoFormat Format:=xlRangeAuto FormatAccounting2` instruction, which will format the worksheet data to the Accounting2 format. Although you could type the entire instruction on one line in the Code window, the line will be longer than the width of the Code window, so you won't be able to read the entire instruction without scrolling the Code window. To improve the procedure's readability, you will use the VBA **line continuation character**, which is simply a space followed by the underscore (_), to enter the instruction on two lines in the Code window.

To enter the instruction that formats the worksheet:

1   Type **'format worksheet data for district sales manager** and press the **Enter** key.

2   Type **shtfirstq.range("a1.d13").autoformat** and press the **spacebar**. Type **_** (the underscore) and press the **Enter** key. See Figure 3-20.

line
continuation
(a space and
an underscore)

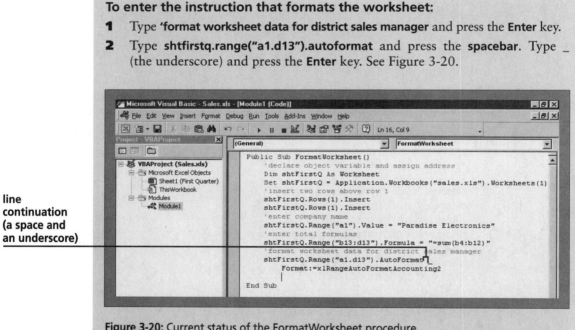

Figure 3-20: Current status of the FormatWorksheet procedure

Although the AutoFormat instruction appears on two lines in the Code window, the line continuation character tells VBA to treat the instruction as though it were entered on the same line.

3   Press the **Tab** key to indent this portion of the instruction. Type **format:=** and then select **xlRangeAutoFormatAccounting2** from the drop-down list and press the **Enter** key.

Step 5 in the pseudocode shown in Figure 3-15 is to print the worksheet.

Previewing and Printing a Worksheet Object

You can use the Worksheet object's **PrintPreview method** to preview a worksheet, allowing you to see how the worksheet will look when printed. To print a worksheet, you use the Worksheet object's **PrintOut method**. The syntax of the PrintPreview method is *expression*.**PrintPreview**, and the syntax of the PrintOut method is *expression*.**PrintOut**. In the syntax for both methods, *expression* is the name of a Worksheet object.

To complete the FormatWorksheet procedure, then save and run the procedure:

1 Press the **Backspace** key to remove the indentation, then type **'print worksheet for district sales manager** and press the **Enter** key. If your computer is connected to a printer, type **shtfirstq.printout** and press the **Enter** key. If your computer is not connected to a printer, type **shtfirstq.printpreview** and press the **Enter** key.

The last steps shown in Figure 3-15's pseudocode are to format the range A1:D13 to the Classic2 format and then print the worksheet for the regional sales manager.

2 Enter the additional instructions shown in Figure 3-21, which shows the completed FormatWorksheet procedure. (Again, if your computer is not connected to a printer, use the PrintPreview method rather than the PrintOut method in the last instruction.)

use PrintPreview if your computer is not connected to a printer

enter these five lines of code

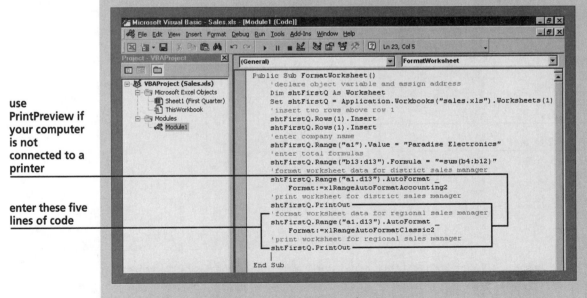

Figure 3-21: Completed FormatWorksheet procedure

3 Verify the accuracy of your code before continuing by comparing your code to the code shown in Figure 3-21.

4 Save the Sales workbook. Click **Tools** on the menu bar, and then click **Macros** to open the Macros dialog box. Click the **Run** button to run the FormatWorksheet macro.

5 If you used the PrintOut method in the FormatWorksheet procedure, the procedure will print two versions of the worksheet: one using the Accounting2 format and one using the Classic2 format. If you used the PrintPreview method rather than the PrintOut method in the FormatWorksheet procedure, click the **Close** button to close the Print Preview window showing the worksheet formatted to the Accounting2 format, then click the **Close** button to close the Print Preview window showing the worksheet formatted to the Classic2 format.

6 Click the **View Microsoft Excel** button 🗷 on the Standard toolbar to return to Excel. Figure 3-22 shows the First Quarter worksheet after running the FormatWorksheet macro.

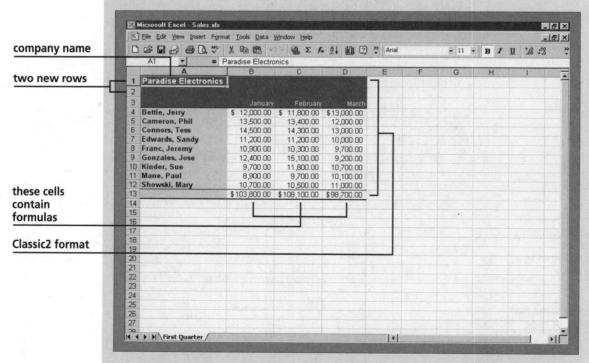

company name

two new rows

these cells contain formulas

Classic2 format

Figure 3-22: First Quarter worksheet after running the FormatWorksheet macro

7 Click **cell B13**. Notice that the cell contains the =SUM("B4:B12") formula.

8 Click **cell C13**. Notice that the formula in this cell is =SUM("C4:C12"). Click **cell D13** and verify that its formula is =SUM("D4:D12").

The FormatWorksheet macro is working correctly, so you can save the workbook and then close Excel.

> **tip**
>
> If you want to run the FormatWorksheet macro again, you first will need to delete the two rows that the macro inserted at the top of the worksheet.

9 Click **cell A1**. Save the Sales workbook, then close Excel.

You now have completed Tutorial 3's Excel lesson. You can either take a break or complete the end-of-lesson exercises before moving on to the next lesson.

EXERCISES

1. In this exercise, you will create a macro procedure that formats a worksheet.
   a. Open the T3-EX-E1 (T3-EX-E1.xls) workbook, which is located in the Tut03\Excel folder on your Data Disk. Save the workbook as T3-EX–E1D.
   b. Open the Visual Basic Editor. Insert a module and a macro procedure named FormatInventory into the project. Use the pseudocode shown in Figure 3-23 to code the FormatInventory procedure.

---

1. Insert three rows at the top of the worksheet.

2. Enter "Parrot Manufacturers" in cell A1.

3. Enter "Inventory Worksheet" in cell A2.

4. Enter "Totals" in the cell below December.

5. Enter formulas in column D that calculate the difference between the year 2000 inventory and the year 1999 inventory.

6. Enter formulas in the row below the December figures. The formulas should total the amounts in the respective columns.

7. Format the worksheet data to the Accounting3 format.

Figure 3-23

   c. Save the workbook, then run the FormatInventory macro. When the macro is working correctly, save and then close the workbook.

2. In this exercise, you will create a macro procedure that enters formulas into a worksheet.
    a. Open the T3-EX-E2 (T3-EX-E2.xls) workbook, which is located in the Tut03\Excel folder on your Data Disk. Save the workbook as T3-EX-E2D.
    b. Open the Visual Basic Editor. Insert a module and a macro procedure named EnterFormulas into the project. Use the pseudocode shown in Figure 3-24 to code the EnterFormulas procedure.

---

1. Insert a row after Apples, Oranges, and Bananas.

2. Enter "Difference" in cell D1.

3. Enter formulas in column D that calculate the difference between the year 2000 fruit inventory and the year 1999 fruit inventory.

4. Two rows below Pears, enter "Totals" in column A and then enter formulas in columns B, C, and D to total the amounts in the respective columns.

5. Display the worksheet in Print Preview.

Figure 3-24

    c. Save the workbook, then run the EnterFormulas macro. When the macro is working correctly, save and then close the workbook.

Exercises 3 through 5 are Discovery Exercises. Discovery Exercises, which may include topics that are not covered in the lesson, allow you to "discover" the solutions to problems on your own.

discovery ▶ 3. In this exercise, you will code the Workbook object's BeforePrint event procedure.
    a. Open the T3-EX-E3 (T3-EX-E3.xls) workbook, which is located in the Tut03\Excel folder on your Data Disk. Save the workbook as T3-EX-E3D.
    b. Open the Visual Basic Editor, then display a Help screen for the Workbook object's BeforePrint event. When does the BeforePrint event occur? Close the Help window.
    c. Open the Workbook object's BeforePrint event procedure. Code the procedure so that it formats the Second Quarter worksheet using the Accounting2 format.
    d. Return to Excel and save the workbook. To test the BeforePrint event procedure, print the Second Quarter worksheet; this will invoke the Workbook object's BeforePrint event procedure. The BeforePrint event formats the worksheet to the Accounting2 format before the worksheet is printed.
    e. When the procedure is working correctly, save and then close the workbook.

discovery ▶ 4. In this exercise, you will create a macro procedure that formats four worksheets. You also will learn how to use the Worksheet object's Protect and Unprotect methods.
    a. Open the T3-EX-E4 (T3-EX-E4.xls) workbook, which is located in the Tut03\Excel folder on your Data Disk. Save the workbook as T3-EX-E4D.
    b. Currently, each worksheet in the workbook is protected.
    c. Open the Visual Basic Editor, then display the Help screen for the Worksheet object's Unprotect and Protect methods. Close the Help window.

d. Create a macro procedure named FormatSheets. The macro should format each of the four worksheets to the Accounting2 format.

e. Save the workbook and run the FormatSheets macro. When the macro is working correctly, save and then close the workbook.

discovery ▶ **5.** In this exercise, you will create a macro procedure that inserts a column into a worksheet and then uses the Range object's AutoFit method to size the column to fit its current contents.

a. Open the T3-EX-E5 (T3-EX-E5.xls) workbook, which is located in the Tut03\Excel folder on your Data Disk. Save the workbook as T3-EX-E5D.

b. Open the Visual Basic Editor. Display the Help screens for the Range object's Columns property, and the AutoFit and Insert methods. Close the Help window.

c. Create a macro procedure named AddNewYear. The macro should insert a new column B. It then should insert, into cell B1, a number that is one greater than the number in cell C1. For example, the first time the macro is run, the procedure will insert 2002 in cell B1. When the macro is run the second time, it will insert 2003 in cell B1, and so on.

d. Return to Excel and save the workbook. Run the AddNewYear macro two times. When the macro is working correctly, save and then close the workbook.

A computer program is good only if it works. Errors in programming code can cause a program to run incorrectly. Therefore, a programmer needs to know how to locate and fix any errors in his or her code. Exercise 6 is a Debugging Exercise. Debugging Exercises allow you to practice recognizing and solving errors in code.

debugging **6.** What is wrong with the following line of code?

```
shtAnnual.Range("a1:f25").AutoFormat Name:=xlAutoFormatClassic2
```

Word Lesson

Creating and Using Object Variables in Word

case ▶ Each month, Pat Jones, the manager of Willowton Health Club, e-mails a document to each club member outlining the free seminars being offered that month. Because Pat has just recently learned how to use Microsoft Word, she is not yet able to incorporate some of the features of Word that make a document look more professional. She has asked you to create a procedure that she can use to dress up the document. You will make the procedure a macro so that Pat can run the procedure from the Macros dialog box in Word whenever she chooses to do so.

Creating the FormatPromo Macro Procedure

Begin by opening Pat's document, which is located in the Tut03\Word folder on your Data Disk.

To open Pat's document, and then insert a module and a procedure:

1 Start Microsoft Word. Open the **T3-WD-1** (T3-WD-1.doc) document, which is located in the Tut03\Word folder on your Data Disk. Save the document as **Promo**.

View the nonprinting characters in the document.

2 Click **Tools** on the menu bar, then click **Options**. When the Options dialog box appears, click the **View** tab, if necessary, then click the **All** check box in the Formatting marks section, if necessary, to select that option. Click the **OK** button to close the Options dialog box. Figure 3-25 shows the Promo document.

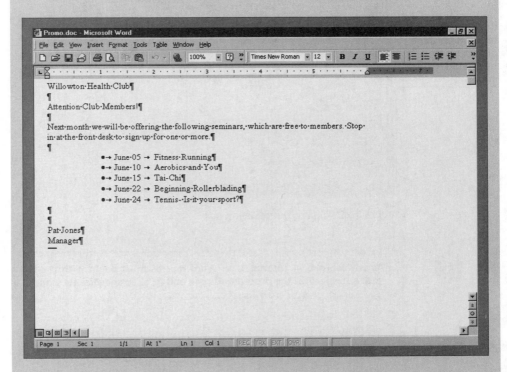

Figure 3-25: Promo document

3 Press **Alt + F11** to open the Visual Basic Editor. If necessary, open the Project Explorer window and close the Properties window, the Immediate window, and any open Code windows.

4 Click **Project (Promo)** in the Project Explorer window, then click **Insert** on the menu bar and then click **Module**. The Visual Basic Editor inserts the Modules folder and the Module1 module into the current project. The General Declarations section of the Module1 module appears in the Code window.

5 Click **Insert** on the menu bar and then click **Procedure**. When the Add Procedure dialog box appears, type **FormatPromo** in the Name text box.

Also verify that the Sub option button and the Public option button are selected, as shown in Figure 3-26.

these must be selected for the procedure to be a Word macro

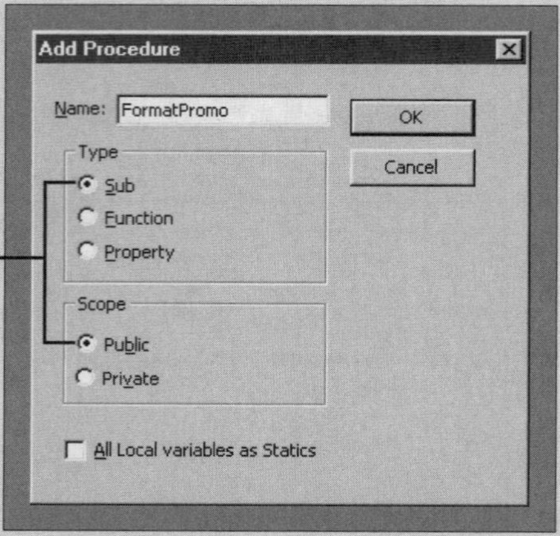

Figure 3-26: Add Procedure dialog box

▶ **tip**

As you learned in Tutorial 1, all Word macros must begin with the keywords `Public Sub`. `Sub` specifies the procedure's type and `Public` specifies its scope.

6 Click the **OK** button to close the Add Procedure dialog box. The FormatPromo procedure is inserted into the Module1 module, and its code template appears in the Code window.

Before entering instructions into a procedure, you should write down on a piece of paper what you want the procedure to accomplish, and the steps it will need to do so. For example, Pat wants the FormatPromo procedure to make the Promo document look more professional. She supplies you with an example of how she wants the formatted document to appear. This example is shown in Figure 3-27.

You can determine the steps the FormatPromo procedure will need to take to accomplish its overall task simply by comparing the original document shown in Figure 3-25 with the formatted document shown in Figure 3-27. For example, notice that the formatted document has a different background. One way of changing the background of a document is to apply a theme to the document. A **theme** in Microsoft Word is a set of unified design elements and color schemes for background images, bullets, fonts, horizontal lines, and other document elements. A theme helps you easily create professional and well-designed documents for viewing in Word, in e-mail, or on the Web. The theme used in Figure 3-27's document is called Rice Paper.

hyperlink to
Willowton's
web site

larger font size

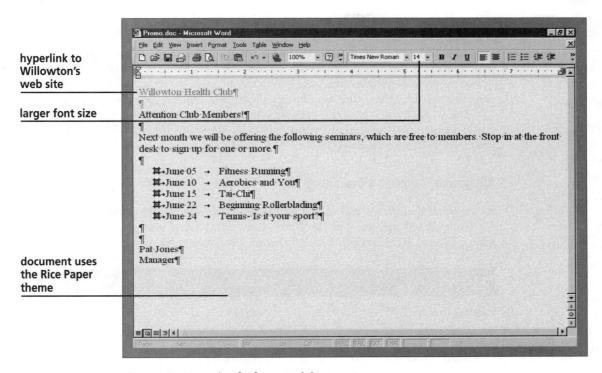

document uses
the Rice Paper
theme

Figure 3-27: Example of a formatted document

A theme does not appear when the document is printed.

Also notice that the size of the font used in the document is larger in Figure 3-27 than it is in Figure 3-25. In Figure 3-25, the size is 12 points, while in Figure 3-27 it is 14 points. In addition, the club's name appears as a hyperlink in Figure 3-27, but it doesn't in Figure 3-25. A **hyperlink** is colored and underlined text or a graphic that you click to go to a file, a location in a file, an HTML page on the World Wide Web, or an HTML page on an intranet. Figure 3-28 lists the steps Pat needs the FormatPromo procedure to follow in order to make the original document look more professional. In programming terms, the list of steps shown in Figure 3-28 is called pseudocode.

1. Apply the Rice Paper theme to the document.

2. Change the font size used in the document to 14.

3. Make the club's name into a hyperlink.

Figure 3-28: Pseudocode for the FormatPromo procedure

Pseudocode, which is composed of short English statements, is a tool programmers use to help them plan the steps that a procedure must take in order to perform its assigned task. Even though the term *pseudocode* might be unfamiliar to you, you've already written pseudocode without even realizing it. Think about the last time you gave someone directions. You wrote each direction down on paper, in your own words; these directions were a form of pseudocode.

The programmer uses the pseudocode as a guide when coding the procedure. For example, the first step in Pat's pseudocode shown in Figure 3-28 is to apply the Rice Paper theme to the document.

Applying a Theme to a Document

As mentioned earlier, a theme is a set of unified design elements and color schemes for background images, bullets, fonts, horizontal lines, and other document elements. Figure 3-29 lists some of the themes available in Microsoft Word.

Theme	Name
Artsy	"artsy"
Blends	"blends"
Blueprint	"blueprnt"
Bold Stripes	"boldstr"
Capsules	"capsules"
Citrus Punch	"citrus"
Rice Paper	"ricepapr"

Figure 3-29: Partial listing of themes available in Microsoft Word

You use the ApplyTheme method to apply a theme to a document. The syntax of the ApplyTheme method is *documentObject*.**ApplyTheme Name:=** *themeName*, where *documentObject* is the name of a Document object and *themeName* is the name of a theme. As you learned in Tutorial 1, the word following the := operator in the syntax is called an argument, and the word preceding the := operator is the argument's name. In this case, Name is the name of the *themeName* argument, and it specifies that what follows the := is the name of a theme. In the FormatPromo procedure, you will use the instruction, `docPromo.ApplyTheme Name:="ricepapr"`, to apply the Rice Paper theme to the Promo document.

As you learned in the Concept lesson, instructions that use object variables to point to objects in memory are much more efficient, as well as easier to enter and understand, than are instructions that contain the full path to the object. In the next set of steps, you will create an object variable named docPromo and assign the address of the Promo document to it. You then will enter the instruction to apply the Rice Paper theme to the document.

To create an object variable named docPromo and then use it in the ApplyTheme instruction:

1 The insertion point should be positioned in the blank line between the Public Sub and End Sub lines in the Code window. Press the **Tab** key, then type **'declare object variable and assign address** and press the **Enter** key. As you learned in Tutorial 1, good programmers both indent and document their code for readability.

2 Type **dim docPromo as document** and press the **Enter** key to create the docPromo object variable. Recall that the Dim statement initializes the object variable to the keyword Nothing.

The *doc* in the name represents the variable's data type (Document), and the *Promo* represents the variable's purpose; in this case, the purpose is to store the address of the Promo document. Recall that it is a common practice to type the three-character ID in lowercase and capitalize the first letter in the part of the name that identifies the purpose.

3 Type **set docpromo = application.documents("promo.doc")** and press the **Enter** key to assign the address of the Promo document object to the object variable.

HELP? If the Application object's member list does not appear when you type the period, click Tools on the menu bar, and then click Options to open the Options dialog box. Click the Editor tab's Auto List Members and Auto Quick Info check boxes to select each one, then click the OK button to close the Options dialog box.

After pressing the Enter key in Step 3, notice that the Visual Basic Editor changes the object variable's name to match the case used in the Dim statement. In other words, it changes the name from docpromo to docPromo. Always type the variable's name using the correct case in the Dim statement. After that, you can type the name using any case. If the Visual Basic Editor does not correct the case in a subsequent instruction, it means that you mistyped the variable's name in that instruction.

Now that you have created the object variable and assigned the appropriate address to it, you can use the object variable in the ApplyTheme instruction.

4 Type **'apply theme to document** and press the **Enter** key, then type **docpromo.applytheme name:= "ricepapr"** and press the **Enter** key.

According to the pseudocode shown in Figure 3-28, the next step is to change the document's font size to 14 points.

Changing the Document's Font Size

You use the following syntax to change the size of the font used in the document: *documentObject*.**Content.Font.Size** = *fontSize*. The Content property of the Document object refers to the entire document, excluding document elements such as footnotes, headers, and footers.

To change the document's font size to 14 points:

1   Type **'change document's font size** and press the **Enter** key.

2   Type **docpromo.content.font.size = 14** and press the **Enter** key.

The next step in the pseudocode shown in Figure 3-28 is to format the health club's name as a hyperlink that links to the Willowton Health Club's Web site.

Adding a Hyperlink to a Document

As mentioned earlier, a hyperlink is the colored and underlined text or graphic that you click to go to a file, a location in a file, an HTML page on the World Wide Web, or an HTML page on an intranet. You use the Add method of the Document object's Hyperlinks collection to add a hyperlink to a document. The syntax of the Add method is *documentObject*.**Hyperlinks.Add Anchor:=**rangeObject, **Address:=**linkAddress. Notice that the Add method's syntax contains two named arguments: **Anchor:=**rangeObject and **Address:=**linkAddress. The Anchor argument is a Range object that represents the text or graphic that you want to convert to a hyperlink. The Address argument is the address of the specified link, and it can be an e-mail address, an address (known as a Uniform Resource Locator, or URL) for a Web page on the Internet or an intranet, or a filename.

Pat wants to make the club's name, which appears as the first sentence in the document, a hyperlink to Willowton's Web site. You will use the `docPromo.Hyperlinks.Add Anchor:=docPromo.Sentences(1),Address:= "http://www.willowton.com"` instruction to do so. Although you could type the entire instruction on one line in the Code window, the line will be longer than the width of the Code window, so you won't be able to read the entire instruction without scrolling the Code window. To improve the procedure's readability, you will use the VBA **line continuation character**, which is simply a space followed by the underscore (_), to enter the instruction on three lines in the Code window.

To convert the club's name to a hyperlink:

1   Type **'add hyperlink** and press the **Enter** key.

2   Type **docpromo.hyperlinks.add** and press the **spacebar**, then type _ (the underscore) and press the **Enter** key.

---

3 Press the **Tab** key to indent this portion of the instruction. Type **anchor:=docpromo.sentences(1),** and press the **spacebar.** (Be sure to type the comma after the closing parentheses.) Type _ (the underscore) and press the **Enter** key.

4 Type **address:= "http://www.willowton.com"** and press the **Enter** key.

Figure 3-30 shows the completed FormatPromo procedure.

line continuation character (a space and an underscore)

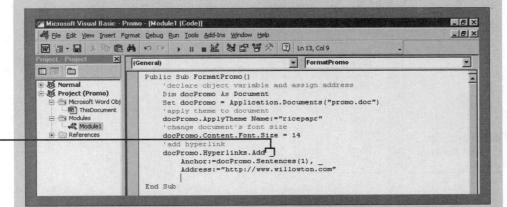

```
Microsoft Visual Basic - Promo - [Module1 (Code)]
File  Edit  View  Insert  Format  Debug  Run  Tools  Add-Ins  Window  Help
                                                    Ln 13, Col 9
Project - Project                  (General)                    FormatPromo
  Normal                     Public Sub FormatPromo()
  Project (Promo)                'declare object variable and assign address
    Microsoft Word Obj           Dim docPromo As Document
      ThisDocument               Set docPromo = Application.Documents("promo.doc")
    Modules                      'apply theme to document
      Module1                    docPromo.ApplyTheme Name:="ricepapr"
    References                   'change document's font size
                                 docPromo.Content.Font.Size = 14
                                 'add hyperlink
                                 docPromo.Hyperlinks.Add _
                                     Anchor:=docPromo.Sentences(1), _
                                     Address:="http://www.willowton.com"

                             End Sub
```

Figure 3-30: Completed FormatPromo procedure

HELP? If the Code window appears in Full Module View, click its Procedure View button 🗐.

Although the instruction that sets the hyperlink appears on three lines in the Code window, the line continuation character tells VBA to treat the instruction as though it were entered on the same line.

5 Verify the accuracy of your code before continuing by comparing your code with the code shown in Figure 3-30.

6 Save the Promo document. Click **Tools** on the menu bar, and then click **Macros** to open the Macros dialog box. Click the **Run** button to run the FormatPromo macro.

7 Click the **View Microsoft Word** button 🔲 on the Standard toolbar to return to Word. Place the mouse pointer on the hyperlink. The 🖑 pointer should appear, as shown in Figure 3-31.

hyperlink to Willowton's Web site

larger font size

document uses the Rice Paper theme

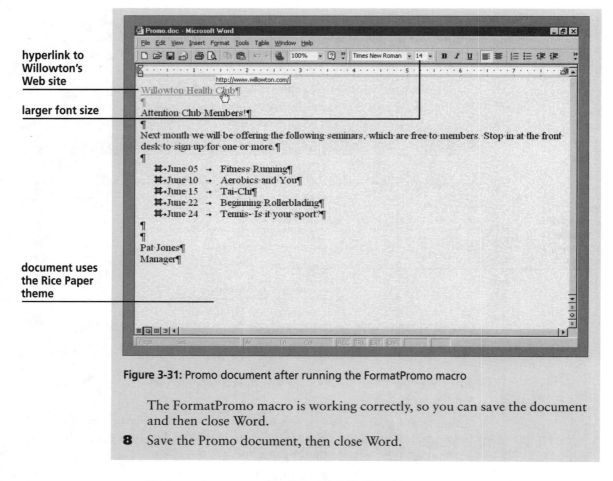

Figure 3-31: Promo document after running the FormatPromo macro

The FormatPromo macro is working correctly, so you can save the document and then close Word.

8 Save the Promo document, then close Word.

You now have completed Tutorial 3's Word lesson. You can either take a break or complete the end-of-lesson exercises before moving on to the next lesson.

 # EXERCISES

1. In this exercise, you will create a macro procedure that formats a document.

   a. Open the T3-WD-E1 (T3-WD-E1.doc) document, which is located in the Tut03\Word folder on your Data Disk. Save the document as T3-WD-E1D.

   b. View the nonprinting characters in the document, if necessary.

   c. Open the Visual Basic Editor. Insert a module and a macro procedure named FormatLions into the project. Use the pseudocode shown in Figure 3-32 to code the FormatLions procedure. (Refer to Figure 3-29 in this lesson for the name of the Citrus Punch theme.)

1. Apply the Citrus Punch theme to the document.

2. Change the font size used in the document to 14.

3. Make the Jacksonville Lions name into a hyperlink to Microsoft's Web site at http://www.microsoft.com.

Figure 3-32

    d. Save the document, then run the FormatLions macro. Return to Word. Place the mouse pointer on the hyperlink. The 🖑 pointer should appear. When the macro is working correctly, save and then close the document.

2. In this exercise, you will create a macro procedure that formats a document.
    a. Open the T3-WD-E2 (T3-WD-E2.doc) document, which is located in the Tut03\Word folder on your Data Disk. Save the document as T3-WD-E2D.
    b. View the nonprinting characters in the document, if necessary.
    c. Open the Visual Basic Editor. Insert a module and a macro procedure named FormatLetter into the project. Use the pseudocode shown in Figure 3-33 to code the FormatLetter procedure. (Refer to Figure 3-29 in this lesson for the name of the Blends theme.)

1. Apply the Blends theme to the document.

2. Change the font size used in the document to 10.

3. Change the font name to Arial.

4. Make the first occurrence of the word Microsoft into a hyperlink to the Microsoft Web site at http://www.microsoft.com.
(Hints: Commas, periods, and paragraph markers are considered words. You can use the Immediate window to help you determine the word's location.)

Figure 3-33

    d. Save the document, then run the FormatLetter macro. Return to Word. Place the mouse pointer on the hyperlink. The 🖑 pointer should appear. When the macro is working correctly, save and then close the document.

3. In this exercise, you will code the Document object's Open event procedure.
    a. Open the T3-WD-E3 (T3-WD-E3.doc) document, which is located in the Tut03\Word folder on your Data Disk. Save the document as T3-WD-E3D.
    b. Open the Visual Basic Editor, then open the Document object's Open event procedure. Code the procedure so that it changes the document's font size to 12.

   c. Save the document. Close the document, then open the document to invoke its Open event procedure. The document's font size should be 12.

   d. When the macro is working correctly, save and then close the document.

Exercises 4 and 5 are Discovery Exercises. Discovery Exercises, which may include topics that are not covered in the lesson, allow you to "discover" the solutions to problems on your own.

discovery ▶ 4. In this exercise, you will create a macro procedure that makes a graphic into a hyperlink.

   a. Open the T3-WD-E4 (T3-WD-E4.doc) document, which is located in the Tut03\Word folder on your Data Disk. Save the document as T3-WD-E4D.

   b. Open the Visual Basic Editor. Create a macro procedure named AddHyper. The AddHyper macro should make the currently selected item in the document into a hyperlink that links to the Microsoft Web site at http://www.microsoft.com. (*Hint*: Display the Hyperlinks Collection Object Help screen, then display the Help screen pertaining to the collection's Add method. Click <u>Example</u> in the Help screen to view examples of how to use the Add method.)

   c. Save the document. Return to Word and select the lion graphic. Click Tools on the Word menu bar, point to Macro, and then click Macros. Click the Run button to run the AddHyper macro. Place the mouse pointer on the lion graphic. The 🖑 pointer should appear, indicating that the graphic is a hyperlink.

   d. When the macro is working correctly, save and then close the document.

discovery ▶ 5. In this exercise, you will learn how to remove a document's theme, set the document's top margin, and add a footer to the document.

   a. Open the T3-WD-E5 (T3-WD-E5.doc) document, which is located in the Tut03\Word folder on your Data Disk. Save the document as T3-WD-E5D.

   b. Open the Visual Basic Editor. Create a macro procedure named ForSchool. The macro should remove the document's theme, set the top margin to 2 inches, and add your name as the primary footer. (*Hint*: Display and study the following Help screens: RemoveTheme Method, PageSetup Object, TopMargin Property, InchesToPoints Method, Section Object, and HeaderFooter Object.)

   c. Save the document, then run the ForSchool macro.

   d. When the macro is working correctly, save and then close the document.

A computer program is good only if it works. Errors in programming code can cause a program to run incorrectly. Therefore, a programmer needs to know how to locate and fix any errors in his or her code. Exercise 6 is a Debugging Exercise. Debugging Exercises allow you to practice recognizing and solving errors in code.

debugging **6.** The following instructions should make into a hyperlink the first word in the first document in the Documents collection. What is wrong with the following instructions? Correct any errors.

```
Dim docMain as Document
Set docMain = Application.Documents
docMain.Hyperlinks.Insert _
    Anchor:=docMain.Words(1), _
    Address:= http://www.course.com
```

Access Lesson

Creating and Using Object Variables in Access

case ▶ Jose Martinez, an economics professor at Snowville College, uses a Microsoft Access database to manage the information he keeps on his Economics 201 students. Specifically, the database contains a table named Students and a report named StudentReport, which he uses to display each student's name and grade. Professor Martinez has asked you to create a procedure that will allow him to display the report in grade order. You will make the procedure a macro so that Professor Martinez can run the procedure from the Database window in Access whenever he chooses to do so.

Creating the DisplayByGrade Procedure

Begin by opening Professor Martinez's database, which is located in the Tut03\Access folder on your Data Disk. Then view the StudentReport.

To open Professor Martinez's database, then view the StudentReport report:

1 Start Microsoft Access, then open the **Econ201** (Econ201.mdb) database. Click the **Maximize** button ☐ on the Microsoft Access title bar to maximize the Microsoft Access window, if necessary.

2 Click **Reports** in the Objects bar of the Database window to display the Reports list. The Reports list box shows that the database contains one report named StudentReport. Right-click **StudentReport** and then click **Print Preview** to view the report. Maximize the report window. Figure 3-34 shows the maximized StudentReport report.

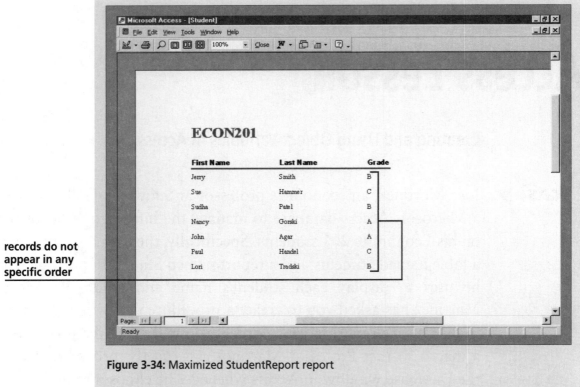

records do not appear in any specific order

Figure 3-34: Maximized StudentReport report

Notice that the records shown in the report are not in any specific order.

3 Close the report.

Now that you have opened the Econ201 database and viewed the report, you can begin creating the DisplayByGrade procedure.

To begin creating the DisplayByGrade procedure:

1 Press **Alt + F11** to open the Visual Basic Editor. If necessary, open the Project Explorer window and close the Properties window, the Immediate window, and any open Code windows.

The Econ201 (Econ201) project already is selected in the Project Explorer window.

2 Click **Insert** on the menu bar, and then click **Module**. The Visual Basic Editor inserts the Modules folder and the Module1 module into the current project.

The General Declarations section of the Module1 module appears in the Code window.

3 Click **Insert** on the menu bar and then click **Procedure**. When the Add Procedure dialog box appears, type **DisplayByGrade** in the Name text box, then click the **Function** option button to select it. Also verify that the Public option button is selected, as shown in Figure 3-35.

these must be selected for the procedure to be run by a macro

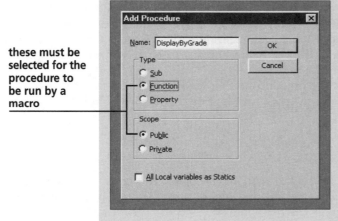

Figure 3-35: Add Procedure dialog box

> As you learned in Tutorial 1, only procedures that begin with the keywords `Public Function` can be run by an Access macro. `Function` specifies the procedure's type and `Public` specifies its scope.

4 Click the **OK** button to close the Add Procedure dialog box. The DisplayByGrade procedure is inserted into the Module1 module, and its code template appears in the Code window.

Before entering instructions into a procedure, you should write down on a piece of paper what you want the procedure to accomplish, and the steps it will need to do so. For example, Professor Martinez wants the DisplayByGrade procedure to display the StudentReport report in grade order. Figure 3-36 shows the steps the procedure will need to take to do so. In programming terms, the list of steps shown in Figure 3-36 is called pseudocode.

1. Open the Student report.

2. Order the records by grade.

Figure 3-36: Pseudocode for the DisplayByGrade procedure

Pseudocode, which is composed of short English statements, is a tool programmers use to help them plan the steps that a procedure must take in order to perform its assigned task. Even though the word *pseudocode* might be unfamiliar to you, you've already written pseudocode without even realizing it. Think about the last time you gave someone directions. You wrote each direction down on paper, in your own words; these directions were a form of pseudocode.

The programmer uses the pseudocode as a guide when coding the procedure. For example, the first step in the pseudocode shown in Figure 3-36 is to open the StudentReport report.

Opening an Access Report

You use the OpenReport method of the DoCmd object to open an Access report. As you learned in Tutorial 2, the DoCmd object is the Access object that allows you to perform tasks such as closing windows, opening forms, and opening and printing reports. The syntax of the OpenReport method is **DoCmd.OpenReport Reportname:=** *reportName,* **View:=***viewName*, where *reportName* is the name of a report and *viewName* is the name of a view. As you learned in Tutorial 1, the word following the := operator in the syntax is called an argument, and the word preceding the := operator is the argument's name. In this case, Reportname is the name of the *reportName* argument, and it specifies that what follows the := is the name of a report. View, on the other hand, is the name of the *viewName* argument, and it specifies that what follows the := is the name of a view. The viewName argument can be any of the view names shown in Figure 3-37.

View name	Meaning
acViewDesign	Opens the report and displays it in Design View
acViewNormal	(default) Opens the report and also prints it immediately
acViewPreview	Opens the report and displays it in Print Preview View

Figure 3-37: Valid view names for the OpenReport method's View argument

You will use the `DoCmd.OpenReport Reportname:="studentreport",` `View:=acViewPreview` instruction to open the report and then display it in Print Preview View.

As you learned in the Concept lesson, instructions that use object variables to point to objects in memory are much more efficient, as well as easier to enter and understand, than are instructions that contain the full path to the object. In the next set of steps, you will create an object variable named rptStudent and assign the address of the StudentReport Report object to it.

To create an object variable named rptStudent and then assign the StudentReport object's address to it:

1 The insertion point should be positioned in the blank line between the `Public Function` and `End Function` lines in the Code window. Press the **Tab** key, then type **'declare object variable** and press the **Enter** key. As you learned in Tutorial 1, good programmers both indent and document their code for readability.

2 Type **dim rptStudent as report** and press the **Enter** key to create the rptStudent object variable. Recall that the Dim statement initializes the object variable to the keyword `Nothing`.

> The *rpt* in the name represents the variable's data type (Report), and the *Student* represents the variable's purpose; in this case, the purpose is to store the address of the StudentReport report. Recall that it is a common practice to type the three-character ID in lowercase letters and capitalize the first letter in the part of the name that identifies the purpose.

You cannot assign a Report object to an object variable unless the report is open. Therefore, you will need to open the StudentReport report before you can assign its address to the rptStudent object variable. Although you could type the entire `DoCmd.OpenReport Reportname:="studentreport",` `View:=acViewPreview` instruction on one line in the Code window, the line will be longer than the width of the Code window, so you won't be able to read the entire instruction without scrolling the Code window. To improve the procedure's readability, you will use the VBA **line continuation character**, which is simply a space followed by the underscore (_), to enter the instruction on two lines in the Code window.

3 Type **'open report** and press the **Enter** key. Type **docmd.openreport** and press the **spacebar**. Type _ (the underscore) and press the **Enter** key.

HELP? If the DoCmd object's member list does not appear when you type the period, click Tools on the menu bar, and then click Options to open the Options dialog box. Click the Editor tab's Auto List Members and Auto Quick Info check boxes to select each one, then click the OK button to close the Options dialog box.

4 Press the **Tab** key to indent this portion of the instruction, then type **reportname:="studentreport", view:=acviewpreview** and press the **Enter** key.

Now you can assign the address of the open report to the rptStudent object variable. Open reports in Access belong to the Application object's Reports collection.

5 Press the **Backspace** key to remove the indentation, then type **'assign address to object variable** and press the **Enter** key. Type **set rptstudent = application.reports("studentreport")** and press the **Enter** key.

tip

After pressing the Enter key in Step 3, notice that the Visual Basic Editor changes the object variable's name to match the case used in the Dim statement. In other words, it changes the name from rptstudent to rptStudent. Always type the variable's name using the correct case in the Dim statement. After that, you can type the name using any case. If the Visual Basic Editor does not correct the case in a subsequent instruction, it means you mistyped the variable name in that instruction.

According to the pseudocode shown in Figure 3-36, the next step is to order the records in the report by the grade.

Ordering the Records in a Report

To change the order of the records that appear in a report, you need first to set the Report object's OrderByOn property to the Boolean value True. Then you need to set the Report object's OrderBy property to the name of the field or fields on which you want to sort the records. In this case, you want to sort the records by the Grade field. The OrderBy property will automatically sort the records in ascending order.

To complete the DisplayByGrade procedure:

1 Type **'order records by grade** and press the **Enter** key.

2 Type **rptstudent.orderbyon = true** and press the **Enter** key.

3 Type **rptstudent.orderby = "grade"** and press the **Enter** key.

Figure 3-38 shows the completed DisplayByGrade procedure.

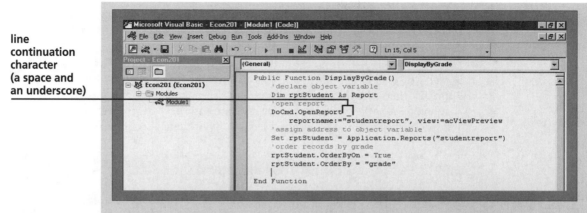

line continuation character (a space and an underscore)

Figure 3-38: Completed DisplayByGrade procedure

HELP? If the Code window appears in Full Module View, click its Procedure View button ▤.

Although the OpenReport instruction appears on two lines in the Code window, the line continuation character tells VBA to treat the instruction as though it were entered on the same line.

4 Verify the accuracy of your code before continuing by comparing your code to the code shown in Figure 3-38.

5 Save the DisplayByGrade procedure. When you are asked for a name for the module, click the **OK** button to accept the default name, Module1.

Now create the macro that Professor Martinez can use to run the DisplayByGrade procedure.

Creating the DisplayByGradeMacro Macro

As you learned in Tutorial 1, you use the Macro window to create an Access macro. The macro then can be run from either the Macro window or the Database window in Access.

To create the DisplayByGradeMacro macro, and then save and run the macro:

1 Click the **View Microsoft Access** button ▣ on the Visual Basic Editor Standard toolbar to return to Access. Click **Macros** in the Objects bar of the Database window, then click the **New** button ▣ in the Database window's toolbar to open the Macro window.

Recall that in the Macro window, you record the tasks that you want the macro to perform. You do so by selecting one or more actions from the Action combo box.

2   Click the **Action list arrow** that appears in the first line of the Macro window. Scroll down the list until you see RunCode, then click **RunCode**. Click **Function Name** in the Action Arguments section of the window, then type **DisplayByGrade()** (be sure to type the parentheses) as the function name. Figure 3-39 shows the completed DisplayByGradeMacro macro.

runs the
Function
procedure code

Function
procedure's
name

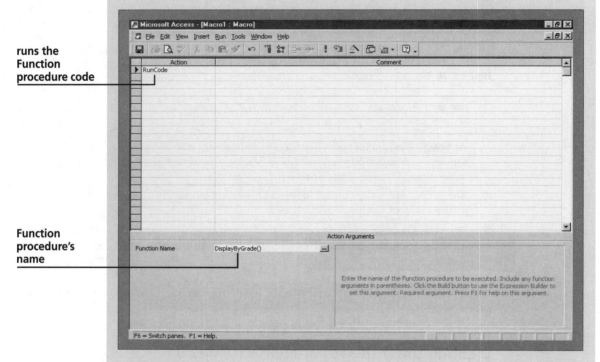

Figure 3-39: Macro window showing the completed DisplayByGradeMacro macro

3   Click the **Save** button 🖫 on the Standard toolbar. When you are asked for the macro name, type **DisplayByGradeMacro** and press the **Enter** key to select the **OK** button, then close the Macro window.

4   Right-click **DisplayByGradeMacro** in the Macros list, then click **Run**. The StudentReport report appears with the records in grade order, as shown in Figure 3-40.

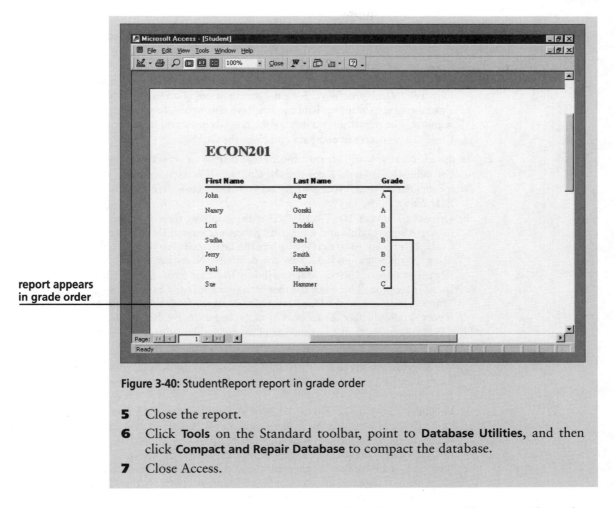

report appears
in grade order

Figure 3-40: StudentReport report in grade order

5 Close the report.

6 Click **Tools** on the Standard toolbar, point to **Database Utilities**, and then click **Compact and Repair Database** to compact the database.

7 Close Access.

You now have completed Tutorial 3's Access lesson. You can either take a break or complete the end-of-lesson exercises.

EXERCISES

1. In this exercise, you will create a macro that displays a report in ascending order.

   a. Use Windows to make a copy of the Econ201 (Econ201.mdb) database that you completed in this lesson. The file is located in the Tut03\Access folder on your Data Disk. Rename the copy T3-AC-E1D.mdb.

b. Open the T3-AC-E1D (T3-AC-E1D.mdb) database, then open the Visual Basic Editor. Add a function procedure named DisplayByName to the Module1 module. Code the procedure so that it displays the StudentReport report in ascending order using the last name field. Save the database.

c. Return to Access. Use the Macro window to create a macro that runs the DisplayByName procedure. Save the macro, naming it DisplayByNameMacro, then close the Macro window. Run the DisplayByNameMacro macro from the Database window. The report should display the records in ascending order by last name.

d. Close the report, then compact and close the database.

2. In this exercise, you will create a macro that displays a report in ascending order.

a. Use Windows to make a copy of the Contacts (Contacts.mdb) database, which is located in the Tut03\Access folder on your Data Disk. Rename the copy T3-AC-E2D.mdb.

b. Open the T3-AC-E2D (T3-AC-E2D.mdb) database, then open the Visual Basic Editor. Add a module and a function procedure named DuesOrder to the project. Code the procedure so that it displays the ListReport report in ascending order using the dues amount field. Save the database. Name the module Module1.

c. Return to Access. Use the Macro window to create a macro that runs the DuesOrder procedure. Save the macro, naming it DuesOrderMacro, then close the Macro window. Run the DuesOrderMacro macro from the Database window. The report should display the records in ascending order by the dues amount field.

d. Close the report, then compact and close the database.

3. In this exercise, you will code the Report object's Open event.

a. Use Windows to make a copy of the Contacts (Contacts.mdb) database, which is located in the Tut03\Access folder on your Data Disk. Rename the copy T3-AC-E3D.mdb.

b. Open the T3-AC-E3D (T3-AC-E3D.mdb) database. Open the ListReport report in Design View. To include the report's name in the Project Explorer window, you need simply to set the report's Has Module property to Yes. You do so using the report's property sheet. Right-click the report selector box on the Design View window, and then click Properties on the shortcut menu. Click the Other tab on the property sheet, then change the value of the Has Module property to Yes. Close the property sheet. Save the report, then close the report.

c. Open the Visual Basic Editor, then open the Report object's Open event procedure. Code the procedure so that it displays the ListReport report in ascending order using the organization name field. Save the database.

d. Return to Access. Open the report in Print Preview, which will invoke the Report object's Open event procedure. The report should display the records in ascending order by the organization name field.

e. Close the report, then compact and close the database.

Exercises 4 through 6 are Discovery Exercises. Discovery Exercises, which may include topics that are not covered in the lesson, allow you to "discover" solutions to problems on your own.

discovery ▶ 4. In this exercise, you will learn how to order the report records in descending order. You will use the database that you completed in Exercise 2.

a. Use Windows to make a copy of the T3-AC-E2D (T3-AC-E2D.mdb) database that you completed in Exercise 2. The file is located in the Tut03\Access folder on your Data Disk. Rename the copy T3-AC-E4D.mdb.

b. Open the T3-AC-E4D (T3-AC-E4D.mdb) database. Open the Visual Basic Editor. Display the Help screen for the OrderBy property. In the Help screen, locate the information pertaining to displaying records in descending order. Close the Help window.

c. Open the DuesOrder procedure. Modify the procedure so that it displays the records in descending order by the dues amount field. Save the database.

d. Return to Access. Run the DuesOrderMacro macro from the Database window. The report should display the records in descending order by the dues amount field.

e. Close the report, then compact and close the database.

discovery ▶ 5. In this exercise, you will learn how to order records by more than one field. You will use the database that you completed in Exercise 3.

a. Use Windows to make a copy of the T3-AC-E3D (T3-AC-E3D.mdb) database that you completed in Exercise 3. The file is located in the Tut03\Access folder on your Data Disk. Rename the copy T3-AC-E5D.mdb.

b. Open the T3-AC-E5D (T3-AC-E5D.mdb) database. Open the Visual Basic Editor. Display the Help screen for the OrderBy property. In the Help screen, locate the information pertaining to displaying records in order by more than one field. Close the Help window.

c. Open the Report object's Open event procedure. Modify the procedure so that it displays the records in ascending order by first name within last name. In other words, if two records have the same last name, then those records should be ordered according to the first name field. (For example, the Harry Barnes record should precede the Mabel Barnes record because, alphabetically, the H in Harry comes before the M in Mabel.) Save the database.

d. Return to Access. Open the report in Print Preview. The report should display the records in ascending order by first name within last name.

e. Close the report, then compact and close the database.

discovery ▶ 6. In this exercise, you will learn how to order the records displayed in an entry form.

a. Use Windows to make a copy of the Contacts (Contacts.mdb) database, which is located in the Tut03\Access folder on your Data Disk. Rename the copy T3-AC-E6D.mdb.

b. Open the T3-AC-E6D (T3-AC-E6D.mdb) database. Open the ListForm form in Design View. To include the form's name in the Project Explorer window, you need simply to set the form's Has Module property to Yes. You do so using the form's property sheet. Right-click the form selector box on the Design View window, and then click Properties on the shortcut menu. Click the Other tab on the property sheet, then change the value of the Has Module property to Yes. Close the property sheet. Save the form, then close the form.

c. Open the Visual Basic Editor, then open the Form object's Open event procedure. Code the procedure so that it displays the records in ascending order using the organization name field. (*Hints*: Open forms belong to the Application object's Forms collection. The three-character ID for a form object is *frm*.) Save the database.

d. Return to Access. Open the form and browse through the database records. The report should display the records in ascending order by the organization name field.

e. Close the form, then compact and close the database.

A computer program is good only if it works. Errors in programming code can cause a program to run incorrectly. Therefore, a programmer needs to know how to locate and fix any errors in his or her code. Exercise 7 is a Debugging Exercise. Debugging Exercises allow you to practice recognizing and solving errors in code.

debugging

7. The following code should assign the ProfGreyReport report to an object variable, but it is not working correctly. What is wrong with the following code? Correct any errors.

```
Dim rptGrade as Report
Set rptGrade = Application.Reports("ProfGreyReport")
DoCmd.OpenReport Reportname:="ProfGreyReport", _
    View:=acViewPreview
```

String
Variables

In this tutorial, you will learn how to:

- Reserve a String variable
- Use an assignment statement to assign a value to a String variable
- Use the InputBox function to get information from the user at the keyboard
- Concatenate strings
- Use the Val function
- Use strings in calculations
- Use the Option Explicit statement
- Use a form field in Word
- Create a custom toolbar in Word

Concept Lesson

Variables

In Tutorial 3, you learned that the memory cells reserved by a programmer are called variables. You also learned how to reserve an object variable, which is a memory cell in the computer that can store the address of an object. In addition to reserving object variables, programmers also can reserve other types of variables, such as numeric variables, Date variables, Boolean variables, and String variables. A **numeric variable** is a memory cell that can store a number—for example, it can store an employee's gross pay amount. A **Date variable** is a memory cell that can store a date, such as a birth date or a hire date. A **Boolean variable** is a memory cell that can store the Boolean values True and False. A **String variable** is a memory cell that can store a **string**, which is zero or more characters enclosed in quotation marks (""). The term *string* refers to the fact that the characters enclosed within the quotation marks are strung together, one after another, in a row. You would use a String variable to store an employee's name—for example, the name "John Smith".

In this tutorial, you will learn how to reserve procedure-level String variables. You will learn how to reserve procedure-level Date variables in Tutorial 5, numeric variables in Tutorial 6, and Boolean variables in Tutorial 11.

Reserving a Procedure-level String Variable

As you learned in Tutorial 3, you reserve a procedure-level variable by entering the appropriate Dim statement within a procedure. Recall that only the procedure containing the Dim statement can use the procedure-level variable, and the variable remains in memory only while that procedure is running. When the procedure ends, VBA removes the procedure-level variable from memory.

> In addition to the Dim statement, you also can use the Public and Static statements to declare a variable.

As you learned in Tutorial 3, the syntax of the Dim statement is **Dim** *variablename* **As** *datatype*, where *variablename* is the name of the variable, and *datatype* represents the type of data the variable can store. When creating a String variable, *datatype* is always the keyword `String`. The `Dim strName As String` statement, for example, reserves a variable named strName that can store a string—zero or more characters enclosed in quotation marks. Figure 4-1 shows examples of strings that could be stored in a String variable.

"Visual Basic"
"$8.34"
"1999 Sales"
"5%"
"1-800-111-1111"

Figure 4-1: Examples of strings

Notice that the strings shown in Figure 4-1 contain letters, numbers, spaces, the period, the hyphen, the dollar sign ($), and the percent sign (%). A string can contain any character that you can type at the keyboard.

The more technical term for a string is **string literal constant**. *Literal* refers to the fact that the characters enclosed within the quotation marks should be taken literally—in other words, exactly as shown. *Constant* refers to the fact that the string's value does not change while a procedure is running. For example, the string literal constant "Jim" will always have the same value—"Jim".

Be careful not to confuse a String variable with a string literal constant. You store string literal constants in String variables, which are memory cells. As suggested in Tutorial 3, it may be helpful to picture a variable (memory cell) as a box inside the computer. A string literal constant is then an item that you can place inside the box. The item's (string literal constant's) value cannot change, but the contents of the box (String variable) can. For example, at one point in the procedure the variable can store the string literal constant "Jim", while later in the procedure the variable can store the string literal constant "Beth". Figure 4-2 illustrates a String variable and a string literal constant.

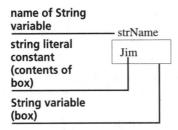

name of String variable — strName
string literal constant (contents of box) Jim
String variable (box)

Figure 4-2: Illustration of a String variable and a string literal constant

As Figure 4-2 indicates, only the characters within the string literal constant's quotation marks are stored in the String variable. The quotation marks themselves are not stored in the variable.

When you use the Dim statement to reserve a String variable in memory, VBA automatically initializes the variable to a zero-length string. A **zero-length string,** often referred to as an **empty string,** is simply two quotation marks with nothing between them, like this: "". Figure 4-3 shows examples of Dim statements that reserve String variables.

> Recall that object variables are initialized to the keyword Nothing.

```
Dim strEmployName As String

Dim strStateCode As String

Dim strPhone As String
```

Figure 4-3: Examples of Dim statements that reserve String variables

> Be sure always to include the **As** *datatype* portion of the Dim statement. If you neglect to assign a specific data type to a variable, VBA assigns a default data type, called Variant, to it. Although Variant is the most flexible data type because variables created with it can contain any type of data, it is not the most efficient data type. A Variant variable typically uses more memory space than is required. Variant variables also increase the time it takes to process a procedure because, before a procedure can use the variable's data, it first must ascertain the type of data the variable stores—numeric, string, date, and so on. You should avoid using the Variant data type.

Notice that the name of each of the String variables shown in Figure 4-3 begins with *str*, which is the three-character ID associated with a String variable. As you learned in Tutorial 3, you should assign a descriptive name to each variable that you reserve. The name should reflect both the variable's data type and purpose. Recall that one popular naming convention is to have the first three characters in the name represent the data type—in this case, *str* for String—and the remainder of the name represent the variable's purpose. The names strEmployName, strStateCode, and strPhone indicate that the variables are String variables that store an employee's name, a state code, and a phone number, respectively.

> It is a common practice to type the variable's three-character ID in lowercase letters and capitalize the first letter in the part of the name that identifies the purpose.

Recall that variable names must begin with a letter and can contain only letters, numbers, and the underscore (_). Variable names cannot be longer than 255 characters and they cannot be reserved words, such as Print or MsgBox.

After using the Dim statement to reserve and initialize a String variable, you can use an assignment statement to assign a different value to the variable.

Using an Assignment Statement to Assign a Value to a String Variable

Unlike object variables, whose values are assigned by the Set statement, numeric, Date, Boolean, and String variables get their values from assignment statements. **Assignment statements** are so named because they *assign* values to the memory cells inside the computer. The syntax of an assignment statement that assigns a value to a variable is *variablename = value*. Figure 4-4 shows examples of assignment statements that assign string literal constants to String variables.

```
strEmployName = "Mary Jones"

strStateCode = "NM"

strPhone = "1-800-111-1111"
```

Figure 4-4: Examples of assignment statements that assign string literal constants to String variables

As you learned in Tutorial 3, when you assign a new value to a memory cell, the new value replaces the old value, because a memory cell can store only one value at a time. To illustrate this, assume that a procedure contains the following five lines of code:

```
Dim strEmployName As String
strEmployName = "Mary Jones"
MsgBox Prompt:=strEmployName
strEmployName = "Bill Murtez"
MsgBox Prompt:=strEmployName
```

When you run the procedure, the five lines of code are processed as follows:

■ The `Dim strEmployName As String` statement creates the strEmployName variable in memory. Because the strEmployName variable is a String variable, it is initialized to a zero-length string ("").
■ The `strEmployName = "Mary Jones"` assignment statement removes the zero-length string from the strEmployName variable and stores the string literal constant "Mary Jones" there instead. The variable now contains only the name "Mary Jones" (without the quotation marks).
■ The `MsgBox Prompt:=strEmployName` statement displays "Mary Jones" (without the quotes) in a message box.

- The `strEmployName = "Bill Murtez"` assignment statement removes "Mary Jones" from the strEmployName variable and stores the string literal constant "Bill Murtez" there instead. The variable now contains only the name "Bill Murtez" (without the quotation marks).
- The `MsgBox Prompt:=strEmployName` statement displays "Bill Murtez" (without the quotation marks) in a message box.

In addition to assigning a string literal constant to a String variable, you also can use an assignment statement to assign the value returned by VBA's InputBox function.

Using the InputBox Function

A common task performed by many VBA procedures is to get information from the user at the keyboard. For example, a procedure that calculates an employee's gross pay will need the user to enter the number of hours the employee worked and his or her pay rate. Similarly, a procedure that replaces one word in a document with another word will need the user to enter both the original word and the replacement word. VBA provides the InputBox function for getting keyboard input from the user.

 tip

> The InputBox function is only one of many ways of getting input from the user at the keyboard. Additional ways to obtain input from the user will be explored in future tutorials.

The **InputBox function** displays one of VBA's predefined dialog boxes. The dialog box contains a title, a message, an OK button, a Cancel button, and an input area in which the user can enter information. The InputBox function allows the programmer to specify the title, the message, and, if necessary, a default value in the input area. Figure 4-5 shows two examples of the dialog box created by the InputBox function.

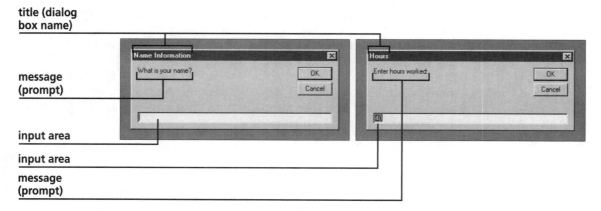

Figure 4-5: Examples of the dialog box created by the InputBox function

Notice in Figure 4-5 that the words "Name Information" appear in the first dialog box's title bar, and the word "Hours" appears in the second dialog box's title bar. "Name Information" and "Hours" are the names of the dialog boxes, similar to the way that Open and Save As are the names of the dialog boxes that allow you to open and save a document in a Windows application. The name you assign to a dialog box should be indicative of the dialog box's purpose.

The message that you display in the dialog box should prompt the user to enter the appropriate information in the input area of the dialog box. The prompt messages used in Figure 4-5's dialog boxes are "What is your name?" and "Enter hours worked:". After the user enters the appropriate information—in this case, either a name or the number of hours worked—he or she then clicks either the OK button or the Cancel button, which removes the dialog box from the screen and allows the procedure to continue.

The syntax of the InputBox function is **InputBox(Prompt:=** *prompt* [, **Title:=** *title*] [, **Default:=***defaultValue*]), where *prompt* is the message displayed inside the dialog box, *title* is the text (name) displayed in the dialog box's title bar, and *defaultValue* is the value that appears in the input area when the dialog box first opens. As you learned in Tutorial 1, the italicized items appearing to the right of the := operator are called arguments, and the bold items appearing to the left of the := operator are the names of the arguments. For example, *prompt, title,* and *defaultValue* are arguments of the InputBox function, and their names are Prompt, Title, and Default, respectively.

Notice that the Title and Default arguments appear in square brackets ([]) in the syntax, indicating that they are optional parts of the syntax. If you do not include the Title argument within the InputBox function, the name of the application (for example, Microsoft Word) will appear in the dialog box's title bar. If you do not include the Default argument, the input area will be blank when the dialog box first opens; otherwise the *defaultValue* will appear in the input area. Figure 4-6 shows the InputBox functions used to create the dialog boxes shown in Figure 4-5.

```
InputBox(Prompt:= "What is your name?", Title:="Name Information")

InputBox(Prompt:= "Enter hours worked:", Title:="Hours", Default:="40")
```

Figure 4-6: InputBox functions used to create the dialog boxes shown in Figure 4-5

As Figure 4-6 indicates, the *prompt, title,* and *defaultValue* arguments must be enclosed in quotation marks. The standard in Windows is to use sentence capitalization for the *prompt,* and book title capitalization for the *title.* **Sentence capitalization** means that you capitalize only the first word and any words that are customarily capitalized— for example, both *prompts* shown in Figure 4-6—"What is your name:" and "Enter hours worked:"—are entered using sentence capitalization. **Book title capitalization** means that you capitalize the first letter in each word, except for articles, conjunctions, and prepositions that do not occur at either the beginning or the end of the *title.* Both the "Name Information" and "Hours" *title*s shown in Figure 4-6 are entered using book title capitalization. You can use any style of capitalization for the *defaultValue.*

Like a procedure, a **function** is a set of instructions that performs a task. However, unlike a procedure, a function returns a value after the task has been performed. The InputBox function's task, for example, is to display a dialog box that prompts the user to enter some information. After the user does so, the InputBox function returns the value entered by the user. The value returned by the InputBox function is always a string literal constant, so you typically will assign the returned value (the user's response) to a String variable. Figure 4-7 shows examples of assignment statements that use the InputBox function to prompt the user to enter information, and then store the user's response in a String variable.

```
strName = InputBox(Prompt:="What is your name?", Title:="Name
Information")

strHours = InputBox(Prompt:="Enter hours worked:", Title:="Hours",
Default:="40")
```

Figure 4-7: Examples of assignment statements that include the InputBox function

The `strName = InputBox(Prompt:="What is your name?", Title:="Name  Information")` instruction will display the first dialog box shown in Figure 4-5. When the user enters a name in the input area of the dialog box and then clicks the OK button, the name is assigned to the strName variable. If the user clicks the OK button without entering any information in the input area, or if he or she clicks the Cancel button, an empty string ("") is assigned to the strName variable.

The `strHours  =  InputBox(Prompt:="Enter hours worked:", Title:="Hours", Default:="40")` instruction will display the second dialog box shown in Figure 4-5. Notice that the *defaultValue* 40 appears in the input area of that dialog box. If the user clicks the OK button without entering a different value into the input area, the *defaultValue* 40 is assigned to the strHours variable; otherwise the value the user entered is assigned to the variable. If, on the other hand, the user clicks the Cancel button, an empty string ("") is assigned to the strHours variable.

To summarize, if the user clicks the OK button, the InputBox function returns the value that appears in the dialog box's input area. If no value appears in the input area, or if the user clicks the Cancel button, the InputBox function returns the empty string ("").

In the next section, you will learn how to concatenate strings (link them together). You may need to do so to display a message along with the user's input—for example, to display the message "The name you entered was " along with the contents of the strName variable.

Concatenating Strings

Connecting (or linking) strings together is called **concatenating**. In VBA, you concatenate strings with the **concatenation operator**—the ampersand (&). Figure 4-8 shows some examples of string concatenation.

Assume you have the following String variables:			
strFirst	strLast	strCity	strName
Sue	Chen	Westmont	Ned Turner

Examples

This instruction: `MsgBox Prompt:="The name you entered was " & strName`
(Note that there is a space before the ending quotation mark.)

Results in a message box containing the concatenated string "The name you entered was Ned Turner"

This instruction: `strFull = strFirst & " " & strLast`
(Note that there is a space between the quotation marks.)

Results in the concatenated string "Sue Chen" assigned to the strFull variable

---

This instruction: `MsgBox Prompt:=strFirst & " lives in " & strCity & "."`
(Note that there is a space before the letter l in the word lives and after the letter n in the word in.)

Results in a message box containing the concatenated string "Sue lives in Westmont."

This instruction: `strMsg = strCity & "'s zip code is 60559."`

Results in the concatenated string "Westmont's zip code is 60559." assigned to the strMsg variable

Figure 4-8: Examples of string concatenation

The `MsgBox Prompt:="The name you entered was " & strName` instruction first concatenates the string literal constant "The name you entered was " with the contents of the strName variable (Ned Turner), and then displays the concatenated string in a message box. The concatenated string "The name you entered was Ned Turner" (without the quotation marks), will appear in the message box.

The `strFull = strFirst & " " & strLast` instruction concatenates the contents of the strFirst variable (Sue), a space, and the contents of the strLast variable (Chen). The concatenated string—in this case, "Sue Chen"—is then assigned to the strFull variable.

The `MsgBox Prompt:=strFirst & " lives in " & strCity & "."` instruction concatenates the contents of the strFirst variable (Sue), the string literal constant " lives in ", the contents of the strCity variable (Westmont), and a period. The concatenated string, "Sue lives in Westmont.", will appear, without the quotation marks, in a message box.

The `strMsg = strCity & "'s zip code is 60559."` instruction concatenates the contents of the strCity variable (Westmont) with the string literal constant "'s zip code is 60559." and then assigns the concatenated string ("Westmont's zip code is 60559.") to the strMsg variable.

When concatenating strings, you must be sure to include a space before and after the concatenation operator—the ampersand (&). If you do not enter a space before and after the ampersand, VBA will not recognize the ampersand as the concatenation operator.

> You also can use the plus sign (+) to concatenate strings. To avoid confusion, however, you should use the plus sign for addition and the ampersand for concatenation.

In addition to concatenating strings, you also can use strings in calculations, as long as the strings contain only numbers and the period. For example, you may need to use the string returned by the InputBox function—in this case, a string that represents the number of hours an employee works—in an expression that calculates the employee's gross pay. Before using a string in a calculation, you should use VBA's Val function to convert the string to a number.

Using the Val Function

As you learned earlier, a function is a predefined procedure that performs a task and then returns a value after the task is performed. For example, the **Val function** converts a *string* into a number, and it then returns the number. The syntax of the Val function is **Val(String:=*string*)**. Because VBA must be able to interpret the *string* as a numeric value, the *string* can contain only numbers and the period; it cannot include a letter or a special character, such as the dollar sign, the comma, or the percent sign. When the Val function encounters an invalid character in its *string*, it stops converting the *string* to a number at that point. Figure 4-9 shows some examples of how the Val function would convert various string literal constants to numbers.

This Val function:	Would convert the string to the number:
Val(String:="456")	456
Val(String:="24,500")	24
Val(String:="123X")	123
Val(String:="25%")	25
Val(String:="$56.88")	0
Val(String:="Abc")	0
Val(String:="")	0

Figure 4-9: Examples of using the Val function to convert string literal constants to numbers

> When a command has only one argument, it is a common practice to omit the argument's name when entering the command in the Code window. For example, rather than entering Val(String:="456"), you simply can enter Val("456").

In the first example, `Val(String:="456")`, the Val function correctly converts the *string* ("456") to the number 456. The second, third, and fourth examples shown in Figure 4-9 indicate that when the Val function encounters an invalid character in the *string*, it stops converting the *string* to a number at that point. For example, notice that "24,500" is converted to the number 24, "123X" is converted to 123, and "25%" is converted to 25; this happens because a comma, a letter, and the percent sign are invalid characters for the Val function. In cases where the *string* begins with an invalid character, as in the last three examples shown in Figure 4-9, the Val function converts the *string* to the number 0. Notice, for example, that the Val function converts "$56.88", "Abc", and "" (the empty string) to the number 0.

In addition to string literal constants, the *string* in a Val function also can be a String variable. When you use the Val function to convert the contents of a String variable to a number, VBA first creates a temporary copy of the String variable in memory; it then converts the contents of the copy to a number. In other words, using the Val function to convert the contents of a String variable to a number does not change the contents of the String variable itself. For example, assume that the strCode variable contains the string "123X". Although `Val(String:=strCode)` returns the number 123, the strCode variable still contains the string "123X". Figure 4-10 shows examples of using the Val function in equations containing String variables.

Assume you have the following String variables:			
strHours	strRate	strRaise	strAge
32	10	2	21

Examples
This instruction: `MsgBox Prompt:=Val(String:=strHours) * Val(String:=strRate)` Results in a message box containing the value 320
This instruction: `docPay.Words(1).Text = Val(String:=strRate) + Val(String:=strRaise)` Results in the value 12 assigned to the first word in the docPay document
This instruction: `shtEmploy.Range("B1").Value = Val(String:=strAge) + 1` Results in the value 22 assigned to cell B1 in the shtEmploy worksheet

Figure 4-10: Examples of using the Val function to convert the contents of String variables to numbers

The `MsgBox Prompt:=Val(String:=strHours) * Val(String:= strRate)` instruction multiplies the contents of the strHours variable, treated as a number, by the contents of the strRate variable, also treated as a number. The instruction displays 320 (32 times 10) in a message box. The `docPay.Words(1).Text = Val(String:=strRate) + Val(String:=strRaise)` instruction converts the contents of the strRate and strRaise variables to numbers, adds both numbers together, and then assigns the sum to the first word in the docPay Document object; the instruction assigns the value 12 (10 plus 2). The `shtEmploy.Range("B1").Value = Val(String:=strAge) + 1` instruction adds the number 1 to the contents of the strAge variable, treated as a number, and then assigns the sum to cell B1 in the shtEmploy Worksheet object. This instruction assigns the number 22 (21 plus 1) to cell B1.

It is very easy to inadvertently misspell a variable's name as you are entering it in the Code window; doing so will cause the procedure to run incorrectly. You can use VBA's Option Explicit statement to prevent this type of error from occurring.

The Option Explicit Statement

One common error made when coding a procedure is to misspell a variable's name. For example, study the code shown in Figure 4-11.

```
Dim strName As String

strName = "Yolanda"

MsgBox Prompt:=strName

strNames = "Patty"

MsgBox Prompt:=strName
```

variable name misspelled

Figure 4-11: Code containing a misspelled variable name

Notice that the variable name strName appears in all of the instructions shown in Figure 4-11, with the exception of the fourth instruction, where strName was mistakenly entered as strNames. Although the variable name used in the fourth instruction is obviously misspelled, this typing mistake is not treated as an error, so no error message will appear to alert you that you have misspelled the name. Rather, when the `strNames = "Patty"` instruction is processed, VBA automatically will reserve a variable named strNames for you, and it is in the strNames variable, rather than the strName variable, that the string literal constant "Patty" will be stored. Therefore, when VBA processes the `MsgBoxPrompt:=strName` instruction that appears at the end of the procedure, the message box displays "Yolanda" rather than "Patty".

It is considered poor programming practice to allow VBA to reserve variables "on the fly"—in other words, to reserve variables that you did not declare in a Dim statement—because it makes finding errors in your program more difficult. You can use the Option Explicit statement to prevent VBA from reserving variables that you did not explicitly declare, but you must be sure to enter the statement in each of the project's modules. The Option Explicit statement tells the Visual Basic Editor to display an error message if your code contains the name of an undeclared variable.

tip

Variables created by VBA "on the fly" are assigned the default data type Variant.

You can type the Option Explicit statement in each module yourself, or you can have the Visual Basic Editor do it for you by selecting the Require Variable Declaration check box that appears on the Editor tab in the Options dialog box, as shown in Figure 4-12.

automatically enters the Option Explicit statement

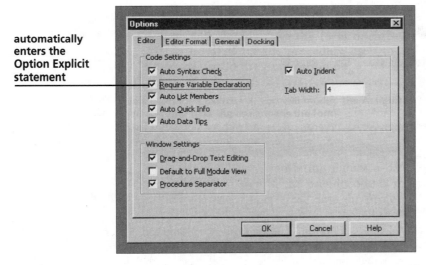

Figure 4-12: Options dialog box showing the Require Variable Declaration check box

It is important to remember that the Require Variable Declaration option will enter the Option Explicit statement in the General Declarations section of new modules only; it will not enter the statement in the project's existing modules. You must manually enter the Option Explicit statement in the General Declarations section of existing modules.

tip

It is a good practice to verify that the Require Variable Declaration check box is selected *before* you insert any modules into a project.

You now have completed Tutorial 4's Concept lesson. You can either take a break or complete the end-of-lesson questions and exercises before moving on to the next lesson.

S U M M A R Y

To reserve a procedure level String variable:

- Use the Dim statement. The syntax of the Dim statement is **Dim** *variablename* **As** *datatype*, where *variablename* represents the name of the variable (memory cell) and *datatype* is the keyword `String`. The three-character ID used to name String variables is *str*.

- Variable names must begin with a letter and can contain only letters, numbers, and the underscore (_). Variable names cannot be longer than 255 characters and cannot be a reserved word, such as Print or MsgBox.

To assign a value to a variable:

- Use an assignment statement with the following syntax: *variablename = value*.

To get input from the user at the keyboard:

- Use the InputBox function. The syntax of the InputBox function is **InputBox(Prompt:=** *prompt* [, **Title:=** *title*] [, **Default:=** *defaultValue*)**, where *prompt* is the message you want displayed inside the dialog box, *title* is the text (name) you want displayed in the dialog box's title bar, and *defaultValue* is the value you want to appear in the input area when the dialog box first opens.

- The *prompt*, *title*, and *defaultValue* must be enclosed in quotation marks. The standard in Windows is to use sentence capitalization for the *prompt*, and book title capitalization for the *title*. The *defaultValue* can be entered in any case.

- If the user clicks the OK button in the dialog box, the InputBox function returns a string that corresponds to the value that appears in the dialog box's input area. If no value appears in the input area, or if the user clicks the Cancel button, the InputBox function returns an empty string ("").

To concatenate (link together) strings:

- Use the concatenation operator, which is the ampersand (&). To ensure the ampersand is recognized as the concatenation operator, be sure to include a space before and after it.

To convert a string into a number:

- Use the Val function. The syntax of the Val function is **Val(String:=***string***)**. The Val function converts the *string* into a number; it then returns the number. The *string* must contain only numbers and the period; it cannot include a letter or a special character, such as the dollar sign, the comma, or the percent sign. When the Val function encounters an invalid character in its *string*, it stops converting the *string* to a number at that point.

To prevent VBA from reserving undeclared variables:

■ Enter the Option Explicit statement in each module's General Declarations section. The Option Explicit statement tells the Visual Basic Editor to display an error message if your code contains the name of an undeclared variable.

■ To have the Visual Basic Editor enter the Option Explicit statement automatically in every new module, click Tools on the menu bar and then click Options to display the Options dialog box. Select the Require Variable Declaration check box, which is located on the Editor tab.

 # R E V I E W   Q U E S T I O N S

1. Which of the following are valid string literal constants?
   a. Tom Smith
   b. "45"
   c. $5.67
   d. None of the above

2. A(n) _____ is an item of data whose value does not change while the procedure in which it is used is running.
   a. assignment variable
   b. constant value
   c. literal constant
   d. variable

3. A(n) _____ is a memory cell whose contents can change while a procedure is running.
   a. assignment variable
   b. constant value
   c. literal constant
   d. variable

4. Which of the following is a valid name for a variable?
   a. strCity
   b. 2000Party
   c. strBirth.Month
   d. January Sales

5. Which of the following is false?
   a. A procedure level variable is created in a procedure.
   b. When you declare a variable using the String data type, VBA initializes the variable to a space.
   c. A procedure level variable can be used only by the procedure in which it is declared.
   d. A procedure level variable remains in memory only while the procedure in which it is declared is running.

6. Which of the following is false?
   a. You use VBA's Dim statement to create a procedure level variable.
   b. When a procedure ends, the variables created within the procedure remain in memory until you close the application.
   c. After a variable is created and initialized, you can use either an assignment statement or the InputBox function to store other data in it.
   d. None of the above is false.

7. Which of the following InputBox functions will display a dialog box that shows "Enter the month:" as the message and "Month" as the dialog box's name?
   a. `InputBox(Prompt:="Enter the month:", Title:="Month")`
   b. `InputBox(Prompt = "Enter the month:", Title = "Month")`
   c. `InputBox(Prompt "Enter the month:", Title "Month")`
   d. `InputBox(Prompt:="Month", Title:="Enter the month:")`

8. _____ capitalization means that you capitalize the first letter in each word, except for articles, conjunctions, and prepositions that do not occur at either the beginning or the end of the *title*.
   a. Book title
   b. Proper
   c. Sentence
   d. None of the above

9. "Enter the day of the week" is an example of _____ capitalization.
   a. book title
   b. paragraph
   c. sentence
   d. None of the above

10. The InputBox function returns a _____.
   a. numeric literal constant
   b. numeric variable
   c. string literal constant
   d. string variable

11. Which of the following is the concatenation operator?
   a. &
   b. *
   c. @
   d. $

12. Assume the strReg1 variable contains the string "North" and the strReg2 variable contains the string "West". Which of the following will display the string "NorthWest" in a message box?
   a. `MsgBox = Prompt:=strReg1 & strReg2`
   b. `MsgBox = Prompt:="strReg1" & "strReg2"`
   c. `MsgBox Prompt:=strReg1 & strReg2`
   d. `MsgBox Prompt:=strReg1 @ strReg2`

13. Assume the strCity variable contains the string "Boston" and the strState variable contains the string "MA". Which of the following will display the string "Boston, MA" (the city, a comma, a space, and the state) in a message box?

    a. `MsgBox = Prompt:=strCity & , & strState`
    b. `MsgBox Prompt:=strCity & ", " & strState`
    c. `MsgBox Prompt:="strCity, strState"`
    d. `MsgBox Prompt:="strCity, " & "strState"`

14. Which of the following correctly adds the contents of the strNum1 variable to the contents of the strNum2 variable, and then displays the sum in a message box?

    a. `MsgBox Prompt:=strNum1 + strNum2`
    b. `MsgBox Prompt:=Val(String:=strNum1 + strNum2)`
    c. `MsgBox Prompt:=Val(String:=strNum1) + Val(String:=strNum2)`
    d. Both b and c

15. Val(String:="$4.50") would convert the *string* "$4.50" to the number _____.

    a. 0
    b. 4
    c. 4.5
    d. 4.50

16. Selecting the Require Variable Declaration check box that appears on the Editor tab in the Options dialog box tells VBA to enter the _____ statement in every new module.

    a. Explicit Definition
    b. Explicit Option
    c. Option Explicit
    d. Require Definition

    Use the following lines of code to answer questions 17 through 19.

```
Dim strCity As String
strCity = "New York"
MsgBox Prompt:=strCity
strCity = "Boston"
MsgBox Prompt:=stCity
```

17. What value is stored in the strCity variable after the `Dim strCity As String` instruction is processed?

    a. A space
    b. A zero-length string
    c. 0 (zero)
    d. None of the above

18. What will the `MsgBox Prompt:=strCity` instruction display in the message box?

    a. A zero-length string
    b. Boston
    c. New York
    d. "New York"

19. What will the `MsgBox Prompt:=stCity` instruction display in the message box?
    a. A zero-length string
    b. Boston
    c. "Boston"
    d. New York

EXERCISES

1. a. Write a Dim statement that reserves a String variable named strPetName.
    b. Write an assignment statement that assigns the string literal constant "Lassie" to the strPetName variable.
    c. Write an assignment statement that assigns the value returned by the InputBox function to the strPetName variable. Use "What is your pet's name?" as the *prompt*, and use "Pet Name" as the *title*.

2. a. Write a Dim statement that reserves a String variable named strPayRate.
    b. Write an assignment statement that assigns the string literal constant "6.55" to the strPayRate variable.
    c. Write an assignment statement that assigns the value returned by the InputBox function to the strPayRate variable. Use "Enter the pay rate:" as the *prompt*, and use "Pay Rate" as the *title*. Use the string literal constant "5" as the *defaultValue*.

3. Write the InputBox function that corresponds to the dialog box shown in Figure 4-13. Use "Y" as the *defaultValue*.

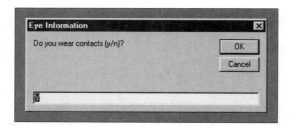

Figure 4-13

Use the information shown in Figure 4-14 to complete Exercises 4 through 9.

strCity	strState	strZip	strMsg	strSales	strRate	strBonus
Madison	WI	53711	My zip code is	10000	.05	200

Figure 4-14

4. Use the information shown in Figure 4-14 to write a VBA instruction that will display the string "Madison, WI" in a message box.

5. Use the information shown in Figure 4-14 to write a VBA instruction that will display the string "The capital of WI is Madison." in a message box.

6. Use the information shown in Figure 4-14 to write a VBA instruction that will display the string "My zip code is 53711." in a message box.

7. Use the information shown in Figure 4-14 to write a VBA instruction that will display, in a message box, the result of multiplying the contents of the strSales variable by the contents of the strRate variable.

8. Use the information shown in Figure 4-14 to write a VBA instruction that will display, in a message box, the result of adding the contents of the strSales variable to the contents of the strBonus variable.

9. Use the information shown in Figure 4-14 to write a VBA instruction that will display, in a message box, the result of adding the number 10 to the contents of the strBonus variable.

Exercise 10 is a Discovery Exercise. Discovery Exercises, which may include topics that are not covered in this lesson, allow you to "discover" the solutions to problems on your own.

discovery ▶

10. Start either Word, Excel, Access, or PowerPoint. Open the Visual Basic Editor. Display the Option Explicit Statement Help screen. Use the Help screen to complete the following statements.

   a. If you attempt to use an undeclared variable name, an error occurs at

   _____.

   b. Compile time is _____.

   c. If you don't use the Option Explicit statement, all undeclared variables are assigned the _____ data type.

   d. You can use the keywords _____, _____, _____, _____, or _____ to explicitly declare a variable.

You also can use VBA in PowerPoint to create procedures that enhance your presentations. Exercise 11 allows you to apply this tutorial's programming concept in a PowerPoint presentation.

powerpoint

11. Assume that a procedure contains a String variable named strFifthName and a Slide object variable named sldFifth, which contains the address of the fifth slide in the PowerPoint presentation. First write an assignment statement that uses the InputBox function to prompt the user to enter the name of the fifth slide, and then stores the user's response in the strFifthName variable. Use "Enter name of fifth slide:" as the *prompt* and "Get Name" as the *title*. Then write an assignment statement that assigns the contents of the strFifthName variable to the fifth slide's Name property.

A computer program is good only if it works. Errors in programming code can cause a program to run incorrectly. Therefore, a programmer needs to know how to locate and fix any errors in his or her code. Exercise 12 is a Debugging Exercise. Debugging Exercises allow you to practice recognizing and solving errors in code.

debugging 🐞

12. The following code should add the contents of the strJanSales variable to the contents of the strFebSales variable, and then display the sum in a message box. What is wrong with the following code? Correct any errors.

```
MsgBox Prompt:=strJanSales + strFebSales
```

Excel Lesson

Using String Variables in Excel

case ▶ Martin Washington, the accountant at Paradise Electronics, is going on vacation next week. Jason Wells, from Temporary Help Inc., has been hired to take over Martin's duties while he is away. One of those duties is to calculate the January commission for the sales staff. Martin already has entered the January sales data into an Excel worksheet. Jason needs simply to enter his own name and the commission rate for the month. Martin has decided to code the workbook's Open event so that it first prompts Jason for the missing information, and then enters the information in the appropriate cells in the workbook's January worksheet.

Coding the Workbook's Open Event Procedure

Begin by opening Martin's commission workbook, which is located in the Tut04\Excel folder on your Data Disk.

To open Martin's workbook and view its formulas, then open the Visual Basic Editor and view the workbook's Open event procedure:

1 Start Microsoft Excel. Open the **T4-EX-1** (T4-EX-1.xls) workbook, which is located in the Tut04\Excel folder on your Data Disk, then save the workbook as **Commission**. The Commission workbook contains a worksheet named January, as shown in Figure 4-15.

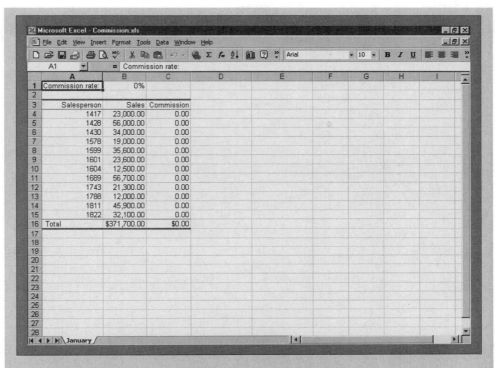

Figure 4-15: Commission workbook showing January worksheet

View the formulas contained in the January worksheet.

2 Click **Tools** on the menu bar and then click **Options** to open the Options dialog box. Click the **View** tab, if necessary, and then click the **Formulas** check box, which is located in the Window options section, to select it. Click the **OK** button to return to the worksheet. The formulas appear in the worksheet, as shown in Figure 4-16.

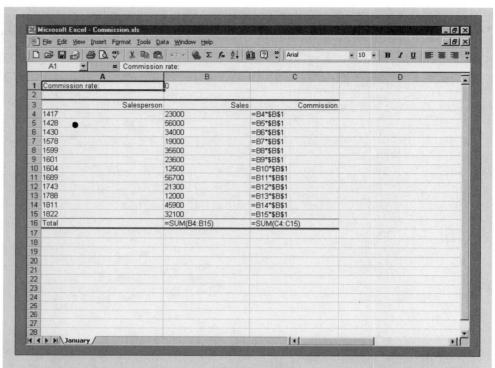

Figure 4-16: Formulas displayed in the January worksheet

Notice that cells B16 and C16, and cells C4 through C15, contain formulas. Cell B16, for example, contains the =SUM(B4:B15) formula, which totals the sales amounts entered in column B of the worksheet. Cell C16 contains a similar formula, =SUM(C4:C15), which totals the commission amounts entered in column C. The formulas entered in cells C4 through C15 calculate each salesperson's commission amount. Notice that each formula in the range C4:C15 multiplies a sales amount found in column B by the commission rate, which is located in cell B1. For example, cell C4 contains the =B4*$B$1 formula, which multiplies the sales amount entered in cell B4 (23000) by the commission rate entered in cell B1 (0); the result is 0.

tip

Notice that the absolute cell reference $B$1 appears in each of the commission formulas in column C. An absolute cell reference is used so that the location of the commission rate remains constant when the original formula entered in cell C4 is copied to other cells—in this case, to cells C5 through C15.

Return the worksheet to its original state.

3 Click **Tools** on the menu bar and then click **Options** to open the Options dialog box. Click the **Formulas** check box on the View tab to deselect it. Click the **OK**

button to close the Options dialog box. The worksheet displays the values shown earlier in Figure 4-15.

Now open the Visual Basic Editor.

4 Press **Alt+F11** to open the Visual Basic Editor. Open the Project Explorer window, if necessary, and close the Properties window, the Immediate window, and any open Code windows.

5 Right-click **ThisWorkbook** in the Project Explorer window and then click **View Code**. The Workbook object's General Declarations section appears in the Code window. Type **option explicit** and press the **Enter** key. Recall that the Option Explicit statement tells the Visual Basic Editor to display an error message if your code contains the name of an undeclared variable.

6 Click the **Object box list arrow**, then click **Workbook** in the list. The Workbook object's Open event procedure appears in the Code window.

7 Close the Project Explorer window so that you can view more of the Code window.

As you learned in Tutorial 3, before entering instructions into a procedure, you should write down on a piece of paper what you want the procedure to accomplish, and the steps it will need to do so. Recall that these steps are called pseudocode. Figure 4-17 shows the pseudocode for the Commission workbook's Open event procedure.

1. Use the InputBox function to prompt the user to enter his or her name. Store the user's response in a String variable named strName.

2. Use the InputBox function to prompt the user to enter the commission rate as a whole number. Store the user's response in a String variable named strRate.

3. Convert the rate stored in the strRate variable to its decimal equivalent by dividing the rate by 100. Assign the result to cell B1 in the January worksheet.

4. Concatenate the string literal constant "Prepared by " to the name stored in the strName variable. Assign the result to cell A19 in the January worksheet.

Figure 4-17: Pseudocode for the Commission workbook's Open event procedure

After determining the steps you want the procedure to take, you can begin coding the procedure. First examine the pseudocode to determine what variables, if any, the procedure will need to use. For example, Steps 1 and 2 in the pseudocode indicate that the Open event procedure will use the InputBox function to get the user's name and the commission rate. As you learned in the Concept lesson, the InputBox function returns a string literal constant, so you will need to reserve two String variables in which to store the name and rate information.

Slightly less obvious in the pseudocode are the object variables that the procedure will use. You can determine that information by looking for the objects mentioned in the pseudocode. In Figure 4-17's pseudocode, for example, you will notice that the January worksheet is mentioned in the last two steps. You can make the Open event procedure easier to write and understand, as well as run more efficiently, by assigning the address of the January Worksheet object to an object variable. You will name the object variable shtJan.

Now you can declare the appropriate variables, and then translate each line in the pseudocode into one or more VBA statements.

To code the Open event procedure:

1 The insertion point should be positioned in the blank line between the `Private Sub` and `End Sub` lines in the Code window. To declare the variables for the procedure, enter the documentation and the Dim and Set statements shown in Figure 4-18, then position the insertion point as shown in the figure. (Be sure to enter the line continuation character—a space followed by the underscore—after the equal sign in the Set statement.)

enter these lines of code

position the insertion point here

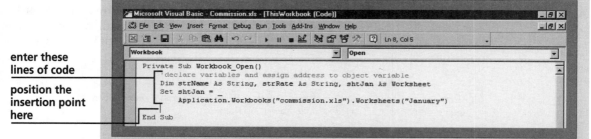

Figure 4-18: Code window showing documentation and Dim and Set statements

The first step in the pseudocode shown in Figure 4-17 is to use the InputBox function to prompt the user to enter his or her name, and then assign the user's response to the strName variable. Recall that the syntax of the InputBox function is **InputBox(Prompt:=***prompt* [**, Title:=***title*] [**, Default:=***defaultValue*]**)**, where *prompt* is the message you want displayed inside the dialog box, *title* is the text (name) you want displayed in the dialog box's title bar, and *defaultValue* is the value you want to appear in the input area when the dialog box first opens.

2 With the insertion point positioned as shown in Figure 4-18, type **'enter name** and press the **Enter** key. Type **strname = inputbox(prompt:= "Enter your name:", title:="Name")** and press the **Enter** key.

The next step is to prompt the user for the commission rate, and then assign the user's response to the strRate variable. You will use the current value stored in cell B1, multiplied by 100, as the *defaultValue* in the InputBox function.

3   Type **'enter rate** and press the **Enter** key. Type **strrate = _** (be sure to type the equal sign followed by a space and the underscore) and press the **Enter** key. Press the **Tab** key, then type **inputbox(prompt:= "Enter rate as a whole number:", _** (be sure to type the comma followed by a space and the underscore) and press the **Enter** key. Type **title:="Rate", default:= shtjan.range("b1").value * 100)** and press the **Enter** key.

Step 3 in the pseudocode is to divide the number stored in the strRate variable by 100, and then assign the result to cell B1 in the January worksheet. As you learned in the Concept lesson, before using a string in a calculation, you should use VBA's Val function to convert the string to a number.

4   Press the **Backspace** key to remove the indentation, then type **'convert rate to decimal** and press the **Enter** key. Type **shtjan.range("b1").value = val(string:=strrate) / 100** and press the **Enter** key.

The last step in the pseudocode is to concatenate the "Prepared by " message to the name stored in the strName variable, and then assign the result to cell A19 in the January worksheet.

5   Type the additional two lines of code shown in Figure 4-19, which shows the completed Open event procedure.

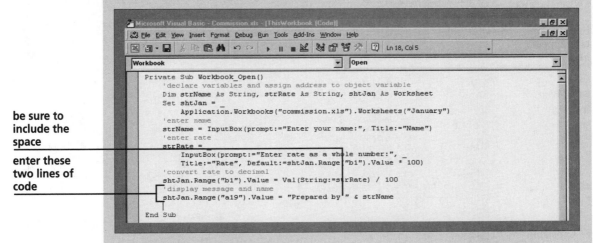

be sure to include the space

enter these two lines of code

Figure 4-19: Completed Open event procedure

6   Verify the accuracy of your code by comparing it to the code shown in Figure 4-19, then save the Commission.xls workbook.

Now that you have translated the pseudocode shown in Figure 4-17 into VBA statements, you need to test the Open event procedure to verify that it is working correctly.

To test the workbook's Open event procedure from within the Visual Basic Editor:

1 Click the **Run Sub/UserForm** button ▶ on the toolbar to run the Open event procedure.

> **tip**
>
> You also can run a procedure by clicking Run on the Visual Basic Editor menu bar and then clicking Run Sub/UserForm. You also can press the F5 key.

2 When the Name dialog box appears and prompts you to enter your name, type **Jason Wells** and then click the **OK** button.

You also can select the OK button in the InputBox function's dialog box by pressing the Enter key when the insertion point is in the input area of the dialog box.

3 When the Rate dialog box appears, type **10** and then press the **Enter** key.

4 Click the **View Microsoft Excel** button ▣ to return to Excel. Figure 4-20 shows the January worksheet after running the workbook's Open event procedure.

commission
rate appears
here

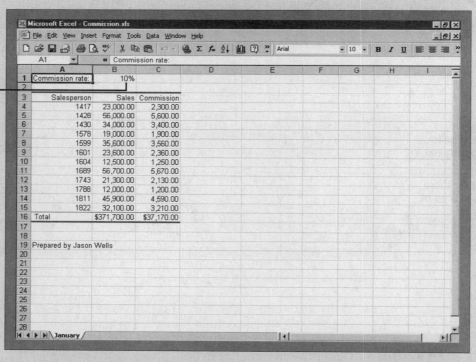

Figure 4-20: January worksheet after running the workbook's Open event procedure

5 Save the Commission workbook.

Now test the Open event procedure by closing and then opening the Commission workbook.

6 Close the Commission workbook, then open the workbook. Click the **Enable Macros** button, if necessary. When the Name dialog box appears, type your name and then click the **OK** button. When the Rate dialog box appears, type **7** and press the **Enter** key. The January worksheet calculates each salesperson's commission using a 7 percent rate.

7 Save the workbook, then close Excel.

You now have completed Tutorial 4's Excel lesson. You can either take a break or complete the end-of-lesson exercises before moving on to the next lesson.

 # E X E R C I S E S

1. In this exercise, you will create a macro procedure that prompts the user to enter two items of information, and then enters the information into the worksheet.
   a. Open the T4-EX-E1 (T4-EX-E1.xls) workbook, which is located in the Tut04\Excel folder on your Data Disk. Save the workbook as T4-EX-E1D.
   b. Study the formulas entered in the worksheet.
   c. Open the Visual Basic Editor. Create a macro procedure named GetYearAndRate. Be sure to enter the Option Explicit statement in the Module1 module's General Declarations section. Use the pseudocode shown in Figure 4-21 to code the procedure.

---

1. Use the InputBox function to prompt the user to enter the current year. Store the user's response in a String variable named strYear.

2. Use the InputBox function to prompt the user to enter the increase rate as a whole number. Store the user's response in a String variable named strRate.

3. Convert the rate stored in the strRate variable to its decimal equivalent by dividing the rate by 100. Assign the result to cell B15 in the Sales Forecast worksheet.

4. Concatenate the string literal constant "Year ", the contents of the strYear variable, and the string literal constant " Sales". Assign the result (for example, Year 2001 Sales) to cell B4 in the Sales Forecast worksheet.

5. Concatenate the string literal constant "Year ", the contents of the strYear variable increased by 1, and the string literal constant " Sales". Assign the result (for example, Year 2002 Sales) to cell D4 in the Sales Forecast worksheet.

Figure 4-21

d. Save the workbook. Return to Excel and run the GetYearAndRate macro. Enter 2001 as the year, and enter 4 as the increase rate.

e. When the macro is working correctly, save and then close the workbook.

2. In this exercise, you will code a workbook's Open event procedure so that it prompts the user to enter three items of information. The procedure enters the information into the worksheet.

a. Open the T4-EX-E2 (T4-EX-E2.xls) workbook, which is located in the Tut04\Excel folder on your Data Disk. Save the workbook as T4-EX-E2D.

b. Study the formulas entered in the worksheet.

c. Compare the worksheet on your screen to the one shown in Figure 4-22.

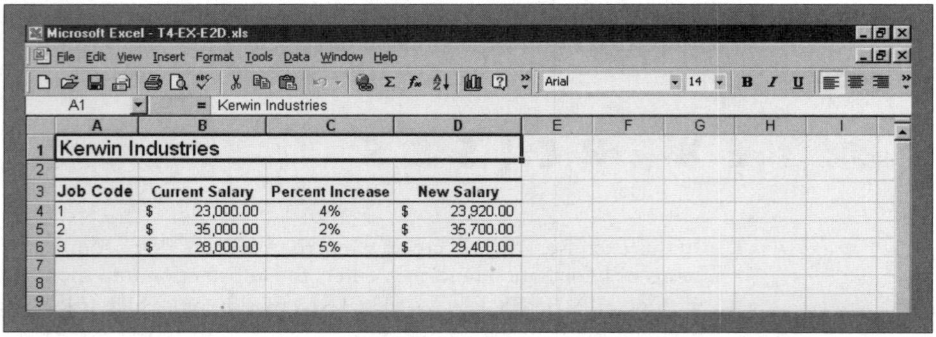

Figure 4-22

d. Open the Visual Basic Editor and view the workbook's Code window. Verify that the General Declarations section contains the Option Explicit statement.

e. Open the workbook's Open event procedure. Code the procedure so that it allows the user to enter each job code's current salary amount. The procedure should assign the information to the appropriate cells in the Salary worksheet, as shown in Figure 4-22. Use the current contents of cells B4, B5, and B6 as the *defaultValue* in the InputBox functions.

f. Save the workbook, then run the workbook's Open event procedure from within the Visual Basic Editor. Use the information shown in Figure 4-22 to enter the appropriate salaries.

g. When the procedure is working correctly, save and then close the workbook.

3. In this exercise, you will create a macro procedure that prompts the user to enter five items of information, and then enters the information into the worksheet.

a. Open the T4-EX-E3 (T4-EX-E3.xls) workbook, which is located in the Tut04\Excel folder on your Data Disk. Save the workbook as T4-EX-E3D.

b. Study the formulas entered in the worksheet.

c. Compare the worksheet on your screen to the one shown in Figure 4-23.

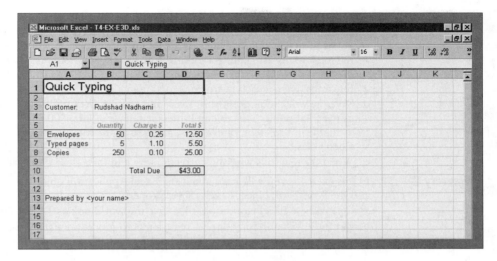

Figure 4-23

   d. Open the Visual Basic Editor. Create a macro procedure named GetNameAndQuantity. Be sure to enter the Option Explicit statement in the Module1 module's General Declarations section. The GetNameAndQuantity procedure should allow the user to enter the customer name, the number of envelopes, the number of typed pages, the number of copies, and the clerk's name. The procedure should assign the information to the appropriate cells in the Billing worksheet. Use the number 0 as the *defaultValue* in the InputBox functions that get the number of envelopes, typed pages, and copies. Use your name as the *defaultValue* in the InputBox function that gets the clerk's name.

   e. Save the workbook. Return to Excel and run the GetNameAndQuantity macro. Use the information shown in Figure 4-23 to enter the appropriate names and quantities.

   f. When the macro is working correctly, save and then close the workbook.

Exercises 4 through 6 are Discovery Exercises. Discovery Exercises, which may include topics that are not covered in this lesson, allow you to "discover" the solutions to problems on your own.

discovery ▶   **4.** In this exercise, you will create a macro procedure that prompts the user to enter three items of information, and then enters each item in a separate worksheet.

   a. Open the T4-EX-E4 (T4-EX-E4.xls) workbook, which is located in the Tut04\Excel folder on your Data Disk. Save the workbook as T4-EX-E4D.

   b. Study the formulas entered in the three worksheets.

   c. Open the Visual Basic Editor. Create a macro procedure named GetTotalPoints. The procedure should allow the user to enter the total points available in Professor

Carver's course, the total points available in Professor Patel's course, and the total points available in Professor Chen's course. The procedure should assign the total points available in each course to cell B3 in the appropriate worksheet. (For example, the total points available in Professor Carver's course should be assigned to cell B3 in the Carver worksheet.) Use the number 0 as the *defaultValue* in the InputBox functions that get each instructor's total points.

d. Save the workbook. Return to Excel and run the GetTotalPoints macro. Enter 300 as the total points available in Professor Carver's class, 500 as the total points available in Professor Patel's class, and 450 as the total points available in Professor Chen's class.

e. When the macro is working correctly, save and then close the workbook.

discovery ▶ 5. In this exercise, you will learn about the Excel Application object's InputBox method and the Workbook object's ActiveSheet property.

a. Open a new Excel workbook, then save the workbook as T4-EX-E5D.

b. Open the Visual Basic Editor. Create a macro procedure named ZeroFill.

c. View the Help screen for the Workbook object's ActiveSheet property.

d. View the Help screen for the Application object's InputBox method. What does the Type argument specify? What is the meaning of the *type* values 0, 1, 2, and 8? Click Example at the top of the Help screen to view an example of using the InputBox method to select a range. Close the Help window.

e. Code the ZeroFill macro so that it uses the InputBox method to get a range from the user. You will need to include only the *prompt*, *title*, and *type* arguments in the InputBox method. Use "Select a range:" as the *prompt*, and "Range" as the *title*. Use the appropriate value for the *type*. The macro should assign the number 0 to the cells contained in the selected range.

f. Save the workbook. Return to Excel and run the ZeroFill macro. When the InputBox method's dialog box appears and prompts you to enter a range, use the mouse to select the range A1:A10 on Sheet1, then click the dialog box's OK button. The number 0 appears in cells A1 through A10.

g. Run the ZeroFill macro again. This time select the range A12:D12 on Sheet1, then click the OK button.

h. Run the ZeroFill macro again. This time select the range A1:A4 on Sheet2, then click the OK button.

i. When the macro is working correctly, save and then close the workbook.

discovery ▶ 6. In this exercise, you will learn about VBA's Call statement.

a. Open the Commission (Commission.xls) workbook that you created in this lesson. The workbook is located in the Tut04\Excel folder on your Data Disk. Click the Enable Macros button, if necessary. Enter Sue Jones as the name and 7 as the commission rate. Save the workbook as T4-EX-E6D.

b. Open the Visual Basic Editor. View the Help screen for the Call statement. Close the Help window.

c. Create a macro procedure named GetNameAndRate. Move the code from the workbook's Open event to the GetNameAndRate procedure. Modify the Set statement so that it uses "t4-ex-e6d.xls" as the workbook's name.

d. In the Open event, enter a Call statement that calls the GetNameAndRate procedure.

e. Save the workbook, then return to Excel. Close the workbook, then open the workbook to invoke its Open event. Click the Enable Macros button, if necessary. When prompted, enter Nancy Smith as the name and enter 10 as the commission rate.

f. Now assume that the user wants to change the name and rate. Rather than having to close and then open the workbook to invoke its Open event, he or she simply can run the GetNameAndRate macro. Run the GetNameAndRate macro. When prompted, enter Harry Hou as the name and enter 5 as the commission rate.

g. When the Open event and macro are working correctly, save and then close the workbook.

A computer program is good only if it works. Errors in programming code can cause a program to run incorrectly. Therefore, a programmer needs to know how to locate and fix any errors in his or her code. Exercise 7 is a Debugging Exercise. Debugging Exercises allow you to practice recognizing and solving errors in code.

debugging   **7.** In this exercise, you will debug an existing macro procedure.

a. Open the T4-EX-E7 (T4-EX-E7.xls) workbook, which is located in the Tut04\Excel folder on your Data Disk. Click the Enable Macros button, if necessary. Save the workbook as T4-EX-E7D.

b. Open the Visual Basic Editor. Right-click Module1 in the Project Explorer window, then click View Code on the shortcut menu. Use the Code window's Procedure box to view the CalcEndInv macro procedure. Study the code, then run the procedure. Enter 100 as the beginning inventory, 10 as the purchases, and 5 as the sales. Return to Excel. You will notice that the procedure does not calculate the ending inventory correctly.

c. Return to the Visual Basic Editor. What is wrong with the code? Correct any errors.

d. Save the workbook, then run the procedure again, using 100, 10, and 5 as the beginning inventory, purchases, and sales, respectively.

e. When the procedure is working correctly, save and then close the workbook.

Word Lesson

Using String Variables in Word

case ▶ As a way to increase membership, Willowton Health Club now offers free health seminars to area businesses. At the beginning of each month, Pat Jones, the manager of Willowton Health Club, faxes each of the businesses a schedule of the free seminars being offered. Pat has decided to create a macro that generates a facsimile transmittal sheet that can easily be customized for sending to each business.

Creating a Facsimile Transmittal Sheet

Begin by opening the T4-WD-1 document, which is located in the Tut04\Word folder on your Data Disk. The document contains Pat's partially completed facsimile transmittal sheet.

To open the T4-WD-1 document, then save the document as Fax:

1 Start Microsoft Word. Open the **T4-WD-1** (T4-WD-1.doc) document, which is located in the Tut04\Word folder on your Data Disk. Save the document as **Fax**. Display the nonprinting characters in the document.

2 Click **Tools** on Word's menu bar and then click **Options** to display the Options dialog box. If necessary, click the **All** check box, which is located in the Formatting marks section on the View tab, to select it, then click the **OK** button. Figure 4-24 shows the partially completed facsimile sheet.

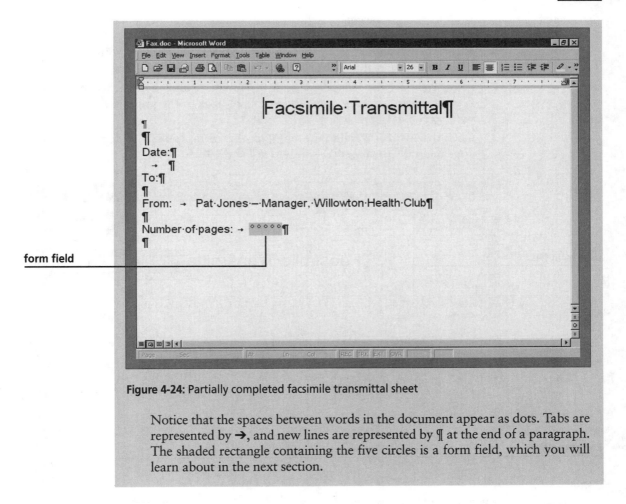

form field

Figure 4-24: Partially completed facsimile transmittal sheet

Notice that the spaces between words in the document appear as dots. Tabs are represented by →, and new lines are represented by ¶ at the end of a paragraph. The shaded rectangle containing the five circles is a form field, which you will learn about in the next section.

Before you can begin creating the macro procedure, which you will name FaxTransmittal, you will need to complete the facsimile transmittal sheet by entering two additional form fields.

Using Form Fields

A **form field** is a special area in the document reserved for entering and displaying information. Although the form field shown in Figure 4-24 appears shaded when you view the document, the shading will not appear when you print the document.

You will use three form fields in the facsimile transmittal sheet. The first form field, which you will name CurrentDate, will display the date, and the second form field, which you will name ToNames, will display the recipient's name and also his or her company name. The third form field, named NumPages, is already included in the document, and displays the number of pages being faxed.

To add the first form field to the Fax document:

1 Click after the colon (:) in Date: and then press the **Tab** key to position the insertion point at the location where you want to place the first form field.

2 Click **View** on the menu bar, point to **Toolbars**, and then click **Forms**. The Forms toolbar appears. Drag the Forms toolbar to the upper right corner of your screen, if necessary.

3 Click the **Text Form Field** button [abl] on the Forms toolbar. A Text form field appears in the document, as shown in Figure 4-25.

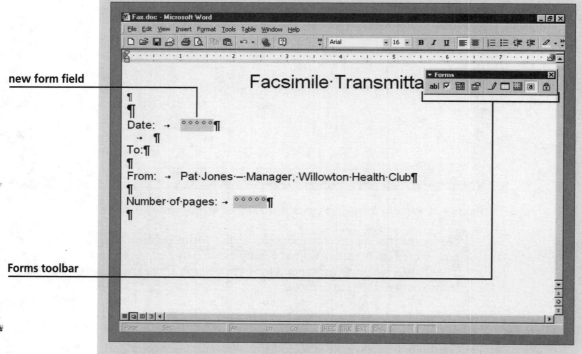

new form field

Forms toolbar

Figure 4-25: Text form field added to the Fax document

 tip

> You can turn the form field shading off by clicking the Form Field Shading button [📷] on the Forms toolbar.

4 Click the **Form Field Options** button [📑] on the Forms toolbar. The Text Form Field Options dialog box appears, as shown in Figure 4-26.

form field's
type

form field's
format

form field's
name

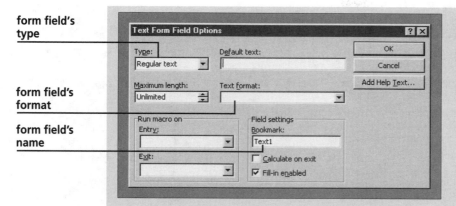

Figure 4-26: Text Form Field Options dialog box

The Bookmark text box, which is located in the Field settings section of the dialog box, shows that the name of the form field is Text1. To help document the purpose of the form field, you should change its default name to a more meaningful one.

5 Double-click **Text1** in the Bookmark text box, and then type **CurrentDate**.

The CurrentDate form field should display the current date whenever the Fax document is opened. To have Word automatically display the current date in the CurrentDate form field, you need to change the field's type from Regular text to Current date, and also select the Calculate on exit check box.

6 Click the **Type** list arrow and then click **Current date** in the list. Click the **Calculate on exit** check box to select it.

You can use the Date format list box to select a format for displaying the date. You will select the M/d/yyyy format, which will display the December 15, 2002 date as 12/15/2002.

If you don't select a format in the Date format list box, the default date format (M/d/yy) will be used to display the date. Using this format, the December 15, 2002 date will appear as 12/15/02.

7 Click the **Date format** list arrow and then click **M/d/yyyy** in the list. Figure 4-27 shows the completed Text Form Field Options dialog box for the CurrentDate field.

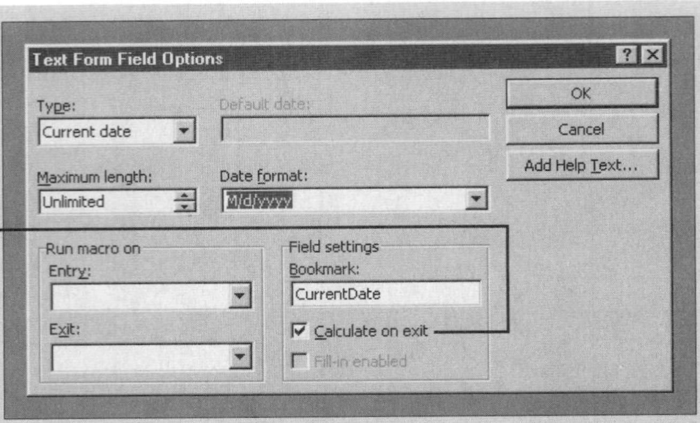

displays the current date automatically

Figure 4-27: Completed Text Form Field Options dialog box for the CurrentDate field

8 Click the **OK** button to close the Text Form Field Options dialog box. The current date appears in the M/d/yyyy format.

Now create a form field that you can use to display the name of both the recipient and his or her company.

To add the second form field to the form:

1 Click after the colon (:) in To: and then press the **Tab** key twice. Click the **Text Form Field** button [abl] on the Forms toolbar to insert another form field in the document. Click the **Form Field Options** button [🖭] on the Forms toolbar to display the Text Form Field Options dialog box.

This form field will contain text—the name of both the recipient and his or her company—so you do not need to change the field's type; Regular text is the correct field type for this situation. You should, however, give this form field a more meaningful name.

2 Double-click **Text1** in the Bookmark text box and then type **ToNames**. Click the **OK** button to close the Text Form Field Options dialog box.

When using form fields in a document, it is customary to protect the document so that changes can be made only to the form fields.

3 Click the **Protect Form** button [🔒] on the Forms toolbar to protect the document and allow changes only to the form fields.

4 Close the Forms toolbar, then save the Fax document. Figure 4-28 shows the completed facsimile transmittal sheet.

your date might be different

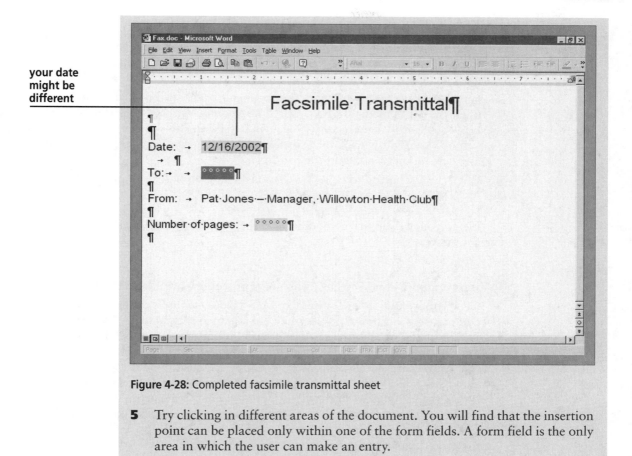

Figure 4-28: Completed facsimile transmittal sheet

5   Try clicking in different areas of the document. You will find that the insertion point can be placed only within one of the form fields. A form field is the only area in which the user can make an entry.

You now can open the Visual Basic Editor and begin creating the FaxTransmittal macro procedure.

Creating the FaxTransmittal Macro Procedure

Recall that Pat wants to create a facsimile transmittal form that she can fax to local businesses along with information about Willowton's free health seminars. Before you can create the FaxTransmittal macro procedure, you need to open the Visual Basic Editor.

To open the Visual Basic Editor:

1   Press **Alt+F11** to open the Visual Basic Editor. If necessary, open the Project Explorer window and close the Properties window, the Immediate window, and any open Code windows.

2   Click **Tools** on the Visual Basic Editor menu bar, and then click **Options** to open the Options dialog box. Click the **Require Variable Declaration** check box to select it, if necessary. Recall that selecting this check box tells the Visual Basic Editor to automatically enter the Option Explicit statement in any new modules added to the project.

3   Click the **OK** button to close the Options dialog box.

Next, you will insert a module and the FaxTransmittal procedure into the current project.

To insert a module and the FaxTransmittal procedure into the current project:

1   Click **Project (Fax)** in the Project Explorer window to insert the module into the Fax project. Click **Insert** on the menu bar and then click **Module**. As the Project Explorer window shows, the Visual Basic Editor creates a Modules folder in the Fax project and it inserts the Module1 module into the folder. Also notice that the General Declarations section of the Module1 module appears in the Code window. Because you selected the Require Variable Declaration check box in the previous set of steps, the Option Explicit statement is automatically entered into the module's General Declarations section. Recall that the Option Explicit statement tells the Visual Basic Editor to display an error message if the code contains the name of an undeclared variable.

2   Click **Insert** on the menu bar and then click **Procedure**. When the Add Procedure dialog box appears, type **FaxTransmittal** in the Name text box. Also verify that the Sub option button and the Public option button are selected.

3   Click the **OK** button to close the Add Procedure dialog box. The FaxTransmittal procedure is inserted into the Module1 module, and the FaxTransmittal procedure's code template appears in the Code window.

4   Close the Project Explorer window so that you can view more of the Code window.

As you learned in Tutorial 3, before entering instructions into a procedure, you should write down on a piece of paper what you want the procedure to accomplish, and the steps it will need to do so. Recall that these steps are called pseudocode. Figure 4-29 shows the pseudocode for the FaxTransmittal procedure.

1. Use the InputBox function to prompt the user to enter the recipient's name. Store the user's response in a String variable named strName.

2. Use the InputBox function to prompt the user to enter the recipient's company name. Store the user's response in a String variable named strCompany.

3. Use the InputBox function to prompt the user to enter the number of pages being faxed, excluding the fax transmittal sheet. Store the user's response in a String variable named strPages.

4. Concatenate the contents of the strName variable, the string literal constant " - " (a space, a hyphen, and a space), and the contents of the strCompany variable. Assign the result to the ToNames form field in the Fax document.

5. Assign the contents of the strPages variable, plus 1 for the fax transmittal sheet, to the NumPages form field in the Fax document.

Figure 4-29: Pseudocode for the FaxTransmittal macro procedure

After determining the steps you want the procedure to take, you can begin coding the procedure. First examine the pseudocode to determine what variables, if any, the procedure will need to use. For example, Steps 1 through 3 in the pseudocode indicate that the FaxTransmittal procedure will use the InputBox function to get the recipient's name, his or her company name, and the number of pages being faxed. As you learned in the Concept lesson, the InputBox function returns a string literal constant, so you will need to reserve three String variables in which to store that information.

Slightly less obvious in the pseudocode are the object variables that a procedure will use. You can determine that information by looking for the objects mentioned in the pseudocode. In Figure 4-29's pseudocode, for example, notice that the Fax document is mentioned in the last two steps. You can make the FaxTransmittal procedure easier to write and understand, as well as run more efficiently, by assigning the address of the Fax Document object to an object variable. You will name the object variable docFax.

Now you can declare the appropriate variables, and then translate each line in the pseudocode into one or more VBA statements.

To code the FaxTransmittal procedure:

1 The insertion point should be positioned in the blank line between the `Public Sub` and `End Sub` lines in the Code window. To declare the variables for the procedure, enter the documentation and the Dim and Set statements shown in Figure 4-30.

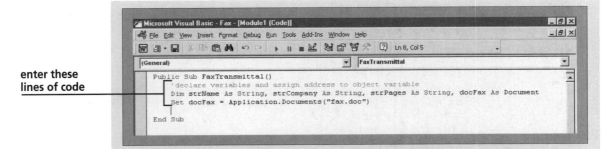

enter these lines of code

```
Public Sub FaxTransmittal()
    'declare variables and assign address to object variable
    Dim strName As String, strCompany As String, strPages As String, docFax As Document
    Set docFax = Application.Documents("fax.doc")

End Sub
```

Figure 4-30: Code window showing documentation and Dim and Set statements

The first step in the pseudocode shown in Figure 4-29 is to use the InputBox function to prompt the user to enter the recipient's name, and then assign the user's response to the strName variable. Recall that the syntax of the InputBox function is **InputBox(Prompt:=** *prompt* [**, Title:=** *title*] [**, Default:=***defaultValue*]**)**, where *prompt* is the message you want displayed inside the dialog box, *title* is the text (name) you want displayed in the dialog box's title bar, and *defaultValue* is the value you want to appear in the input area when the dialog box first opens.

2 Type **'enter recipient's name** and press the **Enter** key. Type **strname = inputbox (prompt:="Enter name:", title:="Recipient's Name")** and press the **Enter** key.

The next step is to prompt the user to enter the recipient's company, and then assign the user's response to the strCompany variable.

3 Type **'enter recipient's company** and press the **Enter** key. Type **strcompany = _** (be sure to type the equal sign followed by a space and the underscore) and press the **Enter** key. Press the **Tab** key, then type **inputbox(prompt:= "Enter company:", title:="Recipient's Company")** and press the **Enter** key.

The next step is to prompt the user to enter the number of pages being faxed, excluding the fax transmittal sheet, and then assign the user's response to the strPages variable.

4 Press the **Backspace** key to remove the indentation, then type **'enter number of pages, excluding fax transmittal sheet** and press the **Enter** key. Type **strpages = _** (be sure to type the equal sign followed by a space and the underscore) and press the **Enter** key. Press the **Tab** key, then type **inputbox(prompt:= "Enter number of pages, excluding fax transmittal sheet:", _** (be sure to type the comma followed by a space and the underscore) and press the **Enter** key. Type **title:="Pages")** and press the **Enter** key.

The fourth step in the pseudocode is to concatenate the contents of the strName variable, the string literal constant " - "(a space, a hyphen, and a space), and the contents of the strCompany variable, and then assign the result to the ToNames form field. You use the following syntax to assign a value to a form field: *documentObject* **.FormFields(***formFieldName***).Result** = *value*. In the syntax, *documentObject* is the name of a Document object, *formFieldName* is the name of a form field, and *value* is the value you want assigned to the form field. The name of the form field must be enclosed in quotation marks.

5   Press the **Backspace** key to remove the indentation. Type **'display recipient and company** and press the **Enter** key. Type **docfax.formfields("tonames").result = strname & " – " & strcompany** and press the **Enter** key.

The last step in the pseudocode is to assign the contents of the strPages variable, plus one for the fax transmittal sheet, to the NumPages form field.

6   Type the additional lines of code shown in Figure 4-31, which shows the completed FaxTransmittal macro procedure.

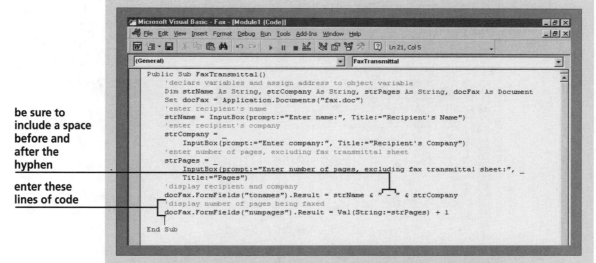

be sure to include a space before and after the hyphen

enter these lines of code

```
Public Sub FaxTransmittal()
    'declare variables and assign address to object variable
    Dim strName As String, strCompany As String, strPages As String, docFax As Document
    Set docFax = Application.Documents("fax.doc")
    'enter recipient's name
    strName = InputBox(prompt:="Enter name:", Title:="Recipient's Name")
    'enter recipient's company
    strCompany = _
        InputBox(prompt:="Enter company:", Title:="Recipient's Company")
    'enter number of pages, excluding fax transmittal sheet
    strPages = _
        InputBox(prompt:="Enter number of pages, excluding fax transmittal sheet:", _
        Title:="Pages")
    'display recipient and company
    docFax.FormFields("tonames").Result = strName & " – " & strCompany
    'display number of pages being faxed
    docFax.FormFields("numpages").Result = Val(String:=strPages) + 1

End Sub
```

Figure 4-31: Completed FaxTransmittal macro procedure

7   Verify the accuracy of your code by comparing it to the code shown in Figure 4-31, then save the Fax document.

Now that you have translated the pseudocode shown in Figure 4-29 into VBA statements, you can test the FaxTransmittal procedure to verify that it is working correctly.

To test the FaxTransmittal procedure:

1   Click the **Run Sub/UserForm** button ▶ on the toolbar to run the FaxTransmittal procedure from within the Visual Basic Editor.

tip

2   When the Recipient's Name dialog box appears and prompts you to enter a name, type **Julie Caines** and click the **OK** button.

You also can select the OK button in the InputBox function's dialog box by pressing the Enter key when the insertion point is in the input area of the dialog box.

3   When you are prompted to enter the company name, type **ABC Typing Company** and then press the **Enter** key. When you are prompted to enter the number of pages, type **4** and press the **Enter** key.

4   Click the **View Microsoft Word** button 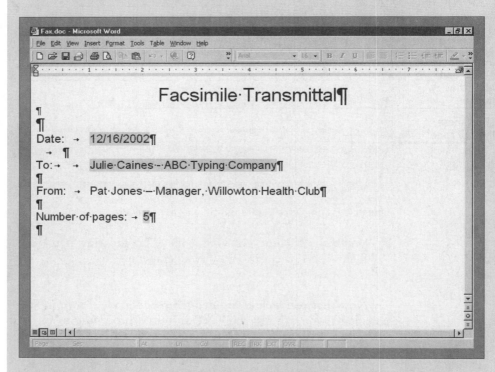 to return to Word. Figure 4-32 shows the Fax document after running the FaxTransmittal macro. Notice that the information you entered appears in the appropriate form fields in the document. (Your date might be different.)

Figure 4-32: Fax document after running the FaxTransmittal macro

Now try running the FaxTransmittal macro from Word.

5   Click **Tools** on Word's menu bar and then point to **Macro**. Notice that the Macros option is dimmed, which means that it is not currently available. When a document is protected, you cannot run a macro from the Tools menu.

6   Click the document to close the Tools menu.

You can make a macro in a protected document available to the user by adding a macro button to a toolbar. In the next section, you will learn how to create a custom toolbar named Macros that includes a custom macro button.

Creating a Custom Toolbar and Button

As you learned in the previous set of steps, you cannot use the Tools menu in Word to run a macro when a document is protected. You can give the user access to the macro by adding a button to either one of Office 2000's existing toolbars, or you can create your own toolbar and add it there. In the next set of steps, you will learn how to create a custom toolbar named Macros that includes a button that represents the FaxTransmittal macro.

To create a custom toolbar, and then add to it a button that represents a macro:

1   Click **Tools** on Word's menu bar and then click **Unprotect Document** to unprotect the Fax document.

2   Click **Tools** and then click **Customize** to open the Customize dialog box. Click the **Toolbars** tab, if necessary, and then click the **New** button. The New Toolbar dialog box appears.

You will change the custom toolbar's name from Custom 1 to Macros. The Macros toolbar should be available only to the Fax.doc document.

3   Custom 1 should be selected in the Toolbar name text box, so you need simply to type **Macros** to change the toolbar's name. Click the **Make toolbar available to** list arrow and then select **Fax.doc** in the list, as shown in Figure 4-33.

Figure 4-33: New Toolbar dialog box

tip

To make a toolbar available to all documents, select Normal.dot in the Make toolbar available to list box.

4   Click the **OK** button to close the New Toolbar dialog box. The Macros toolbar appears next to the Customize dialog box, as shown in Figure 4-34.

Macros toolbar (your toolbar's location might be different)

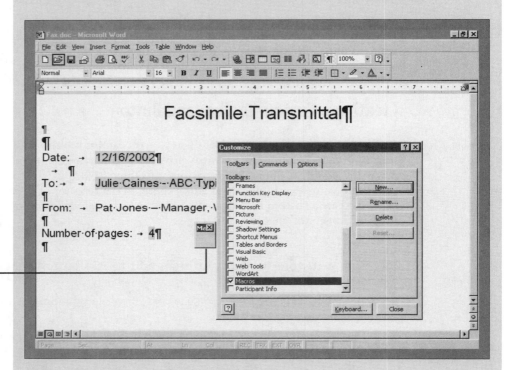

Figure 4-34: Macros toolbar added to the document

HELP? Do not be concerned if your toolbar appears in a different location on the screen.

Next you will add a FaxTransmittal button to the Macros toolbar.

5   Click the **Commands** tab in the Customize dialog box. Scroll down the Categories list box and then click **Macros** in the list.

The FaxTransmittal macro is located in the Fax.doc document.

6   Click the **Save in** list arrow and then click **Fax.doc** in the list, if necessary. Project.Module1.FaxTransmittal appears in the Commands list box.

7   Click **Project.Module1.FaxTransmittal** in the Commands list box and hold down the mouse button as you drag **Project.Module1.FaxTransmittal** to the Macros toolbar, as shown in Figure 4-35.

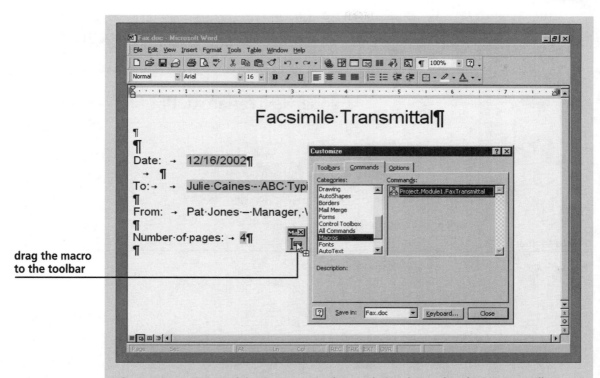

drag the macro to the toolbar

Figure 4-35: Project.Module1.FaxTransmittal macro being dragged to the Macros toolbar

8 Release the mouse button. The Project.Module1.FaxTransmittal button appears on the Macros toolbar.

Now shorten the name that appears on the button and add an icon to the button.

9 Right-click the **Project.Module1.FaxTransmittal** button on the Macros toolbar. Click **Name** on the shortcut menu, then type **FAX** and press the **Enter** key.

10 Right-click the **FAX** button on the Macros toolbar, then point to **Change Button Image**. A palette of icons is displayed. Click the **telephone icon** (second row, fifth button from the left) in the icon palette, then click the **Close** button in the Customize dialog box. Drag the Macros toolbar to the upper-right corner of the document, as shown in Figure 4-36.

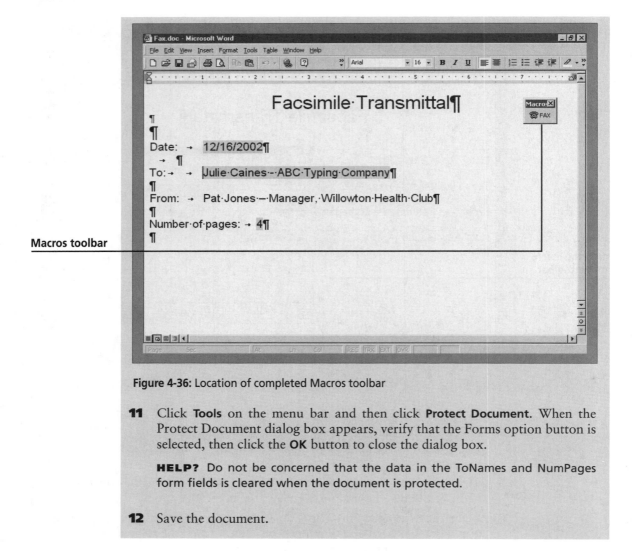

Macros toolbar

Figure 4-36: Location of completed Macros toolbar

11 Click **Tools** on the menu bar and then click **Protect Document**. When the Protect Document dialog box appears, verify that the Forms option button is selected, then click the **OK** button to close the dialog box.

HELP? Do not be concerned that the data in the ToNames and NumPages form fields is cleared when the document is protected.

12 Save the document.

Now test the FAX button to see if it runs the FaxTransmittal macro.

To test the FAX button:

1 Click the **FAX** button on the Macros toolbar. Enter your name as the recipient name, **Henderson Inc.** as the company name, and **2** as the number of pages.

2 Save the Fax document, then exit Word.

You now have completed Tutorial 4's Word lesson. You can either take a break or complete the end-of-lesson exercises before moving on to the next lesson.

E X E R C I S E S

1. In this exercise, you will add form fields to a document. You also will create a macro procedure that prompts the user for the form field information. Additionally, you will create a custom toolbar.

    a. Open the T4-WD-E1 (T4-WD-E1.doc) document, which is located in the Tut04\Word folder on your Data Disk. Save the document as T4-WD-E1D.doc.

    b. Display the nonprinting characters in the document. View the Forms toolbar. Add four form fields to the document, as shown in Figure 4-37. Name the form fields as shown in the figure. Have the CurrentDate form field display the current date in the MMMM d, yyyy format. (Your current date might be different from the one shown in the figure.)

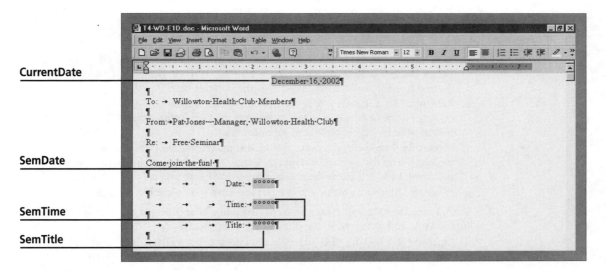

Figure 4-37

    c. Close the Forms toolbar. Open the Visual Basic Editor. Create a macro procedure named GetSemInfo. The procedure's pseudocode is shown in Figure 4-38.

1. Use the InputBox function to prompt the user to enter the seminar date in the mm/dd/yy format. Store the user's response in a String variable named strSemDate.

2. Use the InputBox function to prompt the user to enter the time that the seminar begins (for example, 5 p.m.). Store the user's response in a String variable named strBegTime.

3. Use the InputBox function to prompt the user to enter the time that the seminar ends (for example, 7:30 p.m.). Store the user's response in a String variable named strEndTime.

4. Use the InputBox function to prompt the user to enter the seminar title. Store the user's response in a String variable named strTitle.

5. Assign the contents of the strSemDate variable to the SemDate form field in the document.

6. Concatenate the contents of the strBegTime variable, the string literal constant " - " (a space, a hyphen, and a space), and the contents of the strEndTime variable. Assign the result to the SemTime form field in the document.

7. Assign the contents of the strTitle variable to the SemTitle form field in the document.

Figure 4-38

d. Save the document, then run the GetSemInfo procedure from within the Visual Basic Editor. Enter 4/2/02 as the seminar date, 5 p.m. as the beginning time, 7:30 p.m. as the ending time, and "Eating Right" as the seminar title.

e. Return to Word. Create a Macros toolbar that is available only to the T4-WD-E1D.doc document, then add a button that represents the GetSemInfo procedure to it. Name the button Seminar and select an appropriate icon.

f. Protect the document, then save the document. Use the Seminar button on the Macros toolbar to run the GetSemInfo macro. Enter 4/3/02 as the seminar date, 7 p.m. as the beginning time, 9 p.m. as the ending time, and "Exercising is Fun" as the seminar title.

g. When the macro is working correctly, save and then close the document.

2. In this exercise, you will create a macro procedure that prompts the user for the information to be entered in the document's form fields.

a. Open the T4-WD-E2 (T4-WD-E2D.doc) document, which is located in the Tut04\Word folder on your Data Disk. Click the Enable Macros button, if necessary. If the Macros toolbar is not displayed, click View, point to Toolbars, and then click Macros. Save the document as T4-WD-E2D.

b. The document contains five form fields, named CurrentDate, Name, Grade, Course, and Professor.

c. Open the Visual Basic Editor. Open the Module1 module's Code window, then view the GetGradeInfo procedure. Code the procedure so that it allows the user to enter the student's name and his or her grade, and also the course ID and the professor's name. The procedure should assign the information to the appropriate form fields in the document.

d. Save the document, then return to Word. Use the Grade button on the Macros toolbar to run the GetGradeInfo macro. Enter your name, grade, course ID, and professor's name.

e. When the macro is working correctly, save and then close the document.

Exercises 3 and 4 are Discovery Exercises. Discovery Exercises, which may include topics that are not covered in this lesson, allow you to "discover" the solutions to problems on your own.

discovery ▶

3. In this exercise, you will create a macro procedure that calculates the total amount owed based on information entered by the user. The procedure then assigns the information and the result of the calculation to the document's form fields.

    a. Open the T4-WD-E3 (T4-WD-E3.doc) document, which is located in the Tut04\Word folder on your Data Disk. Click the Enable Macros button, if necessary. If the Macros toolbar is not displayed, click View, point to Toolbars, and then click Macros. Save the document as T4-WD-E3D. Figure 4-39 shows the document with the nonprinting characters displayed. (Your date might be different from the one shown in the figure.)

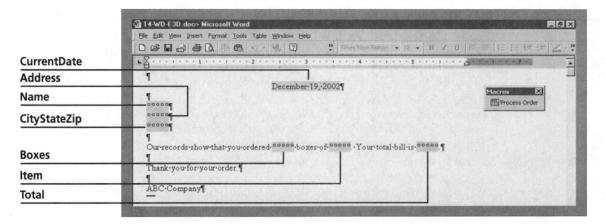

Figure 4-39

    b. Open the Visual Basic Editor. Open the Module1 module's Code window, then view the ProcessOrder procedure. Code the procedure so that it will allow the user to enter the customer's name, address, city, state, and zip code. Use the current value of the appropriate form field as the *defaultValue* in the InputBox functions that get this information. The user also will need to enter the number of boxes ordered, the item ordered, and the price of one box of the item. The procedure should calculate the total amount owed (number of boxes ordered times the price of one box). The procedure should assign the necessary information (name, address, city, state, zip code, number of boxes ordered, item ordered, and total amount due) to the appropriate form fields in the document.

    c. Save the document, then test the document from within the Visual Basic Editor. Enter your name, address, city, state, and zip code. Enter 25 as the number of boxes, enter paper clips as the item, and enter 4 as the box price.

    d. Return to Word. Use the Process Order button on the Macros toolbar to run the ProcessOrder macro. Enter your name, address, city, state, and zip code. Enter 20 as the number of boxes, enter pencils as the item, and enter 8 as the box price.

    e. When the macro is working correctly, save and then close the document.

discovery ▶ 4. In this exercise, you will learn about the VBA Call statement.

   a. Open the Fax (Fax.doc) document that you created in this lesson. The document is located in the Tut04\Word folder on your Data Disk. Click the Enable Macros button, if necessary. Save the document as T4-WD-E4D.

   b. Open the Visual Basic Editor. View the Help screen for the Call statement. Close the Help window.

   c. Right-click the ThisDocument that appears in the T4-WD-E4D project in the Project Explorer window, then click View Code. View the Document object's Open event procedure.

   d. In the Document object's Open event procedure, enter a Call statement that calls the FaxTransmittal procedure.

   e. Open the FaxTransmittal procedure, which is located in the Module1 module. Change the file name in the Set statement from "fax.doc" to "t4-wd-e4d.doc".

   f. Save the document. Return to Word and close the document.

   g. Open the T4-WD-E4D (T4-WD-E4D.doc) document, which will invoke the Document object's Open event. Click the Enable Macros button, if necessary. The Open event calls (runs) the FaxTransmittal procedure. Enter your name as the recipient name. Enter XYZ Company as the company name, and enter 2 as the number of pages.

   h. When the Open event is working correctly, save and then close the document.

A computer program is good only if it works. Errors in programming code can cause a program to run incorrectly. Therefore, a programmer needs to know how to locate and fix any errors in his or her code. Exercise 5 is a Debugging Exercise. Debugging Exercises allow you to practice recognizing and solving errors in code.

debugging   5. In this exercise, you will debug an existing macro procedure.

   a. Open the T4-WD-E5 (T4-WD-E5.doc) document, which is located in the Tut04\Word folder on your Data Disk. Click the Enable Macros button, if necessary. Save the document as T4-WD-E5D.

   b. Open the Visual Basic Editor. Open the Module1 module's Code window, then view the BookInfo procedure. Study the procedure's code, then run the procedure. Enter "Paris in the Summer" (without the quotation marks) as the book title, "Jack Perkins" (without the quotation marks) as the author, and "Course Technology" (without the quotation marks) as the publisher. When the error message appears in the dialog box, click the Debug button to locate the error. Click the Reset button ■ on the standard toolbar to stop the procedure.

   c. Correct the error in the `docBook.FormFields("booktitle").Result = strTitle` instruction. (*Hint*: You will need to return to Word and unprotect the document to verify the form field's name. Be sure to protect the document before returning to the Visual Basic Editor.)

   d. Save the document and run the procedure again. Enter "Paris in the Summer" as the book title, "Jack Perkins" as the author, and "Course Technology" as the publisher.

   e. Return to Word. Although the procedure did not end in an error, you will notice that it still is not working correctly. Return to the Visual Basic Editor and correct the BookInfo procedure.

   f. Save the document, then run the procedure again, using "Paris in the Summer", "Jack Perkins", and "Course Technology" as the title, author, and publisher, respectively. When the procedure is working correctly, save and then close the document.

Access Lesson

Using String Variables in Access

case▶ In Tutorial 3's Access lesson, you created the DisplayByGrade macro for Professor Martinez of Snowville College. Recall that the macro allowed Professor Martinez to display an Access report named StudentReport in ascending order by the Grade field. Professor Martinez now would like a procedure that will allow him to display the report in either ascending or descending order by any field he chooses.

Creating the SelectFieldOrder Procedure

Begin by opening Professor Martinez's database, which is located in the Tut04\Access folder on your Data Disk, then view the StudentReport report.

To open Professor Martinez's database, then view the StudentReport report:

1 Start Microsoft Access, then open the **Econ201** (Econ201.mdb) database. Click the **Maximize** button ☐ on the Microsoft Access title bar to maximize the Microsoft Access window, if necessary.

2 Click **Reports** in the Objects bar of the Database window to display the Reports list. The Reports list box shows that the database contains one report named StudentReport.

3 Right-click **StudentReport** and then click **Print Preview** to view the report. Maximize the report window. Figure 4-40 shows the maximized StudentReport report.

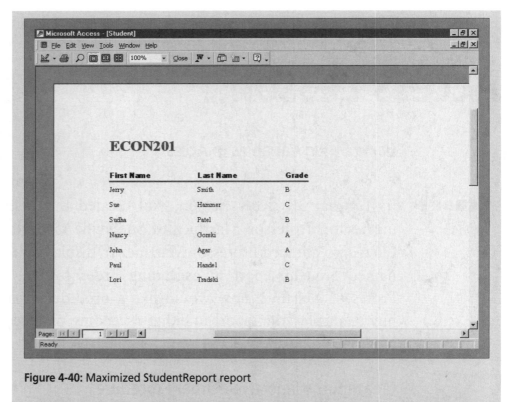

Figure 4-40: Maximized StudentReport report

Notice that the records shown in the report are not in any specific order.

4   Close the report.

Now open the Visual Basic Editor and insert a module and the SelectFieldOrder procedure into the current project.

To open the Visual Basic Editor and insert a module and a procedure into the Econ201 project:

1   Press **Alt+F11** to open the Visual Basic Editor. Open the Project Explorer window, if necessary, and close the Properties window, the Immediate window, and any open Code windows.

2   Click **Tools** on the Visual Basic Editor menu bar, and then click **Options** to open the Options dialog box. Click the **Require Variable Declaration** check box to select it, if necessary. Recall that selecting this check box tells the Visual Basic Editor to automatically enter the Option Explicit statement in any new modules added to the project. Click the **OK** button to close the Options dialog box.

3 The Econ201 (Econ201) project should already be selected in the Project Explorer window. Click **Insert** on the menu bar and then click **Module**. The Visual Basic Editor inserts the Modules folder and the Module1 module into the current project. The General Declarations section of the Module1 module appears in the Code window. Because you selected the Require Variable Declaration check box, the Option Explicit statement is automatically entered into the module's General Declarations section for you. Recall that the Option Explicit statement tells the Visual Basic Editor to display an error message if your code contains the name of an undeclared variable.

► **tip**

The Option Compare statement designates the technique Access uses to compare and sort text data. The default, Database, means that Access compares and sorts letters in normal alphabetical order.

4 Click **Insert** on the menu bar and then click **Procedure**. When the Add Procedure dialog box appears, type **SelectFieldOrder** in the Name text box. Click the **Function** option button to select it. Also verify that the Public option button is selected. Click the **OK** button to close the Add Procedure dialog box. The Visual Basic Editor inserts the SelectFieldOrder procedure into the Module1 module, and the SelectFieldOrder procedure's code template appears in the Code window.

5 Close the Project Explorer window so that you can view more of the Code window.

As you learned in Tutorial 3, before entering instructions into a procedure, you should write down on a piece of paper what you want the procedure to accomplish, and the steps it will need to do so. Recall that these steps are called pseudocode. Figure 4-41 shows the pseudocode for the SelectFieldOrder procedure.

1. Open the StudentReport report.

2. Use the InputBox function to prompt the user to enter the field name. Store the user's response in a String variable named strField.

3. Use the InputBox function to prompt the user to enter the order, either asc for ascending or desc for descending. Store the user's response in a String variable named strOrder.

4. Display the StudentReport report with the records sorted according to the field (strField) and order (strOrder) entered by the user.

Figure 4-41: Pseudocode for the SelectFieldOrder procedure

After determining the steps you want the procedure to take, you can begin coding the procedure. First examine the pseudocode to determine what variables, if any, the procedure will need to use. For example, Steps 2 and 3 in the pseudocode indicate that the SelectFieldOrder procedure will use the InputBox function to get the field name and the sort order—either asc for ascending or desc for descending. As you learned in the Concept lesson, the InputBox function returns a string literal constant, so you will need to reserve two String variables in which to store that information.

Slightly less obvious in the pseudocode are the object variables that a procedure will use. You can determine that information by looking for the objects mentioned in the pseudocode. In Figure 4-41's pseudocode, for example, notice that the StudentReport report is mentioned in the last step. You can make the SelectFieldOrder procedure easier to write and understand, as well as run more efficiently, by assigning the address of the StudentReport Report object to an object variable. You will name the object variable rptStudent.

Now you can declare the appropriate variables, and then translate each line in the pseudocode into one or more VBA statements.

To code the SelectFieldOrder procedure:

1 The insertion point should be positioned in the blank line between the `Public Function` and `End Function` lines in the Code window. Press the **Tab** key, then type **'declare variables** and press the **Enter** key, then type **dim strField as string, strOrder as string, rptStudent as report** and press the **Enter** key.

As you learned in Tutorial 3, you cannot assign a Report object to an object variable unless the report is open. Opening the StudentReport report is Step 1 in the pseudocode.

2 Type **'open the report** and press the **Enter** key, then type **docmd.openreport** and press the **spacebar**. Type _ (the underscore) and press the **Enter** key. Press the **Tab** key to indent this portion of the instruction, then type **reportname:="studentreport", view:=acviewpreview** and press the **Enter** key.

Now assign the address of the open report to the rptStudent object variable. Recall that open reports in Access belong to the Application object's Reports collection.

3 Press the **Backspace** key to remove the indentation, then type **'assign address to object variable** and press the **Enter** key. Type **set rptstudent = application.reports("studentreport")** and press the **Enter** key.

Step 2 in Figure 4-41's pseudocode is to use the InputBox function to prompt the user to enter the field name, and then assign the user's response to the strField variable. Recall that the syntax of the InputBox function is **InputBox(Prompt:=***prompt* [**, Title:=***title*] [**, Default:=***defaultValue*]**), where *prompt* is the message you want displayed inside the dialog box, *title* is the text (name) you want displayed in the dialog box's title bar, and *defaultValue* is the value you want to appear in the input area when the dialog box first opens.

Because Professor Martinez typically displays the report in ascending order by the Grade field, you will make "grade" the *defaultValue* in the InputBox function.

4 Type **'enter field name** and press the **Enter** key. Type **strfield = _** (be sure to type the equal sign followed by a space and the underscore) and press the **Enter** key. Press the **Tab** key, then type **inputbox(prompt:="Enter the field name (StudentID, LastName, FirstName, Grade):", _** (be sure to type the comma followed by a space and the underscore) and press the **Enter** key. Type **title:="Field", default:="grade")** and press the **Enter** key.

The next step is to prompt the user to enter the sort order, either asc for ascending or desc for descending, and then assign the user's response to the strOrder variable. As mentioned earlier, Professor Martinez typically arranges the records in ascending order, so you will make the keyword asc the default value.

5 Press the **Backspace** key to remove the indentation, then type **'enter order** and press the **Enter** key. Type **strorder = inputbox(prompt:="Enter sort order (either asc or desc):", _** (be sure to type the comma followed by a space and the underscore) and press the **Enter** key. Press the **Tab** key, then type **title:="Order", default:="asc")** and press the **Enter** key.

The next step in Figure 4-41's pseudocode is to arrange the records in the proper order, based on the contents of the strField and strOrder variables. As you learned in Tutorial 3, you change the order of the records that appear in a report first by setting the Report object's OrderByOn property and then setting its OrderBy property. The syntax of the OrderByOn property is *objectName*.**OrderByOn** = *booleanValue*, where *objectName* is the name of either a Report or Form object, and *booleanValue* is either the Boolean value True or the Boolean value False. The syntax of the OrderBy property is *objectName*.**OrderBy** = *"fieldNames order"*, where *objectName* is the name of either a Report or Form object, and *fieldNames* is one or more field names, separated by commas. *Order* in the syntax is either the keyword asc or the keyword desc, or a String variable that contains either keyword. To sort the StudentReport report according to the field and sort order entered by the user, you will need to concatenate the contents of the strField variable, a space, and the contents of the strOrder variable, and then assign the result to the StudentReport Report object's OrderBy property.

6 Press the **Backspace** key to remove the indentation, then type the additional three lines of code shown in Figure 4-42, which shows the completed SelectFieldOrder procedure.

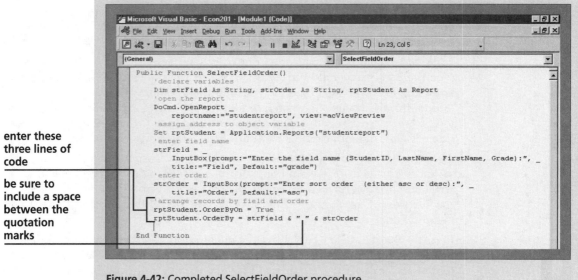

enter these
three lines of
code

be sure to
include a space
between the
quotation
marks

```
Microsoft Visual Basic - Econ201 - [Module1 (Code)]
File  Edit  View  Insert  Debug  Run  Tools  Add-Ins  Window  Help

(General)                                          SelectFieldOrder

Public Function SelectFieldOrder()
    'declare variables
    Dim strField As String, strOrder As String, rptStudent As Report
    'open the report
    DoCmd.OpenReport _
        reportname:="studentreport", view:=acViewPreview
    'assign address to object variable
    Set rptStudent = Application.Reports("studentreport")
    'enter field name
    strField = _
        InputBox(prompt:="Enter the field name (StudentID, LastName, FirstName, Grade):", _
        title:="Field", Default:="grade")
    'enter order
    strOrder = InputBox(prompt:="Enter sort order  (either asc or desc):", _
        title:="Order", Default:="asc")
    'arrange records by field and order
    rptStudent.OrderByOn = True
    rptStudent.OrderBy = strField & " " & strOrder

End Function
```

Figure 4-42: Completed SelectFieldOrder procedure

7 Verify the accuracy of your code before continuing, then save the database.
When you are asked for a name for the module, click the **OK** button to accept
the default name, Module1.

Now that you have translated the pseudocode shown in Figure 4-41 into VBA
statements, you can create the macro that Professor Martinez can use to run the
SelectFieldOrder procedure.

Creating the SelectFieldOrderMacro Macro

As you learned in Tutorial 1, you use the Macro window to create an Access macro,
which can be run from either the Macro window or the Database window in Access.

To create the SelectFieldOrderMacro macro, and then save and run the macro:

1 Click the **View Microsoft Access** button 📷 on the Visual Basic Editor's
Standard toolbar to return to Access. Click **Macros** in the Objects bar of the
Database window, then click the **New** button 🔲 in the Database window's
toolbar to open the Macro window.

Recall that in the Macro window, you record the tasks that you want the
macro to perform. You do so by selecting one or more actions from the
Action combo box.

2 Click the **Action list arrow** that appears in the first line of the Macro window. Scroll down the list until you see RunCode, then click **RunCode**. Click **Function Name** in the Action Arguments section of the window, then type **SelectFieldOrder()** (be sure to type the parentheses) as the function name.

3 Click the **Save** button 🖫 on the Standard toolbar. When you are asked for the macro name, type **SelectFieldOrderMacro** and click the **OK** button, then close the Macro window.

4 Right-click **SelectFieldOrderMacro** in the Macros list, then click **Run**. When the Field dialog box appears, type **lastname** and click the **OK** button.

You also can select the OK button in the InputBox function's dialog box by pressing the Enter key when the insertion point is in the input area of the dialog box.

5 When the Order dialog box appears, type **desc** and press the **Enter** key. The StudentReport report appears with the records in descending order by the LastName field, as shown in Figure 4-43.

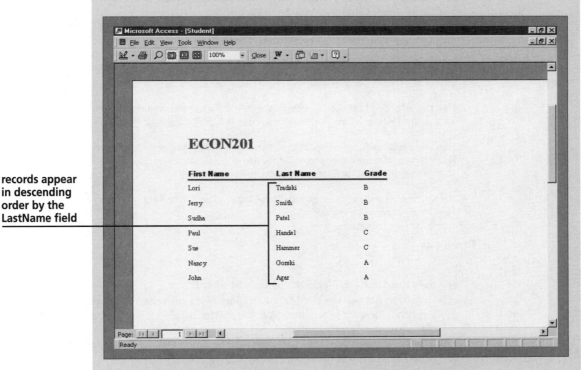

records appear in descending order by the LastName field

Figure 4-43: StudentReport report in descending order by the LastName field

6 Close the report, then compact the database and close Access.

You now have completed Tutorial 4's Access lesson. You can either take a break or complete the end-of-lesson exercises.

 # EXERCISES

1. In this exercise, you will create a function procedure and a macro. The function procedure will allow the user to specify the field and order to use when displaying the records in a report.
    a. Use Windows to make a copy of the Members (Members.mdb) database, which is located in the Tut04\Access folder on your Data Disk. Rename the copy T4-AC-E1D.mdb.
    b. Open the T4-AC-E1D (T4-AC-E1D.mdb) database in Access. Open the Members table in design view. Notice that the field names are ID, FirstName, LastName, OrganizationName, and DuesAmount. Close the table.
    c. Preview the MemberReport report. Notice that the report is in ascending order by the ID field. Close the report.
    d. Open the Visual Basic Editor. Create a function procedure named ReportFieldOrder. The pseudocode for the procedure is shown in Figure 4-44.

---

1. Open the MemberReport report.

2. Use the InputBox function to prompt the user to enter the field name. Make ID the default field name. Store the user's response in a String variable named strField.

3. Use the InputBox function to prompt the user to enter the order, either asc for ascending or desc for descending. Make asc the default order. Store the user's response in a String variable named strOrder.

4. Display the report with the records sorted according to the field (strField) and order (strOrder) entered by the user.

Figure 4-44

    e. Save the database. Name the module Module1.
    f. Return to Access. Use the Macro window to create a macro that runs the ReportFieldOrder procedure. Save the macro, naming it ReportFieldOrderMacro, then close the Macro window.
    g. Run the ReportFieldOrderMacro macro from the Database window. Display the report in ascending order by the OrganizationName field.
    h. Close the report, then compact and close the database.
2. In this exercise, you will create a function procedure and a macro. The function procedure will allow the user to specify the field and order to use when displaying the records in a form.

a. Use Windows to make a copy of the Members (Members.mdb) database, which is located in the Tut04\Access folder on your Data Disk. Rename the copy T4-AC-E2D.mdb.

b. Open the T4-AC-E2D (T4-AC-E2D.mdb) database in Access. Open the Members table in design view. Notice that the field names are ID, FirstName, LastName, OrganizationName, and DuesAmount. Close the table.

c. Open the MemberForm form. Scroll through the records, then close the form.

d. Open the Visual Basic Editor. Create a function procedure named FormOrder that will allow the user to control the arrangement of the records in the MemberForm entry form. Allow the user to select the field and the order, either ascending or descending. Make the ID field the default field, and make descending order the default order. (*Hints*: You must open a form before you can assign its address to an object variable. Open forms belong to the Application object's Forms collection. The three-character ID for a Form object is *frm*. Use acNormal as the *view* argument.)

e. Save the database. Name the module Module1.

f. Return to Access. Use the Macro window to create a macro that runs the FormOrder procedure. Save the macro, naming it FormOrderMacro, then close the Macro window.

g. Run the FormOrderMacro macro from the Database window. Display the records in the entry form in descending order by the LastName field. Scroll through the records to verify that they appear in the appropriate order in the form. Add your record to the end of the table.

h. Close the form, then compact and close the database.

Exercises 3 and 4 are Discovery Exercises. Discovery Exercises, which may include topics that are not covered in this lesson, allow you to "discover" the solutions to problems on your own.

discovery ▶ **3.** In this exercise, you will create a function procedure and a macro. The function procedure will use the contents of two fields to sort the records in a report.

a. Use Windows to make a copy of the Members (Members.mdb) database, which is located in the Tut04\Access folder on your Data Disk. Rename the copy T4-AC-E3D.mdb.

b. Open the T4-AC-E3D (T4-AC-E3D.mdb) database in Access. Open the Members table in design view. Notice that the field names are ID, FirstName, LastName, OrganizationName, and DuesAmount. Close the table.

c. Preview the MemberReport report. You will notice that the report is in ascending order by the ID field. Close the report.

d. Open the Visual Basic Editor. Create a function procedure named TwoFields. The procedure should allow the user to select both a primary and a secondary field on which to sort. Make the LastName field the default for the primary field, and make the FirstName field the default for the secondary field. Always sort the records in ascending order.

e. Save the database. Name the module Module1.

f. Return to Access. Use the Macro window to create a macro that runs the TwoFields procedure. Save the macro, naming it TwoFieldsMacro, then close the Macro window.

g. Run the TwoFieldsMacro macro from the Database window. Display the report in ascending order by the LastName and FirstName fields. (The LastName field should be the primary field, and the FirstName field should be the secondary field.)

h. Close the report, then compact and close the database.

discovery ▶ 4. In this exercise, you will learn about the VBA Call statement.
   a. Use Windows to make a copy of the Econ201 (Econ201.mdb) database that you completed in this lesson. The database is located in the Tut04\Access folder on your Data Disk. Rename the copy T4-AC-E4D.mdb.
   b. Open the T4-AC-E4D (T4-AC-E4D.mdb) database in Access. Open the StudentReport report in design view. Right-click the report selector box on the Design View window, and then click Properties on the shortcut menu. Click the Other tab on the property sheet, then change the value of the Has Module property to Yes. Close the property sheet. Save and then close the report.
   c. Open the Visual Basic Editor. View the Help screen for the Call statement. Close the Help window.
   d. Open the StudentReport report's Open event procedure. In the Open event procedure, enter a Call statement that calls the SelectFieldOrder procedure.
   e. Save the database. Return to Access. Close the report, if necessary, then open the report in print preview. Display the report in ascending order by the Grade field.
   f. Close the report, then compact and close the database.

A computer program is good only if it works. Errors in programming code can cause a program to run incorrectly. Therefore, a programmer needs to know how to locate and fix any errors in his or her code. Exercise 5 is a Debugging Exercise. Debugging Exercises allow you to practice recognizing and solving errors in code.

debugging 5. In this exercise, you will debug an existing macro procedure.
   a. Use Windows to make a copy of the T4-AC-E5 (T4-AC-E5.mdb) database, which is located in the Tut04\Access folder on your Data Disk. Rename the copy T4-AC-E5D.mdb.
   b. Open the T4-AC-E5D (T4-AC-E5D. mdb) database in Access.
   c. Open the Visual Basic Editor. Open the Module1 module's Code window. Use the Code window's Procedure box to view the GetField procedure. Study the code.
   d. Return to Access and run the GetFieldMacro macro. When you are prompted to enter the field name, type grade and press the Enter key. When the error message appears in a dialog box, click the Debug button to locate the error. Click the Reset button ■ on the Standard toolbar to stop the procedure, then click the Halt button. Close the report, then return to the Visual Basic Editor and fix any errors.
   e. Run the GetFieldMacro macro again. When the macro is working correctly, display the report in ascending order by the Grade field.
   f. Close the report, then compact and close the database.

Date
Variables

objectives

In this tutorial, you will learn how to:

- Reserve a Date variable
- Use an assignment statement to assign a value to a Date variable
- Assign the VBA Date, Time, and Now functions to a Date variable
- Control the appearance of dates and times using the Format function
- Perform calculations using Date variables
- Convert a string to a Date data type using the DateValue and TimeValue functions
- Refer to the active cell in Excel
- Use the Range object's Offset property in Excel
- Preview and print a document in Word
- Refer to a control on an Access form
- Create a custom toolbar in Access

Concept Lesson

Date Variables

In Tutorial 4, you learned how to reserve a procedure-level String variable. Recall that a String variable is a memory cell that can store a string—zero or more characters enclosed in quotation marks—and that a procedure-level variable is one that can be used only by the procedure in which it is declared. A procedure-level variable remains in memory until the procedure in which it is declared ends. In this tutorial, you will learn how to reserve a procedure-level **Date variable**, which is a variable that can store date and time information.

Reserving a Procedure-level Date Variable

As you learned in Tutorial 3, you reserve a procedure-level variable by entering the appropriate Dim statement within a procedure. Recall that the syntax of the Dim statement is **Dim** *variablename* **As** *datatype*, where *variablename* is the name of the variable, and *datatype* represents the type of data the variable can store. When creating a Date variable, *datatype* is always the keyword **Date**. Date variables are automatically initialized to the number 0. Figure 5-1 shows examples of Dim statements that reserve Date variables.

```
Dim dtmPay As Date

Dim dtmEmploy As Date

Dim dtmStart As Date

Dim dtmEnd As Date

Dim dtmBirth As Date
```

Figure 5-1: Examples of Dim statements that reserve Date variables

Notice that the name of each of the Date variables shown in Figure 5-1 begins with *dtm*, which is the three-character ID associated with a Date variable; the *d* stands for *date* and the *tm* stands for *time*. The *dtm* ID indicates that the variable is a Date variable, which can store date and time information.

After using the Dim statement to both reserve and initialize a Date variable, you can use an assignment statement to assign a different value to the variable.

Using An Assignment Statement to Assign a Value to a Date Variable

Recall that the format of an assignment statement that assigns a value to a variable is *variablename* = *value*. Figure 5-2 shows examples of assignment statements that assign date and time values, more technically referred to as **date literal constants**, to the Date variables reserved in Figure 5-1.

```
dtmPay = #January 7, 2003#

dtmEmploy = #12/31/2002#

dtmStart = #11:05:00 AM#

dtmEnd = #7:30:07 PM#

dtmBirth = #July 4, 1980 12:05:00 PM#
```

Figure 5-2: Assignment statements that assign date literal constants to the Date variables declared in Figure 5-1

As Figure 5-2 indicates, date literal constants are enclosed in number signs (#). A date literal constant can be a date (such as #January 7, 2003# and #12/31/2002#), or it can be a time (such as #11:05:00 AM# and #7:30:07 PM#). Date literal constants also can include both a date and a time—for example, #July 4, 1980 12:05:00 PM#. Notice that you use a space to separate the date and time within the number signs. Date variables can store dates that range from January 1, 100 through December 31, 9999, and times that range from 0:00:00 (12:00:00 AM) through 23:59:59 (11:59:59 PM).

●●

VBA recognizes dates and times entered in many different formats. You can experiment with the different formats by completing this lesson's Exercise 4.

●●

Similar to the way VBA does not store the quotation marks ("") surrounding a string literal constant in a String variable, VBA also does not store the number signs (#) surrounding a date literal constant in a Date variable, as illustrated in Figure 5-3.

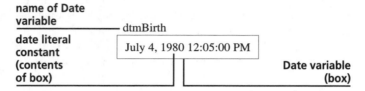

Figure 5-3: Illustration of a date literal constant stored in a Date variable

In addition to assigning date literal constants to Date variables, you also can assign the value returned by VBA's Date, Time, and Now functions.

Using VBA's Date, Time, and Now Functions

Recall that a function is a procedure that returns a value. VBA's **Date function**, for example, returns the system date, which is the date maintained by your computer's internal clock. VBA's **Time function** returns the system time, which is the time maintained by your computer's internal clock. VBA's **Now function** returns both the system date and time. You can use an assignment statement to assign the values returned by these functions to Date variables, as shown in Figure 5-4's AssignDisplayDate procedure.

```
Public Sub AssignDisplayDate()
    'declare Date variables
    Dim dtmCurDate As Date
    Dim dtmCurTime As Date
    Dim dtmCurDateTime As Date

    'assign values to Date variables
    dtmCurDate = Date
    dtmCurTime = Time
    dtmCurDateTime = Now

    'display contents of Date variables
    MsgBox Prompt:=dtmCurDate & vbNewLine _
        & dtmCurTime & vbNewLine & dtmCurDateTime
End Sub
```

Figure 5-4: AssignDisplayDate procedure

The AssignDisplayDate procedure first reserves three Date variables named dtmCurDate, dtmCurTime, and dtmCurDateTime. The `dtmCurDate = Date` instruction assigns the current system date to the dtmCurDate variable, and the `dtmCurTime = Time` instruction assigns the current system time to the dtmCurTime variable. The `dtmCurDateTime = Now` instruction assigns both the system date and the system time to the dtmCurDateTime variable. The last instruction shown in Figure 5-4 uses the MsgBox statement, along with string concatenation and the intrinsic constant `vbNewLine`, to display the contents of the three Date variables in a message box. The `vbNewLine` constant causes the insertion point to move to the next line in the message box. Figure 5-5 shows the message box that will appear on the screen when the AssignDisplayDate procedure is run.

 tip

As you learned in Tutorial 2, an intrinsic constant is a word that is defined by the application and typically represents a numeric value. Constants are more meaningful than the numbers they represent, so they are easier to understand and remember.

each item
appears on a
different line

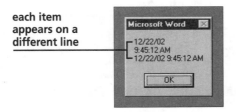

Figure 5-5: Message box displayed by the AssignDisplayDate procedure

Notice that the first line in the message box displays the date in the mm/dd/yy format, which is called the Short Date format. The second line displays the time in the hh:mm:ss AM/PM format, known in VBA as the Long Time format. The third line displays both the date and time; here again, the date appears in the Short Date format and the time appears in the Long Time format. You can use the VBA Format function to display dates and times in formats other than Short Date and Long Time.

 tip

The default formats used to display dates and times are system dependent. The formats are controlled by the values selected on the Date and Time tabs on the Windows Control Panel's Regional Settings Properties dialog box.

Using the Format Function

You can use the VBA **Format function** to control the appearance of dates and times. The syntax of the Format function is **Format(Expression:=**_expression_**, Format:=**_format_**)**. In the syntax, _expression_ specifies the number, date, time, or string whose appearance you want to format, and _format_ is the name of a predefined VBA format. Figure 5-6 shows the Help screen for the predefined date/time formats in VBA.

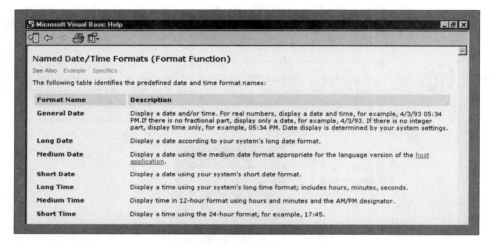

Figure 5-6: Help screen showing the VBA predefined date/time formats

If you want greater control over the appearance of the Format function's _expression_, you can use a string containing special symbols, rather than a predefined format, as the _format_ argument. You can learn more about these special symbols by completing this lesson's Exercise 5.

Figure 5-7 shows some examples of using the Format function to control the display of dates and times.

Format function and result
`Format(Expression:=#1/3/2002#, Format:="General Date")` Result: 1/3/02
`Format(Expression:=#1/3/2002#, Format:="Long Date")` Result: Thursday, January 03, 2002
`Format(Expression:=#1/3/2002#, Format:="Medium Date")` Result: 03-Jan-02
`Format(Expression:=#1/3/2002#, Format:="Short Date")` Result: 1/3/02
`Format(Expression:=#5:09:00 PM#, Format:="General Date")` Result: 05:09:00 PM
`Format(Expression:=#5:09:00 PM#, Format:="Long Time")` Result: 05:09:00 PM
`Format(Expression:=#5:09:00 PM#, Format:="Medium Time")` Result: 05:09 PM
`Format(Expression:=#5:09:00 PM#, Format:="Short Time")` Result: 17:09

Figure 5-7: Examples of using the Format function to control the display of dates and times

Notice that the Short Time format displays a time using a 24-hour, rather than a 12-hour, format. The 24-hour format is sometimes referred to as military time.

In the next section, you will learn how to use dates and times in calculations.

Using Dates and Times in Calculations

At times, you may need to include dates and times in the calculations performed by a procedure. For example, a procedure designed to determine an invoice's due date, which is 15 days from the invoice date, will need to add the number 15 to the invoice date. Similarly, a procedure designed to determine the number of years an employee has been with a company will need to subtract the employee's hire date from the current date.

VBA provides two functions called DateAdd and DateDiff that you can use to perform calculations involving dates and times. The **DateAdd function** allows you to add a specified time interval to a date or time, and it returns the new date or time. You could use the DateAdd function, for example, to add 15 days to an invoice date and then return the due date. The **DateDiff function**, on the other hand, allows you to determine the time interval that occurs between two dates—for example, the number of years between an employee's hire date and the current date. Unlike the DateAdd function, which returns a date or time, the DateDiff function returns an integer (a whole number).

The syntax of the DateAdd function is **DateAdd(Interval:=***interval***, Number:=** *number***, Date:=***date***)**, where *interval* is one of the settings shown in Figure 5-8.

interval setting	Description
"yyyy"	Year
"q"	Quarter
"m"	Month
"y"	Day of year
"d"	Day
"w"	Weekday
"ww"	Week
"h"	Hour
"n"	Minute
"s"	Second

Figure 5-8: Valid settings for the *interval* argument

To specify the number of days to add to a date using the DateAdd function, you need to use "d" as the function's *interval* argument. You use an *interval* of "m", on the other hand, to add a specified number of months to a date, and you use "n" to add a specified number of minutes to a time.

In the DateAdd function's syntax, *number* is the number of *intervals* (days, months, minutes, and so on) you want to add to the date or time specified in the function's *date* argument. The *number* argument can be either a positive or negative number. A positive *number* will give you dates and times occurring after the date or time specified in the *date* argument, and a negative *number* will give you dates and times occurring before the date or time specified in the *date* argument. Figure 5-9 shows examples of using the DateAdd function to calculate dates and time.

DateAdd function and result
`dtmNew = DateAdd(Interval:="yyyy", Number:=2, Date:=#1/1/2001#)`
Result: Assigns 1/1/2003 to the dtmNew variable
`dtmDue = DateAdd(Interval:="d", Number:=15, Date:=dtmInvDate)`
Result: If the dtmInvDate variable contains 1/1/2002, then 1/16/2002 is assigned to the dtmDue variable
`dtmFinish = DateAdd(Interval:="h", Number:=4, Date:=Time)`
Result: If the current time is 3:54:11 PM, then 7:54:11 PM is assigned to the dtmFinish variable
`MsgBox Prompt:=DateAdd(Interval:="n", Number:=-5, _`   `Date:=#10:25:00 AM#)`
Result: Displays 10:20:00 AM in a message box

Figure 5-9: Examples of the DateAdd function

tip

You will learn about other functions that operate on dates and times in this lesson's Exercises 6 through 8.

The first example shown in Figure 5-9, `dtmNew = DateAdd(Interval:="yyyy", Number:=2, Date:=#1/1/2001#)`, adds two years to the date literal constant #1/1/2001#, and then assigns the resulting date—in this case, 1/1/2003—to the dtmNew variable. The second example shown in the figure, `dtmDue = DateAdd(Interval:="d", Number:=15, Date:=dtmInvDate)`, adds 15 days to the contents of the dtmInvDate variable, and then assigns the resulting date to the dtmDue variable. Assuming that the dtmInvDate variable contains 1/1/2002, the date 1/16/2002 will be assigned to the dtmDue variable.

The third example shown in Figure 5-9, `dtmFinish = DateAdd(Interval:="h", Number:=4, Date:=Time)`, adds four hours to the current time, and then assigns the resulting time to the dtmFinish variable. If the current time is 3:54:11 PM, then the statement will assign 7:54:11 PM to the dtmFinish variable. The last example shown in the figure, `MsgBox Prompt:=DateAdd(Interval:="n", Number:=-5, Date:= #10:25:00 AM#)`, adds a negative five minutes to the date literal constant #10:25:00#, and then displays the resulting time—in this case, 10:20:00 AM—in a message box. (Adding a negative number is the same as subtracting a positive number.) Notice that the *date* argument in the DateAdd function can be a Date variable, a date literal constant, or one of the VBA date and time functions, and the *number* argument can be either a positive or negative number.

Unlike the DateAdd function, which returns either a future or past date or time, the DateDiff function returns an integer (whole number) that represents the number of time intervals between two specified dates or times. The syntax of the DateDiff function is **DateDiff(Interval:=**_interval_, **Date1:=**_date1_, **Date2:=**_date2_**)**, where _interval_ is one of the settings shown earlier in Figure 5-8, and _date1_ and _date2_ are the dates you want to use in the calculation. The DateDiff function subtracts _date1_ from _date2_, and then returns the difference as an integer. If the date or time specified in _date1_ occurs before the date or time specified in _date2_, the difference will be a positive number; otherwise, it will be a negative number. Figure 5-10 shows examples of the DateDiff function.

DateDiff function and result

`MsgBox Prompt:=DateDiff(Interval:="yyyy", Date1:=#1/1/2001#, _`
 	
`        Date2:=#1/1/2003#)`
 	
Result: Displays 2 in a message box

`MsgBox Prompt:=DateDiff(Interval:="yyyy", Date1:=#1/1/2003#, _`
 	
`        Date2:=#1/1/2001#)`
 	
Result: Displays -2 in a message box

`intDay = DateDiff(Interval:="d", Date1:=dtmInvDate, _`
 	
`        Date2:=dtmDue)`
 	
Result: If the dtmInvDate variable contains 1/1/2002 and the dtmDue variable contains 1/31/2002, then 30 is assigned to the intDay variable

`intHour = DateDiff(Interval:="h", Date1:=#3:54:11 PM#, _`
 	
`        Date2:=Time)`
 	
Result: If the current time is 7:54:00 PM, then 4 is assigned to the intHour variable

`MsgBox Prompt:=DateDiff(Interval:="n", Date1:=#10:25:00 AM#, _`
 	
`        Date2:=#10:20:00 AM#)`
 	
Result: Displays -5 in a message box

Figure 5-10: Examples of the DateDiff function

The first example shown in Figure 5-10, `MsgBox Prompt:=DateDiff(Interval:="yyyy", Date1:=#1/1/2001#, Date2:=#1/1/2003#)`, calculates the number of years ("yyyy") occurring between _date1_ (#1/1/2001#) and _date2_ (#1/1/2003#), and then displays the resulting integer in a message box. Because _date1_'s date occurs before _date2_'s date, the DateDiff function returns a positive 2 as the number of years between both dates. The second example shown in the figure is identical to the first example, except *date1* and *date2* are reversed in the DateDiff function. In this case, because *date1* (#1/1/2003#) occurs after *date2* (#1/1/2001#), the DateDiff function returns a –2 as the number of years between both dates.

The third example shown in Figure 5-10, `intDay = DateDiff (Interval:="d", Date1:=dtmInvDate, Date2:=dtmDue)`, calculates the number of days occurring between the date specified in the dtmInvDate variable and the date specified in the dtmDue variable. Assuming that the dtmInvDate variable contains 1/1/2002 and the dtmDue variable contains 1/31/2002, the number 30 will be assigned to an Integer variable named intDay. (You will learn about Integer variables in Tutorial 6.) The fourth example shown in the figure, `intHour = DateDiff(Interval:="h", Date1:=#3:54:11 PM#, Date2: =Time)`, calculates the number of hours occurring between the date literal constant #3:54:11 PM# and the current time. Assuming the current time is 7:54:00 PM, the number 4 will be assigned to the intHour variable. The last example shown in Figure 5-10, `MsgBox Prompt:=DateDiff(Interval:="n", Date1:=#10:25:00 AM#, Date2:=#10:20:00 AM#)`, calculates the number of minutes occurring between the date literal constants 10:25:00 AM and 10:20:00 AM, and then displays the result—in this case, –5—in a message box. Notice that the *date1* and *date2* arguments in the DateDiff function can be a Date variable, a date literal constant, or one of the VBA date and time functions. Also notice that the DateDiff function returns an integer, rather than a date or time.

In the next section, you will learn how to convert a string to a date.

Converting Strings to Dates

In Tutorial 4, you learned how to use the InputBox function to display a dialog box that prompts the user to enter information. As you may remember, the InputBox function returns the user's response as a string, which is typically assigned to a String variable. Before using a string that represents a date or time in a calculation, you should use either the VBA DateValue function or the TimeValue function to convert the string to a date or time, respectively.

··
tip

As you learned in Tutorial 4, you use the VBA Val function to return the numeric equivalent of a string.
··

The syntax of the DateValue function is **DateValue(Date:=*stringExpression*)**, where *stringExpression* represents a valid date ranging from January 1, 100 through December 31, 9999. The **DateValue function** returns the date equivalent of the *stringExpression* argument. The syntax of the TimeValue function is **TimeValue(Time:=*stringExpression*)**, where *stringExpression* represents a valid time ranging from 0:00:00 (12:00:00 AM) through 23:59:59 (11:59:59 PM). The **TimeValue function** returns the time equivalent of the *stringExpression* argument. Figure 5-11 shows examples of using the DateValue and TimeValue functions to convert strings to dates and times.

DateValue function	Result
dtmShip = DateValue(Date:="3/5/2002")	Converts the "3/5/2002" string to a date, and then assigns the resulting date, 3/5/2002, to the dtmShip Date variable
dtmBirth = DateValue(Date:=strBirth)	Assuming the strBirth variable contains the string "October 11, 1950", the statement converts the string to a date and then assigns the result, 10/11/1950, to the dtmBirth Date variable

TimeValue function	Result
dtmIn = TimeValue(Time:="5:30pm")	Converts the "5:30pm" string to a time, and then assigns the resulting time, 5:30:00 PM, to the dtmIn Date variable
dtmOut = TimeValue(Time:=strOut)	Assuming the strOut variable contains the string "3:45am", the statement converts the string to a time and then assigns the result, 3:45:00 AM, to the dtmOut Date variable

Figure 5-11: Examples of using the DateValue and TimeValue functions to convert strings to dates and times

> When a function has only one argument, as do the DateValue and TimeValue functions, it is a common practice to omit the argument's name and the := operator when entering the function in the Code window. For example, rather than entering DateValue(Date:="3/5/2002"), you simply can enter DateValue("3/5/2002").

The dtmShip = DateValue(Date:="3/5/2002") statement shown in Figure 5-11 first converts the string literal constant "3/5/2002" to a date, and then assigns the date to the dtmShip Date variable. The dtmBirth = DateValue(Date:=strBirth) statement converts the string stored in the strBirth variable to a date before assigning the date to the dtmBirth variable. (Keep in mind that this statement does not change the contents of the strBirth variable.) The third statement shown in Figure 5-11, dtmIn = TimeValue(Time:="5:30pm"), converts the string literal constant "5:30pm" to a time, which it assigns to the dtmIn variable. The last example shown in the figure, dtmOut = TimeValue(Time:=strOut), assigns the contents of the strOut variable, converted to a time, to the dtmOut variable. (Again, this statement does not change the contents of the strOut variable.)

You now have completed Tutorial 5's Concept lesson. You can either take a break or complete the end-of-lesson questions and exercises before moving on to the next lesson.

S U M M A R Y

To reserve a procedure-level Date variable:

■ Use the Dim statement. The syntax of the Dim statement is **Dim** *variablename* **As** *datatype*, where *variablename* represents the name of the variable (memory cell) and *datatype* is the type of data the variable can store.

■ When reserving a Date variable, *datatype* is always the keyword **Date**. The three-character ID used to name Date variables is *dtm*. A Date variable can store date and time information.

■ Variable names must begin with a letter and they can contain only letters, numbers, and the underscore (_). Variable names cannot be longer than 255 characters and they cannot be reserved words.

To assign a value to a variable:

■ Use an assignment statement in the following syntax: *variablename* = *value*.

To access the current system date and time:

■ Use the VBA Date, Time, and Now functions. The Date function returns the system date. The Time function returns the system time. The Now function returns both the system date and time. (The system date and time are the date and time maintained by your computer's internal clock.)

To control the appearance of dates and times:

■ Use the VBA Format function, the syntax of which is **Format(Expression:=***expression,* **Format:=***format*). In the syntax, *expression* specifies the number, date, time, or string whose appearance you want to format, and *format* is the name of a predefined VBA format. Refer to Figure 5-6 for a listing of the VBA predefined date/time formats.

To add a specified time interval to a date or time, and then return the new date or time:

■ Use the VBA DateAdd function. The syntax of the DateAdd function is **DateAdd(Interval:=***interval***, Number:=***number***, Date:=***date***)**, where *interval* is one of the settings shown in Figure 5-8, and *number* is the number of intervals you want to add to the date or time specified in the function's *date* argument. *Number* can be either negative (for past dates and times) or positive (for future dates and times). The DateAdd function returns a date or time.

To calculate the number of time intervals between two specified dates or times:

■ Use the VBA DateDiff function. The syntax of the DateDiff function is **DateDiff(Interval:=***interval***, Date1:=***date1***, Date2:=***date2***)**, where *interval* is one of the settings shown in Figure 5-8, and *date1* and *date2* are the dates you want to use in the calculation. The DateDiff function subtracts *date1* from *date2* and returns the difference as an integer. If the date or time specified in *date1* occurs before the date or time specified in *date2*, the difference will be a positive number; otherwise, it will be a negative number.

To convert a string to a Date data type:

■ Use the DateValue function to return the date equivalent of a string. The syntax of the DateValue function is **DateValue(Date:=***stringExpression***)**, where *stringExpression* represents a valid date ranging from January 1, 100 through December 31, 9999.

■ Use the TimeValue function to return the time equivalent of a string. The syntax of the TimeValue function is **TimeValue(Time:=***stringExpression***)**, where *stringExpression* represents a valid time ranging from 0:00:00 (12:00:00 AM) through 23:59:59 (11:59:59 PM).

 # R E V I E W   Q U E S T I O N S

1. Which of the following are valid date literal constants?
   a. #12/03/2002#
   b. %January 3, 2002%
   c. &6/5/2002&
   d. None of the above

2. Which of the following assigns the date 6/5/2002 to the dtmPay Date variable?
   a. dtmPay = #6/5/2002#
   b. dtmPay = 6/5/2002
   c. dtmPay = &6/5/2002&
   d. #6/5/2002# = dtmPay

3. Which of the following displays the current date and time in a message box?
   a. `MsgBox Prompt:=CurrentDateTime`
   b. `MsgBox Prompt:=DateTime`
   c. `MsgBox Prompt:=NowDtm`
   d. `MsgBox Prompt:=Now`

4. What will be returned by the following Format function?
   `Format(Expression:=#12/30/2002#, Format:="Short Date")`
   a. Monday, December 30, 2002
   b. 12/30/02
   c. 30-Dec-02
   d. December 30, 2002

5. Which of the following adds 15 days to the contents of the dtmPay variable, and then displays the resulting date in a message box?
   a. `MsgBox Prompt:=Add(Interval:="d", Number:=15, Date:=dtmPay)`
   b. `MsgBox Prompt:=AddDate(Interval:="d", Number:=15, Date:=dtmPay)`
   c. `MsgBox Prompt:=Date(Interval:="d", Number:=15, Date:=dtmPay)`
   d. `MsgBox Prompt:=DateAdd(Interval:="d", Number:=15, Date:=dtmPay)`

6. Which of the following displays the number of minutes between January 1, 2002 and January 2, 2002?
   a. `MsgBox Prompt:=Date(Interval:="m", Date1:=#1/1/2002#, Date2:=#1/2/2002#)`
   b. `MsgBox Prompt:=DateDiff(Interval:="m", Date1:=#1/1/2002#, Date2:=#1/2/2002#)`
   c. `MsgBox Prompt:=DateDiff(Interval:="n", Date1:=#1/1/2002#, Date2:=#1/2/2002#)`
   d. `MsgBox Prompt:=DiffDate(Interval:="n", Date1:=#1/1/2002#, Date2:=#1/2/2002#)`

7. Which of the following converts the contents of the strStart variable to a time?
   a. `DateValue(Date:=strStart)`
   b. `DateValue(Time:=strStart)`
   c. `TimeValue(Date:=strStart)`
   d. `TimeValue(Time:=strStart)`

 # E X E R C I S E S

1. a. Write a Dim statement that reserves two Date variables named dtmDepart and dtmReturn, and a String variable named strDepartDate.
   b. Write an assignment statement that assigns the system date to the dtmDepart variable.
   c. Write an assignment statement that assigns the date January 5, 2002 to the dtmDepart variable.

   d. Write an assignment statement that assigns the value returned by the InputBox function to the strDepartDate variable. Use "When do you leave?" as the *prompt*, and use "Depart Date" as the *title*.

   e. Write an assignment statement that assigns the date equivalent of the strDepartDate variable to the dtmDepart variable.

   f. Write an assignment statement that adds seven days to the dtmDepart variable. Assign the result to the dtmReturn variable.

   g. Write a MsgBox statement that displays the contents of the dtmReturn variable using the Long Date format.

   h. Write a MsgBox statement that displays the number of days between the dtmDepart and dtmReturn dates. Display the result as a positive number.

2. a. Write a Dim statement that reserves two Date variables named dtmCheckIn and dtmCheckOut, and a String variable named strTime.

   b. Write an assignment statement that assigns the system time to the dtmCheckIn variable.

   c. Write an assignment statement that assigns the time 6:35PM to the dtmCheckIn variable.

   d. Write an assignment statement that assigns the value returned by the InputBox function to the strTime variable. Use "Enter arrival time:" as the *prompt*, and use "Arrival Time" as the *title*.

   e. Write an assignment statement that assigns the time equivalent of the strTime variable to the dtmCheckIn variable.

   f. Write an assignment statement that adds eight hours to the dtmCheckIn variable. Assign the result to the dtmCheckOut variable.

   g. Write a MsgBox statement that displays the contents of the dtmCheckOut variable using the Short Time format.

   h. Write a MsgBox statement that displays the number of hours between the dtmCheckIn and dtmCheckOut times. Display the result as a positive number.

3. In this exercise, you will experiment with the DateValue and TimeValue functions.

   a. Start either Word, Excel, Access, or PowerPoint. Open the Visual Basic Editor, then open the Immediate window. Enter the following statements in the Immediate window. (Recall that when a function has only one argument, it is a common practice to omit the argument's name and the := operator when entering the function; in this case, Date:= and Time:= are omitted.)

```
MsgBox Prompt:=DateValue("Jan 4, 2002 5:30 am")
MsgBox Prompt:=TimeValue("Jan 4, 2002 5:30 am")
```

   b. What does the DateValue function return when the *stringExpression* contains both a date and a time? What does the TimeValue function return when the *stringExpression* contains both a date and a time?

4. In this exercise, you will experiment with the different date and time formats recognized by VBA.

   a. Start either Word, Excel, Access, or PowerPoint. Open the Visual Basic Editor, then open the Immediate window. Enter each of the commands shown in Figure 5-12 in the Immediate window, then record the date or time displayed in each message box.

Command	Result
MsgBox Prompt:=#Oct 4, 1980#	
MsgBox Prompt:=#30/4/1999#	
MsgBox Prompt:=#6/7#	
MsgBox Prompt:=#4-Jun-01#	
MsgBox Prompt:=#5 7 2002#	
MsgBox Prompt:=#7 Nov#	
MsgBox Prompt:=#99 11 5#	
MsgBox Prompt:=#2000 May 3#	
MsgBox Prompt:=#1:03#	
MsgBox Prompt:=#4:50:00 AM#	
MsgBox Prompt:=#15:00#	
MsgBox Prompt:=#7:00#	
MsgBox Prompt:=#7pm#	

Figure 5-12

    b. If a date literal constant does not include a year, what year does VBA use when it displays the date? (*Hint*: Refer to the MsgBox Prompt:=#6/7# and MsgBox Prompt:=#7 Nov# examples in the table.)

    c. If AM or PM is not included in a date literal constant that represents a time, which does VBA use—AM or PM? (*Hint*: Refer to the MsgBox Prompt:=#1:03#, MsgBox Prompt:=#15:00#, and MsgBox Prompt:=#7:00# examples in the table.)

Exercises 5 through 8 are Discovery Exercises. Discovery Exercises, which may include topics that are not covered in the lesson, allow you to "discover" the solutions to problems on your own.

discovery ▶ 5. In this exercise, you will learn how to create user-defined formats for displaying dates and times.

    a. Start either Word, Excel, Access, or PowerPoint. Open the Visual Basic Editor. Display the Help screen for the Format function. When the Help screen appears, click See Also at the top of the Help screen, then click User-Defined Date/Time Formats (Format Function) in the Topics Found dialog box, and then click the Display button. Read the Help screen, then click Example at the top of the User-Defined Date/Time Formats (Format Function) Help screen. Study the examples shown in the Help screen, then close the Help window.

b. Open the Immediate window. Enter the commands shown in Figure 5-13 in the Immediate window, then record the date or time displayed in each message box. (If you are entering only the *prompt* argument in the MsgBox function, you can omit the argument's name and the := operator. In other words, you can omit the Prompt:= when entering the function. You also can omit the names of the *expression* and *format* arguments, as well as the := operator, when entering the Format function, but you must be sure to enter the *expression* argument first, followed by the *format* argument, as shown in Figure 5-13.)

Command	Result
MsgBox Format(#3/12/02#,"m/d/yy")	
MsgBox Format(#3/12/02#,"d-mmm")	
MsgBox Format(#3/12/02#,"d-mmmm-yy")	
MsgBox Format(#3/12/02#,"d mmmm")	
MsgBox Format(#3/12/02#,"mmmm yy")	
MsgBox Format(#2:05:00 AM#, "hh:mm AM/PM")	
MsgBox Format(#2:05:00 AM#, "h:mm:ss a/p")	
MsgBox Format(#2:05:00 AM#, "h:mm")	
MsgBox Format(#2:05:00 AM#, "hh:mm:ss")	
MsgBox Format(Now, "m/d/yy h:mm")	
MsgBox Format(Now, "m/d/yy h:mm am/pm")	

Figure 5-13

c. Record the following on a piece of paper:
   1) Write the user-defined format that will display the date literal constant #3/1/2002# as 3-2002.
   2) Write the user-defined format that will display the date literal constant #3/1/2002# as March 2002.
   3) Write the user-defined format that will display the date literal constant #6/4/2002# as June 4.
   4) Write the user-defined format that will display the date literal constant #6/4/2002# as June 04.
   5) Write the user-defined format that will display the date literal constant #13:30:00# as 1:30 PM.
d. In the Immediate window, enter the appropriate MsgBox statements to verify the accuracy of the user-defined formats you wrote in Step c.
e. Close the application.

discovery ▶ **6.** In this exercise, you will learn about the DatePart, DateSerial, and TimeSerial functions in VBA.

    a. Start either Word, Excel, Access, or PowerPoint. Open the Visual Basic Editor. Display the Help screens for the DatePart, DateSerial, and TimeSerial functions. Read the Help screens. Also view and study the examples that each Help screen provides, then close the Help window.

    b. Record the following on a piece of paper:

       1) Write the DatePart function that will return the quarter of the year in which the date literal constant #6/15/2002# occurs.

       2) Write the DateSerial function that will return the date corresponding to a year of 2002, a month of 10, and a day of 25.

       3) Write the TimeSerial function that will return the time corresponding to six hours, 30 minutes, and 10 seconds.

    c. In the Immediate window, enter the appropriate MsgBox statements to verify the accuracy of the functions you wrote in Step b.

    d. Close the application.

discovery ▶ **7.** In this exercise, you will learn about the Hour, Minute, and Second functions in VBA.

    a. Start either Word, Excel, Access, or PowerPoint. Open the Visual Basic Editor. Display the Help screens for the Hour, Minute, and Second functions. Read the Help screens. Also view and study the examples that each Help screen provides, then close the Help window.

    b. Enter the following three MsgBox statements in the Immediate window. On a piece of paper, record what each MsgBox statement displays.

       1) What will the `MsgBox Prompt:=Hour(#4:30:10AM#)` statement display?

       2) What will the `MsgBox Prompt:=Minute(#4:30:10AM#)` statement display?

       3) What will the `MsgBox Prompt:=Second(#4:30:10AM#)` statement display?

    c. Close the application.

discovery ▶ **8.** In this exercise, you will learn about the Day, Month, Year, and Weekday functions in VBA.

    a. Start either Word, Excel, Access, or PowerPoint. Open the Visual Basic Editor. Display the Help screens for the Day, Month, Year, and Weekday functions. Read the Help screens. Also view and study the examples that each Help screen provides, then close the Help window.

    b. Enter the following four MsgBox statements in the Immediate window. On a piece of paper, record what each MsgBox statement displays.

       1) What will the `MsgBox Prompt:=Day(#10/22/2002#)` statement display?

       2) What will the `MsgBox Prompt:=Month(#10/22/2002#)` statement display?

       3) What will the `MsgBox Prompt:=Year(#10/22/2002#)` statement display?

       4) What will the `MsgBox Prompt:=Weekday(Date:=#10/22/2002#)` statement display? What is the meaning of the number returned by the Weekday function?

    c. Close the application.

You also can use VBA in PowerPoint to create procedures that enhance your presentations. Exercise 9 allows you to apply this tutorial's programming concept in a PowerPoint presentation.

powerpoint   9.   In this exercise, you will create a macro procedure in PowerPoint that uses a Date variable.

   a. Open the T5-PP-E9 (T5-PP-E9.ppt) presentation, which is located in the Tut05\Concept folder on your Data Disk. Save the presentation as T5-PP-E9D.

   b. Open the Visual Basic Editor. Insert a module into the project, then insert a macro procedure named DisplayDate.

   c. Declare a date variable named dtmToday. Assign the system date to the dtmToday variable. Use the MsgBox function to display the contents of the dtmToday variable, formatted to Long Date, in a message box.

   d. Save the presentation, then run the procedure. When the procedure is working correctly, close the Visual Basic Editor.

   e. Return to PowerPoint. Select the *Click here to display date* text that appears on the first slide, then right-click the selected text. Click Action Settings on the shortcut menu to display the Action Settings dialog box. Click the Run macro option button on the dialog box's Mouse Click tab, then click the OK button.

   f. Save the presentation. Click View on the menu bar and then click Slide Show. When the slide appears, click the *Click here to display date* text. The system date appears in a message box. Click the message box's OK button, then press the Esc key to stop the slide show.

   g. Close PowerPoint.

A computer program is good only if it works. Errors in programming code can cause a program to run incorrectly. Therefore, a programmer needs to know how to locate and fix any errors in his or her code. Exercise 10 is a Debugging Exercise. Debugging Exercises allow you to practice recognizing and solving errors in code.

debugging 🐞   10. The following code should add 10 days to the date stored in the dtmOrig variable, and then assign the result to the dtmNew variable. What is wrong with the following code? Correct any errors.

```
dtmNew = AddDays(Interval:="10", Date:=dtmOrig)
```

Excel Lesson

Using Date Variables in Excel

case ▶ Paradise Electronics employs three part-time employees who are paid every two weeks. The employees keep track of their hours worked using electronic timecards, which they then turn in to Martin Washington, Paradise's accountant, at the end of each week. The electronic timecards record each of the employee's starting and ending times, and Martin uses this information to calculate the number of hours worked each day and the total number of hours worked during the two-week period—a very time-consuming process. Recently, Martin has begun tracking the part-time employees' hours using an Excel workbook. He has decided to create a macro procedure to record the necessary information and make the required calculations.

Creating the CalcHours Macro Procedure

Your Data Disk contains the workbook that Martin uses to record the part-time employee information. Begin by opening Martin's workbook and viewing the code template for the CalcHours procedure, which has already been inserted into a module.

To open Martin's workbook and view the code template for the CalcHours procedure:

1 Start Microsoft Excel. Open the **T5-EX-1** (T5-EX-1.xls) workbook, which is located in the Tut05\Excel folder on your Data Disk. Click the **Enable Macros** button, if necessary, then save the workbook as **Hours Worked**. The Hours Worked workbook contains three worksheets, one for each of the part-time workers, as shown in Figure 5-14.

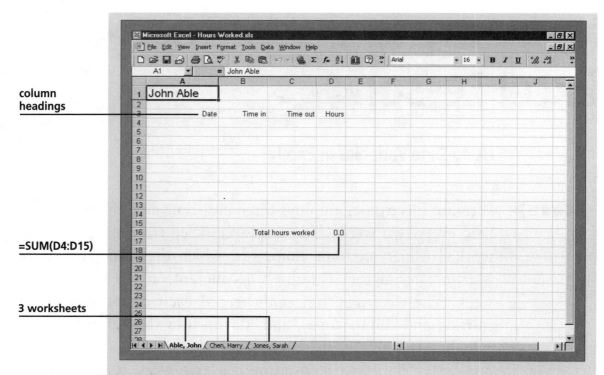

column
headings

=SUM(D4:D15)

3 worksheets

Figure 5-14: Hours Worked workbook

Each worksheet contains the employee's name in cell A1, as well as column headings (Date, Time In, Time Out, Hours) in row 3 of columns A, B, C, and D. As the column headings indicate, column A will show the dates the employee worked during the two-week period. Columns B and C will contain each day's starting and ending time, respectively, and column D will show the number of hours worked for that day. Each worksheet also contains a formula that calculates the total number of hours the employee worked during the two-week period. The formula, =SUM(D4:D15), is located in cell D16 in each worksheet.

Next, open the Visual Basic Editor.

2   Press **Alt+F11** to open the Visual Basic Editor. If necessary, open the Project Explorer window and close the Properties window, the Immediate window, and any open Code windows.

3   Open the Module1 module's Code window, then view the CalcHours procedure.

4   Close the Project Explorer window so that you can view more of the Code window.

As you learned in Tutorial 3, before entering instructions into a procedure, you should write down on a piece of paper what you want the procedure to accomplish, and the steps it will need to do so. Recall that these steps are called pseudocode. Figure 5-15 shows the pseudocode for the CalcHours procedure.

1. Use the InputBox function to prompt the user to enter the starting time. Store the user's response in a String variable named strIn.

2. Use the InputBox function to prompt the user to enter the ending time. Store the user's response in a String variable named strOut.

3. Use the TimeValue function to convert the string stored in the strIn variable to a time, and then assign the result to a Date variable named dtmIn.

4. Use the TimeValue function to convert the string stored in the strOut variable to a time, and then assign the result to a Date variable named dtmOut.

5. Assign the system date to the active cell in column A.

6. Assign the starting time, which is contained in the dtmIn variable, to the cell located one column to the right of the active cell. This cell is located in column B.

7. Assign the ending time, which is contained in the dtmOut variable, to the cell located two columns to the right of the active cell. This cell is located in column C.

8. Use the DateDiff function to calculate the number of hours worked. Assign the result to the cell located three columns to the right of the active cell. This cell is located in column D.

Figure 5-15: Pseudocode for the CalcHours procedure

After determining the steps you want the procedure to take, you can begin coding the procedure. First examine the pseudocode to determine what variables, if any, the procedure will need to use. For example, Steps 1 and 2 in the pseudocode indicate that the CalcHours procedure will use the InputBox function to get the starting and ending times. As you learned in Tutorial 4, the InputBox function returns a string, so you will need to reserve two String variables in which to store the time information; you will name the String variables strIn and strOut. The next two instructions in the pseudocode convert the contents of the String variables to times, and then assign the results to two Date variables named dtmIn and dtmOut.

As you learned in Tutorial 4, slightly less obvious in the pseudocode are the object variables that a procedure will use. You can determine that information by looking for the objects mentioned in the pseudocode. In Figure 5-15's pseudocode, for example, you will notice that the active cell is mentioned in Steps 5 through 8. You can make the CalcHours procedure easier to write and understand, and also make it run more efficiently, by assigning the address of the active cell to an object variable. As you learned in Tutorial 2, a cell is considered a Range object, so you will need to reserve a Range object variable to store the active cell's address; you will name the Range object rngActive.

In the next set of steps, you will reserve the appropriate variables (strIn, strOut, dtmIn, dtmOut, and rngActive), and then begin translating each line in Figure 5-15's pseudocode into one or more VBA statements.

To begin coding the CalcHours procedure:

1 The insertion point should be positioned in the blank line between the `Public Sub` and `End Sub` lines in the CalcHours procedure's Code window. Enter the documentation and the Dim statements shown in Figure 5-16.

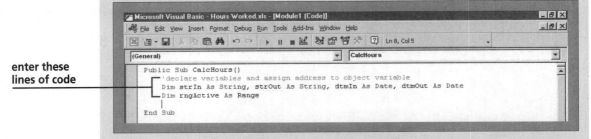

enter these lines of code

Figure 5-16: Code window showing documentation and Dim statements

Now assign the address of the active cell to the rngActive object variable. You can do so using the Excel Application object's ActiveCell property.

2 Type **set rngactive = application.activecell** and press the **Enter** key.

You now can begin translating Figure 5-15's pseudocode into VBA statements. The first two steps in the pseudocode are to use the InputBox function to prompt the user to enter the starting and ending times, and then assign the user's response to the strIn and strOut variables, respectively. Recall that the syntax of the InputBox function is **InputBox(Prompt:=**_prompt_ [**, Title:=**_title_] [**, Default:=**_defaultValue_]**)**.

3 Type **'enter starting and ending time** and press the **Enter** key. Type **strin = inputbox(prompt:="Enter the starting time:",** _ (be sure to type the comma followed by a space and the underscore) and press the **Enter** key. Press the **Tab** key, then type **title:="Start Time", default:=#9am#)** and press the **Enter** key. Notice that the Visual Basic Editor changes the #9am# to #9:00:00 AM# after you press the Enter key.

4 Press the **Backspace** key to remove the indentation, then type **strout = inputbox (prompt:="Enter the ending time:",** _ (be sure to type the comma followed by a space and the underscore) and press the **Enter** key. Press the **Tab** key, then type **title:="End Time", default:=#5pm#)** and press the **Enter** key. Notice that the Visual Basic Editor changes the #5pm# to #5:00:00 PM# after you press the Enter key.

Steps 3 and 4 in the pseudocode use the TimeValue function to convert the contents of the strIn and strOut variables to times, and then assign the results to the dtmIn and dtmOut variables, respectively.

5 Press the **Backspace** key to remove the indentation, then type **'convert strings to times** and press the **Enter** key. Type **dtmin = timevalue(time:=strin)** and press the **Enter** key. Type **dtmout = timevalue(time:=strout)** and press the **Enter** key.

 tip

Recall that when a function has only one argument, you can omit the argument's name and the := operator when entering the function in the Code window; in this case, you can omit Time:= from the TimeValue function.

Now assign the system date to the active cell.

6 Type **'assign values to worksheet cells** and press the **Enter** key, then type **rngactive.value = date** and press the **Enter** key.

7 Verify the accuracy of your code by comparing the code on your screen with the code shown in Figure 5-17.

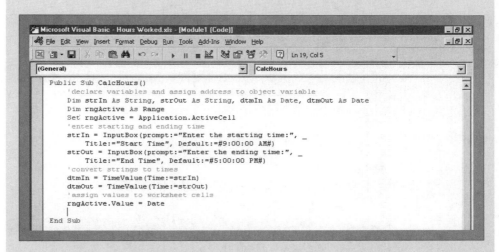

Figure 5-17: Partially completed CalcHours procedure

8 Save the workbook.

Before you can code Steps 6 through 8 of the pseudocode, you need to learn about a Range object's Offset property within Excel.

The Offset Property

You can use a Range object's Offset property to refer to a cell located a certain number of rows or columns away from the range itself. The syntax of the Offset property is *rangeObject*.**Offset([***rowOffset***] [,***columnOffset***])**, where *rowOffset* represents the number of rows above or below the *rangeObject*, and *columnOffset* is the number of columns to the right or left of the *rangeObject*. Notice that both *rowOffset* and *columnOffset* are optional, as indicated by the square brackets in the syntax.

You use a positive *rowOffset* to refer to rows found below the *rangeObject*, and you use a negative *rowOffset* to refer to rows above the *rangeObject*. For example, if the *rangeObject* is cell B5, then a *rowOffset* of 1 refers to cell B6, which is located one row below cell B5. A *rowOffset* of –1, on the other hand, refers to cell B4, which is one row above cell B5. Similarly, you use a positive *columnOffset* to refer to a column located to the right of the *rangeObject*, and you use a negative *columnOffset* to refer to a column located to the left of the *rangeObject*. For example, if the *rangeObject* is cell B5, then a *columnOffset* of 1 refers to cell C5, which is located one column to the right of cell B5. A *columnOffset* of –1, on the other hand, refers to cell A5, which is located one column to the left of cell B5. Following this logic, a *rowOffset* of 2 along with a *columnOffset* of 3 would refer to cell E7, which is located two rows down and three columns to the right of cell B5. The Offset property is illustrated in Figure 5-18.

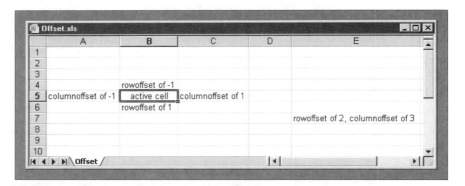

Figure 5-18: Illustration of the Offset property

You will use the Offset property to assign the starting and ending times, as well as the number of hours worked, to the cells located one column, two columns, and three columns to the right of the active cell in the Hours Worked worksheet.

To use the Offset property to complete the CalcHours procedure:

1   Type **rngactive.offset(columnoffset:=1).value = dtmin** and press the **Enter** key. This instruction assigns the starting time, which is stored in the dtmIn variable, to the cell located one column to the right of the active cell, whose address is stored in the rngActive variable.

2 Type **rngactive.offset(columnoffset:=2).value = dtmout** and press the **Enter** key. This instruction assigns the ending time, which is stored in the dtmOut variable, to the cell located two columns to the right of the active cell, whose address is stored in the rngActive variable.

The last step in the pseudocode shown in Figure 5-15 is to use the DateDiff function to calculate the number of hours worked for the day. Your first thought might be to use the `DateDiff(Interval:="h", Date1:=dtmIn, Date2:=dtmOut)` statement to calculate the hours worked. However, recall that the DateDiff function subtracts *date1* from *date2*, and then returns the difference as an integer. Assuming *date1* is 5:00pm and *date2* is 6:30pm, the `DateDiff(Interval:="h", Date1:=dtmIn, Date2:=dtmOut)` statement will return 1 (the integer difference between 5:00 and 6:30) rather than 1.5 (the number of hours the employee actually worked). The correct way to calculate the number of hours worked is to first use the DateDiff function to calculate the total minutes worked, and then divide that difference by 60 (the number of minutes in an hour). In other words, you will need to use the `DateDiff(Interval:="n", Date1:=dtmIn, Date2:=dtmOut)/60` statement to calculate the number of hours worked for the day. Assuming *date1* is 5:00pm and *date2* is 6:30pm, the `DateDiff(Interval:="n", Date1:=dtmIn, Date2:=dtmOut)` part of the statement will return the integer 90 as the number of minutes between 5:00pm and 6:30pm. The remaining part of the statement then will divide the 90 minutes by 60, resulting in 1.5 hours worked.

3 Type the additional code shown in Figure 5-19, which shows the completed CalcHours macro procedure.

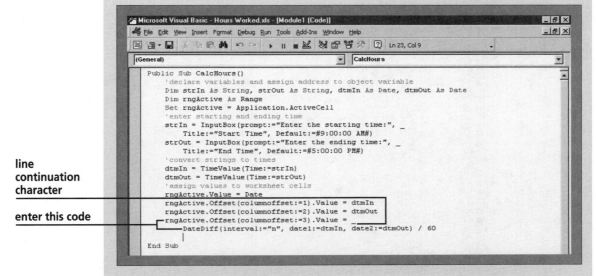

line
continuation
character

enter this code

Figure 5-19: Completed CalcHours macro procedure

4 Verify the accuracy of your code by comparing the code on your screen with the code shown in Figure 5-19, then save the workbook.

Now that you have translated the pseudocode shown in Figure 5-15 into VBA statements, you should test the CalcHours procedure to verify that it is working correctly.

To test the CalcHours procedure:

1 Click the **View Microsoft Excel** button ⊠ on the Standard toolbar to return to Excel. Select cell **A4** in the Able, John worksheet to make that cell the active cell.

2 Run the **CalcHours** macro.

3 When the Start Time dialog box appears and prompts you to enter the starting time, click the **OK** button to accept the default value of 9:00:00 AM. When you are prompted to enter the ending time, type **3:30pm** and then press the **Enter** key to select the OK button. Figure 5-20 shows the Able, John worksheet after running the CalcHours macro. (Your date might be different from that shown in the figure.)

active cell

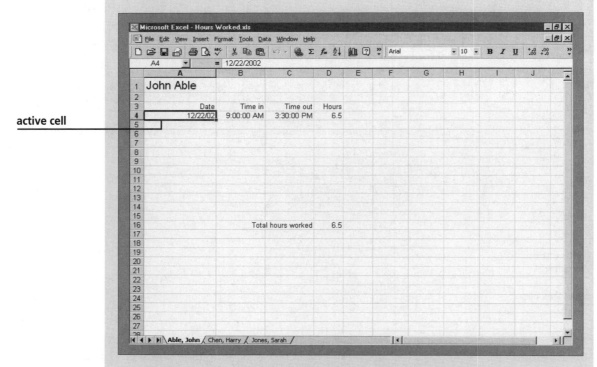

Figure 5-20: Able, John worksheet after running the CalcHours macro

4   Save the workbook, then exit Excel.

You now have completed Tutorial 5's Excel lesson. You can either take a break or complete the end-of-lesson exercises before moving on to the next lesson.

 **E X E R C I S E S**

1.   In this exercise, you will modify the CalcHours procedure that you created in this lesson. The modified procedure will prompt the user to enter the date.

   a. Open the Hours Worked (Hours Worked.xls) workbook, which is located in the Tut05\Excel folder on your Data Disk. Click the Enable Macros button, if necessary, then save the workbook as T5-EX-E1D.

   b. Open the Visual Basic Editor, then view the CalcHours procedure's code. Currently, the procedure enters the system date in the active cell. Modify the procedure so that it uses the InputBox function to prompt the user to enter the date. Use Work Day as the InputBox function's *title* argument, and use the system date as the *defaultValue*. Store the user's response in a String variable named strDate, then assign the contents of the strDate variable, formatted to Medium Date, to the active cell. (*Hint*: You will not be using the strDate variable in a calculation, so it is not necessary to convert its contents to a date.)

   c. Save the workbook. Return to Excel. Click cell A4 in the Chen, Harry worksheet, then run the CalcHours macro. When the Work Day dialog box appears, type 5/6/2002, then press the Enter key. When the Start Time dialog box appears, type 10am and then press the Enter key. When the End Time dialog box appears, type 1pm and then press the Enter key.

   d. Click cell A4 in the Jones, Sarah worksheet, then run the CalcHours macro. When the Work Day dialog box appears, press the Enter key to accept the system date. When the Start Time dialog box appears, type 2pm and press the Enter key. When the End Time dialog box appears, type 9pm and press the Enter key.

   e. Save and then close the workbook.

2.   In this exercise, you will create a macro procedure that calculates an invoice's due date.

   a. Open the T5-EX-E2 (T5-EX-E2.xls) workbook, which is located in the Tut05\Excel folder on your Data Disk. Save the workbook as T5-EX-E2D.

   b. Create a macro procedure named AssignDates. The procedure should accomplish the steps shown in Figure 5-21. (*Hint*: You learned how to assign a value to a multi-cell range in Tutorial 2.)

1. Use the InputBox function to prompt the user to enter the invoice date. Use the current date as the InputBox function's *defaultValue*. Store the user's response in a String variable named strInvDate.

2. Convert the contents of the strInvDate variable to a date. Store the result in a Date variable named dtmInvDate.

3. Calculate the invoice's due date by adding three weeks to the invoice date stored in the dtmInvDate variable. Store the result in a Date variable named dtmDueDate.

4. Assign the contents of the dtmInvDate variable, formatted to Short Date, to cells C4 through C9.

5. Assign the contents of the dtmDueDate variable, formatted to Short Date, to cells D4 through D9.

Figure 5-21

    c. Save the workbook. Return to Excel and run then AssignDates macro. Enter 9/15/2002 as the invoice date.

    d. When the macro is working correctly, save and then close the workbook.

3. In this exercise, you will create a macro procedure that calculates a discount date and a penalty date.

    a. Open the T5-EX-E3 (T5-EX-E3.xls) workbook, which is located in the Tut05\Excel folder on your Data Disk. Save the workbook as T5-EX-E3D.

    b. Create a macro procedure named CalcDiscAndPenalty. The macro should accomplish the tasks shown in Figure 5-22.

1. Use the InputBox function to prompt the user to enter the date. Store the user's response in a String variable named strOrigDate.

2. Convert the string stored in the strOrigDate variable to a date. Assign the result to a Date variable named dtmOrigDate.

3. Subtract 7 days from the contents of the dtmOrigDate variable. Assign the result to a Date variable named dtmDiscDate.

4. Add 7 days to the contents of the dtmOrigDate variable. Assign the result to a Date variable named dtmPenDate.

5. Assign the contents of the dtmOrigDate variable, formatted to Short Date, to the active cell in column A in the worksheet.

6. Assign the contents of the dtmDiscDate variable, formatted to Short Date, to the cell located two columns to the right of the active cell.

7. Assign the contents of the dtmPenDate variable, formatted to Short Date, to the cell located four columns to the right of the active cell.

Figure 5-22

c. Save the workbook. Return to Excel. Click cell A4, then run the CalcDiscAndPenalty macro. Enter 2/1/2002 as the date. Click cell A5, then run the CalcDiscAndPenalty macro. Enter 12/20/2002 as the date.

d. When the macro is working correctly, save and then close the workbook.

4. In this exercise, you will create a macro procedure that calculates the dates for a patient's six-month and one-year checkup.

a. Open the T5-EX-E4 (T5-EX-E4.xls) workbook, which is located in the Tut05\Excel folder on your Data Disk. Save the workbook as T5-EX-E4D.

b. Create a macro procedure named CheckUps. The macro should accomplish the tasks shown in Figure 5-23. (*Hint:* You learned how to select a cell in Tutorial 2, and how to insert a row in Tutorial 3.)

---

1. Select cell A5.

2. Insert a row above row 5.

3. Use the InputBox function to prompt the user to enter the patient's name. Store the user's response in a String variable named strPatient.

4. Use the InputBox function to prompt the user to enter the date of the patient's last exam. Use the system date as the InputBox function's *defaultValue*. Store the user's response in a String variable named strExamDate.

5. Convert the string stored in the strExamDate variable to a date. Store the result in a Date variable named dtmExamDate.

6. Calculate the date of the patient's six-month checkup. Assign the result to a Date variable named dtmSixMonth.

7. Calculate the date of the patient's one-year checkup. Assign the result to a Date variable named dtmOneYear.

8. Assign the patient's name to the active cell in column A.

9. Assign the exam date, formatted to Short Date, to the appropriate cell in column B.

10. Assign the six-month checkup date, formatted to Short Date, to the appropriate cell in column C.

11. Assign the one-year checkup date, formatted to Short Date, to the appropriate cell in column D.

Figure 5-23

c. Save the workbook, then return to Excel. Use the CheckUps macro to enter Sam Adams as the name and 7/11/02 as the exam date. You will notice that the range A5:D5 appears in bold. Select the range A5:D5, then click the Bold button **B** on the Standard toolbar.

d. Return to the Visual Basic Editor. Modify the CheckUps procedure so that it turns the Bold feature off for the range A5:D5. (*Hint*: Display the Help screen for the Bold property.) Save the workbook, then return to Excel. Use the CheckUps macro to enter the following names and exam dates: Jesse Juarez, 10/9/02, Frank Friar, 11/5/02.

e. When the macro is working correctly, save and then close the workbook.

5. In this exercise, you will create a macro procedure that calculates an invoice's due date.

a. Open the T5-EX-E5 (T5-EX-E5.xls) workbook, which is located in the Tut05\Excel folder on your Data Disk. Save the workbook as T5-EX-E5D.

b. Compare the worksheet on your screen to the one shown in Figure 5-24.

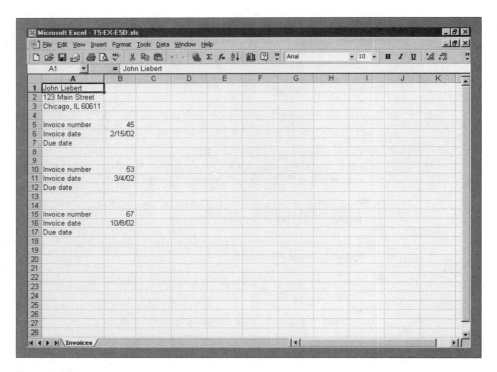

Figure 5-24

c. Create a macro procedure named CalcDueDate that will allow the user to enter the invoice number and invoice date. The macro should calculate the invoice's due date, which is 10 days after the invoice date. The macro should assign the "Invoice number" row heading to the active cell in column A. The remaining row headings ("Invoice date" and "Due date") should be assigned to the rows below the active cell, and the invoice number, invoice date, and due date should be assigned to the appropriate cells in column B.

d. Save the workbook. Return to Excel. Use the CalcDueDate macro to enter the information shown in Figure 5-24. (*Hint*: The macro should calculate the correct due date for each invoice. The correct due dates are not shown in the figure.)

e. When the macro is working correctly, save and then close the workbook.

6. In this exercise, you will create a macro procedure that calculates the beginning time for a trip.

   a. Open the T5-EX-E6 (T5-EX-E6.xls) workbook, which is located in the Tut05\Excel folder on your Data Disk. Save the workbook as T5-EX-E6D.

   b. Create a macro procedure named CalcBeginTime that will allow the user to enter an arrival time and the number of minutes necessary to reach the user's destination. The procedure should use this information to calculate the beginning time for the trip. (In other words, if the user enters 7:18pm as the arrival time, and 10 as the number of minutes for the trip, then the user will need to leave his or her home at 7:08pm.) The procedure should assign the beginning and arrival times, formatted to Medium Time, to cells A4 and B4, respectively.

   c. Save the workbook. Return to Excel. Use the CalcBeginTime macro to answer the following questions:

   1) Assume that a trip takes 54 minutes and you want to arrive at the destination at 3:45pm. What time would you need to leave home?

   2) Assume that a trip takes 133 minutes and you want to arrive at the destination at 7am. What time would you need to leave home?

   d. When the macro is working correctly, save and then close the workbook.

Exercises 7 and 8 are Discovery Exercises. Discovery Exercises, which may include topics that are not covered in the lesson, allow you to "discover" the solutions to problems on your own.

discovery ▶ 7. In this exercise, you will learn about the Application object's Selection property.

   a. Open the T5-EX-E7 (T5-EX-E7.xls) workbook, which is located in the Tut05\Excel folder on your Data Disk. Click the Enable Macros button, if necessary. Save the workbook as T5-EX-E7D.

   b. Open the Visual Basic Editor. View the partially completed EnterDate procedure, which is located in the Module1 module. Study the code. The procedure should allow you to enter a date, and then assign the date to the cells currently selected in the worksheet. You can use the Application object's Selection property, whose syntax is Application.Selection, to determine which cells are currently selected in the worksheet.

   c. Complete the EnterDate procedure by declaring a Range object variable and assigning the address of the current selection to it. Also assign the date entered by the user to the current selection. Format the date to Long Date.

   d. Save the workbook. Return to Excel. Select cells B4 through B6, then run the EnterDate macro. When the Date dialog box appears, click the OK button to accept the system date.

   e. Select cells B7 through B9, then run the EnterDate macro. Enter 12/20/02 as the date, then press the Enter key to enter this date in the selected cells.

   f. When the macro is working correctly, save and then close the workbook.

discovery ▶ 8. In this exercise, you will learn about the Excel Application object's InputBox method. You will use the Hours Worked workbook that you created in this lesson.

   a. Open the Hours Worked (Hours Worked.xls) workbook, which is located in the Tut05\Excel folder on your Data Disk. Click the Enable Macros button, if necessary, then save the workbook as T5-EX-E8D.

   b. Open the Visual Basic Editor. View the CalcHours procedure, which is located in the Module1 module. Currently, the procedure requires the user to select the appropriate cell in column A before running the macro.

c. View the Help screen on the Application object's InputBox method. Modify the CalcHours procedure so that it first prompts the user to select the appropriate cell in column A. (*Hint*: Recall that a cell is considered a Range object.)

d. Save the workbook. Return to Excel. Click cell A1. Run the CalcHours macro. When the InputBox method's dialog box appears and prompts you to select the appropriate cell in column A, use the mouse to select cell A5 in the Able, John worksheet, then click the OK button. Use 8:05am and 1:10pm as the starting and ending times, respectively.

e. Run the CalcHours macro again. This time select cell A4 in the Jones, Sarah worksheet, then click the OK button. Use 10:30am and 1:00pm as the starting and ending times, respectively. Activate the Jones, Sarah worksheet to verify that the starting and ending times were entered correctly.

f. When the macro is working correctly, save and then close the workbook.

A computer program is good only if it works. Errors in programming code can cause a program to run incorrectly. Therefore, a programmer needs to know how to locate and fix any errors in his or her code. Exercise 9 is a Debugging Exercise. Debugging Exercises allow you to practice recognizing and solving errors in code.

debugging   **9.** In this exercise, you will debug an existing macro procedure.

a. Open the T5-EX-E9 (T5-EX-E9.xls) workbook, which is located in the Tut05\Excel folder on your Data Disk. Click the Enable Macros button, if necessary. Save the workbook as T5-EX-E9D.

b. Open the Visual Basic Editor. View the SetEmployDate procedure, which is located in the Module1 module. Study the code, then return to Excel and run the macro. Notice that the macro enters the system date in cell A6, rather than in cell C4. Delete the date from cell A6, then return to the Visual Basic Editor and correct the macro.

c. Save the workbook, then return to Excel and run the macro again.

d. When the macro is working correctly, save and then close the workbook.

Word Lesson

Using Date Variables in Word

case ▶ Four times per year, Willowton Health Club invites 10 members, selected at random, to a member appreciation dinner at Julie's Lobster and Steak House. Pat Jones, the manager of Willowton Health Club, wants to create a procedure that she can use to print a professional-looking invitation to send to the members. The procedure will need to prompt Pat for the dinner date and then calculate the RSVP date, which is the date by which the member must respond to the invitation.

Coding the PrintInvitation Procedure

Pat's invitation to Willowton Health Club's member appreciation dinner is stored on your Data Disk. Begin by opening the document and viewing the code template for the PrintInvitation procedure, which has already been inserted into a module.

To open Pat's document and view the code template for the PrintInvitation procedure:

1 Start Microsoft Word. Open the **T5-WD-1** (T5-WD-1.doc) document, which is located in the Tut05\Word folder on your Data Disk. Click the **Enable Macros** button, if necessary, then save the document as **Invitation**.

View the entire Invitation document.

2 Click **File** on the menu bar and then click **Print Preview**. See Figure 5-25.

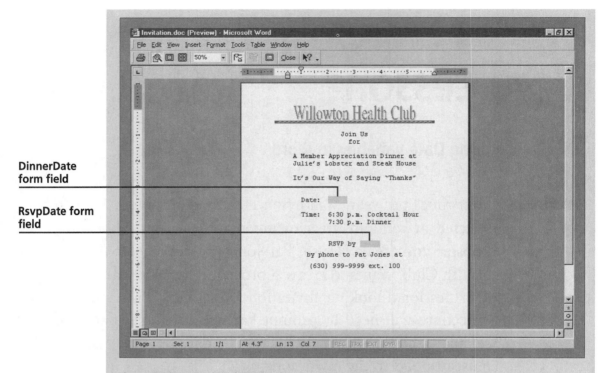

DinnerDate form field

RsvpDate form field

Figure 5-25: Invitation document

The Invitation document contains two form fields named DinnerDate and RsvpDate.

···

As you learned in Tutorial 4, a form field is a special area in the document reserved for entering and displaying information.

···

3 Close the Print Preview window.

Next, open the Visual Basic Editor.

4 Press **Alt+F11** to open the Visual Basic Editor. If necessary, open the Project Explorer window and close the Properties window, the Immediate window, and any open Code windows.

5 Open the Module1 module's Code window, then view the code template for the PrintInvitation procedure.

6 Close the Project Explorer window so that you can view more of the Code window.

As you learned in Tutorial 3, before entering instructions into a procedure, you should write down on a piece of paper what you want the procedure to accomplish, and the steps it will need to do so. Recall that these steps are called pseudocode. Figure 5-26 shows the pseudocode for the PrintInvitation procedure.

1. Use the InputBox function to prompt the user to enter the dinner date. Store the user's response in a String variable named strDinDate.

2. Use the DateValue function to convert the string stored in the strDinDate variable to a date, and then assign the result to a Date variable named dtmDinDate.

3. Use the DateAdd function to calculate the RSVP date, which is six days prior to the dinner date. Store the result in a Date variable named dtmRsvpDate.

4. Assign the dinner date, which is stored in the dtmDinDate variable, to the DinnerDate form field in the Invitation document. Format the dinner date to Long Date.

5. Assign the RSVP date, which is stored in the dtmRsvpDate variable, to the RsvpDate form field in the Invitation document. Format the RSVP date to Long Date.

6. Print the Invitation document.

Figure 5-26: Pseudocode for the PrintInvitation procedure

After determining the steps you want the procedure to take, you can begin coding the procedure. First examine the pseudocode to determine what variables, if any, the procedure will need to use. For example, Steps 1 through 3 in the pseudocode indicate that the PrintInvitation procedure will need a String variable named strDinDate and two Date variables named dtmDinDate and dtmRsvpDate.

As you learned in Tutorial 4, slightly less obvious in the pseudocode are the object variables that a procedure will use. You can determine that information by looking for the objects mentioned in the pseudocode. In Figure 5-26's pseudocode, for example, notice that the Invitation document is mentioned in the last three steps. You can make the PrintInvitation procedure easier to write and understand, and also make it run more efficiently, by assigning the address of the Invitation document object to an object variable. You will name the object variable docInvitation.

In the next set of steps, you will declare the appropriate variables, and then begin translating each line in Figure 5-26's pseudocode into one or more VBA statements.

To begin coding the PrintInvitation procedure:

1   The insertion point should be positioned in the blank line between the `Public Sub` and `End Sub` lines in the Code window. Enter the documentation and the Dim and Set statements shown in Figure 5-27.

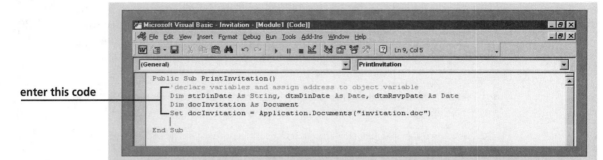

enter this code

Figure 5-27: Code window showing documentation and Dim and Set statements

You now can begin translating Figure 5-26's pseudocode into VBA statements. The first step in the pseudocode is to use the InputBox function to prompt the user to enter the dinner date. Recall that the syntax of the InputBox function is **InputBox(Prompt:=***prompt* [, **Title:=***title*] [, **Default:=***defaultValue*]).

2   Type **'enter dinner date** and press the **Enter** key. Type **strdindate = _** (be sure to type the equal sign followed by a space and the underscore) and press the **Enter** key. Press the **Tab** key, then type **inputbox(prompt:="Enter the dinner date in m/d/yy format:", title:="Dinner Date")** and press the **Enter** key.

The next step in the pseudocode is to convert the string stored in the strDinDate variable to a date, and then assign the result to the dtmDinDate variable.

3   Press the **Backspace** key to remove the indentation. Type **'convert string to a date** and press the **Enter** key, then type **dtmdindate = datevalue(date:=strdindate)** and press the **Enter** key.

> **tip**
>
> Recall that when a function has only one argument, you can omit the argument's name and the := operator when entering the function in the Code window; in this case, you can omit Date:= from the DateValue function.

Step 3 in the pseudocode is to use the DateAdd function to calculate the RSVP date, which is six days prior to the dinner date, and then assign the result to the dtmRsvpDate variable.

4   Type **'calculate RSVP date** and press the **Enter** key, then type **dtmrsvpdate = dateadd(interval:="d", number:=-6, date:=dtmdindate)** and press the **Enter** key. (Be sure to type the minus sign before the 6 in the *number* argument.)

Steps 4 and 5 in the pseudocode are to assign the dinner and RSVP dates, formatted to Long Date, to the form fields in the document. As you learned in Tutorial 4, you use the following syntax to assign a value to a form field: *documentObject*.**FormFields(***formFieldName***).Result = ***value*.

5 Type **'assign values to form fields** and press the **Enter** key. Type **docinvitation.formfields("dinnerdate").result = _** (be sure to type the equal sign followed by a space and the underscore) and press the **Enter** key. Press the **Tab** key, then type **format(expression:=dtmdindate, format:="long date")** and press the **Enter** key.

6 Press the **Backspace** key to remove the indentation, then type **docinvitation.formfields("rsvpdate").result = _** (be sure to type the equal sign followed by a space and the underscore) and press the **Enter** key. Press the **Tab** key, then type **format(expression:=dtmrsvpdate, format:="long date")** and press the **Enter** key.

The last step in the pseudocode is to print the document, which you will learn how to do in the next section.

7 Save the Invitation document.

Printing a Document

You can use the Document object's **PrintPreview method** to preview a document on the screen before printing it, and you can use the Document object's **PrintOut method** to print the document on the printer. The syntax of the PrintPreview method is *documentObject*.**PrintPreview**. The syntax of the PrintOut method is *documentObject*.**PrintOut**, which prints one copy of the entire *documentObject*. While you are creating and testing a macro, it is a common practice to use the PrintPreview method, rather than the PrintOut method, in the code; this is done mainly to conserve paper, but it also allows you to test a macro in cases where your computer is not connected to a printer. When you are sure that the macro is working correctly, you simply replace the PrintPreview method with the PrintOut method in the code.

tip

• •

The PrintOut method's full syntax contains many optional arguments that give you greater control over the printing of the document. For example, the PrintOut method contains arguments that you can use to specify the range of pages to print and the number of copies to print. You can learn more about the Printout method by completing this lesson's Exercise 4.

• •

To complete the PrintInvitation procedure, then test the procedure:

1 Press the **Backspace** key to remove the indentation, then type **'print the document** and press the **Enter** key.

Use the PrintPreview method to preview the document until you are sure that the macro is working correctly.

2 Type **docinvitation.printpreview** and press the **Enter** key. Figure 5-28 shows the PrintInvitation procedure.

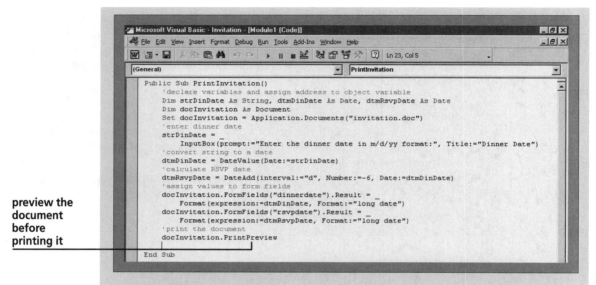

preview the document before printing it

Figure 5-28: The PrintInvitation procedure

3 Verify the accuracy of your code by comparing the code on your screen to the code shown in Figure 5-28.

4 Save the document.

Now that you have translated the pseudocode shown in Figure 5-26 into VBA statements, you should test the PrintInvitation procedure to verify that it is working correctly. You will test the procedure from Word.

5 Click the **View Microsoft Word** button ⊞ on the Standard toolbar to return to Word.

The Invitation document contains a customized toolbar named Dinner Macro. On the Dinner Macro toolbar is a button that will allow you to run the PrintInvitation macro. View the Dinner Macro toolbar.

6 Click **View** on Word's menu bar, point to **Toolbars**, and then click **Dinner Macro** to display the Dinner Macro toolbar. See Figure 5-29. (Your toolbar might be located in a different area of the screen.)

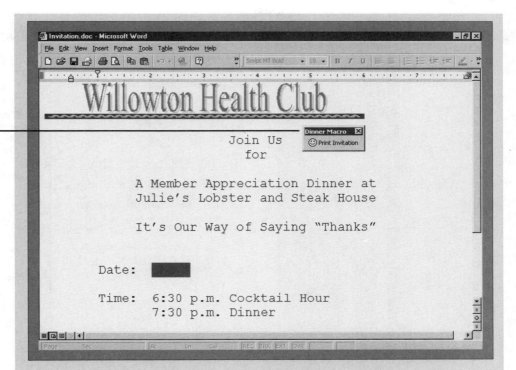

Dinner Macro toolbar

Figure 5-29: The Dinner Macro toolbar

7 Click the **Print Invitation** button on the Dinner Macro toolbar. When the Dinner Date dialog box prompts you to enter the dinner date, type **3/4/02** and press the **Enter** key. The macro calculates the RSVP date (2/26/02) and assigns the dinner and RSVP dates, formatted to Long Date, to the form fields in the document. The Invitation document appears in Print Preview, as shown in Figure 5-30.

8 Close the Print Preview window.

9 Press **Alt+F11** to return to the Visual Basic Editor. Change the `docInvitation.PrintPreview` instruction to **docInvitation.PrintOut**.

Now that you have made a change to the procedure, you will need to test the procedure again to be sure that it still is working correctly.

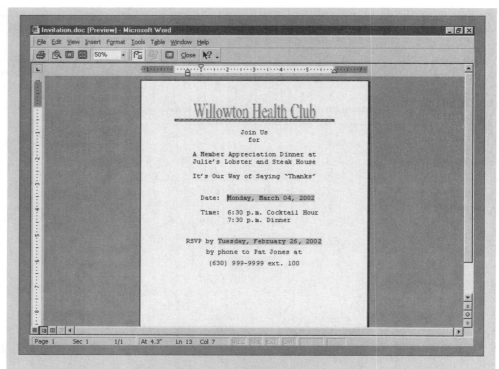

Figure 5-30: Invitation document shown in Print Preview

10 Save the document. Click the **View Microsoft Word** button ![W] to return to Word, then click the **Print Invitation** button on the Dinner Macro toolbar to run the PrintInvitation macro. In the Dinner Date dialog box, type **6/23/02** as the dinner date, then press the **Enter** key. The macro calculates the RSVP date (6/17/02) and assigns the dinner and RSVP dates, formatted to Long Date, to the form fields in the document. The macro then prints the document.

11 Save the document, then exit Word.

You now have completed Tutorial 5's Word lesson. You can either take a break or complete the end-of-lesson exercises before moving on to the next lesson.

E X E R C I S E S

1. In this exercise, you will modify the PrintInvitation procedure that you created in this lesson. The modified procedure will prompt the user for the cocktail time and then calculate the dinner time.

a. Open the Invitation (Invitation.doc) document, which is located in the Tut05\Word folder on your Data Disk. Click the Enable Macros button, if necessary, then save the document as T5-WD-E1D.doc.

b. Use the Tools menu to unprotect the document. Display the Forms toolbar. Replace the 6:30 pm time with a form field named CocktailTime, and replace the 7:30 pm time with a form field named DinnerTime. (Do not remove the words "Cocktail Hour" and "Dinner" from the document.) Close the Forms toolbar.

c. Use the Tools menu to protect the document.

d. Open the Visual Basic Editor, then view the PrintInvitation procedure. Change the document name in the Set statement from "invitation.doc" to "t5-wd-e1d.doc". Replace the macro's `docInvitation.PrintOut` instruction with `docInvitation.PrintPreview` until you are sure the macro is working correctly.

e. Modify the PrintInvitation macro so that it prompts the user to enter the cocktail time. The macro should calculate the dinner time by adding one hour to the cocktail time. Display the cocktail and dinner times using the "h:mm am/pm" format in the appropriate form fields in the document.

f. Save the document, then return to Word. Display the Dinner Macro toolbar, if necessary. Click the PrintInvitation button on the Dinner Macro toolbar. Enter 4/2/02 as the dinner date and enter 6pm as the cocktail time.

g. When the macro is working correctly, change the macro's `docInvitation.PrintPreview` instruction to `docInvitation.PrintOut`.

h. Save the document and then return to Word and run the PrintInvitation macro again. Enter 11/4/02 as the dinner date and enter 5:30pm as the cocktail time.

i. Save and then close the document.

2. In this exercise, you will create a macro procedure that calculates the number of days until Christmas.

a. Open the T5-WD-E2 document, which is located in the Tut05\Word folder on your Data Disk. Click the Enable Macros button, if necessary, then save the document as T5-WD-E2D.

b. View the customized Xmas Macro toolbar, if necessary.

c. Open the Visual Basic Editor. Open the Module1 module's Code window, then view the code template for the CalcXmasDays procedure. The CalcXmasDays procedure should calculate the number of days between the current date and December 25th, Christmas Day. Display the number of days in the Days form field in the document. Also have the macro print the document.

d. Save the document, then return to Word. Click the Calculate Xmas Days button on the Xmas Macro toolbar. When the macro is working correctly, save and then close the document.

3. In this exercise, you will create a macro procedure that calculates an order's pickup date.

a. Open the T5-WD-E3 (T5-WD-E3.doc) document, which is located in the Tut05\Word folder on your Data Disk. Click the Enable Macros button, if necessary, then save the document as T5-WD-E3D. Figure 5-31 shows the T5-WD-E3D document. (Your date might be different from the one shown in the figure.)

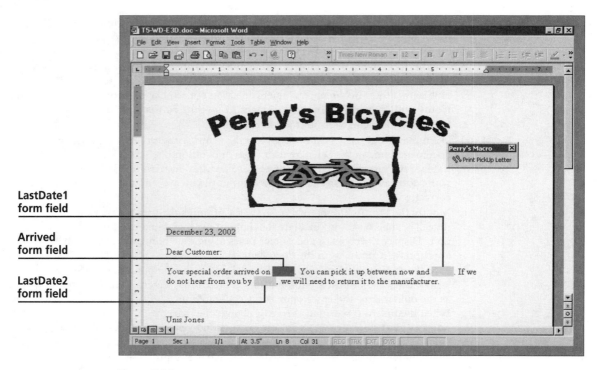

**LastDate1
form field**

**Arrived
form field**

**LastDate2
form field**

Figure 5-31

b. View the customized Perry's Macro toolbar, if necessary.
c. Open the Visual Basic Editor. Open the Module1 module's Code window, then view
    the code template for the PrintPickUp procedure. The procedure should allow the user
    to enter the arrival date; use the current date as the *defaultValue* in the InputBox func-
    tion. After getting the arrival date, the procedure should calculate the last pickup date
    by adding 30 days to the arrival date. The macro should assign the arrival date to the
    Arrived form field in the document, and it should assign the last pickup date to both
    the LastDate1 and LastDate2 form fields. Also have the macro print the document.
d. Save the document, then return to Word. Click the Print PickUp Letter button on
    the Perry's Macro toolbar. Enter 12/7/02 as the arrival date.
e. When the macro is working correctly, save and then close the document.

Exercise 4 is a Discovery Exercise. Discovery Exercises, which may include topics that are
not covered in the lesson, allow you to "discover" the solutions to problems on your own.

discovery ▶ **4.** In this exercise, you will learn more about the Document object's PrintOut method.
a. Open the T5-WD-E4 (T5-WD-E4.doc) document, which is located in the Tut05\Word
    folder on your Data Disk. Click the Enable Macros button, if necessary, then save the
    document as T5-WD-E4D.
b. View the customized Books Macro toolbar, if necessary.

c. Open the Visual Basic Editor. Open the Module1 module's Code window, then view the PrintBooks procedure. Study the existing code. Notice that the instruction to print the document is missing from the code.

d. View the Help screen for the Document object's PrintOut method. The title of the Help screen is PrintOut Method (Application, Document, and Window Objects). Notice that the PrintOut method allows many optional arguments.

e. Click Example, which appears at the top of the PrintOut method's Help screen. Study the examples, then return to the PrintOut method's Help screen. Use the Help screen to answer the following questions:

   1) To print pages 2 through 4, set the PrintOut method's Range argument to the constant _____, and set its From argument to _____ and its To argument to _____.

   2) To specify the number of copies to print, set the PrintOut method's _____ argument.

   3) To collate the printed pages, set the PrintOut method's Collate argument to _____.

f. Close the Help window. Modify the PrintBooks macro so that it prints the pages whose page numbers are specified in the strBegPage and strEndPage variables. Print the number of copies specified in the strNumPage and collate the pages. (*Hint:* You can use String variables in the PrintOut method's arguments.)

g. Save the document, then return to Word and run the PrintBooks macro using the Print Book Document button on the Books Macro toolbar. When the From Page Number dialog box appears, type 2 and press the Enter key. When the To Page Number dialog box appears, type 3 and press the Enter key. When the Number of Copies dialog box appears, type 2 and press the Enter key.

h. When the macro is working correctly, save and then close the document.

A computer program is good only if it works. Errors in programming code can cause a program to run incorrectly. Therefore, a programmer needs to know how to locate and fix any errors in his or her code. Exercise 5 is a Debugging Exercise. Debugging Exercises allow you to practice recognizing and solving errors in code.

debugging **5.** In this exercise, you will debug an existing macro procedure.

a. Open the T5-WD-E5 (T5-WD-E5.doc) document, which is located in the Tut05\Word folder on your Data Disk. Click the Enable Macros button, if necessary, then save the document as T5-WD-E5D.

b. Open the Visual Basic Editor. Open the Module1 module's Code window, then view the EnterDates procedure. Study the existing code, then run the procedure. When the error message appears in the dialog box, click the Debug button to locate the error, then click the Reset button ■ on the Standard toolbar to stop the procedure.

c. Correct the error in the `dtmTomorrow = DateAdd(interval:="dd", Number:=-1, Date:=dtmToday)` instruction, then save the document and run the procedure again. Return to Word. Although the procedure did not end in an error, notice that it still is not working correctly.

d. Return to the Visual Basic Editor and correct the procedure.

e. Save the document, then run the procedure again. When the procedure is working correctly, save and then close the document.

Access Lesson

Using Date Variables in Access

case ▶ Professor Andrew Carlisle of Snowville College uses an Access database to keep track of the 10 projects he assigns in his Introduction to Programming course. The database contains a Projects table that includes fields for the project number, the date Professor Carlisle assigned the project, and the project's due date, which is always seven days after the assigned date. The database also includes a form named ProjectsForm. Professor Carlisle has decided to create a procedure that he can use to calculate a project's due date based on the assigned date he enters in the form.

Creating the AssignDates Procedure

Professor Carlisle's database is stored on your Data Disk. Begin by opening the database and viewing the ProjectsForm form. Then open the Visual Basic Editor and view the code template for the AssignDates procedure.

To open the database, view the form, and then view the AssignDates procedure in the Visual Basic Editor:

1 Start Microsoft Access. Open the **Carlisle** (Carlisle.mdb) database, which is located in the Tut05\Access folder on your Data Disk. Click the **Maximize** button ☐ on the Microsoft Access title bar to maximize the Microsoft Access window, if necessary.

2 Click **Forms** in the Objects bar of the Database window to display the Forms list. Right-click **ProjectsForm** and then click **Design View** to view the design of the form. Maximize the form. See Figure 5-32.

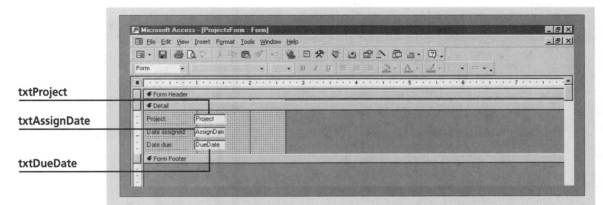

Figure 5-32: Open ProjectsForm form

The form contains three text boxes in which the user can enter the project number, assigned date, and due date. As Figure 5-32 shows, the names of the text boxes are txtProject, txtAssignDate, and txtDueDate.

> **tip**
>
> The three-character ID used to name text boxes is *txt*. You will learn more about a form's controls in Tutorial 12.

3   Click the form's **Restore Window** button 🖽, then close the form.

Next, open the Visual Basic Editor.

4   Press **Alt+F11** to open the Visual Basic Editor. If necessary, open the Project Explorer window and close the Properties window, the Immediate window, and any open Code windows.

5   Open the Module1 module's Code window, then view the code template for the AssignDates function procedure.

6   Close the Project Explorer window so that you can view more of the Code window.

As you learned in Tutorial 3, before entering instructions into a procedure, you should write down on a piece of paper what you want the procedure to accomplish, and the steps it will need to do so. Recall that these steps are called pseudocode. Figure 5-33 shows the pseudocode for the AssignDates procedure.

1. Use the InputBox function to prompt the user to enter the assigned date. Store the user's response in a String variable named strAssign.

2. Use the DateValue function to convert the string stored in the strAssign variable to a date, and then assign the result to a Date variable named dtmAssign.

3. Use the DateAdd function to calculate the due date, which is seven days from the assigned date. Assign the result to a Date variable named dtmDue.

4. Assign the assigned date, which is contained in the dtmAssign variable, to the txtAssignDate text box in the ProjectsForm form.

5. Assign the due date, which is contained in the dtmDue variable, to the txtDueDate text box in the ProjectsForm form.

Figure 5-33: Pseudocode for the AssignDates procedure

After determining the steps you want the procedure to take, you can begin coding the procedure. First examine the pseudocode to determine what variables, if any, the procedure will need to use. For example, Steps 1, 2, and 3 in the pseudocode indicate that the AssignDates procedure will use one String variable named strAssign and two Date variables named dtmAssign and dtmDue.

As you learned in Tutorial 4, slightly less obvious in the pseudocode are the object variables that a procedure will use. You can determine that information by looking for the objects mentioned in the pseudocode. In Figure 5-33's pseudocode, for example, notice that the ProjectsForm form is mentioned in the last two steps. You can make the AssignDates procedure easier to write and understand, and also make it run more efficiently, by assigning the address of the ProjectsForm Form object to an object variable. You will name the object variable frmProjects.

Recall from Tutorial 3's Concept lesson that the three-character ID for a Form object is *frm*.

In the next set of steps, you will declare the appropriate variables, and then translate each line in Figure 5-33's pseudocode into one or more VBA statements.

To code the AssignDates procedure:

1 The insertion point should be positioned in the blank line between the `Public Function` and `End Function` lines in the Code window. Enter the documentation and the Dim statement shown in Figure 5-34.

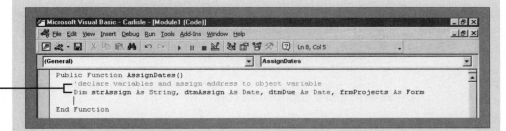

enter these
lines of code

```
Microsoft Visual Basic - Carlisle - [Module1 (Code)]                    _ 8 X
File  Edit  View  Insert  Debug  Run  Tools  Add-Ins  Window  Help        _ 8 X

                                                    Ln 8, Col 5

(General)                                    AssignDates

   Public Function AssignDates()
       'declare variables and assign address to object variable
      Dim strAssign As String, dtmAssign As Date, dtmDue As Date, frmProjects As Form

   End Function
```

Figure 5-34: Code window showing documentation and Dim statement

Next, you need to assign the address of the ProjectsForm Form object to the frmProjects object variable. As is true of reports, a form must be open before its address can be assigned to an object variable. In this case, Professor Carlisle will already have the form open before he runs the procedure, so there is no need for the procedure itself to open the form. Open forms in Access belong to the Application object's Forms collection.

> In this lesson's Exercise 3, you will modify the AssignDates procedure so that the procedure, rather than the user, opens the form.

2 Type **set frmprojects = application.forms("projectsform")** and press the **Enter** key.

You now can begin translating Figure 5-33's pseudocode into VBA statements. The first step in the pseudocode is to use the InputBox function to prompt the user to enter the date the project was assigned. Recall that the syntax of the InputBox function is **InputBox(Prompt:=**_prompt_ [**, Title:=**_title_] [**, Default:=**_defaultValue_]).

3 Type **'enter date assigned** and press the **Enter** key. Type **strassign = inputbox(prompt:="Enter date assigned:", title:="Date Assigned", default:= date)** and press the **Enter** key.

The next step in the pseudocode is to convert the string stored in the strAssign variable to a date, and then assign the result to the dtmAssign variable.

4 Type **'convert string to a date** and press the **Enter** key. Type **dtmassign = datevalue(date:=strassign)** and press the **Enter** key.

> Recall that when a function has only one argument, you can omit the argument's name and the := operator when entering the function in the Code window; in this case, you can omit Date:= from the DateValue function.

Next, use the DateAdd function to calculate the due date, which is seven days after the assigned date; assign the result to the dtmDue variable.

5 Type **'calculate the due date** and press the **Enter** key. Type **dtmdue = dateadd(interval:="d", number:=7, date:=dtmassign)** and press the **Enter** key.

The last two steps in the pseudocode are to assign the appropriate dates to the Form object's txtAssignDate and txtDueDate text boxes. You will learn how to do so in the next section.

Referring to a Control on a Form

Each of the text boxes on a form is considered a Control object in VBA, and each belongs to the Form object's Controls collection. You can use the *formObject*.**Controls**(*controlName*) syntax to refer to a control on a form. In the syntax, *controlName* is the name of the control and is enclosed in quotation marks. For example, `frmProjects.Controls("txtAssignDate")` refers to the txtAssignDate text box on the frmProjects form, and `frmProjects.Controls("txtDueDate")` refers to the form's txtDueDate text box.

You can change the value stored in a text box by assigning a new value to the text box's Value property. For example, you can use the `frmProjects.Controls ("txtAssignDate").Value = #10/30/02#` statement to assign the date literal constant #10/30/02# to the txtAssignDate text box's Value property. In the current procedure, you will need to assign the contents of the dtmAssign variable to the txtAssignDate text box, and assign the contents of the dtmDue variable to the txtDueDate text box.

To complete the AssignDates procedure:

1 Type the three lines of code shown in Figure 5-35, which shows the completed AssignDates procedure.

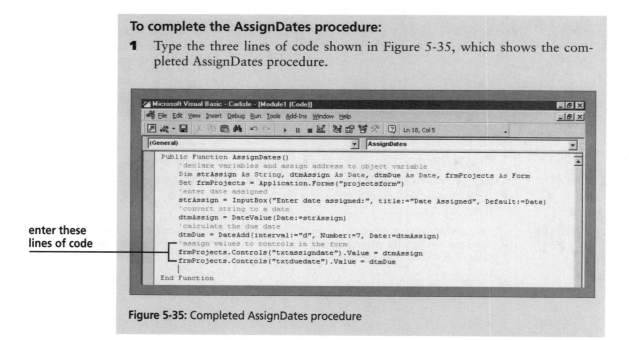

enter these
lines of code

Figure 5-35: Completed AssignDates procedure

2 Verify the accuracy of your code by comparing the code on your screen with the code shown in Figure 5-35.

3 Save the database.

Now that you have translated the pseudocode into VBA statements, you can create the macro that Professor Carlisle can use to run the AssignDates procedure.

To create the AssignDatesMacro macro:

1 Click the **View Microsoft Access** button 🖉 on the Standard toolbar to return to Access. Click **Macros** in the Objects bar of the Database window, then click the **New** button 🗷 in the Database window's toolbar to open the Macro window.

2 Click the **Action list arrow** that appears in the first line of the Macro window. Scroll down the list until you see RunCode, then click **RunCode**. Click **Function Name** in the Action Arguments section of the window, then type **AssignDates()** (be sure to type the parentheses) as the function name.

3 Click the **Save** button 🖫 on the Standard toolbar. When you are asked for the macro name, type **AssignDatesMacro** and press the **Enter** key, then close the Macro window.

In the next section, you will learn how to create a custom toolbar named Projects that includes a custom macro button.

Creating a Custom Toolbar and Button

Rather than running a macro from the Database window, as you have done in previous Access lessons, you can give a user access to the macro by adding a button to either one of Office 2000's existing toolbars, or you can create your own toolbar and add it there. In the next set of steps, you will learn how to create a custom toolbar named Projects that includes a button that represents the AssignDatesMacro macro.

To create a custom toolbar, and then add to it a button that represents a macro:

1 Click **Tools** on the Access menu bar and then click **Customize** to open the Customize dialog box. Click the **Toolbars** tab, if necessary, and then click the **New** button. The New Toolbar dialog box appears.

You will change the custom toolbar's name from Custom 1 to Projects.

2 Custom 1 should be selected in the Toolbar name text box, so you need simply to type **Projects** to change the toolbar's name.

3 Click the **OK** button to close the New Toolbar dialog box. The Projects toolbar appears next to the Customize dialog box, as shown in Figure 5-36.

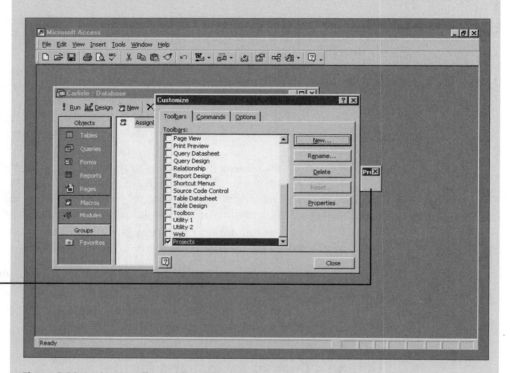

Projects toolbar

Figure 5-36: Projects toolbar added to the database

> **HELP?** Do not be concerned if your toolbar appears in a different location on the screen.

Next, you will add an Assign Project Dates button to the Projects toolbar.

4 Click the **Commands** tab in the Customize dialog box. Scroll down the Categories list box and then click **All Macros** in the list.

5 Click **AssignDatesMacro** in the Commands list box and hold down the mouse button as you drag **AssignDatesMacro** to the Projects toolbar, as shown in Figure 5-37.

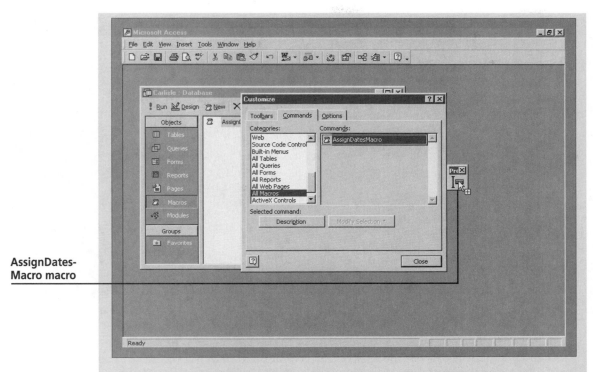

AssignDates-Macro macro

Figure 5-37: AssignDatesMacro macro being dragged to the Projects toolbar

6 Release the mouse button. The AssignDatesMacro button appears on the Projects toolbar.

Now change the name that appears on the button and add an icon to the button.

7 Click the **Modify Selection** button on the Commands tab. Click **Image and Text** on the shortcut menu to select that option.

8 Click the **Modify Selection** button, then click **Name,** and then type **Assign Project Dates** and press the **Enter** key.

9 Click the **Modify Selection** button, then point to **Change Button Image**. A palette of icons is displayed. Click the **hourglass icon,** which is the last icon in row six in the icon palette, then click the **Close** button in the Customize dialog box. Drag the Projects toolbar to the upper-right corner of the Microsoft Access window, as shown in Figure 5-38.

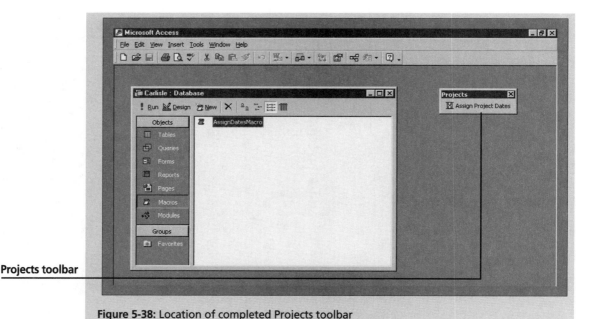

Projects toolbar

Figure 5-38: Location of completed Projects toolbar

Now use the Assign Project Dates button to test the macro and the AssignDates procedure.

To test the macro and the AssignDates procedure:

1 Click **Forms** in the Objects bar of the Database window to display the Forms list. Right-click **ProjectsForm** and then click **Open** to open the form. The insertion point is positioned in the first record's Project field.

2 Click the **Assign Project Dates** button on the Projects toolbar. When the Date Assigned dialog box appears, type **9/16/02** and then press the **Enter** key. The macro enters the assigned date (9/16/02) in the txtAssignDate text box, and it enters the due date (9/23/02) in the txtDueDate text box, as shown in Figure 5-39.

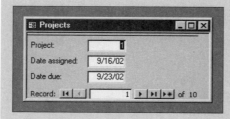

Figure 5-39: Projects form showing dates entered in first record

3 Click the **Next Record** button ▶ on the form to make the second record the current record. Click the **Assign Project Dates** button on the Projects toolbar. Type **9/25/02** as the assigned date, then press the **Enter** key. The macro enters 9/25/02 as the assigned date and 10/2/02 as the due date.

4 Close the form, then compact the database and exit Access.

You now have completed Tutorial 5's Access lesson. You can either take a break or complete the end-of-lesson exercises.

EXERCISES

1. In this exercise, you will create a function procedure, a macro, and a custom toolbar. The function procedure will calculate the date to send reminder notices to seminar participants.

   a. Use Windows to make a copy of the T5-AC-E1 (T5-AC-E1.mdb) database, which is located in the Tut05\Access folder on your Data Disk. Rename the copy T5-AC-E1D.mdb.

   b. Open the T5-AC-E1D (T5-AC-E1D.mdb) database in Access. Open the Seminars table in design view. Notice that the field names are SemID, SemName, SemDate, and ReminderDate, and that the SemDate and ReminderDate fields are Date/Time fields. Close the table.

   c. Open the SeminarsForm form. The four text boxes are named txtSemID, txtSemName, txtSemDate, and txtReminderDate. Scroll through the seven records. Notice that only the SemID and SemName fields contain data. Close the form.

   d. Open the Visual Basic Editor. Open the Module1 module's Code window, then view the Reminder function procedure.

   e. Use the pseudocode shown in Figure 5-40 to code the Reminder procedure.

---

1. Use the InputBox function to prompt the user to enter the seminar date. Store the user's response in a String variable named strSemDate.

2. Use the DateValue function to convert the string stored in the strSemDate variable to a date, and then assign the result to a Date variable named dtmSemDate.

3. Use the DateAdd function to calculate the reminder date, which is 10 days prior to the seminar date. Assign the result to a Date variable named dtmRemind.

4. Assign the seminar date, which is contained in the dtmSemDate variable, to the txtSemDate text box in the Seminars form.

5. Assign the reminder date, which is contained in the dtmRemind variable, to the txtReminderDate text box in the Seminars form.

Figure 5-40

f. Save the database, then return to Access. Create a macro named ReminderMacro that can be used to run the Reminder function procedure. Also create a custom toolbar that contains a custom macro button Drag the ReminderMacro macro to the button. Name the button Calculate Reminder Date.

g. Open the SeminarsForm form. Use the Calculate Reminder Date button on the custom toolbar to enter the following seminar dates:

Seminar ID	Seminar Date
1	6/1/02
2	7/3/02
3	7/28/02
4	8/15/02
5	9/1/02
6	9/5/02
7	9/15/02

h. Close the form. Compact and then close the database.

2. In this exercise, you will create a function procedure that calculates the number of days from the date an order is placed to the date the order is shipped.

a. Use Windows to make a copy of the T5-AC-E2 (T5-AC-E2.mdb) database, which is located in the Tut05\Access folder on your Data Disk. Rename the copy T5-AC-E2D.mdb.

b. Open the T5-AC-E2D (T5-AC-E2D.mdb) database in Access. Open the Invoices table in design view. Notice that the field names are InvNo, OrderDate, ShipDate, and Days, and that the OrderDate and ShipDate fields are Date/Time fields. Close the table.

c. Open the InvoicesForm form. The four text boxes are named txtInvNo, txtOrderDate, txtShipDate, and txtDays. Scroll through the five records. Notice that the Days field is empty in each of the records. Close the form.

d. Open the Visual Basic Editor. Open the Module1 module's Code window, then view the ShipDays function procedure. The ShipDays procedure should calculate the number of days between the order date and the ship date, and then assign the result to the txtDays control on the InvoicesForm form. Code the ShipDays procedure appropriately. (*Hint*: This procedure requires only a Form object variable. You do not need to create any String or Date variables.)

e. Save the database, then return to Access and open the InvoicesForm form. Display the Invoices toolbar, if necessary. Use the Calculate Days button on the Invoices toolbar to calculate the number of days between each record's order date and ship date.

f. Close the form. Compact and then close the database.

Exercises 3 through 5 are Discovery Exercises. Discovery Exercises, which may include topics that are not covered in the lesson, allow you to "discover" the solutions to problems on your own.

discovery ▶ 3. In this exercise, you will learn how to use the *wherecondition* argument in the DoCmd object's OpenForm method. You will modify the AssignDates procedure that you created in this lesson.

a. Use Windows to make a copy of the Carlisle (Carlisle.mdb) database, which is located in the Tut05\Access folder on your Data Disk. Rename the copy T5-AC-E3D.mdb.

b. Open the T5-AC-E3D (T5-AC-E3D.mdb) database in Access.

c. Open the Visual Basic Editor and view the Help screen for the DoCmd object's OpenForm method. Also view the example that the Help screen provides. Close the Help window.

d. View the AssignDates procedure. Modify the procedure so that it performs the tasks shown in Figure 5-41. The changes made to the original pseudocode shown in Figure 5-33 are shaded in Figure 5-41. (*Hints*: Be sure to use the names of the appropriate arguments in the OpenForm method; in this case, you will need to use the FormName and WhereCondition arguments. Use string concatenation to concatenate the Project field name and an equal sign with the strProjNum variable. You will need to use the OpenForm method before the Set statement.)

1. Use the InputBox function to prompt the user to enter the project number. Store the user's response in a String variable named strProjNum.

2. Open the ProjectsForm form, showing only the project requested by the user.

3. Use the InputBox function to prompt the user to enter the assigned date. Store the user's response in a String variable named strAssign.

4. Use the DateValue function to convert the string stored in the strAssign variable to a date, and then assign the result to a Date variable named dtmAssign.

5. Use the DateAdd function to calculate the due date, which is seven days from the assigned date. Assign the result to a Date variable named dtmDue.

6. Assign the assigned date, which is contained in the dtmAssign variable, to the txtAssignDate text box in the ProjectsForm form.

7. Assign the due date, which is contained in the dtmDue variable, to the txtDueDate text box in the ProjectsForm form.

Figure 5-41

e. Save the database, then return to Access. Use the Assign Project Dates button on the Projects toolbar to enter 7/2/02 as the assigned date for Project 6. Then use the Assign Project Dates button to enter 8/1/02 as the assigned date for Project 3.

f. Close the form, then compact and close the database.

discovery ▶ 4. In this exercise, you will learn how to use the *wherecondition* argument in the DoCmd object's OpenReport method.

a. Use Windows to make a copy of the T5-AC-E4 (T5-AC-E4.mdb) database, which is located in the Tut05\Access folder on your Data Disk. Rename the copy T5-AC-E4D.mdb.

b. Open the T5-AC-E4D (T5-AC-E4D.mdb) database in Access. Open the Orders report in Print Preview. Maximize the report to view its contents. Click the report's Restore Window button 🔲, then close the report.

c. Open the Visual Basic Editor and view the Help screen for the DoCmd object's OpenReport method. Also view the example that the Help screen provides. Close the Help window.

d. Open the Module1 module's Code window, then view the PrintReport function procedure. The procedure should prompt the user to enter the name of one of the date fields (Ordered, Required, Promised) and a date. It then should open the report, in print preview, showing only the records whose field and date matches the user's input. Code the procedure appropriately. Make the Ordered field name the *defaultValue* in the InputBox function that gets the field name, and make the system date the *defaultValue* in the InputBox function that gets the date. (*Hints*: Use string concatenation in the *wherecondition*. You will need to enclose, in number signs [#], the String variable that stores the date input by the user.)

e. Save the database. Return to Access. Display the Print Macro toolbar, if necessary. Use the Print Report button on the Print Macro toolbar to preview the report showing only the records whose order date is 2/1/02. Close the report.

f. Use the Print Report button on the Print Macro toolbar to preview the report showing only the records whose required date is 3/20/02.

g. Close the report, then compact and close the database.

discovery ▶ 5. In this exercise, you will modify the procedure that you created in Exercise 4 so that it prompts the user to enter the comparison operator for the OpenReport method's *wherecondition* argument.

a. Use Windows to make a copy of the T5-AC-E4D (T5-AC-E4D.mdb) database that you created in Exercise 4. The database is located in the Tut05\Access folder on your Data Disk. Rename the copy T5-AC-E5D.mdb.

b. Open the T5-AC-E5D (T5-AC-E5D.mdb) database in Access.

c. Open the Visual Basic Editor. Open the Module1 module's Code window, then view the PrintReport function procedure. Modify the procedure's code so that it prompts the user to enter the appropriate comparison operator (=, >, >=, <, <=, or <>). Make the equal sign (=) the *defaultValue* in the InputBox function. Modify the OpenReport method's *wherecondition* so that it uses the comparison operator entered by the user.

d. Save the database. Return to Access. Display the Print Macro toolbar, if necessary. Use the Print Report button on the Print Macro toolbar to preview the report showing only the records whose promised date is 3/1/02. Close the report.

e. Use the Print Report button on the Print Macro toolbar to preview the report showing only the records whose promised date is on or after 3/1/02. Close the report.

f. Compact and then close the database.

A computer program is good only if it works. Errors in programming code can cause a program to run incorrectly. Therefore, a programmer needs to know how to locate and fix any errors in his or her code. Exercise 6 is a Debugging Exercise. Debugging Exercises allow you to practice recognizing and solving errors in code.

debugging 6. The following code should add one year to the system date, and then display the new date in a message box. What is wrong with the code? Correct the error(s).

```
MsgBox Prompt:=DateAdd(Interval:="y", Number:=1, Date:=Date)
```

Numeric Variables

In this tutorial, you will learn how to:

- Reserve a numeric variable
- Use an assignment statement to assign a value to a numeric variable
- Perform calculations using arithmetic operators
- Add a list box to an Excel worksheet
- Use the Excel VLookup function in a procedure
- Search a table in Word
- Refer to the Access ADO object model in code
- Use the Recordset Object's Find method

Concept Lesson

Reserving a Procedure-level Numeric Variable

In Tutorials 3 through 5, you used the Dim statement to reserve procedure-level object, String, and Date variables. In this tutorial, you will learn how to use the Dim statement to reserve a procedure-level **numeric variable**, which is a memory cell that can store a number only. Recall that the syntax of the Dim statement is **Dim** *variablename* **As** *datatype*. When reserving a numeric variable, *datatype* can be any of the data types listed in Figure 6-1.

datatype Keyword	Name ID	Stores	Memory required	Range of values
Integer	int	Integers (whole numbers)	2 bytes	-32,768 to 32,767
Long	lng	Integers (whole numbers)	4 bytes	+/- 2 billion
Single	sng	Numbers with a decimal portion	4 bytes	0 Negative numbers: -3.402823E38 to -1.401298E-45 Positive numbers: 1.401298E-45 to 3.402823E38
Currency	cur	Numbers with a decimal portion	8 bytes	-922,337,203,685,477.5808 to 922,337,203,685,477.5807

Figure 6-1: Data types used to reserve numeric variables

Figure 6-1 shows only the most commonly used numeric data types. VBA also has Byte, Boolean, and Double data types. To view a full list of VBA data types, view the Dim Statement Help screen. Click See Also, then click Data Type Summary in the Topics Found dialog box, and then click the Display button.

The first two columns shown in Figure 6-1 list the VBA keyword and three-character ID associated with each numeric data type. As the figure indicates, you use the keywords `Integer`, `Long`, `Single`, and `Currency` to reserve numeric variables, and you use the three-character IDs *int*, *lng*, *sng*, and *cur* when naming the variables.

In addition to showing both the keyword and three-character ID associated with each numeric data type, Figure 6-1 also shows the range of values that each numeric data type can store and the amount of memory required to do so. For instance, variables assigned either the Integer or the Long data type can store integers, which are whole numbers—numbers without any decimal places. The differences between the two data types are in the range of numbers each type can store and the amount of memory each type needs to store the numbers. The memory requirement of a data type is an important consideration when coding a procedure. If you want to optimize a procedure's code, and thereby conserve system resources, you should use variables with smaller memory requirements wherever possible. For example, although a Long type variable can store a number in the Integer type range of −32,768 to 32,767, the Long data type takes twice as much memory to do so; the Long data type uses 4 bytes of memory, while the Integer data type uses only 2 bytes. (A byte is equivalent to a character.) Therefore, it would be more efficient to store a person's age in an Integer variable. You would need to use a Long variable, however, to store the population of a large city.

According to Figure 6-1, a Single type variable can store a number that has a decimal portion, and it uses 4 bytes to do so. A Single variable can contain the number 0, as well as negative numbers in the range of -3.402823E38 to -1.401298E-45, and positive numbers in the range of 1.401298E-45 to 3.402823E38. You would use a Single variable to store a sales tax rate—for example, .05.

The E shown in the range of Single numbers represents **exponential notation**—a convenient way of writing both extremely small and extremely large numbers. The positive number after the E indicates how many places to the right to move the decimal point. For example, 3.402823E38 indicates that you should move the decimal point 38 places to the right—an extremely large positive number. The negative number after the E indicates how many places to the left to move the decimal point. For example, 1.401298E-45 tells you to move the decimal point 45 places to the left—an extremely small positive number.

According to Figure 6-1, the Currency type variable also stores numbers with a decimal portion, but it uses 8 bytes to do so and the numbers that it can store range from -922,337,203,685,477.5808 to 922,337,203,685,477.5807. The Currency data type is provided for the express purpose of holding monetary values, such as sales amounts and gross pay amounts.

When you use the Dim statement to reserve a numeric variable, the variable is automatically initialized to the number 0. Figure 6-2 shows examples of Dim statements that reserve numeric variables.

Recall that object variables are initialized to the keyword `Nothing`, and String variables to a zero-length (empty) string. Date variables are initialized to the number 0.

Dim statement	Result
`Dim intAge As Integer`	Declares an Integer variable named intAge
`Dim lngPop As Long`	Declares a Long variable named lngPop
`Dim sngRate As Single`	Declares a Single variable named sngRate
`Dim curGross As Currency`	Declares a Currency variable named curGross

Figure 6-2: Examples of Dim statements that reserve numeric variables

Recall that variable names must begin with a letter and can contain only letters, numbers, and the underscore (_). Variable names cannot be longer than 255 characters and they cannot be reserved words. If you neglect to include the **As** *datatype* portion of the Dim statement, the default data type, Variant, is assigned to the variable. Recall that you should not use the Variant data type because it is not an efficient data type.

After using the Dim statement to both reserve and initialize a numeric variable, you can use an assignment statement to assign a different value to the variable.

Using an Assignment Statement to Assign a Value to a Numeric Variable

Recall that the format of an assignment statement that assigns a value to a variable is *variablename = value*. When *variablename* is the name of a numeric variable, *value* can be a number, more technically referred to as a numeric literal constant, or it can be a numeric expression. First learn how to assign a numeric literal constant to a numeric variable.

Assigning a Numeric Literal Constant to a Numeric Variable

A **numeric literal constant** is simply a number. Figure 6-3 shows examples of valid and invalid numeric literal constants.

Valid numeric literal constants	Invalid numeric literal constants
0	2%
.3	$4.56
4.5	123A
5	5,678
3200.67	"45"

Figure 6-3: Examples of valid and invalid numeric literal constants

As Figure 6-3 indicates, numeric literal constants can contain only numbers and the period. A numeric literal constant cannot contain a letter, except for the letter E, which is used in exponential notation. (Refer to the tip below Figure 6-4 for more information about exponential notation.) Numeric literal constants also cannot contain special symbols, such as the % sign, the $ sign, or the comma. They also cannot be enclosed in quotation marks ("") or number signs (#), because numbers enclosed in quotation marks are considered string literal constants, and numbers enclosed in number signs are considered date literal constants.

···

You learned about string literal constants in Tutorial 4 and about date literal constants in Tutorial 5.

···

Figure 6-4 shows examples of assignment statements that assign numeric literal constants to the numeric variables reserved in Figure 6-2.

```
intAge = 21

lngPop = 60450

sngRate = 0.05

curGross = 300.75
```

Figure 6-4: Examples of assignment statements that assign numeric literal constants to variables

···

You also can assign a number written in exponential notation to a numeric variable. For example, you can type `sngTotal = 3.45E2` **in a procedure's Code window. When you move to the next line in the Code window, the Visual Basic Editor will change the 3.45E2 to 345.**

···

Next, learn how to assign a numeric expression to a numeric variable.

Assigning a Numeric Expression to a Numeric Variable

As mentioned earlier, the *value* assigned to a numeric variable can be a numeric expression. **Numeric expressions** can contain items such as numeric literal constants, variable names, functions, and arithmetic operators. Figure 6-5 lists the arithmetic operators you can use in a numeric expression, along with each operator's precedence number. The precedence numbers represent the order in which the arithmetic operations are processed in an expression. However, you can use parentheses to override the order of precedence because operations within parentheses always are performed before operations outside of parentheses.

Operator	Operation	Order of precedence
^	exponentiation (raises a number to a power)	1
-	negation	2
*, /	multiplication and division	3
+, -	addition and subtraction	4
Important Note: You can use parentheses to override the order of precedence. Operations within parentheses are always performed before operations outside parentheses.		

Figure 6-5: Arithmetic operators and their order of precedence

When you create a numeric expression that contains more than one arithmetic operator, keep in mind that VBA follows the same order of precedence as you do when evaluating the expression; that is, operations with a precedence number of 1 are performed before operations with a precedence number of 2, and so on. If the expression contains more than one operator having the same priority, those operators are evaluated from left to right. For example, in the equation 3+9/3*5, the division (/) would be performed first, then the multiplication (*), and then the addition (+). In other words, VBA first would divide 9 by 3, then multiply by 5, and then add 3. The expression evaluates to 18. You can use parentheses to change the order in which the operators will be evaluated. For example, the expression (3+9)/3*5 evaluates to 20, not 18. That's because the parentheses tell VBA to add 3 + 9 first, then divide by 3, and then multiply by 5. Figure 6-6 shows examples of assignments statements that contain numeric expressions.

Statement	Result
`intNum = 8 / 2 + 6 * 3`	The number 22 assigned to the intNum variable
`intNum = 8 / (2 + 6) * 3`	The number 3 assigned to the intNum variable
`curGross = intHours * curRate`	If the intHours variable contains 40 and the curRate variable contains 5.75, then the number 230 is assigned to the curGross variable
`sngAvg = intN1 + intN2 / 2`	If the intN1 variable contains 5 and the intN2 variable contains 10, then the number 10 is assigned to the sngAvg variable
`sngAvg = (intN1 + intN2) / 2`	If the intN1 variable contains 5 and the intN2 variable contains 10, then the number 7.5 is assigned to the sngAvg variable
`lngSquare = intNum ^ 2`	If the intNum variable contains 1000, then the number 1,000,000 is assigned to the lngSquare variable
`sngHours = Val(String:=strHours)`	Assigns the numeric equivalent of the string stored in the strHours variable to the sngHours variable

Figure 6-6: Examples of assignment statements containing numeric expressions

The assignment statement `intNum = 8 / 2 + 6 * 3` tells VBA first to divide 8 by 2 (giving 4), and then multiply 6 by 3 (giving 18), and then add 4 to 18 (giving 22). The statement assigns the number 22 to the intNum variable. Notice that the second example shown in Figure 6-6 is identical to the first example, except parentheses are placed around the 2 + 6. The second example results in the number 3 being assigned to the intNum variable. This is because the 8 / (2 + 6) * 3 expression tells VBA first to add 2 to 6 (giving 8), then divide 8 by 8 (giving 1), and then multiply 1 by 3 (giving 3).

The third example shown in Figure 6-6, `curGross = intHours * curRate`, tells VBA to multiply the contents of the intHours variable (40) by the contents of the curRate variable (5.75), and then assign the product (230) to the curGross variable. Figure 6-6's fourth example, `sngAvg = intN1 + intN2 / 2`, tells VBA first to divide the contents of the intN2 variable (10) by 2, and then add the quotient (5) to the contents of the intN1 variable (5). The statement assigns the result (10) to the sngAvg variable. The fifth example is identical to the fourth example, except parentheses are placed around the intN1 + intN2. In this case, the `sngAvg = (intN1 + intN2)` `/ 2` assignment statement tells VBA first to add the contents of the intN1 variable (5) to the contents of the intN2 variable (10), and then divide the sum (15) by 2. The statement assigns the result (7.5) to the sngAvg variable. The sixth example shown in Figure 6-6, `lngSquare = intNum ^ 2`, tells VBA to multiply the contents of the intNum variable (1000) by itself—in other words, it tells VBA to square the contents of the intNum variable. The statement assigns the result (1,000,000) to the lngSquare variable. The last example shown in Figure 6-6, `sngHours = Val(String:=strHours)`, uses the Val function to assign the numeric equivalent of the string stored in the strHours variable to the sngHours variable.

You now have completed Tutorial 6's Concept lesson. You can either take a break or complete the end-of-lesson questions and exercises before moving on to the next lesson.

SUMMARY

To reserve a procedure-level numeric variable:

- Use the Dim statement. The syntax of the Dim statement is **Dim** *variablename* **As** *datatype*, where *variablename* represents the name of the variable (memory cell) and *datatype*, which can be any of the keywords shown in Figure 6-1, is the type of data the variable can store. Figure 6-1 also shows the three-character ID associated with each numeric data type. Numeric variables can store only numbers and the period.

- Variable names must begin with a letter and they can contain only letters, numbers, and the underscore (_). Variable names cannot be longer than 255 characters and they cannot be reserved words.

To assign a value to a numeric variable:

- Use an assignment statement in the following syntax: *variablename* = *value*. In the syntax, *value* can be a numeric literal constant or a numeric expression containing items such as numeric literal constants, variable names, functions, or arithmetic operators.

REVIEW QUESTIONS

1. Assume that you want to store whole numbers in the range of 5 through 100 in a numeric variable. The most efficient data type to use for the variable is _____.
   a. Currency
   b. Integer
   c. Long
   d. Single

2. Assume that you want to store numbers in the range of 0 through 0.75 in a numeric variable. The most efficient data type to use for the variable is _____.
   a. Currency
   b. Integer
   c. Long
   d. Single

3. Which of the following are valid numeric literal constants?
   a. 1.2
   b. 3,500
   c. "5.67"
   d. None of the above

4. Which of the following are valid numeric literal constants?
   a. "85"
   b. 100%
   c. $45
   d. None of the above

5. The ID associated with names of Single variables is _____.
   a. sgl
   b. sin
   c. slg
   d. sng

6. The expression 5 – 4 / 4 * 6 + 3 will result in the number _____.
   a. 2
   b. 4.5
   c. 7.833
   d. None of the above

7. The expression 2 * 4 ^ 3 - 1 will result in the number _____.
   a. 32
   b. 127
   c. 511
   d. None of the above

8. Which of the following statements should you use to assign the contents of the strNum variable to the sngNum variable? (Recall that `String:=` is not required in the Val function.)
   a. `sngNum = Val(strNum)`
   b. `strNum = sngNum`
   c. `strNum = Val(sngNum)`
   d. `Val(strNum) = sngNum`

EXERCISES

1. a. Write a Dim statement that reserves an Integer variable named intQuantity.
    b. Write an assignment statement that assigns the numeric literal constant 5 to the intQuantity variable.

2. Write an assignment statement that assigns the numeric equivalent of the value stored in the strAge variable to the intAge variable.

3. a. Write a Dim statement that reserves a Currency variable named curPayRate and a String variable named strPayRate.
    b. Write an assignment statement that assigns the value returned by the InputBox function to the strPayRate variable. Use "Enter the pay rate:" as the *prompt*, and use "Pay Rate" as the *title*. Display the number 5 as the *defaultValue*.
    c. Write an assignment statement that assigns the contents of the strPayRate variable, treated as a number, to the curPayRate variable.

4. Write an assignment statement that multiplies the contents of the curSales variable by the contents of the curRate variable, and then assigns the result to the curCommission variable.

5. Write an assignment statement that adds the contents of the curRegular variable to the contents of the curOvertime variable, and then assigns the result to the curTotal variable.

6. Write an assignment statement that adds the number 10 to the contents of the sngBonus variable, and then displays the result in a message box.

7. Write an assignment statement that cubes the number 5, and then assigns the result to the lngCubed variable.

8. Write an assignment statement that finds the average of the numbers stored in the curNorth, curSouth, curEast, and curWest variables, and then assigns the result to the curAvg variable.

Exercises 9 and 10 are Discovery Exercises. Discovery Exercises, which may include topics that are not covered in the lesson, allow you to "discover" the solutions to problems on your own.

discovery ▶ 9. In this exercise, you will learn about the \ and Mod arithmetic operators.
    a. Start either Word, Excel, Access, or PowerPoint. Open the Visual Basic Editor. Display the \ Operator Help screen. The \ operator is referred to as the integer division operator. Use the Help screen to complete the following two statements.
    The \ operator is used to _____.
    Its syntax is _____.
    b. Click Example at the top of the Help screen. Study the examples shown in the Help screen.
    c. Display the Mod Operator Help screen. Use the Help screen to complete the following two statements.
    The Mod operator is used to _____.
    Its syntax is _____.

d. Click Example at the top of the Help screen. Study the examples shown in the Help screen, then close the Help window.

e. Open the Immediate window. Enter the commands shown in Figure 6-7 in the Immediate window. Notice that the commands include the division (/), integer division (\), and Mod operators. Record the results.

Command	Result
? 7 / 3	
? 7 \ 3	
? 7 Mod 3	
? 23 / 4	
? 23 \ 4	
? 23 Mod 4	
? 8.4 / 2	
? 8.4 \ 2	
? 8.4 Mod 2	
? 8.6 / 2	
? 8.6 \ 2	
? 8.6 Mod 2	

Figure 6-7

f. Assume that a company has 5125 cups in inventory, and that the company can pack 33 cups in a box. Use the \ operator in an expression to calculate the number of full boxes that can be packed, then use the Mod operator to calculate the number of cups left over. Verify the accuracy of the expressions by entering each expression in the Immediate window, preceded by the ?. Record the expressions and their results on a piece of paper.

g. Close the Visual Basic Editor. Also close either Word, Excel, Access, or PowerPoint.

discovery ▶ 10. In this exercise, you will learn about the type conversion functions.

a. Start either Word, Excel, Access, or PowerPoint. Open the Visual Basic Editor. Display the Type Conversion Functions Help screen. Use the Help screen to complete the following three statements.

The conversion functions coerce an _____ to a specific _____.

You should use the conversion functions instead of Val to _____.

When the fractional part of a number is exactly 0.5, CInt and CLng always round the number to the _____. For example, CInt and CLng would round 1.5 to _____ and they would round 2.5 to _____.

b. Click Example at the top of the Help screen. Display the examples for the CCur, CInt, CLng, and CSng functions. Study the examples shown in the Help screens, then close the Help window.

c. Open the Immediate window. Enter the commands shown in Figure 6-8 in the Immediate window. Record the results. (Recall that when a function has only one argument, it is a common practice to omit the argument's name and the := operator when typing the function.)

Command	Result
? Val(1.5)	
? CInt(1.5)	
? Val(2.5)	
? CInt(2.5)	
? Val(a)	
? CLng(a)	
? Val("a")	
? CSng("a")	
? Val("$4.50")	
? CSng("$4.50")	
? Val("2,300"))	
? CCur("2,300")	

Figure 6-8

d. Close the Visual Basic Editor. Also close either Word, Excel, Access, or PowerPoint.

You also can use VBA in PowerPoint to create procedures that enhance your presentations. Exercise 11 allows you to apply this tutorial's programming concept in a PowerPoint presentation.

powerpoint ▬ 11. In this exercise, you will create a procedure in PowerPoint that calculates and displays the commission for the year.

a. Open the T6-PP-E11 (T6-PP-E11.ppt) presentation, which is located in the Tut06\Concept folder on your Data Disk. Click the Enable Macros button, if necessary, then save the presentation as T6-PP-E11D.

b. Open the Visual Basic Editor. Open the Module1 module's Code window, then view the partially completed CalcCommission procedure. Study the existing code. The last assignment statement will display the sales and commission amounts on separate lines on the presentation's first slide. (As you learned in Tutorial 4, the vbNewLine constant causes the insertion point to move to the next line.)

c. To complete the CalcCommission procedure, declare two Currency variables named curSales and curComm and a Single variable named sngRate. Use the Val function to convert the contents of the strSales variable to a number; assign the result to the curSales variable. Also use the Val function to convert the contents of the strRate variable to a decimal number; assign the result to the sngRate variable. Calculate the commission by multiplying the contents of the curSales variable by the contents of the sngRate variable; assign the result to the curComm variable.

d. Save the presentation, then run the procedure. Enter 1000 as the sales and 10 as the rate. Return to PowerPoint to verify that the sales and commission appear on the first slide.

e. Return to the Visual Basic Editor and run the CalcCommission procedure. This time enter the letter A as the sales and the letter B as the rate. Return to PowerPoint. The first slide displays $0.00 as the sales and commission amounts. On a piece of paper, explain why $0.00 appears on the first slide.

f. Right-click the picture that appears on the first slide, then click Action Settings on the shortcut menu to display the Action Settings dialog box. Click the Run macro option button on the dialog box's Mouse Click tab, then click the OK button.

g. Save the presentation. Click View on the menu bar and then click Slide Show. When the slide appears, click the picture. Enter 250500 as the sales and 10 as the rate. The message box displays $25,000.00 as the commission amount. Press the Esc key to stop the slide show.

h. Save the presentation, then close PowerPoint.

A computer program is good only if it works. Errors in programming code can cause a program to run incorrectly. Therefore, a programmer needs to know how to locate and fix any errors in his or her code. Exercise 12 is a Debugging Exercise. Debugging Exercises allow you to practice recognizing and solving errors in code.

debugging

12. The following code should assign the average of the numbers stored in the curRegion1 and curRegion2 variables to the curAvg variable. It then should display the average in a message box. However, when curRegion1 is 1000 and curRegion2 is 2000, the number 2000, rather than the number 1500, appears in the message box. What is wrong with the following code? Correct any errors.

```
curAvg = curRegion1 + curRegion2 / 2
MsgBox Prompt:=curAvg
```

Excel Lesson

Using Numeric Variables in Excel

case ▶ In an effort to boost sales in its Jackson store, Paradise Electronics mailed a discount coupon to each of the customers on the store's mailing list. The discounts, which range from 10 percent to 25 percent, apply to new computers purchased between May 1st and June 30th. The model numbers and prices of the computers are stored in an Excel workbook. Jake Yardley, the Jackson store manager, has decided to create a list box and a procedure that the clerks can use to calculate the discounted price when a customer uses the coupon to purchase a computer.

Viewing the Paradise Electronics Price List

Your Data Disk contains the Paradise Electronics price list in an Excel workbook. Begin by opening that workbook and viewing the price list.

To open Jake's workbook and view the Paradise Electronics price list:

1 Start Microsoft Excel. Open the **T6-EX-1** (T6-EX-1.xls) workbook, which is located in the Tut06\Excel folder on your Data Disk. Save the workbook as **Price List**. The Price List workbook contains one worksheet, named Computers, as shown in Figure 6-9.

The Computers worksheet contains the Paradise Electronics price list in cells F3 through G13; column F in that range shows each computer's unique model number, and column G shows each computer's price. To make it easier to refer to the price list when coding, you will assign the name PriceList to the range F3:G13.

Name Box

price list

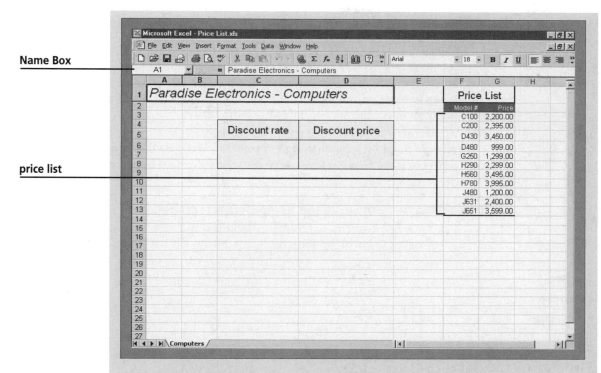

Figure 6-9: Price List workbook showing the Computers worksheet

2   Select the range of cells **F3:G13**, which contains the price list. Click the **Name Box**, which is located immediately above column A in the worksheet, then type **PriceList** and press the **Enter** key. PriceList appears in the Name Box. Click cell **A1** to make it the active cell.

> You also can click Insert on the menu bar, point to Name, and then click Define to add and delete range names from a worksheet.

When a range has a name, you can use its name rather than its cell addresses in a VBA statement; doing so makes the statement more self-documenting and, therefore, easier to understand. For example, the range name PriceList is much more meaningful than are the cell addresses F3:G13, because the range name makes it clear as to what data the statement refers.

Before you can create the procedure that the clerks will use to calculate a computer's discounted price, you first must add a list box to the worksheet. The clerks will use the list box to select the model number of the computer whose price should be discounted.

Creating a List Box

A **list box** is one of several objects, called **controls**, that can be added to a worksheet. You typically use a list box to display a set of choices from which the user can select only one. List boxes help prevent errors from occurring in the worksheet because, rather than relying on the user to enter the data correctly, the list box allows the user simply to select the appropriate data from its list.

> **tip**
>
> You also can create list boxes that allow the user to select more than one item in the list.

To add a list box control to the Computers worksheet:

1 Click **View** on the menu bar, point to **Toolbars**, and then click **Control Toolbox** to display the Control Toolbox toolbar, which is shown in Figure 6-10.

Text Box
Properties
Design Mode
View Code
Check Box
Command Button
List Box
Toggle Button
Scroll bar
Image
More Controls
Label
Spin Button
Combo Box
Option Button

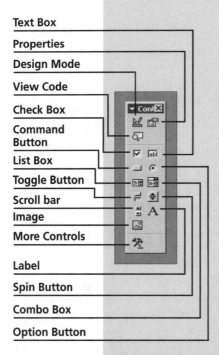

Figure 6-10: Control Toolbox toolbar

> **tip**
>
> You will learn more about the tools on the Control Toolbox toolbar in Tutorials 12 and 13.

The Control Toolbox toolbar is separated into three sections. The top section contains three buttons named Design Mode, Properties, and View Code. The middle section contains 11 buttons; each button represents a tool that you can use to draw a control—such as a text box, command button, and list box—on the worksheet. The bottom section contains one button named More Controls. You can use the More Controls button to add additional tools to the toolbar.

When the Design Mode button 🖾 is selected in the top section of the Control Toolbox toolbar, you can use the toolbar tools to draw new controls on the worksheet and also edit existing controls. Selecting the Properties button 🖻 displays the Properties window. As you learned in Tutorial 1, the Properties window lists the properties that control an object's appearance and behavior; it also lists the default value assigned to each property. Selecting the View Code button 🖳 opens the selected object's Code window in the Visual Basic Editor. You will use the Control Toolbox toolbar to add a list box control to the Computers worksheet.

2 Click the **List Box** button 🖼 on the Control Toolbox toolbar. Notice that selecting 🖼 also selects the Design Mode button 🖾. (You can tell that the buttons are selected because both buttons appear indented.)

3 When you move the mouse pointer onto the worksheet, the mouse pointer becomes a crosshair ✛. Place the ✛ as shown in Figure 6-11.

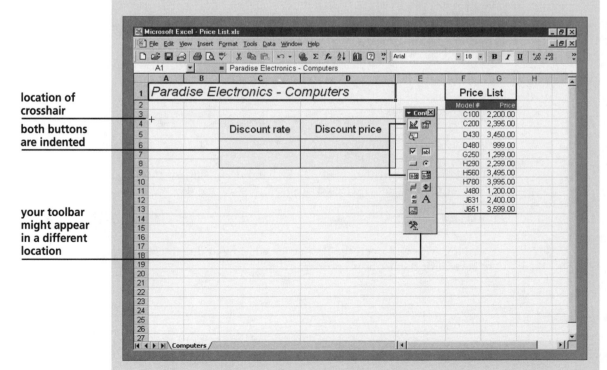

location of crosshair

both buttons are indented

your toolbar might appear in a different location

Figure 6-11: Placement of crosshair

HELP? Do not be concerned if your Control Toolbox toolbar appears in a different location from that shown in the figure. You can reposition the toolbar by dragging it by its title bar.

4 Drag the mouse down and to the right. When the list box control is about the size shown in Figure 6-12, release the mouse button.

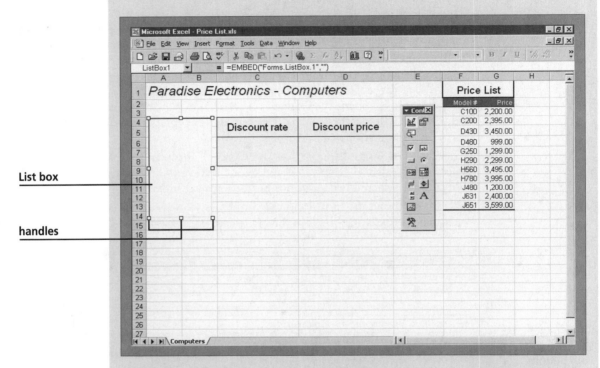

Figure 6-12: List box control drawn on the worksheet

As indicated in the figure, eight handles appear on the list box, indicating that the list box is selected. You can use the handles to change the size of the list box.

Next you will open the Properties window and then change the value assigned to several of the list box's properties.

To change the value assigned to several of the list box's properties:

1 Click the **Properties** button 🖹 on the Control Toolbox toolbar to open the Properties window. If necessary, click **(Name)** to select the Name property. See Figure 6-13.

Settings box

Object box

Properties list

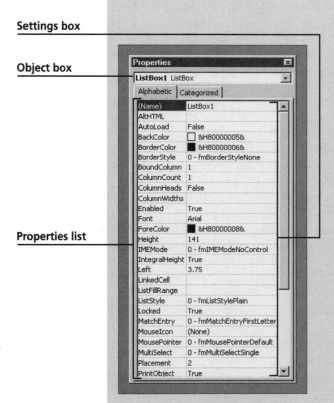

Figure 6-13: Properties window

As indicated in the figure, the Properties window includes an Object box and a Properties list. The **Object box**, located immediately below the Properties window's title bar, displays the name and type of the selected object—in this case, **ListBox1** ListBox. When you click the Object list arrow, a list of objects included in the worksheet will appear. You can use the list to select a different object in the worksheet. You must select an object before you can either display or change the value of its properties.

The **Properties list**, which can be displayed either alphabetically or by category, has two columns. The left column displays all the properties associated with the selected object (in this case, the list box). The right column, called the **Settings box**, displays the current value, or setting, of each of those properties. For example, the current value of the list box's Name property is ListBox1.

You can change the setting for many of the listed properties simply by typing a new value in the property's Settings box. Some properties, however, have predefined settings. If a property has predefined settings, either a list arrow button or an ellipsis (...) button will appear in the Settings box when the property is selected. When you click the list arrow button, either a list or a color palette appears containing the valid predefined settings for that property; you then select the setting you want from that list or color palette. Clicking the ellipsis button in the Settings box displays a dialog box in which you select the settings for the property.

First change the list box's default name (ListBox1) to lstModel, which is a more descriptive name for a list box that will display the model numbers of the computers. In this case, the lst identifies the control as a list box, and Model reminds you of the list box's purpose.

The rules for naming controls are the same as the rules for naming variables, which are listed in Tutorial 3's Figure 3-7. The three-character prefix for list box names is lst.

2   (Name) is already selected in the Properties list, so you just need to type **lstModel** (be sure to type the letter l and not the number 1) and then press the **Enter** key.

You can use the list box's **ListFillRange property** to specify the range of data you want the list box to display. In this case, you want the list box to display the model numbers contained in the range F3:F13 in the worksheet.

3   Click **ListFillRange** in the Properties list, then type **f3:f13** and press the **Enter** key. The list box displays the model numbers contained in the range F3:F13, as shown in Figure 6-14.

If you change a value stored in the range F3:F13, the new value will replace the previous value in the list box.

You can make the list box more descriptive by including the column heading contained in cell F2, Model #, in the list box.

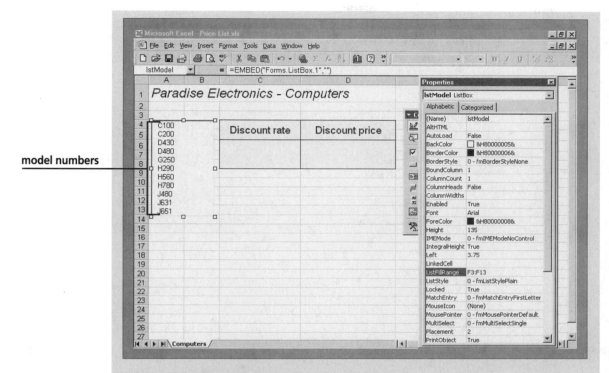

model numbers

Figure 6-14: Model numbers displayed in the list box

4   Click **ColumnHeads** in the Properties list. Notice that the default value of this property is the Boolean value False and that a list arrow button appears in this property's Settings box. To display, in the list box, the column heading that appears above the range F3:F13, click the **list arrow** button in the Settings box, then click **True** in the list. Model # appears above the model numbers in the list box.

Now change the size of the font used to display the list box data.

5   Click **Font** in the Properties list, then click the ... (ellipsis) button in the Settings box. When the Font dialog box appears, click **14** in the Size list box, then click the **OK** button.

Notice that a vertical scroll bar now appears on the list box. When the list box is too small to display all of its data, either a vertical scroll bar or a horizontal scroll bar, or both, will appear automatically on the list box. You can use the scroll bars to view the complete list of items.

Now close the Properties window, and then use the handles that appear on the list box to change the height and width of the list box.

6 Close the Properties window. Drag the center handle that appears on the bottom of the list box until the list box displays all 11 of its items, then drag the center handle that appears on the right side of the list box until the list box is approximately the size shown in Figure 6-15.

Exit Design Mode button

correct size of list box

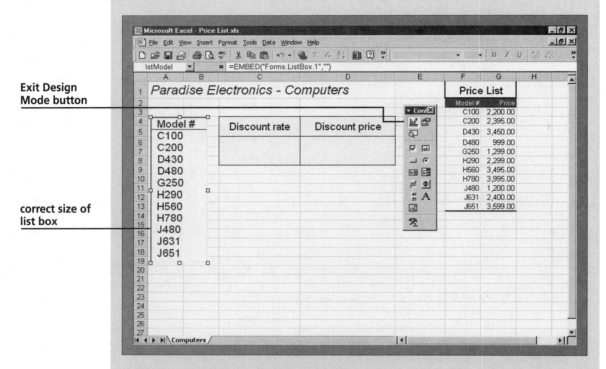

Figure 6-15: List box shown in the correct size

Now that the list box has been created and the appropriate properties set, you can exit Design Mode and then close the Control Toolbox toolbar.

7 Click the **Exit Design Mode** button ![icon] on the Control Toolbox toolbar to exit Design Mode. Notice that doing so removes the eight handles from the list box. Close the Control Toolbox toolbar.

 tip

Before you can make subsequent changes to the lstModel control, you will need first to display the Control Toolbox toolbar and then click the Design Mode button ![icon].

Now protect the worksheet so that the user cannot inadvertently change its contents.

8 Click **Tools** on the menu bar, point to **Protection**, and then click **Protect Sheet**. Verify that the Contents, Objects, and Scenarios check boxes are selected in the Protect Sheet dialog box, then click the **OK** button.

9   Save the workbook.

Now that the list box has been created and the appropriate properties set, you can begin coding the procedure that will calculate the discounted price of a computer. The procedure that you will code is the list box's DblClick event procedure.

Coding the List Box's DblClick Event Procedure

A list box's **DblClick event procedure** occurs when the user double-clicks an item in the list. Figure 6-16 shows the pseudocode for the list box's DblClick event procedure.

---

1. Unprotect the Computers worksheet.
2. Use the InputBox function to prompt the user to enter the discount rate as a whole number. Store the user's response in a String variable named strRate.
3. Convert the rate stored in the strRate variable to its decimal equivalent by dividing the rate by 100. Store the result in a Single variable named sngRate.
4. Use the VLookup worksheet function to search the first column of the price list for the model number that is selected in the lstModel list box. Assign the computer's price from the second column of the price list to a Currency variable named curPrice.
5. Calculate the discounted price first by subtracting the discount rate, which is stored in the sngRate variable, from the number 1, and then multiplying that difference by the computer's price, which is stored in the curPrice variable. Assign the discounted price to a Currency variable named curDiscPrice.
6. Display the discount rate, which is stored in the sngRate variable, in cell C6 in the Computers worksheet.
7. Display the discounted price, which is stored in the curDiscPrice variable, in cell D6 in the Computers worksheet.
8. Protect the Computers worksheet.

Figure 6-16: Pseudocode for the list box's DblClick event procedure

Figure 6-17 lists the variables that the DblClick event procedure will use.

Variables	datatype
strRate	String
sngRate	Single
curPrice	Currency
curDiscPrice	Currency
shtComputers	Worksheet

Figure 6-17: Variables used by the list box's DblClick event procedure

In the next set of steps, you will declare the appropriate variables.

To begin coding the DblClick event procedure:

1 Press Alt+F11 to open the Visual Basic Editor. If necessary, open the Project Explorer window and close the Properties window, the Immediate window, and any open Code windows.

2 Right-click **Sheet1 (Computers)** in the Project Explorer window, and then click **View Code**. Click the **Object box list arrow**, then click **lstModel** in the list. The code template for the lstModel control's Click event procedure appears in the Code window.

3 Click the **Procedure box list arrow**, then click **DblClick** in the list to view the code template for the lstModel control's DblClick event procedure. At this point, you do not need to be concerned about the information contained in the parentheses after the event procedure's name. Items inside an event procedure's parentheses are called arguments, and they are used by VBA to pass information to the event procedure. You will learn about event procedure arguments in Tutorial 13.

4 Close the Project Explorer window so that you can view more of the Code window, then enter the documentation and the Dim and Set statements shown in Figure 6-18.

enter these lines of code

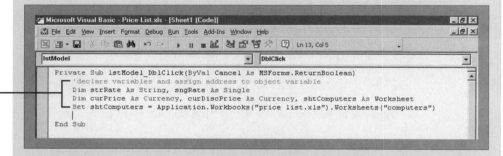

Figure 6-18: Code window showing documentation and Dim and Set statements

You now can begin translating the pseudocode shown in Figure 6-16 into VBA statements. The first step is to unprotect the Computers worksheet so the macro can display the discount rate and the discounted price in the appropriate worksheet cells.

5 Type **'unprotect worksheet** and press the **Enter** key, then type **shtcomputers.unprotect** and press the **Enter** key.

> **tip**
>
> A procedure cannot enter data into a protected worksheet.

The second step in the pseudocode is to use the InputBox function to get the discount rate (entered as a whole number) from the user, and then assign the user's response to the strRate variable. You will make the number 0 the *defaultValue* in the InputBox function.

6 Type **'enter discount rate** and press the **Enter** key. Type **strrate = inputbox(prompt:="Enter discount rate (whole number):", _** (be sure to type the comma followed by a space and the underscore) and press the **Enter** key. Press the **Tab** key, then type **title:="Rate", default:=0)** and press the **Enter** key.

Next, convert the discount rate to its decimal equivalent by dividing the rate by 100, and then assign the result to the sngRate variable.

7 Press the **Backspace** key, then type the additional two lines of code shown in Figure 6-19.

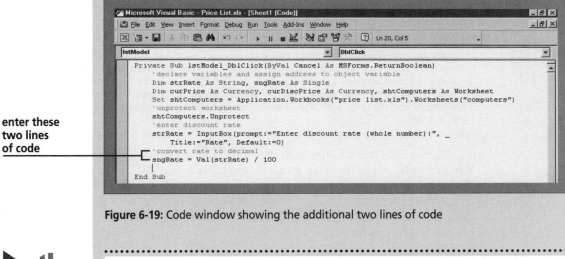

enter these
two lines
of code

Figure 6-19: Code window showing the additional two lines of code

8 Save the workbook.

Step 4 in the pseudocode is to use the VLookup worksheet function to search the price list for the model number selected in the list box, and then return its price. Before you can code this step, you need to learn how to use Excel's VLookup function in a VBA procedure.

Using the Excel VLookup Function in a Procedure

You can use most of the Excel worksheet functions—for example, Sum, Min, Max, Average, Vlookup, HLookup, and so on—in a VBA statement. The Excel worksheet functions are available through the WorksheetFunction object, which is contained within the Excel Application object.

> To view a listing of Excel functions available to VBA, display the WorksheetFunction Object Help screen. Click Methods to open the Topics Found dialog box, then click List of Worksheet Functions Available to Visual Basic, and then click the Display button.

You can use Excel's VLookup function to search for, or "look up," a value located in the first column of a vertical list, and then return a value located in one or more columns to its right. The values listed in the first and subsequent columns of the list form a **table**, which is simply a group of related facts arranged in rows and columns.

> The V in the VLookup function's name stands for "vertical." Excel also has an HLookup function, which performs a horizontal lookup. You use the VLookup function to search tables that are arranged vertically, with the information to be looked up appearing in the first column of the table. You use the HLookup function to search tables that are arranged horizontally, with the information to be looked up appearing in the first row of the table.

You already are familiar with the concept of looking up information in a table. For example, a phone book is an example of a vertical table; names are listed alphabetically in the first column and the corresponding phone numbers are listed in the second column. To locate a person's phone number, you first look up his or her name in the first column of the table, then you look one column to the right to get the phone number. You use a vertical table—the federal income tax table—to determine your yearly income tax. Recall that you first must look up your taxable income in the first column of the table, which contains income amounts arranged in ascending numerical order. After locating your taxable income, you then look one or more columns to the right, depending on your filing status, to find the amount of your income tax. Similarly, the list box's DblClick event procedure will need to look up the model number in the first column of the price list in order to determine the computer's price, which is located in the second column.

Figure 6-20 shows the syntax of the VLookup function.

Syntax: **Application.WorksheetFunction.VLookup(***lookup_value,* **Range(***table*)**,** *col_index_num, range_lookup***)**	
lookup_value	The value to be found in the first column of *table*.
Range(*table*)	The location of the range that contains the table of information. *Table* must be enclosed in quotation marks.
col_index_num	A number that indicates the *table* column from which the desired value is returned. A *col_index_num* of 1 returns the value located in the first column of the table. A *col_index_num* of 2 returns the value located in the second colum of the table, and so on.
range_lookup	A Boolean value that specifies whether you want the function to find an exact match (False) or an approximate match (True or omitted).

Figure 6-20: Syntax of the VLookup function

In the VLookup function's syntax, *lookup_value* is the value to be found in the first column of *table*, which is the location of the range that contains the table of information. *Col_index_num* is the number of the column from which the desired value—for example, the phone number, income tax, and computer's price—is returned. A *col_index_num* of 1 returns the value located in the first column in the table—in other words, it returns the *lookup_value* itself. A *col_index_num* of 2 returns the value located in the second column in the table, and so on.

In the syntax, *range_lookup* is a Boolean value (False or True) that specifies the type of search—either exact or approximate—you want the VLookup function to perform. When *range_lookup* is False, the VLookup function performs an exact search, which means that the function searches the first column of the table for a value that is identical to the *lookup_value*. A value is considered to be identical if it contains the same characters as in *lookup_value*, ignoring case. In other words, the VLookup function treats the words "Basic", "BASIC", and "basic" as being identical. If an exact match is found, the VLookup function stops the search at that point; otherwise, an error occurs.

When *range_lookup* is True, or when the argument is omitted, the VLookup function performs a case-insensitive approximate search, stopping when it reaches the largest value that is less than or equal to the *lookup_value*. For example, assume that a table contains the values 1, 3, 4, and 6 in the first column. If *lookup_value* is the number 3 and *range_lookup* is True, then the VLookup function will discontinue the search when it finds the number 3, which is the largest value that is less than or equal to the *lookup_value* 3. However, if *lookup_value* is the number 5 and *range_lookup* is True, the VLookup function will stop the search when it reaches the number 4, which is the largest value that is less than or equal to the *lookup_value* 5. In order for the VLookup function to work correctly when *range_lookup* is True, the values listed in the first column of the table should be arranged in ascending order. Figure 6-21 shows examples of the VLookup function using the data contained in the PriceList range in the Computers worksheet.

VLookup Function	Result
Application.WorksheetFunction.VLookup("D430", Range("PriceList"), 1, False)	D430
Application.WorksheetFunction.VLookup("D430", Range("PriceList"), 2, False)	3450
Application.WorksheetFunction.VLookup("j480", Range("PriceList"), 2, False)	1200
Application.WorksheetFunction.VLookup("F100", Range("PriceList"), 2, False)	error
Application.WorksheetFunction.VLookup("F100", Range("PriceList"), 1, True)	D480

table

col_index.num

range_lookup

lookup_value

Figure 6-21: Examples of the VLookup function

The first instruction in Figure 6-21, `Application.WorksheetFunction.VLookup("D430", Range("PriceList"), 1, False)`, searches the first column of the PriceList range for an exact match to the model number D430, and then returns the contents of the first column. This instruction will return the model number D430, which is the *lookup_value* itself.

The second instruction in the figure, `Application.WorksheetFunction.VLookup("D430", Range("PriceList"), 2, False)`, is identical to the first instruction except the *col_index_num* was changed from 1 to 2. The instruction looks up model number D430 in the first column of the PriceList range, and then returns the contents of the second column. This instruction will return the number 3450, which is the price corresponding to model number D430.

The `Application.WorksheetFunction.VLookup("j480", Range("PriceList"), 2, False)` instruction searches the first column of the PriceList range for an exact match to model number j480, and then returns the contents of the second column. This instruction will return 1200, which is the price of model number J480. (Recall that the VLookup function always performs a case-insensitive search.)

The `Application.WorksheetFunction.VLookup("F100", Range("PriceList"), 2, False)` instruction searches the first column of the PriceList range for an exact match to the model number F100, and then returns the contents of the second column. This instruction will result in an error because the table does not contain an exact match to the *lookup_value* F100.

The `Application.WorksheetFunction.VLookup("F100", Range("PriceList"), 1, True)` instruction searches the first column of the PriceList range for an approximate match to the model number F100, and then return the contents of the first column. This instruction will return D480, which is the largest value that is less than or equal to F100.

Now use the VLookup function in the DblClick event procedure to search for the computer model number selected in the lstModel list box, and then return its corresponding price.

To complete the DblClick event procedure:

1 Type **'search for model number and return price** and press the **Enter** key.

When the user selects an item in a list box, the item is stored automatically in the list box's Text property, so you will use lstModel.Text as the *lookup_value* in the VLookup function. You will use PriceList as *table*, which is the location of the range that contains the price list table.

2 Type **curprice = application.worksheetfunction.vlookup(lstmodel.text, _** (be sure to type the comma followed by a space and the underscore) and press the **Enter** key. Press the **Tab** key, then type **range("pricelist"), 2, false)** and press the **Enter** key. This instruction uses the Excel VLookup function to look up the model number (lstModel.Text) in the first column of the PriceList range, and then return its corresponding price, which is located in the second column of the range. Notice that the *range_lookup* argument has a value of False, which tells the VLookup function to search the price list for an exact match, rather than for an approximate match, to the model number selected in the list box.

Step 5 in the pseudocode is to calculate the discounted price. You do so by subtracting the contents of the sngRate variable from the number 1, and then multiplying that difference by the contents of the curPrice variable.

3 Press the **Backspace** key to remove the indention, then type **'calculate the discounted price** and press the **Enter** key.

4 Type **curdiscprice = (1 – sngrate) * curprice** and press the **Enter** key.

The last steps in the pseudocode are to display the discount rate and discounted price in the appropriate cells in the worksheet, and then protect the worksheet again.

5   Type the additional five lines of code shown in Figure 6-22, which shows the completed DblClick event procedure.

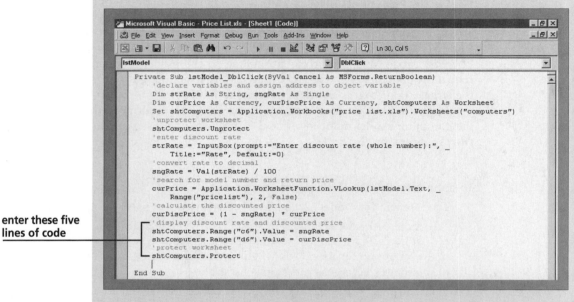

enter these five
lines of code

Figure 6-22: Completed DblClick event procedure

6   Verify the accuracy of your code by comparing the code on your screen to the code shown in Figure 6-22, then save the workbook.

Now that you have translated the pseudocode shown in Figure 6-16 into VBA statements, you can test the list box's DblClick event procedure to verify that it is working correctly.

To test the list box's DblClick event procedure:

1   Click the **View Microsoft Excel** button [×] on the Standard toolbar to return to Excel.

Calculate the price for model number D430 using a 10 percent discount rate.

2   Double-click **D430** in the list box. When you are prompted to enter the discount rate as a whole number, type **10** and then press the **Enter** key. The discount rate of 10.00% and the discounted price of $3,105.00 (the original price of 3450 multiplied by .90) are displayed, as shown in Figure 6-23.

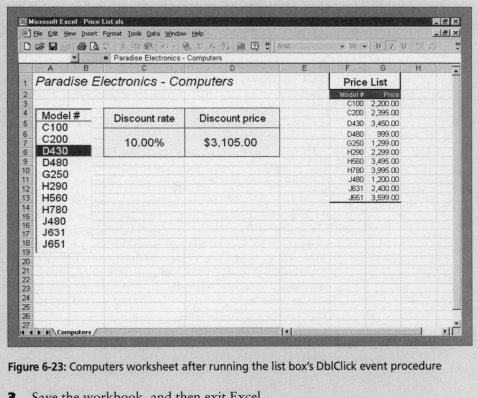

Figure 6-23: Computers worksheet after running the list box's DblClick event procedure

3 Save the workbook, and then exit Excel.

You now have completed Tutorial 6's Excel lesson. You can either take a break or complete the end-of-lesson exercises before moving on to the next lesson.

EXERCISES

1. In this exercise, you will code the list box's Click event procedure.
   a. Open the Price List (Price List.xls) workbook that you created in this lesson. The workbook is located in the Tut06\Excel folder on your Data Disk. Click the Enable Macros button, if necessary, then save the workbook as T6-EX-E1D.
   b. Open the Visual Basic Editor. Open the Sheet1 (Computers) Code window, then view the lstModel control's DblClick event procedure. Change the workbook name in the Set statement from "price list.xls" to "t6-ex-e1d.xls".
   c. Save the workbook, then return to Excel. Double-click C100 in the list box. When the Rate dialog box appears, type 10 and press the Enter key. The DblClick event procedure displays the discount rate and the discounted price in the worksheet.

Now click (don't double-click) D430 in the list box. Notice that clicking a different item in the list does not change the discount rate or discounted price, which can be misleading. You should clear the discount rate and discounted price when the user clicks a different item in the list.

d. Return to the Visual Basic Editor. View the lstModel control's Click event procedure. Code the procedure so that it removes the discount rate and discounted price from cells C6 and D6. (*Hint*: Assign the empty string to the range C6:D6.)

e. Save the workbook, then return to Excel. Double-click C100 in the list box. When the Rate dialog box appears, type 10 and press the Enter key. The DblClick event procedure displays the discount rate and the discounted price in the worksheet.

f. Click (don't double-click) D430 in the list box. The Click event procedure clears the cells containing the discount rate and discounted price.

g. When the procedure is working correctly, save and then close the workbook.

2. In this exercise, you will modify the list box's DblClick event procedure that you created in this lesson. Rather than prompting the user to enter the discount rate, the event procedure will search the price list for the discount rate.

a. Open the T6-EX-E2 (T6-EX-E2.xls) workbook, which is located in the Tut06\Excel folder on your Data Disk. Click the Enable Macros button, if necessary, then save the workbook as T6-EX-E2D. Notice that the price list contains an additional column named Disc. Rate, which lists the discount rate for each computer model. The PriceList range name was redefined to refer to the F3:H13 range, rather than the F3:G13 range used in this lesson.

b. Open the Visual Basic Editor. Open the Sheet1 (Computers) Code window and view the lstModel control's DblClick event procedure. Currently, the procedure prompts the user to enter the discount rate. Modify the procedure so that it uses the rates shown in the Disc. Rate column as the discount rate. (In other words, do not prompt the user to enter the discount rate. Rather, use the rates shown in column G.)

c. Save the workbook. Return to Excel. Double-click C200 in the list box. The list box's DblClick event procedure displays the discount rate (10.00%) and discounted price ($2,155.50) in the worksheet.

d. When the procedure is working correctly, save and then close the workbook.

3. In this exercise, you will create a procedure that searches a table for a model number, and then returns either the model's retail price or its educational price.

a. Open the T6-EX-E3 (T6-EX-E3.xls) workbook, which is located in the Tut06\Excel folder on your Data Disk. Click the Enable Macros button, if necessary, then save the workbook as T6-EX-E3D.

Column A in the Computers worksheet lists the model numbers of the computers sold at Paradise Electronics, and columns B and C list the prices of each model; column B shows the retail price and column C shows the educational price.

b. Assign the following range names:

Range	Range Name
A5:C15	PriceList
F2	Model
F3	Status
F4	Price

c. Protect the worksheet.

   d. Open the Visual Basic Editor. Open the Module1 module's Code window, then view the code template for the DisplayPrice procedure. Code the procedure so that it prompts the user to enter the model number and the pricing status—either 2 for retail or 3 for educational. Use C100 as the *defaultValue* for the model number, and use 2 as the *defaultValue* for the status. Display the model number in the Model range, the status (2 or 3) in the Status range, and the price, formatted to Currency, in the Price range.

   e. Save the workbook. Return to Excel and run the DisplayPrice macro. Enter g250 as the model number, then enter 2 as the status.

   f. Run the DisplayPrice macro again. Enter c200 as the model number, then enter 3 as the status.

   g. When the macro is working correctly, save and then close the workbook.

4. In this exercise, you will create a procedure that searches a table for an inventory number and returns the daily rental fee. The procedure also calculates the discount and the total due.

   a. Open the T6-EX-E4 (T6-EX-E4.xls) workbook, which is located in the Tut06\Excel folder on your Data Disk. Click the Enable Macros button, if necessary, then save the workbook as T6-EX-E4D. The workbook contains two worksheets named Receipt and Daily Rental Fee.

   b. Assign the following range names in the Receipt worksheet:

Cell	Range Name
C3	CustName
C4	InvNum
C5	Days
C6	Disc
C7	Total

   c. Protect the Receipt worksheet.

   d. Assign the name DailyFee to cells A4:B15 in the Daily Rental Fee worksheet, then protect the Daily Rental Fee worksheet.

   e. Open the Visual Basic Editor. Open the Module1 module's Code window, then view the code template for the PrintReceipt procedure. Code the procedure so that it prompts the user to enter the customer's name, the inventory number, the number of days the computer was rented, and the discount rate (entered as a whole number). Use Comp1 as the *defaultValue* for the inventory number. Use 1 as the *defaultValue* for the number of days rented, and use 0 as the *defaultValue* for the discount rate.

   f. After getting the input data from the user, the PrintReceipt procedure should calculate the rental fee by multiplying the number of days the computer was rented by the daily fee shown in the Daily Rental Fee worksheet. It also should calculate the discount amount and the total due.

   g. After making the appropriate calculations, the PrintReceipt procedure should display the customer's name, the inventory number, the number of days rented, the discount amount, and the total due in the appropriate ranges in the Receipt worksheet. Format the discount amount and the total due to Currency. The PrintReceipt procedure also should print the Receipt worksheet.

h. Save the workbook. Return to Excel. Activate the Receipt worksheet, if necessary, then run the PrintReceipt macro. Enter your name as the customer name, then enter HP1 as the inventory number, 25 as the number of days the computer was rented, and 0 as the discount rate.

i. Run the PrintReceipt macro again. Enter your name as the customer name, then enter IBM3 as the inventory number, 10 as the number of rental days, and 25 as the discount rate.

j. When the macro is working correctly, save and then close the workbook.

5. In this exercise, you will add a list box to a worksheet. You also will create a procedure that searches two tables.

a. Open the T6-EX-E5 (T6-EX-E5.xls) workbook, which is located in the Tut06\Excel folder on your Data Disk. Click the Enable Macros button, if necessary, then save the workbook as T6-EX-E5D.

The workbook contains one worksheet named Monthly Fee. The range G3:I4 is named Membership, and the range G9:I12 is named Options. The Membership range lists the monthly fees for Single (S) and Family (F) memberships. The Options range lists the additional monthly fee for four different membership options.

b. View the Control Toolbox toolbar. Draw a list box in the range C3:C8 in the worksheet.

c. Open the Properties window. Name the list box lstOptions. The list box should display the membership options contained in the range G9:G12; it also should display the heading contained in cell G8. When you are finished creating the list box and setting its properties, close the Properties window and then exit design mode and close the Control Toolbox toolbar.

d. Protect the worksheet.

e. Open the Visual Basic Editor. Open the Sheet1 (Monthly Fee) Code window, then view the code template for the list box's DblClick event procedure. Code the DblClick event procedure so that it prompts the user to enter the membership type (S or F); use S as the *defaultValue* in the InputBox function. Calculate the total monthly fee by adding the membership type fee to the option fee. Display the membership type (S or F) in cell B3. Display the total monthly fee, formatted to Currency, in cell B4.

f. Save the workbook. Return to Excel. Double-click 0 in the list box. When the Membership dialog box appears, type F and press the Enter key.

g. Double-click 2 in the list box. When the Membership dialog box appears, press the Enter key to accept the *defaultValue*, S.

h. When the procedure is working correctly, save and then close the workbook.

6. In this exercise, you will create a procedure that searches a table for the total points earned by a student, and then returns his or her grade.

a. Open the T6-EX-E6 (T6-EX-E6.xls) workbook, which is located in the Tut06\Excel folder on your Data Disk. Click the Enable Macros button, if necessary, then save the workbook as T6-EX-E6D.

The workbook contains one worksheet named Grade. The Grade worksheet has been protected using the following password: Valdez. (*Hint*: To learn how to unprotect and protect a worksheet containing a password, display the Help screens for the Unprotect and Protect methods.) The range A5:C9 is named GradingScale. The GradingScale range lists the minimum and maximum points corresponding to each grade.

b. Open the Visual Basic Editor. Open the Module1 module's Code window, then view the code template for the DisplayGrade procedure. Code the procedure so that it prompts the user to enter the student's name, as well as his or her three test scores and two assignment scores. Use 0 as the *defaultValue* for each test and assignment score. Calculate the total points earned, then use this information to display the appropriate grade in cell F5. Display the student's name in cell E5.

c. Save the workbook. Return to Excel and run the DisplayGrade macro. Enter your name as the student's name, then enter 90, 80, and 75 as the test scores, and then enter 50 and 45 as the assignment scores. Your name should appear in cell E5; B should appear in cell F5.

d. When the macro is working correctly, save and then close the workbook.

Exercises 7 through 9 are Discovery Exercises. Discovery Exercises, which may include topics that are not covered in the lesson, allow you to "discover" the solutions to problems on your own.

discovery ▶ **7.** In this exercise, you will use the Excel Hlookup function in a procedure.

a. Open the T6-EX-E7 (T6-EX-E7.xls) workbook, which is located in the Tut06\Excel folder on your Data Disk. Click the Enable Macros button, if necessary, then save the workbook as T6-EX-E7D.

The workbook contains one worksheet named Stores. The Stores worksheet contains the store numbers in row 3, and the locations and manager names in rows 4 and 5. The worksheet has been protected. The range B3:F5 is named StoreInfo.

b. Open the Visual Basic Editor. Open the Module1 module's Code window, then view the code template for the DisplayInfo procedure. Code the DisplayInfo procedure so that it prompts the user to enter the store number; use store number 1 as the *defaultValue* in the InputBox function. The procedure then should display the store location and the store manager's name on two separate lines in a message box. For example, if the user enters store number 1, display "Location: Jacksonville" (without the quotation marks) on the first line in the message box, then display "Manager: Janet Paige" (without the quotation marks) on the second line.

c. Save the workbook. Return to Excel and run the DisplayInfo macro. Enter 3 as the store number. When the macro is working correctly, save and then close the workbook.

discovery ▶ **8.** In this exercise, you will learn about the Excel Match worksheet function and the Cells property of a Range object.

a. Open the T6-EX-E8 (T6-EX-E8.xls) workbook, which is located in the Tut06\Excel folder on your Data Disk. Click the Enable Macros button, if necessary, then save the workbook as T6-EX-E8D.

The workbook contains one worksheet named Inventory. The Inventory worksheet contains part numbers in column A and quantities on hand in column B. The worksheet has been protected. The range A5:A16 is named PartNums.

b. Open the Visual Basic Editor. Open the Module1 module's Code window, then view the partially completed UpdateQuantity procedure. Notice that two instructions are missing from the procedure.

c. View the Help screen for Excel's Match worksheet function. Study the information in the Help screen. Also view the Help screen for the Range object's Cells property. (*Hint*: View the Range Object Help screen first, then use the Help screen to view the Cells Property Help screen.) Study the Help screen, then close the Help window.

d. Complete the UpdateQuantity procedure by entering the two missing instructions. The first instruction should use the Match worksheet function to return the location of the part number in the PartNums range. Assign the location to the intRow variable. The second instruction should use the Range object's Cells property to add the contents of the intUpdate variable to the appropriate part number's quantity on hand.

e. Save the workbook. Return to Excel and run the UpdateQuantity macro. Enter 456m as the part number, then enter 2 as the update quantity. The quantity on hand for this part number should be 20.

f. Run the UpdateQuantity macro again. When the Part Number dialog box appears, press the Enter key to accept the *defaultValue*, 123D, then enter −3 (notice the negative sign before the 3) as the update quantity. The quantity on hand for this part number should be 7.

g. When the macro is working correctly, save and then close the workbook.

discovery ▶ 9. In this exercise, you will learn about a Range object's Find method and a Range object's Offset property.

a. Open the T6-EX-E9 (T6-EX-E9.xls) workbook, which is located in the Tut06\Excel folder on your Data Disk. Click the Enable Macros button, if necessary, then save the workbook as T6-EX-E9D.

The workbook contains one worksheet named Inventory. The Inventory worksheet contains part numbers in column A and quantities on hand in column B. The worksheet has been protected. The range A5:A16 is named PartNums.

b. Open the Visual Basic Editor, then view the partially completed UpdateQuantity procedure. Notice that two instructions are missing from the procedure.

c. View the Help screen for the Range object's Find method. Study the Help screen. Also view the Help screen for the Range object's Offset property. Study the Help screen, then close the Help window.

d. Complete the UpdateQuantity procedure by entering the two missing instructions. The first instruction should use the Find method to locate the part number in the PartNums range; assign the location to the rngFind object variable. The second instruction should use the Offset property to add the contents of the intUpdate variable to the appropriate part number's quantity on hand.

e. Save the workbook. Return to Excel and run the UpdateQuantity macro. Enter 675x as the part number, then enter 5 as the update quantity. The quantity on hand for this part number should be 29.

f. Run the UpdateQuantity macro again. When the Part Number dialog box appears, press the Enter key to accept the *defaultValue*, 123D, then enter −3 (notice the negative sign before the 3) as the update quantity. The quantity on hand for this part number should be 7.

g. When the macro is working correctly, save and then close the workbook.

A computer program is good only if it works. Errors in programming code can cause a program to run incorrectly. Therefore, a programmer needs to know how to locate and fix any errors in his or her code. Exercise 10 is a Debugging Exercise. Debugging Exercises allow you to practice recognizing and solving errors in code.

debugging 10. In this exercise, you will debug an existing macro procedure.

a. Open the T6-EX-E10 (T6-EX-E10.xls) workbook, which is located in the Tut06\Excel folder on your Data Disk. Click the Enable Macros button, if necessary. Save the workbook as T6-EX-E10D. The Grade worksheet contains two range names: GradeInfo (A4:C7) and Message (F4:G7).

b. Open the Visual Basic Editor. Open the Module1 module's Code window, then view the DisplayMsg procedure. Study the code, then return to Excel and run the DisplayMsg macro. Enter 80 as the total points. The Above Average message appears in the Message range.

c. Run the DisplayMsg macro again. This time, enter 75 as the total points. An error message appears in a dialog box. Read the message, then click the Debug button in the dialog box. Notice that the instruction containing the Vlookup function is causing the error. Click the Reset button ■ on the Standard toolbar.

d. What is wrong with the worksheet and/or procedure? Correct any errors in the worksheet and the procedure.

e. Save the workbook, then return to Excel and run the DisplayMsg macro. Use 80 as the total points. The Above Average message should appear in the Message range. Run the macro again using 75 as the total points. The Average message should appear in the Message range.

f. When the macro is working correctly, save and then close the workbook.

Word Lesson

Using Numeric Variables in Word

case▶ Willowton Health Club offers two types of memberships: full and matinee. A full membership allows the member full use of the facilities, while a matinee membership allows the member to use the facilities only during the hours from 2 p.m. to 5 p.m. Pat Jones, the manager of Willowton Health Club, uses a Word document to keep track of the number of full and matinee memberships sold by each salesperson during the year. At the end of each week, she updates the yearly information in the document by adding the current week's sales to it. Pat has decided to create a macro that will automate the entry and totalling process.

Coding the UpdateMembership Procedure

Your Data Disk contains the document that Pat uses to record the number of memberships sold by each salesperson during the year. Begin by opening this document and viewing the code template for the UpdateMembership procedure, which already has been inserted into a module.

To open Pat's document and view the UpdateMembership procedure:

1 Start Microsoft Word. Open the **T6-WD-1** (T6-WD-1.doc) document, which is located in the Tut06\Word folder on your Data Disk. Click the **Enable Macros** button, if necessary, then save the document as **Membership**. Figure 6-24 shows the Membership document.

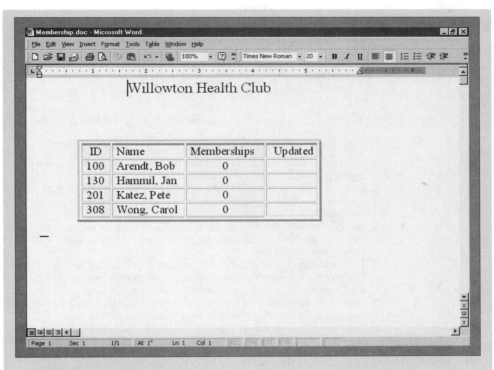

Figure 6-24: Membership document

Notice that the Membership document contains a table that has five rows and four columns. The first row in the table contains the column headings—ID, Name, Memberships, and Updated—and the remaining rows contain the corresponding information about each of Willowton's four salespeople. For example, each salesperson's ID is listed in the first column of his or her row, and his or her name is listed in the second column. The third column in each of rows 2 through 5 shows the total number of memberships sold by the salesperson, and the fourth column lists the date that the salesperson's information was last updated (the updated information has not yet been entered into the table).

The intersection of a row and a column in a table is called a **cell**. You refer to an individual cell in a table by using the cell's row and column numbers. The first row in a table is row 1, and the first column is column 1. For example, the column heading "ID" is entered in the cell located at the intersection of row 1 and column 1 in the Membership document's table. The name "Wong, Carol," on the other hand, is entered in the cell located in row 5, column 2.

Next, open the Visual Basic Editor.

2 Press **Alt+F11** to open the Visual Basic Editor. If necessary, open the Project Explorer window and close the Properties window, the Immediate window, and any open Code windows.

3 Open the Module1 module's Code window, then view the code template for the UpdateMembership procedure.

4 Close the Project Explorer window so that you can view more of the Code window.

Figure 6-25 shows the pseudocode for the UpdateMembership procedure.

1. Use the InputBox function to prompt the user to enter the salesperson's ID. Store the user's response in a String variable named strId.
2. Use the InputBox function to prompt the user to enter the number of full memberships sold during the week. Store the user's response in a String variable named strFull.
3. Use the InputBox function to prompt the user to enter the number of matinee memberships sold during the week. Store the user's response in a String variable named strMatinee.
4. Calculate the weekly total by adding together the contents of the strFull variable (treated as a number) to the contents of the strMatinee variable (treated as a number). Assign the sum to an Integer variable named intWeekTotal.
5. Search the first column of the table for the ID stored in the strId variable. Assign the number of the row that contains the ID to an Integer variable named intRow.
6. Use the intRow variable to update the appropriate cell located in the third column of the table. Update the cell by adding the weekly total stored in the intWeekTotal variable to the sales amount, treated as a number, currently stored in the cell.
7. Use the intRow variable and the Date function to update the appropriate cell in the fourth column of the table.
8. Place the insertion point at the beginning of the document.

Figure 6-25: Pseudocode for the UpdateMembership procedure

Figure 6-26 lists the variables that the UpdateMembership procedure will use.

Variables	datatype
strId	String
strFull	String
strMatinee	String
intWeekTotal	Integer
intRow	Integer
tblSales	Table

Figure 6-26: Variables used by the UpdateMembership procedure

In the next set of steps, you will declare the appropriate variables, and then translate each line in Figure 6-25's pseudocode into one or more VBA statements.

To begin coding the UpdateMembership procedure:

1   Enter the documentation and the Dim and Set statements shown in Figure 6-27.

enter these lines of code →

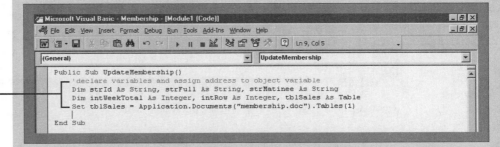

```
Microsoft Visual Basic - Membership - [Module1 {Code}]
 File  Edit  View  Insert  Format  Debug  Run  Tools  Add-Ins  Window  Help

(General)                                      UpdateMembership

    Public Sub UpdateMembership()
        'declare variables and assign address to object variable
        Dim strId As String, strFull As String, strMatinee As String
        Dim intWeekTotal As Integer, intRow As Integer, tblSales As Table
        Set tblSales = Application.Documents("membership.doc").Tables(1)

    End Sub
```

Figure 6-27: Code window showing documentation and Dim and Set statements

You now can begin translating the pseudocode shown in Figure 6-25 into VBA statements. The first three steps are to use the InputBox function to get the salesperson's ID, as well as the number of full and matinee memberships sold during the week. You should assign the user's responses to the strId, strFull, and strMatinee variables, respectively. You will make the first salesperson's ID (100) the *defaultValue* in the InputBox function that gets the ID, and you will make the number 0 the *defaultValue* in the InputBox functions that get the number of full and matinee memberships.

2   Type **'enter ID and number of full and matinee memberships** and press the **Enter** key. Type **strid = inputbox(prompt:="ID:", title:="ID", default:="100")** and press the **Enter** key.

3   Type **strfull = inputbox(prompt:="Full memberships:", title:="Full", default:=0)** and press the **Enter** key.

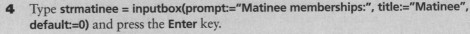

When the *defaultValue* is a number, you do not need to enclose it in quotation marks.

4   Type **strmatinee = inputbox(prompt:="Matinee memberships:", title:="Matinee", default:=0)** and press the **Enter** key.

Step 4 in the pseudocode is to calculate the total number of memberships sold during the week. Recall that you do so by adding the contents of the strFull variable, treated as a number, to the contents of the strMatinee variable, also treated as a number.

5   Type the additional two lines of code shown in Figure 6-28.

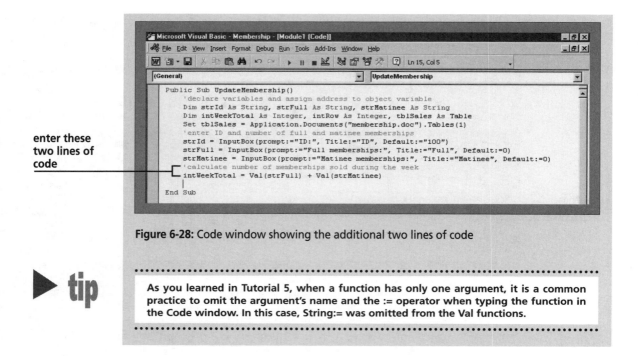

Figure 6-28: Code window showing the additional two lines of code

▶ **tip**

As you learned in Tutorial 5, when a function has only one argument, it is a common practice to omit the argument's name and the := operator when typing the function in the Code window. In this case, String:= was omitted from the Val functions.

Step 5 in the pseudocode is to search for the salesperson's ID in the first column of the table, and then assign the number of the row that contains the ID to the intRow variable. You will learn how to search a table in the next section.

Searching a Table

In Word, you can search a column in a table first by selecting the column, and then using the Execute method of the Find object to locate the desired value. As you learned in Tutorial 2, you select a range by using the Select method. For example, you could use the `Application.Documents("membership.doc").Words(1).Select` instruction to select the first word in the Membership document, and you could use the `tblSales.Select` instruction to select the first table. (Recall that the UpdateMembership procedure assigns the address of the first table in the document to a Table object named tblSales.) To select the first column in the tblSales table, you use the instruction `tblSales.Columns(1).Select`.

To continue coding the UpdateMembership procedure:

1 Type **'search table for ID, then assign row number to intRow** and press the **Enter** key. Type **tblsales.columns(1).select** and press the **Enter** key. This instruction selects the first column in the tblSales table.

When a range is selected in a document, that range is considered an object, and it is referred to as the Selection object. You learned about the Selection object in Tutorial 2. You can use the following syntax to search for text contained in the Selection object: **Selection.Find.Execute FindText:=**_string_. The syntax uses the Execute method of the Find object, which is a member of the Selection object, to search the selected text for the _string_ contained in the FindText argument. If the _string_ is found, it is selected, and it becomes the new value of the Selection object. For example, the `Selection.Find.Execute FindText:="201"` instruction searches the Selection object—in this case, the first column of the Membership document's table—for the _string_ "201". If the Execute method finds "201" in the first column of the table, it will deselect the first column of the table and will select only the "201" _string_; in other words, the Selection object will include only the cell that contains the ID "201".

Use the Execute method of the Find object to search the Selection object for the _string_ stored in the strId variable.

2 Type **selection.find.execute findtext:=strid** and press the **Enter** key. When the Execute method finds the salesperson's ID in the first column of the table, it will select the ID.

The Selection object's Information property, whose syntax is **Selection.Information(Type:=**_type_**)**, stores information about the Selection object. In the syntax, _type_ is a VBA constant that represents the type of information you want to return. For example, you use the wdStartOfRangeRowNumber constant to return the number of the row containing the selected text, and you use the wdStartOfRangeColumnNumber constant to return the column number. In this case, you want to return the number of the row containing the salesperson's ID, which is currently selected.

To learn how to return other information about the Selection object, display the Help screen for the Selection object's Information property.

3 Type **introw = selection.information(type:=wdstartofrangerownumber)** and press the **Enter** key.

Step 6 in the pseudocode is to update the salesperson's annual sales amount by adding to it his or her weekly sales amount. To do so you will need to access the cell that contains the salesperson's annual sales amount—specifically, you will need to access the cell located at the intersection of column 3 and the row containing the salesperson's information. Recall that the number of the appropriate row is stored in the intRow variable.

You can use the following syntax to refer to the contents of an individual cell in a table: _expression_.**Cell(Row:=**_rowNum_, **Column:=**_colNum_**).Range.Text**. In the syntax, _expression_ is a Table object and _rowNum_ and _colNum_ are numbers that represent the row and column location of the cell. For example, `tblSales.Cell(Row:=2, Column:=3).Range.Text` refers to Bob Arendt's sales amount, which is located in row 2, column 3 in the table.

`TblSales.Cell(Row:=5, Column:=3).Range.Text`, on the other hand, refers to Carol Wong's sales amount, which is located in row 5, column 3. In the current procedure, you want to update the sales amount located at the intersection of row intRow and column 3.

4 Type **'update the membership and updated columns** and press the **Enter** key, then type **tblsales.cell(row:=introw, column:=3).range.text = _** (be sure to type the equal sign followed by a space and the underscore) and press the **Enter** key. Press the **Tab** key, then type **val(tblsales.cell(row:=introw, column:=3).range.text) + intweektotal** and press the **Enter** key.

Step 7 in the pseudocode is to display the current date in the appropriate cell located in the fourth column of the table. The appropriate cell is found at the intersection of row intRow and column 4.

5 Press the **Backspace** key to remove the indentation, then type **tblsales.cell(row:=introw, column:=4).range.text = date** and press the **Enter** key.

6 Save the document.

The last step in the pseudocode is to place the insertion point at the beginning of the document; doing so will cancel the selection of the ID.

Moving the Insertion Point to the Beginning of the Document

You can use the Selection object's HomeKey method to move the insertion point to a different area in the document. The HomeKey method, whose syntax is *expression*.**HomeKey Unit:**=*unit*, corresponds to the functionality of the Home key on your keyboard. In the syntax, *expression* is a Selection object. The Unit argument, which represents the unit to which the selection is to be moved, can be one of the following VBA constants: wdStory, wdColumn, wdLine, or wdRow. For example, the `Selection.HomeKey Unit:=wdLine` instruction moves the insertion point to the beginning of the current line. The `Selection.HomeKey Unit:=wdStory` instruction, on the other hand, moves the insertion point to the beginning of the current story. In Microsoft Word, a **story** is defined as an area of a document that contains a range of text that is distinct from other areas of text in the document. For example, if a document contains body text, footnotes, and headers, then it contains a main text story, a footnotes story, and a headers story. If the Selection object is located in the headers story, then `Selection.HomeKey Unit:=wdStory` will move the insertion point to the beginning of the header. If, on the other hand, the Selection object is located in the main text story, then `Selection.HomeKey Unit:=wdStory` will move the insertion point to the beginning of the document.

 tip

You also can use the Selection object's HomeKey method to extend the selection. To learn how to do so, view the HomeKey method's Help screen.

To complete the UpdateMembership procedure, then test the procedure:

1 Type the additional comment and instruction shown in Figure 6-29, which shows the completed UpdateMembership procedure.

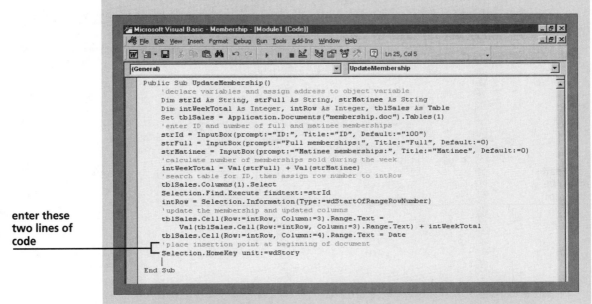

enter these
two lines of
code

Figure 6-29: Completed UpdateMembership procedure

2 Verify the accuracy of your code by comparing the code on your screen to the code shown in Figure 6-29, then save the document.

Now that you have translated the pseudocode into VBA statements, you can test the UpdateMembership macro to verify that it is working correctly.

3 Click the **View Microsoft Word** button 🔳 on the Standard toolbar to return to Word.

4 Run the **UpdateMembership** macro. When the ID dialog box appears and prompts you to enter the salesperson's ID, type **130** and press the **Enter** key. When you are prompted to enter the number of full memberships sold, type **2** and press the **Enter** key. When you are prompted to enter the number of matinee memberships sold, type **1** and press the **Enter** key.

HELP? To run the UpdateMembership macro, click Tools on the Word menu bar, point to Macro, then click Macros. When the Macros dialog box appears, click UpdateMembership in the list of macro names, then click the Run button. You also can use Alt+F8 to open the Macros dialog box.

5 Run the macro again. Enter the following weekly sales for salesperson 308: 0 full memberships and 2 matinee memberships.

Figure 6-30 shows the updated Membership document. (Your dates in column 4 of the table might be different.)

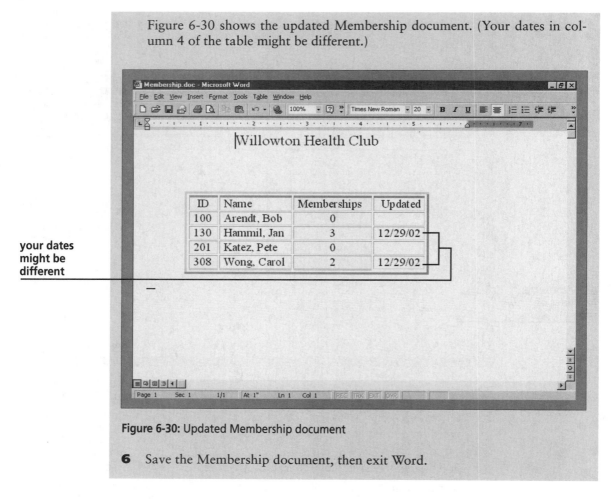

your dates might be different

Figure 6-30: Updated Membership document

6 Save the Membership document, then exit Word.

You now have completed Tutorial 6's Word lesson. You can either take a break or complete the end-of-lesson exercises before moving on to the next lesson.

EXERCISES

1. In this exercise, you will modify the UpdateMembership procedure that you created in this lesson.

    a. Open the T6-WD-E1 (T6-WD-E1.doc) document, which is located in the Tut06\Word folder on your Data Disk. Click the Enable Macros button, if necessary, then save the document as T6-WD-E1D.

Notice that the document's table contains two additional columns named Full and Matinee, and that the Memberships column has been replaced with a column named Total.

b. Open the Visual Basic Editor. Open the Module1 module's Code window, then view the UpdateMembership procedure's code. Modify the code so that it displays the number of full and matinee memberships sold during the year in the Full and Matinee columns, respectively. Display the total number of memberships sold in the Total column.

c. Save the document, then return to Word. Use the UpdateMembership macro to enter the following data:

ID	Full	Matinee
100	3	4
130	1	0
201	0	2
308	2	1
100	1	0
308	2	3

d. When the macro is working correctly, save and then close the document.

2. In this exercise, you will create a procedure that calculates the total points earned on two tests and two assignments. It also calculates the percentage of total points earned.

a. Open the T6-WD-E2 (T6-WD-E2.doc) document, which is located in the Tut06\Word folder on your Data Disk. Click the Enable Macros button, if necessary, then save the document as T6-WD-E2D. View the customized Carlisle Macros toolbar, if necessary. The document contains nine form fields, as shown in Figure 6-31.

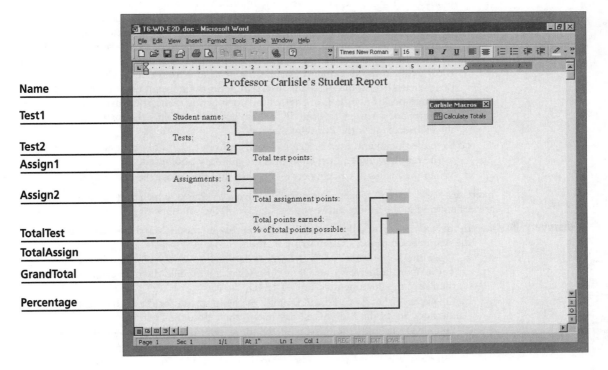

Figure 6-31

b. Open the Visual Basic Editor. Open the Module1 module's Code window, then view the code template for the CalcTotals procedure's code. Code the procedure so that it prompts the user to enter the student's name, two test scores, and two assignment scores. (Each test is worth 100 points, and each assignment is worth 50 points.) Use the number 0 as the *defaultValue* in the InputBox functions that get the test and assignment scores. The procedure should calculate the total test points, total assignment points, total points earned, and percentage of total points possible. Display the input and calculated data in the appropriate form fields in the document.

c. Save the document, then return to Word. Use the Calculate Totals button on the Carlisle Macros toolbar to enter the following data:

Name	Test 1	Test 2	Assign 1	Assign 2
George Mai	100	95	45	40
Pamela Chu	75	83	39	50

d. When the macro is working correctly, save and then close the document.

3. In this exercise, you will create a procedure that calculates the total due based on the model number and quantity purchased entered by the user.

a. Open the T6-WD-E3 (T6-WD-E3.doc) document, which is located in the Tut06\Word folder on your Data Disk. Click the Enable Macros button, if necessary, then save the document as T6-WD-E3D. The document contains four form fields, named Number, Price, Quantity, and Total.

b. Open the Visual Basic Editor. Open the Module1 module's Code window, then view the code template for the FillInForm procedure's code. Code the procedure so that it prompts the user to enter the model number and the quantity purchased. Use model number 111 as the *defaultValue* in the InputBox function that gets the model number, and use the number 0 as the *defaultValue* in the InputBox function that gets the quantity purchased. The procedure should calculate the total due by multiplying the quantity purchased by the model's price, which is listed in the document's table. Display the model number, price, quantity purchased, and total due in the appropriate form fields in the document. Format the price and total due to Currency. The procedure also should place the insertion point at the beginning of the document, and then print only the first page of the document. (*Hint*: You learned how to print an entire document in Tutorial 5. To learn how to print only the current page, display the Help screen for the PrintOut method.)

c. Save the document, then return to Word and run the FillInForm macro. Enter 124 as the model number, then enter 3 as the quantity purchased.

d. When the macro is working correctly, save and then close the document.

Exercises 4 and 5 are Discovery Exercises. Discovery Exercises, which may include topics that are not covered in the lesson, allow you to "discover" the solutions to problems on your own.

discovery ▶ 4. In this exercise, you will learn about the Execute method's MatchCase argument and the Application object's CleanString method.

a. Open the T6-WD-E4 (T6-WD-E4.doc) document, which is located in the Tut06\Word folder on your Data Disk. Click the Enable Macros button, if necessary, then save the document as T6-WD-E4D.

b. Open the Visual Basic Editor. Display the Help screen for the Find object's Execute method. Study the MatchCase argument, then close the Help window.

c. Open the Module1 module's Code window, then view the code template for the BirthDate procedure's code. Code the procedure so that it prompts the user to enter a name. The name can be entered in any case—lowercase, uppercase, or any combination. The procedure should search for the name in the first column of the table, and then display the message "Birth date:" along with the person's birth date in a message box. The procedure then should move the insertion point to the beginning of the document.

d. Save the document, then return to Word and run the BirthDate macro. When the Name dialog box appears, type hou, sarah and press the Enter key. Figure 6-32 shows the resulting message box.

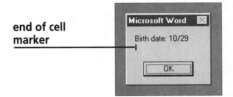

end of cell marker

Figure 6-32

e. Notice that the end of cell marker appears in the message box. (Each cell in a table contains an end of cell marker.) Click the OK button to close the message box.

f. You can use the Application object's CleanString method to remove the end of cell marker before displaying the birth date in the message box. Return to the Visual Basic Editor and display the Help screen for the Application object's CleanString method. Read and then close the Help window.

g. Use the CleanString method in the BirthDate procedure to remove the end of cell marker before displaying the birth date in the message box.

h. Save the document, then return to Word. Use the BirthDate macro to display Sarah Hou's birth date. Figure 6-33 shows the resulting message box. Notice that the end of cell marker does not appear in the message box.

Figure 6-33

i. Click the OK button to close the message box. When the macro is working correctly, save and then close the document.

discovery ▶ 5. In this exercise, you will learn how to use the Document object's Content property, as well as how to use the Find object's Execute method to find and replace text in a document.

a. Open the T6-WD-E5 (T6-WD-E5.doc) document, which is located in the Tut06\Word folder on your Data Disk. Click the Enable Macros button, if necessary, then save the document as T6-WD-E5D. Notice that the word "story" is misspelled as "stori" in the document.

b. Open the Visual Basic Editor. Display the Help screen for the Document object's Content property. Read the Help screen. Notice that the Content property refers to the main story in the document.

c. Display the Help screen for the Find object's Execute method. Study the FindText, MatchCase, MatchWholeWord, ReplaceWith, and Replace arguments. Click Example at the top of the Help screen. Study the second example. Notice that the Execute method can be used with either a Selection or Range object. Close the Help window.

d. View the code template for the FindAndReplace procedure. Code the procedure so that it performs the tasks shown in Figure 6-34. (*Hint*: In this exercise, you will not need to select the text in the document before using the Execute method.)

---

1. Declare a Document object variable named docStory and a Range object variable named rngContent.
2. Assign the address of the document to the docStory variable, and then assign the address of the main story to the rngContent variable.
3. Print the document.
4. Search for the word "stori" in the document and replace it with the word "story".
5. Print the document.

Figure 6-34

e. Save the document, then return to Word. Run the FindAndReplace macro. (*Hint*: If the macro did not work correctly, you can use the Undo option on the Edit menu to undo the changes made by the macro.)

f. When the macro is working correctly, save and then close the document.

A computer program is good only if it works. Errors in programming code can cause a program to run incorrectly. Therefore, a programmer needs to know how to locate and fix any errors in his or her code. Exercise 6 is a Debugging Exercise. Debugging Exercises allow you to practice recognizing and solving errors in code.

debugging

6. In this exercise, you will debug an existing macro procedure.

a. Open the T6-WD-E6 (T6-WD-E6.doc) document, which is located in the Tut06\Word folder on your Data Disk. Click the Enable Macros button, if necessary, then save the document as T6-WD-E6D.

b. Open the Visual Basic Editor. Open the Module1 module's Code window, then view the code template for the DisplayQuantity procedure. The procedure should prompt the user to enter the code. The first letter in the code can be entered in either upper-case or lowercase letters. The procedure should display the code in the Code form field, and it should display the quantity, which is listed in the document's table, in the Quantity form field.

c. Return to Word. Run the DisplayQuantity macro. When the Code dialog box appears, press the Enter key to accept the *defaultValue*, A123. Notice that the macro is not working correctly.

d. Return to the Visual Basic Editor. What is wrong with the DisplayQuantity procedure? Correct any errors.

e. Save the document, then return to Word and run the DisplayQuantity macro. Enter b345 as the code.

f. When the macro is working correctly, save and then close the document.

Access Lesson

Using Numeric Variables in Access

case▶ The Spanish Club at Snowville College is offering a one-week trip to Spain for a cost of $1200 per student. A $200 deposit is due from the student within one week of registering for the trip, and then additional payments are due periodically until the entire $1200 is paid. Professor Martinez, who has agreed to help coordinate the trip, has decided to use an Access database with an appropriate procedure to keep track of the money collected from each student.

The ADO Object Model

The procedure that Professor Martinez will use to keep track of the money collected for the Spain trip will need to access the student records stored in the Payments table, which is contained in the professor's Trip database. Before you can create the procedure for Professor Martinez, you need to learn how to use the ADO object model. The ADO (ActiveX Data Objects) object model contains all of the objects needed to manage the records contained in one or more tables. The process of managing records includes tasks such as creating new records and editing and deleting existing records. Figure 6-35 shows the portion of the ADO object model that includes the most commonly used ADO objects.

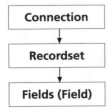

Figure 6-35: Portion of the ADO object model showing the most commonly used ADO objects

Notice that the Connection object appears at the top of the ADO object model. A **Connection object** represents the physical connection between an Access database and a **data provider**, which is a set of complex interfaces that allows ADO objects to use the data stored in a database. In other words, the data provider is the middleman between the database and the ADO objects; as such, it is responsible for providing the database data in a format that can be utilized by the objects in the ADO model. You do not need to be concerned with the data provider at this point. When you open an Access database, Access automatically creates a Connection object that connects the database to the appropriate data provider.

The name of the data provider that allows ADO to access the data stored in an Access database is OLE DB Provider for Microsoft Jet. Jet refers to the database engine found in Microsoft Access.

Immediately below the Connection object in the ADO object model is the **Recordset object**, which represents either all or a portion of the records (rows) contained in one or more tables. Notice that the Recordset object contains a Fields collection, which is composed of individual Field objects. Each Field object represents a field (column) in the recordset.

Now that you are familiar with the ADO object model, you can begin coding the PaymentUpdate procedure.

Coding the PaymentUpdate Procedure

Professor Martinez's database is stored on your Data Disk. Begin by opening this database and viewing the Payments table.

To open Professor Martinez's database and view the Payments table:

1   Start Microsoft Access. Open the **Trip** (Trip.mdb) database, which is located in the Tut06\Access folder on your Data Disk. Click the **Maximize** button ⬜ on the Microsoft Access title bar to maximize the Microsoft Access window, if necessary.

The Trip database contains one table named Payments and one report named PayReport. It also contains a macro named PaymentUpdateMacro. View the structure of the Payments table.

2 Click **Tables** in the Objects bar of the Database window, if necessary. Right-click **Payments** in the Database window and then click **Design View**. Notice that each record contains five fields: ID, LastName, FirstName, Paid, and Updated. The ID, LastName, and FirstName fields are Text fields. The Paid field, which will store the total amount paid by each student, is a Currency field. The Updated field, which will store the date the student's information was last updated, is a Date/Time field.

3 Close the Design View window.

Next, view the records contained in the Payments table.

4 Right-click **Payments** in the Database window and then click **Open**. See Figure 6-36.

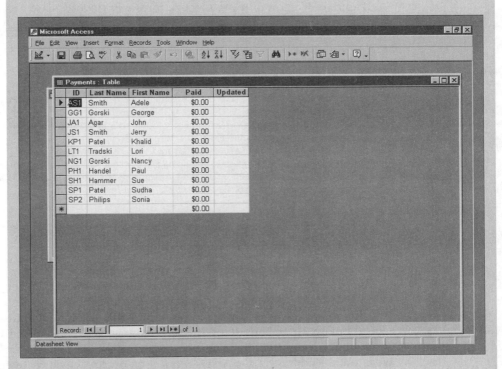

Figure 6-36: Records contained in the Payments table

Notice that the Paid field contains $0.00, and the Updated field is empty. This is because no payments as yet have been collected.

5 Close the Payments table.

Now open the Visual Basic Editor.

6 Press **Alt+F11** to open the Visual Basic Editor. If necessary, open the Project Explorer window and close the Properties window, the Immediate window, and any open Code windows.

7 Open the Module1 module's Code window, then view the code template for the PaymentUpdate function procedure.

8 Close the Project Explorer window so that you can view more of the Code window.

Figure 6-37 shows the pseudocode for the PaymentUpdate procedure.

1. Open a recordset that contains all of the records stored in the Trip database's Payments table.
2. Use the InputBox function to prompt the user to enter the student's ID. Store the user's response in a String variable named strId.
3. Use the InputBox function to prompt the user to enter the current payment. Store the user's response in a String variable named strPayment.
4. Convert the contents of the strPayment variable to a number, and assign the result to a Currency variable named curPayment.
5. Search the ID field for the student ID stored in the strId variable.
6. Calculate the total amount paid by adding the contents of the curPayment variable to the contents of the student's Paid field. Assign the sum to the student's Paid field.
7. Assign the current date to the student's Updated field.
8. Save the changes made to the student's record.
9. Close the recordset.

Figure 6-37: Pseudocode for the PaymentUpdate procedure

In addition to the String (strId and strPayment) and Currency (curPayment) variables mentioned in the pseudocode, the PaymentUpdate procedure also will use two object variables—a Connection object named cnnTrip and a Recordset object named rstPays. (*cnn* and *rst* are the three-character IDs associated with the names of Connection and Recordset objects, respectively.) The cnnTrip Connection object will store the address of the ADO Connection object, which represents the physical connection between the Trip database and its data provider. The rstPays Recordset object will store the address of an ADO Recordset object that contains all of the records stored in the Payments table. Figure 6-38 shows the variables that the PaymentUpdate procedure will use.

Variables	datatype
strId	String
strPayment	String
curPayment	Currency
cnnTrip	ADODB.Connection
rstPays	ADODB.Recordset

Figure 6-38: Variables used by the PaymentUpdate procedure

As Figure 6-38 shows, you use the *datatype* ADODB.Connection to create an ADO Connection object, and you use the *datatype* ADODB.Recordset to create an ADO Recordset object.

In the next set of steps, you will declare the appropriate variables. Then you will translate each line in Figure 6-37's pseudocode into one or more VBA statements.

To begin coding the PaymentUpdate procedure:

1   Enter the documentation and the Dim statements shown in Figure 6-39.

enter these lines of code

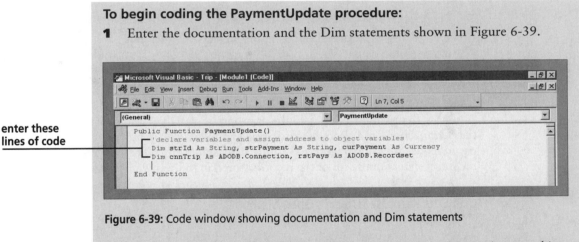

Figure 6-39: Code window showing documentation and Dim statements

As you learned in Tutorial 3, after using the Dim statement to create an object variable, you then use the Set statement to assign the address of an object to it. In this case, you need to assign to the cnnTrip Connection object variable the address of the current Connection object—the one that is created automatically when the Trip database is opened. You can use the CurrentProject object's Connection property to refer to the current Connection object. For example, the appropriate Set statement to use in the PaymentUpdate procedure is

`Set cnnTrip = Application.CurrentProject.Connection`. This Set statement will assign the address of the Trip database's Connection object to the cnnTrip Connection object variable.

You learned about the CurrentProject object in Tutorial 2. Recall that the CurrentProject object is a member of the Access Application object, and it refers to the project that contains the current Access database.

2 Type **set cnntrip = application.currentproject.connection** and press the **Enter** key.

In addition to assigning an address to the Connection object variable, you also need to assign an address—in this case, the address of an existing Recordset object—to the rstPays Recordset object variable. Unlike the Connection object, a Recordset object is not created automatically when a database is opened; rather, the programmer must create the Recordset object through code. You can use the **Set** *objectvar* **= New** *datatype* syntax, where *objectvar* is the name of a Recordset object variable and *datatype* is ADODB.Recordset, to create a Recordset object and, at the same time, assign its address to a Recordset object variable. Notice the use of the keyword New in the syntax. When used in a Set statement, the New keyword creates an object whose data type is *datatype*.

3 Type **set rstpays = new adodb.recordset** and press the **Enter** key.

You will learn more about creating objects in Tutorials 14 and 15, which cover Automation.

4 Save the database.

Now that you have reserved the appropriate variables and assigned addresses to the Connection and Recordset object variables, you can begin translating the pseudocode shown in Figure 6-37 into VBA statements. The first step is to open a recordset that contains all of the records stored in the Trip database's Payments table.

Using the Recordset Object's Open Method

You use the Recordset object's **Open method** to open a recordset. The syntax of the Open method is *recordset*.**open Source:=***datasource*, **ActiveConnection:=***connection*, **CursorType:=***cursortype*, **LockType:=***locktype*, where *recordset* is the name of a Recordset object variable, *datasource* specifies the data source, and *connection* is the name of a Connection object variable. The *cursortype* and *locktype* arguments in the syntax can be one of the constants shown in Figure 6-40.

CursorType Constant	Description
adOpenForwardOnly	(Default) Forward-only cursor. Identical to a static cursor except that you can only scroll forward through records. This improves performance in situations when you need to make only a single pass through a recordset.
adOpenKeyset	Keyset cursor. Like a dynamic cursor, except you cannot see records that other users add. However, records that other users delete are inaccessible from your recordset. Data changes by other users are still visible.
adOpenDynamic	Dynamic cursor. Additions, changes, and deletions by other users are visible, and all types of movement through the recordset are allowed (except for book-marks if the provider doesn't support them).
adOpenStatic	Static cursor. A static copy of a set of records that you can use to find data or generate reports. Additions, changes, or deletions by other users are not visible.
LockType Constant	**Description**
adLockReadOnly	(default) Read-only—you cannot alter the data contained in the recordset.
adLockPessimistic	The provider locks a record immediately upon editing.
adLockOptimistic	The provider locks the record only when you call the Update method to save the changes made to the record.
adLockBatchOptimistic	Required for batch update mode.

Figure 6-40: Valid constants for the Open method's CursorType and LockType arguments

The LockType argument is particularly important in multiuser environments, where more than one user can access a recordset concurrently. The LockType argument prevents more than one user from editing a specific record at the same time by **locking** the record, making it unavailable to other users.

To use the Open method to open a recordset that contains all of the records stored in the Trip database's Payments table, you will use the name of the table (Payments) as the Source argument. You will use the name of the Connection object variable (cnnTrip) as the ActiveConnection argument. Because the PaymentUpdate procedure will need to make only a single pass through the recordset each time it is run, you will use the adOpenForwardOnly constant as the CursorType argument. You will use the adLockPessimistic constant as the LockType argument, which will lock the record as soon as you begin editing it.

To continue coding the PaymentUpdate procedure:

1 Type **'open the recordset** and press the **Enter** key. Type **rstpays.open source:="payments", activeconnection:=cnntrip, _** (be sure to type the comma followed by a space and the underscore) and press the **Enter** key. Press the **Tab** key, then type **cursortype:=adopenforwardonly, locktype:=adlockpessimistic** and press the **Enter** key.

Steps 2 through 4 in the pseudocode are to use the InputBox function to get the student's ID and the amount of his or her payment, and then convert the payment amount to a number and store it in the curPayment variable.

2 Enter the additional four lines of code shown in Figure 6-41.

enter these
four lines of
code

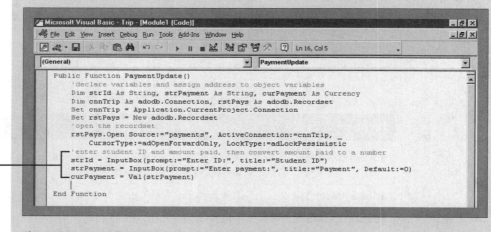

```
Public Function PaymentUpdate()
    'declare variables and assign address to object variables
    Dim strId As String, strPayment As String, curPayment As Currency
    Dim cnnTrip As adodb.Connection, rstPays As adodb.Recordset
    Set cnnTrip = Application.CurrentProject.Connection
    Set rstPays = New adodb.Recordset
    'open the recordset
    rstPays.Open Source:="payments", ActiveConnection:=cnnTrip, _
        CursorType:=adOpenForwardOnly, LockType:=adLockPessimistic
    'enter student ID and amount paid, then convert amount paid to a number
    strId = InputBox(prompt:="Enter ID:", title:="Student ID")
    strPayment = InputBox(prompt:="Enter payment:", title:="Payment", Default:=0)
    curPayment = Val(strPayment)

End Function
```

Figure 6-41: Partially completed PaymentUpdate procedure

3 Verify the accuracy of your code by comparing the code on your screen to the code shown in Figure 6-41, then save the database.

Step 5 in the pseudocode is to search the ID field for the student's ID. Before you can code this step, you need to learn about the Recordset object's Find method.

Using the Recordset Object's Find Method

You can use the Recordset Object's **Find method** to search for a value contained in a field in the recordset. The syntax of the Find method is *recordset.***Find Criteria:=***criteria*, where *criteria* is a string expression that specifies which record or records to locate. The *criteria*, which must be enclosed in quotation marks, includes both the name of the field you want to search and the data for which you want to search. Figure 6-42 shows six examples of using the Find method to search the rstPays recordset.

1. To find the first record whose Paid field contains the numeric literal constant 200, use:
   ```
   rstPays.Find Criteria:="paid = 200"
   ```

2. To find the first record whose ID field contains the string literal constant "gg1", use:
   ```
   rstPays.Find Criteria:="ID = 'gg1'"
   ```

3. To find the first record whose Updated field contains the date literal constant #10/10/02#, use:
   ```
   rstPays.Find Criteria:="Updated = #10/10/02#"
   ```

4. To find the first record whose Paid field contains the value stored in the curPayment Currency variable, use:
   ```
   rstPays.Find Criteria:="Paid = curPayment"
   ```

5. To find the first record whose ID field contains the value stored in the strId String variable, use:
   ```
   rstPays.Find Criteria:="ID = '" & strId & "'"
   ```

6. To find the first record whose Updated field contains the value stored in the dtmDate Date variable, use:
   ```
   rstPays.Find Criteria:="Updated = #" & dtmDate & "#"
   ```

Figure 6-42: Examples of using the Find method to search the rstPays recordset

As the first example shows, you use the instruction `rstPays.Find Criteria:="Paid = 200"` to find the first record whose Paid field contains the numeric literal constant 200. Notice that the entire *criteria*, "Paid = 200", is enclosed in quotation marks to indicate that it is a string expression.

Example 2 indicates that you need to use the instruction `rstPays.Find Criteria:="ID = 'gg1'"` to find the first record whose ID field contains the string literal constant "gg1". Notice the use of both the double and single quotation marks. When the Find method's *criteria* compares a Text field with a string literal constant, you enclose the *criteria* in double quotation marks, and you enclose the string literal constant in single quotation marks.

As Example 3 shows, you use the instruction `rstPays.Find Criteria:="Updated = #10/10/02#"` to locate the first record whose Updated field contains the date literal constant #10/10/02#. As you learned in Tutorial 4, date literal constants must be enclosed in number signs (#).

In addition to using literal constants in the Find method's *criteria*, you also can use variables. Example 4, for example, shows that you can use the instruction `rstPays.Find Criteria:="Paid = curPayment"` to find the first record whose Paid field value is equal to the value stored in the curPayment variable. Notice that this instruction compares the Paid field to a Currency variable.

The fifth example shown in Figure 6-42 indicates that you would need to use string concatenation to include a String variable in the Find method's *criteria*. The `rstPays.Find Criteria:="ID = '" & strId & "'"` instruction first concatenates the string "ID = '" with the strId variable, then concatenates the result with the string "'". This instruction will locate the first record whose ID field value is equal to the value stored in the strId variable. Assuming the strId variable contains the ID gg1, this instruction is identical to the one shown in Example 2 in the figure.

The last example shown in Figure 6-42 indicates that you also would need to use string concatenation to include a Date variable in the *criteria*. Notice that the instruction `rstPays.Find Criteria:="Updated = #" & dtmDate & "#"` concatenates the string "Updated = #" with the dtmDate variable, and then concatenates this result with the string "#". Assuming that the dtmDate variable contains 10/10/02, this instruction is identical to the one shown in Example 3 in the figure.

In the PaymentUpdate procedure, you will use the instruction `rstPays.Find Criteria:="id = '" & strId & "'"` to search the ID field for the student ID stored in the strId variable.

To complete the PaymentUpdate procedure:

1 Type **'search for ID in ID field, then update the record's Paid and Updated fields** and press the **Enter** key, then type **rstpays.find criteria:="id = '" & strid & "'"** and press the **Enter** key.

Step 6 in the pseudocode is to calculate the total amount paid by adding the current payment amount to the value contained in the student's Paid field.

2 Type **'calculate total amount paid** and press the **Enter** key, then type **rstpays.fields("paid").value = rstpays.fields("paid").value + curpayment** and press the **Enter** key.

The next step in the pseudocode is to assign the current date to the student's Updated field.

3 Type **'assign current date** and press the **Enter** key, then type **rstpays.fields("updated").value = date** and press the **Enter** key.

Step 8 in the pseudocode is to save the changes made to the current record; you use the Recordset object's **Update method** to do so. The syntax of the Update method is *recordset*.**Update**, where *recordset* is the name of a Recordset object.

4 Type **'save changes to record** and press the **Enter** key, then type **rstpays.update** and press the **Enter** key.

The last step in the pseudocode is to close the recordset. You use the Recordset object's **Close method**, whose syntax is *recordset*.**Close**, to do so.

5 Type **'close the recordset** and press the **Enter** key, then type **rstpays.close** and press the **Enter** key.

Closing an object created with the keyword New does not remove the object variable associated with the object from memory. To discontinue the association between an object and its object variable, you need to set the object variable to the keyword Nothing. As you learned in Tutorial 3, when an object variable contains the keyword Nothing, it means that the object variable does not point to any object in memory. Before ending a procedure, you should assign the keyword Nothing to any object variables that the procedure created using the keyword New.

6 Type the additional line of code shown in Figure 6-43, which shows the completed PaymentUpdate procedure. (Notice that you can include a comment on the same line as an instruction, as long as the comment comes after the instruction on that line.)

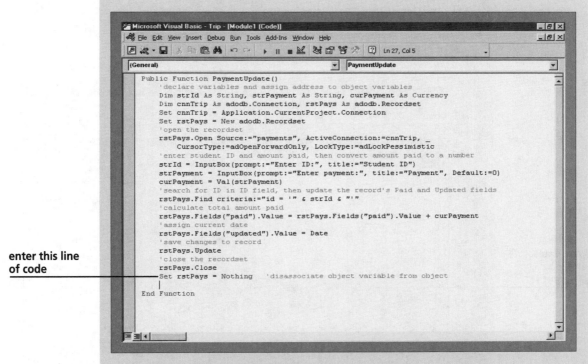

enter this line
of code

Figure 6-43: Completed PaymentUpdate procedure

7 Verify the accuracy of your code by comparing the code on your screen to the code shown in Figure 6-43, then save the database.

Now that you have translated the pseudocode shown in Figure 6-37 into VBA statements, you should test the PaymentUpdate procedure to verify that it is working correctly. You can test the procedure by running the PaymentUpdateMacro macro from the Database window in Access.

To test the PaymentUpdate procedure:

1 Click the **View Microsoft Access** button 🗗 on the Standard toolbar to return to Access, then run the **PaymentUpdateMacro** macro.

2 When the Student ID dialog box appears, type **gg1** and press the **Enter** key. When you are prompted to enter the payment amount, type **125** and press the **Enter** key.

3 On your own, use the PaymentUpdateMacro macro to record the Sonia Phillips payment of $500. Sonia's ID is sp2.

4 Open the Payments table to view the two updated records. See Figure 6-44. (Your dates might be different.)

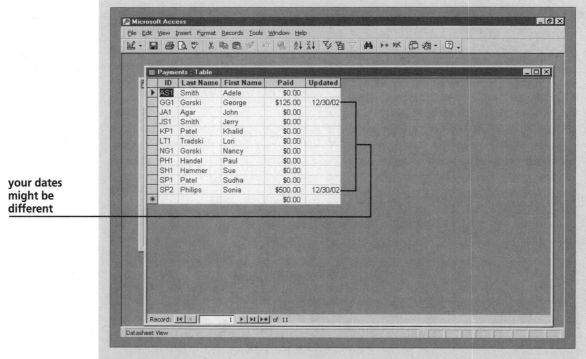

your dates
might be
different

Figure 6-44: Payments table showing the two updated records

5 Close the table, then compact the database and exit Access.

You now have completed Tutorial 6's Access lesson. You can either take a break or complete the end-of-lesson exercises.

 E X E R C I S E S

1. In this exercise, you will modify the PaymentUpdate procedure that you created in the lesson.

   a. Open the T6-AC-E1D (T6-AC-E1D.mdb) database. Open the Payments table. Notice that the Paid field, which stores the total amount paid by each student, contains $0.00. Also notice that the table contains an additional field named Due. The Due field, which stores the amount each student still owes for the trip, contains $1200.00. Close the table.

   b. Open the Visual Basic Editor. Open the Module1 module's Code window, then view the PaymentUpdate function procedure. Modify the procedure so that it calculates the amount the student owes after each payment is made, and then displays the amount in the Due column. For example, if George Gorski pays $400, then the Paid field should show $400.00 and the Due field should show $800.00 (1200-400).

   c. Save the database, then return to Access. Use the PaymentUpdateMacro macro to enter the following information. (The IDs contain two initials followed by a number.)

ID	Paid
js1	300
gg1	400
kp1	1000
js1	900

   d. Preview the PayReport report, then close the report.

   e. When the macro is working correctly, compact and then close the database.

2. In this exercise, you will create a procedure that displays a salary based on the code entered by the user.

   a. Open the T6-AC-E2D (T6-AC-E2D.mdb) database. Open the Codes table. The table contains two fields: a Text field named Code and a Currency field named Salary. Close the table.

   b. Open the Visual Basic Editor. Open the Module1 module's Code window, then view the code template for the DisplaySalary function procedure. Code the procedure so that it prompts the user to enter the salary code. The valid salary codes are C1 through C6. Use C1 as the InputBox function's *defaultValue*. Search for the salary code in the Code field, and then display the corresponding salary from the Salary field. Display the salary in a message box, as shown in Figure 6-45.

Figure 6-45

c. Save the database, then return to Access. Use the DisplaySalaryMacro macro to display the salary for code C3. The message box shown in Figure 6-45 should appear. Click the OK button to close the message box.

d. When the macro is working correctly, compact and then close the database.

3. In this exercise, you will create a procedure that calculates the price increase and new price of a product.

a. Open the T6-AC-E3D (T6-AC-E3D.mdb) database. Open the Products table. The table contains two fields: a Text field named Code and a Currency field named Price. Close the table.

b. Open the Visual Basic Editor. Open the Module1 module's Code window, then view the code template for the PriceIncrease function procedure. Code the procedure so that it prompts the user to enter the product code (A through F) and the price increase rate (entered in decimal form). Use "A" as the *defaultValue* for the InputBox function that gets the code, and use ".00" as the *defaultValue* for the InputBox function that gets the price increase. Search for the product code in the Code field. Calculate the price increase by multiplying the current price by the price increase, and then calculate the new price. Display the new price in the Price field.

c. Save the database, then return to Access. Use the PriceIncreaseMacro macro to enter the following information:

Code	Price Increase
A	.10
F	.05

d. Preview the ProductsReport report. The new price for product code A should be $55.00. The new price for product code F should be $78.75. Close the report.

e. When the macro is working correctly, compact and then close the database.

4. In this exercise, you will create a procedure that enters a date in a field in the recordset.

a. Open the T6-AC-E4D (T6-AC-E4D.mdb) database. Open the Invoices table in Design View. The table contains three fields: a Long field named InvNum and two Date/Time fields named InvDate and ShipDate. Close the Design View window, then open the Invoices table. Notice that the ShipDate field is empty. Close the table.

b. Open the Visual Basic Editor. Open the Module1 module's Code window, then view the code template for the ShipDate function procedure. Code the procedure so that it prompts the user to enter the invoice number and the shipping date. Use the system date as the *defaultValue* in the InputBox function that gets the shipping date. Search for the invoice number in the InvNum field, then assign the shipping date to the ShipDate field.

c. Save the database, then return to Access. Use the ShipDateMacro macro to enter the following information:

Invoice Number	Shipping Date
1	4/2/02
2	3/9/02
3	3/20/02
4	3/11/02
5	3/25/02

d. Preview the InvoicesReport report, then close the report.

e. When the macro is working correctly, compact and then close the database.

Exercise 5 is a Discovery Exercise. Discovery Exercises, which may include topics that are not covered in the lesson, allow you to "discover" the solutions to problems on your own.

discovery ▶ **5.** In this exercise, you will create a procedure that searches a Date/Time field.

a. Open the T6-AC-E5D (T6-AC-E5D.mdb) database. Open the Seminars table. The table contains a Date/Time field named SeminarDate and a Text field named Speaker. Close the table.

b. Open the Visual Basic Editor. Open the Module1 module's Code window, then view the code template for the EnterSpeaker function procedure. Code the procedure so that it prompts the user to enter the seminar date and the speaker's name. Search for the seminar date in the SeminarDate field, then assign the speaker's name to the Speaker field.

c. Save the database, then return to Access. Use the EnterSpeakerMacro macro to enter the following information:

Seminar Date	Speaker
5/1/02	Inez Martinez
5/3/02	Mamta Nadkarni

d. Preview the SeminarsReport report, then close the report.

e. When the macro is working correctly, compact and then save the database.

A computer program is good only if it works. Errors in programming code can cause a program to run incorrectly. Therefore, a programmer needs to know how to locate and fix any errors in his or her code. Exercise 6 is a Debugging Exercise. Debugging Exercises allow you to practice recognizing and solving errors in code.

debugging **6.** In this exercise, you will debug an existing procedure.

a. Open the T6-AC-E6D (T6-AC-E6D.mdb) database. Open the IdNames table. The table contains two Text fields named ID and Name. Close the table.

b. Open the Visual Basic Editor. Open the Module1 module's Code window, then view the DisplayName function procedure. The procedure should prompt the user to enter the ID. It then should display the corresponding name in a message box.

c. Study the code, then return to Access. Run the DisplayNameMacro macro. When the ID dialog box appears, type the letter a and then press the Enter key. When the error message appears in a dialog box, click the Debug button to locate the error. Click the Reset button ■ in the Standard toolbar to stop the procedure, then click the Halt button in the Action Failed dialog box. What is wrong with the procedure? Correct any errors, and then save the database.

d. Return to Access and run the DisplayNameMacro macro again. When the macro is working correctly, compact and then close the database.

The Selection Structure

In this tutorial, you will learn how to:

- Perform selection using the If...Then...Else statement
- Write instructions that use comparison operators and logical operators
- Use the UCase function
- Nest If...Then...Else statements
- Use the PublishObjects collection and PublishObject objects in Excel to publish data to a Web page
- Use the TablesOfContents collection and the TableOfContents objects in Word

Concept Lesson

Using the If...Then...Else Statement

The procedures you created in the previous six tutorials used the sequence programming structure only, where each of the procedure's instructions was processed, one after another, in the order in which they appeared in the Code window. In many procedures, however, the next instruction to be processed will depend on the result of a decision or a comparison that the program must make. For example, a procedure that calculates an employee's weekly gross pay typically will need to compare the number of hours the employee worked with the number 40 to determine if the employee should receive overtime pay. Based on the result of that comparison, the procedure then will select either an instruction that computes regular pay only, or an instruction that computes regular pay plus overtime pay.

You use the **selection structure**, also called the **decision structure**, when you want a procedure to make a decision or comparison and then, based on the result of that decision or comparison, select one of two paths. You can use the VBA If...Then...Else statement, whose syntax is shown in Figure 7-1, to include a selection structure in a procedure. Notice that the instructions following the word "Then" in the syntax are referred to as the **Then clause**, and the instructions following the word "Else" are referred to as the **Else clause**.

If *condition* **Then**

    [*Then clause instructions, which will be processed when the condition evaluates to True*]

[**Else**

    [*Else clause instructions, which will be processed when the condition evaluates to False*]]

End If

Figure 7-1: Syntax of the If...Then...Else statement

 tip

> You also can use the VBA Select Case statement to perform selection in a procedure. You will learn how to use the Select Case statement in Tutorial 8.

The items appearing in square brackets ([]) in the syntax are optional. For example, you don't need to include the Else clause in the If...Then...Else statement. Words in **bold**, however, are essential components of the statement. Thus, the words If, Then, and End If must be included in the statement. (The word Else must be included only if the statement uses the Else clause.) Items in *italics* indicate where the programmer must supply information pertaining to the current procedure. For instance, the programmer must supply the *condition* to be evaluated. The *condition*, which can contain variables, constants, functions, arithmetic operators, comparison operators, and logical operators, must evaluate to either the Boolean value True or the Boolean value False. If the *condition* evaluates to True, the instructions within the Then clause are processed, followed by the instructions appearing after the End If. If, on the other hand, the *condition* evaluates to False, only the instructions within the Else clause are processed, followed by the instructions appearing after the End If. If the If...Then...Else statement does not include an Else clause, then only the instructions following the End If are processed when the *condition* evaluates to False.

As mentioned earlier, the If...Then...Else statement's *condition* can contain variables, constants, functions, arithmetic operators, comparison operators, and logical operators. You already know about variables, constants, functions, and arithmetic operators. In this lesson you will learn about comparison operators and logical operators.

Comparison Operators

You use **comparison operators**, sometimes referred to as relational operators, to compare two values. Figure 7-2 lists the most commonly used comparison operators, along with an example of using each in a *condition*.

Operator	Meaning	Example of a *condition*	Result
=	Equal to	7 = 3	False
>	Greater than	sngHours > 40	True if sngHours contains a value that is greater than 40; otherwise, False
>=	Greater than or equal to	6 >= 6	True
<	Less than	"A" < "B"	True
<=	Less than or equal to	dtmShip <= Date	True if dtmShip contains a value that is less than or equal to the current date; otherwise, False
<>	Not equal to	intAge <> 21	True if intAge contains a value that is not equal to 21; otherwise, False

Figure 7-2: Most commonly used comparison operators

tip

You will learn about another comparison operator, Like, in this lesson's Exercise 14.

As Figure 7-2 indicates, *conditions* containing a comparison operator result in an answer of either True or False only.

Unlike the arithmetic operators that you learned about in Tutorial 6, the comparison operators do not have an order or precedence. When a *condition* contains more than one comparison operator, the comparison operators are evaluated from left to right in the *condition*. Keep in mind, however, that comparison operators are evaluated after any arithmetic operators. In other words, in the *condition* 9 – 4 > 2 * 2, the two arithmetic operators (- and *) will be evaluated before the comparison operator (>). The result of the *condition* is True, as shown in Figure 7-3.

Condition: 9 – 4 > 2 * 2	
Evaluation steps:	**Result of evaluation:**
2 * 2 is evaluated first	9 – 4 > 4
9 – 4 is evaluated second	5 > 4
5 > 4 is evaluated last	True

Figure 7-3: Evaluation steps for a *condition* containing arithmetic and comparison operators

Figure 7-4 shows examples of If...Then...Else statements whose *conditions*, which are shaded in the figure, contain comparison operators.

If...Then...Else statement	Result

`If intQuantity < 25 then`
`    MsgBox Prompt:="Reorder"`
`End If`
	Displays "Reorder" if the intQuantity variable contains a value that is less than 25

`If sngHours <= 40 Then`
`    MsgBox Prompt:="Regular pay"`
`Else`
`    MsgBox Prompt:="Overtime pay"`
`End If`
	Displays "Regular pay" if the sngHours variable contains a value that is less than or equal to 40; otherwise, displays "Overtime pay"

`If curSales > 10000 Then`
`    curBonus = curSales * .1`
`Else`
`    curBonus = curSales * .05`
`End If`
	Calculates a 10% bonus on sales that are greater than $10,000; otherwise, calculates a 5% bonus

Figure 7-4: Examples of If...Then...Else statements whose *conditions* contain comparison operators

The first If...Then...Else statement shown in Figure 7-4 displays "Reorder" if the *condition* `intQuantity < 25` evaluates to True. The second If...Then...Else statement displays "Regular pay" when the *condition* `sngHours <= 40` evaluates to True; it displays "Overtime pay" when the *condition* evaluates to False. The third If...Then...Else statement calculates a 10% bonus when the *condition* `curSales > 10000` evaluates to True; otherwise, it calculates a 5% bonus.

The *conditions* shown in Figure 7-4 compare the contents of numeric variables to numeric literal constants. A *condition* also can compare the contents of a String variable to a string literal constant. In the next section, you will learn how to use the VBA UCase function in *conditions* that involve string comparisons.

UCase Function

As is true in many programming languages, string comparisons in VBA are case sensitive, which means that the uppercase version of a letter is not the same as its lowercase counterpart. So, although a human recognizes "P" and "p" as being the same letter, a computer does not; to a computer, a "P" is different from a "p". A problem occurs when you need to include a string, entered by the user, in a comparison. The problem occurs because you can't control the case in which the user enters the string.

One way of handling the string comparison problem is to include the UCase function, whose syntax is **UCase(String:=*string*)**, in your string comparisons. As you learned in Tutorial 4, a function is a set of instructions that returns a value. The UCase function, for example, returns the uppercase equivalent of its *string* argument. Figure 7-5, on the next page, shows examples of If...Then...Else statements whose *conditions*, which are shaded in the figure, use the UCase function to compare strings.

Because the UCase function has only one argument, you can omit the argument's name and the := operator when typing the function.

The U in UCase stands for "upper." Also included in the VBA language is a function named LCase that returns the lowercase equivalent of a string. The L in LCase stands for "lower."

In the first If...Then...Else statement in Figure 7-5, the *condition* `UCase (String:=strName) = UCase(String:=strEmp)` compares the uppercase equivalents of the string stored in the strName variable with the uppercase equivalent of the string stored in the strEmp variable. If the uppercase equivalents of both strings are equal, then the *condition* evaluates to True and the Then clause displays "Employee".

```
Statement:    If UCase(String:=strName) = UCase(String:=strEmp) Then
                  MsgBox "Employee"
              End If
```
Result: Displays "Employee" if the uppercase versions of the strings stored in the strName and strEmp variables are equal.

```
Statement:    If UCase(String:=strAnswer) = "Y" Then
                  intCorrect = intCorrect + 1
              Else
                  intWrong = intWrong + 1
              End If
```
Result: Adds 1 to the contents of the intCorrect variable if the uppercase version of the string stored in the strAnswer variable is equal to the letter "Y"; otherwise, it adds 1 to the contents of the intWrong variable.

```
Statement:    If UCase(String:=strName1) > UCase(String:=strName2) Then
                  strTemp = strName1
                  strName1 = strName2
                  strName2 = strTemp
              End If
```
Result: Swaps the values stored in the strName1 and strName2 variables when the uppercase version of the string stored in the strName1 variable is greater than (comes after in the alphabet) the uppercase version of the string stored in the strName2 variable

Figure 7-5: Examples of If...Then...Else statements whose *conditions* contain the UCase function

The *condition* `UCase(String:=strAnswer) = "Y"` contained in the second If...Then...Else statement shown in Figure 7-5 compares the uppercase version of the string stored in the strAnswer variable to the uppercase letter "Y". The statement will add the number one to the contents of the intCorrect variable when the *condition* evaluates to True; otherwise, it will add the number one to the contents of the intWrong variable.

The third If...Then...Else statement's *condition*, `UCase(String:=strName1) > UCase(String:=strName2)`, checks to see if the uppercase version of the string stored in the strName1 variable is greater than (comes after in the alphabet) the uppercase version of the string stored in the strName2 variable. If the *condition* evaluates to True, then the contents of both variables are interchanged.

Notice that each of the three *conditions* shown in Figure 7-5 compares the uppercase equivalent of one string to the uppercase equivalent of another string. For the UCase function to work correctly, both strings included in the comparison must be in uppercase letters.

 tip

You also can use the UCase function in an assignment statement. For example, you can use the assignment statement `strState = UCase(String:=strState)` to change the contents of the strState variable to uppercase.

As mentioned earlier, in addition to the arithmetic and comparison operators, the If...Then...Else statement's *condition* also can contain logical operators.

Logical Operators

The two most commonly used logical operators are And and Or. You use the And and Or operators to combine several *conditions* into one compound *condition*. Figure 7-6 lists the two logical operators, their meaning, and their order of precedence.

Operator	Meaning	Order of Precedence
And	All *conditions* connected by the And operator must be true for the compound *condition* to be true	1
Or	Only one of the *conditions* connected by the Or operator needs to be true for the compound *condition* to be true	2

Figure 7-6: Most commonly used logical operators

As is true of all *conditions* containing a comparison operator, all compound *conditions* containing a logical operator will evaluate to an answer of either True or False only. The tables shown in Figure 7-7, called truth tables, summarize how the And and Or logical operators are evaluated in a compound *condition*.

Truth Table for the And Operator		
Value of *condition1*	Value of *condition2*	Value of *condition1* And *condition2*
True	True	True
True	False	False
False	True	False
False	False	False
Truth Table for the Or Operator		
Value of *condition1*	Value of *condition2*	Value of *condition1* Or *condition2*
True	True	True
True	False	True
False	True	True
False	False	False

Figure 7-7: Truth tables for the And and Or logical operators

As Figure 7-7 indicates, when you use the And operator to combine two *conditions*, *condition1* And *condition2*, the resulting compound *condition* is True only when both *conditions* are True. If either *condition* is False or if both *conditions* are False, then the compound *condition* is False. Compare that to the Or operator. When you combine *conditions* using the Or operator, *condition1* Or *condition2*, notice that the compound *condition* is False only when both *conditions* are False. If either *condition* is True or if both *conditions* are True, then the compound *condition* is True.

Figure 7-8 shows examples of If...Then...Else statements whose *conditions*, which are shaded in the figure, contain logical operators.

Statement: If `intQuantity > 0 And intQuantity < 101` Then
        MsgBox Prompt:="Valid quantity"
    Else
        MsgBox Prompt:="Quantity error"
    End If
Result: Displays "Valid quantity" if the intQuantity variable contains a value that is greater than 0 and, at the same time, less than 101; otherwise, displays "Quantity error"

Statement: If `dtmShip = Date And intStock > intOrder` Then
        intStock = intStock - intOrder
    End If
Result: Subtracts the contents of the intOrder variable from the contents of the intStock variable if the dtmShip variable contains today's date and, at the same time, the intStock variable contains a value that is greater than the value stored in the intOrder variable

Statement: If `intCode = 1 Or intCode = 3` Then
        strRaise = "Y"
    Else
        strRaise = "N"
    End If
Result: Assigns the letter "Y" to the strRaise variable if the intCode variable contains either the number 1 or the number 3; otherwise, assigns the letter "N" to the strRaise variable

Statement: If `UCase(String:=strCo) = "A" Or curSales > 10000` Then
        sngBonus = .15
    Else
        sngBonus = .14
    End If
Result: Assigns a 15% bonus rate to the sngBonus variable if either the strCo variable contains the letter "A" or the curSales variable contains a value that is greater than $10,000; otherwise, assigns a 14% bonus rate to the sngBonus variable

Figure 7-8: Examples of If...Then...Else statements whose *conditions* contain logical operators

The first two examples shown in Figure 7-8 use the And operator to combine two *conditions* into one compound *condition*. Notice that the first If...Then...Else statement will display "Valid quantity" only if the intQuantity variable contains a value that is both greater than 0 and, at the same time, less than 101; otherwise, it will display "Quantity error". The second If...Then...Else statement will subtract the contents of the intOrder variable from the contents of the intStock variable only if the dtmShip variable contains today's date and, at the same time, the intStock variable contains a value that is greater than the value stored in the intOrder variable.

The third and fourth examples shown in Figure 7-8 use the Or operator to combine two *conditions* into one compound *condition*. The third If...Then...Else statement will assign the letter "Y" to the strRaise variable if the intCode variable contains either the number 1 or the number 3. If the intCode variable contains a value other than the numbers 1 or 3, it will assign the letter "N" to the strRaise variable. The fourth If...Then...Else statement will assign a 15% bonus rate to the sngBonus variable if either the strCo variable contains the letter "A" or the curSales variable contains a value that is greater than $10,000; otherwise, it will assign a 14% bonus rate to the sngBonus variable.

When a *condition* contains arithmetic, comparison, and logical operators, the arithmetic operators are evaluated first, then the comparison operators are evaluated, and then the logical operators are evaluated. Figure 7-9 illustrates this concept.

Condition: 6 / 3 < 2 Or 2 * 3 > 5	
Evaluation steps:	**Result of evaluation:**
6 / 3 is evaluated first	2 < 2 Or 2 * 3 > 5
2 * 3 is evaluated second	2 < 2 Or 6 > 5
2 < 2 is evaluated third	False Or 6 > 5
6 > 5 is evaluated fourth	False Or True
False Or True is evaluated last	True

Figure 7-9: Evaluation steps for a *condition* containing arithmetic, comparison, and logical operators

Now that you understand the use of comparison and logical operators in the If...Then...Else statement, you will learn how to include a second If...Then...Else statement within another If...Then...Else statement, a technique referred to as **nesting.**

Nesting If...Then...Else Statements

A nested If...Then...Else statement is one in which either the Then clause or the Else clause includes yet another If...Then...Else statement. Figure 7-10 shows the syntax of a nested If...Then...Else statement, first with the second If...Then...Else statement in the Then clause and then with the second If...Then...Else statement in the Else clause.

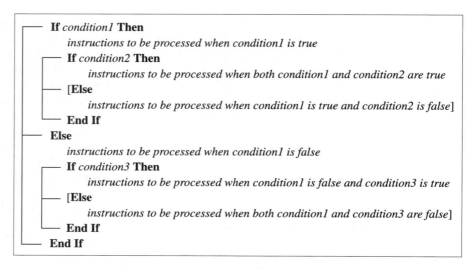

Figure 7-10: Syntax of a nested If...Then...Else statement

Notice that each If...Then...Else statement is matched with an End If, which marks the end of that If...Then...Else statement. Figure 7-11 shows two examples of nested If...Then...Else statements.

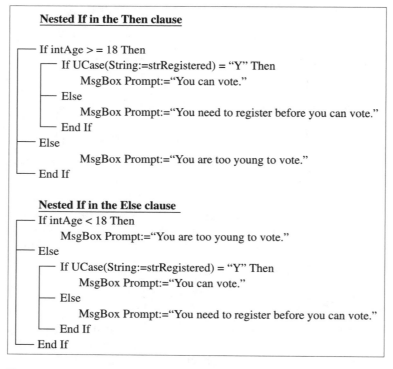

Figure 7-11: Two examples of nested If...Then...Else statements

In the first example in Figure 7-11, the entire nested If...Then...Else statement—which includes the Then clause, the Else clause, and the End If—is contained within the Then clause of the first If...Then...Else statement. In the second example, the entire nested If...Then...Else statement is contained within the Else clause of the first If...Then...Else statement. Both examples will display the "You are too young to vote." message when the intAge variable contains a value that is less than (not greater than or equal to) the number 18. The examples will display either the "You can vote." message or the "You need to register before you can vote." message when the intAge variable contains a value that is greater than or equal to the number 18. The contents of the strRegistered variable determines which message appears. If the strRegistered variable contains the letter Y (in either uppercase or lowercase letters), then the examples will display the "You can vote." message; otherwise, they will display the "You need to register before you can vote." message.

You now have completed Tutorial 7's Concept lesson. You can either take a break or complete the end-of-lesson questions and exercises before moving on to the next lesson.

SUMMARY

To use the If...Then...Else statement to code the selection structure:

■ Use the syntax shown in Figure 7-1, where *condition* can contain variables, constants, functions, arithmetic operators, comparison operators, and logical operators.

To compare two values:

■ Use the comparison operators (=, >, <, >=, <=, <>)

To return the uppercase equivalent of a string:

■ Use the UCase function, whose syntax is **UCase(String:=***string***)**.

To create a compound *condition*:

■ Use the logical operators (And and Or)

To nest If...Then...Else statements:

■ Use the syntax shown in Figure 7-10.

REVIEW QUESTIONS

1. Which of the following is a valid *condition* for an If...Then...Else statement?
   a. `curSales > 500 And curSales < 1000`
   b. `UCase(String:=strState) <> "Alaska"`
   c. `Val(String:=strAge > 65)`
   d. `Val(String:=strAge) >= 18 And < 21`

2. Which of the following statements should you use to compare the string contained in the strName variable with the name Ann? (You do not know the case of the string contained in the strName variable.)
   a. `If strName = "ANN" Then`
   b. `If strName = UCase(String:="ANN") Then`
   c. `If strName = UCase(String:="Ann") Then`
   d. `If UCase(String:=strName) = "ANN" Then`

3. Which of the following will change the contents of the strName variable to uppercase letters?
   a. `strName = UCase(String:=strName)`
   b. `strName = UCase(String:="strName")`
   c. `strName = Upper(String:=strName)`
   d. `UpperCase(String:=strName) = strName`

4. Evaluate the following expression: $3 > 6$ And $7 > 4$
   a. True   b. False

5. Evaluate the following expression: $4 > 6$ Or $10 < 2 * 6$
   a. True   b. False

Use the following information to answer questions 6 through 11.

   intHours = 41, sngRate = 5.5, strName = "John"

6. What will the following If...Then...Else statement display in a message box?

```
If intHours > 40 And UCase(String:=strName) = "John" Then
  MsgBox Prompt:="Condition evaluates to True"
Else
  MsgBox Prompt:="Condition evaluates to False"
End If
```
   a. Condition evaluates to True   b. Condition evaluates to False

7. What will the following If...Then...Else statement display in a message box?

```
If intHours > 40 Or UCase(String:=strName) = "CARL" Then
  MsgBox Prompt:="Condition evaluates to True"
Else
  MsgBox Prompt:="Condition evaluates to False"
End If
```
   a. Condition evaluates to True   b. Condition evaluates to False

8. What will the following If...Then...Else statement display in a message box?

```
If intHours <= 40 Or sngRate > 5 Then
  MsgBox Prompt:="Condition evaluates to True"
Else
  MsgBox Prompt:="Condition evaluates to False"
End If
```
a. Condition evaluates to True   b. Condition evaluates to False

9. What will the following If...Then...Else statement display in a message box? (Remember that you can omit the String:= from the UCase function.)

```
If intHours>40 Or sngRate>5 And UCase(strName)="ANN" Then
  MsgBox Prompt:="Condition evaluates to True"
Else
  MsgBox Prompt:="Condition evaluates to False"
End If
```
a. Condition evaluates to True   b. Condition evaluates to False

10. What will the following nested If...Then...Else statement display in a message box? (Remember that you can omit the String:= from the UCase function.)

```
If UCase(strName) = "JOHN" Then
    If sngRate < 5 Then
        MsgBox Prompt:="Needs a raise"
    Else
        MsgBox Prompt:="No raise"
    End If
Else
    MsgBox Prompt:="It's not John"
End If
```
a. Needs a raise   b. No raise   c. It's not John

11. What will the following nested If...Then...Else statement display in a message box?

```
If intHours < 40 Then
    MsgBox Prompt:="You left early"
Else
    If intHours = 40 Then
        MsgBox Prompt:="You worked 40 hours"
    Else
        MsgBox Prompt:="You worked overtime"
    End If
End If
```
a. You left early   b. You worked 40 hours   c. You worked overtime

E X E R C I S E S

1. Write an If...Then...Else statement that displays the string "Microsoft" in a message box if the strProgram variable contains the string "Word" (in either uppercase or lowercase).

2. Write an If...Then...Else statement that displays the string "Reorder" in a message box if the intUnits variable contains a number that is less than 100; otherwise, display the string "OK".

3. Write an If...Then...Else statement that assigns the number 10 to the curBonus variable if the curSales variable contains a number that is less than or equal to 250; otherwise, assign the number 15.

4. Write an If...Then...Else statement that assigns the number 25 to the intShip variable if the strState variable contains the string "Hawaii" (in either uppercase or lowercase letters); otherwise, assign the number 50.

5. Assume you want to calculate a 5% sales tax if the strState variable contains the string "Kentucky" (in either uppercase or lowercase letters); otherwise, you want to calculate a 7% sales tax. You can calculate the sales tax by multiplying the tax rate by the contents of the curSales variable. Assign the appropriate sales tax rate to the sngRate variable, then assign the sales tax to the curTax variable. Write the VBA code.

6. Assume you want to calculate an employee's gross pay. Employees working more than 40 hours should receive overtime pay (time and one-half) for the hours over 40. Use the variables sngHours, sngRate, and sngGross. Display the contents of the sngGross variable in a message box. Write the VBA code.

7. Assume you want to calculate a 10% discount on the price of two models of computers (Models AX1 and SD2); all other models get a 5% discount. In addition to calculating the discount, also calculate the new price (the original price minus the discount). Use the variables strModelNum, curOrigPrice, sngRate, curDiscount, and curNewPrice. Display the contents of the curNewPrice variable in a message box. Write the VBA code.

8. Assume that all Code 3 employees who have been with the company at least five years are to receive a 5% raise. Employees having other job codes, or those who have been with the company for less than five years, get a 4.5% raise. Calculate the employee's raise and new salary. Use the variables strCode, sngYears, curCurrentSalary, sngRaiseRate, curRaise, and curNewSalary. Display the contents of the curNewSalary variable in a message box. Write the VBA code.

9. Write an If...Then...Else statement that displays the string "Dog" in a message box if the intAnimal variable contains the number 1. Display the string "Cat" if the intAnimal variable contains the number 2. Display the string "Unknown" if the intAnimal variable contains a number other than 1 or 2.

10. Assume you offer programming seminars to companies. Your price per person depends on the number of people the company registers, as per the table shown below. (For example, if the company registers seven people, then the total amount owed by the company is $560.)

Number of registrants	Charge
1 – 4	$100 per person
5 or more	$ 80 per person
less than 1	$ 0 per person (*Note*: Keep in mind that it is

possible that a user may inadvertently type a letter, special symbol, or a negative number as the number of registrants.)
The number of people registered is stored in the intReg variable. Calculate the total amount owed by the company. Store the total amount in the curTotal variable. Write the VBA code.

11. The price of a concert ticket depends on the seat location entered in the strSeat variable, as per the chart shown below. (Keep in mind that you do not know the case of the value stored in the strSeat variable.) Write the VBA code that will display the appropriate price in a message box.

Seat location	Concert ticket price
Box	$75
Pavilion	$30
Lawn	$21
Other	$ 0 (*Note*: Keep in mind that it is possible that

a user may inadvertently misspell the seat location.)

12. Assume you want to calculate a 10% discount on sales made to customers in California and in Texas, a 7% discount on sales made to customers in Oregon and New Mexico, and a 6% discount on sales made to customers in all other states. The state is stored in the strState variable, and the sales amounts are stored in the curSales variable. Assign the appropriate discount rate to the sngRate variable. Calculate the discount amount and assign it to the curDiscount variable. Calculate the discounted sales amount and assign it to the curDiscountedSales variable. Display the contents of the curDiscountedSales variable in a message box.

Exercises 13 and 14 are Discovery Exercises. Discovery Exercises, which may include topics that are not covered in the lesson, allow you to "discover" the solutions to problems on your window.

discovery ▶ 13. In this exercise, you will learn about the IsNumeric function, which you can use to verify that an expression can be converted to a number.
a. Start either Word, Excel, Access, or PowerPoint. Open the Visual Basic Editor. Display the IsNumeric Function Help screen. Use the Help screen to complete the following statements by filling in the blanks.
The syntax of the IsNumeric function is _____. The IsNumeric function returns _____ if the entire *expression* is recognized as a number; otherwise it returns _____. The IsNumeric function returns _____ if the expression is a date.

b. Insert a module, then create a procedure named TestIsNumeric. Enter the following three statements in the TestIsNumeric procedure:

```
Dim strTest As String
strTest = InputBox(prompt:="Number?", title:="Number")
MsgBox Prompt:=IsNumeric(expression:=strTest)
```

c. Run the procedure five times, entering the values 5, 6.78, $2,333.45, 4%, and A. Record the results of the `MsgBox Prompt:=IsNumeric (expression =strTest)` statement on a piece of paper.

d. Place an apostrophe at the beginning of the `MsgBox Prompt:=IsNumeric (expression:=strTest)` statement, then add the following three commands above the `End Sub` statement in the procedure:

```
If IsNumeric(expression:=strTest) = True Then
    MsgBox Prompt:=Val(string:=strTest)
End If
```

e. Run the procedure five times, entering the values 5, 6.78, $2,333.45, 4%, and A. Record the results of the `MsgBox Prompt:=Val(string:=strTest)` statement.

f. Change the `MsgBox Prompt:=Val(string:=strTest)` statement to `MsgBox Prompt:=CSng(strTest)`. (CSng is one of the VBA type conversion functions. It is used to convert a string to a Single data type. To learn more about the type conversion functions, complete Discovery Exercise 10 in Tutorial 6's Concept lesson.)

g. Run the procedure five times, entering the values 5, 6.78, $2,333.45, 4%, and A. Record the results of the `MsgBox Prompt:=CSng(strTest)` statement on a piece of paper.

h. What is the difference between using the Val function and using the CSng function?

discovery ▶ 14. In this exercise, you will learn about the Like comparison operator.

a. Start either Word, Excel, Access, or PowerPoint. Open the Visual Basic Editor. Display the Like Operator Help screen. Use the Help screen to complete the following statements by filling in the blanks.
The Like operator is used to _____. Its syntax is _____. The Like operator returns _____ if *string* matches *pattern*. If string does not match *pattern*, the Like operator returns _____.

b. Open the Immediate window. Enter the following commands in the Immediate window. For each command, record the results and the reason for the results.

```
? "Hat" like "Hat"
? "Hat" like "hat"
? "Coat" like "C"
? "Coat" like "C*"
? "Jim" like "J?"
? "Jim" like "J?m"
```

You also can use VBA in PowerPoint to create procedures that enhance your presentations. Exercise 15 allows you to apply this tutorial's programming concept in a PowerPoint presentation.

powerpoint **15.** In this exercise, you will finish coding a procedure in PowerPoint. The procedure will allow the user to print one or more of a presentation's slides.

    a. Open the T7-PP-E15 (T7-PP-E15.ppt) presentation, which is located in the Tut07\Concept folder on your Data Disk. Click the Enable Macros button, if necessary, then save the presentation as T7-PP-E15D.

    b. Open the Visual Basic Editor. Open the Module1 module's Code window, then view the partially completed PrintSlide procedure. The procedure should allow the user to print one or more of the presentation's slides. Notice that the PrintSlide procedure declares five variables and uses the InputBox function to verify that the user wants to print. Complete the procedure by adding the code that will accomplish the following: If the user does not want to print, then display "No slides will be printed." in a message box. However, if the user wants to print, first prompt him or her for the number of the first slide to print, then prompt the user for the number of the last slide to print. Use the number 1 as the *defaultValue* in both InputBox functions. Convert the user's responses to integers. Use the Presentation object's PrintOut method to print the range of slides.

    c. Save the presentation, then return to PowerPoint. Click View on the menu bar and then click Slide Show. When the slide appears, click the image that appears on the first slide. Enter the letter n in response to the "Do you want to print?" prompt. The message "No slides will be printed." appears in a message box. Click the OK button to close the message box.

    d. Click the image again, then press the Enter key in response to the "Do you want to print?" prompt. Print slides 2 and 3 only, then press the Esc key to stop the slide show.

    e. Close PowerPoint.

A computer program is good only if it works. Errors in programming code can cause a program to run incorrectly. Therefore, a programmer needs to know how to locate and fix any errors in his or her code. Exercise 16 is a Debugging Exercise. Debugging Exercises allow you to practice recognizing and solving errors in code.

debugging **16.** Assume that employees having a job rating of either "A" or "B" are to receive a 5% raise, but only if the employee has been with the company for more than 10 years. All other employees should receive a 3% raise. (The job rating and number of years employed are stored in the strJob and sngYear variables, respectively.) The procedure shown in Figure 7-12 (on the next page) should display the appropriate raise rate, but it is not working correctly; it displays .05 for all employees with a job rating of "A". What is wrong with the procedure? Correct any errors.

```
Public Sub DisplayRate()
      Dim strJob As String, sngYear As Single, sngRate As Single
      strJob = InputBox(Prompt:="Job rating:", Title:="Rating")
      sngYear = InputBox(Prompt:="Years with company:", _
            Title:="Years")
      If UCase(String:=strJob) = "A" Or UCase(String:=strJob) = "B" _
            And sngYear > 10 Then
                  sngRate = 0.05
      Else
                  sngRate = 0.03
      End If
      MsgBox Prompt:=sngRate
End Sub
```

Figure 7-12

Excel Lesson

Using the Selection Structure in Excel

case ▶ Paradise Electronics allows its customers to finance the purchase of new computer equipment. Currently, the store clerk uses an Excel worksheet named Calculator to calculate the appropriate monthly payment (including interest) for the customer. Martin Washington, the accountant at Paradise Electronics, would like to make the worksheet available on the Paradise Electronics Web site on the World Wide Web, which would allow all the Paradise clerks to access up-to-date interest rates, and would also allow customers to calculate their own payments. The **World Wide Web** (also called the "Web" or "WWW") is a global information-sharing system, which is part of the **Internet**, a worldwide network made up of millions of interconnected computers. Information is stored on the Web in the form of electronic documents called **Web pages**. Each Web page can contain a variety of information ranging from simple text to complex multimedia elements such as graphics, sound, and video clips. Web pages are formatted using a special programming language called HTML, or HyperText Markup Language. The HTML language tells a **Web browser**, a special program that allows you to view a Web page, how the Web page should look on the user's screen. (Internet Explorer and Netscape Navigator are two popular Web browsers.) The process of saving one or more document items to a Web page is referred to as **publishing**.

Viewing the Calculator Worksheet

The workbook that Martin created and that Paradise Electronics uses to calculate a customer's monthly payment is stored on your Data Disk. Before creating the macro for publishing the workbook's Calculator worksheet to a Web page, view the worksheet and the code template for the PublishCalculator procedure.

To view the Calculator worksheet and the code template for the PublishCalculator procedure:

1 Start Microsoft Excel. Open the **T7-EX-1** (T7-EX-1.xls) workbook, which is located in the Tut07\Excel folder on your Data Disk. Click the **Enable Macros** button, if necessary, then save the workbook as **Payment Calculator**.

The Payment Calculator workbook contains one worksheet, named Calculator, as shown in Figure 7-13. Notice that cells B3, B4, B5, B7, and E19 are named Principal, Term, Rate, MthlyPay, and Updated, respectively. The entire worksheet, except for the Principal and Term cells, is protected. Martin protected the worksheet in this fashion because he wants to limit the areas of the worksheet that the user can manipulate. In this case, he wants the user to be able to enter data in the Principal and Term cells only.

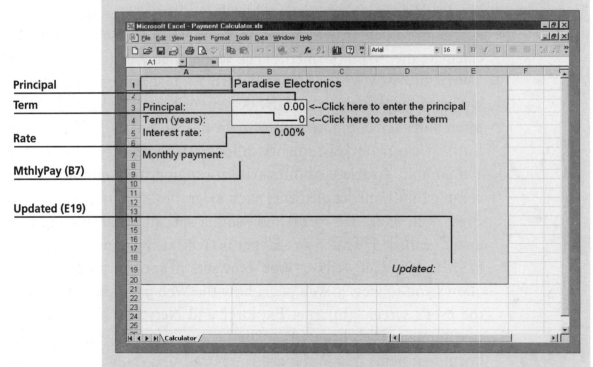

Figure 7-13: Payment Calculator workbook showing the Calculator worksheet

To allow the user to enter data in one or more cells in a protected worksheet, first use the Protection option on the Tools menu to unprotect the worksheet. Select the cells in which you want the user to be able to enter data. Click Format on the menu bar, and then click Cells. When the Format Cells dialog box appears, click the Protection tab, then remove the check mark from the Locked check box, and then click the OK button to close the dialog box. Use the Protection option on the Tools menu to protect the remainder of the worksheet.

As Figure 7-13 indicates, three items of information are necessary to calculate a payment on a loan—the principal, term, and interest rate. The principal is the amount of the loan, and the term is the number of years the customer has to pay off the loan. To calculate his or her monthly payment, the customer will need simply to enter the principal and term information on the Web page created by the PublishCalculator macro.

The interest rate, which will change periodically, is a percentage of the principal, and it represents the additional amount the customer owes for the privilege of borrowing money. The customer will not need to enter the interest rate, as this information already will be entered on the Web page by Martin. Each time the interest rate changes, the PublishCalculator macro will need to be run so that the Web page always reflects the current interest rate. The macro will enter the date the macro was last run in the Updated cell in the worksheet.

The Calculator worksheet contains one formula, which is located in the MthlyPay cell. The formula, IF(Term=0, "", -PMT(Rate/12,Term*12,Principal)), uses the Excel PMT function to calculate the monthly payment based on the principal, term, and interest rate entered in the worksheet.

The PMT function uses the contents of the Term cell as the divisor in the payment calculation formula. The IF function prevents the MthlyPay cell from displaying the #DIV/0! (division by zero) error value when the Term cell is blank or when it contains a zero.

2 Press **Alt+F11** to open the Visual Basic Editor. If necessary, open the Project Explorer window and close the Properties window, the Immediate window, and any open Code windows. Open the Module1 module's Code window, then view the code template for the PublishCalculator procedure.

3 Close the Project Explorer window so that you can view more of the Code window.

Before you can publish the Calculator worksheet's data—in other words, before you can save it to a Web page—you need to learn about Excel's PublishObjects collection and its associated PublishObject objects.

The PublishObjects Collection and PublishObject Objects

Figure 7-14 shows the portion of the Excel object model that includes the PublishObjects collection and its associated PublishObject objects.

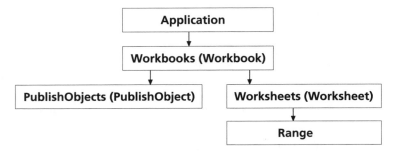

Figure 7-14: The PublishObjects collection and PublishObject objects shown in the Excel object model

As you learned in Tutorial 2, the Excel Application object contains the Workbooks collection along with the individual Workbook objects that make up the collection. Contained within each Workbook object is a PublishObjects collection, made up of individual PublishObject objects. Each PublishObject object represents a workbook item—for example, a worksheet, a range, or a chart—that has been saved to a Web page.

Saving a workbook item to a Web page requires two steps: first you use the PublishObjects collection's Add method to create a PublishObject object that represents the item you want to publish, and then you use the PublishObject object's Publish method to actually create the Web page. First learn about the Add method.

The Add Method

Figure 7-15 shows the syntax and two examples of the PublishObjects collection's Add method.

The Add method's SourceType argument identifies the type of data the PublishObject object will represent, and it can be any of the seven intrinsic constants shown in Figure 7-15. For example, a *sourcetype* of xlSourceSheet indicates that the PublishObject object will represent the entire worksheet, while a *sourcetype* of xlSourceRange indicates that the object corresponds to only a range in the worksheet; the range will be specified in the Add method's Source argument.

Syntax: Application.Workbooks(*name* or *index*).PublishObjects.Add (SourceType:=*sourcetype*, Filename:=*filename*[, Sheet:=*sheetname*][, Source:=*source*][, HtmlType:=htmltype])		

SourceType	Identifies the type of data to be published	
	Constant	**Description**
	`xlSourceAutoFilter`	An AutoFilter range
	`xlSourceChart`	A chart
	`xlSourcePivotTable`	A PivotTable report
	`xlSourcePrintArea`	A range of cells selected for printing
	`xlSourceQuery`	A query table (external data range)
	`xlSourceRange`	A range of cells
	`xlSourceSheet`	An entire worksheet
Filename	The location and name of the Web page to which the data should be published.	
Sheet	The name of the worksheet that contains the data to be published	
Source	The range, chart, PivotTable report, or query table to be published. Not required if SourceType is xlSourceSheet.	
HtmlType	Specifies whether the item is saved as an interactive Microsoft Office Web component or as static text and images	
	Constant	**Description**
	`xlHTMLCalc`	A spreadsheet component
	`xlHTMLChart`	A chart component
	`xlHTMLList`	A PivotTable component
	`xlHTMLStatic`	Static (noninteractive) HTML

Examples:

```
Application.Workbooks("payment calculator.xls").PublishObjects.Add _
        (SourceType:=xlSourceSheet, _
         Filename:="C:\Tut07\Excel\Calculator.htm", _
         Sheet:="Calculator", _
         HtmlType:=xlHTMLStatic)

Application.Workbooks("payment calculator.xls").PublishObjects.Add _
        (SourceType:=xlSourceRange, _
         Filename:="C:\Tut07\Excel\Calculator.htm", _
         Sheet:="Calculator", _
         Source:="a1:e20", _
         HtmlType:=xlHTMLCalc)
```

Figure 7-15: Syntax and two examples of the PublishObjects collection's Add method

The Add method's Filename argument specifies the location and name of the file to which the data will be published—in other words, it specifies the location and name of the Web page. Recall that Web pages are formatted using a language called HTML (Hypertext Markup Language), which uses special codes to describe how the Web page should appear on the screen. Documents created using HTML are called HTML files and the documents are saved using the htm extension. Therefore, the filename you provide in the Add method's Filename argument should have an htm extension to indicate that it contains HTML.

tip

An HTML file also can be saved with the extension html.

tip

If you don't include the location of the Web page in the Filename argument, the Add method will save the file in the current folder, which is the folder in which you currently are working.

The Add method's Sheet argument specifies the name of the worksheet that contains the data you want to publish, and the Source argument identifies which item in the worksheet—for example, which range, chart, PivotTable report, or query table—is to be published. Notice that the Source argument is omitted when the SourceType argument is set to xlSourceSheet; this is because a SourceType setting of xlSourceSheet tells the Add method to save the entire worksheet to a Web page. In other words, the Source argument is necessary only when a portion of the worksheet, rather than the entire worksheet, is being published.

The Add method's HtmlType argument, which can be any of the four intrinsic constants listed in Figure 7-15, specifies whether the published item is interactive or static in the Web page. **Interactive data** can be manipulated by the user—for example, the user can enter new values, as well as format and sort the data. **Static data** can be viewed only and can't be manipulated by the user in any way.

tip

If the HTMLType argument is set to xlHTMLCalc, then the user will be allowed to interact only with data stored in unprotected cells in the worksheet or range being published.

tip

If you omit the HtmlType argument from the Add method, the default value is xlHTMLStatic.

Now study the two examples shown at the bottom of Figure 7-15. Both examples use the Add method to create a PublishObject object. In the first example, the SourceType and Sheet arguments tell the Add method to create a PublishObject object that represents the entire Calculator worksheet. The Filename and HtmlType arguments specify that the worksheet data should be saved as static text in the C:\Tut07\Excel\Calculator.htm file.

tip

Notice that the Source argument is omitted in the first example shown in Figure 7-15. Recall that you omit the Source argument when the SourceType argument is xlSourceSheet.

In Figure 7-15's second example, the SourceType, Sheet, and Source arguments tell the Add method to create a PublishObject object that contains only the range A1:E20 in the Calculator worksheet. The Filename and HtmlType arguments indicate that the data should be saved as interactive text in the C:\Tut07\Excel\Calculator.htm file.

After using the PublishObjects collection's Add method to create a PublishObject object, you then use the PublishObject object's Publish method to write the HTML necessary to create the Web page. The syntax of the Publish method is *expression*.**Publish Create:**=*booleanValue*, where *expression* is a PublishObject object and the **Create** argument is a Boolean value, either True or False, that controls how the data represented by the PublishObject object is saved to the HTML file specified in the Add method's Filename argument. If the HTML file exists and the Create argument is set to True, then the data represented by the PublishObject object replaces the existing data in the file. However, if the HTML file exists and the Create argument is set to False, then the data represented by the PublishObject object is inserted at the end of the file. If the HTML file specified in the Add method's Filename argument does not exist, then the file is created regardless of the value of the Create argument.

Now that you have learned about the PublishObjects collection and its associated PublishObject objects, as well as the Add and Publish methods, you can begin coding the PublishCalculator procedure.

Coding the PublishCalculator Procedure

Recall that it is a good idea to write down the steps the procedure needs to take before you begin coding it. For example, Figure 7-16 shows the pseudocode for the PublishCalculator procedure.

---

1. Use the InputBox function to prompt the user to enter the current interest rate. Store the user's response in a String variable named strRate.
2. Convert the contents of the strRate variable to a number and store the result in a Single variable named sngRate.
3. If the sngRate variable contains a number that is greater than or equal to 1, then
   a. Convert the number to its decimal equivalent by dividing the number by 100.
4. Unprotect the worksheet.
5. Display the interest rate, which is stored in the sngRate variable, in the Rate cell in the Calculator worksheet.
6. Display the current date in the Updated cell in the Calculator worksheet.
7. Protect the worksheet.
8. Use the InputBox function to ask the user if he or she wants to publish the payment calculator. Store the user's response in a String variable named strPublish.
9. If the strPublish variable contains the letter Y (in either uppercase or lowercase), then
   a. Save the range A1:E20 to a Web page.
   b. Use the MsgBox function to display a message indicating that the data was published.
   Else
   a. Use the MsgBox function to display a message indicating that the data was not published.

Figure 7-16: Pseudocode for the PublishCalculator procedure

Figure 7-17 lists the variables that the PublishCalculator procedure will use.

Variables	datatype
strRate	String
sngRate	Single
strPublish	String
shtCalc	Worksheet
pubCalc	PublishObject

Figure 7-17: Variables used by the PublishCalculator procedure

Notice that Figure 7-17 contains a PublishObject object variable named pubCalc. As you learned earlier, a PublishObject object represents a workbook item that is saved to a Web page. In this case, the PublishObject object will represent the range A1:E20 in the Calculator worksheet.

In the next set of steps, you will declare the appropriate variables and then translate each line in Figure 7-16's pseudocode into one or more VBA statements.

To begin coding the PublishCalculator procedure:

1 Enter the documentation and the Dim and Set statements shown in Figure 7-18, then position the insertion point as shown in the figure.

enter this code

make sure you type the drive that contains your Data Disk

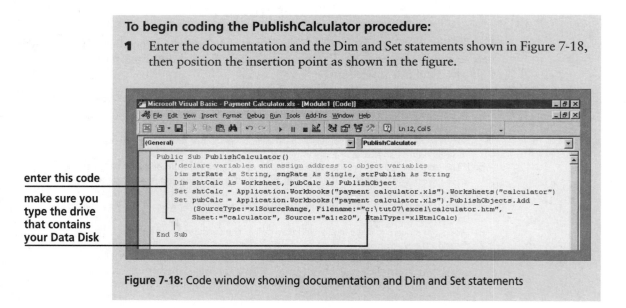

Figure 7-18: Code window showing documentation and Dim and Set statements

Look closely at the second Set statement shown in Figure 7-18. The Set statement assigns the address of the PublishObject object created by the Add method to the pubCalc object variable. As discussed earlier, the Add method creates a PublishObject object that represents the data stored in the range A1:E20 in the Calculator worksheet. Because the HtmlType argument is set to xlHTMLCalc, the user will be allowed to interact with the data that appears in the Web page. In the case of Martin's worksheet however, the user will be able to work with the Principal and Term cells only, as these are the only unprotected cells in the worksheet. Recall that the user can interact only with data stored in unprotected cells.

You now can begin translating the pseudocode shown in Figure 7-16 into VBA statements. The first step is to use the InputBox function to get the interest rate, and then assign the user's response to the strRate variable. You will make the current interest rate, which is entered in the Rate range, the *defaultValue* in the InputBox function.

2 Type **'enter interest rate, then convert to a number** and press the **Enter** key. Type **strrate:=inputbox(prompt:="Enter the interest rate:", title:="Rate",** _ (be sure to type the comma followed by a space and the underscore) and press the **Enter** key. Press the **Tab** key, then type

default:=format(expression:=shtcalc.range("rate").value, format:="fixed")) and press the **Enter** key.

Now assign the numeric equivalent of the interest rate to the sngRate variable.

3 Press the **Backspace** key to remove the indentation, then type **sngrate = val(string:=strrate)** and press the **Enter** key.

If necessary, convert the rate to its decimal equivalent.

4 Type **'if necessary, convert rate to decimal** and press the **Enter** key, then type **if sngrate >= 1 then** and press the **Enter** key. Press the **Tab** key to indent the instructions in the Then clause, then type **sngrate = sngrate / 100** and press the **Enter** key. Press the **Backspace** key to remove the indentation, then type **end if** and press the **Enter** key.

Next, unprotect the worksheet, then display the interest rate and the current date in the Rate and Updated ranges, respectively, and then protect the worksheet.

5 Type **'unprotect worksheet, display rate and current date, then protect worksheet** and press the **Enter** key.

6 Type **shtcalc.unprotect** and press the **Enter** key. Type **shtcalc.range("rate").value = sngrate** and press the **Enter** key. Type **shtcalc.range("updated").value = date** and press the **Enter** key. Type **shtcalc.protect** and press the **Enter** key.

Now use the InputBox function to ask the user if he or she wants to publish the worksheet data. Use the letter "Y" as the function's *defaultValue*.

7 Type **'ask if user wants to publish the data** and press the **Enter** key, then type **strpublish = inputbox(prompt:="Publish calculator now?", title:="Publish", default:="Y")** and press the **Enter** key.

According to Step 9 in the pseudocode shown in Figure 7-16, if the user wants to publish the data, then you need to save the range A1:E20 to a Web page and then display a message indicating that the data was published; otherwise, you need to display a message indicating that the data was not published. Recall that you use the PublishObject object's Publish method to save data, as an HTML document, to a Web page. Each time the PublishCalculator macro is run, you will want the PublishObject object's data to replace the existing data in the Calculator.htm file, so you should set the Publish method's Create argument to True.

8   Enter the additional lines of code shown in Figure 7-19, which shows the completed PublishCalculator procedure.

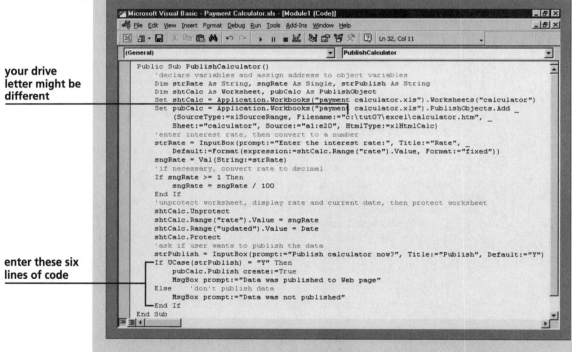

your drive letter might be different

enter these six lines of code

Figure 7-19: Completed PublishCalculator procedure

9   Verify the accuracy of your code by comparing the code on your screen to the code shown in Figure 7-19, then save the procedure.

Now that you have translated the pseudocode shown in Figure 7-16 into VBA statements, you can test the PublishCalculator macro procedure to verify that it is working correctly.

To test the PublishCalculator macro procedure:

1   Return to Excel and run the **PublishCalculator** macro.

> **HELP?** To run a macro from Excel, press Alt+F8 to open the Macro dialog box. Click the name of the macro you want to run, then click the Run button.

2   When the Rate dialog box appears and prompts you to enter the interest rate, type **5** and then press the **Enter** key. Because the number you entered is greater than 1, the PublishCalculator procedure divides the number by 100 to convert it to its decimal equivalent; 5.00% appears in the Rate cell, which was formatted to Percentage.

> **HELP?** You may need to drag the Rate dialog box to another location on the screen to see the Rate cell.

3   When the Publish dialog box appears and asks if you want to publish the calculator, type **n** and press the **Enter** key. A message indicating that the data was not published appears. Press the **Enter** key to close the message box.

4   Run the **PublishCalculator** macro again. When you are prompted to enter the interest rate, type **.06** and then press the **Enter** key. Because the number you entered is less than one, the PublishCalculator procedure does not divide the number by 100. Rather, the number you entered is displayed in Percentage format (6.00%) in the Rate cell.

5   When you are asked if you want to publish the calculator, press the **Enter** key to accept the *defaultValue* "Y". A message indicating that the data was published to the Web page appears. Press the **Enter** key to close the message box.

Now use Internet Explorer to view the Calculator.htm Web page created by the PublishCalculator macro.

6   Start Internet Explorer. If the Work Offline dialog box appears, click the **Work Offline** button, which will allow you to view the Web page without being connected to the Internet.

> **HELP?** To start Internet Explorer, click Start, point to Programs, and then click Internet Explorer. You also can click the Launch Internet Explorer Browser button 🌐 on the Quick Launch toolbar. To view the Quick Launch toolbar, right-click the Windows taskbar, point to Toolbars, and then click Quick Launch.

7   Click **File** on the Internet Explorer menu bar, then click **Open**. When the Open dialog box appears, click the **Browse** button. When the Microsoft Internet Explorer dialog box appears, open the Tut07\Excel folder on your Data Disk, click **Calculator** (Calculator.htm), and then click the **Open** button. When the Open dialog box appears, click the **OK** button to open the Calculator.htm file in Internet Explorer.

Use the Web page to display the monthly payment for a principal of $5000 and a term of 2 years.

8 Click cell **B3** on the Web page, then type **5000** and press the **Enter** key. Type **2** in cell B4 and press the **Enter** key. The Web page indicates that the monthly payment is $221.60, as shown in Figure 7-20.

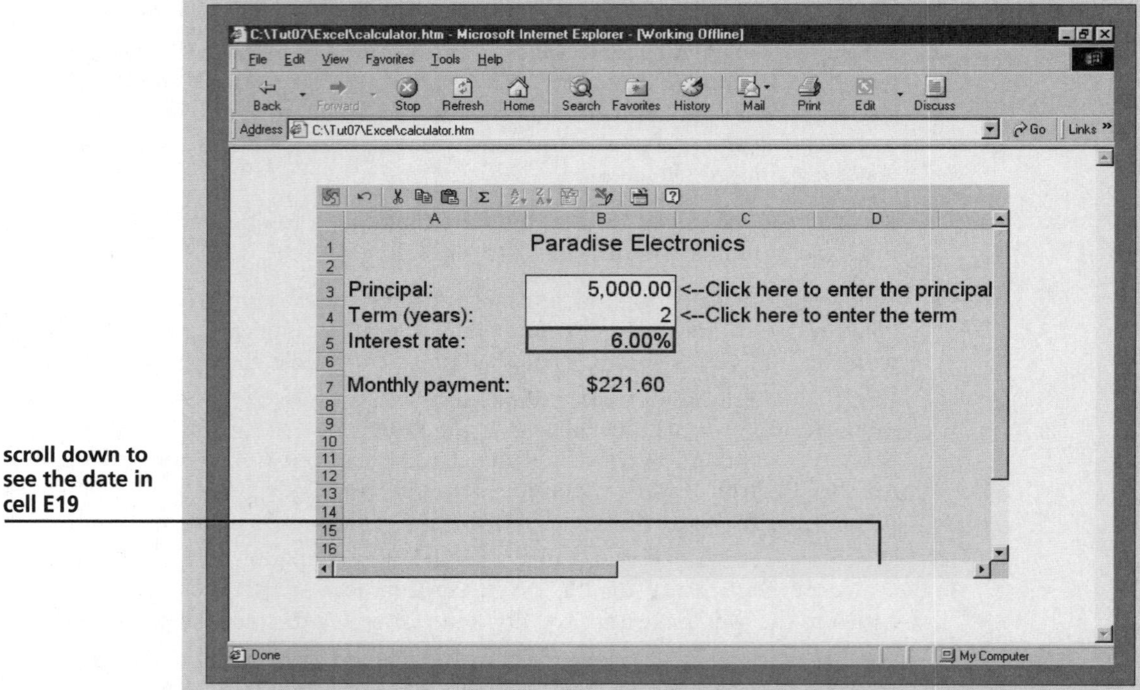

scroll down to see the date in cell E19

Figure 7-20: Web page shown in Internet Explorer

▶ **tip**

> Because only cells B3 and B4 are unprotected in the worksheet, these are the only cells in which the user can enter data.

9 Close Internet Explorer. When you return to Excel, save the Payment Calculator workbook, then close Excel.

You now have completed Tutorial 7's Excel lesson. You can either take a break or complete the end-of-lesson exercises before moving on to the next lesson.

EXERCISES

1. In this exercise, you will modify the PublishCalculator procedure that you created in this lesson.

    a. Open the Payment Calculator (Payment Calculator.xls) workbook, which is located in the Tut07\Excel folder on your Data Disk. Click the Enable Macros button, if necessary, then save the workbook as T7-EX-E1D. Currently, the interest rate shown in the Rate cell is 6.00%.

    b. Open the Visual Basic Editor. View the Help screen for a Workbook object's Saved property. Notice that you can set this property to the Boolean value True if you want to close a modified workbook without either saving it or being prompted to save it. Close the Help window.

    c. Open the Module1 module's Code window, then view the PublishCalculator procedure. Change "payment calculator.xls" to "t7-ex-e1d.xls" in the two Set statements, then modify the PublishCalculator procedure so that it also performs the tasks that are shaded in Figure 7-21. (Use "Y" as the InputBox function's *defaultValue*.)

---

1. Use the InputBox function to prompt the user to enter the current interest rate. Store the user's response in a String variable named strRate.
2. Convert the contents of the strRate variable to a number and store the result in a Single variable named sngRate.
3. If the sngRate variable contains a number that is greater than or equal to 1, then
    a. Convert the number to its decimal equivalent by dividing the number by 100.
4. Unprotect the worksheet.
5. Display the interest rate, which is stored in the sngRate variable, in the Rate cell in the Calculator worksheet.
6. Display the current date in the Updated cell in the Calculator worksheet.
7. Protect the worksheet.
8. Use the InputBox function to ask the user if he or she wants to publish the payment calculator. Store the user's response in a String variable named strPublish.
9. If the strPublish variable contains the letter Y (in any case), then
    a. Save the range A1:E20 to a Web page.
    b. Use the MsgBox function to display a message indicating that the data was published.
    Else
    a. Use the MsgBox function to display a message indicating that the data was not published.
10. Use the InputBox function to ask the user if he or she wants to save the workbook.
11. If the user wants to save the workbook, then
    a. Use the Workbook object's Save method to save the workbook.
    b. Use the MsgBox function to display a message indicating that the workbook was saved.
    Else
    a. Assign the Boolean value True to the workbook's Saved property.
    b. Use the MsgBox function to display a message indicating that the workbook was not saved.
12. Quit the Excel application.

Figure 7-21

d. Save the workbook. Return to Excel and run the PublishCalculator macro. Publish the worksheet data using an interest rate of 2%. When you are asked if you want to save the workbook, type n and press the Enter key. A message indicating that the workbook was not saved appears. Press the Enter key to close the message box. The Excel application should end.

e. Open the T7-EX-E1D workbook again. Click the Enable Macros button, if necessary. The Rate cell should still contain 6.00%, which indicates that the workbook was not saved after the rate was changed in Step d. Run the PublishCalculator macro again. Publish the worksheet using an interest rate of 7%. When you are asked if you want to save the workbook, press the Enter key to accept the *defaultValue* "Y". A message indicating that the workbook was saved appears. Press the Enter key to close the message box. The Excel application should end.

f. Open the T7-EX-E1D workbook again. Click the Enable Macros button, if necessary. The Rate cell should contain 7.00%, which indicates that the workbook was saved after the rate was changed in Step e.

g. Close the workbook.

2. In this exercise, you will create a procedure that publishes a workbook as an interactive and static Web page.

a. Open the T7-EX-E2 (T7-EX-E2.xls) workbook, which is located in the Tut07\Excel folder on your Data Disk. Click the Enable Macros button, if necessary, then save the workbook as T7-EX-E2D. The Prices worksheet within the workbook contains the Paradise Electronics price list.

b. Open the Visual Basic Editor. Open the Module1 module's Code window, then view the code template for the CreateWebPage procedure. Code the procedure so that it prompts the user to enter the store location—either H for the home office, J for the Jackson store, or G for the Glen Park store. Use the letter H as the *defaultValue* in the InputBox function. If the user enters the letter H, then save the entire workbook as an interactive Web page to a file named T7-EX-Inter-E2D.htm. If the user enters either the letter J or the letter G, then save the entire workbook as a static Web page to a file named T7-EX-Static-E2D.htm. Save the files in the Tut07\Excel folder on your Data Disk. Display an appropriate message alerting the user that the data was published. Also display an appropriate error message if the user enters a location other than H, J, or G.

c. Save the workbook. Return to Excel and run the CreateWebPage macro. Enter the letter Y as the store location. An appropriate error message should appear. Click the OK button to close the message box.

d. Run the CreateWebPage macro again. Enter the letter J as the store location. A message box is displayed indicating that the data was published. Click the OK button to close the message box. Start Internet Explorer and open the T7-EX-Static-E2D.htm file.

e. Return to Excel and run the CreateWebPage macro again. When you are prompted to enter the store location, press the Enter key to accept the *defaultValue* H. Return to Internet Explorer and open the T7-EX-Inter-E2D.htm file.

f. Click cell B3 on the Web page. Click the Sort Ascending button ![Sort Ascending], then click Price in the drop-down list to sort the data in ascending order by the Price column. Close Internet Explorer.

g. When you return to Excel, save and then close the workbook.

3. In this exercise, you will create a procedure that updates the value stored in a cell.

   a. Open the T7-EX-E3 (T7-EX-E3.xls) workbook, which is located in the Tut07\Excel folder on your Data Disk. Click the Enable Macros button, if necessary, then save the workbook as T7-EX-E3D. The workbook contains one worksheet named YTD. Column A in the worksheet lists each salesperson's ID, column B lists his or her name, and column C lists his or her year-to-date sales. Column D shows the date that the year-to-date sales were last updated. The entire worksheet is protected.

   b. Open the Visual Basic Editor. Open the Module1 module's Code window, then view the code template for the CalcYtd procedure. Code the CalcYtd procedure so that it prompts the user to enter a monthly sales amount, which must be greater than zero. It then should add the monthly sales amount to the amount contained in the active cell. In other words, the user will need to select the appropriate salesperson's YTD sales amount in column C before running the macro. Display an appropriate error message if the monthly sales amount is not greater than zero.

   c. Save the workbook. Return to Excel. Click cell C4, then run the CalcYtd macro. Enter 0 as the monthly sales amount. An appropriate error message should appear.

   d. Run the CalcYtd macro again. Enter 200 as the monthly sales amount. John Philad's YTD sales should be $200.00, and the current date should appear in cell D4. Run the CalcYtd macro again. This time enter 500 as the monthly sales amount. John Philad's YTD sales now should be $700.00. Lastly, use the CalcYtd macro to update Jill Strait's YTD sales by 1000. (Be sure to click cell C6 before running the macro.)

   e. Save and then close the workbook.

Exercises 4 and 5 are Discovery Exercises. Discovery Exercises, which may include topics that are not covered in the lesson, allow you to "discover" the solutions to problems on your own.

discovery ▶ 4. In this exercise, you will create a procedure that prints a worksheet using either Landscape or Portrait page orientation.

   a. Open the T7-EX-E3 (T7-EX-E3.xls) workbook, which is located in the Tut07\Excel folder on your Data Disk. Click the Enable Macros button, if necessary, and then save the workbook as T7-EX-E3D.

   b. Open the Visual Basic Editor. Display the Help screens for the Workbook object's BeforePrint event procedure, the PageSetup object, and the PageSetup object's Orientation property. Study the Help screens, then close the Help window.

   c. Open the ThisWorkbook object's Code window, then view the Workbook object's BeforePrint event procedure. Code the procedure so that it prompts the user to enter either the letter L or the letter P. Use the letter L as the InputBox function's *defaultValue*. If the user enters the letter L, print the worksheet using Landscape orientation. If the user enters the letter P, print the worksheet using Portrait orientation. If the user enters a letter other than L or P, display a message indicating that the print operation was canceled, then cancel the print operation.

   d. Save the workbook, then return to Excel. Click the Print button 🖨 on the Standard toolbar. When you are prompted for the orientation, type X and press the Enter key. A message indicating that the print operation was canceled should appear. Click the OK button.

   e. Click the Print button 🖨 again. When you are prompted for the orientation, press the Enter key to accept the *defaultValue* L. The worksheet prints using Landscape orientation. Print the workbook again; this time print it using Portrait orientation.

   f. Close the workbook.

discovery ▶ 5. In this exercise, you will create a procedure that publishes a chart to a Web page.

a. Open the T7-EX-E5 (T7-EX-E5.xls) workbook, which is located in the Tut07\Excel folder on your Data Disk. Click the Enable Macros button, if necessary, then save the workbook as T7-EX-E5D.

The workbook contains one worksheet named Sales. In addition to listing the four regions in which Jacksonville Pianos sells and the sales made in each region, the Sales worksheet contains a chart named Chart 1.

b. Open the Visual Basic Editor. Open the Module1 module's Code window, then view the code template for the CreateWebPage procedure. Code the procedure so that it publishes the Chart 1 chart to a Web page named T7-EX-E5D.htm in the Tut07\Excel folder on your Data Disk.

c. Save the workbook. Return to Excel and run the CreateWebPage macro.

d. Start Internet Explorer and open the T7-EX-E5D.htm file. Enter 400 as the North sales, 300 as the South sales, 500 as the East sales, and 800 as the West sales. Close Internet Explorer.

e. When you return to Excel, save and then close the workbook.

A computer program is good only if it works. Errors in programming code can cause a program to run incorrectly. Therefore, a programmer needs to know how to locate and fix any errors in his or her code. Exercise 6 is a Debugging Exercise. Debugging Exercises allow you to practice recognizing and solving errors in code.

debugging 6. In this exercise, you will debug an existing macro procedure.

a. Open the T7-EX-E6 (T7-EX-E6.xls) workbook, which is located in the Tut07\Excel folder on your Data Disk. Click the Enable Macros button, if necessary. Save the workbook as T7-EX-E6D.

b. Open the Visual Basic Editor. Open the Module1 module's Code window, then view the DisplayCost procedure. The procedure should display the code corresponding to the insurance plan in the Plan range, and it should display the cost of the insurance plan in the Cost range. The valid codes for the insurance plans are A, B, and C only. The cost of plans A and B is $35 and the cost of plan C is $50.

c. Study the DisplayCost procedure's code, then return to Excel and run the macro. Enter b as the plan code. "Error", rather than the $35 cost, appears in the Cost cell.

d. Return to the Visual Basic Editor and correct the macro. Save the workbook, then run the macro several times to be sure that it is working correctly.

e. When the macro is working correctly, save and then close the workbook.

Word Lesson

Using the Selection Structure in Word

case ▶ Each year, the personal trainers at Willowton Health Club meet with each of their clients to determine the client's progress. Cardiovascular and strength tests are administered during the meeting, and the trainer and client discuss the client's goals for the following year. Shortly after the meeting, the personal trainer provides the client with a Personal Assessment document that includes the results of the cardiovascular and strength tests, a recommended exercise regime and, if a client's goal is to lose weight, a dietary plan. The Personal Assessment document also summarizes the client's overall goals for the following year.

Pat Jones, the manager of Willowton Health Club, would like to include a table of contents in the Personal Assessment document. In Microsoft Word, a table of contents gives the reader an overview of the topics discussed in a document by listing the headings found in the document. Pat wants to create a macro that will add a table of contents to the Personal Assessment document.

Viewing the Personal Assessment Document

Your Data Disk contains Pat's Personal Assessment document. Begin by opening and viewing the document and the code template for the CreateToc procedure.

To view the personal assessment document:

1 Start Microsoft Word. Open the **T7-WD-1** (T7-WD-1.doc) document, which is located in the Tut07\Word folder on your Data Disk. Click the **Enable Macros** button, if necessary, then save the document as **Assessment**.

Next, display the nonprinting characters in the document.

2 Click **Tools** on the menu bar and then click **Options** to display the Options dialog box. Click the **All** check box in the Formatting marks section on the View tab, if necessary, to select it.

When you create a table of contents in a Word document, a special code, called a field code, is inserted into the document. The **field code** contains the instructions used to generate the table of contents, referred to as the **field results**. You can display either the field code or the field results in the document; the element displayed is controlled by the Field codes check box located in the Show section on the View tab in the Options dialog box. If the Field codes check box is selected, Word displays the field codes in the document; otherwise, it displays the field results, which is the actual table of contents. In the Assessment document, you want the table of contents (the field results) to appear rather than the field codes, so you will deselect the Field codes check box.

3 Click the **Field codes** check box in the Show section of the Options dialog box to deselect it, if necessary, then click the **OK** button to close the Options dialog box.

Figure 7-22 shows the beginning of the Assessment document, which contains four pages.

In this lesson's Exercise 4, you will learn how to set the value of the Field codes check box using VBA code.

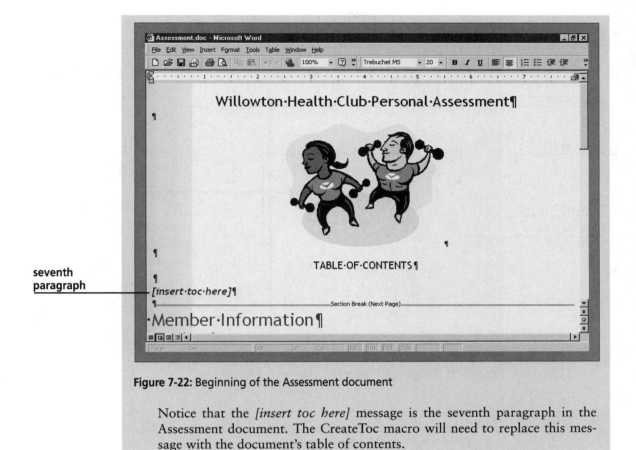

seventh paragraph

Figure 7-22: Beginning of the Assessment document

Notice that the *[insert toc here]* message is the seventh paragraph in the Assessment document. The CreateToc macro will need to replace this message with the document's table of contents.

As mentioned earlier, a table of contents is a list of the headings found in the document. Before you can create a table of contents, you need to specify the text you want treated as a heading; you do so by assigning one of the Word heading styles (Heading 1 through Heading 9) to the text. Word uses the styles when compiling the table of contents. Figure 7-23, which shows the Assessment document's four pages in Print Preview, indicates the heading styles used in the Assessment document.

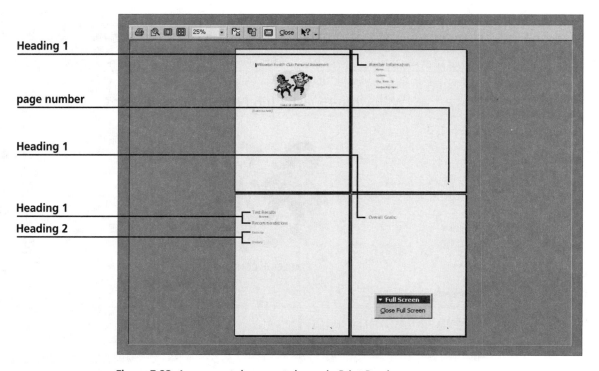

Heading 1

page number

Heading 1

Heading 1
Heading 2

Figure 7-23: Assessment document shown in Print Preview

> You assign a style to text by selecting the text and then selecting the appropriate style from the Style list on the Formatting toolbar.

As indicated in the figure, the Member Information, Test Results, Recommendations, and Overall Goals headings are assigned the Heading 1 style, and the Exercise and Dietary headings are assigned the Heading 2 style.

Notice that only the pages following the first page in the Assessment document contain page numbers, and those pages are numbered 1, 2, and 3, even though they physically are pages 2, 3, and 4 in the document. This page numbering scheme was accomplished first by dividing the document into two sections: one containing the first page only, and the other containing the remaining pages. Page numbers, beginning with number 1, then were inserted into the footer of the second section only.

> To divide a document into sections, position the insertion point to the left of the first character that you want to appear in the new section. Click Insert on the menu bar, and then click Break to open the Break dialog box. Click the Next Page option button in the Section breaks area of the dialog box, then click the OK button.

Now open the Visual Basic Editor and view the code template for the CreateToc procedure.

To open the Visual Basic Editor and view the code template for the CreateToc procedure:

1 Press **Alt+F11** to open the Visual Basic Editor. If necessary, open the Project Explorer window and close the Properties window, the Immediate window, and any open Code windows.

2 Open the Module1 module's Code window, then view the code template for the **CreateToc** procedure.

3 Close the Project Explorer window so that you can view more of the Code window.

Before you can add a table of contents to the Assessment document, you need to learn about the TablesOfContents collection and its associated TableOfContents objects in the Word object model.

The TablesOfContents Collection and TableOfContents Objects

Figure 7-24 shows the portion of the Word object model that includes the TablesOfContents collection and its associated TableOfContents objects.

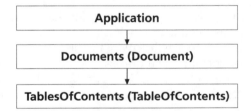

Figure 7-24: The TablesOfContents collection and TableOfContents objects shown in the Word object model

> Notice that the collection name uses the plural word "Tables", whereas the object name uses the singular word "Table".

As you learned in Tutorial 2, the Word Application object contains the Documents collection along with the individual Document objects that make up the collection. Contained within each Document object is a TablesOfContents collection, made up of individual TableOfContents objects. Each TableOfContents object represents a single table of contents in the document.

> Recall that each Document object also contains the Characters, Words, Sentences, and Paragraphs collections.

You use the TablesOfContents collection's Add method to add a TableOfContents object to a document.

The Add Method

Figure 7-25 shows the syntax of the TablesOfContents collection's Add method, along with three examples.

Syntax: *docObject*.**TablesOfContents.Add Range:**=*range*

Examples:
```
docLetter.TablesOfContents.Add Range:=docLetter.Characters(1)
docSmith.TablesOfContents.Add Range:=docSmith.Sentences(5)
docAssess.TablesOfContents.Add Range:=docAssess.Paragraphs(7).Range
```

Figure 7-25: Syntax and three examples of the TablesOfContents collection's Add method

You also can include other arguments in the TablesOfContents collection's Add method. To learn more about the Add method, view its Help screen.

In the Add method's syntax, *docObject* is the name of a Document object variable, and *range*, which must be a Range object, represents the area where you want the table of contents to appear in the document. In the first example, for instance, the `docLetter.Characters(1)` *range* will replace the first character in the docLetter document with the table of contents. The `docSmith.Sentences(5)` *range* in the second example will replace the fifth sentence in the docSmith document with the table of contents. The third example uses the `docAssess.Paragraphs(7).Range` *range* to replace the seventh paragraph in the docAssess document with the table of contents.

As you learned in Tutorial 2, the individual objects included in the Characters and Sentences collections are Range objects. Characters(1), for example, is a Range object that represents the first character in the document, and Sentences(5) is a Range object that represents the fifth sentence. Unlike the Characters and Sentences collections, the Paragraphs collection is made up of Paragraph objects rather than Range objects. Because the Add method's *range* argument requires a Range object, you need to use the Paragraph object's Range property to return a Range object that represents the paragraph.

In this lesson's Exercise 5 you will learn how to add a table of contents to a document without replacing the Range object specified in the Add method's *range* argument.

After adding a table of contents to a document, you can use the TablesOfContents collection's Format property to format the table of contents to one of the predesigned formats available in Word.

The Format Property

The syntax of the Format property is *docObject*.**TablesOfContents.Format** = *constant*, where *docObject* is the name of a Document object and *constant* is one of the intrinsic constants shown in Figure 7-26.

```
wdTOCClassic
wdTOCDistinctive
wdTOCFancy
wdTOCFormal
wdTOCModern
wdTOCSimple
wdTOCTemplate
```

Figure 7-26: Valid constants for the TablesOfContents collection's Format property

Each constant represents one of the predesigned formats available for tables of contents in Word. For example, assuming that the address of the Assessment document is assigned to a Document object variable named docAssess, the instruction `docAssess.TablesOfContents.Format = wdTOCClassic` will display the document's tables of contents using the Classic format.

Now that you have learned about the TablesOfContents collection and its associated TableOfContents objects, as well as the Add method and the Format property, you can begin coding the CreateToc procedure.

Coding the CreateToc Procedure

Figure 7-27 shows the pseudocode for the CreateToc procedure.

1. Use the TablesOfContents Add method to replace the *[insert toc here]* message, which is the seventh paragraph in the document, with the table of contents.
2. Use the InputBox function to ask the user which format to use for the table of contents—C for Classic or D for Distinctive. Store the user's response in a String variable named strFormat.
3. Convert the contents of the strFormat variable to uppercase letters.
4. If the contents of the strFormat variable is equal to the letter C, then
   a. Use the TablesOfContents Format property to format the table of contents to wdTOCClassic.
   Else
   a. Use the TablesOfContents Format property to format the table of contents to wdTOCDistinctive.

Figure 7-27: Pseudocode for the CreateToc procedure

Figure 7-28 lists the variables that the CreateToc procedure will use.

Variables	datatype
strFormat	String
docAssess	Document
rngToc	Range

Figure 7-28: Variables used by the CreateToc procedure

The strFormat variable will store the user's format choice—either C for Classic or D for Distinctive. The docAssess Document object variable will store the address of the Assessment document, and the rngToc Range object variable will store the address of the *[insert toc here]* message, which is the seventh paragraph in the document.

In the next set of steps, you will declare the appropriate variables, and then translate each line in Figure 7-27's pseudocode into one or more VBA statements.

To code the CreateToc procedure, then save and run the procedure:

1 Enter the documentation and the Dim and Set statements shown in Figure 7-29.

enter this code ──────

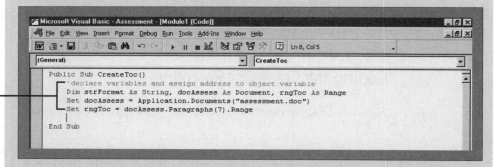

Figure 7-29: Code window showing documentation and Dim and Set statements

You now can begin translating the pseudocode shown in Figure 7-27 into VBA statements. The first step is to replace the *[insert toc here]* message with a table of contents.

2 Type **'add table of contents** and press the **Enter** key.

3 Type **docassess.tablesofcontents.add range:=rngToc** and press the **Enter** key.

Next, ask the user if he or she wants to format the table of contents using the Classic or the Distinctive format. Use the letter "C" as the InputBox function's *defaultValue*.

4 Type **'enter format choice** and press the **Enter** key.

5 Type **strformat = inputbox(prompt:="Format (C for Classic or D for Distinctive):",** _ (be sure to type the comma followed by a space and the underscore) and press the **Enter** key. Press the **Tab** key, then type **title:="Format", default:="C")** and press the **Enter** key.

Step 3 in the pseudocode is to convert the contents of the strFormat variable to uppercase letters.

6 Press the **Backspace** key to remove the indentation. Type **'convert input to uppercase** and press the **Enter** key. Type **strformat = ucase(string:=strformat)** and press the **Enter** key.

According to Step 4 in the pseudocode, if the user enters the letter C, the procedure should format the table of contents using the Classic format; otherwise, it should format the table of contents using the Distinctive format.

7 Type the additional code shown in Figure 7-30, which shows the completed CreateToc procedure.

enter these six
lines of code

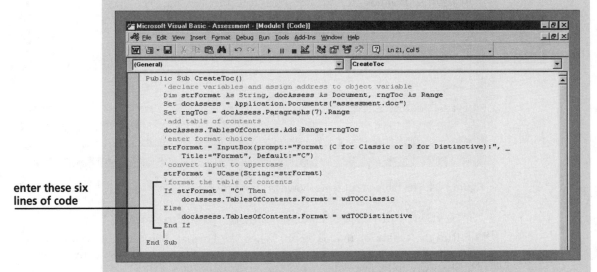

Figure 7-30: Completed CreateToc procedure

8 Verify the accuracy of your code by comparing the code on your screen to the code shown in Figure 7-30, then save the document.

Now that you have translated the pseudocode shown in Figure 7-27 into VBA statements, you should test the CreateToc macro procedure to verify that it is working correctly.

9 Return to Word and run the **CreateToc** macro.

HELP? To run a macro from Word, press Alt+F8 to open the Macros dialog box. Click the name of the macro you want to run, then click the Run button.

10 When the Format dialog box appears, press the **Enter** key to select the default format, Classic. Scroll the document window to view the table of contents, as shown in Figure 7-31.

Classic format —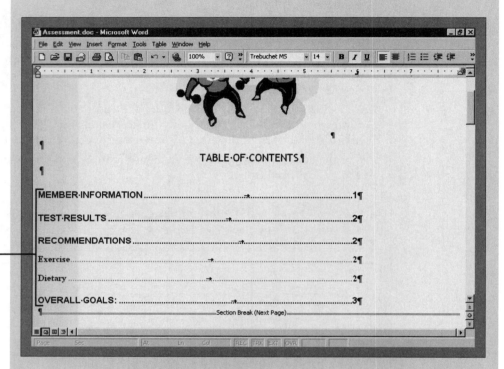

Figure 7-31: The table of contents shown in Classic format

Next, view the table of contents using the Distinctive format.

11 Run the **CreateToc** macro again. When the Format dialog box appears, type **d** and press the **Enter** key. The table of contents appears in the Distinctive format, as shown in Figure 7-32.

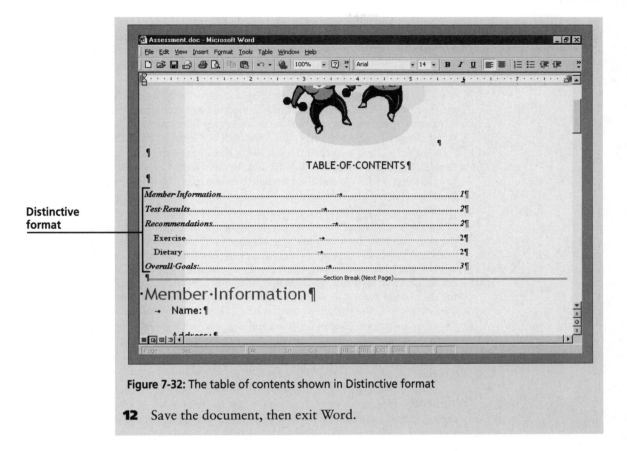

Distinctive format

Figure 7-32: The table of contents shown in Distinctive format

12 Save the document, then exit Word.

You now have completed Tutorial 7's Word lesson. You can either take a break or complete the end-of-lesson exercises before moving on to the next lesson.

 # EXERCISES

1. In this exercise, you will modify the CreateToc procedure that you created in this lesson.
   a. Open the Assessment (Assessment.doc) document, which is located in the Tut07\Word folder on your Data Disk. Click the Enable Macros button, if necessary, then save the document as T7-WD-E1D.
   b. Open the Visual Basic Editor. Open the Module1 module's Code window, then view the CreateToc procedure's code. Change the filename in the Set statement to "t7-wd-e1d.doc". Modify the code so that it allows the user to format the table of contents to either Classic, Distinctive, or Simple.
   c. Save the document, then return to Word and run the CreateToc macro. Display the table of contents using the Simple format.
   d. Save and then close the document.

2. In this exercise, you will create a procedure that adds two tables of contents to a document.

    a. Open the T7-WD-E2 (T7-WD-E2.doc) document, which is located in the Tut07\Word folder on your Data Disk. Click the Enable Macros button, if necessary, then save the document as T7-WD-E2D. If necessary, display the nonprinting characters in the document.

    b. View the document in Print Preview. The document contains eight pages. Notice that the first page contains a graphic and the second page contains a WordArt object. Also notice that both pages contain the *[insert toc here]* message, and that the third through eighth pages are numbered 1 through 6. Close the Print Preview window.

    c. Assign the Heading 1 style to the following three headings in the document: "Visual Basic, VBA, and VBScript," "BASIC and the Microsoft Corporation," and "Reasons for Learning VBA." Assign the Heading 2 style to the "The Beginning of Microsoft" heading. If necessary, left-align the "The Beginning of Microsoft" heading.

    d. Click View on the Word menu bar, then click Print Layout.

    e. Open the Visual Basic Editor. Open the Module1 module's Code window, then view the code template for the AddToc procedure's code. Code the procedure so that it adds two tables of contents to the document. The first table of contents should appear on the first page, and the second table of contents should appear on the second page. (The tables of contents will be identical on both pages.) Prompt the user for the type of format to use for the tables of contents—either Formal, Modern, or Distinctive. Use the letter F as the InputBox function's *defaultValue*.

    f. Save the document. Return to Word and run the AddToc procedure. Format the tables of contents using the Formal format.

    g. Save and then close the document.

3. In this exercise, you will create a procedure that calculates and displays a student's grade.

    a. Open the T7-WD-E3 (T7-WD-E3.doc) document, which is located in the Tut07\Word folder on your Data Disk. Click the Enable Macros button, if necessary, then save the document as T7-WD-E3D. If necessary, display the nonprinting characters in the document. Also display the customized Grade Macro toolbar, if necessary.

    b. Open the Visual Basic Editor. Open the Module1 module's Code window, then view the code template for the DisplayGrade procedure's code. Code the procedure so that it prompts the user to enter the semester, the student's name, and the total number of points earned in the class. The procedure should assign the grade based on the following information:

Points earned	Grade
210 or more	P
less than 210	F
negative value	Error

Display the semester, name, and grade in the Semester, Name, and Grade form fields, respectively. (*Hint:* Before displaying information in the form fields, you will need to unprotect the document. Be sure to protect the document at the end of the procedure. When protecting the document, set the Protect method's *type* argument to wdAllowOnlyFormFields and set its *noreset* argument to True.) If the user enters a negative value, display an appropriate error message in a dialog box. Also display the word "Error" in the Grade form field.

    c. Save the document. Return to Word. Click the Display Grade button on the Grade Macro toolbar. Enter Fall as the semester, your name as the student's name, and 300 as the total points. The grade should be a P.

   d. Click the Display Grade button again. This time enter Spring as the semester, Roger York as the student's name, and 180 as the total points. The grade should be an F.
   e. Click the Display Grade button again. Enter Fall as the semester, Jill Oslo as the student's name, and –2 as the total points. When the error message appears in a dialog box, click the OK button. "Error" should appear in the Grade form field.
   f. Save and then close the document.

Exercises 4 through 7 are Discovery Exercises. Discovery Exercises, which may include topics that are not covered in the lesson, allow you to "discover" the solutions to problems on your own.

discovery ▶ **4.** In this exercise, you will modify the CreateToc procedure that you created in this lesson. You will learn how to use VBA code to set the value of the Field codes check box, which is located in the Show section on the View tab in the Options dialog box.

   a. Open the Assessment (Assessment.doc) document, which is located in the Tut07\Word folder on your Data Disk. Click the Enable Macros button, if necessary, then save the document as T7-WD-E4D. If necessary, display the nonprinting characters in the document.
   b. Open the Visual Basic Editor. Open the Module1 module's Code window, then view the CreateToc procedure. Change the filename in the Set statement to "t7-wd-e4d.doc". The View object's ShowFieldCodes property controls the setting of the Field codes check box. Figure 7-33 shows the portion of the Word object model that contains the View object.

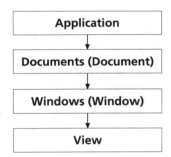

Figure 7-33

   c. Use the Help screens to research the View object and its ShowFieldCodes property, then modify the CreateToc procedure so that it deselects the Field codes check box before adding the table of contents to the document.
   d. Save the document. Return to Word. Click Tools, then click Options. When the Options dialog box appears, click the Field codes check box to select it, if necessary, then click the OK button to close the dialog box. Notice that the document's table of contents was replaced with the field code {TOC \O "1-9"}.
   e. Run the CreateToc macro. Display the table of contents using the Classic format. The table of contents, rather than the field code, appears in the document. (You also can verify that the CreateToc procedure deselected the Field codes check box by opening the Options dialog box.)
   f. Save and then close the document.

discovery ► **5.** In this exercise, you will modify a procedure so that it adds a table of contents to a document without replacing the Add method's *range* argument.

    a. Open the T7-WD-E5 (T7-WD-E5.doc) document, which is located in the Tut07\Word folder on your Data Disk. Click the Enable Macros button, if necessary, then save the document as T7-WD-E5D. If necessary, display the nonprinting characters in the document.

    b. Open the Visual Basic Editor. Open the Module1 module's Code window, then view the AddToc procedure. Study the code, then return to Word and run the AddToc macro. Notice that the macro replaces the graphic with the table of contents, which is not what you wanted. To return the document to its original state, click the Undo button 🔙 on the Standard toolbar twice, then click at the beginning of the document.

    c. Use the Help screens to research a Range object's Collapse method. Use the Collapse method to collapse the *range* before adding the table of contents to the document. Insert the table of contents below the graphic in the document—in other words, insert it at the end of the *range*.

    d. Return to Word and save the document. Run the AddToc macro. The table of contents should appear below the graphic.

    e. Save and then close the document.

discovery ► **6.** In this exercise, you will learn how to use the TableOfContents object's Update and UpdatePageNumbers methods. You will use the Assessment document that you created in this lesson.

    a. Open the Assessment (Assessment.doc) document, which is located in the Tut07\Word folder on your Data Disk. Click the Enable Macros button, if necessary, then save the document as T7-WD-E6D. If necessary, display the nonprinting characters in the document.

    b. Open the Visual Basic Editor. Open the Module1 module's Code window, then view the CreateToc procedure. Change the filename in the Set statement to "t7-wd-e6d.doc".

    c. Insert a macro procedure into the Module1 module. Name the procedure UpdateToc.

    d. Display the Help screens for the TableOfContents object's Update and UpdatePageNumbers methods. When you are done reading the information in the Help screens, close the Help window.

    e. Code the UpdateToc procedure so that it asks the user if he or she wants to update either the entire table of contents or just the page numbers in the table of contents.

    f. Return to Word. Insert a page break before the "Recommendations" section in the document. Change the "Exercise" heading to "Exercise Plan".

    g. Save the document, then run the UpdateToc macro. Update the entire table of contents. Confirm that the "Exercise" heading changed to "Exercise Plan" in the table of contents. Also verify that the page number for the "Recommendations" section changed in the table of contents. (The page number should be 3 rather than 2.)

    h. Remove the page break that you inserted before the "Recommendations" section, then run the UpdateMacro again. This time, update only the page numbers for the table of contents. Verify that the page number for the "Recommendations" section is now 2.

    i. Save and then close the document.

discovery ▶ 7. In this exercise, you will create a macro procedure that adds a table of figures to a document.

    a. Open the T7-WD-E7 (T7-WD-E7.doc) document, which is located in the Tut07\Word folder on your Data Disk. Click the Enable Macros button, if necessary, then save the document as T7-WD-E7D. If necessary, display the nonprinting characters in the document.

    b. Click the first graphic in the document. Click Insert on the menu bar and then click Caption. When the Caption dialog box appears, type Figure 1: Faces in the Caption text box. Also select Figure in the Label list box, and select Below selected item in the Position list box, as shown in Figure 7-34.

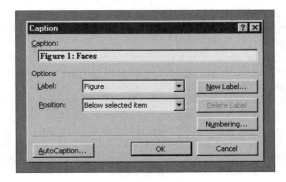

Figure 7-34

    c. Click the OK button to close the Caption dialog box. Click the second graphic in the document and use the Insert menu to insert the Figure 2: Lion caption below the graphic. Insert the Figure 3: People caption below the third graphic.

    d. Open the Visual Basic Editor. Open the Module1 module's Code window, then view the code template for the AddTof macro procedure.

    e. Display the Help screens for the TablesOfFigures collection and its TableOfFigures object. Also research the TablesOfFigures collection's Add method. Close the Help window.

    f. Code the AddTof procedure so that it replaces the [insert table of figures here] message with a table of figures.

    g. Save the document. Return to Word and run the AddTof macro.

    h. Save and then close the document.

A computer program is good only if it works. Errors in programming code can cause a program to run incorrectly. Therefore, a programmer needs to know how to locate and fix any errors in his or her code. Exercise 8 is a Debugging Exercise. Debugging Exercises allow you to practice recognizing and solving errors in code.

debugging **8.** In this exercise, you will debug an existing macro procedure.

a. Open the T7-WD-E8 (T7-WD-E8.doc) document, which is located in the Tut07\Word folder on your Data Disk. Click the Enable Macros button, if necessary, then save the document as T7-WD-E8D. If necessary, display the nonprinting characters in the document.

b. Open the Visual Basic Editor and view the AddToc procedure's code. Study the code, then return to Word and run the AddToc macro. When the error message appears in a dialog box, click the Debug button. The Visual Basic Editor highlights the instruction that is causing the error. Stop the procedure, then correct the error in the procedure.

c. After correcting the error, return to Word, then save the document and run the AddToc macro again. When you are prompted to enter the format type, type the letter d and press the Enter key. The procedure formats the table of contents using the Modern, rather than the Distinctive, format. Also, the *[insert toc here]* message still appears in the document (below the table of contents).

d. Use the Undo button ⟲ on the Standard toolbar to return the document to its original state, then return to the Visual Basic Editor and correct the AddToc procedure. After correcting the error, return to Word, then save the document and run the AddToc macro again. Display the table of contents using the Distinctive format.

e. When the macro is working correctly, save and then close the document.

Access Lesson

Using the Selection Structure in Access

case ▶ In Tutorial 6, you created a procedure named PaymentUpdate for Professor Martinez of Snowville College. This procedure allowed Professor Martinez to record the payments made by the students going on the Spanish Club's trip to Spain. Recall that the total cost of the trip is $1200, and that $200 is due within one week of registering. Additional payments then are due periodically until the entire $1200 is paid.

Professor Martinez wants to modify the PaymentUpdate procedure. After entering the student's payment into the database, Professor Martinez would like the PaymentUpdate procedure to display the amount the student owes. You will make the appropriate modifications to the procedure in this lesson.

Modifying the PaymentUpdate Procedure

Before modifying the PaymentUpdate procedure, open the Trip database and view the Payments table.

To open the Trip database and view the Payments table:

1 Start Microsoft Access. Open the **Trip** (Trip.mdb) database, which is located in the Tut07\Access folder on your Data Disk. Click the **Maximize** button ☐ on the Microsoft Access title bar to maximize the Microsoft Access window, if necessary.

The Trip database contains one table named Payments and one report named PayReport. The Payments table contains five fields: ID, LastName, FirstName, Paid, and Updated. The ID, LastName, and FirstName fields are Text fields. The Paid field, which stores the total amount paid by each student, is a Currency field. The Updated field, which stores the date the student's information was last updated, is a Date/Time field.

View the records contained in the Payments table.

2 Click **Tables** in the Objects bar of the Database window, if necessary. Right-click **Payments** in the Database window and then click **Open**. See Figure 7-35.

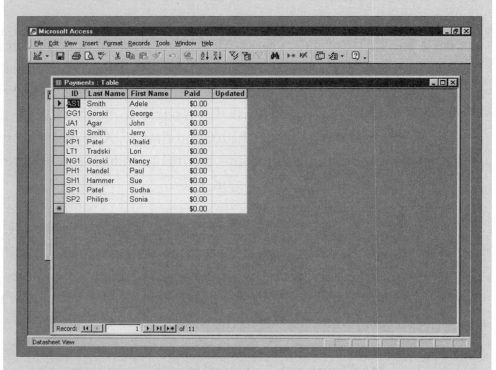

Figure 7-35: Records contained in the Payments table

Notice that for all records, the Paid field contains $0.00 and the Updated field is empty.

3 Close the Payments table.

Now open the Visual Basic Editor.

4   Press **Alt+F11** to open the Visual Basic Editor. If necessary, open the Project Explorer window and close the Properties window, the Immediate window, and any open Code windows.

5   Open the Module1 module's Code window, then view the **PaymentUpdate** procedure. Close the Project Explorer window. The PaymentUpdate procedure that you created in Tutorial 6 appears in the Code window, as shown in Figure 7-36.

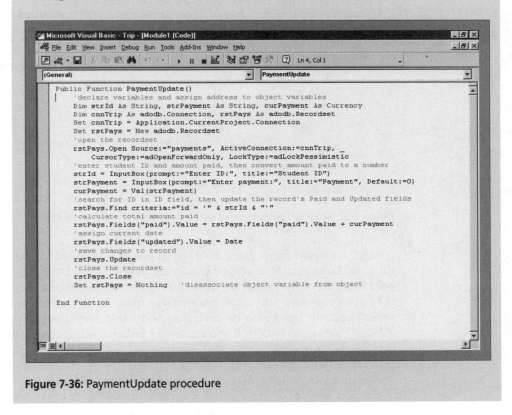

```
Public Function PaymentUpdate()
    'declare variables and assign address to object variables
    Dim strId As String, strPayment As String, curPayment As Currency
    Dim cnnTrip As adodb.Connection, rstPays As adodb.Recordset
    Set cnnTrip = Application.CurrentProject.Connection
    Set rstPays = New adodb.Recordset
    'open the recordset
    rstPays.Open Source:="payments", ActiveConnection:=cnnTrip, _
        CursorType:=adOpenForwardOnly, LockType:=adLockPessimistic
    'enter student ID and amount paid, then convert amount paid to a number
    strId = InputBox(prompt:="Enter ID:", title:="Student ID")
    strPayment = InputBox(prompt:="Enter payment:", title:="Payment", Default:=0)
    curPayment = Val(strPayment)
    'search for ID in ID field, then update the record's Paid and Updated fields
    rstPays.Find criteria:="id = '" & strId & "'"
    'calculate total amount paid
    rstPays.Fields("paid").Value = rstPays.Fields("paid").Value + curPayment
    'assign current date
    rstPays.Fields("updated").Value = Date
    'save changes to record
    rstPays.Update
    'close the recordset
    rstPays.Close
    Set rstPays = Nothing    'disassociate object variable from object

End Function
```

Figure 7-36: PaymentUpdate procedure

Figure 7-37 shows the modified pseudocode for the PaymentUpdate procedure; the modifications are shaded in the figure.

1. Open a recordset that contains all of the records stored in the Trip database's Payments table.
2. Use the InputBox function to prompt the user to enter the student's ID. Store the user's response in a String variable named strId.
3. Use the InputBox function to prompt the user to enter the current payment. Store the user's response in a String variable named strPayment.
4. Convert the contents of the strPayment variable to a number, and assign the result to a Currency variable named curPayment.
5. Search the ID field for the student ID stored in the strId variable.
6. Calculate the total amount paid by adding the contents of the curPayment variable to the contents of the student's Paid field. Assign the sum to the student's Paid field.
7. Calculate the remaining balance by subtracting the contents of the student's Paid field from 1200. Assign the difference to a Currency variable named curBalance.
8. If the curBalance variable contains a value that is greater than 0, then
   a. Display a message along with the balance due
   Else
   a. If the curBalanace variable contains a value that is equal to 0, then
      1) Display a "Paid" message
   Else
      1) Display a message along with the amount overpaid
9. Assign the current date to the student's Updated field.
10. Save the changes made to the student's record.
11. Close the recordset.

Figure 7-37: Modified pseudocode for the PaymentUpdate procedure

According to Steps 7 and 8 in the figure, the modified PaymentUpdate procedure will calculate the student's remaining balance by subtracting the total amount paid from the cost of the trip—$1200. If the remaining balance is greater than zero, then the procedure will display a message along with the balance due. If, on the other hand, the remaining balance is equal to zero, then the procedure will display a "Paid" message. Finally, if the remaining balance is less than zero, the procedure will display a message along with the amount the student overpaid. The modified procedure will require one additional variable—a Currency variable named curBalance—in which you will store the remaining balance.

In the next set of steps, you will declare the additional variable, and then translate Steps 7 and 8 in the pseudocode shown in Figure 7-37 into VBA statements.

To modify the PaymentUpdate procedure, then save and run the procedure:

1 Position the insertion point at the end of the first Dim statement and press the **Enter** key to insert a blank line. Type **dim curBalance as currency**. (Do not type the period at the end of the sentence.)

Now add the code to calculate the remaining balance.

2 Position the insertion point at the end of the `rstPays.Update` instruction and press the **Enter** key to insert a blank line. Type **'calculate balance due, then display appropriate message** and press the **Enter** key. Type **curbalance = 1200 - rstpays.fields("paid").value** and press the **Enter** key.

Now display the appropriate message.

3 Type the nested If...Then...Else statement shown in Figure 7-38.

the figure does not show the beginning of the procedure

enter this code

include a space

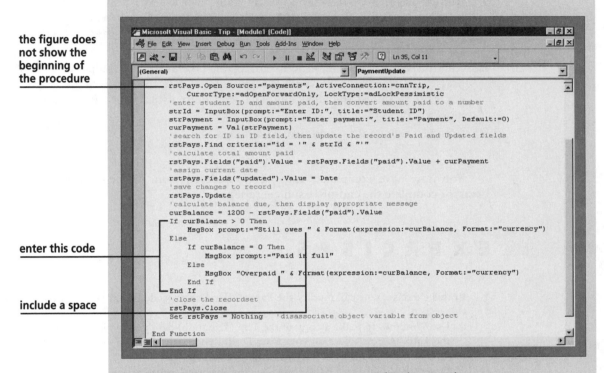

Figure 7-38: Nested If...Then...Else statement entered in the procedure.

You have completed the modifications to the PaymentUpdate procedure, so you can save the file.

4 Verify the accuracy of your code by comparing the code on your screen to the code shown in Figure 7-38, then save the Trip file. (Figure 7-38 does not show the code entered at the beginning of the procedure. Be sure to verify that you entered the `Dim curBalance As Currency` instruction below the first Dim statement in the procedure.)

Next, return to Access and test the procedure to verify that it is working correctly.

5 Return to Access, then run the **PaymentUpdateMacro** macro. When the ID dialog box appears and prompts you to enter the student's ID, type **as1** in the dialog box's input area, and then press the **Enter** key. When you are prompted to enter the payment amount, type **900** and press the **Enter** key.

The procedure displays a message indicating that the student still owes $300.00. Press the **Enter** key to close the message box.

6 Run the **PaymentUpdateMacro** macro again. Type **as1** as the student's ID and press the **Enter** key, then type **300** as the payment and press the **Enter** key. The procedure displays the "Paid in full" message. Press the **Enter** key to close the message box.

7 Run the **PaymentUpdateMacro** macro again. Type **as1** as the student's ID and press the **Enter** key, then type **100** as the payment and press the **Enter** key. The procedure displays a message indicating that the student overpaid ($100.00). Press the **Enter** key.

8 Run the **PaymentUpdateMacro** macro again. Type **as1** as the student's ID and press the **Enter** key, then type **-100** (be sure to type the minus sign) as the payment and press the **Enter** key. The procedure displays the "Paid in full" message. Press the **Enter** key.

9 Compact the database and then exit Access.

You now have completed Tutorial 7's Access lesson. You can either take a break or complete the end-of-lesson exercises.

EXERCISES

1. In this exercise, you will modify the PaymentUpdate procedure that you created in this lesson.
   a. Use Windows to make a copy of the Trip (Trip.mdb) database, which is located in the Tut07\Access folder on your Data Disk. Rename the copy T7-AC-E1D.mdb.
   b. Open the T7-AC-E1D (T7-AC-E1D.mdb) database.
   c. Open the Visual Basic Editor and view the PaymentUpdate procedure. Professor Martinez would like the procedure to verify that the payment amount he enters is greater than zero before the amount is added to the student's record. If he inadvertently enters either a negative number or a letter, the procedure should display an appropriate message and it should not update the student's record. Modify the procedure accordingly.
   d. Save the database, then return to Access. Run the PaymentUpdateMacro macro. Enter gg1 as the student's ID, and enter the letter b as the payment amount. The procedure should display an error message in a message box. Click the OK button to close the message box.
   e. Run the PaymentUpdateMacro macro again. Enter gg1 as the student's ID, and enter −45 as the payment amount. The procedure should display an error message in a message box. Click the OK button to close the message box.
   f. Run the PaymentUpdateMacro macro again. Enter gg1 as the student's ID, and enter 500 as the payment amount. The procedure should display a message indicating that the student still owes $700.00. Click the OK button to close the message box.
   g. Compact and then close the database.

2. In this exercise, you will create a procedure that updates a field and displays an appropriate message.

   a. Open the T7-AC-E2D (T7-AC-E2D.mdb) database, which is located in the Tut07\Access folder on your Data Disk, then open the Products table in Design View. The table contains two fields: a Text field named ProductID and a Number field named UnitsInStock. Close the Design View window. Open the Products table and view the existing records, then close the table.

   b. Open the Visual Basic Editor. Open the Module1 module's Code window, then view the code template for the CheckInv procedure. Code the procedure so that it prompts the user to enter the product ID and the number of units the customer ordered.

   If the number of units in stock is greater than the number ordered, subtract the number ordered from the number of units in stock, then display the message "Entire order shipped" in a message box.

   If, on the other hand, the number of units in stock is less than the number ordered, display the word "Only" followed by the number of units that can be shipped, followed by the words "units shipped". (For example, if the number of units in stock is 100 and the customer ordered 150, then display the message "Only 100 units shipped".) Also assign the number 0 to the record's UnitsInStock field.

   If the number of units in stock is equal to the number of units ordered, then assign the number 0 to record's UnitsInStock field, then display the message "Entire order shipped - Time to reorder."

   c. Save the database, then return to Access and run the CheckInvMacro macro three times, using the following information:

ID	Amount ordered	
AB345	400	("Entire order shipped" should appear.)
TR457	100	("Only 50 units shipped" should appear.)
YY756	300	("Entire order shipped – Time to reorder" should appear.)

   d. Compact and then close the database.

3. In this exercise, you will create a procedure that updates a field in a database.

   a. Open the T7-AC-E3D (T7-AC-E3D.mdb) database which is located in the Tut07\Access folder on your Data Disk, then open the Products table in Design View. The table contains four fields: a Text field named ProductID, a Number field named UnitsInStock, a Number field named ReorderAmt, and a Text field named Reorder. Close the Design View window. Open the Products table and view the existing records, then close the table.

   b. Open the Visual Basic Editor. Open the Module1 module's Code window, then view the code template for the RecordSales procedure. Code the procedure so that it prompts the user to enter the product ID and the number of units ordered. Subtract the number of units ordered from the number of units in stock. (For this exercise, you can assume that the number of units ordered always will be less than or equal to the number of units in stock.) If the number of units in stock is less than or equal to the reorder amount, assign the letter "Y" to the Reorder field.

   c. Save the database, then return to Access and run the RecordSalesMacro macro five times using the following information:

ID	Amount Ordered
KLM2	100
ABX3	50
CDC4	200
XPQ4	25
CBA3	50

d. Open the Products table and verify that "Y" appears in the Reorder field for any Product ID whose UnitsInStock field contains a value that is less than or equal to the value in its ReorderAmt field.

e. Compact and then close the database.

Exercise 4 is a Discovery Exercise. Discovery Exercises, which may include topics that are not covered in the lesson, allow you to "discover" the solutions to problems on your own.

discovery ▶ **4.** In this exercise, you will create a procedure that compares the value stored in a Date field.

a. Open the T7-AC-E4D (T7-AC-E4D.mdb) database, which is located in the Tut07\Access folder on your Data Disk.

b. Open the Shipping table. The table contains a Text field named Item and a Date/Time field named ShipDate. Close the table.

c. Open the Visual Basic Editor. Open the Module1 module's Code window, then view the code template for the VerifyDate procedure. Code the procedure so that it prompts the user to enter the item number and the date the item is required by the customer. (Use the system date as the *defaultValue* in the InputBox function that gets the date.) Search for the item number in the Item field. If the shipping date is later than the required date, display the message "Item won't be available"; otherwise, display the message "Item will be available".

d. Save the database, then return to Access. Run the VerifyDateMacro three times, using the following information:

Item	Required Date
A	5/1/02 ("Item will be available" should appear.)
B	6/4/02 ("Item will be available" should appear.)
C	7/20/02 ("Item won't be available" should appear.)

e. Compact and then close the database.

A computer program is good only if it works. Errors in programming code can cause a program to run incorrectly. Therefore, a programmer needs to know how to locate and fix any errors in his or her code. Exercise 5 is a Debugging Exercise. Debugging Exercises allow you to practice recognizing and solving errors in code.

debugging **5.** In this exercise, you will debug an existing procedure.

a. Open the T7-AC-E5D (T7-AC-E5D. mdb) database, which is located in the Tut07\Access folder on your Data Disk.

b. Open the Code table. The table contains two Text fields named Code and JobTitle. Notice that the valid Codes are the letters A through E. Close the table.

c. Open the Visual Basic Editor. Open the Module1 module's Code window, then view the DisplayTitle procedure. The procedure should prompt the user to enter the code, then verify that the code is valid. It then should display the corresponding job title in a message box.

d. Study the code, then return to Access. Run the DisplayTitleMacro macro three times, using the codes A, b, and X. The A code should display "President". The b code should display "Vice President". The X code should display "Invalid code entered." What is wrong with the DislayTitle procedure? Return to the Visual Basic Editor and correct any errors in the procedure, then save the database and run the DisplayTitleMacro macro again using the codes A, b, and X.

e. When the macro is working correctly, compact and then close the database.

The Select Case Statement and the MsgBox Function

objectives

In this tutorial, you will learn how to:

- Perform selection using the Select Case statement
- Use a message box to communicate with the user
- Use the QueryTables collection and QueryTable object in Excel to retrieve external data
- Use the SQL SELECT statement in Excel, Word, and Access to select records
- Use the MailMerge object in Word to create labels

Concept Lesson

More on the Selection Structure

In Tutorial 6, you learned how to use the If…Then…Else statement to tell the computer to make a decision and then, based on the result of that decision, to select one of two paths—either the Then path (if the *condition* evaluates to True) or the Else path (if the *condition* evaluates to False). In many procedures, however, you might have more than two paths from which a selection structure must choose. When a selection structure has several paths from which to choose, it is usually simpler and clearer to use the Case form of the selection structure instead of the nested If form. The Case form is sometimes referred to as an **extended selection structure**. You can use the VBA Select Case statement to include an extended selection structure in a procedure.

The Select Case Statement

Figure 8-1 shows the syntax of the Select Case statement along with an example that displays a message based on the grade stored in the strGrade variable.

The Select Case statement begins with the Select Case clause and ends with the End Select clause. Between the Select Case and End Select clauses are the individual Case clauses. Each Case clause represents a different path that the selection structure can follow. You can have as many Case clauses as necessary in a Select Case statement. If the Select Case statement includes a Case Else clause, the Case Else clause must be the last clause in the statement.

Notice that the Select Case clause must include a *testexpression*. The *testexpression* can be any numeric, string, or Boolean expression, which means it can contain a combination of variables, constants, functions, and operators. In the example shown in Figure 8-1, the *testexpression* is the String variable strGrade.

tip

A Boolean expression is an expression that evaluates to either the Boolean value True or the Boolean value False. You will learn how to include a Boolean expression in a Select Case statement in this lesson's Exercise 8.

Each of the individual Case clauses, except the Case Else, must contain an *expressionlist*, which can include one or more numeric, string, or Boolean expressions. You include more than one expression in an *expressionlist* simply by separating each expression from the next with a comma, as in Case "D", "F".

Syntax	Example
Select Case *testexpression*	Select Case strGrade
[**Case** *expressionlist1*	Case "A"
[instructions for the first Case]]	MsgBox Prompt:="Excellent"
[**Case** *expressionlist2*	Case "B"
[instructions for the second Case]]	MsgBox Prompt:="Above Average"
[**Case** *expressionlistn*	Case "C"
[instructions for the nth Case]]	MsgBox Prompt:="Average"
[**Case Else**	Case "D", "F"
[instructions for when the *textexpression*	MsgBox Prompt:="Below Average"
does not match any of the *expressionlists*]]	Case "I"
End Select	MsgBox Prompt:="Incomplete"
	Case "W"
	MsgBox Prompt:="Withdrawal"
	Case Else
	MsgBox Prompt:="Incorrect Grade"
	End Select

Figure 8-1: Syntax and an example of the Select Case statement

tip

....
The comma included in an *expressionlist* represents an implicit Or. In other words, Case "D", "F" means "either D Or F".
....

The data type of the expressions included in the *expressionlist*s must be compatible with the data type of the *testexpression*. In other words, if the *testexpression* is numeric, the expressions must be numeric. Likewise, if the *testexpression* is a string, the expressions must be strings. In the example shown in Figure 8-1, the *testexpression* (strGrade) is a string, and so are the expressions—"A", "B", "C", "D", "F", "I", "W"—as the surrounding quotation marks indicate.

When the Select Case statement is processed, the value of the *testexpression* is first compared with the values listed in *expressionlist1*. If a match is found, the instructions for the first Case clause are processed and then the instruction following the End Select clause is processed. If a match is not found in *expressionlist1*, the value of the *testexpression* is compared with the values listed in *expressionlist2*. If a match is found in *expressionlist2*, the instructions for the second Case clause are processed and then the instruction following the End Select clause is processed. If a match is not found in *expressionlist2*, the value of the *testexpression* is compared with the values listed in *expressionlist3*, and so on. If the *testexpression* does not match any of the values listed in any of the *expressionlist*s, the instruction listed in the Case Else clause is processed or, if there is no Case Else clause, the instruction following the End Select clause is processed. Keep in mind that if the *testexpression* matches a value in more than one Case clause, only the instructions in the first match are processed.

In addition to specifying specific values in the *expressionlist*s, as in Figure 8-1's example, you also can specify a range of values in an *expressionlist*. You do so using the Select Case statement's To and Is keywords.

Using To and Is in an Expressionlist

You can use either the keyword To or the keyword Is to specify a range of values in an *expressionlist*; the values included in the range can be either numeric or a string. You use the To keyword when you know both the upper and lower bounds of the range, and you use the Is keyword when you know only one end of the range—either the upper or lower end. For example, assume that the price of an item sold by ABC Corporation depends on the number of items ordered, as shown in the following table.

Number of items ordered	Price per item
1 – 5	$ 25
6 – 10	$ 23
More than 10	$ 20

Figure 8-2 shows the Select Case statement that will assign the appropriate price per item to the intPrice variable.

```
Select Case intNumOrdered
    Case 1 To 5
         intPrice = 25
    Case 6 To 10
         intPrice = 23
    Case Is > 10
         intPrice = 20
    Case Else
         intPrice = 0
         MsgBox Prompt:="Incorrect number ordered"
End Select
```

Figure 8-2: Example of using the To and Is keywords in a Select Case statement

• •

Notice in Figure 8-2 that the *testexpression*, intNumOrdered, is numeric, and so are the values listed in the *expressionlist*s.

• •

According to the ABC Corporation table, the price for one to five items is $25 each. You could, therefore, have written the first Case clause as Case 1, 2, 3, 4, 5. However, a more convenient way of writing that range of numbers is to use the keyword **To** in the Case clause, but you must follow this syntax to do so: **Case** *smallest value in the range* **To** *largest value in the range*. The expression 1 To 5 in the first Case clause, for example, specifies the range of numbers from one to five, inclusive. The expression 6 To 10 in the second Case clause specifies the range of numbers from six to 10, inclusive. Notice that both Case clauses state both the lower (1 and 6) and upper (5 and 10) ends of each range.

▶ **tip**
> When you use the To keyword in a Case clause, the value preceding the To always must be smaller than the value following the To; in other words, 10 To 6 is not a correct expression. An error message will *not* appear if the value preceding the To is greater than the value following the To; instead, the Case statement simply will not give the correct results. This is another reason why it is important to test your code to verify that it is working correctly.

Notice that the third Case clause in Figure 8-2, Case Is > 10, contains the Is keyword rather than the To keyword. Recall that you use the Is keyword when you know only one end of the range of values—either the upper or lower end. In this case, for example, you know only the lower end of the range, 10. This Case clause will handle all intNumOrdered values that are greater than 10.

▶ **tip**
> Because intNumOrdered is an Integer variable, you also can write the third Case clause as Case Is >= 11.

You always use the Is keyword in combination with a comparison operator, like this: **Is** comparison operator *value*. As you learned in Tutorial 7, the comparison operators are >, >=, <, <=, =, <>.

▶ **tip**
> In Discovery Exercise 14 in Tutorial 7's Concept lesson, you learned about the Like comparison operator. You cannot use the Like operator with the Is keyword.

▶ **tip**
> If you neglect to type the keyword Is in an expression, the Visual Basic Editor will type it in for you. In other words, if you enter Case > 10, the Visual Basic Editor will change the clause to Case Is > 10.

Notice that the Case Else clause shown in Figure 8-2 first assigns the number 0 to the intPrice variable and then uses the MsgBox statement to display the message "Incorrect number ordered" when the intNumOrdered variable contains a value that is not included in any of the Case clauses—namely, a zero or a negative number. In addition to the MsgBox statement, VBA also has a MsgBox function, which you will learn about in the next section.

The MsgBox Function

In the previous tutorials, you used the MsgBox statement to display a message in a message box. In addition to the MsgBox statement, VBA also has a MsgBox function. Like the MsgBox statement, the MsgBox function allows you to display a dialog box that contains a message, one or more command buttons, and an icon. After displaying the dialog box, both the MsgBox statement and the MsgBox function wait for the user to choose one of the command buttons. However, unlike the MsgBox statement, the MsgBox function returns a value that indicates which button the user chose.

Recall from Tutorial 4 that all functions return a value.

The syntax of the MsgBox function is almost identical to the syntax of the MsgBox statement, as shown in Figure 8-3.

MsgBox statement

MsgBox Prompt:=*prompt*[, **Buttons:**=*buttons*[, **Title:**=*title*]

```
MsgBox Prompt:="File saved.", _
        Buttons:=vbOKOnly + vbInformation, Title:="Saved"
```

MsgBox function

MsgBox(Prompt:=*prompt*[, **Buttons:**=*buttons*[, **Title:**=*title*]**)**

```
intButton = MsgBox(Prompt:="Do you want to continue?", _
        Buttons:=vbYesNo + vbExclamation + vbDefaultButton1, _
        Title:="Continue")
```

notice the parentheses

Figure 8-3: Syntax and examples of the MsgBox statement and the MsgBox function

Like the MsgBox statement's syntax, the MsgBox function's syntax also includes the optional *helpfile* and *context* arguments, which allow you to provide context-sensitive help for the dialog box. You can learn more about these arguments by displaying the MsgBox function Help screen.

Notice in Figure 8-3 that, unlike the MsgBox statement, the MsgBox function requires its arguments to be enclosed in a set of parentheses. Also unlike the MsgBox statement, which always appears on its own line in a Code window, the MsgBox function always appears as part of another statement, typically an assignment statement that assigns the function's return value to an Integer variable. For example, in Figure 8-3 the MsgBox function's return value is assigned to the intButton variable.

> **Many VBA commands can be used either as a statement, which does not return a value, or as a function, which does return a value. To use the function form of a command, you must enclose the command's arguments in parentheses, and you must provide a storage location for the function's return value.**

You already are familiar with the MsgBox's *prompt* argument, which contains the message you want displayed in the dialog box. The *title* argument is the text (name) displayed in the dialog box's title bar. The *prompt* argument should be entered using sentence capitalization, and *title* should be entered using book title capitalization. If you omit the *title* argument, the application's name—for example, Microsoft PowerPoint—will be displayed in the dialog box's title bar.

> **Recall that you learned about sentence and book title capitalization in Tutorial 4's Concept lesson.**

Next, learn about the MsgBox's *buttons* argument.

The Buttons Argument

The *buttons* argument is an optional numeric expression that represents the sum of values specifying the number and type of buttons to display in the dialog box, the icon style to use, and the identity of the default button. If you omit the *buttons* argument, the dialog box contains an OK button only; it does not contain an icon. Figure 8-4 on the next page shows most, but not all, of the valid settings for the *buttons* argument.

> **You can learn about the *buttons* argument settings not shown in Figure 8-4 by viewing the MsgBox Function Help screen.**

As Figure 8-4 indicates, each setting has an intrinsic constant and a numeric value associated with it. When entering the *buttons* argument in the MsgBox function, you can use either the setting's numeric value or its constant. Using the constant makes the program more self-documenting, so it is the preferred way of entering the *buttons* argument.

> **As you learned in Tutorial 2, an intrinsic constant is a word, built into an application, that typically represents a numeric value. Constants are more meaningful than the numbers they represent, so they are easier to understand and remember. For example, the constant vbYesNo is more meaningful than its numeric equivalent, 4.**

Notice that the *buttons* argument's settings are divided into three groups. The first group controls the number and type of buttons displayed in the dialog box. The vbOKOnly setting, for example, displays one button, the OK button. The vbYesNoCancel setting, on the other hand, displays three buttons—Yes, No, and Cancel.

Settings for the MsgBox's *buttons* argument		
Constant	Value	Description
vbOKOnly	0	Display OK button only
vbOKCancel	1	Display OK and Cancel buttons
vbAbortRetryIgnore	2	Display Abort, Retry, and Ignore buttons
vbYesNoCancel	3	Display Yes, No, and Cancel buttons
vbYesNo	4	Display Yes and No buttons
vbRetryCancel	5	Display Retry and Cancel buttons
vbCritical	16	Display Critical Message icon
vbQuestion	32	Display Warning Query icon
vbExclamation	48	Display Warning Message icon
vbInformation	64	Display Information Message icon
vbDefaultButton1	0	First button is default
vbDefaultButton2	256	Second button is default
vbDefaultButton3	512	Third button is default
vbDefaultButton4	768	Fourth button is default

Group 1 corresponds to vbOKOnly through vbRetryCancel. Group 2 corresponds to vbCritical through vbInformation. Group 3 corresponds to vbDefaultButton1 through vbDefaultButton4.

Figure 8-4: Valid settings for the *buttons* argument

The second group of settings controls the style of the icon displayed in the message box. The vbCritical setting, for example, displays the Critical Message icon ⊗, which alerts the user to a serious problem that requires intervention or correction before the procedure can continue. For example, you would use the Critical Message icon in a dialog box that alerts the user that the disk in the disk drive is write-protected.

The vbQuestion setting displays the Warning Query icon ⑦. Although the Warning Query icon is available, it is not used extensively in dialog boxes to avoid confusing it with the Help icon, which also is a question mark.

The vbExclamation setting displays the Warning Message icon ⚠. You use the Warning Message icon to alert the user that he or she first must make a decision and then enter a response before the application can continue. The message to the user can be phrased as a question—for example, "Do you want to continue?"

The vbInformation setting displays the Information Message icon ⓘ, which you use in a dialog box whose purpose is to display information only. The dialog box should display the OK button only; it should not offer the user any choices. The user acknowledges the informational message by clicking the OK button.

The third group of settings for the *buttons* argument identifies the default button, which is the button that is chosen automatically when the user presses the Enter key. The default button should be the one that represents the user's most likely action, as long as that action is not destructive.

The *buttons* argument is the sum of one of the numbers from each group. The default value for the *buttons* argument is 0 (vbOKOnly + vbDefaultButton1). A *buttons* argument of 0 means that the message box will display an OK button only, and the button will be the default button; no icon will appear in the message box. Suppose that you want the dialog box to display Yes and No buttons along with the Warning Message icon. Additionally, you want the No button to be the default button. To display a dialog box matching that description, you would enter, as the *buttons* argument, either the expression `vbYesNo + vbExclamation + vbDefaultButton2`, or the number 308 (4 + 48 + 256). To make your procedures more self-documenting, it is a good practice to enter the expression that contains the constants instead of the numeric value.

 tip

If you do not want to display an icon in the message box, you do not need to include a number from the second group in the *buttons* argument.

As mentioned earlier, the dialog box produced by the MsgBox function remains on the screen until the user selects a button, at which time the MsgBox function returns a value that represents the button that was selected.

Values Returned by the MsgBox Function

Figure 8-5 shows the MsgBox function's buttons and their corresponding constants and numeric values.

Values returned by the MsgBox function		
Button	Constant	Numeric value
OK	vbOK	1
Cancel	vbCancel	2
Abort	vbAbort	3
Retry	vbRetry	4
Ignore	vbIgnore	5
Yes	vbYes	6
No	vbNo	7

Figure 8-5: MsgBox function's buttons

According to Figure 8-5, if the user selects the Yes button in the dialog box, the MsgBox function returns the integer 6, which can be referred to by the intrinsic constant vbYes. If, on the other hand, the user selects the Retry button, the MsgBox function returns the integer 4, represented by the intrinsic constant vbRetry. To make your procedures more self-documenting, you always should use the constant rather than the integer value when referring to the MsgBox function's return value, as shown in Figure 8-6. Notice that the constants are shaded in the figure.

Example 1

```
Dim intResponse As Integer
intResponse = MsgBox(Prompt:="Do you want to continue", _
    Buttons:=vbYesNo + vbExclamation + vbDefaultButton1, _
    Title:="Continue")
If intResponse = vbYes then
    [instructions to process when Yes button is selected]
Else
    [instructions to process when No button is selected]
End If
```

Example 2

```
Dim intButton As Integer
intButton = MsgBox(Prompt:="Error when saving file", _
    Buttons:=vbAbortRetryIgnore + vbExclamation + _
    vbDefaultButton2, Title:="Error")
    Title:="Error")
Select Case intButton
    Case vbAbort
        [instructions to process when Abort button is selected]
    Case vbRetry
        [instructions to process when Retry button is selected]
    Case vbIgnore
        [instructions to process when Ignore button is selected]
End Select
```

Figure 8-6: Examples of using the MsgBox function's return values

In the first example shown in Figure 8-6, the value returned by the MsgBox function is assigned to an Integer variable named intResponse. Notice that the MsgBox function will display Yes and No buttons and the Warning Message icon ⚠, and that the first button in the dialog box, the Yes button, will be the default button. The example then uses an If...Then...Else statement to determine which button the user selected. If the user selected the Yes button, the *condition* intResponse = vbYes will evaluate to True and the instructions contained in the True path will be processed. If the user selected the No button, the instructions contained in the False path will be processed.

In Figure 8-6's second example, the value returned by the MsgBox function is assigned to an Integer variable named intButton. In this example, the MsgBox will display three buttons—Abort, Retry, and Ignore—along with the Warning Message icon ; the second button, Retry, will be the default button. The example then uses a Select Case statement to determine which button the user selected. If the user selected the Abort button, the instructions in the first Case clause will be processed. If the user selected the Retry button, the second Case clause's instructions will be processed. Finally, if the user selected the Ignore button, the instructions in the third Case clause will be processed.

You now have completed Tutorial 8's Concept lesson. You can either take a break or complete the end-of-lesson questions and exercises before moving on to the next lesson.

SUMMARY

To use the Select Case statement to code the selection structure:

■ Use the syntax shown in Figure 8-1, where the *testexpression* and the *expressionlist*s can contain a numeric, string, or Boolean expression composed of a combination of variables, constants, functions, and operators.

To specify a range of values in a Case clause's *expressionlist*:

■ Use the keyword To in the following syntax: *smallest value in the range* **To** *largest value in the range*. Examples: Case 1 To 4, Case "A" To "C".

■ Use the keyword Is in the following syntax: **Is** relational operator *value*. Examples: Case Is > 10, Case Is <= "JONES".

To display VBA's predefined message box, and then return a value that indicates the button that was selected in the message box:

■ Use the MsgBox function. Its syntax and an example are shown in Figure 8-3. The message box contains a message, one or more command buttons, and an icon. After displaying the message box, the MsgBox function waits for the user to choose a button. It then returns a value that indicates which button the user chose. Figure 8-5 shows the values returned by the MsgBox function, and Figure 8-6 shows two examples of using the return values in a selection structure.

R E V I E W   Q U E S T I O N S

1. If the Select Case statement's *testexpression* is the numeric variable intNumOrdered, which two of the following Case clauses are valid?
   a. `Case 2, 4, 6, 8`
   b. `Case "1" To "3"`
   c. `Case Is <= 6`
   d. `Case Is 4 To 7`
   e. `Case 4 Through 8`

2. If the Select Case statement's *testexpression* is the String variable strCode, which two of the following Case clauses are valid?
   a. `Case A, B, C`
   b. `Case "C To F"`
   c. `Case Is < "D"`
   d. `Case "A" To "H"`
   e. `Case "J" Through "P"`

3. If the Select Case's *testexpression* is the expression UCase(strState), which two of the following Case clauses are valid?
   a. `Case "TEXAS To VERMONT"`
   b. `Case "ALABAMA" And "ARKANSAS"`
   c. `Case Is > "Illinois"`
   d. `Case "COLORADO", "CALIFORNIA"`
   e. `Case "ALABAMA" To "ARKANSAS"`

4. The MsgBox function displays a message box that contains _____.
   a. a message
   b. one or more command buttons
   c. an icon
   d. all of the above

5. The MsgBox function's *buttons* argument controls _____.
   a. the number and type of buttons displayed in the dialog box
   b. the style of the icon displayed in the dialog box
   c. the dialog box's default button
   d. all of the above

6. The MsgBox function returns the value _____ when the user clicks the Yes button in the message box.
   a. msgBoxYes
   b. msgYes
   c. yes
   d. vbYes

7. Which of the following MsgBox functions will display the "Do you want to exit?" message, along with the ⚠ icon and the Yes and No buttons? The No button should be the default button, and the function should assign the user's response to the intAnswer variable.

   a. `intAnswer = MsgBox(Prompt:="Do you want to exit?",`
      `Buttons:=vbYesNo + vbExclamation + vbDefaultButton2,`
      `Title:="Exit")`

   b. `intAnswer = MsgBox(Prompt:="Do you want to exit?",`
      `Buttons:=vbYesNo, vbExclamation, vbDefaultButton2,`
      `Title:="Exit")`

   c. `intAnswer = MsgBox(Prompt:="Do you want to exit?",`
      `Buttons:=vbYesNo + vbCritical + vbDefaultButton1,`
      `Title:="Exit")`

   d. `intAnswer = MsgBox(Prompt:="Do you want to exit?",`
      `Buttons:=vbExclamation, Title:="Exit")`

8. You use the _____ icon in the MsgBox function's dialog box to alert the user that he or she first must make a decision and then enter a response before the procedure can continue.

   a. Critical Message ❌
   b. Warning Message ⚠
   c. Information Message ⓘ

9. A message box used for informational purposes only should contain _____ button only.

   a. a Cancel
   b. an OK
   c. a Yes
   d. either an OK or a Cancel button

E X E R C I S E S

1. Write a Select Case statement that displays the string "Dog" in a message box if the intAnimal variable contains the number 1. Display the string "Cat" if the intAnimal variable contains the number 2. Display the string "Unknown" if the intAnimal variable contains a number other than 1 or 2. (Use the MsgBox statement for this exercise.)

2. Write a Select Case statement that will assign the appropriate shipping charge to the intShip variable. The shipping charge is based on the state stored in the strState variable, as shown in the following table.

State stored in strState	Shipping charge
Hawaii	30
California	30
Oregon	40
New Mexico	50
Other	75

   (*Hint*: Notice that both Hawaii and California have the same shipping charge. Also keep in mind that the state could be stored in any case—either uppercase letters, lowercase letters, or a combination.)

3. Assume you offer programming seminars to companies. Your price per person depends on the number of people the company registers, as per the table shown below. (For example, if the company registers seven people, then the total amount owed by the company is $560.)

Number of registrants	Charge
1 – 4	$100 per person
5 or more	$ 80 per person
less than 1	$ 0 per person

The number of people registered is stored in the intReg variable. Calculate the total amount owed by the company. Store the total amount in the curTotal variable. Write the VBA code. Be sure to use the Select Case statement in the code.

4. Write a Select Case statement that assigns the appropriate bonus amount to the curBonus variable. The bonus amount is based on the sales amount stored in the intSales variable, as shown in the following table. Also use the MsgBox statement to display an appropriate error message when the sales amount is less than zero.

Sales amount stored in curSales	Bonus
0 – 250	0
Over 250, but less than or equal to 1000	10
Over 1000, but less than or equal to 3000	25
Over 3000	50
Less than 0	0

5. Write a Select Case statement that assigns a 10% discount rate to customers in California and Texas, a 7% discount rate to customers in Oregon and New Mexico, and a 6% discount rate to customers in all other states. The state is stored in the strState variable. Assign the rate to the sngRate variable. (*Hint*: Remember that the state could be stored in any case—uppercase letters, lowercase letters, or a combination.)

6. Write the MsgBox function that displays the dialog box shown in Figure 8-7. Assign the user's response to an Integer variable named intAnswer. If the user clicks the Cancel button, what value is assigned to the intAnswer variable?

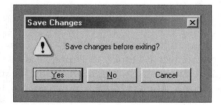

Figure 8-7

7. Complete the following code:

```
Dim intAnswer As Integer
intAnswer = MsgBox(Prompt:="Delete record?", _
    Buttons:=_____ + vbExclamation,
    Title:="Delete")
Select Case _____
    Case _____
        [instructions to process when Yes button
         is selected]
    Case _____
        [instructions to process when No button
         is selected]
    Case _____
        [instructions to process when Cancel button
         is selected]
End Select
```

Exercises 8 through 10 are Discovery Exercises. Discovery Exercises, which may include topics that are not covered in the lesson, allow you to "discover" the solutions to problems on your own.

discovery ▶ 8. In this exercise, you will learn how to use a Boolean value as the *testexpression*.
   a. Start either Word, Excel, Access, or PowerPoint. Open the Visual Basic Editor. Insert a module, then create a procedure named DisplayRaiseRate. The DisplayRaiseRate procedure should assign the appropriate raise rate based on the following information:
      ■ Employees coded A who have been with the company for more than three years get a 4% raise.
      ■ Employees coded B who have been with the company for more than five years get a 5% raise.
      ■ All other employees get a 3% raise.
   b. Enter the partially completed code shown in Figure 8-8. Complete the procedure by entering the appropriate expressions for both *expressionlist1* and *expressionlist2*. (*Hint*: You can use the logical operators And and Or in the *expressionlists*.)

```
'declare variables
Dim strCode As String, strYears As String
Dim intYears As Integer, sngRaise As Single
'enter employee code and years employed
strCode = InputBox(prompt:="Enter the employee code:", Title:="Code")
strYears = InputBox(prompt:="Enter the number of years employed:", _
    Title:="Years")
'convert years to a number and convert code to uppercase
intYears = Val(strYears)
strCode = UCase(strCode)
'assign raise rate
Select Case True
    Case <enter expressionlist1 here>
        sngRaise = 0.04
    Case <enter expressionlist2 here>
        sngRaise = 0.05
    Case Else
        sngRaise = 0.03
End Select
MsgBox Prompt:=Format(expression:=sngRaise, Format:="percent"), _
    Buttons:=vbOKOnly + vbInformation, Title:="Raise Rate"
```

Figure 8-8

c. Save the procedure, then run the procedure five times. First enter A as the code and 2 as the number of years. The message box should display 3.00%. Next, enter A as the code and 10 as the number of years. The message box should display 4.00%. Next, enter B as the code and 8 as the number of years. The message box should display 5.00%. Finally, enter B as the code and 5 as the number of years. The message box should display 3.00%.

d. Exit the application.

discovery ▶ 9. Assume that all Code 3 employees and all employees who have been with the company at least five years are to receive a 5% raise. Employees having other job codes or those who have been with the company for less than five years get a 4.5% raise. Write a Select Case statement that will assign the appropriate rate to the sngRate variable. The employee code and number of years employed are stored in the intCode and intYears variables, respectively. (*Hint*: It may help to complete Exercise 8 first.)

discovery ▶ 10. In this exercise, you will learn about the If...Then...Else statement's ElseIf clause. You can use the If...Then...Else statement, along with the ElseIf clause, to write an extended selection structure.

a. Start either Word, Excel, Access, or PowerPoint. Open the Visual Basic Editor and view the If...Then...Else statement's Help screen. Read the Help screen, then click Example at the top of the screen. Study the examples, then close the Help window, and exit the application.

b. Rewrite the example shown in this lesson's Figure 8-1 using the If...Then...Else statement rather than the Select Case statement. Be sure to use the ElseIf clause.

c. Close the application.

You also can use VBA in PowerPoint to create procedures that enhance your presentations. Exercise 11 allows you to apply this tutorial's programming concept in a PowerPoint presentation.

powerpoint **11.** In this exercise, you will finish coding a procedure in PowerPoint.

   a. Open the T8-PP-E11 (T8-PP-E11.ppt) presentation, which is located in the Tut08\Concept folder on your Data Disk. Click the Enable Macros button, if necessary, then save the presentation as T8-PP-E11D.

   b. Open the Visual Basic Editor and view the PrintSlide procedure, which allows the user to print one or more of the presentation's slides. Make the following modifications to the procedure:

      1) Use the MsgBox function, rather than the InputBox function, to ask the user if he or she wants to print. (*Hint*: Keep in mind that, unlike the InputBox function, which returns a string, the MsgBox function returns an integer.) Display the Yes and No buttons, along with the Warning Message icon, in the message box.

      2) Modify the MsgBox statement shown in the Then clause so that it displays the OK button, the Information icon, and the words "Cancel Print" in its title bar.

      3) Change the If...Then...Else statement to a Select Case statement.

   c. Save the presentation, then return to PowerPoint. Click View on the menu bar and then click Slide Show. When the slide appears, click the image that appears on the first slide. Click the No button in response to the "Do you want to print?" prompt. The message "No slides will be printed." should appear in a message box. Click the OK button to close the message box.

   d. Click the image again, then click the Yes button in response to the "Do you want to print?" prompt. Print slides 2 and 3 only, then press the Esc key to stop the slide show.

   e. Close PowerPoint.

A computer program is good only if it works. Errors in programming code can cause a program to run incorrectly. Therefore, a programmer needs to know how to locate and fix any errors in his or her code. Exercise 12 is a Debugging Exercise. Debugging Exercises allow you to practice recognizing and solving errors in code.

debugging 🐞 **12.** Assume that employees having a job rating of either A or B are to receive a 5% raise. All other employees should receive a 3% raise. (The job rating is stored in the strJob variable.) The following Select Case statement should assign the appropriate raise rate to the sngRate variable, but it is not working correctly. What is wrong with the statement? Correct any errors.

```
Select Case UCase(strJob)
    Case "A" Or "B"
        sngRate = .05
    Case Else
        sngRate = .03
End Select
```

Excel Lesson

Using the Select Case Statement and the MsgBox Function in Excel

case ▶ Martin Washington, the accountant at Paradise Electronics, records each store's monthly sales goal and actual sales made in an Access database named MthSales. Martin would like to display the sales information for either all of the stores or a specific store in an Excel worksheet, along with the difference between the monthly sales goal and the actual sales made. He has decided to create a macro that he can use to retrieve the database information and make the appropriate calculations.

Viewing the MthSales Database and the Sales Worksheet

Your Data Disk contains the Access database that Martin uses to record each store's monthly sales information. The database is named MthSales, and it is stored in the Tut08\Excel folder. Figure 8-9 shows the records contained in the database's 2002Sales table.

Store	Month	Goal	Actual
J	01	$23,000.00	$22,000.00
G	01	$12,250.00	$12,250.00
W	01	$14,500.00	$16,000.00
J	02	$10,500.00	$10,500.00
G	02	$15,000.00	$16,500.00
W	02	$15,400.00	$14,600.00
J	03	$9,500.00	$10,250.00
G	03	$13,400.00	$12,000.00
W	03	$11,000.00	$12,000.00
J	04	$16,000.00	$17,200.00
G	04	$14,250.00	$14,500.00
W	04	$16,300.00	$14,800.00
J	05	$17,250.00	$18,300.00
G	05	$16,700.00	$17,000.00
W	05	$20,000.00	$21,000.00
J	06	$12,000.00	$14,000.00
G	06	$15,000.00	$14,000.00
W	06	$11,500.00	$14,000.00
		$0.00	$0.00

Figure 8-9: Records contained in the 2002Sales table

Your Data Disk also contains the workbook that Martin will use to display and calculate the appropriate sales information. Before creating Martin's macro, view the workbook.

To view the workbook:

1 Start Microsoft Excel.

2 Open the **T8-EX-1** (T8-EX-1.xls) workbook, which is located in the Tut08\Excel folder on your Data Disk. Click the **Enable Macros** button, if necessary, then save the workbook as **Monthly Sales**. The Monthly Sales workbook contains one worksheet, named Sales, as shown in Figure 8-10.

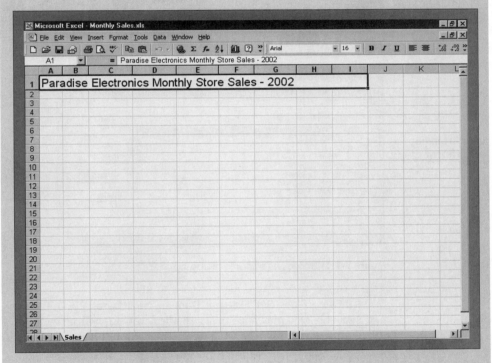

Figure 8-10: Monthly Sales workbook showing the Sales worksheet

Before you can create Martin's macro, you need to learn how to use Microsoft Query to retrieve data from a database and display it in an Excel worksheet.

Using Microsoft Query

Microsoft Query is a separate program that comes with Microsoft Excel, and it is used to bring data from a database into an Excel worksheet. By using Query to retrieve the data stored in a database, you do not have to retype the data in order to

analyze it in Excel. Query also allows you to update the information contained in
the worksheet, automatically, whenever the data in the database changes.

tip

Microsoft Query can retrieve data from the following database sources: Microsoft SQL
Server OLAP Services, Microsoft Access 2000, dBASE, Microsoft FoxPro, Microsoft Excel,
Oracle, Paradox, SQL Server, and text file databases.

**To use Microsoft Query to retrieve the sales information from the Access
database:**

1   Click **cell A3** in the Sales worksheet, which is where you want to begin displaying the sales information. Click **Data** on the menu bar, point to **Get
External Data**, and then click **New Database Query**. The Choose Data Source
dialog box opens. Click the **Databases** tab, if necessary. See Figure 8-11.
(Your list of data sources might be different.)

**your list might
be different**

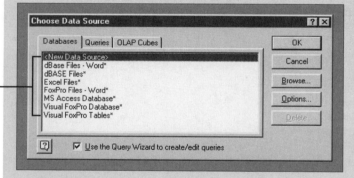

Figure 8-11: Choose Data Source dialog box

HELP? If the Get External Data or New Database Query commands are not
available, you may have to install Microsoft Query from your installation disk. See
online Help, your instructor, or a technical support person for more information.

2   Click **MS Access Database*** in the list, and then click the **OK** button. The
Select Database dialog box opens, and a "Connecting to data source" message appears on the screen.

3   Use the Select Database dialog box to locate the MthSales.mdb database, which
is stored in the Tut08\Excel folder on your Data Disk. Click **MthSales.mdb** in the
list, and then click the **OK** button. The Query Wizard – Choose Columns dialog
box opens. Click the **plus sign** that appears next to the 2002Sales table name in
the Available tables and columns list box. See Figure 8-12.

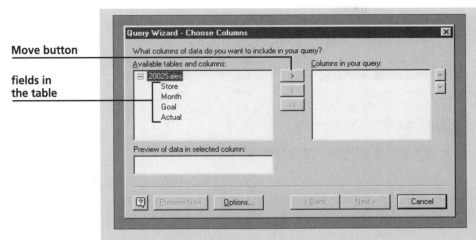

Move button

fields in the table

Figure 8-12: Query Wizard – Choose Columns dialog box

Notice that the 2002Sales table contains four fields named Store, Month, Goal, and Actual. To include a single field in the query, click the field's name and then click the Move button $\boxed{>}$. To include all the fields in the query, click the table's name and then click $\boxed{>}$. In this case, because you want all of the sales information to appear in the Sales worksheet, you will include all of the fields in the query.

4 The name of the table, 2002Sales, should be selected in the Available tables and columns list box. Click the **Move** button $\boxed{>}$ to move all of the field names to the Columns in your query list box, then click the **Next** button. The Query Wizard – Filter Data dialog box opens. You do not need to make any selections in this dialog box because the macro that you will create will select the appropriate records to display in the worksheet.

5 Click the **Next** button in the Query Wizard – Filter Data dialog box. The Query Wizard – Sort Order dialog box opens. You do not need to make any selections in this dialog box because the macro will sort the sales information in the appropriate order before displaying it in the worksheet.

6 Click the **Next** button in the Query Wizard – Sort Order dialog box. The Query Wizard – Finish dialog box opens.

7 Verify that the Return Data to Microsoft Excel option button is selected in the Query Wizard – Finish dialog box, then click the **Finish** button. The Returning External Data to Microsoft Excel dialog box opens, as shown in Figure 8-13. Notice that the dialog box prompts you to enter the location where you want the external data displayed in the worksheet.

this option
button should
be selected

be sure this
says =$A$3

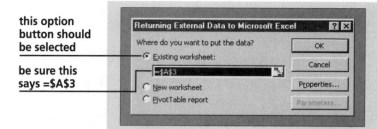

Figure 8-13: Returning External Data to Microsoft Excel dialog box

8   Verify that the Existing Worksheet option button is selected, and that =$A$3 appears in the box below the option button, as shown in Figure 8-13.

HELP? If =$A$3 does not appear in the box, click cell A3 in the worksheet. Do not be concerned that =Sales!$A$3 appears in the box rather than =$A$3.

Before completing the query definition, you will give the query a meaningful name.

9   Click the **Properties** button in the Returning External Data to Microsoft Excel dialog box. The External Data Range Properties dialog box opens. Select **Query from MS Access Database** in the Name text box, then type **SalesQuery** in the box. See Figure 8-14.

table query
name

be sure these
check boxes
and option
buttons are
selected/
deselected

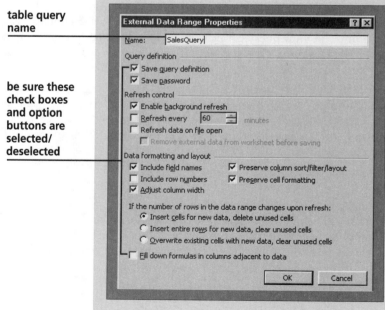

Figure 8-14: External Data Range Properties dialog box

10 Compare the External Data Range Properties dialog box on your screen to the one shown in Figure 8-14. If necessary, select and deselect the check boxes and option buttons on your screen to match the ones shown in Figure 8-14.

11 Click the **OK** button to close the External Data Range Properties dialog box. The Returning External Data to Microsoft Excel dialog box opens.

12 Click the **OK** button to close the Returning External Data to Microsoft Excel dialog box. The sales information from the Access database appears in the Sales worksheet, as shown in Figure 8-15. Notice that the field headings appear in row 3 in the worksheet.

QueryTable object

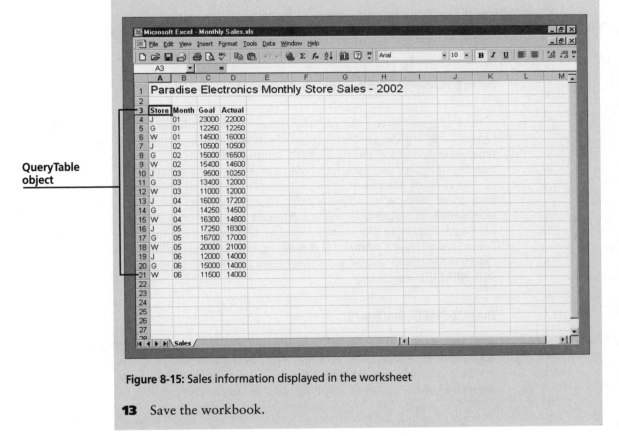

Figure 8-15: Sales information displayed in the worksheet

13 Save the workbook.

As Figure 8-15 indicates, the range of data that contains the retrieved data—in this case, the sales information—is considered an object, called a QueryTable object. QueryTable objects are members of the QueryTables collection in Excel.

The QueryTables Collection and QueryTable Objects

Figure 8-16 shows the portion of the Excel object model that includes the QueryTables collection and its associated QueryTable objects.

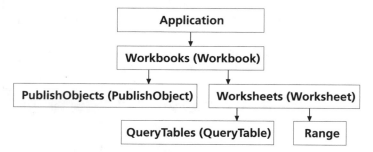

Figure 8-16: The QueryTables collection and QueryTable objects shown in the Excel object model

As Figure 8-16 shows, the QueryTables collection and its associated QueryTable objects are members of the Worksheet object. Each **QueryTable object** represents a worksheet table built from data retrieved from an external data source—for example, data retrieved from an Access database.

After using Microsoft Query to retrieve data from a database—in other words, after using it to create a QueryTable object—you can use the QueryTable object's **CommandText property** to select a different set of records to retrieve from the database and display in the worksheet. The syntax of the CommandText property is *queryTableObject*.**CommandText** = *query*, where *queryTableObject* is the name of a QueryTable object in the worksheet, and *query* is a string that represents a valid SQL SELECT statement.

The SQL SELECT Statement

SQL, pronounced like the word "sequel," stands for **Structured Query Language**. **SQL** is a set of commands, or statements, that allow you to access and manipulate the data stored in many database management systems on computers of all sizes, from large mainframes to small microcomputers. You can use SQL commands to store, retrieve, update, and sequence data.

The most commonly used SQL command is the **SELECT statement**, which allows you to select which database fields and records you want to view, as well as control the order in which the fields and records appear when displayed. Figure 8-17 shows the basic syntax of the SELECT statement. It also shows seven examples of using the SELECT statement to select the fields and records to display in a query table.

Different applications handle the capitalization of SQL keywords in different ways. In this book, you will be entering all SQL keywords in uppercase letters.

tip

The full syntax of the SELECT statement contains other clauses and options that are beyond the scope of this book.

Syntax of the SQL SELECT statement:
SELECT *fieldsList* **FROM** *table* [**WHERE** *condition*] [**ORDER BY** *field*]

Example 1:
```
qtbSales.CommandText = "SELECT Store, Actual FROM 2002Sales"
```

Example 2:
```
qtbSales.CommandText = "SELECT * FROM 2002Sales"
```

Example 3:
```
qtbSales.CommandText = "SELECT * FROM 2002Sales WHERE Store = 'J'"
```

Example 4:
```
qtbSales.CommandText = _
     "SELECT * FROM 2002Sales WHERE Store = 'J' ORDER BY Month"
```

Example 5:
```
qtbSales.CommandText = _
     "SELECT * FROM 2002Sales WHERE Store = '" & strStore & "'"
```

Example 6:
```
qtbSales.CommandText = _
     "SELECT * FROM 2002Sales WHERE Actual > " & curSales
```

Example 7:
```
qtbAccounts.CommandText = _
     "SELECT * FROM Accounts WHERE DueDate = #" & dtmDue & "#"
```

Figure 8-17: Basic syntax and examples of the SQL SELECT statement

In the syntax, *fieldsList* is one or more field names (separated by commas), and *table* is the name of the database table that contains the fields. The *query* `"SELECT Store, Actual FROM 2002Sales"` shown in Figure 8-17's first example will select only the store ID and actual sales from the records stored in the 2002Sales table. Notice that the entire *query* is enclosed in quotation marks to indicate that it is a string.

If you want to select all of the fields in a table, you can enter an asterisk (*) rather than the field names in the *fieldsList* portion of the SELECT statement. The * tells the SELECT statement to display all of the table fields in the order in which the fields appear in the table. In other words, rather than using the *query* `"SELECT Store, Month, Goal, Actual FROM 2002Sales"`, you could use the *query* `"SELECT * FROM 2002Sales"`, as shown in Figure 8-17's second example. Although both *queries* will produce the same result, the latter *query* requires less typing.

The **WHERE** *condition* part of the Select statement's syntax is referred to as the **WHERE clause**, and it allows you to limit the records that will be included, in this case, in the query table. In Figure 8-17's third example, for instance, the WHERE clause indicates that only the records for the Jackson store should be included in the query table. Notice that when a *query* includes a string literal constant, you enclose the string literal constant in single quotation marks. Also notice that the WHERE clause is optional in the SELECT statement, as indicated by the square brackets ([]) in the syntax.

The **ORDER BY** *field* part of the syntax—referred to as the **ORDER BY clause**— allows you to control the order in which the records appear when displayed. The ORDER BY clause in Figure 8-17's fourth example orders (sorts) the selected records in ascending order by the Month field. Like the WHERE clause, the ORDER BY clause is optional in the SELECT statement.

••

To display records in descending order, add the keyword DESC after *field* in the ORDER BY clause. For example, to display the table records in descending order by the Month field, use ORDER BY Month DESC. To display records in order by multiple fields, use a comma to separate each field from the next in the ORDER BY clause. For example, to display records in ascending order by the Month and Goal fields, use ORDER BY Month, Goal. This ORDER BY clause will sort the records in month order. If more than one record has the same month, those records will be sorted by the goal.

••

Examples 5, 6, and 7 in Figure 8-17 show how you can include a String variable, a numeric variable, and a Date variable, respectively, in a SELECT statement. Notice that you must use string concatenation, which you learned about in Tutorial 4, to do so.

After assigning a SELECT statement to the CommandText property, you then must use the QueryTable object's Refresh method to update the query table. The **Refresh method** tells Microsoft Excel to connect to the query table's data source, execute the *query* that appears in the CommandText property, and then return the appropriate data to the query table. The syntax of the Refresh method is *queryTableObject*.**Refresh BackgroundQuery:**=*backgroundQuery*, where *queryTableObject* is the name of a QueryTable object in the worksheet. The BackgroundQuery argument can be set to either the Boolean value True or the Boolean value False. When *backgroundQuery* is True, the Refresh method returns control to the procedure as soon as a database connection is made and the *query* is submitted (the *query* is updated in the background); this allows the procedure to continue processing before the data appears in the worksheet. When *backgroundQuery* is False, the Refresh method returns control to the procedure only after all the requested data has been displayed in the worksheet.

Now that the Sales worksheet contains a QueryTable object, and you know how to use the object's CommandText property and Refresh method, you can begin creating the macro that Martin will use to display the appropriate sales information.

Creating the DisplaySales Macro Procedure

Recall that the DisplaySales macro should allow Martin to display, in the Sales worksheet, the sales for either all of the stores or only a specific store. It also should calculate the difference between the monthly sales goals and the actual sales made. Figure 8-18 shows the pseudocode for the DisplaySales procedure.

1. Use the InputBox function to prompt the user to enter which store's sales he or she wants to display (A for All, G for Glen Park, J for Jackson, or W for Warren). Store the user's response in a String variable named strStore.
2. Value stored in the strStore variable:

= "A"	Assign to the CommandText property a SQL SELECT statement that selects all of the fields and records in the 2002Sales table. Order the records by month within store.
= "G", "J", "W"	Assign to the CommandText property a SQL SELECT statement that selects all of the fields for only the records whose Store field value matches the value stored in the strStore variable. Order the records by month.
Other	Use the MsgBox statement to display an error message in a message box, then exit the procedure.

3. Enter the column heading "Difference" in cell E3 in the worksheet.
4. Enter the formula =D4-C4 in cell E4 in the worksheet.
5. Set the QueryTable object's FillAdjacentFormulas property to True.
6. Use the QueryTable object's Refresh method to update the query table.
7. Use the MsgBox function to ask the user if he or she wants to print the worksheet. Assign the user's response to an Integer variable named intPrint.
8. If intPrint = vbYes, then print the worksheet.

Figure 8-18: Pseudocode for the DisplaySales procedure.

Figure 8-19 lists the variables that the DisplaySales procedure will use.

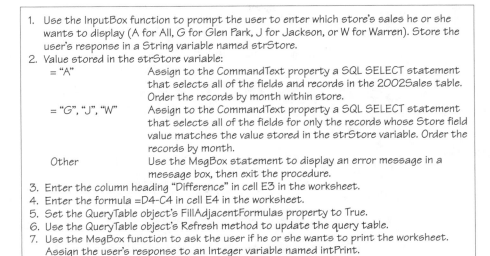

Variables	datatype
strStore	String
intPrint	Integer
shtSales	Worksheet
qtbSales	QueryTable

Figure 8-19: Variables used by the DisplaySales procedure

In the next set of steps, you will declare the appropriate variables and then translate each line in Figure 8-18's pseudocode into one or more VBA statements.

To begin coding the DisplaySales procedure:

1 Press **Alt+F11** to open the Visual Basic Editor. If necessary, open the Project Explorer window and close the Properties window, the Immediate window, and any open Code windows. Open the Module1 module's Code window, then view the code template for the **DisplaySales** procedure.

2 Close the Project Explorer window so that you can view more of the Code window.

3 Enter the documentation and the Dim and Set statements shown in Figure 8-20.

enter these instructions

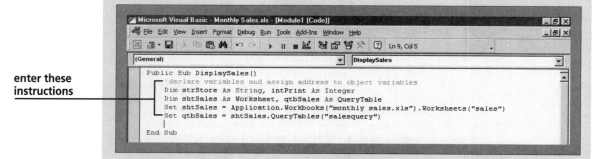

Figure 8-20: Code window showing documentation and Dim and Set statements

You now can begin translating the pseudocode shown in Figure 8-18 into VBA statements. The first step is to use the InputBox function to prompt the user to enter which store's sales he or she wants to display (A for All, G for Glen Park, J for Jackson, or W for Warren). The user's response should be assigned to the strStore variable. You will use the letter "A" as the *defaultValue* in the InputBox function.

4 Type **'enter which store's sales to display** and press the **Enter** key. Type **strStore = inputbox(prompt:="Sales? A(ll), G(len Park), J(ackson), W(arren)", _** (be sure to type the comma followed by a space and the underscore) and press the **Enter** key. Press the **Tab** key, then type **title:="Store Sales", default:="A")** and press the **Enter** key.

Now use the Select Case statement to select the appropriate records based on the value contained in the strStore variable.

5 Press the **Backspace** key, then type **'select appropriate records from database** and press the **Enter** key. Type **select case ucase(strstore)** and press the **Enter** key.

According to the pseudocode, if the user enters the letter "A", the procedure should assign to the QueryTable object's CommandText property a SQL SELECT statement that selects all of the fields and records contained in the 2002Sales table. Additionally, the records should be ordered (sorted) by month within store. In other words, the records should be sorted in store order, and then within each store, the records should be sorted by month.

To sort records in order by more than one field, you simply separate the field names with a comma in the ORDER BY clause. The primary sort field should be listed first, followed by a comma and the secondary sort field. In this case, the primary sort field is Store, and the secondary sort field is Month.

6 Press the **Tab** key, then type **case "A"** and press the **Enter** key. Press the **Tab** key, then type **qtbsales.commandtext = "SELECT * FROM 2002sales ORDER BY store, month"** and press the **Enter** key.

> It is a common programming practice to indent each Case clause within the Select Case statement. Programmers also indent the instructions contained within each Case clause.

If the user enters either G, J, or W, the procedure should select only the records whose Store field value matches the value entered by the user and stored in the strStore variable. The store records should be ordered (sorted) by month.

7   Press the **Backspace** key, then type **case "G", "J", "W"** and press the **Enter** key. Press the **Tab** key, then type **qtbsales.commandtext = "SELECT * FROM 2002sales WHERE store = '"** _ (be sure to type a single quotation mark, followed by a double quotation mark, a space, and the underscore) and press the **Enter** key. Press the **Tab** key, then type **& strstore & "' ORDER BY month"** (be sure to type the double quotation mark followed by a single quotation mark and a space before the ORDER BY clause) and press the **Enter** key.

According to Step 2 in the pseudocode, if the user enters a character other than A, G, J, or W, the procedure should display an appropriate error message and then exit the DisplaySales procedure. You can use VBA's **Exit Sub statement** to exit the sub procedure immediately.

8   Press the **Backspace** key twice, then type the additional instructions shown in Figure 8-21. Position the insertion point as shown in the figure.

make sure you typed the single quotation mark, double quotation mark, space, and underscore

enter these four lines of code

make sure you typed the double quotation mark, single quotation mark, and space

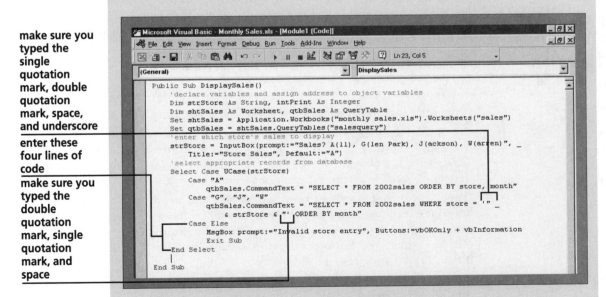

Figure 8-21: Partially completed DisplaySales procedure

9   Verify the accuracy of your code by comparing the code on your screen to the code shown in Figure 8-21, then save the workbook.

Recall that, in addition to retrieving the sales information from the Access database, the DisplaySales macro also needs to display the column heading "Difference" in cell E3 in the worksheet; this is Step 3 in the pseudocode. Additionally, the procedure needs to calculate the difference between the monthly sales goals and the actual sales made. Steps 4 and 5 in the pseudocode accomplish this task first by entering the formula "=D4-C4" in cell E4 in the worksheet, and then by assigning the Boolean value True to the QueryTable object's FillAdjacentFormulas property. When the FillAdjacentFormulas property is set to True, the Refresh method copies any formulas located to the right of the query table to the remaining cells in the same column of the table. In this case, for example, the formula contained in cell E4 will be copied to—or used to "fill"—the remaining cells in column E in the query table. The formulas will be automatically updated whenever the query table is refreshed.

To complete the DisplaySales procedure, then test it:

1 The insertion point should be positioned as shown in Figure 8-21. Type **'enter difference heading and formula** and press the **Enter** key. Type **shtsales.range("e3").value = "Difference"** and press the **Enter** key.

2 Type **shtsales.range("e4").formula = "=d4-c4"** and press the **Enter** key, then type **qtbsales.filladjacentformulas = true** and press the **Enter** key.

Next, use the QueryTable object's Refresh method to update the query table. Set the BackgroundQuery argument to False so that the procedure will not continue processing until all of the requested data is displayed in the worksheet.

tip

In this lesson's Exercise 5, you will observe why this procedure will not work correctly when the BackgroundQuery argument is set to True.

3 Type **qtbsales.refresh backgroundquery:=false** and press the **Enter** key.

Next, use the MsgBox function to ask the user if he or she wants to print the worksheet. Display Yes and No buttons and the Warning Message icon in the message box, and make the No button the default button. Assign the MsgBox function's return value to the intPrint variable.

4 Type **'ask if user wants to print worksheet** and press the **Enter** key. Type **intprint = msgbox(prompt:="Print worksheet?", _** (be sure to type the comma followed by a space and the underscore) and press the **Enter** key. Press the **Tab** key, then type **buttons:=vbyesno + vbexclamation + vbdefaultbutton2, title:="Print")** and press the **Enter** key.

If the user selects the Yes button in the message box, then the procedure should print the worksheet.

5 Press the **Backspace** key, then type the additional instructions shown in Figure 8-22, which shows the completed DisplaySales procedure.

the code in the Code window was compressed so that you could see the entire procedure

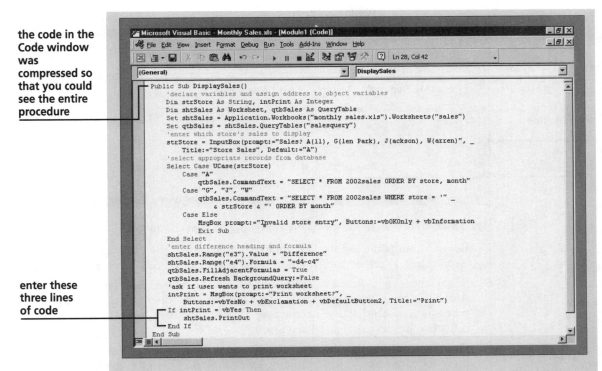

```vb
Public Sub DisplaySales()
    'declare variables and assign address to object variables
    Dim strStore As String, intPrint As Integer
    Dim shtSales As Worksheet, qtbSales As QueryTable
    Set shtSales = Application.Workbooks("monthly sales.xls").Worksheets("sales")
    Set qtbSales = shtSales.QueryTables("salesquery")
    'enter which store's sales to display
    strStore = InputBox(prompt:="Sales? A(ll), G(len Park), J(ackson), W(arren)", _
        Title:="Store Sales", Default:="A")
    'select appropriate records from database
    Select Case UCase(strStore)
        Case "A"
            qtbSales.CommandText = "SELECT * FROM 2002sales ORDER BY store, month"
        Case "G", "J", "W"
            qtbSales.CommandText = "SELECT * FROM 2002sales WHERE store = '" _
                & strStore & "' ORDER BY month"
        Case Else
            MsgBox prompt:="Invalid store entry", Buttons:=vbOKOnly + vbInformation
            Exit Sub
    End Select
    'enter difference heading and formula
    shtSales.Range("e3").Value = "Difference"
    shtSales.Range("e4").Formula = "=d4-c4"
    qtbSales.FillAdjacentFormulas = True
    qtbSales.Refresh BackgroundQuery:=False
    'ask if user wants to print worksheet
    intPrint = MsgBox(prompt:="Print worksheet?", _
        Buttons:=vbYesNo + vbExclamation + vbDefaultButton2, Title:="Print")
    If intPrint = vbYes Then
        shtSales.PrintOut
    End If
End Sub
```

enter these three lines of code

Figure 8-22: Completed DisplaySales procedure

6 Verify the accuracy of your code by comparing the code on your screen to the code shown in Figure 8-22, then save the workbook.

HELP? The code in the Code window shown in Figure 8-22 was compressed so that you could see the entire procedure. If you want to compress the code shown on your screen, click Tools on the Visual Basic Editor's Standard toolbar, then click Options, and then click the Editor Format tab. Select 9 in the Size list box, then click the OK button.

7 Return to Excel and run the **DisplaySales** macro. When the Store Sales dialog box appears, type **w** and press the **Enter** key. When the Print dialog box appears, click the **No** button. The sales information for the Warren store appears in the worksheet, as shown in Figure 8-23. Notice that the information is ordered by month.

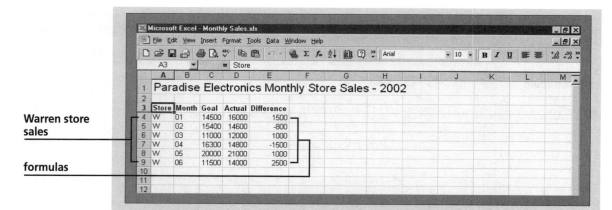

Warren store sales

formulas

Figure 8-23: Worksheet showing only the Warren store's sales information

Before running the DisplaySales macro again, format the query table using the Accounting 1 format, which will make the worksheet look more professional.

8 Select the range **A3:E9**. Click Format on the menu bar, and then click AutoFormat. When the AutoFormat dialog box opens, click the **sample worksheet located above Accounting 1** and then click the **OK** button. Click **cell A1** to cancel the range selection.

9 Run the **DisplaySales** macro again. When the Store Sales dialog box appears, press the **Enter** key to accept the *defaultValue*, A. When the Print dialog box appears, click the **No** button. The sales information for all of the stores appears in the worksheet, as shown in Figure 8-24. Notice that the information is ordered by month within store.

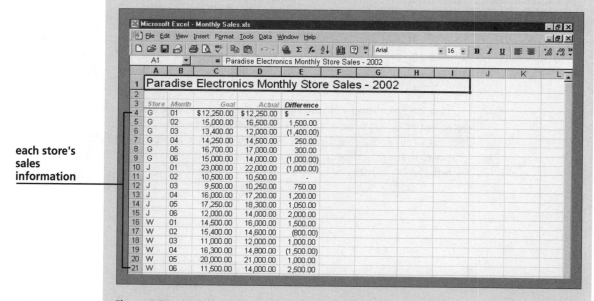

each store's sales information

Figure 8-24: Worksheet showing the sales information for all stores

You now have completed Tutorial 8's Excel lesson. You can either take a break or complete the end-of-lesson exercises before moving on to the next lesson.

EXERCISES

1. In this exercise, you will create a QueryTable object. You then will create a procedure that retrieves the appropriate database information based on the user's input.
   a. Open the T8-EX-E1 (T8-EX-E1.xls) workbook, which is located in the Tut08\Excel folder on your Data Disk. Click the Enable Macros button, if necessary, then save the workbook as T8-EX-E1D.
   b. Create a QueryTable object named MemberQuery. The query should retrieve the information stored in an Access database named Members.mdb, which is located in the Tut08\Excel folder on your Data Disk. The name of the table within the database is MemberList. Display the member information beginning in cell A3 in the worksheet.
   c. Open the Visual Basic Editor. Open the Module1 module's Code window, then view the code template for the DisplayMemberInfo procedure. Code the procedure so that it allows the user to display either all of the database records or only the records for a specific trainer. Use the Select Case statement in your code. If the user chooses to display all of the records, order the records by the MemberID field. If the user chooses to display the records for a specific trainer, order the records by the members' last and first names. Display an appropriate error message in a message box if the user enters something other than A, 101, 102, or 103. Include the OK button and the Information icon in the message box.
   d. Save the workbook, then return to Excel and run the DisplayMemberInfo macro. Display only the records for trainer 101.
   e. Run the DisplayMemberInfo macro again. This time, display all of the records.
   f. Run the DisplayMemberInfo macro again. When prompted for the records that you want to display, type X and press the Enter key. An appropriate error message should appear. Click the OK button to close the message box.
   g. Save and then close the workbook.

2. In this exercise, you will modify the DisplayMemberInfo procedure that you created in Exercise 1.
   a. Open the T8-EX-E1D (T8-EX-E1D.xls) workbook that you created in Exercise 1. The file is located in the Tut08\Excel folder on your Data Disk. Click the Enable Macros button, if necessary, then save the workbook as T8-EX-E2D.
   b. Open the Visual Basic Editor. Open the Module1 module's Code window, then view the DisplayMemberInfo procedure. Change the filename in the Set statement to "t8-ex-e2d.xls". Modify the procedure so that it allows the user to display the records for all of the members (ordered by MemberID) or for only members who have trainers (ordered by TrainerId).
   c. Save the workbook, then return to Excel and run the DisplayMemberInfo macro. Display the records for all members who have trainers.
   d. Save and then close the workbook.

3. In this exercise, you will create a QueryTable object. You then will create a procedure that retrieves the appropriate database information based on the user's input.
   a. Open the T8-EX-E3 (T8-EX-E3.xls) workbook, which is located in the Tut08\Excel folder on your Data Disk. Click the Enable Macros button, if necessary, then save the workbook as T8-EX-E3D.

    b. Create a QueryTable object named TripQuery. The query should retrieve only the ID, LastName, FirstName, and Paid fields from an Access database named Trip.mdb, which is contained in the Tut08\Excel folder on your Data Disk. The name of the table within the database is Payments. Display the trip information beginning in cell A3 in the worksheet.

    c. Open the Visual Basic Editor. Open the Module1 module's Code window, then view the code template for the DisplayTripInfo procedure. Code the procedure so that it allows the user to display all of the database records, only the records for students who still owe money (those whose Paid field contains a value that is less than 1200), and only the records for students whose trip is paid in full (those whose Paid field contains a value that is greater than or equal to 1200). Use the Select Case statement in your code. Always order the records by student ID. Display an appropriate error message in a message box if the user makes an incorrect entry. Include the OK button and the Information icon in the message box. The procedure also should ask the user if he or she wants to print the worksheet. Use the MsgBox function with Yes and No buttons and the Exclamation icon; make the No button the default button. Also have the procedure change the column headings in row 3 to ID, Last, First, and Paid.

    d. Save the workbook, then return to Excel and run the DisplayTripInfo macro. Display only the records for students who still owe money.

    e. Run the DisplayTripInfo macro again. This time, display only the records for students whose trip is paid in full.

    f. Run the DisplayTripInfo macro again. When prompted for which records you want to appear, type X and press the Enter key. An appropriate error message should appear. Click the OK button to close the message box.

    g. Save and then close the workbook.

4. In this exercise, you will modify the DisplayTripInfo procedure that you created in Exercise 3. The modified procedure will calculate the amount due and display it in column E in the worksheet.

    a. Open the T8-EX-E3D (T8-EX-E3D.xls) workbook that you created in Exercise 3. The file is located in the Tut08\Excel folder on your Data Disk. Click the Enable Macros button, if necessary, then save the workbook as T8-EX-E4D.

    b. Select the range A3:E6. Format the range to the Accounting 2 format, then click cell A1.

    c. Open the Visual Basic Editor. Open the Module1 module's Code window, then view the DisplayTripInfo procedure. Change the filename in the Set statement to "t8-ex-e4d.xls". Modify the procedure so that it displays the column heading "Balance Due" in cell E3. The procedure also should enter a formula in cell E4 that calculates a student's balance due; the total cost of the trip is $1200. Use the QueryTable object's FillAdjacentFormulas property to copy the formula to the remaining cells in column E of the query table.

    d. Save the workbook, then return to Excel and run the DisplayTripInfo macro. Display the records for all students who still owe money.

    e. Save and then close the workbook.

Exercises 5 and 6 are Discovery Exercises. Discovery Exercises, which may include topics that are not covered in the lesson, allow you to "discover" the solutions to problems on your own.

discovery ▶   **5.** In this exercise, you will modify the DisplaySales procedure that you created in this lesson. You will observe the effect of setting the Refresh method's BackgroundQuery argument to True.

    a. Open the Monthly Sales (Monthly Sales.xls) workbook that you created in this lesson. The file is located in the Tut08\Excel folder on your Data Disk. Click the Enable Macros button, if necessary, then save the workbook as T8-EX-E5D.

    b. Open the Visual Basic Editor. Open the Module1 module's Code window, then view the DisplaySales procedure. Change the filename in the Set statement to "t8-ex-e5d.xls".

    c. Save the workbook, then return to Excel and run the DisplaySales macro several times. Notice when the worksheet data changes and when the Print dialog box appears. (You do not need to print the worksheet.)

    d. Return to the DisplaySales procedure in the Visual Basic Editor. Change the BackgroundQuery argument in the Refresh method to True.

    e. Save the workbook, then return to Excel and run the DisplaySales macro several times. (You do not need to print the worksheet.) Here again, notice when the worksheet data changes and when the Print dialog box appears. What happens when you use True rather than False as the BackgroundQuery argument?

    f. Save and then close the workbook.

discovery ▶ **6.** In this exercise, you will modify the DisplaySales procedure that you created in this lesson. This time, you will use the If...Then...Else statement rather than the Select Case statement.

    a. Open the Monthly Sales (Monthly Sales.xls) workbook, which is located in the Tut08\Excel folder on your Data Disk. Click the Enable Macros button, if necessary, then save the workbook as T8-EX-E6D.

    b. Open the Visual Basic Editor. Open the Module1 module's Code window, then view the DisplaySales procedure. Change the filename in the Set statement to "t8-ex-e6d.xls".

    c. Display the If...Then...Else statement's Help screen. Read the Help screen, then click Example at the top of the Help screen. Study the examples, then close the Help window.

    d. Modify the DisplaySales procedure so that it uses the If...Then...Else statement rather than the Select Case statement. Be sure to use the ElseIf clause in your code.

    e. Save the workbook, then return to Excel and run the DisplaySales macro. Use the macro to display the Jackson store's sales.

    f. Save and then close the workbook.

A computer program is good only if it works. Errors in programming code can cause a program to run incorrectly. Therefore, a programmer needs to know how to locate and fix any errors in his or her code. Exercise 7 is a Debugging Exercise. Debugging Exercises allow you to practice recognizing and solving errors in code.

debugging **7.** In this exercise, you will debug an existing macro procedure.

    a. Open the T8-EX-E7 (T8-EX-E7.xls) workbook, which is located in the Tut08\Excel folder on your Data Disk. Click the Enable Macros button, if necessary, then save the workbook as T8-EX-E7D.

    b. Open the Visual Basic Editor. Open the Module1 module's Code window, then view the DisplayCost procedure. The procedure should display the code corresponding to the insurance plan in the Plan range, and it should display the cost of the insurance plan in the Cost range. The valid codes for the insurance plans are A, B, and C only. The cost of plans A and B is $35 and the cost of plan C is $50.

    c. Study the DisplayCost procedure's code, then return to Excel and run the DisplayCost macro.

    d. Return to the DisplayCost procedure in the Visual Basic Editor. What is wrong with the procedure? Correct any errors.

    e. When the macro is working correctly, save and then close the workbook.

Word Lesson

Using the Select Case Statement and the MsgBox Function in Word

case ▶ Nancy Manley is the secretary at Willowton Health Club. As such, she is responsible for mailing the club's newsletter, *Healthbeat*, to each member. She also is responsible for mailing monthly statements to those members who prefer to be billed for their membership fee rather than have their credit card charged automatically. Currently, Nancy addresses the mailing envelopes by hand—a very time-consuming and tedious job. She has decided to use the mail merge feature in Word to create labels for the envelopes. The mail merge feature can merge the member names and addresses, which are stored in a Microsoft Access database, with a Word document that specifies the type and size of the labels, as well as the information to include on each label. Nancy has decided to create a GenerateLabels macro to generate the labels required for each mailing.

Viewing the Data Source and the Main Document

The mail merge feature in Word allows you to merge a Word document, called the **main document**, with the data contained in a data source. The **data source** can be another Word document, an Access database, an Outlook contact list, an Excel worksheet, or some other source. In this lesson, the data source will be a Microsoft Access database named Members. The Members database contains one table, named MemberList. Figure 8-25 shows the structure of the MemberList table, and Figure 8-26 shows the records contained in the table.

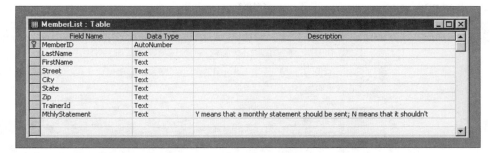

Figure 8-25: Structure of the MemberList table

Member	Last Name	First Name	Street	City	State	Zip	Trainer	Mthly Statement
1	Lin	Susan	111 Main Street	Glen Ellyn	IL	60137	101	Y
2	Poulos	Inez	75 Rose Street	Glen Ellyn	IL	60137		N
3	Lopez	Margaret	6803 Rice Road	Lombard	IL	60148	101	Y
4	Tunner	Jennifer	567 Jackson Street	Glen Ellyn	IL	60137		N
5	Nadkarni	Carol	2 N Harvey Road	Lombard	IL	60148	102	N
6	Lin	Jack	145 Main Street	Glen Ellyn	IL	60137	103	N
7	Lopez	Paul	22 Lambert Road	Glen Ellyn	IL	60137		Y
8	Chen	Linda	6819 Rice Road	Lombard	IL	60148	101	N
9	Jones	Harry	75 River Street	Lisle	IL	60532		Y
10	Williams	Penny	124 Able Lane	Lisle	IL	60532	102	N
11	Utes	Ingrid	345 Jackson Street	Glen Ellyn	IL	60137		Y
12	Avinez	Jose	120 Rose Street	Glen Ellyn	IL	60137	103	N
13	Baker	John	5819 Water Way	Lisle	IL	60532		N
14	Nunez	Carlos	6934 Paulette Road	Lombard	IL	60148	102	Y
15	Donner	August	45 S Jefferson Street	Lisle	IL	60532		N

Figure 8-26: Records contained in the MemberList table

Notice that the MemberList table contains nine fields and 15 records.

Before creating the procedure, open Nancy's main document, which is a Word document stored on your Data Disk. You will use this document to generate the Willowton Health Club labels.

To open the main document, and then view the code template for the GenerateLabels procedure:

1 Start Microsoft Word. Open the **T8-WD-1** (T8-WD-1.doc) document, which is located in the Tut08\Word folder on your Data Disk. Click the **Enable Macros** button, if necessary. The T8-WD-1 document opens in Word. This is not an ordinary Word document, but rather the main document created using the Mail Merge command in Word.

When you open a mail merge's main document, the data source attached to the document—in this case, an Access database named Members—also opens.

2 Click the **Microsoft Access** button that appears on the Windows taskbar. When the Microsoft Access window opens, notice that the Members database is open. Minimize the Microsoft Access window.

3 Save the T8-WD-1 document as **Main Labels**. Figure 8-27 shows the Main Labels document.

each label contains six merge fields

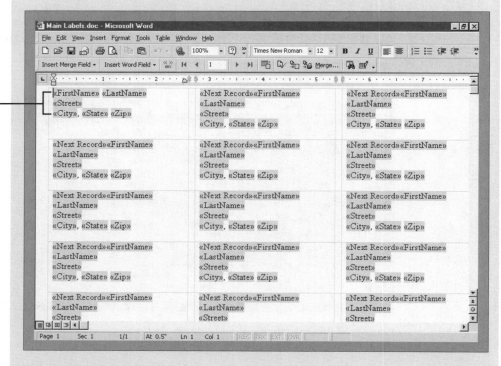

Figure 8-27: Main Labels document

HELP? If the word MERGEFIELD appears before each field name in the document, click Tools on the menu bar, and then click Options. Click the View tab, if necessary, and then click the Field codes check box to deselect it.

As Figure 8-27 indicates, each label in the main document contains six merge fields. A **merge field** is a placeholder that directs Word where to display specific information from the data source. In this case, for example, the merge fields tell Word to display the information stored in each member's FirstName, LastName, Street, City, State, and Zip fields in the Members database.

4 Press **Alt+F11** to open the Visual Basic Editor. If necessary, open the Project Explorer window and close the Properties window, the Immediate window, and any open Code windows. Open the **Module1** module's Code window, then view the code template for the **GenerateLabels** procedure.

5 Close the Project Explorer window so that you can view more of the Code window.

Before you can code the GenerateLabels procedure, you need to learn about Word's MailMerge object. You also need to learn how to use the SQL (Structured Query Language) SELECT command. You will use the SELECT command to select the records for which you want to create labels. First learn about the MailMerge object.

The MailMerge Object

Figure 8-28 shows the portion of the Word object model that includes the MailMerge object.

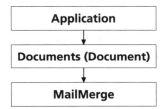

Figure 8-28: The MailMerge object shown in the Word object model

> Notice that the MailMerge object is not a member of a collection. In other words, there is no MailMerges collection. This is because a document can contain only one MailMerge object.

As you learned in Tutorial 2, the Word Application object contains the Documents collection along with the individual Document objects that make up the collection. Contained within each Document object is a MailMerge object that represents the mail merge feature in Word.

> As you learned in prior tutorials, the Document object also contains the Characters, Words, Sentences, Paragraphs, and TablesOfContents collections and their associated objects.

You use the MailMerge object's **Destination property** to control the destination of the merged documents—in other words, to specify where the merged documents are sent when the mail merge completes its task. Figure 8-29 shows the valid settings for the Destination property. Notice that you can send the merged documents to e-mail addresses, fax machines (designated by a fax number), a new document, or the printer.

Constant	Meaning
wdSendToEmail	Sends the merged documents to an e-mail address
wdSendToFax	Sends the merged documents to a fax number
wdSendToNewDocument	Sends the merged documents to a new document
wdSendToPrinter	Sends the merged documents to the printer

Figure 8-29: Valid settings for the MailMerge object's Destination property

To select the records to be merged with the main document, you use the syntax *mailMergeObject*.**DataSource.QueryString** = *query*, where *query* is a string that represents a valid SQL SELECT statement.

The SQL SELECT Statement

SQL, pronounced like the word "sequel," stands for **Structured Query Language**. **SQL** is a set of commands, or statements, that allows you to access and manipulate the data stored in many database management systems on computers of all sizes, from large mainframes to small microcomputers. You can use SQL commands to store, retrieve, update, and sequence data.

The most commonly used SQL command is the **SELECT statement**, which allows you to select which database fields and records you want to view, as well as control the order in which the fields and records appear when displayed. Figure 8-30 shows the basic syntax of the SELECT statement. It also shows seven examples of using the SELECT statement to select records for a mail merge.

Different applications handle the capitalization of SQL keywords in different ways. In this book, you will be entering all SQL keywords in uppercase letters.

The full syntax of the SELECT statement contains other clauses and options that are beyond the scope of this book.

In the syntax, *fieldsList* is one or more field names (separated by commas), and *table* is the name of the database table that contains the fields. The *query* `"SELECT FirstName, LastName FROM MemberList"` shown in Figure 8-30's first example will merge only the first and last names from the records stored in the MemberList table. Notice that the entire *query* is enclosed in quotation marks to indicate that it is a string.

If you want to select all of the fields in a table, you can enter an asterisk (*) rather than the field names in the *fieldsList* portion of the SELECT statement. The * tells the SELECT statement to display all of the table fields in the order in which the fields appear in the table. In other words, rather than using the *query*

Syntax of the SQL SELECT statement:
SELECT *fieldsList* **FROM** *table* [**WHERE** *condition*] [**ORDER BY** *field*]

Example 1:
```
mmgLabels.DataSource.QueryString = _
  "SELECT FirstName, LastName FROM MemberList"
```

Example 2:
```
mmgLabels.DataSource.QueryString = "SELECT * FROM MemberList"
```

Example 3:
```
mmgLabels.DataSource.QueryString = _
  "SELECT * FROM MemberList WHERE TrainerId = '101'"
```

Example 4:
```
mmgLabels.DataSource.QueryString = _
  "SELECT * FROM MemberList WHERE LastName = 'Chu' ORDER BY FirstName"
```

Example 5:
```
mmgLabels.DataSource.QueryString = _
  "SELECT * FROM MemberList WHERE LastName = '" & strLast & "'"
```

Example 6:
```
mmgLabels.DataSource.QueryString = _
  "SELECT * FROM Accounts WHERE Balance > " & curBal
```

Example 7:
```
mmgLabels.DataSource.QueryString = _
  "SELECT * FROM Accounts WHERE DueDate = #" & dtmDue & "#"
```

Figure 8-30: Basic syntax and examples of the SQL SELECT statement

"SELECT MemberId, LastName, FirstName, Street, City, State, Zip, TrainerId, MthlyStatement FROM MemberList", you could use the *query* "SELECT * FROM MemberList", as shown in Figure 8-30's second example. Although both *queries* will produce the same result, the latter *query* requires less typing.

The **WHERE** *condition* part of the Select statement's syntax is referred to as the **WHERE clause**, and it allows you to limit the records that will be included, in this case, in the mail merge. In Figure 8-30's third example, for instance, the WHERE clause indicates that only the records for trainer ID 101 should be merged with the main document. Notice that, when a *query* includes a string literal constant, you enclose the string literal constant in single quotation marks. Also notice that the WHERE clause is optional in the SELECT statement, as indicated by the square brackets ([]) in the syntax.

The **ORDER BY** *field* part of the syntax—referred to as the **ORDER BY clause**—allows you to control the order in which the records appear when displayed. The ORDER BY clause in Figure 8-30's fourth example orders (sorts) the selected records in ascending order by the FirstName field. Like the WHERE clause, the ORDER BY clause is optional in the SELECT statement.

> **tip**
>
> To display records in descending order, add the keyword DESC after *field* in the ORDER BY clause. For example, to display the table records in descending order by the TrainerId field, use ORDER BY TrainerId DESC. To display records in order by multiple fields, use a comma to separate each field from the next in the ORDER BY clause. For example, to display records in ascending order by the LastName and FirstName fields, use ORDER BY LastName, FirstName. This ORDER BY clause will sort the records in last name order. If more than one record has the same last name, those records will be sorted by the first name.

Examples 5, 6, and 7 in Figure 8-30 show how you can include a String variable, a numeric variable, and a Date variable, respectively, in a SELECT statement. Notice that you must use string concatenation, which you learned about in Tutorial 4, to do so.

After selecting the appropriate records to merge, you use the MailMerge object's **Execute method** to perform the mail merge. The syntax of the Execute method is *mailMergeObject*.**Execute**.

Now that you have learned about the MailMerge object and the SQL SELECT statement, you can begin coding the GenerateLabels procedure.

Coding the GenerateLabels Procedure

Figure 8-31 shows the pseudocode for the GenerateLabels procedure.

```
1. Use the InputBox function to ask the user which labels to generate (A for All or B for
   Billing). Store the user's response in a String variable named strWhichLabels.
2. Value stored in the strWhichLabels variable:
      = "A"      Assign to the QueryString property a SQL SELECT statement that
                 selects all of the fields and records in the MemberList table
      = "B"      Assign to the QueryString property a SQL SELECT statement that
                 selects all of the fields for only the records whose MthlyStatement field
                 contains the letter "Y"
      Other      Use the MsgBox statement to display an error message in a message
                 box, then exit the procedure
3. Use the MsgBox function to ask the user if he or she wants to print the labels. Assign
   the user's response to an Integer variable named intAnswer.
4. If intAnswer = vbYes, then
      a. Set the MailMerge object's Destination property to xlSendToPrinter
   Else
      a. Set the MailMerge object's Destination property to xlSendToNewDocument
5. Use the MailMerge object's Execute method to perform the mail merge.
```

Figure 8-31: Pseudocode for the GenerateLabels procedure

Figure 8-32 lists the variables that the GenerateLabels procedure will use.

Variables	datatype
strWhichLabels	String
intAnswer	Integer
mmgLabels	MailMerge

Figure 8-32: Variables used by the GenerateLabels procedure

In the next set of steps, you will declare the appropriate variables and then translate each line in Figure 8-31's pseudocode into one or more VBA statements.

To code the GenerateLabels procedure, then save the procedure:

1 In the GenerateLabels procedure, enter the documentation and the Dim and Set statements shown in Figure 8-33.

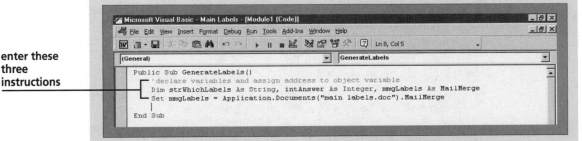

enter these
three
instructions

```
Public Sub GenerateLabels()
    'declare variables and assign address to object variable
    Dim strWhichLabels As String, intAnswer As Integer, mmgLabels As MailMerge
    Set mmgLabels = Application.Documents("main labels.doc").MailMerge

End Sub
```

Figure 8-33: Code window showing documentation and Dim and Set statements

You now can begin translating the pseudocode shown in Figure 8-31 into VBA statements. The first step is to use the InputBox function to ask the user which labels he or she wants to generate.

2 Type **'enter which labels to generate** and press the **Enter** key, then type **strwhichlabels = inputbox(prompt:="Which labels? (A for All, B for Billing)", _** (be sure to type the comma followed by a space and the underscore) and press the **Enter** key. Press the **Tab** key, then type **title:="Labels", default:="A")** and press the **Enter** key.

Next, use the Select Case statement to assign the appropriate SQL SELECT statement to the QueryString property.

3 Press the **Backspace** key to remove the indentation, then type **'select appropriate records** and press the **Enter** key.

If the user enters the letter "A", you need to select all of the fields and records in the MemberList table.

4 Type **select case ucase(strwhichlabels)** and press the **Enter** key. Press the **Tab** key, then type **case "A"** and press the **Enter** key. Press the **Tab** key, then type **mmglabels.datasource.querystring = "SELECT * FROM memberlist"** and press the **Enter** key.

 tip

> It is a common programming practice to indent each Case clause within the Select Case statement. Programmers also indent the instructions contained within each Case clause.

If the user enters the letter "B", you need to select all of the fields in the MemberList table, but only for the members who are sent a monthly statement.

5 Press the **Backspace** key, then type **case "B"** and press the **Enter** key. Press the **Tab** key, then type **mmglabels.datasource.querystring = _** (be sure to type the equal sign followed by a space and the underscore) and press the **Enter** key. Press the **Tab** key, then type **"SELECT * FROM memberlist WHERE mthlystatement = 'Y'"** and press the **Enter** key. Be sure to type single quotation marks around the string literal constant Y in the statement, and type double quotation marks around the entire SELECT statement.

Recall that the procedure should display an error message if the user enters a value other than "A" or "B".

6 Press the **Backspace** key twice, then type **case else** and press the **Enter** key. Press the **Tab** key, then type **msgbox prompt:="Invalid entry", buttons:=vbokonly + vbinformation, title:="Error"** and press the **Enter** key.

According to Step 2 in the pseudocode, if the user enters an invalid label type, you should exit the GenerateLabels procedure. You can do so using VBA's **Exit Sub statement**, which tells VBA to exit the sub procedure immediately.

7 Type **exit sub** and press the **Enter** key. Press the **Backspace** key twice and type **end select** to end the Select Case statement. Press the **Enter** key.

Now use the MsgBox function to display a message box that asks the user if he or she wants to print the labels. Display Yes and No buttons and the Warning Message icon in the message box, and make the No button the default button. Assign the function's return value to the intAnswer variable.

8 Type **'ask if user wants to print the labels** and press the **Enter** key. Type **intanswer = msgbox(prompt:="Do you want to print the labels?", _** (be sure to type the comma followed by a space and the underscore) and press the **Enter** key. Press the **Tab** key, then type **buttons:=vbyesno + vbexclamation + vbdefaultbutton2, title:="Print Labels")** and press the **Enter** key.

If the user clicks the Yes button in the message box, send the labels to the printer; otherwise, send them to a new document. Then use the Execute method to perform the mail merge.

9 Type the additional instructions shown in Figure 8-34, which shows the completed GenerateLabels procedure.

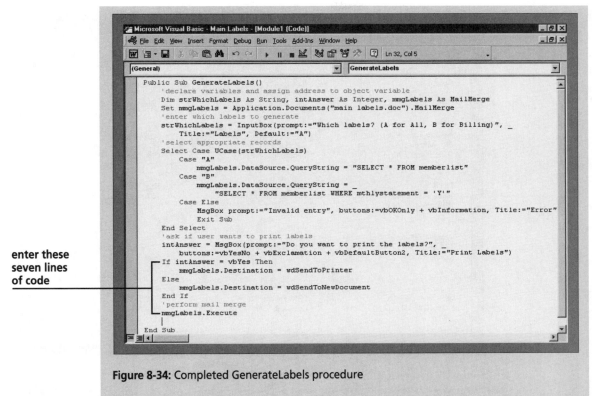

enter these
seven lines
of code

Figure 8-34: Completed GenerateLabels procedure

10 Verify the accuracy of your code by comparing the code on your screen to the code shown in Figure 8-34, then save the document.

Now that you have translated the pseudocode into VBA statements, you should test the GenerateLabels macro to verify that it is working correctly.

To test the GenerateLabels macro:

1 Return to Word, then run the **GenerateLabels** macro.

2 When the Labels dialog box appears and asks you "Which labels?", click the **OK** button to accept the default label choice, A. When you are asked if you want to print the labels, click the **No** button. The labels for all of the members appear in a new document, as shown in Figure 8-35. Notice that Word gives the document a default name—in this case, Labels1.

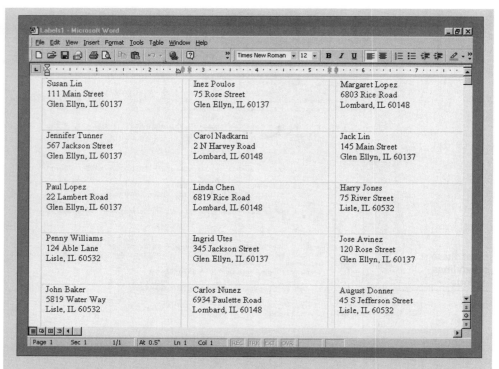

Figure 8-35: New document showing labels for all members

3 Close the Labels1 document without saving it.

4 Run the **GenerateLabels** macro again. When the "Which labels?" prompt appears, type **b** and press the **Enter** key. When you are asked if you want to print the labels, click the **Yes** button, then click the **OK** button. The procedure prints the labels for the six members who are sent monthly statements.

HELP? If your computer is not connected to a printer, click the No button, then close the Labels2 document without saving it.

5 Run the **GenerateLabels** macro again. When the "Which labels?" prompt appears, type **x** and press the **Enter** key. "Invalid entry" appears in a message box. Click the **OK** button to close the message box.

6 Save the Main Labels document, then exit Word.

You now have completed Tutorial 8's Word lesson. You can either take a break or complete the end-of-lesson exercises before moving on to the next lesson.

EXERCISES

1. In this exercise, you will modify the GenerateLabels procedure that you created in this lesson.
    a. Open the Main Labels (Main Labels.doc) document, which is located in the Tut08\Word folder on your Data Disk. Click the Enable Macros button, if necessary, then save the document as T8-WD-E1D.
    b. Open the Visual Basic Editor. Open the Module1 module's Code window, then view the GenerateLabels procedure's code. Change the filename in the Set statement to "t8-wd-e1d.doc". Modify the code so that it prompts the user to enter A for All, B for Billing, and T for Trainer. If the user enters the letter T, prompt the user for the trainer's ID, then display only the labels for that trainer's clients. (*Hint*: Be sure to study the examples shown in Figure 8-30 in this lesson.)
    c. Save the document. Return to Word, then run the GenerateLabels macro. Display the labels for trainer 102's clients. Save the document that contains the labels as T8-WD-E1DLabels, then close the document. Also save and then close the T8-WD-E1D document.

2. In this exercise, you will create a procedure that performs a mail merge.
    a. Open the T8-WD-E2 (T8-WD-E2.doc) document, which is located in the Tut08\Word folder on your Data Disk. Click the Enable Macros button, if necessary, then save the document as T8-WD-E2D. The document was created as a main document for a mail merge. The data source is the MemberList table in the Members.mdb database.
    b. Open the Visual Basic Editor. Open the Module1 module's Code window, then view the code template for the CreditCardLetter procedure. The procedure should generate a form letter for each member whose monthly fee is charged automatically to his or her credit card. Recall that the MthlyStatement field in the MemberList table indicates whether the monthly fee is billed (Y) or charged to a credit card (N). Code the procedure appropriately. The procedure should allow the user either to print the form letters or send them to a new document.
    c. Save the document. Return to Word, then run the CreditCardLetter macro. Send the results to a new document. Save the document containing the form letters as T8-WD-E2DLetters, then close the document. Also save and then close the T8-WD-E2D document.

3. In this exercise, you will create a macro procedure that performs a mail merge.
    a. Open the T8-WD-E3 (T8-WD-E3.doc) document, which is located in the Tut08\Word folder on your Data Disk. Click the Enable Macros button, if necessary, then save the document as T8-WD-E3D. The document was created as a main document. The data source is the Payments table in the Trip database.
    b. View the Trip database and Payments table in Access. Close the table, then minimize the Access window.
    c. Open the Visual Basic Editor. Open the Module1 module's Code window, then view the code template for the StudentLetter procedure. Code the procedure so that it allows the user to choose one of the following three options (use the Select Case statement):
    1) Generate a form letter for each student
    2) Generate a form letter only for students who have paid less than $1200
    3) Generate a form letter only for students who have paid $1200 or more

Allow the user to send the merged documents to either the printer or a new document.

d. Save the document. Return to Word, then run the StudentLetter macro. Generate a form letter only for students who have paid less than $1200. Send the form letters to a new document. Save the new document as T8-WD-E3DLetters, then close the document. Also save and then close the T8-WD-E3D document.

Exercise 4 is a Discovery Exercise. Discovery Exercises, which may include topics that are not covered in the lesson, allow you to "discover" the solutions to problems on your own.

discovery ▶ **4.** In this exercise, you will modify the GenerateLabels procedure that you completed in this lesson's Exercise 1. This time, you will use the If...Then...Else statement rather than the Select Case statement.

a. Open the T8-WD-E1D (T8-WD-E1D.doc) document, which is located in the Tut08\Word folder on your Data Disk. Click the Enable Macros button, if necessary, then save the document as T8-WD-E4D.

b. Open the Visual Basic Editor. Open the Module1 module's Code window, then view the GenerateLabels procedure. Change the filename in the Set statement to "t8-wd-e4d.doc".

c. Display the If...Then...Else statement's Help screen. Read the Help screen, then click Example at the top of the Help screen. Study the examples, then close the Help window.

d. Modify the GenerateLabels code so that it uses the If...Then...Else statement rather than the Select Case statement. Be sure to use the ElseIf clause in your code.

e. Save the document. Return to Word, then run the GenerateLabels macro. Test the macro appropriately. When you are sure the macro is working correctly, display only trainer 101's client labels in a new document. Save the new document as T8-WD-E4DLabels, then close the document. Also save and then close the T8-WD-E4D document.

A computer program is good only if it works. Errors in programming code can cause a program to run incorrectly. Therefore, a programmer needs to know how to locate and fix any errors in his or her code. Exercise 5 is a Debugging Exercise. Debugging Exercises allow you to practice recognizing and solving errors in code.

debugging **5.** In this exercise, you will debug an existing macro procedure.

a. Open the T8-WD-E5 (T8-WD-E5.doc) document, which is located in the Tut08\Word folder on your Data Disk. Click the Enable Macros button, if necessary, then save the document as T8-WD-E5D. Display the nonprinting characters in the document.

b. Open the Visual Basic Editor. Open the Module1 module's Code window, then view the AddToc procedure's code. Study the code, then return to Word and run the AddToc macro. When you are prompted for the format type, press the Enter key to accept the *defaultValue*, C. The "Invalid format type" message appears in a message box. Click the OK button to close the message box, then click the Undo button 🔄.

c. Return to the Visual Basic Editor and correct any errors in the AddToc procedure. When the procedure is working correctly, save and then close the document.

Access Lesson

Using the Select Case Statement and the MsgBox Function in Access

case ▶ In Tutorials 6 and 7, you created and then modified a procedure named PaymentUpdate for Professor Martinez of Snowville College. Recall that the procedure allowed Professor Martinez to record the payments made by the students registered for the Spanish Club's trip to Spain. The total cost of the trip is $1200, and $200 is due within one week of registering. Additional payments then are due periodically until the entire $1200 is paid.

Professor Martinez has decided to create an additional procedure that will give him the following three display options for the database's PayReport report:

1. Display all of the students
2. Display only students who still owe money
3. Display only students whose trip is paid in full

Creating the DisplayReport Procedure

Professor Martinez's database is stored on your Data Disk. Begin by opening the database and viewing the Payments table.

To open the Trip database and view the Payments table:

1   Start Microsoft Access. Open the **Trip** (Trip.mdb) database, which is located in the Tut08\Access folder on your Data Disk. Click the **Maximize** button ☐ on the Microsoft Access title bar to maximize the Microsoft Access window, if necessary.

The database contains one table named Payments and one report named PayReport. The Payments table contains five fields: ID, LastName, FirstName, Paid, and Updated. The ID, LastName, and FirstName fields are Text fields. The Paid field, which stores the total amount paid by each student, is a Currency field. The Updated field, which stores the date the student's information was last updated, is a Date/Time field.

View the records contained in the Payments table.

2   Click **Tables** in the Objects bar of the Database window, if necessary. Right-click **Payments** in the Database window and then click **Open**. See Figure 8-36.

ID	Last Name	First Name	Paid	Updated
AS1	Smith	Adele	$900.00	3/2/02
GG1	Gorski	George	$750.00	2/4/02
JA1	Agar	John	$1,200.00	5/11/02
JS1	Smith	Jerry	$340.00	3/2/02
KP1	Patel	Khalid	$1,000.00	3/12/02
LT1	Tradski	Lori	$200.00	1/4/02
NG1	Gorski	Nancy	$200.00	1/4/02
PH1	Handel	Paul	$600.00	2/22/02
SH1	Hammer	Sue	$500.00	3/22/02
SP1	Patel	Sudha	$1,200.00	5/1/02
SP2	Philips	Sonia	$1,200.00	4/15/02
*			$0.00	

Figure 8-36: Records contained in the Payments table

Notice that some of the students still owe money, while others are paid in full. (Recall that the total cost of the trip is $1200.)

3   Close the Payments table.

Now open the Visual Basic Editor.

4   Press **Alt+F11** to open the Visual Basic Editor. If necessary, open the Project Explorer window and close the Properties window, the Immediate window, and any open Code windows. Open the Module1 module's Code window, then view the code template for the **DisplayReport** function procedure.

5   Close the Project Explorer window so that you can view more of the Code window.

Figure 8-37 shows the pseudocode for the DisplayReport procedure.

1. Use the InputBox function to ask the user which records to include in the report (A for All, O for Owes money, and P for Paid in full). Store the user's response in a String variable named strWhichRecords.
2. Value contained in strWhichRecords variable
   ="A"   Assign to the strSelect variable a SQL SELECT statment that selects all of the fields and records in the Payments table
   ="O"   Assign to the strSelect variable a SQL SELECT statment that selects all of the fields for only the records whose Paid field contains a value that is less than 1200
   ="P"   Assign to the strSelect variable a SQL SELECT statement that selects all of the fields for only the records whose Paid field contains a value that is greater than or equal to 1200
   Other Use the MsgBox statement to display an error message, then exit the procedure
3. Use the MsgBox function to ask the user if he or she wants to print the report. Assign the user's response to an Integer variable named intAnswer.
4. If intAnswer = vbYes, then
   a. Open and then print the report. Use the value stored in the strSelect variable to select the appropriate records to print.
   Else
   a. Open and then display the report in print preview. Use the value stored in the strSelect variable to select the appropriate records to display.

Figure 8-37: Pseudocode for the DisplayReport procedure

Figure 8-38 lists the variables that the DisplayReport procedure will use.

Variables	datatype
strWhichRecords	String
strSelect	String
intAnswer	Integer

Figure 8-38: Variables used by the DisplayReport procedure

In the next set of steps, you will declare the appropriate variables and then begin translating the pseudocode shown in Figure 8-37 into VBA statements.

To begin coding the DisplayReport procedure:

1 The insertion point should be positioned between the `Public Function` and `End Function` lines in the Code window. Press the **Tab** key, then type **'declare variables** and press the **Enter** key. Type **dim strWhichRecords as string, strSelect as string, intAnswer as integer** and press the **Enter** key.

> Step 1 in the pseudocode is to ask the user which student records he or she wants to include in the report. Use the letter "A" as the InputBox function's *defaultValue*.
>
> **2** Type **'enter which records to include in report** and press the **Enter** key. Type **strwhichrecords = inputbox(prompt:="Enter A(ll), O(we), P(aid)", _** (be sure to type the comma followed by a space and the underscore) and press the **Enter** key. Press the **Tab** key, then type **title:="Which Records", default:="A")** and press the **Enter** key.
>
> Now use the Select Case statement to select the appropriate records based on the value entered in the strWhichRecords variable.
>
> **3** Press the **Backspace** key, then type **'select appropriate records** and press the **Enter** key. Type **select case ucase(strwhichrecords)** and press the **Enter** key.

According to the pseudocode, if the user enters the letter "A", the procedure needs to assign to the strSelect variable a SQL SELECT statement that selects all of the fields and records contained in the Payments table. Before you can code this step, you need to learn how to use the SQL SELECT statement to select records.

The SQL SELECT Statement

SQL, pronounced like the word "sequel," stands for **Structured Query Language**. **SQL** is a set of commands, or statements, that allow you to access and manipulate the data stored in many database management systems on computers of all sizes, from large mainframes to small microcomputers. You can use SQL commands to store, retrieve, update, and sequence data.

The most commonly used SQL command is the **SELECT statement**, which allows you to select the database fields and records that you want to view, as well as control the order in which the fields and records appear when displayed. Figure 8-39 shows the basic syntax of the SELECT statement. It also shows seven examples of using the SELECT statement to select records.

Different applications handle the capitalization of SQL keywords in different ways. In this book, you will be entering all SQL keywords in uppercase letters.

The full syntax of the SELECT statement contains other clauses and options that are beyond the scope of this book.

Syntax of the SQL SELECT statement:
SELECT *fieldsList* **FROM** *table* **[WHERE** *condition*] **[ORDER BY** *field*]

Example 1:
```
strSelect = "SELECT FirstName, LastName FROM Payments"
```

Example 2:
```
strSelect = "SELECT * FROM Payments"
```

Example 3:
```
strSelect = "SELECT * FROM Payments WHERE LastName = 'Smith'"
```

Example 4:
```
strSelect = "SELECT * FROM Payments WHERE LastName = 'Smith'
ORDER BY FirstName"
```

Example 5:
```
strSelect = "SELECT * FROM Payments WHERE LastName = '" &
strLast & "'"
```

Example 6:
```
strSelect = "SELECT * FROM Payments WHERE Paid = " & curPaid
```

Example 7:
```
strSelect = "SELECT * FROM Payments WHERE Updated > #" &
dtmPaid & "#"
```

Figure 8-39: Basic syntax and examples of the SQL SELECT statement

In the syntax, *fieldsList* is one or more field names (separated by commas), and *table* is the name of the database table that contains the fields. The statement `"SELECT FirstName, LastName FROM Payments"` shown in Figure 8-39's first example will select only the first and last names from the records stored in the Payments table. Notice that, when assigning a SELECT statement to a String variable, you enclose the entire SELECT statement in quotation marks to indicate that it is a string.

If you want to select all of the fields in a table, you can enter an asterisk (*) rather than the field names in the *fieldsList* portion of the SELECT statement. The * tells the SELECT statement to display all of the table fields in the order in which the fields appear in the table. In other words, rather than using the statement `"SELECT ID, LastName, FirstName, Paid, Updated FROM Payments"`, you could use the statement `"SELECT * FROM Payments"`, as shown in Figure 8-39's second example. Although both statements will produce the same result, the latter statement requires less typing.

The **WHERE** *condition* part of the Select statement's syntax is referred to as the **WHERE clause**, and it allows you to limit the records that will be included, in this case, in the report. In Figure 8-39's third example, for instance, the WHERE clause indicates that only the records for students having a last name of Smith should be included in the report. Notice that, when the SELECT statement includes a string literal constant, you enclose the string literal constant in single quotation marks. Also notice that the WHERE clause is optional in the SELECT statement, as indicated by the square brackets ([]) in the syntax.

The **ORDER BY** *field* part of the syntax—referred to as the **ORDER BY clause**—allows you to control the order in which the records appear when displayed or printed. The ORDER BY clause in Figure 8-39's fourth example orders (sorts) the selected records in ascending order by the FirstName field. Like the WHERE clause, the ORDER BY clause is optional in the SELECT statement.

> **tip**
>
> To display records in descending order, add the keyword DESC after *field* in the ORDER BY clause. For example, to display the table records in descending order by the Paid field, use `ORDER BY Paid DESC`. **To display records in order by multiple fields, use a comma to separate each field from the next in the ORDER BY clause. For example, to display records in ascending order by the LastName and FirstName fields, use `ORDER BY LastName, FirstName`. This ORDER BY clause will sort the records in last name order. If more than one record has the same last name, those records will be sorted by the first name.**

Examples 5, 6, and 7 in Figure 8-39 show how you can include a String variable, a numeric variable, and a Date variable, respectively, in a SELECT statement. Notice that you must use string concatenation, which you learned about in Tutorial 4, to do so.

To complete the DisplayReport procedure, then test the procedure:

1 Press the **Tab** key, then type **case "A"** and press the **Enter** key. Press the **Tab** key, then type **strselect = "SELECT * FROM payments"** and press the **Enter** key. This SELECT statement will select all of the fields and records contained in the Payments table.

> **tip**
>
> It is a common programming practice to indent each Case clause within the Select Case statement. Programmers also indent the instructions contained within each Case clause.

According to the pseudocode, if the user enters the letter "O", the procedure should select all of the fields for only the records whose Paid field contains a value that is less than 1200.

2 Press the **Backspace** key, then type **case "O"** and press the **Enter** key. Press the **Tab** key, then type **strselect = "SELECT * FROM payments WHERE paid < 1200"** and press the **Enter** key.

If the user enters the letter P, the procedure should select all of the fields for only the records whose Paid field contains a value that is greater than or equal to 1200.

3   Press the **Backspace** key, then type **case "P"** and press the **Enter** key. Press the **Tab** key, then type **strselect = "SELECT * FROM payments WHERE paid >= 1200"** and press the **Enter** key.

If the user enters a character other than A, O, or P, the procedure should display an error message and then exit the function procedure. You can use VBA's **Exit Function statement** to exit the function procedure immediately.

4   Press the **Backspace** key, then type the additional instructions shown in Figure 8-40. Also position the insertion point as shown in the figure.

enter these four lines of code

position insertion point here

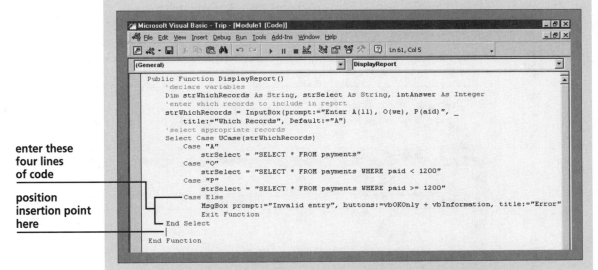

```
Microsoft Visual Basic - Trip - [Module1 (Code)]
File  Edit  View  Insert  Debug  Run  Tools  Add-Ins  Window  Help
                                                        Ln 61, Col 5
(General)                                    DisplayReport

Public Function DisplayReport()
    'declare variables
    Dim strWhichRecords As String, strSelect As String, intAnswer As Integer
    'enter which records to include in report
    strWhichRecords = InputBox(prompt:="Enter A(ll), O(we), P(aid)", _
        title:="Which Records", Default:="A")
    'select appropriate records
    Select Case UCase(strWhichRecords)
        Case "A"
            strSelect = "SELECT * FROM payments"
        Case "O"
            strSelect = "SELECT * FROM payments WHERE paid < 1200"
        Case "P"
            strSelect = "SELECT * FROM payments WHERE paid >= 1200"
        Case Else
            MsgBox prompt:="Invalid entry", buttons:=vbOKOnly + vbInformation, title:="Error"
            Exit Function
    End Select

End Function
```

Figure 8-40: Partially completed DisplayReport procedure

Next, use the MsgBox function to ask the user if he or she wants to print the report. Display Yes and No buttons and the Warning Message icon in the message box, and make the No button the default button. Assign the MsgBox function's return value to the intAnswer variable.

5   Type **'ask if user wants to print report** and press the **Enter** key. Type **intanswer = msgbox(prompt:="Print report?",** _ (be sure to type the comma followed by a space and the underscore) and press the **Enter** key. Press the **Tab** key, then type **buttons:=vbyesno + vbexclamation + vbdefaultbutton2, title:="Print")** and press the **Enter** key.

According to Step 4 in the pseudocode, if the user clicks the Yes button, the procedure should open and then print the PayReport report; otherwise, it should open the report in Print Preview. In either case, the procedure should use the value stored in the strSelect variable to select the appropriate records to print or display.

In Tutorial 3, you learned how to open a report using the syntax **DoCmd.OpenReport Reportname:=** *reportName,* **View:=***viewName*. Recall that *reportName* is the name of the report you want to open and *viewName* is the name of a view—either acViewDesign, acViewNormal, or acViewPreview. In addition to the Reportname and View arguments, the OpenReport method also has an argument named Filtername, which allows you to select the records to include in the report. The Filtername argument must be a string that represents either a SQL SELECT statement or the name of an existing query. In the DisplayReport procedure, you will use the String variable strSelect as the Filtername argument. Recall that the strSelect variable contains a SELECT statement that indicates which student records to include in the PayReport report.

You will learn how to include a query in the OpenReport method's Filtername argument in this lesson's Exercise 1.

6 Press the **Backspace** key, then type the additional instructions shown in Figure 8-41, which shows the completed DisplayReport procedure.

```
Microsoft Visual Basic - Trip - [Module1 (Code)]
File  Edit  View  Insert  Debug  Run  Tools  Add-Ins  Window  Help
                                                          Ln 69, Col 5
(General)                                    DisplayReport

Public Function DisplayReport()
    'declare variables
    Dim strWhichRecords As String, strSelect As String, intAnswer As Integer
    'enter which records to include in report
    strWhichRecords = InputBox(prompt:="Enter A(ll), O(we), P(aid)", _
        title:="Which Records", Default:="A")
    'select appropriate records
    Select Case UCase(strWhichRecords)
        Case "A"
            strSelect = "SELECT * FROM payments"
        Case "O"
            strSelect = "SELECT * FROM payments WHERE paid < 1200"
        Case "P"
            strSelect = "SELECT * FROM payments WHERE paid >= 1200"
        Case Else
            MsgBox prompt:="Invalid entry", buttons:=vbOKOnly + vbInformation, title:="Error"
            Exit Function
    End Select
    'ask if user wants to print report
    intAnswer = MsgBox(prompt:="Print report?", _
        buttons:=vbYesNo + vbExclamation + vbDefaultButton2, title:="Print")
    If intAnswer = vbYes Then
        DoCmd.OpenReport reportname:="payreport", view:=acViewNormal, filtername:=strSelect
    Else
        DoCmd.OpenReport reportname:="payreport", view:=acViewPreview, filtername:=strSelect
    End If

End Function
```

enter these five lines of code

Figure 8-41: Completed DisplayReport procedure

7 Verify the accuracy of your code by comparing the code on your screen to the code shown in Figure 8-41, then save the database.

8 Return to Access, then run the **DisplayReportMacro** macro. When the Which Records dialog box appears and prompts you to enter A, O, or P, type **p** and press the **Enter** key. When the message box asks if you want to print the report, click the **No** button. The report shows that three students have paid in full.

9 Close the report. Run the **DisplayReportMacro** macro again. When the Which Records dialog box appears, type **o** and press the **Enter** key. When the message box asks if you want to print the report, click the **Yes** button. The report lists the eight students who still owe money.

HELP? If your computer is not connected to a printer, click the No button, then close the report.

10 Run the **DisplayReportMacro** macro again. When the Which Records dialog box appears, type **x** and press the **Enter** key. "Invalid entry" appears in a message box. Click the **OK** button to close the message box.

11 Compact the database, then exit Access.

You now have completed Tutorial 8's Access lesson. You can either take a break or complete the end-of-lesson exercises.

E X E R C I S E S

1. In this exercise, you will modify the DisplayReport procedure that you created in this lesson.
   a. Use Windows to make a copy of the Trip (Trip.mdb) database, which is located in the Tut08\Access folder on your Data Disk. Rename the copy T8-AC-E1D.mdb.
   b. Open the T8-AC-E1D (T8-AC-E1D.mdb) database. Create three queries. The first query should select all of the fields and records in the Payment table; name the query AllQry. The second query should select all of the fields for only the records whose Paid field contains a value that is less than 1200; name the query OweMoneyQry. The third query should select all of the fields for only the records whose Paid field contains a value that is greater than or equal to 1200; name the query PaidInFullQry.
   c. Open the Visual Basic Editor. Open the Module1 module's Code window, then view the DisplayReport procedure. Modify the Select Case statement so that it assigns the name of the appropriate query to the strSelect variable.
   d. Save the database, then return to Access and run the DisplayReportMacro macro. Use the macro to view the records for students who still owe money.
   e. Close the report, then compact and close the database.

2. In this exercise, you will create a procedure that updates records.
   a. Open the T8-AC-E2D (T8-AC-E2D.mdb) database, which is located in the Tut08\Access folder on your Data Disk, then open the Products table in Design View. The table contains two fields: a Text field named ProductID and a Number field named UnitsInStock. Close the Design View window. Open the Products table and view the existing records, then close the table.

b. Open the Visual Basic Editor. Open the Module1 module's Code window, then view the code template for the CheckInv procedure. Code the procedure so that it prompts the user to enter the product ID and the number of units the customer ordered.

If the number of units in stock is greater than the number ordered, subtract the number ordered from the number of units in stock, then display the message "Entire order shipped" in a message box.

If, on the other hand, the number of units in stock is less than the number ordered, display the word "Only" followed by the number of units that can be shipped, followed by the words "units shipped". (For example, if the number of units in stock is 100 and the customer ordered 150, then display the message "Only 100 units shipped".) Also assign the number 0 to the record's UnitsInStock field.

If the number of units in stock is equal to the number of units ordered, then assign the number 0 to record's UnitsInStock field, and display the message "Entire order shipped - Time to reorder." Use the Select Case statement to compare the number of units in stock to the number of units ordered.

c. Save the database, then return to Access and run the CheckInvMacro macro three times, using the following data:

ID	Amount ordered	
AB345	400	("Entire order shipped" should be displayed.)
TR457	100	("Only 50 units shipped" should be displayed.)
YY756	300	("Entire order shipped – Time to reorder." should be displayed.)

d. When the macro is working correctly, compact and then close the database.

3. In this exercise, you will create a procedure that updates records.

a. Open the T8-AC-E3D (T8-AC-E3D.mdb) database, which is located in the Tut08\Access folder on your Data Disk, then open the Products table in Design View. The table contains four fields: a Text field named ProductID, a Number field named UnitsInStock, a Number field named ReorderAmt, and a Text field named Reorder. Close the Design View window. Open the Products table and view the existing records, then close the table.

b. Open the Visual Basic Editor. Open the Module1 module's Code window, then view the code template for the RecordSales procedure. Code the procedure so that it prompts the user to enter the product ID and the number of units ordered. Subtract the number of units ordered from the number of units in stock. (For this exercise, you can assume that the number of units ordered always will be less than or equal to the number of units in stock.) If the number of units in stock is less than or equal to the reorder amount, assign the letter "Y" to the Reorder field; otherwise, assign the letter "N". Use the Select Case statement to assign the appropriate letter to the Reorder field.

c. Save the database, then return to Access and run the RecordSalesMacro macro five times using the following information:

ID	Amount ordered
KLM2	100
ABX3	50
CDC4	200
XPQ4	25
CBA3	50

d. Open the Products table and verify that "Y" appears in the Reorder field for any Product ID whose UnitsInStock field contains a value that is less than or equal to the value in its ReorderAmt field.

e. When the macro is working correctly, compact and then close the database.

4. In this exercise, you will create a procedure that displays a report based on the date entered by the user.

a. Open the T8-AC-E4D (T8-AC-E4D.mdb) database, which is located in the Tut08\Access folder on your Data Disk, then open the Shipping table. The table contains a Text field named Item and a Date/Time field named ShipDate. Close the table.

b. Open the Visual Basic Editor. Open the Module1 module's Code window, then view the code template for the DisplayReport procedure. Code the procedure so that it prompts the user to enter a date. Use the system date as the *defaultValue* in the InputBox function. Use the SELECT statement to select the records that match the date entered by the user. Have the procedure open the ShipReport report in Print Preview, using the SELECT statement to select the appropriate records to display.

c. Save the database, then return to Access and run the DisplayReportMacro macro two times, using 4/30/02 and 8/2/02 as the date.

d. When the macro is working correctly, compact and then close the database.

Exercises 5 and 6 are Discovery Exercises. Discovery Exercises, which may include topics that are not covered in the lesson, allow you to "discover" the solutions to problems on your own.

discovery ▶ 5. In this exercise, you will modify the DisplayReport procedure that you completed in this lesson. This time, you will use the If…Then…Else statement rather than the Select Case statement.

a. Use Windows to make a copy of the Trip (Trip.mdb) database, which is located in the Tut08\Access folder on your Data Disk. Rename the copy T8-AC-E5.mdb.

b. Open the T8-AC-E5D (T8-AC-E5D.mdb) database. Open the Visual Basic Editor and view the DisplayReport procedure, which is contained in the Module1 module.

c. Display the If…Then…Else statement's Help screen. Read the Help screen, then click Example at the top of the Help screen. Study the examples, then close the Help window.

d. Modify the DisplayReport code so that it uses the If…Then…Else statement rather than the Select Case statement. Be sure to use the ElseIf clause in your code.

e. Save the database, then return to Access and run the DisplayReportMacro macro. Test the macro appropriately. When the macro is working correctly, compact and then close the database.

discovery ▶ 6. In this exercise, you will create a procedure that compares the value stored in a Date field.

a. Open the T8-AC-E6D (T8-AC-E6D.mdb) database, which is located in the Tut08\Access folder on your Data Disk.

b. Open the Shipping table. The table contains a Text field named Item and a Date field named ShipDate. Close the table.

c. Open the Visual Basic Editor. Open the Module1 module's Code window, then view the code template for the VerifyDate procedure. Code the procedure so that it prompts the user to enter the item number and the date the customer requires the item. (Use the system date as the *defaultValue* in the InputBox function that gets the date.) Search for the item number in the Item field. If the shipping date is later than the required date, display the message "Item won't be available"; otherwise, display the message "Item will be available". Use the Select Case statement.

d. Save the database, then return to Access. Run the VerifyDateMacro three times, using the following information:

Item	Required date
A	5/1/02 ("Item will be available" should be displayed.)
B	6/4/02 ("Item will be available" should be displayed.)
C	7/20/02 ("Item won't be available" should be displayed.)

e. When the macro is working correctly, compact and then close the database.

A computer program is good only if it works. Errors in programming code can cause a program to run incorrectly. Therefore, a programmer needs to know how to locate and fix any errors in his or her code. Exercise 7 is a Debugging Exercise. Debugging Exercises allow you to practice recognizing and solving errors in code.

debugging 7. In this exercise, you will debug an existing procedure.

a. Open the T8-AC-E7D (T8-AC-E7D.mdb) database, which is located in the Tut08\Access folder on your Data Disk.

b. Open the Code table. The table contains two Text fields named EmpCode and JobTitle. Close the table.

c. Open the Visual Basic Editor. Open the Module1 module's Code window, then view the DisplayTitle procedure. The procedure should prompt the user to enter the employee code. It then should display the appropriate records in the CodeReport report.

d. Study the code, then return to Access. Run the DisplayTitleMacro macro three times, using the codes a, 1, and 5. Correct the error(s) in the procedure, then save the database and run the macro again using the codes a, 1, and 5.

e. When the macro is working correctly, compact and then close the database.

The Repetition Structure and the With Statement

Concept Lesson

The Repetition Structure

In the first six tutorials, you used the sequence programming structure, in which each of the procedure's instructions was processed, one after another, in the order in which each appeared in the Code window. In Tutorials 7 and 8, you learned about the selection structure, which you use when you want a procedure to make a decision or comparison and then, based on the result of that decision or comparison, select one of two paths. In this tutorial, as well as in Tutorial 10, you will learn about the third programming structure, repetition.

Like the sequence and selection structures, you already are familiar with the repetition structure. You use it nearly every day. Figure 9-1 shows examples of repetition structures that you may have encountered today. Example 1's instructions are similar to those found on a shampoo bottle. Example 2's instructions, which indicate how to make a glass of chocolate milk, are similar to those found on a can of chocolate syrup.

Example 1	Example 2

Repeat two times:
    apply shampoo to wet hair
    lather
    rinse
	Pour 8 ounces of milk into a glass
	Pour 2 teaspoons of chocolate syrup into
	    the glass
	Repeat the following until milk and syrup are
	mixed thoroughly:
	    stir

Figure 9-1: Examples of the repetition structure

Notice that the examples direct the user to repeat one or more instructions either a precise number of times (Example 1) or until a specified condition is met (Example 2). The repetition structure shown in Example 1, for instance, tells you to repeat the "apply shampoo to wet hair", "lather", and "rinse" instructions twice. In Example 2, the repetition structure tells you to repeat the "stir" instruction until the milk and syrup are mixed thoroughly.

Programmers use the **repetition structure**, also called **looping** or **iteration**, to direct the computer to repeat one or more instructions either a precise number of times or until some condition is met. For example, you may need the computer to process a set of instructions four times, once for each of the worksheets within an Excel workbook. Or, you may want a set of instructions processed until the user enters a negative sales amount, which indicates that the user has no more sales amounts to enter.

In this tutorial, you will learn how to use the VBA For...Next and For Each...Next statements to code the repetition structure. (You will learn how to use the VBA Do...Loop statement to code the repetition structure in Tutorial 10.) In addition to the For...Next and For Each...Next statements, you also will learn how to use the VBA With statement, which provides a convenient way of referring to the properties and methods of an object.

The For...Next Statement

You can use the VBA **For...Next statement** to include a repetition structure in a procedure. Figure 9-2 shows the syntax and an example of the For...Next statement.

<u>Syntax:</u>
For *counter* = *startvalue* **To** *endvalue* [**Step** *stepvalue*]
    [*statements*]
    [**Exit For**]
    [*statements*]
Next *counter*

<u>Example:</u>
```
Dim intCount As Integer, strCity as String
For intCount = 1 To 3 Step 1
    strCity = InputBox(Prompt:="Enter the city:", Title:="City")
    MsgBox Prompt:=strCity & " is city number " & intCount, _
        Buttons:=vbOKOnly + vbInformation, Title:="City Number"
Next intCount
```

Figure 9-2: Syntax and an example of the For...Next statement

The For...Next statement begins with the For clause and ends with the Next clause. Between those two clauses, you enter the instructions you want the loop to repeat, as shown in Figure 9-2's example.

tip

You can use the Exit For statement to exit the For...Next loop prematurely—in other words, to exit it before it has finished processing. You may need to do so if the loop encounters an error when processing its instructions. You also may need to stop the loop when a certain condition is met, as shown in the second example in Figure 9-4.

tip

You can nest For...Next statements, which means that you can place one For...Next statement within another For...Next statement. You may need to do so, for example, if you want to italicize every other paragraph in each open Word document. You will learn how to nest a For...Next statement in this lesson's Exercise 8.

In the syntax, *counter* is the name of the numeric variable that will be used to keep track of the number of times the loop instructions are processed. In Figure 9-2's example, the name of the numeric variable is intCount.

The *startvalue*, *endvalue*, and *stepvalue* items control how many times the loop instructions should be processed. The *startvalue* tells the loop where to begin, the *endvalue* tells the loop when to stop, and the *stepvalue* tells the loop how much to add to (or subtract from if the *stepvalue* is a negative number) the *counter* each time the loop is processed. If you omit the *stepvalue*, a *stepvalue* of positive 1 is used. In the example shown in Figure 9-2, the *startvalue* is 1, the *endvalue* is 3, and the *stepvalue* is 1. Those values tell the loop to start counting at 1 and, counting by 1s, stop at 3—in other words, count 1, 2, and then 3. The example will repeat the InputBox function and MsgBox statement three times.

The For clause's *startvalue*, *endvalue*, and *stepvalue* values must be numeric and they can be either positive or negative, integer or non-integer. If *stepvalue* is positive, then *startvalue* must be less than or equal to *endvalue* for the loop instructions to be processed. In other words, the instruction For intCount = 1 To 3 Step 1 is correct, but the instruction For intCount = 3 To 1 Step 1 is not correct because you can't count from 3 (the *startvalue*) to 1 (the *endvalue*) by adding increments of 1 (the *stepvalue*). If, on the other hand, *stepvalue* is negative, then *startvalue* must be greater than or equal to *endvalue* for the loop instructions to be processed. For example, the instruction For intCount = 3 To 1 Step −1 is correct, but the instruction For intCount = 1 To 3 Step −1 is not correct because you can't count from 1 to 3 by subtracting increments of 1.

When processed, the For...Next loop performs the following three tasks:

1. The loop initializes the *counter* (the numeric variable) to the *startvalue*. This is done only once, at the beginning of the loop.
2. If the *stepvalue* is positive, the loop checks to determine if the value in the *counter* is greater than the *endvalue*. (Or, if the *stepvalue* is negative, the loop checks to determine if the value in the *counter* is less than the *endvalue*.) If it is, the loop stops; if it's not, the instructions within the loop are processed and the next task, task 3, is performed.
3. The loop adds the *stepvalue* to the *counter*. It then repeats tasks 2 and 3 until the *counter* is greater than (or less than, if the *stepvalue* is negative) the *endvalue*.

Figure 9-3 describes how the code shown in Figure 9-2's example will be processed.

1. VBA creates and initializes the intCount and strCity variables in memory.

2. The For...Next statement initializes the counter, intCount, to 1 (*startvalue*).

3. The For...Next statement checks to determine if the value in intCount is greater than 3 (*endvalue*). It's not.

4. The InputBox function prompts the user to enter a city. Assume the city "Paris" is entered.

5. The MsgBox statement displays the message "Paris is city number 1".

6. The For...Next statement adds 1 (*stepvalue*) to intCount, giving 2.

7. The For...Next statement checks to determine if the value in intCount is greater than 3 (*endvalue*). It's not.

8. The InputBox function prompts the user to enter a city. Assume the city "London" is entered.

9. The MsgBox statement displays the message "London is city number 2".

10. The For...Next statement adds 1 (*stepvalue*) to intCount, giving 3.

11. The For...Next statement checks to determine if the value in intCount is greater than 3 (*endvalue*). It's not.

12. The InputBox function prompts the user to enter a city. Assume the city "Madrid" is entered.

13. The MsgBox statement displays the message "Madrid is city number 3".

14. The For...Next statement adds 1 (*stepvalue*) to intCount, giving 4.

15. The For...Next statement checks to determine if the value in intCount is greater than 3 (*endvalue*). It is, so the For...Next statement ends.

Figure 9-3: Processing steps for the code shown in Figure 9-2

Figure 9-4 shows two additional examples of the For...Next statement. In both examples, the For...Next statement is used to repeat a block of instructions for each object in a collection—in this case, each Document object in Microsoft Word's Documents collection.

```
Example 1:
Dim intCount As Integer, docX As Document
For intCount = 1 To Application.Documents.Count
   Set docX = Application.Documents(intCount)
   docX.PrintOut
Next intCount
```

```
Example 2:
Dim intCount As Integer, docX As Document
For intCount = 1 To Application.Documents.Count
   Set docX = Application.Documents(intCount)
   If UCase(docX.Name) = "SMITH.DOC" Then
      docX.PrintOut
      Exit For
   End If
Next intCount
```

Figure 9-4: For...Next loops that repeat instructions for each object in a collection

In both examples, the *startvalue* and *stepvalue* are 1, and the *endvalue* is the number returned from the `Application.Documents.Count` instruction. As you learned in Tutorial 2's Word lesson, this instruction returns the number of documents in the Documents collection. For example, if the Documents collection contains five documents, the instruction returns the number 5, which then becomes the *endvalue* in the For clause.

Notice that a Set statement appears within the loop in both examples. In the first example, the Set statement uses the *counter* variable intCount to assign each Document object's address, one at a time, to the docX object variable before the document is printed. If the Documents collection contains five documents, the loop first will assign the first document's address to docX and then it will print the document. It then will assign the second document's address and then print the document, and so on. Example 1's loop will repeat its instructions for each Document object in the Documents collection—in other words, it will print each open document.

If you want to print only a specific document in the Documents collection, you can use the loop shown in Figure 9-4's Example 2 to do so. As in Example 1's loop, the Set statement within Example 2's loop uses the *counter* variable intCount to assign each Document object's address to the docX object variable. However, unlike the loop in Example 1, the loop in Example 2 contains a selection structure that compares the value stored in the object's Name property to the string "SMITH.DOC". If a match is found, the document is printed and the Exit For statement stops the loop at that point—in other words, the Exit For statement prevents the loop from looking at any more objects in the collection. Processing would continue with the instruction following the Next clause.

In addition to the For...Next statement, you also can use the VBA For Each...Next statement to create a loop that will repeat its instructions for each object in a collection.

The For Each...Next statement

As with the For...Next statement, you can use the VBA **For Each...Next statement** to repeat a group of instructions for each object in a collection. Figure 9-5 shows the syntax and two examples of the For Each...Next statement. The two examples are the same as those shown in Figure 9-4, except that they are written using the For Each...Next statement rather than the For...Next statement.

Syntax:
For Each *element* **In** *group*
   [*statements*]
   [Exit For]
   [*statements*]
Next *element*

Example 1:
```
Dim docX As Document
For Each docX In Application.Documents
   docX.PrintOut
Next docX
```

Example 2:
```
Dim docX As Document
For Each docX In Application.Documents
   If UCase(docX.Name) = "SMITH.DOC" Then
      docX.PrintOut
      Exit For
   End If
Next docX
```

Figure 9-5: Syntax and two examples of the For Each...Next statement

The For Each...Next statement begins with the For Each clause and ends with the Next clause. Between those two clauses you enter the instructions that you want the loop to repeat.

 tip

The For Each...Next statement can be nested, which means you can place one For Each...Next statement within another.

In the syntax, *element* is the name of the object variable used to refer to each object in the collection, and *group* is the name of the collection in which the object is contained. In Figure 9-5's examples, *element* is the docX Document object variable and *group* is the Documents collection.

The For Each clause first verifies that the *group* contains at least one object. If the *group* is empty—in other words, if the collection doesn't contain any objects—the instructions within the loop are skipped, and processing continues with the instruction following the Next clause. However, if the *group* does contain at least one object, the For Each clause assigns the address of the first object to the *element* variable, and then it processes the instructions within the loop. The For Each clause then checks to determine if the *group* contains another object; if it does, the loop instructions are processed again. Unless you use an Exit For statement to exit the loop prematurely, as in Figure 9-5's second example, the For Each...Next statement will process the loop instructions for each object in the *group*. Figure 9-6 describes how the code shown in Figure 9-5's Example 1 will be processed, and Figure 9-7 describes how the code shown in Figure 9-5's Example 2 will be processed.

Note: Assume that the Documents collection contains three Document objects named SalesMemo.doc, Smith.doc, and Brochure.doc.

1. VBA creates and initializes the docX Document object variable in memory.

2. The For Each...Next statement checks to determine if the Documents collection contains at least one Document object. It does.

3. The For Each...Next statement assigns the address of the first Document object to the docX object variable.

4. The PrintOut method prints the first Document object.

5. The For Each...Next statement checks to determine if the Documents collection contains another Document object. It does.

6. The For Each...Next statement assigns the address of the second Document object to the docX object variable.

7. The PrintOut method prints the second Document object.

8. The For Each...Next statement checks to determine if the Document collection contains another Document object. It does.

9. The PrintOut method prints the third Document object.

10. The For Each...Next statement checks to determine if the Document collection contains another Document object. It doesn't, so the For Each...Next statement ends.

Figure 9-6: Processing steps for the code shown in Example 1 in Figure 9-5

> *Note:* Assume that the Documents collection contains three Document objects named SalesMemo.doc, Smith.doc, and Brochure.doc.
>
> 1. VBA creates and initializes the docX Document object variable in memory.
>
> 2. The For Each...Next statement checks to determine if the Documents collection contains at least one Document object. It does.
>
> 3. The For Each...Next statement assigns the address of the first Document object to the docX object variable.
>
> 4. The If...Then...Else statement checks to determine if the first Document object's Name property contains the string "SMITH.DOC". It doesn't.
>
> 5. The For Each...Next statement checks to determine if the Documents collection contains another Document object. It does.
>
> 6. The For Each...Next statement assigns the address of the second Document object to the docX object variable.
>
> 7. The If...Then...Else statement checks to determine if the second Document object's Name property contains the string "SMITH.DOC". It does.
>
> 8. The PrintOut method prints the second Document object.
>
> 9. The Exit For statement stops the loop.

Figure 9-7: Processing steps for the code shown in Example 2 in Figure 9-5

When you compare the examples shown in Figure 9-5 with those shown in Figure 9-4, you will notice that the For Each...Next statement provides a more convenient way of repeating a block of instructions for each object in a collection. For example, one fewer variable—the *counter* variable—is needed in the For Each...Next statement, and the Set statement is unnecessary because the For Each clause assigns the address of each object to the object variable for you.

As mentioned earlier, in addition to learning about the VBA For...Next and For Each...Next statements, which allow you to code the repetition structure, you also will learn about the VBA With statement in this tutorial. You can use the With statement to refer to the properties and methods of an object.

The With Statement

Unlike the For...Next and For Each...Next statements, the VBA With statement is not used to code the repetition structure. Rather, the **With statement** provides a convenient way of accessing the properties and methods of a single object. Figure 9-8 shows the syntax and an example of the With statement.

```
Syntax:
With object
    [statements]
End With
```

```
Example:
Dim shtJuly As Worksheet
Set shtJuly = Application.Workbooks(1).Worksheets(1)
With shtJuly
        .Range("B1").Value = "Bonus"
        .Range("B2:B20").Formula = "=A2 * .1"
        .Name = "July Bonus"
        MsgBox Prompt:="The sheet's name is " & .Name, _
            Buttons:=vbOKOnly + vbInformation, Title:="Name"
        .PrintOut
End With
```

Figure 9-8: Syntax and an example of the With statement

In the syntax, *object* is the name of the object whose properties or methods you want to access. You enter the appropriate instructions—for example, instructions that assign values to the object's properties or invoke its methods—between the With and End With clauses. The example shown in Figure 9-8 illustrates how you can access the properties and methods of an Excel Worksheet object named shtJuly. Notice that you do not need to preface the shtJuly object's properties (Range, Name) and methods (PrintOut) with the object's name; the With statement handles that for you. However, it is necessary to place a period before the object's properties and methods within the With statement—for example, `.Range`, `.Name`, and `.Printout`.

You now have completed Tutorial 9's Concept lesson. You can either take a break or complete the end-of-lesson questions and exercises before moving on to the next lesson.

 # S U M M A R Y

To use the For...Next statement to code the repetition structure:

■ Use the syntax shown in Figure 9-2, where *counter* is the name of the numeric variable used to keep track of the number of times the loop instructions are processed. The *startvalue*, *endvalue*, and *stepvalue* items control how many times to process the loop instructions. The values for *startvalue*, *endvalue*, and *stepvalue* must be numeric and they can be either positive or negative, integer or non-integer. If *stepvalue* is positive, then *startvalue* must be less than or equal to *endvalue* for the loop instructions to be processed. If, on the other hand, *stepvalue* is negative, then *startvalue* must be greater than or equal to *endvalue* for the loop instructions to be processed. If *stepvalue* is omitted, the loop uses a *stepvalue* of positive 1.

To use the For Each...Next statement to code the repetition structure:

■ Use the syntax shown in Figure 9-5, where *element* is the name of the object variable that will be used to refer to each object in the collection, and *group* is the name of the collection in which the object is contained. The collection must contain at least one object for the For Each...Next loop instructions to be processed.

To use the With statement to access the properties and methods of an object:

■ Use the syntax shown in Figure 9-8, where *object* is the name of the object whose properties and methods you want to access. Place a period before the object's property or method within the With statement.

REVIEW QUESTIONS

1. How many times will the MsgBox statement shown in the following code be processed?

    ```
    Dim intCount As Integer
    For intCount = 1 To 6
        MsgBox Prompt:="Number: " & intCount
    Next intCount
    ```
    a. 1
    b. 5
    c. 6
    d. 7

2. What is the value of intCount when the loop in Question 1 stops?
    a. 1
    b. 5
    c. 6
    d. 7

3. How many times will the MsgBox statement shown in the following code be processed?

    ```
    Dim intCount As Integer
    For intCount = 4 To 10 Step 2
        MsgBox Prompt:="Number: " & intCount
    Next intCount
    ```
    a. 0
    b. 3
    c. 4
    d. 5

4. What is the value of intCount when the loop in Question 3 stops?
    a. 6
    b. 10
    c. 11
    d. 12

5. When the *stepvalue* in a For...Next statement is positive, the instructions within the loop are processed only when the *counter* is _____ the *endvalue*.
    a. greater than
    b. greater than or equal to
    c. less than
    d. less than or equal to

6. When the *stepvalue* in a For...Next statement is negative, the instructions within the loop are processed only when the *counter* is _____ the *endvalue*.
    a. greater than
    b. greater than or equal to
    c. less than
    d. less than or equal to

7. Which two of the following are valid For clauses?
    a. `For intTemp = 1.5 To 5 Step .5`
    b. `For intTemp = 3 To 1`
    c. `For intTemp = 1 To 10`
    d. `For sngTemp = 0 To 3.5 Step .5`

8. If you omit the *stepvalue* in a For...Next statement, the statement uses a *stepvalue* of _____ .
    a. −1
    b. 0
    c. 1
    d. None of the above. If you omit the *stepvalue*, an error message appears.

9. Assuming that a procedure declares a Worksheet object variable named shtMonth, which of the following is a valid For Each clause? (*Hint*: An Excel Worksheet object belongs to the Worksheets collection, which is a member of the Application object's Workbooks collection.)
    a. `For Each Sheet In shtMonth`
    b. `For Each shtMonth In Application.Workbooks(1).Worksheets`
    c. `For Each Worksheet In shtMonth`
    d. `For Each shtMonth In Application.WorksheetsCollection`

10. Which of the following will display the name of the open Word documents in a message box? (*Hint*: A Word Document object belongs to the Documents collection.)

    a. ```
Dim docCurrent As Document
For Each docCurrent In Application.Documents
     MsgBox Prompt:=docCurrent.Name
Next docCurrent
```

    b. ```
Dim docCurrent As Documents
For Each docCurrent In Application.Documents
     MsgBox Prompt:=docCurrent.Name
Next docCurrent
```

    c. ```
Dim docCurrent As Document
For Each Document In Documents.docCurrent
     MsgBox Prompt:=docCurrent.Name
Next Document
```

    d. ```
Dim docCurrent As Document
For Each Document In Documents
     MsgBox Prompt:=docCurrent.Name
Next Document
```

11. Which one of the following With statements is correct? (*Hint*: shtCalc is a Worksheet object variable.)

    a. ```
With shtCalc
     Unprotect
     Range("Rate").Value = .25
     Protect
End With
```

    b. ```
With shtCalc
     .Unprotect
     .Range("Rate").Value = .25
     .Protect
End With
```

    c. ```
With Each shtCalc
     .Unprotect
     .Range("Rate").Value = .25
     .Protect
End With
```

    d. ```
With shtCalc.
     Unprotect
     Range("Rate").Value = .25
     Protect
End With
```

EXERCISES

1. Write a For...Next statement that will display the numbers 1 through 10 in a message box. Use intX as the *counter* variable.

2. Write a For...Next statement that will display the even numbers from 2 through 100 in a message box. Use intNum as the *counter* variable.

3. Write a For...Next statement that performs the following two tasks five times:
    a. Use the InputBox function to get a name from the user. Store the user's response in a String variable named strName.
    b. Display the name in a message box.

4. Write a For...Next statement that performs the following four tasks three times:
    a. Use the InputBox function to get a sales amount from the user. Store the user's response in a String variable named strSales.
    b. Convert the contents of the strSales variable to a number. Store the result in a Currency variable named curSales.
    c. Calculate the bonus by multiplying the contents of the curSales variable by 10%. Store the result in a Currency variable named curBonus.
    d. Display the contents of the curBonus variable in a message box.

5. Write the appropriate Dim statement to declare an Excel Worksheet object named shtName. Then write the For Each...Next statement that will display the name of each worksheet contained in the first workbook's Worksheets collection. (*Hint*: The Worksheets collection is a member of the Workbooks collection.)

6. Write the appropriate Dim statement to declare a Word Document object named docTemp. Then write the For Each...Next statement that will close all of the documents contained in the Word Documents collection. (*Hint*: You can use a Document object's Close method to close a document.)

7. Complete the following code, which should assign the name "Seminar Ad" to the worksheet whose address is stored in the shtAd variable and then display the worksheet's name in a message box.

```
Dim shtAd As Worksheet
Set shtAd = Application.Workbooks(1).Worksheets(1)
With _____
    _____
    _____
End With
```

Exercise 8 is a Discovery Exercise. Discovery Exercises, which may include topics that are not covered in the lesson, allow you to "discover" the solutions to problems on your own.

discovery ▶
8. In this exercise, you will learn how to nest For...Next statements—in other words, you will learn how to place one For...Next loop inside another.
    a. Start either Word, Excel, Access, or PowerPoint. Open the Visual Basic Editor. Insert a module, then create a procedure named DisplayNumbers. The DisplayNumbers procedure should display the numbers 0 through 9 in a message box five times, as shown in Figure 9-9. Separate each group of 10 numbers with a space. (*Hint*: View the For...Next Statement Help screen, then click Example at the top of the Help screen. Use the example, which shows nested For...Next statements, as your guide.)

include a space
between each
group of 10
numbers

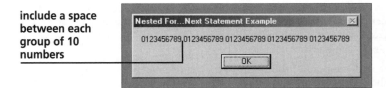

Figure 9-9

   b. Save the procedure, then run the procedure. Your message box should look like the one shown in Figure 9-9. Click the OK button to close the message box, then close the application.

You also can use VBA in PowerPoint to create procedures that enhance your presentations. Exercise 9 allows you to apply this tutorial's programming concept in a PowerPoint presentation.

powerpoint   **9.** In this exercise, you will finish coding a procedure in PowerPoint. The procedure will allow the user to change the address of each hyperlink on a slide.

   a. Open the T9-PP-E9 (T9-PP-E9.ppt) presentation, which is located in the Tut09\Concept folder on your Data Disk. Click the Enable Macros button, if necessary, then save the presentation as T9-PP-E9D.

   b. Click View on the menu bar and then click Slide Show. Click the first slide, being careful not to click the image that appears on the slide. When the second slide appears, place the mouse pointer over each of the four hyperlinks. Notice that each hyperlink contains the same address, http://www.cod.edu. Stop the slide show.

   c. Open the Visual Basic Editor. Open the Module1 module's Code window and view the partially completed ChangeHyperlinkAddress procedure. The procedure should allow the user to change the address of the second slide's hyperlinks. Make the following modifications to the procedure:

     1) Use the InputBox function to display a dialog box that asks the user for the new address. Use "Hyperlink Address" as the dialog box's title. Store the address in the strAddress String variable.

     2) Use the For Each...Next statement to change the address of each hyperlink on the second slide to the address stored in the strAddress variable. (*Hints*: A Hyperlink object is a member of the Hyperlinks collection, and each slide has its own Hyperlinks collection. Also, each Hyperlink object has an Address property.)

     3) Use the `Application.SlideShowWindows(1).View.Next` command to select the second slide.

   d. Save the presentation, then return to PowerPoint. Click View on the menu bar and then click Slide Show. When the slide appears, click the image that appears on the first slide. When the Hyperlink Address dialog box appears, type http://www.course.com and press the Enter key. When the second slide appears, place the mouse pointer over each hyperlink. Notice that the address for each hyperlink is now http://www.course.com.

   e. Stop the presentation, then save the presentation and close PowerPoint.

A computer program is good only if it works. Errors in programming code can cause a program to run incorrectly. Therefore, a programmer needs to know how to locate and fix any errors in his or her code. Exercise 10 is a Debugging Exercise. Debugging Exercises allow you to practice recognizing and solving errors in code.

debugging

10. The following procedure should prompt the user to enter five different sales amounts. The procedure should sum these amounts and then display the total sales immediately before the procedure ends. The procedure is not working as intended. Rewrite the code correctly.

```
Dim intCount As Integer, strSales As String
Dim curTotal As Currency
strSales = InputBox(Prompt:="Enter sales amount:", _
    Title:="Sales")
For intCount = 1 To 5
    curTotal = curTotal + Val(strSales)
    MsgBox Prompt:="Total sales " & strSales, _
        Buttons:=vbOKOnly + vbInformation
Next strSales
```

Excel Lesson

Using the Repetition Structure and the With Statement in Excel

case ▶ In Tutorial 8, you created the DisplaySales macro for Martin Washington, the accountant at Paradise Electronics. Recall that the macro uses the SalesQuery query table to access the sales data stored in an Access database named MthSales, and it allows Martin to display this information in an Excel worksheet, along with the difference between each store's monthly sales goal and its actual sales.

Martin wants to make two modifications to the DisplaySales macro. First, he would like the macro to display the negative numbers that appear in the Difference column in red when a store's actual sales are less than its sales goal. Second, he would like the macro to change the column headings "Goal" and "Actual" to "Sales Goal" and "Actual Sales", respectively. You will make this modification to the DisplaySales macro in this lesson.

Modifying the DisplaySales Macro Procedure

The T9-EX-1 file on your Data Disk contains the same Excel workbook that you used in Tutorial 8 to display the monthly sales for each of Paradise Electronics' stores. Begin by opening and viewing the workbook and the DisplaySales procedure that you created in Tutorial 8.

To view the workbook and the DisplaySales procedure:

1 Start Microsoft Excel. Open the **T9-EX-1** (T9-EX-1.xls) workbook, which is located in the Tut09\Excel folder on your Data Disk. Click the **Enable Macros** button, if necessary, then save the workbook as **Monthly Sales**.

The Monthly Sales workbook contains one worksheet named Sales, as shown in Figure 9-10.

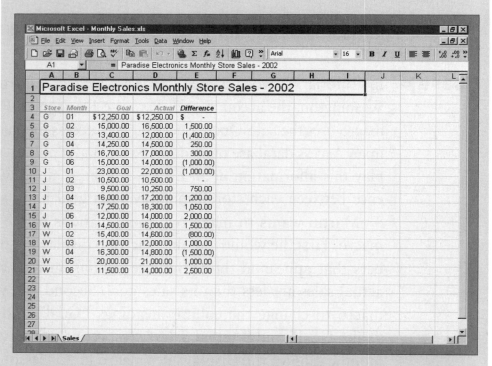

Figure 9-10: The Sales worksheet in the Monthly Sales workbook

2 Press **Alt+F11** to open the Visual Basic Editor. If necessary, open the Project Explorer window and close the Properties window, the Immediate window, and any open Code windows. Open the Module1 module's Code window, then view the **DisplaySales** procedure.

3 Close the Project Explorer window so that you can view more of the Code window.

Figure 9-11 shows the modified pseudocode for the DisplaySales procedure. The modifications made to the original pseudocode shown in Figure 8-18 are shaded in the figure.

1. Use the InputBox function to prompt the user to indicate which store's sales he or she wants to display (A for All, G for Glen Park, J for Jackson, or W for Warren). Store the user's response in a String variable named strStore.
2. Value stored in the strStore variable:

    = "A"   Assign to the CommandText property a SQL SELECT statement that selects all of the fields and records in the 2002Sales table. Order the records by month within store.

    = "G", "J", "W"   Assign to the CommandText property a SQL SELECT statement that selects all of the fields for only the records whose Store field value matches the value stored in the strStore variable. Order the records by month.

    Other   Use the MsgBox statement to display an error message in a message box, then exit the procedure.
3. Enter the column heading "Difference" in cell E3 in the worksheet.
4. Enter the formula =D4-C4 in cell E4 in the worksheet.
5. Set the QueryTable object's FillAdjacentFormulas property to True.
6. Use the QueryTable object's Refresh method to update the query table.
7. Change the column heading "Goal", which appears in cell C3 in the worksheet, to "Sales Goal" and change the column heading "Actual", which appears in cell D3 in the worksheet, to "Actual Sales".
8. Repeat the following for each cell in the Difference column (column E):
    a. If the value stored in the cell's Value property is less than 0, then change the color of the cell's font to red.
9. Use the MsgBox function to ask the user if he or she wants to print the worksheet. Assign the user's response to an Integer variable named intPrint.
10. If intPrint = vbYes, then print the worksheet.

Figure 9-11: Modified pseudocode for the DisplaySales procedure

Notice that two additional steps are necessary to accomplish the changes requested by Paradise Electronics. Step 7, for example, indicates that the modified DisplaySales procedure will need to change the "Goal" and "Actual" column headings to "Sales Goal" and "Actual Sales", respectively. Step 8 indicates that the procedure also will need to compare the Value property of each cell in the Difference column to the number 0. If a cell's Value property contains a negative number—a number that is less than zero—then the procedure should change the color of that cell's font to red.

The modified DisplaySales procedure will need two additional Range object variables, which you will name rngCell and rngCurrent. Both variables will be used in a loop that compares each cell in the Difference column to the number 0.

 tip

As you learned in Tutorial 2, a cell in an Excel worksheet is a Range object. Excel does not have a Cell object.

In the next set of steps, you will declare the appropriate variables and then begin translating Steps 7 and 8 in Figure 9-11's pseudocode into one or more VBA statements.

To begin modifying the DisplaySales procedure:

1   Click at the end of the second Dim statement in the Code window, then type **,** (a comma) and press the **Spacebar**. Type **rngCell as range, rngCurrent as range** to declare the rngCell and rngCurrent Range object variables.

Step 7 in the pseudocode is to change the column headings that appear in cells C3 and D3 in the worksheet; you will use the With statement to do so.

2   Type the additional instructions shown in Figure 9-12 in the blank line below the `qtbSales.Refresh BackgroundQuery:=False` instruction, then position the insertion point as shown in the figure.

the code in the Code window was compressed

scroll to view the remaining instructions

enter these five lines of code

position the insertion point here

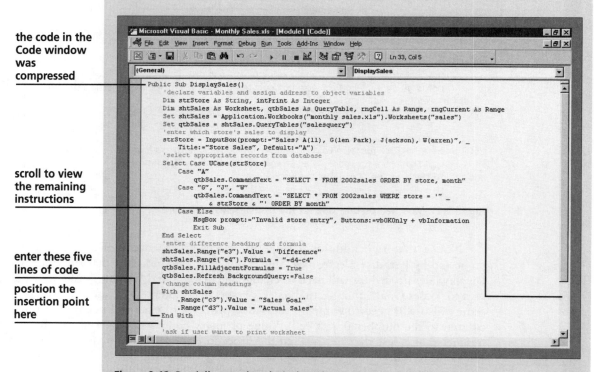

Figure 9-12: Partially completed DisplaySales procedure

HELP? The code in the Code window shown in Figure 9-12 was compressed so that you could view more of the procedure. If you want to compress the code shown on your screen, click Tools on the Visual Basic Editor's Standard toolbar, then click Options, and then click the Editor Format tab. Select 9 in the Size list box, then click the OK button.

3 Save the procedure.

According to Step 8 in the modified pseudocode, the procedure needs to compare the Value property of each cell (Range object) in the Difference column to the number 0. As you learned in the Concept lesson, you can use either the For...Next statement or the For Each...Next statement to repeat one or more instructions for each object in a collection. In this case, you will use the For Each...Next statement simply because it provides a more convenient way to refer to the objects in a collection.

You will modify the DisplaySales procedure to use the For...Next statement in this lesson's Exercise 5.

Although you could repeat the loop instructions for each and every cell in the Difference column, beginning with cell E1 and ending with cell E65536, that would be extremely inefficient. Rather, you should repeat the loop instructions only for the cells in column E that contain the difference amounts. For example, when the worksheet displays the information for all of Paradise's stores, as it does in Figure 9-10, the loop instructions should be processed 18 times, once for each of the cells located in the range E4:E21. However, when the worksheet displays only a specific store's information, the loop instructions should be processed only for the six cells located in the range E4:E9.

In the next section, you will learn two new properties of a Range object—CurrentRegion and Resize. You will use these properties to set the appropriate range to loop through in the For Each...Next statement.

The CurrentRegion and Resize Properties

You can use a Range object's **CurrentRegion property** to return a range that contains the entire region in which the Range object resides. The syntax of the CurrentRegion property is *rangeObject*.**CurrentRegion**. A **region** is defined as a block of cells bounded by any combination of empty rows, empty columns, and the edges of the worksheet. For example, if the Sales worksheet contains the sales data for all of Paradise's stores, as shown earlier in Figure 9-10, then the instruction `shtSales.Range("A3").CurrentRegion` would return the range A3:E21 because that is the region that contains the Range object, A3. Notice that the range A3:E21 is bounded by the edge of the worksheet on the left side, a blank column on the right side, and blank rows at the top and bottom. The instruction `shtSales.Range("C10").CurrentRegion` would return the same range, as would the instruction `shtSales.Range("E4").CurrentRegion`. The instruction `shtSales.Range("A1").CurrentRegion`, on the other hand, would return the range A1:I1.

Now assume that the Sales worksheet contains only the data for the Jackson store, as shown in Figure 9-13.

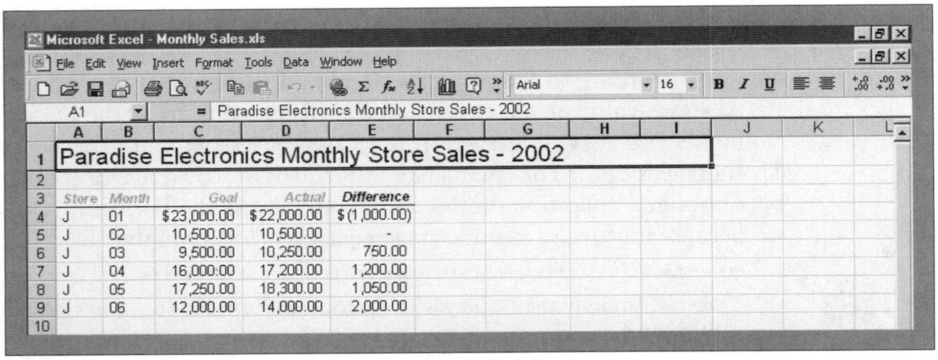

Figure 9-:13: Sales worksheet showing Jackson store data

In this case, the instruction `shtSales.Range("A3").CurrentRegion` would return the range A3:E9, as would the instructions `shtSales.Range("D8").CurrentRegion` and `shtSales.Range("E4").CurrentRegion`.

If you want to determine the number of columns in the current region, you can use the instruction `shtSales.Range("A3").CurrentRegion.Columns.Count` to do so; this instruction will return the number 5. You can use the instruction shtSales.Range("A3").CurrentRegion.Rows.Count to determine the number of rows in the current range. This instruction will return the number 19 when the Sales worksheet contains the data for all of Paradise's stores, and it will return the number 7 when the worksheet contains only one store's data.

You can use a Range object's **Resize property** to resize a range. Figure 9-14 shows the syntax and five examples of the Resize property.

In the syntax, *rangeObject* is the original range, and *rowsize* and *columnsize* are the number of rows and columns, respectively, you want in the new range. The RowSize and ColumnSize arguments are optional, as indicated by the square brackets ([]) in the syntax. If the RowSize argument is omitted, the number of rows in the range remains the same. Likewise, if the ColumnSize argument is omitted, the number of columns in the range remains the same.

Syntax:
rangeObject.**Resize([RowSize:=***rowsize***], [ColumnSize:=***columnsize***])**

Example 1:
```
shtsales.Range("A3:E21").Resize(ColumnSize:=1)
```
Returns range A3:A21

Example 2:
```
shtsales.Range("D5:E10").Resize(RowSize:=4)
```
Returns range D5:E8

Example 3:
```
shtSales.Range("A3").Resize(RowSize:=3, ColumnSize:=2)
```
Returns range A3:B5

Example 4:
```
shtSales.Range("D4:D21") _
   .Resize(ColumnSize:=shtSales.Range("D4:D21").Columns.Count + 1)
```
Returns range D4:E21

Example 5:
```
Dim rngCurrent As Range
Set rngCurrent = shtSales.Range("A3").CurrentRange
rngCurrent.Resize(ColumnSize:=rngCurrent.Columns.Count — 1)
```
Returns either range A3:D21 (if the Sales worksheet contains the data for all of Paradise's stores) or range A3:D9 (if the Sales worksheet contains the data for only one store)

Figure 9-14: Syntax and examples of the Resize property

Example 1 in Figure 9-14 will scale down the range A3:E21 to one column—the leftmost column in the range. In other words, it will resize the range to include only cells A3 through A21. Example 2 will resize the range D5:E10 to include only the cells appearing in the first four rows in the range; those cells are contained in the range D5:E8. Example 3 will expand the range A3 to include three rows and two columns—the range A3:B5. Example 4 will resize the range D4:D21 to the range D4:E21. Notice that the new range (D4:E21) contains one column more than the original range (D4:D21). Example 5 in Figure 9-14 shows how you can contract the current region so that it includes one less column. Example 5 will return either the range A3:D21 (if the Sales worksheet contains the data for all of the stores) or the range A3:D9 (if the Sales worksheet contains only one store's data).

You can't use the Resize property to remove rows and columns from, or add rows and column to, the top and left side, respectively, of a range. You can use it only to remove rows and columns from, and add rows and columns to, the bottom and right side of a range.

You can practice with the CurrentRegion and Resize properties by completing this lesson's Exercise 3.

You will use the Range object's CurrentRegion and Resize properties, as well as its Offset property, to set the range—either E4:E21 or E4:E9—through which the For Each...Next statement should loop.

Recall from Tutorial 5 that you use the Offset property to refer to a cell located either a certain number of rows or columns away from the range itself.

To complete the DisplaySales procedure:

1 The insertion point should be positioned below the End With statement in the Code window. Type **'display negative differences in red** and press the **Enter** key.

First use the Range object's CurrentRegion property to determine the region that contains the sales information. Use cell A3, the upper-left corner of the region, as the Range object. Assign the current region to the rngCurrent object variable.

2 Type **set rngcurrent = shtsales.range("a3").currentregion** and press the **Enter** key. This instruction will return the range A3:E21 when the worksheet displays the sales data for all of Paradise's stores. It will return the range A3:E9 when the worksheet displays only one store's data.

Recall that you want the For Each...Next statement to process its instructions only for the difference amounts shown in column E. However, notice that the CurrentRegion property returns the entire region containing the sales data—all of the columns and all of the rows, including the header row. You can use the Range object's Offset property to exclude row 3 and columns A through D from the current region, and then use the Resize property to resize the current region to include only the appropriate cells in column E.

Recall that you can't use the Resize property to remove columns and rows from the top and left side of a range.

3 Type **set rngcurrent = rngcurrent.offset(rowoffset:=1, columnoffset:=4)** _ (be sure to type the closing parenthesis followed by a space and the underscore) and press the **Enter** key. If the rngCurrent variable contains the range A3:E21, the Offset property will assign to the rngCurrent variable the range located one row below and four columns to the right of range A3:E21; that range is E4:I22. If, on the other hand, the rngCurrent variable contains the range A3:E9, the Offset property will assign the range E4:I10.

Now resize the E4:I22 (or E4:I10) range so that it excludes the last row (either row 22 or row 10) in the range, and includes only one column, column E, which is the first column in the range.

4 Press the **Tab** key, then type **.resize(rowsize:=rngcurrent.rows.count - 1, columnsize:=1)** (be sure to type the period before the word "resize") and press the **Enter** key.

Now enter the For Each clause that directs the loop to repeat its instructions for each cell in the rngCurrent range.

5 Press the **Backspace** key to remove the indentation, then type **for each rngcell in rngcurrent** and then press the **Enter** key.

If a cell's Value property contains a number that is less than zero, the procedure should display the number using a red font.

6 Enter the additional instructions shown in Figure 9-15, which shows the completed DisplaySales procedure.

enter these
four lines
of code

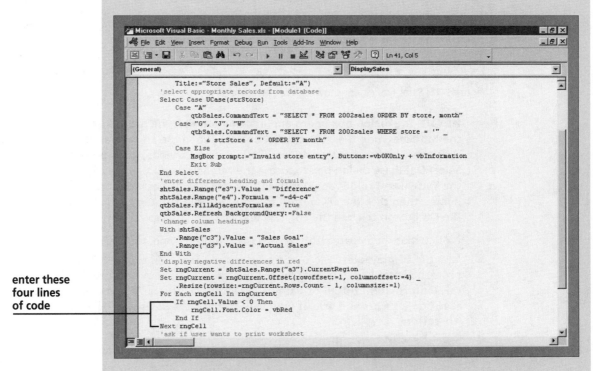

Figure 9-15: Completed DisplaySales procedure

7 Verify the accuracy of your code before continuing by comparing the code on your screen to the code shown in Figure 9-15, then save the workbook.

Now that you have finished modifying the procedure, you should test it to verify that it is working correctly.

To test the DisplaySales macro procedure:

1 Return to Excel, then run the **DisplaySales** macro.

2 When the Store Sales dialog box appears, type **w** and press the **Enter** key to display the sales information for the Warren store. The Print message box appears and asks if you want to print the Sales worksheet. Click the **No** button. Figure 9-16 shows the sales information for the Warren store.

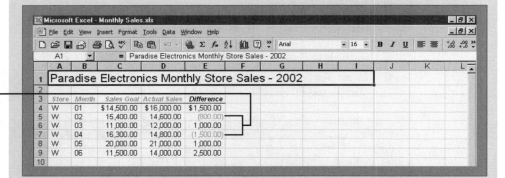

negative values appear in red

Figure 9-16: Sales worksheet showing Warren store data

HELP? If a dialog box opens and informs you that the procedure cannot find the MthSales.mdb file, click the OK button. When the Login dialog box opens, click the Database button to open the Select Database dialog box. Use the Select Database dialog box to locate the MthSales.mdb file, which is located in the Tut09\Excel folder on your Data Disk. Click MthSales.mdb in the list of filenames, then click the OK button to close the Select Database dialog box. Click the OK button to close the Login dialog box.

Notice that the negative differences in column E appear in red.

3 Run the **DisplaySales** macro again. When the Store Sales dialog box appears, press the **Enter** key to accept the default value, A. The procedure displays the sales information for all of Paradise Electronics' stores. When the Print message box appears and asks if you want to print the Sales worksheet, click the **No** button.

4 Save the workbook, then close Excel.

You now have completed Tutorial 9's Excel lesson. You can either take a break or complete the end-of-lesson exercises before moving on to the next lesson.

 # E X E R C I S E S

1. In this exercise, you will modify the DisplaySales procedure that you created in this lesson so that it displays each store's name in column A of the worksheet. The modified procedure also will insert a blank row between the Glen Park and Jackson store data, and between the Jackson and Warren store data.
    a. Open the Monthly Sales (Monthly Sales.xls) workbook, which you created in this lesson. The workbook is located in the Tut09\Excel folder on your Data Disk. Click the Enable Macros button, if necessary, then save the workbook as T9-EX-E1D.
    b. Open the Visual Basic Editor. Open the Module1 module's Code window, then view the DisplaySales procedure.
    c. Make the following modifications to the DisplaySales procedure:
        1) Change the filename in the Set statement to "t9-ex-e1d.xls".
        2) Change the G, J, and W in the Store column to Glen Park, Jackson, and Warren, respectively. Be sure to use the For Each...Next statement. (*Hint*: You will need to reset the rngCurrent variable so the loop repeats its instructions only for the cells in column A.)
        3) Use the Range object's AutoFit property to automatically adjust the width of column A to fit its new values.
        4) When the worksheet displays the sales for all of the stores, insert a blank row to separate the Glen Park store's sales amounts from the Jackson store's sales amounts. Also insert a blank row to separate the Jackson store's sales amounts from the Warren store's sales amounts.
    d. Save the workbook. Return to Excel and run the DisplaySales macro. Use the macro to display the sales for all of Paradise Electronics' stores.
    e. When the macro is working correctly, save and then close the workbook.

2. In this exercise, you will modify the DisplaySales procedure that you created in this lesson so that it uses the With statement to display the negative differences in red and to change the interior color of a cell to yellow.
    a. Open the Monthly Sales (Monthly Sales.xls) workbook, which you created in this lesson. The workbook is located in the Tut09\Excel folder on your Data Disk. Click the Enable Macros button, if necessary, then save the workbook as T9-EX-E2D.
    b. Open the Visual Basic Editor. Open the Module1 module's Code window, then view the DisplaySales procedure.
    c. Change the filename in the Set statement to "t9-ex-e2d.xls".

  d. Remove the `If rngCell.Value < 0 Then,`
     `rngCell.Font.Color = vbRed`, and `End If` instructions from the procedure.
     Use the With statement to do the following:
     1) Determine if the rngCell's Value property contains a value that is less than 0. If
        it does,
        (1) change the font to red
        (2) change the interior color of the cell, as well as the interior color of the corre-
            sponding cells in columns A and B, to yellow. For example, if cell E7 contains
            a negative number, then the interior color of cells E7, A7, and B7 should be
            changed to yellow. (*Hint*: Use the Interior property of a Range object, and use
            vbYellow as the Color constant.)
  e. Save the workbook. Return to Excel and run the DisplaySales macro. Use the macro
     to display the sales for all of Paradise's stores.
  f. When the macro is working correctly, save and then close the workbook.

3. In this exercise, you will experiment with the Range object's CurrentRegion and Resize
   properties.
   a. Open the T9-EX-E3 (T9-EX-E3.xls) workbook, which is located in the Tut09\Excel
      folder on your Data Disk. Click the Enable Macros button, if necessary, then save
      the workbook as T9-EX-E3D.
   b. Open the Visual Basic Editor. Open the Module1 module's Code window, then view
      the CurRegTest procedure. Study the code, then run the procedure. The message
      "Current region: B1:C7" appears in a message box. Click the OK button to close
      the message box.
   c. Change the Range object in the second Set statement from "b1" to each of the fol-
      lowing: C5, F11, G7, G6, B10, C12; then record the address of the current region,
      which appears in the message box.
   d. View the ResizeTest procedure. Study the code, then run the procedure. The mes-
      sage "Current region: B1:C7" appears in a message box. Close the message box.
      The message "Resized region: B1" appears in a message box. Close the message
      box. Change the last Set statement so that it resizes the current region as follows:
      1) Include only cells B1 and C1
      2) Include only cells B1 through B7
      3) Include only cells B1 through C11
      4) Include only cells C1 through G14 (*Hint*: You will need to use the Offset property.)
      5) Include only cells C1 through C4 (*Hint*: You will need to use the Offset property.)
      6) Include only cells C2 through C7 (*Hint*: You will need to use the Offset property.)
   e. Return to Excel. Save and then close the workbook.

4. In this exercise, you will create a macro procedure that calculates each employee's raise
   and new pay.
   a. Open the T9-EX-E4 (T9-EX-E4.xls) workbook, which is located in the Tut09\Excel
      folder on your Data Disk. Click the Enable Macros button, if necessary, then save
      the workbook as T9-EX-E4D.
   b. Open the Visual Basic Editor and view the code template for the CalculateIncrease
      procedure. Code the procedure so that it calculates each employee's raise and new
      pay. If an employee is hourly, give the employee a 7% raise; otherwise, give the
      employee a 5% raise. Keep in mind that employee names may be added or deleted
      to the worksheet. (*Hint*: Use the CurrentRegion property to determine the appropri-
      ate range to use in the For Each…Next statement.)

c. Save the workbook. Return to Excel and run the CalculateIncrease macro to verify that it is working correctly.

d. Return to the Visual Basic Editor. Modify the CalculateIncrease procedure so that it changes the color of the font used in the rows containing salaried employees to blue. (*Hint*: Use vbBlue as the Color constant.)

e. Save the workbook. Return to Excel and run the CalculateIncrease macro. The font used in the three rows that display the information for salaried employees should be blue.

f. When the macro is working correctly, save and then close the workbook.

Exercises 5 through 8 are Discovery Exercises. Discovery Exercises, which may include topics that are not covered in the lesson, allow you to "discover" the solutions to problems on your own.

discovery ▶ **5.** In this exercise, you will modify the DisplaySales procedure that you created in this lesson so that it uses the For...Next statement rather than the For Each...Next statement to display the negative differences in red.

a. Open the Monthly Sales (Monthly Sales.xls) workbook, which you created in this lesson. The workbook is located in the Tut09\Excel folder on your Data Disk. Click the Enable Macros button, if necessary, then save the workbook as T9-EX-E5D.

b. Open the Visual Basic Editor. Display the Cells Property Help screen. Read the Help screen, then click Example at the top of the Help screen. Study the examples, then close the Help window.

c. Open the Module1 module's Code window, then view the DisplaySales procedure. Change the filename in the Set statement to "t9-ex-e5d.xls". Modify the DisplaySales procedure so that it uses the For...Next statement rather than the For Each...Next statement to display the negative differences in red.

d. Save the workbook. Return to Excel and run the DisplaySales macro. Use the macro to display the sales information for only the Glen Park store.

e. Save and then close the workbook.

discovery ▶ **6.** In this exercise, you will learn how to use the Names collection and its Name object members to delete range names from a worksheet.

a. Open the T9-EX-E6 (T9-EX-E6.xls) workbook, which is located in the Tut09\Excel folder on your Data Disk. Click the Enable Macros button, if necessary, then save the workbook as T9-EX-E6D.

b. Click the Name Box arrow. Notice that the Sales worksheet contains eight range names.

c. Open the Visual Basic Editor. View the Names Collection Object Help screen. Study the Help screen, then view the Name Object Help screen and study it. Close the Help window.

d. Open the Module1 module's Code window, then view the code template for the RemoveRangeNames procedure. First code the RemoveRangeNames procedure so that it displays each range name, one at a time, in a message box. Use the For Each...Next statement in your code. Run the procedure, which should display eight message boxes, one for each of the eight range names.

e. Next, modify the procedure so that it displays only range names beginning with the three letters "Reg". (*Hint*: Use the UCase function and the Like operator.) Run the procedure, which now should display only four message boxes.

f. Remove the MsgBox statement from the procedure. Then modify the procedure so that it deletes all range names that do not begin with the three letters "Reg". Run the procedure. Return to Excel and click the Name Box arrow. Only four range names—RegE, RegN, RegS, and RegW—should appear in the list.

g. When the macro is working correctly, save and then close the workbook.

discovery ▶ **7.** In this exercise, you will learn how to use the End property of a Range object to select a range with a variable size.

a. Open the Monthly Sales (Monthly Sales.xls) workbook, which you created in this lesson. The workbook is located in the Tut09\Excel folder on your Data Disk. Click the Enable Macros button, if necessary, then save the workbook as T9-EX-E7D.

b. Open the Visual Basic Editor. Display and then read the End Property Help screen. Click Example at the top of the Help screen. Study the examples, then close the Help window.

c. Open the Module1 module's Code window, then view the DisplaySales procedure. Change the filename in the Set statement to "t9-ex-e7d.xls". Remove the two Set statements that appear below the comment `'display negative differences in red` in the DisplaySales procedure. Replace both Set statements with one that assigns the appropriate range to the rngCurrent variable.

d. Save the workbook. Return to Excel and run the DisplaySales macro. Use the macro to display the sales information for only the Warren store.

e. When the macro is working correctly, save and then close the workbook.

discovery ▶ **8.** In this exercise, you will learn how to use the Range object's FormatConditions property to format a range.

a. Open the Monthly Sales (Monthly Sales.xls) workbook, which you created in this lesson. The workbook is located in the Tut09\Excel folder on your Data Disk. Click the Enable Macros button, if necessary, then save the workbook as T9-EX-E8D.

b. Open the Visual Basic Editor. Display and then read the Add Method (FormatConditions Collection) Help screen. Notice that the Add method contains four arguments: Type, Operator, Formula1, and Formula2. Click Example at the top of the Help screen. Study the example, then close the Help window.

c. Open the Module1 module's Code window, then view the DisplaySales procedure. Change the filename in the Set statement to "t9-ex-e8d.xls". Remove the five instructions beginning with the instruction `For Each rngCell In rngCurrent` and ending with the instruction `Next rngCell`. Replace those five instructions with the following three instructions: `rngCurrent.FormatConditions.Delete`, `rngCurrent.FormatConditions.Add xlCellValue, xlLess, "0"` and `rngCurrent.FormatConditions(1).Font.Color = vbRed`.

d. Save the workbook. Return to Excel and run the DisplaySales macro. Use the macro to display the sales information for only the Warren store.

e. When the macro is working correctly, save and then close the workbook.

A computer program is good only if it works. Errors in programming code can cause a program to run incorrectly. Therefore, a programmer needs to know how to locate and fix any errors in his or her code. Exercise 9 is a Debugging Exercise. Debugging Exercises allow you to practice recognizing and solving errors in code.

debugging

9. In this exercise, you will debug two existing procedures.

   a. Open the T9-EX-E9 (T9-EX-E9.xls) workbook, which is located in the Tut09\Excel folder on your Data Disk. Click the Enable Macros button, if necessary, then save the workbook as T9-EX-E9D.

   b. Open the Visual Basic Editor. Open the Module1 module's Code window, then view the PrintWorksheets1 procedure. The procedure should loop through each worksheet in the workbook, asking the user if he or she wants to print the worksheet, but it is not working correctly. (To conserve paper, use the PrintPreview method rather than the Print method.)

   c. Study the PrintWorksheets1 procedure's code, then return to Excel and run the PrintWorksheets1 macro. Return to the Visual Basic Editor and correct any errors in the procedure. When the macro is working correctly, save the workbook.

   d. Open the Visual Basic Editor and view the PrintWorksheets2 procedure. Like the PrintWorksheets1 procedure, this procedure should loop through each worksheet in the workbook, asking the user if he or she wants to print the worksheet, but it is not working correctly. (To conserve paper, use the PrintPreview method rather than the Print method.)

   e. Study the PrintWorksheets2 procedure's code, then return to Excel and run the PrintWorksheets2 macro. Return to the Visual Basic Editor and correct any errors in the PrintWorksheets2 procedure. When the macro is working correctly, save and then close the workbook.

Word Lesson

Using the Repetition Structure and the With Statement in Word

case ▶ Willowton Health Club is sponsoring a 10K walk/run on July 20th at 9 a.m. All proceeds from the event, which is open to members of the club as well as nonmembers, will be donated to the Fund for Cancer Research. To participate, one needs simply to stop by the club's front desk and fill out a registration form, a copy of which is given to the participant.

At the end of each week, the club's secretary, Nancy Manley, uses the registration forms to compile a list of the names and addresses of the participants. She has decided to create a macro that will print the registration form and also compile the list of participants for her.

Viewing the Registration Form and Participant List Documents

The PrintAndRecordInfo macro will require the use of two Word documents: a Registration Form document and a Participant List document. You will find both document files on your Data Disk. Begin by viewing both files and the code template for the PrintAndRecordInfo procedure.

To view the files and the PrintAndRecordInfo procedure:

1 Start Microsoft Word.

2 Open the **T9-WD-1** (T9-WD-1.doc) document, which is located in the Tut09\Word folder on your Data Disk. Click the **Enable Macros** button, if necessary, then save the document as **Registration Form**. Figure 9-17 shows the Registration Form document.

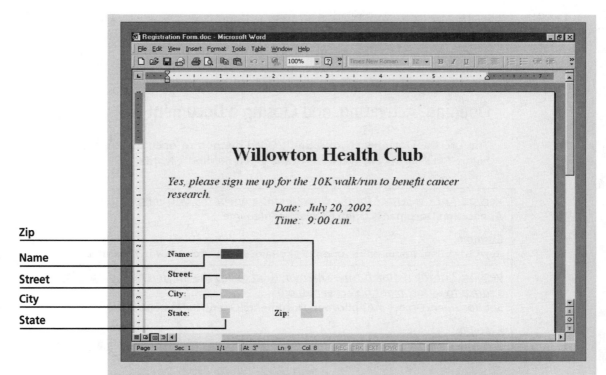

Zip

Name

Street

City

State

Figure 9-17: Registration Form document

As Figure 9-17 indicates, the Registration Form document contains five form fields named Name, Street, City, State, and Zip. The PrintAndRecordInfo macro will need to print this document for the participant, and also record the name and address information in the Participant List document, which you will view next.

3 Open the **T9-WD-2** (T9-WD-2.doc) document, which is located in the Tut09\Word folder on your Data Disk, then save the document as **Participant List**. Notice that the Participant List document contains only the "List of Participants for the 10K Walk/Run" title. The PrintAndRecordInfo macro will record the participant information below this title.

4 Close the Participant List document.

5 Press **Alt+F11** to open the Visual Basic Editor. If necessary, open the Project Explorer window and close the Properties window, the Immediate window, and any open Code windows. Open the Module1 module's Code window, then view the code template for the **PrintAndRecordInfo** procedure.

6 Close the Project Explorer window so that you can view more of the Code window.

Before you can code the PrintAndRecordInfo procedure, you need to learn how to open, activate, and close a document. You also need to learn how to refer to the main text story in a document and how to insert information into a document. First learn about opening, activating, and closing a document

Opening, Activating, and Closing a Document

You use the Documents collection's **Open method** to open an existing document. Figure 9-18 shows two versions of the Open method's syntax.

Version 1 of the syntax for the Open method opens the document:
Application.Documents.Open FileName:=_filename_

Example:
```
Application.Documents.Open FileName:="C:\Tut09\Word\Sample.doc"
```

Version 2 of the syntax for the Open method opens the document and assigns its address to a Document object variable:
Set _documentObject_ = **Application.Documents.Open(FileName:=**_filename_**)**

Example:
```
Set docSample = Application.Documents.Open(FileName:="Sample.doc")
```

Figure 9-18: Two versions of the Open method's syntax

··

Figure 9-18 shows only the basic syntax of the Open method. To learn more about this method, view its Help screen.

··

As Figure 9-18 indicates, the first version of the Open method's syntax merely opens the document while the second version opens the document and immediately assigns its address to a Document object variable. Notice that the second version of the syntax requires you to enclose the FileName argument in a set of parentheses.

In both versions of the syntax, *filename* is the name of the file you want to open and it can include the file's path, as shown in Figure 9-18's first example. If you do not specify the file's path, as in the second example, the Open method will search for the file in the current folder. If the Open method cannot locate *filename*, an error message is displayed.

When multiple documents are open, only one can be the active document, which is the document in which you currently are working. You can use the Document object's **Activate method** to activate (switch the focus to) another document. The syntax of the Activate method is *documentObject*.**Activate**. For example, the instruction `docList.Activate` activates the document whose address is contained in the docList object variable.

You use the **Close method** to close one or more open documents. Figure 9-19 shows the syntax and three examples of the Close method.

Syntax: *expression*.**Close SaveChanges:**=*constant*	
SaveChanges *constant* **settings**	**Meaning**
`wdDoNotSaveChanges`	Close the document without saving any changes made to it since the last time it was saved.
`wdPromptToSaveChanges`	If the document was changed since the last time it was saved, then display a prompt that asks the user if he or she wants to save the document before closing the document.
`wdSaveChanges`	If the document was changed since the last time it was saved, then save the document before closing the document.

Examples:
 `Application.Documents.Close SaveChanges:=wdPromptToSaveChanges`
 `docTemp.Close SaveChanges:=wdDoNotSaveChanges`
 `docList.Close SaveChanges:=wdSaveChanges`	

Figure 9-19: Syntax and examples of the Close method

In the syntax, *expression* can be either the Documents collection or a Document object. If *expression* is the Documents collection, as it is in the first example shown in Figure 9-19, all open documents are closed. If, on the other hand, *expression* is a Document object, as it is in the figure's second and third examples, only the document associated with that object is closed.

The Close method's SaveChanges argument indicates whether changes made to a document should be saved before the document is closed. As Figure 9-19 shows, the SaveChanges argument can be set to either of the intrinsic constants `wdDoNotSaveChanges`, `wdPromptToSaveChanges`, or `wdSaveChanges`.

The PrintAndRecordInfo procedure will need to insert each participant's name and address information below the title in the Participant List document. To do so, the procedure will need to refer to the Participant List document's main text story. It also will need to use the Range object's InsertAfter method. First learn how to refer to a document's main text story.

Referring to the Main Text Story in a Document

As you learned in Tutorial 6's Word lesson, a story is defined as a document area containing a range of text that is distinct from other areas of text in the document. For example, if a document contains body text, footnotes, and headers, then it contains a main text story, a footnotes story, and a headers story.

You can use the Document object's **Content property** to return a Range object that contains the document's main text story. The syntax of the Content property is *documentObject*.**Content**. For example, `docList.Content` returns the main text story of the document whose address is stored in the docList variable. You could use the instruction `Set rngBody = docList.Content` to assign the address of the main text story to the rngBody Range object variable, then use the instruction `rngBody.CheckSpelling` to check the spelling in the main text story.

Next, learn how to use the InsertAfter and InsertBefore methods to insert text in a document.

Inserting Text in a Document

You can use the InsertBefore and InsertAfter methods to insert text in a document. Figure 9-20 shows the syntax and five examples of these methods.

Syntax:
expression.**InsertBefore Text:**=*string*
expression.**InsertAfter Text:**=*string*

Examples:
```
Selection.InsertBefore Text:="Microsoft"

Selection.InsertAfter Text:="Microsoft"

Set rngFirst = docBook.Sentences(1)
rngFirst.InsertBefore Text:="Table of Contents" & vbNewLine

Set rngBody = docBook.Content
rngBody.InsertAfter Text:="The End" & vbNewLine
```

Figure 9-20: Syntax and examples of the InsertBefore and InsertAfter methods

In the syntax, *expression* is either a Selection object or a Range object, and *string* is the text you want to insert either before (**InsertBefore method**) or after (**InsertAfter method**) the object. For example, the instruction `Selection.InsertBefore Text:="Microsoft"` shown in Figure 9-20 inserts the word "Microsoft" (without the quotation marks) before the selection in the document, while the instruction `Selection.InsertAfter Text:="Microsoft"` inserts "Microsoft" after the selection.

In the third example shown in Figure 9-20, the instruction `Set rngFirst = docBook.Sentences(1)` assigns the first sentence in the document whose address is stored in the docBook variable to a Range object variable named rngFirst. The instruction `rngFirst.InsertBefore Text:="Table of Contents" & vbNewLine` then inserts "Table of Contents" (without the quotation marks) and a blank line before the first sentence in the document.

In Figure 9-20's fourth example, the instruction `Set rngBody = docBook.Content` assigns the main text story in the document whose address is stored in the docBook variable to a Range object variable named rngBody. The instruction `rngBody.InsertAfter Text:="The End" & vbNewLine` then will insert "The End" (without the quotation marks) and a blank line after the main text story in the document.

tip

As you learned in Tutorial 5, `vbNewLine` is a VBA intrinsic constant that causes the insertion point to move to the next line in a document.

Now that you know how to open, close, and activate a document, as well as how to refer to a document's main text story and how to insert text in a document, you can begin coding the PrintAndRecordInfo procedure.

Coding the PrintAndRecordInfo Procedure

Recall that the PrintAndRecordInfo procedure will need to print the Registration Form document and also record each participant's name and address in the Participant List document. The participant information should be recorded in the Participant List document using the format shown in Figure 9-21.

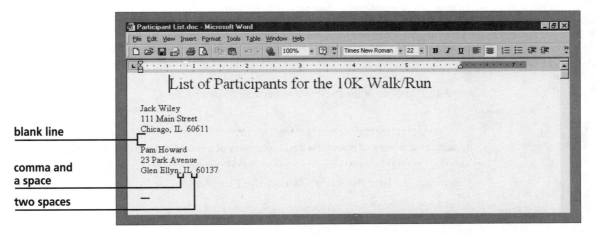

Figure 9-21: Name and address information shown in the Participant List document

Notice that each participant's name and address information occupies three lines in the document: the participant's name appears on the first line, his or her street address appears on the second line, and the city, state, and zip code appear on the third line. As Figure 9-21 indicates, a comma and a space separate the city from the state, and two spaces separate the state from the zip code. Also notice that a blank line separates each participant from the next.

Figure 9-22 shows the pseudocode for the PrintAndRecordInfo procedure.

---

1. Open the Participant List document.
2. Insert the value of the Name form field's Result property at the end of the Participant List document, then move the insertion point to the next line. The form field is contained in the Registration Form document.
3. Insert the value of the Street form field's Result property at the end of the Participant List document, then move the insertion point to the next line. The form field is contained in the Registration Form document.
4. Insert the value of the City form field's Result property, a comma, and a space at the end of the Participant List document. The form field is contained in the Registration Form document.
5. Insert the value of the State form field's Result property and two spaces at the end of the Participant List document. The form field is contained in the Registration Form document.
6. Insert the value of the Zip form field's Result property at the end of the Participant List document, then move the insertion point down two lines. The form field is contained in the Registration Form document.
7. Activate the Registration Form document.
8. Print the Registration Form document.
9. Use the MsgBox function to ask the user if he or she wants to enter another participant's information. Store the user's response in an Integer variable named intAnother.
10. If intAnother = vbYes, then
    a. Repeat the following for each form field in the Registration Form document:
        1) Clear each form field's Result property.
    b. Select the Name form field.
   Else
    a. Close the Participant List document, saving the changes made to it.
    b. Close the Registration Form document without saving the changes made to it.

Figure 9-22: Pseudocode for the PrintAndRecordInfo procedure

···

Recall that you learned about the Result property of a form field in Tutorial 4's Word lesson.

···

Figure 9-23 lists the variables that the PrintAndRecordInfo procedure will use.

Variable	datatype
intAnother	Integer
docRegis	Document
docList	Document
rngListBody	Range
ffdInfo	FormField

Figure 9-23: Variables used by the PrintAndRecordInfo procedure

The PrintAndRecordInfo procedure will use the intAnother variable to store the value returned by the MsgBox function. It will use the docRegis and docList object variables to store the address of the Registration Form and Participant List documents, respectively. The rngListBody variable will store the address of the Participant List document's main text story, and the ffdInfo object variable will be used in a loop that repeats its instructions for each form field in the Registration Form document.

In the next set of steps, you will declare the appropriate variables and then translate each line in Figure 9-22's pseudocode into one or more VBA statements.

To begin coding the PrintAndRecordInfo procedure::

1 Enter the documentation and the Dim and Set statements shown in Figure 9-24.

**enter these six
lines of code**

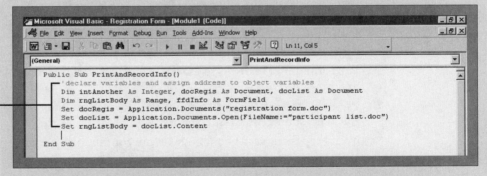

```
Microsoft Visual Basic - Registration Form - [Module1 [Code]]
File Edit View Insert Format Debug Run Tools Add-Ins Window Help

(General)                                    PrintAndRecordInfo

    Public Sub PrintAndRecordInfo()
        'declare variables and assign address to object variables
        Dim intAnother As Integer, docRegis As Document, docList As Document
        Dim rngListBody As Range, ffdInfo As FormField
        Set docRegis = Application.Documents("registration form.doc")
        Set docList = Application.Documents.Open(FileName:="participant list.doc")
        Set rngListBody = docList.Content

    End Sub
```

Figure 9-24: Code window showing documentation and Dim and Set statements

Notice that the first Set statement assigns the address of the open Registration Form document to the docRegis variable. The second Set statement opens the Participant List document, which is Step 1 in the pseudocode, and also assigns its address to the docList object variable. The third Set statement then assigns the Participant List's main text story to the rngListBody variable.

Steps 2 through 6 in the pseudocode are to insert the name and address information at the end of the Participant List document—in other words, insert it after the document's main text story, the address of which is stored in the rngListBody variable.

2 Type **'insert participant information** and press the **Enter** key, then type **with rnglistbody** and press the **Enter** key.

First, insert the value stored in the Name form field's Result property followed by the `vbNewLine` constant, which will move the insertion point to the next line in the document.

3 Press the **Tab** key, then type **.insertafter text:=docregis.formfields("name").result & vbnewline** (be sure to type the period before the word "insertafter") and press the **Enter** key.

Next, insert the value stored in the Street form field's Result property followed by the `vbNewLine` constant.

4 Type **.insertafter text:=docregis.formfields("street").result & vbnewline** and press the **Enter** key.

Now insert the value stored in the City form field's Result property, as well as the comma and space that separates the city from the state.

5 Type **.insertafter text:=docregis.formfields("city").result & ", "** (be sure to type a comma and a space between the quotation marks) and press the **Enter** key.

Now insert the value stored in the State form field's Result property, as well as the two spaces that separate the state from the zip code.

6 Type **.insertafter text:=docregis.formfields("state").result & "** (be sure to type the quotation mark) and press the **Spacebar** twice, then type **"** (a quotation mark) and press the **Enter** key.

Finally, insert the value stored in the Zip form field's Result property followed by two `vbNewLine` constants, which will move the insertion point down two lines in the document.

7 Type **.insertafter text:=docregis.formfields("zip").result & vbnewline & vbnewline** and press the **Enter** key.

8 Press the **Backspace** key to remove the indentation, then type **end with** to end the With statement. Press the **Enter** key.

9 Verify the accuracy of your code before continuing by comparing the code on your screen to the code shown in Figure 9-25.

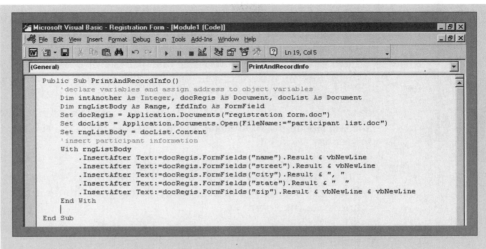

Figure 9-25: Partially completed PrintAndRecordInfo procedure

10 Save the document.

Now that you have entered the code that records the participant's information in the Participant List document, you need to enter the code that will activate and print the Registration Form document.

To finish coding the procedure:

1 Type **'activate and print registration form** and press the **Enter** key, then type **docregis.activate** and press the **Enter** key.

2 If your computer is connected to a printer, type **docregis.printout** and press the **Enter** key. If your computer is not connected to a printer, type **docregis.printpreview** and press the **Enter** key.

According to Step 9 in the pseudocode, the next step is to use the MsgBox function to ask the user if he or she wants to enter another participant's information. You should assign the user's response to the intAnother variable.

3 Type **'ask user if he or she wants to enter another participant's info** and press the **Enter** key, then type **intanother = msgbox(prompt:="Enter another participant?", _** (be sure to type the comma followed by a space and the underscore) and press the **Enter** key. Press the **Tab** key, then type **buttons:=vbyesno + vbexclamation, title:="Participant Information")** and press the **Enter** key.

If the user clicks the Yes button in the message box, the procedure should clear the value stored in each form field's Result property. As you learned in the Concept lesson, you can use either the For...Next statement or the For Each...Next statement to repeat one or more instructions for each object in a collection. In this case, you will use the For Each...Next statement simply because it provides a more convenient way to refer to the objects in a collection.

> You will modify the PrintAndRecordInfo procedure to use the For...Next statement in this lesson's Exercise 1.

4 Press the **Backspace** key, then type **if intanother = vbyes then** and press the **Enter** key. Press the **Tab** key, then type **for each ffdinfo in docregis.formfields** and press the **Enter** key.

You can clear the value stored in each form field by assigning a zero-length string ("") to the form field's Result property.

> Recall that you learned about a zero-length string, often called an empty string, in Tutorial 4's Concept lesson.

5 Press the **Tab** key, then type **ffdinfo.result = ""** (two quotation marks with no space between) and press the **Enter** key. Press the **Backspace** key, then type **next ffdinfo** and press the **Enter** key.

According to the pseudocode, after clearing the form fields, the procedure should select the Name form field so that the user can begin typing the next participant's information.

6 Type **docregis.formfields("name").select** and press the **Enter** key.

If the user does not want to enter information for another participant, the procedure should close both documents, saving the changes made to the Participant List document, but not saving the changes made to the Registration Form document.

7 Press the **Backspace** key, then type the additional instructions shown in Figure 9-26, which shows the completed PrintAndRecordInfo procedure.

the code in the
Code window
was
compressed

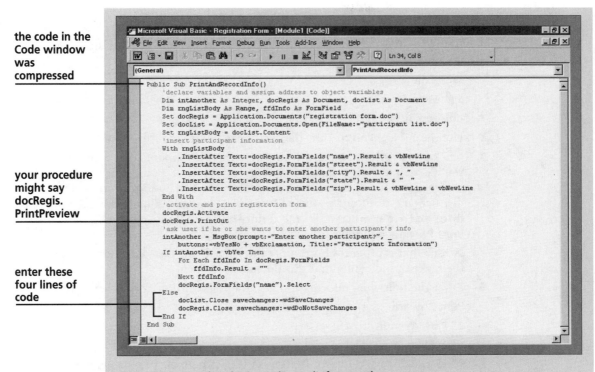

your procedure
might say
docRegis.
PrintPreview

enter these
four lines of
code

```
Microsoft Visual Basic - Registration Form - [Module1 [Code]]
File  Edit  View  Insert  Format  Debug  Run  Tools  Add-Ins  Window  Help

(General)                                                      PrintAndRecordInfo

Public Sub PrintAndRecordInfo()
    'declare variables and assign address to object variables
    Dim intAnother As Integer, docRegis As Document, docList As Document
    Dim rngListBody As Range, ffdInfo As FormField
    Set docRegis = Application.Documents("registration form.doc")
    Set docList = Application.Documents.Open(FileName:="participant list.doc")
    Set rngListBody = docList.Content
    'insert participant information
    With rngListBody
        .InsertAfter Text:=docRegis.FormFields("name").Result & vbNewLine
        .InsertAfter Text:=docRegis.FormFields("street").Result & vbNewLine
        .InsertAfter Text:=docRegis.FormFields("city").Result & ", "
        .InsertAfter Text:=docRegis.FormFields("state").Result & "  "
        .InsertAfter Text:=docRegis.FormFields("zip").Result & vbNewLine & vbNewLine
    End With
    'activate and print registration form
    docRegis.Activate
    docRegis.PrintOut
    'ask user if he or she wants to enter another participant's info
    intAnother = MsgBox(prompt:="Enter another participant?", _
        buttons:=vbYesNo + vbExclamation, Title:="Participant Information")
    If intAnother = vbYes Then
        For Each ffdInfo In docRegis.FormFields
            ffdInfo.Result = ""
        Next ffdInfo
        docRegis.FormFields("name").Select
    Else
        docList.Close savechanges:=wdSaveChanges
        docRegis.Close savechanges:=wdDoNotSaveChanges
    End If
End Sub
```

Figure 9-26: Completed PrintAndRecordInfo procedure

HELP? The code in the Code window shown in Figure 9-26 was compressed so that you could view the entire procedure. If you want to compress the code shown on your screen, click Tools on the Visual Basic Editor's Standard toolbar, then click Options, and then click the Editor Format tab. Select 9 in the Size list box, then click the OK button.

8 Verify the accuracy of your code before continuing by comparing the code on your screen to the code shown in Figure 9-26, then save the document.

Now that you have translated the pseudocode shown in Figure 9-22 into VBA statements, you should test the PrintAndRecordInfo macro to verify that it is working correctly.

To test the PrintAndRecordInfo macro:

1 Return to Word. Enter the following information into the Registration Form document:

Jack Wiley

111 Main Street

Chicago, IL 60611

2 Use the View menu to view the customized Participant Info toolbar.

3 Click the **Print and Record** button on the Participant Info toolbar. When the Participant Information dialog box asks if you want to enter the information for another participant, click the **Yes** button. If you entered the instruction `docRegis.PrintPreview` rather than the instruction `docRegis.PrintOut` in the PrintAndRecordInfo procedure, close the **Print Preview** window.

Notice that a program button for the Participant List document appears on the taskbar, indicating that this document is open.

4 Enter the following information into the Registration Form document:

Pam Howard

23 Park Avenue

Glen Ellyn, IL 60137

5 Click the **Print and Record** button on the Participant Info toolbar. When the Participant Information dialog box asks if you want to enter the information for another participant, click the **No** button.

The procedure closes the Registration Form and Participant List documents, saving the changes made to the Participant List document, but not saving the changes made to the Registration Form document. You will open both documents to verify that fact.

6 Open the **Participant List** (Participant List.doc) document. The document contains the two names and addresses you entered into the Registration Form document, as shown in Figure 9-27.

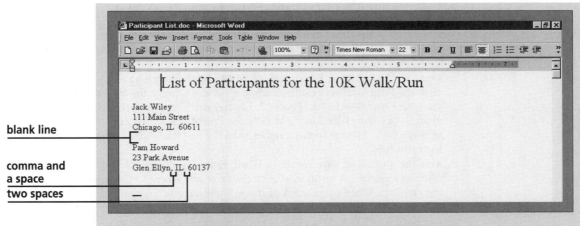

blank line

**comma and
a space**

two spaces

Figure 9-27: Participant List document showing participant information

Notice that each participant's name and address information occupies three lines in the document. A comma and a space separate the city from the state, and two spaces separate the state from the zip code. Also notice that a blank line separates the first participant's information from the second participant's information.

7 Close the **Participant List** document and open the **Registration Form** (Registration Form.doc) document. Click the **Enable Macros** button, if necessary. Notice that the form fields are empty—in other words, the procedure did not save the participant information you entered into the document.

8 Close Word.

You now have completed Tutorial 9's Word lesson. You can either take a break or complete the end-of-lesson exercises before moving on to the next lesson.

 # EXERCISES

1. In this exercise, you will modify the PrintAndRecordInfo procedure that you created in this lesson so that it uses the For...Next statement rather than the For Each...Next statement to clear the form fields.

a. Open the T9-WD-2 (T9-WD-2.doc) document, which is located in the Tut09\Word folder on your Data Disk. Save the document as T9-WD-E1DList, then close the document.

b. Open the Registration Form (Registration Form.doc) document, which you created in this lesson. The document is located in the Tut09\Word folder on your Data Disk. Click the Enable Macros button, if necessary, then save the document as T9-WD-E1DRegis. If necessary, use the View menu to view the customized Participant Info toolbar.

c. Open the Visual Basic Editor. Open the Module1 module's Code window, then view the PrintAndRecordInfo procedure's code. Change the filename in the first Set statement to "t9-wd-e1dregis.doc". Change the filename in the second Set statement to "t9-wd-e1dlist.doc". Modify the PrintAndRecordInfo procedure so that it uses the For...Next statement rather than the For Each...Next statement to clear the form fields.

d. Save the document, then return to Word. Enter your name and address information into the registration form, then click the Print and Record button on the Participant Info toolbar. When you are asked if you want to enter another participant's information, click the No button.

e. Open the T9-WD-E1DList (T9-WD-E1DList.doc) document to verify that it contains your name and address, then close the document.

2. In this exercise, you will create a macro procedure that allows the user to print a permit for either the Cycling or Yoga class.

a. Open the Yoga (Yoga.doc) document, which is located in the Tut09\Word folder on your Data Disk. The document represents a permit for the Beginning Yoga class. Notice that the document's third paragraph says "[insert name and address information here]." Save the document as T9-WD-E2DYoga, then close the document.

b. Open the Cycling (Cycling.doc) document, which is located in the Tut09\Word folder on your Data Disk. The document represents a permit for the Beginning Cycling class. Notice that the document's third paragraph says "[insert name and address information here]." Save the document as T9-WD-E2DCycling, then close the document.

c. Open the T9-WD-E2 (T9-WD-E2.doc) document, which is located in the Tut09\Word folder on your Data Disk. Click the Enable Macros button, if necessary, then save the document as T9-WD-E2D. View the customized Macros toolbar, if necessary. The document has five form fields named Name, Street, City, State, and Zip.

d. Open the Visual Basic Editor. Open the Module1 module's Code window, then view the PrintClassPermit procedure. The procedure should allow the user to enter the name and address information in either of the two permit documents—either the T9-WD-E2DCycling document or the T9-WD-E2DYoga document. Use the InputBox function to prompt the user to enter the appropriate document—either C for Cycling or Y for Yoga. Insert the name and address information from the form fields into the appropriate permit document, then print the permit document. Close the permit document without saving the changes made to it. Clear the form fields in the T9-WD-E2D document, and then select the Name form field.

e. Save the document, then return to Word. Enter your name and address information into the form fields, then click the Print Class Permit button on the Macros toolbar. Print the permit for the Yoga class. Save and then close the T9-WD-E2D document.

3. In this exercise, you will practice with the For...Next statement. You also will learn how to animate the text in a document.

a. Open the T9-WD-E3 (T9-WD-E3.doc) document, which is located in the Tut09\Word folder on your Data Disk. Click the Enable Macros button, if necessary, then save the document as T9-WD-E3D.

b. Open the Visual Basic Editor. Open the Module1 module's Code window and view the AnimateWords1 procedure. Study the procedure's code. Below the `'animate only some words` comment, enter a For...Next statement that will animate every other word to the wdAnimationMarchingRedAnts setting.

c. Save the document. Return to Word and run the AnimateWords1 macro to verify that it is working correctly. (Every other word should be surrounded by a moving red border.)

d. Return to the Visual Basic Editor. Open the AnimateWords2 procedure. Code the procedure so that it uses a For...Next statement to display every third word using the wdAnimationSparkleText setting.

e. Save the document. Return to Word and run the AnimateWords2 macro to verify that it is working correctly.

f. Close the document.

4. In this exercise, you will modify the PrintAndRecordInfo procedure that you created in this lesson. The modified procedure will verify that all of the form fields have been completed before the participant's information is entered into the Participant List document.

a. Open the T9-WD-2 (T9-WD-2.doc) document, which is located in the Tut09\Word folder on your Data Disk. Save the document as T9-WD-E4DList, then close the document.

b. Open the Registration Form (Registration Form.doc) document, which you created in this lesson. The document is located in the Tut09\Word folder on your Data Disk. Click the Enable Macros button, if necessary, then save the document as T9-WD-E4DRegis. Display the customized Participant Info toolbar, if necessary.

c. Open the Visual Basic Editor. Open the Module1 module's Code window, then view the PrintAndRecordInfo procedure's code. Change the filename in the first Set statement to "t9-wd-e4dregis.doc". Change the filename in the second Set statement to "t9-wd-e4dlist.doc".

d. Currently, if the user clicks the Print and Record button on the Participant Info toolbar without first entering data into the form fields, the PrintAndRecordInfo procedure will print the registration form and also insert three lines (two blank lines and one line that contains only a comma) in the participant list document. Modify the procedure so that it uses a For Each...Next loop to determine if each form field contains a value. If at least one of the form fields is blank, prevent the procedure from doing the following: inserting the participant information into the participant list document, activating and printing the registration form, asking the user if he or she wants to enter another participant's information, clearing the form fields, and closing the documents. Rather, have the procedure display an appropriate message alerting the user that all of the form fields must be completed. (*Hint*: View the Trim function's Help screen.)

e. Save the document, then return to Word. Click the Print and Record button on the Participant Info toolbar without entering any information into the form fields. An appropriate message should appear in a message box. Close the message box.

f. Enter your name, street, city, and state information into the registration form, then press the Spacebar twice to enter two spaces in the Zip form field. Click the Print and Record button. An appropriate message should appear in a message box. Close the message box.

g. Enter your name and address information into the registration form, then click the Print and Record button. When you are asked if you want to enter another participant's information, click the No button.

h. Open the T9-WD-E4DList document to verify that it contains your name and address, then close the document.

Exercises 5 through 7 are Discovery Exercises. Discovery Exercises, which may include topics that are not covered in the lesson, allow you to "discover" the solution to the problem on your own.

discovery ▶ 5. In this exercise, you will modify the PrintAndRecordInfo procedure that you created in this lesson. You will learn about the Application object's FileSearch and FoundFiles objects, as well as the Documents collection's Add method.

a. Open the Registration Form (Registration Form.doc) document, which you created in this lesson. The file is located in the Tut09\Word folder on your Data Disk. Click the Enable Macros button, if necessary, then save the document as T9-WD-E5DRegis. Display the customized Participant Info toolbar, if necessary.

b. Open the Visual Basic Editor. Open the Module1 module's Code window, then view the PrintAndRecordInfo procedure. Change the filename in the first Set statement to "t9-wd-e5dregis.doc". Change the filename in the second Set statement to "t9-wd-e5dlist.doc".

c. Display and study the following Help screens: FileSearch Object, LookIn property, FileName property, Execute method, FoundFiles property, FoundFiles object. Also display the Documents Collection Object Help screen, then use this Help screen to display the Add method's Help screen. Close the Help window.

d. Modify the PrintAndRecordInfo procedure so that it checks if the T9-WD-E5DList.doc document exists in the Tut09\Word folder on your Data Disk. Use the With statement to set the FileSearch object's LookIn and FileName properties, as well as to invoke its Execute method. If the T9-WD-E5DList document exists, open the existing document. However, if the T9-WD-E5DList document does not exist, use the Add method to add a document to the Documents collection. Enter the "List of Participants for the 10K Walk/Run" title and two new blank lines into the document. Also, change the title's font size to 22, and change its alignment to center. Use the Document object's SaveAs method to save the new file as T9-WD-E5DList.doc.

e. Save the document, then return to Word. Enter your name and address information into the registration form, then click the Print and Record button on the Participant Info toolbar. When you are asked if you want to enter another participant's information, click the No button.

f. Open the T9-WD-E5DList document to verify that it contains your name and address, then close the document.

discovery ▶ 6. In this exercise, you will create a macro procedure that updates the values contained in a table.

     a. Open the T9-WD-E6 (T9-WD-E6.doc) document, which is located in the Tut09\Word folder on your Data Disk. Click the Enable Macros button, if necessary, then save the document as T9-WD-E6D.

     b. Open the Visual Basic Editor. Open the Module1 module's Code window. The module contains the code template for two procedures named ForEachUpdate and ForNextUpdate. Each procedure should use the InputBox function to allow the user to enter a number, which then will be used to increase each of the amounts shown in the second column of the table. Use the Format function to format the amounts to "Fixed". The ForEachUpdate procedure should use the For Each...Next statement to refer to the appropriate cells, and the ForNextUpdate procedure should use the For...Next statement to refer to the cells.

     c. Save the document. Return to Word and run the ForEachUpdate macro. Use the ForEachUpdate macro to update each table amount by $2. Save the document, then run the ForNextUpdate macro. Use the ForNextUpdate macro to update each table amount by $5.

     d. Save and then close the document.

discovery ▶ 7. In this exercise, you will create a macro procedure that searches for a product ID in a table and then updates the product's price.

     a. Open the T9-WD-E7 (T9-WD-E7.doc) document, which is located in the Tut09\Word folder on your Data Disk. Click the Enable Macros button, if necessary, then save the document as T9-WD-E7D.

     b. Open the Visual Basic Editor. The document contains the code template for two procedures named ForEachUpdate and ForNextUpdate. Each procedure should use the InputBox function to allow the user to enter a product ID and a number. The procedure will need to search for the product ID in the first column in the table, and then use the number entered by the user to update the product's price. (For example, if the user enters product ID EF455 and the number 2, the procedure should increase product ID EF455's price from 25.00 to 27.00.) Use the Format function to format the new price to "Fixed". The ForEachUpdate procedure should use the For Each...Next statement to search for the product ID, and the ForNextUpdate procedure should use the For...Next statement to search for the product ID. Code each procedure appropriately.

     c. Return to Word. Save the document. Use the ForEachUpdate procedure to update product ID EF455 by $2. Save the document. Use the ForNextUpdate procedure to update the BD203 product by $6.

     d. Save and then close the document.

A computer program is good only if it works. Errors in programming code can cause a program to run incorrectly. Therefore, a programmer needs to know how to locate and fix any errors in his or her code. Exercise 8 is a Debugging Exercise. Debugging Exercises allow you to practice recognizing and solving errors in code.

debugging

8. In this exercise, you will debug an existing macro procedure.

   a. Open the T9-WD-E8 (T9-WD-E8.doc) document, which is located in the Tut09\Word folder on your Data Disk. Click the Enable Macros button, if necessary, then save the document as T9-WD-E8D. You will notice that each sentence is separated from the next with a period, rather than with a period and a space. The document's AddASpace procedure was supposed to remedy this situation by inserting a space after each period, but it is not working correctly.

   b. Open the Visual Basic Editor. Open the Module1 module's Code window, then view the AddASpace procedure's code. Study the code, then return to Word and run the AddASpace macro.

   c. Return to the Visual Basic Editor and correct any errors in the AddASpace procedure. When the macro is working correctly, save and then close the document.

Access Lesson

Using the Repetition Structure and the With Statement in Access

case ▶ This semester, Professor Carlisle of Snowville College is teaching three courses over the Internet: CIS100, CIS110, and CIS260. The CIS100 and CIS110 courses require the student to complete a number of projects and tests, while the CIS260 course requires the student to take quizzes and give a presentation. Professor Carlisle records the scores earned by each student in an Access database named InternetCourses. The database contains three tables, one for each course. Each table is associated with a report that can be used to display the student information—student ID, name, and scores—stored in the table. At the beginning of each week, Professor Carlisle uses the Export command on the Microsoft Access File menu to save a copy of each report in the HTML format. The HTML files then are posted to a Web page on the college's Web site.

The **Web** is a global information-sharing system, which is part of the **Internet**, a worldwide network made up of millions of interconnected computers. Information is stored on the Web in the form of electronic documents called **Web pages**. Each Web page can contain a variety of information ranging from simple text to complex multimedia such as graphics, sound, and video clips. Web pages are formatted using a special programming language called HTML, or HyperText Markup Language. The HTML language tells a **Web browser**, a special program that allows you to view a Web page, how the Web page should look on the screen. (Internet Explorer and Netscape Navigator are two popular Web browsers.)

Professor Carlisle has decided to create a macro that will generate the HTML files for him. The macro also will allow him to have one of his teaching assistants post the scores when he is too busy to do so.

Creating the PostScores Procedure

Professor Carlisle's database is stored on your Data Disk. Begin by viewing the three reports contained therein, and the code template for the PostScores procedure.

To view the database's three reports and the PostScores procedure:

1 Start Microsoft Access. Open the **InternetCourses** (InternetCourses.mdb) database, which is located in the Tut9\Access folder on your Data Disk. Click the **Maximize** button ☐ on the Microsoft Access title bar to maximize the Microsoft Access window, if necessary.

The InternetCourses database contains three tables named CIS100, CIS110, and CIS260. It also contains three reports named Report100, Report110, and Report260.

2 Click **Reports** in the Objects bar of the Database window. Right-click **Report100**, then click **Design View**. See Figure 9-28.

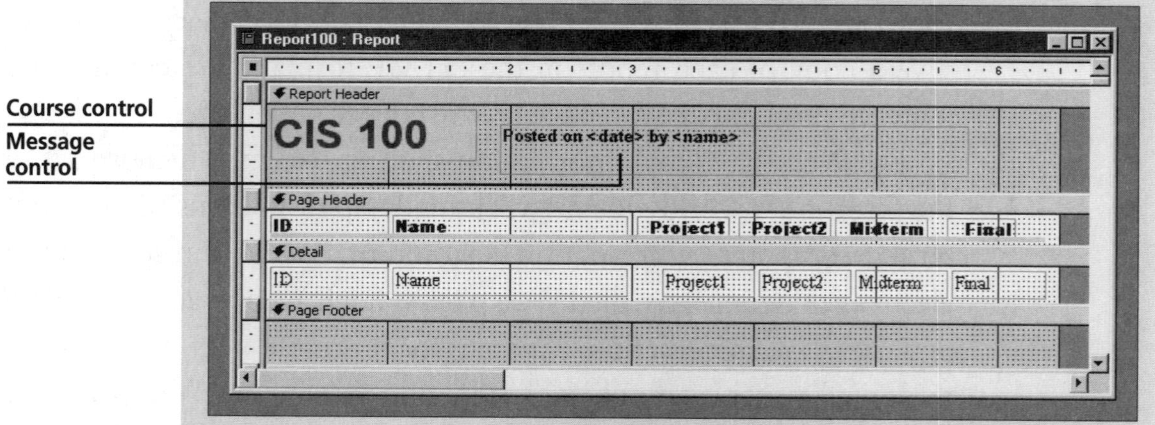

Course control
Message control

Figure 9-28: Report100 report shown in Design View

Each item on a report in Design View is called a **control**. For example, the Report Header section shown in Figure 9-28 contains two label controls named Course and Message. The Course control displays the caption "CIS 100", and the Message control displays the caption "Posted on <date> by <name>". The remaining two reports in the database, Report110 and Report260, contain the same two label controls in their Report Header section. Only the Course control's caption is different in those reports; it is "CIS 110" in the Report110 report and "CIS 260" in the Report260 report. Before the PostScores procedure generates the HTML files for these reports, it will need to enter the appropriate date and name in the Message control.

You can verify the name of a control in the report by right-clicking the control and then clicking Properties on the shortcut menu.

Next, view the report in Print Preview.

3 Close the Design View window. Right-click **Report100** in the Database window, then click **Print Preview**. Maximize the Report100 window. Scroll the Print Preview window until the report appears as shown in Figure 9-29.

scroll the window, if necessary, to view the entire report

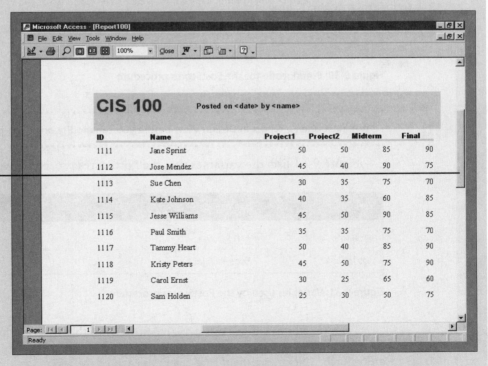

Figure 9-29: Report100 report shown in Print Preview

Notice that the report lists each student's ID, name, and scores.

4   Close the Print Preview window. Click the Database window's **Restore** button ⊡, if necessary, to restore the Database window.

5   Press **Alt+F11** to open the Visual Basic Editor. If necessary, open the Project Explorer window and close the Properties window, the Immediate window, and any open Code windows. Open the Module1 module's Code window, then view the code template for the PostScores procedure.

6   Close the Project Explorer window so that you can view more of the Code window.

Figure 9-30 shows the pseudocode for the PostScores procedure.

1. Use the InputBox function to prompt the user to enter the name of the person posting the scores. Store the user's response in a String variable named strName.
2. Repeat the following for each report in the database:
    a. Open the report in Design View.
    b. Enter the "Posted on <date> by <name>" message in the report's Message control. Use the Date function for the <date> and use the contents of the strName variable for the <name>.
    c. Save a copy of the report in HTML format.
    d. Close the report.

Figure 9-30: Pseudocode for the PostScores procedure

tip

You must open a report in Design View before you can modify one of its controls.

Figure 9-31 lists the variables that the PostScores procedure will use.

Variable	datatype
strName	String
aobToPost	AccessObject

Figure 9-31: Variables used by the PostScores procedure

The procedure will use the strName String variable to store the value returned by the InputBox function. It will use the aobToPost AccessObject object variable in a For Each...Next statement that refers to each of the reports in the database.

tip

As you learned in Tutorial 2's Access lesson, database reports, both opened and closed, are contained in the **AllReports** collection. Recall that each report in the collection is an **AccessObject** object.

In the next set of steps, you will declare the appropriate variables and then begin translating the pseudocode shown in Figure 9-30 into VBA statements.

To begin coding the PostScores procedure:

1   The insertion point should be positioned between the `Public Function` and `End Function` lines in the Code window. Press the **Tab** key, then type **'declare variables** and press the **Enter** key. Type **dim strName as string, aobToPost as accessobject** and press the **Enter** key.

Now use the InputBox function to prompt the user to enter the name of the person posting the scores. Use "Professor Carlisle" as the function's *defaultValue*.

2   Type **'enter name of person posting scores** and press the **Enter** key. Type **strname = _** (be sure to type the equal sign followed by a space and the underscore) and press the **Enter** key. Press the **Tab** key, then type **inputbox(prompt:="Enter name:", title:="Posted By", default:="Professor Carlisle")** and press the **Enter** key.

According to Step 2 in the pseudocode, you now need to perform four tasks for each report in the database. As you learned in the Concept lesson, you can use either the For…Next or the For Each…Next statement to refer to each object in a collection. In this case, you will use the For Each…Next statement to refer to each report, an AccessObject object, in the AllReports collection. Recall from Tutorial 2 that the AllReports collection is a member of the CurrentProject object, which is contained within the Access Application object. (You are using the For Each…Next statement in this case simply because it provides a more convenient way to refer to the objects in a collection.)

---

tip

You will modify the PostScores procedure to use the For…Next statement in this lesson's Exercise 1.

---

3   Press the **Backspace** to remove the indentation, then type **'open each report, insert message, save in HTML format, close report** and press the **Enter** key. Type **for each aobtopost in application.currentproject.allreports** and press the **Enter** key.

The first instruction in the loop should open the report in Design View. As you learned in Tutorial 3's Access lesson, you can use the DoCmd object's OpenReport method to do so.

4 Press the **Tab** key, then type **docmd.openreport reportname:=aobtopost.name, view:=acviewdesign** and press the **Enter** key. This command will open the report and also add a Report object that represents the report to the Application object's Reports collection.

 tip

Recall from Tutorial 3's Access lesson that an open report is a Report object, and all Report objects belong to the Application object's Reports collection.

The next instruction in the loop should enter the current date and the contents of the strName variable in the open report's Message control. The controls on a report belong to the Report object's Controls collection. For example, `Application.Reports("Report100").Controls ("Course")` refers to the Course control on the Report100 report, and `Application.Reports(aobToPost.Name).Controls ("Message")` refers to the Message control on the current report—the one whose address is stored in the aobToPost variable.

5 Type the additional instructions shown in Figure 9-32, then position the insertion point as shown in the figure.

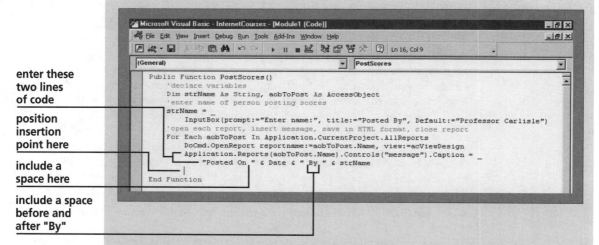

enter these
two lines
of code

position
insertion
point here

include a
space here

include a space
before and
after "By"

Figure 9-32: Partially completed PostScores procedure

6 Verify the accuracy of your code before continuing by comparing the code on your screen to the code shown in Figure 9-32, then save the database.

Steps 2c and 2d in the pseudocode are to save a copy of the report in HTML format and then close the report. Before you can code these steps, you need to learn about the DoCmd object's OutputTo and Close methods. First learn about the OutputTo method.

The DoCmd Object's OutputTo Method

You can use the DoCmd object's **OutputTo method** to save a report in HTML format, allowing the report to be published on the World Wide Web and then viewed with a Web Browser, such as Microsoft Internet Explorer. HTML, which stands for HyperText Markup Language, uses special codes to describe how the Web page should appear in a Web browser, the software used to access and view files (Web pages) on the World Wide Web. Files created using HTML are called HTML files and the files are saved using the htm extension. Figure 9-33 (on the next page) shows the syntax of the OutputTo method.

In addition to using the OutputTo method to output a report to an HTML file, you also can use it to output other Access database objects (datasheets, forms, modules, and data access pages) using other formats—such as Microsoft Excel 98 (*.xls), MS-DOS text (*.txt), and rich-text format (*.rtf).

An HTML file also can be saved with the extension html.

As Figure 9-33 indicates, the ObjectType argument specifies the type of object containing the data you want to output, and it can be one of the intrinsic constants shown in the figure. For example, an *objecttype* of `acOutputReport` indicates that the data resides in a report, whereas an *objecttype* of `acOutputTable` indicates that it resides in a table.

You enter the name of the object you want to output in the ObjectName argument. The output object must be of the same type specified in the ObjectType argument. If you omit the ObjectName argument, the name of the active object is used as the *objectname*.

You use the OutputFormat argument to specify the type of format you want used to output the data, and it can be one of the intrinsic constants shown in the figure. For example, an *outputformat* of `acFormatXLS` will output the data in Microsoft Excel format, whereas an *outputformat* of `acFormatHTML` will output the data in HTML format. If you omit the OutputFormat argument, Microsoft Access will prompt you for the *outputformat* to use.

DoCmd.OutputTo ObjectType:=*objecttype* [, ObjectName:=*objectname*] _ [, OutputFormat:=*outputformat*][, OutputFile:=*outputfile*][, AutoStart:=*autostart*] _ [, TemplateFile:=*templatefile*]	
Argument	**Explanation**
ObjectType	The type of object containing the data to output. Can be one of the following intrinsic constants: 　　　acOutputDataAccessPage 　　　acOutputForm 　　　acOutputModule 　　　acOutputQuery 　　　acOutputReport 　　　acOutputServerView 　　　acOutputStoredProcedure 　　　acOutputTable
ObjectName	A string expression that specifies the name of the object you want to output. The output object must be of the type specifed in the ObjectType argument. If you omit the ObjectName argument, the OutputTo method will use the name of the active object.
OutputFormat	The type of format you want used to output the data. Can be one of the following intrinsic constants. If you omit the OutputFormat argument, Microsoft Access will prompt you for the output format. 　　acFormatASP　　　(Active Server Page) 　　acFormatDAP　　　(Data Access Page) 　　acFormatHTML　　(Hypertext Markup Language) 　　acFormatIIS　　　(Internet Information Server) 　　acFormatRTF　　　(Rich-text Format) 　　acFormatSNP　　　(Snap) 　　acFormatTXT　　　(Text) 　　acFormatXLS　　　(Excel)
OutputFile	A string expression that specifies the name of the file to which you want the output data saved. The expression can include a path. If you omit the OutputFile argument, Microsoft Access will prompt you for the name of the *outputfile*.
AutoStart	Use True to start the appropriate Microsoft Windows-based application and load the file specified in the OutputFile argument when the output is completed. Use False if you don't want to start the application and load the file immediately.
TemplateFile	A string expression that specifes the path and name of the file to use as a template for HTML, HTX, and ASP files. The template file contains HTML tags. (HTX and ASP files are used with Microsoft Internet Information Server and Microsoft Active Server, respectively.)

Figure 9-33: Syntax of the DoCmd object's OutputTo method

In the OutputFile argument, you enter a string expression that specifies the name of the file to which you want the output data saved. If you omit the OutputFile argument, Microsoft Access will prompt you for the name of the *outputfile*.

You use the AutoStart argument, which can be set to either the Boolean value True or the Boolean value False, to indicate whether you want Access to open the *outputfile* immediately after the OutputTo method completes its task. The file will be opened using the appropriate Windows-based application, which is determined by the extension that appears in the *outputfile* name. For example, if AutoStart is set to True and the *outputfile* name ends with .xls, which indicates that the file is an Excel file, then Access will open *outputfile* in Microsoft Excel. However, if AutoStart is set to True and the *outputfile* name ends with .html (or .htm), which indicates that the file is an HTML file, then Access will open *outputfile* in your default Web browser. Setting the AutoStart argument to False indicates that you do not want the *outputfile* opened immediately after the OutputTo method completes its task.

You use the TemplateFile argument to specify the path and name of an HTML template, which is simply a text file that includes HTML tags and tokens unique to Microsoft Access. A **token** is a special code that indicates where to insert output and other information in the *outputfile*. The token <!—AccessTemplate_Title—>, for example, places the object name (Report100, for instance) in the Web browser's title bar. You may want to use a template file to include a company logo or a company-approved background in the *outputfile*. When you output a table, query, form, or report, and you specify an HTML template file in the TemplateFile argument, Microsoft Access merges the HTML template file with the object when creating the *outputfile*.

▶ **tip**

You will learn how to use the OutputTo method's TemplateFile argument in this lesson's Exercise 6.

Figure 9-34 shows the syntax and two examples of the OutputTo method. (The syntax is included in the figure for your convenience in comparing it to the examples.)

Syntax:
DoCmd.OutputTo ObjectType:=*objecttype* [, **ObjectName:**=*objectname*] _
    [, **OutputFormat:**=*outputformat*][, **OutputFile:**=*outputfile*][, **AutoStart:**=*autostart*] _
    [, **TemplateFile:**=*templatefile*]

Example 1:
```
DoCmd.OutputTo ObjectType:=acOutputReport, _
   ObjectName:="Report100", OutputFormat:=acFormatHTML, _
   OutputFile:="C:\Tut09\Access\Report100.htm", AutoStart:=False
```

Example 2:
```
DoCmd.OutputTo ObjectType:=acOutputTable, _
   ObjectName:="CIS260", OutputFormat:=acFormatXLS, _
   OutputFile:="C:\Tut09\Access\CIS260.xls", AutoStart:=True
```

Figure 9-34: Syntax and examples of the DoCmd object's OutputTo method

The OutputTo method shown in Figure 9-34's Example 1 will save a copy of the Report100 report, written in HTML format, to the Report100.htm file. Example 2's OutputTo method will save a copy of the CIS260 table, written in Microsoft Excel format, to the CIS260.xls file. Immediately thereafter, the CIS260.xls file will be opened in Microsoft Excel.

Next, learn about the DoCmd object's Close method.

The DoCmd Object's Close Method

You can use the DoCmd object's **Close method** to close an open report. Figure 9-35 shows the syntax and two examples of the Close method.

DoCmd.Close [ObjectType:=*objecttype*, **ObjectName:**=*objectname*], [**Save:**=*save*]	

ObjectType	The type of object whose window you want to close. Can be one of the following intrinsic constants. If you omit this argument, the active window is closed.
	
	        acDataAccessPage
	        acDefault
	        acDiagram
	        acForm
	        acMacro
	        acModule
	        acQuery
	        acReport
	        acServerView
	        acStoredProcedure
	        acTable

Save	Indicates whether to save changes to the object before it is closed. Can be one of the following intrinsic constants. The default is acSavePrompt.
	
	        acSaveNo
	        acSavePrompt
	        acSaveYes

Example 1:
```
DoCmd.Close ObjectType:=acReport, ObjectName:="Report100", _
    Save:=acSaveNo
```

Example 2:
```
DoCmd.Close ObjectType:=acTable, ObjectName:="CIS260"
```

Figure 9-35: Syntax and examples of the DoCmd object's Close method

The Close method's ObjectType argument specifies the type of object whose window you want to close, and it can be one of the intrinsic constants shown in Figure 9-35. For example, you use an *objecttype* of `acReport` to close a report, but you use an *objecttype* of `acTable` to close a table.

You use the Close method's Save argument to specify whether you want to save the changes made to the object before it is closed. The Save argument can be set to one of the following intrinsic constants: `acSaveNo`, `acSavePrompt`, or `acSaveYes`. The `acSaveNo` setting closes the object without saving any changes made to it, while the `acSaveYes` setting automatically saves the changes before closing the object. The `acSavePrompt` setting, which is the default setting for the Save argument, displays a dialog box that prompts you to save any changes made to the object before it is closed.

The Close method shown in Figure 9-35's Example 1 will close the Report100 report without saving any changes made to it. Example 2's Close method first will prompt you to save any changes made to the table before the table is closed. (Recall that the acSavePrompt setting is the default setting for the Save argument.)

Now that you know how to use the DoCmd object's OutputTo and Close methods, you can complete the PostScores procedure by coding Steps 2c and 2d in the pseudocode.

Completing the PostScores Procedure

According to Steps 2c and 2d in the pseudocode shown in Figure 9-30, you need to save a copy of each report in HTML format and also close each report. You can use the DoCmd object's OutputTo and Close methods in the procedure to accomplish these tasks.

To complete the PostScores procedure:

1 Type the additional instructions shown in Figure 9-36, which shows the completed PostScores procedure.

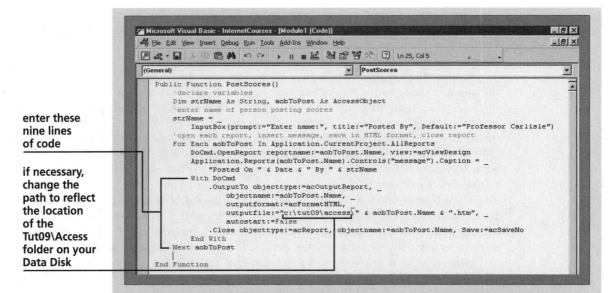

enter these nine lines of code

if necessary, change the path to reflect the location of the Tut09\Access folder on your Data Disk

```
Microsoft Visual Basic - InternetCourses - [Module1 (Code)]
File  Edit  View  Insert  Debug  Run  Tools  Add-Ins  Window  Help                 Ln 25, Col 5

(General)                                              PostScores

Public Function PostScores()
    'declare variables
    Dim strName As String, aobToPost As AccessObject
    'enter name of person posting scores
    strName = _
        InputBox(prompt:="Enter name:", title:="Posted By", Default:="Professor Carlisle")
    'open each report, insert message, save in HTML format, close report
    For Each aobToPost In Application.CurrentProject.AllReports
        DoCmd.OpenReport reportname:=aobToPost.Name, view:=acViewDesign
        Application.Reports(aobToPost.Name).Controls("message").Caption = _
            "Posted On " & Date & " By " & strName
        With DoCmd
            .OutputTo objecttype:=acOutputReport, _
                objectname:=aobToPost.Name, _
                outputformat:=acFormatHTML, _
                outputfile:="c:\tut09\access\" & aobToPost.Name & ".htm", _
                autostart:=False
            .Close objecttype:=acReport, objectname:=aobToPost.Name, Save:=acSaveNo
        End With
    Next aobToPost

End Function
```

Figure 9-36: Completed PostScores procedure

2 Verify the accuracy of your code before continuing by comparing the code on your screen to the code shown in Figure 9-36, then save the database.

3 Return to Access and run the **PostScoresMacro** macro.

4 When the Posted By dialog box appears and prompts you to enter the name of the person posting the scores, click the **OK** button to accept the *defaultValue*, Professor Carlisle.

The procedure opens the first report, enters the appropriate message in the report's Message control, saves the report as an HTML file, and then closes the report. The procedure then repeats the same four steps for the second and third reports in the database. Notice that Access displays a Printing message box that tells you which report is currently being output.

Now use Internet Explorer to view the CIS100.htm Web page created by the PostScores procedure.

5 Start Internet Explorer, if necessary. If the Work Offline dialog box appears, click the **Work Offline** button, which will allow you to view the Web page without being connected to the Internet.

6 Click **File** on the menu bar, then click **Open**. When the Open dialog box opens, click the **Browse** button. When the Microsoft Internet Explorer dialog box opens, locate the Report100 (Report100.htm) file, which is located in the Tut09\Access folder on your Data Disk, then click **Report100** (Report100.htm) in the list. Click the **Open** button. When the Open dialog box appears, click the **OK** button to open the file in Internet Explorer. See Figure 9-37.

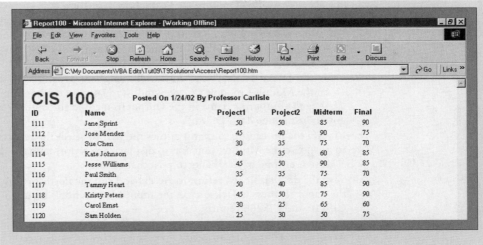

Figure 9-37: Report100.htm file displayed in Internet Explorer

7 Close Internet Explorer. Compact the database, and then close Access.

You now have completed Tutorial 9's Access lesson. You can either take a break or complete the end-of-lesson exercises.

EXERCISES

1. In this exercise, you will modify the PostScores procedure that you created in this lesson so that it uses the For...Next statement rather than the For Each...Next statement to refer to each report in the AllReports collection.

   a. Use Windows to make a copy of the InternetCourses (InternetCourses.mdb) database, which is located in the Tut09\Access folder on your Data Disk. Rename the copy T9-AC-E1D.

   b. Open the T9-AC-E1D (T9-AC-E1D.mdb) database. Open the Visual Basic Editor. Open the Module1 module's Code window, then view the PostScores procedure. Modify the procedure so that it uses the For...Next statement, rather than the For Each...Next statement, to refer to each object in the AllReports collection. (*Hint*: The first report in the AllReports collection has an index of 0.)

   c. Save the database, then return to Access and run the PostScoresMacro macro. When the Posted By dialog box appears, click the OK button to accept the *defaultValue*, Professor Carlisle.

   d. Start Internet Explorer, if necessary, then open the Report100.htm, Report110.htm, and Report260.htm files to verify that the macro worked correctly.

   e. Close Internet Explorer, then compact and close the database.

2. In this exercise, you will modify the PostScores procedure that you created in this lesson so that it allows the user to select the reports he or she wants to post.

   a. Use Windows to make a copy of the InternetCourses (InternetCourses.mdb) database, which is located in the Tut09\Access folder on your Data Disk. Rename the copy T9-AC-E2D.

   b. Open the T9-AC-E2D (T9-AC-E2D.mdb) database. Open the Visual Basic Editor. Open the Module1 module's Code window, then view the PostScores procedure. Change the *outputfile* name in the OutputTo method to "c:\tut09\access\" & aobToPost.Name & "2D.htm".

   c. Modify the procedure so that it allows the user to select the reports he or she wants to post. Use the MsgBox function to display each report name, one at a time, and to ask the user if he or she wants to post that report.

   d. Save the database, then return to Access and run the PostScoresMacro macro. Enter the name "Professor Jackson" in the InputBox function's input area. Post only the CIS110 and CIS260 reports.

   e. Start Internet Explorer, if necessary, then open the Report1102D.htm and Report2602D.htm files to verify that the macro worked correctly.

   f. Close Internet Explorer, then compact and close the database.

3. In this exercise, you will create a procedure that sends database reports to Excel.

   a. Open the T9-AC-E3D (T9-AC-E3D.mdb) database, which is located in the Tut09\Access folder on your Data Disk. Open the Visual Basic Editor, then open the Module1 module's Code window and view the code template for the OutputReportToExcel procedure. Code the procedure so that it saves a copy of both reports to your Data Disk in Microsoft Excel format. (*Hint*: You do not need to open the report in this exercise, because you will not be modifying any of its controls.)

   b. Save the database, then return to Access and run the OutputReportToExcelMacro macro. Start Excel, if necessary, and open the 2001Sales.xls and 2002Sales.xls workbooks to verify that the macro worked correctly. (If you set the AutoStart argument to True, Excel and the two workbooks already will be open.)

   c. Close Excel, then compact and close the database.

4. In this exercise, you will create a procedure that saves a copy of an Access query in rich-text format so that the query can be used by Microsoft Word.

   a. Open the T9-AC-E4D (T9-AC-E4D.mdb) database, which is located in the Tut09\Access folder on your Data Disk. Open the Visual Basic Editor, then open the Module1 module's Code window and view the code template for the QueryToRTF procedure. Code the procedure so that it saves a copy of each query, in rich-text format, to your Data Disk. (*Hint*: Access queries belong to the AllQueries collection. Unlike the AllReports collection, which is a member of the CurrentProject object, the AllQueries collection is a member of the CurrentData object.)

   b. Save the database, then return to Access and run the QueryToRTFMacro macro. Start Word, if necessary, and open the AllQry.rtf, OweMoneyQry.rtf, and PaidInFullQry.rtf files to verify that the macro worked correctly. (If you set the AutoStart argument to True, Word and the three documents already will be open.)

   c. Close Word, then compact and close the database.

Exercises 5 and 6 are Discovery Exercises. Discovery Exercises, which may include topics that are not covered in the lesson, allow you to "discover" the solutions to problems on your own.

discovery ▶ **5.** In this exercise, you will create a procedure that saves a copy of an Access table in HTML format.

a. Open the T9-AC-E5D (T9-AC-E5D.mdb) database, which is located in the Tut09\Access folder on your Data Disk. Open the Visual Basic Editor, then open the Module1 module's Code window and view the code template for the TableToHTML procedure. Code the procedure so that it uses the MsgBox statement to display the name of each database table, one at a time.

b. Save the database, then return to Access and run the TableToHTMLMacro macro. Record the names of the tables on a piece of paper. Notice that the database contains seven tables: two created by the user and five created by Access. Notice that the names of the tables created by Access begin with the four letters MSys.

c. Return to the Visual Basic Editor and remove the MsgBox statement from the TableToHTML procedure. Code the procedure so that it saves, in HTML format, only tables whose names do not begin with the letters "MSys". (*Hint*: Access tables belong to the AllTables collection. Unlike the AllReports collection, which is a member of the CurrentProject object, the AllTables collection is a member of the CurrentData object. Also, it may help to complete Exercise 14 in Tutorial 7's Concept lesson, which covers the Like comparison operator and wildcards.)

d. Save the database, then return to Access and run the TableToHTMLMacro macro. Start Internet Explorer, if necessary, and open the Advanced Seminars.htm and Intro Seminars.htm files to verify that the macro worked correctly. (If you set the AutoStart argument to True, Internet Explorer and the Intro Seminars.htm file already will be open.)

e. Close Internet Explorer, then compact and close the database.

discovery ▶ **6.** In this exercise, you will learn how to use the OutputTo method's TemplateFile argument. You will modify the PostScores procedure that you created in the lesson.

a. Use Windows to make a copy of the InternetCourses (InternetCourses.mdb) database, which is located in the Tut09\Access folder on your Data Disk. Rename the copy T9-AC-E6D.

b. Open the T9-AC-E6D (T9-AC-E6D.mdb) database. Open the Visual Basic Editor, then open the Module1 module's Code window and view the PostScores procedure. Change the *outputfile* name in the OutputTo method to "c:\tut09\access\" & aobToPost.Name & "6D.htm".

c. Open the Help window. Open the Importing, Exporting and Linking book that appears on the Contents tab, then open the Exporting Data or Objects book, and then click "About HTML template files" to display its Help screen. Study the Help screen, then click the "an example of an HTML template file" link to see an example of an HTML template file. Close the Help window.

d. Open the T9-Temp-E6.txt file, which is located in the Tut09\Access folder on your Data Disk, in Notepad. You will use this file as the template file in the PostScores procedure. Study the contents of the file. If necessary, change the "c:\tut09\access\postL.ico" that appears in the fourth instruction to reflect the location of your Data Disk. Close Notepad.

e. Include the TemplateFile argument in the PostScores procedure's OutputTo method.

f. Save the database, then return to Access and run the PostScoresMacro macro. Enter your name in the InputBox function's input area.

g. Start Internet Explorer, if necessary, then open the Report1006D.htm, Report1106D.htm, and Report2606D.htm files to verify that the macro worked correctly.

h. Close Internet Explorer, then compact and close the database.

A computer program is good only if it works. Errors in programming code can cause a program to run incorrectly. Therefore, a programmer needs to know how to locate and fix any errors in his or her code. Exercise 7 is a Debugging Exercise. Debugging Exercises allow you to practice recognizing and solving errors in code.

debugging   7.   In this exercise, you will debug an existing procedure.

a. Open the T9-AC-E7D (T9-AC-E7D.mdb) database, which is located in the Tut09\Access folder on your Data Disk. Open the Visual Basic Editor. Open the Module1 module's Code window, then view the DisplayNames procedure. The procedure should display the name of each of the 11 controls in the 2002Report report in a message box. Study the code, then run the procedure. Correct any errors in the procedure.

b. When the procedure is working correctly, compact and close the database.

More on the Repetition Structure and String Functions

objectives

In this tutorial, you will learn how to:

- Perform repetition using the Do...Loop statement
- Manipulate a string using string functions
- Search for a string within another string
- Sort a table in Word using the Sort method

Concept Lesson

More on the Repetition Structure

In Tutorial 9, you learned how to use the VBA For...Next and For Each...Next statements to code a repetition structure that repeats a set of instructions a precise number of times. As you learned in that tutorial, you also can use the repetition structure to repeat one or more instructions until some condition is met. You can use the VBA Do...Loop statement to code that type of repetition structure.

The Do...Loop Statement

You can use the VBA **Do...Loop statement** to code a repetition structure that repeats its instructions either while some condition is true or until some condition becomes true. Figure 10-1 shows the syntax and four examples of the Do...Loop statement.

> You can use the Exit Do statement to exit the Do...Loop loop prematurely—in other words, to exit it before it has finished processing. You may need to do so if the loop encounters an error when processing its instructions. As is true of the For...Next and For Each...Next statements, you can nest the Do...Loop statement, which means that you can place one Do...Loop statement within another Do...Loop statement.

> VBA also has another version of the Do...Loop statement, where the {While|Until} appears in the Loop clause rather than in the Do clause. You can learn about this version of the Do...Loop statement by completing this lesson's Exercise 12.

The Do...Loop statement begins with the Do clause and it ends with the Loop clause. Between those two clauses, you enter the instructions you want the loop to repeat, as shown in Figure 10-1's examples.

Look closely at the Do clause's syntax. The {**While | Until**} indicates that you can select only one of the keywords appearing within the braces—in this case, you can choose either While or Until. Also appearing in the Do clause is the *condition* that determines if the loop instructions will be processed. The *condition* can contain variables, constants, functions, mathematical operators, comparison operators, and logical operators. Like the *condition* used in the If...Then...Else statement, which you learned about in Tutorial 7, the *condition* in the Do clause also must evaluate to a Boolean value—either True or False.

```
Syntax:
Do {While | Until} condition
    [statements]
    [Exit Do]
    [statements]
Loop
```

```
Example 1:
Dim strName As String
strName = InputBox(Prompt:="Enter name:", Title:="Name")
Do While UCase(strName) <> "X"
    MsgBox Prompt:="You entered " & strName, _
        Buttons:=vbOKOnly + vbInformation
    strName = InputBox(Prompt:="Enter name:", Title:="Name")
Loop
```

```
Example 2:
Dim strName As String
strName = InputBox(Prompt:="Enter name:", Title:="Name")
Do Until UCase(strName) = "X"
    MsgBox Prompt:="You entered " & strName, _
        Buttons:=vbOKOnly + vbInformation
    strName = InputBox(Prompt:="Enter name:", Title:="Name")
Loop
```

```
Example 3:
Dim intCount As Integer, strCity As String
intCount = 1
Do While intCount <= 3
    strCity = InputBox(Prompt:="Enter the city:", Title:="City")
    MsgBox Prompt:=strCity & " is city number " & intCount, _
        Buttons:=vbOKOnly + vbInformation, Title:="City Number"
    intCount = intCount + 1
Loop
```

```
Example 4:
Dim docX as Document, intCount As Integer
intCount = 1
Do While intCount <= Application.Documents.Count
    Set docX = Application.Documents(intCount)
    docX.PrintOut
    intCount = intCount + 1
Loop
```

Figure 10-1: Syntax and examples of the Do...Loop statement

If you use the keyword While in the Do clause, the loop instructions are processed only when the *condition* evaluates to True. For instance, the loop instructions shown in Figure 10-1's Example 1 will be processed only when the name entered by the user is not equal to the letter "X". When the user enters the letter "X" as the name, the *condition* will evaluate to False and the loop will stop.

If you use the keyword Until in the Do clause, the loop instructions are processed only when the *condition* evaluates to False; as soon as the *condition* becomes true, the loop stops. This is illustrated in Figure 10-1's second example, whose loop instructions will be processed only until the name entered by the user is equal to the letter "X". When the user enters the letter "X" as the name, the *condition* will evaluate to True and the loop will stop. Notice that the first two examples shown in Figure 10-1 are just two different ways of writing the same loop.

Figure 10-1's third example shows how you can use the Do...Loop statement, rather than the For...Next statement, to repeat one or more instructions a precise number of times. If you compare this example with the one shown in Tutorial 9's Figure 9-2, you will notice that the For...Next statement requires less coding. For this reason, most programmers use the For...Next statement when they know how many times a set of instructions should be processed.

Figure 10-1's fourth example shows how you can use the Do...Loop statement, rather than the For Each...Next statement, to repeat one or more instructions for each object in a collection. If you compare this example with Example 1 shown in Tutorial 9's Figure 9-5, you will notice that the For Each...Next statement requires less coding. For this reason, most programmers use the For Each...Next statement to loop through the objects in a collection.

In addition to learning about the VBA Do...Loop statement, which allows you to code the repetition structure, in this tutorial you also will learn how to manipulate strings.

The VBA String Manipulation Functions

In many procedures, your code will need to manipulate (process) string data. For example, the code may need to verify that an inventory part number begins with a specific letter; or the code may need to determine if the last three characters in the part number are valid. You also may need to locate a string contained within another string. VBA provides a set of functions that makes string manipulation an easy task. In this lesson, you will learn how to use four of the most frequently used string manipulation functions: Left, Right, Mid, and Instr. First learn about the Left and Right functions.

The Left and Right Functions

As you already know, all functions return a value. The Left and Right functions return one or more characters from a string, starting at either the left or right end of the string. Figure 10-2 shows the syntax and examples of both functions.

Syntax:	*Purpose:*
Left(String:=*string*, **Length:=***length*)	Returns the left-most *length* number of characters in the *string*.
Right(String:=*string*, **Length:=***length*)	Returns the right-most *length* number of characters in the *string*.
Examples: Left(String:="PowerPoint", Length:=5) Right(String:="PowerPoint", Length:=5) Note: For the following examples, assume that the strLanguage variable contains the string "VBA". Left(String:=strLanguage, Length:=1) Right(String:=strLanguage, Length:=1)	*Returns:* Power Point V A

Figure 10-2: Syntax and examples of the Left and Right functions

In the first two examples, the Left and Right functions are used to return five characters from the string literal constant "PowerPoint". In the first example, the Left function returns the left-most five characters in the string—Power. In the second example, the Right function returns the right-most five characters in the string—Point.

In the last two examples shown in Figure 10-2, a string variable containing the three letters "VBA" is used as the *string* in each function. When *string* is a string variable, the Left and Right functions use the contents of the variable, not the variable name itself. For example, the left-most character in the string contained in the strLanguage variable is "V", and the right-most character is "A".

Now learn about the Mid function.

The Mid Function

The Mid function, which has the syntax **Mid(String:=***string*, **Start:=***start*[, **Length:=***length*]), returns *length* number of characters from the *string*, beginning with the *start* character. Figure 10-3 shows the syntax and examples of the Mid function.

Syntax: **Mid(String:**=*string*, **Start:**=*start*[, **Length:**=*length*])	
Purpose: Returns *length* number of characters in the *string* beginning at position *start*. If *length* is omitted, the function returns all characters from the *start* position through the end of the *string*.	

Examples:
`Mid(String:="Excel", Start:=3, Length:=1)`
`Mid(String:="Excel", Start:=4, Length:=2)`
 	
Note: For the following examples, assume that the strLanguage variable contains the string "Visual Basic for Applications".
 	
`Mid(String:=strLanguage, Start:=8, Length:=5)`
`Mid(String:=strLanguage, Start:=8)`
	Returns:
	c
	el
	
	Basic
	Basic for Applications

Figure 10-3: Syntax and examples of the Mid function

In the first two examples, the Mid function is used to return one or more characters from the string "Excel". The first example, for instance, returns one character beginning with the third character in the string—the letter "c". The second example returns two characters beginning with the fourth character in the string—the letters "el".

In the last two examples shown in Figure 10-3, the strLanguage variable, which contains the string "Visual Basic for Applications", is used as the *string* in the Mid function. As the `Mid(String:=strLanguage, Start:=8,Length:=5)` example shows, the five characters beginning with the eighth character in the *string* is the word "Basic". Notice that the `Mid(String:=strLanguage, Start:=8)` function returns "Basic for Applications". When you do not specify the *length* in a Mid function, the function returns all of the characters from the *start* position (8) through the end of the *string*.

The last string function you will learn about is the VBA Instr function.

The Instr Function

You can use the Instr function to search a string to determine if it contains another string. For example, you can use the Instr function to determine if the string "Park" appears within the string "123 Park Avenue". The syntax of the Instr function is **Instr(**start, string1, string2[, compare]**)**, where *start* is a numeric expression that sets the starting position for the search—in other words, the character at which the search should begin. The first character in a string is in position 1, the second character is in position 2, and so on.

▶ **tip**

The Instr function does not support the use of named arguments.

String1 in the syntax is the string expression being searched, and *string2* is the string expression being sought. In the example, "123 Park Avenue" is *string1* and "Park" is *string2*.

The typical setting for the *compare* argument, which is optional, is either the intrinsic constant **vbBinaryCompare** or the intrinsic constant **vbTextCompare**. The **vbBinaryCompare** setting performs a case-sensitive search, whereas the **vbTextCompare** setting performs a case-insensitive search. For example, if *string2* is the word "park" (entered in lowercase letters) and *compare* is set to **vbBinaryCompare**, the Instr function searches *string1* for the word "park" entered in lowercase letters only. If *compare* is set to **vbTextCompare**, on the other hand, the function searches *string1* for the word "park" entered in either lowercase letters, or uppercase letters, or a combination of both cases.

If you omit the *compare* argument in the Instr function, the function performs a case-sensitive search—in other words, it uses **vbBinaryCompare** as the default setting for the *compare* argument. The only exception to this is in Microsoft Access, where the method used to compare strings is determined by the Option Compare statement. For example, if Option Compare is set to Binary, an Instr function that does not contain a *compare* argument will perform a case sensitive search; however, if Option Compare is set to either Text or Database, it will perform a case-insensitive search.

▶ **tip**

If you have completed the Access lessons in the previous tutorials, you may recall seeing the `Option Compare Database` **statement in each module's General Declarations section.**

If *string2* is contained within *string1*, then the Instr function returns the starting position of *string2*. The function returns the number 0 if *string2* is not contained within *string1*. Figure 10-4 (on the next page) shows the syntax and some examples of the Instr function.

Notice that the first example shown in Figure 10-4, `Instr(1, "123 Park Avenue", "Park", vbBinaryCompare)`, returns the number 5, which is the starting position of the string "Park" within the string "123 Park Avenue". Because the *compare* argument is set to **vbBinaryCompare**, the function performs a case-sensitive search.

Figure 10-4's second example, `Instr(1, "123 Park Avenue", "park")`, returns the number 0 in all Office applications except Microsoft Access. This is because the Instr function performs a case-sensitive search when the *compare* argument is omitted, and the string "park" does not appear in the string "123 Park Avenue". The number returned by the Instr function in Microsoft Access depends on the setting of the Option Compare statement. If Option Compare is set to Binary, the Instr function will return 0. However, if Option Compare is set to either Text or Database, the Instr function will return the number 5.

Syntax: **Instr**(*start, string1, string2*[, *compare*]) Purpose: Returns a number that represents the starting position of *string2* within *string1*. If *string2* is not contained within *string1*, the function returns the number 0. The Instr function does not support the use of named arguments.	

Examples:
`Instr(1, "123 Park Avenue", "Park", vbBinaryCompare)`
`Instr(1, "123 Park Avenue", "park")`
 	
`Instr(1, "123 Park Avenue", "park", vbTextCompare)`
`Instr(3, "123 Park Avenue", "park", vbTextCompare)`
`Instr(10, "123 Park Avenue", "Park")`
 	
Note: For the following example, assume that the strFull variable contains the string "Pamela Smith" and the strLast variable contains the string "Smith".
 	
`Instr(1, strFull, strLast, vbTextCompare)`
	Returns:
	5
	0 in all Office applications except Access, where it will return either 0 or 5, depending on the setting of the Option Compare statement
	
	5
	5
	0
	
	8

Figure 10-4: Syntax and examples of the Instr function

Both the third and fourth examples shown in Figure 10-4 perform a case-insensitive search and both return the number 5, which is the starting position of the string "park" within the string "123 Park Avenue". The only difference between both examples is that the third example begins the search with the first character in *string1*, while the fourth example begins the search with the third character in *string1*.

Figure 10-4's fifth example, `Instr(10, "123 Park Avenue", "Park")` returns the number 0, indicating that "Park" is not contained within "Avenue" (the tenth through the last character in *string1*). The last example shown in Figure 10-4, `Instr(1, strFull, strLast, vbTextCompare)`, performs a case-insensitive search and returns the number 8—the starting position of "Smith" within "Pamela Smith".

You now have completed Tutorial 10's Concept lesson. You can either take a break or complete the end-of-lesson questions and exercises before moving on to the next lesson.

S U M M A R Y

To use the Do...Loop statement to code the repetition structure:

■ Use the syntax shown in Figure 10-1, where *condition*, which must evaluate to either True or False, can contain variables, constants, functions, mathematical operators, comparison operators, and logical operators. If you use the keyword `While` in the Do clause, the loop instructions are processed only when the *condition* evaluates to True. If you use the keyword `Until` in the Do clause, the loop instructions are processed only when the *condition* evaluates to False.

To return characters from a string:

■ Use the Left, Right, or Mid functions.

■ The Left function, the syntax of which is **Left(String:=***string*, **Length:=***length***)**, returns the left-most *length* number of characters from the *string*.

■ The Right function, the syntax of which is **Right(String:=***string*, **Length:=***length***)**, returns the right-most *length* number of characters from the *string*.

■ The Mid function, the syntax of which is **Mid(String:=***string*, **Start:=***start*[, **Length:=***length*]**)**, returns *length* number of characters from the *string*, beginning at position *start*.

To search a string to determine if it contains another string:

■ Use the Instr function, the syntax of which is **Instr(***start, string1, string2*[, *compare*]**)**. The Instr function does not support the use of named arguments.

■ *Start* is a numeric expression that sets the starting position for the search. *String1* is the string being searched, and *string2* is the string being sought. *Compare* can be set to either `vbBinaryCompare` or `vbTextCompare`. If *compare* is set to `vbBinaryCompare`, the Instr function performs a case-sensitive search. If *compare* is set to `vbTextCompare`, the Instr function performs a case-insensitive search. If *compare* is omitted in an Instr function, the function performs a case-sensitive search in all the Office applications except Microsoft Access, where the method used to compare strings is determined by the Option Compare statement. If Option Compare is set to Binary, an Instr function that does not contain a *compare* argument will perform a case sensitive search; however, if Option Compare is set to either Text or Database, it will perform a case-insensitive search.

■ If *string2* is contained within *string1*, then the Instr function returns the starting position of *string2*. If *string2* is not contained within *string1*, the Instr function returns the number 0.

REVIEW QUESTIONS

1. What numbers, if any, will appear in a message box when the following code is processed?

    ```
    Dim intX as Integer
    Do While intX < 5
        MsgBox Prompt:=intX
        intX = intX + 1
    Loop
    ```
    a. 0, 1, 2, 3, 4
    b. 0, 1, 2, 3, 4, 5
    c. 1, 2, 3, 4, 5
    d. No numbers will appear, because the loop will not be processed.

2. What is the value of intX when the loop in Question 1 stops?
    a. 0
    b. 1
    c. 5
    d. 6

3. What numbers, if any, will appear in a message box when the following code is processed?

    ```
    Dim intX as Integer
    Do Until intX < 5
        MsgBox Prompt:=intX
        intX = intX + 1
    Loop
    ```
    a. 0, 1, 2, 3, 4
    b. 0, 1, 2, 3, 4, 5
    c. 1, 2, 3, 4, 5
    d. No numbers will appear, because the loop will not be processed.

4. What is the value of intX when the loop in Question 3 stops?
    a. 0
    b. 1
    c. 5
    d. 6

5. Assuming that the strMsg variable contains the string "Have a great time", the `Left(String:=strMsg, Length:=2)` function would return _____.
    a. a
    b. av
    c. ave a great time
    d. Ha

6. Assuming that the strMsg variable contains the string "Have a great time", the `Right(Right:=strMsg, Length:=4)` function would return _____.
   a. e
   b. Have
   c. t
   d. time

7. Assuming that the strMsg variable contains the string "Have a great time", the `Mid(String:=strMsg, Start:=14, Length:=4)` function would return _____.
   a. e a great time
   b. Have
   c. time
   d. a great time

8. The `Left(String:=strName, Length:=3)` function is equivalent to which of the following?
   a. `Mid(String:=strName, Start:=3, Length:=1)`
   b. `Mid(String:=strName, Start:=1, Length:=3)`
   c. `Mid(String:=strName, Start:=3, Length:=0)`
   d. `Mid(String:=strName, Start:=0, Length:=3)`

9. Assuming that the strName variable contains the name "Thomas Jefferson", the `Right(strName, 3)` function is equivalent to which of the following?
   a. `Mid(String:=strName, Start:=14, Length:=3)`
   b. `Mid(String:=strName, Start:=3, Length:=14)`
   c. `Mid(String:=strName, Start:=3)`
   d. `Mid(String:=strName, Start:=13)`

10. Assuming that the strMsg variable contains the string "Have a GREAT day", the `Instr(1, strMsg, "great", vbBinaryCompare)` function would return _____.
    a. 0
    b. 8
    c. G
    d. True

11. Assuming that the strMsg variable contains the string "Have a GREAT day", the `Instr(1, strMsg, "great", vbTextCompare)` function would return _____.
    a. 0
    b. 8
    c. G
    d. False

12. Assuming that the strMsg variable contains the string "Have a GREAT day", the `Instr(6, strMsg, "great", vbTextCompare)` function would return _____.
    a. 0
    b. 8
    c. G
    d. False

13. Assuming that the strMsg variable contains the string "Have a GREAT day", the `Instr(9, strMsg, "great", vbTextCompare)` function would return

_____.

   a. 0
   b. 8
   c. G
   d. True

EXERCISES

1. Rewrite Figure 10-1's Example 3 and Example 4 using the keyword `Until`.

2. Write a Do...Loop statement whose processing will stop when the value in the curSales variable is equal to the number 0. First use the keyword `While`, and then rewrite the statement using the keyword `Until`.

3. Write a Do...Loop statement whose processing will stop when the value in the strName variable is equal to the string "Done" (in either uppercase or lowercase letters). First use the keyword `While`, and then rewrite the statement using the keyword `Until`.

4. Write the code that corresponds to the pseudocode shown in Figure 10-5. Use the keyword `While` in the Do...Loop statement. (Be sure to declare the appropriate variables.)

---

1. Use the InputBox function to get a number from the user. Store the user's response in a String variable named strNum.
2. Repeat the following while the strNum variable does not equal "−1":
   a. Square the contents of the strNum variable. Assign the result to a Long variable named lngNumSquared.
   b. Display the contents of the lngNumSquared variable in a message box.
   c. Use the InputBox function to get another number from the user. Store the user's response in the strNum variable.

Figure 10-5

5. Write the code that corresponds to the pseudocode shown in Figure 10-6. Use the keyword `Until` in the Do...Loop statement. (Be sure to declare the appropriate variables.)

1. Use the InputBox function to get a sales amount from the user. Store the user's response in a String variable named strSales.
2. Repeat the following until the strSales variable equals "0":
   a. Convert the contents of the strSales variable to a number. Store the result in a Currency variable named curSales.
   b. Calculate the bonus by multiplying the contents of the curSales variable by 10%. Store the result in a Currency variable named curBonus.
   c. Display the contents of the curBonus variable in a message box.
   d. Use the InputBox function to get a sales amount from the user. Store the user's response in the strSales variable.

Figure 10-6

6. Write the code that corresponds to the pseudocode shown in Figure 10-7. Use the keyword `While` in the Do...Loop statement. (Be sure to declare the appropriate variables.)

1. Use the MsgBox function to ask the user if he or she wants to enter a name. Store the user's response in an Integer variable named intEnter.
2. Repeat the following while the intEnter variable equals vbYes:
   a. Use the InputBox function to get a name from the user. Store the result in a String variable named strName.
   b. Display the contents of the strName variable in a message box.
   c. Use the MsgBox function to ask the user if he or she wants to enter another name. Store the user's response in the intEnter variable.

Figure 10-7

7. Rewrite the Do...Loop statement in Exercise 6 so that it uses the keyword `Until` rather than the keyword `While`.

8. Write the appropriate code to display, in a message box, the name of each worksheet contained in the open Excel workbook. Use the Do...Loop statement with the keyword `While`. (*Hint*: An Excel Worksheet object belongs to the Worksheets collection, which is a member of the Application object's Workbooks collection.) Use shtX as the name of the Worksheet object variable, and use intCount as the name of the loop variable. Use the number 1 as the index for the Workbooks collection.

9. Write the appropriate code to add together the numbers 1 through 10. Use the Do...Loop statement with the keyword `Until`. Display the sum in a message box.

10. Evaluate the Left, Right, Mid, and Instr functions shown in Figure 10-8. Determine what the returned value will be for each function.

Function	Returns
`Left(String:="Kristen Jacobs", Length:=4)`	
`Right(String:="Sam Johnson", Length:=2)`	
`Mid(String:="Bobby Moriarty", Start:=1, Length:=3)`	
`Mid(String:="Carolyn", Start:=4, Length:=2)`	
`Instr(1, "$45.67", "$")`	
`Instr(1, "VBA", "b")` (in Word, Excel, and PowerPoint)	
`Instr(1, "VBA", "b", vbTextCompare)`	
Note: For the following examples, assume that the strState variable contains the string "California".	
`Left(String:=strState, Length:=2)`	
`Right(String:=strState, Length:=5)`	
`Mid(String:=strState, Start:=5, Length:=3)`	
`Mid(String:=strState, Start:=6)`	
`Instr(1, strState, "a")`	
`Instr(3, strState, "a", vbTextCompare)`	

Figure 10-8

11. Complete the table shown in Figure 10-9 by writing the appropriate functions.

Note: Assume that the strState variable contains the string "Kentucky".	Function
Write the Left function that will return the string "Ken".	
Write the Right function that will return the string "tucky".	
Write the Mid function that will return the string "ntu".	
Write the Mid function that will return the string "Ken".	

Figure 10-9

Write the Instr function that will search the strState variable for the letter "T". Perform a case-insensitive search.	Function
Write the Instr function that will search the strState variable for the letters "ken". Perform a case-sensitive search.	

Figure 10-9 (*continued*)

Exercise 12 is a Discovery Exercise. Discovery Exercises, which may include topics that are not covered in the lesson, allow you to "discover" the solutions to problems on your own.

discovery ▶ **12.** In this exercise, you will learn about another version of the Do...Loop statement.

    a. Start either Word, Excel, Access, or PowerPoint. Open the Visual Basic Editor, then view the Do...Loop Statement Help screen. Read the Help screen, then use the Answer Wizard to display the Using Do...Loop Statements Help screen. Read the Help screen. What is the difference between including the keywords `While` and `Until` in the Do clause and including them in the Loop clause?

    b. Close the Help window, then close the application.

You also can use VBA in PowerPoint to create procedures that enhance your presentations. Exercise 13 allows you to apply this tutorial's programming concept in a PowerPoint presentation.

powerpoint **13.** In this exercise, you will create a procedure that prints only the even-numbered slides contained in a presentation.

    a. Start PowerPoint. Open the T10-PP-E13 (T10-PP-E13.ppt) presentation, which is located in the Tut10\Concept folder on your Data Disk. Save the presentation as T10-PP-E13D.

    b. Open the Visual Basic Editor and view the PrintEvenSlides procedure, which is contained in the Module1 module. Complete the procedure by writing a Do...Loop statement that will print only the even numbered slides contained in the presentation. Use the keyword `Until` in the Do...Loop statement.

    c. Save the presentation, then return to PowerPoint and run the PrintEvenSlides macro.

    d. When the macro is working correctly, save and then close the presentation.

A computer program is good only if it works. Errors in programming code can cause a program to run incorrectly. Therefore, a programmer needs to know how to locate and fix any errors in his or her code. Exercise 14 is a Debugging Exercise. Debugging Exercises allow you to practice recognizing and solving errors in code.

debugging 🐞 **14.** The following procedure should prompt the user to enter one or more sales amounts. The procedure should sum these amounts and then display the total sales immediately before the procedure ends. The procedure is not working as intended. Rewrite the code correctly.

```
Dim strSales As String, curTotal As Currency
strSales = InputBox(Prompt:="Enter sales amount:", _
    Title:="Sales")
Do While strSales = "-1"
    curTotal = curTotal + Val(strSales)
Loop
MsgBox Prompt:="Total sales " & curTotal, _
    Buttons:=vbOKOnly + vbInformation
```

Excel Lesson

Using the Repetition Structure and String Functions in Excel

case ▶ Paradise Electronics is opening a new store in Franklin. The manager of the new Franklin store has given Martin Washington, the accountant at Paradise Electronics, an Excel workbook that contains the names, addresses, and phone numbers of computer consultants in the Franklin area. Upon opening the workbook in Excel, Martin notices that each consultant's full name—first name followed by last name—has been entered in column A of the Consultants worksheet, making it impossible to use the Sort command on the Excel menu to sort the list in order by the last name. Martin decides to create a macro that will separate each full name into two parts—first name and last name—listing the last names in column A and the first names in column B. Separating the names in this manner will allow him to sort the list in last name order.

Viewing the Consultants Worksheet and the BreakNameApart Procedure

The workbook containing the consultant information is stored on your Data Disk. Before creating the macro that will separate each consultant's full name into his or her first and last name, view the workbook and the code template for the BreakNameApart procedure.

To view the workbook and the BreakNameApart procedure:

1 Start Microsoft Excel. Open the **T10-EX-1** (T10-EX-1.xls) workbook, which is located in the Tut10\Excel folder on your Data Disk. Click the **Enable Macros** button, if necessary, and then save the workbook as **Franklin Consultants**.

The Franklin Consultants workbook contains one worksheet named Consultants, as shown in Figure 10-10.

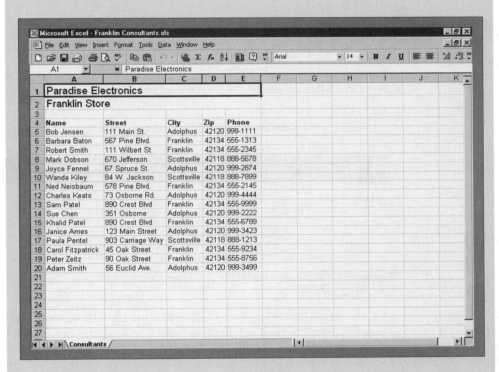

Figure 10-10: The Consultants worksheet in the Franklin Consultants workbook

Notice that column A contains each consultant's full name.

2 Press **Alt+F11** to open the Visual Basic Editor. If necessary, open the Project Explorer window and close the Properties window, the Immediate window, and any open Code windows. Open the Module1 module's Code window, then view the code template for the **BreakNameApart** procedure.

3 Close the Project Explorer window so that you can view more of the Code window.

Figure 10-11 shows the pseudocode for the BreakNameApart procedure.

1. Insert a new column B.
2. Change cell A4's heading to "Last Name" and change cell B4's heading to "First Name".
3. Change range A4:B4 to bold.
4. Repeat the following for each cell in column A that contains a name:
   a. Use the Instr function to locate the space that separates the first name from the last name. Assign the value returned by the function to an Integer variable named intLocation.
   b. Use the Left function to return only the first name. Assign the first name to the cell located to the immediate right of the current cell.
   c. Use the Mid function to return only the last name. Assign the last name to the current cell.
5. Use the Range object's AutoFit method to adjust the width of columns A and B to fit their current contents.

Figure 10-11: Pseudocode for the BreakNameApart procedure

Figure 10-12 shows the variables that the BreakNameApart procedure will use.

Variable	datatype
intLocation	Integer
shtConsult	Worksheet
rngCell	Range

Figure 10-12: Variables used by the BreakNameApart procedure

The BreakNameApart procedure will use the intLocation variable to store the value returned by the Instr function, and it will use the shtConsult variable to store the address of the Consultants worksheet. The rngCell variable will be used in a Do...Loop statement that repeats its instructions for each cell in column A that contains a name.

In the next set of steps, you will declare the appropriate variables and then begin translating Figure 10-11's pseudocode into one or more VBA statements.

To begin coding the BreakNameApart procedure:

1 The insertion point should be located between the `Public Sub` and `End Sub` lines in the Code window. Press the **Tab** key, then type **'declare variables and assign address to Worksheet object variable** and press the **Enter** key.

2 Type **dim intLocation as integer, shtConsult as worksheet, rngCell as range** and press the **Enter** key.

3 Type **set shtconsult = _** (be sure to type the equal sign followed by a space and the underscore) and press the **Enter** key. Press the **Tab** key, then type **application.workbooks("franklin consultants.xls").worksheets("consultants")** and press the **Enter** key.

Now insert a new column B and display the appropriate column headings in cells A4 and B4.

4 Press the **Backspace** key to remove the indentation. Type the additional lines of code shown in Figure 10-13, then position the insertion point as shown in the figure.

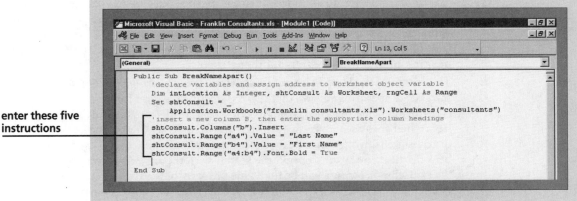

enter these five instructions

```
Microsoft Visual Basic - Franklin Consultants.xls - [Module1 (Code)]
File  Edit  View  Insert  Format  Debug  Run  Tools  Add-Ins  Window  Help

Ln 13, Col 5

(General)                              BreakNameApart

Public Sub BreakNameApart()
    'declare variables and assign address to Worksheet object variable
    Dim intLocation As Integer, shtConsult As Worksheet, rngCell As Range
    Set shtConsult = _
        Application.Workbooks("franklin consultants.xls").Worksheets("consultants")
    'insert a new column B, then enter the appropriate column headings
    shtConsult.Columns("b").Insert
    shtConsult.Range("a4").Value = "Last Name"
    shtConsult.Range("b4").Value = "First Name"
    shtConsult.Range("a4:b4").Font.Bold = True

End Sub
```

Figure 10-13: Partially completed BreakNameApart procedure

According to Step 4 in the pseudocode, the procedure needs to repeat a set of instructions for each cell in column A that contains a name. In Tutorial 9's Concept lesson, you learned that you can use either the For...Next statement or the For Each...Next statement to repeat one or more instructions for each object in a collection; you also can use the Do...Loop statement, which you will do in this lesson. You will have the Do...Loop statement repeat its instructions for each cell in column A, beginning with cell A5, which contains the first consultant name, and ending when the loop encounters an empty cell.

To complete the BreakNameApart procedure:

1 Type **'beginning in cell A5, separate each full name into last and first name** and press the **Enter** key.

First assign the address of cell A5, the location of the first consultant name, to the rngCell variable.

2 Type **set rngcell = shtconsult.range("a5")** and press the **Enter** key.

Now enter a Do clause that instructs the loop to stop when the cell whose address is contained in the rngCell variable is empty. You can determine if a cell is empty by comparing its Value property to a zero-length string (" ").

3   Type **do until rngcell.value = " "** (two quotation marks with no space between) and press the **Enter** key.

tip

> You also could have used the following **Do clause:** `Do While rngCell.Value <> " "`.

According to the pseudocode shown in Figure 10-11, the first loop instruction should use the Instr function to locate the space that separates the consultant's first name from his or her last name, and it should assign the return value, a number, to the intLocation variable. As you learned in the Concept lesson, the number returned by the Instr function represents the beginning position of one string within another string.

The syntax of the Instr function is **Instr(**start, string1, string2 [, compare]**)**, where *start* is a numeric expression that sets the starting position for the search, *string1* is the string being searched, *string2* is the string being sought, and *compare* controls whether the search is case-sensitive (*compare* is set to `vbBinaryCompare`) or case-insensitive (*compare* is set to `vbTextCompare`). In this case, *start* will be 1 because you want to begin the search with the first character contained in the rngCell cell. *String1* will be the Value property of the rngCell cell, and *string2* will be a space enclosed in quotation marks. You will not need to set the *compare* argument, because a space does not have a case.

4   Press the **Tab** key. Type **'find location of space** and press the **Enter** key. Type **intlocation = instr(1, rngcell.value, " ")** (be sure to include one space between the quotation marks) and press the **Enter** key. If the cell's Value property contains the name "Bob Jensen", this instruction will assign the number 4—the location of the space that separates the first name from the last name—to the intLocation variable. However, if the cell's Value property contains the name "Barbara Baton", this instruction will assign the number 8 to the intLocation variable.

Now use the Left function to return the first name from the rngCell cell's Value property. Recall that the syntax of the Left function is **Left(String:=**string, **Length:=**length**)**, where *length* is the number of characters to return from the *string*. In this case, *string* will be the Value property of the rngCell cell. But how will you know how many characters to return when the number of characters in each first name differs? The answer is quite simple: the number of characters to return is always one less than the value stored in the intLocation variable. This is because the first name ends with the character located to the immediate left of the space, as illustrated in Figure 10-14.

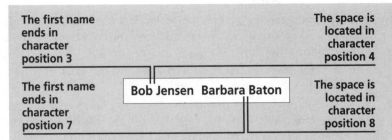

Figure 10-14: Location of space within full name

You should assign the first name to the cell that is one column to the right of the rngCell cell.

5 Type **'assign first name to appropriate cell in column B** and press the **Enter** key. Type **rngcell.offset(columnoffset:=1).value = _** (be sure to type the equal sign followed by a space and the underscore) and press the **Enter** key. Press the **Tab** key, then type **left(string:=rngcell.value, length:=intlocation – 1)** and press the **Enter** key.

Next, use the Mid function to return the last name from the rngCell cell's Value property. Recall that the syntax of the Mid function is **Mid(String:=*string*, Start:=*start*[, Length:=*length*])**, where *length* is the number of characters to return from the *string*, beginning at position *start*. In this case, *string* will be the Value property of the rngCell cell. *Start* will be the position of the character to the immediate right of the space—in other words, *start* will be intLocation + 1, as illustrated in Figure 10-15.

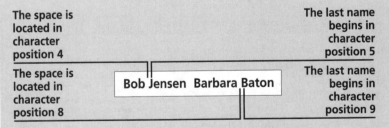

Figure 10-15: Location of last name and space within full name

Because you want the Mid function to return all of the characters that follow the space in the name, you will not specify the *length* in the Mid function. You should assign the last name returned by the Mid function to the rngCell cell, replacing the full name contained therein.

tip

As you learned in the Concept lesson, when you do not specify a *length* in a Mid function, the function returns all of the characters from the *start* position through the end of the *string*.

6   Press the **Backspace** key, then type **'assign last name to current cell** and press the **Enter** key. Type **rngcell.value = mid(string:=rngcell.value, start:=intlocation + 1)** and press the **Enter** key.

Finally, reset the rngCell object variable so that it contains the address of the cell immediately below the current cell.

7   Type **'assign the address of the cell in the next row to the rngCell variable** and press the **Enter** key. Type **set rngcell = rngcell.offset(rowoffset:=1)** and press the **Enter** key. Press the **Backspace** key, then type **loop** and press the **Enter** key.

Now use the Range object's AutoFit method to automatically adjust the width of columns A and B to fit their current contents.

8   Enter the additional instructions shown in Figure 10-16, which shows the completed BreakNameApart procedure.

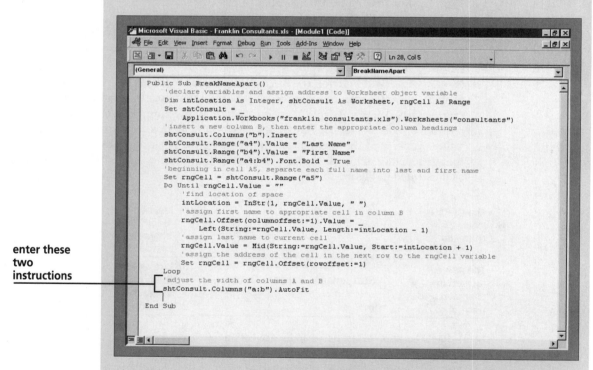

enter these two instructions

Figure 10-16: Completed BreakNameApart procedure

9   Verify the accuracy of your code by comparing the code on your screen to the code shown in Figure 10-16, then save the procedure.

Now that you have translated the pseudocode into VBA statements, you can test the BreakNameApart procedure to verify that it is working correctly.

To test the BreakNameApart procedure:

1 Return to Excel, then run the **BreakNameApart** macro. Figure 10-17 shows the Consultants worksheet after running the BreakNameApart macro.

Notice that each consultant's last name appears in column A and his or her first name appears in column B. Martin now can use the Sort command on the Excel Data menu to sort the list in order by the last name.

You will learn how to create a procedure that sorts the data in this lesson's Exercise 6.

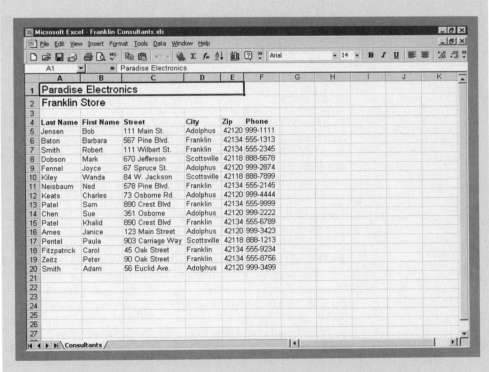

Figure 10-17: Consultants worksheet after running the BreakNameApart macro

2 Save the workbook, then close Excel.

You now have completed Tutorial 10's Excel lesson. You can either take a break or complete the end-of-lesson exercises before moving on to the next lesson.

EXERCISES

1. In this exercise, you will create a procedure that separates a name into two parts—first name and last name.
   a. Open the T10-EX-E1 (T10-EX-E1.xls) workbook, which is located in the Tut10\Excel folder on your Data Disk. Click the Enable Macros button, if necessary, then save the workbook as T10-EX-E1D.
   b. Open the Visual Basic Editor. Open the Module1 module's Code window, then view the code template for the SplitName procedure. Code the procedure so that it separates each name into two parts—first name and last name. Display the first names in column A and display the last names in column B. Use the Do...Loop statement. Display the column headings "First Name" and "Last Name" in cells A5 and B5, respectively. Display the column headings in bold. Be sure to adjust the width of columns A and B to fit their current contents.
   c. Save the workbook. Return to Excel and run the SplitName macro. When the macro is working correctly, save and then close the workbook.

2. In this exercise, you will create a procedure that separates an address into street, city, and zip code.
   a. Open the T10-EX-E2 (T10-EX-E2.xls) workbook, which is located in the Tut10\Excel folder on your Data Disk. Click the Enable Macros button, if necessary, then save the workbook as T10-EX-E2D.
   b. Open the Visual Basic Editor. Open the Module1 module's Code window, then view the code template for the SplitAddress procedure. Code the procedure so that it displays the street address in column B, the city in column C, and the zip code in column D. Display appropriate column headings, in bold, in cells B1, C1, and D1.
   c. Save the workbook. Return to Excel and run the SplitAddress macro. When the macro is working correctly, save and then close the workbook.

3. In this exercise, you will modify a procedure so that it allows the user to calculate and display the price for as many items as desired.
   a. Open the T10-EX-E3 (T10-EX-E3.xls) workbook, which is located in the Tut10\Excel folder on your Data Disk. Click the Enable Macros button, if necessary, then save the workbook as T10-EX-E3D.
   b. Open the Visual Basic Editor. Open the Module1 module's Code window, then view the CalcPrice procedure. Study the procedure's code, then modify the procedure so that it allows the user to calculate and display the price for as many model numbers as desired, without having to run the CalcPrice macro each time. Use the Do...Loop statement. Stop the loop when the user clicks the Cancel button in the InputBox function that requests the model number. (*Hint*: Recall that the InputBox function returns the empty string when the user clicks the Cancel button.)
   c. Save the workbook. Return to Excel and run the CalcPrice macro. Calculate and display the price for model number H560 with a 10% discount, then calculate and display the price for model number J651 with a 5% discount. (You may need to drag the dialog box to a different location on the screen to view the discounted price.)
   d. When the macro is working correctly, save and then close the workbook.

4. In this exercise, you will modify the DisplaySales procedure that you created in Tutorial 9's Excel Lesson.

   a. Open the T10-EX-E4 (T10-EX-E4.xls) workbook, which is located in the Tut10\Excel folder on your Data Disk. Click the Enable Macros button, if necessary, then save the workbook as T10-EX-E4D.

   b. Open the Visual Basic Editor. Open the Module1 module's Code window, then view the DisplaySales procedure. Study the code, then modify the procedure so that it will process the InputBox function until the user enters one of the following letters: A, G, J, or W. Use the Do...Loop statement.

   c. Save the workbook. Return to Excel and run the DisplaySales macro. When the Store Sales dialog box appears, type the letter p and press the Enter key. The Store Sales dialog box should appear again. This time, type the number 2 and press the Enter key. The Store Sales dialog box should appear again. This time, type the letter w and press the Enter key. When you are asked if you want to print, click the No button. (*Hint*: If a dialog box opens and informs you that the procedure cannot find the MthSales.mdb file, click the OK button. When the Login dialog box opens, click the Database button to open the Select Database dialog box. Use the Select Database dialog box to locate the MthSales.mdb file, which is located in the Tut10\Excel folder on your Data Disk. Click MthSales.mdb in the list of filenames, then click the OK button to close the Select Database dialog box. Click the OK button to close the Login dialog box.)

   d. When the macro is working correctly, save and then close the workbook.

Exercises 5 through 8 are Discovery Exercises. Discovery Exercises, which may include topics that are not covered in the lesson, allow you to "discover" the solutions to problems on your own.

discovery ▶ 5. In this exercise, you will learn about the VBA Len and IsNumeric functions.

   a. Open the T10-EX-E5 (T10-EX-E5.xls) workbook, which is located in the Tut10\Excel folder on your Data Disk. Click the Enable Macros button, if necessary, then save the workbook as T10-EX-E5D.

   b. Open the Visual Basic Editor. Open the Module1 module's Code window, then view the code template for the VerifyPartNumber procedure. Code the procedure so that it verifies the part numbers listed in column A. Each part number should be exactly five characters in length. (*Hint*: Use the VBA Len function to determine the length.) If the part number is not five characters, display the message "Does not meet length requirement" in column B. If the part number is five characters in length, verify that the first two characters are numeric. (*Hint*: Use the VBA IsNumeric function, which you learned about in Exercise 13 in Tutorial 7's Concept lesson.) If the first two characters are not numeric, display the message "First two characters are not numeric" in column B. If the first two characters are numeric, then verify that the third character is either the letter A or the letter X. If the third character is not one of those two letters, then display the message "Incorrect middle character" in column B. Have the procedure adjust the width of column B to fit its current contents.

   c. Save the workbook. Return to Excel and run the VerifyPartNumber macro. When the macro is working correctly, save and then close the workbook.

discovery ▶ 6. In this exercise, you will create a procedure that uses the Range object's Sort method to sort a range of data. You will use the Franklin Consultants workbook that you created in this lesson.

    a. Open the Franklin Consultants (Franklin Consultants.xls) workbook, which you created in this lesson. The workbook is located in the Tut10\Excel folder on your Data Disk. Click the Enable Macros button, if necessary, then save the workbook as T10-EX-E6D.

    b. Open the Visual Basic Editor and display the Sort Method Help screen. Read the Help screen, then click Example at the top of the Help screen. Study the examples, then close the Help window.

    c. Create a macro procedure named SortByName. The procedure should use the Sort method to sort the worksheet in ascending order by the last name. If more than one consultant has the same last name, sort those records in ascending order by the first name.

    d. Save the workbook, then return to Excel. Enter the following record in row 21 of the worksheet: Apak, Carol, 23 Main Street, Franklin, 42134, 555-2222. Run the SortByName macro. The new record should appear in row 6 of the worksheet.

    e. When the macro is working correctly, save and then close the workbook.

discovery ▶ 7. In this exercise, you will learn about the Range object's EntireRow property and its Delete method.

    a. Open the T10-EX-E7 (T10-EX-E7.xls) workbook, which is located in the Tut10\Excel folder on your Data Disk. Click the Enable Macros button, if necessary, then save the workbook as T10-EX-E7D. Notice that the worksheet data is sorted in order by name. The data will need to be sorted in this manner for the RemoveDuplicateRows procedure, which you will create in this exercise, to work correctly.

    b. Open the Visual Basic Editor. Open the Module1 module's Code window, then view the code template for the RemoveDuplicateRows procedure. Code the procedure so that it removes rows with duplicate names from the worksheet. For example, notice that the name "Ames, Janice" appears three times in the worksheet; the name should appear only once. (*Hint*: View the Help screens for a Range object's EntireRow property and its Delete method.)

    c. Save the workbook. Return to Excel and run the RemoveDuplicateRows macro. When the macro is working correctly, save and then close the workbook.

discovery ▶ 8. In this exercise, you will modify the CalcHours procedure that you created in Tutorial 5's Excel Lesson. You will use the VBA IsDate function in the procedure.

    a. Open the T10-EX-E8 (T10-EX-E8.xls) workbook, which is located in the Tut10\Excel folder on your Data Disk. Click the Enable Macros button, if necessary, then save the workbook as T10-EX-E8D.

    b. Open the Visual Basic Editor. Open the Module1 module's Code window, then view the CalcHours procedure. Study the procedure's code, then modify the procedure so that it will process the first InputBox function until the user enters a valid starting time, and it will process the second InputBox function until the user enters a valid ending time. Use the Do...Loop statement in both instances. (*Hint*: Use the VBA IsDate function to verify that the user entered a valid time.)

    c. Save the workbook, then return to Excel. Click cell A5 on John Able's worksheet, then run the CalcHours macro. When the Start Time dialog box appears, type the letter p and press the Enter key. The Start Time dialog box should appear again. This time, type 11am and press the Enter key. When the End Time dialog box appears, type the number 7 and press the Enter key. The End Time dialog box should appear again. This time, type 1pm and press the Enter key.

    d. When the macro is working correctly, save and then close the workbook.

A computer program is good only if it works. Errors in programming code can cause a program to run incorrectly. Therefore, a programmer needs to know how to locate and fix any errors in his or her code. Exercise 9 is a Debugging Exercise. Debugging Exercises allow you to practice recognizing and solving errors in code.

debugging **9.** In this exercise, you will debug an existing procedure.

    a. Open the T10-EX-E9 (T10-EX-E9.xls) workbook, which is located in the Tut10\Excel folder on your Data Disk. Click the Enable Macros button, if necessary, then save the workbook as T10-EX-E9D.

    b. Open the Visual Basic Editor. Open the Module1 module's Code window, then view the PrintWorksheets procedure. The procedure should loop through each worksheet in the workbook, asking the user if he or she wants to print the worksheet, but it is not working correctly. (To conserve paper, the procedure uses the PrintPreview method rather than the Print method.)

    c. Study the PrintWorksheets procedure's code, then return to Excel and run the PrintWorksheets macro. Return to the Visual Basic Editor and correct any errors in the procedure.

    d. When the macro is working correctly, save and then close the workbook.

Word Lesson

Using the Repetition Structure and String Functions in Word

case ▶ During Willowton Health Club's semi-annual membership promotion, each member is mailed three complimentary guest passes, which can be used to bring guests to the club. Nancy Manley, the club's secretary, enters each guest's name and address, as well as the date that he or she visited the club, in a Word document. At the end of the promotion, Nancy sorts the guest list in ascending order by name. She then scans the list, searching for and removing any duplicate names. The resulting document is given to the sales manager, who sends membership information and a coupon worth $100 toward the initiation fee to each name on the list. Nancy has decided to create a macro that will sort the guest list and also remove any duplicate names.

Viewing the Guest Document

Nancy's document containing the guest list is stored on your Data Disk. Before creating the procedure that will sort the list and then remove any duplicate names, view the document and the code template for the SortAndRemoveDuplicates procedure.

To view the document and the code template for the SortAndRemoveDuplicates procedure:

1 Start Microsoft Word. Open the **T10-WD-1** (T10-WD-1.doc) document, which is located in the Tut10\Word folder on your Data Disk. Click the **Enable Macros** button, if necessary, and then save the document as **Guest List**. Figure 10-18 shows the Guest List document.

these rows contain duplicate names and addresses

this row contains a duplicate name, but not a duplicate address

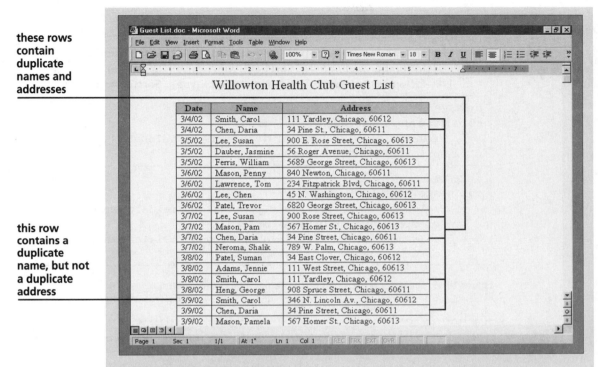

Figure 10-18: The Guest List document

Notice that the document contains a table that has three columns and 21 rows. As the figure indicates, some of the rows contain duplicate names and addresses. One of the rows, row 19, contains a duplicate name (Smith, Carol) only.

2 Press **Alt+F11** to open the Visual Basic Editor. If necessary, open the Project Explorer window and close the Properties window, the Immediate window, and any open Code windows. Open the Module1 module's Code window, then view the code template for the **SortAndRemoveDuplicates** procedure.

3 Close the Project Explorer window so that you can view more of the Code window.

Before you can code the SortAndRemoveDuplicates procedure, you need to learn how to sort the contents of a table.

Sorting a Table

You can use the Table object's **Sort method** to sort the entries in a table in either ascending or descending order. Figure 10-19 shows the syntax and two examples of the Sort method.

```
Syntax:
tableObject.Sort ExcludeHeader:=booleanValue, _
     FieldNumber:=number[, SortFieldType:=type][, SortOrder:=order] _
     [, FieldNumber2:=number][, SortFieldType2:=type][, SortOrder2:=order] _
     [, FieldNumber3:=number][, SortFieldType3:=type][, SortOrder3:=order]
```
```
Example 1:
tblGuests.Sort ExcludeHeader:=True, _
     FieldNumber:=1, SortFieldType:=wdSortFieldDate, _
     SortOrder:=wdSortOrderDescending
```
```
Example 2:
tblGuests.Sort ExcludeHeader:=True, _
     FieldNumber:=2, SortFieldType:=wdSortFieldAlphanumeric, _
     SortOrder:=wdSortOrderAscending, _
     FieldNumber2:=3, SortFieldType2:=wdSortFieldAlphanumeric, _
     SortOrder2:=wdSortOrderAscending
```

Figure 10-19: Syntax and examples of the Table object's Sort method

 tip

Figure 10-19 shows only the basic syntax of the Sort method. To learn more about this method, view its Help screen.

The Sort method's ExcludeHeader argument, which can be set to either the Boolean value True or the Boolean value False, controls whether the first row in the table is sorted along with the remaining table rows. You would set this argument to True if the first row contained headings, because you typically would not want the headings included in the sort; otherwise, you would set the argument to False. In both examples shown in Figure 10-19, the ExcludeHeader argument is set to True.

You can sort the table entries based on the values stored in one, two, or three different columns. As the syntax indicates, you specify the columns in the Sort method's FieldNumber, FieldNumber2, and FieldNumber3 arguments, where *number* represents the column number. The first column in a table is column number 1.

You use the SortFieldType, SortFieldType2, and SortFieldType3 arguments to indicate the type of data contained in the FieldNumber, FieldNumber2, and FieldNumber3 columns, respectively. The sort field type arguments can be set to one of the following intrinsic constants: `wdSortFieldAlphanumeric`, `wdSortFieldDate`, or `wdSortFieldNumeric`. In Figure 10-19's Example 1, the SortFieldType argument is set to `wdSortFieldDate` because column 1, which is the column on which the sort is based, contains dates. In Example 2, the SortFieldType and SortFieldType2 arguments are set to `wdSortFieldAlphanumeric` to indicate that columns 2 and 3 may contain letters, numbers, and special characters (such as the comma).

You indicate the order in which the FieldNumber, FieldNumber2, and FieldNumber3 columns should be sorted in the SortOrder, SortOrder2, and SortOrder3 arguments, respectively. These arguments can be set to either the intrinsic constant **wdSortOrderAscending** or the intrinsic constant **wdSortOrderDescending**. The first example shown in Figure 10-19, for instance, will sort the table in descending order by the entries in the first column in the table—the Date column. Notice that the figure's second example specifies two columns to use when sorting the table—the second column (Name) and the third column (Address). This example will sort the table in ascending order by name. However, if the Sort method encounters two or more names that are the same, it will sort those names in ascending order by address.

Now that you know how to use the Sort method to sort the entries in a table, you can begin coding the SortAndRemoveDuplicates procedure.

Coding the SortAndRemoveDuplicates Procedure

Figure 10-20 shows the pseudocode for the SortAndRemoveDuplicates procedure.

1. Use the Sort method to sort the table in ascending order by the Name column. If the Sort method encounters two or more names that are the same, sort those names in ascending order by the Address column.
2. Repeat the following for each table row that contains guest information:
   a. Assign the current row's name to a String variable named strCurrentName.
   b. Assign the previous row's name to a String variable named strPreviousName.
   c. Assign vbNo to an Integer variable named intDuplicate.
   d. If the first four characters stored in the strCurrentName variable are equal to the first four characters stored in the strPreviousName variable, then
      1) Select the current row.
      2) Use the MsgBox function to ask the user if the current row contains a duplicate name. Assign the user's response to the intDuplicate variable.
   e. If intDuplicate = vbYes, then
      1) Delete the current row.
      Else
      1) Continue processing with the next row in the table.
3. Place the insertion point at the beginning of the document.

Figure 10-20: Pseudocode for the SortAndRemoveDuplicates procedure

Figure 10-21 lists the variables that the SortAndRemoveDuplicates procedure will use.

Variable	*datatype*
intRow	Integer
strCurrentName	String
strPreviousName	String
intDuplicate	Integer
docGuestList	Document
tblGuests	Table

Figure 10-21: Variables used by the SortAndRemoveDuplicates procedure

The SortAndRemoveDuplicates procedure will use the intRow variable in a Do...Loop statement that repeats its instructions for each table row that contains guest information. It will use the strCurrentName and strPreviousName variables to store the names entered in the current and previous rows, respectively, in the table. It will use the intDuplicate variable to store the value returned by the MsgBox function. The docGuestList variable will store the address of the Guest List document, and the tblGuests variable will store the address of the document's table.

In the next set of steps, you will declare the appropriate variables and then translate each line in Figure 10-20's pseudocode into one or more VBA statements.

To code the SortAndRemoveDuplicates procedure, then save the procedure:

1 Enter the documentation and the Dim and Set statements shown in Figure 10-22.

enter these five
lines of code

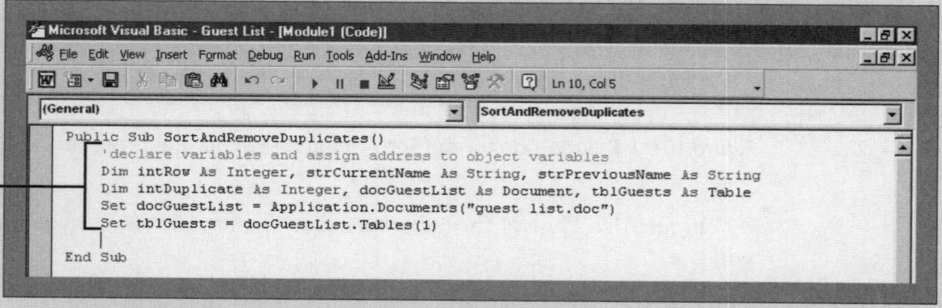

```
Microsoft Visual Basic - Guest List - [Module1 (Code)]
File  Edit  View  Insert  Format  Debug  Run  Tools  Add-Ins  Window  Help                    Ln 10, Col 5
(General)                                          SortAndRemoveDuplicates

Public Sub SortAndRemoveDuplicates()
    'declare variables and assign address to object variables
    Dim intRow As Integer, strCurrentName As String, strPreviousName As String
    Dim intDuplicate As Integer, docGuestList As Document, tblGuests As Table
    Set docGuestList = Application.Documents("guest list.doc")
    Set tblGuests = docGuestList.Tables(1)

End Sub
```

Figure 10-22: Code window showing documentation and Dim and Set statements

Now use the Sort method to sort the table in ascending order by the Name column, which is the second column in the table. If the Sort method encounters two or more names that are the same, sort those names in ascending order by the Address column, which is the third column in the table.

2 Type **'sort table in ascending order by name and address** and press the **Enter** key.

3 Type **tblguests.sort excludeheader:=true, _** (be sure to type the comma followed by a space and the underscore) and press the **Enter** key. Press the **Tab** key, then type **fieldnumber:=2, sortfieldtype:=wdsortfieldalphanumeric, sortorder:=wdsortorderascending, _** (be sure to type the comma followed by a space and the underscore) and press the **Enter** key. Type **fieldnumber2:=3, sortfieldtype2:=wdsortfieldalphanumeric, sortorder2:=wdsortorderascending** and press the **Enter** key.

According to Step 2 in the pseudocode, you need to repeat a set of instructions for each row in the table that contains guest information; these are rows 2 through 21. (Recall that the first row in the table contains the column headings.) In Tutorial 9's Concept lesson, you learned that you can use either the For...Next statement or the For Each...Next statement to repeat one or more instructions for each object in a collection; you also can use the Do...Loop statement, which you will do in this lesson.

> **A Row object is a member of the Table object's Rows collection. You will use the For Each...Next statement to code the SortAndRemoveDuplicates procedure in this lesson's Exercise 5. In this lesson's Exercise 6, you will learn why you can't use the For...Next statement to code this procedure.**

4 Press the **Backspace** key, then type **'search for and remove duplicate entries** and press the **Enter** key. Type **introw = 2** and press the **Enter** key to start processing the loop instructions with row 2 in the table, then type **do while introw <= tblguests.rows.count** and press the **Enter** key.

Now assign the names appearing in the second column in the current and previous rows to the appropriate String variables. As you learned in Tutorial 6's Word lesson, the intersection of a row and column in a table is called a **cell**. Recall that you can use the following syntax to refer to the contents of an individual cell in a table: *expression*.**Cell(Row:=**rowNum, **Column:=**colNum**).Range.Text**. In the syntax, *expression* is a Table object and rowNum and colNum are numbers that represent the row and column location of the cell.

5 Press the **Tab** key, then type **'assign current and previous names to String variables** and press the **Enter** key. Type **strcurrentname = tblguests.cell(row:=introw, column:=2).range.text** and press the **Enter** key, then type **strpreviousname = tblguests.cell(row:=introw – 1, column:=2).range.text** and press the **Enter** key.

Step 2c in the pseudocode is to assign the intrinsic constant vbNo to the intDuplicate variable.

6 Type **'assume names are not the same** and press the **Enter** key, then type **intduplicate = vbno** and press the **Enter** key.

Step 2d in the pseudocode is to compare the first four characters in the current name with the first four characters in the previous name. If the first four characters in each name are equal, the procedure should select the current row and then ask the user if the row contains a duplicate name.

▶ **tip**

> The procedure will compare only the first four characters in the last name, rather than compare the entire name, because a guest may sign in as "Mason, Pam" on one visit, but as "Mason, Pamela" on the next visit.

7 Type the additional instructions shown in Figure 10-23, then position the insertion point as shown in the figure.

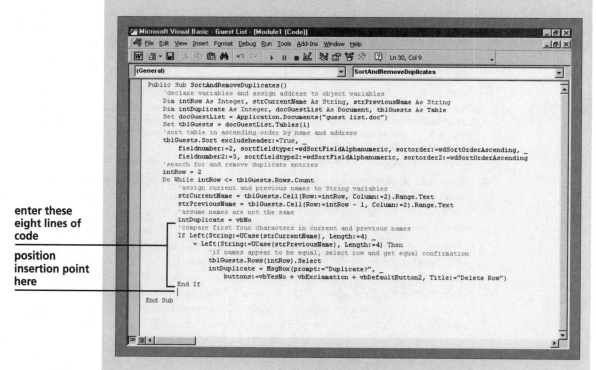

enter these eight lines of code

position insertion point here

Figure 10-23: Partially completed SortAndRemoveDuplicates procedure

HELP? The code in the Code window shown in Figure 10-23 was compressed so that you could view more of the procedure. If you want to compress the code shown on your screen, click Tools on the Visual Basic Editor's Standard toolbar, then click Options, and then click the Editor Format tab. Select 9 in the Size list box, then click the OK button.

According to Step 2e in the pseudocode, if the value stored in the intDuplicate variable is equal to the intrinsic constant **vbYes**, then the procedure should delete the current row. You can use the Row object's Delete method to delete a row in a table.

8 Type **'if duplicate, then delete row; otherwise, move to next row** and press the **Enter** key.

9 Type **if intduplicate = vbyes then** and press the **Enter** key. Press the **Tab** key, then type **tblguests.rows(introw).delete** and press the **Enter** key.

If the value stored in the intDuplicate variable is not equal to vbYes, then the procedure should continue processing with the next row in the table.

10 Press the **Backspace** key, then type **else** and press the **Enter** key. Press the **Tab** key, then type **introw = introw + 1** and press the **Enter** key. Press the **Backspace** key, then type **end if** and press the **Enter** key.

Now enter the Loop clause, which marks the end of the Do...Loop statement.

11 Press the **Backspace** key, and then type **loop** and press the **Enter** key.

Finally, position the insertion point at the beginning of the document.

12 Type **selection.homekey unit:=wdstory** and press the **Enter** key.

13 Verify the accuracy of your code before continuing by comparing the code on your screen to the code in Figure 10-24, which shows the completed SortAndRemoveDuplicates procedure, then save the document. (Not all of the procedure is displayed in the figure.)

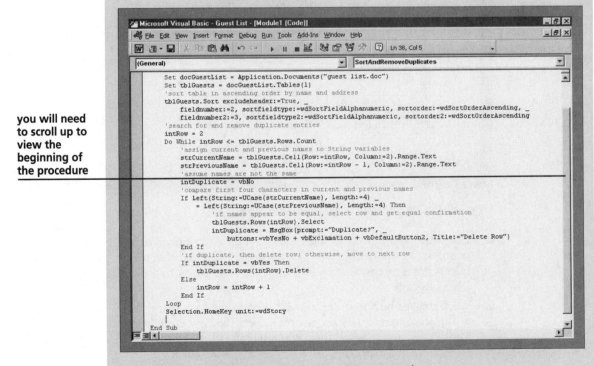

you will need to scroll up to view the beginning of the procedure

```
Set docGuestList = Application.Documents("guest list.doc")
Set tblGuests = docGuestList.Tables(1)
'sort table in ascending order by name and address
tblGuests.Sort excludeheader:=True, _
    fieldnumber:=2, sortfieldtype:=wdSortFieldAlphanumeric, sortorder:=wdSortOrderAscending, _
    fieldnumber2:=3, sortfieldtype2:=wdSortFieldAlphanumeric, sortorder2:=wdSortOrderAscending
'search for and remove duplicate entries
intRow = 2
Do While intRow <= tblGuests.Rows.Count
    'assign current and previous names to String variables
    strCurrentName = tblGuests.Cell(Row:=intRow, Column:=2).Range.Text
    strPreviousName = tblGuests.Cell(Row:=intRow - 1, Column:=2).Range.Text
    'assume names are not the same
    intDuplicate = vbNo
    'compare first four characters in current and previous names
    If Left(String:=UCase(strCurrentName), Length:=4) _
        = Left(String:=UCase(strPreviousName), Length:=4) Then
            'if names appear to be equal, select row and get equal confirmation
            tblGuests.Rows(intRow).Select
            intDuplicate = MsgBox(prompt:="Duplicate?", _
                buttons:=vbYesNo + vbExclamation + vbDefaultButton2, Title:="Delete Row")
    End If
    'if duplicate, then delete row; otherwise, move to next row
    If intDuplicate = vbYes Then
        tblGuests.Rows(intRow).Delete
    Else
        intRow = intRow + 1
    End If
Loop
Selection.HomeKey unit:=wdStory

End Sub
```

Figure 10-24: Completed SortAndRemoveDuplicates procedure

Now that you have translated the pseudocode into VBA statements, you should test the SortAndRemoveDuplicates procedure to verify that it is working correctly.

To test the SortAndRemoveDuplicates procedure:

1 Return to Word and run the **SortAndRemoveDuplicates** procedure. The procedure sorts the table in ascending order by the Name and Address columns. It then selects the fourth row in the table because the first four characters in this row's name (Chen, Daria) are equal to the first four characters in the previous row's name (Chen, Daria). The procedure also displays a message asking if this name is a duplicate, as shown in Figure 10-25.

this row contains a duplicate name and address

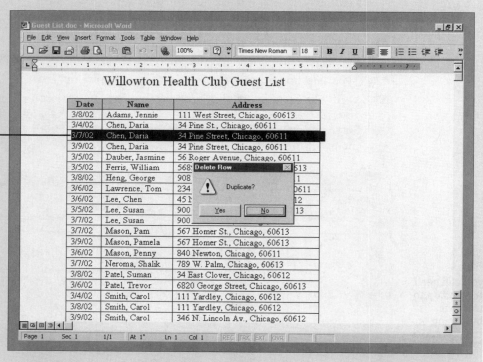

Figure 10-25: Current status of Guest List document

2 Click the **Yes** button in the message box to confirm that the current row contains a duplicate name. The procedure deletes the current row and then selects the next row that contains a name whose first four characters match the letters "Chen".

3 Click the **Yes** button in the message box to confirm that this row also contains a duplicate name. The procedure selects the row containing the name "Lee, Susan" because the first four characters in the name are equal to the first four characters in the previous row's name ("Lee, Chen").

4 Click the **No** button in the message box because both names are not the same. The procedure selects the next row containing "Lee," as the first four characters. Both "Lee, Susan" records in the table appear to be the same; their address differs only slightly.

5 Click the **Yes** button in the message box to confirm that the current row contains a duplicate name.

6 On your own, confirm the deletion only of the "Mason, Pamela" record and the "Smith, Carol" record dated 3/8/02. Figure 10-26 shows the Guest List document after running the SortAndRemoveDuplicates procedure.

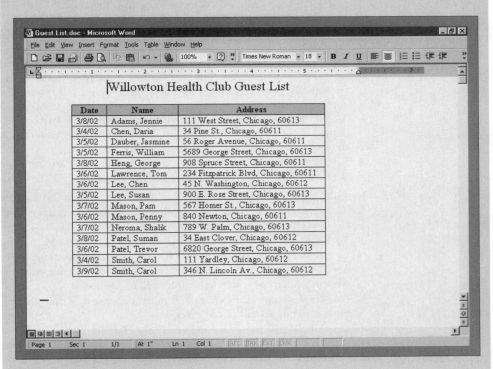

Figure 10-26: Guest List document after running the SortAndRemoveDuplicates procedure

7 Save the document and then close Word.

You now have completed Tutorial 10's Word lesson. You can either take a break or complete the end-of-lesson exercises before moving on to the next lesson.

E X E R C I S E S

1. In this exercise, you will create a procedure that separates an inventory ID into manufacturer, color, and description.

   a. Open the T10-WD-E1 (T10-WD-E1.doc) document, which is located in the Tut10\Word folder on your Data Disk. Click the Enable Macros button, if necessary, then save the document as T10-WD-E1D. Notice that the document contains a table that has 10 rows and four columns. Column A contains inventory IDs that consist of three characters. The first character in each ID indicates the item's manufacturer: the letter "A" signifies Adams Company and the letter "B" signifies Baltic Inc. The second character in each ID indicates the item's color: 1 is Blue, 2 is Red, 3 is Green, and 4 is White. The third character in each ID indicates the item's description: the letter "J" indicates a Jacket and the letter "S" indicates a Sweater.

   b. Display the nonprinting characters in the document. Notice that each cell in the table contains an end of cell marker.

   c. Open the Visual Basic Editor. Open the Module1 module's Code window, then view the code template for the SplitPartNumber procedure. Code the procedure so that it splits the IDs into three parts (Manufacturer, Color, and Description) and then enters each part in the appropriate column in the table. In other words, for ID "A2J", the procedure should enter "Adams Company" (without the quotation marks) in the Manufacturer column, "Red" in the Color column, and "Jacket" in the Description column.

   d. Save the document. Return to Word and run the SplitPartNumber macro.

   e. When the macro is working correctly, save and then close the document.

2. In this exercise, you will create a procedure that changes a full name from first name followed by last name to last name followed by a comma, a space, and the first.

   a. Open the T10-WD-E2 (T10-WD-E2.doc) document, which is located in the Tut10\Word folder on your Data Disk. Click the Enable Macros button, if necessary, then save the document as T10-WD-E2D. The document contains a table that has 11 rows and six columns. Notice that the second table column contains each student's full name—first name followed by last name.

   b. Display the nonprinting characters in the document. Notice that each cell in the table contains an end of cell marker.

   c. Open the Visual Basic Editor. Display the Help screen for the Len function. You will need to use this function in the procedure that you will be creating in this exercise. Read the Help screen. Notice that you can use the Len function to determine the number of characters contained in a string. Close the Help window.

   d. Open the Module1 module's Code window, then view the code template for the ReverseName procedure. Code the procedure so that it displays each student's last name, a comma, a space, and the student's first name in the second column of the table. In other words, display "Sprint, Jane" rather than "Jane Sprint". (*Hint*: Use the Mid function to separate the last name from the first name. You can calculate the number of characters to return by subtracting the length of the first name from the length of the cell's contents, and then subtracting 3—one for the space and two for the end of cell information—from that difference.)

   e. Save the document. Return to Word and run the ReverseName procedure.

   f. When the macro is working correctly, save and then close the document.

3. In this exercise, you will modify the UpdateMembership procedure that you created in Tutorial 6's Word lesson.

   a. Open the T10-WD-E3 (T10-WD-E3.doc) document, which is located in the Tut10\Word folder on your Data Disk. Click the Enable Macros button, if necessary, then save the document as T10-WD-E3D.

   b. Open the Visual Basic Editor. Open the Module1 module's Code window, then view the UpdateMembership procedure. Study the code, then modify the procedure so that it allows the user to update the membership information for as many salespeople as desired. Use the Do...Loop statement to code the appropriate loop. Stop the loop when the user clicks the Cancel button in the ID dialog box. (Recall that the InputBox function returns the empty string when the user clicks the Cancel button.)

   c. Save the document. Return to Word and run the UpdateMembership macro. Record these sales: salesperson 100 sold three full memberships and two matinee memberships; salesperson 201 sold two full memberships and one matinee membership.

   d. When the macro is working correctly, save and then close the document.

Exercises 4 through 6 are Discovery Exercises. Discovery Exercises, which may include topics that are not covered in the lesson, allow you to "discover" the solutions to problems on your own.

discovery ▶ 4. In this exercise, you will create a procedure that allows the user to enter information into a table.

   a. Open the T10-WD-E4 (T10-ED-E4.doc) document, which is located in the Tut10\Word folder on your Data Disk. Click the Enable Macros button, if necessary, then save the document as T10-WD-E4D. Notice that the document contains a four-column table. Currently, only the column headings appear in the table.

   b. Open the Visual Basic Editor. Display and study the Help screens for the Rows Collection object and its Add method. Also display and study the Help screens for the Row object and its Cells property. Close the Help window.

   c. Open the Module1 module's Code window, then view the code template for the AddActivity procedure. The procedure should ask the user if he or she has an activity to enter. If the user has an activity to enter, the procedure should add a row to the table and then get the activity information from the user. The procedure should allow the user to enter the information for as many activities as desired without having to run the macro each time. Use the Do...Loop statement to code the loop. The procedure should adjust the width of the columns to fit their current contents.

   d. Save the document. Return to Word and run the AddActivity macro. Use the macro to enter the following information into the table:

7/1/02	Bicycle		3 miles
7/2/02	Step Class		50 minutes
7/3/02	Hip Abductor	3/12	
7/3/02	Sit-ups	2/25	
7/3/02	Free Weights	2/15	

   e. When the macro is working correctly, save and then close the document.

discovery ▶ 5. In this exercise, you will modify the SortAndRemoveDuplicates procedure that you created in this lesson so that the procedure uses the For Each...Next statement rather than the Do...Loop statement.

    a. Open the Guest List (Guest List.doc) document, which you created in this lesson. The document is located in the Tut10\Word folder on your Data Disk. Click the Enable Macros button, if necessary, then save the document as T10-WD-E5D.

    b. Add the following two records to the end of the table:

4/1/02	Chen, Daria	34 Pine Street, Chicago, 60611
4/1/02	Smith, Carol	111 Yardley, Chicago, 60612

    c. Open the Visual Basic Editor. Display and study the Help screens for the Rows Collection object, as well as for the Row object and its Cells property. Close the Help window.

    d. Open the Module1 module's Code window, then view the SortAndRemoveDuplicates procedure. Change the filename in the first Set statement to "t10-wd-e5d.doc".

    e. Modify the procedure so that it uses the For Each...Next statement, rather than the Do...Loop statement, to refer to each row in the table. (*Hints*: Declare a Row object variable, and then use the For Each...Next statement to loop through each row in the Rows collection. Use the Row object's Cells property to assign the current name to the appropriate String variable.)

    f. Save the document. Return to Word and run the SortAndRemoveDuplicates macro. Confirm the deletion only of the two records you entered in Step b.

    g. When the macro is working correctly, save and then close the document.

discovery ▶ 6. In this exercise, you will learn why you cannot use the For...Next statement to code the SortAndRemoveDuplicates procedure that you created in this lesson.

    a. Open the T10-WD-E6 (T10-WD-E6.doc) document, which is located in the Tut10\Word folder on your Data Disk. Click the Enable Macros button, if necessary, then save the document as T10-WD-E6D. Notice that the table contains three "Chen, Daria" records.

    b. Open the Visual Basic Editor. Open the Module1 module's Code window and view the SortAndRemoveDuplicates procedure. Notice that the procedure uses the For...Next statement rather than the Do...Loop statement to refer to each table row that contains guest information.

    c. Return to Word and run the SortAndRemoveDuplicates macro. When you are asked if the selected record is a duplicate, click the Yes button. Notice that the macro does not work correctly. Click the Debug button, then click the Reset button on the Visual Basic Editor's Standard toolbar to stop the procedure. Return to Word and use the Undo button to undo the changes made to the document.

    d. Return to the Visual Basic Editor and try various ways to make the procedure work with the For...Next loop. When you have given up trying, think about why the `Do While intRow <= tblGuests.Row.Count` clause works correctly, but the `For intRow = 2 To tblGuests.Rows.Count` clause does not. What does this exercise imply about how VBA processes the Do...Loop and For...Next statements?

    e. Close the document.

A computer program is good only if it works. Errors in programming code can cause a program to run incorrectly. Therefore, a programmer needs to know how to locate and fix any errors in his or her code. Exercise 7 is a Debugging Exercise. Debugging Exercises allow you to practice recognizing and solving errors in code.

debugging 7. In this exercise, you will debug an existing macro procedure.

a. Open the T10-WD-E7 (T9-WD-E7.doc) document, which is located in the Tut10\Word folder on your Data Disk. Click the Enable Macros button, if necessary, then save the document as T10-WD-E7D. Notice that each sentence is separated from the next with a period rather than with a period and a space. The AddASpace procedure is supposed to remedy this situation by inserting a space after each period, but it is not working correctly.

b. Open the Visual Basic Editor. Open the Module1 module's Code window, then view the AddASpace procedure's code. Study the code, then return to Word and run the AddASpace macro. (*Hint*: If the procedure is in an endless loop, press Ctrl+Break, then click the End button.)

c. Return to the Visual Basic Editor and correct the errors in the procedure. When the macro is working correctly, save and then close the document.

Access Lesson

Using the Repetition Structure and String Functions in Access

case ▶ Professor Carlisle, who has recently become chair of the CIS department at Snowville College, records the names and phone numbers of the adjunct CIS instructors, as well as the courses that each instructor teaches, in an Access database. Professor Carlisle has decided to create a macro that he can use to quickly display the names of the instructors that teach a particular course.

Viewing the Database and the LocateInstructor Procedure

Professor Carlisle's Access database containing information about the adjunct CIS faculty is stored on your Data Disk. Before creating the macro that will display the names of instructors teaching a particular course, you will view the records contained in the database's AdjunctFaculty table.

To view the AdjunctFaculty table and the LocateInstructor procedure:

1 Start Microsoft Access. Open the **AdjFac** (AdjFac.mdb) database, which is located in the Tut10\Access folder on your Data Disk. Click the **Maximize** button ▢ on the Microsoft Access title bar to maximize the Microsoft Access window, if necessary. Click **Tables** in the Objects bar of the Database window, if necessary. Notice that the database contains one table named AdjunctFaculty. Right-click **AdjunctFaculty**, then click **Open**. See Figure 10-27.

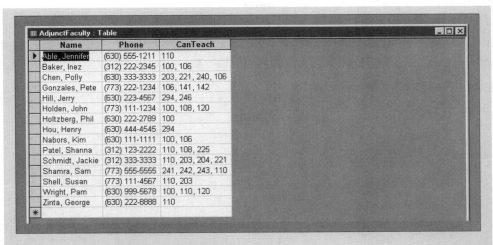

Figure 10-27: Records contained in the AdjunctFaculty table

Each record contains three Text fields: Name, Phone, and CanTeach.

2 Close the table.

3 Press **Alt+F11** to open the Visual Basic Editor. If necessary, open the Project Explorer window and close the Properties window, the Immediate window, and any open Code windows. Open the Module1 module's Code window, then view the code template for the LocateInstructor function procedure.

4 Close the Project Explorer window so that you can view more of the Code window.

Figure 10-28 shows the pseudocode for the LocateInstructor procedure.

1. Use the InputBox function to get the course number from the user. Store the user's response in a String variable named strCourseNum.
2. Open a recordset that includes all of the records stored in the AdjunctFaculty table.
3. Repeat the following for each record in the recordset:
   a. If the course number entered by the user is included in the current record's CanTeach field, then
      1) Use the MsgBox function to display the current record's name and phone number.
      2) Assign "Y" to a String variable named strFound.
   b. Move the record pointer to the next record.
4. If the strFound variable does not contain the letter "Y", then
   a. Use the MsgBox function to display the "No instructors were found" message.
5. Close the recordset.

Figure 10-28: Pseudocode for the LocateInstructor procedure

Figure 10-29 lists the variables that the LocateInstructor procedure will use.

Variable	datatype
strCourseNum	String
strFound	String
cnnAdjFac	ADODB.Connection
rstAdjFac	ADODB.Recordset

Figure 10-29: Variables used by the LocateInstructor procedure

The procedure will use the String variable strCourseNum to store the course number entered by the user. It will use the String variable strFound to store the letter "Y", indicating that the procedure located at least one instructor who teaches the course. The cnnAdjFac and rstAdjFac object variables will be used to store the addresses of the Connection and Recordset objects, respectively.

> **tip**
>
> As you learned in Tutorial 6's Access lesson, the ADO object model contains all of the objects needed to manage the records contained in an Access database. Recall that the Connection object, which appears at the top of the ADO object model, represents the physical connection between an Access database and a data provider. Immediately below the Connection object is the Recordset object, which represents either all or a portion of the records (rows) contained in one or more tables.

In the next set of steps, you will declare the appropriate variables and then begin translating the pseudocode shown in Figure 10-28 into VBA statements.

To begin coding the LocateInstructor procedure:

1 Enter the documentation and Dim and Set statements shown in Figure 10-30.

```
Microsoft Visual Basic - AdjFac - [Module1 (Code)]
File  Edit  View  Insert  Debug  Run  Tools  Add-Ins  Window  Help
                                                    Ln 10, Col 5
(General)                                LocateInstructor

    Public Function LocateInstructor()
        'declare variables and assign address to object variables
        Dim strCourseNum As String, strFound As String
        Dim cnnAdjFac As ADODB.Connection, rstAdjFac As ADODB.Recordset
        Set cnnAdjFac = Application.CurrentProject.Connection
        Set rstAdjFac = New ADODB.Recordset

    End Function
```

enter these five lines of code

Figure 10-30: Code window showing documentation and Dim and Set statements

tip

Recall from Tutorial 6 that you can use the CurrentProject object's Connection property to refer to the Connection object that Access automatically creates when you open a database. Also recall that, unlike the Connection object, a Recordset object is not created automatically when a database is opened; rather, the programmer must create the Recordset object through code. As you learned earlier, you can use the Set *objectvar* = New *datatype* syntax, where *objectvar* is the name of a Recordset object variable and *datatype* is ADODB.Recordset, to create a Recordset object and, at the same time, assign its address to a Recordset object variable.

Now use the InputBox function to prompt the user to enter the course number.

2 Type **'enter course number** and press the **Enter** key. Type **strcoursenum = inputbox(prompt:="Enter the 3-character course number:", _** (be sure to type the comma followed by a space and the underscore) and press the **Enter** key. Press the **Tab** key, then type **title:="Course Number")** and press the **Enter** key.

Next, open a recordset that will include all of the records contained in the AdjunctFaculty table. As you learned in Tutorial 6, you use the Recordset object's Open method to do so.

3 Press the **Backspace** key, then type **'open recordset** and press the **Enter** key.

4 Type **rstadjfac.open source:="adjunctfaculty", activeconnection:=cnnadjfac, _** (be sure to type the comma followed by a space and the underscore) and press the **Enter** key. Press the **Tab** key, then type **cursortype:=adopenforwardonly, locktype:=adlockpessimistic** and press the **Enter** key.

5 Verify the accuracy of your code before continuing by comparing the code on your screen to the code in Figure 10-31, then save the database.

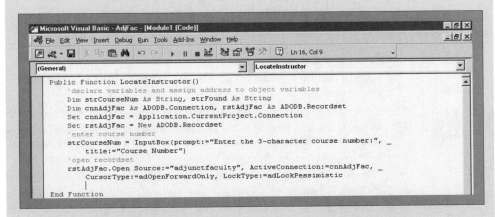

```
Microsoft Visual Basic - AdjFac - [Module1 (Code)]
File  Edit  View  Insert  Debug  Run  Tools  Add-Ins  Window  Help
                                                    Ln 16, Col 9
(General)                                           LocateInstructor

Public Function LocateInstructor()
    'declare variables and assign address to object variables
    Dim strCourseNum As String, strFound As String
    Dim cnnAdjFac As ADODB.Connection, rstAdjFac As ADODB.Recordset
    Set cnnAdjFac = Application.CurrentProject.Connection
    Set rstAdjFac = New ADODB.Recordset
    'enter course number
    strCourseNum = InputBox(prompt:="Enter the 3-character course number:", _
        title:="Course Number")
    'open recordset
    rstAdjFac.Open Source:="adjunctfaculty", ActiveConnection:=cnnAdjFac, _
        CursorType:=adOpenForwardOnly, LockType:=adLockPessimistic

End Function
```

Figure 10-31: Partially completed LocateInstructor procedure

According to Step 3 in the pseudocode, the procedure needs to repeat a set of instructions for each record in the recordset. You will use the Do...Loop statement along with the Recordset object's EOF property to code the appropriate loop. The Recordset object's **EOF property** returns the Boolean value True if the record pointer, which Access uses to keep track of the current record, is positioned after the last record in the recordset. The EOF property returns the Boolean value False if the record pointer is positioned on or before the last record. In this case, the loop should process its instructions while the EOF property contains the value False; it should stop processing its instructions when the EOF property contains the value True.

> **tip**
>
> Because a Recordset is an object rather than a collection, you cannot use the For Each...Next statement that you learned about in Tutorial 9 to code the loop; however, you can use the For...Next statement, which you will do in this lesson's Exercise 1.

To complete the LocateInstructor procedure:

1 Press the **Backspace** key to remove the indentation, then type **'search for course number in each record's CanTeach field** and press the **Enter** key, then type **do until rstadjfac.eof = true** and press the **Enter** key.

> **tip**
>
> You also could have written the Do clause in one of the following three ways: `Do While rstAdjFac.EOF <> True`, `Do Until rstAdjFac.EOF`, `Do While Not rstAdjFac.EOF`.

According to the pseudocode, the first instruction in the loop should search the CanTeach field for the course number entered by the user; you can use the Instr function to perform the search. As you learned in the Concept lesson, the Instr function, which has the syntax **Instr(**start, string1, string2[, compare]**)**, returns a number that represents the location of string2 within string1. If string2 is not located within string1, the function returns 0; otherwise, it returns a number that is greater than 0.

2 Press the **Tab** key, then type **if instr(1, rstadjfac.fields("canteach"), strcoursenum) > 0 then** and press the **Enter** key.

> **tip**
>
> As you learned in Tutorial 6, the Recordset object contains a Fields collection composed of individual Field objects, each of which represents a field in the recordset.

If the course number is contained within the CanTeach field, the procedure should display the contents of the record's Name and Phone fields in a message box, and the letter "Y" should be assigned to the strFound variable.

3 Press the **Tab** key, then type **'display current record's name and phone number** and press the **Enter** key. Type **msgbox prompt:=rstadjfac.fields("name").value _** (be sure to type a space followed by the underscore after the letter e) and press the **Enter** key. This part of the MsgBox statement will display the instructor's name in the message box.

Before displaying the phone number in the message box, you will use the VBA intrinsic constant `vbNewLine` to insert two blank lines into the message box.

4 Press the **Tab** key, then type **& vbnewline & vbnewline & rstadjfac.fields("phone").value, _** (be sure to type the comma followed by a space and the underscore) and press the **Enter** key.

You will display the OK button and the Information icon in the message box, and you will display the letters "CIS" followed by the course number in the message box's title bar.

5 Type **buttons:=vbokonly + vbinformation, title:="CIS" & strcoursenum** and press the **Enter** key.

6 Press the **Backspace** key, then type **'assign value to strFound variable** and press the **Enter** key, then type **strfound = "Y"** and press the **Enter** key. Press the **Backspace** key, then type **end if** to end the If…Then…Else statement, and then press the **Enter** key.

The next instruction in the loop should move the record pointer to the next record in the recordset; you can use the Recordset object's MoveNext method to do so.

> VBA also has MovePrevious, MoveFirst, and MoveLast methods. These methods move the record pointer to the previous, first, and last records, respectively, in the recordset.

7 Type **'move record pointer to next record** and press the **Enter** key, then type **rstadjfac.movenext** and press the **Enter** key. Press the **Backspace** key, then type **loop** to end the Do…Loop statement, and then press the **Enter** key.

After the loop processes its instructions for each record in the recordset, the procedure should check the value stored in the strFound variable, displaying the message "No instructors were found" if the variable does not contain the letter "Y".

8 Type **'check if an instructor was found** and press the **Enter** key, then type **if strfound <> "Y" then** (be sure to type an uppercase letter Y) and press the **Enter** key. Press the **Tab** key, then type **msgbox prompt:="No instructors were found.", _** (be sure to type the comma followed by a space and the underscore) and press the **Enter** key. Press the **Tab** key, then type **buttons:=vbokonly + vbinformation, title:="CIS" & strcoursenum** and press the **Enter** key. Press the **Backspace** key twice, then type **end if** and press the **Enter** key.

The last step in the pseudocode is to close the recordset. However, as you learned in Tutorial 6, closing an object created with the keyword `New` does not remove the object variable associated with the object from memory.

To discontinue the association between an object and its object variable, you need to set the object variable to the keyword `Nothing`. Recall that when an object variable contains the keyword `Nothing`, it means that the object variable does not point to any object in memory. Before ending a procedure, you should assign the keyword `Nothing` to any object variables that the procedure created using the keyword `New`.

9 Type the additional instructions shown in Figure 10-32, which shows the completed LocateInstructor procedure. (The figure does not show the beginning of the procedure.)

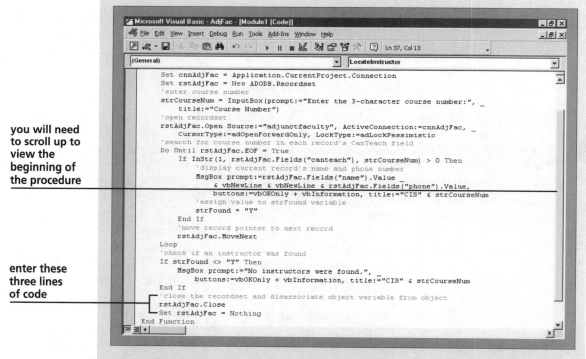

you will need to scroll up to view the beginning of the procedure

enter these three lines of code

Figure 10-32: Completed LocateInstructor procedure

10 Verify the accuracy of your code before continuing by comparing the code on your screen to the code shown in Figure 10-32, then save the database.

Now that you have finished coding the LocateInstructor procedure, you should run the procedure to verify that it is working correctly.

To test the LocateInstructor procedure:

1   Return to Access and run the **LocateInstructorMacro** macro.

2   When the Course Number dialog box appears, type **120** and press the **Enter** key.

The procedure displays John Holden's name and phone number in a message box, as shown in Figure 10-33. Notice that the course number, CIS120, appears in the message box's title bar.

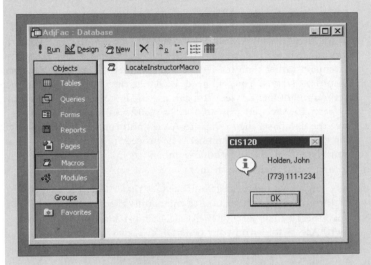

Figure 10-33: Message box showing John Holden's name and phone number

3   Press the **Enter** key to close the message box. Pam Wright's name and phone number appear in a message box. Press the **Enter** key to close the message box. The LocateInstructor procedure ends because these are the only two instructors that teach the CIS120 course.

Now enter a course number that does not appear in any instructor's CanTeach field.

4   Run the **LocateInstructorMacro** macro again. Type **345** as the course number and press the **Enter** key. The message "No instructors were found." appears in a message box. Press the **Enter** key to close the message box.

5   Compact the database, then close Access.

You now have completed Tutorial 10's Access lesson. You can either take a break or complete the end-of-lesson exercises.

EXERCISES

1. In this exercise, you will modify the LocateInstructor procedure that you created in this lesson so that it uses the For...Next statement, rather than the Do...Loop statement, to refer to each record in the Recordset.

   a. Use Windows to make a copy of the AdjFac database that you used in this lesson. The database is located in the Tut10\Access folder on your Data Disk. Rename the copy T10-AC-E1D.

   b. Open the T10-AC-E1D (T10-AC-E1D.mdb) database. Open the Visual Basic Editor, then open the Module1 module's Code window and view the LocateInstructor procedure. Modify the procedure so that it uses the For...Next statement, rather than the Do...Loop statement, to refer to each record in the Recordset. (*Hints*: You will need to change the CursorType argument in the Open method to adOpenKeyset. You can use the Recordset object's RecordCount property to determine the number of records in the recordset.)

   c. Save the database, then return to Access and run the LocateInstructorMacro macro. Enter 120 as the course number. The procedure should display John Holden's and Pam Wright's name and phone number.

   d. Compact and then close the database.

2. In this exercise, you will create a procedure that allows the user to display an instructor's full name after the user enters only the first few characters of the last name.

   a. Open the T10-AC-E2D (T10-AC-E2D.mdb) database, which is located in the Tut10\Access folder on your Data Disk. View the records contained in the Faculty table, then close the table.

   b. Open the Visual Basic Editor. Open the Module1 module's Code window, then view the code template for the GetFullName procedure. Code the procedure so that it prompts the user to enter one or more characters in the instructor's last name. The procedure then should search the LastName field for the matching records. (*Hint*: Display the Like Operator Help screen, or complete Exercise 14 in Tutorial 7's Concept lesson.) Display the first and last name of each matching record, one at a time, in a message box. Use the Do...Loop statement.

   c. Save the database, then return to Access and run the GetFullNameMacro macro. Enter the letters sm. The procedure should display three names.

   d. Compact and then close the database.

Exercises 3 through 6 are Discovery Exercises. Discovery Exercises, which may include topics that are not covered in the lesson, allow you to "discover" the solutions to problems on your own.

discovery ▶ 3. In this exercise, you will create a procedure that removes duplicate records from a table. You will learn how to use the SQL Delete statement and the Connection object's Execute method. (You learned about SQL commands in Tutorial 8.)

   a. Open the T10-AC-E3D (T10-AC-E3D.mdb) database, which is located in the Tut10\Access folder on your Data Disk. View the records contained in the Tutors table. Notice that the table contains 16 names, and some names appear more than once in the Name field. Also notice that the names are in alphabetical order, which must be true for the RemoveDuplicates procedure, which you will code in this exercise, to work correctly. Close the table.

b. Open the Visual Basic Editor. Open the Module1 module's Code window, then view the code template for the RemoveDuplicates procedure.

c. You can use the ADO Connection object's Execute method to execute a SQL statement. The syntax of the Execute method is *connection.***Execute** ***CommandText:=****commandtext*, where *commandtext* is the SQL statement. You can use the SQL Delete statement, whose syntax is **Delete From** *table* [**Where** *condition*] to delete records from a table. (*Hint*: When you find a duplicate record, assign a character—for example, assign the letter "X"—to its Name field. When the loop completes its processing, use the Execute method to execute a Delete statement that deletes records whose Name field contains the letter "X".) Use the Do…Loop statement.

d. Save the database, then return to Access and run the RemoveDuplicatesMacro macro. View the records contained in the Tutors table. The table should contain 10 unique names.

e. Close the table, then compact and close the database.

discovery ▶ **4.** In this exercise, you will modify the LocateInstructor procedure that you created in this lesson. Rather than using a selection structure to search for the course number in each record's CanTeach field, you will use a SQL SELECT statement to include only the appropriate records in the recordset. (You learned about the SQL SELECT statement in Tutorial 8's Access lesson.)

a. Open the T10-AC-E4D (T10-AC-E4D.mdb) database, which is located in the Tut10\Access folder on your Data Disk. Open the Visual Basic Editor. Open the Module1 module's Code window, then view the LocateInstructor procedure.

b. Create a SQL SELECT statement that selects only the records whose CanTeach field contains the course number stored in the strCourseNum variable; arrange the records in ascending order by name. Assign the SELECT statement to the strSql variable. Enter the appropriate statement below the 'create SQL string comment in the procedure.

c. Study the procedure's existing code. Notice that the strSql variable, rather than the table name (AdjunctFaculty), is used in the Open method, and the CursorType argument is set to adOpenKeyset. Also notice that the loop does not have to search for the course number in each record's CanTeach field; this is because the SELECT statement will already have selected the appropriate records. (*Hint*: You will need to use string concatenation in the SELECT statement. This is because you can include a field name, but not a variable name, within the quotation marks.)

d. Save the database, then return to Access and run the LocateInstructorMacro macro. Enter 203 as the course number. The procedure should display the names and phone numbers of three instructors.

e. Compact and then close the database.

discovery ▶ **5.** In this exercise, you will complete a procedure that separates a full name into two parts— first name and last name—and then enters both parts of the name into another table.

a. Open the T10-AC-E5 (T10-AC-E5.mdb) database, which is located in the Tut10\Access folder on your Data Disk. Open the Instructors1 table. Notice that the table contains one field named Name and 10 records. The Name field contains the full name of each instructor. Close the table.

b. Open the Instructors2 table. Notice that the table contains two fields, LastName and FirstName. Currently, the table does not contain any records. Close the table.

c. Open the Visual Basic Editor. Open the Module1 module's Code window, then view the partially completed SplitName procedure. Study the existing code, then complete the procedure so that it separates each full name entered in the Instructors1 table into its last name and first name components. Store each last name and first name in the appropriate fields in the Instructors2 table. (*Hint*: View the ADO Recordset object's AddNew and Update methods. You will need to use the AddNew method to add a new record to the Instructors2 table. You will need to use the Update method to save the data entered in the new record.)

d. Save the database, then return to Access and run the SplitNameMacro macro. Open the Instructors1 table. The table should still contain the original 10 records. Close the table. Open the Instructors2 table. The table should contain the 10 last names in the LastName field and it should contain the 10 first names in the FirstName field. Close the table.

e. Compact and then close the database.

discovery ▶ 6. In this exercise, you will create a procedure that removes the zip code from an Address field and stores it in the Zip field.

a. Open the T10-AC-E6 (T10-AC-E6.mdb) database, which is located in the Tut10\Access folder on your Data Disk. Open the Contacts table. Notice that the table contains three fields (Name, Address, and Zip) and five records. The Address field contains the full street address, and the Zip field is currently empty. Close the table.

b. Open the Visual Basic Editor. Open the Module1 module's Code window, then view the code template for the SeparateZip procedure. Code the procedure so that it removes the zip code from the Address field and stores it in the Zip field. Be sure also to remove the comma and space that separate the city from the zip code in the Address field. (*Hint*: You will need to use the ADO Recordset object's Update method to save the changes made to each record.)

c. Save the database, then return to Access and run the SeparateZipMacro macro. Open the Contacts table. The Address field should contain only the street address, followed by a space, a comma, and the city name. The zip code should appear in the Zip field. Close the table.

d. Compact and then close the database.

A computer program is good only if it works. Errors in programming code can cause a program to run incorrectly. Therefore, a programmer needs to know how to locate and fix any errors in his or her code. Exercise 7 is a Debugging Exercise. Debugging Exercises allow you to practice recognizing and solving errors in code.

debugging 7. In this exercise, you will debug an existing procedure.

a. Open the T10-AC-E7 (T10-AC-E7.mdb) database, which is located in the Tut10\Access folder on your Data Disk. Open the Contacts table, which contains three fields and six records. Close the table.

b. Open the Visual Basic Editor. Open the Module1 module's Code window, then view the FindStreetOrCity procedure. The procedure should search the Address field for the characters entered by the user, and it should display the name and address of each matching record. Study the code, then run the procedure. When the Street Or City dialog box appears, type pueblo and press the Enter key. Correct any errors in the procedure. (*Hint*: If the procedure is in an endless loop, press Ctrl+Break.)

c. When the procedure is working correctly, save, compact, and then close the database.

Built-in Dialog Boxes and the Office Assistant

In this tutorial, you will learn how to:

- Use the dialog boxes contained in the Excel and Word Dialogs collections
- Declare and assign a value to a Boolean variable
- Create a customized balloon for the Office Assistant
- Use the Sort dialog box in Excel to sort a range of data
- Access an individual cell in an Excel range
- Insert database information into a Word document
- Apply the OpenReport method's WhereCondition argument in Access

Concept Lesson

Communicating with the User

One of the most common tasks performed by a procedure is to communicate with the user either by displaying a message for the user to read or by prompting for and then getting user input. In previous tutorials, many of the procedures you created accomplished this task by displaying the predefined dialog boxes created by the MsgBox statement, MsgBox function, and InputBox function.

VBA also provides other ways of interacting with the user while a procedure is running. For example, you can use the Office Assistant, which is available in all of the Microsoft Office applications. You also can use the predefined dialog boxes contained in the Dialogs collection in both Microsoft Excel and Microsoft Word. Additionally, you can create a custom dialog box. In this tutorial, you will learn how to use the Office Assistant and the Dialogs collection. You will learn how to create custom dialog boxes in Tutorial 12. Begin by learning about the Dialogs collection.

The Dialogs Collection

The Application object in both the Microsoft Excel and Microsoft Word object models contains a **Dialogs collection** composed of individual Dialog objects. Each **Dialog object** represents one of the application's built-in dialog boxes. The Excel Dialogs collection, for example, contains Dialog objects that represent the Open, Print, and Save As dialog boxes, as well as the Sort and Consolidate dialog boxes. Examples of dialog boxes included in the Word Dialogs collection are the Open, Print, Save As, Merge, and Paragraph dialog boxes.

··

The following Microsoft Office applications currently do not have a Dialogs collection: Access, PowerPoint, Outlook, and FrontPage.

··

You refer to an individual Dialog object using the syntax **Application.Dialogs(*index*)**, where *index* is an intrinsic constant that identifies the Dialog object within the Dialogs collection. Excel's intrinsic constants begin with "xlDialog"—for example, `xlDialogOpen`, `xlDialogPrint`, `xlDialogSaveAs`, `xlDialogSort`, and `xlDialogConsolidate`. Word's intrinsic constants, on the other hand, begin with "wdDialog"—for example, `wdDialogFileOpen`, `wdDialogFilePrint`, `wdDialogFileSaveAs`, `wdDialogMailMerge`, and `wdDialogFormatParagraph`.

You use the Dialog object's **Show method**, which has the syntax *dialogObject*.**Show**, to display the dialog box on the screen. For example, the `Application.Dialogs(xlDialogSaveAs).Show` instruction will display Excel's Save As dialog box, and the `Application.Dialogs(wdDialogFileSaveAs).Show` instruction will display Word's Save As dialog box. Both dialog boxes are shown in Figure 11-1.

default file type in Excel

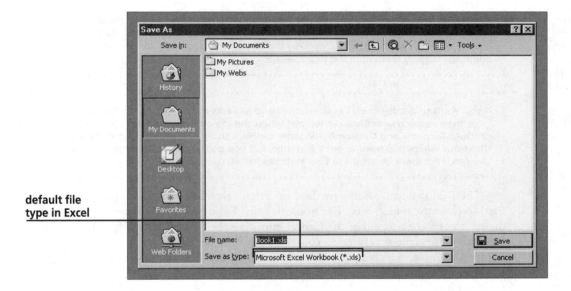

default file type in Word

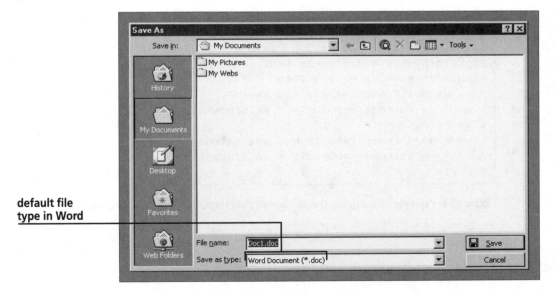

Figure 11-1: The Save As dialog boxes built into Excel and Word

Notice that the default file format in the Excel Save As dialog box is "Microsoft Excel Workbook (*.xls)", while in Word the default is "Word Document (*.doc)."

The Save As dialog box will remain on the screen until the user closes it by clicking the Save button, the Cancel button, or the Close button ☒. If the user clicks the Save button, the file will be saved before the dialog box closes; otherwise, the dialog box will close without saving the file.

▸ tip

In Microsoft Word, you also can use the Dialog object's Display method to display a built-in dialog box. Different from using the Show method, VBA does not carry out the dialog box's actions when the dialog box displayed by the Display method is closed. You will learn more about the Display method in the Word lesson.

▸ tip

If you want to display Excel's built-in Open and Save As dialog boxes, but do not want to have their respective actions carried out when the dialog box is closed, you can use the GetOpenFilename and GetSaveAsFilename methods to do so. These methods are useful in situations where you need to get a filename, but you don't want the file opened or saved. You can learn more about these two methods in Exercise 5 in the Excel lesson.

The Dialog object's Show method returns a value that indicates which button was used to close the dialog box. The Boolean value False is returned if the user closed the dialog box by clicking either the Cancel button or the Close button ☒; otherwise, the Boolean value True is returned. You can assign the Show method's return value to a **Boolean variable**, which is a variable that can store either the Boolean value True or the Boolean value False. The code shown in Figure 11-2, for example, assigns the value returned by the Save As dialog box to a Boolean variable named blnReturnValue.

```
Dim blnReturnValue As Boolean, dlgSaveAs As Dialog
Set dlgSaveAs = Application.Dialogs(xlDialogSaveAs)
blnReturnValue = dlgSaveAs.Show
If blnReturnValue = True Then
    MsgBox Prompt:="File was saved", _
         Buttons:=vbOKOnly + vbInformation
Else
    MsgBox Prompt:="File was not saved", _
         Buttons:=vbOKOnly + vbInformation
End If
```

Figure 11-2: Example of assigning the Show method's return value to a Boolean variable

First, the Dim statement shown in Figure 11-2 declares two variables: a Boolean variable named blnReturnValue and a Dialog object variable named dlgSaveAs. The Set statement then assigns the address of Excel's built-in Save As dialog box to the dlgSaveAs variable. The instruction `blnReturnValue = dlgSaveAs.Show` displays the Save As dialog box on the screen and, when the user closes the dialog box, it assigns the Show method's return value to the blnReturnValue variable. If the user clicks the Save button, the instruction assigns True to the blnReturnValue variable; otherwise, it assigns False. The If...Then...Else statement uses the value stored in the blnReturnValue variable to determine the appropriate message to display. In this case, the message "File was saved" will be displayed if the blnReturnValue variable contains the Boolean value True; otherwise, the message "File was not saved" will be displayed.

Next, learn how you can use the Office Assistant to communicate with the user.

The Office Assistant

The Office Assistant, usually referred to simply as the Assistant, is one of several objects that Microsoft Office makes available to each of its applications. You can use the Assistant to display messages, such as tips or instructions for completing a task. You also can use the Assistant to get user input; you do so by displaying labels, buttons, or check boxes that represent choices from which the user can select. Figure 11-3 shows the Overview of the Office Assistant Help screen, which contains an illustration of the Office Assistant and its components.

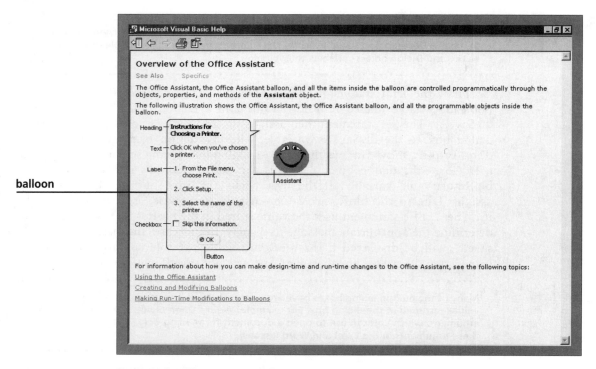

Figure 11-3: Office Assistant Help screen

▶ **tip**

....

To view a complete listing of objects available to all of the Microsoft Office applications, view the Microsoft Office Objects Help screen.

....

Notice that the Assistant displays its information in a balloon, and that the balloon can contain a heading, text, labels, check boxes, and buttons. It also can contain an icon, which is not included in the illustration. When used, the icon appears to the left of the heading.

Figure 11-4 shows the Assistant's object model.

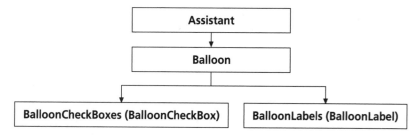

Figure 11-4: Assistant's object model

As Figure 11-4 indicates, the Assistant object contains a **Balloon object**, which represents a customized balloon that you want the Assistant to display. Included within the Balloon object are the BalloonCheckBoxes and BalloonLabels collections, composed of BalloonCheckBox and BalloonLabel objects, respectively.

In the next section, you will review several of the properties of the Assistant object. You also will learn how to use the Assistant object's NewBalloon property to create a Balloon object.

Properties of the Assistant Object

Figure 11-5 lists the most commonly used properties of the Assistant object. Each of these properties, except for the NewBalloon property, was covered in Tutorial 1.

Property	Purpose
FileName	Controls the character used to display the Assistant
Left	Controls the position of the Assistant's left border; measured in points
NewBalloon	Creates a customized balloon for the Assistant
On	Setting this property to True turns the Assistant feature on; setting it to False turns the Assistant feature off
Top	Controls the position of the Assistant's top border; measured in points
Visible	Setting this property to True displays the Assistant on the screen; setting it to False hides the Assistant

Figure 11-5: Most commonly used properties of the Assistant object

As Figure 11-5 shows, you use the FileName property to control the character used to display the Assistant. For example, the instruction `Assistant.FileName = "Dot.acs"` tells Microsoft Office to display the character The Dot, which is pictured in Figure 11-3, as the Assistant.

You use the Left and Top properties to position the Assistant's Left and Top borders, respectively, on the screen. Recall that the setting for these properties is measured in points, with one point equivalent to 1/72 of an inch. For example, the two instructions `Assistant.Left = 504` and `Assistant.Top = 216` will position the Assistant seven inches from the left side of the screen and three inches from the top of the screen.

You turn the Assistant feature on by setting the Assistant object's On property to the Boolean value True, and you disable the Assistant feature by setting the On property to the Boolean value False. You use the Visible property, which also can be set to either True or False, to display or hide the Assistant.

You create a Balloon object—a customized balloon—by using the Assistant object's **NewBalloon property** in the following syntax: **Set** *balloonObject* = **Assistant.NewBalloon**, where *balloonObject* is the name of a Balloon object variable. For example, the instruction `Set balOptions = Assistant.NewBalloon` will create a Balloon object and also assign its address to the balOptions Balloon object variable. The Balloon object created by the NewBalloon property contains only an OK button. You can display other information in the balloon by setting the Balloon object's properties. You will learn how to set these properties, as well as how to use the Balloon object's Show method to display the balloon, in the next section.

> To create a Balloon object variable, use the Dim statement in the following syntax: **Dim** *variablename* **As Balloon**. The three-character ID used to name a Balloon object variable is *bal*.

Properties and Methods of the Balloon Object

Figure 11-6 shows the most commonly used properties of the Balloon object.

Property	Purpose

BalloonType	Controls the format of the labels that appear in the balloon; can be set to one of the following intrinsic constants:
	`msoBalloonTypeButtons` (default)
	`msoBalloonTypeBullets`
	`msoBalloonTypeNumbers`

Button	Controls the type of button displayed at the bottom of the balloon; can be set to one of the following intrinsic constants:
	`msoButtonSetAbortRetryIgnore` `msoButtonSetOkCancel`
	`msoButtonSetBackClose` `msoButtonSetRetryCancel`
	`msoButtonSetBackNextClose` `msoButtonSetSearchClose`
	`msoButtonSetBackNextSnooze` `msoButtonSetTipsOptionsClose`
	`msoButtonSetCancel` `msoButtonSetYesAllNoCancel`
	`msoButtonSetNextClose` `msoButtonSetYesNoCancel`
	`msoButtonSetNone` `msoButtonSetYesNo`
	`msoButtonSetOK` (default)

Checkboxes(*index*)	Creates a BalloonCheckBox object; *index* is a number from 1 through 5
Heading	Controls the heading that appears in the balloon

Figure 11-6: Most commonly used properties of the Balloon object

Property	Purpose

Icon	Controls the type of icon that appears in the upper-left portion of the balloon; can be set to one of the following intrinsic constants:
	`msoIconAlert` `msoIconAlertWarning`
	`msoIconAlertCritical` `msoIconNone` (default)
	`msoIconAlertInfo` `msoIconTip`
	`msoIconAlertQuery`

Labels(*index*)	Creates a BalloonLabel object; *index* is a number from 1 through 5
Text	Controls the text displayed after the heading but before any labels or check boxes in the balloon

Figure 11-6: Most commonly used properties of the Balloon object (*continued*)

••

The *mso* that appears before each of the intrinsic constants shown in Figure 11-6 stands for "Microsoft Office."

••

Notice that the **Button property** specifies which buttons (if any) should appear at the bottom of the balloon. The default value for this property is `msoButtonSetOK`, which displays only an OK button in the balloon.

The Balloon object's **Icon property** indicates which icon should appear in the upper-left portion of the balloon. If you do not assign a value to this property, no icon will appear in the balloon; this is because the default value for this property is `msoIconNone`.

The Balloon object's **Heading property** specifies the text to display at the top of the balloon, and the **Text property** specifies the text to display after the heading but before any labels or check boxes.

You use the Balloon object's **Checkboxes property** to create a BalloonCheckBox object. The syntax of the Checkboxes property is *balloonObject*.**Checkboxes(***index***)**, where *balloonObject* is the name of a Balloon object variable and *index* is a number from 1 through 5. You can create a maximum of five BalloonCheckBox objects for a balloon. The first BalloonCheckBox object has an *index* of 1, the second an *index* of 2, and so on. Each **BalloonCheckBox object** is a member of the **BalloonCheckBoxes collection**.

You select a BalloonCheckBox object in a balloon simply by clicking it; a check mark will appear in the object to indicate that it is selected. You deselect a BalloonCheckBox object by clicking it again; this will remove the check mark. After selecting and deselecting the desired BalloonCheckBox objects, the user then clicks the button that appears at the bottom of the balloon both to register his or her check box selections and to dismiss (or close) the balloon.

You can determine if a check box is selected by using the BalloonCheckBox object's Checked property. The **Checked property** returns the Boolean value True if the check box is selected, and it returns the Boolean value False if the check box is not selected. Figure 11-7 shows an example of using the Checked property to determine which of three check boxes (if any) are selected.

```
For intX = 1 To 3
   If balOptions.Checkboxes(intX).Checked = True Then
      MsgBox Prompt:="Check box " & intX & " is selected", _
          Buttons:=vbOKOnly + vbInformation
   Else
      MsgBox Prompt:="Check box " & intX & " is not selected", _
          Buttons:=vbOKOnly + vbInformation
   End If
Next intX
```

Figure 11-7: Example of using the BalloonCheckBox object's Checked property

The code shown in Figure 11-7 uses a For...Next loop to compare the Checked property of the three BalloonCheckBox objects to the Boolean value True. If the first check box is selected, the message "Check box 1 is selected" will be displayed; otherwise, the message "Check box 1 is not selected" will be displayed. If the second check box is selected, the message "Check box 2 is selected" will be displayed; otherwise, the message "Check box 2 is not selected" will be displayed. Finally, if the third check box is selected, the message "Check box 3 is selected" will be displayed; otherwise, the message "Check box 3 is not selected" will be displayed.

You use the Balloon object's **Labels property** to create a maximum of five BalloonLabel objects for a balloon. The syntax of the Labels property is *balloonObject*.**Labels**(*index*), where *balloonObject* is the name of a Balloon object variable and *index* is a number from 1 through 5. The first BalloonLabel object has an *index* of 1, the second an *index* of 2, and so on. Each **BalloonLabel object** is a member of the **BalloonLabels collection**.

As Figure 11-6 indicates, the **BalloonType property** controls the format of the BalloonLabel objects, which can appear as buttons or as a list of bulleted or numbered items. If the BalloonLabel objects appear as buttons, the balloon closes immediately after the user clicks one of the buttons; otherwise, the user must click the button that appears at the bottom of the balloon to dismiss the balloon.

You can view the different formats for the BalloonLabel object, as well as the various icons you can include in a balloon, by completing this lesson's Exercise 6.

Like the Balloon object, the BalloonCheckBox and BalloonLabel objects also have a Text property. When used with the BalloonCheckBox and BalloonLabel objects, the **Text property** controls the text displayed next to the check box or label. Figure 11-8 shows examples of using the Text property to display the appropriate text next to each check box and label.

```
Example 1:

With balOptions
     .Checkboxes(1).Text = "January"
     .Checkboxes(2).Text = "February"
     .Checkboxes(3).Text = "March"
End With
```

```
Example 2:

With balOptions
     .ButtonType = msoBalloonTypeBullets
     .Labels(1).Text = "Print"
     .Labels(2).Text = "Save"
End With
```

Figure 11-8: Examples of using the Text property for BalloonCheckBox and BalloonLabel objects

The first example shown in Figure 11-8 will display three check boxes and an OK button in the Assistant's balloon. The check boxes will be labeled January, February, and March. The second example will display an OK button along with a bulleted list containing the Print and Save labels.

Recall that the default setting for the Balloon object's Button property is `msoButtonSetOK`, which displays only an OK button.

After creating the Balloon object and setting its properties, you then need to use the Balloon object's **Show method**, which has the syntax *balloonObject*.**Show**, to display the balloon on the screen. When the user dismisses the balloon, the Show method returns a value that indicates which button the user selected. For example, if the Balloon object's Button property is set to `msoButtonSetOkCancel`, which will display the OK and Cancel buttons, the Show method will return the intrinsic constant `msoBalloonButtonOK` if the user clicks the OK button, but it will return the intrinsic constant `msoBalloonButtonCancel` if the user clicks the Cancel button. Figure 11-9 shows the intrinsic constants that correspond to the various buttons that can appear at the bottom of a balloon.

```
msoBalloonButtonAbort
msoBalloonButtonBack
msoBalloonButtonCancel
msoBalloonButtonClose
msoBalloonButtonIgnore
msoBalloonButtonNext
msoBalloonButtonNo
msoBalloonButtonNull
msoBalloonButtonOK
msoBalloonButtonOptions
msoBalloonButtonRetry
msoBalloonButtonSearch
msoBalloonButtonSnooze
msoBalloonButtonTips
msoBalloonButtonYes
msoBalloonButtonYesToAll
```

Figure 11-9: Intrinsic constants returned by the Balloon object's Show method

In addition to the buttons that appear at the bottom of the balloon, the BalloonLabel objects that you create also can be buttons. Recall that you display BalloonLabel objects as buttons by setting the Balloon object's BalloonType property to the intrinsic constant `msoBalloonTypeButtons`. If the user clicks the first BalloonLabel button, the Show method returns the number 1. If he or she clicks the second BalloonLabel button, the Show method returns the number 2, and so on. Figure 11-10 shows examples of using the value returned by the Balloon object's Show method.

Example 1:
```
intReturnValue = balOptions.Show
If intReturnValue = msoBalloonButtonOK Then
    [instructions to be processed when the user clicks the OK button]
End If
```

Example 2:
```
intReturnValue = balOptions.Show
Select Case intReturnValue
   Case 1
      [instructions to be processed when the user clicks the first ButtonLabel object]
   Case 2
      [instructions to be processed when the user clicks the second ButtonLabel object]
   Case 3
      [instructions to be processed when the user clicks the third ButtonLabel object]
End Select
```

Figure 11-10: Examples of using the value returned by the Balloon object's Show method

Example 1 in Figure 11-10 uses an If…Then…Else statement to determine if the user clicked the OK button in the Assistant's balloon. Example 2 uses a Select Case statement to process the appropriate instructions based on which of three ButtonLabel objects the user selected in the Assistant's balloon.

You now have completed Tutorial 11's Concept lesson. You can either take a break or complete the end-of-lesson questions and exercises before moving on to the next lesson.

SUMMARY

To create a variable that can store a Dialog object:

■   Use the Dim statement in the following syntax: *variablename* **As Dialog**. The Dim statement initializes Dialog object variables to `Nothing`. The three-character ID used to name a Dialog object variable is *dlg*.

To refer to an individual Dialog object in Excel's or Word's Dialogs collection:

■   Use the syntax **Application.Dialogs(***index***)**, where *index* is an intrinsic constant that identifies the Dialog object within the Dialogs collection. The Excel intrinsic constants begin with "xlDialog". The Word intrinsic constants begin with "wdDialog".

To display one of Excel's or Word's built-in dialog boxes, and then wait for the user to close the dialog box:

■   Use the Dialog object's Show method, which has the syntax *dialogObject*.**Show.** The Show method returns the Boolean value False if the user closes the dialog box by clicking either the Cancel button or the Close button ✕ ; otherwise, it returns the Boolean value True.

To create a variable that can store a Boolean value:

■   Use the Dim statement, which initializes Boolean variables to `False`. The three-character ID used to name a Boolean variable is *bln*.

To customize the Office Assistant:

■   Use the FileName property to control the character used to display the Assistant.

■   Use the Left and Top properties to position the left and top borders, respectively, on the screen. The setting for both properties is measured in points, with one point equivalent to 1/72 of an inch.

■   Use the On property to turn the Assistant feature on (True) or off (False).

■   Use the Visible property to display (True) or hide (False) the Assistant.

To create a variable that can store a Balloon object:

■   Use the Dim statement in the following syntax: *variablename* **As Balloon.** The Dim statement initializes Balloon object variables to `Nothing`. The three-character ID used to name a Balloon object variable is *bal*.

To create a Balloon object:

■   Use the Assistant object's NewBalloon property in the following syntax: **Set** *balloonObject* = **Assistant.NewBalloon.**

To display buttons, an icon, a heading, and text in a Balloon object:

■   Use the Balloon object's Button property to specify which buttons, if any, should appear at the bottom of the balloon. Refer to Figure 11-6 for a list of intrinsic constants applicable to this property. You can use the value returned by the Balloon object's Show method to determine which button the user selected.

■ Use the Balloon object's Icon property to specify which icon, if any, should appear in the upper-left portion of the balloon. Refer to Figure 11-6 for a list of intrinsic constants applicable to this property.

■ Use the Balloon object's Heading property to specify the text to display at the top of the balloon.

■ Use the Balloon object's Text property to specify the text to display after the heading but before any labels or check boxes.

To create a BalloonCheckBox object:

■ Use the Balloon object's Checkboxes property, which has the syntax **Checkboxes(***index***)**. *Index* is a number from 1 through 5.

■ The BalloonCheckBox object's Checked property returns the Boolean value True if the check box is selected; it returns the Boolean value False if the check box is not selected.

■ Use the BalloonCheckBox object's Text property to specify the text that should appear next to the check box.

To create a BalloonLabel object:

■ Use the Balloon object's Labels property, which has the syntax **Labels(***index***)**. *Index* is a number from 1 through 5.

■ Use the Balloon object's BalloonType property to control the format of the balloon labels, which can appear as buttons or as a list of bulleted or numbered items. If the BalloonType property is set to `msoBalloonTypeButtons`, you can use the value returned by the Balloon object's Show method to determine which BalloonLabel object the user selected.

■ Use the BalloonLabel object's Text property to specify the text that should appear next to the button, bullet, or number.

To display a Balloon object:

■ Use the Balloon object's Show method, which has the syntax *balloonObject*.**Show**. The Show method returns a value that indicates which button the user selected in the balloon.

REVIEW QUESTIONS

1. The Dialogs collection is not included in the _____ object model.
   a. Access
   b. Excel
   c. Word
   d. None of the above. Each application in Microsoft Office contains a Dialogs collection.

2. Which of the following intrinsic constants refers to the built-in Print dialog box in Word?
   a. `vbPrint`
   b. `wdDialogFilePrint`
   c. `wdPrint`
   d. `dlgWordPrint`

3. Which of the following will display Excel's built-in Open dialog box?
   a. `Application.Dialogs(dlgDialogOpen).Display`
   b. `Application.Dialogs(exDialogOpen).Show`
   c. `Application.Dialogs(xlDialogOpen).Show`
   d. `Application.Dialogs(xlOpen).Display`

4. If the user clicks the Open button in the built-in Open dialog box, the Show method returns _____.
   a. False
   b. the empty string
   c. the intrinsic constant `Open`
   d. True

5. Which of the following instructions creates a Balloon object and assigns its address to the balMsg object variable?
   a. `Set balMsg = Assistant.Balloon.New`
   b. `Set balMsg = Assistant.Balloon.NewBalloon`
   c. `Set balMsg = Assistant.New.Balloon`
   d. `Set balMsg = Assistant.NewBalloon`

6. The Balloon object created by the NewBalloon property contains _____.
   a. an OK button
   b. a heading
   c. labels
   d. All of the above.

7. The Balloon object's _____ property indicates which buttons, if any, should appear at the bottom of the balloon.
   a. Button
   b. ButtonType
   c. TypeButton
   d. None of the above.

8. Which of the following instructions will create a check box for the balChoices Balloon object?
   a. `balChoices.Checkbox(1).Create`
   b. `balChoices.Checkboxes.Label = "Choice 1"`
   c. `balChoices.Checkboxes(1).Text = "Choice 1"`
   d. `balChoices.CreateCheckBox = "Choice 1"`

9. Each check box in the Assistant's balloon is a(n) _____ object, and each is a member of the _____ collection.
   a. AssistantBalloonCheckBox, AssistantBalloonCheckBoxes
   b. BalloonCheckBox, BalloonCheckBoxes
   c. CheckBox, CheckBoxes
   d. CheckBoxBalloon, CheckBoxBalloons

10. You use the _____ property to determine if a balloon's check box is selected.
    a. Balloon object's Checked
    b. BalloonCheckBox object's Checked
    c. CheckBoxBalloon object's Selected
    d. CheckBox object's Selected

11. You can create a maximum of _____ BalloonLabel objects for a balloon.
    a. 2
    b. 3
    c. 4
    d. 5

12. Which of the following will display the BalloonLabel objects as a numbered list?
    a. `balChoices.Balloon = msoBalloonTypeNumbers`
    b. `balChoices.BalloonLabels = msoBalloonTypeNumbers`
    c. `balChoices.BalloonLabelType = msoBalloonTypeNumbers`
    d. `balChoices.BalloonType = msoBalloonTypeNumbers`

13. Which of the following will display the balChoices Balloon object on the screen?
    a. `balChoices.Display`
    b. `balChoices.Show`
    c. `balChoices.ShowBalloon`
    d. `balChoices.View`

14. If the user clicks the first BalloonLabel button in a balloon, the Show method returns _____.
    a. the intrinsic constant `msoBalloonButton1`
    b. the intrinsic constant `msoBalloonLabelButton1`
    c. the number 0
    d. the number 1

15. If the user clicks the Yes button in a balloon, the Show method returns _____.
    a. the intrinsic constant `msoBalloonButtonYes`
    b. the intrinsic constant `msoButtonYes`
    c. the string "Yes"
    d. the number 0

EXERCISES

1. Write the instruction that displays Excel's built-in Open dialog box, and then waits for the user to close the dialog box. Use the intrinsic constant `xlDialogOpen`.

2. Write the instruction that displays Word's built-in Paragraph dialog box, and then waits for the user to close the dialog box. Use the intrinsic constant `wdDialogFormatParagraph`.

3. Assume that a procedure uses the Show method to display the built-in Open dialog box. The value returned by the Show method is assigned to a Boolean variable named blnSelection. Write an If...Then...Else statement that uses the blnSelection variable to determine if the user clicked the Open button in the Open dialog box. Display the message "File opened" if the user clicked the Open button; otherwise, display the message "No file was opened." (Display the message in a message box, along with an OK button and the Information icon.)

4. Assume that a procedure contains the instruction `Dim balReminder As Balloon`.
   a. Write the instruction that will create a Balloon object and assign its address to the balReminder variable.
   b. Write the instructions that will display the following in the balReminder balloon. (*Hint*: Use the With statement.)
      1) The heading "End of Day Reminders".
      2) The text "Be sure to".
      3) The Tip icon.
      4) Three BalloonLabel objects, which should appear as bulleted items. The objects should say "Save your work", "Turn the computer off", and "Turn the lights off".
      5) The OK button.
   c. Write the instruction that will display the balReminder Balloon object on the screen.

5. Assume that a procedure contains the instruction `Dim balDirections As Balloon`. Write the instructions that will create and display the Balloon object that appears in Figure 11-11.

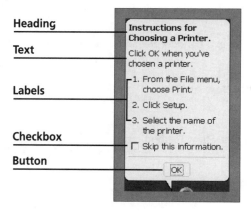

Figure 11-11

6.   In this exercise, you will experiment with the Balloon object's Icon, BalloonType, and Button properties.

a. Start either Word, Excel, Access, or PowerPoint. Open the Visual Basic Editor and insert a module. Create a procedure named Test that contains the instructions shown in Figure 11-12.

```
Dim balOptions As Balloon
Set balOptions = Assistant.NewBalloon
Assistant.On = True
With balOptions
      .Heading = "User Options"
      .Text = "Here are your options:"
      .Labels(1).Text = "Option 1"
      .Labels(2).Text = "Option 2"
      .Labels(3).Text = "Option 3"
      .Icon = msoIconNone
      .BalloonType = msoBalloonTypeButtons
      .Button = msoButtonSetNone
      .Show
End With
```

Figure 11-12

b. Run the procedure. Click any one of the three BalloonLabel objects to dismiss the balloon.

c. Assign each of the following intrinsic constants, one at a time, to the Icon property: msoIconAlert, msoIconAlertWarning, msoIconAlertCritical, msoIconAlertInfo, msoIconAlertQuery, and msoIconTip. Run the procedure after each change. When you are finished, assign the msoIconNone to the Icon property.

d. Assign the intrinsic constant msoButtonSetOk to the Button property, then assign the intrinsic constant msoBalloonTypeBullets to the BalloonType property. Run the procedure. Click the OK button to dismiss the balloon.

e. Assign the intrinsic constant msoBalloonTypeNumbers to the BalloonType property. Run the procedure. Click the OK button to dismiss the balloon.

f. Close the application. You do not need to save this file.

Exercise 7 is a Discovery Exercise. Discovery Exercises, which may include topics that are not covered in the lesson, allow you to "discover" the solutions to problems on your own.

discovery ▶   7.   In this exercise, you will learn about an additional property of the Dialogs, BalloonCheckBoxes, and BalloonLabels collections.

a. Start either Word or Excel. Open the Visual Basic Editor. Use the Object Browser to display the Help screens for the Dialogs, BalloonCheckBoxes, and BalloonLabels collections. Which property can you use to display the number of built-in dialog boxes, as well as the number of BalloonCheckBox and BalloonLabel objects contained in a balloon?

b. Close the application.

You also can use VBA in PowerPoint to create procedures that enhance your presentations. Exercise 8 allows you to apply this tutorial's programming concept in a PowerPoint presentation.

powerpoint   8.   In this exercise, you will create a customized balloon for the Office Assistant.

     a. Start PowerPoint. Open the T11-PP-E8 (T11-PP-E8.ppt) file, which is located in the Tut11\Concept folder on your Data Disk. Click the Enable Macros button, if necessary, then save the file as T11-PP-E8D.

     b. Open the Visual Basic Editor and view the DisplayDirections procedure. The procedure creates and displays a customized balloon that contains options for printing one or more of the presentation's slides. Notice that "Enter the missing instruction(s) here" appears in four places in the procedure. Complete the procedure by entering the missing instructions. Use the comments as your guide.

     c. Save the presentation, then return to PowerPoint and view the slide show. Click the icon that appears on the first slide to display the Assistant and Balloon objects. Click the first and third check boxes, then click the OK button. Press the Esc key to stop the slide show.

     d. When the procedure is working correctly, close PowerPoint.

A computer program is good only if it works. Errors in programming code can cause a program to run incorrectly. Therefore, a programmer needs to know how to locate and fix any errors in his or her code. Exercise 9 is a Debugging Exercise. Debugging Exercises allow you to practice recognizing and solving errors in code.

debugging 🐞   9.   The code shown in Figure 11-13 is not working correctly. Test the code by entering it into a procedure in either Word, Excel, PowerPoint, or Access and then running the procedure. Correct the error(s). When the procedure is working correctly, close the application. You do not need to save the file.

```
Dim balTips As Balloon
Set balTips = Assistant.Balloon
Assistant.On = True
With balTips
    .Heading = "Tips"
    .Labels(1) = "Exercise daily"
    .Labels(2) = "Eat right"
    .Labels(3) = "Smile"
    .BalloonType = msoBalloonTypeNumbers
    .Show
End With
```

Figure 11-13

Excel Lesson

Using Built-in Dialog Boxes and the Office Assistant in Excel

case ▶ Martin Washington, the accountant at Paradise Electronics, has given each of the four Paradise store managers an Excel workbook to keep track of their store's daily sales. At the end of each week, the store managers submit the workbook tracking the daily sales for that week to Martin. To make this workbook easier for the managers to use, Martin has decided to create a macro that first sorts the sales information in order by the salesperson ID, and then shades every other salesperson's records, making it easier to distinguish each salesperson's information. He decides to create the macro and test it in the workbook that the Franklin store manager just submitted to him, which contains the sales for the first week in March.

Viewing the Franklin Store Worksheet and the SortAndShade Procedure

The workbook containing the Franklin store's sales information for the first week in March is stored on your Data Disk. Before creating the macro that will group the sales information by salesperson ID and then shade every other group, view the workbook and the code template for the SortAndShade procedure.

To view the workbook and the SortAndShade procedure:

1 Start Microsoft Excel. Open the **T11-EX-1** (T11-EX-1.xls) workbook, which is located in the Tut11\Excel folder on your Data Disk. Click the **Enable Macros** button, if necessary, and then save the workbook as **Franklin Sales**.

The Franklin Sales workbook contains one worksheet named March 1-7, as shown in Figure 11-14.

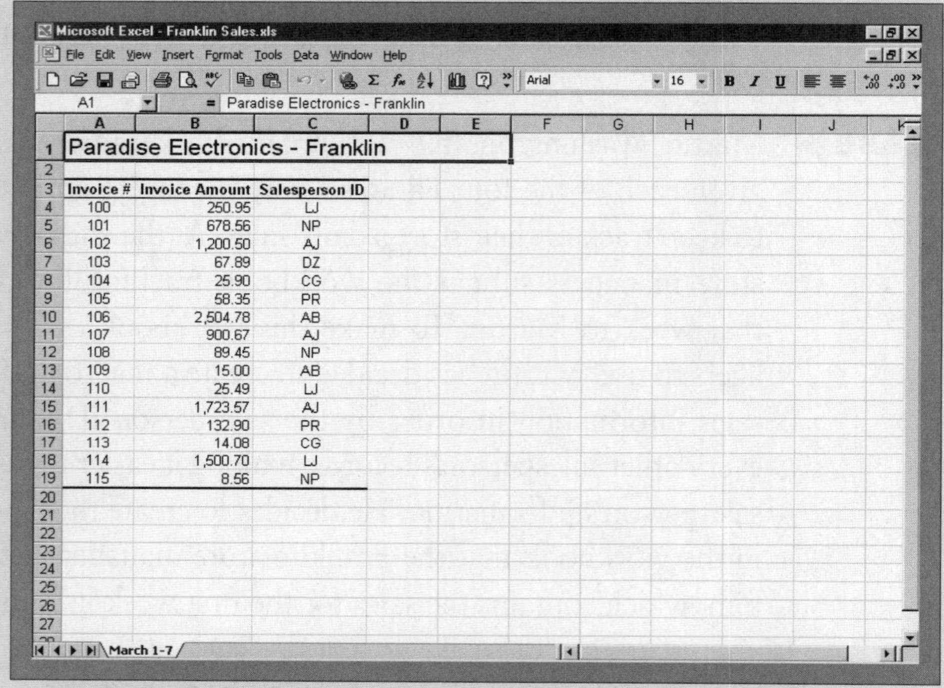

Figure 11-14: The March 1-7 worksheet in the Franklin Sales workbook

Notice that the worksheet contains the invoice number, invoice amount, and salesperson ID, and that the data is in order by the invoice number..

2 Press **Alt+F11** to open the Visual Basic Editor. If necessary, open the Project Explorer window and close the Properties window, the Immediate window, and any open Code windows. Open the Module1 module's Code window, then view the code template for the **SortAndShade** procedure.

3   Close the Project Explorer window so that you can view more of the Code
window.

Figure 11-15 shows the pseudocode for the SortAndShade procedure.

1. Turn the Assistant feature on, and then make the Assistant visible.
2. Select the sales information, then display Excel's built-in Sort dialog box. Sort the
    sales information in ascending order by ID.
3. Deselect the sales information by selecting cell A1.
4. Create a Balloon object for the Assistant. The balloon should contain three
    BalloonLabel objects, labeled "Blue", "Pink", and "Yellow."
5. Display the Balloon object. Assign its return value to an Integer variable named
    intReturnValue.
6. Value of intReturnValue:
    = 1   assign color-index 15 (blue) to an Integer variable named intColor.
    = 2   assign color-index 7 (pink) to an Integer variable named intColor.
    = 3   assign color-index 6 (yellow) to an Integer variable named intColor.
7. Repeat the following for each row in the sales information range:
    a. If the ID in the current row is equal to the ID in the previous row, then
       1)   Shade the current row using the previous row's color
       Else
            (1) If the previous row is shaded white, then
                 (a) shade the current row using the color value stored in the intColor
                      variable
            Else
                 (a) shade the current row white
8. Display Excel's built-in Print dialog box. Assign the return value to a Boolean
    variable named blnPrint.
9. If the blnPrint variable contains the Boolean value False, then
    a. Display the message "Printing was cancelled."

Figure 11-15: Pseudocode for the SortAndShade procedure

Important Note: The color-index values for the various colors are system dependent.

As Figure 11-15 indicates, the SortAndShade procedure will use Excel's built-in Sort and Print dialog boxes to sort and print the worksheet, respectively. It also will use a Balloon object to offer the user three color choices (blue, pink, and yellow) for shading every other salesperson's information.

Figure 11-16 shows the variables that the SortAndShade procedure will use.

Variable	datatype
balColors	Balloon
intReturnValue	Integer
intColor	Integer
blnPrint	Boolean
shtMarWeek1	Worksheet
rngData	Range
rngRow	Range

Figure 11-16: Variables used by the SortAndShade procedure

The procedure will store the address of the Balloon object in the balColors variable, and it will assign the Balloon object's return value to the intReturnValue variable. The intColor variable will be used to store a number that identifies the shading color chosen by the user. As you will learn later in this lesson, each color available in Excel is identified by a number, referred to as its color-index.

When the user closes the Print dialog box, the procedure will assign the dialog box's return value to the Boolean variable blnPrint. The shtMarWeek1 variable will store the address of the March1-7 worksheet, and the rngData variable will store the address of the range containing the sales information (A3:C19). The procedure will use the rngRow variable in a For Each...Next statement that repeats its instructions for each row in the rngData range.

In the next set of steps, you will declare the appropriate variables and then begin translating Figure 11-15's pseudocode into one or more VBA statements.

To begin coding the SortAndShade procedure:

1 Type the documentation and Dim and Set statements shown in Figure 11-17.

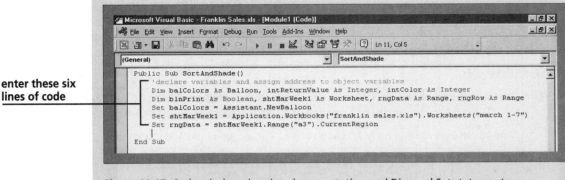

enter these six lines of code ──────

Figure 11-17: Code window showing documentation and Dim and Set statements

You learned about the Range object's CurrentRegion property in Tutorial 9's Excel lesson. Recall that the property returns a range that contains the entire region in which the Range object—in this case, cell A3—resides. Recall that a region is defined as a block of cells bounded by any combination of empty rows, empty columns, and the edges of the worksheet.

Step 1 in the pseudocode is to turn the Assistant feature on, and then make the Assistant visible.

2   Type **'display Assistant** and press the **Enter** key. Type **assistant.on = true** and press the **Enter** key, then type **assistant.visible = true** and press the **Enter** key.

Step 2 in the pseudocode is to select the sales information range and then display Excel's built-in Sort dialog box, which should sort the information in ascending order by ID. First, enter the instruction that will select the sales information range; the address of that range is stored in the rngData variable.

3   Type **'select sales information, then display Sort dialog box** and press the **Enter** key, then type **rngdata.select** and press the **Enter** key.

4   Save the workbook.

Before you can finish coding Step 2, you need to learn how to display the Sort dialog box in Excel.

Displaying the Sort Dialog Box in Excel

The **Sort dialog box** is one of the built-in dialog boxes contained in Excel's Dialogs collection. As you learned in the Concept lesson, you can use the Show method to display a built-in dialog box. Figure 11-18, for example, shows the syntax and three examples of using the Show method to display Excel's Sort dialog box.

Syntax:

Application.Dialogs(xlDialogSort).Show [**arg1:**=*orientation*][, **arg2:**=*key1*][, **arg3:**=*order1*]
[, **arg4:**=*key2*][, **arg5:**=*order2*][, **arg6:**=*key3*][, **arg7:**=*order3*][, **arg8:**=*header*]

Examples:

```
Application.Dialogs(xlDialogSort).Show arg1:=xlSortColumns, _
            arg2:="Invoice #", arg3:=xlDescending, arg8:=xlYes

Application.Dialogs(xlDialogSort).Show arg1:=xlSortColumns, _
            arg2:="Salesperson ID", arg3:=xlAscending, _
            arg4:="Invoice Amount", arg5:=xlAscending, _
            arg8:=xlYes

Application.Dialogs(xlDialogSort).Show arg1:=xlSortColumns, _
            arg2:=shtMarWeek1.Range("C4"), _
            arg3:=xlAscending, arg8:=xlNo
```

Figure 11-18: Syntax and examples of displaying Excel's Sort dialog box

....

To determine the arguments that each built-in dialog box provides, display the Built-In Dialog Box Argument Lists Help screen in the Visual Basic Editor.

....

Notice that the Sort dialog box provides eight arguments, each of which is optional. You use the arg1 argument, whose *orientation* value can be set to either xlSortColumns or xlSortRows, to specify whether the sort is based on data contained in columns or rows in the worksheet. If *orientation* is set to xlSortColumns, you can sort the data based on the values stored in one, two, or three different columns. If *orientation* is set to xlSortRows, on the other hand, the data can be sorted based on the values stored in one, two, or three different rows. You specify the columns (rows) in the arg2, arg4, and arg6 arguments. You use the arg3, arg5, and arg7 arguments, whose values can be set to either xlAscending or xlDescending, to indicate the order in which the data in each column (row) should be sorted.

You use the arg8 argument, whose *header* value can be set to either xlYes or xlNo, to specify whether the first row (or column) in the sort range contains headers. Setting *header* to xlYes indicates that headers are present, and it prevents the headers from being sorted along with the other data. Setting *header* to xlNo indicates that the sort range does not contain headers and, therefore, the entire range should be sorted.

Assuming that the sales data contained in the range A3:C19 is selected, the first example shown in Figure 11-18 will sort the sales data in descending order by the invoice number. Notice that the example uses the column header "Invoice #" as the *key1* value for the arg2 argument. Because the first row in the selected range contains column headers, the *header* value for the arg8 argument is set to xlYes to exclude the headers from the sort.

The second example will sort the selected range (A3:C19) in ascending order by the salesperson ID. However, if more than one row contains the same salesperson's ID, the data in those rows will be sorted in ascending order by the invoice amount. As in the first example, the *header* value for the arg8 argument in this example is set to `xlYes` to exclude the headers in row 3 from the sort.

Assuming the range A4:C19, rather than A3:C19, is selected, Figure 11-18's third example will sort the selected range in ascending order by the salesperson ID. Because the first row in the selected range does not contain column headers, the example uses a cell reference, rather than a column header, as the *key1* value for the arg2 argument. The cell reference, C4, tells the Sort dialog box that you want to sort the data based on the values in column C. Notice that the *header* value for the arg8 argument is set to `xlNo` to indicate that, in this case, the first row in the selected range should be included in the sort.

Now that you know how to display the Sort dialog box, you can complete Step 2 in the pseudocode, which is to display the Sort dialog box, allowing the user to sort the sales information in ascending order by the salesperson ID.

To continue coding the SortAndShade procedure:

1 Type **application.dialogs(xldialogsort).show arg1:=xlsortcolumns, _** (be sure to type the comma followed by a space and the underscore) and press the **Enter** key. Press the **Tab** key, then type **arg2:="salesperson id", arg3:=xlascending, arg8:=xlyes** and press the **Enter** key.

As you learned in the Concept lesson, when the user clicks the OK button in a built-in dialog box displayed by the Show method, the dialog box's actions are carried out. In this case, the Sort dialog box will sort the sales data in ascending order by the salesperson ID.

Now cancel the selection of the sales information range by selecting cell A1 in the worksheet.

2 Press the **Backspace** key to remove the indentation, type **'deselect range** and press the **Enter** key, then type **shtmarweek1.range("a1").select** and press the **Enter** key.

Steps 4 and 5 in the pseudocode are to create a Balloon object that contains three BalloonLabel objects, labeled "Blue", "Pink", and "Yellow", and then display the Balloon object. You are to assign the Balloon object's return value to the intReturnValue variable.

3 Type the additional code shown in Figure 11-19.

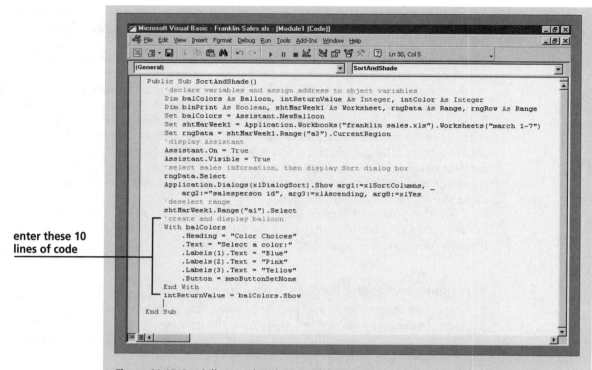

enter these 10 lines of code

Figure 11:19: Partially completed SortAndShade procedure

4   Verify the accuracy of your code by comparing the code on your screen to the code shown in Figure 11-19, then save the workbook.

Step 6 in the pseudocode is to assign the appropriate color-index to the intColor variable.

Color-Indexes

As mentioned earlier in this lesson, each color available in Excel's color palette is identified by a number, referred to as its **color-index**. You can determine the color-index assigned to a color by displaying the ColorIndex Property Help screen.

To display the ColorIndex Property Help screen, then continue coding the SortAndShade procedure:

1   Click **Help** on the Visual Basic Editor menu bar, and then click **Microsoft Visual Basic Help**. Maximize the Microsoft Visual Basic Help screen, then click the **Index** tab, if necessary.

HELP? If the Assistant appears when you click Help, click Options in the Assistant's balloon, then click the Use the Office Assistant check box to deselect it, and then click the OK button. Then repeat Step 1.

HELP? If the Help window's Selection pane is not visible, click the Show button ⊲ on the Microsoft Visual Basic Help toolbar.

2   Type **colorindex** in the Type keywords text box, then click the **Search** button. Click the **Hide** button ⊲ to hide the Selection pane. Figure 11-20 shows the ColorIndex Property Help screen.

color-index values

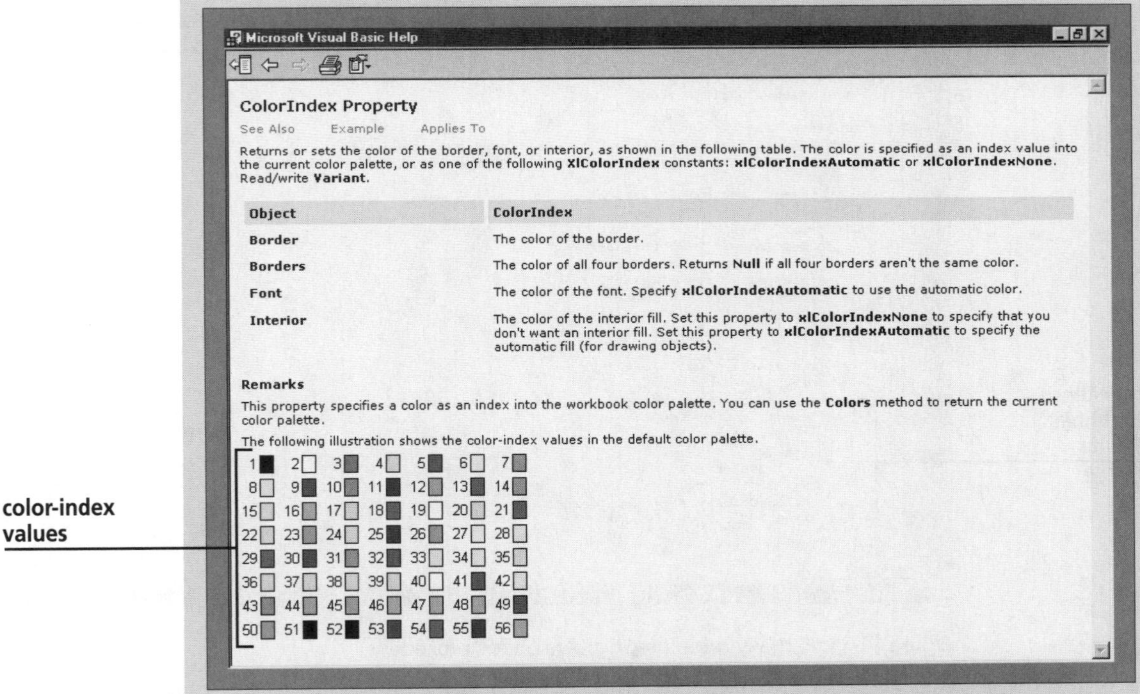

Figure 11-20: ColorIndex Property Help screen

The illustration at the bottom of the Help screen shows the color-index values assigned to the colors in Excel's default color palette. You will use color-indexes 2, 6, 7, and 15 to represent the colors white, yellow, pink, and blue, respectively. (Recall that only every other salesperson's information will be shaded using the color chosen by the user—either yellow, pink, or blue. The remaining rows will be colored white.)

Important Note: Color-index values for the various colors are system dependent. If your color-index numbers do not correspond with the ones described above, select appropriate color-index numbers.

3 Click the **Show** button 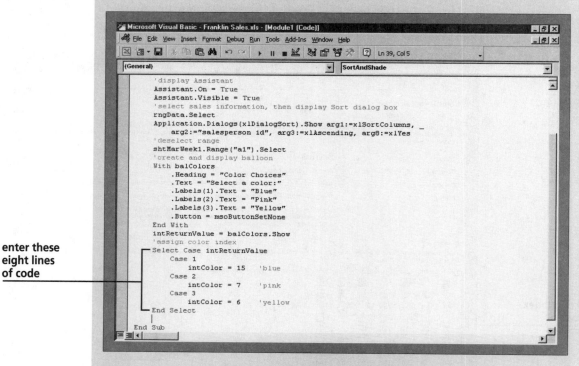 to display the Selection pane, then close the Help window.

4 Type **'assign color index** and press the **Enter** key, then type the additional instructions shown in Figure 11-21. (Notice that you can include a comment on the same line as an instruction, as long as the comment comes after the instruction on that line.)

```
Microsoft Visual Basic - Franklin Sales.xls - [Module1 (Code)]
File  Edit  View  Insert  Format  Debug  Run  Tools  Add-Ins  Window  Help       Ln 39, Col 5
(General)                                    SortAndShade
        'display Assistant
        Assistant.On = True
        Assistant.Visible = True
        'select sales information, then display Sort dialog box
        rngData.Select
        Application.Dialogs(xlDialogSort).Show arg1:=xlSortColumns, _
            arg2:="salesperson id", arg3:=xlAscending, arg8:=xlYes
        'deselect range
        shtMarWeek1.Range("a1").Select
        'create and display balloon
        With balColors
            .Heading = "Color Choices"
            .Text = "Select a color:"
            .Labels(1).Text = "Blue"
            .Labels(2).Text = "Pink"
            .Labels(3).Text = "Yellow"
            .Button = msoButtonSetNone
        End With
        intReturnValue = balColors.Show
        'assign color index
        Select Case intReturnValue
            Case 1
                intColor = 15     'blue
            Case 2
                intColor = 7      'pink
            Case 3
                intColor = 6      'yellow
        End Select

    End Sub
```

enter these
eight lines
of code

Figure 11-21: Partially completed SortAndShade procedure

Next, the procedure needs to repeat a set of instructions for each row in the sales information range (A3:C19). Recall that the address of that range is stored in the rngData variable. You will use a For Each...Next loop to repeat the appropriate instructions.

5 Type **'shade appropriate rows** and press the **Enter** key, then type **for each rngrow in rngdata.rows** and press the **Enter** key.

According to the pseudocode shown in Figure 11-15, the first loop instruction should compare the ID stored in column C in the current row with the one stored in column C in the previous row. You can do so using the Range object's Cells property.

The Range Object's Cells Property

You can use the Range object's Cells property to refer to an individual cell in a range. The syntax to do so is *rangeObject*.**Cells([RowIndex:**=*row*][, **ColumnIndex:**=*column*]), where *row* and *column* are numbers that represent the location of the cell within the range. For example, you would use `rngData.Cells(RowIndex:=1, ColumnIndex:=3)` to refer to cell C3, which is the cell located in the first row, third column of the rngData range (A3:C19), and you would use `rngData.Cells(RowIndex:=3, ColumnIndex:=2)` to refer to cell B5. In the SortAndShade procedure, you will use `rngRow.Cells(ColumnIndex:=3)` to refer to the cell located in column C of the current row. You will use `rngRow.Offset(RowOffset:=-1).Cells(ColumnIndex:=3)` to refer to the cell located in column C of the previous row.

To complete the SortAndShade procedure, then test the procedure:

1 Press the **Tab** key.

First, check to see if the ID in the current row is equal to the ID in the previous row.

2 Type **if rngrow.cells(columnindex:=3).value = _** (be sure to type the equal sign followed by a space and the underscore) and press the **Enter** key. Press the **Tab** key, then type **rngrow.offset(rowoffset:=-1).cells(columnindex:=3).value then** (be sure to type the minus sign before the 1 in the RowOffset argument) and press the **Enter** key.

If the ID in the current row is the same as the ID in the previous row, the procedure should shade the current row to match the previous one. You can use the following syntax to change the background color of a row: *rowObject*.**Interior.ColorIndex** = *number*, where *number* is the color-index corresponding to the desired color. For example, the instruction `rngRow.Interior.ColorIndex = 15` will shade the current row blue. In this case, however, you want to shade the current row using the same color used in the previous row, so you will use `rngrow.offset(rowoffset:=-1).interior.colorindex` as *number*.

• •

The Interior property returns an Interior object that represents the interior portion of a range, and the ColorIndex property refers to the Interior object's color.

• •

3 Press the **Tab** key, then type **rngrow.interior.colorindex = rngrow.offset(rowoffset:=-1).interior.colorindex** (be sure to type the minus sign before the 1 in the RowOffset argument) and press the **Enter** key.

If the ID in the current row is not equal to the ID in the previous row, then the procedure needs to determine the previous row's color. If the previous row is shaded white, then the procedure should use the color chosen by the user to shade the current row; otherwise, it should shade the current row white.

4 Press the **Backspace** key twice, then type the additional lines of code shown in Figure 11-22.

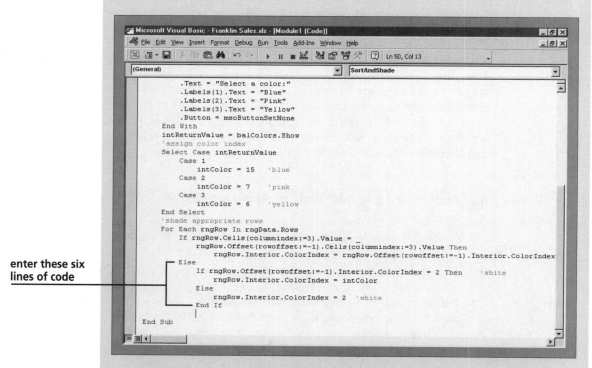

enter these six lines of code

Figure 11-22: Current status of the SortAndShade procedure

Now you can end both the outer If…Then…Else statement and the For Each…Next loop.

5 Press the **Backspace** key, then type **end if** and press the **Enter** key. Press the **Backspace** key, then type **next rngrow** and press the **Enter** key.

Step 8 in the pseudocode is to display Excel's built-in Print dialog box and assign its return value to the blnPrint variable.

6 Type **'display Print dialog box** and press the **Enter** key, then type **blnprint = application.dialogs(xldialogprint).show** and press the **Enter** key.

If the user clicks either the Cancel button or the Close button, the procedure should display the message "Printing was cancelled."

7 Type the additional lines of code shown in Figure 11-23, which shows the completed SortAndShade procedure. (Not all of the procedure is displayed in the figure.)

the figure does not show the beginning of the procedure

enter these four lines of code

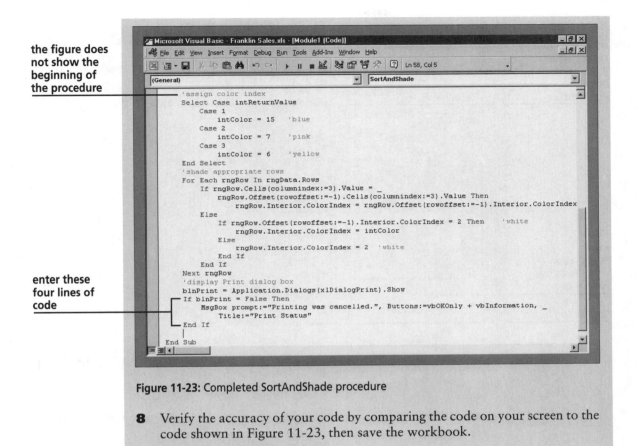

```
Microsoft Visual Basic - Franklin Sales.xls - [Module1 (Code)]
File  Edit  View  Insert  Format  Debug  Run  Tools  Add-Ins  Window  Help
                                                    Ln 58, Col 5

(General)                                          SortAndShade

        'assign color index
        Select Case intReturnValue
            Case 1
                intColor = 15    'blue
            Case 2
                intColor = 7     'pink
            Case 3
                intColor = 6     'yellow
        End Select
        'shade appropriate rows
        For Each rngRow In rngData.Rows
            If rngRow.Cells(columnindex:=3).Value = _
                rngRow.Offset(rowoffset:=-1).Cells(columnindex:=3).Value Then
                    rngRow.Interior.ColorIndex = rngRow.Offset(rowoffset:=-1).Interior.ColorIndex
            Else
                If rngRow.Offset(rowoffset:=-1).Interior.ColorIndex = 2 Then    'white
                    rngRow.Interior.ColorIndex = intColor
                Else
                    rngRow.Interior.ColorIndex = 2  'white
                End If
            End If
        Next rngRow
        'display Print dialog box
        blnPrint = Application.Dialogs(xlDialogPrint).Show
        If blnPrint = False Then
            MsgBox prompt:="Printing was cancelled.", Buttons:=vbOKOnly + vbInformation, _
                Title:="Print Status"
        End If

    End Sub
```

Figure 11-23: Completed SortAndShade procedure

8   Verify the accuracy of your code by comparing the code on your screen to the code shown in Figure 11-23, then save the workbook.

Now that you have translated the pseudocode into VBA statements, you can test the SortAndShade macro procedure to verify that it is working correctly.

To test the SortAndShade procedure:

1   Return to Excel, then run the **SortAndShade** macro. The Assistant and the Sort dialog box appear, as shown in Figure 11-24.

Assistant (your character and its location might be different)

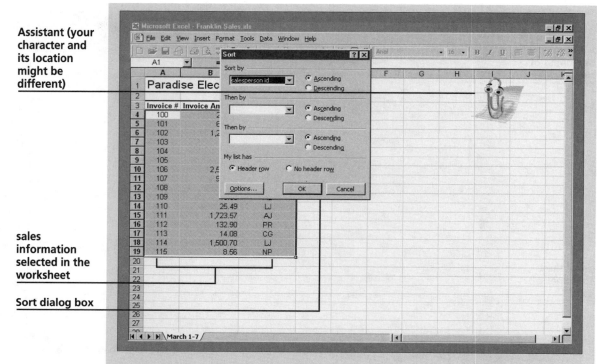

sales information selected in the worksheet

Sort dialog box

Figure 11-24: The Assistant and Sort dialog box

HELP? Do not be concerned if your screen shows a different Assistant, or if the Assistant is located in a different area of the screen.

When the Show method displays the Sort dialog box, notice that it enters the value of the arg2 argument (salesperson id) in the Sort by list box. It also selects the Ascending option button that appears next to the Sort by list box, and the Header row option button that appears in the My list has section of the dialog box. Both option buttons are selected as a result of the arg3 and arg8 arguments.

tip

You can verify the result of setting the arg1 argument, which controls the sort orientation, by clicking the Options button in the Sort dialog box. When the Sort Options dialog box appears, you will notice that the Sort top to bottom option button is selected. Click the Cancel button to return to the Sort dialog box.

2 Click the **OK** button. The Sort dialog box sorts the data in ascending order by the salesperson ID, and then the dialog box closes. The Assistant's balloon appears, as shown in Figure 11-25.

Balloon object

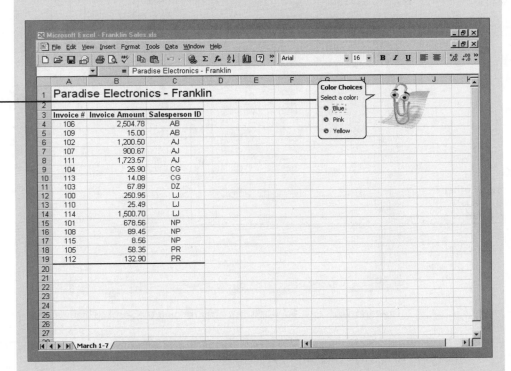

Figure 11-25: Assistant's balloon

3 Click **Blue** in the Assistant's balloon. The rows containing every other salesperson's data are shaded blue; the remaining rows are shaded white. Then the Print dialog box appears.

4 Click the **Cancel** button in the Print dialog box. The message "Printing was cancelled." appears in the Print Status message box. Click the **OK** button to close the message box. Figure 11-26 shows the March 1-7 worksheet after running the SortAndShade macro.

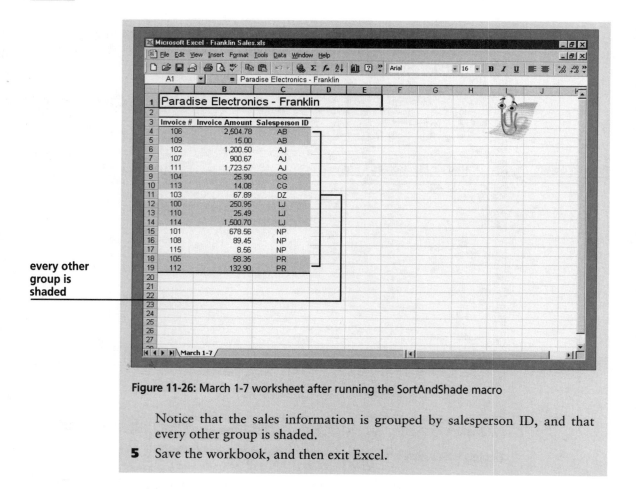

every other group is shaded

Figure 11-26: March 1-7 worksheet after running the SortAndShade macro

Notice that the sales information is grouped by salesperson ID, and that every other group is shaded.

5 Save the workbook, and then exit Excel.

You now have completed Tutorial 11's Excel lesson. You can either take a break or complete the end-of-lesson exercises before moving on to the next lesson.

EXERCISES

1. In this exercise, you will modify the SortAndShade procedure that you created in this lesson so that it uses the Assistant to offer saving and printing options to the user.

    a. Open the Franklin Sales (Franklin Sales.xls) workbook, which is located in the Tut11\Excel folder on your Data Disk. Click the Enable Macros button, if necessary, then save the workbook as T11-EX-E1D.

b. Open the Visual Basic Editor, then open the Module1 module's Code window and view the SortAndShade procedure. Change the filename in the Set statement to "t11-ex-e1d.xls". Remove the six lines of code that appear before the End Sub. (The six lines begin with 'display Print dialog box and end with End If.)

c. Modify the procedure so that it uses a Boolean variable to record the current status of the Assistant's On property before turning the Assistant feature on. (This will allow you to return the Assistant to its initial setting when the procedure ends.) Create another balloon for the Assistant. This balloon should include two check boxes, labeled "Print" and "Save", and an OK button. If the user wants to print the worksheet, use the PrintOut method to do so. If the user wants to save the worksheet, display Excel's built-in Save As dialog box. (*Hint*: Use the intrinsic constant xlDialogSaveAs.) Before ending the procedure, return the Assistant's On property to its initial setting.

d. Save the workbook, then return to Excel and run the SortAndShade macro. When the Sort dialog box appears, click the OK button. Click Yellow in the Assistant's balloon. When the second balloon appears, select both check boxes, then click the OK button. When the Save As dialog box appears, save the worksheet using the name t11-ex-e1d, then close the workbook.

2. In this exercise, you will modify the SortAndShade procedure that you created in this lesson so that it allows the user to publish the worksheet as a Web page.

a. Open the Franklin Sales (Franklin Sales.xls) workbook, which is located in the Tut11\Excel folder on your Data Disk. Click the Enable Macros button, if necessary, then save the workbook as T11-EX-E2D.

b. Open the Visual Basic Editor, then open the Module1 module's Code window and view the SortAndShade procedure. Change the filename in the Set statement to "t11-ex-e2d.xls". Remove the six lines of code that appear before the End Sub. (The six lines begin with 'display Print dialog box and end with End If.)

c. Before the procedure ends, use the Assistant to ask the user if he or she wants to publish the worksheet as a Web page. (Provide Yes and No buttons in the balloon.) If the user wants to publish the worksheet, then the procedure should display Excel's built-in PublishAsWebPage dialog box. (*Hint*: Use the intrinsic constant xlDialogPublishAsWebPage.)

d. Save the workbook, then return to Excel and run the SortAndShade macro. When the Sort dialog box appears, click the OK button. Click Pink in the Assistant's balloon. When the second balloon appears, click the Yes button. When the Publish as Web Page dialog box appears, publish the range A1:E19 as a Web page named T11-EX-E2D.htm. Close the Web page browser, if necessary, then click cell A1 to deselect the selected range.

e. Save and then close the workbook.

3. In this exercise, you will create a macro procedure that sorts the worksheet data in order by the last and first names.

a. Open the T11-EX-E3 (T11-EX-E3.xls) workbook, which is located in the Tut11\Excel folder on your Data Disk. Click the Enable Macros button, if necessary, then save the workbook as T11-EX-E3D.

b. Open the Visual Basic Editor, then open the Module1 module's Code window and view the code template for the SortByName procedure. Code the procedure so that it uses the Sort dialog box to sort the worksheet data in ascending order by the employee last name. If more than one employee has the same last name, sort those records in order by the first name.

    c. Save the workbook, then return to Excel and run the SortByName procedure.

    d. Save and then close the workbook.

Exercises 4 and 5 are Discovery Exercises. Discovery Exercises, which may include topics that are not covered in the lesson, allow you to "discover" the solutions to problems on your own.

discovery ▶ **4.** In this exercise, you will learn how to include arguments in the Save As dialog box's Show method.

    a. Open a new workbook. Enter your name in cell A1, then save the workbook as T11-EX-E4D in the Tut11\Excel folder on your Data Disk.

    b. Open the Visual Basic Editor and insert a module. Add a macro procedure named DisplayNumberOfDialogBoxes. Code the procedure so that it displays, in a message box, the number of Dialog objects included in Excel's Dialogs collection. Run the procedure. How many Dialog objects are included in the Dialogs collection? Close the message box.

    c. Use the Object Browser to view the Dialogs Collection Object Help screen. Click Show in the Help screen to display the Show Method Help screen. Read the section that pertains to the Dialog object. Click Built-In Dialog Box Argument Lists in the Help screen. Scroll the Help screen to view the arguments for the `xlDialogSaveAs` constant. On a piece of paper, record the six arguments, then close the Help window and the Object Browser.

    d. Add a macro procedure named SaveTheFile to the module. Enter the following line of code in the procedure: `Application.Dialogs(xlDialogSaveAs).Show arg1:="Test"`. Save the workbook, and then run the procedure. When the Save As dialog box appears, notice that "Test" appears as the suggested filename. Click the Cancel button.

    e. Modify the SaveTheFile procedure so that it saves the Test file using the word "dog" as the password. (*Hint*: Use arg3.) Save the workbook, and then run the procedure. When the Save As dialog box appears, click the Save button. To verify that the macro saved the workbook correctly, close the workbook, then open the Test workbook. Click the Enable Macros button, if necessary. When prompted, enter "dog" (without the quotation marks) as the password. Close the workbook.

discovery ▶ **5.** In this exercise, you will learn about Excel's GetOpenFilename, GetSaveAsFilename, SaveAs, and Open methods.

    a. Open the Franklin Sales (Franklin Sales.xls) workbook, which is located in the Tut11\Excel folder on your Data Disk. Click the Enable Macros button, if necessary, then save the workbook as T11-EX-E5D.

    b. Open the Visual Basic Editor, then open the Module1 module's Code window and view the SortAndShade procedure. Change the filename in the Set statement to "t11-ex-e5d.xls".

    c. Display the GetSaveAsFilename Method Help screen. Use the Help screen to answer/complete the following:

       1) What is the difference between using the Show method to display the Save As dialog box and using the GetSaveAsFilename method?

       2) GetSaveAsFilename is a method of the _____ object.

    3) Write an instruction that uses the GetSaveAsFilename method to display the Save As dialog box. Display "T11-EX-E5D.xls" as the suggested filename. Include a file filter that displays only Excel workbook files. Assign the filename chosen by the user to a String variable named strFname.

    4) The GetSaveAsFilename method returns _____ if the user cancels the dialog box; otherwise it returns _____ .

d. Display the SaveAs Method Help screen. Use the Help screen to complete the following:

    1) You use the SaveAs method's Syntax 2 to _____ .

    2) Write an instruction that uses the SaveAs method to save the active workbook as "Current.xls".

    3) Write an instruction that uses the SaveAs method to save the active workbook using the name stored in the strFname variable.

e. Display the GetOpenFilename Method Help screen. Use the Help screen to answer/complete the following:

    1) What is the difference between using the Show method to display the Open dialog box and using the GetOpenFilename method?

    2) GetOpenFilename is a method of the _____ object.

    3) Write an instruction that uses the GetOpenFilename method to display the Open dialog box, showing only Excel workbook files. Assign the filename chosen by the user to a String variable named strFname.

    4) When set to True, the MultiSelect argument allows the user to _____ . The default setting for this argument is _____ .

    5) The GetOpenFilename method returns _____ if the user cancels the dialog box; otherwise it returns _____ .

f. Display the Open Method Help screen (the one that applies to opening a workbook). Use the Help screen to complete the following:

    1) You set the Open method's ReadOnly argument to _____ to open the workbook in read-only mode.

    2) Write an instruction that uses the Open method to open the "Current.xls" workbook in read-only mode.

    3) Write an instruction that uses the Open method to open the workbook whose name is stored in the strFname variable.

g. Close the Help window. Modify the SortAndShade procedure so that it uses the GetSaveAsFilename method to display the Save As dialog box before the procedure ends. If the user clicks the Save button, use the SaveAs method to save the file. (*Hint*: Use the instructions you wrote in Steps c3 and d3.)

h. Save the workbook, then return to Excel and run the SortAndShade macro. When the Sort dialog box appears, click the OK button. Click Blue in the Assistant's balloon. When the Print dialog box appears, click the Cancel button, then click the OK button in the Print Status dialog box. When the Save As dialog box appears, click the Save button, then click the Yes button.

i. Return to the Visual Basic Editor. Modify the SortAndShade procedure so that it uses the GetOpenFilename method to display the Open dialog box before the procedure ends. If the user clicks the Open button, use the Open method to open the file whose name is selected in the dialog box. (*Hint*: Use the instructions you wrote in Steps e3 and f3.)

j. Save the workbook, then return to Excel and run the SortAndShade macro. When the Sort dialog box appears, click the OK button. Click Yellow in the Assistant's balloon. When the Print dialog box appears, click the Cancel button, then click the OK button in the Print Status dialog box. When the Save As dialog box appears, click the Save button, then click the Yes button. When the Open dialog box appears, click T11-EX-1.xls and then click the Open button.

k. Save and then close the open workbooks.

A computer program is good only if it works. Errors in programming code can cause a program to run incorrectly. Therefore, a programmer needs to know how to locate and fix any errors in his or her code. Exercise 6 is a Debugging Exercise. Debugging Exercises allow you to practice recognizing and solving errors in code.

debugging   **6.** In this exercise, you will debug an existing procedure.

a. Open the T11-EX-E6 (T11-EX-E6.xls) workbook, which is located in the Tut11\Excel folder on your Data Disk. Click the Enable Macros button, if necessary. Save the workbook as T11-EX-E6D.

b. Open the Visual Basic Editor. Open the Module1 module's Code window and view the DisplaySortOptions procedure. The procedure should use the Assistant to display options that allow the user to sort the worksheet in ascending order by date, name, or hours worked. Study the procedure's code, then return to Excel and run the DisplaySortOptions macro. Return to the Visual Basic Editor and correct any errors. Keep running the macro and correcting the errors until the macro is working correctly.

c. When the macro is working correctly, sort the data in ascending order by the hours worked, and then save and close the workbook.

Word Lesson

Using Built-in Dialog Boxes and the Office Assistant in Word

case ▶ Each personal trainer at Willowton Health Club records the names and addresses of his or her clients in their own Access database. Every so often, Nancy Manley, the club's secretary, uses the information stored in the Client table in these databases to print a client list for each personal trainer. Rather than using an Access report to print the listings, Nancy would prefer to use a Word document. She has decided to create a macro that will allow her to do so.

Viewing the Client Document

The document Nancy will use to print each client list is stored on your Data Disk. Before creating the macro that will insert the database information into the document and then print the document, view the document and the code template for the PrintClientList procedure.

To view the document and the PrintClientList procedure:

1 Start Microsoft Word. Open the **T11-WD-1** (T11-WD-1.doc) document, which is located in the Tut11\Word folder on your Data Disk. Click the **Enable Macros** button, if necessary, and then save the document as **Client List**. Figure 11-27 shows the Client List document.

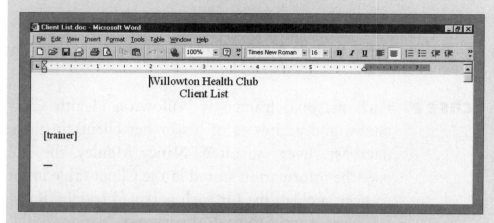

Figure 11-27: Client List document

2 Press **Alt+F11** to open the Visual Basic Editor. If necessary, open the Project Explorer window and close the Properties window, the Immediate window, and any open Code windows. Open the Module1 module's Code window, then view the code template for the **PrintClientList** procedure.

3 Close the Project Explorer window so that you can view more of the Code window.

Figure 11-28 shows the pseudocode for the PrintClientList procedure. As the figure indicates, the PrintClientList procedure will use Word's built-in Open and Print dialog boxes. The Open dialog box will allow the user to select the name of the appropriate database to display in the document, and the Print dialog box will allow the user to print the document. The procedure also will use a Balloon object to display the names of the three trainers: George, Nora, and Pam.

1. Turn the Assistant feature on, and then make the Assistant visible.
2. Create a Balloon object for the Assistant. The balloon should contain three BalloonLabel objects, labeled "George", "Nora", and "Pam."
3. Display the Balloon object. Assign its return value to an Integer variable named intReturnValue.
4. Value of intReturnValue:
    = 1   replace the sixth paragraph in the document with "Trainer:", a tab, "George", and a blank line.
    = 2   replace the sixth paragraph in the document with "Trainer:", a tab, "Nora", and a blank line.
    = 3   replace the sixth paragraph in the document with "Trainer:", a tab, "Pam", and a blank line.
5. Delete any existing tables from the document.
6. Display Word's built-in Open dialog box, showing only Access database filenames ending in .mdb. Assign the filename selected by the user to a String variable named strFileName.
7. If the user clicks the Open dialog box's Open button after selecting an .mdb file, then
    a. Place the insertion point at the end of the document.
    b. Use the Range object's InsertDatabase method to insert the database information into the document. The name of the database is stored in the strFileName variable.
    c. Display Word's built-in Print dialog box.

Figure 11-28: Pseudocode for the PrintClientList procedure

Figure 11-29 lists the variables that the PrintClientList procedure will use.

Variable	datatype
balTrainer	Balloon
intReturnValue	Integer
blnOpen	Boolean
strFileName	String
docClient	Document
tblClient	Table

Figure 11-29: Variables used by the PrintClientList procedure

The procedure will store the address of the Balloon object in the balTrainer variable, and it will assign the Balloon object's return value to the intReturnValue variable. When the user closes the Open dialog box, the procedure will assign the dialog box's return value to the Boolean variable blnOpen. The filename selected by the user in the Open dialog box will be assigned to the String variable strFileName. The docClient variable will store the address of the Client List document, and the tblClient variable will be used in a For Each...Next loop that deletes any existing tables from the document.

In the next set of steps, you will declare the appropriate variables and then translate each line in Figure 11-28's pseudocode into one or more VBA statements.

To begin coding the PrintClientList procedure:

1 Enter the documentation and the Dim and Set statements shown in Figure 11-30.

enter these five lines of code

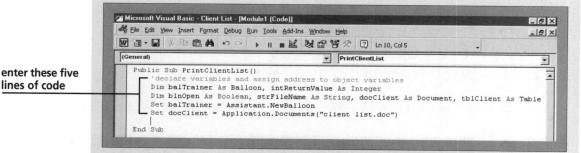

Figure 11-30: Code window showing documentation and Dim and Set statements

The first step in the pseudocode is to turn the Assistant feature on, and then make the Assistant visible.

2 Type **'display Assistant** and press the **Enter** key. Type **assistant.on = true** and press the **Enter** key, then type **assistant.visible = true** and press the **Enter** key.

Steps 2 and 3 in the pseudocode are to create a Balloon object that contains three BalloonLabel objects, labeled "George", "Nora", and "Pam", and then display the Balloon object. You are to assign the Balloon object's return value to the intReturnValue variable.

3 Type the additional code shown in Figure 11-31.

Step 4 in the pseudocode is to replace the sixth paragraph in the document (the paragraph that contains [trainer]) with the word "Trainer:", a tab, the trainer's name, and a blank line. You can use the Balloon object's return value, which is stored in the intReturnValue variable, to determine the appropriate name to display.

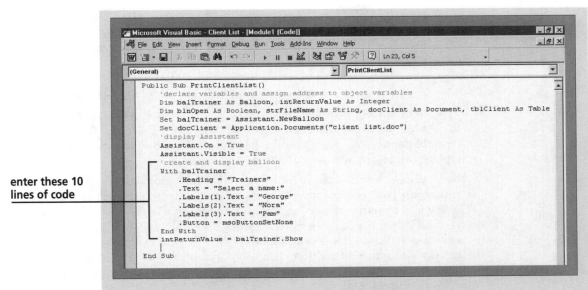

Figure 11-31: Partially completed PrintClientList procedure

4 Type the additional code shown in Figure 11-32.

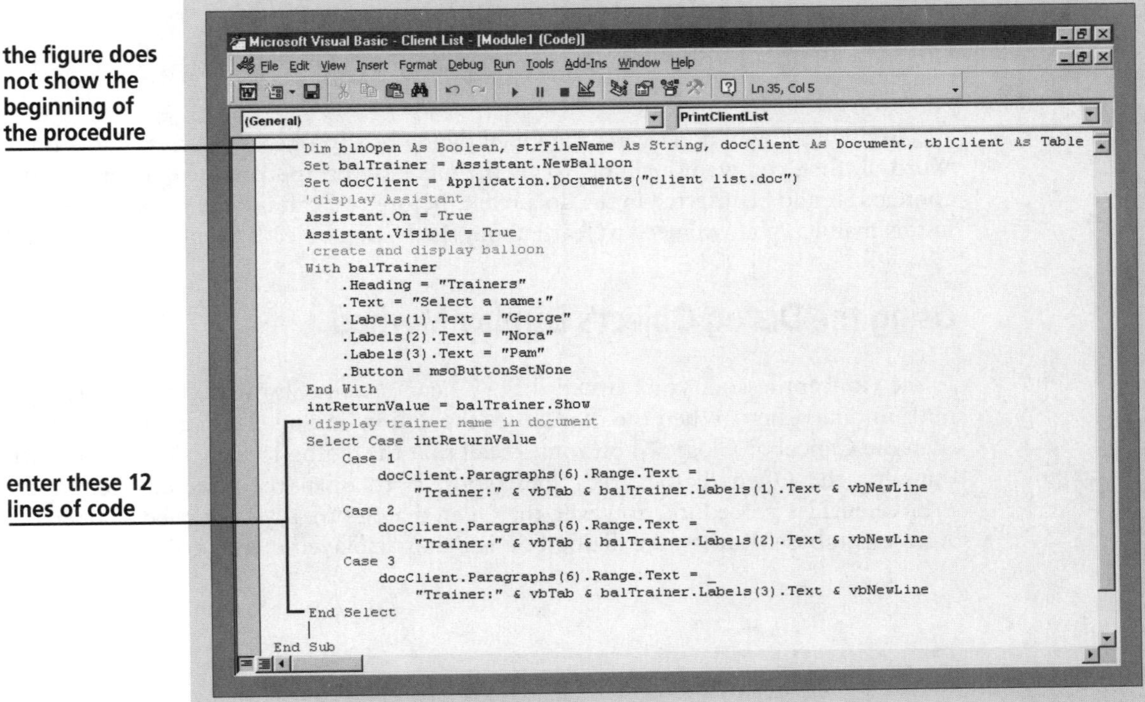

the figure does not show the beginning of the procedure

enter these 12 lines of code

Figure 11-32: Current status of the PrintClientList procedure

Step 5 in the pseudocode is to delete any existing tables from the document.

5   Type **'delete existing tables** and press the **Enter** key, then type **for each tblclient in docclient.tables** and press the **Enter** key. Press the **Tab** key, then type **tblclient.delete** and press the **Enter** key. Press the **Backspace** key, then type **next tblclient** and press the **Enter** key.

Next, display Word's built-in Open dialog box, showing only filenames ending with .mdb. You can control the types of files initially displayed in the Open dialog box by setting the dialog box's Name property. In this case, for example, you will set the Name property to the string "*.mdb". The asterisk (*) is known as a wildcard character because, similar to a wild card in a game of poker, you can use it to represent anything you want. In this case, the "*" indicates that it doesn't matter what the beginning of the filename is; all that matters is that the filename ends in .mdb.

6   Type **'get the name of the Access database** and press the **Enter** key.

7   Type **with application.dialogs(wddialogfileopen)** and press the **Enter** key. Press the **Tab** key, then type **.name = "*.mdb"** (be sure to type the period before the word "name") and press the **Enter** key.

8   Save the document.

In this case, you don't want the Open dialog box to open the Access database in Word. Rather, you want it simply to get the name of the appropriate database whose contents should be inserted in the document. Before you can use the Open dialog box in this manner, you will need to learn about the Dialog object's Display method.

Using the Dialog Object's Display Method

In the Concept lesson, you learned that you can use the Show method to display a built-in dialog box. When the user closes the dialog box by clicking a button other than the Cancel or Close ☒ buttons, recall that the dialog box's actions are carried out—for the Open dialog box, that action is to open the selected file. In the PrintClientList procedure, however, the Open dialog box does not need to open the Access database. Rather, the dialog box is being displayed merely to give the user a convenient way of selecting the appropriate filename. In situations where you want Word to display a built-in dialog box, but you don't want the actions of the dialog box to be carried out, you use the **Display method**, rather than the Show method, to display the dialog box on the screen.

The syntax of the Display method is *dialogObject*.**Display**. Like the Show method, the Display method returns the Boolean value False if the user closes the dialog box by clicking either the Cancel button or the Close button ☒; otherwise, it returns the Boolean value True. The PrintClientList procedure will assign the returned value to the blnOpen variable.

To continue coding the PrintClientList procedure:

1 Type **blnopen = .display** and press the **Enter** key.

The filename selected by the user is stored in the Open dialog box's Name property, the value of which you will assign to the strFileName variable.

2 Type **strfilename = .name** and press the **Enter** key. Press the **Backspace** key, then type **end with** and press the **Enter** key to end the With statement.

According to Step 7 in the pseudocode, the procedure needs to determine if the user clicked the Open dialog box's Open button after selecting an .mdb file. You can determine if the Open button was clicked by comparing the value stored in the blnOpen variable to the Boolean value True. You can use the Right function, which you learned about in Tutorial 10, to determine if the name stored in the strFileName variable ends with .mdb.

3 Type **if blnopen = true and right(strfilename, 4) = ".mdb" then** and press the **Enter** key.

If the user clicked the Open button in the Open dialog box, then the procedure needs to complete three tasks, which are to move the insertion point to the end of the document, insert the database information, and display Word's built-in Print dialog box.

4 Press the **Tab** key, then type **'insert database information and display Print dialog box** and press the **Enter** key.

First, position the insertion point at the end of the Client List document, which is where you want to begin inserting the database information.

5 Type **selection.endkey unit:=wdstory** and press the **Enter** key.

6 Verify the accuracy of your code by comparing the code on your screen to the code shown in Figure 11-33.

the figure does
not show the
beginning of
the procedure

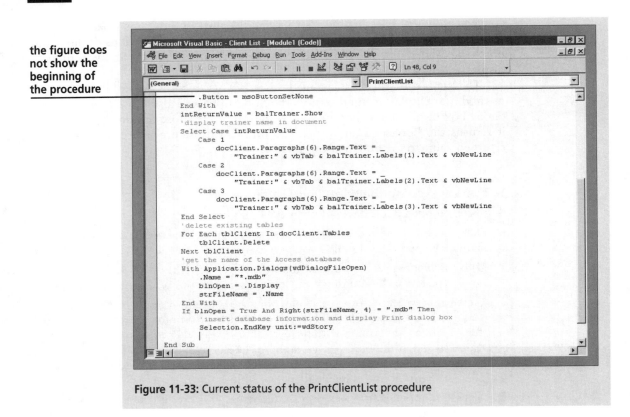

Figure 11-33: Current status of the PrintClientList procedure

The next task is to insert the database information into the document. Before
you can do so, you will need to learn about the Range object's InsertDatabase
method.

Using the Range Object's InsertDatabase Method

You can use the Range object's **InsertDatabase method** to retrieve data from a data
source and insert the data as a table in a document. The data source can be another
Word document, an Excel worksheet, or an Access database. Figure 11-34 shows
the basic syntax and three examples of the InsertDatabase method.

Syntax: *rangeObject*.**InsertDatabase(Format:**=*format*, **Style**:=*style*, **Connection**:=*connectionString*, _ **SQLStatement**:=*sqlStatementString*, **DataSource**:=*dataSourceName*)	
Format	Controls the table formatting. Can be any of the intrinsic constants listed in the AutoFormatType Property Help screen—for example, `wdTableFormatSimple1`, `wdTableFormatClassic2`, and so on.

Style	Controls which attributes of the format, specified in the *format* argument, are applied to the table. Use the sum of any combination of the following values:
	
	     0 (zero) None
	        1 Borders
	        2 Shading
	        4 Font
	        8 Color
	      16 Auto Fit
	      32 Heading Rows
	      64 Last Row
	     128 First Column
	     256 Last Column

Connection	A string that identifies the name of the table or query containing the records to insert
SQLStatement	A SQL statement, entered as a string, that specifies the records to insert
DataSource	A string that identifies the name of the file that contains the data source

Example 1:
 	
`Selection.Range.InsertDatabase _`
`        Format:= wdTableFormatSimple1, Style:=57, _`
`        Connection:="Table Client", DataSource:=strFileName`	

Example 2:
 	
`Selection.Range.InsertDatabase _`
`        Format:= wdTableFormatClassic2, Style:=57, _`
`        Connection:="Query Paid", DataSource:=strFileName`	

Example 3:
 	
`Selection.Range.InsertDatabase _`
`        Format:=wdTableFormatClassic2, Style:=63, _`
`        SQLStatement:="SELECT * FROM client", _`
`        DataSource:=strFileName`	

Figure 11-34: Basic syntax and examples of the Range object's InsertDatabase method

Figure 11-34 shows only a few of the InsertDatabase method's arguments. You can learn more about this method by viewing its Help screen.

As Figure 11-34 indicates, the Format argument controls the formatting for the table, and it can be set to any of the intrinsic constants listed in the AutoFormatType Property Help screen. Examples of these intrinsic constants are `wdTableFormatSimple1` and `wdTableFormatClassic2`. Each constant corresponds to one of the settings listed in the Table AutoFormat dialog box, which is shown in Figure 11-35. For example, the `wdTableFormatSimple1` constant corresponds to the Simple 1 setting shown in the dialog box's Formats list box.

controlled by the Format argument

controlled by the Style argument

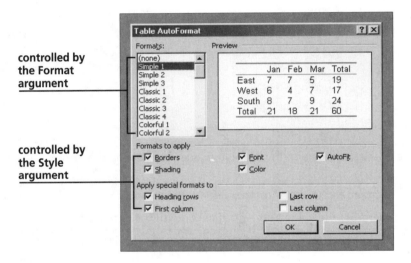

Figure 11-35: Table AutoFormat dialog box

The InsertDatabase method's Style argument specifies which attributes of the Format argument's *format* are applied to the table. You set the Style argument to an integer that represents the sum of any combination of the numbers listed in Figure 11-34. Each number corresponds to one of the check boxes in the Table AutoFormat dialog box. For example, the number 4 corresponds to the Font check box, and the number 16 corresponds to the AutoFit check box. Including the number in the integer sum assigned to the Style argument selects the corresponding check box. In other words, assigning the integer 20 to the Style argument will select the Font and AutoFit check boxes. To select the Borders, Color, AutoFit, and Heading rows check boxes, you would need to set the Style argument to the number 57 (1 + 8 + 16 + 32). A Style argument setting of 151 would select the Borders, Shading, Font, AutoFit, and First column check boxes.

You use the DataSource argument to specify the name of the file that contains the data source. In the examples shown in Figure 11-34, the filename is stored in the String variable strFileName.

When the source file is a Microsoft Access database, as it is in Figure 11-34's examples, you can use the Connection argument to specify the name of the table or query that contains the records you want to insert. You indicate that the Connection argument is a table by entering a *connectionString* that includes the keyword `Table` followed by a space and the table name; this is illustrated in the first example shown in Figure 11-34. The *connectionString* `"Table Client"` tells the InsertDatabase method to insert all of the records contained in the Client table.

To indicate that the Connection argument is a query, you enter a *connectionString* that includes the keyword `Query` followed by a space and the query name, as shown in Figure 11-34's second example. The *connectionString* "Query Paid" tells the InsertDatabase method to insert only records matching the Paid query's specifications.

Besides using the Connection argument, you also can use the SQLStatement argument to specify the records you want to insert. The SQLStatement argument must be a string that represents a valid SQL statement. Example 3 in Figure 11-34, for instance, uses the SQL SELECT statement, which you learned about in Tutorial 8, to select all of the records stored in the Client table. These are the records that the InsertDatabase method will insert into the document.

Now, include the InsertDatabase method in the PrintClientList procedure. Use `wdTableFormatClassic2` as the Format argument, and the number 63 as the Style argument. (The number 63 will select the Borders, Shading, Font, Color, AutoFit, and Heading rows check boxes in the Table AutoFormat dialog box.) Use the variable strFileName, which contains the name of the appropriate database, as the DataSource argument. The name of the table in each trainer's database is Client, so use "`Table Client`" as the Connection argument.

To complete the PrintClientList procedure, then save and test the procedure:

1 Type **selection.range.insertdatabase format:=wdtableformatclassic2, style:=63, _** (be sure to type the comma followed by a space and the underscore) and press the **Enter** key. Press the **Tab** key, then type **connection:="table client", datasource:=strfilename** and press the **Enter** key.

Finally, display Word's built-in Print dialog box. In this case, you do want the dialog box's actions carried out when the user clicks the OK button, so you will use the Show method to display the dialog box.

2 Type the additional instructions shown in Figure 11-36, which shows the completed PrintClientList procedure. (Not all of the procedure is displayed in the figure.)

the figure does
not show the
beginning of
the procedure

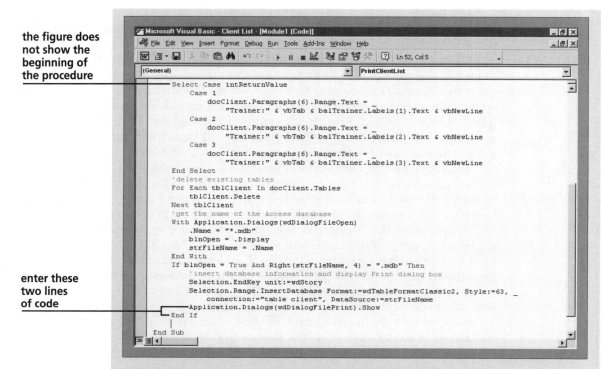

```
Select Case intReturnValue
    Case 1
        docClient.Paragraphs(6).Range.Text = _
            "Trainer:" & vbTab & balTrainer.Labels(1).Text & vbNewLine
    Case 2
        docClient.Paragraphs(6).Range.Text = _
            "Trainer:" & vbTab & balTrainer.Labels(2).Text & vbNewLine
    Case 3
        docClient.Paragraphs(6).Range.Text = _
            "Trainer:" & vbTab & balTrainer.Labels(3).Text & vbNewLine
End Select
'delete existing tables
For Each tblClient In docClient.Tables
    tblClient.Delete
Next tblClient
'get the name of the Access database
With Application.Dialogs(wdDialogFileOpen)
    .Name = "*.mdb"
    blnOpen = .Display
    strFileName = .Name
End With
If blnOpen = True And Right(strFileName, 4) = ".mdb" Then
    'insert database information and display Print dialog box
    Selection.EndKey unit:=wdStory
    Selection.Range.InsertDatabase Format:=wdTableFormatClassic2, Style:=63, _
        connection:="table client", DataSource:=strFileName
    Application.Dialogs(wdDialogFilePrint).Show
End If

End Sub
```

enter these
two lines
of code

Figure 11-36: Completed PrintClientList procedure

Now that you have translated the pseudocode into VBA statements, you can test the PrintClientList procedure to verify that it is working correctly.

3 Verify the accuracy of your code by comparing the code on your screen to the code shown in Figure 11-36, then save the document. Return to Word and run the PrintClientList macro.

Use the macro to display Pam's client list.

4 Click **Pam** in the Assistant's balloon. When the Open dialog box opens, click **Pam** (Pam.mdb), which is located in the Tut11\Word folder on your Data Disk, and then click the **Open** button. A table containing the names and addresses of Pam's clients appears in the document, and the Print dialog box opens. Click the **Cancel** button to close the Print dialog box without printing the document. See Figure 11-37.

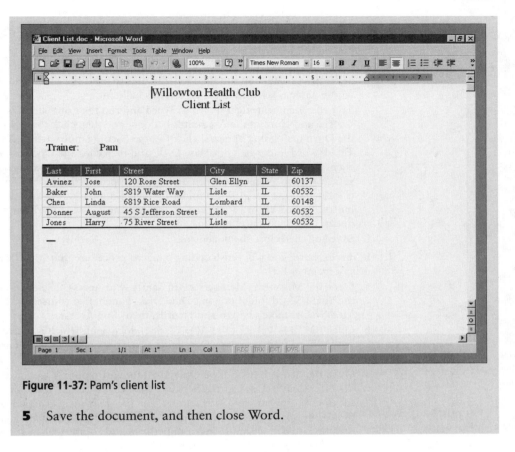

Figure 11-37: Pam's client list

5 Save the document, and then close Word.

You now have completed Tutorial 11's Word lesson. You can either take a break or complete the end-of-lesson exercises before moving on to the next lesson.

E X E R C I S E S

1. In this exercise, you will modify the PrintClientList procedure that you created in this lesson so that it allows the user to print the client list for as many trainers as desired.

    a. Open the Client List (Client List.doc) document, which is located in the Tut11\Word folder on your Data Disk. Click the Enable Macros button, if necessary, then save the document as T11-WD-E1D.

    b. Open the Visual Basic Editor. Open the Module1 module's Code window and view the PrintClientList procedure. Change the filename in the Set statement to "t11-wd-e1d.doc".

    c. Modify the Assistant's balloon so that it uses BalloonCheckbox objects labeled "George", "Nora", and "Pam", rather than BalloonLabel objects. Also include an OK button in the balloon.

    d. Modify the procedure so that it uses a loop to determine which, if any, check boxes are selected. The loop should allow the user to print the client list for each trainer whose name is selected in the Assistant's balloon.

    e. Save the document, then return to Word and run the PrintClientList macro. Click George and Nora in the Assistant's balloon, and then click the OK button. When the Open dialog box appears, click George (George.mdb), which is located in the Tut11\Word folder on your Data Disk, and then click the Open button. George's client list appears in the document. When the Print dialog box opens, click the Cancel button. When the Open dialog box appears, click Nora (Nora.mdb), which is located in the Tut11\Word folder on your Data Disk, and then click the Open button. Nora's client list appears in the document. When the Print dialog box opens, click the Cancel button.

    f. Save and then close the document.

2. In this exercise, you will finish coding a macro procedure that will allow the user to print a member list.

    a. Open the Members (Members.mdb) database in Access. The database is located in the Tut11\Word folder on your Data Disk. Familiarize yourself with the MemberList table's design and records, then close Access.

    b. Open the T11-WD-E2 (T11-WD-E2.doc) document, which is located in the Tut11\Word folder on your Data Disk. Click the Enable Macros button, if necessary, then save the document as T11-WD-E2D.

    c. Open the Visual Basic Editor. Open the Module1 module's Code window and view the PrintMemberList procedure. Study the existing code. Notice that the Select Case statement is missing two instructions. The first missing instruction should insert all of the information from the Members database into the document. The second missing instruction should insert only the records of members whose Trainer field entry matches the ID stored in the strList variable. Complete the procedure by entering the missing instructions. Use `wdTableFormatClassic2` as the Format argument, and 63 as the Style argument.

    d. Save the document, then return to Word and run the PrintMemberList macro four times, entering A, 101, 102, and 103 in the Member List dialog box. Print only trainer 101's listing. (Do not be concerned if the Print dialog box opens before the client list is displayed on the screen. You can learn how to fix this problem by completing Exercise 3.)

    e. Save and then close the document.

Exercises 3 through 6 are Discovery Exercises. Discovery Exercises, which may include topics that are not covered in the lesson, allow you to "discover" the solutions to problems on your own.

discovery ▶ 3. In this exercise, you will learn about the Application object's ScreenRefresh method. You will use the document that you completed in Exercise 2 to do so.

    a. Open the T11-WD-E2D (T11-WD-E2D.doc) document, which you completed in Exercise 2. The document is located in the Tut11\Word folder on your Data Disk. Click the Enable Macros button, if necessary, then save the document as T11-WD-E3D.

b. Open the Visual Basic Editor. Open the Module1 module's Code window and view the PrintMemberList procedure. Change the filename in the Set statement to "t11-wd-e3d.doc".

As you observed when you ran the PrintMemberList procedure in Exercise 2, the Print dialog box appears on the screen before the client list appears in the document, even though the InsertDatabase method occurs before the Show method in the procedure. You can use the Application object's ScreenRefresh method to fix this problem. The ScreenRefresh method updates the display on the monitor with the information currently stored in the video memory buffer.

c. Enter the instruction `Application.ScreenRefresh` below the `End Select` instruction in the procedure.

d. Save the document, then return to Word and run the PrintMemberList macro two times, entering A and 101 in the Member List dialog box. You do not need to print either listing.

e. Save and then close the document.

discovery ▶ **4.** In this exercise, you will finish coding a macro procedure. You will learn how to insert a range of records contained in an Access database.

a. Open the Members (Members.mdb) database in Access. The database is located in the Tut11\Word folder on your Data Disk. Familiarize yourself with the MemberList table's design and records, then close Access.

b. Open the T11-WD-E4 (T11-WD-E4.doc) document, which is located in the Tut11\Word folder on your Data Disk. Click the Enable Macros button, if necessary, then save the document as T11-WD-E4D.

c. Open the Visual Basic Editor. Open the Module1 module's Code window and view the DisplayRecords procedure. Study the existing code. Notice that the procedure prompts the user to enter the number of both the first and last record he or she wants to display. The procedure should insert only these records into the document; the instruction to do so, however, is missing from the procedure.

d. Display the InsertDatabase Method Help screen. Study the Help screen, then close the Help window.

e. Complete the DisplayRecords procedure by entering the missing instruction. Use `wdTableFormatClassic2` as the Format argument, and 63 as the Style argument.

f. Save the document, then return to Word and run the DisplayRecords macro. Display records 1 through 5, then display records 5 through 15.

g. Save and then close the document.

discovery ▶ **5.** In this exercise, you will learn about the Document object's Open event and the Call statement. You will use the Client List document that you created in this lesson.

a. Open the Client List (Client List.doc) document, which is located in the Tut11\Word folder on your Data Disk. Click the Enable Macros button, if necessary, then save the document as T11-WD-E5D.

b. Open the Visual Basic Editor. Open the Module1 module's Code window and view the PrintClientList procedure. Change the filename in the Set statement to "t11-wd-e5d.doc", then close the Code window.

c. Display the Open Event Help screen. Study the Help screen, then close the Help window.

    d. Right-click ThisDocument in the Project Explorer window, then click View Code on the shortcut menu. Click the Object list arrow in the Code window, then click Document. Click the Procedure list arrow, then click Open.

    e. Display the Call Statement Help screen. Study the Help screen, then close the Help window.

    f. In the Open event, enter an instruction that calls the PrintClientList procedure.

    g. Save the document, then return to Word. To test the Open event, close the document, then open the document. Click the Enable Macros button, if necessary. Display Nora's client list, which is stored in the Nora (Nora.mdb) database located in the Tut11\Word folder on your Data Disk. You do not need to print the document.

    h. Save and then close the document.

discovery ▶ 6. In this exercise, you will finish coding a macro procedure that inserts database records contained in an Excel workbook.

    a. Open the Computer (Computer.xls) file in Excel. The file is located in the Tut11\Word folder on your Data Disk. Familiarize yourself with the Consultants worksheet, then close Excel.

    b. Open the T11-WD-E6 (T11-WD-E6.doc) document, which is located in the Tut11\Word folder on your Data Disk. Click the Enable Macros button, if necessary, then save the document as T11-WD-E6D.

    c. Open the Visual Basic Editor. Open the Module1 module's Code window and view the DisplayConsultants procedure. Study the existing code. The procedure should insert the database records stored in the Computer workbook. However, the instruction to accomplish this task is missing from the procedure.

    d. Display the InsertDatabase Method Help screen. Study the Help screen, then close the Help window. Complete the DisplayRecords procedure by entering the missing instruction. Use `wdTableFormatClassic2` as the Format argument, and 63 as the Style argument.

    e. Save the document, then return to Word and run the DisplayConsultants macro. You do not need to print the document.

    f. Save and then close the document.

A computer program is good only if it works. Errors in programming code can cause a program to run incorrectly. Therefore, a programmer needs to know how to locate and fix any errors in his or her code. Exercise 7 is a Debugging Exercise. Debugging Exercises allow you to practice recognizing and solving errors in code.

debugging 7. In this exercise, you will debug an existing macro procedure.

    a. Open the T11-WD-E7 (T11-WD-E7.doc) document, which is located in the Tut11\Word folder on your Data Disk. Click the Enable Macros button, if necessary, then save the document as T11-WD-E7D.

    b. Open the Visual Basic Editor. Open the Module1 module's Code window and view the SortConsultants procedure. Study the code, then return to Word and run the SortConsultants macro.

    c. When the Sort dialog box appears, click the Sort by list arrow, and then click City in the list. Click the OK button. Notice that the procedure does not sort the table information in order by the City. Return to the Visual Basic Editor and correct any errors in the procedure. Test the macro twice, sorting the table information in order by the City and then by the Name.

    d. When the macro is working correctly, save and then close the document.

Access Lesson

Using the Office Assistant in Access

case ▶ Professor Carlisle, the chair of the CIS department at Snowville College, has decided to rewrite the LocateInstructor procedure created in Tutorial 10's Access lesson. Recall that the procedure first prompts Professor Carlisle to enter a course number. It then locates instructors in the AdjFac database who teach the course, and it displays each instructor's name and phone number in a message box.

The new LocateInstructor procedure will display the instructor information—in this case, the name, phone number, and courses taught—in a report rather than in message boxes. Additionally, the procedure will allow Professor Carlisle to preview the report showing either all of the instructors or only those who teach a specific course.

Viewing the Database and the LocateInstructor Procedure

Professor Carlisle's Access database containing information about the adjunct CIS faculty is stored on your Data Disk. Before coding the LocateInstructor procedure, which will display the requested instructor information, you will view the records contained in the database's AdjunctFaculty table.

To view the AdjunctFaculty table and the LocateInstructor procedure:

1 Start Microsoft Access. Open the **AdjFac** (AdjFac.mdb) database, which is located in the Tut11\Access folder on your Data Disk. The AdjFac database contains one table named AdjunctFaculty. Click the **Maximize** button 🔲 on the Microsoft Access title bar to maximize the Microsoft Access window, if necessary. Click **Tables** in the Objects bar of the Database window, if necessary. Right-click **AdjunctFaculty**, then click **Open**. See Figure 11-38.

Name	Phone	CanTeach
▶ Able, Jennifer	(630) 555-1211	110
Baker, Inez	(312) 222-2345	100, 106
Chen, Polly	(630) 333-3333	203, 221, 240, 106
Gonzales, Pete	(773) 222-1234	106, 141, 142
Hill, Jerry	(630) 223-4567	294, 246
Holden, John	(773) 111-1234	100, 108, 120
Holtzberg, Phil	(630) 222-2789	100
Hou, Henry	(630) 444-4545	294
Nabors, Kim	(630) 111-1111	100, 106
Patel, Shanna	(312) 123-2222	110, 108, 225
Schmidt, Jackie	(312) 333-3333	110, 203, 204, 221
Shamra, Sam	(773) 555-5555	241, 242, 243, 110
Shell, Susan	(773) 111-4567	110, 203
Wright, Pam	(630) 999-5678	100, 110, 120
Zinta, George	(630) 222-8888	110

Figure 11-38: Records contained in the AdjunctFaculty table

Each record contains three Text fields: Name, Phone, and CanTeach.

2 Close the table.

3 Press **Alt+F11** to open the Visual Basic Editor. If necessary, open the Project Explorer window and close the Properties window, the Immediate window, and any open Code windows. Open the Module1 module's Code window, then view the code template for the LocateInstructor function procedure.

4 Close the Project Explorer window so that you can view more of the Code window.

Before you can refer to the Assistant's object model in Microsoft Access, you need to add the Microsoft Office 9.0 object library to the project.

5 Click **Tools** on the Visual Basic Editor's menu bar, and then click **References** to display the References – AdjFac dialog box. Scroll the Available References list box until you see the Microsoft Office 9.0 Object Library check box, then, if necessary, click the **Microsoft Office 9.0 Object Library** check box to select it. Click the **OK** button.

Figure 11-39 shows the pseudocode for the LocateInstructor procedure.

1. Store the current value of the Assistant object's On property in a Boolean variable named blnInitialState.
2. Turn the Assistant feature on, and then make the Assistant visible.
3. Create a Balloon object for the Assistant. The balloon should contain two BalloonLabel objects, labeled "All Instructors" and "By Course Number". Also include a Cancel button in the balloon.
4. Display the Balloon object. Assign its return value to an Integer variable named intChoice.
5. Value of intChoice:
   = 1   display the report showing all of the AdjunctFaculty table's records.
   = 2   use the InputBox function to get the course number from the user. Store the user's response in a String variable named strCourseNum.
          Display the report showing only the information for instructors whose CanTeach field contains the course number entered by the user.
   = msoBalloonButtonCancel
          use the MsgBox statement to display the message "Report preview canceled."
6. Return the Assistant to its original state by assigning the value stored in the blnInitialState variable to the Assistant object's On property.

Figure 11-39: Pseudocode for the LocateInstructor procedure

As Figure 11-39 indicates, the LocateInstructor procedure will use a Balloon object to display the "All Instructors" and "By Course Number" options.

Figure 11-40 lists the variables that the LocateInstructor procedure will use.

Variable	datatype
blnInitialState	Boolean
intChoice	Integer
strCourseNum	String
balOptions	Balloon

Figure 11-40: Variables used by the LocateInstructor procedure

The procedure will store the current value of the Assistant object's On property in the Boolean variable blnInitialState. It will assign the value returned by the Balloon object to the Integer variable intChoice, and it will assign the course number entered by the user to the String variable strCourseNum. The balOptions object variable will be used to store the address of the Balloon object.

In the next set of steps, you will declare the appropriate variables and then begin translating the pseudocode shown in Figure 11-39 into VBA statements.

To begin coding the LocateInstructor procedure:

1   Enter the documentation and Dim and Set statements shown in Figure 11-41.

enter these
four lines
of code

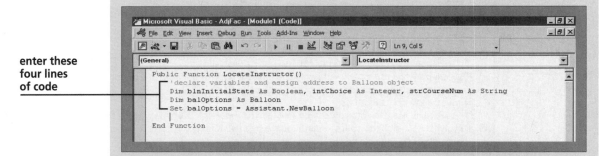

```
Public Function LocateInstructor()
    'declare variables and assign address to Balloon object
    Dim blnInitialState As Boolean, intChoice As Integer, strCourseNum As String
    Dim balOptions As Balloon
    Set balOptions = Assistant.NewBalloon

End Function
```

Figure 11-41: Code window showing documentation and Dim and Set statements

The first step in the pseudocode is to store the current value of the Assistant object's On property in the blnInitialState variable.

2   Type **'save initial state of Assistant** and press the **Enter** key, then type **blninitialstate = assistant.on** and press the **Enter** key.

Step 2 in the pseudocode is to turn the Assistant feature on, and then make the Assistant visible.

3   Type **'display Assistant** and press the **Enter** key. Type **assistant.on = true** and press the **Enter** key, then type **assistant.visible = true** and press the **Enter** key.

Step 3 in the pseudocode is to create a Balloon object for the Assistant. You will display the Alert Query icon (a question mark), the heading "Print Preview", and the text "Preview which report?" in the Balloon object. You also will display two BalloonLabel objects and a Cancel button.

4   Type **'create and display balloon** and press the **Enter** key, then type **with baloptions** and press the **Enter** key.

5   Press the **Tab** key, and then type **.icon = msoiconalertquery** and press the **Enter** key. Type **.heading = "Print Preview"** and press the **Enter** key, and then type **.text = "Preview which report?"** and press the **Enter** key.

6   Type **.labels(1).text = "All Instructors"** and press the **Enter** key, then type **.labels(2).text = "By Course Number"** and press the **Enter** key.

7   Type **.button = msobuttonsetcancel** and press the **Enter** key. Press the **Backspace** key, then type **end with** and press the **Enter** key.

Next, display the Balloon object and assign its return value to the intChoice variable.

8   Type **intchoice = baloptions.show** and press the **Enter** key.

9   Save the database.

According to Step 5 in the pseudocode, the procedure should use the contents of the intChoice variable either to display or cancel the report.

To complete the LocateInstructor procedure:

1   Type **'display or cancel report** and press the **Enter** key, then type **select case intchoice** and press the **Enter** key.

If the intChoice variable contains the number 1, it means that the user clicked the first BalloonLabel object and the procedure should display all of the instructor information in the report. Recall from Tutorial 3's Access lesson that you open a report using the DoCmd object's OpenReport method.

2   Press the **Tab** key. Type **case 1** and press the **Tab** key, then type **'display all instructors** and press the **Enter** key.

3   Press the **Tab** key, then type **docmd.openreport reportname:="adjfacreport", view:=acviewpreview** and press the **Enter** key.

If the intChoice variable contains the number 2, it means that the user clicked the second BalloonLabel object. In that case, the procedure should prompt the user to enter the course number, and then display the report showing only instructors who teach the course.

4   Press the **Backspace** key. Type **case 2** and press the **Tab** key, then type **'display only instructors teaching a specific course** and press the **Enter** key.

5   Press the **Tab** key, then type **strcoursenum = inputbox(prompt:="Enter the 3-character course number:", _** (be sure to type the comma followed by a space and the underscore) and press the **Enter** key. Press the **Tab** key, then type **title:="Course Number")** and press the **Enter** key.

6   Verify the accuracy of your code by comparing the code on your screen to the code shown in Figure 11-42.

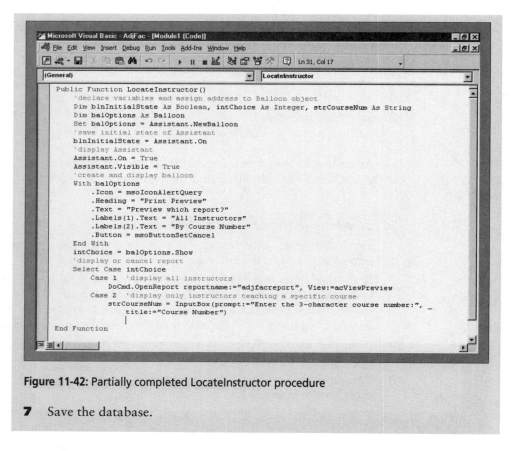

```
Microsoft Visual Basic - AdjFac - [Module1 (Code)]                                    _ 8 X
File  Edit  View  Insert  Debug  Run  Tools  Add-Ins  Window  Help                    _ 8 X
                                                          Ln 31, Col 17

(General)                                     LocateInstructor

Public Function LocateInstructor()
    'declare variables and assign address to Balloon object
    Dim blnInitialState As Boolean, intChoice As Integer, strCourseNum As String
    Dim balOptions As Balloon
    Set balOptions = Assistant.NewBalloon
    'save initial state of Assistant
    blnInitialState = Assistant.On
    'display Assistant
    Assistant.On = True
    Assistant.Visible = True
    'create and display balloon
    With balOptions
        .Icon = msoIconAlertQuery
        .Heading = "Print Preview"
        .Text = "Preview which report?"
        .Labels(1).Text = "All Instructors"
        .Labels(2).Text = "By Course Number"
        .Button = msoButtonSetCancel
    End With
    intChoice = balOptions.Show
    'display or cancel report
    Select Case intChoice
        Case 1  'display all instructors
            DoCmd.OpenReport reportname:="adjfacreport", View:=acViewPreview
        Case 2  'display only instructors teaching a specific course
            strCourseNum = InputBox(prompt:="Enter the 3-character course number:", _
                title:="Course Number")

End Function
```

Figure 11-42: Partially completed LocateInstructor procedure

7 Save the database.

Before you enter the instruction that displays only instructors teaching a specific course, you will learn about the OpenReport method's WhereCondition argument.

Using the OpenReport Method's WhereCondition Argument

In addition to the Reportname and View arguments, the OpenReport method also has a WhereCondition argument, which you can use to limit the records displayed in the report. Figure 11-43 shows this argument in the OpenReport method's syntax; it also shows eight examples of using the WhereCondition argument.

Syntax:

DoCmd.OpenReport Reportname:=*reportname*, **View:=***viewname*, _
          WhereCondition:=*wherecondition*

Example 1 – numeric field and numeric constant:

```
DoCmd.OpenReport Reportname:="janrpt", View:=acViewPreview, _
                 WhereCondition:="sales > 1000"
```

Example 2 – numeric field and numeric variable:

```
DoCmd.OpenReport Reportname:="janrpt", View:=acViewPreview, _
                 WhereCondition:="sales > " & curSales
```

Example 3 – Date/Time field and Date constant:

```
DoCmd.OpenReport Reportname:="janrpt", View:=acViewPreview, _
                 WhereCondition:="duedate = #10/25/2002#"
```

Example 4 – Date/Time field and Date variable:

```
DoCmd.OpenReport Reportname:="janrpt", View:=acViewPreview, _
                 WhereCondition:="duedate = #" & dtmDue & "#"
```

Example 5 – Text field and String constant:

```
DoCmd.OpenReport Reportname:="adjfacrpt", View:=acViewPreview, _
                 WhereCondition:="name = 'Hill, Jerry'"
```

Example 6 – Text field and String variable:

```
DoCmd.OpenReport Reportname:="adjfacrpt", View:=acViewPreview, _
                 WhereCondition:="name = '" & strName & "'"
```

---

*Example 7 – Like operator and * wildcard:*

```
DoCmd.OpenReport Reportname:="adjfacrpt", View:=acViewPreview, _
                 WhereCondition:="name like 'Sh*'"
```

---

*Example 8 – Like operator and * wildcard:*

```
DoCmd.OpenReport Reportname:="adjfacrpt", View:=acViewPreview, _
                 WhereCondition:="phone like '*111-*'"
```

Figure 11-43: Syntax and examples of the OpenReport method

In the syntax, *wherecondition* is a string expression that represents a valid SQL WHERE clause, but without the word WHERE. The first example shown in the figure indicates how you use a numeric field and numeric constant in the *wherecondition*.

Notice that you need simply to enclose the field name (sales), a comparison operator (>), and the constant (1000) within a set of quotation marks (""").

You learned about the SQL WHERE clause in Tutorial 8.

Example 2 in Figure 11-43 shows how you include a numeric field and numeric variable in the *wherecondition*. To do so, you enclose the field name and a comparison operator within the quotation marks, and you concatenate that string with the numeric variable, like this: `"sales > " & curSales`.

The *wherecondition* shown in Example 3, `"duedate = #10/25/2002#"`, includes a Date/Time field and a Date constant. Notice that the Date constant is enclosed within number signs (#), and the entire *wherecondition* is enclosed in quotation marks.

Example 4's *wherecondition*, `"duedate = #" & dtmDue & "#"`, indicates how you use a Date/Time field and a Date variable in the *wherecondition*. Notice that you enclose the field name, a comparison operator, and a number sign within quotation marks. The resulting string is then concatenated with the Date variable, which is then concatenated with a number sign enclosed within quotation marks.

The *wherecondition* shown in Example 5, `"name = 'Hill, Jerry'"`, includes a Text field and a String constant. Notice that the String constant is enclosed within single quotation marks, and the entire *wherecondition* is enclosed in double quotation marks.

Example 6's *wherecondition*, `"name = '" & strName & "'"`, indicates how you use a Text field and a String variable in the *wherecondition*. Notice that you enclose the field name, a comparison operator, and a single quotation mark within double quotation marks. The resulting string is then concatenated with the String variable, which is then concatenated with a single quotation mark enclosed within double quotation marks.

In addition to the =, >, <, >=, <=, and <> operators, you also can use the Like operator and the asterisk (*) wildcard in the *wherecondition*, as shown in Examples 7 and 8 in Figure 11-43. In Example 7, the *wherecondition* `"name like 'Sh*'"` tells the OpenReport method to include only records whose Name field contains a value that begins with the two letters Sh. The asterisk (*) is known as a wildcard character because, similar to a wild card in a game of poker, you can use it to represent anything you want. In this case, the "*" indicates that you are not concerned either with the number of characters that occur after the Sh in the Name field, or which characters they are.

You can learn more about the Like operator and the * wildcard by completing Exercise 14 in Tutorial 7's Concept lesson.

Example 8 in Figure 11-43 shows how you can use the Like operator and the asterisk wildcard to locate one or more characters appearing somewhere within a Text field. In addition to placing an asterisk wildcard after the characters, as in Example 7, you also place an asterisk wildcard before the characters. For example, the *wherecondition* `"phone like '*111-*'"` tells the OpenReport method to include only records containing the four characters `111-` somewhere in their Phone field. The first asterisk indicates that you don't care how many characters, or which characters, appear before the `111-`. The second asterisk indicates that you don't care how many characters, or which characters, appear after the `111-`.

Now that you know how to use the OpenReport method's WhereCondition argument, you can complete the LocateInstructor procedure.

To complete the LocateInstructor procedure, then save and run the procedure:

1 Press the **Backspace** key. Then type **docmd.openreport reportname:= "adjfacreport", view:=acviewpreview, _** (be sure to type the comma followed by a space and the underscore) and press the **Enter** key.

Display all records whose CanTeach field contains the course number stored in the strCourseNum variable.

2 Press the **Tab** key, then type **wherecondition:="canteach like '*" & strcoursenum & "*'"** and press the **Enter** key.

According to Step 5 in the pseudocode, if the user clicks the Cancel button in the Assistant's balloon, the procedure should display the message "Report preview canceled."

3 Press the **Backspace** key twice, then type **case msoballoonbuttoncancel** and press the **Enter** key.

4 Press the **Tab** key, then type **msgbox prompt:="Report preview canceled.", _** (be sure to type the comma followed by a space and the underscore) and press the **Enter** key. Press the **Tab** key, then type **buttons:=vbokonly + vbinformation, title:="Preview"** and press the **Enter** key.

5 Press the **Backspace** key three times, then type **end select** and press the **Enter** key.

The last step in the pseudocode is to return the Assistant feature to the state it was in—either on or off—before the procedure was run. You can do so by assigning the value stored in the blnInitialState variable to the Assistant's On property.

6 Type the additional instructions shown in Figure 11-44, which shows the completed LocateInstructor procedure. (Not all of the procedure is displayed in the figure.)

the figure does not show the beginning of the procedure

be sure that you type the single and double quotation marks correctly

enter these two lines of code

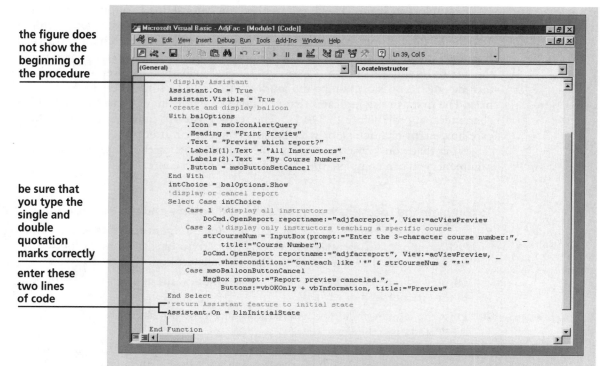

```
'display Assistant
Assistant.On = True
Assistant.Visible = True
'create and display balloon
With balOptions
    .Icon = msoIconAlertQuery
    .Heading = "Print Preview"
    .Text = "Preview which report?"
    .Labels(1).Text = "All Instructors"
    .Labels(2).Text = "By Course Number"
    .Button = msoButtonSetCancel
End With
intChoice = balOptions.Show
'display or cancel report
Select Case intChoice
    Case 1 'display all instructors
        DoCmd.OpenReport reportname:="adjfacreport", View:=acViewPreview
    Case 2 'display only instructors teaching a specific course
        strCourseNum = InputBox(prompt:="Enter the 3-character course number:", _
            title:="Course Number")
        DoCmd.OpenReport reportname:="adjfacreport", View:=acViewPreview, _
            wherecondition:="canteach like '*' & strCourseNum & '*'"
    Case msoBalloonButtonCancel
        MsgBox prompt:="Report preview canceled.", _
            Buttons:=vbOKOnly + vbInformation, title:="Preview"
End Select
'return Assistant feature to initial state
Assistant.On = blnInitialState

End Function
```

Figure 11-44: Completed LocateInstructor procedure

7 Verify the accuracy of your code by comparing the code on your screen to the code shown in Figure 11-44, then save the database.

Now that you have finished coding the LocateInstructor procedure, you will run the LocateInstructorMacro macro to verify that the procedure is working correctly.

8 Return to Access, then run the **LocateInstructorMacro** macro. The Office Assistant and its customized balloon appear on the screen, as shown in Figure 11-45.

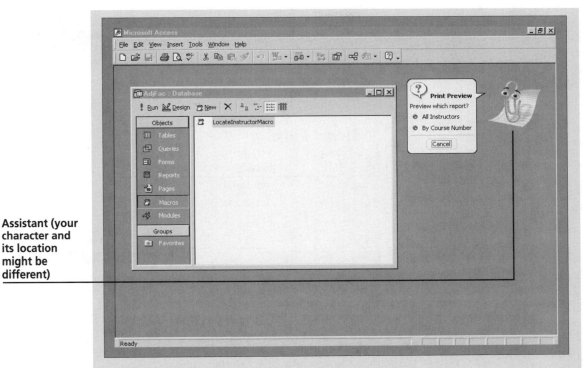

Assistant (your character and its location might be different)

Figure 11-45: The Office Assistant and its customized balloon

> **HELP?** Do not be concerned if your screen shows a different Assistant, or if the Assistant is located in a different area of the screen.

9 Click the **Cancel** button in the Office Assistant's balloon. The message "Report preview canceled." appears in a message box. Click the **OK** button to close the message box. Notice that the procedure ends without displaying the report.

10 Run the **LocateInstructorMacro** macro again. Click the **By Course Number** button in the balloon. When the Course Number dialog box appears, type **108** as the course number and press the **Enter** key. The procedure displays the report shown in Figure 11-46.

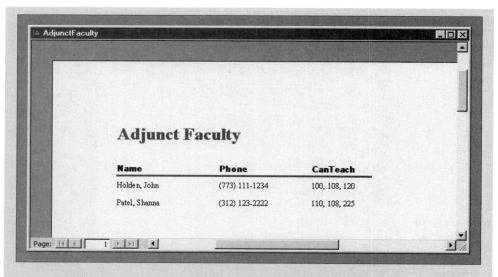

Figure 11-46: Report showing instructors who teach course number 108

11 Close the report, then run the **LocateInstructorMacro** macro again. Click the **All Instructors** button in the balloon. The information pertaining to all 15 instructors appears in the report.

12 Close the report, then compact the database and exit Access.

You now have completed Tutorial 11's Access lesson. You can either take a break or complete the end-of-lesson exercises.

 # E X E R C I S E S

1. In this exercise, you will modify the LocateInstructor procedure that you created in this lesson. The procedure now will allow the user to preview the report showing only those instructors whose name matches the characters entered by the user.
    a. Use Windows to make a copy of the AdjFac database, which is located in the Tut11\Access folder on your Data Disk. Rename the copy T11-AC-E1D.
    b. Open the T11-AC-E1D (T11-AC-E1D.mdb) database. Open the Visual Basic Editor, then open the Module1 module's Code window and view the LocateInstructor procedure.
    c. Include another BalloonLabel object in the Assistant's balloon. Label the object By Name. If the user clicks the By Name button, the procedure should prompt the user to enter one or more characters in the instructor's name. The procedure should display only records whose Name field contains these characters.

    d. Save the database, then return to Access and run the LocateInstructorMacro macro. Click the By Name button. When the InputBox function's dialog box appears, type Hou and press the Enter key. The report should display only Harry Hou's information.

    e. Run the LocateInstructorMacro macro again. Click the By Name button. When the InputBox function's dialog box appears, type Je and press the Enter key. The report should display the information for Jennifer Able and Jerry Hill.

    f. Compact and then close the database.

2. In this exercise, you will modify the PostScores procedure that you created in Tutorial 9's Access lesson. The procedure now will allow the user to select zero or more reports to publish.

    a. Open the T11-AC-E2D (T11-AC-E2D.mdb) database, which is located in the Tut11\Access folder on your Data Disk. Familiarize yourself with each of the tables and reports included in the database.

    b. Open the Visual Basic Editor. Open the Module1 module's Code window and view the PostScores procedure. Use the Tools menu to add the Microsoft Office 9.0 Object Library reference to the project.

    c. Modify the PostScores procedure so that it allows the user to post zero or more reports to the Web. Use the Office Assistant to display the choices for the user. Use an appropriate icon, heading, and text in the balloon. Display the choices as check boxes labeled Report100, Report110, and Report260. Display an OK button at the bottom of the balloon. Return the Office Assistant to its original state—either on or off—before the procedure ends.

    d. Save the database, then return to Access and run the PostScoresMacro macro. When the Posted By dialog box appears, click the OK button to accept Professor Carlisle's name. Post the Report100 and Report110 reports only.

    e. Compact and then close the database.

Exercise 3 is a Discovery Exercise. Discovery Exercises, which may include topics that are not covered in the lesson, allow you to "discover" the solutions to problems on your own.

discovery ▶ **3.** In this exercise, you will learn how to use the OpenReport method's FilterName argument.

    a. Open the T11-AC-E3D (T11-AC-E3D.mdb) database, which is located in the Tut11\Access folder on your Data Disk. View the records contained in the CIS100 table, then close the table. Also familiarize yourself with the five queries and one report included in the database.

    b. Open the Visual Basic Editor. Open the Module1 module's Code window and view the code template for the DisplayGrades procedure. Use the Tools menu to add the Microsoft Office 9.0 Object Library reference to the project.

    c. View the OpenReport Method Help screen. Study the portion of the Help screen for the FilterName argument, then close the Help window.

    d. Code the DisplayGrades procedure so that it gives the user two options: to preview all of the records in the report or to preview the report showing only records for a specific grade entered by the user. Use the Office Assistant to offer the user both options. Include a Cancel button at the bottom of the Assistant's balloon. Also include a heading, text, and two BalloonLabel objects labeled "All" and "Grade."

   e. If the user clicks the Cancel button, the procedure should display the message "Report preview canceled." If the user clicks the "All" button, display all of the records in the report. If the user clicks the "Grade" button, use the InputBox function to ask the user to enter the grade: A, B, C, D, or F. If the user enters the letter A, use the OpenReport method's FilterName argument to display the report using the QryA query. If the user enters the letter B, display the report using the QryB query, and so on. Before the procedure ends, it should return the Office Assistant to its original state—either on or off.

   f. Save the database, then return to Access and run the DisplayGradesMacro macro. Click the All button to preview the report showing all of the records. Close the report.

   g. Run the DisplayGradesMacro macro again. Click the Grade button, then enter the letter B and press the Enter key. The report should display only the two records whose Grade field contains the letter B. Close the report.

   h. Run the DisplayGradesMacro macro again. Click the Cancel button. The message "Report preview canceled." should be displayed in a message box. Click the OK button to close the message box.

   i. Compact and then close the database.

A computer program is good only if it works. Errors in programming code can cause a program to run incorrectly. Therefore, a programmer needs to know how to locate and fix any errors in his or her code. Exercise 4 is a Debugging Exercise. Debugging Exercises allow you to practice recognizing and solving errors in code.

debugging 4. In this exercise, you will debug an existing procedure.

   a. Open the T11-AC-E4D (T11-AC-E4D.mdb) database, which is located in the Tut11\Access folder on your Data Disk. Familiarize yourself with the Contacts table and the ContactsReport report.

   b. Open the Visual Basic Editor. Open the Module1 module's Code window and view the FindAddressOrZip procedure. The procedure should allow the user to display the report showing records that match a partial address or a zip code. Study the code, then return to Access.

   c. Run the FindAddressOrZipMacro macro. Click the Address button in the balloon, then type "west" (without the quotation marks) in the Address dialog box and press the Enter key. Although two of the records in the Contacts table contain "West" in their Address field, no records appear in the report. Close the report.

   d. Run the FindAddressOrZipMacro macro again. This time, click the Zip button in the balloon, then type 60133 in the Zip dialog box. When the error dialog box appears, click the End button, then click the Halt button.

   e. Return to the Visual Basic Editor and correct the errors in the FindAddressOrZip procedure.

   f. Save the database, then return to Access. Run the FindAddressOrZipMacro macro two times, first displaying records containing "west" in their address field and then displaying records whose zip code is 60133.

   g. When the macro is working correctly, compact and then close the database.

Custom Dialog Boxes

objectives

In this tutorial, you will learn how to:

- Follow the Windows standards for creating a custom dialog box
- Explain the use of text box, label, and command button controls
- Set the tab order for controls
- Provide keyboard access to controls using accelerator keys
- Add new and existing forms to a project
- Add controls to a form
- Display and remove a custom dialog box
- Code a custom dialog box

Concept Lesson

Custom Dialog Boxes

In previous tutorials, you learned how to use the MsgBox and InputBox functions, as well as the Office Assistant and Word's and Excel's built-in dialog boxes, to get user input. Additionally, you can create a custom dialog box. To do so, you first add a **form**—the foundation of a dialog box—to the project, and then you add objects, called **controls**, to the form. This form and its controls are what constitute a dialog box.

> If a procedure needs to perform a task for which a built-in dialog box exists, it is better to use the built-in dialog box rather than a customized dialog box. The benefit to the programmer lies in the fact that, because the built-in dialog boxes are ready-made, he or she does not need to spend time creating and testing them. Additionally, the built-in dialog boxes allow the user to use something with which he or she is already familiar.

Design Standards for Dialog Boxes

While the design of a custom dialog box's interface is open to creativity, there are some guidelines to which you should adhere so that the dialog box is consistent with the Windows standards. This consistency will make the dialog box easier for the user to use because the interface will have a familiar look to it. Before you can create a custom dialog box, you need to understand the Windows standards for dialog boxes. The custom dialog boxes shown in Figure 12-1 illustrate many of these design standards.

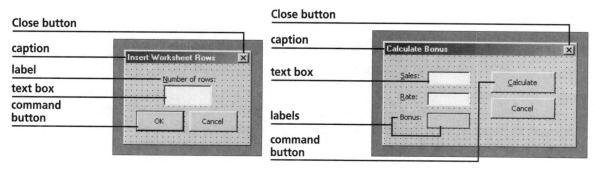

Figure 12-1: Insert Worksheet Rows and Calculate Bonus custom dialog boxes

While you are designing the dialog box, dots appear in the form to assist you in aligning the controls. You should try to align the controls wherever possible to minimize the number of different margins in the dialog box, making it easier for the user to scan the dialog box's information. When positioning the controls, be sure to maintain a consistent margin from the edge of the form; a margin of two or three dots is recommended.

Because a dialog box is a window, it has a title bar and borders. The title bar typically contains a caption that identifies the purpose of the dialog box. For example, the caption "Insert Worksheet Rows" indicates that the dialog box can be used to insert one or more rows in a worksheet. The caption "Calculate Bonus" indicates that the dialog box calculates a bonus amount. The dialog box's caption should be entered using **book title capitalization**, which means you capitalize the first letter in each word, except for articles, conjunctions, and prepositions that do not occur at either the beginning or the end of the caption.

In addition to the caption, a dialog box's title bar always contains a Close button ☒. It is a Windows standard that dialog boxes cannot be sized; therefore, the title bar does not contain the Minimize and Maximize buttons, and the user will not be able to drag the borders to make the dialog box either smaller or larger.

Dialog Box Controls

The Insert Worksheet Rows and Calculate Bonus dialog boxes contain three different types of controls: text box, label, and command button. You use a **text box control** to provide an area in the dialog box where data can be entered, edited, and displayed. The text box in the Insert Worksheet Rows dialog box, for example, allows the user to specify the number of rows to insert. The two text boxes in the Calculate Bonus dialog box allow the user to enter the sales amount and bonus rate.

You use a **label control** to display text that you don't want the user to modify, such as text that identifies another control in the dialog box or text that represents the result of a calculation.

The Insert Worksheet Rows dialog box in Figure 12-1 contains one label control, captioned "Number of rows:", whose sole purpose is to identify the text box located immediately below it. The Calculate Bonus dialog box contains four label controls; three of these—the ones captioned "Sales:", "Rate:", and "Bonus:"—identify the controls located to their immediate right. The fourth label control, situated to the right of the "Bonus:" label, is used to display the result of the bonus calculation.

If a label control is used as an identifier for another control, its caption should be no more than three words in length and entered using **sentence capitalization**, which means that you capitalize only the first letter in the first word and in any words that are customarily capitalized. Additionally, the entire caption should appear on one line in the control and it should end with a colon (:). The Windows standard is to left-align the caption within the label control, and to position the label control either above or to the left of the control it identifies. In the Insert Worksheet Rows dialog box, the "Number of rows:" label is positioned above the text box. The identifying labels in the Calculate Bonus dialog box are positioned to the left of their associated controls.

The third control type included in Figure 12-1's dialog boxes is the command button control. You use a **command button control** to process one or more instructions when the user clicks the button. Most dialog boxes, like the Insert Worksheet Rows dialog box, contain the familiar OK and Cancel command buttons. When the user clicks the OK button, the button first performs the dialog box's action—in this case, it will insert the desired number of rows—and then it closes the dialog box. When the user clicks the Cancel button, on the other hand, the button closes the dialog box without performing the dialog box's action.

Command buttons other than the OK and Cancel buttons also can appear in a dialog box. For example, notice that the Calculate Bonus dialog box contains a Calculate button rather than an OK button. The button's caption—Calculate—specifies the action the button will perform when clicked. You typically use such a button, rather than the OK button, to indicate that the dialog box will remain open after the action is performed. In this case, for example, the Calculate button will calculate the bonus amount, but it will not close the dialog box after completing the calculation, allowing the user to calculate another bonus amount without having to reopen the dialog box. The user can close the Calculate Bonus dialog box by clicking either the Cancel button or the Close button ☒.

> In some dialog boxes, a button whose caption is Close replaces the Cancel button. A Cancel button closes the dialog box without saving the changes made to options within the dialog box. A Close button also closes the dialog box, but it retains the changes made to options within the dialog box.

A command button's caption should be no more than three words in length and entered using book title capitalization. The entire caption should appear on one line in the button.

Command buttons should be positioned either at the bottom or on the right side of the dialog box. The buttons can be placed side by side (as in the Insert Worksheet Rows dialog box) or they can be stacked (as in the Calculate Bonus dialog box). If the buttons appear side by side, then each should be the same height; their widths, however, may vary. If the buttons are stacked, then each should be the same height and the same width.

You should group related command buttons together by placing them close to each other in the dialog box. The most commonly used command button in the group should be placed first, which means it should be the left-most button in the group when the buttons are side by side, and it should be the top-most button in the group when the buttons are stacked. Buttons unrelated to a specific group can be situated away from the group, if desired.

> One way to learn the Windows standards for dialog boxes is to study the dialog boxes built into the Microsoft Office applications; however, don't be surprised if you find some inconsistencies in the standards. For example, the Options tab on the Customize dialog box (which you open by clicking Tools on the application's menu bar and then clicking Customize) contains a command button whose caption, Reset my usage data, is entered using sentence capitalization rather than book title capitalization.

After adding the necessary controls to a custom dialog box, you need to specify the order in which each control should receive the focus. This order is referred to as the tab order.

Setting the Tab Order

The **tab order** is the order in which the focus moves from one essential control in a dialog box to the next essential control as you press the Tab key. An **essential control** is one that can receive input from the user. For example, the text boxes and command buttons contained in the Insert Worksheet Rows and Calculate Bonus dialog boxes in Figure 12-2 (on the next page) are essential controls because each accepts user input; the user can enter information into the text boxes and he or she can select the command buttons. The label controls in both dialog boxes are not considered essential controls because the user does not have access to them.

The first essential control in the tab order typically is located in the upper-left area of the dialog box; this is where the focus should appear when the dialog box first opens. In the Insert Worksheet Rows dialog box, the text box labeled "Number of rows:" will have the initial focus. When you press the Tab key, the focus will move from the text box to the OK command button. Pressing the Tab key two more times will send the focus to the Cancel command button and then back to the text box. Notice that the Number of rows: label control never gets the focus; this is to prevent the user from making any modifications to the label control's contents.

In the Calculate Bonus dialog box, the text box labeled "Sales:" will have the focus when the dialog box first appears on the screen. Pressing the Tab key four times will send the focus to the second text box, then to the Calculate command button, the Cancel command button, and back to the first text box. Here again, notice that none of the labels gets the focus. You will need to specify the correct tab order for the controls contained in the custom dialog boxes you create. You do so by setting each control's TabIndex property. The use of this property is illustrated in the Excel, Word, and Access lessons.

Next you will learn how to provide keyboard access to a control in the dialog box.

Providing Keyboard Access to a Control

Providing keyboard access to the controls in a dialog box allows the user to work with the dialog box using the keyboard rather than the mouse. The user may need to use the keyboard if his or her mouse becomes inoperative. Or, the user simply may prefer to use the keyboard if he or she is a fast typist. Another important reason for providing keyboard access to controls is that it allows people with disabilities, which may prevent them from using a mouse, to work with the dialog box.

You should provide keyboard access to the essential controls in a dialog box—those controls that can accept user input. As noted earlier, the text boxes and command buttons contained in the Insert Worksheet Rows and Calculate Bonus dialog boxes are essential controls, but the label controls contained in those dialog boxes are not. You can provide keyboard access to a control by assigning an accelerator key to it.

Assigning Accelerator Keys

When you look closely at the dialog boxes shown in Figure 12-2, you will notice that an underlined letter appears in the Calculate button's caption and also in the captions of the labels that identify the three text boxes.

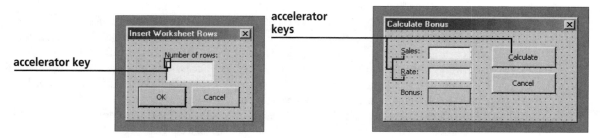

Figure 12-2: Insert Worksheet Rows and Calculate Bonus custom dialog boxes

The underlined letter is called an **accelerator key** and it is used in combination with the Alt key as a shortcut for selecting a control. For example, you can use Alt+C to select the Calculate command button in the Calculate Bonus dialog box because the letter C is that button's accelerator key. Accelerator keys are not case sensitive, so you can use either Alt+c or Alt+C to select the Calculate command button.

The Microsoft Access Help screens use the term *access key* **rather than** *accelerator key* **to refer to the underlined letter in a control's caption.**

Alt+N would send the focus to the Number of rows: label control in the Insert Worksheet Rows dialog box. However, because label controls cannot receive the focus, the focus would be sent to the next control in the tab order—in this case, it would be sent to the text box located below the Number of rows: label.

Each accelerator key in a dialog box must be unique. The first choice for an accelerator key is the first letter of the caption, unless another letter provides a more meaningful association. For example, the letter X is typically the accelerator key for an Exit button because the letter X provides a more meaningful association than does the letter E. If you can't use the first letter (perhaps because it already is used as the accelerator key for another control) and no letter provides a more meaningful association, then use a distinctive consonant in the caption. The last choices for an accelerator key are a vowel or a number in the caption.

In all Microsoft Office applications but Access, you use a control's Accelerator property to assign an accelerator key to the control. In Access, you place an ampersand (&) to the left of the appropriate letter in the control's Caption property.

Notice that the OK and Cancel buttons in Figure 12-2's dialog boxes do not have accelerator keys, as indicated by the lack of an underlined letter in their caption. Rather than, or in addition to, assigning an accelerator key to a command button, you can provide keyboard access to the button by setting either its Default property or its Cancel property.

Using the Default and Cancel Properties

In most dialog boxes, one of the command buttons (typically the OK button) is designated as the default button, while another command button (typically the Cancel button) is designated as the cancel button. The **default button** is the one that is selected automatically when the user presses the Enter key, even when the button does not have the focus. In the Insert Worksheet Rows dialog box, the user can type the number of rows in the text box and then press the Enter key to select the default button, OK, which will insert the appropriate number of rows and then close the dialog box. You make a command button the default button by setting its **Default property** to the Boolean value True. Only one command button in a dialog box can be the default button. Command buttons that perform destructive actions, such as deleting files and records, should never be designated as the default button unless the dialog box also provides a way to reverse the action.

tip

If another command button has the focus when the user presses the Enter key, that command button, rather than the default button, will be selected.

The **cancel button** is the one that is selected automatically when the user presses the Esc key, and it is usually the button that closes the dialog box without performing any action. In both dialog boxes shown in Figure 12-2, the command button captioned Cancel is designated as the cancel button. You make a command button the cancel button by setting its **Cancel property** to the Boolean value True. Only one of the command buttons in a dialog box can be the cancel button.

Now that you understand the guidelines for creating and designing a custom dialog box, you next will learn how to add a form to a project.

Important Note: The following sections on adding a form and controls to a project apply to all of the Microsoft Office applications except Access. Please refer to the Access lesson in this tutorial for detailed information on using forms and controls in Access.

Adding a Form to the Project

Before you can create a custom dialog box, you first must add a form to the project. The form will serve as the foundation of the dialog box. **Unlike in the previous Concept lessons in this book, you will need to complete the following steps while working at your computer.**

To add a form to the project:

1 Start either PowerPoint, Excel, or Word, opening a blank presentation, workbook, or document, respectively. Press **Alt+F11** to open the Visual Basic Editor. (The remaining figures in this lesson will show the Visual Basic Editor opened in PowerPoint, but the concepts illustrated apply to Excel and Word as well.)

2 If necessary, open the Project Explorer window and close the Properties window, the Immediate window, and any open Code windows.

3 Click **Insert** on the menu bar, and then click **UserForm**. The Visual Basic Editor adds a form to the project and also displays the Toolbox window.

HELP? If the Toolbox window does not appear on the screen, click View on the Standard toolbar and then click Toolbox.

4 Place the mouse pointer on the Toolbox window's title bar and then drag the Toolbox window to the location shown in Figure 12-3.

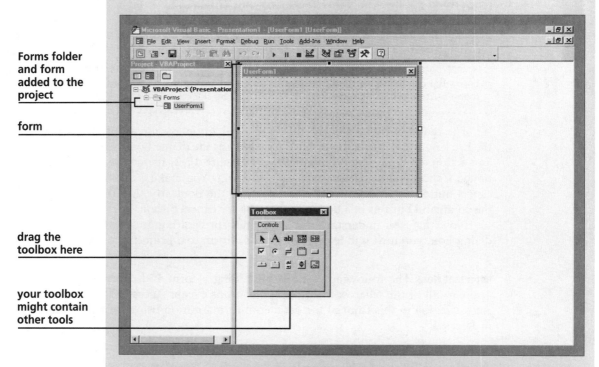

Forms folder and form added to the project

form

drag the toolbox here

your toolbox might contain other tools

Figure 12-3: Form and Toolbox window shown in the Visual Basic Editor

HELP? The text that appears in the Visual Basic Editor's title bar, as well as the contents of the Project Explorer window, will differ from that shown in Figure 12-3 if you are using Excel or Word rather than PowerPoint.

HELP? Don't be concerned if your Toolbox window is not identical to the one shown in Figure 12-3.

Notice that the Project Explorer window now contains a Forms folder, and that the Forms folder contains one form named UserForm1. The Visual Basic Editor assigns a default name to each form added to a project. The default name for the first form in a project is UserForm1, the default name for the second form is UserForm2, and so on. Because a project can contain many forms, it is a good practice to give each one a more descriptive name to help you keep track of the various forms.

Naming the Form

Each form in a project must have a unique name. The rules for naming forms are the same as the rules for naming variables, which are listed in Tutorial 3's Figure 3-7. The three-character ID used in form names is *frm*. For example, a more descriptive name for the current form would be frmUpdateInv. The *frm* identifies the object as a form, and the *UpdateInv* reminds you of the form's purpose. You can use the Properties window to change the current form's name from UserForm1 to frmUpdateInv.

To change the form's name:

1 Right-click the **form**, then click **Properties** on the shortcut menu. The Visual Basic Editor hides the Toolbox window and opens the Properties window. If necessary, place the mouse pointer on the Properties window's title bar and then drag the Properties window to the location shown in Figure 12-4.

To display the Toolbox window again, you need simply to click the form.

The Properties window lists only the properties that can be set at design time, which is when you are creating the form in the Visual Basic Editor. It does not list the properties that can be set only at run time, through code. Run time occurs when a procedure is running. To view a complete listing of an object's properties, display the object's Help screen.

Other ways of displaying the Properties window include pressing the F4 key, using the Properties Window command on the View menu, and clicking the Properties Window button 📄 on the Standard toolbar.

Properties window

Object box

Properties list

Settings box

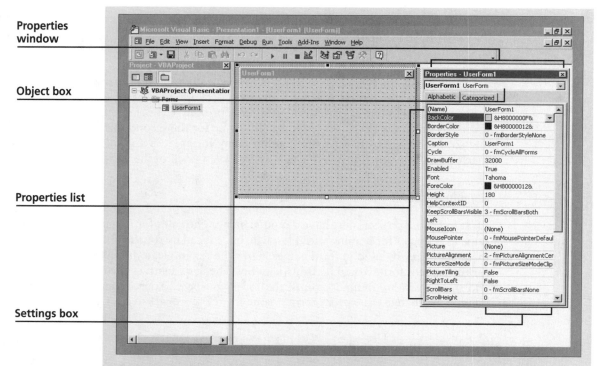

Figure 12-4: The Properties window

As you learned in Tutorial 1, the Properties window lists the set of character-istics, called **properties**, that control an object's appearance and behavior. Currently, the Properties window displays the properties of the form.

Notice that the Properties window includes an Object box and a Properties list. The **Object box**, located immediately below the Properties window's title bar, displays the name and type of the selected object—in this case, UserForm1 UserForm. When you click the Object list arrow, a list of objects included in the dialog box appears. You can use the list to select an object in the dialog box. You must select an object before you can either display or change the value of its properties.

The **Properties list**, which can be displayed either alphabetically or by category, has two columns. The left column displays all the properties associated with the selected object (in this case, the form). The right column contains the **Settings box** for each of the object's properties, and it displays the current value, or setting, of each of those properties. For example, the Settings box indicates that the current value of the form's Name property is UserForm1.

You can change the setting for many of the listed properties simply by typing a new value in the property's Settings box. Some properties, however, have predefined settings. If a property has predefined settings, either a list arrow or an ellipsis (...) will appear in the property's Settings box. When you click the list arrow, either a list or a color palette appears containing the valid predefined settings for that property; you then select the setting you want from that list or color palette. Clicking the ellipsis in the Settings box displays a dialog box in which you select the settings for the property.

2   Click **(Name)** in the Properties list. Notice that the (Name) Settings box does not contain either a list arrow or an ellipsis, which means that this property does not have any predefined settings. Type **frmUpdateInv** and press the **Enter** key. The new name appears in the (Name) Settings box and in the Forms folder in the Project Explorer window. Notice that you do not have to delete the old name before entering the new name. You need simply to select the appropriate property and then type the new value.

3   Click the **form** to make it the active window. The Toolbox window reappears.

Notice that the default caption UserForm1 appears in the form's title bar. As you learned earlier, the text appearing in a dialog box's title bar should indicate the purpose of the dialog box, and it should be entered using book title capitalization. You will change the title bar text, which is controlled by the form's Caption property, from UserForm1 to Update Inventory.

4   Click **Caption** in the Properties list, then type **Update Inventory** and press the **Enter** key. The new caption appears in the Settings box and in the form's title bar.

Notice that the form's title bar contains only the caption and a Close button ⊠. As you learned earlier, dialog boxes do not contain the Minimize and Maximize buttons, and they can't be sized by dragging their borders. Although you can't size the dialog box while it is running, you can size it while you are designing it in the Visual Basic Editor.

5   Place the mouse pointer on the form's lower-right handle until the mouse pointer becomes a double arrow ⬉, then drag the handle until the form is slightly smaller than its current size, which is known as the default size. (You don't need to worry about the exact size.) When the form is the desired size, release the mouse button.

It can be very easy to confuse an object's Name property with its Caption property. The Caption property controls the text displayed inside the object—for example, the text displayed in the form's title bar. The Name property, however, assigns a name to an object. When writing VBA instructions, you use an object's name, not its caption, to refer to the object. In other words, the name is used by the programmer, whereas the caption is read by the user.

Next, learn how to use the Toolbox window to add a control to the form.

Using the Toolbox Window to Add a Control to the Form

The **Toolbox window**, also referred to simply as the **toolbox**, contains the set of tools you use to place objects, called controls, on the form. Figure 12-5 shows each of the basic tools contained in the toolbox and it describes the purpose of each tool. It also gives the three-character ID used to name the controls associated with each tool.

Tool	Name	Purpose	Control ID
☑	Check Box	Displays a box that is either checked or unchecked	chk
	Combo Box	Combines and displays a text box with a list box	cbo
	Command Button	Performs instructions when clicked	cmd
	Frame	Provides a visual and functional container for controls	fra
	Image	Displays a picture	img
A	Label	Displays text that the user cannot change	lbl
	List Box	Displays a list of choices from which a user can select	lst
	Multi Page	Presents multiple screens of information as a single set	mpg
	Option Button	Displays a button that can be either on or off	opt
	Scroll Bar	Displays a scroll bar containing a range of values	scr
	Select Objects	Selects objects; this tool does not create a control	
	Spin Button	Increments and decrements numbers	spn
	Tab Strip	Presents a set of related controls as a visual group	tab
abl	Text Box	Accepts or displays text that the user can change	txt
	Toggle Button	Shows the selection state of an item	tog

Figure 12-5: Basic tools included in the toolbox

> If you have trouble distinguishing the tools in the toolbox, you can display a ToolTip containing the tool's name by resting the mouse pointer on the tool.

> The toolbox in Access will differ from that shown in Figure 12-5.

Figure 12-5 lists only the basic tools included in the toolbox. You can add additional tools to the toolbox by right-clicking an empty area on the Controls tab in the Toolbox window and then clicking Additional Controls on the shortcut menu. You can delete existing tools by right-clicking the tool in the toolbox and then clicking Delete <toolname> on the shortcut menu.

You can add a control to a form simply by dragging the appropriate tool to the desired location on the form. For example, dragging the Label tool $\boxed{A}$ from the toolbox to the form will place a default-size label control on the form.

> You will learn other ways of adding a control to a form, as well as how to select, align, and size more than one control at a time, in this lesson's Exercise 3.

To add a default-size label, text box, and command button to the form:

1 Drag the **Label** tool $\boxed{A}$ from the toolbox to the upper-left corner of the form, then release the mouse button. (Don't worry about the exact location.) The Visual Basic Editor adds a default-size label control to the form, as shown in Figure 12-6 (on the next page).

HELP? If a different control appears, press the Delete key to remove the incorrect control, then repeat Step 1.

The Visual Basic Editor assigns Label1 as the default setting for the first label control's Name and Caption properties. (You can verify this by looking in the Properties window.) The caption appears inside the label control.

2 Drag the **TextBox** tool $\boxed{abl}$ from the toolbox to the lower-right corner of the form, then release the mouse button. (Don't worry about the exact location.) The Visual Basic Editor adds a default-size text box control, named TextBox1, to the form.

Notice that, unlike a label control, no text appears inside a text box control when the text box is added to the form. Scanning the Properties list also shows that a text box control does not have a Caption property, as does a label control. The contents of a text box are controlled by the Text box's Text property, whose Settings box is currently empty.

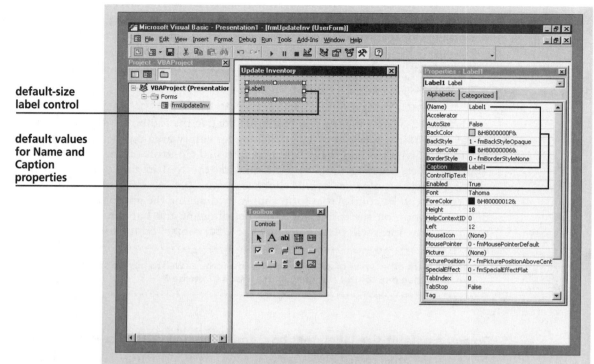

default-size label control

default values for Name and Caption properties

Figure 12-6: Default-size label control

3   Drag the **CommandButton** tool ⬛ from the toolbox to the center of the form, then release the mouse button. (Don't worry about the exact location.) The Visual Basic Editor adds a default-size command button control to the form, setting its Caption and Name properties to CommandButton1. The caption appears inside the command button control.

Change the command button's caption to Exit, and assign the letter x as the button's accelerator key.

4   Click **Caption** in the Properties list, and then type **Exit** and press the **Enter** key. Click **Accelerator** in the Properties list, and then type **x** and press the **Enter** key. The letter x appears underlined in the button's caption.

Programmers typically give meaningful names to the form and to any controls that will be either coded or referred to in code. Programmers leave the names of those controls that are not coded and are not referred to in code at their default values. Later in this lesson, you will code the Exit command button, so you should assign a more meaningful name to it. Recall from Figure 12-5 that the three-character ID used in command button names is *cmd*.

5   Click **(Name)** in the Properties list, and then type **cmdExit** and press the **Enter** key. The name, cmdExit, appears in the Object box and in the Settings box, as shown in Figure 12-7.

Object box

handles appear around the control to indicate that it is selected

caption and accelerator key

current values of properties

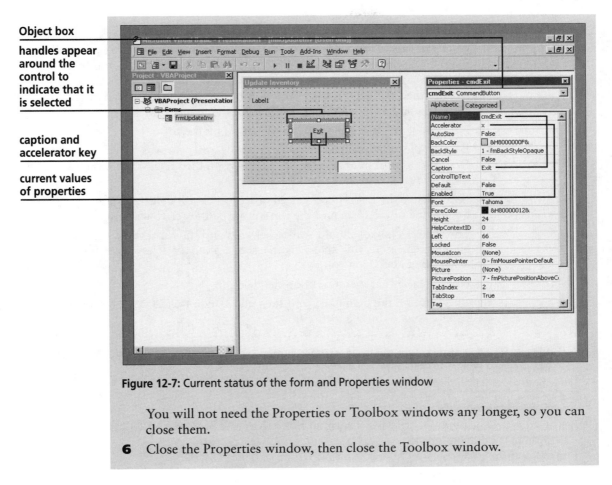

Figure 12-7: Current status of the form and Properties window

You will not need the Properties or Toolbox windows any longer, so you can close them.

6 Close the Properties window, then close the Toolbox window.

Now practice sizing, moving, deleting, and restoring a control.

Sizing, Moving, Deleting, and Restoring a Control

You size, move, and delete an object in the Visual Basic Editor in the same manner as you do in any Windows application. First, you must select the object that you want to size, move, or delete; you can select a control by clicking it. When a control is selected, handles appear around it. For example, notice the handles around the command button control in Figure 12-7 indicating that the control is selected.

If you inadvertently delete a control, you can use the Undo Delete Object option on the Edit menu to restore the control on the form.

To size, move, delete, and restore the Label1 control:

1   Click the **Label1 control** to select it. Handles appear around the control. Place the mouse pointer on the control's lower-right handle until the mouse pointer becomes a double arrow ⬊, then drag the handle until the label is slightly smaller than the default size. (You don't need to worry about the exact size.) When the label is the desired size, release the mouse button.

Now move the label to a different location on the form.

2   Position the mouse pointer anywhere on the Label1 control, except on a handle. Drag the control to another area of the screen, then release the mouse button. (Don't worry about the exact location.)

Next, delete the Label1 control. In order to delete a control, the control must be selected in the form and the form must be the active window.

3   The Label1 control should still be selected and the form's title bar should be highlighted, indicating that it is the active window. Press the **Delete** key to delete the Label1 control.

Now use the Edit menu to undo the deletion.

4   Click **Edit** on the menu bar, and then click **Undo Delete Object** to restore the Label1 control on the form.

You also can use the Undo *<action>* button 🔄 on the Visual Basic Editor's Standard toolbar to undo your last action.

If you want to use a form in more than one project, you will need to save it to a file on a disk.

Saving a Form

The process of saving a form to a file on a disk is referred to as **exporting**. After a form has been exported—in other words, after it has been saved to a file on a disk—you can add the form to one or more projects.

To save the current form to a file on a disk:

1   Right-click **frmUpdateInv** in the Project Explorer window, and then click **Export File** on the shortcut menu. The Export File dialog box opens.

You also can use the Export File option on the File menu to open the Export File dialog box.

2   If necessary, open the Tut12 folder on your Data Disk, then open the Concept folder located in the Tut12 folder. Change the filename in the File name text box to **Update Inventory,** as shown in Figure 12-8.

open the
Concept folder
contained in
the Tut12
folder on your
Data Disk

filename

default file
format

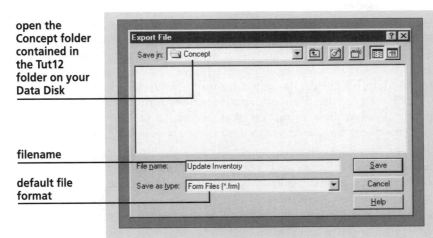

Figure 12-8: Export File dialog box

> When you click the Save button in the Export File dialog box, the file will be saved with an .frm extension on its name; the .frm stands for form.
>
> **3** Click the **Save** button to save (export) the file as Update Inventory.frm in the Tut12\Concept folder on your Data Disk.

Next, learn how to remove a form from the current project, and also how to add an existing form to the current project.

Removing and Adding an Existing Form

You can remove an existing form from a project by right-clicking the form's name in the Project Explorer window and then clicking Remove *<formname>* on the shortcut menu. You can add an existing form to a project, a process referred to as **importing,** by right-clicking the Project Explorer window and then clicking Import File on the shortcut menu.

 tip

> You also can use the Remove *<formname>* option on the File menu to remove a form from a project, and you can use the Import File option on the File menu to add an existing form to a project.

To remove the frmUpdateInv form from the project, and then add an existing form to the project:

1 Right-click **frmUpdateInv** in the Project Explorer window, then click **Remove frmUpdateInv** on the shortcut menu. A dialog box containing the message "Do you want to export frmUpdateInv before removing it?" appears. The dialog box also contains four buttons: Yes, No, Cancel, and Help.

Clicking the Yes button displays the Export File dialog box, allowing you to save the form before it is removed from the project. Clicking the No button removes the form from the current project without saving the form. Clicking the Cancel button closes the dialog box without removing the form, and clicking the Help button displays an appropriate Help screen. In this case, you will click the No button to remove the form without saving it. The form was already saved in the previous set of steps and, since you have made no changes to it since it was saved, there is no reason to save it again.

2 Click the **No** button to remove the form without saving it. The Project Explorer window shows that the frmUpdateInv form was removed from the project. Because the project no longer contains any forms, the Forms folder also was removed from the project.

Now add to the project the form that you just removed. Recall that the name of the form file on your Data Disk is Update Inventory.frm.

3 Right-click the **Project Explorer window**, and then click **Import File** on the shortcut menu. The Import File dialog box opens and shows the contents of the Concept folder contained in the Tut12 folder on your Data Disk. Click **Update Inventory** (Update Inventory.frm) in the list of filenames, as shown in Figure 12-9.

select this
filename

open the
Concept folder
contained in
the Tut12
folder on your
Data Disk

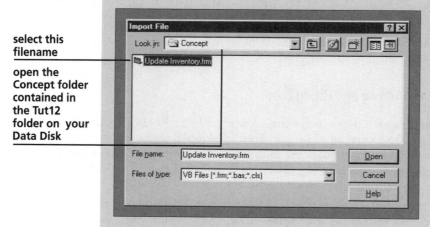

Figure 12-9: Import File dialog box

HELP? If the Tutorial 12's Concept folder is not open, use the Look in list box to open it.

4 Click the **Open** button to add the form contained in the Update Inventory file to the project. A Forms folder appears in the Project Explorer window.

5 Open the **Forms** folder in the Project Explorer window. Notice that the name of the form contained in the Update Inventory file, frmUpdateInv, appears in the Forms folder.

6 Right-click **frmUpdateInv** in the Project Explorer window, and then click **View Object** on the shortcut menu to view the form.

You will not need the Project Explorer window any longer, so you can close it.

7 Close the Project Explorer window.

Next, learn how to have a procedure display a custom dialog box on the screen, and also remove a custom dialog box from the screen and the computer's memory, while the procedure is running.

Displaying and Removing a Custom Dialog Box

You use the form's **Show method** to bring the custom dialog box into the computer's memory and then display it on the screen, and you use the **Unload statement** to remove the dialog box from both the screen and memory. The syntax of the Show method is *formName*.**Show**, and the syntax of the Unload statement is **Unload** *formName*. Notice that the method name (Show) comes *after* the form name and the dot member selection operator in the syntax. The statement name (Unload), on the other hand, comes *before* the form name, and no dot member selection operator appears in the syntax.

The Show method also has a Style argument that specifies whether the form is modal or modeless. A modal form is one that requires the user to close the dialog box before he or she can continue working in the current application. The Open dialog box is an example of a modal dialog box. A modeless dialog box is one that can remain open while the user is working in the current application. The Help window is an example of a modeless dialog box. To learn more about the Style argument, view the Help screen for a form's Show method.

Recall that the method for displaying and removing a dialog box in Access differs from the methods you are learning in this lesson.

For a custom dialog box to perform one or more tasks, you need to code it. In the next section, you will learn some general information about coding a custom dialog box. You also will code the current form's Exit button so that it uses the Unload statement to remove the dialog box from the screen and memory.

Coding a Custom Dialog Box

Think about the Windows environment for a moment. Did you ever wonder why the OK and Cancel buttons respond the way they do when you click them? The answer to this question is very simple: a programmer gave the buttons explicit instructions on how to respond to the user's action—in this case, the action of clicking the button.

Actions performed by the user—such as clicking, double-clicking, and scrolling—are called **events**. You tell an object how to respond to an event by writing an event procedure. Similar to the procedures created in previous tutorials, **event procedures** are blocks of instructions that perform a task. However, event procedures run in response to an event rather than in response to running a macro.

As you learned earlier, a dialog box is composed of a form and controls. The form, as well as each of the controls on the form, has its own set of event procedures—one procedure for each of the events the object can recognize. Each procedure has a code template that can be viewed in the Visual Basic Editor's Code window. You can open an object's Code window by right-clicking the object and then clicking View Code on the shortcut menu.

To open, code, and then run the Exit command button's Click event procedure:

1 Right-click the **Exit** command button on the current form, and then click **View Code** on the shortcut menu. The Code window opens and displays the code template for the cmdExit control's Click event procedure, as shown in Figure 12-10.

event name

object name

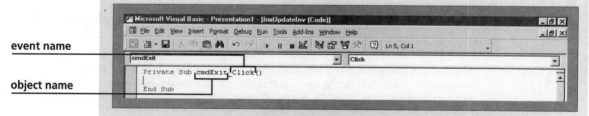

Figure 12-10: Code template for the cmdExit control's Click event procedure

> **tip**
>
> You also can double-click an object to open its Code window.

The code template indicates the name of the object (cmdExit) as well as the name of the event (Click). Between the `Private Sub` and `End Sub` lines, you enter the VBA instructions that should be processed when the event occurs on the object.

> **tip**
>
> UserForm, rather than the name of the form, appears in the code templates for a form. For example, the Click event procedure for a form begins with `Private Sub UserForm_Click`.

Now code the Exit button's Click event procedure so that it removes the form from the screen and from the computer's memory when the user clicks the button. Recall that you use the Unload statement to do so.

2 Press the **Tab** key, then type **unload frmupdateinv** and press the **Enter** key.

Keep in mind that a command button's Click event occurs when the user clicks the command button or when he or she presses the Enter key when the command button has the focus. If the command button is the default button, and no other command button in the dialog box has the focus, pressing the Enter key also will invoke the default button's Click event.

As you learned in Tutorial 1, you can use the Code window's Procedure list box to view the other event procedures an object can recognize.

3   Click the **Procedure box list arrow** to display the event procedures recognized by a command button control.

The scroll bars on the list box indicate that not all of the event procedures are currently displayed. You would need to scroll up and down the list box to view the remaining event procedures. To change to another event procedure, you simply click the one you want in the list.

4   Click the **Procedure box list arrow** to close the list of event procedures.

You can use the Code window's Object box to switch to another object.

5   Click the **Object box list arrow**, then click **TextBox1** in the list. The text box's Code window opens and displays its Change event.

Now return to the cmdExit control's Code window.

6   Click the **Object box list arrow**, then click **cmdExit** in the list. The cmdExit control's Click event appears in the Code window.

Before testing the Click event procedure to verify that it will work correctly, save the form to your Data Disk.

7   Click **File** on the menu bar, and then click **Export File**. If necessary, open the **Concept** folder contained in the Tut12 folder on your Data Disk. Click **Update Inventory** (Update Inventory.frm) in the list of filenames, and then click the **Save** button. When you are asked if you want to replace the file, click the **Yes** button.

Now test the Click event procedure to verify that it will work correctly.

8   Click the **Run Sub/UserForm** button ▶ on the Standard toolbar. The custom dialog box appears on the screen, as shown in Figure 12-11.

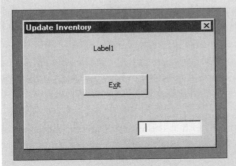

Figure 12-11: Custom dialog box

9 Click the **Exit** button to unload the custom dialog box. The dialog box closes and you are returned to the Visual Basic Editor.

10 Close the Visual Basic Editor, then close the application. You do not need to save the PowerPoint presentation, Excel workbook, or Word document.

You now have completed Tutorial 12's Concept lesson. You can either take a break or complete the end-of-lesson questions and exercises before moving on to the next lesson.

SUMMARY

To create a custom dialog box:

■ Add a form to the project, then add controls to the form. The form's title bar should contain a caption, entered using book title capitalization, that identifies the purpose of the dialog box. It also should contain a Close button , but no Minimize or Maximize buttons. The user should not be able to size the dialog box by dragging its borders.

■ Align the controls wherever possible to minimize the number of different margins on the form.

To follow the Windows standards for controls:

■ Use a label control to display text that you don't want the user to modify. Label controls used to identify other controls should have captions that are no more than three words in length and entered using sentence capitalization. The entire caption should appear on one line in the control and it should end with a colon (:). Left-align the caption within the label control and position the label control either above or to the left of the control it identifies. The information displayed in a label control is contained in the control's Caption property.

■ Use a text box control to provide an area in the dialog box where data can be entered. The information is stored in the control's Text property. Use a label control to identify the text box.

■ Use a command button control to process one or more instructions as soon as the button is clicked. The caption, which is stored in the control's Caption property, should be no more than three words in length and entered using book title capitalization. The entire caption should appear on one line in the control.

■ Position the command buttons either at the bottom or on the right side of the dialog box. The command buttons can be placed side by side or they can be stacked.

- Group related command buttons together by positioning them close to each other in the dialog box. The most commonly used command button in the group should be placed first. Buttons unrelated to a specific group can be situated away from the group, if desired.

- Provide keyboard access to the essential controls in the dialog box using accelerator keys.

To select an appropriate accelerator key for a control:

- Use the first letter of the control's caption, unless another letter provides a more meaningful association. If you can't use the first letter and no letter provides a more meaningful association, then use a distinctive consonant in the caption. The last choices for an accelerator key are a vowel or a number in the caption.

To specify a command button as the default button:

- Set the command button's Default property to True. The default button can be selected by pressing the Enter key, even when the button does not have the focus. (However, if another command button has the focus, pressing the Enter key will select that button rather than the default button.)

To specify a command button as the cancel button:

- Set the command button's Cancel property to True. The cancel button can be selected by pressing the Esc key.

To add a form to the project in all Microsoft Office applications except Access:

- Click Insert on the menu bar, and then click UserForm.

To change the properties of an object:

- Use the Properties window.

To add a control to a form:

- Drag the appropriate tool from the toolbox to the form.

To size a control:

- Drag one of the handles that appears around the control.

To move a control to another location on the screen:

- Position the mouse pointer anywhere on the control, except on a handle, and then drag the control to the desired location.

To delete a control:

■ Select the control on the form, and then press the Delete key. In order to delete a control, the control must be selected in the form and the form must be the active window.

To restore a control that was deleted:

■ Click Edit on the menu bar, and then click Undo Delete Object. You also can use the Undo Delete Object button ⟳ on the Visual Basic Editor's Standard toolbar.

To save a form to a file on a disk:

■ Right-click the form's name in the Project Explorer window, and then click Export File. Enter the location and name of the file in the Export File dialog box, and then click the Save button.

To remove an existing form from a project:

■ Right-click the form's name in the Project Explorer window and then click Remove *<formname>*.

To add an existing form to a project:

■ Right-click the Project Explorer window and then click Import File. Click the filename in the Import File dialog box and then click the Open button.

To have a procedure display a custom dialog box on the screen:

■ Use the Show method, whose syntax is *formName.***Show**.

To have a procedure remove a form from both the screen and the computer's memory:

■ Use the Unload statement, whose syntax is **Unload** *formName*.

To open an object's Code window:

■ Right-click the object, and then click View Code. You also can double-click an object to open its Code window.

To have an object respond to an event in a particular way:

■ Enter VBA instructions in the appropriate event procedure for the object.

 **R E V I E W   Q U E S T I O N S**

1. Which of the following is false?
   a. A dialog box's title bar contains the Close, Minimize, and Maximize buttons.
   b. A dialog box's title bar contains a caption that identifies the purpose of the dialog box.
   c. Custom dialog boxes are created using a form and controls.
   d. A dialog box's caption is entered using book title capitalization.

2. Which of the following controls provides an area in which the user can enter data?
   a. command button
   b. label
   c. text box
   d. All of the above.

3. You use the _____ control to display text that identifies other controls in the dialog box.
   a. command button
   b. label
   c. text box
   d. All of the above.

4. Command button captions should be entered using _____.
   a. book title capitalization
   b. sentence capitalization
   c. Either of the above.

5. The OK button typically is the _____ button in a dialog box.
   a. cancel
   b. default
   c. first
   d. last

6. The _____ brings a form into the computer's memory and also displays it on the screen.
   a. Display statement
   b. Display method
   c. Load statement
   d. Show method

7. The _____ removes a form from the computer's memory and from the screen.
   a. Erase method
   b. Hide method
   c. Remove statement
   d. Unload statement

8. Actions performed on an object by the user are called _____.
   a. events
   b. happenings
   c. occurrences
   d. procedures

9. The information entered into a text box control is stored in the control's
    _____ property.
    a. Caption
    b. Entry
    c. Text
    d. Words

10. The information appearing in a label control is stored in the control's _____
    property.
    a. Caption
    b. Entry
    c. Text
    d. Words

11. Saving a form to a file on a disk is referred to as _____.
    a. archiving
    b. exporting
    c. filing
    d. importing

E X E R C I S E S

1. Figure 12-12 shows a custom dialog box that does not follow the Windows standards.
    Identify what is wrong with the dialog box's design.

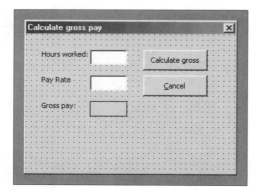

Figure 12-12

2. Figure 12-13 shows a custom dialog box that does not follow the Windows standards.
    Identify what is wrong with the dialog box's design.

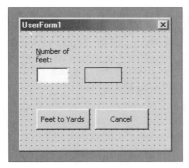

Figure 12-13

3. In this exercise, you will learn other ways of adding a control to a form. You also will learn how to select, align, and size more than one control at a time.

   a. Start PowerPoint, Excel, or Word, opening a new presentation, workbook, or document, respectively.

   b. Open the Visual Basic Editor. Click Insert on the menu bar, and then click UserForm.

   As you learned in this lesson, you can add a default-size control to the form by dragging a tool from the toolbox.

   c. Drag the Label tool **A** from the toolbox to the upper-left corner of the form.

   You also can add a default-size control to the form by clicking the tool and then clicking the form.

   d. Click the Label tool **A** in the toolbox, then click an area located in the lower-right corner of the form.

   Another way of adding a control to the form is to click the tool, place the mouse pointer on the form, and then drag.

   e. Click the Label tool **A** in the toolbox. Place the mouse pointer in the center of the form, then hold down the left mouse button as you drag down and to the right. When the control is the desired size, release the mouse button.

   Now select the three controls on the form.

   f. Click one of the label controls on the form, then press and hold down the Ctrl key as you click the remaining two label controls.

   Notice that, when you select more than one control, the handles for the last control selected are white, whereas the handles for the other selected controls are black. The Format menu's Align and Make Same Size commands use the control with the white handles as the reference control when aligning and sizing the selected controls. Use the Format menu's Align command to align the three label controls by their left-most edges.

   g. Click Format, point to Align, and then click Lefts. The Visual Basic Editor aligns the left border of the first two controls you selected with the left border of the reference control, which is the last control you selected.

   The Format menu's Make Same Size command makes the selected controls the same height *or* width, or it makes the selected controls the same height *and* width. Here again, the size is determined by the last control you select, which is the one with the white handles.

h. If the label controls on the form are the same size, use their handles to size them differently. Select the three label controls, if necessary. Click Format, point to Make Same Size, and then click Both. The Visual Basic Editor changes the height and width of the first two controls you selected to match the height and width of the reference control. Click the form to deselect the label controls.

i. Close the application. You do not need to save the presentation, workbook, or document.

Exercise 4 is a Discovery Exercise. Discovery Exercises, which may include topics that are not covered in the lesson, allow you to "discover" the solutions to problems on your own.

discovery ▶ 4. In this exercise, you will use the Help screens to research properties of the label, text box, and command button controls.

a. Start PowerPoint, Excel, or Word, opening a new presentation, workbook, or document, respectively.

b. Open the Visual Basic Editor. Click Insert on the menu bar and then click UserForm. The Visual Basic Editor adds a form to the project; it also displays the Toolbox window. (If the Toolbox window is not displayed, click View on the menu bar and then click Toolbox.)

c. Place the mouse pointer on the ⒜ tool in the toolbox. A ToolTip appears and indicates that this is the Label tool. Drag the Label tool to the form. The Visual Basic Editor adds a label control to the form. Press the F1 key to display the Label Control Help screen. Read the Help screen, then display the Help screens for a label control's AutoSize, BorderStyle, and Caption properties. Briefly describe the purpose of these properties. Close the Help window.

d. Locate the TextBox tool ⒜bl in the toolbox, then drag the TextBox tool to the form. Press the F1 key to display the TextBox Control Help screen. Read the Help screen, then display the Help screens for a text box control's ControlTipText and Text properties. Briefly describe the purpose of these properties. Close the Help window.

e. Locate the CommandButton tool ▭ in the toolbox, then drag the CommandButton tool to the form. Press the F1 key to display the CommandButton Control Help screen. Read the Help screen, then display the Help screens for a command button control's Cancel and Default properties. Briefly describe the purpose of these properties. Close the Help window.

f. Close the application. You do not need to save the presentation, workbook, or document.

You also can use VBA in PowerPoint to create procedures that enhance your presentations. Exercise 5 allows you to apply this tutorial's programming concept in a PowerPoint presentation.

powerpoint ▬ 5. In this exercise, you will display a custom dialog box that will allow the user to enter a company name on a slide.

a. Start PowerPoint. Open the T12-PP-E5 (T11-PP-E5.ppt) presentation, which is located in the Tut12\Concept folder on your Data Disk. Click the Enable Macros button, if necessary, then save the presentation as T12-PP-E5D.

b. Open the Visual Basic Editor, then open the Project Explorer window. If necessary, right-click frmCompany in the Forms folder, and then click View Object to view the form. The custom dialog box allows the user to enter the company name. If necessary, close the Toolbox window.

c. Right-click the OK button on the form, and then click Properties. Notice that this command button's Default property is set to True, which means the user will be able to select this button by pressing the Enter key, even when the button does not have the focus.

d. Click the Cancel button on the form. Notice that this command button's Cancel property is set to True, which means the user will be able to select this button by pressing the Esc key.

e. Close the Properties window. Right-click the OK button on the form, then click View Code. The OK command button's Click event procedure assigns the company name, entered by the user, to the second shape on the first slide. The procedure then removes the form from both the computer's memory and the screen. Close the Code window.

f. Right-click the Cancel button on the form, and then click View Code. The Cancel button's Click event procedure should remove the form from both the computer's memory and the screen. Enter the appropriate command, then close the Code window.

g. Open the Module1 module's Code window, then view the code template for the EnterCompany procedure. Enter the instruction that will display the frmCompany form on the screen. Close the Code window.

h. Save the presentation, then return to PowerPoint and view the slide show. Click the *Click to enter company name* hyperlink that appears on the first slide. When the Enter Company Name dialog box appears, press the Esc key to select the Cancel button, which closes the dialog box, removing it from both the computer's memory and the screen.

i. View the slide show again. Click the *Click to enter company name* hyperlink. When the Enter Company Name dialog box appears, enter ABC Company as the company name, then press the Enter key to select the OK button. The OK button enters ABC Company on the first slide and then it closes the dialog box.

j. Press the Esc key to stop the slide show. Save and then close the presentation.

A computer program is good only if it works. Errors in programming code can cause a program to run incorrectly. Therefore, a programmer needs to know how to locate and fix any errors in his or her code. Exercise 6 is a Debugging Exercise. Debugging Exercises allow you to practice recognizing and solving errors in code.

debugging 　**6.** The procedure shown in Figure 12-14 is not working correctly. It should remove the frmUpdate form from the screen and memory when the user clicks the Cancel command button, the name of which is cmdCancel. Correct any errors in the procedure.

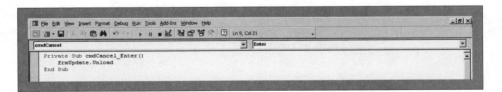

Figure 12-14

Excel Lesson

Using Custom Dialog Boxes in Excel

case▶ Jake Yardley, the manager of the Paradise Electronics store in Jackson, uses an Excel workbook to keep track of the store's computer inventory. At the end of each day, Jake updates each computer's inventory amount by subtracting the number sold from the number in stock. Jake has decided to create a macro that uses a custom dialog box to help him perform the updates.

Viewing the Inventory Worksheet

The workbook in which Jake records the store's computer inventory is stored on your Data Disk. Before creating the macro and custom dialog box that Jake will use to update the inventory amounts, view the workbook.

To view the workbook:

1 Start Microsoft Excel. Open the **T12-EX-1** (T12-EX-1.xls) workbook, which is located in the Tut12\Excel folder on your Data Disk.

2 Save the workbook as **Computer Inventory**.

The Computer Inventory workbook contains one worksheet named Inventory, as shown in Figure 12-15.

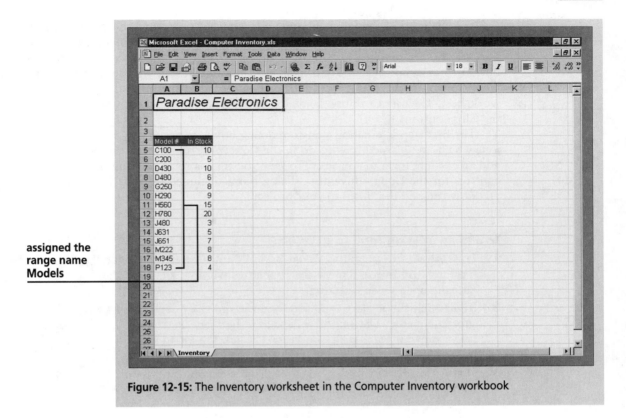

Figure 12-15: The Inventory worksheet in the Computer Inventory workbook

The Inventory worksheet shows the model number of each type of computer sold at Paradise Electronics. It also shows the current quantity in stock for each model. The range A5:A18 was assigned the range name Models to make it easier to refer to this range in code. (The code will need to search the Models range for the model number whose inventory amount should be updated.)

Figure 12-16 shows a sketch of the custom dialog box that you will create in this lesson.

```
Update Inventory

    Model number:    [          ]        Update

    Number sold:     [          ]        Cancel


    Updated amount:  [          ]
```

Figure 12-16: Sketch of the custom dialog box

The dialog box shown in Figure 12-16 consists of a form and eight controls: four labels, two text boxes, and two command buttons. After entering the model number and the number sold in the two text boxes, the user can click the Update button to calculate the updated inventory amount, which will be displayed in a label control in the dialog box and also entered into the appropriate cell in the worksheet. The user can close the dialog box by clicking either the Cancel button or the Close button ☒.

The first step in creating a custom dialog box is to add a new form to the project, which you learned how to do in the Concept lesson. Recall that you also can add an existing form to a project. To save you time, a form containing the required controls for the Update Inventory dialog box is included on your Data Disk, and you now can add that form to your project.

To add an existing form to a project:

1 Press **Alt+F11** to open the Visual Basic Editor. If necessary, open the Project Explorer window and close the Properties window, the Immediate window, and any open Code windows.

2 Right-click the **Project Explorer window** and then click **Import File** on the shortcut menu. The Import File dialog box opens. Open the Tut12\Excel folder on your Data Disk, if necessary. Click **T12-EX-1** (T12-EX-1.frm) in the list of filenames and then click the **Open** button.

3 Open the **Forms folder** in the Project Explorer window. Right-click **frmUpdateInv** in the Forms folder and then click **View Object** on the shortcut menu. If necessary, close the Toolbox window. The partially completed frmUpdateInv form appears, as shown in Figure 12-17.

form name

consistent
margin of
two dots

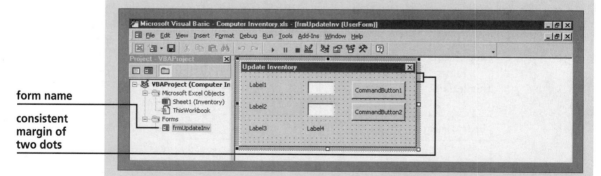

Figure 12-17: The partially completed frmUpdateInv form

Following the Windows standard, the form maintains a consistent margin—in this case, a margin of two dots—around its border. Also, the controls are aligned to minimize the number of different margins appearing in the interface.

You will not need the Project Explorer window anymore, so you can close it.

4 Close the Project Explorer window.

Now set the appropriate properties for each control. The first property you will set is the Name property.

> Some programmers create the entire interface before setting each object's properties, while others change the properties of each object as the object is added to the form. Either way will work, so it's really just a matter of preference.

Setting the Name Property

As you learned in the Concept lesson, the form and any controls that will be either coded or referred to in code should have their default name changed to a more meaningful one. The form's name already has been changed from UserForm1 to frmUpdateInv; you now need to change the appropriate control names. Figure 12-18 lists the eight controls, their status (whether they will be coded or referred to in code), and their new names, if applicable.

Default Name	Status	New Name
CommandButton1	Coded	cmdUpdate
CommandButton2	Coded	cmdCancel
Label1	Not coded or referred to in code	
Label2	Not coded or referred to in code	
Label3	Not coded or referred to in code	
Label4	Referred to in code	lblUpdated
TextBox1	Referred to in code	txtModel
TextBox2	Referred to in code	txtNumSold

Figure 12-18: Controls included in the Update Inventory dialog box

Notice that only five of the eight controls will need to have their name changed. You will not need to change the names of the three identifying labels (Label1, Label2, and Label3), because those controls will not be coded or referred to in code.

To set the Name property for five of the controls:

1 Right-click the **CommandButton1** control, then click **Properties** on the short-cut menu. Click **(Name)** in the Properties list, then type **cmdUpdate** and press the **Enter** key.

2 Change the CommandButton2 control's name to **cmdCancel** and change the Label4 control's name to **lblUpdated**. Also change the names of the TextBox1 and TextBox2 controls to **txtModel** and **txtNumSold**, respectively.

> You can select a control by clicking the control on the form, or you can use the Object list box in the Properties window to select the control.

3 Save the workbook.

Next, you will set the Caption property for the command button and label controls.

Setting the Caption Property

Label controls and command buttons have a Caption property that controls the text appearing inside the control. When a label or command button is added to the form, its default name is assigned to the Caption property. In the next set of steps, you will change the captions of the labels and command buttons appropriately.

> Recall that text boxes do not have a Caption property. The text appearing inside a text box is stored in the control's Text property, which is empty when a text box is added to the form.

To set the Caption property for the label and command button controls:

1 Click the **Label1** control to select it. Recall that a label control's caption should end with a colon and it should be entered using sentence capitalization. Click **Caption** in the Properties list, and then type **Model number:** and press the **Enter** key.

2 Change the Label2 control's Caption property to **Number sold:** and change the Label3 control's Caption property to **Updated amount:**.

3 Click the **Label4** control to select it. This time, double-click **Caption** in the Properties list; this selects the Label4 caption in the Settings box. Press the **Delete** key to remove the selected caption, then press the **Enter** key.

HELP? If the Label4 caption is not selected in the Settings box, double-click the Caption property again until the Label4 caption is selected. You also can drag the mouse over the caption in the Settings box to select it.

> Be sure to use either the Delete key or the Backspace key, rather than the Spacebar, to delete the highlighted text in the Settings box. Pressing the Spacebar does not clear the property's contents; rather, it replaces the highlighted text with a space.

4 Change the CommandButton1 caption to **Update** and change the CommandButton2 caption to **Cancel**.

5 Save the workbook.

Next, you will learn about the BorderStyle property.

Setting the BorderStyle Property

Many objects have a BorderStyle property that determines the style of the object's border. Label controls, for example, have a **BorderStyle property** that can be set to either 0 - fmBorderStyleNone or 1 - fmBorderStyleSingle. The 0 - fmBorderStyleNone setting displays the label control without a border, while the 1 - fmBorderStyleSingle setting displays the label control with a thin line around its border.

Label controls used as identifying labels should have their BorderStyle property left at the default setting, 0 - fmBorderStyleNone. However, you will typically set to 1 - fmBorderStyleSingle the BorderStyle property for label controls that display the results of calculations, such as the lblUpdated label in the Update Inventory dialog box.

To set the BorderStyle property of the lblUpdated label:

1 Click the **Object box** list arrow, located immediately below the Properties window's title bar, to display both the name and type of objects included in the dialog box. Click **lblUpdated Label** in the list. The lblUpdated control is selected on the form and its properties are displayed in the Properties window.

2 Click **BorderStyle** in the Properties list. A list arrow appears in the Settings box, indicating that this property has predefined settings.

3 Click the **Settings box list arrow** to view the valid settings for the BorderStyle property, then click **1 - fmBorderStyleSingle** in the list. A border appears around the lblUpdated control on the form.

Many controls also have an **AutoSize property**, which does just what its name implies: it automatically sizes the control to fit its current contents. You will use the AutoSize property to size the three identifying labels, which are slightly longer than their captions.

Changing the AutoSize Property for More Than One Control at a Time

You can set the AutoSize property for the three identifying labels individually, or you can change the property for the three controls at the same time. Before you can change a property for a group of controls, you need to select the controls. You do so by clicking one of the controls in the group and then pressing and holding down the Ctrl key as you click the other controls in the group. To deselect one of the selected controls, you press and hold down the Ctrl key as you click the control. To deselect all of the selected controls, you click the form or any unselected control on the form.

To set the AutoSize property for the three identifying labels:

1   Click the **Model number:** label. Press and hold down the **Ctrl** key as you click the **Number sold:** and **Updated amount:** labels, then release the Ctrl key. The three label controls now are selected, as the handles shown in Figure 12-19 indicate.

selected
controls

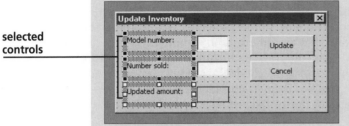

Figure 12-19: Three controls selected in the dialog box

> When more than one control is selected, the Properties window displays only the properties common to the selected controls.

Notice that the handles on the Updated amount: label are white, while the handles on the other selected labels are black. When you select more than one control, the last control you select will have white handles; the other selected controls will have black handles. The Format menu uses the control with the white handles as the reference control when aligning and sizing a group of controls. You can learn more about the reference control by completing Exercise 3 in this tutorial's Concept lesson.

> You also can select a group of contiguous controls on the form by placing the mouse pointer ⍾ slightly above and to the left of the first control you want to select, then pressing the left mouse button and dragging. A dotted rectangle will appear as you drag. When all of the controls you want to select are within the dotted rectangle, release the mouse button. All of the controls surrounded by the dotted rectangle will be selected.

2   Click **AutoSize** in the Properties list, and then click the **Settings box list arrow**. Click **True** in the list and then press the **Enter** key. The Visual Basic Editor sizes each of the selected controls to fit its current contents.

3   Click the **form** to deselect the selected controls.

Now move the text boxes and the lblUpdated control closer to their identifying labels.

4   Select the two text boxes and the lblUpdated label control. Position the mouse pointer on one of the controls, except on a handle, then drag the controls one dot to the left.

5   Click the **form** to deselect the controls, then save the workbook.

Next, provide keyboard access to the essential controls in the dialog box.

Providing Keyboard Access to Essential Controls

As you learned in the Concept lesson, you should provide keyboard access to each essential control on the form. Recall that a control is considered essential if it accepts user input. In the Update Inventory dialog box, the two text boxes and the two command buttons are essential controls. The four labels are not considered essential because the user does not have access to them.

You will use accelerator keys to provide keyboard access to the text boxes and to the Update command button. You will provide keyboard access to the Cancel button by designating it as the cancel button.

To provide keyboard access to the essential controls in the Update Inventory dialog box:

1 Click the **Cancel** button on the form, then click **Cancel** in the Properties list. Set the Cancel property to **True**.

Now use the Accelerator property to designate the letter U as the accelerator key for the Update command button.

2 Click the **Update** button on the form. Click **Accelerator** in the Properties list, then type **U** and press the **Enter** key. The letter U now is underlined in the button's caption.

3 Click the **txtModel** text box to select it.

Notice that, unlike command buttons, text boxes do not have an Accelerator property, nor do they have a Caption property. So how then can you provide keyboard access to a text box? You do so first by assigning the accelerator key to the text box's identifying label, which has both an Accelerator and a Caption property. You then use the TabIndex property, which you will learn about in the next section, to place the label control immediately before the text box in the tab order.

4 Click the **Model number:** label to select it, then set its Accelerator property to **M** (be sure to type an uppercase letter M). The letter M now is underlined in the label control's caption, indicating to the user that pressing the Alt key and the M key will access the Model number text box.

tip

> Entering a lowercase letter m as the Accelerator property would underline the m in the word "number."

5 Click the **Number sold:** label, then set its Accelerator property to the letter **N**.

To complete the dialog box's interface, you need only to set the tab order for the controls in the dialog box.

Setting the Tab Order

As you learned in the Concept lesson, the tab order is the order in which the focus moves from one essential control to the next essential control as you press the Tab key in a dialog box. The tab order is determined by the TabIndex property of the controls included in the dialog box. When you add a control to a form, the control's TabIndex property is set to a number that represents the order in which the control was added to the form. The TabIndex value for the first control added to a form is 0 (zero), the TabIndex value for the second control is 1, and so on.

The control whose TabIndex value is 0 will receive the focus first, because it is the first control in the tab order. When you press the Tab key, the focus will move to the second control in the tab order—the control whose TabIndex is 1—and so on. If a control cannot receive the focus (for example, label controls cannot receive the focus), the focus moves to the next control in the tab order.

Before you can set the TabIndex property of the controls, you need to determine where each essential control should fall in the tab order. In the Update Inventory dialog box, for example, the first essential control in the tab order should be the first text box, followed by the second text box, the Update command button, and the Cancel command button. It appears, then, that these controls should have TabIndex values of 0, 1, 2, and 3, respectively. However, recall that giving keyboard access to a text box requires that you not only assign an accelerator key to the text box's identifying label, but you also place the identifying label immediately before the text box in the tab order. Therefore, in addition to setting the TabIndex property of the essential controls, you also need to set the TabIndex property of label controls that identify essential controls, such as label controls that identify text boxes. The TabIndex property of controls other than these do not need to be changed. Figure 12-20 shows the TabIndex values for the appropriate controls in the Update Inventory dialog box.

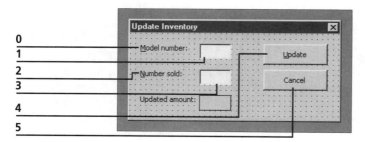

Figure 12-20: TabIndex values for essential controls and their identifying labels

Notice that each text box's identifying label has a TabIndex value that is one number less than its own TabIndex value; this places the identifying label before its corresponding text box in the tab order.

To set the TabIndex property of the controls, then run the dialog box to test it:

1 Click the **Model number:** label to select it, then click **TabIndex** in the Properties list. Verify that this label control's TabIndex value is set to the number 0.

2 Click the **txtModel** text box to select it, then click **TabIndex** in the Properties list. Type **1** (the number one) and press the **Enter** key.

3 Set the TabIndex property of the Number Sold: label, the txtNumSold textbox, the cmdUpdate command button, and the cmdCancel command button controls to **2**, **3**, **4**, and **5**, respectively.

 tip

You also can use the Tab Order dialog box to set the TabIndex property. To learn more about the Tab Order dialog box, complete this lesson's Exercise 5.

4 Save the workbook. Click the **form** to make it the active window, then click the **Run Sub/UserForm** button ▶ on the toolbar.

HELP? If the button says Run Macro rather than Run Sub/UserForm, click the form to select it. The form must be the active window for you to run it.

When the dialog box opens, the focus is sent to the control whose TabIndex value is 0; in this case, the focus is sent to the Model number: label control. Because a label control cannot receive the focus, the focus moves to the next control in the tab order; in this case, it moves to the txtModel text box.

5 Type **40** in the txtModel text box, then press the **Tab** key four times. The focus moves to the second text box, the Update button, the Cancel button, and then back to the first text box.

Notice that the txtModel control's existing text (40) is selected automatically when you tab to that control. It is customary in Windows applications for the existing text in a text box to be selected when the text box receives the focus. By doing so, the new text entered by the user will automatically replace the selected text.

Now verify that the accelerator keys and the Esc key work as intended.

6 Press **Alt+u**. The focus moves to the Update command button. Press **Alt+n** to move the focus to the txtNumSold text box. Press **Alt+m** to move the focus to the txtModel text box. Press the **Esc** key. The focus moves to the Cancel button.

7 Click the dialog box's **Close** button ✕. The dialog box closes and you return to the Visual Basic Editor.

You will not need the Properties window anymore, so you can close it.

8 Close the Properties window.

Now that you have completed the dialog box's interface, you can begin coding the necessary controls in the dialog box.

Coding the Controls in the Update Inventory Dialog Box

The first control you will code is the Cancel button, which should remove the form from both the screen and the computer's memory when the user selects the button. In this case, the user can select the Cancel button by clicking it, or by pressing the Esc key (recall that the button's Cancel property is set to True), or by pressing the Enter key when the button has the focus. When any of these actions occurs, the button's Click event is invoked.

To code the Cancel button's Click event, then test the procedure:

1   Right-click the **Cancel** button, then click **View Code** on the shortcut menu. The Code window opens and shows the code template for the cmdCancel button's Click event procedure.

Recall from the Concept lesson that you use the Unload statement to remove a form from both the screen and the computer's memory.

2   Press the **Tab** key, then type **unload frmupdateinv** and press the **Enter** key.

3   Close the Code window, then click the **Run Sub/UserForm** button [▶] to run the dialog box. Press the **Esc** key to select the Cancel button, thereby invoking its Click event procedure. The procedure closes the dialog box, removing the form from both the screen and the computer's memory.

The next control you will code is the Update command button, which the user can select either by clicking it or by pressing the Enter key when the button has the focus. In this case, the button's Click event should perform the tasks listed in Figure 12-21's pseudocode.

1. Assign the contents of the txtModel control, in uppercase letters, to a String variable named strModel.
2. Assign the contents of the txtNumSold control, treated as a number, to an Integer variable named intNumSold.
3. Repeat the following for each cell in the Models range:
   a. If the model number stored in the current cell is equal to the model number stored in the strModel variable, then
      1) Calculate the updated inventory amount by subtracting the contents of the intNumSold variable from the model's current inventory amount, which is contained in the cell located to the immediate right of the current cell in the worksheet. Assign the result to an Integer variable named intUpdated.
      2) Assign the contents of the intUpdated variable both to the lblUpdated control in the dialog box and to the cell located to the immediate right of the current cell in the worksheet.
      3) Exit the loop.

Figure 12-21: Pseudocode for the Update button's Click event procedure

Figure 12-22 lists the variables that the Update button's Click event procedure will use.

Variable	datatype
strModel	String
intNumSold	Integer
intUpdated	Integer
shtInventory	Worksheet
rngCell	Range

Figure 12-22: Variables used by the Update button's Click event procedure

The procedure will assign the user's input to the strModel and intNumSold variables, and it will assign the updated inventory amount, calculated by subtracting the number sold from the current inventory amount, to the intUpdated variable. The shtInventory variable will store the address of the Inventory worksheet. The rngCell variable will be used in a For Each...Next statement that repeats its instructions for each cell in the Models range.

In the next set of steps, you will declare the appropriate variables and then translate each line in Figure 12-21's pseudocode into one or more VBA statements.

To code the Update button's Click event procedure, then test the procedure:

1   Right-click the **Update** button, then click **View Code** on the shortcut menu to open the code template for the cmdUpdate control's Click event procedure. Enter the documentation and the Dim and Set statements shown in Figure 12-23.

enter these five
lines of code

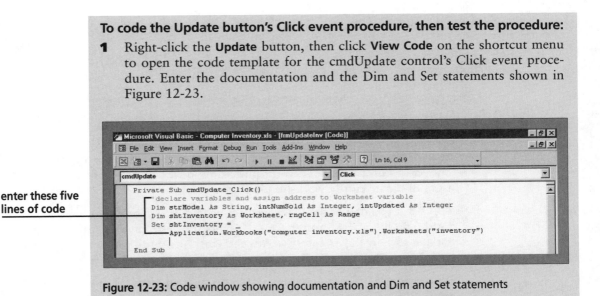

Figure 12-23: Code window showing documentation and Dim and Set statements

According to the pseudocode, you should assign the contents of both text boxes to variables. Recall that a text box control's contents are stored in the control's Text property.

2 Press the **Backspace** key to remove the indentation, then type **'assign user input to variables** and press the **Enter** key. Type **strmodel = ucase(txtmodel.text)** and press the **Enter** key, then type **intnumsold = val(txtnumsold.text)** and press the **Enter** key.

Next, enter the code that searches for the model number in the Models range and then calculates the model's updated inventory amount. Assign the updated amount to the Caption property of the lblUpdated control and also to the appropriate cell in the worksheet.

3 Type the additional instructions shown in Figure 12-24, which shows the completed Click event procedure for the cmdUpdate control.

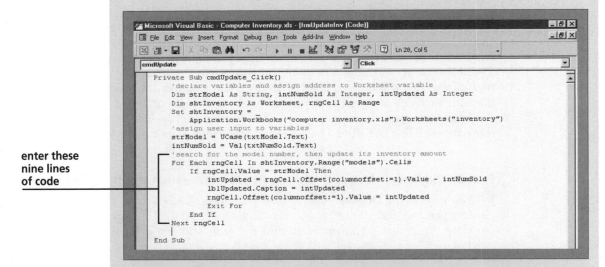

enter these nine lines of code

```
Private Sub cmdUpdate_Click()
    'declare variables and assign address to Worksheet variable
    Dim strModel As String, intNumSold As Integer, intUpdated As Integer
    Dim shtInventory As Worksheet, rngCell As Range
    Set shtInventory = _
        Application.Workbooks("computer inventory.xls").Worksheets("inventory")
    'assign user input to variables
    strModel = UCase(txtModel.Text)
    intNumSold = Val(txtNumSold.Text)
    'search for the model number, then update its inventory amount
    For Each rngCell In shtInventory.Range("models").Cells
        If rngCell.Value = strModel Then
            intUpdated = rngCell.Offset(columnoffset:=1).Value - intNumSold
            lblUpdated.Caption = intUpdated
            rngCell.Offset(columnoffset:=1).Value = intUpdated
            Exit For
        End If
    Next rngCell

End Sub
```

Figure 12-24: Completed Click event procedure for the cmdUpdate control

4 Save the workbook, then close the Code window. Click the **Run Sub/UserForm** button ▶ on the toolbar to run the dialog box. The dialog box appears in front of the Inventory worksheet in Excel.

HELP? If you do not see the worksheet behind the dialog box, close the dialog box. Click the Microsoft Excel - Computer Inventory.xls button on the taskbar to view the Inventory worksheet. Press Alt+F11 to return to the Visual Basic Editor, then run the dialog box again.

Notice that 10 C100 computers are currently in stock. Record the sale of two C100 computers.

5 In the Update Inventory dialog box, type **c100** as the model number. Press the **Tab** key, then type **2** as the number sold. Press the **Tab** key to move the focus to the Update button, then press the **Enter** key to select the Update button. The Update button's Click event procedure calculates the updated inventory amount (8) and displays the amount in the dialog box and in the worksheet, as shown in Figure 12-25.

updated inventory amount

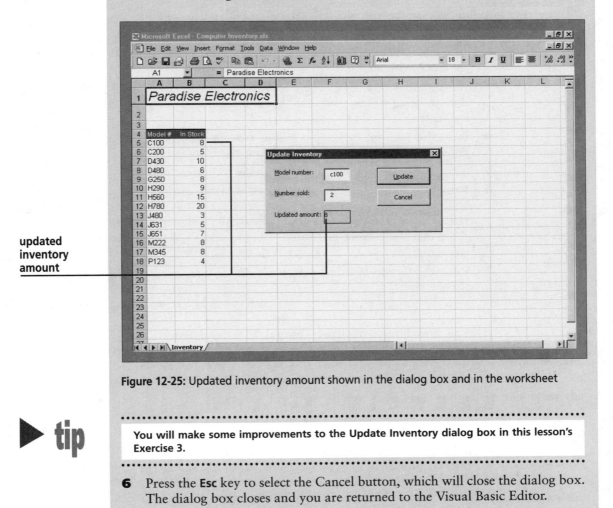

Figure 12-25: Updated inventory amount shown in the dialog box and in the worksheet

▶ **tip**

You will make some improvements to the Update Inventory dialog box in this lesson's Exercise 3.

6 Press the **Esc** key to select the Cancel button, which will close the dialog box. The dialog box closes and you are returned to the Visual Basic Editor.

Now that the custom dialog box has been created and tested, all that remains is to create a macro that will display the dialog box on the screen.

To create a macro that will display the Update Inventory dialog box, then test the macro:

1 In the Visual Basic Editor, click **Insert** on the menu bar and then click **Module** to add a module to the project.

2 Click **Insert** on the menu bar and then click **Procedure** to add a procedure to the module.

3 In the Add Procedure dialog box, type **UpdateInventory** as the procedure's name. Be sure the Sub and Public option buttons are selected, then click the **OK** button. The code template for the UpdateInventory procedure appears in the Code window.

As you learned in the Concept lesson, you use the Show method in a procedure to bring a dialog box into the computer's memory and also show it on the screen.

4 Press the **Tab** key, then type **'display custom dialog box** and press the **Enter** key. Type **frmupdateinv.show** and press the **Enter** key.

5 Close the Code window, then save the workbook.

6 Return to Excel and run the **UpdateInventory** macro. The custom Update Inventory dialog box appears on the screen. Use the dialog box to record the sale of three H560 computers and one P123 computer. The worksheet should show that the current inventory of H560 and P123 computers is 12 and 3, respectively.

7 Click the **Cancel** button to close the dialog box. Save the workbook, then close Excel.

You now have completed Tutorial 12's Excel lesson. You can either take a break or complete the end-of-lesson exercises before moving on to the next lesson.

 **EXERCISES**

1. In this exercise, you will create and code a custom dialog box that allows the user to enter an interest rate and to indicate whether he or she wants to publish the worksheet. You will use the workbook and macro created in Tutorial 7's Excel lesson.

   a. Open the T12-EX-E1 (T12-EX-E1.xls) workbook, which is located in the Tut12\Excel folder on your Data Disk. Click the Enable Macros button, if necessary, then save the workbook as T12-EX-E1D.

   b. Open the Visual Basic Editor. Open the Module1 module's Code window and view the PublishCalculator procedure. Study the procedure's code. (The filenames in the Set statements have already been changed for you. If necessary, change the drive and/or directory information.)

    c. Notice that the procedure uses two InputBox functions—one to get the rate and another to ask the user if he or she wants to publish the worksheet. Create one custom dialog box in which the user can enter both items of information. Include OK and Cancel buttons in the dialog box. The text box should display the letter Y when the custom dialog box first appears on the screen.

    d. Move the code from the PublishCalculator procedure to the OK button's Click event procedure. Remove the InputBox functions from the procedure, then make any other necessary changes to the Click event procedure. (Recall that the OK button should unload the dialog box after completing its task.)

    e. Code the Cancel button so that it unloads the custom dialog box.

    f. Code the PublishCalculator procedure so that it simply displays the custom dialog box.

    g. Return to Excel and save the workbook. Run the PublishCalculator macro. Publish the worksheet using 3 as the rate. When the message "Data was published to Web page" appears in a message box, click the OK button.

    h. Save and then close the workbook.

2. In this exercise, you will create and code a custom dialog box that allows the user to enter starting and ending times. You will use the workbook and macro created in Tutorial 5's Excel lesson.

    a. Open the T12-EX-E2 (T12-EX-E2.xls) workbook, which is located in the Tut12\Excel folder on your Data Disk. Click the Enable Macros button, if necessary, then save the workbook as T12-EX-E2D.

    b. Open the Visual Basic Editor. Open the Module1 module's Code window, then view the CalcHours procedure. Study the procedure's code. Notice that the procedure uses InputBox functions to get both the starting and ending time. Create one custom dialog box in which the user can enter both items of information. Include OK and Cancel buttons in the dialog box.

    c. Move the code from the CalcHours procedure to the OK button's Click event. Remove the InputBox functions from the procedure, then make any other necessary changes to the Click event procedure. Also change the CalcHours procedure so that it simply displays the form. Code the Cancel button appropriately.

    d. Save the workbook, then return to Excel. Click cell A4 in John Able's worksheet. Run the CalcHours macro. Enter 9am as the starting time and enter 3pm as the ending time, then click the OK button. The appropriate information appears in the worksheet, and the form is unloaded.

    e. Save and then close the workbook.

Exercises 3 through 5 are Discovery Exercises. Discovery Exercises, which may include topics that are not covered in the lesson, allow you to "discover" the solutions to problems on your own.

discovery ▶ **3.** In this exercise, you will make two improvements to the dialog box created in this lesson. Specifically, you will center the contents of the lblUpdated control and you will clear its contents when a change is made to either text box.

    a. Open the Computer Inventory (Computer Inventory.xls) workbook, which is located in the Tut12\Excel folder on your Data Disk. Click the Enable Macros button, if necessary, then save the workbook as T12-EX-E3D.

b. Open the Visual Basic Editor. Use the Project Explorer window to view the frmUpdateInv form. Click the lblUpdated control on the form. Display the Properties window, if necessary. Scan the Properties window, looking for a property that you can use to align the text that appears in the label control. Use the appropriate property to center the contents of the lblUpdated control. Close the Properties window.

c. Open the Update button's Click event procedure. Change the filename in the Set statement to "t12-ex-e3d.xls". Close the Code window.

d. When the user makes a change to the contents of either text box, the procedure should clear the contents of the lblUpdated control. Open the txtModel control's Change event procedure and enter the appropriate instruction. Also enter the instruction in the txtNumSold control's Change event procedure. Close the Code window.

e. Save the workbook, then return to Excel and run the UpdateInventory macro. Use the Update Inventory dialog box to record the sale of one C100 computer. The updated inventory amount (7) should be centered in the lblUpdated control.

f. Use the Update Inventory dialog box to record the sale of one C200 computer. (When you enter the model number, the txtModel control's Change event removes the contents of the lblUpdated control.) The updated inventory amount (4) appears centered in the lblUpdated control.

g. Click the Cancel button to close the dialog box. Save and then close the workbook.

discovery ▶ **4.** In this exercise, you will learn about the IsDate function. You will use the workbook and procedure you created in this lesson's Exercise 2.

a. Open the T12-EX-E2D (T12-EX-E2D.xls) workbook, which is located in the Tut12\Excel folder on your Data Disk. Click the Enable Macros button, if necessary, then save the workbook as T12-EX-E4D.

b. Open the Visual Basic Editor. Use the Project Explorer window to view the custom dialog box that you created in this lesson's Exercise 2. Open the OK button's Click event procedure.

c. Display the IsDate Function Help screen. Study the Help screen, then close the Help window.

d. Modify the OK button's Click event procedure so that it converts the strings to times and also enters the appropriate values in the worksheet only if the contents of both text boxes can be converted to a time. Use the IsDate function to determine if the contents of the text boxes can be converted. If either text box contains a value that cannot be converted to a time, use the MsgBox statement to display an appropriate message.

e. Save the workbook, then return to Excel. Click cell A5 in John Able's worksheet. Run the CalcHours macro. Enter the letter T as the starting time, then click the OK button. When the error message appears in a message box, click the OK button to close the message box. The procedure unloads the custom dialog box.

f. Run the CalcHours macro again. Enter 9am as the starting time and enter 2pm as the ending time, then click the OK button. The appropriate information appears in the worksheet, and the form is unloaded.

g. Save and then close the workbook.

discovery ▶ 5. In this exercise, you will learn about the StartUpPosition property and the Tab Order dialog box. You will use the Computer Inventory workbook that you created in this lesson.

    a. Open the Computer Inventory (Computer Inventory.xls) workbook, which is located in the Tut12\Excel folder on your Data Disk. Click the Enable Macros button, if necessary, then save the workbook as T12-EX-E5D.

    b. Open the Visual Basic Editor. Use the Project Explorer window to view the frmUpdateInv form. Open the Update button's Click event procedure. Change the filename in the Set statement to "t12-ex-e5d.xls". Close the Code window.

    c. Right-click the form, then click Tab Order. Use the Tab Order dialog box to place the cmdUpdate and cmdCancel buttons first and second in the tab order. Close the Tab Order dialog box, then run the form. The initial focus appears on the Update button. Press the Tab key several times to observe the new tab order, then press the Esc key to close the dialog box.

    d. Display the Properties window, if necessary. Use the Help window to research the form's StartUpPosition property. What is the purpose of this property? What are the valid settings for this property? Change the Update Inventory dialog box's StartUpPosition property to each of these settings, then run the dialog box and note the differences on a piece of paper. Change the StartUpPosition property to 2 - Center Screen.

    e. Save and then close the workbook.

A computer program is good only if it works. Errors in programming code can cause a program to run incorrectly. Therefore, a programmer needs to know how to locate and fix any errors in his or her code. Exercise 6 is a Debugging Exercise. Debugging Exercises allow you to practice recognizing and solving errors in code.

debugging 6. The following line of code should display the frmInput custom dialog box on the screen. What, if anything, is wrong with the code?

```
frmInput.Display
```

Word Lesson

Using Custom Dialog Boxes in Word

case▶ Nancy Manley, the secretary at Willowton Health Club, has decided to revise the PrintClientList macro created in Tutorial 11. As you may remember, the macro displayed the names of the Willowton Health Club trainers in the Office Assistant's balloon. After Nancy selected a trainer's name in the balloon, the macro displayed Word's built-in Open dialog box, which Nancy used to select the appropriate database. The macro inserted the contents of the database's Client table in the document, and then it displayed Word's built-in Print dialog box. Nancy could click either the OK button in the Print dialog box to print the client list, or she could click the Cancel button to close the dialog box without printing the client list. Rather than using the Office Assistant to display each trainer's name, the revised PrintClientList macro will use a custom dialog box that allows Nancy to enter the trainer's name. The custom dialog box also will allow Nancy to specify whether the built-in Print dialog box is displayed.

Viewing the Client Document

The document Nancy uses to print each client list is stored on your Data Disk. Before creating the appropriate macro and custom dialog box, view the document.

To view the document:

1 Start Microsoft Word. Open the **T12-WD-1** (T12-WD-1.doc) document, which is located in the Tut12\Word folder on your Data Disk.

2 Click the **Enable Macros** button, if necessary, and then save the document as **Client List**. The Client List document is shown in Figure 12-26.

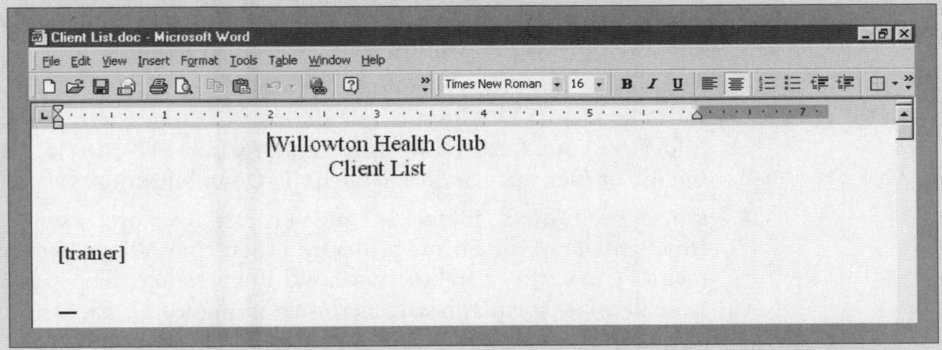

Figure 12-26: The Client List document

Figure 12-27 shows a sketch of the custom dialog box that you will create in this lesson.

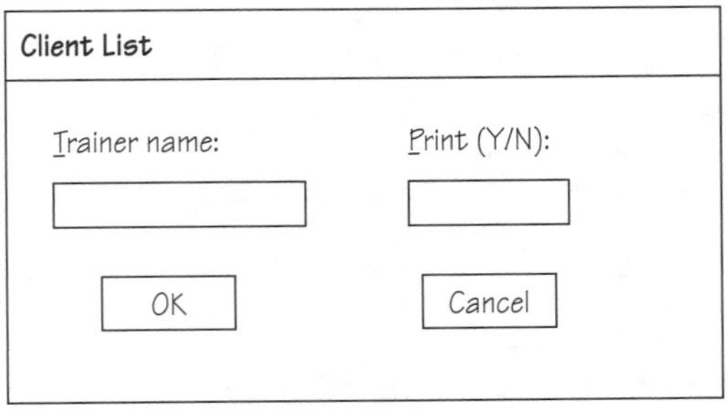

Figure 12-27: Sketch of the custom dialog box

The dialog box shown in Figure 12-27 consists of a form and six controls: two labels, two text boxes, and two command buttons. The user will need to enter the trainer's name in the first text box and then either the letter Y or the letter N in the second text box. When the user clicks the OK button, the button's Click event first will display Word's built-in Open dialog box. It then will insert the appropriate database information into the document and then, optionally, display Word's built-in Print dialog box. The user can close the dialog box by clicking either the Cancel button or the Close button ☒.

The first step in creating a custom dialog box is to add a new form to the project, which you learned how to do in the Concept lesson. Recall that you also can add an existing form to a project. To save you time, a form containing the required controls for the Client List dialog box is included on your Data Disk, and you now can add that form to your project.

To add an existing form to a project:

1 Press **Alt+F11** to open the Visual Basic Editor. If necessary, open the Project Explorer window and close the Properties window, the Immediate window, and any open Code windows.

2 Right-click the **Project Explorer window** and then click **Import File** on the shortcut menu. The Import File dialog box appears. Open the Tut12\Word folder on your Data Disk, if necessary. Click **T12-WD-1** (T12-WD-1.frm) in the list of filenames and then click the **Open** button.

3 Open the **Forms folder** in the Project Explorer window. Right-click **frmClientList** in the Forms folder and then click **View Object** on the shortcut menu. Close the Toolbox window, if necessary. The partially completed frmClientList form appears, as shown in Figure 12-28.

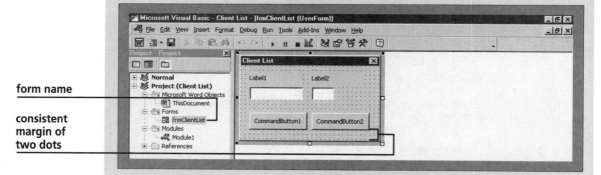

Figure 12-28: The partially completed frmClientList form

Following the Windows standard, the form maintains a consistent margin—in this case, a margin of two dots—around its border. Also, the controls are aligned to minimize the number of different margins appearing in the interface.

You will not need the Project Explorer window for awhile, so you can close it.

4 Close the Project Explorer window.

Now set the appropriate properties for each control. The first property you will set is the Name property.

> Some programmers create the entire interface before setting each object's properties, while others change the properties of each object as the object is added to the form. Either way will work, so it's really just a matter of preference.

Setting the Name Property

As you learned in the Concept lesson, the form and any controls that will be either coded or referred to in code should have their default name changed to a more meaningful one. The form's name already has been changed from UserForm1 to frmClientList; you now need to change the appropriate control names. Figure 12-29 lists the six controls, their status (whether they will be coded or referred to in code), and their new names, if applicable.

Default Name	Status	New Name
CommandButton1	Coded	cmdOk
CommandButton2	Coded	cmdCancel
Label1	Not coded or referred to in code	
Label2	Not coded or referred to in code	
TextBox1	Referred to in code	txtTrainer
TextBox2	Referred to in code	txtPrint

Figure 12-29: Controls included in the Client List dialog box

Notice that only four of the six controls will need to have their name changed. You will not need to change the names of the two identifying labels (Label1 and Label2), because those controls will not be coded or referred to in code.

To set the Name property for four of the controls:

1 Right-click the **CommandButton1** control, then click **Properties** on the short-cut menu. Click **(Name)** in the Properties list, then type **cmdOk** and press the **Enter** key.

2 Change the CommandButton2 control's name to **cmdCancel** and change the names of the TextBox1 and TextBox2 controls to **txtTrainer** and **txtPrint**, respectively.

••
tip

You can select a control by clicking the control on the form, or you can use the Properties window's Object list box to select the control.
••

3 Save the document.

The next property you will set is the Text property of the txtPrint control.

Setting the Text Property

Most of the time, Nancy will want to print the client list. Rather than having her enter the letter Y into the txtPrint text box, you will have the text box display the letter Y automatically when the dialog box first appears. You display information in a text box by setting the text box's Text property.

To display the letter Y in the txtPrint text box:

1   Click the **txtPrint** text box to select it, if necessary.

2   Scroll down the Properties window until you see the Text property. Click **Text** in the Properties list, then type **Y** and press the **Enter** key. The letter Y appears in the Settings box and in the text box on the form.

Now set the Caption property for the command button and label controls.

Setting the Caption Property

Label controls and command buttons have a Caption property that controls the text appearing inside the control. When a label or command button is added to the form, its default name is assigned to the Caption property. In the next set of steps, you will change the captions of the labels and command buttons appropriately.

To set the Caption property for the label and command button controls:

1   Click the **Label1** control to select it. Recall that a label control's caption should end with a colon and it should be entered using sentence capitalization. Click **Caption** in the Properties list, and then type **Trainer name:** and press the **Enter** key.

2   Change the Label2 control's Caption property to **Print (Y/N):**.

3   Change the Caption property of the CommandButton1 and CommandButton2 controls to **OK** and **Cancel**, respectively.

4   Save the document.

Many controls have an **AutoSize property**, which does just what its name implies: it automatically sizes the control to fit its current contents. You will use the AutoSize property to size the two identifying labels, which are slightly longer than their captions.

Changing the AutoSize Property for More Than One Control at a Time

You can set the AutoSize property for the two identifying labels individually, or you can change the property for both controls at the same time. Before you can change a property for a group of controls, you need to select the controls. You do so by clicking one of the controls in the group and then pressing and holding down the Ctrl key as you click the other controls in the group. To deselect one of the selected controls, you press and hold down the Ctrl key as you click the control. To deselect all of the selected controls, you click the form or any unselected control on the form.

> **To set the AutoSize property for the two identifying labels:**
>
> **1**   Click the **Trainer name:** label. Press and hold down the **Ctrl** key as you click the **Print (Y/N):** label, then release the Ctrl key. The two label controls now are selected, as the handles shown in Figure 12-30 indicate.

selected
controls

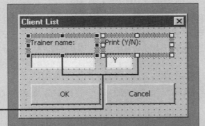

Figure 12-30: Two controls selected in the dialog box

> When more than one control is selected, the Properties window displays only the properties common to the selected controls.

Notice that the handles on the Print (Y/N): label are white, while the handles on the Trainer name: label are black. When you select more than one control, the last control you select will have white handles; the other selected controls will have black handles. The Format menu uses the control with the white handles as the reference control when aligning and sizing a group of controls. You can learn more about the reference control by completing Exercise 3 in this tutorial's Concept lesson.

> You also can select a group of contiguous controls on the form by placing the mouse pointer ⍚ slightly above and to the left of the first control you want to select, then pressing the left mouse button and dragging. A dotted rectangle will appear as you drag. When all of the controls you want to select are within the dotted rectangle, release the mouse button. All of the controls surrounded by the dotted rectangle will be selected.

2   Click **AutoSize** in the Properties list, and then click the **Settings box list arrow**. Click **True** in the list and then press the **Enter** key. The Visual Basic Editor sizes each of the selected controls to fit its current contents.

3   Click the **form** to deselect the selected controls.

Now move the text boxes closer to their identifying labels.

4   Select the two text box controls. Position the mouse pointer on one of the controls, except on a handle, then drag the controls up one dot.

5   Click the **form** to deselect the controls, then save the document.

You also can size a control by setting its Height and Width properties.

Setting the Height and Width Properties

In addition to using the handles and the AutoSize property, a third method of sizing a control is by setting its Height and Width properties. The height and width of an object is measured in points, with one **point** being the equivalent of 1/72 of an inch. You will set the Width property of both command buttons to 50 points.

To set the Width property of both command buttons, then reposition the buttons and size the form:

1   Select both command buttons, then set their Width property to **50**.

2   Click the **form** to deselect the controls.

As you learned in the Concept lesson, you should align the controls wherever possible to minimize the number of different margins appearing in the dialog box. You also should maintain a consistent margin around the form's borders; recall that two or three dots is recommended.

3   Drag the Cancel button to the left, as shown in Figure 12-31. Then, click the **form** and size its right border as shown in the figure.

size this border

drag to this location

Figure 12-31: Current status of the form

Next, provide keyboard access to the essential controls in the dialog box.

Providing Keyboard Access to the Essential Controls

As you learned in the Concept lesson, you should provide keyboard access to each essential control on the form. Recall that a control is considered essential if it accepts user input. In the Client List dialog box, the two text boxes and the two command buttons are essential controls. The two labels are not considered essential, because the user does not have access to them.

You will use accelerator keys to provide keyboard access to the text boxes. You will provide keyboard access to the OK and Cancel buttons by designating them as the default and cancel buttons, respectively.

To provide keyboard access to the essential controls in the Client List dialog box:

1 Click the **OK** button on the form, then click **Default** in the Properties list. Set the Default property to **True**.

2 Click the **Cancel** button on the form, then click **Cancel** in the Properties list. Set the Cancel property to **True**.

3 Click the **txtTrainer** text box to select it.

Notice that, unlike command buttons, text boxes do not have an Accelerator property, nor do they have a Caption property. So how then can you provide keyboard access to a text box? You do so first by assigning the accelerator key to the text box's identifying label, which has both an Accelerator and a Caption property. You then use the TabIndex property, which you will learn about in the next section, to place the label control immediately before the text box in the tab order.

4 Click the **Trainer name:** label to select it, then click **Accelerator** in the Properties list. Type **T** and press the **Enter** key. The letter T now is underlined in the label control's caption.

5 Click the **Print (Y/N):** label, then set its Accelerator property to **P**.

To complete the dialog box's interface, you need only to set the tab order for the controls in the dialog box.

Setting the Tab Order

As you learned in the Concept lesson, the tab order is the order in which the focus moves from one essential control to the next essential control as you press the Tab key in a dialog box. The tab order is determined by the TabIndex property of the controls included in the dialog box. When you add a control to a form, the control's TabIndex property is set to a number that represents the order in which the control was added to the form. The TabIndex value for the first control added to a form is 0 (zero), the TabIndex value for the second control is 1, and so on.

The control whose TabIndex value is 0 will receive the focus first, because it is the first control in the tab order. When you press the Tab key, the focus will move to the second control in the tab order—the control whose TabIndex is 1—and so on. If a control cannot receive the focus (for example, label controls cannot receive the focus), the focus moves to the next control in the tab order.

Before you can set the TabIndex property of the controls, you need to determine where each essential control should fall in the tab order. In the Client List dialog box, for example, the first essential control in the tab order should be the first text box, followed by the second text box, the OK command button, and the Cancel command button. It appears, then, that these controls should have TabIndex values of 0, 1, 2, and 3, respectively. However, recall that giving keyboard access to a text box requires that you not only assign an accelerator key to the text box's identifying label, but that you also place the identifying label immediately before the text box in the tab order. Therefore, in addition to setting the TabIndex property of the essential controls, you also need to set the TabIndex property of label controls that identify essential controls, such as label controls that identify text boxes. The TabIndex property of controls other than these do not need to be changed. Figure 12-32 shows the TabIndex values for the appropriate controls in the Client List dialog box.

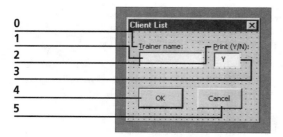

Figure 12-32: TabIndex values for essential controls and their identifying labels

Notice that each text box's identifying label has a TabIndex value that is one number less than its own TabIndex value; this places the identifying label before its corresponding text box in the tab order.

To set the TabIndex property of the controls, then run the dialog box to test it:

1 Click the **Trainer name:** label to select it, then click **TabIndex** in the Properties list. Type **0** (the number zero) and press the **Enter** key.

2 Click the **txtTrainer** text box to select it, then click **TabIndex** in the Properties list. Verify that this text box's TabIndex value is set to 1 (the number one).

3 Set the TabIndex property of the Print (Y/N): label, the txtPrint text box, the cmdOk command button, and the cmdCancel command button controls to **2**, **3**, **4**, and **5**, respectively.

You also can use the Tab Order dialog box to set the TabIndex property. You can open the Tab Order dialog box by right-clicking the form and then clicking Tab Order on the shortcut menu.

4 Save the document. Click the **form** to make it the active window, then click the **Run Sub/UserForm** button ▶ on the toolbar.

HELP? If the button says Run Macro rather than Run Sub/UserForm, click the form to select it. The form must be the active window for you to run it.

When the dialog box opens, the focus is sent to the control whose TabIndex value is 0; in this case, the focus is sent to the Trainer name: label control. Because a label control cannot receive the focus, the focus moves to the next control in the tab order; in this case, it moves to the txtTrainer text box.

5 Press the **Tab** key. The focus moves to the txtPrint text box, because the Print (Y/N): label cannot receive the focus.

Notice that the txtPrint control's existing text (Y) is selected automatically when the text box receives the focus. Any new text entered by the user will automatically replace the selected text.

6 Press the **Tab** key three times. The focus moves to the OK button, the Cancel button, and then back to the first text box.

Now verify that the accelerator keys work as intended.

7 Press **Alt+p**. The focus moves to the txtPrint text box. Press **Alt+t** to move the focus to the txtTrainer text box.

Finally, verify that the Enter key will select the OK button and that the Esc key will select the Cancel button.

8 Press the **Enter** key. The focus moves to the OK button. Press the **Esc** key. The focus moves to the Cancel button.

9 Click the dialog box's **Close** button ✕. The dialog box closes and you return to the Visual Basic Editor.

You will not need the Properties window anymore, so you can close it.

10 Close the Properties window.

Now that you have completed the dialog box's interface, you can begin coding the necessary controls in the dialog box.

Coding the Controls in the Client List Dialog Box

The first control you will code is the Cancel button, which should remove the form from both the screen and the computer's memory when the user selects the button. In this case, the user can select the Cancel button by clicking it, or by pressing the Esc key (recall that the button's Cancel property is set to True), or by pressing the Enter key when the button has the focus. When any of these actions occurs, the button's Click event is invoked.

To code the Cancel button's Click event, then test the procedure:

1   Right-click the **Cancel** button, then click **View Code** on the shortcut menu. The Code window opens and shows the code template for the cmdCancel button's Click event procedure.

Recall from the Concept lesson that you use the Unload statement to remove a form from both the screen and the computer's memory.

2   Press the **Tab** key, then type **unload frmclientlist** and press the **Enter** key.

3   Close the Code window, then click the **Run Sub/UserForm** button ▶ to run the dialog box. Press the **Esc** key to select the Cancel button, thereby invoking its Click event procedure. The procedure closes the dialog box, removing the form from both the screen and the computer's memory.

The next control you will code is the OK command button, which the user can select either by clicking it or by pressing the Enter key even when the button does not have the focus. (Recall that the OK button's Default property is set to True.) In this case, the button's Click event should perform the tasks listed in Figure 12-33's pseudocode.

---

1. Replace the sixth paragraph in the document with "Trainer:", a tab, the text entered in the txtTrainer text box, and a blank line.
2. Delete any existing tables from the document.
3. Display Word's built-in Open dialog box, showing only Access database filenames ending in .mdb. Assign the filename selected by the user to a String variable named strFileName.
4. If the user clicks the Open dialog box's Open button after selecting an .mdb file, then
   a. Place the insertion point at the end of the document.
   b. Use the Range object's InsertDatabase method to insert the database information into the document. The name of the database is stored in the strFileName variable.
   c. If the text entered in the txtPrint text box is equal to the letter "Y" (in any case), then
      1) Display Word's built-in Print dialog box.
5. Unload the dialog box.

Figure 12-33: Pseudocode for the OK button's Click event procedure

Figure 12-34 lists the variables that the OK button's Click event procedure will use.

Variable	datatype
blnOpen	Boolean
strFileName	String
docClient	Document
tblClient	Table

Figure 12-34: Variables used by the OK button's Click event procedure

The procedure will use the Boolean variable blnOpen to store the value returned by Word's built-in Open dialog box. The filename selected by the user in the Open dialog box will be assigned to the String variable strFileName. The docClient variable will store the address of the Client List document, and the tblClient variable will be used in a For Each…Next loop that deletes any existing tables from the document.

In the next set of steps, you will declare the appropriate variables and then translate each line in Figure 12-33's pseudocode into one or more VBA statements.

To code the OK button's Click event procedure, then test the procedure:

1   Right-click the **OK** button, then click **View Code** on the shortcut menu to open the cmdOk control's Click event procedure. Enter the documentation and the Dim and Set statements shown in Figure 12-35.

enter these
three lines
of code

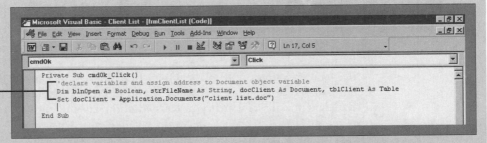

Figure 12-35: Code window showing documentation and Dim and Set statements

Step 1 in the pseudocode is to replace the sixth paragraph in the document, which is the paragraph that contains the text [trainer], with the word "Trainer:", a tab, the text entered in the txtTrainer text box, and a blank line.

2   Type **'display trainer name in document** and press the **Enter** key. Type **docclient.paragraphs(6).range.text = _** (be sure to type the equal sign followed by a space and the underscore) and press the **Enter** key. Press the **Tab** key, then type **"Trainer:" & vbtab & txttrainer.text & vbnewline** and press the **Enter** key.

Next, delete any existing tables in the document.

3 Press the **Backspace** key to remove the indentation, then type **'delete existing tables** and press the **Enter** key. Type **for each tblclient in docclient.tables** and press the **Enter** key.

4 Press the **Tab** key, then type **tblclient.delete** and press the **Enter** key. Press the **Backspace** key, then type **next tblclient** and press the **Enter** key.

Now display Word's built-in Open dialog box, showing only Access database filenames. Assign the filename selected by the user to the strFileName variable.

5 Type the additional instructions shown in Figure 12-36.

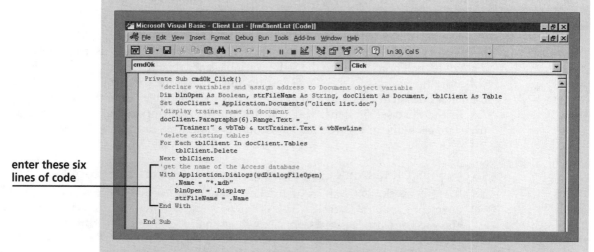

enter these six
lines of code

Figure 12-36: Partially completed cmdOk Click event procedure

According to Step 4 in the pseudocode, the procedure needs to determine if the user clicked the Open dialog box's Open button after selecting an .mdb file. You can determine if the Open button was clicked by comparing the value stored in the blnOpen variable to the Boolean value True. You can use the Right function, which you learned about in Tutorial 10, to determine if the name stored in the strFileName variable ends with .mdb.

6 Type **if blnopen = true and right(strfilename, 4) = ".mdb" then** and press the **Enter** key.

If the user clicked the Open button in the Open dialog box, then the procedure needs to complete three tasks, which are to move the insertion point to the end of the document, insert the database information, and then determine if the text entered in the txtPrint text box is equal to the letter "Y". If it is, the procedure should display Word's built-in Print dialog box.

7 Type the additional instructions shown in Figure 12-37. Also verify the accuracy of your code by comparing the code on your screen to the code shown in the figure. (Be sure to type an uppercase letter Y in the second If...Then...Else statement's *condition*.)

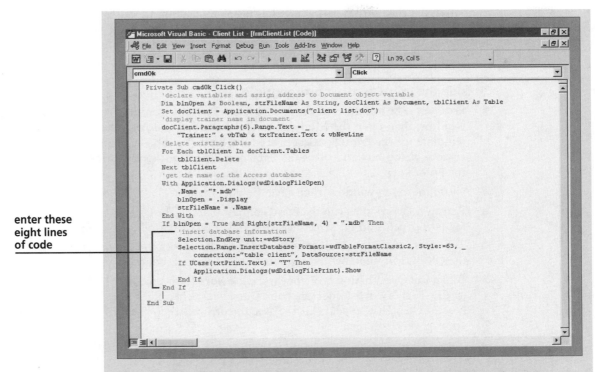

enter these eight lines of code

Figure 12-37: Partially completed Click event procedure for the cmdOk control

The last instruction in the pseudocode is to unload the dialog box.

8 Type **'unload the form** and press the **Enter** key, then type **unload frmclientlist** and press the **Enter** key.

9 Save the document, then close the Code window. Click the **Run Sub/UserForm** button ▸ on the toolbar to run the dialog box. The dialog box appears in front of the Client List document in Word.

HELP? If you do not see the document behind the dialog box, close the dialog box. Click the Client List.doc - Microsoft Word button on the taskbar to view the Client List document. Press Alt+F11 to return to the Visual Basic Editor, then run the dialog box again.

10 Type **Pam** in the Trainer name text box. Press the **Tab** key, then **n** in the Print (Y/N) text box and click the **OK** button.

11 When the Open dialog box appears, open the Tut12\Word folder on your Data Disk, if necessary. Click **Pam** (Pam.mdb) in the list of filenames, and then click the **Open** button. The procedure inserts Pam's client list in the document, and then it unloads the dialog box and you are returned to the Visual Basic Editor. Because you entered a letter other than the letter Y in the Print (Y/N) text box, the procedure does not display Word's built-in Print dialog box.

12 Return to Word to verify that Pam's client list appears in the document.

Now that the custom dialog box has been created and tested, all that remains is to code the PrintClientList procedure so that it will display the Client List dialog box on the screen.

To code the PrintClientList procedure:

1   Press **Alt+F11** to return to the Visual Basic Editor. Open the Project Explorer window, then open the Module1 module's Code window and view the code template for the **PrintClientList** procedure. Press the **Tab** key, then type **'display custom dialog box** and press the **Enter** key. Type **frmclientlist.show** and press the **Enter** key.

2   Close the Code window, then save the document.

3   Return to Word, then run the **PrintClientList** macro. The custom Client List dialog box appears on the screen. Use the dialog box to display Nora's client list.

4   Type **Nora** in the txtTrainer text box, and then press the **Enter** key to select the **OK** button, thereby invoking its Click event procedure.

5   When the Open dialog box appears, click **Nora** (Nora.mdb), which is located in the Tut12\Word folder on your Data Disk, then click the **Open** button. Nora's client list appears in the document, and then the Print dialog box appears on the screen.

6   If your computer is connected to a printer, click the **OK** button in the Print dialog box to print the document; otherwise, click the **Cancel** button. Figure 12-38 shows Nora's clients listed in the document.

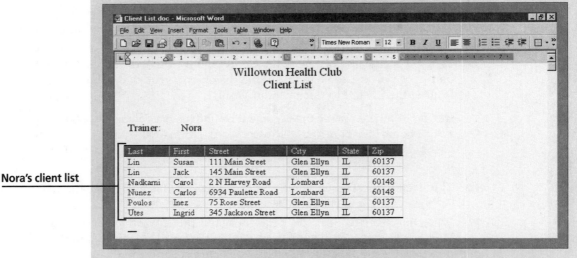

Nora's client list

Figure 12-38: Nora's client list shown in the document

7   Save the document, then close Word.

You now have completed Tutorial 12's Word lesson. You can either take a break or complete the end-of-lesson exercises before moving on to the next lesson.

EXERCISES

1. In this exercise, you will modify the custom dialog box that you created in this lesson.
   a. Open the Client List (Client List.doc) document, which is located in the Tut12\Word folder on your Data Disk. Click the Enable Macros button, if necessary, then save the document as T12-WD-E1D.
   b. Open the Visual Basic Editor. Use the Project Explorer window to view the frmClientList form. Open the Toolbox window, then add a label control and a text box to the form. The text box should allow the user to specify whether the document should be saved. Set the size, position, and properties of the label and text box appropriately. (You can reposition the other controls, if desired.) Display the letter Y in the text box. Close the Properties window.
   c. Open the OK button's Click event procedure. Change the filename in the Set statement to "t12-wd-e1d.doc". If the user indicates that the document should be saved, the procedure should display Word's built-in Save As dialog box. (Display the Save As dialog box before displaying the Print dialog box.) Modify the code accordingly.
   d. Save the document, then return to Word and run the PrintClientList macro. Save (using the current name, t12-wd-e1d.doc), but don't print, the client list for George. George's clients are listed in the George (George.mdb) file, which is located in the Tut12\Word folder on your Data Disk.
   e. Close the document.

2. In this exercise, you will create and code a custom dialog box. You will use the document and macro created in Tutorial 6's Word lesson.
   a. Open the T12-WD-E2 (T12-ED-E2.doc) document, which is located in the Tut12\Word folder on your Data Disk. Click the Enable Macros button, if necessary, then save the document as T12-WD-E2D.
   b. Open the Visual Basic Editor. Open the Module1 module's Code window and view the UpdateMembership procedure. Study the procedure's code. (The filename in the Set statement has already been changed for you.) Notice that the procedure uses three InputBox functions to get the trainer ID and the number of full and matinee memberships sold. Create one custom dialog box in which the user can enter the three items of information. Include Update and Cancel command buttons in the dialog box. Display the number 0 in the full and matinee text boxes. Close the Properties window.
   c. Move the code from the UpdateMembership procedure to the Update button's Click event procedure. Remove the InputBox functions from the procedure, then make any other necessary changes to the Click event procedure. (Recall that the command button used in place of the OK button—in this case, the Update button—typically does not close the form after completing its task.)
   d. Change the UpdateMembership procedure so that it simply displays the form. Code the Cancel button so that it removes the form from both the screen and memory.

e. Save the document, then return to Word and run the UpdateMembership procedure. Record Jan's sale of three full memberships and two matinee memberships; Jan's trainer ID is 130. Press the Esc key to select the Cancel button, which unloads the dialog box.

f. Save and then close the document.

Exercises 3 and 4 are Discovery Exercises. Discovery Exercises, which may include topics that are not covered in the lesson, allow you to "discover" the solutions to problems on your own.

discovery ▶ **3.** In this exercise, you will learn about the Frame control.

a. Open the Client List (Client List.doc) document, which is located in the Tut12\Word folder on your Data Disk. Click the Enable Macros button, if necessary, then save the document as T12-WD-E3D.

b. Open the Visual Basic Editor. Use the Help screens to research the Frame tool. What is the purpose of the tool? Close the Help window.

c. Use the Project Explorer window to view the frmClientList form. Open the Toolbox window. Add a frame control to the form. Drag the two labels and two text boxes inside the frame. Adjust the size of the frame accordingly.

d. Save the document, then return to Word and run the PrintClientList macro. When the Client List dialog box appears, click the Cancel button, then close the document.

discovery ▶ **4.** In this exercise, you will learn about the TabStop property.

a. Open the Client List (Client List.doc) document, which is located in the Tut12\Word folder on your Data Disk. Click the Enable Macros button, if necessary, then save the document as T12-WD-E4D.

b. Open the Visual Basic Editor. Use the Project Explorer window to view the frmClientList form. Use the Help screens to research the TabStop property. (Be sure to research the TabStop property, not the TabStops property.) What is the purpose of the TabStop property?

c. Open the Properties window, if necessary, then set the txtPrint control's TabStop property to False. Save the document, then return to Word and run the PrintClientList macro. Press the Tab key. Where does the Tab key send the focus? How does this differ from the dialog box used in the lesson? If the user usually will print the client list, how does changing the txtPrint control's TabStop property make the dialog box more convenient to use when tabbing? Click the txtPrint text box. When you click a control whose TabStop property is set to False, does the control receive the focus?

d. Click the Cancel button to close the custom dialog box, then close the document.

A computer program is good only if it works. Errors in programming code can cause a program to run incorrectly. Therefore, a programmer needs to know how to locate and fix any errors in his or her code. Exercise 5 is a Debugging Exercise. Debugging Exercises allow you to practice recognizing and solving errors in code.

debugging **5.** The instruction `lblSum.Text = Val(txtFirst.Text) + Val(txtSecond.Text)` should add the contents of the txtFirst text box to the contents of the txtSecond text box, and then display the sum in the lblSum control. Correct the instruction.

Access Lesson

Using Custom Dialog Boxes in Access

case ▶ Professor Carlisle, the chair of the CIS department at Snowville College, has decided to revise the LocateInstructor procedure created in Tutorial 11. As you may remember, the procedure allows Professor Carlisle to preview the AdjFacReport report showing the name, phone number, and courses taught for either all of the CIS adjunct faculty or only those who teach a specific course. Rather than using the Office Assistant and the InputBox function to display the report choices and to get the course number from the user, the revised procedure will use a custom dialog box.

Viewing the Database

Professor Carlisle's Access database containing the adjunct CIS faculty information is stored on your Data Disk. Before creating the custom dialog box and the LocateInstructor procedure, view the records contained in the database's AdjunctFaculty table.

To view the AdjunctFaculty table:

1 Start Microsoft Access. Open the **AdjFac** (AdjFac.mdb) database, which is located in the Tut12\Access folder on your Data Disk. Click the **Maximize** button ▣ on the Microsoft Access title bar to maximize the Microsoft Access window, if necessary. Click **Tables** in the Objects bar of the Database window, if necessary. Right-click **AdjunctFaculty**, then click **Open**. See Figure 12-39.

Figure 12-39: Records contained in the AdjunctFaculty table

Each record contains three Text fields: Name, Phone, and CanTeach.

2 Close the table.

Before creating the custom dialog box, you will learn how to add a form and controls to the database.

Adding a Form and Controls

The first step in creating a custom dialog box is to add a new form—the foundation of the dialog box—to the database. Before creating the custom dialog box that Professor Carlisle will use in the LocateInstructor procedure, you will create a generic custom dialog box to familiarize yourself with the process in Access.

To add a form to the database:

1 Click **Forms** in the Objects bar of the Database window. Right-click **Create form in Design view** and then click **Design View**. Access adds a form to the database.

··

You can also add a form by clicking the New button ▦ on the Database window's toolbar.

··

> ▶ **tip**

2   If necessary, click the **Toolbox** button 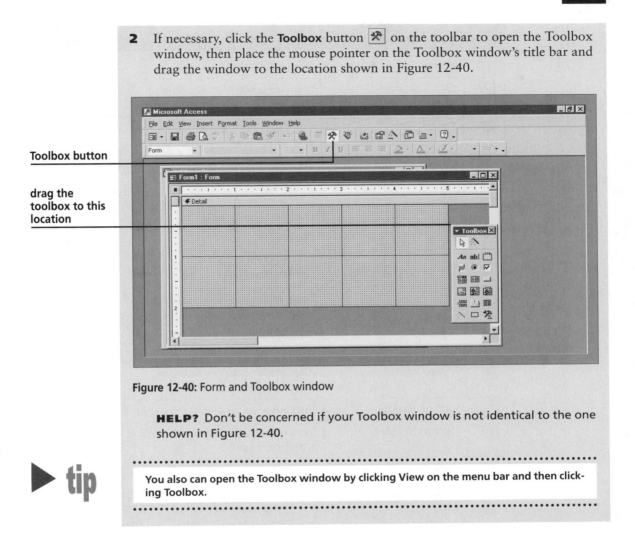 on the toolbar to open the Toolbox window, then place the mouse pointer on the Toolbox window's title bar and drag the window to the location shown in Figure 12-40.

Toolbox button

drag the toolbox to this location

Figure 12-40: Form and Toolbox window

> **HELP?** Don't be concerned if your Toolbox window is not identical to the one shown in Figure 12-40.

▶ **tip**

> You also can open the Toolbox window by clicking View on the menu bar and then clicking Toolbox.

The **Toolbox window,** also referred to simply as the **toolbox,** contains the set of tools you use to place objects, called **controls,** on the form. Figure 12-41 shows each of the basic tools contained in the toolbox and it describes the purpose of each tool. It also gives the three-character ID used to name the controls associated with each tool.

Tool	Name	Purpose	ID
	Bound Object Frame	Displays a bound OLE object	bof
	Check Box	Displays a box that is either checked or unchecked	chk
	Combo Box	Combines and displays a text box with a list box	cbo
	Command Button	Performs instructions when clicked	cmd
	Control Wizards	Displays a control wizard; does not create a control	
	Image	Displays a picture	img
	Label	Displays text that the user cannot change	lbl
	Line	Emphasizes or divides a form, report, or page	lin
	List Box	Displays a list of choices from which a user can select	lst
	More Controls	Adds controls to the toolbox; does not create a control	
	Option Group	Displays a set of alternative values	ogr
	Option Button	Displays a button that can be either on or off	opt
	Page Break	Inserts a page break in a form or report	pgb
	Rectangle	Visually groups a set of controls or emphasizes a portion of a form, report, or page	rec
	Select Objects	Selects objects; does not create a control	
	Subform/Subreport	Displays data from more than one table on a form or report	sub
	Tab Control	Creates a tabbed form with one or more pages	tab
	Text Box	Accepts or displays text that the user can change	txt
	Toggle Button	Shows the selection state of an item	tog
	Unbound Object Frame	Displays an unbound OLE object	uof

Figure 12-41: Basic tools included in the toolbox

tip

Figure 12-41 lists only the basic tools included in the toolbox. Notice that you can use the More Controls button 🔧 to add additional tools to the toolbox. You can delete existing tools by clicking the More Buttons button ▼ on the toolbox's title bar and then clicking Add or Remove Buttons.

You add a control to a form simply by clicking the appropriate tool in the toolbox and then clicking the desired location on the form. Some tools—for example, the Command Button tool—have wizards. The Command Button tool wizard creates command buttons that perform common tasks, such as locating records and closing forms. Whether a wizard appears depends on which tool is selected and it also depends on the current status of the Control Wizards button 🪄. If the Control Wizards button is selected, a wizard will appear for any control that has one; no wizards will appear if the Control Wizards button is not selected.

To practice adding controls to a form:

1 You will not use the control wizards in this lesson. If necessary, click the **Control Wizards** button 🪄 to deselect it. (The button should appear as shown in Figure 12-42.)

2 Click the **Text Box** tool `ab|` in the toolbox, then position the mouse pointer as shown in Figure 12-42.

position the pointer here

control appears indented

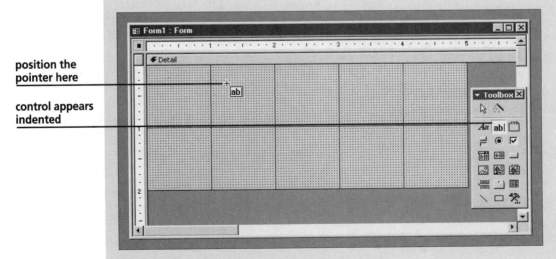

Figure 12-42: Position of mouse pointer on the form

3 Click the **form**. A default-size text box control and a label control appear on the form, as shown in Figure 12-43.

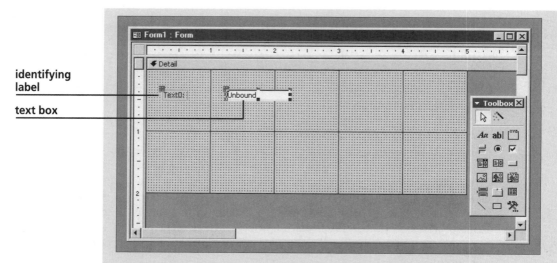

identifying
label

text box

Figure 12-43: Default-size text box and label control added to the form

HELP? If a different control appears, press the Delete key to remove the incorrect control, then repeat Steps 1 through 3.

As you learned in the Concept lesson, label controls are used to identify text box controls in a dialog box. Notice that Access automatically provides the identifying label control when you add a text box to a form.

The word "Unbound" appearing in the text box indicates that the control is not linked to any table field in the database. The text box's name and a colon—in this case, Text0:—appear as the caption in the text box's indentifying label.

4   Click the **Label** tool *Aa* in the toolbox, then click the lower-left area of the form to place a default-size label control on the form. (Don't worry about the control's exact location.) Type **The label control will size itself as you type.** and press the **Enter** key.

5   Click the **Command Button** tool ⬜ in the toolbox, then click the **center of the form** to place a default-size command button control on the form. (Don't worry about the control's exact location.) Figure 12-44 shows the current status of the form.

HELP? If the Command Button Wizard dialog box appears, click the Cancel button, then click the Control Wizards button 🔲 to deselect it.

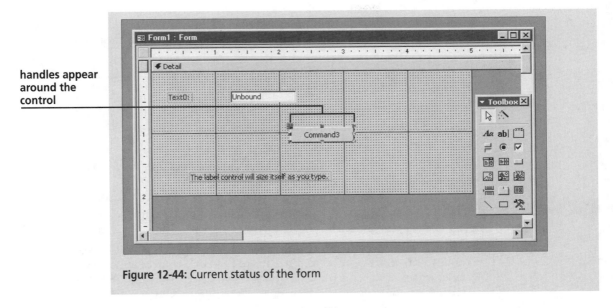

handles appear around the control

Figure 12-44: Current status of the form

Now practice sizing, moving, deleting, and restoring a control.

Sizing, Moving, Deleting, and Restoring a Control

You size, move, and delete an object in the Visual Basic Editor in the same manner as you do in any Windows application. First, you must select the object that you want to size, move, or delete; you can select a control simply by clicking it. When a control is selected, handles appear around it. For example, notice the handles around the command button control in Figure 12-44, indicating that the control is selected. You can use either of the seven smaller handles to size the control. You use the larger handle, which appears in the upper-left corner of the control, to move the control. If you inadvertently delete a control, you can use the Undo Delete Object option on the Edit menu to restore the control on the form.

To size, move, delete, and restore a control:

1 Place the mouse pointer on the command button control's lower-right handle until the mouse pointer becomes a double arrow ↘, then drag the handle until the button is slightly larger than the default size. (You don't need to worry about the exact size.) When the control is the desired size, release the mouse button.

Now move the text box control to a different location on the form.

2 Click the **text box control** (the control that contains the word "Unbound"). Position the mouse pointer on the text box until the pointer changes to ✋, then drag the text box to the upper-right corner of the form. Release the mouse button. Notice that the text box's identifying label moves with the text box.

If you want to move the text box or its identifying label independently, you use the large handle that appears in the upper-left corner of the control to do so.

3 Position the mouse pointer on the large handle located in the upper-left corner of the text box. The pointer changes to 👆. Drag the text box closer to its identifying label, then release the mouse button.

Next, delete the command button control from the form.

4 Click the **command button control** to select it, then press the **Delete** key.

Now use the Edit menu to undo the deletion.

5 Click **Edit** on the menu bar and then click **Undo Delete** to restore the command button control on the form.

> You also can use the Undo *<action>* button 🔄 on the Visual Basic Editor's Standard toolbar to undo your last action.

You also can delete, move, and size more than one control at a time, but first you must select the controls that you want to delete, move, or size. You select a group of controls by clicking one of the controls in the group and then pressing and holding down the Shift key as you click the other controls in the group. You can use the Shift+click method to select as many controls as you want. To deselect one of the selected controls, you press and hold down the Shift key as you click the control. To deselect all of the selected controls, you click the form or any unselected control on the form. Practice selecting and deselecting the controls on the form.

6 The command button control already should be selected on the form. Press and hold down the **Shift** key as you click the remaining controls. Handles appear around each control, indicating that each is selected.

7 Press and hold down the **Shift** key as you click the **command button control**; this will deselect the command button control. Click the **form** to deselect all of the controls.

8 Practice sizing the form, which you can do by placing the mouse pointer on either the right or bottom edge of the form until the pointer changes to ↔ or ↕, respectively. You then drag the edge to the desired location.

This form was just for practice, so you can close it without saving it.

9 Close the form without saving it.

You now can begin creating Professor Carlisle's custom dialog box.

Creating the Locate an Instructor Dialog Box

Figure 12-45 shows a sketch of the custom dialog box that you will create in this lesson.

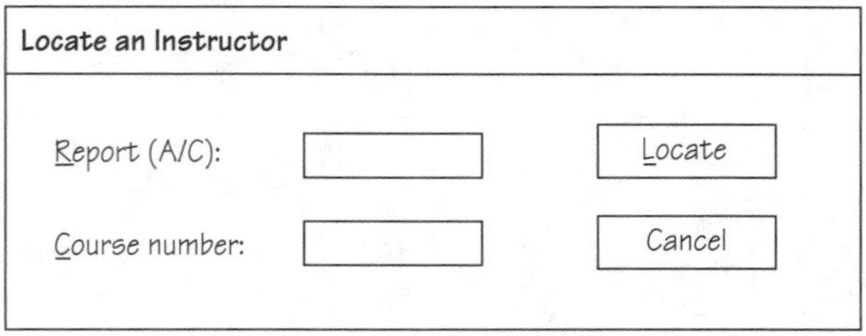

```
┌─────────────────────────────────────────────────────────┐
│ Locate an Instructor                                      │
├─────────────────────────────────────────────────────────┤
│                                                           │
│   Report (A/C):    ┌──────────┐      ┌──────────┐        │
│                    │          │      │  Locate  │        │
│                    └──────────┘      └──────────┘        │
│   Course number:   ┌──────────┐      ┌──────────┐        │
│                    │          │      │  Cancel  │        │
│                    └──────────┘      └──────────┘        │
│                                                           │
└─────────────────────────────────────────────────────────┘
```

Figure 12-45: Sketch of the custom dialog box

The dialog box shown in Figure 12-45 consists of a form and six controls: two labels, two text boxes, and two command buttons. The user can display the report showing the information for all of the instructors simply by entering the letter A in the first text box and then clicking the Locate button. To display the report showing the information for instructors that teach a specific course, the user needs to enter C in the first text box and also enter the course number in the second text box before he or she clicks the Locate button. To save you time, a form containing the required controls for the Locate an Instructor dialog box is included in the database.

To open the partially completed LocateInstructor form, then change some of its properties:

1 Right-click **LocateInstructor** in the list of forms and then click **Design View** to open the LocateInstructor form in the Design View window. Close the Toolbox window. Figure 12-46 (on the next page) shows the partially completed LocateInstructor form.

HELP? If the Form Design toolbar is not displayed on the screen, click View on the menu bar, point to Toolbars, and then click Form Design.

Following the Windows standard, the form maintains a consistent margin—in this case three dots—around its border, and the controls are aligned to minimize the number of different margins appearing in the interface.

As you learned in Tutorial 1, every object has a set of characteristics, called **properties,** that control the object's appearance and behavior. You can view the properties associated with a form by displaying the form's property sheet.

Form Design toolbar

form selector box

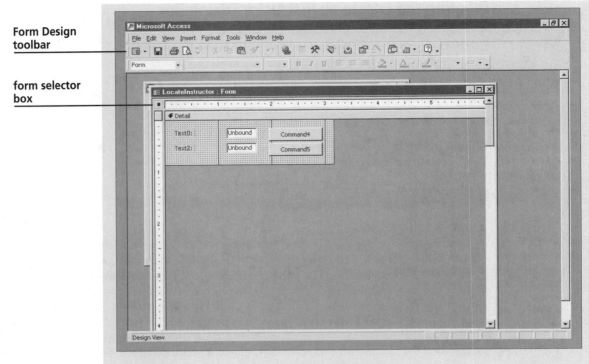

Figure 12-46: Partially completed LocateInstructor form

2 Right-click the **form selector box** in the Design View window and then click **Properties** on the shortcut menu. (Refer to Figure 12-46 for the location of the form selector box, if necessary.) The Form property sheet appears. If necessary, click the **Format** tab in the property sheet, and drag the property sheet to the location shown in Figure 12-47.

HELP? If the property sheet's title bar says Section: Detail, you inadvertently selected the section selector box. Click the form selector box, which is located above the section selector box.

▶ **tip**

You also can use the Properties window in the Visual Basic Editor to change the properties for the form and its controls. However, it is easier to use the property sheet to change the properties, because it allows you to view the form at the same time.

form selector box

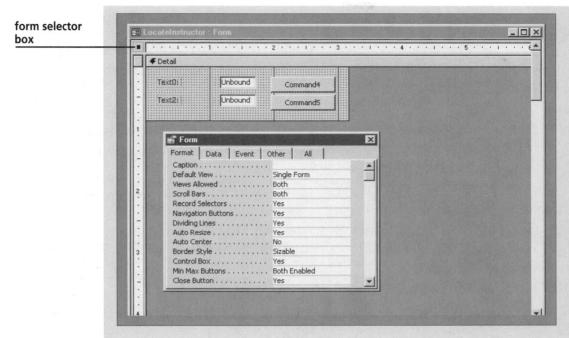

Figure 12-47: The Form property sheet

The property sheet contains five tabs: Format, Data, Event, Other, and All. The properties listed on the Format tab affect the form's appearance. For example, the value of the Close Button property determines whether the Close button appears in the form's title bar. The properties listed on the Data tab specify the table to which the form is associated, and also whether the form can be used to add, edit, and delete records. The Event tab lists the properties associated with events that a form can recognize, and the Other tab lists properties that do not fit in either of these categories. The All tab shows a complete listing of the object's properties.

Each tab on the property sheet has two columns. The left column displays the properties associated with the selected object (in this case, the form). The right column contains the **Settings box** for each of the object's properties, and it displays the current value, or setting, of each of those properties. For example, the Settings box indicates that the current value of the form's Close Button property is Yes. You can change the setting for many of the listed properties simply by typing a new value in the property's Settings box. Some properties, however, have predefined settings. If a property has predefined settings, either a list arrow or an ellipsis (...) will appear in the Settings box when the property is selected. When you click the list arrow, either a list or a color palette appears containing the valid predefined settings for that property; you then select the setting you want from that list or color palette. Clicking the ellipsis in the Settings box displays a dialog box in which you select the settings for the property.

Notice that the form's name and type—in this case, LocateInstructor Form—appear in the Design View window's title bar. If you do not enter a value in the form's Caption property, the form's name and type also will appear in the custom dialog box's title bar. As you learned in the Concept lesson, the text appearing in a dialog box's title bar should indicate the purpose of the dialog box.

3   Click **Caption** on the Format tab, if necessary. Recall that the title bar text should be entered using book title capitalization. Type **Locate an Instructor** and press the **Enter** key. The new caption appears in the Form property sheet.

Also recall that a dialog box should have a Close button, but no Minimize and Maximize buttons, and that the user should not be able to size the dialog box by dragging its borders. You can make the current form follow these standards simply by changing the form's Border Style property from Sizable to Dialog.

4   Click **Border Style** on the Format tab. The list arrow in the Settings box indicates that this property has predefined settings. Click the **Settings box list arrow**, then click **Dialog** in the list. This setting will display the form with a Close button, but no Minimize and Maximize buttons. It also will prevent the user from sizing the form by dragging its borders.

HELP? Don't be concerned that the Min Max Buttons property is currently set to Both Enabled. The Min Max Buttons property is ignored when the Border Style property is set to Dialog.

You can switch to Form View to see the effect of changing the Caption and Border Style properties.

5   Click the **View** button ▦ list arrow on the Form Design toolbar, and then click **Form View**. See Figure 12-48.

HELP? Don't be concerned about the size of the form in Form View. Form View displays the form using the same size as the Design View window.

Notice that the form's title bar contains the Locate an Instructor caption and the Close button only.

You will need to make some further modifications to the form shown in Figure 12-48. For example, because the dialog box will not be used to display records, you can remove the record selector and the navigation buttons from the form. You also can remove the dividing line that divides the different sections in the form. Additionally, you will center the form on the screen.

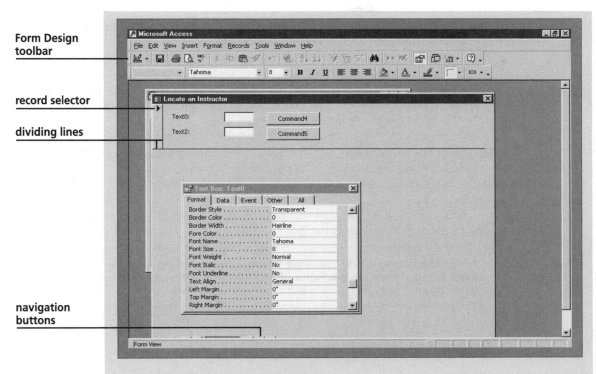

Form Design toolbar

record selector

dividing lines

navigation buttons

Figure 12-48: The form shown in Form View

6 Click the **View** button 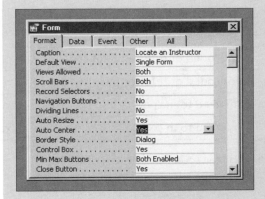 list arrow on the Form Design toolbar, and then click **Design View** to return to the Design View window.

7 Set the Record Selectors, Navigation Buttons, and Dividing Lines properties, located on the Format tab, to **No**.

8 Set the Auto Center property, located on the Format tab, to **Yes**.

Figure 12-49 shows the status of the Format tab on the Form property sheet.

Figure 12-49: Current status of the Format tab

9 Save the database. Click the **View** button ⊞ list arrow on the Form Design toolbar, and then click **Form View**. Notice that the record selector, navigation buttons, and dividing lines no longer appear in the form.

> When viewing the form in Form View, you will not see the effect of the Auto Center property, which centers the form on the screen. The form is centered only when you open it, which you will do in a later set of steps.

10 Click the **View** button ⊠ list arrow on the Form Design toolbar, and then click **Design View** to return to the Design View window.

Next, you will set the appropriate properties for each control on the form. The first property you will set is the Name property.

> Some programmers create the entire interface before setting each object's properties, while others change the properties of each object as the object is added to the form. Either way will work, so it's really just a matter of preference.

Setting the Name Property

Programmers typically give meaningful names to any controls that will be either coded or referred to in code. Controls that are not coded and are not referred to in code are not given meaningful names; programmers leave the names of these controls at their default values. Figure 12-50 lists the six controls included in the Locate an Instructor dialog box; it also shows their status (whether they are coded or referred to in code), and their new names, if applicable.

Default Name	Status	New Name
Command4	Coded	cmdLocate
Command5	Coded	cmdCancel
Label1	Not coded or referred to in code	
Label3	Not coded or referred to in code	
Text0	Referred to in code	txtReport
Text2	Referred to in code	txtCourse

Figure 12-50: Controls included in the Locate an Instructor dialog box

Notice that only four of the six controls will need to have their name changed. You will not need to change the names of the two identifying labels, because those controls will not be coded or referred to in code.

To set the Name property for four of the controls:

1 Click the **Command4** control to display its properties in the property sheet. Set the control's Name property, which is located on the Other tab, to **cmdLocate**.

HELP? If the property sheet is not displayed on the screen, right-click the Command4 control and then click Properties.

2 Set the Command5 control's Name property to **cmdCancel**.

3 Click the **text box located to the right of the Text0: label**. Change the text box's Name property from Text0 to **txtReport**.

HELP? If the Name property says Label1, you mistakenly selected the label control whose caption is Text0. Click the text box located to the right of the label control.

4 Change the name of the Text2 text box from Text2 to **txtCourse**.

The next property you will set is the Caption property for the command button and label controls.

Setting the Caption Property

Label controls and command buttons have a Caption property that controls the text appearing inside the control. In the next set of steps, you will change the captions of the labels and command buttons to match the captions shown earlier in Figure 12-45. As you learned in the Concept lesson, you use sentence capitalization for label control captions, but book title capitalization for command button captions. Also recall that a label control's caption should end with a colon and be entered on one line.

To set the Caption property for the label and command button controls:

1 Click the **label control whose caption is Text0:**. Set the control's Caption property, which is located on the Format tab, to **Report (A/C):**.

2 Set the Caption property of the label control whose caption is Text2: to **Course number:**.

3 Size the label controls to fit their captions.

4 Set the Command4 control's Caption property to **Locate** and set the Command5 control's Caption property to **Cancel**.

5 Save the database.

Next, provide keyboard access to the essential controls in the dialog box.

Providing Keyboard Access to the Essential Controls

As you learned in the Concept lesson, you should provide keyboard access to each essential control on the form. Recall that a control is considered essential if it accepts user input. In the Locate an Instructor dialog box, the two text boxes and the two command buttons are essential controls. The two labels are not considered essential, because the user does not have access to them.

You will use accelerator keys to provide keyboard access to the text boxes and to the Locate button. You will provide keyboard access to the Cancel button by designating it as the cancel button.

> The Microsoft Access Help screens use the term *access key* rather than *accelerator key* to refer to the underlined letter in a control's caption.

To provide keyboard access to the essential controls in the Locate an Instructor dialog box:

1   Set the Cancel button's Cancel property, which is located on the Other tab, to **Yes**.

2   Click the **Locate** button on the form, then click the property sheet's **Format** tab.

In Access, you can assign an accelerator key to any control that has a Caption property. You assign the accelerator key by including an ampersand (&) in the control's caption. The ampersand is entered to the immediate left of the character you want to designate as the accelerator key.

3   Click to the **left of the L in the Caption property,** then type & (the ampersand) and press the **Enter** key. The Caption property now should say &Locate, and the letter L should be underlined in the control's caption.

4   Click the **txtReport** text box on the form.

Notice that, unlike command buttons, text boxes do not have a Caption property. So how then can you provide keyboard access to a text box? You do so by assigning the accelerator key to the text box's identifying label, which does have a Caption property.

5   Click the **Report (A/C):** label on the form, then change its Caption property to **&Report (A/C):** and press the **Enter** key. The letter R now is underlined in the label control's caption.

6   Set the Caption property for the **Course number:** label, which identifies the txtCourse text box, to **&Course number:**. The letter C now is underlined in the label control's caption.

To complete the dialog box's interface, you need only to set the tab order for the controls in the dialog box.

Setting the Tab Order

As you learned in the Concept lesson, the tab order is the order in which the focus moves from one essential control to the next essential control as you press the Tab key in a dialog box. In Access, the tab order is determined by the Tab Index property, which is located on the Other tab in the property sheet. Not all controls have a Tab Index property. Label controls, for example, do not have a Tab Index property, because the user cannot access a label control.

When you add a control that does have a Tab Index property to a form, its Tab Index property is set to a number representing the order in which the control was added. The Tab Index value for the first control is 0 (zero), the Tab Index value for the second control is 1, and so on. The control whose Tab Index value is 0 will receive the focus first, because it is the first control in the tab order. When you press the Tab key, the focus will move to the second control in the tab order—the control whose Tab Index is 1—and so on.

Before you can set the Tab Index property of the controls, you need to determine where each essential control should fall in the tab order. In the Locate an Instructor dialog box, for example, the first essential control in the tab order should be the first text box, followed by the second text box, the Locate command button, and the Cancel command button. You can use a control's property sheet to set its Tab Index property, or you can use the Tab Order dialog box. You will use the Tab Order dialog box.

 tip

The Tab Index property is listed on the Other tab in the property sheet.

To use the Tab Order dialog box to set the Tab Index property of the controls, then run the dialog box to test it:

1 Right-click the **form**, then click **Tab Order**. The Tab Order dialog box opens, as shown in Figure 12-51.

row selectors

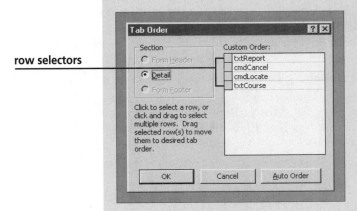

Figure 12-51: Tab Order dialog box

2 Click the **txtCourse row selector** in the Custom Order list box to select that row. Drag the txtCourse row selector until it is below the txtReport row, then release the mouse button. The txtCourse row appears below the txtReport row in the list box.

3 Click the **cmdLocate row selector**. Drag the cmdLocate row selector until it is below the txtCourse row, then release the mouse button. Figure 12-52 shows the correct tab order for the controls.

sets the Tab Index property to 0

sets the Tab Index property to 3

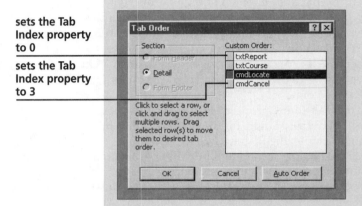

Figure 12-52: Correct tab order for controls

4 Click the **OK** button to close the Tab Order dialog box.

5 Close the property sheet, then save the database.

6 Click the **View** button 🖳 list arrow, and then click **Form View**.

When the dialog box opens, the focus is sent to the txtReport control, because that is the control whose Tab Index value is 0.

7 Type **a** and press the **Tab** key four times. The focus moves to the txtCourse text box, the Locate button, the Cancel button, and then back to the first text box. Notice that the letter "a" is selected in the txtReport text box. It is customary in Windows applications for the existing text in a text box to be selected when the text box receives the focus. By doing so, the new text entered by the user will automatically replace the selected text.

Now verify that the accelerator keys and the Esc key work as intended.

8 Press **Alt+l** (the letter l). The focus moves to the Locate command button. Press **Alt+r** to move the focus to the txtReport text box. Press **Alt+c** to move the focus to the txtCourse text box. Press the **Esc** key. The focus moves to the Cancel button.

9 Click the **View** button 🖳 list arrow, and then click **Design View**.

Now that you have completed the dialog box's interface, you can begin coding the necessary controls in the dialog box.

Coding the Controls in the Locate an Instructor Dialog Box

The first control you will code is the Cancel button, which should close the custom dialog box when the button is selected by the user. In this case, the user can select the Cancel button by clicking it, or by pressing the Esc key (recall that the button's Cancel property is set to True), or by pressing the Enter key when the button has the focus. When any of these actions occurs, the button's Click event is invoked.

To code the Cancel button's Click event, then test the procedure:

1 Press **Alt+F11** to open the Visual Basic Editor. If necessary, open the Project Explorer window and close the Properties window, the Immediate window, and any open Code windows. Click any plus boxes appearing in the Project Explorer window, if necessary.

The Project Explorer window indicates that the project contains one module, named Module1. No mention of the form appears in the Project Explorer window because, up to this point, you have not entered any code in any of the event procedures for the form or its controls. You can include the form's name in the Project Explorer window by setting the form's Has Module property to Yes.

2 Return to Access. Right-click the **form selector box** ■ in the Design View window, then click **Properties** to display the form's property sheet. Set the Has Module property, which is located on the Other tab, to **Yes**.

3 Close the property sheet, then save the database and close the form.

4 Press **Alt+F11** to return to the Visual Basic Editor. Open the Microsoft Access Class Objects folder, if necessary. Form_LocateInstructor appears in the folder. Right-click **Form_LocateInstructor** in the folder, then click **View Code**.

5 Close the Project Explorer window so that you can view more of the Code window.

6 Use the Object box in the Code window to open the cmdCancel control's Click event. The code template for the cmdCancel control's Click event procedure appears in the Code window.

In Access, you use the DoCmd object's **Close method** to remove a custom dialog box from the screen and from memory. The basic syntax of the Close method is **DoCmd.Close**.

> You can learn about the additional arguments available in the Close method by displaying the method's Help screen. Using the Close method without any arguments closes the active window, which, in Step 7, is the custom dialog box.

7 Press the **Tab** key, then type **docmd.close** and press the **Enter** key.

8 Save the database, then return to Access. If the form appears either behind or in front of the Database window, click the form's **Close** button ☒ to close the form.

9   Right-click **LocateInstructor** in the Database window's list of forms, then click **Open**. The Locate an Instructor dialog box appears centered on the screen, as shown in Figure 12-53.

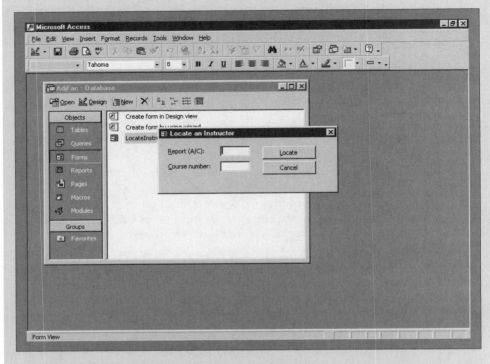

Figure 12-53: The Locate an Instructor dialog box

10   Press the **Esc** key to select the dialog box's Cancel button, thereby invoking the button's Click event procedure. The procedure closes the dialog box.

The next control you will code is the Locate command button, which the user can select either by clicking it or by pressing the Enter key when the button has the focus.

Coding the Locate Button

The Locate button's Click event procedure should perform the tasks listed in Figure 12-54.

1. Assign the contents of the txtReport control, in uppercase letters, to a String variable named strReport.
2. Value contained in strReport variable:
   = "A"   Display the report showing all of the AdjunctFaculty table's records.
   = "C"   Assign the contents of the txtCourse control to a String variable named strCourseNum.
           Display the report showing only the information for instructors whose CanTeach field contains the course number stored in the strCourseNum variable.
   Other
           Use the MsgBox statement to display the message "Report preview canceled."

Figure 12-54: Pseudocode for the Locate button's Click event procedure

The Locate button's Click event procedure will use two String variables, named strReport and strCourseNum. The procedure will assign the contents of the txtReport control, in uppercase letters, to the strReport variable. It will assign the contents of the txtCourse control to the strCourseNum variable. Figure 12-55 shows the variables used by the Locate button's Click event procedure.

Variable	datatype
strReport	String
strCourseNum	String

Figure 12-55: Variables used by the Locate button's Click event procedure

To code the Locate button's Click event:

1 Press **Alt+F11** to return to the Visual Basic Editor. Use the Object box in the Code window to open the code template for the cmdLocate control's Click event procedure.

2 Press the **Tab** key, then type **'declare variables** and press the **Enter** key. Type **dim strReport as string, strCourseNum as string** and press the **Enter** key.

Step 1 in the pseudocode is to assign the contents of the txtReport control, in uppercase letters, to the strReport variable.

3 Type **'assign report type to variable** and press the **Enter** key, then type **strreport = ucase(txtreport)** and press the **Enter** key.

HELP? If you completed either the Excel or Word lessons, you may be surprised that the assignment statement in Step 3 does not mention the text box's Text property. In Access, you can refer to a text box's Text property only when the text box has the focus. If the text box does not have the focus, you refer to its contents simply by using its name.

According to Step 2 in the pseudocode, the procedure should use the contents of the strReport variable either to display or cancel the report.

4 Type the additional instructions shown in Figure 12-56, which shows the completed Click event procedure for the Locate button.

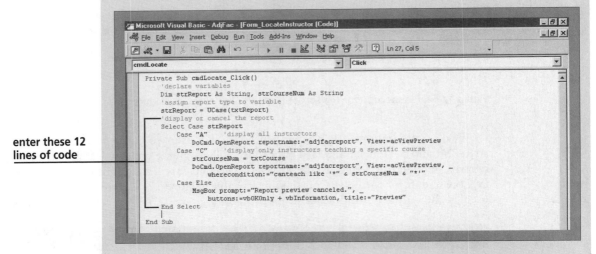

enter these 12 lines of code

```
Private Sub cmdLocate_Click()
    'declare variables
    Dim strReport As String, strCourseNum As String
    'assign report type to variable
    strReport = UCase(txtReport)
    'display or cancel the report
    Select Case strReport
        Case "A"    'display all instructors
            DoCmd.OpenReport reportname:="adjfacreport", View:=acViewPreview
        Case "C"    'display only instructors teaching a specific course
            strCourseNum = txtCourse
            DoCmd.OpenReport reportname:="adjfacreport", View:=acViewPreview, _
                wherecondition:="canteach like '*' & strCourseNum & '*'"
        Case Else
            MsgBox prompt:="Report preview canceled.", _
                buttons:=vbOKOnly + vbInformation, title:="Preview"
    End Select

End Sub
```

Figure 12-56: Completed Click event procedure for the Locate button

5 Verify the accuracy of your code by comparing the code on your screen with the code shown in Figure 12-56.

6 Close the Code window, then save the database.

Next, open the LocateInstructor procedure, which is contained in the Module1 module, and enter the code that will display the Locate an Instructor dialog box.

7 Open the Project Explorer window. Open the Module1 module, then view the code template for the LocateInstructor function procedure.

In Access, you use the DoCmd object's **OpenForm method** to load a custom dialog box into memory and display it on the screen. The basic syntax of the OpenForm method is **DoCmd.OpenForm Formname:=***formName*.

> You can learn about the additional arguments available in the OpenForm method by displaying the method's Help screen.

8 Press the **Tab** key, then type **'display custom dialog box** and press the **Enter** key. Type **docmd.openform formname:="locateinstructor"** and press the **Enter** key.

9 Close the Code window, then save the database.

Now that you have finished coding the custom dialog box and the LocateInstructor procedure, you will test the code you entered to verify that it is working correctly.

To test the code you entered:

1 Return to Access. If the form appears either behind or in front of the Database window, click the form's **Close** button ✕ to close the form.

2 Run the **LocateInstructorMacro** macro.

3 When the Locate an Instructor dialog box appears, type **c** in the Report (A/C) text box. Press the **Tab** key, then type **120** in the Course number text box. Click the **Locate** button, which invokes the button's Click event procedure. The information for the two instructors that teach the 120 course appears in the report.

4 Close the report.

5 On your own, preview the report showing all the instructors. Close the report, then click the Cancel button to close the custom dialog box.

6 Compact the database, then close Access.

You now have completed Tutorial 12's Access lesson. You can either take a break or complete the end-of-lesson exercises.

E X E R C I S E S

1. In this exercise you will modify the Locate an Instructor dialog box that you completed in this lesson.

   a. Use Windows to make a copy of the AdjFac database, which is located in the Tut12\Access folder on your Data Disk. Rename the copy T12-AC-E1D.

   b. Open the T12-AC-E1D (T12-AC-E1D.mdb) database. Open the LocateInstructor form in Design View. Open the Toolbox window. Add a text box that allows the user to control whether the report is printed by entering either the letter Y or the letter N. Set the Default Value property on the Data tab to "N". Close the property sheet, then save and close the form.

   c. Open the Visual Basic Editor and view the form's Code window. Open the Locate button's Click event procedure. If the user enters the letter Y, the Locate button's Click event should print the report; otherwise, it should simply display the report on the screen. Modify the Locate button's Click event procedure accordingly. Also change the prompt in the MsgBox statement to "Report canceled." and change the title to "Report".

   d. Save the database, then return to Access. Close the form, if necessary, then run the LocateInstructorMacro macro. Print the report showing the information for all of the instructors.

   e. Close the custom dialog box, then compact and close the database.

2.   In this exercise, you will modify the DisplayReport procedure that you created in Tutorial 8's Access lesson so that it now uses a custom dialog box.

   a.   Open the T12-AC-E2D (T12-AC-E2D.mdb) database, which is located in the Tut12\Access folder on your Data Disk. Familiarize yourself with the table and the report included in the database.

   b.   Open the Visual Basic Editor and view the DisplayReport procedure. Study the existing code. Notice that the code uses the InputBox function to ask the user which records to include in the report, and it uses the MsgBox function to ask the user if he or she wants to print or preview the report.

   c.   Return to Access. Create a custom dialog box that allows the user to enter the two items of information. Use a text box to get the records (All, Owe, or Paid) that the user wants to include in the report. Use Print and Preview buttons to determine if the user wants to print or preview the report. Also include a Cancel command button on the form. Set the appropriate properties of the form and controls. (Be sure to set the form's Has Module property to Yes.)

   d.   Close the property sheet. Save the form as TripForm, then close the form.

   e.   Return to the Visual Basic Editor. Code the Cancel button so that it closes the custom dialog box.

   f.   Copy the DisplayReport procedure's code to both the Print and Preview command buttons' Click events, then modify the code appropriately. (*Hint*: You will need to change the `Exit Function` statement to `Exit Sub`.)

   g.   Code the DisplayReport procedure so that it merely opens the form.

   h.   Save the database, then return to Access. Close the form, if necessary, then run the DisplayReportMacro macro. Preview the report only for those who still owe money, then print the report for those who have paid. Press the Esc key to select the Cancel button, which closes the dialog box.

   i.   Compact and then close the database.

3.   In this exercise, you will modify the PaymentUpdate procedure that you created in Tutorial 7's Access lesson so that it now uses a custom dialog box.

   a.   Open the T12-AC-E3D (T12-AC-E3D.mdb) database, which is located in the Tut12\Access folder on your Data Disk.

   b.   Familiarize yourself with the table and the report included in the database.

   c.   Open the Visual Basic Editor. Open the Module1 module's Code window, then view the PaymentUpdate procedure. Study the existing code. Notice that the code uses the InputBox function to get the student ID and the payment amount.

   d.   Return to Access. Create a custom dialog box that allows the user to enter the two items of information. Include Update and Cancel command buttons on the form. Set the appropriate properties of the form and controls. (Be sure to set the form's Has Module property to Yes.)

   e.   Close the property sheet. Save the form as UpdateForm, then close the form.

   f.   Return to the Visual Basic Editor. Code the Cancel button so that it closes the custom dialog box.

   g.   Copy the PaymentUpdate procedure's code to the Update command button's Click event, then modify the code appropriately.

   h.   Code the PaymentUpdate procedure so that it merely opens the form.

   i.   Save the database, then return to Access. Close the form, if necessary, then run the PaymentUpdateMacro macro. Student ID LT1 has paid $400; record the payment. A message indicating that the student still owes $800 appears in a message box. Click the OK button to close the message box.

   j.   Press the Esc key to select the Cancel button, which will close the form.

Exercise 4 is a Discovery Exercise. Discovery Exercises, which may include topics that are not covered in the lesson, allow you to "discover" the solutions to problems on your own.

discovery ▶ **4.** In this exercise, you will modify the Locate an Instructor dialog box that you created in the lesson. You will learn about a control's Enabled property and also its SetFocus method.

a. Use Windows to make a copy of the AdjFac database, which is located in the Tut12\Access folder on your Data Disk. Rename the copy T12-AC-E4D.

b. Open the T12-AC-E4D (T12-AC-E4D.mdb) database.

c. Open the Visual Basic Editor. Use the Help screens to research the SetFocus method and the Enabled property. Study the Help screens, then close the Help window.

d. Return to Access and open the LocateInstructor form in Design View. Set the txtCourse control's Enabled property, located on the Data tab, to No.

e. Close the property sheet. Save and then close the form.

f. Return to the Visual Basic Editor. Open the txtReport control's Change event. Code the event so that it enables the txtCourse control only when the user types the letter C (in any case) in the txtReport control. If the user types a letter other than C, disable the txtCourse control. (*Hint*: Compare the txtReport control's Text property, in uppercase letters, to the letter C. Use the txtCourse control's Enabled property to enable and disable the control.)

g. Open the Locate button's Click event. Before the procedure ends, have the procedure send the focus to the txtReport text box for the user. (*Hint*: Use the txtReport control's SetFocus method.)

h. Save the database, then return to Access. Close the form, if necessary, then run the LocateInstructorMacro macro. You will notice that the Course number label and text box are dimmed, indicating that they are not available at this time.

i. Type the letter c in the txtReport control. Notice that the Course number label and text box controls now are darkened, indicating that the text box will accept user input. Type 120 in the Course number text box, then click the Locate button to display the report showing only instructors who teach the CIS 120 course.

j. Close the report. Notice that the Locate button sends the focus to the txtReport control.

k. Type the letter b in the txtReport control, which will make the txtCourse control unavailable again. Click the Cancel button to close the dialog.

l. Compact and then close the database.

A computer program is good only if it works. Errors in programming code can cause a program to run incorrectly. Therefore, a programmer needs to know how to locate and fix any errors in his or her code. Exercise 5 is a Debugging Exercise. Debugging Exercises allow you to practice recognizing and solving errors in code.

debugging **5.** Assume that an Access database contains a form named CalculateBonus and a function procedure named Calculate. The Calculate procedure, which contains the `CalculateBonus.Show` instruction, should display the CalculateBonus form on the screen, but it is not working correctly. Correct any errors in the line of code.

Option Button, Check Box, and List Box Controls

objectives

In this tutorial, you will learn how to:

- Create and use option button, check box, and list box controls
- Create an option group
- Select the default option button and list box item
- Use the Sort method in Excel
- Use the AddItem method to display items in a list box
- Use the QueryClose event in Word
- Use the List Box Control's Column property in Access

Concept Lesson

More Dialog Box Controls

In addition to text box, label, and command button controls, which you learned about in Tutorial 12, many dialog boxes also contain option button, check box, and list box controls. The custom dialog box shown in Figure 13-1, for example, contains each of these control types.

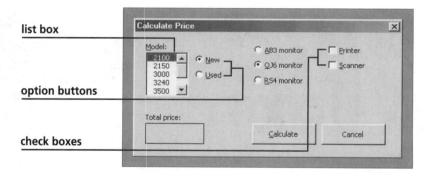

Figure 13-1: The Calculate Price dialog box

Like text box controls, option button, check box, and list box controls provide a means by which the user can enter data into a dialog box. However, unlike text box controls, these controls do not require the user to type the data. Rather, the data is selected from a set of predefined choices, resulting in fewer entry errors.

The Option Button Control

You use the **option button control** in a dialog box when you want to limit the user to only one choice in a group of two or more related and mutually exclusive choices.

You can use the Calculate Price dialog box, shown in Figure 13-1, to calculate the price of either a new or used computer along with a monitor and an optional printer and scanner. The Calculate Price dialog box contains two groups of option buttons. The New and Used option buttons in the first group pertain to the type of computer purchased. The user can select either the New option button or the Used option button, but not both buttons at the same time. The three option buttons in the second group pertain to the monitor type; the user can select only one of these buttons at any one time.

In all Microsoft Office applications except Access, you can create a group of option buttons, called an **option group**, by setting each button's GroupName property to the same value. You create an option group in Microsoft Access by placing the option buttons in an **option group control**, which is a rectangular control in Access that acts as a container for option button, check box, and toggle button controls.

> The other Microsoft Office applications also have a rectangular control, called a frame control, that acts as a container for other controls. You can learn more about the GroupName property and the frame control by completing this lesson's Exercise 7.

The minimum number of option buttons in a group is two, because the only way to deselect an option button is to select another option button. The recommended maximum number of option buttons in a group is seven. The Windows standard is that one option button in each group should be selected automatically when the dialog box first opens. The selected button, referred to as the **default option button**, should be the button that represents the user's most likely choice, or, if neither option button is used more than the others, it should be the first option button in the group. Notice that in Figure 13-1 the first option button, captioned New, is selected in the first group of option buttons in the Calculate Price dialog box, and the QJ6 monitor option button, which represents the most popular monitor, is selected in the second group.

> If you have more than seven choices from which the user can choose, you should consider using a list box control rather than option buttons.

In all Microsoft Office applications except Access, you select the default option button by setting the button's Value property to the Boolean value True. In Access, you set the option group control's DefaultValue property to a number that represents the option button in the group that you want to be the default button. For example, if the option group control contains three option buttons and you want the second button to be the default button, you would set the option group control's DefaultValue property to the number 2.

An option button's caption should be short; no more than four words in length is recommended. The caption should be meaningful and it should be entered using sentence capitalization.

The Check Box Control

You use the **check box control** to allow the user to select any number of choices from a set of one or more independent and nonexclusive choices. Unlike option buttons, where only one button in a group can be selected at any one time, any number of check boxes in a dialog box can be selected at the same time. The Calculate Price dialog box shown in Figure 13-1 contains two check boxes, captioned Printer and Scanner. The user can select one or both of the check boxes, or he or she can leave both check boxes unselected.

The Windows standard is to have all check boxes unselected when the dialog box first opens. However, you can ignore this standard in situations where you know that most times the user will be selecting the check box. For example, you may remember that the Code check box in the Visual Basic Editor's Print – Project dialog box already is selected when the dialog box opens. This is because the Print – Project dialog box is used, most times, to print the project's code. You can have a check box automatically selected when a dialog box first opens by setting the check box's Value property to the Boolean value True.

A check box's caption should be short, meaningful, and entered using sentence capitalization.

The List Box Control

Like option buttons, a **list box control** also can be used to display a set of predefined choices from which the user can select only one of the choices. This type of list box is called a **single selection list box**. The Calculate Price dialog box shown in Figure 13-1 contains one single selection list box that allows the user to select the model number of the computer. Unlike option buttons, a list box does not require you to display all of the choices on the screen at the same time. You can make a list box any size you want, and if you have more items than will fit into the list box, as does the Model list box in the Calculate Price dialog box, scroll bars appear automatically on the box. You can use the scroll bars to view the complete list of items.

••

You also can create both a multicolumn list box, which contains more than one column of data, and a multiselection list box, which allows the user to select more than one item in the list. You will learn about multicolumn and multiselection list boxes in this lesson's Exercise 6.

••

When a user selects an item in a single selection list box, the item is assigned automatically to the list box control's Value property. The only exception to this is in Microsoft Access, where the selected item is assigned to the list box's Column property.

The selected item's location in the list is assigned automatically to the list box control's ListIndex property. Similar to the TabIndex property, which keeps track of the various objects in a form, the **ListIndex property** keeps track of the various items in a list box. The first item in a list box has a ListIndex value of 0 (zero), the second item has a ListIndex value of 1, and so on. Therefore, if the user selects the first item in the list box, the number 0 is recorded automatically in the list box's ListIndex property. If the user selects the second item in the list box, the number 1 is recorded in the ListIndex property.

The Windows standard is to display, in the list box, a minimum of three items and a maximum of eight items at a time. It is customary to have a default item selected in the list when the dialog box first appears. For example, notice that model number 2100 is selected in the Model list box shown in Figure 13-1. In all Microsoft Office applications except Access, you can select the default item by setting the list box's ListIndex property to a number that represents the item's location in the list. To select the first item, for example, you would set the list box control's ListIndex property to the number 0, like this: `lstModel.ListIndex = 0`. In Access, you select the default list box item by assigning the item, entered as a string, to the list box's Default Value property; you can do so either on the property sheet or from code. For example, you can assign "2100" to the Default Value property on the lstModel control's property sheet, or you can use the VBA instruction `lstModel.DefaultValue = "2100"` in a Code window.

Because option button, check box, and list box controls accept user input, they are considered essential controls and, therefore, each should have an accelerator key. As you learned in Tutorial 12, you use the accelerator key in combination with the Alt key as a shortcut for selecting a control. For example, you can use Alt+u to select the Used option button in the Calculate Price dialog box shown in Figure 13-1.

> The Microsoft Access Help screens use the term *access key* rather than *accelerator key* to refer to the underlined letter in a control's caption.

You now have completed Tutorial 13's Concept lesson. You can either take a break or complete the end-of-lesson questions and exercises before moving on to the next lesson.

SUMMARY

To limit the user to only one choice in a group of related and mutually exclusive choices:

■ Use either the option button control or the list box control.

■ The minimum number of option buttons in a group is two; the recommended maximum is seven. Select a default option button in each group of option buttons. An option button's caption should be short, meaningful, and entered using sentence capitalization. An option button should have an accelerator key.

■ Display, in a list box, a minimum of three items and a maximum of eight items at a time. Select a default item in the list box. Use a label control to identify the list box and to provide an accelerator key for the list box.

To create a group of option buttons:

■ In all Microsoft Office applications except Access, set each button's GroupName property to the same value. In Access, place the option buttons in an option group control.

To select the default option button:

■ In all Microsoft Office applications except Access, set the option button control's Value property to the Boolean value True. In Access, set the option group control's Default Value property to a number that represents the option button in the group that you want to be the default button.

To select the default list box item:

- In all Microsoft Office applications except Access, set the list box control's ListIndex property to a number that represents the item's location in the list. The first item in the list has a ListIndex of 0.

- In Access, assign the item, entered as a string, to the list box's Default Value property; you can do so either on the property sheet or from code.

To determine which item is selected in a list box that allows one selection only:

- The list box control's ListIndex property contains a number that represents the item's location in the list.

- In all Microsoft Office applications except Access, the list box control's Value property contains the selected item. In Access, the list box control's Column property contains the selected item.

To allow the user to select any number of choices from a set of one or more independent and nonexclusive choices:

- Use the check box control. Check boxes typically are unselected when the dialog box first opens. A check box's caption should be short, meaningful, and entered using sentence capitalization. A check box should have an accelerator key.

To select a check box:

- Set the check box control's Value property to the Boolean value True.

REVIEW QUESTIONS

1. Which of the following is false?
   a. Text box controls provide an area in a dialog box where the user can enter data.
   b. The advantage of using option button, check box, and list box controls, rather than text box controls, is that these controls prevent the user from making a typing error.
   c. The user can select more than one check box at a time.
   d. If you have more data than can fit into a list box, the list box will automatically size itself so that all of the data shows at the same time.

2. You can use the _____ control to display a group of related and mutually exclusive choices.
   a. check box
   b. list box
   c. option button
   d. both b and c

3. You can use the _____ control to display a group of independent and nonexclusive choices.
   a. check box
   b. list box
   c. option button
   d. both b and c

4. If a dialog box contains two groups of four option buttons, what is the maximum number of option buttons that can be selected at the same time?
   a. 1
   b. 2
   c. 4
   d. 8

5. In all Microsoft Office applications except Access, you can create an option group by setting each option button's _____ property to the same value.
   a. Group
   b. GroupName
   c. GroupOption
   d. OptionGroup

6. You can select a check box control by setting its _____ property to the Boolean value True.
   a. CheckBox
   b. CheckValue
   c. SelectBox
   d. Value

7. If the user selects the first item in a list box, the list box control's _____ property contains the number 0.
   a. ListIndex
   b. ListValue
   c. SelectedItem
   d. ValueItem

8. The minimum number of option buttons in a dialog box is _____.
   a. 1
   b. 2
   c. 3
   d. 7

9. The Windows standard is to display, in a list box, a minimum of _____ items and a maximum of _____ items at a time.
   a. 2, 7
   b. 2, 8
   c. 3, 8
   d. 3, 10

10. Which of the following instructions can you use in Microsoft Word to select the first item in the lstMonths list box? (The first item is the word "January".)
   a. lstMonths.ListIndex = 0
   b. lstMonths.ListIndex = "January"
   c. lstMonths.Select = 0
   d. lstMonths.Select = True

11. When a user selects an item in a list box included on a form in PowerPoint, the item is contained in the list box control's _____ property.
   a. ListIndex
   b. ListItem
   c. Selected
   d. Value

E X E R C I S E S

1. Write an instruction that you can use in Excel to select the default option button, which is named optVanilla.

2. Write an instruction that you can use in Access to select the first option button in a group control named ogrFlavors.

3. Write an instruction that you can use to select the chkPrint check box.

4. Write an instruction that you can use in Word to select the "Republican" item in the lstParty list box. The item is the second item in the list.

5. Write an instruction that you can use in Access to select the "Republican" item in the lstParty list box.

Exercises 6 and 7 are Discovery Exercises. Discovery Exercises, which may include topics that are not covered in the lesson, allow you to "discover" the solutions to problems on your own.

 discovery ▶

6. In this exercise, you will use the Help screens to research properties of the list box control.
   a. Start Word, Excel, or PowerPoint and open a new document, workbook, or presentation.
   b. Open the Visual Basic Editor. Open the Project Explorer window, if necessary. Right-click the Project Explorer window, then click Import File. Open the Tut13\Concept folder on your Data Disk. Use the Import File dialog box to add the T13-E6 (T13-E6.frm) form to the project.
   c. View the frmNames form object. If necessary, close the Toolbox window and open the Properties window.
   d. Display the Help screens for the list box control's ListStyle and MultiSelect properties. What is the purpose of each property? What are the valid settings for the ListStyle property? What does each setting mean? What are the valid settings for the MultiSelect property? How do you select more than one item when the MultiSelect property is set to fmMultiSelectMulti? How do you select more than one item when the MultiSelect property is set to fmMultiSelectExtended? Close the Help window.

e. Run the dialog box. Notice that six names appear in the list box. Click each name in the list. Notice that only one name can be selected at any one time. Close the dialog box.

f. Complete the table shown in Figure 13-2 by setting the list box control's ListStyle and MultiSelect properties in the Properties window, and then running the dialog box to see the effect. (Refer to your answers from Step d to find out how to determine if more than one item can be selected at a time.)

ListStyle	MultiSelect	What appears inside the list box?	Can more than one item be selected at a time?
fmListStylePlain	fmMultiSelectSingle	Six names	No
fmListStylePlain	fmMultiSelectMulti		
fmListStylePlain	fmMultiSelectExtended		
fmListStyleOption	fmMultiSelectSingle		
fmListStyleOption	fmMultiSelectMulti		
fmListStyleOption	fmMultiSelectExtended		

Figure 13-2

g. Close the application. You do not need to save the document, workbook, or presentation.

discovery ▶ 7. In this exercise, you will learn about the GroupName property and the frame control.

a. Start Word, Excel, or PowerPoint and open a new document, workbook, or presentation.

b. Open the Visual Basic Editor. Open the Project Explorer window, if necessary. Right-click the Project Explorer window, then click Import File. Open the Tut13\Concept folder on your Data Disk. Use the Import File dialog box to add the T13-E7 (T13-E7.frm) form to the project.

c. View the frmEmploy form object. If necessary, close the Toolbox window and open the Properties window. The dialog box contains a frame control and two groups of option buttons. The first group contains the Female and Male option buttons, and the second group contains the Hourly and Salaried option buttons.

d. Run the dialog box. Click each option button. Notice that only one option button can be selected at a time. To indicate that the form contains two groups of option buttons, you can either set each group's GroupName property or you can place one of the groups in a frame control.

e. Close the dialog box. Use the Properties window to set the GroupName property for the Female and Male option buttons to Gender, then set the GroupName property for the Hourly and Salaried option buttons to PayType.

f. Run the dialog box. Click each option button. Notice that only one option button in each group can be selected at a time.

g. Close the dialog box, then delete the contents of each option button's GroupName property. Run the dialog box, then click each option button. Notice that only one of the four buttons can be selected at a time.

h. Close the dialog box. Select the Female and Male option buttons, then drag the buttons into the frame control. Run the dialog box, then click each option button. Notice that only one option button in each group can be selected at a time.

i. Close the dialog box, then close the application. You do not need to save the document, workbook, or presentation.

You also can use VBA in PowerPoint to create procedures that enhance your presentations. Exercise 8 allows you to apply this tutorial's programming concept in a PowerPoint presentation.

powerpoint **8.** In this exercise, you will learn about the ControlTipText property.

a. Start PowerPoint. Open the T13-PP-E8 (T13-PP-E8.ppt) file, which is located in the Tut13\Concept folder on your Data Disk. Click the Enable Macros button, if necessary, then save the file as T13-PP-E8D.

b. Open the Visual Basic Editor. Open the Project Explorer window, then view the frmCompany form object. If necessary, close the Toolbox window and open the Properties window. The dialog box allows the user to enter the company name. You can make your custom dialog boxes easier to use by providing control tips for the various controls in the dialog box. A control tip is a message that appears on the screen when the user briefly rests the mouse pointer on a control without clicking. The purpose of a control tip is to provide the user with information about the control. You enter the control tip message in the control's ControlTipText property. The message should be meaningful, yet short—usually no more than five words in length and entered using book title capitalization.

c. Click the Company Name text box, then click ControlTipText in the Properties window. Set the property to "Company Name" (without the quotation marks) and press the Enter key. Set the OK button's ControlTipText property to "Enter Company Name on Slide". Set the Cancel button's ControlTipText property to "Close Dialog Box".

d. Save the presentation, then return to PowerPoint and view the slide show. Click the "Click to enter company name" hyperlink. When the Enter Company Name dialog box appears, verify that the control tips appear correctly by briefly resting the mouse pointer on each control. Enter your name as the company name, then press the Enter key to select the OK button. The OK button enters your name on the first slide and then it closes the dialog box.

e. Stop the presentation. Save and then close the presentation.

A computer program is good only if it works. Errors in programming code can cause a program to run incorrectly. Therefore, a programmer needs to know how to locate and fix any errors in his or her code. Exercise 9 is a Debugging Exercise. Debugging Exercises allow you to practice recognizing and solving errors in code.

debugging 🐛 **9.** Assume that a Word document contains a custom dialog box. In the dialog box is a list box named lstEmployees and two option buttons named optFulltime and optParttime. The following instructions should select both the third item in the list box and the optFulltime option button. Correct any errors in the instructions.

```
lstEmployees.ListIndex = 3

optFulltime.Value = On
```

Excel Lesson

Using Option Button, Check Box, and List Box Controls in Excel

case▶ Jake Yardley, the manager of the Paradise Electronics store in Jackson, uses an Excel workbook to keep track of the store's monthly computer sales. Jake has decided to create a custom dialog box and a macro that he can use to calculate the total and average sales made by each salesperson during the month.

Viewing the Sales Workbook

The workbook in which Jake records the store's monthly computer sales is stored on your Data Disk. Before creating the custom dialog box and macro that Jake will use to calculate a salesperson's total and average sales, view the workbook.

To view the workbook:

1   Start Microsoft Excel.

2   Open the **T13-EX-1** (T13-EX-1.xls) workbook, which is located in the Tut13\Excel folder on your Data Disk. Click the **Enable Macros** button, if necessary, then save the workbook as **January Sales**.

The January Sales workbook contains one worksheet named January, as shown in Figure 13-3 (on the next page).

The January worksheet shows the date and amount of each sale for the first two weeks of January, as well as the computer's stock number and the salesperson's ID. Notice that the sales data is sorted by date.

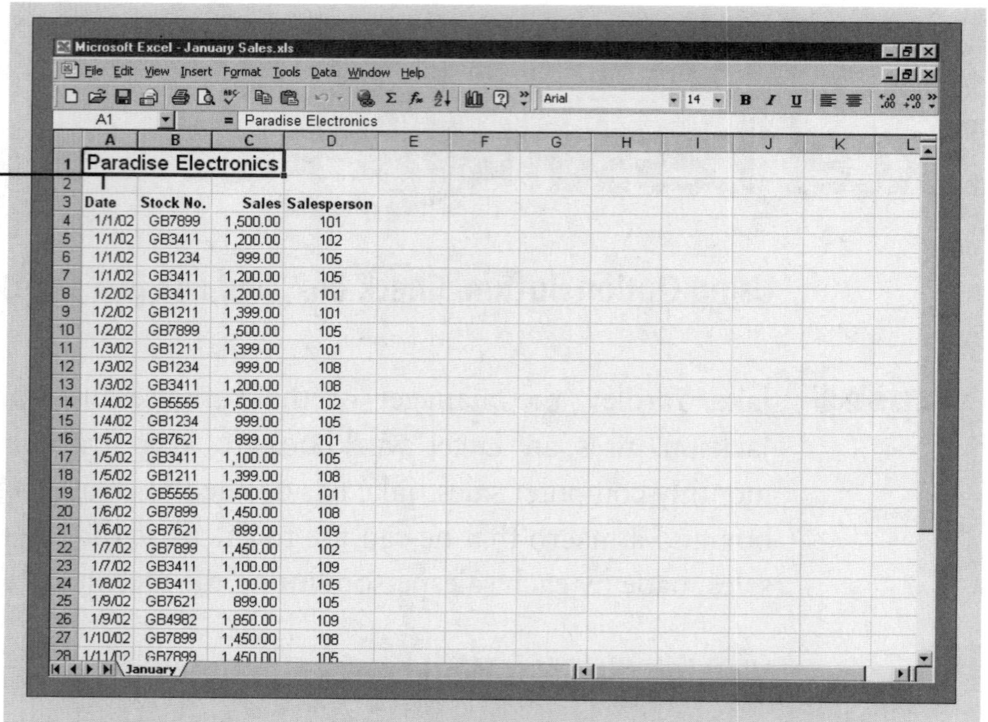

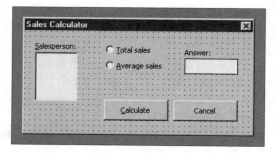

data appears in date order

Figure 13-3: The January worksheet in the January Sales workbook

Figure 13-4 shows the custom dialog box that you will complete in this lesson.

Figure 13-4: The custom dialog box you will complete in this lesson

The dialog box consists of a form and eight controls: three labels, one list box, two option buttons, and two command buttons. After selecting the salesperson's ID in the list box and also selecting the appropriate option button, the user can click the Calculate button to calculate either the salesperson's total sales or his or her average sales. The calculated amount will be displayed in the label control identified by the Answer: caption.

A partially completed Sales Calculator dialog box is included on your Data Disk.

To add the partially completed Sales Calculator dialog box to the project, and then begin completing the dialog box:

1 Press **Alt+F11** to open the Visual Basic Editor. If necessary, open the Project Explorer window and close the Properties window, the Immediate window, and any open Code windows.

2 Right-click the **Project Explorer window** and then click **Import File** on the shortcut menu. The Import File dialog box opens. If necessary, open the Tut13\Excel folder on your Data Disk. Click **T13-EX-1** (T13-EX-1.frm) in the list of filenames and then click the **Open** button.

3 Open the Forms folder in the Project Explorer window. Right-click **frmSalesCalc** in the Forms folder and then click **View Object**. The partially completed frmSalesCalc form appears.

4 If necessary, open the Toolbox and Properties windows, and then drag the windows to the location shown in Figure 13-5. Click the **form** to make it the active window.

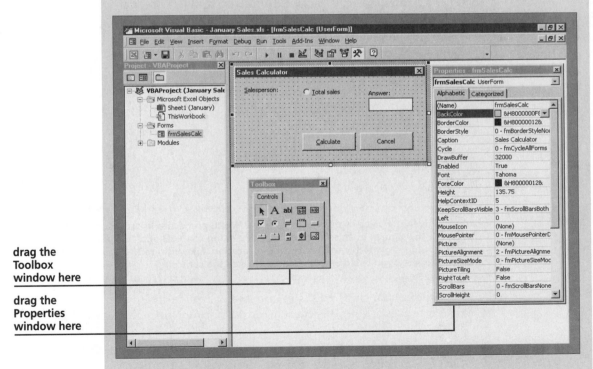

drag the
Toolbox
window here

drag the
Properties
window here

Figure 13-5: Partially completed Sales Calculator dialog box

To complete the dialog box's interface, you need to add one option button and one list box to the form. You then need to set the appropriate properties for those controls.

5 Drag the **OptionButton** tool 🔘 from the toolbox to the form. Place the option button immediately below the other option button. (Don't worry about the exact location or size—you will adjust the position and size of the control in the next set of steps.)

6 Drag the **ListBox** tool 🔳 from the toolbox to the form. Place the list box immediately below the Salesperson: label. (Don't worry about the exact location or size—you will adjust the position and size of the control in the next set of steps.)

7 Close the Toolbox window.

You now will set the appropriate properties for the option button and list box controls.

To set the properties for the option button and list box controls:

1 Click the **OptionButton1** control to select it, then use the Properties window to set the following properties. (The three-character ID used in an option button's name is *opt*.)

Property	Value
Name	**optAverage**
Accelerator	**A**
Caption	**Average sales**
Left	**90**
Top	**30**
Width	**70**

You are given the values for the Left, Top, and Width properties in order for your screen to match the figures in this book. Instead of setting the Left and Top properties, you simply could drag the control to its proper location. Likewise, rather than setting the Width property, you could use the handles to size the control.

To indicate that the Total Sales and Average Sales option buttons belong to the same group, you will set each button's GroupName property to the same value, Calculation.

2 Set the optAverage control's GroupName property to **Calculation**, then set the optTotal control's GroupName property to **Calculation**.

tip

If a form contains only one group of option buttons, it is not essential to set the GroupName property; the option buttons will work correctly even if the GroupName property is not set. However, you must either set the GroupName property or use a frame control to include more than one group of option buttons on a form. You can learn more about the GroupName property and the frame control in the Concept lesson's Exercise 7.

3 Click the **ListBox1** control to select it, then use the Properties window to set the following properties. (The three-character ID used in a list box's name is *lst*.)

Property	Value
Name	**lstId**
Height	**50**
Left	**12**
Top	**24**

4 Click the **form**. Figure 13-6 shows the current status of the form.

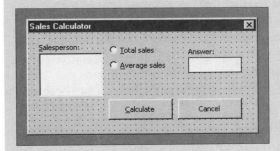

Figure 13-6: Current status of the form

After adding the controls to the form, recall that you then need to determine the appropriate tab order for the essential controls. The Sales Calculator dialog box contains five essential controls: one list box, two option buttons, and two command buttons. The focus should begin in the list box, which is the essential control located in the upper-left corner of the form. Pressing the Tab key should move the focus first to the option buttons and then to the command buttons.

As you learned in Tutorial 12, you specify the tab order by setting each essential control's TabIndex property. If an essential control has an identifying label, recall that you also must set the identifying label's TabIndex property. In this case, you will need to set the TabIndex property for the following six controls: Label1 (the label captioned Salesperson:), lstId, optTotal, optAverage, cmdCalc, and cmdCancel.

To set the tab order, then run the dialog box to test it:

1 Set the TabIndex property for the six controls as follows:

Control	TabIndex value
Label1	**0** (the number 0)
lstId	**1** (the number 1)
optTotal	**2**
optAverage	**3**
cmdCalc	**4**
cmdCancel	**5**

2 Close the Project Explorer and Properties windows.

3 Save the workbook, then click the **Run Sub/UserForm** button ▶ to run the dialog box.

4 Verify that the tab order is set appropriately. Also verify that the accelerator keys work correctly.

HELP? Because the list box does not contain any items, you will not see the focus when the dialog box first appears, nor will you see it when you tab to the list box.

5 Click the **Cancel** button, which already has been coded for you, to close the dialog box. (The Cancel button contains the instruction `Unload frmSalesCalc`, which removes the form from both the screen and the computer's memory.)

Now that you have completed the dialog box's interface, you can begin coding the dialog box. First you will code the form's Initialize event.

Coding the Form's Initialize Event

A form's **Initialize event** occurs after the form is loaded into memory but before it is shown on the screen. In the Initialize event, you enter code that prepares the form for use—for example, code that sets the initial values for controls or code that arranges the worksheet data in a specific order. Figure 13-7 shows the pseudocode for the Sales Calculator form's Initialize event.

1. Fill the list box with unique IDs only. To do so,
   a. Assign the column heading "Salesperson" to a String variable named strId.
   b. Sort the sales data in order by the Salesperson column.
   c. Repeat the following for each cell in the Salesperson column:
      1) If the value stored in the current cell is not equal to the value stored in the strId variable, then
         a) Add the current cell's value to the list box.
         b) Assign the current cell's value to the strId variable.
2. Select the first item in the list box as the default item.
3. Select the default option button (Total sales).

Figure 13-7: Pseudocode for the Sales Calculator form's Initialize event

Figure 13-8 lists the variables that the Initialize event will use.

Variable	datatype
strId	String
rngData	Range
rngCell	Range

Figure 13-8: Variables used by the form's Initialize event procedure

The Initialize event procedure will use the strId variable to store the column heading "Salesperson"; it also will use the variable to store the ID mostly recently added to the list box. The rngData variable will store the address of the sales data range—currently, A3:D36. The rngCell variable will be used in a For Each…Next statement that repeats its instructions for each cell in the Salesperson column.

To begin coding the form's Initialize event:

1 Right-click the **form**, then click **View Code**. The Code window opens and shows the code template for the UserForm's Click event procedure.

2 View the code template for the UserForm's **Initialize** event procedure, then enter the documentation and the Dim and Set statements shown in Figure 13-9.

be sure to
enter the
code in the
Initialize event

enter these five
lines of code

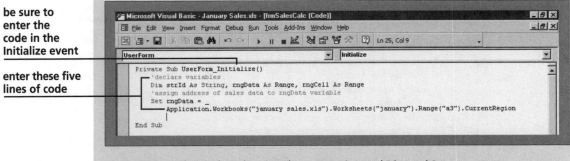

Figure 13-9: Code window showing documentation and Dim and Set statements

Step 1 in the pseudocode is to fill the list box with unique IDs from the worksheet. To do so, you first will assign the column heading "Salesperson" to the
strId variable.

3 Press the **Backspace** key, then type **'assign column heading to strId variable**
and press the **Enter** key.

4 Type **strid = "Salesperson"** and press the **Enter** key. (Be sure to begin the word
"Salesperson" with an uppercase letter "S".)

Next, sort the sales data range in ascending order by the Salesperson column.
You can use the Range object's Sort method to do so.

Using the Sort Method to Sort a Range

You can use the Range object's Sort method to sort a range of values in either
ascending or descending order. Figure 13-10 shows the basic syntax and some
examples of the Sort method.

Syntax:

rangeObject.**Sort Key1:**=*key1*[, **Order1:**=*order1*][, **Key2:**=*key2*][, **Order2:**=*order2*] _
                [, **Key3:**=*key3*][, **Order3:**=*order3*][, **Header:**=*header*]

Examples:

```
rngDsata.Sort Key1:="Salesperson", Order1:=xlAscending, _
          Header:=xlYes

rngData.Sort Key1:="Salesperson", Order1:=xlAscending, _
          Key2:="Sales", Order2:=xlDescending, _
          Header:=xlYes
```

Figure 13-10: Basic syntax and examples of the Range object's Sort method

You can sort a range of data based on the values stored in the one, two, or three different columns specified in the Sort method's Key1, Key2, and Key3 arguments. You use the Order1, Order2, and Order3 arguments, which can be set to either of the intrinsic constants `xlAscending` or `xlDescending`, to indicate the order in which the data in each column should be sorted.

 tip

> You also can use the Sort method to sort data based on the information stored in one, two, or three rows. To learn how to do so, view the Sort Method Help screen.

You use the Header argument, which can be set to the intrinsic constants `xlYes`, `xlNo`, or `xlGuess`, to specify whether the first row in the sort range contains column headers. Setting the Header argument to `xlYes` indicates that the first row in the sort range contains column headers; the headers will not be sorted along with the other data. Setting the Header argument to `xlNo`, which is the default value, indicates that the sort range does not contain headers and, therefore, the entire range should be sorted. You can use the `xlGuess` constant to let Microsoft Excel determine whether the sort range contains headers. (You may need to do so if you are importing data from a database, and you are not sure if the data contains headers.)

The first example shown in Figure 13-10 will sort the rngData range (A3:D36) in ascending order by the salesperson ID. Notice that the example uses the column header "Salesperson" as the Key1 argument. The second example will sort the rngData range in ascending order by the salesperson ID. However, if more than one row contains the same salesperson ID, the data in those rows will be sorted in descending order by the sales amount. Because the first row in the rngData range contains column headers, the Header argument is set to `xlYes` in both examples to exclude the headers from the sort.

Now that you know how to use the Sort method, you can continue coding the form's Initialize event procedure.

To continue coding the form's Initialize event procedure:

1 Type **'sort sales data, then add only unique IDs to list box** and press the **Enter** key, then type **rngdata.sort key1:=strid, header:=xlyes** and press the **Enter** key.

Now begin a For Each...Next loop that will repeat its instructions for each cell in the Salesperson column of the rngData range. The Salesperson column is column 4 in the range.

2 Type **for each rngcell in rngdata.columns(4).cells** and press the **Enter** key.

If the value stored in the current cell is not equal to the value stored in the strId variable, then the procedure should add the current cell's value to the list box.

3   Press the **Tab** key, then type **if rngcell.value <> strid then** and press the **Enter** key. Your code should look like Figure 13-11.

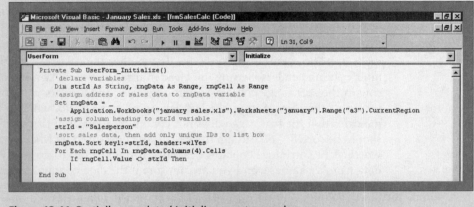

```
Microsoft Visual Basic - January Sales.xls - [frmSalesCalc (Code)]
File  Edit  View  Insert  Format  Debug  Run  Tools  Add-Ins  Window  Help
                                                        Ln 31, Col 9
UserForm                                    Initialize

Private Sub UserForm_Initialize()
    'declare variables
    Dim strId As String, rngData As Range, rngCell As Range
    'assign address of sales data to rngData variable
    Set rngData = _
        Application.Workbooks("january sales.xls").Worksheets("january").Range("a3").CurrentRegion
    'assign column heading to strId variable
    strId = "Salesperson"
    'sort sales data, then add only unique IDs to list box
    rngData.Sort key1:=strId, header:=xlYes
    For Each rngCell In rngData.Columns(4).Cells
        If rngCell.Value <> strId Then

End Sub
```

Figure 13-11: Partially completed Initialize event procedure

4   Save the workbook.

Before you can enter the code that will add an item to a list box, you need to learn how to use the list box's AddItem method.

The AddItem Method

You use the AddItem method to specify the items you want displayed in a list box control. The syntax of the AddItem method is *object*.**AddItem** *item*, where *object* is the name of the control to which you want the item added and *item* is the expression you want displayed in the control. The expression can be either numeric or string; however, if you want to display a string in the list box, you must enclose the string in quotation marks. Figure 13-12 shows some examples of using the AddItem method to display items in a list box.

tip

The AddItem method also allows you to specify the position where the new item will be placed within the control's list. To learn more about the AddItem method, view its Help screen.

Example	Result
`lstAnimal.AddItem "Dog"`	Displays the string "Dog" in the lstAnimal list box
`lstAge.AddItem 35`	Displays the number 35 in the lstAge list box

`For sngCount = 0 To 5 Step .5`
`    lstRate.AddItem sngCount`
`Next sngCount`
	Displays the numbers from 0 through 5, in increments of .5, in the lstRate list box

`lstId.AddItem rngCell.Value`	Displays the contents of the rngCell range in the lstId list box

Figure 13-12: Examples of using the AddItem method

The first two examples shown in Figure 13-12 use the AddItem method to add a string literal constant ("Dog") and a numeric literal constant (35), respectively, to a list box. The third example uses the AddItem method within a loop to display the numbers from 0 through 5, in increments of .5, in a list box. The last example shown in the figure uses the AddItem method to display the contents of a cell in a list box.

To complete the Initialize event procedure, then test the procedure:

1   Press the **Tab** key, then type **lstid.additem rngcell.value** and press the **Enter** key. This instruction will add the current cell's value to the list box.

Now assign the current cell's value to the strId variable to indicate that this ID already has been added to the list box.

2   Type **strid = rngcell.value** and press the **Enter** key.

You now can enter the code that will end the selection and repetition structures.

3   Press the **Backspace** key, then type **end if** and press the **Enter** key. Press the **Backspace** key, then type **next rngcell** and press the **Enter** key.

Step 2 in the pseudocode is to select the default list box item—in this case, the default item will be the first item in the list. You can use the ListIndex property to select the default item. Recall that the first item in a list box has a ListIndex value of 0.

4   Type **'select default list box item** and press the **Enter** key, then type **lstid.listindex = 0** (the number 0) and press the **Enter** key.

The last step in the pseudocode is to select the default option button. You do so by setting the option button's Value property to the Boolean value True.

5   Type the additional code shown in Figure 13-13, which shows the completed Initialize event procedure.

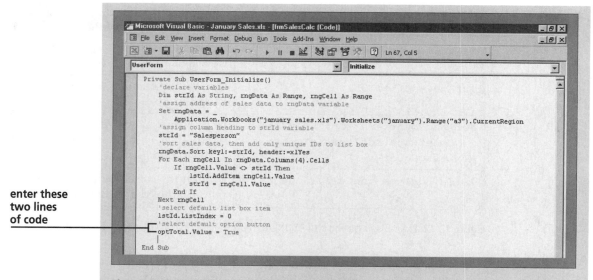

enter these two lines of code

Figure 13-13: Completed Initialize event procedure

6 Verify the accuracy of your code by comparing the code on your screen to the code shown in Figure 13-13, then close the Code window.

7 Save the workbook, then click the **Run Sub/UserForm** button ▶ to run the dialog box. See Figure 13-14.

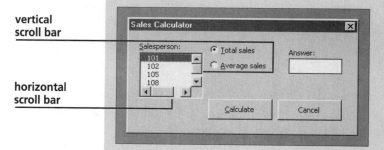

vertical scroll bar

horizontal scroll bar

Figure 13-14: List box showing scroll bars

HELP? If no data appears in your list box and the Total sales option button is not selected, close the dialog box. Verify that you entered the code shown in Figure 13-13 in the UserForm's Initialize procedure, rather than in another procedure. If you entered the code in the wrong procedure, cut the code from the incorrect procedure and then paste it into the Initialize event procedure.

After the form is loaded into memory, but before it appears on the screen, the Initialize event procedure fills the list box with the unique salesperson IDs from the worksheet. It then selects the first item in the list box and it also selects the Total sales option button.

Notice that the list box contains both horizontal and vertical scroll bars. The horizontal scroll bar allows you to scroll the list box horizontally.

8 Use the horizontal scroll bar, which appears along the bottom of the list box, to scroll the list box. Notice that the list box is slightly wider than is needed to show its contents.

The vertical scroll bar indicates that the list box contains more items than can be viewed at the same time.

9 Use the vertical scroll bar, which appears along the right side of the list box, to scroll the list box. Notice that the list box contains one additional ID, 109.

10 Close the dialog box.

You can use the list box's ColumnWidths property, which controls the width of each column in a list box, to remove the horizontal scroll bar, and you can use either the list box's handles or its Width property to decrease the width of the list box. You can eliminate the vertical scroll bar by increasing the height of the list box so that all items can be displayed at the same time. You can increase the height either by dragging the list box's handles or by setting the list box's Height property. In this case, you will remove both scroll bars from the lstId list box.

 tip

As you learned in the Concept lesson, the minimum number of items you should display in a list box at any one time is three, and the maximum number is eight.

To remove the horizontal and vertical scroll bars from the lstId list box:

1 Right-click the **lstId list box**, then click **Properties**. Set the ColumnWidths property to **45**.

HELP? 45 pt will appear as the value of the ColumnWidths property. The "pt" stands for "point". A point is 1/72 of an inch.

 tip

As you will learn in this lesson's Exercise 6, a list box can contain more than one column of data.

2   Set the list box's Height property to **56** and its Width property to **48**.

3   Close the Properties window. Save the workbook, then run the dialog box. Notice that the five IDs appear in the list box, and that the list box does not contain any scroll bars.

4   Close the dialog box.

The next procedure you will code is the Calculate button's Click event.

Coding the Calculate Button's Click Event Procedure

Figure 13-15 shows the pseudocode for the Calculate button's Click event procedure.

1. Assign the ID selected in the list box to a String variable named strId.
2. Search the Salesperson column for the first occurrence of the ID contained in the strId variable. Exclude the column heading from the search.
3. Beginning with the first occurrence of the ID, repeat the following while the ID in the Salesperson column matches the ID stored in the strId variable:
   a.   Add the sales, located in the Sales column, to the curSales variable.
   b.   Add 1 to the number of sales stored in the intNumSales variable.
   c.   Increase the row number by one.
4. If the Total sales option button is selected, then
   a.   Display the total sales, formatted to currency, in the lblAnswer control.
   Else
   a.   Calculate the average sales by dividing the total sales stored in curSales by the number of sales stored in intNumSales.
   b.   Display the average sales, formatted to currency, in the lblAnswer control.

Figure 13-15: Pseudocode for the Calculate button's Click event procedure

Figure 13-16 lists the variables that the Calculate button's Click event procedure will use.

Variable	datatype
rngData	Range
intRow	Integer
strId	String
intNumSales	Integer
curSales	Currency

Figure 13-16: Variables used by the Calculate button's Click event procedure

The procedure will store the address of the sales data—currently, A3:D36—in the rngData variable, and it will use the intRow variable to keep track of each row in the rngData range. It will use the strId variable to store the ID the user selects in the list box, and it will use the intNumSales and curSales variables to count and accumulate, respectively, the salesperson's sales.

To begin coding the Calculate button's Click event procedure:

1 Right-click the **Calculate** button, then click **View Code**. In the Calculate button's Click event procedure, enter the documentation and the Dim and Set statements shown in Figure 13-17.

enter these five lines of code

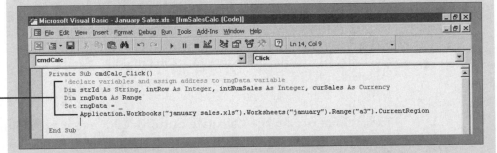

```
Private Sub cmdCalc_Click()
    'declare variables and assign address to rngData variable
    Dim strId As String, intRow As Integer, intNumSales As Integer, curSales As Currency
    Dim rngData As Range
    Set rngData = _
        Application.Workbooks("january sales.xls").Worksheets("january").Range("a3").CurrentRegion

End Sub
```

Figure 13-17: Code window showing documentation and Dim and Set statements

The first step in the pseudocode is to assign, to the strId variable, the item selected in the list box. When the user selects an item in a list box, the selected item is assigned automatically to the list box's Value property.

> **tip**
>
> Recall that the selected item's location in the list is assigned automatically to the list box's ListIndex property.

2 Press the **Backspace** key. Type **'assign selected list box item to strId variable** and press the **Enter** key, then type **strId = lstId.value** and press the **Enter** key.

The next step is to search the Salesperson column, excluding the column heading, for the first occurrence of the selected ID. You will need to use a repetition structure to perform the search. To exclude the column heading, you will begin the search in row 2 of the rngData range.

3 Type **'locate first occurrence of ID** and press the **Enter** key, then type **introw = 2** and press the **Enter** key.

4 Type **do until rngdata.cells(rowindex:=introw, columnindex:=4).value = strid** and press the **Enter** key.

```
You   also   could   have   written   the   Do   clause   as   Do While
rngData.Cells(RowIndex:=intRow, ColumnIndex:=4).Value <> strId.
```

If the ID contained in the current row of the Salesperson column does not match the ID selected by the user and contained in the strId variable, the loop should search the next row in the Salesperson column.

5 Press the **Tab** key, then type **introw = introw + 1** and press the **Enter** key. Press the **Backspace** key, then type **loop** and press the **Enter** key to end the loop.

The Do loop will stop when it locates the first occurrence of the ID in the Salesperson column. At that point, the intRow variable will contain the row number of the row where the ID is located in the column.

After locating the first occurrence of the ID, the procedure will use another Do loop to both accumulate and count the salesperson's sales amounts. This Do loop will stop when it encounters an ID that differs from the one stored in the strId variable. (Recall that the procedure first sorts the sales data in ascending order by the salesperson ID.)

To continue coding the Calculate button's Click event procedure:

1 Type **'accumulate and count salesperson's sales, stop when loop encounters different ID** and press the **Enter** key.

2 Type **do while rngdata.cells(rowindex:=introw, columnindex:=4).value = strid** and press the **Enter** key.

3 Press the **Tab** key, then type **cursales = cursales + rngdata.cells(rowindex:=introw, columnindex:=3).value** and press the **Enter** key.

4 Type **intnumsales = intnumsales + 1** and press the **Enter** key.

Now, increase the row number by one and then end the loop.

5 Type **introw = introw + 1** and press the **Enter** key. Press the **Backspace** key, then type **loop** and press the **Enter** key.

The last step in the pseudocode is to determine which option button is selected, and then display either the total sales or the average sales. If an option button is selected, its Value property will contain the Boolean value True; otherwise, it will contain the Boolean value False.

6 Enter the selection structure shown in Figure 13-18, which shows the completed Click event procedure for the Calculate button.

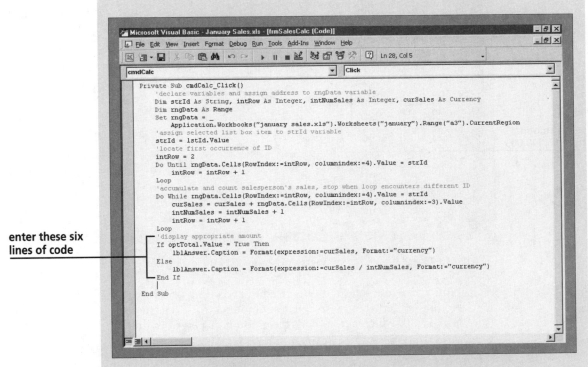

enter these six lines of code

```
Private Sub cmdCalc_Click()
    'declare variables and assign address to rngData variable
    Dim strId As String, intRow As Integer, intNumSales As Integer, curSales As Currency
    Dim rngData As Range
    Set rngData = _
        Application.Workbooks("january sales.xls").Worksheets("january").Range("a3").CurrentRegion
    'assign selected list box item to strId variable
    strId = lstId.Value
    'locate first occurrence of ID
    intRow = 2
    Do Until rngData.Cells(RowIndex:=intRow, columnindex:=4).Value = strId
        intRow = intRow + 1
    Loop
    'accumulate and count salesperson's sales, stop when loop encounters different ID
    Do While rngData.Cells(RowIndex:=intRow, columnindex:=4).Value = strId
        curSales = curSales + rngData.Cells(RowIndex:=intRow, columnindex:=3).Value
        intNumSales = intNumSales + 1
        intRow = intRow + 1
    Loop
    'display appropriate amount
    If optTotal.Value = True Then
        lblAnswer.Caption = Format(expression:=curSales, Format:="currency")
    Else
        lblAnswer.Caption = Format(expression:=curSales / intNumSales, Format:="currency")
    End If
End Sub
```

Figure 13-18: Completed Click event procedure for the Calculate button

7 Verify the accuracy of your code by comparing the code on your screen to the code shown in Figure 13-18.

8 Close the Code window, then save the workbook.

Now that you have finished coding the Calculate button's Click event procedure, you will test it to be sure it is working correctly.

To test the Calculate button's Click event procedure:

1 Run the dialog box. Click **102** in the list box, then click the **Calculate** button. The total sales made by salesperson 102 ($6,149.00) appears in the lblAnswer control. If necessary, drag the dialog box to the location shown in Figure 13-19.

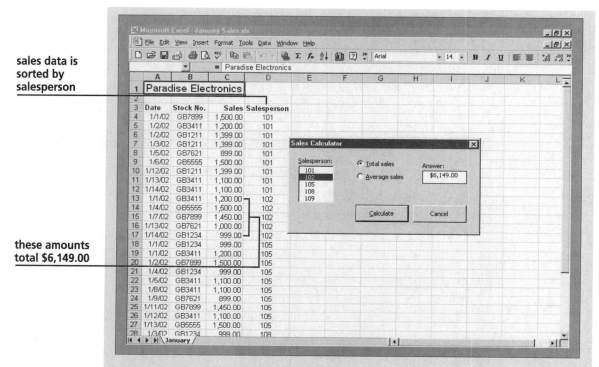

sales data is sorted by salesperson

these amounts total $6,149.00

Figure 13-19: Total sales for salesperson 102 shown in the dialog box

Notice that the sales data is sorted in ascending order by the salesperson ID. Adding together the five sales amounts for salesperson 102 results in $6,149.00, which agrees with the amount displayed in the lblAnswer control.

Use the dialog box to display the average sales for salesperson 109.

2   Click **109** in the list box, then click the **Average sales** option button. Notice that selecting either a different ID or a different option button does not change the value previously displayed in the lblAnswer control, which can be misleading to the user. You will fix this problem in this lesson's Exercise 1.

3   Click the **Calculate** button to calculate and display salesperson 109's average sales. The label control shows that the average sales are $1,424.75.

4   Close the dialog box.

Now that the custom dialog box has been tested, all that remains is to enter the Show method in a macro procedure. Recall that you use the Show method to display a custom dialog box on the screen.

Coding the CalculateSales Macro

The January Sales workbook already contains the code template for the CalculateSales macro procedure.

To code the CalculateSales procedure, then test the macro:

1 Open the Project Explorer window. Open the Module1 module's Code window, then view the code template for the **CalculateSales** procedure.

2 Press the **Tab** key. Type **'display custom dialog box** and press the **Enter** key, then type **frmsalescalc.show** and press the **Enter** key.

3 Save the workbook, then return to Excel.

4 Run the **CalculateSales** macro. Use the Sales Calculator dialog box to calculate the total sales for salesperson 105. The label control should show that the total sales are $11,847.00.

5 Close the dialog box. Save the workbook, then exit Excel.

You now have completed Tutorial 13's Excel lesson. You can either take a break or complete the end-of-lesson exercises before moving on to the next lesson.

E X E R C I S E S

1. In this exercise, you will make some improvements and add a check box to the custom dialog box you created in this lesson. You also will learn about the UserForm's QueryClose event.
    a. Open the January Sales (January Sales.xls) workbook, which is located in the Tut13\Excel folder on your Data Disk. Click the Enable Macros button, if necessary, then save the workbook as T13-EX-E1D.
    b. Open the Visual Basic Editor. Open the Project Explorer window, if necessary, and view the frmSalesCalc form. Change the filename in the Set statements, located in the UserForm's Initialize event and in the Calculate button's Click event, to "t13-ex-e1d.xls".
    c. When the user clicks an item in the list box, the list box should remove the value stored in the lblAnswer control. Code the appropriate list box event.
    d. When the user clicks an option button, the option button should remove the value stored in the lblAnswer control. Code the appropriate option button event.
    e. Add a check box control to the form. Set the check box's Name property to chkDateSort. Set its Caption property to Sort by date, then set its Accelerator property to the letter d. Position the check box below the option buttons, then size the check box appropriately.
    f. Change the tab order of the controls appropriately.

g. Use the Help screens to research the UserForm's QueryClose event. When does this event occur? How can you prevent the UserForm from closing? Close the Help window.

h. Open the UserForm's QueryClose event. If the Sort by date check box is selected, the event should sort the sales data in ascending order by the Date column; otherwise, it should leave the sales data sorted by the Salesperson column. (*Hint*: Like option buttons, check boxes have a Value property that indicates whether the control is selected.)

i. Save the workbook, then return to Excel and run the CalculateSales macro. Click the Calculate button to display the total sales for ID 101 in the lblAnswer control.

j. Click 105 in the list box, which should clear the value displayed in the lblAnswer control. Click the Calculate button to display the total sales for ID 105.

k. Click the Average sales option button, which should clear the value displayed in the lblAnswer control. Click the Calculate button to display the average sales for ID 105.

l. Click the Cancel button to close the dialog box. The sales data should appear in ascending order by the Salesperson column.

m. Run the CalculateSales macro again. Click the Sort by date check box, then click the Cancel button. The UserForm's QueryClose event should sort the sales data in ascending order by the Date column.

n. Save and then close the workbook.

2. In this exercise, you will modify the custom dialog box that you created in Tutorial 12's Excel lesson so that it uses a list box rather than a text box.

a. Open the T13-EX-E2 (T13-EX-E2.xls) workbook, which is located in the Tut13\Excel folder on your Data Disk. Click the Enable Macros button, if necessary, then save the workbook as T13-EX-E2D.

b. Open the Visual Basic Editor. Open the Project Explorer window, if necessary, and view the frmUpdateInv form. Open the Toolbox and Properties windows.

c. Remove the txtModel text box from the form, then add a list box in its place. Name the list box lstModel.

d. Add two option buttons to the form. Name the buttons optSale and optReturn. Change the optSale button's Caption property to "Sale" and set its Accelerator property to "S". Change the optReturn button's Caption property to "Return" and set its Accelerator property to "R". To indicate that the buttons belong to the same group, set each option button's GroupName property to SaleType.

e. Change the Caption property for the Label2 control from "Number sold:" to "Number sold/returned:". Adjust the position of the controls appropriately.

f. Change the tab order of the controls appropriately. Close the Project Explorer, Properties, and Toolbox windows.

g. Open the UserForm's Initialize event. The Initialize event should display, in the lstModel list box, the model numbers located in the worksheet's Models range (A5:A18). It also should select both the first item in the list box and the optSale button. (Notice that the model numbers in the worksheet are unique.)

h. Open the Update button's Click event. Modify the code as follows: Assign the model number selected in the list box to the strModel variable. If the optSale button is selected, the procedure should subtract the number entered in the txtNumSold control from the current inventory; otherwise, it should add the amount to the current inventory.

    i. Save the workbook, then return to Excel and run the UpdateInventory macro. Use the Update Inventory dialog box to record the return of three H560 computers. The updated inventory amount (15) should appear in the lblUpdated control and in cell B11 in the worksheet.

    j. Save and then close the workbook.

3. In this exercise, you will modify the custom dialog box that you created in this lesson so that it works for three worksheets. (It is recommended that you complete Exercise 7 in this tutorial's Concept lesson before completing this exercise.)

    a. Open the T13-EX-E3 (T13-EX-E3.xls) workbook, which is located in the Tut13\Excel folder on your Data Disk. Click the Enable Macros button, if necessary, then save the workbook as T13-EX-E3D.

    b. Open the Visual Basic Editor. Use the Help screens to research the list box control's Clear method and its Click event, then close the Help window.

    c. Open the Project Explorer window, if necessary, and view the frmSalesCalc form. Open the Toolbox and Properties windows, if necessary. Add three option buttons to the form. Position the option buttons to the right of the list box. Name the buttons optJan, optFeb, and optMar, then change each button's Caption, Accelerator, and TabIndex properties appropriately. To indicate that the three buttons belong to the same group, set each of the three button's GroupName property to Month.

    d. Open the UserForm's Initialize event. The Initialize event should select the optJan control and the optAverage control.

    e. When the user clicks either of the option buttons in the Month group, the option button's Click event should activate the appropriate worksheet. It then should clear the contents of the lstId list box before displaying, in the list box, the unique sales-person IDs from the active worksheet. Finally, the procedure should select the first item in the lstId control and remove the contents of the lblAnswer control. Code the appropriate events.

    f. When the user clicks an item in the lstId control, or when he or she clicks either the Total sales or Average sales option buttons, the control should remove the contents of the lblAnswer control. Code the appropriate events.

    g. Open the Calculate button's Click event and make any necessary modifications. (*Hint*: Research the Workbook object's ActiveSheet property.)

    h. Save the workbook, then return to Excel and run the CalculateSales macro. Click the Calculate button to display the total January sales for ID 101 in the lblAnswer control.

    i. Click the optMar button, which should activate the March worksheet before displaying only the worksheet's unique IDs in the list box. The option button also should clear the value displayed in the lblAnswer control. Click 105 in the list box, then click the Calculate button to display the total March sales for ID 105.

    j. Click the Average sales option button, which should clear the value displayed in the lblAnswer control, then click the optFeb button. Click 105 in the list box, and then click the Calculate button to display the average February sales for ID 105.

    k. Click the Cancel button to close the dialog box.

    l. Save and then close the workbook.

4. In this exercise, you will code a custom dialog box so that it displays the total and average sales for any number of worksheets.

    a. Open the T13-EX-E4 (T13-EX-E4.xls) workbook, which is located in the Tut13\Excel folder on your Data Disk. Click the Enable Macros button, if necessary, then save the workbook as T13-EX-E4D.

b. Open the Visual Basic Editor. Open the Project Explorer window, if necessary, and view the frmSalesCalc form object.

c. Use the Help screens to research the list box control's Clear method and its Click event, then close the Help window.

d. Open the form's Initialize event. The Initialize event should display the three worksheet names in the lstMonth control. (The code should work even if the user changes the name of one of the worksheets.) It then should select the first item in the lstMonth control and it also should select the optTotal control. Code the event appropriately.

e. Open the lstMonth control's Click event. When the user clicks an item in the lstMonth list box, the list box should activate the appropriate worksheet. It then should clear the contents of the lstId list box before displaying, in the lstId list box, the unique salesperson IDs from the worksheet. Finally, it should select the first item in the lstId control and remove the contents of the lblAnswer control. Code the event appropriately.

f. When the user clicks an item in the lstId control, or he or she clicks an option button, the control should remove the contents of the lblAnswer control. Code the appropriate events.

g. Open the Calculate button's Click event. Change the Set statement so that it refers to the active worksheet, rather than the "jan" worksheet.

h. Save the workbook, then return to Excel and run the CalculateSales macro. Click the Calculate button to display the total January sales for ID 101 ($11,496.00) in the lblAnswer control.

i. Click Feb in the list box, which should activate the Feb worksheet and also clear the value displayed in the lblAnswer control. Click 105 in the list box, then click the Calculate button to display the total February sales for ID 105 ($11,847.00).

j. Click the Average sales option button, which should clear the value displayed in the lblAnswer control. Click the Calculate button to display the average February sales for ID 105 ($1,184.70)

k. Click the Cancel button to close the dialog box.

l. Save and then close the workbook.

Exercises 5 and 6 are Discovery Exercises. Discovery Exercises, which may include topics that are not covered in the lesson, allow you to "discover" the solutions to problems on your own.

discovery ▶ 5. In this exercise, you will learn about a list box's RowSource property.

a. Open the T13-EX-E5 (T13-EX-E5.xls) workbook, which is located in the Tut13\Excel folder on your Data Disk. Click the Enable Macros button, if necessary, then save the workbook as T13-EX-E5D.

b. Open the Visual Basic Editor. Open the Project Explorer window, if necessary, and view the frmUpdateInv form object. Familiarize yourself with the dialog box's controls.

c. Set the lblUpdated control's TextAlign property so that it centers the contents of the label control.

d. Display the RowSource Property Help screen. Study the Help screen, then close the Help window.

e. Open the UserForm's Initialize event. The Initialize event should display, in the lstModel list box, the model numbers located in the worksheet's Models range (A5:A18). It also should select the first item in the list box. Use the RowSource property to display the appropriate model numbers. (Notice that the model numbers in the worksheet are unique.)

f. Save the workbook, then return to Excel and run the UpdateInventory macro. Use the Update Inventory dialog box to record the sale of two C200 computers. The updated inventory amount (3) should appear in the lblUpdated control and in cell B6 in the worksheet.

g. Close the dialog box. Save and then close the workbook.

discovery ▶ 6. In this exercise, you will learn about a list box's BoundColumn, ColumnCount, ColumnWidths, RowSource, Text, TextColumn, and Value properties.

a. Open the T13-EX-E6 (T13-EX-E6.xls) workbook, which is located in the Tut13\Excel folder on your Data Disk. Click the Enable Macros button, if necessary, then save the workbook as T13-EX-E6D.

b. Open the Visual Basic Editor. Open the Project Explorer window, if necessary, and view the frmInventory form object. Use the Help screens to research the BoundColumn, ColumnCount, ColumnWidths, RowSource, and TextColumn properties for a list box. What is the purpose of each of these properties? Close the Help window.

c. Click the lstInventory list box in the form. Display the Properties window, if necessary. Notice that the BoundColumn and ColumnCount properties are set to 1, and the TextColumn property contains a -1. What does the -1 in the TextColumn property indicate?

d. Open the Display button's Click event and study its code.

e. Open the UserForm's Initialize event. The Initialize event should use the list box's RowSource property to display, in the lstInventory list box, the information located in the worksheet's Models range (A5:C18). It also should select the first item in the list. Code the event procedure appropriately.

f. Save the workbook, then run the dialog box. Only the IDs from the Models range should appear in the list box. Click C200 in the list, then click the Display button. What values are stored in the list box's Text and Value properties? Close the dialog box.

g. In the Properties window, change the list box's ColumnCount property to 3. Run the dialog box. What changes appear in the list box? Click C200 in the list, then click the Display button. What values are stored in the list box's Text and Value properties? Close the dialog box.

h. In the Properties window, change the list box's BoundColumn property to 2. Run the dialog box. Click C200 in the list, then click the Display button. What values are stored in the list box's Text and Value properties? Which of the two properties is controlled by the BoundColumn property? Close the dialog box.

i. In the Properties window, change the list box's TextColumn property to 3. Run the dialog box. Click C200 in the list, then click the Display button. What values are stored in the list box's Text and Value properties? Which of the two properties is controlled by the TextColumn property? Close the dialog box.

j. In the Properties window, change the list box's ColumnWidths property so that only the model numbers appear in the first column. The other two columns should be hidden. Run the dialog box. Click C200 in the list, then click the Display button. Can you still access the Text and Value properties when the columns to which they refer are hidden? Close the dialog box.

k. Save and then close the workbook.

A computer program is good only if it works. Errors in programming code can cause a program to run incorrectly. Therefore, a programmer needs to know how to locate and fix any errors in his or her code. Exercise 7 is a Debugging Exercise. Debugging Exercises allow you to practice recognizing and solving errors in code.

debugging 7. The following code should display, in the lstNum list box, the numbers 1 through 5 in increments of .5. The code results in an endless loop. Correct any errors in the code.

```
Private Sub UserForm_Initialize()
    Dim intNum As Integer
    For intNum = 1 To 5 Step 0.5
        lstNum.AddItem intNum
    Next intNum
End Sub
```

Word Lesson

Using Option Button, Check Box, and List Box Controls in Word

case ▶ Each morning, Nancy Manley, Willowton Health Club's secretary, creates and prints the exercise class schedule for the following day. The schedule lists the beginning and ending times of each class as well as the class activity—either aerobics, cycling, or step. Nancy has decided to create a custom dialog box and a macro that will help her create and print the schedule.

Viewing the Schedule Document

The document that Nancy uses to create and print the exercise class schedule is stored on your Data Disk. Before creating the custom dialog box and macro that Nancy will use to create and print the schedule, view the document.

To view the document:

1 Start Microsoft Word.

2 Open the **T13-WD-1** (T13-WD-1.doc) document, which is located in the Tut13\Word folder on your Data Disk. Click the **Enable Macros** button, if necessary, then save the document as **Schedule**. The Schedule document is shown in Figure 13-20.

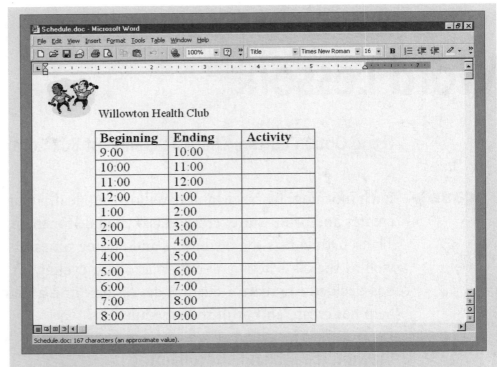

Figure 13-20: Schedule document

The document contains a table that has three columns and 13 rows. The first two columns list the beginning and ending times, respectively, for each class. Notice that, except for the heading in its first row, the third column currently is empty; the dialog box that you will complete in this lesson will enter the class activity in this column.

Figure 13-21 shows the Scheduler custom dialog box that you will complete in this lesson.

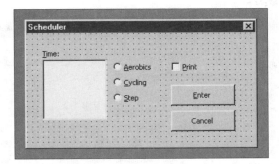

Figure 13-21: The custom dialog box you will complete in this lesson

The Scheduler dialog box consists of a form and eight controls: one label, one list box, one check box, three option buttons, and two command buttons. After selecting the beginning class time in the list box and also selecting the appropriate activity's option button, the user can click the Enter button to record the activity in the table's Activity column.

A partially completed Scheduler dialog box is included on your Data Disk.

To add the partially completed Scheduler dialog box to the project, and then begin completing the dialog box:

1 Press **Alt+F11** to open the Visual Basic Editor. If necessary, open the Project Explorer window and close the Properties window, the Immediate window, and any open Code windows.

2 Right-click the **Project Explorer window** and then click **Import File** on the shortcut menu. The Import File dialog box appears. If necessary, open the Tut13\Word folder on your Data Disk. Click **T13-WD-1** (T13-WD-1.frm) in the list of filenames and then click the **Open** button.

3 Open the Forms folder in the Project Explorer window. Right-click **frmScheduler** in the Forms folder and then click **View Object**. The partially completed frmScheduler form appears.

4 If necessary, open the Toolbox and Properties windows, and then drag the windows to the location shown in Figure 13-22 (on the next page). Click the **form** to make it the active window.

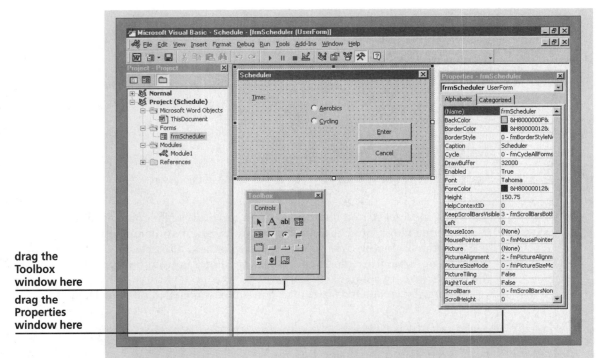

drag the Toolbox window here

drag the Properties window here

Figure 13-22: Partially completed Scheduler form

To complete the dialog box's interface, you need to add one option button, one check box, and one list box to the form. You then need to set the appropriate properties for those controls.

5 Drag the **OptionButton** tool ⦿ from the toolbox to the form. Place the option button below the Cycling option button. (Don't worry about the exact location or size—you will adjust the position and size of the option button, check box, and list box controls in the next set of steps.)

6 Drag the **CheckBox** tool ☑ from the toolbox to the form. Place the check box immediately above the Enter command button. (Don't worry about the exact location or size.)

7 Drag the **ListBox** tool 🔠 from the toolbox to the form. Place the list box immediately below the Time: label. (Don't worry about the exact location or size.)

8 Close the Toolbox window.

You now will set the appropriate properties for the option button, check box, and list box controls.

To set the properties for the option button, check box, and list box controls:

1 Click the **OptionButton1** control to select it, then use the Properties window to set the following properties. (The three-character ID used in an option button's name is *opt.*)

Property	Value
Name	**optStep**
Accelerator	**S**
Caption	**Step**
Left	**96**
Top	**66**
Width	**51**

> **tip**
>
> You are given the values for the Left, Top, and Width properties in order for your screen to match the figures in this book. Instead of setting the Left and Top properties, you simply could drag the control to its proper location. Likewise, rather than setting the Width property, you could use the handles to size the control.

To indicate that the Aerobics, Cycling, and Step option buttons belong to the same group, you will set each button's GroupName property to the same value, Activity.

2 Set the GroupName property for the optStep, optCycling, and optAerobics controls to **Activity**.

> **tip**
>
> If a form contains only one group of option buttons, it is not essential to set the GroupName property; the option buttons will work correctly even if the GroupName property is not set. However, you must either set the GroupName property or use a frame control to include more than one group of option buttons on a form. You can learn more about the GroupName property and the frame control in the Concept lesson's Exercise 7.

3 Click the **CheckBox1** control to select it, then use the Properties window to set the following properties. (The three-character ID used in a check box's name is *chk.*)

Property	Value
Name	**chkPrint**
Accelerator	**P**
Caption	**Print**
Left	**162**
Top	**30**
Width	**40**

4 Click the **ListBox1** control to select it, then use the Properties window to set the following properties. (The three-character ID used in a list box's name is *lst.*)

Property	Value
Name	**lstTime**
Left	**18**
Height	**70**
Top	**30**

5 Click the **form.** Figure 13-23 shows the current status of the form.

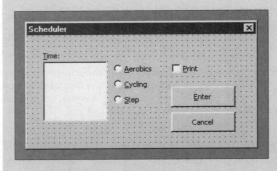

Figure 13-23: Current status of the form

After adding the controls to the form, recall that you then need to determine the appropriate tab order for the essential controls. The Scheduler dialog box contains seven essential controls: the list box, check box, three option buttons, and two command buttons. The focus should begin in the list box, which is the essential control located in the upper-left corner of the form. Pressing the Tab key should move the focus first to the option buttons, then to the check box, and then to the command buttons.

As you learned in Tutorial 12, you specify the tab order by setting each essential control's TabIndex property. If an essential control has an identifying label, recall that you also must set the identifying label's TabIndex property. In this case, you will need to set the TabIndex property for all eight controls: Label1 (the label captioned Time:), lstTime, optAerobics, optCycling, optStep, chkPrint, cmdEnter, and cmdCancel.

To set the tab order, then run the dialog box to test it:

1 Set the TabIndex property for the eight controls as follows:

Control	TabIndex value
Label1	**0** (the number 0)
lstTime	**1** (the number 1)
optAerobics	**2**
optCycling	**3**
optStep	**4**
chkPrint	**5**
cmdEnter	**6**
cmdCancel	**7**

2 Close the Project Explorer and Properties windows.

3 Save the document, then click the **Run Sub/UserForm** button ▶ to run the dialog box.

4 Verify that the tab order is set appropriately. Also verify that the accelerator keys work correctly.

HELP? Because the list box does not contain any items, you will not see the focus when the dialog box first appears, nor will you see it when you tab to the list box.

5 Click the **Cancel** button, which already has been coded for you, to close the dialog box. (The Cancel button contains the instruction `Unload frmScheduler`, which removes the form from both the screen and the computer's memory.)

Now that you have completed the dialog box's interface, you can begin coding the dialog box. First you will code the UserForm's Initialize event.

Coding the UserForm's Initialize Event

A form's **Initialize event** occurs after the form is loaded into memory but before it is shown on the screen. In the Initialize event, you enter code that prepares the form for use—for example, code that sets the initial values for controls. Figure 13-24 shows the pseudocode for the Scheduler form's Initialize event.

1. Fill the list box with the beginning class times from the table. To do so,
   a. Repeat the following for table rows 2 through 13:
      1) Assign the time from the Beginning table column to a String variable named strTableTime.
      2) Add the contents of the strTableTime variable to the list box.
2. Select the first item in the list box (9:00) as the default item.
3. Select the first option button (Aerobics) as the default option button.

Figure 13-24: Pseudocode for the Scheduler form's Initialize event procedure

Figure 13-25 lists the variables that the Initialize event procedure will use.

Variable	datatype
strTableTime	String
intRow	Integer
tblSchedule	Table

Figure 13-25: Variables used by the form's Initialize event procedure

The Initialize event procedure will use the strTableTime variable to store the beginning class times listed in the first column of the table. The intRow variable will be used in a For...Next statement that repeats its instructions for rows 2 through 13 in the table. The tblSchedule variable will store the address of the table.

To begin coding the form's Initialize event procedure:

1 Right-click the **form**, then click **View Code**. The Code window opens and shows the code template for the UserForm's Click event procedure.

2 View the code template for UserForm's Initialize event procedure, then enter the documentation and the Dim and Set statements shown in Figure 13-26.

be sure to
enter the
code in the
Initialize event

enter these
three lines
of code

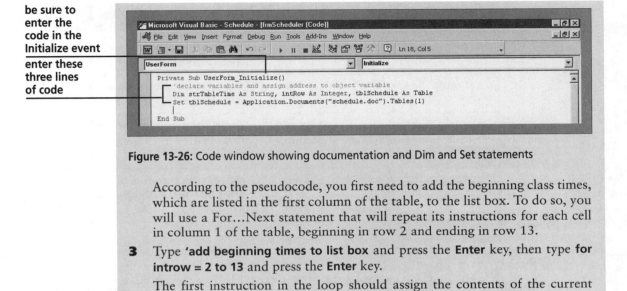

Figure 13-26: Code window showing documentation and Dim and Set statements

According to the pseudocode, you first need to add the beginning class times, which are listed in the first column of the table, to the list box. To do so, you will use a For...Next statement that will repeat its instructions for each cell in column 1 of the table, beginning in row 2 and ending in row 13.

3 Type **'add beginning times to list box** and press the **Enter** key, then type **for introw = 2 to 13** and press the **Enter** key.

The first instruction in the loop should assign the contents of the current table cell to the strTableTime variable.

4 Press the **Tab** key, then type **strtabletime = tblschedule.columns(1).cells (introw).range.text** and press the **Enter** key.

The second instruction in the loop should add the contents of the strTableTime variable to the list box. Before you can code this instruction, you need to learn how to use the list box's AddItem method.

The AddItem Method

You use the AddItem method to specify the items you want displayed in a list box control. The syntax of the AddItem method is *object*.**AddItem** *item*, where *object* is the name of the control to which you want the item added and *item* is the expression you want displayed in the control's list. The expression can be either numeric or string; however, if you want to display a string in the list box, you must enclose the string in quotation marks. Figure 13-27 shows some examples of using the AddItem method to display items in a list box.

tip

The AddItem method also allows you to specify the position within the control where the new item is placed. To learn more about the AddItem method, view its Help screen.

Example	Result
`lstParty.AddItem "Democrat"`	Displays the string "Democrat" in the lstParty list box
`lstHours.AddItem 40`	Displays the number 40 in the lstHours list box

`For sngCount = 1 To 4 Step .5`
`    lstRate.AddItem sngCount`
`Next sngCount`
	Displays the numbers from 1 through 4, in increments of .5, in the lstRate list box

`lstTime.AddItem strTableTime`	Displays the contents of the strTableTime variable in the lstTime list box

Figure 13-27: Examples of using the AddItem method

The first two examples shown in Figure 13-27 use the AddItem method to add a string literal constant ("Democrat") and a numeric literal constant (40), respectively, to a list box. The third example uses the AddItem method within a loop to display the numbers from 1 through 4, in increments of .5, in a list box. The last example shown in the figure uses the AddItem method to display the contents of the strTableTime variable in the lstTime list box.

To complete the Initialize event procedure, then test the procedure:

1   Type **lsttime.additem strtabletime** and press the **Enter** key. This instruction will add the contents of the strTableTime variable to the list box.
    Now end the loop.

2   Press the **Backspace** key, then type **next introw** and press the **Enter** key.
    The next step in the pseudocode is to select the default list box item—in this case, the default item will be the first item in the list. You can use the ListIndex property to select the default item. Recall that the first item in a list box has a ListIndex value of 0.

3   Type **'select default list box item** and press the **Enter** key, then type **lsttime.listindex = 0** (the number 0) and press the **Enter** key.
    The last step in the pseudocode is to select the default option button—in this case, the Aerobics button. You do so by setting the option button's Value property to the Boolean value True.

4   Type **'select default option button** and press the **Enter** key, then type **optaerobics.value = true** and press the **Enter** key. Figure 13-28 shows the current status of the form's Initialize event procedure.

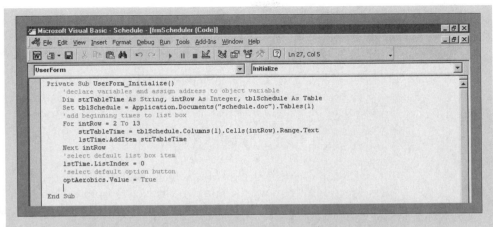

Figure 13-28: Current status of the form's Initialize event procedure

5 Verify the accuracy of your code by comparing the code on your screen to the code shown in Figure 13-28.

6 Close the Code window. Save the document, then click the **Run Sub/UserForm** button ▶ to run the dialog box. See Figure 13-29.

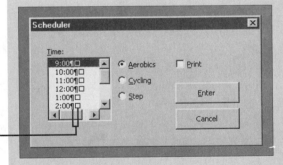

paragraph and end of cell marker

Figure 13-29: List box showing paragraph and end of cell markers

HELP? If no data appears in your list box and the Aerobics option button is not selected, close the dialog box. Verify that you entered the code shown in Figure 13-28 in the UserForm's Initialize procedure, rather than in another procedure. If you entered the code in the wrong procedure, cut the code from the incorrect procedure and then paste it into the Initialize event procedure.

After the form is loaded into memory, but before it appears on the screen, the Initialize event procedure fills the list box with the beginning class times from the table. It then selects the first item in the list box and it also selects the Aerobics option button. Notice that a paragraph marker and a small square, representing the end of cell marker, appear at the end of each list box item. To fix this problem, you will need to modify the Initialize event procedure's code. You will do this next.

7 Close the dialog box.

You can use the Left function, which you learned about in Tutorial 10, and the Len function to remove the last two characters from each beginning time. As you learned, the syntax of the Left function is **Left(String:=*string*, Length:=*length*)**, where *length* is the number of characters you want to return from the *string*. The syntax of the Len function, which returns the number of characters in a string, is **Len(String:=*string*)**.

Len is short for "length."

To modify the form's Initialize event procedure:

1 Open the form's Initialize event procedure, then enter the additional line of code shown in Figure 13-30, which shows the completed Initialize procedure.

enter this line of code

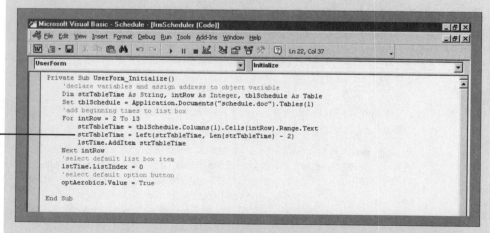

```
Private Sub UserForm_Initialize()
    'declare variables and assign address to object variable
    Dim strTableTime As String, intRow As Integer, tblSchedule As Table
    Set tblSchedule = Application.Documents("schedule.doc").Tables(1)
    'add beginning times to list box
    For intRow = 2 To 13
        strTableTime = tblSchedule.Columns(1).Cells(intRow).Range.Text
        strTableTime = Left(strTableTime, Len(strTableTime) - 2)
        lstTime.AddItem strTableTime
    Next intRow
    'select default list box item
    lstTime.ListIndex = 0
    'select default option button
    optAerobics.Value = True

End Sub
```

Figure 13-30: Completed Initialize event procedure

2 Close the Code window. Save the document, then run the dialog box. The Initialize event removes the paragraph and end of cell markers from each beginning time before adding the time to the list box.

Notice that the list box contains both horizontal and vertical scroll bars. The horizontal scroll bar allows you to scroll the list box horizontally.

3 Use the horizontal scroll bar, which appears along the bottom of the list box, to scroll the list box. Notice that the list box is slightly wider than is needed to show its contents.

The vertical scroll bar indicates that the list box contains more items than can be viewed at the same time.

4 Use the vertical scroll bar, which appears along the right side of the list box, to scroll the list box.

5 Close the dialog box.

You can use the ColumnWidths property, which controls the width of each column in a list box, to remove the horizontal scroll bar, and you can use either the list box's handles or its Width property to decrease the width of the list box. You can eliminate the vertical scroll bar by increasing the height of the list box so that all items can be displayed at the same time. You can increase the height either by dragging the list box's handles or by setting the list box's Height property. In this case, you will remove only the horizontal scroll bar from the lstTime list box. (As you learned in the Concept lesson, the minimum number of items you should display in a list box at any one time is three, and the maximum number is eight.)

To remove the horizontal scroll bar from the lstTime list box:

1 Right-click the **lstTime list box**, then click **Properties**. Set the ColumnWidths property to **45**.

HELP? 45 pt will appear as the value of the ColumnWidths property. The "pt" stands for "point". A point is 1/72 of an inch.

A list box can contain more than one column of data.

2 Set the list box's Width property to **55**.

3 Close the Properties window. Save the document, then run the dialog box. Notice that the horizontal scroll bar does not appear on the list box.

4 Close the dialog box.

The next procedure you will code is the Enter button's Click event.

Coding the Enter Button's Click Event Procedure

Figure 13-31 shows the pseudocode for the Enter button's Click event procedure.

1. Assign the time selected in the list box to a String variable named strInputTime.
2. Search the Beginning table column, excluding the heading, for the time contained in the strInputTime variable. To do so, repeat the following for table rows 2 through 13:
   a. Assign the time from the Beginning table column in the current row to a String variable named strTableTime.
   b. If the contents of the strTableTime and strInputTime variables are equal, then
      1) Selected option button:
         Aerobics: Display "Aerobics" in the table's Activity column.
         Cycling: Display "Cycling" in the table's Activity column.
         Step: Display "Step" in the table's Activity column.
      2) Stop the search by exiting the loop.

Figure 13-31: Pseudocode for the Enter button's Click event procedure

Figure 13-32 lists the variables that the Enter button's Click event procedure will use.

Variable	datatype
strInputTime	String
strTableTime	String
intRow	Integer
tblSchedule	Table

Figure 13-32: Variables used by the Enter button's Click event procedure

The procedure will use the strInputTime variable to store the time selected in the list box, and it will use the strTableTime variable to store the times listed in the Beginning table column. The intRow variable will be used in a For...Next statement that repeats its instructions for table rows 2 through 13. The tblSchedule variable will store the address of the table.

To code the Enter button's Click event procedure:

1   Right-click the **Enter** button, then click **View Code**. In the Enter button's Click event, enter the documentation and the Dim and Set statements shown in Figure 13-33.

enter these three lines of code

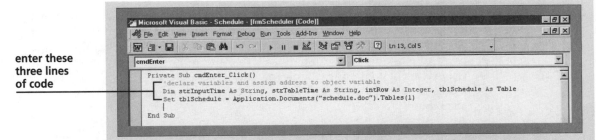

```
Microsoft Visual Basic - Schedule - [frmScheduler (Code)]
File  Edit  View  Insert  Format  Debug  Run  Tools  Add-Ins  Window  Help                Ln 13, Col 5

cmdEnter                                          Click

Private Sub cmdEnter_Click()
    'declare variables and assign address to object variable
    Dim strInputTime As String, strTableTime As String, intRow As Integer, tblSchedule As Table
    Set tblSchedule = Application.Documents("schedule.doc").Tables(1)

End Sub
```

Figure 13-33: Code window showing documentation and Dim and Set statements

The first step in the pseudocode is to assign the selected list box item to the strInputTime variable. When the user selects an item in a list box, the selected item is assigned automatically to the list box's Value property.

> **tip**
>
> Recall that the selected item's location in the list is assigned automatically to the list box's ListIndex property.

2 Type **'assign selected list box item to strInputTime variable** and press the **Enter** key, then type **strinputtime = lsttime.value** and press the **Enter** key.

The next step is to search the Beginning column, excluding the column heading, for the time contained in the strInputTime variable. You will need to use a repetition structure to perform the search. To exclude the column heading, you will begin the search in row 2 of the table.

3 Type **'search table for time, then display activity** and press the **Enter** key, then type **for introw = 2 to 13** and press the **Enter** key.

First assign the time located in the first column of the current row to the strTableTime variable.

4 Press the **Tab** key, then type **strtabletime = tblschedule.columns(1).cells (introw).range.text** and press the **Enter** key.

Now use the Left and Len functions to remove the paragraph and end of cell markers from the string stored in the strTableTime variable.

5 Type **strtabletime = left(strtabletime, len(strtabletime) - 2)** and press the **Enter** key.

Next, compare the values stored in the strTableTime and strInputTime variables to see if they are equal.

6 Type **'compare table time to input time** and press the **Enter** key. Type **if strtabletime = strinputtime then** and press the **Enter** key.

According to the pseudocode, if the contents of both variables are equal, the procedure must determine which option button is selected before it can display the appropriate activity in the table; you will use a Select Case statement to make that determination. If an option button is selected, its Value property will contain the Boolean value True; otherwise, it will contain the Boolean value False. Recall that the Activity column is the third column in the table.

7 Press the **Tab** key, then enter the selection structure shown in Figure 13-34.

enter these eight lines of code

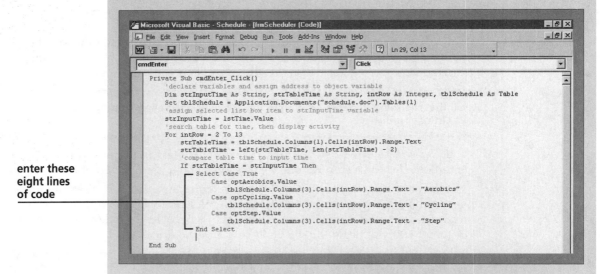

```
Private Sub cmdEnter_Click()
    'declare variables and assign address to object variable
    Dim strInputTime As String, strTableTime As String, intRow As Integer, tblSchedule As Table
    Set tblSchedule = Application.Documents("schedule.doc").Tables(1)
    'assign selected list box item to strInputTime variable
    strInputTime = lstTime.Value
    'search table for time, then display activity
    For intRow = 2 To 13
        strTableTime = tblSchedule.Columns(1).Cells(intRow).Range.Text
        strTableTime = Left(strTableTime, Len(strTableTime) - 2)
        'compare table time to input time
        If strTableTime = strInputTime Then
            Select Case True
                Case optAerobics.Value
                    tblSchedule.Columns(3).Cells(intRow).Range.Text = "Aerobics"
                Case optCycling.Value
                    tblSchedule.Columns(3).Cells(intRow).Range.Text = "Cycling"
                Case optStep.Value
                    tblSchedule.Columns(3).Cells(intRow).Range.Text = "Step"
            End Select

End Sub
```

Figure 13-34: Current status of the Enter button's Click event procedure

After displaying the appropriate activity in the table, the procedure will stop the search by exiting the loop.

8 Type **'stop the search** and press the **Enter** key, then type **exit for** and press the **Enter** key.

Finally, end the If...Then...Else and For...Next statements.

9 Press the **Backspace** key, then type **end if** and press the **Enter** key to end the If...Then...Else statement. Press the **Backspace** key, then type **next introw** and press the **Enter** key to end the For...Next statement.

10   Verify the accuracy of your code by comparing the code on your screen with the code shown in Figure 13-35, which shows the completed Click event procedure for the Enter button.

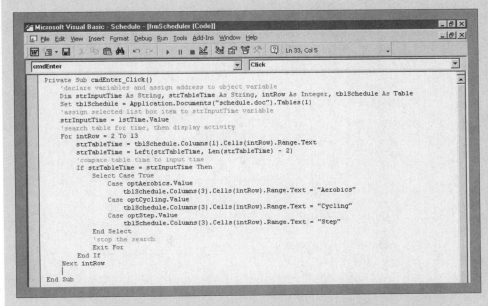

```
Microsoft Visual Basic - Schedule - [frmScheduler [Code]]
File  Edit  View  Insert  Format  Debug  Run  Tools  Add-Ins  Window  Help
                                                                    Ln 33, Col 5
cmdEnter                                        Click

Private Sub cmdEnter_Click()
    'declare variables and assign address to object variable
    Dim strInputTime As String, strTableTime As String, intRow As Integer, tblSchedule As Table
    Set tblSchedule = Application.Documents("schedule.doc").Tables(1)
    'assign selected list box item to strInputTime variable
    strInputTime = lstTime.Value
    'search table for time, then display activity
    For intRow = 2 To 13
        strTableTime = tblSchedule.Columns(1).Cells(intRow).Range.Text
        strTableTime = Left(strTableTime, Len(strTableTime) - 2)
        'compare table time to input time
        If strTableTime = strInputTime Then
            Select Case True
                Case optAerobics.Value
                    tblSchedule.Columns(3).Cells(intRow).Range.Text = "Aerobics"
                Case optCycling.Value
                    tblSchedule.Columns(3).Cells(intRow).Range.Text = "Cycling"
                Case optStep.Value
                    tblSchedule.Columns(3).Cells(intRow).Range.Text = "Step"
            End Select
            'stop the search
            Exit For
        End If
    Next intRow

End Sub
```

Figure 13-35: Completed Click event procedure for the Enter button

11   Close the Code window, then save the document.

Now that you have finished coding the Enter button's Click event procedure, you will test it to be sure it is working correctly.

To test the Enter button's Click event procedure:

1   Run the dialog box. Scroll down the list box and then click **4:00**. Click the **Step** option button, then click the **Enter** button. The Enter button's Click event procedure enters "Step" in the Activity column for the 4:00 row, as shown in Figure 13-36.

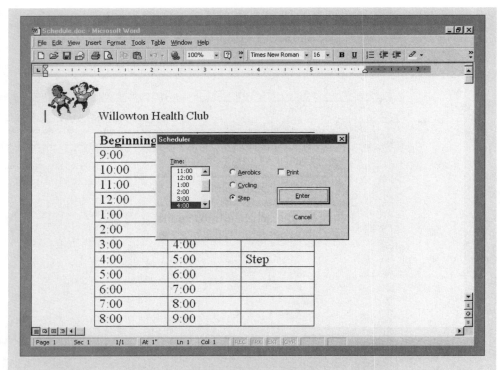

Figure 13-36: Step entered in the 4:00 row's Activity column

HELP? If you do not see the document behind the dialog box, close the dialog box. Click the Schedule.doc - Microsoft Word button in the taskbar to view the Schedule document. Press Alt+F11 to return to the Visual Basic Editor, then repeat Step 1.

2   Click the **Cancel** button to close the dialog box.

The last procedure you will code is the form's QueryClose event.

Coding the UserForm's QueryClose Event

A form's QueryClose event occurs before the form is removed from the computer's memory, and it typically is used to perform last-minute tasks, such as verifying that the user saved the current data. In this case, you will use the QueryClose event to check the status of the chkPrint check box. If the check box is selected, the procedure should print the Schedule document; otherwise, it should not print the document.

Notice that two items of information—`Cancel As Integer` and `CloseMode As Integer`—appear inside the parentheses in the event's `Private Sub` line. Items inside the parentheses are called **arguments**, and they are used by VBA to pass information to the event procedure. In this case, VBA passes the number 0 to the QueryClose event's Cancel argument, indicating that the form should be closed. If you do not enter, into the QueryClose event, an instruction that changes the value contained in the Cancel argument, the form will be removed from both the screen and the computer's memory. You can prevent the removal of the form by setting the QueryClose event's Cancel argument to any nonzero value. For example, you can use the instruction `Cancel = 1` to prevent the form from being closed. You may want to do so if the user neglected to save the current data.

VBA also passes a number to the CloseMode argument. The number indicates the cause of the QueryClose event, as shown in Figure 13-37.

Numeric value	Constant	Meaning
0	vbFormControlMenu	The user clicked the Close button on the form's title bar.
1	vbFormCode	The Unload statement was invoked from code.
2	vbAppWindows	The current Windows operating environment session is ending.
3	vbAppTaskManager	The Windows Task Manager is closing the application.

Figure 13-37: Values passed to the QueryClose event's CloseMode argument

You will use the Scheduler dialog box's QueryClose event simply to check the selection state of the chkPrint check box. You will not need to prevent the form from being closed, nor will you need to know what caused the QueryClose event to occur.

enter these three lines of code

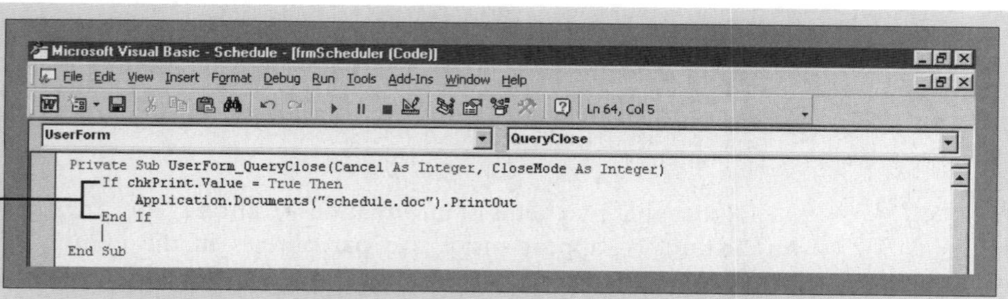

```
Microsoft Visual Basic - Schedule - [frmScheduler (Code)]
File  Edit  View  Insert  Format  Debug  Run  Tools  Add-Ins  Window  Help
                                                    Ln 64, Col 5
UserForm                                    QueryClose

    Private Sub UserForm_QueryClose(Cancel As Integer, CloseMode As Integer)
        If chkPrint.Value = True Then
            Application.Documents("schedule.doc").PrintOut
        End If

    End Sub
```

Figure 13-38: Completed QueryClose event procedure

2 Close the Code window, then save the document and run the dialog box.

3 Scroll down the list box and then click **5:00**. Click the **Enter** button. The Enter button's Click event enters "Aerobics" in the Activity column for the 5:00 row.

4 If your computer is connected to a printer, click the **Print** check box to select it.

5 Close the dialog box. If you selected the Print check box, the form's QueryClose event procedure prints the Schedule document.

Now that the custom dialog box has been tested, all that remains is to enter the Show method in a macro procedure. Recall that you use the Show method to display a custom dialog box on the screen.

Coding the CreateSchedule Macro

The Schedule document already contains the code template for the CreateSchedule macro procedure.

To code the CreateSchedule procedure, then test the macro:

1 Open the Project Explorer window. Open the Module1 module's Code window, then view the code template for the **CreateSchedule** procedure. Close the Project Explorer window so that you can view more of the Code window.

2 Press the **Tab** key. Type **'display custom dialog box** and press the **Enter** key, then type **frmscheduler.show** and press the **Enter** key.

3 Save the document, then return to Word.

4 Run the **CreateSchedule** macro. Use the Scheduler dialog box to enter the Cycling activity in the 9:00 row in the table.

5 Close the dialog box. Save the document, then close Word.

You now have completed Tutorial 13's Word lesson. You can either take a break or complete the end-of-lesson exercises before moving on to the next lesson.

E X E R C I S E S

1. In this exercise, you will modify the custom dialog box that you created in this lesson so that it uses a list box rather than option buttons.
   a. Open the Schedule (Schedule.doc) document, which you created in this lesson. The document is located in the Tut13\Word folder on your Data Disk. Click the Enable Macros button, if necessary, then save the document as T13-WD-E1D.
   b. Open the Visual Basic Editor. Open the Project Explorer window, if necessary, and view the frmScheduler form object. Remove the three option buttons from the form. Replace the option buttons with a label control and a list box. The label control's caption should say Activity:. Assign the letter A to the label control's Accelerator property. Name the list box lstActivity.
   c. Change the tab order of the controls appropriately.
   d. Open the form's Initialize event. Change the filename in the Set statement to "t13-wd-e1d.doc". The Initialize event should fill the lstActivity list box with the following five activity names: Aerobics, Cycling, Step I, Step II, Tai Chi. It also should select the first item in the list. Add the appropriate code to the event.
   e. Open the Enter button's Click event procedure. Change the filename in the Set statement to "t13-wd-e1d.doc". Make the necessary modifications to the code.
   f. Open the form's QueryClose event. Change the filename in the Set statement to "t13-wd-e1d.doc".
   g. Close the Code window. Save the document, then return to Word and run the CreateSchedule macro. Enter the following activities:

10:00	Tai Chi
11:00	Step II
4:00	Step I

   h. Close the dialog box. Save and then close the document.

2. In this exercise, you will modify the custom dialog box you created in Tutorial 12's Word lesson so that it uses a list box and a check box.
   a. Open the T13-WD-E2 (T13-WD-E2.doc) document, which is located in the Tut13\Word folder on your Data Disk. Click the Enable Macros button, if necessary, then save the document as T13-WD-E2D.
   b. Open the Visual Basic Editor. Open the Project Explorer window, if necessary, and view the frmClientList form object.
   c. Modify the form so that it uses a list box, rather than a text box, to get the trainer's name. Use a check box, rather than a text box, to control whether the document is printed.

d. Change the tab order of the controls appropriately.

e. Open the form's Initialize procedure, which should fill the list box with the trainer names—George, Nora, and Pam. The event also should select the first name in the list. Because the user usually will want to print the document, have the Initialize event procedure select the check box.

f. Open the OK button's Click event procedure and make the necessary modifications.

g. Close the Code window. Save the document, then return to Word and run the PrintClientList macro. Print Pam's client list.

h. Save and then close the document.

Exercise 3 is a Discovery Exercise. Discovery Exercises, which may include topics that are not covered in the lesson, allow you to "discover" the solutions to problems on your own.

discovery ▶ 3. In this exercise, you will create a custom dialog box that will calculate the price of either a new or used computer along with a monitor and an optional printer and scanner.

a. Open the T13-WD-E3 (T13-WD-E3.doc) document, which is located in the Tut13\Word folder on your Data Disk. Save the document as T13-WD-E3D.

b. Open the Visual Basic Editor. Open the Project Explorer window, if necessary, and add a UserForm to the project. Name the form frmPrice. Create the dialog box shown in Figure 13-39. (The dialog box contains three label controls, one list box, five option buttons, two check boxes, and two command buttons.)

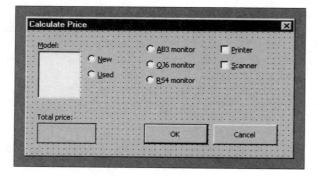

Figure 13-39

c. Code the dialog box so that it displays the appropriate information in the dialog box and document. (The form field names are Model, Type, Monitor, ComputerPrice, MonitorPrice, PrinterPrice, ScannerPrice, and TotalPrice.) Format the dollar amounts in the document as currency. Also format the total price in the dialog box as currency. Figure 13-40 shows the information you will need to create and code the dialog box.

Computer Model	New Price	Used Price
2100	999.00	700.00
2150	1050.00	900.00
3000	2000.00	1600.00
3240	2000.00	1600.00
3500	2000.00	1600.00
4000	3500.00	3000.00
6000	4000.00	3700.00
Monitor	**Price**	
AB3	1200.00	
QJ6	2000.00	
RS4	3500.00	
Other	**Price**	
Printer	350.00	
Scanner	200.00	

Figure 13-40

d. Code the Cancel button so that it unloads the form.
e. Make the OK button the default button, and make the Cancel button the cancel button.
f. Create a macro procedure named CreateReceipt. The macro procedure should display the dialog box on the screen.
g. Save the document, then return to Word and run the CreateReceipt macro. Assume a customer orders a new computer (model number 4000) along with monitor AB3 and a printer. Use the Calculate Price dialog box to create the receipt. (The total price should be $5,050.00.)
h. Save and then close the document.

A computer program is good only if it works. Errors in programming code can cause a program to run incorrectly. Therefore, a programmer needs to know how to locate and fix any errors in his or her code. Exercise 4 is a Debugging Exercise. Debugging Exercises allow you to practice recognizing and solving errors in code.

debugging

4. The following code should save the "test.doc" document before the form is removed from the screen and the computer's memory, but only if the chkSave check box is selected. The code is not working correctly. Correct the errors.

```
Private Sub UserForm_Click()
    If chkSave.Selected = True Then
        Application.Documents("test.doc").Save
    End If
End Sub
```

Access Lesson

Using Option Button, Check Box, and List Box Controls in Access

case ▶ Professor Carlisle, the chair of the CIS department at Snowville College, has decided to modify the custom dialog box created in Tutorial 12 so that it uses a list box and option buttons rather than text boxes. As you may remember, the procedure allows Professor Carlisle to preview the AdjFacReport report showing the name, phone number, and courses taught for either all of the CIS adjunct faculty members or only those who teach a specific course.

Viewing the Database

Professor Carlisle's Access database containing the adjunct CIS faculty information and the custom dialog box created in Tutorial 12 is stored on your Data Disk. Before modifying the dialog box, view the records contained in the database's AdjunctFaculty table. Also view a new table, named CourseNumbers, that contains the number of each CIS course.

To view the AdjunctFaculty and CourseNumbers tables:

1 Start Microsoft Access. Open the **AdjFac** (AdjFac.mdb) database, which is located in the Tut13\Access folder on your Data Disk. Click the **Maximize** button ▢ on the Microsoft Access title bar to maximize the Microsoft Access window, if necessary.

2 Click **Tables** in the Objects bar of the Database window, if necessary. Right-click **AdjunctFaculty**, then click **Open**. See Figure 13-41.

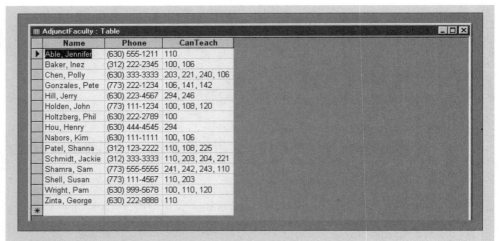

Figure 13-41: Records contained in the AdjunctFaculty table

Each record contains three Text fields: Name, Phone, and CanTeach.

3 Close the AdjunctFaculty table, then open the CourseNumbers table. See Figure 13-42.

CourseNum
100
106
108
110
120
141
142
203
204
221
225
240
241
242
243
246
294

Figure 13-42: Records contained in the CourseNumbers table

The CourseNumbers table contains a listing of the CIS courses offered at Snowville College.

4 Close the CourseNumbers table.

Next, view the custom dialog box created in Tutorial 12.

To view the custom dialog box created in Tutorial 12:

1 Click **Forms** in the Objects bar of the Database window.

2 Right-click **LocateInstructor** in the Database window, then click **Design View**. Figure 13-43 shows the dialog box that you created in Tutorial 12.

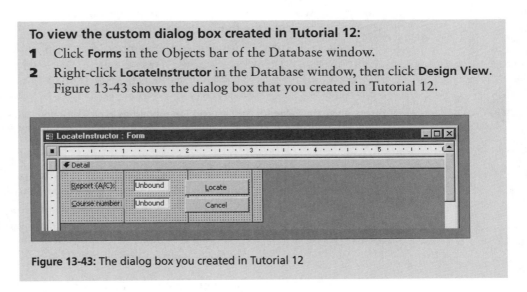

Figure 13-43: The dialog box you created in Tutorial 12

Figure 13-44 shows the modified dialog box that you will complete in this lesson.

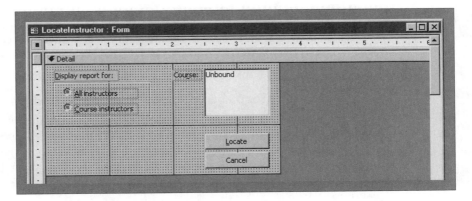

Figure 13-44: The modified dialog box that you will complete in this lesson

The modified dialog box consists of a form and 10 controls: two option buttons, one option group, four labels, one list box, and two command buttons. After selecting the desired option button and course number, the user can click the Locate button to display the AdjFacReport report.

To begin modifying the dialog box:

1 Select the two label controls and the two text box controls, then press the **Delete** key to delete the four controls from the form.

2 Right-click the **Locate** button, then click **Properties** to display the cmdLocate control's property sheet. Click the **Format** tab, if necessary, then set the control's Left property to **2.5** and set its Top property to **1.15**.

▶ **tip**

You are given the value for the Left and Top properties in order for your screen to match the figures in this book. Instead of setting the Left and Top properties, you simply could drag the control to its proper location.

3 Click the **Cancel** button to display the cmdCancel control's property sheet. Set the control's Left property to **2.5** and set its Top property to **1.45**.

4 Open the Toolbox window, if necessary. You will not use the control wizards in this lesson, so you can click the **Control Wizards** button to deselect it, if necessary.

First you will add the option group control and the two option buttons to the form. The option group control is necessary to indicate that both option buttons belong to the same group.

▶ **tip**

If you do not place both option buttons in an option group control, the user will be able to select both buttons at the same time, because each will be treated as a separate group.

To add the option group and option button controls to the dialog box:

1 Click the **Option Group** tool in the toolbox. Position the mouse pointer in the upper-left corner of the form, then click the **form**. (Don't worry about the exact location or size—you will adjust the position and size in the next step.) A default-size option group control, along with its identifying label control, appears on the form. The property sheet now lists the properties of the option group control.

2 Change the following properties for the option group control. All but the Name property are located on the Format tab; the Name property is located on the Other tab. (The three-character ID used in an option group control's name is *ogr*.)

Property	Value
Height	0.55
Left	0.15
Top	0.3
Width	1.5
Name	ogrReportType

3 Click the **Data** tab, then click **Default Value**. Type **1** (the number 1) and press the **Enter** key. This will select the first option button in the group. (You will include the option buttons later in this set of steps.)

4 Click the **option group control's identifying label control**, then set the label control's properties as follows. (All of the properties are located on the Format tab.)

Property	Value
Caption	&Display report for:
Left	0.15
Top	0.1
Width	1.0

5 Click the **Option Button** tool ⊙ in the toolbox, then position the mouse pointer inside the option group control. (Don't worry about the exact location.) Notice that the option group control changes color to indicate that the mouse pointer is within the control's borders. Click **the option group control**. A default-size option button control, along with its identifying label control, appear inside the option group control.

6 Use the Format and Other tabs on the Properties window to set the following properties for the option button control. (The three-character ID used in an option button's name is *opt*.)

Property	Value
Left	0.3
Top	0.4
Name	optAll

7 Click the **Data** tab. Notice that the Option Value property contains the number 1, which indicates that this is the first option button added to the option group control. This is the button that the option group control's Default Value property will select when the dialog box first opens.

8   Click the **option button's identifying label control**, then use the Format tab to set the following properties.

Property	Value
Caption	&All instructors
Left	0.45
Top	0.4
Width	1.0

9   Use the Option Button tool ⊙ to add another option button to the option group control. Set the following properties for this second option button control.

Property	Value
Left	0.3
Top	0.65
Name	optCourse

10   Click the **Data** tab. Notice that the Option Value property contains the number 2, which indicates that this is the second option button added to the option group control.

11   Click the **option button's identifying label control**, then use the Format tab to set the following properties.

Property	Value
Caption	&Course instructors
Left	0.45
Top	0.65
Width	1.0

12   Save the database.

In the next set of steps, you will add a list box control, along with its identifying label, to the form.

To add a list box to the dialog box:

1   Click the **List Box** tool ▦ in the toolbox, then click in the upper-right corner of the **form**. (Don't worry about the exact location or size.) A default-size list box control, along with its identifying label, appear on the form.

2   Use the Format and Other tabs to set the following properties for the list box control. (The three-character ID used in a list box's name is *lst*.)

Property	Value
Left	**2.5**
Height	**0.75**
Top	**0.1**
Width	**1.0**
Name	**lstCourse**

You can display in the lstCourse list box the course numbers contained in the CourseNumbers table by setting the list box's Row Source Type property to Table/Query and setting its Row Source property to CourseNumbers.

3 Click the **Data** tab. The Row Source Type property, which identifies the type of data assigned to the Row Source property, already is set to Table/Query. Click **Row Source** in the property sheet, then click the **Row Source list arrow**. Click **CourseNumbers** in the list of table names.

You can select the first item in the list box—in this case, course number 100—when the dialog box first opens by setting the list box's Default Value property to 100.

4 Click **Default Value** in the property sheet, then type **100** and press the **Enter** key.

5 Click the **list box's identifying label**, then use the Format tab to set its properties as follows:

Property	Value
Caption	**Cou&rse:**
Left	**2.0**
Top	**0.1**
Width	**0.45**

6 Close the Properties window and the Toolbox window. Drag the form's right and bottom borders until the form is approximately the size shown in Figure 13-45.

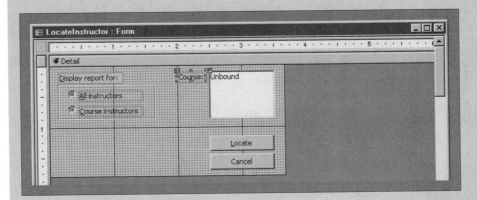

Figure 13-45: Current status of the form

After adding the controls to the form, recall that you then need to determine the appropriate tab order for the essential controls. The Locate an Instructor dialog box contains four essential controls: the list box, two command buttons, and the group control that contains the two option buttons. The focus should begin in one of the option buttons contained in the option group control, which is the control located in the upper-left corner of the form. Pressing the Tab key should move the focus from the option group control to the list box, and then to the command buttons.

As you learned in Tutorial 12, you specify the tab order by setting each essential control's Tab Index property. You can do so using either the property sheet or the Tab Order dialog box.

tip

> When an option button is placed in an option group control, it no longer has a Tab Index property. Rather, it uses the Tab Index property of the option group control.

To use the Tab Order dialog box to set the tab order, then run the dialog box to test it:

1   Right-click the **form**, then click **Tab Order** to open the Tab Order dialog box. Adjust the tab order as shown in Figure 13-46.

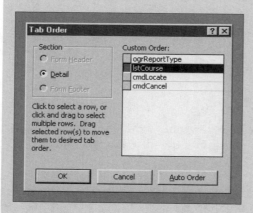

Figure 13-46: Tab Order dialog box showing correct tab order for controls

2   Click the **OK** button to close the Tab Order dialog box, then save the database.

3   Click the **View** button ⊞ list arrow, and then click **Form View**. See Figure 13-47.

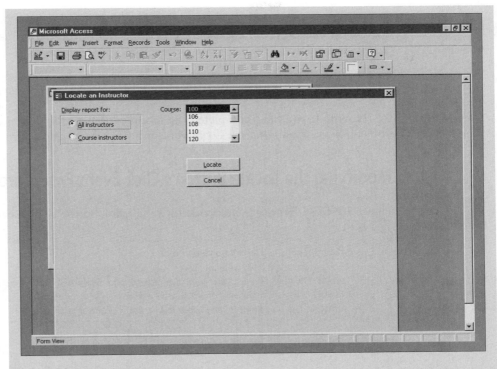

Figure 13-47: Form shown in Form View

When the dialog box opens, the focus is sent to the first option button in the option group control, as indicated by the dotted rectangle around the button's identifying label. Notice that both the first option button and the first item in the list box are selected.

4   Press the **Tab** key to move the focus to the list box, which contains the course numbers from the CourseNumbers table. Because the list box contains more items than can be displayed at the same time, a vertical scroll bar appears along the right side of the box.

5   Use the vertical scroll bar to view the remaining course numbers in the list.

6   Press the **Tab** key three times. The focus moves to the Locate button, the Cancel button, and then back to the first option button in the option group control.

7   Verify that Alt+r, Alt+c, and Alt+a move the focus to the list box, the second option button, and the first option button, respectively.

8   Click the **View** button 🖾 list arrow, then click **Design View**.

Now that you have completed the modifications to the dialog box's interface, you can begin modifying the Locate button's Click event procedure.

Modifying the Locate Button's Click Event Procedure

Figure 13-48 shows the pseudocode for the Locate button's Click event procedure.

1. Option button selected in the option group control:
   = 1   Display the report showing all of the AdjunctFaculty table's records.
   = 2   Assign the selected list box item to a String variable named strCourseNum.
          Display the report showing only the information for instructors whose CanTeach field
          contains the course number stored in the strCourseNum variable.

Figure 13-48: Pseudocode for the Locate button's Click event procedure

Before displaying the appropriate report, the Click event procedure will need to determine which option button is selected in the option group. If the first option button is selected, the procedure will display the report showing the information for all of the instructors. If the second option button is selected, the procedure will assign the course number selected in the list box to the strCourseNum variable, and it will display the report showing only those instructors who teach that course.

To modify the Locate button's Click event procedure:

1   Press **Alt+F11** to open the Visual Basic Editor. If necessary, open the Project Explorer window and close the Properties window, the Immediate window, and any open Code windows.

2   Open the **Microsoft Access Class Objects** folder, if necessary. Right-click **Form_LocateInstructor** in the Project Explorer window, then click **View Code**.

3   Use the Object box in the Code window to open the cmdLocate control's Click event procedure.

4   Close the Project Explorer window.

5 Delete the code specified in Figure 13-49.

delete the enclosed code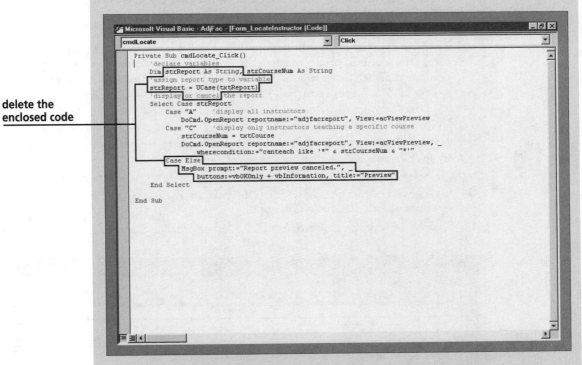

```
Microsoft Visual Basic - AdjFac - [Form_LocateInstructor [Code]]
cmdLocate                                    Click
Private Sub cmdLocate_Click()
    'declare variables
    Dim strReport As String, strCourseNum As String
    'assign report type to variable
    strReport = UCase(txtReport)
    'display or cancel the report
    Select Case strReport
        Case "A"    'display all instructors
            DoCmd.OpenReport reportname:="adjfacreport", View:=acViewPreview
        Case "C"    'display only instructors teaching a specific course
            strCourseNum = txtCourse
            DoCmd.OpenReport reportname:="adjfacreport", View:=acViewPreview, _
                wherecondition:="canteach like '*' & strCourseNum & '*'"
        Case Else
            MsgBox prompt:="Report preview canceled.", _
                buttons:=vbOKOnly + vbInformation, title:="Preview"
    End Select

End Sub
```

Figure 13-49: Code to delete in the cmdLocate control's Click event procedure

> The Click event procedure will no longer need the `Case Else` clause, because the user cannot enter an incorrect report type. This is one advantage of using option buttons rather than text boxes to get user input.

You use the option group control's Value property to determine which option button in the group is selected.

6 Change the Select Case clause from `Select Case strReport` to **Select Case ogrReportType.Value.**

If the first option button in the group—in this case, the optAll button—is selected, the option group control's Value property will contain the number 1. If the optCourse button is selected, the option group control's Value property will contain the number 2.

7 Change `Case "A"` in the Select Case statement to **Case 1** and change `Case "C"` to **Case 2.**

► tip

The value assigned to the option group control is the value stored in the selected option button's Option Value property.

The item selected in a list box is stored in the list box's Column property. You access the Column property using the syntax *listbox*.**Column**(*number*), where *number* represents the number of the column containing the item you want to access. The first column in a list box is numbered 0. In this case, you want to assign the item selected in the first column of the list box to the strCourseNum variable.

► tip

A list box can contain more than one column of data.

8 Change strCourseNum = txtCourse in the Case 2's instructions to **strCourseNum = lstCourse.Column(0)**.

Figure 13-50 shows the completed Click event procedure for the Locate button.

change these
four
instructions

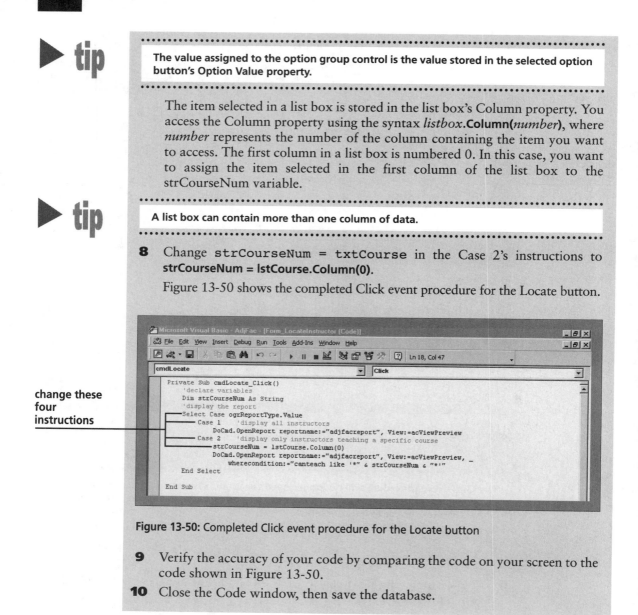

Figure 13-50: Completed Click event procedure for the Locate button

9 Verify the accuracy of your code by comparing the code on your screen to the code shown in Figure 13-50.

10 Close the Code window, then save the database.

Now that you have finished coding the Locate button's Click event procedure, you will test it to verify that it is working correctly.

To test the Locate button's Click event procedure:

1   Return to Access. Close the form.

2   Run the **LocateInstructorMacro** macro. Click the **Locate** button to display the report showing the information for all of the instructors. Close the report.

3   Click the **Course instructors** option button, then click **120** in the **Course** list box. Click the **Locate** button to view the report showing only the two instructors who teach the 120 course.

4   Close the report, then click the **Cancel** button to close the dialog box.

5   Compact the database, then exit Access.

You now have completed Tutorial 13's Access lesson. You can either take a break or complete the end-of-lesson exercises.

EXERCISES

1.   In this exercise, you will modify the Locate an Instructor dialog box that you completed in this lesson so that it uses a check box to allow the user to print the report.

   a.   Use Windows to make a copy of the AdjFac database, which you completed in this lesson. The database is located in the Tut13\Access folder on your Data Disk. Rename the copy T13-AC-E1D.

   b.   Open the T13-AC-E1D (T13-AC-E1D.mdb) database. Open the LocateInstructor form in Design View. Add a check box to the form. Name the check box chkPrint. Use &Print as its Caption property setting. Set the check box's Default Value property to the Boolean value False.

   c.   Adjust the tab order appropriately. Save the database.

   d.   Open the Visual Basic Editor. Open the Project Explorer window, if necessary, and view the Code window for the Form_LocateInstructor form. Open the Locate button's Click event procedure. If the check box is selected, the Locate button's Click event should print the report; otherwise, it should display the report on the screen. Modify the Locate button's Click event procedure accordingly. (*Hint*: If a check box is selected, its Value property will contain the Boolean value True.)

   e.   Save the database, then return to Access. Close the form, if necessary, then run the LocateInstructorMacro macro. Print the report showing the information only for the CIS adjunct faculty teaching the 120 course.

   f.   Close the dialog box, then compact and close the database.

2.   In this exercise, you will code a custom dialog box so that it displays the phone number corresponding to the company name selected in a list box.

   a.   Open the T13-AC-E2D (T13-AC-E2D.mdb) database, which is located in the Tut13\Access folder on your Data Disk. Open the table to familiarize yourself with its contents. Close the table.

b. Open the DisplayPhoneForm form in Design View. Familiarize yourself with the form and its controls. Set the list box's Row Source property so that it displays the company names contained in the Company table. Also set the list box's Default Value property to "Akron Jewelry". Save the database, then close the form.

c. Open the Visual Basic Editor and view the form's Code window. Use the Object box to view the list box's Code window, then use the Procedure box to view the list box's DblClick event procedure. Code the list box's DblClick event procedure so that it displays, in the txtPhone text box, the phone number corresponding to the name selected in the lstNames list box. (*Hint*: Use the Column property of the lstNames control. The phone numbers are contained in the PhoneNumber field, which is the second field in the Company table.)

d. Save the database, then return to Access and run the DisplayPhoneMacro macro. Double-click a company name in the list box. The company's phone number appears in the text box.

e. Close the dialog box, then compact and close the database.

Exercise 3 is a Discovery Exercise. Discovery Exercises, which may include topics that are not covered in the lesson, allow you to "discover" the solutions to problems on your own.

discovery ▶ 3. In this exercise, you will create a dialog box that displays the name and balance due corresponding to the ID selected in a list box. You will learn about the list box control's Column Count and Column Widths properties.

a. Open the T13-AC-E3D (T13-AC-E3D.mdb) database, which is located in the Tut13\Access folder on your Data Disk. Familiarize yourself with the Payments table included in the database. Notice that the table includes five fields. Close the table.

b. Open the DisplayBalance form in Design View. Display the list box control's property sheet. Click the Data tab, if necessary. Notice that the Row Source property is set to the Payments table.

c. Click the Format tab. Set the list box's Column Count property to 5, which is the number of fields in the Payments. This will display the five fields in the list box, and will allow you to access each field.

d. Set the Column Widths property to 1;0;0;0;0 (the number one and four zeros, separated by semicolons). 1";0";0";0";0" will appear in the Column Widths property. This will display just the first field in the list box; the remaining four fields will be hidden in the list box, but they still will be accessible. Close the form.

e. Open the Visual Basic Editor. Open the Project Explorer window, if necessary, and view the form's Code window. Use the Object box to open the cmdDisplay control's Click event procedure. Code the procedure so that it displays, in the txtName text box, the name (first name followed by a space and the last name) of the student whose ID is selected in the lstId list box. (*Hint*: You will need to use string concatenation to append a space and the last name to the end of the first name.) The procedure also should display the balance due in the txtBalance text box. The full cost of the trip is $1200. Code the Display button's Click event procedure appropriately. (*Hint*: You will need to use the list box's Column property.)

f. Save the database, then return to Access and run the DisplayBalanceMacro macro. Click KP1 in the list box, then click the Display button. Khalid Patel appears in the Name text box, and 200 appears in the Balance text box.

g. Close the dialog box, then compact and close the database.

A computer program is good only if it works. Errors in programming code can cause a program to run incorrectly. Therefore, a programmer needs to know how to locate and fix any errors in his or her code. Exercise 4 is a Debugging Exercise. Debugging Exercises allow you to practice recognizing and solving errors in code.

debugging   **4.** What is wrong with the following line of code, which should display the item selected in the lstParty list box? (The list box contains only one column of data.)

```
MsgBox Prompt:=lstParty.Column(1)
```

Automation

In this tutorial, you will learn how to:

■ Differentiate between an Automation server and an Automation controller
■ Perform Automation
■ Set a reference to a server's object library
■ Use the CreateObject function to create an object from a class
■ Use the DLookup function in Access to find and return data

Concept Lesson

The Automation Process

Each of the applications included in Microsoft Office 2000 has a specific purpose. For example, Word provides word processing services, while Excel and Access provide spreadsheet and database management services, respectively. Increasingly, developers and users are finding that they need to create macros that combine the services of two or more applications. For example, a user may need a macro that can create an Excel chart from the sales amounts entered in an Access database, and then include the chart in a document created in Word. You can use Automation (formerly known as OLE Automation) to accomplish this cross-application programming.

Automation is a process that allows one application to control the objects included in another application's object model; the controlling application does so using VBA. For example, you can use VBA to perform Automation between Microsoft Word and Microsoft Excel, allowing the Word application to control the objects contained in the Excel application's object model, and allowing the Excel application to control the objects contained in the Word application's object model.

Automation is a feature of the Component Object Model (COM), an industry-standard technology used to make objects available to applications that support Automation. COM specifies the common interface that enables applications and objects written by different companies and even in different programming languages to interact.

Applications that can **expose** their objects—in other words, applications that can make their objects available—to other applications are called **Automation servers**, while those that can use VBA to control another's exposed objects are called **Automation controllers**. An application can be both an Automation server and an Automation controller. Access, Excel, Word, and PowerPoint, for example, are both Automation servers and Automation controllers, because each can expose its objects to other applications and each can control the objects exposed by other applications.

Automation controllers also are called Automation clients.

To use Automation, you need simply to perform the following steps, each of which will be explained in the sections that follow:

1. Set a reference to the Automation server's object library in the Automation controller.

2. Create an object that can be used for Automation, and assign its address to an object variable.
3. Manipulate the Automation object, as necessary, through its properties and methods.
4. Close the Automation object and release the memory allocated to it.

First, learn how to set a reference to the Automation server's object library.

Referencing an Automation Server's Object Library

Every Automation server provides an **object library,** which is a file that contains information about the objects the Automation server exposes. An Automation server's object library, for example, contains the names of the exposed objects, as well as descriptions of their properties, methods, and events.

Before you can refer to an Automation server's objects from within an Automation controller, the Automation controller must contain a reference to the Automation server's object library. You set the reference using the References dialog box, which is displayed by selecting the References option on the Visual Basic Editor's Tools menu. The settings selected in the References dialog box shown in Figure 14-1, for example, allow you to refer to the objects in the Excel object model from within PowerPoint.

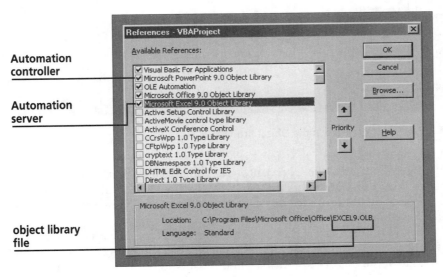

Figure 14-1: References dialog box

Object libraries are stored in files with names that have either an .olb, .tlb, .exe, or .dll extension.

When an Automation controller contains a reference to an Automation server's object library, the Visual Basic Editor will display the properties and methods of an exposed object when you enter the object's name in a Code window. The reference also makes the Automation server's object library available in the Object Browser, as shown in Figure 14-2.

Project/Library list box

Classes list box

Members list box

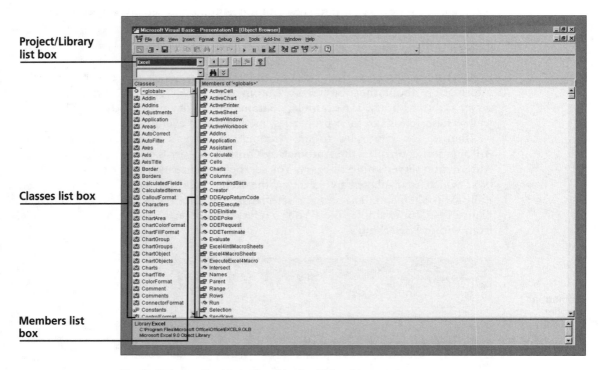

Figure 14-2: Excel's objects listed in the Object Browser

As the figure indicates, the Object Browser contains a Project/Library list box, a Classes list box, and a Members list box. You use the Project/Library list box to select the project or library that you want to examine. In Figure 14-2, the Excel library is selected in the Project/Library list box.

The Classes list box lists the classes included in the selected project or library. A **class** is simply a pattern or blueprint for creating an object. A class defines the properties that control the object's appearance and the methods and events that control the object's behavior. Every object in an application's object model is associated with a class.

tip

....

Classes are identified by the 🖳 icon in the Classes list box.

....

The Members list box lists the properties, methods, and events belonging to the currently selected class. The Members list box shown in Figure 14-3, for example, lists the members of the Excel Application class.

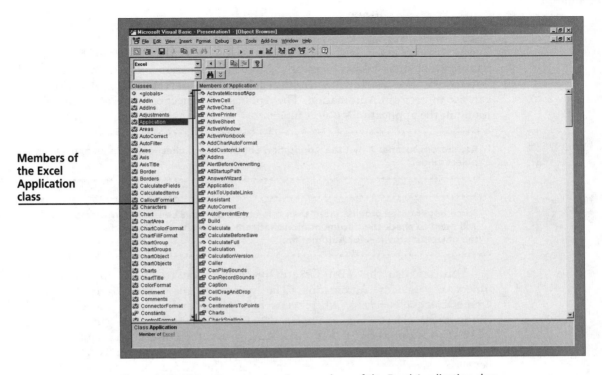

Members of the Excel Application class

Figure 14-3: Object Browser showing members of the Excel Application class

tip

Properties, methods, and events are respectively identified by the [icon], [icon], and [icon] icons in the Members list box.

When you use a class to create an object, the object that is created is referred to as an **instance** of the class. For example, you can use the Excel Application class to create an Excel Application object. Because the object is an instance of the Excel Application class, it will have all of the properties, methods, and events shown in the Members list box in Figure 14-3.

tip

You can think of a class as being similar to a cookie cutter, and an instance of a class (an object) as being similar to a cookie that is made using the cookie cutter.

The second step in the Automation process is to create an object that can be used for Automation, and assign its address to an object variable.

Creating an Object for Automation

Every Automation server provides at least one object that can be used for Automation; that object typically is the Application object. Access, Excel, PowerPoint, and Word, for example, each provide an Application object that you can use to perform Automation. The Application object contains all of the objects found in the application's object model.

> Recall from Tutorial 2 that the Application object is the highest object in an application's object model.

> Some applications provide more than one object that can be used for Automation. You will need to check the documentation that comes with the application for the names of the objects it provides for Automation.

You can use the VBA CreateObject function to create the appropriate object to use for Automation. The syntax of the CreateObject function is **CreateObject(Class:=***class***)**, where *class* is a string that specifies the class of the Automation object. For example, the CreateObject function `CreateObject (Class:="PowerPoint.Application")` uses the PowerPoint Application class to create a PowerPoint Application object, which can be used to perform Automation between PowerPoint and another application. The CreateObject function starts the appropriate Automation server—in this case, it would start PowerPoint—before it creates the object. You assign the resulting object to an object variable that is of the same type as the object. In other words, you would assign a PowerPoint Application object to a PowerPoint Application object variable. Figure 14-4 shows the syntax and two examples of creating an object for Automation.

Syntax:

Dim *variablename* **As** *datatype*
Set *variablename* = **CreateObject(Class:=***class***)**

Example 1:
```
Dim appPowerPoint As PowerPoint.Application
Set appPowerPoint = CreateObject(Class:="PowerPoint.Application")
```

Example 2:
```
Dim appWord As Word.Application
Set appWord = CreateObject(Class:="Word.Application")
```

Figure 14-4: Syntax and examples of creating an object for Automation

tip

•••
In this lesson's Exercise 3, you will learn how to use the keyword New to create an object for Automation.
•••

Example 1 in the figure uses the Dim statement to create an object variable that can store the address of a PowerPoint Application object. It then uses the CreateObject function both to start PowerPoint and to create the object, and it uses the Set statement to assign the object's address to the object variable. In Example 2, the Dim statement creates a Word object variable. The CreateObject function starts Word before it creates the Application object, and the Set statement assigns the object's address to the object variable.

Once the Automation server is started and the Automation object is created, the Automation controller can manipulate the object using the object's properties and methods. This is the third step in the Automation process.

Manipulating the Object Used for Automation

You can manipulate the Automation object by setting its properties and invoking its methods. For instance, assuming the Automation object is a PowerPoint Application object named appPowerPoint, you can use the instruction `appPowerPoint.Presentations.Add` to create a new PowerPoint presentation from within Excel, Access, or Word. Figure 14-5 shows examples of manipulating Automation objects through their properties and methods.

Example	Result
`appPowerPoint.Presentations.Open _` `FileName:="c:\tut14\concept\sales.ppt"`	Opens an existing PowerPoint presentation
`appExcel.ActiveSheet.Name = "Jan"`	Assigns the name Jan to the active worksheet in Excel
`appWord.Visible = True`	Makes the Word application visible
`appAccess.Quit`	Closes the Access Application object

Figure 14-5: Examples of manipulating Automation objects

The final step in the Automation process is to close the Automation object and then release the memory allocated to it.

Closing the Automation Object and Releasing Its Memory

Most Automation servers provide either a Quit method or a Close method that you can use to close the Automation object. The method you use depends on the type of Automation object you are closing. For example, you use the Quit method to close an Application object, but you use the Close method to close an ADO Recordset object. (You learned about the ADO Recordset object in Tutorial 6's Access lesson.)

In addition to closing the Automation object, you also should assign the keyword `Nothing` to the variable that stores the object's address. As you learned in Tutorial 3, when an object variable contains the keyword `Nothing`, it means that the variable does not point to any object in memory. Figure 14-6 shows three examples of closing an Automation object and releasing the memory allocated to it.

Example	Result
`appPowerPoint.Quit` `Set appPowerPoint = Nothing`	Closes the PowerPoint Application object and frees the memory allocated to it
`appWord.Quit` `Set appWord = Nothing`	Closes the Word Application object and frees the memory allocated to it
`rstCustomers.Close` `Set rstCustomers = Nothing`	Closes the ADO Recordset object and frees the memory allocated to it

Figure 14-6: Examples of closing an Automation object and releasing its memory

The DisplayTitleOnSlide procedure shown in Figure 14-7 uses Automation to display, on a PowerPoint slide, information contained in a Word document. The procedure, which is entered in a Code window in PowerPoint, assumes that PowerPoint (the Automation controller) contains a reference to the object library in Word (the Automation server). Recall that setting the reference is the first step in the Automation process.

Recall that Step 2 in the Automation process is to create the object used for Automation and to assign its address to an object variable. The Dim and Set statements in the DisplayTitleOnSlide procedure perform this step by creating a Word Application object and assigning the object's address to an object variable named appWord.

Step 3 in the Automation process is to manipulate the Automation object, as necessary, using its properties and methods. The DisplayTitleOnSlide procedure uses the Word Application object's properties and methods to open a Word document and to display, on the first PowerPoint slide, the text contained in the document's first paragraph.

```
Public Sub DisplayTitleOnSlide()
    'step 2 - create an object for Automation and assign
    'its address to an object variable
    Dim appWord As Word.Application
    Set appWord = CreateObject(Class:="word.application")

    'step 3 - manipulate the Automation object using its
    'properties and methods
    appWord.Documents.Open FileName:="c:\tut14\concept\title.doc"
    ActivePresentation.Slides(1).Shapes(1).TextFrame.TextRange.Text = _
      appWord.ActiveDocument.Paragraphs(1).Range.Text

    'step 4 - close the Automation object, then release
    'the memory allocated to it
    appWord.Quit
    Set appWord = Nothing
End Sub
```

Figure 14-7: DisplayTitleOnSlide procedure

The final step in the Automation process is to close the Automation object and then release the memory allocated to it. The DisplayTitleOnSlide procedure uses the Quit method to close the Word Application object. The procedure then frees the memory allocated to the object by assigning the keyword Nothing to the appWord object variable.

You now have completed Tutorial 14's Concept lesson. You can either take a break or complete the end-of-lesson questions and exercises before moving on to the next lesson.

SUMMARY

To use Automation:

- Set a reference to the Automation server's object library in the Automation controller.

- Create an object that can be used for Automation, and assign its address to an object variable.

- Manipulate the Automation object, as necessary, through its properties and methods.

- Close the Automation object and release the memory allocated to it.

To set a reference to the Automation server's object library:

■ Click Tools on the Visual Basic Editor's menu bar, then click References to display the References dialog box. Click the name of the appropriate object library, then click the OK button.

To create an object that can be used for Automation:

■ Use the CreateObject function. The syntax of the CreateObject function is **CreateObject(Class:=**_class_**)**, where _class_ is a string that specifies the class of the Automation object.

To close the Automation object:

■ Use either the Quit or Close method.

To release the memory allocated to the Automation object:

■ Assign the keyword Nothing to the object variable used to store the Automation object's address.

R E V I E W   Q U E S T I O N S

1. Applications that can expose their objects are called Automation _____.
   a. clients
   b. controllers
   c. exposers
   d. servers

2. Applications that can control the objects exposed by other applications are called Automation _____.
   a. controllers
   b. hosts
   c. rulers
   d. servers

3. The first step in the Automation process is to _____.
   a. create an object that can be used for Automation, and assign its address to an object variable
   b. manipulate the Automation object through its properties and methods
   c. set a reference to the Automation server's object library in the Automation controller
   d. start the Automation server

4. Every Automation server provides an _____, which is a file that contains information about the objects the server exposes.
   a. object library
   b. object list
   c. object server
   d. None of the above.

5. You use a _____ to create an object in VBA.
   a. blueprint
   b. class
   c. pattern
   d. None of the above.

6. The `CreateObject(Class:=Access.Application)` function will _____.
   a. assign the Access Application object to an object variable
   b. create an Access Application object
   c. start Access
   d. b and c only

7. Which of the following will close an Access Application object named appAccess?
   a. `appAccess.End`
   b. `appAccess.Quit`
   c. `appAccess.Stop`
   d. None of the above.

8. Which of the following will free the memory allocated to an Access Application object named appAccess?
   a. `appAccess = Nothing`
   b. `Set appAccess = 0`
   c. `Set appAccess = ""`
   d. None of the above.

EXERCISES

1. Write the statements to do the following:
   a. Declare an object variable that can store an Excel Application object. Name the object appExcel.
   b. Create an Excel Application object and assign its address to the appExcel variable.
   c. Open a workbook named Inventory.xls. Assume that the file is located in the Tut14\Excel folder on your Data Disk. (*Hint*: An Excel workbook is a member of the Workbooks collection.)
   d. Make Excel visible by setting its Visible property to True. (*Hint*: The address of the Excel application is stored in the appExcel variable.)
   e. Close the Excel Application object. (*Hint*: The address of the Excel application is stored in the appExcel variable.)
   f. Release the memory allocated to the appExcel variable.

2. In this exercise, you will perform Automation using PowerPoint and Word. The procedure you create will display, on a PowerPoint slide, the information stored in a Word document.

   a. Start PowerPoint. Open the T14-PP-E2 (T14-PP-E2.ppt) presentation, which is located in the Tut14\Concept folder on your Data Disk. Click the Enable Macros button, if necessary, then save the presentation as T14-PP-E2D.

   b. Open the Visual Basic Editor. Use the Tools menu to set a reference to the Microsoft Word 9.0 object library.

   c. Open the Module1 module's Code window and view the DisplayTitleOnSlide procedure. Complete the procedure by entering the missing code, which is shown in Figure 14-7. If necessary, change the file's path in the Open method's FileName argument. (The Title.doc file is stored in the Tut14\Concept folder on your Data Disk and contains the two words "Automation Procedure".)

   d. Save the presentation, then return to PowerPoint and run the DisplayTitleOnSlide procedure. The words "Automation Procedure" (without the quotation marks) should appear on the slide.

   e. Save the presentation, then close PowerPoint.

Exercise 3 is a Discovery Exercise. Discovery Exercises, which may include topics that are not covered in the lesson, allow you to "discover" the solutions to problems on your own.

discovery ▶ 3. In this exercise, you will learn how to use the keyword New to create an object that can be used for Automation. Before you can complete this exercise, you need to complete Exercise 2.

   a. Start PowerPoint. Open the T14-PP-E2D (T14-PP-E2D.ppt) presentation, which is located in the Tut14\Concept folder on your Data Disk. Click the Enable Macros button, if necessary, then save the presentation as T14-PP-E3D.

   b. Change the title of the slide from Automation Procedure to Title, then click the slide.

   c. Open the Visual Basic Editor. Open the Module1 module's Code window and view the DisplayTitleOnSlide procedure.

   d. Use the Help screens to research the Dim and Set statements. Notice that you can use the keyword New in both statements. Close the Help window.

   e. In the DisplayTitleOnSlide procedure, replace the Set appWord = CreateObject(class:="word.application") instruction with a Set statement that uses the keyword New to create the Word Application object.

   f. Save the presentation, then return to PowerPoint and run the DisplayTitleOnSlide procedure. The macro changes the word "Title" to "Automation Procedure".

   g. Change the slide's title from Automation Procedure to Title.

   h. Return to the Visual Basic Editor. Place an apostrophe (') before the Dim and Set statements to make those statements comments. Enter a Dim statement that creates the Word Application object.

   i. Save the presentation, then return to PowerPoint and run the DisplayTitleOnSlide procedure. The words "Automation Procedure" (without the quotation marks) should appear on the slide.

   j. Save the presentation, then close PowerPoint.

You also can use VBA in PowerPoint to create procedures that enhance your presentations. Exercise 4 allows you to apply this tutorial's programming concept in a PowerPoint presentation.

powerpoint 4. In this exercise, you will perform Automation using PowerPoint and Word. The procedure you create will display, on a PowerPoint slide, the information stored in a Word document.

a. Start Word. Open the AutoProc (AutoProc.doc) document, which is stored in the Tut14\Concept folder on your Data Disk. The first paragraph in the procedure is the title, Automation Procedure. Paragraphs two through five are the four steps needed to perform Automation. Close Word.

b. Start PowerPoint. Open the T14-PP-E4 (T14-PP-E4.ppt) presentation, which is located in the Tut14\Concept folder on your Data Disk. Click the Enable Macros button, if necessary, then save the presentation as T14-PP-E4D.

c. Open the Visual Basic Editor. Use the Tools menu to set a reference to the Microsoft Word 9.0 object library.

d. Open the Module1 module's Code window and view the CreateAutomationProcedureSlide procedure. Complete the procedure based on the comments included in the procedure.

e. Save the presentation, then return to PowerPoint and run the CreateAutomationProcedureSlide procedure. The words "Automation Procedure" (without the quotation marks) should appear as the slide's title. The four steps needed to perform Automation should appear in the Procedure Section on the slide.

f. Save the presentation, then close PowerPoint.

A computer program is good only if it works. Errors in programming code can cause a program to run incorrectly. Therefore, a programmer needs to know how to locate and fix any errors in his or her code. Exercise 5 is a Debugging Exercise. Debugging Exercises allow you to practice recognizing and solving errors in code.

debugging 5. The following code should declare an object variable that can store the address of an Excel Application object. It then should create an Excel Application object and assign its address to the object variable. Finally, it should close Excel's Application object and release the memory allocated to it. What, if anything, is wrong with the following code?

```
Dim appExcel As Excel.Application
appExcel = CreateObject(Class:=Excel.Application)
appExcel.Close
Set appExcel = None
```

Excel Lesson

Using Automation in Excel

case ▶ Jake Yardley, the manager of the Paradise Electronics store in Jackson, uses an Excel workbook to keep track of the quarterly sales made by each salesperson. At the end of each quarter, Jake gives a $50 check along with a Top Salesperson certificate to the salesperson who had the highest quarterly sales. Jake has decided to create a macro that he can use to print the certificate for the appropriate salesperson. The name of the salesperson is stored in an Access database, while the certificate is stored in a Word document.

Viewing the Paradise Documents

The workbook in which Jake records the store's quarterly sales is stored on your Data Disk. Also stored on your Data Disk are both a Word document containing the Top Salesperson certificate and an Access database containing each salesperson's ID and name. Before creating the macro that Jake will use to print the Top Salesperson certificate, view the Excel workbook, the Word document, and the Access database.

To view the Excel workbook, the Word document, and the Access database:

1   Start Microsoft Excel. Open the **T14-EX-1** (T14-EX-1.xls) workbook, which is located in the Tut14\Excel folder on your Data Disk. Click the **Enable Macros** button, if necessary, then save the workbook as **Quarter Sales**.

The Quarter Sales workbook contains one worksheet named First Quarter, as shown in Figure 14-8.

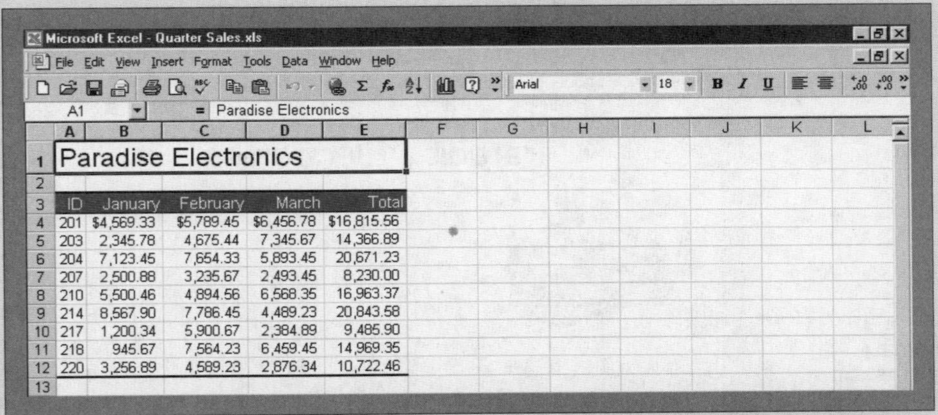

	A	B	C	D	E
1	Paradise Electronics				
2					
3	ID	January	February	March	Total
4	201	$4,569.33	$5,789.45	$6,456.78	$16,815.56
5	203	2,345.78	4,675.44	7,345.67	14,366.89
6	204	7,123.45	7,654.33	5,893.45	20,671.23
7	207	2,500.88	3,235.67	2,493.45	8,230.00
8	210	5,500.46	4,894.56	6,568.35	16,963.37
9	214	8,567.90	7,786.45	4,489.23	20,843.58
10	217	1,200.34	5,900.67	2,384.89	9,485.90
11	218	945.67	7,564.23	6,459.45	14,969.35
12	220	3,256.89	4,589.23	2,876.34	10,722.46
13					

Figure 14-8: The First Quarter worksheet in the Quarter Sales workbook

The First Quarter worksheet shows each salesperson's ID and monthly sales for the first quarter. Notice that the sales data is in ascending order by ID. To determine the salesperson with the highest quarterly sales, the macro will need to sort the sales data in descending order by the Total column.

Next, open the Top Salesperson certificate document in Word.

2 Start Microsoft Word. Open the **Certif** (Certif.doc) document, which is located in the Tut14\Excel folder on your Data Disk. The Top Salesperson certificate is shown in Figure 14-9, which is on the next page.

As Figure 14-9 indicates, the name of the top salesperson should appear in the document's TopName form field. Recall, however, that the First Quarter worksheet contains only the salesperson's ID and sales; it does not contain the salesperson's name. The macro will need to search an Access database for the top salesperson's ID and then return his or her name and insert it into the certificate.

3 Close Word. You are returned to the Quarter Sales workbook in Excel.

Now open the Access database that contains each salesperson's ID and name.

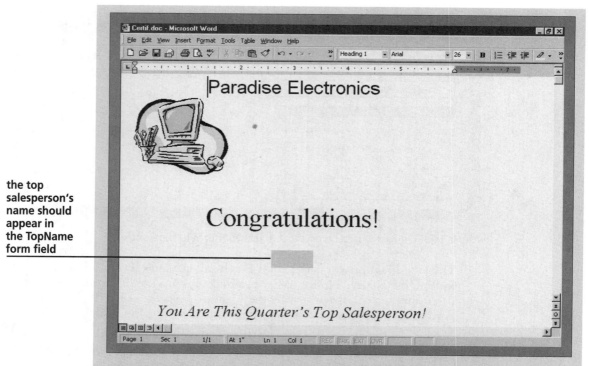

the top salesperson's name should appear in the TopName form field

Figure 14-9: Certificate issued to the top salesperson each quarter

4 Start Microsoft Access. Open the **Sales** (Sales.mdb) database, which is located in the Tut14\Excel folder on your Data Disk. Open the **Salespeople** table, which is shown in Figure 14-10.

Notice that the Salespeople table contains two fields: ID and Name.

5 Close the table, then close Access. You are returned to the Quarter Sales workbook in Excel.

6 Press **Alt+F11** to open the Visual Basic Editor. If necessary, open the Project Explorer window and close the Properties window, the Immediate window, and any open Code windows.

7 Open the Module1 module's Code window, then view the code template for the **IssueCertificate** procedure.

8 Close the Project Explorer window so that you can view more of the Code window.

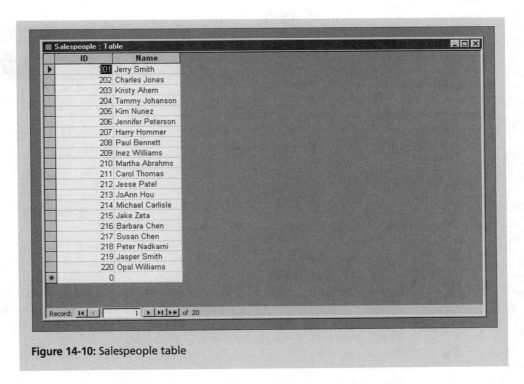

Figure 14-10: Salespeople table

Figure 14-11 shows the pseudocode for the IssueCertificate procedure.

1. Sort the sales data in descending order by the quarterly sales amount entered in the Total column.
2. Create an Access Application object named appAccess to use for Automation.
3. Create a Word Application object named appWord to use for Automation.
4. Open the sales.mdb file in Access.
5. Open the certif.doc file in Word.
6. Use the Access application's DLookup function to look up the top salesperson's ID in the Salespeople table and return his or her name. Assign the name to a String variable named strName.
7. Assign the contents of the strName variable to the TopName form field in the Word document.
8. Print the Word document.
9. Display the message "The certificate was printed." in a message box.
10. Close the Access Application object.
11. Close the Word Application object without saving the changes made to the document.
12. Set the Access and Word Application object variables to Nothing.
13. Return the sales data to its original order by sorting the data in ascending order by ID.

Figure 14-11: Pseudocode for the IssueCertificate procedure

Figure 14-12 lists the variables that the IssueCertificate procedure will use.

Variable	datatype
strName	String
shtFirstQ	Worksheet
rngData	Range
appWord	Word.Application
appAccess	Access.Application

Figure 14-12: Variables used by the IssueCertificate procedure

The IssueCertificate procedure will use the strName variable to store the name of the salesperson having the highest quarterly sales. It will store the address of the First Quarter worksheet in the shtFirstQ variable, and it will store the address of the sales data in the rngData variable. The procedure will assign the address of the objects used for Automation—a Word Application object and an Access Application object—to the appWord and appAccess variables, respectively.

To begin coding the IssueCertificate procedure:

1 Click **Tools** on the Visual Basic Editor's menu bar, then click **References** to display the References dialog box.

Recall that Step 1 in the Automation process is to set a reference to the Automation server's object library. In this case, you will need to set a reference to Access's object library and to Word's object library.

2 Scroll the Available References list box, if necessary, until you see Microsoft Access 9.0 Object Library in the list. Click the **check box that appears to the left of Microsoft Access 9.0 Object Library** in the list. Be sure a check mark appears in the check box.

3 Scroll the Available References list box, if necessary, until you see Microsoft Word 9.0 Object Library in the list. Click the **check box that appears to the left of Microsoft Word 9.0 Object Library** in the list. Be sure a check mark appears in the check box.

4 Click the **OK** button to close the References dialog box.

5 Enter the documentation and the Dim and Set statements shown in Figure 14-13.

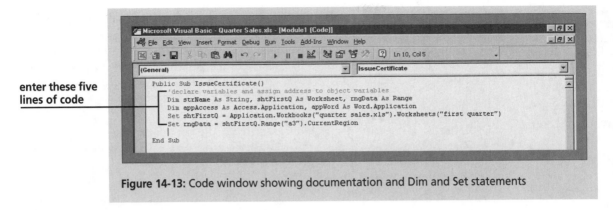

Figure 14-13: Code window showing documentation and Dim and Set statements

The first step in the pseudocode is to sort the sales data in descending order by the quarterly sales amounts, which are listed in the Total column.

To continue coding the IssueCertificate procedure:

1 Type **'sort the sales data in descending order by the Total column** and press the **Enter** key, then type **rngdata.sort key1:="total", order1:=xldescending, header:=xlyes** and press the **Enter** key.

You learned about the Sort method in Tutorial 13's Excel lesson.

After the sales data is sorted, cell E4 will contain the highest sales amount and cell A4 will contain the top salesperson's ID.

Next, create an Access Application object and a Word Application object to use for Automation.

2 Type **'create objects for automation** and press the **Enter** key, then type **set appaccess = createobject(class:="access.application")** and press the **Enter** key. Type **set appword = createobject(class:="word.application")** and press the **Enter** key.

Now open the Access database and the Word document.

3 Type **'open Access database and Word document** and press the **Enter** key. Type **appaccess.opencurrentdatabase "c:\tut14\excel\sales.mdb"** and press the **Enter** key, then type **appword.documents.open "c:\tut14\excel\certif.doc"** and press the **Enter** key. (If necessary, change the path in both statements to reflect the location of the files on your Data Disk.)

Step 6 in the pseudocode is to use the Access application's DLookup function to look up the top salesperson's ID in the Salespeople table and return his or her name. The syntax of the DLookup function is **DLookup(***expr, domain*[, *criteria*]**)**, where *expr* is an expression that identifies the field whose value you want the function to return. In this case, you want the function to return the value stored in the table's Name field. You will store the returned value in the strName variable.

Domain is a string expression identifying the set of records you want to search, and it can be the name of either a table or a query. You will use the table name Salespeople as the *domain*.

Criteria is an optional string expression used to restrict the range of data on which the DLookup function is performed. In this case, you want to restrict the data range to only those records whose ID matches the value stored in cell A4 in the First Quarter worksheet. (Recall that after the sales data is sorted in descending order by the Total column, cell E4 will contain the highest sales amount and cell A4 will contain the ID of the salesperson associated with those sales.)

> **tip**
>
> The *Criteria* argument is often equivalent to the WHERE clause in an SQL expression, but without the word WHERE.

4   Type **'locate ID in Access table and return the name** and press the **Enter** key, then type **strname = appaccess.dlookup("name", "salespeople", "ID = " & shtfirstq.range("a4").value)** and press the **Enter** key.

Step 7 in the pseudocode is to assign the name returned by the DLookup function to the TopName form field in the Word document.

5   Type **'assign name to TopName form field in the Word document** and press the **Enter** key, then type **appword.documents("certif.doc").formfields ("topname").result = strname** and press the **Enter** key.

Next, print the Word document, then display the message "The certificate was printed." in a message box.

6   Type **'print the Word document** and press the **Enter** key, then type **appword.documents("certif.doc").printout** and press the **Enter** key.

7   Type **msgbox prompt:="The certificate was printed.", buttons:=vbokonly + vbinformation** and press the **Enter** key.

Steps 10 through 12 in the pseudocode are to close the Access and Word Application objects, which were used for Automation, and then release the memory allocated to them. Step 13, the last step in the pseudocode, is to return the sales data to its original order by sorting the data in ascending order by ID.

8   Type the additional lines of code shown in Figure 14-14, which shows the completed IssueCertificate procedure.

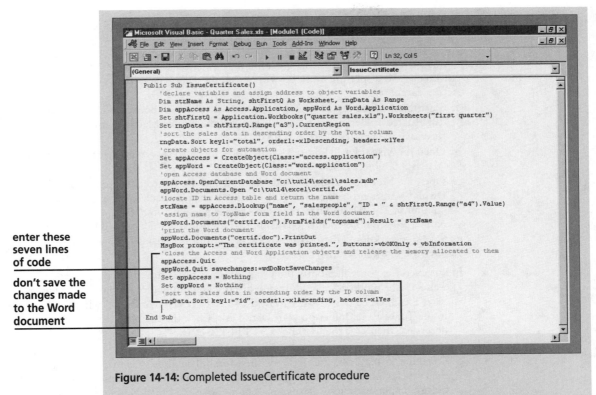

```
Microsoft Visual Basic - Quarter Sales.xls - [Module1 (Code)]
File  Edit  View  Insert  Format  Debug  Run  Tools  Add-Ins  Window  Help                    Ln 32, Col 5

(General)                                           IssueCertificate

    Public Sub IssueCertificate()
        'declare variables and assign address to object variables
        Dim strName As String, shtFirstQ As Worksheet, rngData As Range
        Dim appAccess As Access.Application, appWord As Word.Application
        Set shtFirstQ = Application.Workbooks("quarter sales.xls").Worksheets("first quarter")
        Set rngData = shtFirstQ.Range("a3").CurrentRegion
        'sort the sales data in descending order by the Total column
        rngData.Sort key1:="total", order1:=xlDescending, header:=xlYes
        'create objects for automation
        Set appAccess = CreateObject(Class:="access.application")
        Set appWord = CreateObject(Class:="word.application")
        'open Access database and Word document
        appAccess.OpenCurrentDatabase "c:\tut14\excel\sales.mdb"
        appWord.Documents.Open "c:\tut14\excel\certif.doc"
        'locate ID in Access table and return the name
        strName = appAccess.DLookup("name", "salespeople", "ID = " & shtFirstQ.Range("a4").Value)
        'assign name to TopName form field in the Word document
        appWord.Documents("certif.doc").FormFields("topname").Result = strName
        'print the Word document
        appWord.Documents("certif.doc").PrintOut
        MsgBox prompt:="The certificate was printed.", Buttons:=vbOKOnly + vbInformation
        'close the Access and Word Application objects and release the memory allocated to them
        appAccess.Quit
        appWord.Quit savechanges:=wdDoNotSaveChanges
        Set appAccess = Nothing
        Set appWord = Nothing
        'sort the sales data in ascending order by the ID column
        rngData.Sort key1:="id", order1:=xlAscending, header:=xlYes

    End Sub
```

enter these seven lines of code

don't save the changes made to the Word document

Figure 14-14: Completed IssueCertificate procedure

9 Verify the accuracy of your code by comparing the code on your screen to the code shown in Figure 14-14, then save the workbook.

Now that you have finished coding the IssueCertificate procedure, you will test it to be sure it is working correctly.

To test the IssueCertificate procedure:

1 Return to Excel and run the **IssueCertificate** macro. When the message "The certificate was printed." appears in a message box, click the **OK** button. The name of the top salesperson, Michael Carlisle, appears on the printed certificate.

2 Save the workbook, then close Excel.

You now have completed Tutorial 14's Excel lesson. You can either take a break or complete the end-of-lesson exercises before moving on to the next lesson.

EXERCISES

1. In this exercise, you will perform Automation using Excel and Access. The procedure you create will display, in an Excel worksheet, the salesperson names contained in an Access database.

    a. Start Excel. Open the T14-EX-E1 (T14-EX-E1.xls) workbook, which is located in the Tut14\Excel folder on your Data Disk. Click the Enable Macros button, if necessary, then save the workbook as T14-EX-E1D.

    b. Open the Visual Basic Editor. Use the Tools menu to set a reference to the Microsoft Access 9.0 Object Library.

    c. Open the Module1 module's Code window and view the code template for the DisplayNames procedure. Use Automation to display each salesperson's name in column B. The IDs and names of the salespeople are stored in an Access database named Sales.mdb, which is located in the Tut14\Excel folder on your Data Disk.

    d. Save the workbook, then return to Excel and run the DisplayNames macro.

    e. Save the workbook, then close Excel.

2. In this exercise, you will modify the DisplayNames procedure that you created in Exercise 1. The modified procedure will insert a column before displaying the names.

    a. Start Excel. Open the T14-EX-E1D (T14-EX-E1D.xls) workbook, which is located in the Tut14\Excel folder on your Data Disk. Click the Enable Macros button, if necessary, then save the workbook as T14-EX-E2D.

    b. Delete column B in the worksheet.

    c. Open the Visual Basic Editor. Open the Module1 module's Code window and view the DisplayNames procedure. Modify the procedure so that it inserts a new column B before displaying each salesperson's name. Use the word Name as the title for column B. Left-align the word Name in cell B3. You will need to use the Range object's AutoFit method to adjust the width of column B after the names are displayed.

    d. Save the workbook, then return to Excel and run the DisplayNames macro.

    e. Save the workbook, then close Excel.

3. In this exercise, you will perform Automation using Excel and Word. The procedure you create will display, in a Word document, the payment information contained in an Excel worksheet.

    a. Start Word. Open the Payment (Payment.doc) document, which is located in the Tut14\Excel folder on your Data Disk. The document contains four form fields named Loan, Rate, Term, and MonthPayment. Close Word.

    b. Start Excel. Open the T14-EX-E3 (T14-EX-E3.xls) workbook, which is located in the Tut14\Excel folder on your Data Disk. Click the Enable Macros button, if necessary, then save the workbook as T14-EX-E3D. You can use the Payment worksheet to calculate the monthly payment on a loan. You need simply to enter the loan amount, interest rate, and term in cells B1, B2, and B3, respectively. Cell B4 contains the PMT function that will perform the calculation.

    c. Open the Visual Basic Editor. Use the Tools menu to set a reference to the Microsoft Word 9.0 Object Library.

      d. Open the Module1 module's Code window and view the code template for the SendPaymentInfo procedure. Code the procedure so that it displays the loan information (loan amount, interest rate, term, and monthly payment) in the Payment document's form fields. It then should print the Payment document and display the message "The document was printed." in a message box. When closing the Word Application object, save the changes made to the Payment document. (*Hint*: Use the intrinsic constant `wdSaveChanges`.)

      e. Save the workbook, then return to Excel. Enter 9000 as the loan amount, 6% as the interest rate, and 4 as the term. Run the SendPaymentInfo macro.

      f. Save the workbook, then close Excel.

Exercises 4 and 5 are Discovery Exercises. Discovery Exercises, which may include topics that are not covered in the lesson, allow you to "discover" the solutions to problems on your own.

discovery ▶ **4.** In this exercise, you will learn about the Application object's Visible property.

      a. Start Excel. Open the T14-EX-E4 (T14-EX-E4.xls) workbook, which is located in the Tut14\Excel folder on your Data Disk. Click the Enable Macros button, if necessary, then save the workbook as T14-EX-E4D.

      b. Open the Visual Basic Editor and set a reference to the Microsoft Word 9.0 Object Library.

      c. Open the Module1 module's Code window and view the partially completed ViewWordDocument procedure. The procedure should add a table to a new Word document. It then should assign the contents of cells A1 through A4 in the Excel worksheet to the Word table. Use the procedure's comments to guide you in completing the procedure.

      d. Save the workbook, then return to Excel and run the ViewWordDocument procedure. While the procedure is running, does the sales.doc – Microsoft Word button appear on the taskbar?

      e. Start Word, then open the Sales (Sales.doc) document, which is located in the Tut14\Excel folder on your Data Disk. The document should contain a four-row, one-column table. January should appear in row 1, and 100, 200, and 300 should appear in rows 2, 3, and 4, respectively.

      f. Open the Visual Basic Editor in Word. Use the Help screens to research the Application object's Visible property. Based on what you observed in Step d, what is the default value of the Visible property for an Application object?

      g. Close Word, then use Windows to delete the Sales (Sales.doc) document from your Data Disk.

      h. Return to the ViewWordDocument procedure in Excel. Add an instruction to the procedure that sets the Word Application object's Visible property to True. Enter the instruction immediately after the Set statement in which the object is created.

      i. Save the workbook, then return to Excel and run the ViewWordDocument procedure. While the procedure is running, does the sales.doc – Microsoft Word button appear on the taskbar?

      j. Change the `appWord.Quit` instruction to a comment by beginning the instruction with an apostrophe ('). Save the workbook, then return to Excel and run the ViewWordDocument procedure. What happens to Word and the document? (**Important Note:** You should never remove the Quit or Close instructions when the object's Visible property is set to False. You can learn more about this by completing this lesson's Debugging Exercise.)

      k. Close Word, then close Excel.

discovery ▶   **5.**   In this exercise, you will perform Automation using Excel and the ADO object model in Access.

     a.   Start Access. Open the Nora (Nora.mdb) database, which is located in the Tut14\Excel folder on your Data Disk. Open the Client table in Design View. Notice that the table contains six fields. Close Access.

     b.   Start Excel. Open the T14-EX-E5 (T14-EX-E5.xls) workbook, which is located in the Tut14\Excel folder on your Data Disk. Click the Enable Macros button, if necessary, then save the workbook as T14-EX-E5D.

     c.   Open the Visual Basic Editor. Use the Tools menu to set a reference to the Microsoft ActiveX Data Objects 2.1 Library object library.

     d.   Open the Module1 module's Code window and view the partially completed DisplayNames procedure. The procedure should display the last and first names from the Client table in columns A and B, respectively, in the worksheet. Complete the procedure, using the procedure's comments as a guide. (If necessary, change the location of the Nora.mdb file.)

     e.   Save the workbook, then return to Excel and run the DisplayNames macro. The last and first names from the Client table should appear in columns A and B, respectively, in the worksheet.

     f.   Save the workbook, then close Excel.

A computer program is good only if it works. Errors in programming code can cause a program to run incorrectly. Therefore, a programmer needs to know how to locate and fix any errors in his or her code. Exercise 6 is a Debugging Exercise. Debugging Exercises allow you to practice recognizing and solving errors in code.

debugging   **6.**   In this exercise, you will debug an existing application.

     a.   If Microsoft Word is running, close it.

     b.   Start Excel. Open the T14-EX-E6 (T14-EX-E6.xls) workbook, which is located in the Tut14\Excel folder on your Data Disk. Click the Enable Macros button, if necessary, then save the workbook as T14-EX-E6D.

     c.   Enter your name in cell A1 in the worksheet.

     d.   Press Ctrl+Alt+Del to open the Close Program dialog box. Verify that Winword does not appear in the list of programs, then click the Cancel button. (***Important Note:*** If Winword appears in the list of programs, click it, then click the End Task button. In a short time, the Winword dialog box will appear. When the dialog box appears, click the End Task button.)

     e.   Open the Visual Basic Editor. Open the Module1 module's Code window and view the DisplayName procedure. The procedure should create a new Word document and then display the contents of cell A1 in the document.

     f.   Run the DisplayName procedure. Start Word, then open the Name (Name.doc) document. The text "Do you want to revert to the saved 'name.doc'?" appears in a message box, indicating that the document is already open. Click the No button, then close Word.

     g.   Press Ctrl+Alt+Del to open the Close Program dialog box. You will notice that Winword appears in the list. Why do you think this is so?

h. To remove Winword from the list, click Winword in the Close Program dialog box and then click the End Task button. In a short time, the Winword dialog box will appear. Click the End Task button in the Winword dialog box, then press Ctrl+Alt+Del to open the Close Program dialog box. Verify that Winword no longer appears in the list. Click the Cancel button.

i. In the DisplayName procedure, enter the instruction `docName.Close` above the comment `'release the memory allocated to the appWord object`. This instruction will close the Name document. Run the DisplayName procedure, then start Word and open the Name (Name.doc) document. Are you able to open the document?

j. Close Word, then press Ctrl+Alt+Del to open the Close Program dialog box. Does Winword appear in the list? Remove Winword from the list. (*Hint*: See Step h.) Why do you think Winword appears in the list even when the document is closed?

k. One way to correct the DisplayName procedure is to have the procedure close Word rather than close the document. Change the instruction `docName.Close` to `appWord.Quit`. Run the DisplayName procedure. Press Ctrl+Alt+Del to open the Close Program dialog box. Does Winword appear in the list? Click the Cancel button.

l. Another way to correct the DisplayName procedure is to allow the user to close Word. You can do so by leaving Word open, but making it visible. Change the instruction `appWord.Quit` to `appWord.Visible = True`. Run the DisplayName procedure. Your name appears in the Word document.

m. Close Word, then press Ctrl+Alt+Del to open the Close Program dialog box. Does Winword appear in the list? Click the Cancel button.

n. Save and then close the workbook, then close Excel.

Word Lesson

Using Automation in Word

case▶ Periodically, Nancy Manley, Willowton Health Club's secretary, needs to send a letter, stored as a Word document, to one or more club members. The names and addresses of the club members are stored in an Access database. Nancy has decided to use a custom dialog box to assist her in entering the appropriate name and address in the letter.

Viewing Nancy's Documents

The Word document that Nancy uses to create the member correspondence is stored on your Data Disk. The document already contains Nancy's custom dialog box. Before coding the dialog box, view the database, the Word document, and the dialog box.

To view the database, document, and custom dialog box:

1 Start Microsoft Access. Open the **Members** (Members.mdb) database, which is located in the Tut14\Word folder on your Data Disk. Open the **Client** table. Figure 14-15 shows the 15 records contained in the Client table.

Notice that each record contains six fields: Last, First, Street, City, State, and Zip.

2 Close the table, then close Access.

3 Start Microsoft Word.

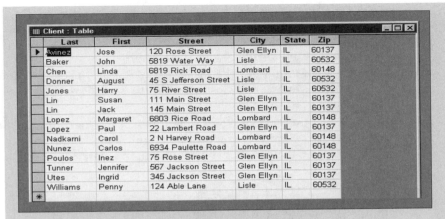

Figure 14-15: Records contained in the Client table

4 Open the **T14-WD-1** (T14-WD-1.doc) document, which is located in the Tut14\Word folder on your Data Disk. Click the **Enable Macros** button, if necessary, then save the document as **Member Letters**. The Member Letters document is shown in Figure 14-16.

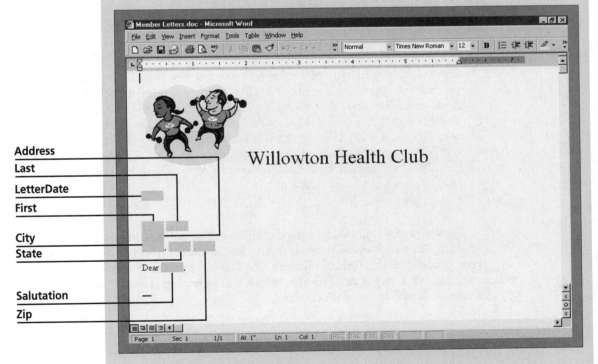

Figure 14-16: The Member Letters document

As the figure indicates, the document contains eight form fields: LetterDate, First, Last, Address, City, State, Zip, and Salutation.

Next, view the custom dialog box.

5   Press **Alt+F11** to open the Visual Basic Editor. If necessary, open the Project Explorer window and close the Properties window, the Immediate window, and any open Code windows.

6   View the **frmMembers** form object, which is located in the Forms folder in the Project Explorer window. The form is the foundation for the Member List custom dialog box, which is shown in Figure 14-17.

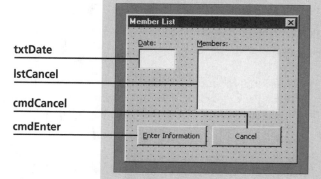

txtDate

lstCancel

cmdCancel

cmdEnter

Figure 14-17: The Member List dialog box

The dialog box consists of a form and six controls: two labels, one text box, one list box, and two command buttons. You will code the form's Initialize event procedure so that it displays the current date in the text box and each member's name in the list box. When the user clicks the Enter Information button, the button's Click event will enter the date and the member's name and address in the document before unloading the form. When the user clicks the Cancel button, the button's Click event simply will unload the form.

7   Close the Project Explorer window.

Now you can begin coding the dialog box. You will need to enter code only in the form's Initialize event procedure and in the Enter Information button's Click event procedure; the Cancel button's Click event procedure already contains the instruction `Unload frmMembers`, which will unload the form. First you will code the form's Initialize event procedure.

Coding the Form's Initialize Event Procedure

As you learned in Tutorial 13's Word lesson, a form's Initialize event occurs after the form is loaded into memory but before it is shown on the screen. Figure 14-18 shows the pseudocode for the frmMembers form's Initialize event procedure.

1. Create an ADODB.Recordset object named rstMembers to use for Automation.
2. Open a recordset that contains all of the Client table's records. Sort the records in ascending order by the last and first names.
3. Repeat the following for each record in the recordset:
   a. Add the last and first names to the list box. Separate the last and first names with a comma.
   b. Move the record pointer to the next record in the recordset.
4. Select the first item in the list box as the default item.
5. Close the ADODB.Recordset object.
6. Set the ADODB.Recordset object variable to Nothing.
7. Display the current date in the txtDate text box.

Figure 14-18: Pseudocode for the frmMembers form's Initialize event

The Initialize event procedure will use one variable: an ADODB.Recordset object variable named rstMembers. The rstMembers variable will store the address of the ADODB.Recordset object used for Automation.

tip

You learned about the ADODB.Recordset object in Tutorial 6's Access lesson.

To begin coding the form's Initialize event procedure:

1 Click **Tools** on the Visual Basic Editor's menu bar, then click **References** to display the References dialog box.

Recall that Step 1 in the Automation process is to set a reference to the Automation server's object library. In this case, you will need to set a reference to the Microsoft ActiveX Data Objects 2.1 Library object library.

2 If necessary, scroll the Available References list box until you see Microsoft ActiveX Data Objects 2.1 Library in the list. Click the **check box that appears to the left of Microsoft ActiveX Data Objects 2.1 Library** in the list. Be sure that a check mark appears in the check box. Click the **OK** button to close the References dialog box.

3 Right-click the **form**, and then click **View Code** on the shortcut menu. The UserForm's Click event procedure appears in the Code window. Use the Code window's Procedure list box to open the UserForm's **Initialize** procedure.

4 Press the **Tab** key, then type **'declare variable** and press the **Enter** key. Type **dim rstMembers as adodb.recordset** and press the **Enter** key.

The first step in the pseudocode is to create an ADODB.Recordset object to use for Automation. You will assign the address of the Recordset object to the rstMembers variable.

5 Type **'create a Recordset object for Automation** and press the **Enter** key, then type **set rstmembers = createobject(class:="adodb.recordset")** and press the **Enter** key.

Step 2 in the pseudocode is to open a recordset that contains all of the Client table's records, sorted in ascending order by the last and first names. You use the Recordset object's Open method to open the recordset. The syntax of the Open method is *recordset*.**open Source:**=*datasource*, **ActiveConnection:**=*connection*, **CursorType:**=*cursortype*, **LockType:**=*locktype*, where *recordset* is the name of a Recordset object variable, *datasource* specifies the data source, and *connection* specifies both the data provider and database name. The *cursortype* and *locktype* arguments in the syntax can be one of the constants shown in Figure 14-19.

CursorType Constant	Description
adOpenForwardOnly	(Default) Forward-only cursor. Identical to a static cursor except that you can only scroll forward through records. This improves performance in situations when you need to make only a single pass through a recordset.
adOpenKeyset	Keyset cursor. Like a dynamic cursor, except that you cannot see records that other users add. However, records that other users delete are inaccessible from your recordset. Data changes by other users are still visible.
adOpenDynamic	Dynamic cursor. Additions, changes, and deletions by other users are visible, and all types of movement through the recordset are allowed (except for book-marks if the provider doesn't support them).
adOpenStatic	Static cursor. A static copy of a set of records that you can use to find data or generate reports. Additions, changes, or deletions by other users are not visible.
LockType Constant	**Description**
adLockReadOnly	(Default) Read-only—you cannot alter the data contained in the recordset.
adLockPessimistic	The provider locks a record immediately upon editing.
adLockOptimistic	The provider locks the record only when you call the Update method to save the changes made to the record.
adLockBatchOptimistic	Required for batch update mode.

Figure 14-19: Valid constants for the Open method's CursorType and LockType arguments

You can use the CursorType argument to control how the records in the recordset can be accessed. You can use the LockType argument, which is important in multiuser environments, to prevent more than one user from editing a specific record at the same time by locking the record, making it unavailable to other users.

▶ **tip**

You may find it helpful to review Tutorial 6's Access lesson, where the Open method is first introduced.

To use the Open method to open a recordset that contains all of the Client table's records, sorted in ascending order by the last and first names, you will use the SQL SELECT statement `"SELECT * FROM client ORDER BY last, first"` as the Source argument, and you will use the string `"provider=microsoft.jet.oledb.4.0;data source=c:\tut14 \word\members.mdb"` as the ActiveConnection argument. Because the Initialize procedure will need to make only a single pass through the recordset, you will use the intrinsic constant `adOpenForwardOnly` as the CursorType argument. You will use the intrinsic constant `adLockReadOnly` as the LockType argument, which will prevent the records from being edited.

To continue coding the form's Initialize event procedure, then test the procedure:

1 Type the comment and the additional instruction shown in Figure 14-20. (Be sure to type an equal sign—but no spaces—after the words "provider" and "data source" in the Open method.) If necessary, change the path to reflect the location of the database on your Data Disk.

enter these four lines of code

your path might be different

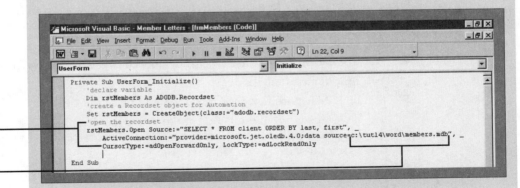

Figure 14-20: Current status of the Initialize event

Step 3 in the pseudocode is to repeat a set of instructions for each record in the recordset. You can use the Recordset object's EOF property to determine if the record pointer is positioned at the end of the file. (EOF stands for *end of file*.) The EOF property returns the Boolean value True if the record pointer is positioned after the last record in the recordset; otherwise, it returns the Boolean value False.

> **You learned about the Recordset object's EOF property in Tutorial 10's Access lesson.**

2   Press the **Backspace** key, then type **'add member names to list box** and press the **Enter** key. Type **do until rstmembers.eof = true** and press the **Enter** key.

The first instruction in the loop should add the current member's last and first name, separated by a comma, to the lstMembers list box.

3   Press the **Tab** key, then type **lstmembers.additem rstmembers.fields("last").value & _** (be sure to type the ampersand followed by a space and the underscore) and press the **Enter** key. Press the **Tab** key, then type **", " & rstmembers.fields("first") . value** (be sure to include a space after the comma) and press the **Enter** key. This instruction will concatenate the member's last name with a comma, a space, and the member's first name. It will display the result in the lstMembers list box.

> **You learned about the list box's AddItem method in Tutorial 13's Excel and Word lessons.**

The second instruction in the loop should move the record pointer to the next record in the recordset. You can use the Recordset object's MoveNext method to do so.

> **You learned about the MoveNext method in Tutorial 10's Access lesson.**

4   Press the **Backspace** key, then type **rstmembers.movenext** and press the **Enter** key. You now can end the loop.

5   Press the **Backspace** key, then type **loop** and press the **Enter** key.

The last steps in the pseudocode are to select the default list box item, close the Recordset object and release the memory allocated to it, and then display the current date in the txtDate text box.

6   Type the additional lines of code shown in Figure 14-21, which shows the completed Initialize event procedure.

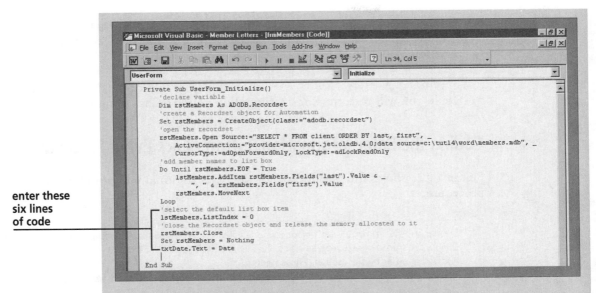

enter these six lines of code

```
Private Sub UserForm_Initialize()
    'declare variable
    Dim rstMembers As ADODB.Recordset
    'create a Recordset object for Automation
    Set rstMembers = CreateObject(class:="adodb.recordset")
    'open the recordset
    rstMembers.Open Source:="SELECT * FROM client ORDER BY last, first", _
        ActiveConnection:="provider=microsoft.jet.oledb.4.0;data source=c:\tut14\word\members.mdb", _
        CursorType:=adOpenForwardOnly, LockType:=adLockReadOnly
    'add member names to list box
    Do Until rstMembers.EOF = True
        lstMembers.AddItem rstMembers.Fields("last").Value & _
            ", " & rstMembers.Fields("first").Value
        rstMembers.MoveNext
    Loop
    'select the default list box item
    lstMembers.ListIndex = 0
    'close the Recordset object and release the memory allocated to it
    rstMembers.Close
    Set rstMembers = Nothing
    txtDate.Text = Date
End Sub
```

Figure 14-21: Completed Initialize event procedure

7 Verify the accuracy of your code by comparing the code on your screen to the code shown in Figure 14-21, then save the document.

Now test the procedure to verify that it is working correctly.

8 Return to Word and run the **GetMemberInfo** macro. (The GetMemberInfo procedure already contains the frmMembers.Show instruction, which will display the custom dialog box on the screen.) When the Member List dialog box appears, the text box displays the current date and the list box displays each club member's name, as shown in Figure 14-22. (Your date might be different from the one shown in the figure.)

your date might be different

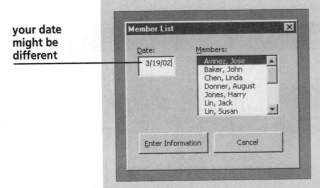

Figure 14-22: Member List dialog box showing the current date and member names

9 Click the **Cancel** button to close the dialog box. Recall that the Cancel button's Click event procedure already contains the instruction `Unload frmMembers`.

Next, you will code the Enter Information button's Click event procedure.

Coding the Enter Information Button's Click Event Procedure

Figure 14-23 shows the pseudocode for the Enter Information button's Click event procedure.

1. Create an ADODB.Recordset object named rstMembers to use for Automation.
2. Open a recordset that contains all of the Client table's records. Sort the records in ascending order by the last and first names.
3. Position the record pointer on the record whose name matches the name selected in the list box.
4. Display the member's name and address in the appropriate form fields in the document.
5. Close the ADODB.Recordset object.
6. Set the ADODB.Recordset object variable to Nothing.
7. Display the contents of the txtDate text box in the LetterDate form field.
8. Unload the frmMembers form.
9. Position the cursor at the end of the document.

Figure 14-23: Pseudocode for the Enter Information button's Click event procedure

Figure 14-24 lists the variables that the Enter Information button's Click event procedure will use.

Variable	datatype
docLetter	Document
rstMembers	ADODB.Recordset

Figure 14-24: Variables used by the Enter Information button's Click event procedure

The Enter Information button's Click event procedure will store the address of the Member Letters document in the docLetter variable, and it will store the address of the ADODB.Recordset object, which is used for Automation, in the rstMembers variable.

To begin coding the Enter Information button's Click event procedure:

1 Press **Alt+F11** to return to the Visual Basic Editor. Use the Object box in the Code window to open the Enter Information button's Click event procedure. (The name of the Enter Information button is cmdEnter.) In the Click event procedure, enter the documentation and Dim and Set statements shown in Figure 14-25.

enter these
three lines
of code

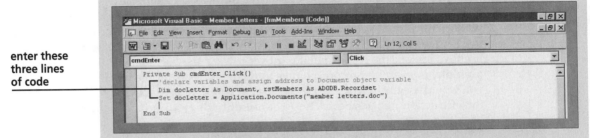

Figure 14-25: Code window showing documentation and Dim and Set statements

The first two steps in the pseudocode are to create an ADODB.Recordset object variable, and then open a recordset that contains all of the Client table's records, sorted in ascending order by the last and first names.

2 Type the additional lines of code shown in Figure 14-26. (Be sure to type only an equal sign after the words "provider" and "data source" in the Open method.) If necessary, change the path in the open statement to reflect the location of the database on your Data Disk.

enter these
six lines
of code

your path
might be
different

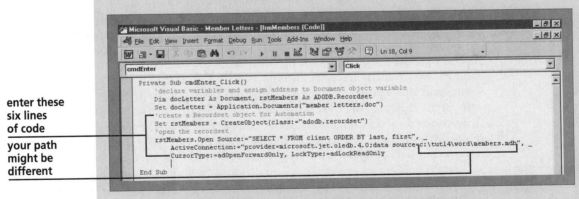

Figure 14-26: Current status of the cmdEnter control's Click event procedure

Step 3 in the pseudocode is to position the record pointer on the record whose name matches the name selected in the list box. You can do so using the Recordset object's Move method.

Moving the Record Pointer

You can use the Recordset object's Move method, which has the syntax *recordset*.**Move NumRecords:**=*numRecords*, to move the record pointer to another record in the *recordset*. In the syntax, *numRecords* is an integer, either positive or negative, that specifies the number of records you want the record pointer to move. If *numRecords* is a positive integer, the record pointer moves toward the end of the recordset. If *numRecords* is a negative integer, the record pointer moves toward the beginning of the recordset. For example, to move the record pointer to the next record in the rstMembers recordset, you would use the instruction `rstMembers.Move NumRecords:=1`. You would use the instruction `rstMembers.Move NumRecords:=-5` to move the record pointer back five records.

Figure 14-27 shows the records that comprise the rstMembers recordset. It also shows each member's name listed in the lstMembers list box, as well as each name's ListIndex value. When a recordset is first opened, the record pointer is pointing to the first record. In the case of the rstMembers recordset, for example, the record pointer will be pointing to the Jose Avinez record. Notice in the figure that the name corresponding to this record also appears as the first item in the list box.

> Recall that the Open method in the form's Initialize procedure sorts the recordset in ascending order by the last and first names before the names are added to the list box.

If the user selects the first item in the list box, the procedure will not need to move the record pointer, because it already is pointing to the appropriate record. However, if the user selects the second item in the list box, the procedure will need to move the record pointer one record from its current location. Similarly, if the user selects the third item in the list box, the procedure will need to move the record pointer two records from its current location. Notice that the number of records you want the record pointer to move corresponds to the list box's ListIndex property. Because of this, you can use the instruction `rstMembers.Move NumRecords:=lstMembers.ListIndex` to move the record pointer to the record whose name is selected in the list box.

> As you learned in Tutorial 13, when the user selects an item in a list box, the item's location is recorded in the list box's ListIndex property. The first item has a ListIndex value of 0 (zero), the second item has a ListIndex value of 1, and so on.

Record	Recordset:					
1 —	Avinez	Jose	120 Rose Street	Glen Ellyn	IL	60137
2	Baker	John	5819 Water Way	Lisle	IL	60532
3	Chen	Linda	6819 Rick Road	Lombard	IL	60148
4	Donner	August	45 S Jefferson Street	Lisle	IL	60532
5	Jones	Harry	75 River Street	Lisle	IL	60532
6	Lin	Susan	111 Main Street	Glen Ellyn	IL	60137
7	Lin	Jack	145 Main Street	Glen Ellyn	IL	60137
8	Lopez	Margaret	6803 Rice Road	Lombard	IL	60148
9	Lopez	Paul	22 Lambert Road	Glen Ellyn	IL	60137
10	Nadkarni	Carol	2 N Harvey Road	Lombard	IL	60148
11	Nunez	Carlos	6934 Paulette Road	Lombard	IL	60148
12	Poulos	Inez	75 Rose Street	Glen Ellyn	IL	60137
13	Tunner	Jennifer	567 Jackson Street	Glen Ellyn	IL	60137
14	Utes	Ingrid	345 Jackson	Glen Ellyn	IL	60137
15	Williams	Penny	124 Able Lane	Lisle	IL	60532

ListIndex	List box:
0 —	Avinez, Jose
1	Baker, John
2	Chen, Linda
3	Donner, August
4	Jones, Harry
5	Lin, Susan
6	Lin, Jack
7	Lopez, Margaret
8	Lopez, Paul
9	Nadkarni, Carol
10	Nunez, Carlos
11	Poulos, Inez
12	Tunner, Jennifer
13	Utes, Ingrid
14	Williams, Penny

Figure 14-27: Records contained in the recordset and in the list box

To complete the Enter Information button's Click event procedure, then test the procedure:

1 Press the **Backspace** key. Type '**move the record pointer to the record whose name matches the one selected in the list box** and press the **Enter** key. Type **rstmembers.move numrecords:=lstmembers.listindex** and press the **Enter** key.

Step 4 in the pseudocode is to display the member's name and address information in the appropriate form fields in the document.

2 Type the additional lines of code shown in Figure 14-28.

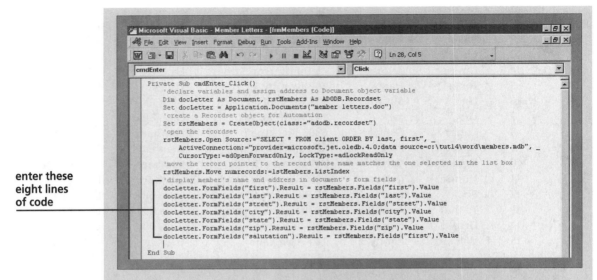

enter these
eight lines
of code

Figure 14-28: Current status of the cmdEnter control's Click event procedure

Steps 5 and 6 in the pseudocode are to close the Recordset object and release the memory allocated to it.

3 Type **'close the Recordset object and release the memory allocated to it** and press the **Enter** key. Type **rstmembers.close** and press the **Enter** key, then type **set rstmembers = nothing** and press the **Enter** key.

The last three steps in the pseudocode are to display the contents of the txtDate text box in the LetterDate form field in the document, unload the frmMembers form, and then position the cursor at the end of the document. You will use the "mmmm d, yyyy" format to display the date. The "mmmm d, yyyy" format will display the month's name, the date, a comma, and four digits in the year.

4 Type the additional lines of code shown in Figure 14-29, which shows the completed Click event procedure for the Enter Information button.

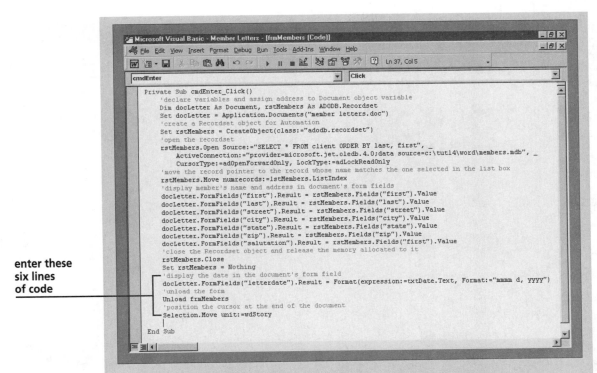

enter these six lines of code

```
Private Sub cmdEnter_Click()
    'declare variables and assign address to Document object variable
    Dim docLetter As Document, rstMembers As ADODB.Recordset
    Set docLetter = Application.Documents("member letters.doc")
    'create a Recordset object for Automation
    Set rstMembers = CreateObject(class:="adodb.recordset")
    'open the recordset
    rstMembers.Open Source:="SELECT * FROM client ORDER BY last, first", _
        ActiveConnection:="provider=microsoft.jet.oledb.4.0;data source=c:\tut14\word\members.mdb", _
        CursorType:=adOpenForwardOnly, LockType:=adLockReadOnly
    'move the record pointer to the record whose name matches the one selected in the list box
    rstMembers.Move numrecords:=lstMembers.ListIndex
    'display member's name and address in document's form fields
    docLetter.FormFields("first").Result = rstMembers.Fields("first").Value
    docLetter.FormFields("last").Result = rstMembers.Fields("last").Value
    docLetter.FormFields("street").Result = rstMembers.Fields("street").Value
    docLetter.FormFields("city").Result = rstMembers.Fields("city").Value
    docLetter.FormFields("state").Result = rstMembers.Fields("state").Value
    docLetter.FormFields("zip").Result = rstMembers.Fields("zip").Value
    docLetter.FormFields("salutation").Result = rstMembers.Fields("first").Value
    'close the Recordset object and release the memory allocated to it
    rstMembers.Close
    Set rstMembers = Nothing
    'display the date in the document's form field
    docLetter.FormFields("letterdate").Result = Format(expression:=txtDate.Text, Format:="mmmm d, yyyy")
    'unload the form
    Unload frmMembers
    'position the cursor at the end of the document
    Selection.Move unit:=wdStory

End Sub
```

Figure 14-29: Completed Click event procedure for the Enter Information button

5 Verify the accuracy of your code by comparing the code on your screen with the code shown in Figure 14-29, then save the document.

Now test the procedure to verify that it is working correctly

6 Return to Word and run the **GetMemberInfo** macro. When the Member List dialog box appears, click **Donner, August** in the list, then click the **Enter Information** button. The current date, along with August Donner's name and address, appear in the document, as shown in Figure 14-30 on the next page. (Your date might be different from the one shown in the figure.)

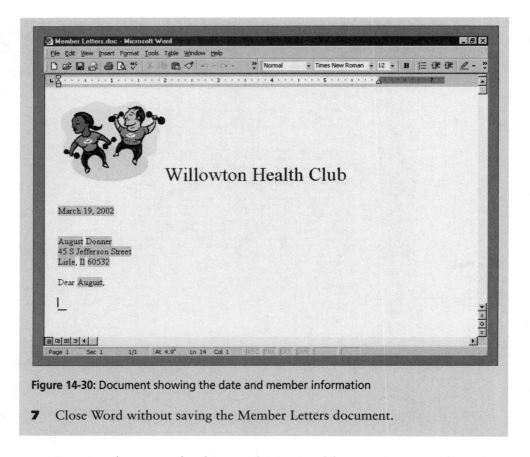

Figure 14-30: Document showing the date and member information

7 Close Word without saving the Member Letters document.

You now have completed Tutorial 14's Word lesson. You can either take a break or complete the end-of-lesson exercises before moving on to the next lesson.

 E X E R C I S E S

1. In this exercise, you will perform Automation using Word and Excel. The procedure you create will display, in a Word document, the name of the salesperson associated with the highest sales amount contained in an Excel worksheet.

    a. Start Excel. Open the Sales.xls workbook, which is located in the Tut14\Word folder on your Data Disk. Familiarize yourself with the First Quarter worksheet.

    b. Open the Visual Basic Editor. Use the Help screens to research the Excel Application object's Quit method. What property of the Application object allows you to close a workbook without being prompted to save the changes made to it? What property of the Workbook object also will allow you to close a workbook without being prompted to save the changes made to it? Close Excel.

    c. Start Word. Open the T14-WD-E1 (T14-WD-E1.doc) document, which is located in the Tut14\Word folder on your Data Disk. Click the Enable Macros button, if necessary, then save the document as T14-WD-E1D. The document contains a form field named TopName.

    d. Open the Visual Basic Editor. Use the Tools menu to set a reference to the Microsoft Excel 9.0 Object Library.

    e. Open the Module1 module's Code window and view the partially completed CreateAward procedure. Use the comments that appear in the procedure to enter the missing statements. The procedure should use Automation to display, in the TopName form field, the name of the salesperson having the highest quarterly sales amount. Use the appropriate property of the Workbook object to prevent Excel from prompting you to save the changes made to the Sales.xls workbook.

    f. Save the document, then return to Word and run the CreateAward macro. Nancy Bean's name should appear in the document.

    g. Save the document, then close Word.

2. In this exercise, you will perform Automation using Word and Access. The procedure you create will display, in a Word document, the information stored in an Access database.

    a. Start Access. Open the Items.mdb database, which is located in the Tut14\Word folder on your Data Disk. Familiarize yourself with the ItemPrices table. Close Access.

    b. Start Word. Open the T14-WD-E2 (T14-WD-E2.doc) document, which is located in the Tut14\Word folder on your Data Disk. Click the Enable Macros button, if necessary, then save the document as T14-WD-E2D. The document contains two form fields named Item and Price.

    c. Open the Visual Basic Editor. Use the Tools menu to set a reference to the Microsoft ActiveX Data Objects 2.1 Library.

    d. View the frmItem form object. The lstItem list box should display the item numbers from the ItemPrices table when the form first appears. Code the UserForm's Initialize event procedure appropriately.

    e. When the user clicks the OK button, the button's Click event procedure should move the record pointer to the record whose item number matches the one selected in the list box. The procedure should enter the item's number and price in the appropriate form fields in the document.

    f. Save the document, then return to Word and run the DisplayPrice macro. The ABC Consolidated dialog box opens. Click AC222 in the dialog box's list box, then click the OK button. AC222 and $15.00 should appear in the Item and Price form fields, respectively.

    g. Save the document, then close Word.

3. In this exercise, you will perform Automation using Word and Excel. The procedure you create will display, in a Word document, the value returned by the Excel PMT function.

    a. Start Word. Open the T14-WD-E3 (T14-WD-E3.doc) document, which is located in the Tut14\Word folder on your Data Disk. Click the Enable Macros button, if necessary, then save the document as T14-WD-E3D. The document contains four form fields named Loan, Rate, Term, and MonthPayment.

    b. View the customized Payment toolbar, if necessary.

    c. Open the Visual Basic Editor. Use the Tools menu to set a reference to the Microsoft Excel 9.0 Object Library.

    d. Use the Help window to research the PMT function in Excel. (It may be helpful to print the Help screen.) Close the Help window.

    e. Open the Module1 module's Code window and view the code template for the CalcPayment procedure. The procedure should use Excel's PMT function to calculate the monthly loan payment based on the loan amount, rate, and term entered in the form fields. (*Hint*: The Excel PMT function is available through the

WorksheetFunction object, which is contained within the Excel Application object. You learned how to access the WorksheetFunction object in Tutorial 6's Excel lesson.)

f. Save the document, then return to Word. In the form fields, enter 9000 as the loan amount, .06 as the annual interest rate, and 4 (years) as the term. Click the Calculate Payment button on the Payment toolbar. The monthly payment of $211.36 should appear in the MonthPayment form field.

g. Save the document, then close Word.

Exercise 4 is a Discovery Exercise. Discovery Exercises, which may include topics that are not covered in the lesson, allow you to "discover" the solutions to problems on your own.

discovery ▶ **4.** In this exercise, you will learn about the Application object's Visible property.

a. Start Word. Open the T14-WD-E4 (T14-WD-E4.doc) document, which is located in the Tut14\Word folder on your Data Disk. Click the Enable Macros button, if necessary, then save the document as T14-WD-E4D.

b. Open the Visual Basic Editor and set a reference to the Microsoft Excel 9.0 Object Library.

c. Open the Module1 module's Code window and view the ViewExcelWorkbook procedure. Familiarize yourself with the code; use the comments as a guide.

d. Run the ViewExcelWorkbook procedure. While the procedure is running, does a Microsoft Excel button appear on the taskbar?

e. Start Excel, then open the Heading (Heading.xls) workbook, which is located in the Tut14\Word folder on your Data Disk. The first worksheet should contain ABC in cell A1, and Corporation in cell A2.

f. Open the Visual Basic Editor in Excel. Use the Help screens to research the Application object's Visible property. Based on what you observed in Step d, what is the default value of the Visible property for an Application object?

g. Close Excel.

h. Return to the ViewExcelWorkbook procedure in Word. Include an instruction that sets the Excel Application object's Visible property to True. Enter the instruction immediately after the Set statement in which the object is created.

i. Save the document, then run the ViewExcelWorkbook procedure. Click the Yes button when asked if you want to replace the Heading.xls file. While the procedure is running, does a Microsoft Excel button appear on the taskbar?

j. Change the `appExcel.Quit` instruction to a comment by beginning the instruction with an apostrophe ('). Save the document, then run the ViewExcelWorkbook procedure. Click the Yes button when asked if you want to replace the Heading.xls file. What happens to Excel and the workbook when the procedure ends? (**Important Note:** You should never remove the Quit or Close instructions when the object's Visible property is set to False. You can learn more about this by completing this lesson's Debugging Exercise.)

k. Close Excel, then close Word.

A computer program is good only if it works. Errors in programming code can cause a program to run incorrectly. Therefore, a programmer needs to know how to locate and fix any errors in his or her code. Exercise 5 is a Debugging Exercise. Debugging Exercises allow you to practice recognizing and solving errors in code.

debugging   **5.** The following code should create a PowerPoint Application object that can be used to perform Automation with Word. Correct any errors in the code.

```
Dim appPower As Application.PowerPoint
appPower = CreateObject(Class:="PowerPoint.Application")
```

Access Lesson

Using Automation in Access

case ▶ At the end of each semester, Professor Carlisle of Snowville College meets individually with each of his CIS100 students to discuss the student's grade in the course. The student's scores on the two projects, midterm, and final are stored in an Access database. Rather than using an Access report to print the student's name and scores, Professor Carlisle has decided to use a Word document.

Viewing the Database and the Word Document

The Access database in which Professor Carlisle records each CIS100 student's name and scores is stored on your Data Disk. The database includes a table and a custom dialog box; both are named CIS100. Your Data Disk also contains a Word document that Professor Carlisle will use to print the student's name and scores. Before you begin coding the custom dialog box, view the Word document, the records contained in the database's CIS100 table, and the CIS100 form.

To view the Word document, the CIS100 table, and the CIS100 form:

1 Start Microsoft Word. Open the **CIS100 Letter** (CIS100 Letter.doc) document, which is located in the Tut14\Access folder on your Data Disk. The document is shown in Figure 14-31.

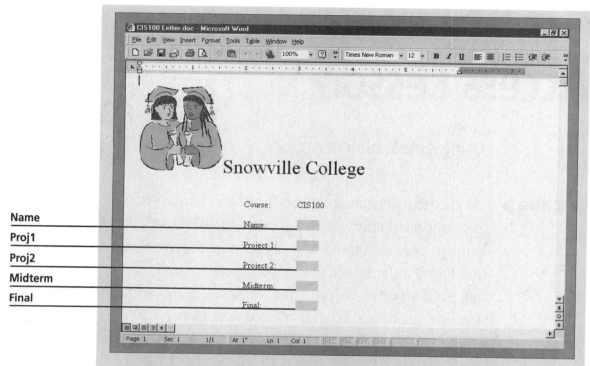

Figure 14-31: CIS100 Letter document

As the figure indicates, the document contains five form fields: Name, Proj1, Proj2, Midterm, and Final.

2   Close Word. Start Microsoft Access. Open the **ProfCarlisle** (ProfCarlisle.mdb) database, which contains one table and one form. Click the **Maximize** button [] on the Microsoft Access title bar to maximize the Microsoft Access window, if necessary.

3   Click **Tables** in the Objects bar of the Database window, if necessary. Right-click **CIS100**, then click **Open**. The records contained in the CIS100 table are shown in Figure 14-32.

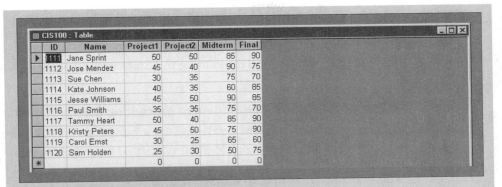

Figure 14-32: Records contained in the CIS100 table

Each record contains six Text fields: ID, Name, Project1, Project2, Midterm, and Final.

4 Close the table.

5 Click **Forms** in the Objects bar of the Database window. Right-click **CIS100**, then click **Design View**. Click the **Maximize** button ☐ on the CIS100 : Form title bar to maximize the form window. See Figure 14-33.

Restore Window button ———

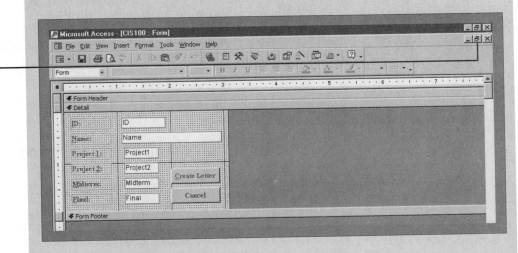

Figure 14-33: CIS100 form

You will need to code only the Cancel button's Click event procedure and the Create Letter button's Click event procedure.

6 Click the form's **Restore Window** button 🗗, then close the form.

First, you will code the Cancel button's Click event procedure.

Coding the Cancel Button's Click Event Procedure

The Cancel button's Click event procedure should close the form. Recall from Tutorial 12 that you can do so using the Close method of the DoCmd object.

To code the Cancel button's event procedure, then test the procedure:

1 Press **Alt+F11** to open the Visual Basic Editor. If necessary, open the Project Explorer window and close the Properties window, the Immediate window, and any open Code windows.

2 Open the **Microsoft Access Class Objects folder**, if necessary. Right-click **Form_CIS100** in the Project window, then click **View Code**. Use the Object box in the Code window to open the code template for the cmdCancel control's Click event procedure.

3 Close the Project Explorer window so that you can view more of the Code window.

4 Press the **Tab** key, then type **'close the form** and press the **Enter** key. Type **docmd.close** and press the **Enter** key.

Now test the Cancel button to see if it is working correctly.

5 Save the database, then return to Access. If the CIS100 Form window appears behind the Database window, close the Form window.

6 Open the CIS100 form, then click the **Cancel** button. The button's Click event procedure closes the form.

Now code the Create Letter button's Click event procedure.

Coding the Create Letter Button's Click Event Procedure

Figure 14-34 shows the pseudocode for the Create Letter button's Click event procedure.

1. Create a Word Application object named appWord to use for Automation.
2. Open the CIS100 Letter document in Word.
3. Assign the current student's name and scores to the appropriate form fields in the document.
4. Make the Word Application object visible.
5. Set the Word Application object variable to Nothing.
6. Close the CIS100 form.

Figure 14-34: Pseudocode for the Create Letter button's Click event procedure

Figure 14-35 lists the variables that the Create Letter button's Click event procedure will use.

Variable	datatype
docLetter	Document
appWord	Word.Application

Figure 14-35: Variables used by the Create Letter button's Click event procedure

The Create Letter button's Click event procedure will store the address of the CIS100 Letter document in the docLetter variable, and it will store the address of the Word.Application object, which is used for Automation, in the appWord variable.

To code the Create Letter button's Click event procedure, then test the procedure:

1 Press **Alt+F11** to return to the Visual Basic Editor. Click **Tools** on the Visual Basic Editor's menu bar, then click **References** to display the References dialog box.

Recall that Step 1 in the Automation process is to set a reference to the Automation server's object library. In this case, you will need to set a reference to Word's object library.

2 Scroll the Available References list box, if necessary, until you see Microsoft Word 9.0 Object Library in the list. Click the **check box that appears to the left of Microsoft Word 9.0 Object Library** in the list. Be sure that a check mark appears in the check box. Click the **OK** button to close the References dialog box

3 Open the code template for the cmdCreate control's Click event procedure. Press the **Tab** key, then type **'declare variables** and press the **Enter** key.

4 Type **dim docLetter as document, appWord as word.application** and press the **Enter** key.

The first step in the pseudocode is to create a Word Application object that can be used for Automation.

5 Type **'create Word Application object for Automation** and press the **Enter** key, then type **set appword = createobject(class:="word.application")** and press the **Enter** key.

Step 2 in the pseudocode is to open the CIS100 Letter document.

6 Type **'open the Word document** and press the **Enter** key, then type **set docletter = appword.documents.open("c:\tut14\access\cis100 letter.doc")** and press the **Enter** key. If necessary, change the path in the open statement to reflect the location of the document on your Data Disk.

Now assign the current student's name and scores, which appear in the text boxes on the CIS100 form, to the appropriate form fields in the Word document. You can use the Form object's Controls collection to refer to a control on the form. For example, you can use `Application.Forms("cis100").Controls("txtName")` to refer to the txtName text box on the CIS100 form.

7 Type the additional lines of code shown in Figure 14-36.

enter these six lines of code

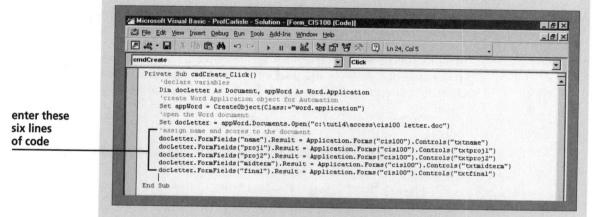

```
Microsoft Visual Basic - ProfCarlisle - Solution - [Form_CIS100 (Code)]
File Edit View Insert Debug Run Tools Add-Ins Window Help
                                           Ln 24, Col 5
cmdCreate                              Click

Private Sub cmdCreate_Click()
    'declare variables
    Dim docLetter As Document, appWord As Word.Application
    'create Word Application object for Automation
    Set appWord = CreateObject(Class:="word.application")
    'open the Word document
    Set docLetter = appWord.Documents.Open("c:\tut14\access\cis100 letter.doc")
    'assign name and scores to the document
    docLetter.FormFields("name").Result = Application.Forms("cis100").Controls("txtname")
    docLetter.FormFields("proj1").Result = Application.Forms("cis100").Controls("txtproj1")
    docLetter.FormFields("proj2").Result = Application.Forms("cis100").Controls("txtproj2")
    docLetter.FormFields("midterm").Result = Application.Forms("cis100").Controls("txtmidterm")
    docLetter.FormFields("final").Result = Application.Forms("cis100").Controls("txtfinal")
End Sub
```

Figure 14-36: Current status of the Create Letter button's Click event procedure

Next, make the Word Application object visible; this will allow you to view the CIS100 Letter document, including the student's name and scores, before printing.

8 Type **'make the Word Application object visible** and press the **Enter** key, then type **appword.visible = true** and press the **Enter** key.

The last two steps in the pseudocode are to set the Word Application object variable to `Nothing` and then close the form.

9 Type the additional lines of code shown in Figure 14-37, which shows the completed Click event procedure for the Create Letter button.

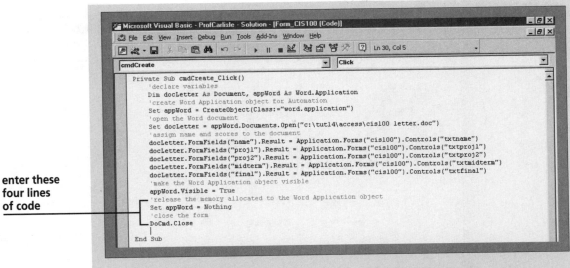

enter these four lines of code

```
Microsoft Visual Basic - ProfCarlisle - Solution - [Form_CIS100 [Code]]
File  Edit  View  Insert  Debug  Run  Tools  Add-Ins  Window  Help
                                                     Ln 30, Col 5
cmdCreate                                    Click

Private Sub cmdCreate_Click()
    'declare variables
    Dim docLetter As Document, appWord As Word.Application
    'create Word Application object for Automation
    Set appWord = CreateObject(Class:="word.application")
    'open the Word document
    Set docLetter = appWord.Documents.Open("c:\tut14\access\cis100 letter.doc")
    'assign name and scores to the document
    docLetter.FormFields("name").Result = Application.Forms("cis100").Controls("txtname")
    docLetter.FormFields("proj1").Result = Application.Forms("cis100").Controls("txtproj1")
    docLetter.FormFields("proj2").Result = Application.Forms("cis100").Controls("txtproj2")
    docLetter.FormFields("midterm").Result = Application.Forms("cis100").Controls("txtmidterm")
    docLetter.FormFields("final").Result = Application.Forms("cis100").Controls("txtfinal")
    'make the Word Application object visible
    appWord.Visible = True
    'release the memory allocated to the Word Application object
    Set appWord = Nothing
    'close the form
    DoCmd.Close

End Sub
```

Figure 14-37: Completed Click event procedure for the Create Letter button

10 Verify the accuracy of your code by comparing the code on your screen to the code shown in Figure 14-37, then save the database.

Notice that the Create Letter button's Click event procedure does not contain an instruction to close the Word Application object. The user can close the object simply by clicking its Close button or by using the File menu. You will see how this works when you test the procedure in the next set of steps.

To test the Create Letter button's Click event procedure:

1 Return to Access. If the CIS100 Form window appears behind the Database window, close the Form window.

2 Run the **SendLetterMacro** macro. When the CIS100 dialog box appears, display the record for ID **1114**, then click the **Create Letter** button. Kate Johnson's information appears in the CIS100 Letter document, as shown in Figure 14-38.

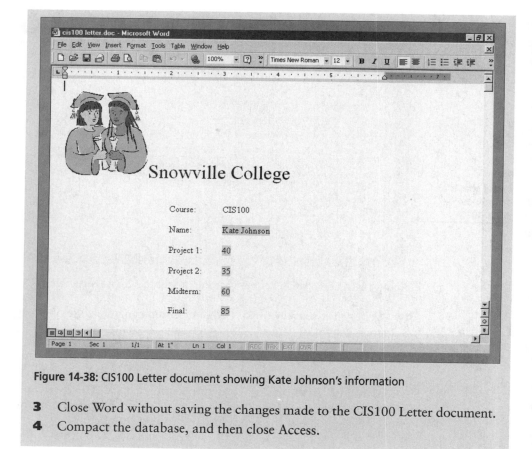

Figure 14-38: CIS100 Letter document showing Kate Johnson's information

3 Close Word without saving the changes made to the CIS100 Letter document.

4 Compact the database, and then close Access.

You now have completed Tutorial 14's Access lesson. You can either take a break or complete the end-of-lesson exercises.

EXERCISES

1. In this exercise, you will modify the Create Letter button's Click event procedure that you completed in this lesson. The procedure will print the CIS100 Letter document before closing Word.
   a. Use Windows to make a copy of the ProfCarlisle database, which is located in the Tut14\Access folder on your Data Disk. Rename the copy T14-AC-E1D.
   b. Start Access. Open the T14-AC-E1D (T14-AC-E1D.mdb) database. Open the Visual Basic Editor and view the cmdCreate control's Click event procedure. Recall that the procedure uses the `appWord.Visible = True` instruction to make the Word Application object visible. When the Application object is visible, the user can close the object using either its File menu or Close button.

c. Change the 'make the Word Application object visible comment to 'close the Word Application object. Remove the appWord.Visible = True instruction. When the Application object is not visible, the procedure must contain an instruction that closes the object. Modify the procedure accordingly.

d. Also modify the procedure so that it automatically prints the CIS100 Letter document. (*Hint*: Use the Document object's PrintOut method. Set the method's Background argument to the Boolean value False.)

e. Save the database, then return to Access. Close the form, if necessary, then run the SendLetterMacro macro. Print the CIS100 letter for Paul Smith. When you are asked if you want to save the changes made to the document, click the No button.

f. Compact and then close the database and Access.

2. In this exercise, you will perform Automation using Access and Word. The procedure you create will display, in a Word document, the information contained in an Access database.

a. Start Word. Open the Sales Letter (Sales Letter.doc) document, which is located in the Tut14\Access folder on your Data Disk. The document contains three form fields named Id, Name, and Sales. Close Word.

b. Start Access. Open the T14-AC-E2D (T14-AC-E2D.mdb) database, which is located in the Tut14\Access folder on your Data Disk. Familiarize yourself with the Salespeople table and the Salespeople form.

c. Open the Visual Basic Editor. Use the Tools menu to set a reference to the Microsoft Word 9.0 Object Library.

d. Open the Form_Salespeople form's Code window, then view the cmdOK control's Click event procedure. Code the procedure so that it uses Automation to send the current record's ID, name, and sales information to the Sales Letter document. The procedure should close the form and leave Word visible. Use the comments that appear in the procedure as a guide.

e. Save the database, then return to Access and open the form. Display the Opal Williams record, then click the OK button to display her information in the Sales Letter document.

f. Close Word without saving the changes made to the Sales Letter document.

g. Compact the database, then close the database and Access.

Exercise 3 is a Discovery Exercise. Discovery Exercises, which may include topics that are not covered in the lesson, allow you to "discover" the solutions to problems on your own.

discovery ▶ 3. In this exercise, you will perform Automation using Access and Excel.

a. Start Access. Open the T14-AC-E3D.mdb database, which is located in the Tut14\Access folder on your Data Disk. Familiarize yourself with the Salespeople table and the Salespeople form.

b. Open the Visual Basic Editor. Use the Tools menu to set a reference to the Microsoft Excel 9.0 Object Library.

c. Open the Form_Salespeople form's Code window, then view the cmdOK control's Click event procedure. Code the procedure so that it uses Automation to send the current record's ID, name, and sales information to a new Excel workbook. (Display the ID in cell A1, the name in cell A2, and the sales amount in cell A3.) The procedure should close the form and leave Excel visible. Use the comments that appear in the procedure as a guide.

d. Save the database, then return to Access and open the form. Display the Charles Jones record, then click the OK button to display his information in the Excel workbook.

e. Close Excel without saving the changes made to the workbook.

f. Compact the database, then close the database and Access.

A computer program is good only if it works. Errors in programming code can cause a program to run incorrectly. Therefore, a programmer needs to know how to locate and fix any errors in his or her code. Exercise 4 is a Debugging Exercise. Debugging Exercises allow you to practice recognizing and solving errors in code.

debugging   4. The following code should create a Word Application object that can be used to perform Automation with Access. Correct any errors in the code.

```
Dim appWord As Word.Application
appWord = NewObject(Class:="Word.Application")
```

Automation and Error Trapping

In this tutorial, you will learn how to:

■ Access an existing Automation object using the GetObject function
■ Access the information stored in the Err object
■ Intercept and handle run-time errors
■ Prevent multiple instances of an application

Concept Lesson

More on Automation

In Tutorial 14, you learned how to use the CreateObject function to create an Automation object. Recall that the syntax of the CreateObject function is **CreateObject(Class:=***class***)**, where *class* is a string that specifies the class of the Automation object. Figure 15-1 shows an example of using the CreateObject function in a procedure named NewWorkbook, which can be used to create a new Excel workbook.

```
Public Sub NewWorkbook()
    'declare object variable for Automation
    Dim appExcel As Excel.Application
    'assign Automation object's address to object variable
    Set appExcel = CreateObject(Class:="Excel.Application")
    'add a new workbook to the Workbooks collection
    appExcel.Workbooks.Add
    'make the Excel application visible
    appExcel.Visible = True
    'release the memory allocated to the appExcel object
    Set appExcel = Nothing
End Sub
```

Figure 15-1: NewWorkbook procedure

Study closely the NewWorkbook procedure's code. First the Dim statement declares an object variable named appExcel. The CreateObject function then creates an Excel Application object, and the Set statement assigns the object's address to the appExcel variable. The `appExcel.Workbooks.Add` instruction adds a new workbook to the Workbooks collection, and the `appExcel.Visible = True` instruction makes the Excel application visible to the user. (If you do not include the `appExcel.Visible = True` instruction in the NewWorkbook procedure, the user will not be able to view the new workbook.) Finally, the `Set appExcel = Nothing` instruction releases the memory allocated to the appExcel object.

As you learned in Tutorial 14, the CreateObject function starts the Automation server before it creates the Automation object; this is true even if the server is already started. For example, if the user starts Excel prior to running the NewWorkbook procedure, the procedure's CreateObject function will start another instance of Excel. As a result, when the NewWorkbook procedure ends, you will have two instances of Excel open at the same time—a waste of computer time and memory. A more efficient approach is to have the NewWorkbook procedure start Excel only if the application is not already open, and to use the existing instance of Excel if the application *is* open. Before you can accomplish this, you will need to learn about the GetObject function.

tip

Some applications—for example, PowerPoint and Outlook—are single-instance applications. A **single-instance application** is one that does not allow multiple instances of itself to be started. In other words, if PowerPoint is already running when the `CreateObject(Class:="PowerPoint.Application")` function is processed, the function will use the current instance of PowerPoint rather than starting a new instance. This concept is illustrated in this lesson's Exercise 2.

Using the GetObject Function

Unlike the CreateObject function, which is used to create an Automation object, the **GetObject function** allows you to access an existing Automation object. The syntax of the GetObject function is **GetObject(Class:=*class*)**, where *class* is a string that specifies the class of the Automation object—in other words, the type of Automation object you want the function to access. To access an Excel Application object, for example, you would use "`Excel.Application`" as the Class argument. If the object specified in the Class argument exists, the function returns the object's address; otherwise, the function results in an error. Figure 15-2 shows the syntax of the GetObject function. It also includes two examples of using the GetObject function to access Automation objects.

Syntax:

Dim *variablename* **As** *datatype*
Set *variablename* = **GetObject(Class:=***class***)**

Example 1:
```
Dim appExcel As Excel.Application
Set appExcel = GetObject(Class:="Excel.Application")
```

Example 2:
```
Dim appWord As Word.Application
Set appWord = GetObject(Class:="Word.Application")
```

Figure 15-2: Syntax and examples of the GetObject function

If the Excel application is already running, Example 1's GetObject function returns the address of the existing instance of Excel's Application object. The function results in an error, however, if the Excel application is not already running. Similarly, if Word is already started, Example 2's GetObject function returns the address of Word's Application object; otherwise, the function produces an error.

The error that occurs when the GetObject function cannot access the Automation object specified in its Class argument is one of many run-time errors that a procedure can intercept and subsequently handle.

Intercepting and Handling Run-time Errors

A **run-time error** is an error that occurs while a procedure's code is running. A run-time error results when a VBA instruction attempts to complete an invalid operation. For example, if the intCount variable contains the number 0, the instruction `sngQuotient = 100 / intCount` will produce a run-time error, because the instruction is attempting to divide a number by zero—an invalid operation. As mentioned earlier, a run-time error also occurs when the GetObject function cannot access the object specified in its Class argument.

When a run-time error occurs, information about the error is recorded in a special object called the **Err object**. Errors recorded in the Err object can be intercepted, or trapped, by a procedure. You trap an error in order to take corrective action, if possible, when the error occurs. Figure 15-3 shows a partial listing of errors that can be trapped while a procedure is running.

assigned to Err object's **Description** property

assigned to Err object's **Number** property

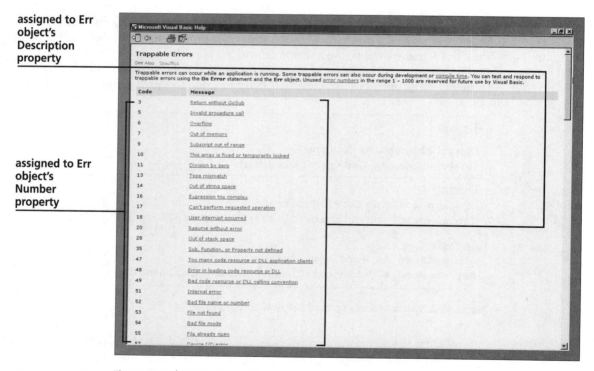

Figure 15-3: Partial listing of trappable errors

Notice that each error is identified by a code and a message. When a trappable error occurs, VBA assigns the error's code to the Err object's Number property, and it assigns the error's message to the Err object's Description property. For example, if a procedure attempts to divide a number by zero, VBA assigns the number 11 (the error code corresponding to a "Division by zero" error) to the Err object's Number property and it assigns the string "Division by zero" to the Err object's Description property. Likewise, if the GetObject function cannot locate the appropriate Automation object, VBA assigns the number 429 and the string "ActiveX component can't create object" to the Err object's Number and Description properties, respectively. You can use the Err object's Description and Number properties to determine which error occurred, and then take the appropriate action, if possible, to fix the error while the procedure is running.

The process of intercepting a trappable error is called **error trapping**, and the set of instructions you enter into a procedure to tell the procedure how to handle any trapped errors is called the **error-handling routine**, or **error handler**. You must use VBA's On Error statement to include error trapping in your VBA code.

The On Error Statement and the Error-handling Routine

For a procedure to perform error trapping, it must include an On Error statement. The **On Error statement** turns the error trapping process on in each procedure in which it is entered. The syntax of the On Error statement is **On Error GoTo** *line*, where *line*, which is either a line label or a line number in the procedure, identifies the location of the procedure's error handler—the set of instructions that tells the procedure how to handle the trapped errors.

tip   You turn the error trapping process off by setting *line* in the On Error statement to 0 (zero).

Most programmers place the On Error statement at the beginning of the procedure, as the statement must be processed before any run-time errors can be trapped. When a trappable error occurs, the On Error statement sends program control to the error-handling routine to determine how to handle the error. How the error is handled depends on the type of error that occurred.

A procedure that includes error trapping typically will follow the structure shown in Figure 15-4.

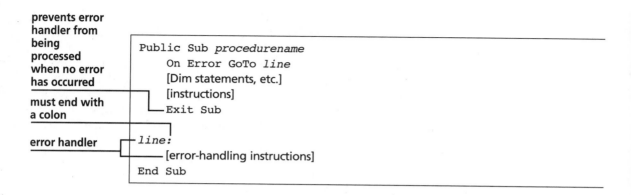

prevents error handler from being processed when no error has occurred

must end with a colon

error handler

```
Public Sub procedurename
     On Error GoTo line
     [Dim statements, etc.]
     [instructions]
     Exit Sub

line:
     [error-handling instructions]
End Sub
```

Figure 15-4: Structure of a procedure that includes error trapping

tip

Error trapping also can be used in function procedures. You use `Exit Function` rather than `Exit Sub` to exit a function procedure.

Notice the `Exit Sub` statement, which is placed immediately above the error handler in the code. The `Exit Sub` statement does exactly what its name implies: it exits the sub procedure immediately. The `Exit Sub` statement prevents the error-handling routine from being processed when no error has occurred. Also notice that *line* located immediately above the error-handling instructions has a colon at the end, but *line* used in the On Error statement does not. Figure 15-5 shows an example of a procedure that includes error trapping.

First the CalcQuotient procedure uses the On Error statement to turn the error trapping process on. Then, after declaring the necessary variables, the procedure prompts the user to enter any number except zero, and it stores the user's response in the strNumber variable.

After converting the contents of the strNumber variable to a number and assigning the result to the intNumber variable, the procedure divides the number 100 by the number stored in the intNumber variable, and it assigns the quotient to the sngQuotient variable. The `MsgBox Prompt:=sngQuotient, Buttons:=vbOKOnly + vbInformation` instruction displays the contents of the sngQuotient variable in a message box, and the `Exit Sub` statement exits the procedure, preventing the error-handling routine from being processed when no error has occurred.

turns error trapping on

exits procedure

error handler

```
Public Sub CalcQuotient()
    'turn error trapping on
    On Error GoTo CalcQuotientErrHandler
    'declare variables
    Dim strNumber As String
    Dim intNumber As Integer, sngQuotient As Single
    'get divisor
    strNumber = InputBox(Prompt:="Enter any number except 0")
    intNumber = Val(strNumber)
    'calculate and display the quotient
    sngQuotient = 100 / intNumber
    MsgBox Prompt:=sngQuotient, Buttons:=vbOKOnly + vbInformation
    Exit Sub

CalcQuotientErrHandler:
    Select Case Err.Number
        Case 11        'division by zero error
            MsgBox Prompt:="Entry error", _
                Buttons:=vbOKOnly + vbInformation
        Case Else      'unforeseen errors
            MsgBox Prompt:="Please record this information: " & _
                Err.Description & "   " & Err.Number, _
                Buttons:=vbOKOnly + vbInformation
    End Select
End Sub
```

Figure 15-5: CalcQuotient procedure

Now look closely at the code in the CalcQuotientErrHandler routine. Notice that the error handler uses a Select Case statement to take the appropriate action when a trappable error occurs. For example, if in the CalcQuotient procedure the user enters a zero, a letter, or a special character in response to the InputBox function, the intNumber variable will contain the number 0 and the sngQuotient = 100 / intNumber instruction will result in trappable error number 11 (Division by zero). When the error occurs, the On Error statement will intercept the error and it will send program control to the CalcQuotientErrHandler routine to determine how the error should be handled. According to the error handler, when error number 11 occurs, the procedure simply should display the "Entry error" message in a message box. When the user clicks the OK button in the message box, the message box will close and the CalcQuotient procedure will end.

The Case Else clause in the error handler's Select Case statement is used to handle any unforeseen errors. When an error that you may not be expecting occurs, the error handler will ask the user to record the error's description and number; you then can modify the procedure to accommodate this error. After recording the error on a piece of paper, the user can click the message box's OK button to close the message box and to end the procedure.

Rather than displaying a message and then simply ending the procedure when an error occurs, as is done in the CalcQuotient procedure shown in Figure 15-5, you can have the error handler take some corrective action and then use the Resume statement to continue processing the procedure's code.

The Resume Statement

You can use the **Resume statement** to continue processing a procedure's code after the error handler has taken some corrective action. Resume, by itself, continues, or resumes, processing with the statement that caused the error. Figure 15-6 shows how you can incorporate the Resume statement in the CalcQuotient procedure. The changes made to the original CalcQuotient procedure are shaded in the figure.

```
Public Sub CalcQuotient()
    'turn error trapping on
    On Error GoTo CalcQuotientErrHandler
    'declare variables
    Dim strNumber As String
    Dim intNumber As Integer, sngQuotient As Single
    'get divisor
    strNumber = InputBox(Prompt:="Enter any number except 0")
    intNumber = Val(strNumber)
    'calculate and display the quotient
    sngQuotient = 100 / intNumber
    MsgBox Prompt:=sngQuotient, Buttons:=vbOKOnly + vbInformation
    Exit Sub

CalcQuotientErrHandler:
    Select Case Err.Number
        Case 11      'division by zero error
          MsgBox Prompt:="Entry error", _
              Buttons:=VBOKOnly + vbInformation
          intNumber = 1
          Resume      'return to statement that caused the error
        Case Else     'unforeseen errors
          MsgBox Prompt:="Please record this information: " & _
              Err.Description & "  " & Err.Number, _
              Buttons:=VBOKOnly + vbInformation
    End Select
End Sub
```

corrects the error ——→ (intNumber = 1)

continues processing with the statement that caused the error ——→ (Resume)

Figure 15-6: CalcQuotient procedure with Resume statement

As before, when error 11 (Division by zero) occurs, the error handler will display the message "Entry error" in a message box. However, after the user closes the message box, the `intNumber = 1` instruction will assign the number 1 to the intNumber variable, and the `Resume` statement will resume processing with the statement that caused the error. In this case, processing will continue with the `sngQuotient = 100 / intNumber` statement, which will divide 100 by one, preventing the Division by zero error from occurring again. The statement will assign the quotient (in this case, 100) to the sngQuotient variable. The next instruction in the procedure—`MsgBox Prompt:=sngQuotient, Buttons:=vbOKOnly + vbInformation`—will display the number 100 in a message box. When the user closes the message box, the `Exit Sub` instruction will be processed and the procedure will end.

You also can use the `Resume` statement with the keyword `Next`. Unlike `Resume`, which continues processing with the statement that caused the error, `Resume Next` resumes processing with the statement immediately following the one that caused the error. Figure 15-7 shows how you can incorporate `Resume Next` in the CalcQuotient procedure. The changes made to the original procedure shown in Figure 15-5 are shaded in Figure 15-7.

```
Public Sub CalcQuotient()
    'turn error trapping on
    On Error GoTo CalcQuotientErrHandler
    'declare variables
    Dim strNumber As String
    Dim intNumber As Integer, sngQuotient As Single
    'get divisor
    strNumber = InputBox(Prompt:="Enter any number except 0")
    intNumber = Val(strNumber)
    'calculate and display the quotient
    sngQuotient = 100 / intNumber
    MsgBox Prompt:=sngQuotient, Buttons:=vbOKOnly + vbInformation
    Exit Sub

CalcQuotientErrHandler:
    Select Case Err.Number
        Case 11      'division by zero error
            MsgBox Prompt:="Entry error", _
                Buttons:=vbOKOnly + vbInformation
            Resume Next      'return to statement below the one
                             'that caused the error
        Case Else    'unforeseen errors
            MsgBox Prompt:="Please record this information: " & _
                Err.Description & "   " & Err.Number, _
                Buttons:=vbOKOnly + vbInformation
    End Select
End Sub
```

continues processing with the statement below the one that caused the error ───

Figure 15-7: CalcQuotient procedure with `Resume Next` statement

As before, the `Case 11` clause will display the message "Entry error" in a message box. When the user closes the message box, the `Resume Next` statement will resume processing with the statement immediately below the one that caused the error. In this case, processing will continue with the `MsgBox Prompt:=sngQuotient, Buttons:=vbOKOnly + vbInformation` statement, which will display the number 0 in a message box. The procedure will end when the `Exit Sub` statement is processed.

You also can include a line label or line number in the `Resume` statement. You would use `Resume` *line* in situations where the procedure cannot resume processing either with the instruction that caused the error or with the one located immediately below that instruction. `Resume` *line* allows the error handler to resume program execution at *line*, which is either a line label or a line number that identifies an instruction located somewhere in the procedure.

Figure 15-8 shows how you can incorporate `Resume` *line* in the CalcQuotient procedure. The changes made to the original procedure shown in Figure 15-5 are shaded in Figure 15-8.

line label →

continues processing with the line labeled Here

```
Public Sub CalcQuotient()
    'turn error trapping on
    On Error GoTo CalcQuotientErrHandler
    'declare variables
    Dim strNumber As String
    Dim intNumber As Integer, sngQuotient As Single
    'get divisor
Here:
    strNumber = InputBox(Prompt:="Enter any number except 0")
    intNumber = Val(strNumber)
    'calculate and display the quotient
    sngQuotient = 100 / intNumber
    MsgBox Prompt:=sngQuotient, Buttons:=vbOKOnly + vbInformation
    Exit Sub

CalcQuotientErrHandler:
    Select Case Err.Number
        Case 11      'division by zero error
            MsgBox Prompt:="Entry error", _
                Buttons:=vbOKOnly + vbInformation
            Resume Here   'return to statement labeled Here
        Case Else    'unforeseen errors
            MsgBox Prompt:="Please record this information: " & _
                Err.Description & "  " & Err.Number, _
                Buttons:=vbOKOnly + vbInformation
    End Select
End Sub
```

Figure 15-8: CalcQuotient procedure with `Resume` *line* statement

After the user closes the message box that contains the "Entry error" message, the `Resume Here` statement in the `Case 11` clause will resume processing with the statement identified by the line label `Here`. That statement, `strNumber = InputBox(Prompt:="Enter any number except 0")`, will prompt the user to enter another number, and it will assign the user's response to the strNumber variable. After converting the contents of the strNumber variable to a number and assigning the result to the intNumber variable, the procedure will attempt to divide 100 by the value stored in intNumber. If a "Division by zero" error occurs, the error handler will once again handle the error; otherwise, the procedure will process the `MsgBox Prompt:=sngQuotient, Buttons:=vbOKOnly + vbInformation` and `Exit Sub` instructions. If an error other than the "Division by zero" error occurs while the CalcQuotient procedure is running, the error handler's `Case Else` clause will be processed. Recall that the `Case Else` clause prompts the user to record the error's description and number before the procedure ends.

Next, you will learn how to use the GetObject function, along with error trapping, to prevent a procedure from starting multiple instances of an application.

Preventing Multiple Instances of an Application

Figure 15-1 showed the NewWorkbook procedure, which uses Automation to add a new workbook to Excel's Workbooks collection. Recall that the procedure has one drawback: its CreateObject function starts Excel even if Excel already is running. You can prevent the NewWorkbook procedure from opening another instance of Excel by using the GetObject function along with error trapping, as shown in Figure 15-9 (on the next page). Changes made to the original procedure are shaded in the figure.

The revised NewWorkbook procedure includes both the `On Error GoTo NewWorkbookErrHandler` statement, which turns the error trapping process on, and the `Exit Sub` statement, which exits the procedure and prevents the error handler from being processed when no error occurs. Notice that the first Set statement now uses the GetObject function rather than the CreateObject function. If Excel already is started, the GetObject function will return the address of the existing Excel Application object, and the Set statement will assign the address to the appExcel variable. The procedure then will process the remaining code, ending when it processes the `Exit Sub` statement.

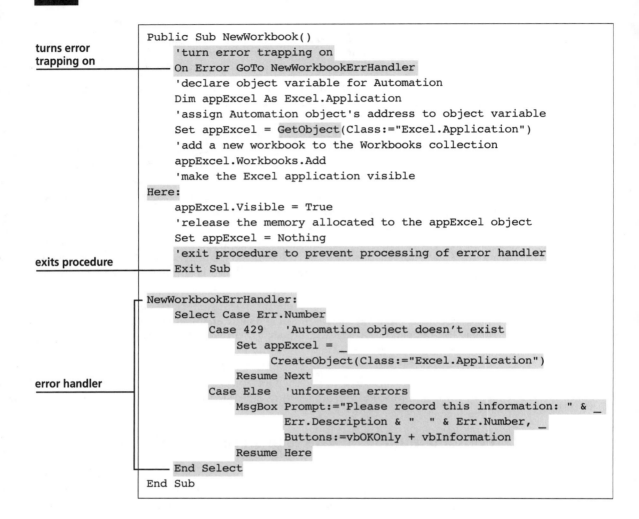

turns error trapping on

exits procedure

error handler

```
Public Sub NewWorkbook()
    'turn error trapping on
    On Error GoTo NewWorkbookErrHandler
    'declare object variable for Automation
    Dim appExcel As Excel.Application
    'assign Automation object's address to object variable
    Set appExcel = GetObject(Class:="Excel.Application")
    'add a new workbook to the Workbooks collection
    appExcel.Workbooks.Add
    'make the Excel application visible
Here:
    appExcel.Visible = True
    'release the memory allocated to the appExcel object
    Set appExcel = Nothing
    'exit procedure to prevent processing of error handler
    Exit Sub

NewWorkbookErrHandler:
    Select Case Err.Number
        Case 429    'Automation object doesn't exist
            Set appExcel = _
                CreateObject(Class:="Excel.Application")
            Resume Next
        Case Else   'unforeseen errors
            MsgBox Prompt:="Please record this information: " & _
                Err.Description & "  " & Err.Number, _
                Buttons:=vbOKOnly + vbInformation
            Resume Here
    End Select
End Sub
```

Figure 15-9: Revised NewWorkbook procedure

If, on the other hand, Excel is not already started, the GetObject function will result in a error, because it can't locate an Excel Application object; more specifically, the function will result in trappable error 429. Recall that when a trappable error occurs, the On Error statement intercepts the error and then it sends control to the error handler to determine what corrective action to take. In the case of error 429, you will notice that the error handler uses the CreateObject function to start Excel and to create an Excel Application object, and it uses the Set statement to assign the object's address to the appExcel variable. The `Resume Next` instruction in the `Case 429` clause resumes processing with the statement immediately following the one that caused the error—in this case, processing will continue with the `appExcel.Workbooks.Add` statement.

If any unforeseen error occurs, the error handler prompts the user to record the error's description and number. It then resumes execution with the line labeled `Here`—the `appExcel.Visible = True` line.

The modified version of the NewWorkbook procedure shown in Figure 15-9 uses error trapping and error handling to make sure that only one instance of the Excel application is running at any time—a much more efficient use of the computer's resources.

You now have completed Tutorial 15's Concept lesson. You can either take a break or complete the end-of-lesson questions and exercises before moving on to the next lesson.

S U M M A R Y

To access an existing Automation object:

■ Use the GetObject function, which has the syntax **GetObject(Class:=***class***)**, where class specifies the *class* of the Automation object.

To turn the error trapping process on:

■ Use the On Error GoTo statement. Its syntax is **On Error GoTo** *line*, where *line*, which is either a line label or a line number in the procedure, identifies the location of the procedure's error handler—the set of instructions that tells the procedure how to handle the trapped errors. If *line* is 0 (zero), the On Error statement turns the error trapping process off.

To include an error-handling routine in a procedure:

■ Use the structure shown in Figure 15-4.

To access information about a run-time error:

■ Use the Err object's Description and Number properties.

To resume processing after an error handler has taken some corrective action:

■ Use the `Resume` statement. `Resume`, by itself, resumes processing with the statement that caused the error. `Resume Next` resumes processing with the statement immediately below the one that caused the error. `Resume` *line* resumes processing at *line*, which is either a line label or a line number that identifies an instruction located somewhere in the procedure.

R E V I E W   Q U E S T I O N S

1. Which of the following functions will allow you to access an existing Access Application object?
   a. `CreateObject(Class:="Access.Application")`
   b. `CreateObject(Class:="Application.Access")`
   c. `GetObject(Class:="Access.Application")`
   d. `GetObject(Class:="Application.Access")`

2. When a trappable error occurs, the error's numeric code is stored in the _____ property.
   a. Err object's Code
   b. Err object's Number
   c. Error object's Code
   d. Error object's Description

3. The process of intercepting and handling a run-time error is called _____.
   a. error interception
   b. error timing
   c. error trapping
   d. None of the above.

4. In VBA, the _____ statement turns the error trapping process on.
   a. Error
   b. On Error GoTo
   c. On Error Process
   d. Trap Error

5. Always enter the _____ statement immediately above the error handler in the procedure.
   a. End
   b. Exit Handler
   c. Exit On Error
   d. None of the above.

6. The line label that identifies the error-handling routine ends with a _____.
   a. colon (:)
   b. comma (,)
   c. period (.)
   d. semicolon (;)

7. Which of the following instructions will continue processing a procedure's code with the statement immediately below the one that caused the error?
   a. Continue Next
   b. On Error Next
   c. Resume Next
   d. None of the above.

EXERCISES

1. Write a procedure named NewDocument that does the following:
   a. Turns error trapping on. Use NewDocumentErrors as the name of the error handler.
   b. Declares an object variable that can store a Word Application object. Name the object appWord.
   c. Assigns the address of a Word Application object to the appWord variable. If Word already is running, use its current instance; otherwise, start a new instance.
   d. Opens a new Word document. (*Hint*: A new document is a member of the Documents collection.)
   e. Makes the Word application visible to the user.
   f. Releases the memory allocated to the appWord variable.
   g. Prevents the procedure from processing the error handler when no error has occurred.
   h. Traps any unforeseen errors. Display a message that prompts the user to record the error's description and number, then continue processing with the instruction that makes the Word application visible.

Exercise 2 is a Discovery Exercise. Discovery Exercises, which may include topics that are not covered in this lesson, allow you to "discover" the solutions to problems on your own.

discovery ▶ 2. In this exercise, you will learn about a single-instance application, which is one that does not allow multiple instances of itself to be started.
   a. If PowerPoint is running, close PowerPoint.
   b. Start Excel or Word, opening a new workbook or document.
   c. Open the Visual Basic Editor. Insert a module into the project, then insert a macro procedure named OpenPowerPoint into the module.
   d. Use the Tools menu to add a reference to the Microsoft PowerPoint 9.0 Object Library.
   e. Enter the following four instructions in the OpenPowerPoint procedure:

```
Dim appPowerPoint As PowerPoint.Application
Set appPowerPoint = CreateObject(class:="powerpoint.application")
appPowerPoint.Visible = True
Set appPowerPoint = Nothing
```

The Dim statement creates a PowerPoint.Application object variable named appPowerPoint. The Set statement uses the CreateObject function to start the PowerPoint application and assign its address to the appPowerPoint variable. The `appPowerPoint.Visible = True` statement makes the PowerPoint application visible, and the `Set appPowerPoint = Nothing` statement releases the memory allocated to the appPowerPoint object.
   f. Run the OpenPowerPoint procedure. How many instances of PowerPoint are currently running? (*Hint*: You can tell by looking at the buttons on the taskbar. You also can press Ctrl+Alt+Del to open the Close Program dialog box, which lists the names of the programs that are currently running; you then can click the Cancel button to close the dialog box.)
   g. Minimize PowerPoint, if necessary, then run the OpenPowerPoint procedure again. How many instances of PowerPoint are running currently? Is PowerPoint a single-instance application?
   h. Close PowerPoint, then close either Excel or Word without saving the workbook or document.

You also can use VBA in PowerPoint to create procedures that enhance your presentations. Exercise 3 allows you to apply this tutorial's programming concept in a PowerPoint presentation.

 powerpoint

3. In this exercise, you will perform Automation using PowerPoint and Word. The procedure you create in PowerPoint will open a new Word document. To complete this exercise, you first must complete Exercise 1.

    a. If Word is running, close Word.

    b. Start PowerPoint. Open the T15-PP-E3 presentation, which is located in the Tut15\Concept folder on your Data Disk. Click the Enable Macros button if necessary, then save the presentation as T15-PP-E3D.

    c. Open the Visual Basic Editor. Use the Tools menu to set a reference to the Microsoft Word 9.0 Object Library.

    d. Open the Module1 module's Code window and view the code template for the NewDocument procedure. In the NewDocument procedure, enter the code you wrote in this lesson's Exercise 1. Include appropriate comments.

    e. Save the presentation, then return to PowerPoint and run the NewDocument macro, which should open a new Word document. Type your first name in the document.

    f. Press Ctrl+Alt+Del to open the Close Program dialog box, which lists the names of the applications that are currently running. How many instances of Word appear in the list? Click the Cancel button to close the Close Program dialog box.

    g. Press Alt+Tab to return to PowerPoint. Run the NewDocument macro again. How many Word documents are open? (*Hint*: Look on the taskbar.)

    h. Press Ctrl+Alt+Del to open the Close Program dialog box. How many instances of Word are currently running? Click the Cancel button to close the Close Program dialog box.

    i. Close PowerPoint. Close Word without saving any changes made to the documents.

A procedure is good only if it works. Errors in programming code can cause a procedure to run incorrectly. Therefore, a programmer needs to know how to locate and fix any errors in his or her code. Exercise 4 is a Debugging Exercise. Debugging Exercises allow you to practice recognizing and solving errors in code.

debugging

4. Correct any errors in the code shown in Figure 15-10.

```
Public Sub OpenExcel()
    'turn error trapping on
    On Error GoTo ErrHandler
    'declare object variable for Automation
    Dim appExcel As Excel.Application
    'assign Automation object's address to object variable
    Set appExcel = GetObject(Class:="Excel.Application")
    'add a new workbook to Workbooks collection
    appExcel.Workbooks.Add
    'make Excel application visible
Here:
    appExcel.Visible = True
    'release the memory allocated to the appExcel object
    Set appExcel = Nothing
    'exit procedure to prevent processing of error handler
    End Sub

ErrHandler
    Select Case Err.Number
        Case 428      'Automation object doesn't exist
            Set appExcel = _
                CreateObject(Class:="Excel.Application")
            Resume
        Case Else     'unforeseen errors
            MsgBox Prompt:="Record this information: " & _
                Err.Description & " " & Err.Number, _
                Buttons:=vbOKOnly + vbInformation
            Resume Here
    End Select
End Sub
```

Figure 15-10

Excel Lesson

Using Automation and Error Trapping in Excel

case ▶ At the end of each quarter, Martin Washington, the accountant at Paradise Electronics, enters the company's quarterly sales data into an Excel workbook. He then sends a copy of the workbook, along with a short memo, to each store manager. The OpenMemo procedure in the workbook allows Martin to open the memo—a Word document—while in Excel. Martin has decided to modify the procedure so that it starts the Word application only if the application is not already running; otherwise, the procedure should use the existing instance of Word.

Viewing Martin's Documents

The workbook in which Martin records the quarterly sales is stored on your Data Disk along with the memo he sends to each store manager. Before modifying the workbook's OpenMemo procedure, view the Word document that contains the memo. Also view the Excel workbook and the OpenMemo procedure.

To view the Word document, the Excel workbook, and the OpenMemo procedure:

1 Start Microsoft Word. Open the **QtrMemo** (QtrMemo.doc) document, which is located in the Tut15\Excel folder on your Data Disk. The document is shown in Figure 15-11.

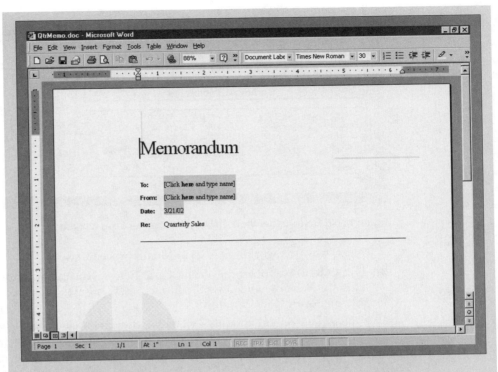

Figure 15-11: QtrMemo document

2   Close Word.

Now view the Excel workbook.

3   Start Microsoft Excel. Open the **T15-EX-1** (T15-EX-1.xls) workbook, which is located in the Tut15\Excel folder on your Data Disk. Click the **Enable Macros** button, if necessary, then save the workbook as **Quarter Sales**.

The Quarter Sales workbook contains one worksheet named First Quarter, as shown in Figure 15-12.

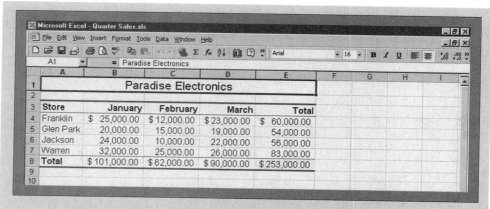

Figure 15-12: First Quarter worksheet in the Quarter Sales workbook

Next, view the workbook's OpenMemo procedure.

4 Press **Alt+F11** to open the Visual Basic Editor. If necessary, open the Project Explorer window and close the Properties Window, the Immediate Window, and any open Code Windows.

5 Open the Module1 module's Code window, then view the OpenMemo procedure. Close the Project Explorer window so that you can view more of the Code window. The OpenMemo procedure is shown in Figure 15-13.

your path
might be
different

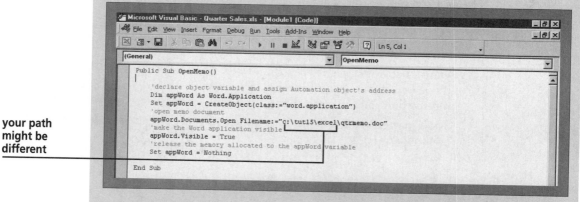

Figure 15-13: OpenMemo procedure

First the OpenMemo procedure declares an object variable named appWord. The instruction `Set appWord = CreateObject(class:="word.application")` then creates a Word Application object to use for Automation and it assigns the object's address to the appWord variable. Recall that the CreateObject function will start the Word application before it creates the Application object.

The next instruction in the procedure, `appWord.Documents.Open Filename:="c:\tut15\excel\qtrmemo.doc"`, opens the QtrMemo document and adds it to the Documents collection in Word. The instruction `appWord.Visible = True` makes the Word application visible, allowing the user to view the QtrMemo document. Finally, the instruction `Set appWord = Nothing` releases the memory allocated to the appWord object.

6 If necessary, change the path in the Open method to reflect the location of the QtrMemo.doc document on your Data Disk.

Before modifying the procedure, you will start Microsoft Word and then return to the Visual Basic Editor in Excel and run the OpenMemo procedure. This will allow you to verify that the CreateObject function starts a new instance of Word even if Word already is open.

To verify that the CreateObject function opens a new instance of Word:

1 Start Microsoft Word. A new document opens. Type your name in the document, then save the document as **First Instance** in the Tut15\Excel folder on your Data Disk.

2 Use the taskbar to return to the Visual Basic Editor. Click the **Run Sub/User Form** button ▶ to run the **OpenMemo** procedure. The OpenMemo procedure starts a new instance of Word and it displays the QtrMemo document on the screen.

You can verify that a new instance of Word was started by viewing the Close Program dialog box, which lists the names of applications that are currently running.

3 Press and hold down the **Ctrl** and **Alt** keys as you press the **Del** key. The Close Program dialog box opens.

HELP? On some keyboards, the Ctrl and Del keys are named Control and Delete.

Notice that two instances of the Word application are open: qtrmemo.doc - Microsoft Word and First Instance.doc - Microsoft Word.

4 Click **qtrmemo.doc - Microsoft Word** in the list, if necessary, and then click the **End Task** button to close this instance of Word.

5 Press **Ctrl+Alt+Del** to open the Close Program dialog box again. Notice that only one instance of Word—First Instance.doc - Microsoft Word—is open. Click the **Cancel** button to close the dialog box.

Now modify the OpenMemo procedure so that it starts Word only if Word is not already running. Figure 15-14 shows the pseudocode for the modified OpenMemo procedure.

---

1. Turn error trapping on.
2. Use the GetObject function to assign the address of an existing Word Application object to an object variable named appWord. If Word is not already started, this function will result in error 429.
3. Open the QtrMemo document in Word.
4. Make the Word application visible.
5. Release the memory allocated to the appWord object.
6. Exit the procedure to prevent processing of the error handler.

OpenMemoErrHandler:
    Case of Err.Number
        = 429 Use the CreateObject function to start Word and create a Word
            Application object. Assign the object's address to the appWord
            variable.
            Resume processing with the statement immediately below the
            one containing the GetObject function.
        Else Prompt the user to record the error's description and code.
            Resume processing with the statement that makes the Word
            application visible.

Figure 15-14: Pseudocode for the modified OpenMemo procedure

Notice that the modified OpenMemo procedure will use the GetObject function to determine if an instance of the Word Application already exists. If Word is already running, the address of its existing instance will be assigned to the appWord object variable. If Word is not running, the OpenMemoErrHandler routine will be called upon to start the Word application and assign the application's address to the appWord variable.

To modify the OpenMemo procedure:

1 In the blank line below the statement `Public Sub OpenMemo()`, type **'turn error trapping on** and press the **Enter** key, then type **on error goto OpenMemoErrHandler**.

2 Change the CreateObject function in the first Set statement to **GetObject**.

3 Insert a blank line above the `appWord.Visible = True` instruction, then type **Here:** (be sure to type the colon).

4 In the blank line above the `End Sub` statement, type **exit sub** and press the **Enter** key twice.

Now begin coding the error handler.

5   Type **OpenMemoErrHandler:** (be sure to type the colon) and press the **Enter** key. After you press the Enter key, notice that the line label moves to the left margin of the Code window.

If the GetObject function produces error 429, which indicates that the function cannot locate an existing Word Application object, the error handler should use the CreateObject function to start Word and to create the Application object. It should assign the object's address to the appWord variable. Processing then should resume with the statement immediately below the one containing the GetObject function.

If any unforeseen errors occur, the error handler should prompt the user to record the error's number and description, then resume processing with the line labeled Here.

6   Type the error handler code shown in Figure 15-15, which shows the modified OpenMemo procedure.

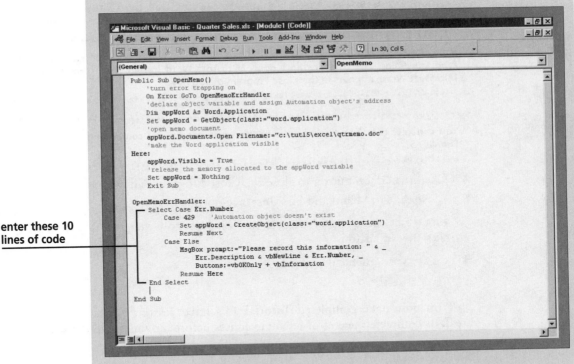

enter these 10
lines of code

```
Public Sub OpenMemo()
    'turn error trapping on
    On Error GoTo OpenMemoErrHandler
    'declare object variable and assign Automation object's address
    Dim appWord As Word.Application
    Set appWord = GetObject(class:="word.application")
    'open memo document
    appWord.Documents.Open Filename:="c:\tut15\excel\qtrmemo.doc"
    'make the Word application visible
Here:
    appWord.Visible = True
    'release the memory allocated to the appWord variable
    Set appWord = Nothing
    Exit Sub

OpenMemoErrHandler:
    Select Case Err.Number
        Case 429    'Automation object doesn't exist
            Set appWord = CreateObject(class:="word.application")
            Resume Next
        Case Else
            MsgBox prompt:="Please record this information: " & _
                Err.Description & vbNewLine & Err.Number, _
                Buttons:=vbOKOnly + vbInformation
            Resume Here
    End Select

End Sub
```

Figure 15-15: Modified OpenMemo procedure

7   Verify the accuracy of your code by comparing the code on your screen to the code shown in Figure 15-15, then save the workbook.

Now that you have finished modifying the OpenMemo procedure, you will test it to be sure it is working correctly.

To test the OpenMemo procedure:

1 Use the taskbar to verify that an instance of Word is still open.

HELP? The taskbar should contain a button labeled First Instance.doc - Microsoft Word.

2 Return to Excel and run the **OpenMemo** macro. Click **qtrmemo.doc - Microsoft Word** on the taskbar, if necessary, to view the QtrMemo document. The taskbar indicates that two Word documents—First Instance.doc and qtrmemo.doc—are currently open.

3 Press **Ctrl+Alt+Del** to open the Close Program dialog box. The dialog box indicates that only one instance of Microsoft Word (qtrmemo.doc - Microsoft Word) is currently running, proving that the Case 429 section of the error handler is working correctly.

> If the First Instance document was the active document when you opened the Close Program dialog box, First Instance.doc - Microsoft Word, rather than qtrmemo.doc - Microsoft Word, appears in the Close Program dialog box.

> You can test the Case Else section of the error handler by completing this lesson's Exercise 5.

4 Click the **Cancel** button to close the Close Program dialog box.

5 Close the QtrMemo and First Instance documents.

HELP? If you are prompted to save changes to either of the documents, click the No button.

6 Close Word, then close Excel.

You now have completed Tutorial 15's Excel lesson. You can either take a break or complete the end-of-lesson exercises before moving on to the next lesson.

EXERCISES

1. In this exercise, you will perform Automation using Excel and Word. The procedure you create will display, in a Word document, the payment information contained in an Excel worksheet.

   a. Start Word. Open the Payment (Payment.doc) document, which is located in the Tut15\Excel folder on your Data Disk. The document contains four form fields named Loan, Rate, Term, and MonthPayment. Close Word.

   b. Start Excel. Open the T15-EX-E1 (T15-EX-E1.xls) workbook, which is located in the Tut15\Excel folder on your Data Disk. Click the Enable Macros button, if necessary, then save the workbook as T15-EX-E1D. You can use the Payment worksheet to calculate the monthly payment on a loan. You need simply to enter the loan amount, interest rate, and term in cells B1, B2, and B3, respectively. Cell B4 contains the PMT function that will perform the calculation.

   c. Open the Visual Basic Editor. Use the Tools menu to set a reference to the Microsoft Word 9.0 Object Library.

   d. Open the Module1 module's Code window and view the code template for the SendPaymentInfo procedure. Code the procedure so that it displays the loan information (loan amount, interest rate, term, and monthly payment) in the Payment document's form fields. The procedure should start Word only if Word is not currently running. Be sure to include an instruction to make the Word application visible, and an instruction that releases the memory allocated to the Word Application object. When the procedure ends, leave Word running.

   e. Save the workbook, then return to Excel. Enter 9000 as the loan amount, 4% as the interest rate, and 2 as the term. Run the SendPaymentInfo macro.

   f. Close Word without saving the Payment document.

   g. Save the workbook, then close Excel.

2. In this exercise, you will modify the OpenMemo procedure that you created in this lesson. The modified procedure will handle the error that occurs when the procedure cannot locate the QtrMemo document.

   a. Start Excel. Open the Quarter Sales (Quarter Sales.xls) workbook, which is located in the Tut15\Excel folder on your Data Disk. Click the Enable Macros button, if necessary, then save the workbook as T15-EX-E2D.

   b. Open the Visual Basic Editor. Open the Module1 module's Code window and view the OpenMemo procedure. If the Open method cannot locate the QtrMemo.doc file, error 5273 occurs. Include a Case clause in the error handler to handle this error. The Case clause should display the message "QtrMemo document not found", along with the OK button and Information icon. It then should resume processing with the `appWord.Visible = True` instruction.

   c. To test the Case clause added in Step b, change the Filename argument in the Open statement to "c:\excel\qtrmemo.doc" (notice that tut15 is missing from the path).

   d. Save the workbook, then return to Excel and run the OpenMemo procedure. When the "QtrMemo document not found" message appears, click the OK button. Close Word.

   e. Return to the Visual Basic Editor. Change the Filename argument in the Open statement to "c:\tut15\excel\qtrmemo.doc" (or, change the path to reflect the location of the QtrMemo.doc file on your Data Disk).

   f. Save the workbook, then close Excel.

Exercises 3, 4 and 5 are Discovery Exercises. Discovery Exercises, which may include topics that are not covered in the lesson, allow you to "discover" the solutions to problems on your own.

discovery ▶ **3.** In this exercise, you will learn about the UserControl property of the Access Application object.

    a. Start Excel. Open the T15-EX-E3 (T15-EX-E3.xls) workbook, which is located in the Tut15\Excel folder on your Data Disk. Click the Enable Macros button, if necessary, then save the workbook as T15-EX-E3D.

    b. Open the Visual Basic Editor. Use the Tools menu to set a reference to the Microsoft Access 9.0 Object Library.

    c. Open the Module1 module's Code window and view the code template for the OpenAccess procedure. Code the procedure so that it uses Automation to open an Access database named Sales.mdb, which is located in the Tut15\Excel folder on your Data Disk. Use the comments that appear in the procedure as a guide. Open the Access application only if Access is not already running.

    d. Save the workbook, then return to Excel and run the OpenAccess macro. Notice that Access appears only briefly on the screen. To keep the Access application open, you will need to set its UserControl property to True.

    e. Return to the Visual Basic Editor. Enter the appropriate instruction below the one that makes the Access application visible.

    f. Save the workbook, then return to Excel and run the OpenAccess macro.

    g. Close Access, then close Excel.

discovery ▶ **4.** In this exercise, you will modify the IssueCertificate procedure that you created in Tutorial 14's Excel lesson so that it includes error trapping. You also will learn about the Access application's CloseCurrentDatabase method.

    a. Start Excel. Open the T15-EX-E4 (T15-EX-E4.xls) workbook, which is located in the Tut15\Excel folder on your Data Disk. Click the Enable Macros button, if necessary, then save the workbook as T15-EX-E4D.

    b. Open the Visual Basic Editor. Open the Module1 module's Code window and view the IssueCertificate procedure. If necessary, modify the path in the OpenCurrentDatabase and Open methods to reflect the location of the Sales.mdb and Certif.doc files on your Data Disk.

    c. Place an apostrophe before the following three instructions to make them into comments: `appWord.Documents("certif.doc").PrintOut`, `appAccess.Quit`, and `appWord.Quit savechanges:=wdDoNotSaveChanges`.

    d. Modify the procedure so that it opens Word only if Word is not already running, and it opens Access only if Access is not already running. (*Hint*: You will need to keep track of which application—Word or Access—caused error 429 to occur. You can use a variable to do so.) Also include error trapping for unforeseen errors. If an unforeseen error occurs, continue processing with the `appAccess.Quit` instruction. (Don't be concerned that this instruction is currently a comment.)

e. Save the workbook, then return to Excel. Start Word, opening a new document. Start Access, opening the Sales.mdb database, which is located in the Tut15\Excel folder on your Data Disk. Run the IssueCertificate macro. A message box appears indicating that an error has occurred. Notice the description and number of the error. Click the OK button to remove the message box.

f. Return to the Visual Basic Editor. Modify the IssueCertificateErrHandler procedure to handle this error. (*Hint*: You can do so using the Access application's CloseCurrentDatabase method, which will close the open database. The procedure then should return to the instruction that caused the error.)

g. Save the workbook, then return to Excel and run the IssueCertificate macro. When the macro is working correctly, return to the Visual Basic Editor and remove the apostrophe before the three instructions `appWord.Documents("certif.doc").PrintOut`, `appAccess.Quit`, and `appWord.Quit savechanges:=wdDoNotSaveChanges`.

h. Save the workbook, then return to Excel and run the IssueCertificate macro.

i. Save the workbook, then close Excel.

discovery ▶ 5. In this exercise, you will learn about the Err object's Raise method. You will use the Quarter Sales workbook that you completed in this lesson.

a. Start Excel. Open the Quarter Sales (Quarter Sales.xls) workbook, which is located in the Tut15\Excel folder on your Data Disk. Click the Enable Macros button, if necessary, then save the workbook as T15-EX-E5D.

b. Open the Visual Basic Editor. Open the Module1 module's Code window and view the OpenMemo procedure. You can use the Err object's Raise method to test the procedure's Case Else clause. The Raise method allows you to generate (raise) an error while a procedure is running. The syntax of the Err object's Raise method is **Err.Raise** *number*, where *number* is the number of the error you want to raise.

c. Insert a blank line below the statement `Set appWord = GetObject(class:="word.application")`. In the blank line, type Err.Raise Number:=61, which will generate the Disk Full error.

d. Save the workbook, then return to Excel and run the OpenMemo procedure. When the "Please record this information: Disk full 61" message appears, click the OK button. Close Word, then close Excel.

A computer program is good only if it works. Errors in programming code can cause a program to run incorrectly. Therefore, a programmer needs to know how to locate and fix any errors in his or her code. Exercise 6 is a Debugging Exercise. Debugging Exercises allow you to practice recognizing and solving errors in code.

debugging   **6.**   Correct any errors in the code shown in Figure 15-16.

```
Public Sub OpenWord()
    'turn error trapping on
    On Error GoTo ErrHandler
    'declare object variable for Automation
    Dim appWord As Word.Application
    'assign Automation object's address to object variable
    Set appWord = GetObject(Class:="Word.Application")
    'add a new document to Documents collection
    appWord.Documents.Add
    'make Word application visible
Here:
    appWord.Visible = True
    'release the memory allocated to the appWord object
    Set appWord = Nothing
    'exit procedure to prevent processing of error handler

ErrHandler
    Select Case Err.Number
        Case 429    'Automation object doesn't exist
            Set appWord = _
                CreateObject(Class:="Word.Application")
            Resume Here
        Case Else    'unforeseen errors
            MsgBox Prompt:="Record this information: " & _
                Err.Description & " " & Err.Number, _
                Buttons:=vbOKOnly + vbInformation
            Resume
    End Select
End Sub
```

Figure 15-16

Word Lesson

Using Automation and Error Trapping in Word

case▶ At the end of each quarter, Nancy Manley, Willowton Health Club's secretary, gives a $25 check along with a Sales Award certificate—a Word document—to the sales associate who sells the most new memberships. The new membership sales information is stored in an Excel workbook. The CreateCertificate procedure in the Word document opens the Excel workbook and inserts, into the document, the name of the top sales associate and the number of memberships he or she sold. Nancy has decided to modify the procedure so that it starts the Excel application only if the application is not currently running; otherwise, the procedure should use the existing instance of Excel.

Viewing Nancy's Documents

The document that Nancy uses to create the Sales Award certificate is stored on your Data Disk along with the Excel workbook containing the new membership sales information. Before modifying the document's CreateCertificate procedure, view the Excel workbook, the Word document, and the CreateCertificate procedure.

To view the Excel workbook, the Word document, and the CreateCertificate procedure:

1   Start Microsoft Excel. Open the **First Qtr** (First Qtr.xls) workbook, which is located in the Tut15\Word folder on your Data Disk. The workbook is shown in Figure 15-17.

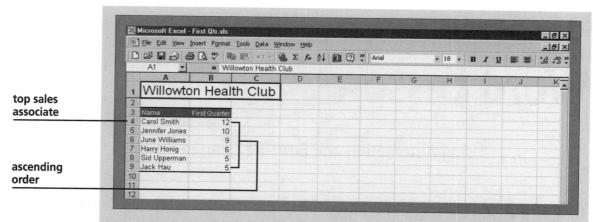

top sales associate

ascending order

Figure 15-17: First Qtr workbook

The workbook contains one worksheet named New Memberships, which lists the name of each sales associate and the number of new memberships he or she sold during the first quarter. Notice that the sales information appears in ascending order by the number of memberships sold. Cell A4 contains the name of the top sales associate (Carol Smith), and cell B4 contains the number of memberships she sold during the first quarter (12).

2 Close Excel.

Now view the Word document.

3 Start Microsoft Word. Open the **T15-WD-1** (T15-WD-1.doc) document, which is located in the Tut15\Word folder on your Data Disk. Click the **Enable Macros** button, if necessary, then save the document as **Certificate**.

Figure 15-18 shows the Certificate document.

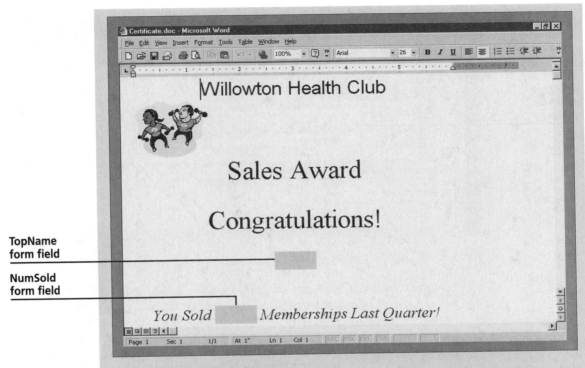

TopName form field

NumSold form field

Figure 15-18: Certificate document

The document contains two form fields named TopName and NumSold. Next, view the document's CreateCertificate procedure.

4 Press **Alt+F11** to open the Visual Basic Editor. If necessary, open the Project Explorer window and close the Properties Window, the Immediate Window, and any open Code Windows.

5 Open the Module1 module's Code window, then view the **CreateCertificate** procedure. Close the Project Explorer window so that you can view more of the Code window. Figure 15-19 shows the CreateCertificate procedure.

your path might be different

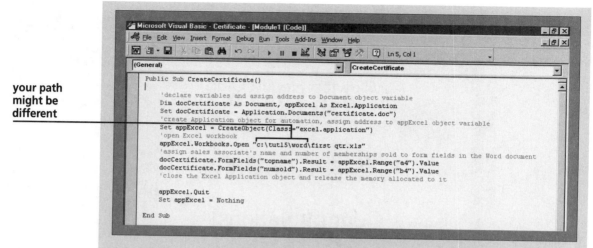

```
Microsoft Visual Basic - Certificate - [Module1 [Code]]
File  Edit  View  Insert  Format  Debug  Run  Tools  Add-Ins  Window  Help                    Ln 5, Col 1

(General)                                                    CreateCertificate

Public Sub CreateCertificate()

        'declare variables and assign address to Document object variable
        Dim docCertificate As Document, appExcel As Excel.Application
        Set docCertificate = Application.Documents("certificate.doc")
        'create Application object for automation, assign address to appExcel object variable
        Set appExcel = CreateObject(Class:="excel.application")
        'open Excel workbook
        appExcel.Workbooks.Open "c:\tut15\word\first qtr.xls"
        'assign sales associate's name and number of memberships sold to form fields in the Word document
        docCertificate.FormFields("topname").Result = appExcel.Range("a4").Value
        docCertificate.FormFields("numsold").Result = appExcel.Range("b4").Value
        'close the Excel Application object and release the memory allocated to it

        appExcel.Quit
        Set appExcel = Nothing

End Sub
```

Figure 15-19: CreateCertificate procedure

First the CreateCertificate procedure declares two object variables: a Document object variable named docCertificate and an Excel.Application object variable named appExcel. The first Set statement, `Set docCertificate = Application.Documents("certificate.doc")`, assigns the address of the Certificate document to the docCertificate variable. The second Set statement, `Set appExcel = CreateObject(Class:="excel. application")`, creates an Excel Application object to use for Automation, and it assigns the object's address to the appExcel variable. Recall that the CreateObject function will start the Excel application before it creates the Application object.

The next instruction in the procedure, `appExcel.Workbooks.Open "c:\tut15\word\first qtr.xls"`, opens the First Qtr workbook and adds it to the Workbooks collection in Excel. The next two instructions assign the top sales associate's name and number of memberships sold to the form fields in the Word document. The last two instructions, `appExcel.Quit` and `Set appExcel = Nothing`, close the Excel application and release the memory allocated to the appExcel object.

6 If necessary, change the path in the Open method to reflect the location of the First Qtr.xls workbook on your Data Disk.

Before modifying the procedure, you will start Microsoft Excel and then return to the Visual Basic Editor in Word and run the CreateCertificate procedure. This will allow you to verify that the CreateObject function starts a new instance of Excel even if Excel already is open.

To verify that the CreateObject function opens a new instance of Excel:

1 Start Microsoft Excel. A new workbook opens. Type your name in cell A1 in the Sheet1 worksheet, then save the workbook as **First Instance** in the Tut15\Word folder on your Data Disk.

2 Use the taskbar to return to the Visual Basic Editor, then enter an apostrophe before the instruction `appExcel.Quit` to make the instruction a comment.

3 In the blank line above the `'appExcel.Quit` comment, type **appexcel.visible = true**.

> Every procedure that uses Automation should include an instruction that either closes the Automation object or makes the Automation object visible so that the user can close it.

4 Click the **Run Sub/User Form** button ▶ to run the **CreateCertificate** procedure. The CreateCertificate procedure starts a new instance of Excel and it displays the First Qtr workbook on the screen.

You can verify that a new instance of Excel was started by viewing the Close Program dialog box, which lists the names of applications that are currently running.

5 Press and hold down the **Ctrl** and **Alt** keys as you press the **Del** key. The Close Program dialog box opens.

HELP? On some keyboards, the Ctrl and Del keys are named Control and Delete.

Notice that two instances of the Excel application are open: Microsoft Excel - First Qtr.xls and Microsoft Excel - First Instance.xls.

6 Click **Microsoft Excel – First Qtr.xls** in the list, if necessary, and then click the **End Task** button to close this instance of Excel.

7 Press **Ctrl+Alt+Del** to open the Close Program dialog box again. Notice that only one instance of Excel— Microsoft Excel - First Instance.xls—is open. Click the **Cancel** button to close the dialog box.

Now modify the CreateCertificate procedure so that it starts Excel only if Excel is not already running. Figure 15-20 shows the pseudocode for the modified CreateCertificate procedure.

1. Turn error trapping on.
2. Use the GetObject function to assign the address of an existing Excel Application object to an object variable named appExcel. If Excel is not already started, this function will result in error 429.
3. Open the First Qtr workbook in Excel.
4. Release the memory allocated to the appExcel object.
5. Exit the procedure to prevent processing of the error handler.

CreateCertificateErrHandler:
    Case of Err.Number
        = 429 Use the CreateObject function to start Excel and create an Excel Application object. Assign the object's address to the appExcel variable.
        Resume processing with the statement immediately below the one containing the GetObject function.
      Else   Prompt the user to record the error's description and code. Resume processing with the statement that closes the Excel application.

Figure 15-20: Pseudocode for the modified CreateCertificate procedure

Notice that the modified CreateCertificate procedure will use the GetObject function to determine if an instance of the Excel Application already exists. If Excel is already running, the address of its existing instance will be assigned to the appExcel object variable. If Excel is not running, the CreateCertificateErrHandler routine will be called upon to start the Excel application and assign the application's address to the appExcel variable.

To modify the CreateCertificate procedure:

1 Return to the Visual Basic Editor, if necessary. In the blank line below the statement `Public Sub CreateCertificate()`, type **'turn error trapping on** and press the **Enter** key, then type **on error goto CreateCertificateErrHandler**.

2 Change the CreateObject function in the second Set statement to **GetObject**.

3 Insert a blank line above the `appExcel.Visible = True` instruction. In the blank line, type **Here:** (be sure to type the colon).

Important Note: You will remove the `appExcel.Visible = True` instruction and the apostrophe that appears before the `appExcel.Quit` instruction later in this lesson. You are leaving both instructions as they are at this point so that you can verify that the CreateCertificate procedure will use the existing instance of Excel if Excel already is running.

When you move the insertion point to another line, the Here: line label will move to the left margin of the Code window.

4 In the blank line above the End Sub statement, type **exit sub** and press the **Enter** key twice.

Now begin coding the error handler.

5 Type **CreateCertificateErrHandler:** (be sure to type the colon) and press the **Enter** key. After you press the Enter key, notice that the line label moves to the left margin of the Code window.

If the GetObject function produces error 429, which indicates that the function cannot locate an existing Excel Application object, the error handler should use the CreateObject function to start Excel and to create the Application object. It should assign the object's address to the appExcel variable. Processing then should resume with the statement below the one containing the GetObject function.

If any unforeseen errors occur, the error handler should prompt the user to record the error's number and description, then resume processing with the line labeled Here.

6 Type the error handler code shown in Figure 15-21, which shows the modified CreateCertificate procedure.

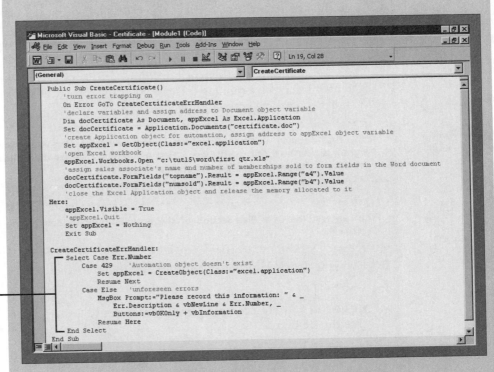

enter these 10 lines of code

```
Public Sub CreateCertificate()
    'turn error trapping on
    On Error GoTo CreateCertificateErrHandler
    'declare variables and assign address to Document object variable
    Dim docCertificate As Document, appExcel As Excel.Application
    Set docCertificate = Application.Documents("certificate.doc")
    'create Application object for automation, assign address to appExcel object variable
    Set appExcel = GetObject(Class:="excel.application")
    'open Excel workbook
    appExcel.Workbooks.Open "c:\tut15\word\first qtr.xls"
    'assign sales associate's name and number of memberships sold to form fields in the Word document
    docCertificate.FormFields("topname").Result = appExcel.Range("a4").Value
    docCertificate.FormFields("numsold").Result = appExcel.Range("b4").Value
    'close the Excel Application object and release the memory allocated to it
Here:
    appExcel.Visible = True
    'appExcel.Quit
    Set appExcel = Nothing
    Exit Sub

CreateCertificateErrHandler:
    Select Case Err.Number
        Case 429    'Automation object doesn't exist
            Set appExcel = CreateObject(Class:="excel.application")
            Resume Next
        Case Else   'unforeseen errors
            MsgBox Prompt:="Please record this information: " & _
                Err.Description & vbNewLine & Err.Number, _
                Buttons:=vbOKOnly + vbInformation
            Resume Here
    End Select
End Sub
```

Figure 15-21: Modified CreateCertificate procedure

7 Verify the accuracy of your code by comparing the code on your screen to the code shown in Figure 15-21, then save the document.

Now that you have finished modifying the CreateCertificate procedure, you will test it to be sure it is working correctly.

To test the CreateCertificate procedure:

1 Use the taskbar to verify that an instance of Excel is still open.

HELP? The taskbar should contain a button labeled Microsoft Excel - First Instance.xls.

2 Return to Word. Carol Smith and the number 12 appear in the document's form fields.

You can clear the form fields by first protecting the document, and then unprotecting it.

3 Click **Tools** on the Standard menu bar, then click **Protect Document**. When the Protect Document dialog box appears, click the **Forms** option button to select it, then click the **OK** button. The information is removed from the form fields. Click **Tools** on the Standard menu bar, then click **Unprotect Document** to unprotect the document once again.

4 Run the **CreateCertificate** macro. Click **First Qtr.xls** on the taskbar, if necessary, to view the First Qtr workbook. The taskbar indicates that two Excel workbooks—First Instance.xls and First Qtr.xls—are currently open.

5 Press **Ctrl+Alt+Del** to open the Close Program dialog box. The dialog box indicates that only one instance of Microsoft Excel (Microsoft Excel - First Qtr.xls) is currently running, proving that the Case 429 section of the error handler is working correctly.

If the First Instance workbook was the active workbook when you opened the Close Program dialog box, Microsoft Excel - First Instance.xls, rather than Microsoft Excel - First Qtr.xls, appears in the Close Program dialog box.

You can test the Case Else section of the error handler by completing this lesson's Exercise 4.

6 Click the **Cancel** button to close the Close Program dialog box.

7 Close Excel.

HELP? If you are prompted to save changes to either of the workbooks, click the No button.

8   Return to the Visual Basic Editor. Delete the apostrophe that appears before the instruction `appExcel.Quit`, then delete the line containing the instruction `appExcel.Visible = True`. The completed CreateCertificate procedure is shown in Figure 15-22.

remove the line that contained the appExcel. Visible = True instruction

remove the apostrophe from this line

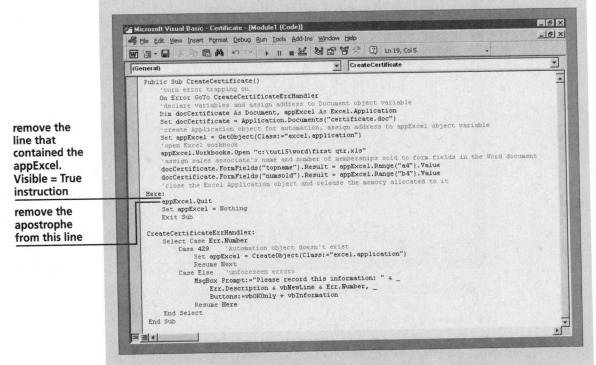

```
Microsoft Visual Basic - Certificate - [Module1 (Code)]
File  Edit  View  Insert  Format  Debug  Run  Tools  Add-Ins  Window  Help

(General)                                    CreateCertificate

Public Sub CreateCertificate()
    'turn error trapping on
    On Error GoTo CreateCertificateErrHandler
    'declare variables and assign address to Document object variable
    Dim docCertificate As Document, appExcel As Excel.Application
    Set docCertificate = Application.Documents("certificate.doc")
    'create Application object for automation, assign address to appExcel object variable
    Set appExcel = GetObject(Class:="excel.application")
    'open Excel workbook
    appExcel.Workbooks.Open "c:\tut15\word\first qtr.xls"
    'assign sales associate's name and number of memberships sold to form fields in the Word document
    docCertificate.FormFields("topname").Result = appExcel.Range("a4").Value
    docCertificate.FormFields("numsold").Result = appExcel.Range("b4").Value
    'close the Excel Application object and release the memory allocated to it
Here:
    appExcel.Quit
    Set appExcel = Nothing
    Exit Sub

CreateCertificateErrHandler:
    Select Case Err.Number
        Case 429    'Automation object doesn't exist
            Set appExcel = CreateObject(Class:="excel.application")
            Resume Next
        Case Else   'unforeseen errors
            MsgBox Prompt:="Please record this information: " & _
                Err.Description & vbNewLine & Err.Number, _
                Buttons:=vbOKOnly + vbInformation
            Resume Here
    End Select
End Sub
```

Figure 15-22: Completed CreateCertificate procedure

9   Save the document, then return to Word. Clear the form fields by protecting and then unprotecting the document.

10 Run the CreateCertificate macro. The document appears as shown in Figure 15-23.

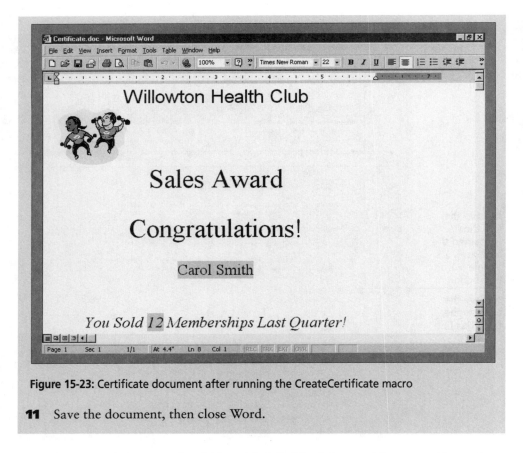

Figure 15-23: Certificate document after running the CreateCertificate macro

11 Save the document, then close Word.

You now have completed Tutorial 15's Word lesson. You can either take a break or complete the end-of-lesson exercises before moving on to the next lesson.

 # EXERCISES

1. In this exercise, you will modify the CreateCertificate procedure that you created in this lesson. The modified procedure will close either the Excel application or the First Qtr workbook.

   a. Start Excel. Open the First Instance (First Instance.xls) workbook, which you created in this lesson. Minimize Excel.

   b. Start Word. Open the Certificate (Certificate.doc) document, which is located in the Tut15\Word folder on your Data Disk. Click the Enable Macros button, if necessary, then save the document as T15-WD-E1D.

   c. Clear the form fields by protecting and then unprotecting the document.

d. Open the Visual Basic Editor. Open the Module1 module's Code window and view the CreateCertificate procedure. Change the filename in the first Set statement to "t15-wd-e1d.doc".

e. Modify the procedure so that it closes the Excel application only if the procedure created an instance of Excel—in other words, only if the CreateObject function was processed in the error handler. If the procedure used an existing instance of Excel, close only the First Qtr workbook, not the Excel application itself. (*Hint*: You can use a Workbook object's Close method to close a workbook.)

f. Save the document, then return to Word and run the CreateCertificate procedure. When the procedure ends, Excel and the First Instance workbook should still be open.

g. Close Excel, then run the CreateCertificate procedure again. This time when the procedure ends, no instances of Excel should be open.

h. Save the document, then close Word.

2. In this exercise, you will modify the CreateCertificate procedure that you created in this lesson. The modified procedure will handle the error that occurs when the procedure cannot locate the First Qtr workbook.

a. Start Word. Open the Certificate (Certificate.doc) document, which is located in the Tut15\Word folder on your Data Disk. Click the Enable Macros button, if necessary, then save the document as T15-WD-E2D.

b. Clear the form fields by protecting and then unprotecting the document.

c. Open the Visual Basic Editor. Open the Module1 module's Code window and view the CreateCertificate procedure. Change the filename in the first Set statement to "t15-wd-e2d.doc".

d. If the Open method cannot locate the First Qtr.xls file, error 1004 occurs. Include a Case clause in the error handler to handle this error. The Case clause should display the message "First Qtr workbook not found", along with the OK button and Information icon. It then should resume processing with the `appExcel.Quit` instruction.

e. To test the Case clause added in Step d, change the Filename argument in the Open method to "c:\word\first qtr.xls" (notice that tut15 is missing from the path).

f. Save the document, then return to Word and run the CreateCertificate procedure. When the "First Qtr workbook not found" message appears, click the OK button.

g. Return to the Visual Basic Editor. Change the Filename argument in the Open method to "c:\tut15\word\first qtr.xls" (or, change the path to reflect the location of the First Qtr.xls file on your Data Disk).

h. Return to Word and run the CreateCertificate procedure.

i. Save the document, then close Word.

Exercises 3 and 4 are Discovery Exercises. Discovery Exercises, which may include topics that are not covered in the lesson, allow you to "discover" the solutions to problems on your own.

discovery ▶ 3. In this exercise, you will learn about the UserControl property of the Access Application object.

a. Start Word. Open the T15-WD-E3 (T15-WD-E3.doc) document, which is located in the Tut15\Word folder on your Data Disk. Click the Enable Macros button, if necessary, then save the document as T15-WD-E3D.

b. Open the Visual Basic Editor. Use the Tools menu to set a reference to the Microsoft Access 9.0 Object Library.

    c. Open the Module1 module's Code window and view the code template for the OpenAccess procedure. Code the procedure so that it uses Automation to open an Access database named Sales.mdb, which is located in the Tut15\Word folder on your Data Disk. Use the comments that appear in the procedure as a guide. Open the Access application only if Access is not already running.

    d. Save the document, then return to Word and run the OpenAccess macro. Notice that Access appears only briefly on the screen. To keep the Access application open, you will need to set its UserControl property to True.

    e. Return to the Visual Basic Editor. Enter the appropriate instruction below the one that makes the Access application visible.

    f. Save the document, then return to Word and run the OpenAccess macro.

    g. Close Access, then close Word.

discovery ▶ **4.** In this exercise, you will learn about the Err object's Raise method. You will use the Certificate document that you completed in this lesson.

    a. Start Word. Open the Certificate (Certificate.doc) document, which is located in the Tut15\Word folder on your Data Disk. Click the Enable Macros button, if necessary, then save the document as T15-WD-E4D.

    b. Clear the form fields by protecting and then unprotecting the document.

    c. Open the Visual Basic Editor. Open the Module1 module's Code window and view the CreateCertificate procedure. Change the filename in the first Set statement to "t15-wd-e4d.doc". You can use the Err object's Raise method to test the procedure's Case Else clause. The Raise method allows you to generate (raise) an error while a procedure is running. The syntax of the Err object's Raise method is **Err.Raise** *number*, where *number* is the number of the error you want to raise.

    d. Insert a blank line below the statement `Set appExcel = GetObject(Class:="excel.application")`. In the blank line, type Err.Raise Number:=61, which will generate the Disk Full error.

    e. Save the document, then return to Word and run the CreateCertificate procedure. When the "Please record this information: Disk full 61" message appears, click the OK button. Close Word.

A computer program is good only if it works. Errors in programming code can cause a program to run incorrectly. Therefore, a programmer needs to know how to locate and fix any errors in his or her code. Exercise 5 is a Debugging Exercise. Debugging Exercises allow you to practice recognizing and solving errors in code.

debugging **5.** Correct any errors in the code shown in Figure 15-24.

```
Public Sub OpenExcel()
    'turn error trapping on
    On Error GoTo OpenExcelErrHandle
    'declare object variable for Automation
    Dim appExcel As Excel.Application
    'assign Automation object's address to object variable
    Set appExcel = CreateObject(Class:="Excel.Application")
    'add a new workbook to Workbooks collection
    appExcel.Workbooks.Add
    'make Excel application visible
Here:
    appExcel.Visible = True
    'release the memory allocated to the appExcel object
    Set appExcel = Nothing
    'exit procedure to prevent processing of error handler
    Exit Sub

OpenExcelErrHandler:
    Select Case Err.Number
        Case 429       'Automation object doesn't exist
            Set appExcel = _
                GetObject(Class:="Excel.Application")
            Resume Next
        Case Else      'unforeseen errors
            MsgBox Prompt:="Record this information: " & _
                Err.Description & " " & Err.Number, _
                Buttons:=vbOKOnly + vbInformation
            Resume Here
    End Select
End Sub
```

Figure 15-24

Access Lesson

Using Automation and Error Trapping in Access

case ▶ In Tutorial 14, you coded a custom dialog box for Professor Carlisle of Snowville College. As you may remember, the Create Letter button in the dialog box inserted, into a Word document, a student's name and scores earned on two projects, a midterm, and a final, all of which are stored in an Access database. Professor Carlisle has decided to modify the Create Letter button's Click event procedure so that it starts the Word application only if the application is not currently running; otherwise, the procedure should use the existing instance of Word.

Viewing the Database and the Word Document

The Access database in which Professor Carlisle records each CIS100 student's name and scores is stored on your Data Disk along with the Word document used to print the student information. Figure 15-25 shows the records contained in the database's CIS100 table.

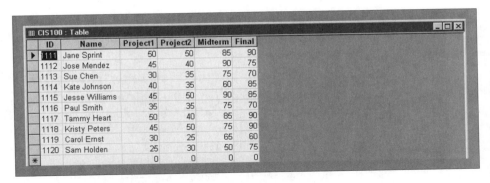

Figure 15-25: Records contained in the database's CIS100 table

Each record in the CIS100 table contains six Text fields: ID, Name, Project1, Project2, Midterm, and Final.

Figure 15-26 shows the Word document that Professor Carlisle uses to print the student information. The document's name is CIS100 Letter.

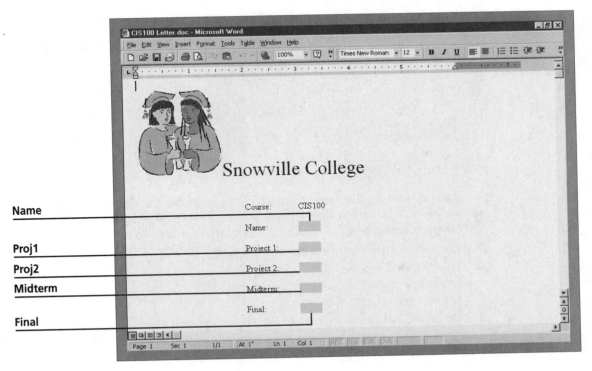

Figure 15-26: CIS100 Letter document

As Figure 15-26 indicates, the CIS100 Letter document contains five form fields.

Now view the custom dialog box—a form named CIS100—as well as the Create Letter button's Click event procedure.

To view the CIS100 form and the Create Letter button's Click event procedure:

1 Start Microsoft Access. Open the **ProfCarlisle** (ProfCarlisle.mdb) database, which is located in the Tut15\Access folder on your Data Disk. Click the **Maximize** button on the Microsoft Access title bar to maximize the Microsoft Access window, if necessary.

2 Click **Forms** in the Objects bar of the Database window. Right-click **CIS100**, then click **Design View**. Click the **Maximize** button ☐ on the CIS100 : Form title bar to maximize the form window. See Figure 15-27.

Restore Window button

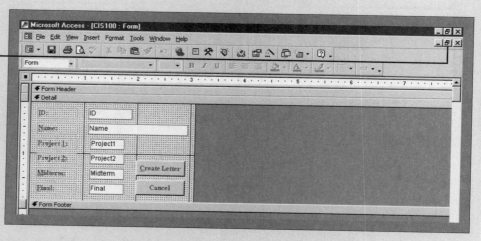

Figure 15-27: CIS100 form

After displaying the appropriate student's record in the form, the user needs simply to click the Create Letter button to start Word, open the CIS100 Letter document, and insert the student information into the document.

3 Click the form's **Restore Window** button 🗗, then close the form.

4 Press **Alt+F11** to open the Visual Basic Editor. If necessary, open the Project Explorer window and close the Properties Window, the Immediate Window, and any open Code Windows.

5 Open the Microsoft Access Class Objects folder, if necessary. Right-click **Form_CIS100** in the Project Explorer window, then click **View Code** on the shortcut menu.

6 Use the Code window's Object box to view the cmdCreate control's Click event procedure. Close the Project Explorer window so that you can view more of the Code window. Figure 15-28 shows the Create Letter button's Click event procedure.

your path might be different

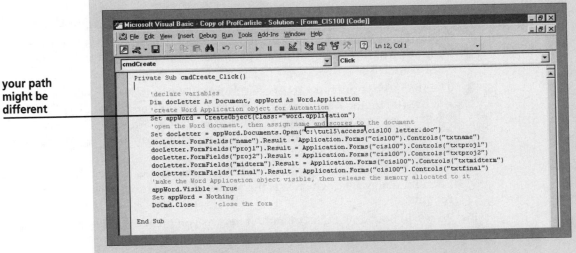

```
Microsoft Visual Basic - Copy of ProfCarlisle - Solution - [Form_CIS100 (Code)]
File  Edit  View  Insert  Debug  Run  Tools  Add-Ins  Window  Help                    Ln 12, Col 1

cmdCreate                                    Click

Private Sub cmdCreate_Click()

    'declare variables
    Dim docLetter As Document, appWord As Word.Application
    'create Word Application object for Automation
    Set appWord = CreateObject(Class:="word.application")
    'open the Word document, then assign name and scores to the document
    Set docLetter = appWord.Documents.Open("c:\tut15\access\cis100 letter.doc")
    docLetter.FormFields("name").Result = Application.Forms("cis100").Controls("txtname")
    docLetter.FormFields("proj1").Result = Application.Forms("cis100").Controls("txtproj1")
    docLetter.FormFields("proj2").Result = Application.Forms("cis100").Controls("txtproj2")
    docLetter.FormFields("midterm").Result = Application.Forms("cis100").Controls("txtmidterm")
    docLetter.FormFields("final").Result = Application.Forms("cis100").Controls("txtfinal")
    'make the Word Application object visible, then release the memory allocated to it
    appWord.Visible = True
    Set appWord = Nothing
    DoCmd.Close       'close the form

End Sub
```

Figure 15-28: Create Letter button's Click event procedure

First the Click event procedure declares two object variables: a Document object variable named docLetter and a Word.Application object variable named appWord. The first Set statement, `Set appWord = CreateObject (Class:="word.application")`, creates a Word Application object to use for Automation, and it assigns the object's address to the appWord variable. Recall that the CreateObject function will start the Word application before it creates the Application object. The second Set statement, `Set docLetter = appWord.Documents.Open("c:\tut15\access\cis100 letter. doc")`, assigns the address of the CIS100 Letter document to the docLetter variable.

The next five instructions assign the student's name and scores earned to the form fields in the Word document. The last three instructions— `appWord.Visible = True, Set appWord = Nothing`, and `DoCmd. Close`—make the Word application visible, release the memory allocated to the appWord object, and close the form, respectively.

7 If necessary, change the path in the Open method to reflect the location of the CIS100 Letter.doc document on your Data Disk, then save the database.

Before modifying the procedure, you will start Microsoft Word and then return to Access and run the SendLetterMacro macro. This will allow you to verify that the CreateObject function in the cmdCreate control's Click event procedure starts a new instance of Word even if Word already is open.

To verify that the CreateObject function opens a new instance of Word:

1 Start Microsoft Word. A new document opens. Type your name in the document, then save the document as **First Instance** in the Tut15\Access folder on your Data Disk.

2 Use the taskbar to return to Access. Run the **SendLetterMacro** macro. When the CIS100 dialog box appears, click the **Create Letter** button. The button's Click event procedure starts a new instance of Word and it displays the CIS100 Letter document, containing the student information for Jane Sprint, on the screen.

You can verify that a new instance of Word was started by viewing the Close Program dialog box, which lists the names of applications that are currently running.

3 Press and hold down the **Ctrl** and **Alt** keys as you press the **Del** key. The Close Program dialog box opens.

HELP? On some keyboards, the Ctrl and Del keys are named Control and Delete.

Notice that two instances of the Word application are open: cis100 letter.doc - Microsoft Word and First Instance.doc - Microsoft Word.

4 Click **cis100 letter.doc - Microsoft Word** in the list, if necessary, and then click the **End Task** button to close this instance of Word. When you are asked if you want to save the changes made to the document, click the **No** button.

5 Press **Ctrl+Alt+Del** to open the Close Program dialog box again. Notice that only one instance of Word—First Instance.doc – Microsoft Word—is open. Click the **Cancel** button to close the dialog box.

Now modify the cmdCreate control's Click event procedure so that it starts Word only if Word is not already running. Figure 15-29 shows the pseudocode for the modified procedure.

1. Turn error trapping on.
2. Use the GetObject function to assign the address of an existing Word Application object to an object variable named appWord. If Word is not already started, this function will result in error 429.
3. Open the CIS100 Letter document in Word.
4. Assign the current student's name and scores to the appropriate form fields in the document.
5. Make the Word Application object visible.
6. Release the memory allocated to the appWord object.
7. Close the CIS100 form.
8. Exit the procedure to prevent processing of the error handler.

CreateLetterErrHandler:
  Case of Err.Number
    = 429   Use the CreateObject function to start Word and create a Word Application object. Assign the object's address to the appWord variable.
             Resume processing with the statement immediately below the one containing the GetObject function.
    Else   Prompt the user to record the error's description and code.
             Resume processing with the statement that makes the Word application visible.

Figure 15-29: Pseudocode for the modified Click event procedure

Notice that the modified cmdCreate control's Click event procedure will use the GetObject function to determine if an instance of the Word Application already exists. If Word is already running, the address of its existing instance will be assigned to the appWord object variable. If Word is not running, the CreateLetterErrHandler routine will be called upon to start the Word application and assign the application's address to the appWord variable.

To modify the cmdCreate control's Click event procedure:

1   Return to the Visual Basic Editor. In the blank line below the statement Private Sub cmdCreate_Click(), type **'turn error trapping on** and press the **Enter** key, then type **on error goto CreateLetterErrHandler.**

2   Change the CreateObject function in the first Set statement to **GetObject.**

3   Insert a blank line above the appWord.Visible instruction. In the blank line, type **Here:** (be sure to type the colon).

....

When you move the insertion point to another line, the Here: line label will move to the left margin of the Code window.

....

 tip

4   In the blank line above the End Sub statement, type **exit sub** and press the **Enter** key twice.

Now begin coding the error handler.

5   Type **CreateLetterErrHandler:** (be sure to type the colon) and press the **Enter** key. After you press the Enter key, notice that the line label moves to the left margin of the Code window.

If the GetObject function produces error 429, which indicates that the function cannot locate an existing Word Application object, the error handler should use the CreateObject function to start Word and to create the Application object. It should assign the object's address to the appWord variable. Processing then should resume with the statement below the one containing the GetObject function.

If any unforeseen errors occur, the error handler should prompt the user to record the error's number and description, then resume processing with the line labeled Here.

6   Type the error handler code shown in Figure 15-30, which shows the modified Click event procedure for the cmdCreate control.

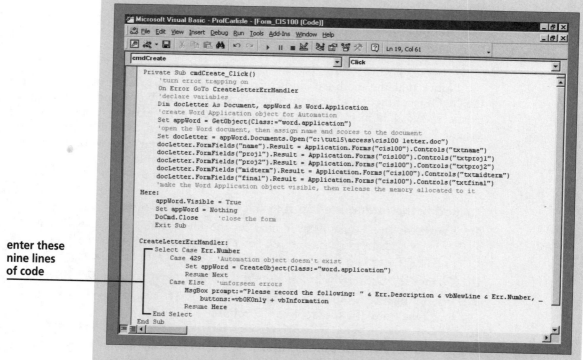

enter these nine lines of code

Figure 15-30: Modified Click event procedure for the cmdCreate control

7   Verify the accuracy of your code by comparing the code on your screen to the code shown in Figure 15-30, then save the database.

Now that you have finished modifying the Create Letter button's Click event procedure, you will test it to be sure it is working correctly.

To test the Create Letter button's Click event procedure:

1 Use the taskbar to verify that an instance of Word is still open.

HELP? The taskbar should contain a button labeled First Instance.doc - Microsoft Word.

2 Return to Access. Close the CIS100 form, if necessary, then run the **SendLetterMacro** macro. When the CIS100 form appears, click the Create Letter button.

3 Click **cis100 letter.doc** on the taskbar, if necessary, to view the CIS100 Letter document, which contains Jane Sprint's information. The taskbar indicates that two Word documents—First Instance.doc and cis100 letter.doc—are currently open.

4 Press **Ctrl+Alt+Del** to open the Close Program dialog box. The dialog box indicates that only one instance of Microsoft Word (cis100 letter.doc - Microsoft Word) is currently running, proving that the Case 429 section of the error handler is working correctly.

If the First Instance document was the active document when you opened the Close Program dialog box, First Instance.doc - Microsoft Word, rather than cis100 letter.doc - Microsoft Word, would appear in the Close Program dialog box.

You can test the Case Else section of the error handler by completing this lesson's Exercise 4.

5 Click the **Cancel** button to close the Close Program dialog box.

6 Close Word. When you are prompted to save changes to the CIS100 Letter document, click the **No** button.

7 Return to Access. Compact the database, then close Access.

You now have completed Tutorial 15's Access lesson. You can either take a break or complete the end-of-lesson exercises.

EXERCISES

1. In this exercise, you will modify the Create Letter button's Click event procedure that you coded in this lesson. The modified procedure will print the CIS100 Letter document and then close either Word or the CIS100 Letter document.

   a. Use Windows to make a copy of the ProfCarlisle (ProfCarlisle.mdb) database, which is located in the Tut15\Access folder on your Data Disk. Rename the copy T15-AC-E1D.

   b. Start Word. Open the First Instance.doc document, which you created in this lesson. The document is located in the Tut15\Access folder on your Data Disk.

   c. Minimize Word. Start Microsoft Access. Open the T15-AC-E1D (T15-AC-E1D.mdb) database, which is located in the Tut15\Access folder on your Data Disk.

   d. Open the Visual Basic Editor and view the cmdCreate control's Click event procedure. Modify the procedure so that it automatically prints the CIS100 Letter document. (*Hint*: You can use a Document object's PrintOut method to print a document. Set the Background argument of the PrintOut method to False.)

   e. Also modify the cmdCreate control's Click event procedure so that it closes the Word application only if the procedure created an instance of Word—in other words, only if the CreateObject function was processed in the error handler. If the procedure used an existing instance of Word, close only the CIS100 Letter document, not the Word application itself. (*Hint*: You can use a Document object's Close method to close a document, and you can use a Word Application object's Quit method to close Word. When closing either Word or the document, do not save the changes made to the CIS100 Letter document.)

   f. Save the database, then return to Access. Close the CIS100 form, if necessary, then run the SendLetterMacro macro. When the CIS100 form appears, click the Create Letter button. When the button's Click event procedure ends, Word and the First Instance document should still be open.

   g. Close Word, then run the SendLetterMacro macro again. When the CIS100 form appears, click the Create Letter button. This time when the button's Click event procedure ends, no instances of Word should be open.

   h. Compact the database, then close Access.

2. In this exercise, you will modify the Create Letter button's Click event procedure that you coded in this lesson. The modified procedure will handle the error that occurs when the procedure cannot locate the CIS100 Letter document.

   a. Use Windows to make a copy of the ProfCarlisle (ProfCarlisle.mdb) database, which is located in the Tut15\Access folder on your Data Disk. Rename the copy T15-AC-E2D.

   b. Start Access. Open the T15-AC-E2D (T15-AC-E2D.mdb) database, which is located in the Tut15\Access folder on your Data Disk.

c. Open the Visual Basic Editor and view the cmdCreate control's Click event procedure. If the Open method cannot locate the CIS100 Letter.doc file, error 5273 occurs. Include a Case clause in the error handler to handle this error. The Case clause should display the message "CIS100 Letter document not found", along with the OK button and Information icon. It then should resume processing with the line labeled Here.

d. To test the Case clause added in Step c, change the Filename argument in the Open method to "c:\access\cis100 letter.doc" (notice that tut15 is missing from the path).

e. Save the database, then return to Access. Close the form, if necessary, then run the SendLetterMacro macro. When the CIS100 form appears, click the Create Letter button. When the "CIS100 Letter document not found" message appears, click the OK button.

f. Return to the Visual Basic Editor. Change the Filename argument in the Open method to "c:\tut15\access\cis100 letter.doc" (or, change the path to reflect the location of the CIS100 Letter.doc file on your Data Disk).

g. Save the database, then return to Access. Close the form, if necessary, then compact the database and close Access. Close Word.

Exercises 3 and 4 are Discovery Exercises. Discovery Exercises, which may include topics that are not covered in the lesson, allow you to "discover" the solutions to problems on your own.

discovery ▶ **3.** In this exercise, you will perform Automation using Access and Excel. The procedure you create will display, in an Excel worksheet, the records stored in an Access database.

a. Start Excel. Open the Sales (Sales.xls) workbook, which is located in the Tut15\Access folder on your Data Disk. Familiarize yourself with the January worksheet, then close Excel.

b. Start Access. Open the T15-AC-E3D (T15-AC-E3D.mdb) database, which is located in the Tut15\Access folder on your Data Disk. Familiarize yourself with the Salespeople table.

c. Open the Visual Basic Editor. Use the Tools menu to set a reference to the Microsoft Excel 9.0 Object Library.

d. Open the Module1 module's Code window and view the partially completed SendToExcel procedure. Code the procedure so that it uses Automation to send each record's ID, name, and sales information to the Sales workbook. Display the first record's ID, name, and sales amount in cells A5, B5, and C5, respectively. Use the comments that appear in the procedure as a guide. When the procedure ends, leave Excel and the Sales workbook open.

e. Save the database, then return to Access and run the SendToExcelMacro macro.

f. View the Sales workbook in Excel, then close Excel without saving the changes made to the workbook.

g. Compact the database, then close Access.

discovery ▶
4. In this exercise, you will learn about the Err object's Raise method. You will use the ProfCarlisle database that you completed in this lesson.

a. Use Windows to make a copy of the ProfCarlisle (ProfCarlisle.mdb) database, which is located in the Tut15\Access folder on your Data Disk. Rename the copy T15-AC-E4D.

b. Start Access. Open the T15-AC-E4D (T15-AC-E4D.mdb) database, which is located in the Tut15\Access folder on your Data Disk.

c. Open the Visual Basic Editor. Right-click Form_CIS100, which is located in the Microsoft Access Class Objects folder, then click View Code. Open the cmdCreate control's Click event procedure. You can use the Err object's Raise method to test the procedure's Case Else clause. The Raise method allows you to generate (raise) an error while a procedure is running. The syntax of the Err object's Raise method is **Err.Raise** *number*, where *number* is the number of the error you want to raise.

d. Insert a blank line below the statement `Set appWord = GetObject(Class:="word.application")`. In the blank line, type Err.Raise Number:=61, which will generate the Disk Full error.

e. Save the database, then return to Access. Close the form, if necessary, then run the SendLetterMacro macro. When the CIS100 form appears, click the Create Letter button. When the "Please record this information: Disk full 61" message appears, click the OK button.

f. Compact the database, then close Access.

A computer program is good only if it works. Errors in programming code can cause a program to run incorrectly. Therefore, a programmer needs to know how to locate and fix any errors in his or her code. Exercise 5 is a Debugging Exercise. Debugging Exercises allow you to practice recognizing and solving errors in code.

debugging
5. Correct any errors in the code shown in Figure 15-31.

```
Public Sub OpenWord()
      'turn error trapping on
      On Error GoTo OpenWordErrHandler
      'declare object variable for Automation
      Dim appWord As Word.Application
      'assign Automation object's address to object variable
      Set appWord = CreateObject(Class:="Word.Application")
      'add a new document to Documents collection
      appWord.Documents.Add
      'make Word application visible
Here:
      appWord.Visible = True
      'release the memory allocated to the appWord object
      Set appWord = Nothing
      'exit procedure to prevent processing of error handler
      Exit Proc

OpenWordErrHandler
      Select Case Err.Code
          Case 429        'Automation object doesn't exist
              Set appWord = _
                  GetObject(Class:="Word.Application")
              Resume Next
          Case Else      'unforeseen errors
              MsgBox Prompt:="Record this information: " & _
                  Err.Description & " " & Err.Number, _
                  Buttons:=vbOKOnly + vbInformation
              Resume Here
      End Select
End Sub
```

Figure 15-31

Index